THE INTERSECTIONS COLLECTION
PEARSON CUSTOM SOCIOLOGY

Formerly published as Intersections, Crossroads & Inequalities

EDITORS

KATHLEEN A. TIEMANN

University of North Dakota
Introduction to Sociology, Social Problems & Issues, Inequalities & Diversity

RALPH B. MCNEAL, JR.

University of Connecticut
Introduction to Sociology

BETSY LUCAL

Indiana University South Bend
Inequalities & Diversity

MORTEN G. ENDER

United States Military Academy, West Point
Inequalities & Diversity

COMPILED BY:

University of Houston

Pearson Custom Publishing

New York   Boston   San Francisco
London   Toronto   Sydney   Tokyo   Singapore   Madrid
Mexico City   Munich   Paris   Cape Town   Hong Kong   Montreal

Senior Vice President, Editorial and Marketing: Patrick F. Boles
Senior Sponsoring Editor: Robin J. Lazrus
Development Editor: Abbey Lee Briggs
Associate Editor: Ana Díaz-Caneja
Marketing Manager: Jack Cooney
Operations Manager: Eric M. Kenney
Database Product Manager: Jennifer Berry
Rights Manager: Katie Huha
Art Director: Renée Sartell
Cover Designer: Renée Sartell

Cover Art: "Figures," courtesy of Eugenie Lewalski Berg; "Abstract Crowd," courtesy of Diana Ong/Superstock; "R&B Figures," courtesy of Diana Ong/Superstock; "Bramante's Staircase," courtesy of Veer/Photodisc Photography; "Hand Prints," courtesy of Veer/Photodisc Photography; "People Running-Falling," courtesy of Veer/Campbell Laird; "Sunbathers on Beach," courtesy of Veer/Scott Barrow.

Please visit our website at *www.pearsoncustom.com.*

Attention bookstores: For permission to return any unsold stock, contact us at *pe-uscustomreturns@pearson.com.*

**Pearson
Custom Publishing**
is a division of

www.pearsonhighered.com   ISBN 10: 0558271111
ISBN 13: 9780558271114

&Ꮿ Contents Ꮢ

iii

Contents

Contents

v

Contents

vi

Contents

Contents

The Sociology of Culture at the University of Houston

. . .

The professors in our department teach and conduct research in a wide range of sociological areas. Among them are family, health, gender, education, religion, organizations, law, immigration, race and ethnic relations, sports, and deviant behavior. A growing area of interest—in the broader discipline as well as in our own department—is the sociological study of culture. The author of our textbook, John J. Macionis, defines *culture* as "the ways of thinking, the ways of acting, and the material objects that together form a people's way of life." In contrast, *culture* is a people's way of life, whereas *society* is the specific group of people who live that way of life everyday. Culture provides the meanings—values, ideas, traditions, rules, laws, and beliefs—for life.

The sociological study of culture examines the many different sources of meaning that comprise a people's way of life. This area is increasing in interest and importance because of the great changes taking place in these sources of meaning. Just a few hundred years ago, the sources of culture consisted of some writing, but much conversation and story telling. In our lifetime—I as a baby boomer and you as a college student—we have witnessed the massive explosion of cultural sources and media: television, the Internet, Internet radio, MySpace, movies, neighborhood newspapers, specialized magazines, iPods, iPhones, and televangelism, just for starters. Culture and society are just about synonymous now: are you what your facebook profile says you are...?

My professors study—and, of course, conduct research on—a wide range of cultural topics. Dr. Russell Curtis is studying examining the ways African-Americans are portrayed in sports films. Dr. Helen Rose Ebaugh is studying the role of Islamic beliefs systems on democratization in the Middle East. Dr. Stella Gregorian is studying the meaning of food in American life.

We now present three complete, scholarly articles as prime examples of this work. Dr. Samantha Kwan's article reports on her very exciting research on the various ways individuals perform *beauty work*, which strengthens a social and cultural system that accentuates youth and attractiveness. Dr. Tracy Karner's intriguing article reports on the way Vietnam veterans interpret the films portraying the war in which the fought and survived. Finally, my article examines the various ways baby boomers—people in my generation—continue their interest in rock'n'roll music. Baby boomers were the first generation to grow up completely with rock'n'roll and its various musical and cultural progeny. Rock'n'roll continue to provide meanings for the everyday life issues—e.g., family, friends, religion, and aging—they continue to face.

Dr. Joseph A. Kotarba
Professor and Chair,
Department of Sociology
University of Houston

The Sociological
Perspective

The sociological perspective shows us that the society around us influences how we act and even what we think and feel. Learning to see the world sociologically is useful in many ways—and it is also fun!

The Sociological Perspective

Mark Scott/Getty Images

If you were to randomly ask 100 people in the United States, "Why do couples marry?" it is a safe bet that at least 90 of them would reply, "People marry because they fall in love." Most of us find it hard to imagine a marriage being happy without love; for the same reason, when people fall in love, we expect them to think about marriage.

But is the decision about whom to marry really just a matter of personal feelings? There is plenty of evidence to show that if love is the key to marriage, Cupid's arrow is carefully aimed by the society around us.

Society has many "rules" about whom we should and should not marry. In all states but Massachusetts, the law rules out half the population, banning people from marrying someone of the same sex, even if a couple is deeply in love. But there are other rules as well. Sociologists have found that people, especially when they are young, are very likely to marry someone close in age, and people of all ages typically marry others in the same racial category, of similar social class background, with about the same level of education, and with the same degree of physical attractiveness (Chapter 18, "Families," gives details). People end up making choices about whom to marry, but society narrows the field long before they do (Gardyn, 2002; Zipp, 2002).

When it comes to love, the decisions people make do not simply result from the process philosophers call "free will." Sociology teaches us that the social world guides all our life choices in much the same way that the seasons influence our clothing and activities.

The Sociological Perspective

Sociology is *the systematic study of human society.* At the heart of sociology is a special point of view called the *sociological perspective.*

Seeing the General in the Particular

Years ago, Peter Berger (1963) described the **sociological perspective** as *seeing the general in the particular.* By this he meant that sociologists look for general patterns in the behavior of particular people. Although every individual is unique, a society shapes the lives of its members. Here in the United States, for example, people expect to be in love with the person they marry, an idea almost unknown among, say, people living in a traditional village in rural Pakistan.

In addition, any society shapes the lives of people in various *categories* (such as children and adults, women and men, the rich and the poor). In a classic study of women's hopes for their marriages, for example, Lillian Rubin (1976) found that higher-income women typically expected the men they married to be sensitive to others, to talk readily, and to share feelings and experiences. Lower-income women, she found, had very different expectations and were looking for men who did not drink too much, were not violent, and held steady jobs.

Obviously, what women think they can expect in a marriage partner has a lot to do with social class position. In general, people who come from more privileged social backgrounds tend to be more confident and optimistic about their lives. This is not surprising when we realize that they have more opportunities as well as the training and skills to take advantage of them. We begin to think sociologically by realizing how the society we live in—as well as the general categories into which we fall within that society—shapes our particular life experiences.

 How do you think your social class background shapes the kind of job you expect to have after you graduate? What effect did your background have on your decision to go to college?

Seeing the Strange in the Familiar

At first, using the sociological perspective is *seeing the strange in the familiar.* Imagine a young woman walking up to a young male friend and saying, "You fit all the right social categories, which means you would make a wonderful husband!" We are used to thinking that people fall in love and decide to marry based on personal feelings. But the sociological perspective reveals the initially strange idea that society shapes what we think and do.

Because we live in an individualistic society, learning to see how society affects us may take a bit of practice. If someone asked you why you "chose" to enroll at your particular college, you might offer one of the following reasons:

"I wanted to stay close to home."

"I got a basketball scholarship."

"With a journalism degree from this university, I can get a good job."

"My girlfriend goes to school here."

"I didn't get into the school I *really* wanted to attend."

Any of these responses may well be true. But do they tell the whole story?

Thinking sociologically about going to college, it's important to realize that only about 5 out of every 100 people in the world earn a college degree. Even in the United States a century ago, going to college was not an option for most people. Today, going to college is

Chapter Overview

This chapter introduces the discipline of sociology. The most important skill to gain from this course is the ability to use what we call the *sociological perspective.* This chapter also introduces *sociological theory,* which helps us build understanding from what we see using the sociological perspective.

We can easily see the power of society over the individual by imagining how different our lives would be had we been born in place of any of these children from, respectively, Bolivia, Ethiopia, Thailand, Botswana, South Korea, and El Salvador.

Caroline Penn/Corbis/Bettmann (*top left*); Minh-Thu Pham (*top middle*); Graham, Neal/ Omni-Photo Communications, Inc. (*top right*); Paul W. Liebhardt (*bottom left*); Alan Evrard/Robert Harding World Imagery (*bottom middle*); Paul W. Liebhardt (*bottom right*)

within the reach of far more people. But a look around the classroom shows that social forces still have much to do with who goes to college. For instance, most U.S. college students are young, generally between eighteen and about thirty. Why? Because in our society, attending college is linked to this period of life. But more than age is involved, because fewer than half of all young men and women actually end up on campus.

Another factor is cost. Because higher education is so expensive, college students tend to come from families with above-average incomes. If you are lucky enough to belong to a family earning more than $75,000 a year, you are almost three times as likely to go to college as someone whose family earns less than $20,000. Is it reasonable, in light of these facts, to say that attending college is simply a matter of personal choice?

Seeing Personal Choice in Social Context

To see how society shapes personal choices, consider the number of children women have. In the United States, as shown in Global Map 1, the average woman has about two children during her lifetime. In India, however, the average is about three; in Cambodia, about four; in Ethiopia, about five; in Yemen, about six; and in Niger, about seven.

What accounts for these striking differences? As later chapters explain, women in poor countries have less schooling and fewer economic opportunities, are more likely to remain in the home, and are less likely to use contraception. Clearly, society has much to do with the decisions women and men make about childbearing.

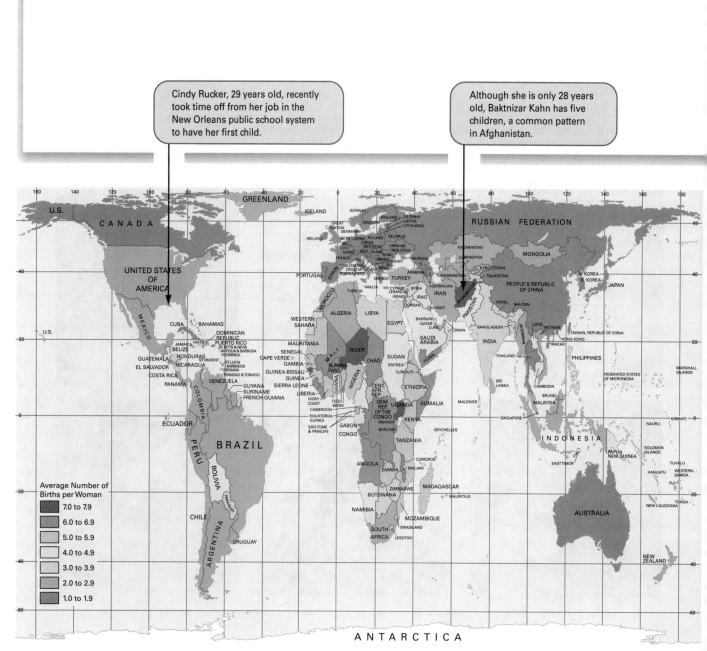

WINDOW ON THE WORLD

GLOBAL MAP 1 Women's Childbearing in Global Perspective

Is childbearing simply a matter of personal choice? A look around the world shows that it is not. In general, women living in poor countries have many more children than women in rich nations. Can you point to some of the reasons for this global disparity? In simple terms, such differences mean that if you had been born into another society (whether you are female or male), your life might be quite different from what it is now.

Sources: Data from Hamilton, Martin, & Ventura (2006) and United Nations (2006b). Map projection from *Peters Atlas of the World* (1990).

Another illustration of the power of society to shape even our most private choices comes from the study of suicide. What could be a more personal choice than the decision to end your own life? But Emile Durkheim (1858–1917), one of sociology's pioneers, showed that even here, social forces are at work.

Examining official records in France, his own country, Durkheim found that some categories of people were more likely than others to take their own lives. Men, Protestants, wealthy people, and the unmarried had much higher suicide rates than women, Catholics and Jews, the poor, and married people. Durkheim explained the differences in

THE SOCIOLOGICAL PERSPECTIVE

terms of *social integration:* Categories of people with strong social ties had low suicide rates, and more individualistic categories of people had high suicide rates.

In Durkheim's time, men had much more freedom than women. But despite its advantages, freedom weakens social ties and thus increases the risk of suicide. Likewise, more individualistic Protestants were more likely to commit suicide than more tradition-bound Catholics and Jews, whose rituals encourage stronger social ties. The wealthy have much more freedom than the poor, but once again, at the cost of a higher suicide rate.

A century later, Durkheim's analysis still holds true (Thorlindsson & Bjarnason, 1998). Figure 1 shows suicide rates for various categories of people in the United States. Keep in mind that suicide is very rare—a rate of 10 suicides for every 100,000 people is about the same as 6 inches in a mile. Even so, we can see some interesting patterns. In 2003, there were 12.1 recorded suicides for every 100,000 white people, more than twice the rate for African Americans (5.1). For both races, suicide was more common among men than among women. White men (19.5) were more than four times as likely as white women (4.7) to take their own lives. Among African Americans, the rate for men (8.8) was about five times higher than for women (1.8). Applying Durkheim's logic helps us understand why this is the case: The higher suicide rate among white people and men reflects their greater wealth and freedom; the lower rate among women and African Americans reflects their limited social choices. Just as Durkheim did a century ago, we can see general patterns in the personal actions of particular individuals.

 Single people are at greater risk of suicide than married people. Can you explain why?

Seeing Sociologically: Marginality and Crisis

Anyone can learn to see the world using the sociological perspective. But two situations help people see clearly how society shapes individual lives: living on the margins of society and living through a social crisis.

From time to time, everyone feels like an "outsider." For some categories of people, however, being an *outsider*—not part of the dominant group—is an everyday experience. The greater people's social marginality, the better they are able to use the sociological perspective.

For example, no African American grows up in the United States without understanding the importance of race in shaping people's

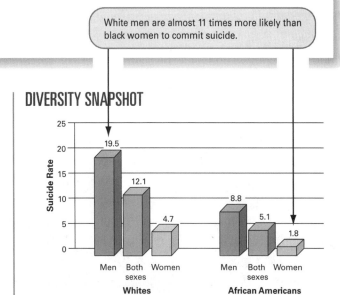

DIVERSITY SNAPSHOT

White men are almost 11 times more likely than black women to commit suicide.

FIGURE 1 Rate of Death by Suicide, by Race and Sex, for the United States

Suicide rates are higher for white people than for black people and higher for men than for women. Rates indicate the number of deaths by suicide for every 100,000 people in each category for 2003.
Source: Hoyert et al. (2006).

lives. Rap lyrics by groups such as Three 6 Mafia, who say that they "Done seen people killed, done seen people deal, done seen people live in poverty with no meals," show that some people of color—especially African Americans living in the inner city—feel like their hopes and dreams are crushed by society. But white people, as the dominant majority, think less often about race and the privileges it provides, believing that race affects only people of color and not themselves as well. People at the margins of social life, including women, gay people, people with disabilities, and the very old, are aware of social patterns that others rarely think about. To become better at using the sociological perspective, we must step back from our familiar routines and look at our lives with a new curiosity.

Periods of change or crisis make everyone feel a little off balance, encouraging us to use the sociological perspective. The sociologist C. Wright Mills (1959) illustrated this idea using the Great Depression of the 1930s. As the unemployment rate soared to 25 percent, people out of work could not help but see general social forces at work in their particular lives. Rather than saying, "Something is wrong with me; I can't find a job," they took a sociological approach and realized, "The economy has collapsed; there are no jobs to be found!" Mills believed that using what he called the "sociological imagination" in this way helps people understand not only their society but also their

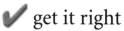

People with the greatest privileges tend to see individuals as responsible for their own lives. Those at the margins of society, by contrast, are quick to see how race, class, and gender can create disadvantages. The rap group Three 6 Mafia has given voice to the frustration felt by many African Americans living in this country's inner cities.

Kevork Djansezian/AP Wide World Photos

own lives, because the two are closely related. The Seeing Sociology in Everyday Life box takes a closer look.

Just as social change encourages sociological thinking, sociological thinking can bring about social change. The more we learn about how "the system" operates, the more we may want to change it in some way. Becoming aware of the power of gender, for example, has caused many women and men to try to reduce gender inequality.

The Importance of a Global Perspective

December 10, Fez, Morocco. This medieval city—a web of narrow streets and alleyways—is alive with the laughter of playing children, the silence of veiled women, and the steady gaze of men leading donkeys loaded with goods. Fez seems to have changed little over the centuries. Here, in northwest Africa, we are just a few hundred miles from the more familiar rhythms of Europe. Yet this place seems a thousand years away. Never have we had such an adventure! Never have we thought so much about home!

As new information technology draws even the farthest reaches of the Earth closer to one another, many academic disciplines are taking a **global perspective,** *the study of the larger world and our society's place in it.* What is the importance of a global perspective for sociology?

First, global awareness is a logical extension of the sociological perspective. Sociology shows us that our place in society shapes our life experiences. It stands to reason, then, that the position of our society in the larger world system affects everyone in the United States. The Thinking Globally box describes a "global village" to show the social shape of the world and the place of the United States within it.

The world's 193 nations can be divided into three broad categories according to their level of economic development. **High-income countries** are the *nations with the highest overall standards of living.* The sixty countries in this category include the United States and Canada, Argentina, the nations of Western Europe, South Africa, Israel, Saudi Arabia, Japan, and Australia. Taken together, these nations produce most of the world's goods and services, and the people who live there own most of the planet's wealth. Economically speaking, people in these countries are very well off, not because they are smarter or work harder than anyone else, but because they were lucky enough to be born in a rich region of the world.

A second category is **middle-income countries**, *nations with a standard of living about average for the world as a whole.* People in any of these seventy-six nations—many of the countries of Eastern Europe, some of Africa, and almost all of Latin America and Asia—are as likely to live in rural villages as in cities and to walk or ride tractors, scooters, bicycles, or animals as to drive automobiles. On average, they receive six to eight years of schooling. Most middle-income countries also have considerable social inequality within their own borders, so that some people are extremely rich (members of the business elite in nations across North Africa, for example), but many more lack safe housing and adequate nutrition (people living in the shanty settlements that surround Mexico City or Lima, Peru).

The remaining fifty-seven nations of the world are **low-income countries**, *nations with a low standard of living in which most people are poor.* Most of the poorest countries in the world are in Africa, and a few are in Asia. Here, again, a few people are very rich, but the majority struggle to get by with poor housing, unsafe water, too little food, and perhaps most serious of all, little chance to improve their lives.

tip
Read and think about the four reasons to take a global perspective. The overall point is that understanding global patterns both helps us understand our own lives (as Peter Berger would say) and increases our awareness of global problems (as C. Wright Mills would say).

tip
The box below suggests that C. Wright Mills hoped the sociological imagination would spark social change toward a more equal society.

Seeing Sociology in Everyday Life
The Sociological Imagination: Turning Personal Problems into Public Issues

The power of the sociological perspective lies not just in changing individual lives but in transforming society. As C. Wright Mills saw it, society, not people's personal failings, is the cause of poverty and other social problems. The sociological imagination brings people together to create change by transforming personal *problems* into public *issues*.

In the following excerpt, Mills (1959:3–5) explains the need for a sociological imagination:*

When a society becomes industrialized, a peasant becomes a worker; a feudal lord is liquidated or becomes a businessman. When classes rise or fall, a man is employed or unemployed; when the rate of investment goes up or down, a man takes new heart or goes broke. When wars happen, an insurance salesman becomes a rocket launcher; a store clerk, a radar man; a wife lives alone; a child grows up without a father. Neither the life of an individual nor the history of a society can be understood without understanding both.

Yet men do not usually define the troubles they endure in terms of historical change. . . . The well-being they enjoy, they do not usually impute to the big ups and downs of the society in which they live. Seldom aware of the intricate connection between the patterns of their own lives and the course of world history, ordinary men do not usually know what this connection means for the kind of men they are becoming and for the kinds of history-making in which they might take part. They do not possess the quality of mind essential to grasp the interplay of men and society, of biography and history, of self and world. . . .

What they need . . . is a quality of mind that will help them to [see] what is going on in the world and . . . what may be happening within themselves. It is this quality . . . that . . . may be called the sociological imagination.

WHAT DO YOU THINK?

1. As Mills sees it, how are personal troubles different from public issues?
2. Living in the United States, why do we often blame ourselves for the personal problems we face?
3. By using the sociological imagination, how do we gain power over our world?

---

*In this excerpt, Mills uses "man" and male pronouns to apply to all people. Note that even an outspoken critic of society such as Mills reflected the conventional writing practices of his time as far as gender was concerned.

Comparisons between the United States and other nations are made for four reasons:

1. **Where we live shapes the lives we lead.** As we saw in Global Map 1, women living in rich and poor countries have very different lives, as suggested by the number of children they have. To understand ourselves and appreciate how others live, we must understand something about how countries differ, which is one good reason to pay attention to the global maps found throughout this text.

2. **Societies throughout the world are increasingly interconnected.** Historically, people in the United States took only passing note of the countries beyond our own borders. In recent decades, however, this country and the rest of the world have become linked as never before. Electronic technology now transmits sounds, pictures, and written documents around the globe in seconds.

One effect of new technology is that people the world over now share many tastes in food, clothing, and music. Rich countries such as the United States influence other nations, whose people are ever more likely to gobble up our Big Macs and Whoppers, dance to the latest hip-hop music, and speak the English language.

But the larger world also has an impact on us. We all know the contributions of famous immigrants such as Arnold Schwarzenegger (who came to the United States from Austria) and Gloria Estefan (who came from Cuba). More than 1 million immigrants enter the United States each year, bringing their skills and talents, along with their fashions and foods, greatly increasing the racial and cultural diversity of this country.

Trade across national boundaries has also created a global economy. Large corporations make and market goods worldwide. Stock traders in New York pay close attention to

Thinking Globally
The Global Village: A Social Snapshot of Our World

The Earth is home to 6.6 billion people who live in the cities and villages of 193 nations. To grasp the social shape of the world, imagine shrinking the planet's population to a "global village" of just 1,000 people. In this village, more than half (610) of the inhabitants are Asian, including 200 citizens of the People's Republic of China. Next, in terms of numbers, we would find 140 Africans, 110 Europeans, 85 people from Latin America and the Caribbean, 5 from Australia and the South Pacific, and just 50 North Americans, including 45 people from the United States.

A close look at this settlement would reveal some startling facts: The village is a rich place, with a spectacular range of goods and services for sale. Yet most of the villagers can only dream about such treasures, because they are so poor: 80 percent of the village's total income is earned by just 200 people.

For most, the greatest problem is getting enough food. Every year, village workers produce more than enough to feed everyone; even so, half the people in the village, including most of the children, do not get enough to eat, and many must go to sleep hungry every night. The worst-off 200 residents (who, together, have less money than the richest person in the village) lack both clean drinking water and safe shelter. Weak and unable to work, their lives are at risk from deadly diseases.

The village has many schools, including a fine university. About 50 inhabitants have completed a college degree, but about one-third of the village's people are not even able to read or write.

We in the United States, on average, would be among the village's richest people.

Although we may think that our comfortable lives are the result of our own talent and hard work, the sociological perspective reminds us that our achievements also result from our nation's privileged position in the worldwide social system.

WHAT DO YOU THINK?

1. Do any of the statistics presented in this box surprise you? Which ones? Why?
2. How do you think the lives of poor people in a lower-income country differ from those typical of people in the United States?
3. Is your "choice" to attend college affected by the country in which you live? How?

Sources: Calculations by the author based on data from Population Reference Bureau (2006) and United Nations Development Programme (2006).

the financial markets in Tokyo and Hong Kong even as wheat farmers in Iowa watch the price of grain in the former Soviet republic of Georgia. Because most new U.S. jobs involve international trade, global understanding has never been more important.

3. **Many social problems that we face in the United States are far more serious elsewhere.** Poverty is a serious problem in the United States, but poverty in Latin America, Africa, and Asia is both more common and more serious. In the same way, although women have lower social standing than men in the United States, gender inequality is even greater in the world's poor countries.

4. **Thinking globally helps us learn more about ourselves.** We cannot walk the streets of a distant city without thinking about what it means to live in the United States. Comparing life in various settings also leads to unexpected lessons. In a squatter settlement in Madras, India, despite desperate poverty, people thrive in the love and support of family members. Why, then, are so many poor people in our own country angry and alone?

Are material things—so central to our definition of a "rich" life—the best way to measure human well-being?

In sum, in an increasingly interconnected world, we can understand ourselves only to the extent that we understand others. Sociology is an invitation to learn a new way of looking at the world around us. But is this invitation worth accepting? What are the benefits of applying the sociological perspective?

How would your life be different if you had been born into an impoverished family in an Asian farming village? What might you be doing right now instead of reading this textbook?

Applying the Sociological Perspective

Applying the sociological perspective is useful in many ways. First, sociology guides many of the laws and policies that shape our lives. Second, on an individual level, making use of the sociological perspective leads to important personal growth and expanded

awareness. Third, for anyone, studying sociology is excellent preparation for the world of work. We will look briefly at these different ways of putting sociology to work.

Sociology and Public Policy

Sociologists have helped shape public policy—the laws and regulations that guide how people in communities live and work—in countless ways, from racial desegregation and school busing to laws regulating divorce. For example, in her study of how divorce affects people's income, the sociologist Lenore Weitzman (1985, 1996) discovered that women who leave marriages typically experience a dramatic loss of income. Recognizing this fact, many states passed laws that have increased women's claims to marital property and enforced fathers' obligations to provide support for women raising their children.

Sociology and Personal Growth

By applying the sociological perspective, we are likely to become more active and aware and to think more critically in our daily lives. Using sociology benefits us in four ways:

1. **The sociological perspective helps us assess the truth of "common sense."** We all take many things for granted, but that does not make them true. One good example is the idea that we are free individuals who are personally responsible for our own lives. If we think we decide our own fate, we may be quick to praise very successful people as superior and consider others with fewer achievements personally deficient. A sociological approach, by contrast, encourages us to ask whether such common beliefs are actually true and, to the extent that they are not, why they are so widely held. The Seeing Sociology in Everyday Life box gives an example of how the sociological perspective sometimes makes us rethink commonsense ideas about other people.

2. **The sociological perspective helps us see the opportunities and constraints in our lives.** Sociological thinking leads us to see that in the game of life, we have a say in how to play our cards, but it is society that deals us the hand. The more we understand the game, the better players we will be. Sociology helps us "size up" our world so that we can pursue our goals more effectively. "In the *Times*" suggests that societal forces play a powerful role in shaping the direction of our lives.

3. **The sociological perspective empowers us to be active participants in our society.** The more we understand how society works, the more active citizens we become. As

One important reason to gain a global understanding is that living in a high-income nation, we can scarcely appreciate the suffering that goes on in much of the world. This family, living in the African nation of Zambia, has none of the security most of us take for granted. In poor nations, children have only a fifty-fifty chance of surviving to adulthood.

Sean Sprague/The Image Works/The Image Works

C. Wright Mills (1959) explained in the box two pages back, it is the sociological perspective that turns a personal problem (such as being out of work) into a public issue (a lack of good jobs). As we come to see how society affects us, we may support society as it is, or we may set out with others to change it.

4. **The sociological perspective helps us live in a diverse world.** North Americans represent just 5 percent of the world's people, and as the remaining chapters of this book explain, many of the other 95 percent live very differently than we do. Still, like people everywhere, we tend to define our own way of life as "right," "natural," and "better." The sociological perspective encourages us to think critically about the relative strengths and weaknesses of all ways of life, including our own.

Careers: The "Sociology Advantage"

Most students at colleges and universities today are very interested in getting a good job. A background in sociology is excellent preparation for the working world. Of course, completing a bachelor's degree in

Seeing Sociology in Everyday Life
Nickel and Dimed: On (Not) Getting By in America

All of us know people who work at low-wage jobs as waitresses at nearby diners, cash register clerks at local drive-throughs, or sales associates at discount stores such as Wal-Mart. We see such people just about every day. Many of us actually *are* such people. In the United States, "common sense" tells us that the jobs people have and the amount of money they make reflect their personal abilities as well as their willingness to work hard.

Barbara Ehrenreich (2001) had her doubts. To find out what the world of low-wage work is really like, the successful journalist and author decided to leave her comfortable middle-class life to live and work in the world of low-wage jobs. She began in Key West, Florida, taking a job as a waitress for $2.43 an hour plus tips. Right away, she found out that she had to work much harder than she ever imagined. By the end of a shift, she was exhausted, but after sharing tips with the kitchen staff, she averaged less than $6 an hour. This was barely above the minimum wage and was just enough to pay the rent on her tiny apartment, buy food, and cover other basic expenses. She had to hope that she didn't get sick, because the job did not provide health insurance and she couldn't afford to pay for a visit to a doctor's office.

After working for more than a year at a number of other low-wage jobs, includ-ing cleaning motels in Maine and working on the floor of a Wal-Mart in Minnesota, she had rejected quite a bit of "common sense." First, she now knew that tens of millions of people with low-wage jobs work very hard every day. If you don't think so, Ehrenreich says, try one of these jobs for yourself. Second, these jobs require not just hard work (imagine thoroughly cleaning three motel rooms per hour all day long) but special skills and real intelligence (try waiting on ten tables in a restaurant at the same time and keeping everybody happy). She found that the people she worked with were, on average, just as smart, clever, and funny as those she knew who wrote books for a living or taught at a college.

Jeff Greenberg/PhotoEdit Inc.

Why, then, do we think of low-wage workers as lazy or as people with less ability? It surprised Ehrenreich to learn that many low-wage workers felt this way about themselves. In a society that teaches us to believe personal ability is everything, we learn to size people up by their jobs. Subject to the constant supervision, random drug tests, and other rigid rules that usually come along with low-wage jobs, Ehrenreich imagined that many people end up feeling unworthy, even to the point of not trying for anything better. Such beliefs, she concludes, help support a society of "extreme inequality," in which some people live better because of the low wages paid to the rest.

WHAT DO YOU THINK?

1. Have you ever held a low-wage job? If so, would you say you worked hard? What was your pay? Were there any benefits?

2. Ehrenreich claims that most well-off people in the United States are dependent on low-wage workers. What do you think she means by this?

3. Do you think most people with jobs at Wendy's or Wal-Mart have a real chance to enroll in college and to work toward a different career? Why or why not?

sociology is the right choice for people who decide they would like to go on to graduate work to eventually become a professor or researcher in this field. Throughout the United States, tens of thousands of men and women teach sociology in universities, colleges, and high schools. But just as many professional sociologists work as researchers for government agencies or private foundations and businesses, gathering important information on social behavior and carrying out evaluation research. In today's cost-conscious world, agencies and companies want to be sure that the programs and policies they set in place get the job done at the lowest cost. Sociologists, especially those with advanced research skills, are in high demand for this kind of work (Deutscher, 1999).

In addition, a smaller but increasing number of professional sociologists work as clinical sociologists. These women and men work, much as clinical psychologists do, with the goal of improving the lives of troubled clients. A basic difference is that sociologists focus on difficulties not in the personality but in the individual's web of social relationships.

The New York Times

E*TRADE B...

MARKET
...ESTATE
AUTOS
ALL CLASSIFIEDS

WORLD
U.S.
Politics
Washington
Education
N.Y./REGION
BUSINESS
TECHNOLOGY
SPORTS
SCIENCE
HEALTH
OPINION
ARTS
Books
Movies
Music
Television
Theater
STYLE
Dining & Wine
Fashion & Style
Home & Garden
Weddings/
Celebrations
TRAVEL

Blogs
Cartoons
Classifieds
Corrections
Crossword/
Games
First Look
Learning
Network
Multimedia
NYC Guide
Obituaries
Podcasts
The Public
Editor
Sunday
Magazine
Weather
Week in Review

NEWSPAPER
Get Home
Delivery
Customer Care
TimesPoints

 NYT Archive Since 1981 | Search

 Get Home Delivery | New York Cloudy 48°F

No Degree, and No Way Back to the Middle Class

By TIMOTHY EGAN
May 24, 2005

SPOKANE, Wash.—Over the course of his adult life, Jeff Martinelli has married three women and buried one of them, a cancer victim. He had a son and has watched him raise a child of his own. Through it all, one thing was constant: a factory job that was his ticket to the middle class.

It was not until that job disappeared, and he tried to find something—anything—to keep him close to the security of his former life that Mr. Martinelli came to an abrupt realization about the fate of a working man with no college degree in 21st-century America.

He has skills developed operating heavy machinery . . . at Kaiser Aluminum, once one of the best jobs in this city of 200,000. His health is fine. He has no shortage of ambition. But the world has changed for people like Mr. Martinelli.

"For a guy like me, with no college, it's become pretty bleak out there," said Mr. Martinelli, who is 50. . . .

His son, Caleb, already knows what it is like out there. Since high school, Caleb has had six jobs, none very promising. Now 28, he may never reach the middle class, he said. But for his father and others of a generation that could count on a comfortable life without a degree, the fall out of the middle class has come as a shock. . . .

They have seen factory gates close and not reopen. They have taken retraining classes for jobs that pay half their old wages. And as they hustle around for work, they have been constantly reminded of the one thing that stands out on their résumés: the education that ended with a high school diploma.

It is not just that the American economy has shed six million manufacturing jobs over the last three decades; it is that the market value of those put out of work . . . has declined considerably over their lifetimes, opening a gap that has left millions of blue-collar workers at the margins of the middle class.

And the changes go beyond the factory floor. Mark McClellan worked his way up from the Kaiser furnaces to management. He did it by taking extra shifts and learning everything he could about the aluminum business.

Still, in 2001, when Kaiser closed, Mr. McClellan discovered that the job market did not value his factory skills nearly as much as it did four years of college. He had the experience, built over a lifetime, but no degree. . . .

He still lives in a grand house in one of the nicest parts of town, and he drives a big white Jeep. But they are a facade.

"I may look middle class," said Mr. McClellan, who is 45 . . . "But I'm not. My boat is sinking fast."

By the time these two Kaiser men were forced out of work, a man in his 50's with a college degree could expect to earn 81 percent more than a man of the same age with just a high school diploma. . . .

Mr. Martinelli refuses to feel sorry for himself. He has a job in pest control now, killing ants and spiders at people's homes, making barely half the money he made at the Kaiser smelter. . . .

Mr. Martinelli and other former factory workers say that, over time, they have come to fear that the fall out of the middle class could be permanent. Their new lives—the frustrating job interviews, the bills that arrive with red warning letters on the outside—are consequences of a decision made at age 18.

. . . Mr. McClellan was a doctor's son. . . . He thought about going to college. But when he got on at Kaiser, he felt he had arrived.

At the time, the decision to skip college was not that unusual, even for a child of the middle class. Despite Mr. McClellan's lack of skills or education beyond the 12th grade, there was good reason to believe that the aluminum factory could get him into middle-class security quicker than a bachelor's degree could, he said.

By 22, he was a group foreman. By 28, a supervisor. By 32, he was in management. Before his 40th birthday, Mr. McClellan hit his earnings peak, making $100,000 with bonuses.

"I had a house with a swimming pool, new cars," he said. "My wife never had to work. I was right in the middle of middle-class America and I knew it and I loved it." . . .

The job lasted just short of 30 years. Kaiser, debt-ridden after a series of failed management initiatives and a long strike, closed the plant in 2001. . . .

Mr. McClellan has yet to find work, living off his dwindling savings and investments from his years at Kaiser. . . .

"Am I scared just a little bit?" he said. "Yeah, I am."

He has vowed that his son David will never do the kind of second-guessing that he is. Even at 16, David knows what he wants to do: go to college and study medicine. . . .

He said he would not make the same choice his father did 27 years earlier. . . .

Mr. McClellan agrees. He is firm in one conclusion, having risen from the factory floor only to be knocked down: "There is no working up anymore."

WHAT DO YOU THINK?

1. In what ways does the operation of society shape what people experience as their personal successes and failures?

2. Why is having a college degree more important now than ever before to increase your job opportunities?

3. Do you think your decision to attend college makes sense in terms of future earnings?

But sociology is not just for people who want to be sociologists. People who work in criminal justice—including jobs in police departments, probation offices, and corrections facilities—gain the "sociology advantage" by learning which categories of people are most at risk of becoming criminals as well as victims, how effective

various policies and programs are at preventing crime, and why people turn to crime in the first place. Similarly, people who work in health care—including doctors, nurses, and technicans—also gain a "sociology advantage" by learning about patterns of health and illness within the population, as well as how factors such as race, gender, and social class affect human health.

The American Sociological Association (2002) reports that sociology is also excellent preparation for jobs in dozens of additional fields, including advertising, banking, business, education, government, journalism, law, public relations, and social work. In almost any type of work, success depends on understanding how various categories of people differ in beliefs, family patterns, and other ways of life. Unless you plan to have a job that never involves dealing with people, you should consider the workplace benefits of learning more about sociology.

Write down five jobs that appeal to you. Then identify ways in which sociological thinking would increase your chances for success in each one.

The Origins of Sociology

Like the "choices" made by individuals, major historical events rarely just "happen." The birth of sociology was itself the result of powerful social forces.

Social Change and Sociology

Striking changes took place in Europe during the eighteenth and nineteenth centuries. Three kinds of change were especially important in the development of sociology: the rise of a factory-based industrial economy, the explosive growth of cities, and new ideas about democracy and political rights.

A New Industrial Economy

During the Middle Ages in Europe, most people plowed fields near their homes or worked in small-scale *manufacturing* (a word derived from Latin words meaning "to make by hand"). By the end of the eighteenth century, inventors used new sources of energy—the power of moving water and then steam—to operate large machines in mills

and factories. Instead of laboring at home, workers became part of a large and anonymous labor force, under the control of strangers who owned the factories. This change in the system of production took people out of their homes, weakening the traditions that had guided community life for centuries.

The Growth of Cities

Across Europe, landowners took part in what historians call the *enclosure movement*—they fenced off more and more farmland to create grazing areas for sheep, the source of wool for the thriving textile mills. Without land, countless tenant farmers had little choice but to head to the cities in search of work in the new factories.

As cities grew larger, these urban migrants faced many social problems, including pollution, crime, and homelessness. Moving through streets crowded with strangers, they found a new, impersonal social world.

Political Change

People in the Middle Ages viewed society as an expression of God's will: From the royalty to the serfs, each person up and down the social ladder played a part in the holy plan. This theological view of society is captured in lines from the old Anglican hymn "All Things Bright and Beautiful":

> The rich man in his castle,
> The poor man at his gate,
> God made them high and lowly
> And ordered their estate.

But as cities grew, tradition came under spirited attack. In the writings of Thomas Hobbes (1588–1679), John Locke (1632–1704), and Adam Smith (1723–1790), we see a shift in focus from a moral obligation to God and king to the pursuit of self-interest. In the new political climate, philosophers spoke of *personal liberty* and *individual rights*. Echoing these sentiments, our own Declaration of Independence states that every person has "certain unalienable rights," including "life, liberty, and the pursuit of happiness."

The French Revolution, which began in 1789, was an even greater break with political and social tradition. The French social analyst Alexis de Tocqueville (1805–1859) thought the changes in society brought about by the French Revolution were so great that they amounted to "nothing short of the regeneration of the whole human race" (1955:13, orig. 1856).

A New Awareness of Society

Huge factories, exploding cities, a new spirit of individualism—these changes combined to make people aware of their surroundings. The new discipline of sociology was born in England, France, and Germany—precisely where the changes were greatest.

Science and Sociology

And so it was that the French social thinker Auguste Comte (1798–1857) coined the term *sociology* in 1838 to describe a new way of looking at society. This makes sociology one of the youngest academic disciplines—far newer than history, physics, or economics, for example.

Of course, Comte was not the first person to think about the nature of society. Such questions fascinated the brilliant thinkers of ancient civilizations, including the Chinese philosopher K'ung Fu-tzu, or Confucius (551–479 B.C.E.), and the Greek philosophers Plato (c. 427–347 B.C.E.) and Aristotle (384–322 B.C.E.).[1] Centuries later, the Roman emperor Marcus Aurelius (121–180), the medieval thinkers Saint Thomas Aquinas (c. 1225–1274) and Christine de Pisan (c. 1363–1431), and the English playwright William Shakespeare (1564–1616) wrote about the workings of society.

Yet these thinkers were more interested in imagining the ideal society than in studying society as it really was. Comte and other pioneers of sociology all cared about how society could be improved, but their major goal was to understand how society actually operates.

Comte (1975, orig. 1851–54) saw sociology as the product of a three-stage historical development. During the earliest, the *theological stage,* from the beginning of human history to the end of the European Middle Ages about 1350 C.E., people took a religious view that society expressed God's will.

With the dawn of the Renaissance in the fifteenth century, the theological approach gave way to a *metaphysical stage* of history in which people saw society as a natural rather than a supernatural system. Thomas Hobbes (1588–1679), for example, suggested that society reflected not the perfection of God so much as the failings of a selfish human nature.

What Comte called the *scientific stage* of history began with the work of early scientists such as the Polish astronomer Copernicus (1473–1543), the Italian astronomer and physicist Galileo (1564–1642), and the English physicist and mathematician Isaac Newton (1642–1727). Comte's contribution came in applying the scien-

Here we see Galileo, one of the great pioneers of the scientific revolution, defending himself before church officials, who were greatly threatened by his claims that science could explain the operation of the universe. Just as Galileo challenged the common sense of his day, pioneering sociologists such as Auguste Comte later argued that society is neither rigidly fixed by God's will nor set by human nature. On the contrary, Comte claimed, society is a system we can study scientifically, and based on what we learn, we can act intentionally to improve our lives.

North Wind Picture Archives

tific approach—first used to study the physical world—to the study of society.[2]

Comte's approach is called **positivism,** *a way of understanding based on science.* As a positivist, Comte believed that society operates according to its own laws, much as the physical world operates according to gravity and other laws of nature.

By the beginning of the twentieth century, sociology had spread to the United States and showed the influence of Comte's ideas. Today, most sociologists still consider science a crucial part of sociology. But we now realize that human behavior is far more complex than the movement of planets or even the actions of other living things. We are creatures of imagination and spontaneity, so human behavior can never fully be explained by rigid "laws of society." In addition, early sociologists such as Karl Marx (1818–1883), whose ideas are discussed

---

[1]The abbreviation B.C.E. means "before the common era." We use this throughout the text instead of the traditional B.C. ("before Christ") to reflect the religious diversity of our society. Similarly, in place of the traditional A.D. (*anno Domini,* or "in the year of our Lord"), we use the abbreviation C.E. ("common era").

[2]Illustrating Comte's stages, the ancient Greeks and Romans viewed the planets as gods; Renaissance metaphysical thinkers saw them as astral influences (giving rise to astrology); by the time of Galileo, scientists understood planets as natural objects moving according to natural laws.

In the Plains and Mountain regions of the country, where population density is very low, people are more isolated and have a higher rate of suicide.

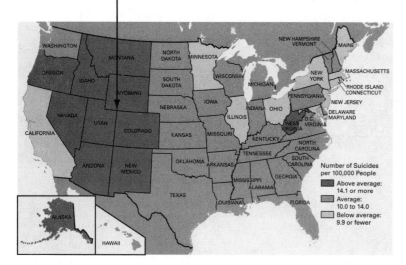

SEEING OURSELVES

NATIONAL MAP 1
Suicide Rates across the United States

This map shows which states have high, average, and low suicide rates. Look for patterns. By and large, high suicide rates occur where people live far apart from one another. More densely populated states have low suicide rates. Do these data support or contradict Durkheim's theory of suicide? Why?

Source: Hoyert et al. (2006).

Number of Suicides per 100,000 People
Above average: 14.1 or more
Average: 10.0 to 14.0
Below average: 9.9 or fewer

---

in Chapter 4 ("Society"), were troubled by the striking inequality of industrial society. They wanted the new discipline of sociology not just to understand society but to bring about change toward social justice.

Sociological Theory

Weaving observations into understanding brings us to another aspect of sociology: theory. A **theory** is *a statement of how and why specific facts are related.* The job of sociological theory is to explain social behavior in the real world. For example, recall Emile Durkheim's theory that categories of people with low social integration (men, Protestants, the wealthy, and the unmarried) are at higher risk of suicide.

As the next chapter ("Sociological Investigation") explains, sociologists test their theories by gathering evidence using various research methods. Durkheim did exactly this, finding out which categories of people were more likely to commit suicide and which were less likely and then devising a theory that best squared with all available evidence. National Map 1 displays the suicide rate for each of the fifty states.

In building theory, sociologists face two fundamental questions: What issues should we study? And how should we connect the facts? In the process of answering these questions, sociologists look to one or more theoretical approaches as "road maps." Think of a **theoretical approach** as *a basic image of society that guides thinking and research.* Sociologists make use of three major theoretical approaches: the structural-functional approach, the social-conflict approach, and the

symbolic-interaction approach, each of which will be explored in the remainder of this chapter.

The Structural-Functional Approach

The **structural-functional approach** is *a framework for building theory that sees society as a complex system whose parts work together to promote solidarity and stability.* As its name suggests, this approach points to **social structure,** *any relatively stable pattern of social behavior.* Social structure gives our lives shape—in families, the workplace, the classroom, and the community. This approach also looks for a structure's **social functions,** *the consequences of any social pattern for the operation of society as a whole.* All social structure, from a simple handshake to complex religious rituals, functions to keep society going, at least in its present form.

The structural-functional approach owes much to Auguste Comte, who pointed out the need to keep society unified at a time when many traditions were breaking down. Emile Durkheim, who helped establish the study of sociology in French universities, also based his work on this approach. A third structural-functional pioneer was the English sociologist Herbert Spencer (1820–1903). Spencer compared society to the human body. Just as the structural parts of the human body—the skeleton, muscles, and various internal organs—function interdependently to help the entire organism survive, social structures work together to preserve society. The structural-functional approach, then, leads sociologists to identify various structures of society and investigate their functions.

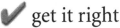 **get it right**

Like the structural-functional approach, the social-conflict approach is concerned with the "functions" or consequences of social patterns. But structural-functional theory looks at the functions of a social pattern for *all* of society; social-conflict theory looks at how a social pattern advantages some categories of people and at the same time harms others.

Robert K. Merton (1910–2003) expanded our understanding of the concept of social function by pointing out that any social structure probably has many functions, some more obvious than others. He distinguished between **manifest functions,** *the recognized and intended consequences of any social pattern,* and **latent functions,** *the unrecognized and unintended consequences of any social pattern.* For example, the manifest function of the U.S. system of higher education is to provide young people with the information and skills they need to perform jobs after graduation. Perhaps just as important, although less often acknowledged, is college's latent function as a "marriage broker," bringing together people of similar social backgrounds. Another latent function of higher education is to limit unemployment by keeping millions of young people out of the labor market, where many of them may not easily find jobs.

But Merton also recognized that the effects of social structure are not all good, and certainly not good for everybody. Thus a **social dysfunction** is *any social pattern that may disrupt the operation of society.* People often disagree about what is helpful and what is harmful to society as a whole. In addition, what is functional for one category of people (say, high profits for factory owners) may well be dysfunctional for another category of people (say, low wages for factory workers).

▶ **CRITICAL REVIEW** The main idea of the structural-functional approach is its vision of society as stable and orderly. The main goal of the sociologists who use this approach, then, is to figure out "what makes society tick."

In the mid-1900s, most sociologists favored the structural-functional approach. In recent decades, however, its influence has declined. By focusing on social stability and unity, critics point out, structural-functionalism ignores inequalities of social class, race, and gender, which cause tension and conflict. In general, its focus on stability at the expense of conflict makes this approach somewhat conservative. As a critical response, sociologists developed the social-conflict approach.

✓ **YOUR LEARNING** How do manifest functions differ from latent functions? Give an example of a manifest function and a latent function of automobiles in the United States.

The Social-Conflict Approach

The **social-conflict approach** is *a framework for building theory that sees society as an arena of inequality that generates conflict and change.* Unlike the structural-functional emphasis on solidarity and stability, this approach highlights inequality and change. Guided by this approach, sociologists investigate how factors such as social class, race,

Applying the structural-functional approach, we look at the functions of various patterns in social life. From this point of view, higher education not only conveys important knowledge and skills to young people but also provides an opportunity for them to gain experience in personal relationships.
Corbis Royalty Free

ethnicity, gender, sexual orientation, and age are linked to a society's unequal distribution of money, power, education, and social prestige. A conflict analysis rejects the idea that social structure promotes the operation of society as a whole, focusing instead on how social patterns benefit some people while hurting others.

Sociologists using the social-conflict approach look at ongoing conflict between dominant and disadvantaged categories of people—the rich in relation to the poor, white people in relation to people of color, and men in relation to women. Typically, people on top try to protect their privileges while the disadvantaged try to gain more for themselves.

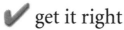
A conflict analysis of our educational system shows how schooling carries class inequality from one generation to the next. For example, secondary schools assign students to either college preparatory or vocational training programs. From a structural-functional point of view, such "tracking" benefits everyone by providing schooling that fits students' abilities. But conflict analysis argues that tracking often has less to do with talent than with social background, so that well-to-do students are placed in higher tracks while poor children end up in the lower tracks.

In this way, young people from privileged families get the best schooling, which leads them to college and, later, to high-income careers. The children of poor families, by contrast, are not prepared for college and, like their parents before them, typically get stuck in low-paying jobs. In both cases, the social standing of one generation is passed on to the next, with schools justifying the practice in terms of individual merit (Bowles & Gintis, 1976; Oakes, 1982, 1985).

Many sociologists use the social-conflict approach not just to understand society but to bring about societal change that would reduce inequality. Karl Marx, whose ideas are discussed at length in Chapter 4 ("Society"), championed the cause of the workers in what he saw as their battle against factory owners. In a well-known statement (inscribed on his monument in London's Highgate Cemetery),

Marx asserted, "The philosophers have only interpreted the world, in various ways; the point, however, is to change it."

Feminism and the Gender-Conflict Approach

One important type of conflict analysis is the **gender-conflict approach,** *a point of view that focuses on inequality and conflict between women and men.* The gender-conflict approach is closely linked to **feminism,** *support of social equality for women and men.*

The importance of the gender-conflict approach lies in making us aware of the many ways in which our way of life places men in positions of power over women: in the home (where men are usually considered the "head of household"), in the workplace (where men earn more income and hold most positions of power), and in the mass media (how many hip-hop stars are women?).

Another contribution of the gender-conflict approach is making us aware of the importance of women to the development of sociology. Harriet Martineau (1802–1876) is regarded as the first woman sociologist. Martineau, who was born to a wealthy English family, made her mark in 1853 by translating the writings of Auguste Comte from French into English. In her own published writings, she documented the evils of slavery and argued for laws to protect factory workers, defending workers' right to unionize. She was particularly concerned about the position of women in society and fought for changes in education policy so that women could look forward to more in life than marriage and raising children.

In the United States, Jane Addams (1860–1935) was a sociological pioneer whose contributions began in 1889 when she helped found Hull House, a Chicago settlement house that provided assistance to immigrant families. Although widely published (she wrote eleven books and hundreds of articles), Addams chose the life of a public activist over that of a university sociologist, speaking out on issues involving immigration and the pursuit of peace. Despite the controversy caused by her pacifism during World War I, she was awarded the Nobel Peace Prize in 1931.

All chapters of this book consider the importance of gender and gender inequality.

The Race-Conflict Approach

Another important type of social-conflict analysis is the **race-conflict approach,** *a point of view that focuses on inequality and conflict between people of different racial and ethnic categories.* Just as men have power over women, white people have numerous social

The social-conflict approach points out patterns of inequality. In general, students are relatively privileged women and men who routinely come into contact with other people who have far fewer opportunities for success. What patterns of social inequality do you see in your everyday life?

David Young-Wolff/PhotoEdit Inc.

tip

A good way to think of a macro-level approach is to imagine yourself using a telescope to look at society from an airplane; you would notice broad patterns, such as whether most people make a living from agriculture, in factories, or in offices. A micro-level approach is more like placing society under a microscope to study in detail how individual people interact in a specific situation.

tip

Harriet Martineau is considered the first woman sociologist.

advantages over people of color, including, on average, higher incomes, more schooling, better health, and longer life.

The race-conflict approach also points out the contributions made by people of color to the development of sociology. Ida Wells Barnett (1862–1931) was born to slave parents but rose to become a teacher and then a journalist and newspaper publisher. She campaigned tirelessly for racial equality and, especially, to put an end to the lynching of black people. She wrote and lectured about racial inequality throughout her life (Lengerman & Niebrugge-Brantley, 1998).

An important contribution to understanding race in the United States was made by William Edward Burghardt Du Bois (1868–1963). Born to a poor Massachusetts family, Du Bois enrolled at Fisk University in Nashville, Tennessee, and then at Harvard University, where he earned the first doctorate awarded by that university to a person of color. Like most people who follow the social-conflict approach (whether focusing on class, gender, or race), Du Bois believed that sociologists should try to solve society's problems. He therefore studied the black community (1967, orig. 1899), spoke out against racial inequality, and served as a founding member of the National Association for the Advancement of Colored People (NAACP). The Thinking About Diversity: Race, Class, & Gender box takes a closer look at the ideas of W. E. B. Du Bois.

We can use the sociological perspective to look at sociology itself. All of the most widely recognized pioneers of the discipline were men. This is because in the nineteenth century, it was all but unheard of for women to be college professors, and few women took a central role in public life. But Harriet Martineau in England, Jane Addams in the United States, and others made contributions to sociology that we now recognize as important and lasting.

Corbis/ Bettmann, (*left*); Brown Brothers, (*right*)

▶ **CRITICAL REVIEW** The various social-conflict approaches have gained a large following in recent decades, but like other approaches, they have met with criticism. Because any conflict analysis focuses on inequality, it largely ignores how shared values and interdependence unify members of a society. In addition, say critics, to the extent that the conflict approaches pursue political goals, they cannot claim scientific objectivity. Supporters of social-conflict approaches respond that *all* theoretical approaches have political consequences.

A final criticism of both the structural-functional and the social-conflict approaches is that they paint society in broad strokes—in terms of "family," "social class," "race," and so on. A third theoretical approach views society less in general terms and more as the everyday experiences of individual people.

✔ **YOUR LEARNING** Why do sociologists characterize the social-conflict approach as "activist"? What is it trying to achieve?

The Symbolic-Interaction Approach

The structural-functional and social-conflict approaches share a **macro-level orientation,** *a broad focus on social structures that shape society as a whole.* Macro-level sociology takes in the big picture, rather like observing a city from high above in a helicopter and seeing how high-

ways help people move from place to place or how housing differs from rich to poor neighborhoods. Sociology also uses a **micro-level orientation,** *a close-up focus on social interaction in specific situations.* Exploring urban life in this way occurs at street level, where you might watch how children invent games on a school playground or how pedestrians respond to homeless people they pass on the street. The **symbolic-interaction approach,** then, is *a framework for building theory that sees society as the product of the everyday interactions of individuals.*

How does "society" result from the ongoing experiences of tens of millions of people? One answer is that society is nothing more than the shared reality that people construct as they interact with one another. That is, human beings live in a world of symbols, attaching *meaning* to virtually everything, from the words on this page to the wink of an eye. "Reality," therefore, is simply how we define our surroundings, our obligations toward others, and even our own identities.

The symbolic-interaction approach has roots in the thinking of Max Weber (1864–1920), a German sociologist who emphasized the need to understand a setting from the point of view of the people in it.

Since Weber's time, sociologists have taken micro-level sociology in a number of different directions. Other contemporary soci-

✤ tip

W. E. B. Du Bois was one of the first persons of color to earn a doctorate in sociology and the first to earn this degree from Harvard University.

Thinking About Diversity: Race, Class, & Gender
An Important Pioneer: Du Bois on Race

One of sociology's pioneers in the United States, William Edward Burghardt Du Bois, did not see sociology as a dry, academic discipline. Rather, he thought of it as the key to solving society's problems, especially racial inequality.

Du Bois spoke out against racial separation and was a founding member of the National Association for the Advancement of Colored People (NAACP). He helped his colleagues in sociology—and people everywhere—see the deep racial divisions in the United States. White people can simply be "Americans," Du Bois pointed out; African Americans, however, have a "double consciousness," reflecting their status as people who are never able to escape identification based on the color of their skin.

In his sociological classic *The Philadelphia Negro: A Social Study,* published in 1899, Du Bois explored Philadelphia's African American community, identifying both the strengths and the weaknesses of people who were dealing with overwhelming social problems on a day-to-day basis. He

challenged the belief—widespread at that time—that blacks were inferior to whites, and he blamed white prejudice for creating the problems that African Americans faced. He also criticized successful people of color for being so eager to win white acceptance that

Brown Brothers

they gave up all ties with the black community, which needed their help.

Du Bois described race as the major problem facing the United States in the twentieth century. Early in his career, he was hopeful about overcoming racial divisions. By the end of his life, however, he had grown bitter, believing that little had changed. At the age of ninety-three, Du Bois left the United States for Ghana, where he died two years later.

WHAT DO YOU THINK?

1. If he were alive today, what do you think Du Bois would say about racial inequality in the twenty-first century?

2. How much do you think African Americans today experience a "double consciousness"?

3. In what ways can sociology help us understand and reduce racial conflict?

Sources: Based in part on Baltzell (1967) and Du Bois (1967, orig. 1899).

---

ologists, including George Homans and Peter Blau, have developed *social-exchange analysis.* In their view, social interaction is guided by what each person stands to gain or lose from the interaction. In the ritual of courtship, for example, people seek mates who offer at least as much—in terms of physical attractiveness, intelligence, and wealth—as they offer in return.

CRITICAL REVIEW Without denying the existence of macro-level social structures such as the family and social class, the symbolic-interaction approach reminds us that society basically amounts to *people interacting.* That is, micro-level sociology tries to show how individuals actually experience society. But on the other side of the coin, by focusing on what is unique in each social scene, this approach risks overlooking the widespread influence of culture, as well as factors such as class, gender, and race.

YOUR LEARNING How does a micro-level analysis differ from a macro-level analysis? Provide an explanation of a social pattern at both levels.

The Applying Theory table summarizes the main characteristics of the structural-functional approach, the social-conflict approach, and the symbolic-interaction approach. Each approach is helpful in answering particular kinds of questions about society. However, the fullest understanding of our social world comes from using all three, as you can see in the following analysis of sports in the United States.

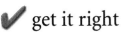

get it right

The Applying Theory table summarizes the three major theoretical approaches in sociology. Study the table to be sure you understand each one.

APPLYING THEORY

Major Theoretical Approaches

	Structural-Functional Approach	Social-Conflict Approach	Symbolic-Interaction Approach
What is the level of analysis?	Macro-level	Macro-level	Micro-level
What image of society does the approach have?	Society is a system of interrelated parts that is relatively stable. Each part works to keep society operating in an orderly way. Members generally agree about what is morally right and morally wrong.	Society is a system of social inequalities based on class (Marx), gender (feminism and gender-conflict approach), and race (race-conflict approach). Society operates to benefit some categories of people and harm others. Social inequality causes conflict that leads to social change.	Society is an ongoing process. People interact in countless settings using symbolic communications. The reality people experience is variable and changing.
What core questions does the approach ask?	How is society held together? What are the major parts of society? How are these parts linked? What does each part do to help society work?	How does society divide a population? How do advantaged people protect their privileges? How do disadvantaged people challenge the system seeking change?	How do people experience society? How do people shape the reality they experience? How do behavior and meaning change from person to person and from one situation to another?

Applying the Approaches: The Sociology of Sports

Who among us doesn't enjoy sports? Children as young as six or seven may play as many as two or three organized sports at a time. For adults, weekend television is filled with sporting events, and whole sections of our newspapers are devoted to reporting the scores. In the United States, top players such as Mark McGwire (baseball), Tiger Woods (golf), and Serena Williams (tennis) are among our most famous celebrities. Sports in the United States are also a multibillion-dollar industry. What sociological insights can the three theoretical approaches give us into this familiar part of everyday life?

The Functions of Sports

A structural-functional approach directs our attention to the ways in which sports help society operate. The manifest functions of sports include providing recreation as well as offering a means of getting in physical shape and a relatively harmless way to let off steam. Sports have important latent functions as well, from building social relationships to creating tens of thousands of jobs across the country. Sports encourage competition and the pursuit of success, both of which are values that are central to our society's way of life.

Sports also have dysfunctional consequences. For example, colleges and universities that try to field winning teams sometimes recruit students for their athletic skill rather than their academic ability. This

Sports and Conflict

A social-conflict analysis of sports begins by pointing out that the games people play reflect their social standing. Some sports—including tennis, swimming, golf, sailing, and skiing—are expensive, so taking part is largely limited to the well-to-do. Football, baseball, and basketball, however, are accessible to people of almost all income levels.

Throughout history, sports have been oriented mostly toward males. For example, the first modern Olympic Games, held in 1896, barred women from competition; in the United States, Little League teams in most parts of the country have only recently let girls play. Traditional ideas that girls and women lack the strength to play sports have now been widely rejected. But our society still encourages men to become athletes while expecting women to be attentive observers and cheerleaders. At the professional level, women also take a back seat to men, particularly in the sports with the most earnings and social prestige.

For decades, big league sports excluded people of color, who were forced to form leagues of their own. Only in 1947 did Major League Baseball admit the first African American player when Jackie Robinson joined the Brooklyn Dodgers. More than fifty years later, professional baseball honored Robinson's amazing career by retiring his number 42 on *all* of the teams in the league. In 2005, African Americans (12 percent of the U.S. population) accounted for 9 percent of Major League Baseball players, 66 percent of National Football League (NFL) players, and 73 percent of National Basketball Association (NBA) players (Lapchick, 2006).

One reason for the increasing number of African Americans in professional sports is that athletic performance—in terms of batting average or number of points scored per game—can be precisely measured and is not influenced by racial prejudice. It is also true that some people of color make a particular effort to excel in athletics, where they see greater opportunity than in other careers (S. Steele, 1990; Hoberman, 1997, 1998; Edwards, 2000; Harrison, 2000). In recent years, in fact, African American athletes have earned higher salaries, on average, than white players.

But racial discrimination still exists in professional sports. For one thing, race is linked to the *positions* athletes play on the field, in a pattern called "stacking." Figure 2 shows the results of a study of race in football. Notice that white athletes are much more likely than African American athletes to play offense and to take the central positions on both sides of the line. More broadly, African Americans have a large share of players in only five sports: baseball, basketball, football, boxing, and track. In all professional sports, the vast majority of managers, head coaches, and owners of sports teams are white (Lapchick, 2006).

DIVERSITY SNAPSHOT

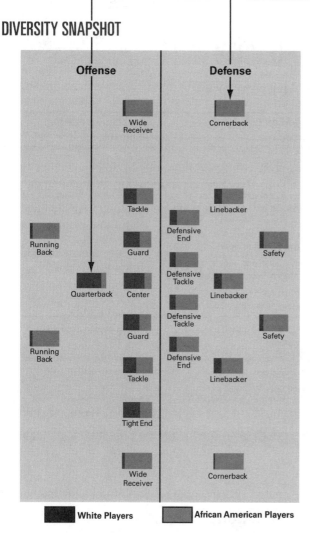

86% of quarterbacks but only 5% of cornerbacks are white.

FIGURE 2 "Stacking" in Professional Football

Does race play a part in professional sports? Looking at the various positions in professional football, we see that white players are more likely to play the central and offensive positions. What do you make of this pattern?

Source: Lapchick (2006).

practice not only lowers the academic standards of a school but also shortchanges athletes who spend little time doing the academic work that will prepare them for later careers (Upthegrove, Roscigno, & Charles, 1999).

get it right

Read this box carefully to understand how sociology's generalizations about social life differ from everyday stereotypes.

 Controversy & Debate

Is Sociology Nothing More than Stereotypes?

JENA: (*raising her eyes from her notebook*) Today in sociology class, we talked about stereotypes.

MARCIA: (*trying to focus on her science lab*) OK, here's one: Roommates don't like to be disturbed when they're studying.

JENA: Seriously, my studious friend, we all have stereotypes, even professors.

MARCIA: (*becoming faintly interested*) Like what?

JENA: Professor Chandler said today in class that Protestants are the people who kill themselves. And then Yannina—this girl from, I think, Ecuador—says something like, "You Americans are rich, you marry, and you love to divorce!"

MARCIA: My brother said to me last week that "Everybody knows you have to be black to play professional basketball." Now there's a stereotype!

College students, like everyone else, are quick to make generalizations about people. And as this chapter has explained, sociologists, too, love to generalize by looking for social patterns. However, beginning students of sociology may wonder if generalizations aren't really the same thing as stereotypes. For example, are the statements reported by Jena and Marcia true generalizations or false stereotypes?

Let's first be clear that a **stereotype** is *a simplified description applied to every person in some category.* Each of the statements made at the beginning of this box is a stereotype that is false for three reasons. First, rather than describing averages, each statement describes every person in some category in exactly the same way; second, even though many stereotypes often contain an element of truth, each statement ignores facts and distorts reality; and third, each statement seems to be motivated by bias, sounding more like a "put-down" than a fair-minded observation.

What about sociology? If our discipline looks for social patterns and makes generalizations, does it express stereotypes? The answer is no, for three reasons. First, *sociologists do not carelessly apply any generalization to everyone in a category.* Second, *sociologists make sure that a generalization squares with the available facts.* And third, *sociologists offer generalizations fair-mindedly, with an interest in getting at the truth.*

Jena remembered her professor saying (although not in quite the same words) that the suicide rate among Protestants is higher than among Catholics or Jews. Based on information presented earlier in this chapter, that is a true statement. However, the way Jena incorrectly reported the classroom remark—"Protestants are the ones who kill themselves"—is not good sociology. It is not a true generalization because the vast majority of Protestants do no such thing. It would be just as wrong to jump to the conclusion that a particular friend, because he is a Protestant male, is about to end his own life.

(Imagine refusing to lend money to a roommate who happens to be a Baptist, explaining, "Well, given the way people like you commit suicide, I might never get paid back!")

Second, sociologists shape their generalizations to the available facts. A more factual version of the statement Yannina made in class is that on average, the U.S. population does have a high standard of living, almost everyone in our society does marry at some point in their lives, and although few people take pleasure in divorcing, our divorce rate is also among the world's highest.

Third, sociologists try to be fair-minded and want to get at the truth. The third statement made by Marcia's brother, about African Americans and basketball, is an unfair stereotype rather than good sociology for two reasons. First, it is simply not true, and second, it seems motivated by bias rather than truth-seeking.

The bottom line is that good sociological generalizations are *not* the same as harmful stereotyping. A college sociology course is an excellent setting for getting at the truth behind common stereotypes. The classroom encourages discussion and offers the factual information you need to decide whether a particular statement is a valid sociological generalization or just a stereotype.

WHAT DO YOU THINK?

1. Can you think of a common stereotype of sociologists? What is it? After reading this box, do you still think it is valid?

2. Do you think taking a sociology course can help correct people's stereotypes? Why or why not?

3. Can you think of a stereotype of your own that might be challenged by sociological analysis?

A sociology classroom is a great place to get at the truth behind common stereotypes.

Photodisc/Getty Images

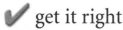 get it right

Both the structural-functional and social-conflict approaches take a broad, or macro-level, view of sports. The symbolic-interaction approach views sports at a micro-level, more the way a particular individual might experience it.

 tip

The Applying Sociology in Everyday Life items provide additional ways for you to connect the ideas found in this chapter with your own life.

As the television show *Friday Night Lights* makes clear, sports are an important element of social life in countless communities across the United States. Sociology's three theoretical approaches all contribute to our understanding of the role of sports in society.

Photofest

Although many individual players get supersized salaries and millions of fans enjoy following their teams, sports are a big business that provides big profits for a small number of people (predominantly white men). In sum, sports in the United States are bound up with inequalities based on gender, race, and economic power.

Sports as Interaction

At the micro-level, a sporting event is a complex, face-to-face interaction. In part, play is guided by the players' assigned positions and the rules of the game. But players are also spontaneous and unpredictable. Following the symbolic-interaction approach, we see sports less as a system than as an ongoing process.

From this point of view, too, we expect each player to understand the game a little differently. Some players enjoy a setting of stiff competition; for others, love of the game may be greater than the need to win.

In addition, the behavior of any single player may change over time. A rookie in professional baseball, for example, may feel self-conscious during the first few games in the big leagues but go on to develop a comfortable sense of fitting in with the team. Coming to feel at home on the field was slow and painful for Jackie Robinson, who knew that many white players, and millions of white fans, resented his presence. In time, however, his outstanding ability and his confident and cooperative manner won him the respect of the entire nation.

The three theoretical approaches—the structural-functional approach, the social-conflict approach, and the symbolic-interaction approach—provide different insights into sports, and none is more correct than the others. Applied to any issue, each approach generates its own interpretations. To appreciate fully the power of the sociological perspective, you should become familiar with all three.

 Apply the three theoretical approaches to the issues that opened this chapter—love and marriage. Consider questions such as these: What categories of people are you most likely to date? Why? Why are today's younger college students likely to wait many more years to marry than students did fifty years ago?

The Controversy & Debate box discusses the use of the sociological perspective and reviews many of the ideas presented in this chapter. This box raises a number of questions that will help you understand how sociological generalizations differ from the common stereotypes we encounter every day.

Applying Sociology in Everyday Life

1. Explore your local area, and draw a sociological map of the community. Include the types of buildings (for example, "big single-family homes," "rundown business area," "new office buildings," "student apartments") found in various places, and guess at the categories of people who live or work there. What patterns do you see?

2. Observe male-female couples holding hands. In almost every case, the male will hold hands with his wrist to the front, and the female will do so with her wrist to the rear. Thinking sociologically, what general societal pattern do you see in this particular situation?

MAKING THE GRADE

The Sociological Perspective

What Is the Sociological Perspective?

The **SOCIOLOGICAL PERSPECTIVE** reveals the power of society to shape individual lives.

- What we comonly think of as personal choice—whether or not to go to college, how many children we will have, even the decision to end our own life—is affected by social forces.
- Peter Berger described the sociological perspective as "seeing the general in the particular."
- C. Wright Mills called this point of view the "sociological imagination," claiming it transforms personal troubles into public issues.
- The experience of being an outsider or of living through a social crisis can encourage people to use the sociological perspective.

sociology the systematic study of human society

sociological perspective the special point of view of sociology that sees general patterns of society in the lives of particular people

The Importance of a Global Perspective

global perspective the study of the larger world and our society's place in it

high-income countries nations with the highest overall standards of living

middle-income countries nations with a standard of living about average for the world as a whole

low-income countries nations with a low standard of living in which most people are poor

Where we live—in a **high-income country** like the United States, a **middle-income country** such as Mexico, or a **low-income country** such as Mali—shapes the lives we lead.

Many social problems that we face in the United States are far more serious in other countries.

Societies throughout the world are increasingly interconnected.

- New technology allows people around the world to share popular trends.
- Immigration from around the world increases the racial and ethnic diversity of the United States.
- Trade across national boundaries has created a global economy.

Learning about life in other societies helps us learn more about ourselves.

Applying the Sociological Perspective

Research by sociologists plays an important role in shaping **public policy**.

On a **personal level**, using the sociological perspective helps us see the opportunities and limits in our lives and empowers us to be active citizens.

A background in sociology is excellent preparation for success in many different **careers**.

Origins of Sociology

positivism a way of understanding based on science

RAPID SOCIAL CHANGE in the eighteenth and nineteenth centuries made people more aware of their surroundings and helped trigger the development of sociology:

- The **rise of an industrial economy** moved work from homes to factories, weakening the traditions that had guided community life for centuries.
- The **explosive growth of cities** created many social problems, such as crime and homelessness.
- **Political change** based on ideas of individual liberty and individual rights encouraged people to question the structure of society.

AUGUSTE COMTE named sociology in 1838 to describe a new way of looking at society.

- Early philosophers had tried to describe the ideal society.
- Comte wanted to understand society as it really is by using **positivism**, a way of understanding based on science.
- Karl Marx and many later sociologists used sociology to try to make society better.

✔ The countries that experienced the most rapid social change were those in which sociology developed first.

MAKING THE GRADE continued . . .

Sociological Theory

A **THEORY** states how facts are related, weaving observations into insight and understanding. Sociologists use three major **THEORETICAL APPROACHES** to describe the operation of society.

 ┌──────── macro-level ────────┐

The **STRUCTURAL-FUNCTIONAL APPROACH** explores how **social structures**—patterns of behavior, such as religious rituals or family life—work together to help society operate.

- Auguste Comte, Emile Durkheim, and Herbert Spencer helped develop the structural-functional approach.
- Thomas Merton pointed out that social structures have both **manifest functions** and **latent functions**; he also identified **social dysfunctions** as patterns that may disrupt the operation of society.

The **SOCIAL-CONFLICT APPROACH** shows how inequality creates conflict and causes change.

- Karl Marx helped develop the social-conflict approach.
- The **gender-conflict approach**, linked to **feminism**, focuses on ways in which society places men in positions of power over women. Harriet Martineau is regarded as the first woman sociologist.
- The **race-conflict approach** focuses on the advantages—including higher income, more schooling, and better health—that society gives to white people over people of color.
- W. E. B. Du Bois identified the "double consciousness" of African Americans.

 micro-level

The **SYMBOLIC-INTERACTION APPROACH** studies how people, in everyday interaction, construct reality.

- Max Weber's claim that people's beliefs and values shape society is the basis of the social-interaction approach.
- Social-exchange analysis states that social life is guided by what each person stands to gain or lose from the interaction.

▦   See the Applying Theory table in the chapter.

✔   *To get the full benefit of the sociological perspective, apply all three approaches.*

Applying the Approaches: The Sociology of Sports

THE FUNCTIONS OF SPORTS

The structural-functional approach looks at how sports help society function smoothly.

- Manifest functions of sports include providing recreation, a means of getting in physical shape, and a relatively harmless way to let off steam.
- Latent functions of sports include building social relationships and creating thousands of jobs.

SPORTS AND CONFLICT

The social-conflict approach looks at the links between sports and social inequality.

- Historically, sports have benefited men more than women.
- Some sports—such as golf, sailing, and skiing— are accessible mainly to affluent people.
- Racial discrimination exists in professional sports.

SPORTS AS INTERACTION

The social-interaction approach looks at the different meanings and understandings people have of sports.

- Within a team, players affect each other's understanding of the sport.
- The reaction of the public can affect how players perceive their sport.

✔   *Sociology helps us understand the difference between well-grounded generalizations and unfair stereotypes.*

---

theory a statement of how and why specific facts are related

theoretical approach a basic image of society that guides thinking and research

structural-functional approach a framework for building theory that sees society as a complex system whose parts work together to promote solidarity and stability

social structure any relatively stable pattern of social behavior

social functions the consequences of any social pattern for the operation of society as a whole

manifest functions the recognized and intended consequences of any social pattern

latent functions the unrecognized and unintended consequences of any social pattern

social dysfunction any social pattern that may disrupt the operation of society

social-conflict approach a framework for building theory that sees society as an arena of inequality that generates conflict and change

gender-conflict approach a point of view that focuses on inequality and conflict between women and men

feminism support of social equality for women and men

race-conflict approach a point of view that focuses on inequality and conflict between people of different racial and ethnic categories

macro-level orientation a broad focus on social structures that shape society as a whole

micro-level orientation a close-up focus on social interaction in specific situations

symbolic-interaction approach a framework for building theory that sees society as the product of the everyday interactions of individuals

stereotype a simplified description applied to every person in some category

MAKING THE GRADE

Sample Test Questions

The Sociological Perspective

These questions are similar to those found in the test bank that accompanies this textbook.

Multiple-Choice Questions

1. **What does the sociological perspective tell us about whom any individual chooses to marry?**
   a. There is no explaining personal feelings like love.
   b. People's actions reflect human free will.
   c. The operation of society guides many of our personal choices.
   d. In the case of love, opposites attract.

2. **Which early sociologist studied patterns of suicide?**
   a. Peter Berger
   b. Emile Durkheim
   c. Auguste Comte
   d. Karl Marx

3. **The personal value of studying sociology includes**
   a. seeing the opportunities and constraints in our lives.
   b. the fact that it is good preparation for a number of jobs.
   c. being more active participants in society.
   d. All of the above are correct.

4. **The discipline of sociology first developed in**
   a. countries experiencing rapid social change.
   b. countries with little social change.
   c. countries with a history of warfare.
   d. the world's poorest countries.

5. **Which early sociologist coined the term *sociology* in 1838?**
   a. Karl Marx
   b. Herbert Spencer
   c. Adam Smith
   d. Auguste Comte

6. **Which theoretical approach is closest to that taken by early sociologists Auguste Comte and Emile Durkheim?**
   a. the symbolic-interaction approach
   b. the structural-functional approach
   c. the social-conflict approach
   d. None of the above is correct.

7. **Which term refers to the recognized and intended consequences of a social pattern?**
   a. manifest functions
   b. latent functions
   c. eufunctions
   d. dysfunctions

8. **Sociology's social-conflict approach draws attention to**
   a. how structure contributes to the overall operation of society.
   b. how people construct meaning through interaction.
   c. patterns of social inequality.
   d. the stable aspects of society.

9. **Which woman, among the first sociologists, studied the evils of slavery and also translated the writings of Auguste Comte?**
   a. Elizabeth Cady Stanton
   b. Jane Addams
   c. Harriet Martineau
   d. Margaret Mead

10. **Which of the following illustrates a micro-level focus?**
    a. the operation of the U.S. political system
    b. patterns of global terrorism
    c. class inequality in the armed forces
    d. two new dormitory roommates getting to know one another

Answers: 1(c); 2(b); 3(d); 4(a); 5(d); 6(b); 7(a); 8(c); 9(c); 10(d).

Essay Questions

1. Explain why applying the sociological perspective can make us seem less in control of our lives. In what ways does it actually give us greater power over our lives?

2. Guided by the discipline's three major theoretical approaches, come up with sociological questions about (a) television, (b) war, and (c) colleges and universities.

Sociological Investigation

Sociology isn't just a way of looking at our surroundings; it is also a system for learning about how society operates and finding out how people experience their world.

© Doranne Jacobson

Sociological Investigation

While on a visit to Atlanta during the winter holiday season, the sociologist Lois Benjamin (1991) called up the mother of an old college friend. Benjamin was eager to learn about Sheba; the two women both had dreamed about earning a graduate degree, landing a teaching job, and writing books. Now a successful university professor, Benjamin had seen her dream come true. But as she soon found out, this was not the case with Sheba.

Benjamin recalled early signs of trouble. After college, Sheba had begun graduate work at a Canadian university. But in letters to Benjamin, Sheba became more and more critical of the world and seemed to be cutting herself off from others. Some wondered if she was suffering from a personality disorder.

Reuben Burrell/Hampton University/Lois Benjamin

But as Sheba saw it, the problem was racism. As an African American woman, she felt she was the target of racial hostility. Before long, she flunked out of school, blaming the failure on her white professors. At this point, she left North America, earning a Ph.D. in England and then settling in Nigeria. In the years since, Benjamin had not heard from her longtime friend.

Benjamin was happy to hear that Sheba had returned to Atlanta. But her delight dissolved into shock when she saw Sheba and realized that her friend had suffered a mental breakdown and was barely responsive to anyone.

For months, Sheba's emotional collapse troubled Benjamin. Obviously, Sheba was suffering from serious psychological problems. Having felt the sting of racism herself, Benjamin wondered if this might have played a part in Sheba's story. Partly as a tribute to her old friend, Benjamin set out to explore the effects of race in the lives of bright, well-educated African Americans in the United States.

Benjamin knew she was calling into question the common belief that race is less of a barrier today than it used to be, especially to talented African Americans (W. J. Wilson, 1978). But her own experiences—and, she believed, Sheba's too—seemed to contradict such thinking.

To test her ideas, Benjamin spent the next two years asking 100 successful African Americans across the country how race affected their lives. In the words of these "Talented One Hundred"[1] men and women, she found evidence that even among privileged African Americans, racism remains a heavy burden.

Later in this chapter, we will take a closer look at Lois Benjamin's research. For now, notice how the sociological perspective helped her spot broad social patterns in the lives of individuals. Just as important, Benjamin's work shows us the *doing* of sociology, the process of *sociological investigation.*

Many people think that scientists work only in laboratories, carefully taking measurements using complex equipment. But as this chapter explains, although some sociologists do conduct scientific research in laboratories, most work on neighborhood streets, in homes and workplaces, in schools and hospitals, in bars and prisons—in short, wherever people can be found.

This chapter examines the methods that sociologists use to conduct research. Along the way, we shall see that research involves not just ways of gathering information but controversies about values: Should researchers strive to be objective? Or should they point to the need for change? Certainly Lois Benjamin did not begin her study just to show that racism exists; she wanted to bring racism out in the open as a way to challenge it. We shall

tackle questions of values after presenting the basics of sociological investigation.

Basics of Sociological Investigation

Sociological investigation starts with two simple requirements. The first was *Apply the sociological perspective.* This point of view reveals curious patterns of behavior all around us that call for further study. It was Lois Benjamin's sociological imagination that prompted her to wonder how race affects the lives of talented African Americans.

This brings us to the second requirement: *Be curious and ask questions.* Benjamin wanted to learn more about how race affects people who are high achievers. She began by asking, Who are the leaders of this nation's black community? What effect does being part of a racial minority have on their view of themselves? On the way white people perceive them and their work?

Seeing the world sociologically and asking questions are basic to sociological investigation. But where do we look for answers? To answer this question, we need to realize that there are various kinds of "truth."

---

[1]W. E. B. Du Bois used the term "Talented Tenth" to refer to African American leaders.

Chapter Overview

This chapter explains how sociologists "do" sociology. First, it looks at science as a way of knowing and then discusses two limitations to scientific sociology that are addressed by two other approaches to knowing—interpretive sociology and critical sociology. Finally, it explains four methods of data collection.

Science as One Form of Truth

Saying that we "know" something can mean many things. Most people in the United States, for instance, say they believe in God. Few claim to have direct contact with God, but they say they believe all the same. We call this kind of knowing "belief" or "faith."

A second kind of truth comes from recognized experts. Students with a health problem, for example, may consult a campus physician or search the Internet for articles written by experts in the field.

A third type of truth is based on simple agreement among ordinary people. Most of us in the United States would probably say we "know" that sexual intercourse among ten-year-old children is wrong. But why? Mostly because just about everyone says it is.

People's "truths" differ the world over, and we often encounter "facts" at odds with our own. Imagine being a Peace Corps volunteer who has just arrived in a small, traditional village in Latin America. Your job is to help local people grow more crops. On your first day in the fields, you observe a strange practice: After planting the seeds, the farmers lay a dead fish on top of the soil. When you ask about this, they explain that the fish is a gift to the god of the harvest. A village elder adds sternly that the harvest was poor one year when no fish were offered.

From that society's point of view, using fish as gifts to the harvest god makes sense. The people believe in it, their experts endorse it, and everyone seems to agree that the system works. But with scientific training in agriculture, you have to shake your head and wonder. The scientific "truth" in this situation is something entirely different: The decomposing fish fertilize the ground, producing a better crop.

Science represents a fourth way of knowing. **Science** is *a logical system that bases knowledge on direct, systematic observation.* Standing apart from faith, the wisdom of "experts," and general agreement, scientific knowledge rests on **empirical evidence,** that is, *information we can verify with our senses.*

Our Peace Corps example does not mean that people in traditional villages ignore what their senses tell them or that members of technologically advanced societies use only science to know things. A medical researcher using science to develop a new drug for treating cancer, for example, may still practice her religion as a matter of faith, turn to financial experts when making decisions about money, and pay attention to the political opinions of her family and friends. In short, we all hold various kinds of truths at the same time.

Common Sense versus Scientific Evidence

Like the sociological perspective, scientific evidence sometimes challenges our common sense. Here are six statements that many North Americans assume are true:

In a complex and ever-changing world, there are many different "truths." This Peace Corps volunteer, who spent a year on a small island in the South Pacific, learned a crucial lesson—that other people often see things in a different way. There is great value in our own scientific approach to truth, but there are also important truths in the ancient traditions of people living around the world.

Rick Rycroft/AP Wide World Photos

1. **"Poor people are far more likely than rich people to break the law."** Not true. If you regularly watch television shows like *Cops,* you might think that police arrest only people from "bad" neighborhoods. Poor people do stand out in the official arrest statistics. But research also shows that police and prosecutors are more likely to treat well-to-do people more leniently, as when a Hollywood celebrity is accused of shoplifting or drunk driving. Some laws are even written in a way that criminalizes poor people more and affluent people less.

2. **"The United States is a middle-class society in which most people are more or less equal."** False. Data show that the richest 5 percent of U.S. families control 60 percent of the nation's total wealth, but almost half of all families have scarcely any wealth at all.

3. **"Most poor people don't want to work."** Wrong. Research indicates that this statement is true of some but not most poor people. In fact, about half of poor individuals in the United States are children and elderly people who are not expected to work.

4. **"Differences in the behavior of females and males are just 'human nature.'"** Wrong again. Much of what we call

student 2 student

"Am I being too far out to say that the world might be a better place if everyone had taken a course in sociology?"

Common sense suggests that in a world of possibilities, people fall in love with that "special someone." Sociological research reveals that the vast majority of people select partners who are very similar in social background to themselves.

Brian Smith/Eyedea Presse/Gamma Press USA, Inc.

"human nature" is constructed by the society in which we live. Further, some societies define "feminine" and "masculine" very differently from the way we do.

5. **"People change as they grow old, losing many interests as they focus on their health."** Not really. Aging changes our personalities very little. Problems of health increase in old age, but by and large, elderly people keep the distinctive personalities they have had throughout their adult lives.

6. **"Most people marry because they are in love."** Not always. To members of our society, few statements are so obvious. Surprisingly, however, in many societies marriage has little to do with love.

These examples confirm the old saying that "it's not what we *don't* know that gets us into trouble as much as the things we *do* know that *just aren't so.*" We have all been brought up believing widely accepted truths, being bombarded by expert advice, and feeling pressure to accept the opinions of people around us. As adults, we need to evaluate more critically what we see, read, and hear. Sociology can help us do just that. "In the *Times*" shows how collecting data leads researchers to a better understanding of recent trends in marriage.

Think of several "commonsense" ideas you were brought up to believe that you later learned were not true.

Three Ways to Do Sociology

"Doing" sociology means learning more about the social world. There is more than one way to do this. Just as sociologists can use one or more theoretical approaches, they may also use different research orientations. The following sections describe three ways to do research: scientific sociology, interpretive sociology, and critical sociology.

Scientific Sociology

Early sociologists such as Auguste Comte and Emile Durkheim applied science to the study of society just as natural scientists investigate the physical world. **Scientific sociology,** then, is *the study of society based on systematic observation of social behavior.* The scientific orientation to knowing, called *positivism,* assumes that an objective reality exists "out there." The job of the scientist is to discover this reality by gathering empirical evidence, facts we can verify with our senses, say, by "seeing," "hearing," or "touching."

Concepts, Variables, and Measurement

A basic element of science is the **concept,** *a mental construct that represents some part of the world in a simplified form.* "Society" is a concept, as are the structural parts of societies, such as "the family" and "the economy." Sociologists also use concepts to describe people, as when we speak of someone's "race" or "social class."

A **variable** is *a concept whose value changes from case to case.* The familiar variable "price," for example, changes from item to item in a supermarket. Similarly, we use the concept "social class" to identify people as "upper-class," "middle-class," "working-class," or "lower-class."

The use of variables depends on **measurement,** *a procedure for determining the value of a variable in a specific case.* Some variables are easy to measure, as when you step on a scale to see how much you weigh. But measuring sociological variables can be far more difficult. For example, how would you measure a person's "social class"? You might look at clothing, listen to patterns of speech, or note a home address. Or trying to be more precise, you might ask about income, occupation, and education.

Because almost any variable can be measured in more than one way, sociologists often have to decide which factors to consider. For example, having a very high income might qualify a person as "upper-class." But what if the income comes from selling automobiles, an occupation most people think of as "middle-class"? Would having only an eighth-grade education make the person "lower-class"? In a case like this, sociologists usually combine these three measures—income, occupation, and education—to assign social class.

The New York Times

Why Are There So Many Single Americans?

BY KATE ZERNIKE
January 21, 2007

The news that 51 percent of all women live without a spouse might be enough to make you invest in cat futures.

But consider, too, the flip side: about half of all men find themselves in the same situation. . . .

When it comes to marriage, the two Americas aren't divided by gender. . . . The emerging gulf is instead one of class—what demographers, sociologists and those who study the often depressing statistics about the wedded state call a "marriage gap" between the well-off and the less so.

Statistics show that college educated women are more likely to marry than non-college educated women—although they marry, on average, two years later. . . . In the past, less educated women often "married up." . . . Now, marriage has become more one of equals; when more highly educated men marry, it tends to be to more highly educated women. . . .

Women with more education also are becoming less likely to divorce, or inclined to divorce, than those with less education. They are even less likely to be widowed all in all, less likely to end up alone.

"Educated women used to have a difficult time," said David Popenoe, co-director of the National Marriage Project at Rutgers University. "Now they're the most desired. . . ."

The difference extends across race lines: black women are significantly less likely to marry than white women, but among blacks, women with a college education are more likely to marry than those who do not.

Among women ages 25–34, 59 percent of college graduates are married, compared with 51 percent of non-college graduates, according to an analysis of the Census Bureau's June 2006 Current Population Survey by Steven P. Martin, a sociologist at the University of Maryland. The same is true at older age groups: the difference is 75 percent to 62 percent for those ages 35–44, and 50 percent to 41 percent among those 65 and older. . . .

Why have things changed so much for women who don't have the choices that educated women have? While marriage used to be something you did before launching a life or career, now it is seen as something you do after you're financially stable —when you can buy a house, say. The same is true for all classes. But the less educated may not get there.

"Women are saying, 'I'm not ready, I want to work for a while, the guys I hang around with don't make enough money . . . ,' " [said Christopher Jencks, professor of social policy at Harvard]. . . .

Women of all education levels figure their earning power will flatten out after they have children, he said. "The longer you wait, the higher the level it flattens out at. That's a good argument to wait. . . ."

Maybe in the past, a man with little education nevertheless had a good-paying manufacturing job, with a health care and pension plan. He was a catch and represented stability.

Today, it may be hyperbolic to talk about the emasculation of the blue-collar man. But it is not only liberals concerned with the wealth gap who are watching these national trends with alarm. Social and religious conservatives have called on society to do more to address economic strains faced by this class.

"Marriage is more difficult today than it was in the past," Mr. Popenoe said. "The people who excel in one area probably excel in that area, too. And people who are high school dropouts probably have a higher propensity to drop out of marriage."

The last 30 years have seen a huge shift in educated women's attitudes about divorce. Mr. Martin, who has written about women and divorce, said that three decades ago, about 30 percent of women who had graduated from college said it should be harder to get a divorce. Now, about 65 percent say so, he said.

But for less educated women and for men, the numbers have not changed; only 40 percent—a minority—say it should be harder to get a divorce.

"The way we used to look at marriage was that if women were highly educated, they had higher earning power, they were more culturally liberal and people might have predicted less marriage among them," Mr. Martin said. "What's becoming more powerful is the idea that economic resources are conducive to stable marriages. Women who have more money or the potential for more money are married to men who have more stable income."

All this leads to a happiness gap, too. According to the Marriage Project, the percentage of spouses who rate their marriage as "very happy" has dropped among those without a college education, while it has risen or held steady among those better educated.

The better educated husbands and wives tend to share intellectual interests and economic backgrounds, as well as ideas about the division of household roles. They also have more earning power. And as in so many other things, in marriage, money helps ease the way.

WHAT DO YOU THINK?

1. What is the class-based "marriage gap"? What are some reasons for this gap?

2. Being economically secure may strengthen marriage, but does being married also help people enjoy higher income? Explain.

3. Have economics played a part in your own decision to marry or not to marry? If so, how?

Adapted from the original article by Kate Zernike published in *The New York Times* on January 21, 2007. Copyright © 2007 by The New York Times Company. Reprinted with permission.

tip

The concepts in this section on scientific sociology are the basic elements of science. They are familiar to anyone doing scientific research not just in sociology but also in other disciplines, including biology, chemistry, and psychology.

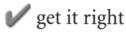

get it right

Be sure you understand the meaning of these concepts: variable, measurement, operationalizing a variable, reliability, and validity.

Seeing Sociology in Everyday Life
Three Useful (and Simple) Descriptive Statistics

The admissions office at your school is preparing a new brochure, and as part of your work-study job in that office, your supervisor asks you to determine the average salary received by last year's graduating class. To keep matters simple, assume that you talk to only seven members of the class (a real study would require contacting many more) and gather the following data on their present incomes:

$30,000	$42,000
$22,000	$165,000
$22,000	$35,000
$34,000	

Sociologists use three different descriptive statistics to report averages. The simplest statistic is the *mode,* the value that occurs most often in a series of numbers. In this example, the mode is $22,000, since that value occurs two times and each of the others occurs only once. If all the values were to occur only once, there would be no mode; if two different values each occurred two or three times, there would be two modes. Although it is easy to identify, sociologists rarely use the mode because it reflects only some of the numbers and is therefore a crude measure of the "average."

A more common statistic, the *mean,* refers to the arithmetic average of a series of numbers, calculated by adding all the values together and dividing by the number of cases. The sum of the seven incomes is $350,000. Dividing by 7 yields a mean income of $50,000. But notice that the mean is not a very good "average" because it is higher than six of the seven incomes and is not particularly close to any of the actual numbers. Because the mean is "pulled" up or down by an especially high or low value (in this case, the $165,000 paid to one graduate, an athlete who signed as a rookie with the Cincinnati Reds farm team), it can give a distorted picture of any data that include one or more extreme scores.

The *median* is the middle case, the value that occurs midway in a series of numbers arranged from lowest to highest. Here the median income for the seven graduates is $34,000, because when the numbers are placed in order from lowest to highest, this value divides the series exactly in half, with three incomes higher and three lower. (With an even number of cases, the median is halfway between the two middle cases.) If there should be any extreme scores, the median (unlike the mean) is not affected by them. In such cases, the median gives a better picture of what is "average" than the mean.

WHAT DO YOU THINK?

1. Your grade point average (GPA) is an example of an average. Is it a mode, a median, or a mean? Explain.

2. Sociologists generally use the median instead of the mean when they study people's incomes. Can you see why?

3. Do a quick calculation of the mean, median, and mode for these simple numbers: 1, 2, 5, 6, 6.

Answers: mode = 6, median = 5, mean = 4.

Sociologists also face the problem of dealing with huge numbers of people. For example, how do you report income for thousands or even millions of U.S. families? Listing streams of numbers would carry little meaning and tells us nothing about the people as a whole. To solve this problem, sociologists use *descriptive statistics* to state what is "average" for a large number of people. The Seeing Sociology in Everyday Life box explains how.

Defining Concepts Measurement is always somewhat arbitrary because the value of any variable partly depends on how it is defined. In addition, deciding how to measure abstract concepts such as "love," "family," or "intelligence" can lead to lengthy debates.

Good research, therefore, requires that sociologists **operationalize a variable** by *specifying exactly what is to be measured before assigning a value to a variable.* Before measuring the concept of social class, for example, you would have to decide exactly what you were

going to measure—say, income level, years of schooling, or occupational prestige. Sometimes sociologists measure several of these things; in such cases, they need to specify exactly how they plan to combine these variables into one overall score. The next time you read the results of a study, notice the way the researchers operationalize each variable. How they define terms can greatly affect the results.

When deciding how to operationalize variables, sociologists often take into account the opinions of the people they study. Since 1977, for example, researchers at the U.S. Census Bureau have defined race and ethnicity as white, black, Hispanic, Asian or Pacific Islander, and American Indian or Alaska Native. One problem with this system is that someone can be *both* Hispanic and white or black; similarly, people of Arab ancestry might not identify with *any* of these choices. Just as important, an increasing number of people in the United States are *multiracial.* Because of the changing face of the U.S. population, the 2000 census was the first one to allow people to describe their

38   SOCIOLOGICAL INVESTIGATION

tip

The reason science places such high value on identifying cause-and-effect relationships is that this knowledge gives us control over the world—the power to change one variable by adjusting another. It also gives us the power to predict; knowing the value of the causal variable, we can predict the value of the effect variable.

 tip

Look at the photo below and carefully read the caption. Notice how this example shows us that in everyday situations, it is often difficult to tell which factor is a "cause" and which is an "effect."

race and ethnicity by selecting more than one category, resulting in a more accurate description of the true diversity of the population.

Reliability and Validity   For a measurement to be useful, it must be reliable and valid. **Reliability** refers to *consistency in measurement*. A measurement is reliable if repeated measurements give the same result time after time. But consistency does not guarantee **validity**, which means *actually measuring exactly what you intend to measure*.

Getting a valid measurement is sometimes tricky. For example, if you want to study how "religious" people are, you might ask the people you are studying how often they attend religious services. But is going to a church, temple, or mosque really the same thing as being religious? People may attend religious services because of deep personal beliefs, but they may also do so out of habit or because others pressure them to go. And what about spiritual people who avoid organized religion altogether? Even when a measurement yields consistent results (making it reliable), it still may not measure what we want it to (and therefore lack validity). Measuring religiosity should take account of not only church attendance but also a person's beliefs and the degree to which a person lives by religious convictions. In sum, careful measurement is important, but it is also often a challenge.

 What specific questions would you ask in order to measure a person's social class position?

Relationships among Variables   Once measurements are made, investigators can pursue the real payoff: seeing how variables are related. The scientific ideal is **cause and effect,** *a relationship in which change in one variable causes change in another.* Cause-and-effect relationships occur around us every day, such as when studying hard for an exam results in a high grade. *The variable that causes the change* (in this case, how much you study) is called the **independent variable.** *The variable that changes* (the exam grade) is called the **dependent variable.** The value of one variable, in other words, depends on the value of another. Why is linking variables in terms of cause and effect important? Because this kind of relationship allows us to *predict* the outcome of future events—if we know one thing, we can accurately predict another. For example, knowing that studying hard results in a better exam grade, we can predict with confidence that if you do study hard for the next exam, you will receive a high grade, and if you do not study hard, your grade will suffer.

Alcohol abuse is common among many homeless people. But knowing that homelessness and alcohol abuse are correlated does not establish cause and effect. Can you see how abusing alcohol could lead to becoming homeless? Can you see how becoming homeless might lead people to abuse alcohol?

argus/Schwarzbach/ Peter Arnold, Inc.

But just because two variables change together does not mean that they are linked by a cause-and-effect relationship. For example, sociologists have long recognized that juvenile delinquency is more common among young people who live in crowded housing. Say we operationalize the variable "juvenile delinquency" as the number of times a person under the age of eighteen has been arrested, and we define "crowded housing" by a home's number of square feet of living space per person. It turns out that these variables are related: Delinquency rates are high in densely populated neighborhoods. But should we conclude that crowding in the home (in this case, the independent variable) is what causes delinquency (the dependent variable)?

Not necessarily. **Correlation** is *a relationship in which two (or more) variables change together.* We know that density and delinquency are correlated because they change together, as shown in part (a) of Figure 1. This relationship *may* mean that crowding causes more arrests, but it could also mean that some third factor is at work causing change in *both* of the variables under observation. To identify a third variable, think what kind of people live in crowded housing: people with less money and few choices—the poor. Poor children are also more likely to end up with police records. In reality, crowded housing and juvenile delinquency are found together because *both* are caused by a third factor—poverty—

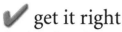 **get it right**

Correlation is not the same as cause and effect. To claim cause and effect, two variables must show correlation, the causal variable must come first, and there can be no evidence that the correlation is spurious.

 tip

Spurious is another way of saying "false."

FIGURE 1   Correlation and Cause: An Example

Correlation is not the same as cause. Here's why.

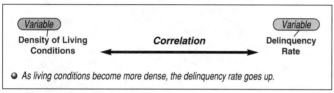

(a) If two variables increase and decrease together, they display correlation.

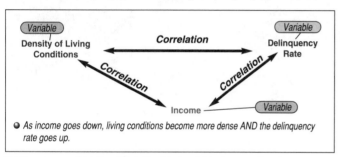

(b) Here we consider the effect of a third variable: income. Low income may cause *both* high-density living conditions *and* a high delinquency rate.

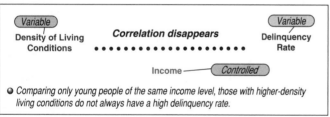

(c) When we control for income—that is, examine only young people of the same income level—we find that density of living conditions and delinquency rate no longer increase and decrease together.

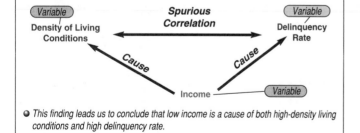

(d) Density of living conditions and delinquency rate are correlated, but their correlation is *spurious* because neither one causes the other.

as shown in part (b) of Figure 1. In short, the apparent connection between crowding and delinquency is "explained away" by a third variable—low income—that causes them both to change. So our original connection turns out to be a **spurious correlation,** *an apparent but false relationship between two (or more) variables that is caused by some other variable.*

Exposing a correlation as spurious requires a bit of detective work, assisted by a technique called **control,** *holding constant all variables except one in order to see clearly the effect of that variable.* In our example, we suspect that income level may be causing a spurious link between housing density and delinquency. To check whether the correlation between delinquency and crowding is spurious, we control for income—that is, we hold income constant by looking at only young people of one income level. If the correlation between density and delinquency remains, that is, if young people of the same income level living in more crowded housing show higher rates of arrest than young people in less crowded housing, we have more reason to think that crowding does, in fact, cause delinquency. But if the relationship disappears when we control for income, as shown in part (c) of Figure 1, then we know we were dealing with a spurious correlation. In fact, research shows that the correlation between crowding and delinquency just about disappears if income is controlled (Fischer, 1984). So we have now sorted out the relationship among the three variables, as illustrated in part (d) of the figure. Housing density and juvenile delinquency have a spurious correlation; evidence shows that both variables rise or fall according to income.

To sum up, correlation means only that two (or more) variables change together. To establish cause and effect, three requirements must be met: (1) a demonstrated correlation, (2) an independent (or causal) variable that occurs before the dependent variable, and (3) no evidence that a third variable could be causing a spurious correlation between the two.

Natural scientists usually have an easier time than social scientists in identifying cause-and-effect relationships because most natural scientists work in laboratories, where they can control other variables. Carrying out research in a workplace or on the streets, however, makes control very difficult, so sociologists often have to settle for demonstrating only correlation. Also, human behavior is highly complex, involving dozens of causal variables at any one time, so establishing all the cause-and-effect relationships in any situation is extremely difficult.

The Ideal of Objectivity

Ten students are sitting around a dorm lounge discussing the dream vacation spot for the upcoming spring break. Do you think one place will end up being everyone's clear favorite? That hardly seems likely.

In scientific terms, each of the ten people probably operationalizes the concept "dream vacation" differently. For one, it might be a

tip

The scientific ideal of researcher objectivity assumes the existence of a reality "out there" that we can understand by using our senses. By contrast, interpretive sociology, discussed below, claims that our subjectivity is the key to a reality that is within our minds.

get it right

Be sure you understand the difference between Weber's concepts of value-free and value-relevant research.

deserted, sunny beach in Mexico; for another, the choice might be New Orleans, a lively city with a very active social scene; for still another, hiking the Rocky Mountains below snow-capped peaks may be the choice. Like so many other "bests" in life, the best vacations turn out to be mostly a matter of individual taste.

Personal values are fine when it comes to choosing travel destinations, but they pose a challenge to scientific research. Remember, science assumes that reality is "out there." Scientists need to study this reality without changing it in any way, and so they strive for **objectivity**, *personal neutrality in conducting research*. Objectivity means that researchers carefully hold to scientific procedures and do not let their own attitudes and beliefs influence the results.

Scientific objectivity is an ideal rather than a reality, of course, because no one can be completely neutral. Even the topic someone chooses to study reflects a personal interest of one sort or another, as Lois Benjamin showed us in the reasons for her decision to investigate race. But the scientific ideal is to keep a professional distance or sense of detachment from the results, however they turn out. With this ideal in mind, you should do your best when conducting research to see that conscious or unconscious biases do not distort your findings. As an extra precaution, many researchers openly state their personal leanings in their research reports so that readers can interpret the conclusions with them in mind.

The influential German sociologist Max Weber expected that people would select their research topics according to their personal beliefs and interests. Why else, after all, would one person study world hunger, another investigate the effects of racism, and still another examine how children manage in one-parent families? Knowing that people select topics that are *value-relevant*, Weber cautioned researchers to be *value-free* in their investigations. Only by controlling their personal feelings and opinions (as we expect any professionals to do) can researchers study the world *as it is* rather than tell us *how they think it should be*. This detachment, for Weber, is a crucial element of science that sets it apart from politics. Politicians are committed to particular outcomes; scientists try to maintain an open mind about the results of their investigations, whatever they may turn out to be.

Weber's argument still carries much weight, although most sociologists admit that we can never be completely value-free or even aware of all our biases. Keep in mind, however, that sociologists are not "average" people: Most are white, highly educated, and more politically liberal than the population as a whole (Klein & Stern, 2004). Remember that sociologists, like everyone else, are influenced by their social backgrounds.

One way to limit distortion caused by personal values is **replication**, *repetition of research by other investigators*. If other researchers repeat a study using the same procedures and obtain the same results, we gain

One principle of scientific research is that sociologists and other investigators should try to be objective in their work, so that their personal values and beliefs do not distort their findings. But such a detached attitude may discourage the relationship needed in order for people to open up and share information. Thus sociologists have to decide how much to pursue objectivity and how much to show their own feelings.

© Doranne Jacobson/International Images

confidence that the results are accurate (both reliable and valid). The need for replication in scientific investigation probably explains why the search for knowledge is called "*re*-search" in the first place.

Keep in mind that the logic of science does not guarantee objective, absolute truth. What science offers is an approach to knowledge that is *self-correcting* so that in the long run, researchers stand a good chance of limiting their biases. Objectivity and truth lie, then, not in any one study but in the scientific process itself as it continues over time.

Why do you think many doctors, teachers, and police officers avoid working professionally with their own children?

Some Limitations of Scientific Sociology

Science is one important way of knowing. Yet, applied to social life, science has several important limitations.

1. **Human behavior is too complex for sociologists to predict any individual's actions precisely.** Astronomers calculate the movement of objects in the skies with remarkable precision, but comets and planets are unthinking objects. Humans, by contrast, have minds of their own, so no two people react to any event (whether it be a sports victory or a natural disaster) in exactly the same way. Sociologists must therefore be satisfied with showing that *categories* of people *typically* act in one way or another. This is not a failing of sociology. It simply reflects the fact that we study creative, spontaneous people.

2. **Because humans respond to their surroundings, the mere presence of a researcher may affect the behavior being studied.** An astronomer's gaze has no effect whatever on a distant comet. But most people react to being observed. Try staring at someone for a few minutes and see for yourself. People being watched may become anxious, angry, or defensive; others may be especially friendly or helpful. We can change people just by studying them.

3. **Social patterns change; what is true in one time or place may not hold true in another.** The same laws of physics will apply tomorrow as today, and they hold true all around the world. But human behavior is so variable that there are no universal sociological laws.

4. **Because sociologists are part of the social world they study, being value-free when conducting social research is difficult.** Barring a laboratory mishap, chemists are rarely personally affected by what goes on in test tubes. But sociologists live in their "test tube," the society they study. Therefore, social scientists may find it difficult to control—or even to recognize—personal values that may distort their work.

Interpretive Sociology

All sociologists agree that studying social behavior scientifically presents some real challenges. But some sociologists go further, suggesting that science as it is used to study the natural world misses a vital part of the social world: *meaning.*

As humans, we do not simply act; we act for a reason. Max Weber, who pioneered this orientation, argued that the proper focus of

A basic lesson of social research is that being observed affects how people behave. Researchers can never be certain precisely how this will occur; some people resent public attention, but others become highly animated when they think they have an audience.

Steve McCurry/Magnum Photos, Inc. (*left*); Argas/Getty Images, Inc—Liaison (*right*)

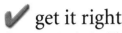 get it right

Be sure you understand the difference between
quantitative and qualitative data.

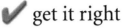 get it right

Pay special attention to the discussion at the
bottom of this column that links theoretical
approaches to research orientations.

sociology must go beyond just observing behavior to include *interpretation*—learning what meaning people find in what they do. **Interpretive sociology** is *the study of society that focuses on the meanings people attach to their social world.*

The Importance of Meaning

Interpretive sociology differs from scientific, or positivist, sociology in three ways. First, scientific sociology focuses on actions, what people do; interpretive sociology, by contrast, focuses on the meaning people attach to their actions. Second, scientific sociology sees an objective reality "out there," but interpretive sociology sees reality constructed by people themselves in the course of their everyday lives. Third, scientific sociology tends to favor *quantitative* data—numerical measurements of people's behavior—and interpretive sociology favors *qualitative* data, or how people understand their surroundings.

The scientific orientation is well suited to research in a laboratory, where investigators stand back and take careful measurements. The interpretive orientation is better suited to research in a natural setting, where investigators interact with people, learning how they make sense of their everyday lives.

Weber's Concept of *Verstehen*

Weber believed the key to interpretive sociology lay in *Verstehen* (pronounced "ver-SHTAY-in"), the German word for "understanding." The interpretive sociologist does not just observe *what* people do but also tries to understand *why* they do it. The thoughts and feelings of subjects—which scientists tend to dismiss because they are difficult to measure—are the focus of the interpretive sociologist's attention.

Critical Sociology

There is a third research orientation in sociology. Like the interpretive orientation, critical sociology developed in reaction to the limitations of scientific sociology. This time, however, the problem was the foremost principle of scientific research: objectivity.

Scientific sociology holds that reality is "out there" and the researcher's task is to study and document this reality. But Karl Marx, who founded the critical orientation, rejected the idea that society exists as a "natural" system with a fixed order. To assume this, he claimed, is the same as saying that society cannot be changed. Scientific sociology, from this point of view, ends up supporting the status quo. **Critical sociology,** by contrast, is *the study of society that focuses on the need for social change.*

The Importance of Change

Rather than asking the scientific question "How does society work?" critical sociologists ask moral and political questions, such as "Should society exist in its present form?" Their answer to this question, typically, is that it should not. One recent account of this orientation, echoing Marx, claims that the point of sociology is "not just to research the social world but to change it in the direction of democracy and social justice" (Feagin & Hernán, 2001:1). In making value judgments about how society should be improved, critical sociology rejects Weber's goal that researchers be value-free and emphasizes instead that they should be social activists in pursuit of desirable change.

Sociologists using the critical orientation seek to change not just society but the character of research itself. They often identify personally with their research subjects and encourage them to help decide what to study and how to do the work. Typically, researchers and subjects use their findings to provide a voice for less powerful people and to advance the political goal of a more equal society (B. B. Hess, 1999; Feagin & Hernán, 2001; Perrucci, 2001).

Sociology as Politics

Scientific sociologists object to taking sides in this way, charging that critical sociology (whether feminist, Marxist, or some other critical orientation) becomes political, lacks objectivity, and cannot correct for its own biases. Critical sociologists reply that *all* research is political or biased—either it calls for change or it does not. Sociologists, they continue, have no choice about their work being political, but they can choose *which* positions to support.

Critical sociology is an activist orientation tying knowledge to action, seeking not just to understand the world but also to improve it. Generally speaking, scientific sociology tends to appeal to researchers with nonpolitical or conservative political views; critical sociology appeals to those whose politics range from liberal to radical left.

Research Orientations and Theory

Is there a link between research orientations and sociological theory? There is no precise connection, but each of the three research orientations—scientific, interpretive, and critical—does stand closer to one of the theoretical approaches. Scientific sociology corresponds to the structural-functional approach, interpretive sociology is related to the symbolic-interaction approach, and critical sociology is linked to the social-conflict approach. The Summing Up table provides a quick review of the differences among the three research orientations. Many sociologists favor one orientation over another; however,

tip

Looking closely at the Summing Up tables is a good way to check how well you understand the material. If you don't understand any of the material in this table, go back and review the section "Three Ways to Do Sociology."

tip

Gender affects almost every aspect of social life—including doing research. The discussion on this page explains how.

SUMMING UP

Three Research Orientations in Sociology

	Scientific	Interpretive	Critical
What is reality?	Society is an orderly system. There is an objective reality "out there."	Society is ongoing interaction. People construct reality as they attach meanings to their behavior.	Society is patterns of inequality. Reality is that some categories of people dominate others.
How do we conduct research?	Researcher gathers empirical, ideally quantitative, data. Researcher tries to be a neutral observer.	Researcher develops a qualitative account of the subjective sense people make of their world. Researcher is a participant.	Research is a strategy to bring about desired social change. Researcher is an activist.
Corresponding theoretical approach	Structural-functional approach	Symbolic-interaction approach	Social-conflict approach

because each provides useful insights, it is a good idea to become familiar with all three (Gamson, 1999).

Gender and Research

In recent years, sociologists have become aware that research is affected by **gender,** *the personal traits and social positions that members of a society attach to being female or male.* Margrit Eichler (1988) identifies five ways in which gender can shape research:

1. **Androcentricity.** Androcentricity refers to approaching an issue from a male perspective (*andro-* in Greek means "male"; *centricity* means "being centered on"). Sometimes researchers act as if only men's activities are important, ignoring what women do. For years, researchers studying occupations focused on the paid work of men and overlooked the housework and child care traditionally performed by women. Clearly, research that seeks to understand human behavior cannot ignore half of humanity.

   Gynocentricity—seeing the world from a female perspective—can also limit good sociological investigation. However, in our male-dominated society, this problem arises less often.

2. **Overgeneralizing.** This problem occurs when researchers use data drawn from people of only one sex to support conclusions about "humanity" or "society." Gathering information by talking to only male students and then drawing conclusions about an entire campus would be an example of overgeneralizing.

3. **Gender blindness.** Failing to consider the variable of gender at all is known as gender blindness. As is evident throughout this book, the lives of men and women differ in countless ways. A study of growing old in the United States might suffer from gender blindness if it overlooked the fact that most elderly men live with their wives but elderly women typically live alone.

4. **Double standards.** Researchers must be careful not to distort what they study by judging men and women differently. For example, a family researcher who labels a couple as "man and wife" may define the man as the "head of household" and treat him accordingly and assume that the woman simply engages in family "support work."

5. **Interference.** Another way gender can distort a study is if a subject reacts to the sex of the researcher, interfering with the research operation. While studying a small community in Sicily, for instance, Maureen Giovannini (1992) found that many men treated her as a woman rather than as a researcher. Some thought it was wrong for any single woman to speak privately with a man. Others denied Giovannini access to places they considered off-limits to women.

There is nothing wrong with focusing research on one sex or the other. But all sociologists, as well as people who read their work, should be aware of the importance of gender in any investigation.

Think of three research topics in U.S. society that might be affected by the gender of the researcher. In each case, explain why.

tip

The following pages describe four methods of sociological research, beginning with the experiment and including survey research, participant observation, and the use of existing data.

get it right

The experiment is the method that comes closest to the logic of science. Experiments are rare in sociology because the high level of control that they require usually can only be achieved in a laboratory rather than in the "real world." The example of an experiment, two pages ahead, was carried out by Philip Zimbardo, a psychologist.

Research Ethics

Like all researchers, sociologists must be aware that research can harm as well as help subjects or communities. For this reason, the American Sociological Association (ASA)—the major professional association of sociologists in North America—has established formal guidelines for conducting research (1997).

Sociologists must try to be skillful and fair-minded in their work. They must disclose all research findings without omitting significant data. They should make their results available to other sociologists who want to replicate a study.

Sociologists must also make sure that the subjects taking part in a research project are not harmed, and they must stop their work right away if they suspect that any subject is at risk of harm. Researchers are also required to protect the privacy of anyone involved in a research project, even if they come under pressure from the police or the courts to release confidential information. Researchers must also get the *informed consent* of participants, which means that subjects understand the responsibilities and risks that the research involves and agree—before the work begins—to take part.

Another important guideline concerns funding. Sociologists must include in their published results the sources of all financial support. They must also avoid taking money that raises concerns of conflicts of interest. For example, researchers must never accept funding from an organization that seeks to influence the research results for its own purposes.

The federal government also plays a part in research ethics. Every college and university that seeks federal funding for research involving human subjects must have an *institutional review board* (IRB) to review grant applications and ensure that research will not violate ethical standards.

Finally, there are global dimensions to research ethics. Before beginning research in another country, an investigator must become familiar enough with that society to understand what people *there* are likely to regard as a violation of privacy or a source of personal danger. In a multicultural society such as the United States, the same rule applies to studying people whose cultural background differs from your own. The Thinking About Diversity: Race, Class, & Gender box offers some tips about how outsiders can effectively and sensitively study Hispanic communities.

Methods of Sociological Research

A **research method** is *a systematic plan for doing research.* The remainder of this chapter introduces four commonly used methods of sociological investigation: experiments, surveys, participant observation,

If you ask only male subjects about their attitudes or actions, you may be able to support conclusions about "men" but not more generally about "society." What would a researcher have to do to ensure that research data support conclusions about all of society?

Jeff Greenberg/The Image Works

and the use of existing data. None is better or worse than any other. Rather, in the same way that a carpenter selects a particular tool for a specific task, researchers choose a method—or mix several methods—according to whom they plan to study and what they wish to learn.

Testing a Hypothesis: The Experiment

The logic of science is most clearly found in the **experiment,** *a research method for investigating cause and effect under highly controlled conditions.* Experimental research is *explanatory;* that is, it asks not just what happens but why. Typically, researchers devise an experiment to test a **hypothesis,** *a statement of a possible relationship between two (or more) variables.* A hypothesis typically takes the form of an *if-then* statement: *If* one thing were to happen, *then* something else will result.

The ideal experiment consists of four steps. First, the researcher specifies the variable that is assumed to cause the change (the independent variable, or the "cause") as well as the variable that is changed (the dependent variable, or the "effect"). Second, the researcher measures the initial value of the dependent variable. Third, the researcher exposes the dependent variable to the independent variable (the "treatment"). Fourth, the researcher again measures the dependent variable to see what change took place. If the expected change did occur, the experiment supports the hypothesis; if not, the hypothesis must be modified.

Thinking About Diversity: Race, Class, & Gender
Studying the Lives of Hispanics

JORGE: If you are going to include Latinos in your research, you need to learn a little about their culture.

MARK: I'm interviewing lots of different families. What's special about interviewing Latinos?

JORGE: Sit down and I'll tell you a few things you need to know . . .

Because U.S. society is racially, ethnically, and religiously diverse, all of us have to work with people who differ from ourselves. The same is true of sociologists. Learning—in advance—the ways of life of any category of people can ease the research process and ensure that there will be no hard feelings when the work is finished.

Gerardo Marín and Barbara Van Oss Marín (1991) have identified five areas of concern in conducting research with Hispanic people:

1. **Be careful with terms.** The Maríns point out that the term "Hispanic" is a label of convenience used by the U.S. Census Bureau. Few people of Spanish descent think of themselves as "Hispanic" or "Latino"; most identify with a particular country (generally, with a Latin American nation, such as Mexico or Argentina, or with Spain).

2. **Be aware of cultural differences.** By and large, the United States is a nation of individualistic, competitive people. Many Hispanics, by contrast, place more value on cooperation and com-

munity. An outsider, then, may judge the behavior of a Hispanic subject as conformist or overly trusting when in fact the person is simply trying to be helpful. Researchers should also realize that Hispanic respondents might agree with a particular statement merely out of politeness.

3. **Anticipate family dynamics.** Generally speaking, Hispanic cultures have strong family loyalties. Asking subjects to reveal information about another family member may make them uncomfortable or even angry. The Maríns add that in the home, a researcher's request to speak privately with a Hispanic woman may provoke suspicion or outright disapproval from her husband or father.

4. **Take your time.** Spanish cultures, the Maríns explain, tend to place the quality of relationships above simply getting a job done. A non-Hispanic researcher who tries to hurry an interview with a Hispanic family, perhaps wishing not to delay the

family's dinner, may be considered rude for not proceeding at a more sociable and relaxed pace.

5. **Think about personal space.** Finally, people of Spanish-speaking ancestry typically maintain closer physical contact than many non-Hispanics. As a result, researchers who seat themselves across the room from their subjects may appear standoffish. Researchers might also wrongly label Hispanics as "pushy" when they move closer than non-Hispanic people find comfortable.

Of course, Hispanics differ among themselves, just like people in every other category, and these generalizations apply to some more than to others. But we need to be aware of them. The challenge of being culturally aware is especially great in the United States, where hundreds of categories of people make up our multicultural society.

WHAT DO YOU THINK?

1. Give a specific example of damage to a study that might take place if researchers are not sensitive to the culture of their subjects.

2. What do researchers need to do to avoid the kinds of problems noted in this box?

3. Discuss the research process with classmates from various cultural backgrounds. How are the concerns raised by people of different cultural backgrounds similar? How do they differ?

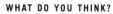
Tony Freeman/PhotoEdit Inc.

tip

Because the Zimbardo research raised the possibility of harm to subjects, it helped launch the development of research ethics in social science.

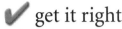

get it right

In the Zimbardo experiment described below, be sure you understand that the independent variable is the prison setting and the dependent variable is the violence that occurs.

But a change in the dependent variable could be due to something other than the supposed cause. (Think back to our discussion of spurious correlations.) To be certain that they identify the correct cause, researchers carefully control other factors that might affect the outcome of the experiment. Such control is easiest in a laboratory, a setting specially constructed to neutralize outside influences.

Another strategy to gain control is dividing subjects into an *experimental group* and a *control group*. Early in the study, the researcher measures the dependent variable for subjects in both groups but later exposes only the experimental group to the independent variable or treatment. (The control group typically gets a *placebo*, a treatment that the members of the group think is the same but really has no effect on the experiment.) Then the investigator measures the subjects in both groups again. Any factor occurring during the course of the research that influences people in the experimental group (say, a news event) would do the same to those in the control group, thus controlling or "washing out" the factor. By comparing the before and after measurements of the two groups, a researcher can learn how much of the change is due to the independent variable.

 YOUR LEARNING How does the experiment allow researchers to reach conclusions about cause and effect?

The Hawthorne Effect

Researchers need to be aware that subjects' behavior may change simply because they are getting special attention, as one classic experiment revealed. In the late 1930s, the Western Electric Company hired researchers to investigate worker productivity in its Hawthorne factory near Chicago (Roethlisberger & Dickson, 1939). One experiment tested the hypothesis that increasing the available lighting would raise worker output. First, researchers measured worker productivity (the dependent variable). Then they increased the lighting (the independent variable) and measured output a second time. The resulting increased productivity supported the hypothesis. But when the research team later turned the lighting back down, productivity increased again. What was going on? In time, the researchers realized that the employees were working harder (even if they could not see as well) simply because people were paying attention to them and measuring their output. From this research, social scientists coined the term **Hawthorne effect** to refer to *a change in a subject's behavior caused simply by the awareness of being studied.*

Illustration of an Experiment: The Stanford County Prison

Prisons can be violent settings, but is this due simply to the "bad" people who end up there? Or as Philip Zimbardo suspected, does the prison itself somehow generate violent behavior? This question led Zimbardo to devise a fascinating experiment, which he called the "Stanford County Prison" (Zimbardo, 1972; Haney, Banks, & Zimbardo, 1973).

Zimbardo thought that once inside a prison, even emotionally healthy people are prone to violence. Thus Zimbardo treated the *prison setting* as the independent variable capable of causing *violence,* the dependent variable.

To test this hypothesis, Zimbardo's research team constructed a realistic-looking "prison" in the basement of the psychology building on the campus of California's Stanford University. Then they placed an ad in the local newspaper, offering to pay young men to help with a two-week research project. To each of the seventy who responded they administered a series of physical and psychological tests and then selected the healthiest twenty-four.

The next step was to randomly assign half the men to be "prisoners" and half to be "guards." The plan called for the guards and prisoners to spend the next two weeks in the mock prison. The prisoners

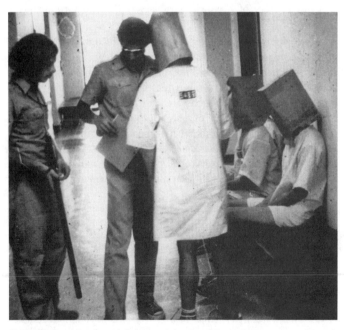

Philip Zimbardo's research helps explain why violence is a common element in our society's prisons. At the same time, his work demonstrates the dangers that sociological investigation poses for subjects and the need for investigators to observe ethical standards that protect the welfare of people who participate in research.

Philip G. Zimbardo, Inc.

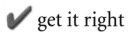

began their part of the experiment soon afterward when the city police "arrested" them at their homes. After searching and handcuffing the men, the police drove them to the local police station, where they were fingerprinted. Then police transported their captives to the Stanford prison, where the guards locked them up. Zimbardo started his video camera rolling and watched to see what would happen next.

The experiment turned into more than anyone had bargained for. Both guards and prisoners soon became embittered and hostile toward one another. Guards humiliated the prisoners by assigning them tasks such as cleaning out toilets with their bare hands. The prisoners resisted and insulted the guards. Within four days, the researchers removed five prisoners who displayed "extreme emotional depression, crying, rage and acute anxiety" (Haney, Banks, & Zimbardo, 1973:81). Before the end of the first week, the situation had become so bad that the researchers had to cancel the experiment. Zimbardo explains:

> The ugliest, most base, pathological side of human nature surfaced. We were horrified because we saw some boys (guards) treat others as if they were despicable animals, taking pleasure in cruelty, while other boys (prisoners) became servile, dehumanized robots who thought only of escape, of their own individual survival and of their mounting hatred for the guards. (Zimbardo, 1972:4)

The events that unfolded at the "Stanford County Prison" supported Zimbardo's hypothesis that prison violence is rooted in the social character of jails themselves, not in the personalities of guards and prisoners. This finding raises questions about our society's prisons, suggesting the need for basic reform. Notice, too, that this experiment shows the potential of research to threaten the physical and mental well-being of subjects. Such dangers are not always as obvious as they were in this case. Therefore, researchers must carefully consider the potential harm to subjects at all stages of their work and end any study, as Zimbardo did, if subjects may suffer harm of any kind.

 How might Zimbardo's findings help explain the abuse of Iraqi prisoners by U.S. soldiers in the Abu Ghraib prison?

Asking Questions: Survey Research

A **survey** is *a research method in which subjects respond to a series of statements or questions in a questionnaire or an interview.* The most widely used of all research methods, surveys are especially good for studying attitudes—such as beliefs about politics, religion, or race—since there is no way to observe directly what people think. Sometimes surveys provide clues about cause and effect, but typically they yield *descriptive* findings, painting a picture of people's views on some issue.

Population and Sample

A survey targets some **population,** *the people who are the focus of research.* Lois Benjamin, in her study of racism described at the beginning of this chapter, studied a select population—talented African Americans. Other surveys such as political polls that predict election results treat every adult in the country as the population.

Obviously, contacting millions of people is impossible for even the best-funded and most patient researcher. Fortunately, there is an easier way that yields accurate results: Researchers collect data from a **sample,** *a part of a population that represents the whole.* Benjamin chose 100 talented African Americans as her sample. National political polls typically survey a sample of about 1,000 people.

Everyone uses the logic of sampling all the time. If you look at students sitting near you and notice five or six heads nodding off, you might conclude that the class finds the day's lecture dull. In reaching this conclusion, you are making a judgment about *all* the people in the class (the "population") from observing *some* of your classmates (the "sample").

But how can we be sure that a sample really represents the entire population? One way is *random sampling,* in which researchers draw a sample from the population randomly so that every person in the population has an equal chance to be selected. The mathematical laws of probability dictate that a random sample is likely to represent the population as a whole. Selecting a random sample usually means listing everyone in the population and using a computer to make a random selection.

Beginning researchers sometimes make the mistake of assuming that "randomly" walking up to people on a street produces a sample that is representative of the entire city. Unfortunately, this technique does not give every person an equal chance to be included in the sample. For one thing, any street, whether in a rich neighborhood or on a college campus, contains more of some kinds of people than others. The fact that some people are more approachable than others is another source of bias.

Although good sampling is no simple task, it offers a considerable savings in time and expense. We are spared the tedious work of contacting everyone in a population, yet we can obtain essentially the same results.

Using Questionnaires

Selecting subjects is just the first step in carrying out a survey. Also needed is a plan for asking questions and recording answers. Most surveys use a questionnaire for this purpose.

A **questionnaire** is *a series of written questions a researcher presents to subjects.* One type of questionnaire provides not only the questions but also a selection of fixed responses (similar to a multiple-choice examination). This *closed-ended format* makes it fairly easy to analyze the results, but by narrowing the range of responses, it can also distort the findings. For example, Frederick Lorenz and Brent Bruton (1996) found that the number of hours per week students say they study for a college course depends on the options offered to them. When the researchers presented students with options ranging from one hour or less to nine hours or more, 75 percent said that they studied four hours or less per week. But when subjects in a comparable group were given choices ranging from four hours or less to twelve hours or longer (a higher figure that suggests students should study more), they suddenly became more studious; only 34 percent reported that they studied four hours or less each week.

A second type of questionnaire, using an *open-ended format,* allows subjects to respond freely, expressing various shades of opinion. The drawback of this approach is that the researcher has to make sense out of what can be a very wide range of answers.

The researcher must also decide how to present questions to subjects. Most often, researchers use a *self-administered survey,* mailing or e-mailing questionnaires to respondents and asking them to complete the form and send it back. Since no researcher is present when subjects read the questionnaire, it must be both inviting and clearly written. *Pretesting* a self-administered questionnaire with a small number of people before sending it to the entire sample can prevent the costly problem of finding out—too late—that instructions or questions were confusing.

Using the mail or e-mail allows a researcher to contact a large number of people over a wide geographic area at minimal expense. But many people treat such questionnaires as junk mail, so typically no more than half are completed and returned (in 2000, just two-thirds of people returned U.S. Census Bureau forms). Researchers must send follow-up mailings (or, as the Census Bureau does, visit people's homes) to urge reluctant subjects to respond.

Finally, keep in mind that many people are not capable of completing a questionnaire on their own. Young children obviously cannot, nor can many hospital patients or a surprising number of adults who simply lack the required reading and writing skills.

Conducting Interviews

An **interview** is *a series of questions a researcher asks respondents in person.* In a closed-format design, researchers read a question or statement and then ask the subject to select a response from several that are presented. More commonly, however, interviews are open-ended so that subjects can respond as they choose and researchers can probe with follow-up questions. In either case, the researcher must guard

Focus groups are a type of survey in which a small number of people representing a target population are asked for their opinions about some issue or product. Here, an organization opposed to cigarette smoking asks teens to judge which cigarette commercials seem most and least likely to get young people to light up.

KRT Photograph/Ron Tarver/*Philadelphia Inquirer*/NewsCom

against influencing a subject, which is as easy as raising an eyebrow when a person begins to answer.

Although subjects are more likely to complete a survey if contacted personally by the researcher, interviews have some disadvantages: Tracking people down is costly and takes time, especially if subjects do not live in the same area. Telephone interviews allow far greater "reach," but the impersonality of cold calls by telephone (and reaching answering machines) can lower the response rate.

In both questionnaires and interviews, how a question is worded greatly affects how people answer. For example, when asked if they support our military, most adults in the United States said yes. Yet when asked if they support what the military is trying to do in Iraq, most said no. Emotionally loaded language can also sway subjects. For instance, using the expression "welfare mothers" rather than "women who receive public assistance" adds an emotional element to a question that encourages people to answer negatively.

Another problem is that researchers may confuse respondents by asking a double question, like "Do you think that the government should reduce the deficit by cutting spending and raising taxes?" The

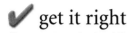

issue here is that a subject could very well agree with one part of the question but not the other, so that forcing a subject to say yes or no distorts the opinion the researcher is trying to measure.

Conducting a good interview means standardizing the technique—treating all subjects in the same way. But this, too, can lead to problems. Drawing people out requires establishing rapport, which in turn depends on responding naturally to the particular person being interviewed, as you would in a normal conversation. In the end, researchers have to decide where to strike the balance between uniformity and rapport (Lavin & Maynard, 2001).

 YOUR LEARNING Provide an example of a research topic that might lead a researcher to use a questionnaire. What about a topic that would call for interviews?

Illustration of Survey Research: Studying the African American Elite

This chapter began by explaining how Lois Benjamin came to investigate the effects of racism on talented African American men and women. Benjamin suspected that personal achievement did not prevent hostility based on color. She believed this because of her own experiences after becoming the first black professor in the history of the University of Tampa. But was she the exception or the rule? To answer this question, Benjamin set out to discover whether—and if so, how—racism affected a number of the most successful African Americans.

Opting to conduct a survey, Benjamin chose to interview subjects rather than distribute a questionnaire because, first, she wanted to enter into a conversation with her subjects, to ask follow-up questions, and to pursue topics that she could not anticipate. A second reason Benjamin favored interviews over questionnaires is that racism is a sensitive topic. A supportive investigator can make it easier for subjects to respond to painful questions (Bergen, 1993).

Choosing to conduct interviews made it necessary to limit the number of people in the study. Benjamin settled for a sample of 100 men and women. Even this small number kept Benjamin busy for more than two years as she scheduled interviews, traveled all over the country, and met with her respondents. She spent two more years analyzing the tapes of her interviews, deciding what the hours of talk told her about racism, and writing up her results.

In selecting her sample, Benjamin first considered using all the people listed in *Who's Who in Black America*. But she rejected this idea in favor of starting out with people she knew and asking them to suggest others. This strategy is called *snowball sampling* because the number of individuals included grows rapidly over time.

Snowball sampling is an easy way to do research—we begin with familiar people who introduce us to their friends and colleagues. But snowball sampling rarely produces a sample that is representative of the larger population. Benjamin's sample probably contained many like-minded individuals, and it was certainly biased toward people willing to talk openly about race and prejudice. She understood these problems, and she did what she could to make her sample diverse in terms of sex, age, and region of the country. The Thinking About Diversity: Race, Class, & Gender box presents a statistical profile of Benjamin's respondents and some tips on how to read tables.

Benjamin based all her interviews on a series of questions with an open-ended format so that her subjects could say whatever they wished. As usually happens, the interviews took place in a wide range of settings. She met subjects in offices (hers or theirs), in hotel rooms, and in cars. In each case, Benjamin tape-recorded the conversation, which lasted from two-and-one-half to three hours, so that she would not be distracted by taking notes.

As research ethics demand, Benjamin offered full anonymity to participants. Even so, many—including notables such as Vernon E. Jordan Jr. (former president of the National Urban League) and Yvonne Walker-Taylor (first woman president of Wilberforce University)—were used to being in the public eye and allowed Benjamin to use their names.

What surprised Benjamin most about her research was how eager many people were to be interviewed. These normally busy men and women seemed to go out of their way to contribute to her project. Benjamin reports, too, that once the interviews were under way, many became very emotional—at some point in the conversation, about 40 of her 100 subjects cried. For them, apparently, the research provided a chance to release feelings long kept inside. How did Benjamin respond? She reports that she cried right along with them.

Of the research orientations described earlier in the chapter, you will see that Benjamin's study fits best under interpretive sociology (she explored what race meant to her subjects) and critical sociology (she undertook the study partly to document that racial prejudice still exists). Many of her subjects reported fearing that race might someday undermine their success, and others spoke of a race-based "glass ceiling" preventing them from reaching the highest positions in our society. Benjamin concluded that despite the improving social standing of African Americans, black people in the United States still feel the sting of racial hostility.

 Do you think this research could have been carried out by a white sociologist? Why or why not?

tip

Throughout this book, you will find tables and figures that summarize data collected about various populations. Most of these data are collected by the government, typically by researchers using questionnaires.

tip

In her study of the African American elite, Lois Benjamin made great effort to explain who her subjects were. Always consider this question when reading anyone's research results.

Thinking About Diversity: Race, Class, & Gender
The African American Elite: Reading Data in a Table

The sociologist Lois Benjamin completed an important study of the African American elite. Who are these people? An easy way for a researcher to answer this question is to provide a table. A table provides a lot of information in a small amount of space, so learning to read tables can increase your reading efficiency.

When you are reading a study and you spot a table, look first at the title to see what information it contains. The title of the table presented here tells you that it provides a profile of the 100 subjects participating in Lois Benjamin's research. Across the top of the table, you see eight variables that describe these men and women. Reading down each column, note the different categories, with the percentages adding up to 100.

Starting at the top left, we see that Benjamin's sample was mostly men (63 percent men, 37 percent women). In terms of age, most of the respondents (68 percent) were in the middle stage of life, and most had grown up in a predominantly black community in the South or in the North or Midwest region of the United States.

Most of these individuals have a lot of schooling. Half earned either a doctorate (32 percent) or a medical or law degree (17 percent). Given their extensive education (and Benjamin's own job as a professor), we should not be surprised that the largest share (35 percent) worked in academic institutions. In terms of income, these people were pretty well off, and most (64 percent) earned more than $50,000 a year back in the 1980s (a salary that only 33 percent of full-time workers make even today).

Finally, we see that these 100 individuals were generally left-of-center in their political views. In part, this reflects their extensive schooling (which encourages progressive thinking) and the tendency of academics to fall on the liberal side of the political spectrum.

WHAT DO YOU THINK?

1. Why are statistical data, such as those in this table, an efficient way to convey lots of information?

2. Looking at the table, can you determine how long it took most people to become part of this elite? Explain your answer.

3. Do you see any ways in which this African American elite might differ from a comparable white elite? If so, what are they?

The Talented One Hundred: Lois Benjamin's African American Elite

Sex	Age	Childhood Racial Setting	Childhood Region	Highest Educational Degree	Job Sector	Income	Political Orientation
Male 63%	35 or younger 6%	Mostly black 71%	West 6%	Doctorate 32%	College or university 35%	More than $50,000 64%	Radical left 13%
Female 37%	36 to 54 68%	Mostly white 15%	North or Midwest 32%	Medical or law 17%	Private for-profit 17%	$35,00 to $50,000 18%	Liberal 38%
	55 or older 26%	Racially mixed 14%	South 38%	Master's 27%	Private nonprofit 9%	$20,000 to $34,999 12%	Moderate 28%
			Northeast 12%	Bachelor's 13%	Government 22%	Less than $20,000 6%	Conservative 5%
			Other 12%	Less 11%	Self-employed 14%		Depends on issue 14%
					Retired 3%		Unknown 2%
100%	100%	100%	100%	100%	100%	100%	100%

Source: Adapted from Lois Benjamin, *The Black Elite: Facing the Color Line in the Twilight of the Twentieth Century* (Chicago: Nelson-Hall, 1991), p. 276.

tip

If the experiment comes closest to the logic of science, participant observation is the method that is used by sociologists engaged in interpretive sociology.

tip

As you read about *Street Corner Society,* notice how participant observation is a great method for understanding everyday life in a social setting.

Participant observation is a method of sociological research that we can apply in our everyday lives. Every time we find ourselves in an interesting social setting, we can try to determine what people are doing and what meaning they find in their actions.

Eric Gaillard/Reuters/Landov LLC

In the Field: Participant Observation

Lois Benjamin's research demonstrates that sociological investigation takes place not only in laboratories but also "in the field," that is, where people carry on their everyday lives. The most widely used strategy for field study is **participant observation,** *a research method in which investigators systematically observe people while joining them in their routine activities.*

Participant observation allows researchers an inside look at social life in settings ranging from nightclubs to religious seminaries. Cultural anthropologists commonly use participant observation (which they call *fieldwork*) to study communities in other societies. They term their descriptions of unfamiliar cultures *ethnographies.* Sociologists prefer to call their accounts of people in particular settings *case studies.*

At the beginning of a field study, most investigators do not have a specific hypothesis in mind. In fact, they may not yet realize what the important questions will turn out to be. Thus most field research is *exploratory* and *descriptive.*

As its name suggests, participant observation has two sides. On one hand, getting an "insider's" look depends on becoming a participant in the setting—"hanging out" with the research subjects, trying

to act, think, and even feel the way they do. Compared to experiments and survey research, participant observation has fewer hard-and-fast rules. But it is precisely this flexibility that allows investigators to explore the unfamiliar and adapt to the unexpected.

Unlike other research methods, participant observation may require that the researcher enter the setting not just for a week or two but for months or even years. At the same time, however, the researcher must maintain some distance as an "observer," mentally stepping back to record field notes and later to interpret them. Because the investigator must both "play the participant" to win acceptance and gain access to people's lives and "play the observer" to maintain the distance needed for thoughtful analysis, there is an inherent tension in this method. Carrying out the twin roles of insider participant and outsider observer often comes down to a series of careful compromises.

Most sociologists carry out participant observation alone, so they—and readers, too—must remember that the results depend on the work of a single person. Participant observation usually falls within interpretive sociology, yielding mostly qualitative data—the researcher's accounts of people's lives and what they think of themselves and the world around them—although researchers sometimes collect some quantitative (numerical) data. From a scientific point of view, participant observation is a "soft" method that relies heavily on personal judgment and lacks scientific rigor. Yet its personal approach is also a strength: A highly visible team of sociologists attempting to administer formal surveys would disrupt many social settings, but a single skillful participant-observer can often gain a lot of insight into people's natural behavior.

 YOUR LEARNING What are several strengths of participant observation? What are several weaknesses of this research method?

Illustration of Participant Observation: *Street Corner Society*

In the late 1930s, a young graduate student at Harvard University named William Foote Whyte (1914–2000) was fascinated by the lively street life of a nearby, rather rundown section of Boston. His curiosity led him to carry out four years of participant observation in this neighborhood, which he called "Cornerville," and in the process to produce a sociological classic.

At the time, Cornerville was home to first- and second-generation Italian immigrants. Many were poor, and many people living in the rest of Boston considered Cornerville a place to avoid: a poor slum that was home to racketeers. Unwilling to accept easy stereotypes, Whyte set out to discover for himself exactly what kind of life went on in this community. His celebrated book, *Street Corner Society* (1981, orig. 1943), describes Cornerville as a complex community with a distinctive code of values and its own social conflicts.

tip
Participant observation requires a lot of time but little money or specialized equipment. For that reason, this method is often chosen by students in college or graduate school.

In beginning his investigation, Whyte considered a range of research methods. Should he take questionnaires to one of Cornerville's community centers and ask local people to fill them out? Should he invite members of the community to come to his Harvard office for interviews? It is easy to see that such formal strategies would have gained little cooperation from the local people. Whyte decided, therefore, to set out on his own, working his way into Cornerville life in the hope of coming to understand this rather mysterious place.

Right away, Whyte discovered the challenges of even getting started in field research. After all, an upper-middle-class WASP graduate student from Harvard did not exactly fit into Cornerville life. Even a friendly overture from an outsider could seem pushy and rude. One night, Whyte dropped in at a local bar, hoping to buy a woman a drink and encourage her to talk about Cornerville. Looking around the room, he could find no woman alone. But then he saw a man sitting down with two women. He walked up to them and asked, "Pardon me. Would you mind if I joined you?" Instantly, he realized his mistake:

> There was a moment of silence while the man stared at me. Then he offered to throw me down the stairs. I assured him that this would not be necessary, and demonstrated as much by walking right out of there without any assistance. (1981:289)

As this incident suggests, gaining entry to a community is the difficult (and sometimes hazardous) first step in field research. "Breaking in" requires patience, quick thinking, and a little luck. Whyte's big break came when he met a young man named "Doc" at a local social service agency. Whyte explained to Doc how hard it was to make friends in Cornerville. Doc responded by taking Whyte under his wing and introducing him to others in the community. With Doc's help, Whyte soon became a neighborhood regular.

Whyte's friendship with Doc illustrates the importance of a *key informant* in field research. Such people not only introduce a researcher to a community but often remain a source of information and help. But using a key informant also has its risks. Because any person has a particular circle of friends, a key informant's guidance is certain to "spin" or bias the study in one way or another. In addition, in the eyes of others, the reputation of the key informant—good or bad—usually rubs off on the investigator. So although a key informant is helpful early on, a participant-observer must soon seek a broader range of contacts.

Having entered the Cornerville world, Whyte quickly learned another lesson: A field researcher needs to know when to speak up and when to shut up. One evening, he joined a group discussing neighborhood gambling. Wanting to get the facts straight, Whyte asked innocently, "I suppose the cops were all paid off?" In a heartbeat, "the gambler's jaw dropped. He glared at me. Then he denied

vehemently that any policeman had been paid off and immediately switched the conversation to another subject. For the rest of that evening I felt very uncomfortable." The next day, Doc offered some sound advice:

> "Go easy on that 'who,' 'what,' 'why,' 'when,' 'where' stuff, Bill. You ask those questions and people will clam up on you. If people accept you, you can just hang around, and you'll learn the answers in the long run without even having to ask the questions." (1981:303)

In the months and years that followed, Whyte became familiar with life in Cornerville and even married a local woman with whom he would spend the rest of his life. In the process, he learned that the common stereotypes were wrong. In Cornerville, most people worked hard, many were quite successful, and some even boasted of sending children to college. Even today, Whyte's book is a fascinating story of the deeds, dreams, and disappointments of immigrants and their children living in one ethnic community, and it contains the kind of rich details that come only from years of participant observation.

 Can you think of a topic you might be interested in studying as a participant-observer?

Using Available Data: Existing Sources

Not all research requires investigators to collect their own data. Sometimes sociologists analyze existing sources, data collected by others.

The most widely used statistics in social science are gathered by government agencies. The U.S. Census Bureau continuously updates a wide range of data about the U.S. population. Comparable data on Canada are available from Statistics Canada, a branch of that nation's government. For international data, there are various publications of the United Nations and the World Bank. In short, data about the whole world are as close as your library or the Internet.

Using available data—whether government statistics or the findings of individual researchers—saves time and money. This approach has special appeal to sociologists with low budgets. For anyone, however, government data are generally more extensive and more accurate than what most researchers could obtain on their own.

But using existing data has problems of its own. For one thing, available data may not exist in the exact form needed. For example, you may be able to find the average salary paid to professors at your school but not separate figures for the amounts paid to women and

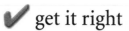
to men. Further, there are always questions about the meaning and accuracy of work done by others. For example, in his classic study of suicide, Emile Durkheim soon discovered that there was no way to know whether a death classified as a suicide was really an accident or vice versa. In addition, various agencies use different procedures and categories in collecting data, so comparisons may be difficult. In the end, then, using existing data is a little like shopping for a used car: There are plenty of bargains out there, but you have to shop carefully.

YOUR LEARNING What are some advantages of using existing data? What are some dangers?

Illustration of the Use of Existing Sources: A Tale of Two Cities

To people stuck in the present, existing data can be used as a key to unlock secrets of the past. The award-winning study *Puritan Boston and Quaker Philadelphia*, by E. Digby Baltzell (1979b), is a good example of how a researcher can use available data to do historical research.

This story starts with Baltzell making a chance visit to Bowdoin College in Maine. As he walked into the college library, he saw up on the wall three large portraits—of the celebrated author Nathaniel Hawthorne, the famous poet Henry Wadsworth Longfellow, and Franklin Pierce, the fourteenth president of the United States. He soon learned that all three great men had been members of the same class at Bowdoin, graduating in 1825. How could it be, Baltzell wondered, that this small college had graduated more famous people in a single year than his own, much bigger University of Pennsylvania had graduated in its entire history? To answer this question, Baltzell was soon paging through historical documents to see whether New England had really produced more famous people than his native Pennsylvania.

What were Baltzell's data? He turned to the *Dictionary of American Biography*, twenty volumes profiling more than 13,000 outstanding men and women in fields such as politics, law, and the arts. The dictionary told Baltzell *who* was great, and he realized that the longer the biography, the more important the person is thought to be.

By the time Baltzell had identified the seventy-five individuals with the longest biographies, he saw a striking pattern. Massachusetts had the most by far, with twenty-one of the seventy-five top achievers. The New England states, combined, claimed thirty-one of the entries. By contrast, Pennsylvania could boast of only two, and all the states in the Middle Atlantic region had just twelve. Looking more closely, Baltzell discovered that most of New England's great achievers had grown up in and around the city of Boston. Again, in stark contrast, almost no one of comparable standing came from his own Philadelphia, a city with many more people than Boston.

What could explain this remarkable pattern? Baltzell drew inspiration from the German sociologist Max Weber (1958, orig. 1904–05), who argued that a region's record of achievement was influenced by its major religious beliefs. In the religious differences between Boston and Philadelphia, Baltzell found the answer to his puzzle. Boston was originally a Puritan settlement, founded by people who highly valued the pursuit of excellence and public achievement. Philadelphia, by contrast, was settled by Quakers, who believed in equality and avoided public notice.

Both the Puritans and the Quakers were fleeing religious persecution in England, but the two religions produced quite different cultural patterns. Boston's Puritans saw humans as innately sinful, so they built a rigid society in which family, church, and school regulated people's behavior. The Puritans celebrated hard work as a means of glorifying God and viewed public success as a reassuring sign of God's blessing. In short, Puritanism fostered a disciplined life in which people both sought and respected achievement.

Philadelphia's Quakers, by contrast, built their way of life on the belief that all human beings are basically good. They saw little need for strong social institutions to "save" people from sinfulness. They believed in equality, so that even those who became rich considered themselves no better than anyone else. Thus rich and poor alike lived modestly and discouraged one another from standing out by seeking fame or even running for public office.

In Baltzell's sociological imagination, Boston and Philadelphia took the form of two social "test tubes": Puritanism was poured into one, Quakerism into the other. Centuries later, we can see that different "chemical reactions" occurred in each case. The two belief systems led to different attitudes toward personal achievement, which in turn shaped the history of each region. Today, we can see that Boston's Kennedys (despite being Catholic) are only one of that city's many families who exemplify the Puritan pursuit of recognition and leadership. By contrast, there has never been even one family with such public stature in the entire history of Philadelphia.

Baltzell's study uses scientific logic, but it also illustrates the interpretive approach by showing how people understood their world. His research reminds us that sociological investigation often involves mixing research orientations to fit a particular problem.

 Why is the use of existing sources especially important in doing historical research? What other questions might you wish to answer using existing sources?

tip

Study this Summing Up table to be sure you understand both the type of research issue that calls for each of the four methods of data collection and the strengths and limitations of each method.

SUMMING UP

Four Research Methods

	Experiment	Survey	Participant Observation	Existing Sources
Application	For explanatory research that specifies relationships between variables Generates quantitative data	For gathering information about issues that cannot be directly observed, such as attitudes and values Useful for descriptive and explanatory research Generates quantitative or qualitative data	For exploratory and descriptive study of people in a "natural" setting Generates qualitative data	For exploratory, descriptive, or explanatory research whenever suitable data are available
Advantages	Provides the greatest opportunity to specify cause-and-effect relationships Replication of research is relatively easy	Sampling, using questionnaires, allows surveys of large populations Interviews provide in-depth responses	Allows study of "natural" behavior Usually inexpensive	Saves time and expense of data collection Makes historical research possible
Limitations	Laboratory settings have an artificial quality Unless the research environment is carefully controlled, results may be biased	Questionnaires must be carefully prepared and may yield a low return rate Interviews are expensive and time-consuming	Time-consuming Replication of research is difficult Researcher must balance roles of participant and observer	Researcher has no control over possible biases in data Data may only partially fit current research needs

The Summing Up table provides a quick review of the four major methods of sociological investigation. We now turn to our final consideration: the link between research results and sociological theory.

The Interplay of Theory and Method

No matter how sociologists collect their data, they have to turn facts into meaning by building theory. They do this in two ways: inductive logical thought and deductive logical thought.

Inductive logical thought is *reasoning that transforms specific observations into general theory.* In this mode, a researcher's thinking runs from the specific to the general and goes something like this: "I have some interesting data here; I wonder what they mean?" Baltzell's research illustrates the inductive logical model. His data showed that one region of the country (the Boston area) had produced many more high achievers than another (the Philadelphia region). He worked "upward" from ground-level observations to the high-flying theory

that religious values were a key factor in shaping people's attitudes toward achievement.

A second type of logical thought moves "downward," in the opposite direction: **Deductive logical thought** is *reasoning that transforms general theory into specific hypotheses suitable for testing.* The researcher's thinking runs from the general to the specific: "I have this hunch about human behavior; let's collect some data and put it to the test." Working deductively, the researcher first states the theory in the form of a hypothesis and then selects a method by which to test it. To the extent that the data support the hypothesis, we conclude that the theory is correct; if the data refute the hypothesis, we know that the theory needs to be revised or perhaps rejected entirely.

Philip Zimbardo's "Stanford County Prison" experiment illustrates deductive logic. Zimbardo began with the general theory that a social environment can change human behavior. He then developed a specific, testable hypothesis: Placed in a prison setting, even emotionally well-balanced young men will behave violently. The violence that erupted soon after his experiment began supported Zimbardo's

tip

The ten steps listed on the next two pages are a summary of what is needed to conduct good sociological research.

Controversy & Debate

Can People Lie with Statistics?

Josh: (*continuing a discussion about job prospects after graduation*) Well, you know, college students today just aren't as smart as they were fifty years ago.

Sam: Come on, that's not true at all.

Josh: (*smugly*) Sorry, pal. I happen to have the data to prove it.

We have all been in arguments when someone has presented us with "data" as if that were "proof." But are numbers the same as "truth"? It is worth remembering the words of the nineteenth-century English politician Benjamin Disraeli, who once remarked, "There are three kinds of lies: lies, damned lies, and statistics!"

In a world that bombards us with numbers—often described as "scientific data" or "official figures"—it is important to realize that "statistical evidence" is not necessarily the same as truth. For one thing, any researcher can make mistakes. More important, because data do not speak for themselves, someone has to decide what they mean. Sometimes people (even sociologists) "dress up" their data almost the way politicians deliver campaign speeches—with an eye more to winning you over than to getting at the truth.

The best way to avoid being fooled is to understand how people can mislead with statistics.

1. **People select their data.** Many times, the data presented are not wrong, but they do not tell the whole story. Let's say someone who thinks that television is ruining our way of life presents statistics indicating that we watch more TV today than people did a generation ago. It also turns out that during the same period, College Board scores have fallen. Both sets of data may be correct, but the suggestion that there is a cause-and-effect

link here—that television viewing is lowering test scores—is not proved. A person more favorable to television might counter with the additional "fact" that the U.S. population spends much more money buying books today than it did a generation ago, suggesting that television creates new intellectual interests. It is possible to find statistics that seem to support just about any argument.

2. **People interpret their data.** People can also "package" their data with a ready-made interpretation, as if the numbers can mean only one thing. Take a look at

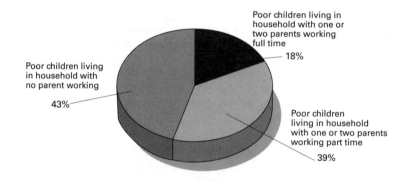

hypothesis. Had his experiment produced friendly behavior between prisoners and guards, his hypothesis clearly would have been wrong.

Just as researchers often employ several methods over the course of one study, they typically use *both* kinds of logical thought. Figure 2 illustrates both types of reasoning: inductively building theory from observations and deductively making observations to test a theory.

Finally, turning facts into meaning usually involves organizing and presenting statistical data. Precisely how sociologists arrange their numbers affects the conclusions they reach. In short, preparing your results amounts to spinning reality in one way or another.

Often we conclude that an argument must be true simply because there are statistics to back it up. However, we must look

at statistics with a cautious eye. After all, researchers choose what data to present, they interpret their statistics, and they may use tables and graphs to steer readers toward particular conclusions. The Controversy & Debate box takes a closer look at this important issue.

Putting It All Together: Ten Steps in Sociological Investigation

We can summarize this chapter by outlining ten steps in the process of carrying out sociological investigation. Each step takes the form of an important question.

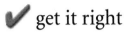
We often think data prove a point. Not so, as the box below explains. Be sure you understand why.

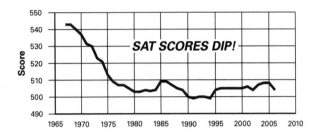

the pie chart, which shows the results of one study of U.S. children living in poverty (National Center for Children in Poverty, cited in *Population Today*, 1995). The researchers reported that 43 percent of these children lived in a household with no working parent, 39 percent lived in a household with one or two parents employed part time, and 18 percent lived in a household with one or two parents working full time. The researchers labeled this figure "Majority of Children in Poverty Live with Parents Who Work." Do you think this interpretation is accurate or misleading? Why or why not?

3. People use graphs to spin the truth.
Especially in newspapers and other popular media, we find statistics in the form of charts and graphs. Graphs, which often show an upward or downward trend over time, are a good way to present data. But using graphs also gives people the opportunity to "spin" data in various ways. The trend depends in part on the time frame used. During the past ten years, for instance, the U.S. crime rate has fallen. But if we were to look at the past fifty years, we would see an opposite trend: The crime rate pushed sharply upward.

The scale used to draw a graph is also important because it lets a researcher "inflate" or "deflate" a trend. Both graphs shown here present identical data for College Board SAT critical reading scores between 1967 and 2006. But the left-hand graph stretches the scale to show a downward trend; the right-hand graph compresses the scale, showing a steady trend. So understanding what statistics mean—or don't mean—depends on being a careful reader!

WHAT DO YOU THINK?

1. Why do you think people are so quick to accept "statistics" as true?

2. From a scientific point of view, is spinning the truth acceptable? Is this practice OK from a critical approach, in which someone is trying to advance social change?

3. Find a news story on some social issue that you think presents biased data or conclusions. What are the biases?

1. **What is your topic?** Being curious and applying the sociological perspective can generate ideas for social research at any time and in any place. Pick a topic you find important to study.

2. **What have others already learned?** You are probably not the first person with an interest in the issue you have selected. Visit the library to see what theories and methods other researchers have applied to your topic. In reviewing the existing research, note problems that have come up to avoid repeating past mistakes.

3. **What, exactly, are your questions?** Are you seeking to explore an unfamiliar social setting? To describe some category of people? To investigate cause and effect among variables? If your study is exploratory or descriptive, identify *whom* you wish to study, *where* the research will take place, and *what* kinds of issues you want to explore. If it is explanatory, you must also formulate the hypothesis to be tested and operationalize each variable.

4. **What will you need to carry out research?** How much time and money are available to you? Is special equipment or training necessary? Can you do the work yourself? You should answer all these questions as you plan the research project.

5. **Are there ethical concerns?** Not all research raises serious ethical questions, but you must be sensitive to this possibility.

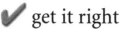

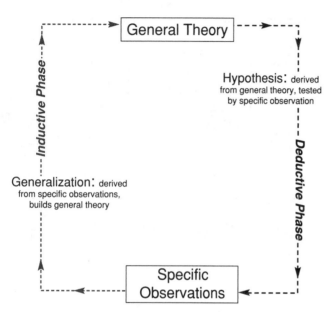

FIGURE 2 Deductive and Inductive Logical Thought

Sociologists link theory and method through both inductive and deductive logic.

Can the research cause harm or threaten anyone's privacy? How might you design the study to minimize the chances for injury? Will you promise anonymity to the subjects? If so, how will you ensure that anonymity is maintained?

6. **What method will you use?** Consider all major research strategies, as well as combinations of approaches. Keep

in mind that the best method depends on the kinds of questions you are asking as well as the resources available to you.

7. **How will you record the data?** Your research method is a plan for data collection. Record all information accurately and in a way that will make sense later (it may be some time before you actually write up the results of your work). Be alert for any bias that may creep into the research.

8. **What do the data tell you?** Study the data in terms of your initial questions and decide how to interpret the data you have collected. If your study involves a specific hypothesis, you must decide whether to confirm, reject, or modify the hypothesis. Keep in mind that there may be several ways to look at your data, depending on which theoretical approach you use, and you should consider all interpretations.

9. **What are your conclusions?** Prepare a final report stating your conclusions. How does your work advance sociological theory? Does it suggest ways to improve research methods? Does your study have policy implications? What would the general public find interesting in your work? Finally, evaluate your own work, noting problems that arose and questions that were left unanswered.

10. **How can you share what you've learned?** Consider sending your research paper to a campus newspaper or magazine or making a presentation to a class, a campus gathering, or perhaps a meeting of professional sociologists. The point is to share what you have learned with others and to let them respond to your work.

Applying Sociology in Everyday Life

1. Observe your instructor in class one day to grade his or her teaching skills. Operationalize the concept "good teaching" in terms of specific traits you can measure. How easy is it to measure "good teaching"?

2. Visit three sociology instructors (or other social science instructors) during their office hours. Ask each whether they think sociology is an objective science. Do they agree? Why or why not?

3. Select a number of primetime television shows, and note the race of major characters. You will have to decide what "primetime" means, what a "major" character is, how to gauge someone's "race," and other issues before you begin. Sketch out a research plan to evaluate the hypothesis that African Americans are not very visible on primetime television.

MAKING THE GRADE

Sociological Investigation

Basics of Sociological Investigation

Two basic requirements for **SOCIOLOGICAL INVESTIGATION** are

- Know how to apply the sociological perspective.
- Be curious and ready to ask questions about the world around you.

What people accept as "truth" differs around the world.

- **SCIENCE**—a logical system that bases knowledge on direct, systematic observation—is one form of truth.
- Scientific evidence gained from sociological research often challenges common sense.

science a logical system that bases knowledge on direct, systematic observation

empirical evidence information we can verify with our senses

Research Orientations: Three Ways to Do Sociology

SCIENTIFIC SOCIOLOGY studies society by systematically observing social behavior.

Scientific sociology

- requires carefully operationalizing variables and ensuring that measurement is both reliable and valid;
- observes how variables are related and tries to establish cause and effect;
- sees an objective reality "out there";
- favors quantitative data;
- is well suited to research in a laboratory;
- demands that researchers try to be objective and suspend their personal values and biases as they conduct research.

✔ Scientific sociology is also called *positivist sociology*.

INTERPRETIVE SOCIOLOGY focuses on the meanings that people attach to behavior.

Interpretive sociology

- sees reality as constructed by people in the course of their everyday lives;
- favors qualitative data;
- is well suited to research in a natural setting.

✔ Weber's concept of *Verstehen* refers to learning how people understand their world.

CRITICAL SOCIOLOGY uses research to bring about social change.

Critical sociology

- asks moral and political questions;
- focuses on inequality;
- rejects the principle of objectivity, claiming that all research is political.

✔ Marx, who founded the critical orientation, criticized scientific sociology as supporting the status quo.

scientific sociology the study of society based on systematic observation of social behavior

concept a mental construct that represents some part of the world in a simplified form

variable a concept whose value changes from case to case

measurement a procedure for determining the value of a variable in a specific case

operationalize a variable specifying exactly what is to be measured before assigning a value to a variable

reliability consistency in measurement

validity actually measuring exactly what you intend to measure

cause and effect a relationship in which change in one variable causes change in another

independent variable the variable that causes the change

dependent variable the variable that changes

correlation a relationship in which two (or more) variables change together

spurious correlation an apparent but false relationship between two (or more) variables that is caused by some other variable

control holding constant all variables except one in order to see clearly the effect of that variable

objectivity personal neutrality in conducting research

replication repetition of research by other investigators

interpretive sociology the study of society that focuses on the meanings people attach to their social world

critical sociology the study of society that focuses on the need for social change

Research Orientations and Theory

- Scientific sociology is loosely linked to the structural-functional approach.
- Interpretive sociology is related to the symbolic-interaction approach.
- Critical sociology corresponds to the social-conflict approach.

⊞ See the Summing Up table in this chapter.

MAKING THE GRADE *continued . . .*

Gender and Research

Gender, involving both researcher and subjects, can affect research in five ways:
- androcentricity
- overgeneralizing
- gender blindness
- double standards
- interference

Research Ethics

Researchers must
- protect the privacy of subjects
- obtain the informed consent of subjects
- indicate all sources of funding
- submit research to an institutional review board (IRB) to ensure it doesn't violate ethical standards

gender the personal traits and social positions that members of a society attach to being female or male

Methods: Strategies for Doing Research

The **EXPERIMENT** allows researchers to study cause and effect between two or more variables in a controlled setting.
- Researchers conduct an experiment to test a **hypothesis**, a statement of a possible relationship between two (or more) variables.
- ✔ Example of an experiment: Zimbardo's "Stanford County Prison"

SURVEY research uses questionnaires or interviews to gather subjects' responses to a series of questions.
- Surveys typically yield descriptive findings, painting a picture of people's views on some issue.
- ✔ Example of a survey: Benjamin's "Talented One Hundred"

Through **PARTICIPANT OBSERVATION**, researchers join with people in a social setting for an extended period of time.
- Participant observation, also called fieldwork, allows researchers an "inside look" at a social setting. Because researchers are not attempting to test a specific hypothesis, their research is exploratory and descriptive.
- ✔ Example of participant observation: Whyte's *Street Corner Society*

Sometimes researchers analyze **EXISTING SOURCES**, data collected by others.
- Using existing sources, especially the widely available data collected by government agencies, can save researchers time and money.
- Existing sources are the basis of historical research.
- ✔ Example of using existing sources: Baltzell's *Puritan Boston and Quaker Philadelphia*

research method a systematic plan for doing research

experiment a research method for investigating cause and effect under highly controlled conditions

hypothesis a statement of a possible relationship between two (or more) variables

Hawthorne effect a change in a subject's behavior caused simply by the awareness of being studied

survey a research method in which subjects respond to a series of statements or questions in a questionnaire or an interview

population the people who are the focus of research

sample a part of a population that represents the whole

questionnaire a series of written questions a researcher presents to subjects

interview a series of questions a researcher asks respondents in person

participant observation a research method in which investigators systematically observe people while joining them in their routine activities

inductive logical thought reasoning that transforms specific observations into general theory

deductive logical thought reasoning that transforms general theory into specific hypotheses suitable for testing

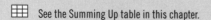

See the Summing Up table in this chapter.

✔ *Which method the researcher uses depends on the question being asked.*

✔ *Researchers combine these methods depending on the specific goals of their study.*

Sample Test Questions

These questions are similar to those found in the test bank that accompanies this textbook.

Multiple-Choice Questions

1. *Science* is defined as
   a. a logical system that bases knowledge on direct, systematic observation.
   b. belief based on faith in some ultimate truth.
   c. knowledge based on a society's traditions.
   d. information that comes from recognized "experts."

2. *Empirical evidence* refers to
   a. quantitative rather than qualitative data.
   b. what people consider "common sense."
   c. information people can verify with their senses.
   d. patterns found in every known society.

3. When trying to measure people's "social class," you would have to keep in mind that
   a. your measurement can never be both reliable and valid.
   b. there are many ways to operationalize this variable.
   c. there is no way to measure "social class."
   d. in the United States, everyone agrees on what "social class" means.

4. What is the term for the value that occurs most often in a series of numbers?
   a. the mode
   b. the median
   c. the mean
   d. All of the above are correct.

5. When measuring any variable, *reliability* refers to
   a. whether you are really measuring what you want to measure.
   b. how dependable the researcher is.
   c. results that everyone would agree with.
   d. whether repeating the measurement yields consistent results.

6. We can correctly say that two variables are *correlated* if
   a. change in one causes no change in the other.
   b. one occurs before the other.
   c. their values vary together.
   d. both measure the same thing.

7. Which of the following is *not* one of the defining traits of a cause-and-effect relationship?
   a. The independent variable must happen before the dependent variable.
   b. Each variable must be shown to be independent of the other.
   c. The two variables must display correlation.
   d. There must be no evidence that the correlation is spurious.

8. Interpretive sociology is a research orientation that
   a. focuses on action.
   b. sees an objective reality "out there."
   c. focuses on the meanings people attach to behavior.
   d. seeks to increase social justice.

9. To study the effects on test performance of playing soft music during an exam, a researcher conducts an experiment in which one test-taking class hears music and another does not. According to the chapter discussion of the experiment, the class hearing the music is called
   a. the placebo.
   b. the control group.
   c. the dependent variable.
   d. the experimental group.

10. In participant observation, the problem of "breaking in" to a setting is often solved with the help of a
    a. key informant.
    b. research assistant.
    c. bigger budget.
    d. All of the above are correct.

ANSWERS: 1 (a); 2 (c); 3 (b); 4 (a); 5 (d); 6 (c); 7 (b); 8 (c); 9 (d); 10 (a).

Essay Questions

1. Explain the idea that there are various types of truth. What are the advantages and limitations of science as a way of discovering truth?

2. Compare and contrast scientific sociology, interpretive sociology, and critical sociology. Which of these approaches best describes the work of Durkheim, Weber, and Marx?

Culture

Culture

WHAT is culture?

WHY is it so important to understand people's cultural differences?

HOW does culture support social inequality?

Whether we look at dancers in Cuzco, Peru, or students on a U.S. college campus, we find distinctive lifestyles. The way we dress, the jobs we do, what we believe, and the things we have are all part of a way of life we call culture.

Hugh Sitton/Corbis Zefa Collection

65

Charles Schwab & Company, Inc.

Back in 1990, executives of Charles Schwab & Co., a large investment brokerage corporation, gathered at the company's headquarters in San Francisco to discuss ways they could expand their business. One idea was that the company would profit by giving greater attention to the increasing racial and ethnic diversity of the United States. In particular, they pointed to Census Bureau data showing the rising number of Asian Americans, not just in San Francisco but throughout the country. The data showed (then as now) that Asian Americans are also, on average, wealthy, with more than one-third of households earning more than $75,000 a year (in today's dollars).

This meeting led Schwab to launch a diversity initiative, assigning three executives to work just on building awareness of the company among Asian Americans. In the years since then, the scope of the program grew and Schwab now employs as many as 300 people speaking Chinese, Japanese, Korean, Vietnamese, or another Asian language. Knowing these languages is important because research shows that most Asian Americans who come to the United States prefer to communicate in their first language. In addition, the company has launched Web sites using Chinese and other Asian languages. Finally, the company has opened branch offices in many Asian American neighborhoods in cities on both coasts.

Has this diversity program succeeded? Schwab has gained a much larger share of investments made by Asian Americans. Because Asian Americans spend more than $300 billion a year, any company would be smart to follow Schwab's lead. Other ethnic and racial categories that represent even larger markets in the United States are Hispanics (who spend $580 billion each year) and African Americans ($600 billion) (Fattah, 2002; Karrfalt, 2003).

Businesses like Schwab are taking note of the fact that the United States is the most *multicultural* of all the world's nations. This cultural diversity reflects the country's long history of receiving immigrants from all over the world. The ways of life found around the world differ, not only in forms of dress, preferred foods, and musical tastes but also in family patterns and beliefs about right and wrong. Some of the world's people have many children, while others have few; some honor the elderly, while others seem to glorify youth. Some societies are peaceful, while others are warlike; and segments of humanity embrace a thousand different religious beliefs as well as particular ideas about what is polite and rude, beautiful and ugly, pleasant and repulsive. This amazing human capacity for so many different ways of life is a matter of human culture.

What Is Culture?

Culture is *the ways of thinking, the ways of acting, and the material objects that together form a people's way of life.* Culture includes what we think, how we act, and what we own. Culture is both our link to the past and our guide to the future.

To understand all that culture is, we must consider both thoughts and things. **Nonmaterial culture** is *the ideas created by members of a society,* ideas that range from art to Zen. **Material culture,** by contrast, is *the physical things created by members of a society,* everything from armchairs to zippers.

Culture shapes not only what we do but also what we think and how we feel—elements of what we commonly, but wrongly, describe as "human nature." The warlike Yanomamö of the Brazilian rain forest think aggression is natural, but halfway around the world, the Semai of Malaysia live quite peacefully. The cultures of the United States and Japan both stress achievement and hard work, but members of our society value individualism more than the Japanese, who value collective harmony.

Given the extent of cultural differences in the world and people's tendency to view their own way of life as "natural," it is no wonder that travelers often find themselves feeling uneasy as they enter an unfamiliar culture. This uneasiness is **culture shock,** *personal disorientation when experiencing an unfamiliar way of life.* People can experience culture shock right here in the United States when, say, African Americans explore an Iranian neighborhood in Los Angeles, college students venture into the Amish countryside in Ohio, or New Yorkers travel through small towns in the Deep South. But culture shock is most intense when we travel abroad: The Thinking Globally box on page 60 tells the story of a U.S. researcher making his first visit to the home of the Yanomamö people living in the Amazon region of South America.

Can you describe specific practices or social patterns familiar to us in the United States that would shock people from another society?

Chapter Overview

This chapter focuses on the concept of "culture," which refers to a society's entire way of life. Notice that the root of the word "culture" is the same as that of the word "cultivate," suggesting that people living together actually "grow" their way of life over time.

Human beings around the globe create diverse ways of life. Such differences begin with outward appearance: Contrast the women shown here from Brazil, Kenya, New Guinea, South Yemen, and the United States and the men from Taiwan (Republic of China), India, Canada, and New Guinea. Less obvious but of even greater importance are internal differences, since culture also shapes our goals in life, our sense of justice, and even our innermost personal feelings.

student 2 student

"I like the way the text points out that as human beings, it is our nature to create culture."

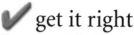

get it right

Humans are not the only creatures who have culture, but we are the only creatures who *depend on* culture to survive.

Thinking Globally
Confronting the Yąnomamö: The Experience of Culture Shock

A small aluminum motorboat chugged steadily along the muddy Orinoco River, deep within South America's vast tropical rain forest. The anthropologist Napoleon Chagnon was nearing the end of a three-day journey to the home territory of the Yąnomamö, one of the most technologically simple societies on Earth.

Some 12,000 Yąnomamö live in villages scattered along the border of Venezuela and Brazil. Their way of life could not be more different from our own. The Yąnomamö wear little clothing and live without electricity, automobiles, or other familiar conveniences. Their traditional weapon, used for hunting and warfare, is the bow and arrow. Most of the Yąnomamö knew little about the outside world, so Chagnon would be as strange to them as they would be to him.

By 2:00 in the afternoon, Chagnon had almost reached his destination. The heat and humidity were almost unbearable. He was soaked with perspiration, and his face and hands swelled from the bites of gnats swarming around him. But he hardly noticed, so excited was he that in just a few moments, he would be face to face with people unlike any he had ever known.

Chagnon's heart pounded as the boat slid onto the riverbank. He and his guide climbed from the boat and headed toward the sounds of a nearby village, pushing their way through the dense undergrowth. Chagnon describes what happened next:

> I looked up and gasped when I saw a dozen burly, naked, sweaty, hideous men staring at us down the shafts of their drawn arrows! Immense wads of green tobacco were stuck between their lower teeth and lips, making them look even more hideous, and strands of dark green slime dripped or hung from their nostrils—strands so long that they clung to their [chests] or drizzled down their chins.

My next discovery was that there were a dozen or so vicious, underfed dogs snapping at my legs, circling me as if I were to be their next meal. I just stood there holding my notebook, helpless and pathetic. Then the stench of the decaying vegetation and filth hit me and I almost got sick. I was horrified. What kind of welcome was this for the person who came here to live with you and learn your way of life, to become friends with you? (1992:11–12)

Fortunately for Chagnon, the Yąnomamö villagers recognized his guide and lowered their weapons. Though reassured that he would survive the afternoon, Chagnon was still shaken by his inability to make any sense of the people surrounding him. And this was to be his home for a year and a half! He wondered why he had given up physics to study human culture in the first place.

WHAT DO YOU THINK?

1. As they came to know Chagnon, might the Yąnomamö, too, have experienced culture shock? Why?

2. Can you think of an experience you had that is similar to the one described here?

3. How can studying sociology help reduce the experience of culture shock?

Herve Collart Odinetz/Corbis/Sygma

January 2, high in the Andes Mountains of Peru. In the rural highlands, people are poor and depend on one another. The culture is built on cooperation among family members and neighbors who have lived nearby for generations. Today, we spent an hour watching a new house being built. A young couple invited their families and friends, who arrived at about 6:30 in the morning, and right away they began building. By midafternoon, most of the work was done, and the couple then provided a large meal, drinks, and music that continued for the rest of the day.

No way of life is "natural" to humanity, even though most people around the world view their own behavior that way. The cooperation that comes naturally to people in the Andes Mountains of Peru is very different from the competitive living that comes

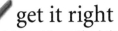

get it right

Carefully read the section below that defines the concepts "culture," "society," and "nation" so that you clearly understand the meaning of each and how each one differs from the others.

tip

The United States is culturally diverse, reflecting our historically high level of immigration.

naturally to many people in, say, Chicago or New York City. Such variations come from the fact that as human beings, we join together to create our own way of life. Every other animal—from ants to zebras—behaves very much the same all around the world because behavior is guided by *instincts,* biological programming over which the species has no control. A few animals—notably chimpanzees and related primates—have the capacity for limited culture, as researchers have noted by observing them using tools and teaching simple skills to their offspring. But the creative power of humans is far greater than that of any other form of life and has resulted in countless ways of being "human." In short, *only humans rely on culture rather than instinct to create a way of life and ensure our survival* (M. Harris, 1987). To understand how human culture came to be, we need to look back at the history of our species.

Culture and Human Intelligence

Scientists tell us that our planet is 4.5 billion years old (see the timeline inside the front cover of this text). Life appeared about 1 billion years later. Fast-forward another 2 to 3 billion years, and we find dinosaurs ruling Earth. It was after these giant creatures disappeared, some 65 million years ago, that our history took a crucial turn with the appearance of the animals we call primates.

The importance of primates is that they have the largest brains relative to body size of all living creatures. About 12 million years ago, primates began to evolve along two different lines, setting humans apart from the great apes, our closest relatives. Then, some 3 million years ago, our distant human ancestors climbed down from the trees of Central Africa to move about in the tall grasses. There, walking upright, they learned the advantages of hunting in groups and made use of fire, tools, and weapons; built simple shelters; and fashioned basic clothing. These Stone Age achievements may seem modest, but they mark the point at which our ancestors set off on a distinct evolutionary course, making culture their primary strategy for survival. By about 250,000 years ago, our own species, *Homo sapiens* (derived from the Latin meaning "thinking person"), finally emerged. Humans continued to evolve so that by about 40,000 years ago, people who looked more or less like ourselves roamed the planet. With larger brains, these "modern" *Homo sapiens* developed culture rapidly, as the wide range of tools and cave art from this period suggests.

About 12,000 years ago, the founding of permanent settlements and the creation of specialized occupations in the Middle East (in what today is Iraq and Egypt) marked the "birth of civilization." At this point, the biological forces we call instincts had mostly disappeared, replaced by a more efficient survival scheme: *fashioning the natural environment for ourselves.* Ever since, humans have made and remade

All societies contain cultural differences that can provoke a mild case of culture shock. This woman traveling on a British subway is not sure what to make of the woman sitting next to her, who is wearing the Muslim full-face veil known as the niqab.

iWitness Photos/Alamy Images

their world in countless ways, resulting in today's fascinating cultural diversity.

Culture, Nation, and Society

The term "culture" calls to mind other similar terms, such as "nation" and "society," although each has a slightly different meaning. *Culture* refers to a shared way of life. A *nation* is a political entity, a territory with designated borders, such as the United States, Canada, Peru, or Zimbabwe. *Society,* the topic of Chapter 4, is the organized interaction of people who typically live in a nation or some other specific territory.

The United States, then, is both a nation and a society. But many nations, including the United States, are *multicultural;* that is, their people follow various ways of life that blend (and sometimes clash).

How Many Cultures?

In the United States, how many cultures are there? One indicator of culture is language; the Census Bureau lists more than 200 languages spoken in this country, most of which were brought by immigrants from nations around the world.

Globally, experts document almost 7,000 languages, suggesting the existence of as many distinct cultures. Yet the number of languages spoken around the world is declining, and roughly half now are spoken by fewer than 10,000 people. Experts expect that the coming decades may see the disappearance of hundreds of these languages, from Gullah, Pennsylvania German, and Pawnee (all spoken in the United States) to Han (spoken in northwestern Canada), Oro (spoken in the Amazon region of Brazil), Sardinian (spoken on the European island of Sardinia), Aramaic (the language of Jesus of Nazareth, still spoken in the Middle East), Nu Shu (a language spoken in southern China that is the only one known to be used exclusively by women), and Wakka Wakka and several other Aboriginal tongues spoken in Australia. What accounts for the decline? Likely causes include high-technology communication, increasing international migration, and an expanding global economy (UNESCO, 2001; Barovick, 2002; Hayden, 2003).

The Elements of Culture

Although cultures vary greatly, they all have common elements, including symbols, language, values, and norms. We begin our discussion with the one that is the basis for all the others: symbols.

People throughout the world communicate not just with spoken words but also with bodily gestures. Because gestures vary from culture to culture, they can occasionally be the cause of misunderstandings. For instance, the commonplace "thumbs up" gesture we use to express "Good job!" can get a person from the United States into trouble in Greece, Iran, and a number of other countries, where people take it to mean "Up yours!"

Stone/Getty Images

Symbols

Like all creatures, humans use their senses to experience the surrounding world, but unlike others, we also try to give the world *meaning*. Humans transform elements of the world into *symbols*. A **symbol** is *anything that carries a particular meaning recognized by people who share a culture*. A word, a whistle, a wall of graffiti, a flashing red light, a raised fist—all serve as symbols. We can see the human capacity to create and manipulate symbols reflected in the very different meanings associated with the simple act of winking an eye, which can convey interest, understanding, or insult.

Societies create new symbols all the time. The Seeing Sociology in Everyday Life box describes some of the cyber-symbols that have developed along with our increasing use of computers for communication.

We are so dependent on our culture's symbols that we take them for granted. However, we become keenly aware of the importance of a symbol when someone uses it in an unconventional way, as when a person burns a U.S. flag during a political demonstration. Entering an unfamiliar culture also reminds us of the power of symbols; culture shock is really the inability to "read" meaning in new surroundings. Not understanding the symbols of a culture leaves a person feeling lost and isolated, unsure of how to act, and sometimes frightened.

Culture shock is a two-way process. On one hand, travelers *experience* culture shock when encountering people whose way of life is different. For example, North Americans who consider dogs beloved household pets might be put off by the Masai of eastern Africa, who ignore dogs and never feed them. The same travelers might be horrified to find that in parts of Indonesia and the northern regions of the People's Republic of China, people roast dogs for dinner.

On the other hand, a traveler may *inflict* culture shock on local people by acting in ways that offend them. A North American who asks for a steak in an Indian restaurant may unknowingly offend Hindus, who consider cows sacred and never to be eaten. Global travel provides almost endless opportunities for this kind of misunderstanding.

Symbolic meanings also vary within a single society. To some people in the United States, a fur coat represents a prized symbol of success, but to others, it represents the inhumane treatment of animals. In the debate about flying the Confederate flag over the South Carolina state house a few years ago, some people saw the flag as a symbol of regional pride, but others saw it as a symbol of racial oppression.

Language

An illness in infancy left Helen Keller (1880–1968) blind and deaf. Without these two senses, she was cut off from the symbolic world, and her social development was greatly limited. Only when her

get it right

Symbols and language involve attaching meaning to action, as well as to sounds and writing. Values, beliefs, and norms involve not just meaning but also moral judgments.

✿ tip

As the box below explains, people create new cultural elements all the time.

Seeing Sociology in Everyday Life
New Symbols in the World of Instant Messaging

Soc was Gr8!
   What happened?
I was :'-D
   Y?
The prof looks like =(_8^(1)
   Maybe his wife looks like >@@@@8^)
GMTA
   See you B4 class. B4N
BCNU

The world of symbols changes all the time. One reason that people create new symbols is that we develop new ways to communicate. Today, almost 100 million people in the United States (most of them young and many of them students) communicate using an instant messaging (IM) program. All you need to have is a computer and a connection to the Internet. About 200 million people also stay connected away from home using a cellular phone.

The exchange above starts with one friend telling the other how much she enjoyed her new sociology class. It makes use of some of the new "shorthand" symbols that have emerged in the IM world. Here is a sampling of IM symbols. (To appreciate the "emoticon" faces, rotate the page 90° to the right.)

:'-D I'm laughing so hard I'm crying.
:-(I am sad.
:-() I am shocked.
:-) I am smiling.
:-)8 I am smiling and wearing a bow tie.
:-O Wow!
:-|| I am angry with you.

:- P I'm sticking my tongue out at you!
%-} I think I've had too much to drink.
:-x My lips are sealed!
-:(Somebody cut my hair into a mohawk!
@}———>——— Here's a rose for you!
=(_8^(1) Homer Simpson
>@@@@8^) Marge Simpson
AFAIK As far as I know
AWHFY Are we having fun yet?
B4 Before
B4N 'Bye for now
BBL Be back later

BCNU Be seeing you
CU See you!
GAL Get a life!
GMTA Great minds think alike.
Gr8 Great
HAGN Have a good night.
H&K Hugs and kisses
IMBL It must be love.
J4F Just for fun
KC Keep cool.
L8r Later
LTNC Long time no see
MYOB Mind your own business.
PCM Please call me.
QPSA ¿Que pasa?
U You
UR You are
Wan2 Want to
X! Typical woman!
Y! Typical man!
Y Why
2bctd To be continued
2g4u Too good for you
2L8 Too late

WHAT DO YOU THINK?

1. What does the creation of symbols such as these suggest about culture?

2. Do you think that using such symbols is a good way to communicate? Does it lead to confusion or misunderstanding? Why or why not?

3. What other kinds of symbols can you think of that are new to your generation?

Sources: J. Rubin (2003) and Berteau (2005).

Corbis Royalty Free

teacher, Anne Mansfield Sullivan, broke through Keller's isolation using sign language did Helen Keller begin to realize her human potential. This remarkable woman, who later became a famous educator herself, recalls the moment she first understood the concept of language:

We walked down the path to the well-house, attracted by the smell of honeysuckle with which it was covered. Someone was drawing water, and my teacher placed my hand under the spout. As the cool stream gushed over one hand, she spelled into the other the word *water*, first slowly, then rapidly. I stood still, my whole attention fixed upon the motions of her fingers. Suddenly I felt a misty consciousness as of

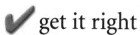
something forgotten—a thrill of returning thought; and somehow the mystery of language was revealed to me. I knew then that "w-a-t-e-r" meant the wonderful cool something that was flowing over my hand. That living word awakened my soul; gave it light, hope, joy, set it free! (1903:24)

Language, the key to the world of culture, is *a system of symbols that allows people to communicate with one another.* Humans have created many alphabets to express the hundreds of languages we speak. Several examples are shown in Figure 1. Even rules for writing differ: Most people in Western societies write from left to right, but people in northern Africa and western Asia write from right to left, and people in eastern Asia write from top to bottom. Global Map 1 shows where we find the world's three most widely spoken languages.

Language not only allows communication but is also the key to **cultural transmission,** *the process by which one generation passes culture to the next.* Just as our bodies contain the genes of our ancestors, our culture contains countless symbols of those who came before us. Language is the key that unlocks centuries of accumulated wisdom.

List three cultural elements that were passed on to you from earlier generations. List three different cultural elements that have emerged in your own generation; do you think these will last to be passed on to your children and grandchildren?

Throughout human history, every society has transmitted culture through speech, a process sociologists call the "oral cultural tradi-

tion." Some 5,000 years ago, humans invented writing, although at that time only a privileged few learned to read and write. Not until the twentieth century did high-income nations boast of nearly universal literacy. Still, at least 10 percent of U.S. adults (more than 20 million people) are functionally illiterate, unable to read and write in a society that increasingly demands such skills. In low-income countries of the world, 30 percent of men and 50 percent of women are illiterate (World Bank, 2007).

Language skills may link us with the past, but they also spark the human imagination to connect symbols in new ways, creating an almost limitless range of future possibilities. Language sets humans apart as the only creatures who are self-conscious, aware of our limitations and ultimate mortality, yet able to dream and to hope for a future better than the present.

Does Language Shape Reality?

Does someone who speaks Cherokee, an American Indian language, experience the world differently from other North Americans who think in, say, English or Spanish? Edward Sapir and Benjamin Whorf claimed that the answer is yes, since each language has its own distinctive symbols that serve as the building blocks of reality (Sapir, 1929, 1949; Whorf, 1956, orig. 1941). Further, they noted that each language has words or expressions not found in any other symbolic system. Finally, all languages fuse symbols with distinctive emotions so that, as multilingual people know, a single idea may "feel" different when spoken in Spanish rather than in English or Chinese.

Formally, the **Sapir-Whorf thesis** states that *people see and understand the world through the cultural lens of language.* In the decades since Sapir and Whorf published their work, however, scholars have taken issue with this thesis. Current thinking is that although we do fashion reality from our symbols, evidence does not support the notion that language *determines* reality the way Sapir and Whorf claimed. For example, we know that children understand the idea of "family" long before they learn that word; similarly, adults can imagine new ideas or things before inventing a name for them (Kay & Kempton, 1984; Pinker, 1994).

Values and Beliefs

What accounts for the popularity of Hollywood film characters such as James Bond, Neo, Erin Brockovich, Lara Croft, and Rocky Balboa? Each is ruggedly individualistic, going it alone and relying on personal skill and savvy to challenge "the system." We are led to admire such characters by certain **values,** *culturally defined standards that people use to decide what is desirable, good, and beautiful and that serve*

إقرأواو Arabic	**Read** English	독서 Korean
Կարդա Armenian	διαβάζω Greek	بخوانيد. Persian
Cambodian	אקרא Hebrew	читать Russian
閲讀 Chinese	पढ़ना Hindi	¡Ven a leer! Spanish

FIGURE 1   **Human Languages: A Variety of Symbols**

Here the English word "read" is written in twelve of the hundreds of languages humans use to communicate with one another.

Chinese is spoken as a native language by twice as many people in the world as English, but English is a widely spoken second language almost everywhere in the world.

Chinese
- Official language
- Widely spoken second language

English
- Official language
- Widely spoken second language

Spanish
- Official language
- Widely spoken second language

WINDOW ON THE WORLD

GLOBAL MAP 1
Language in Global Perspective

Chinese (including Mandarin, Cantonese, and dozens of other dialects) is the native tongue of one-fifth of the world's people, almost all of whom live in Asia. Although all Chinese people read and write with the same characters, they use several dozen dialects. The "official" dialect, taught in schools throughout the People's Republic of China and the Republic of Taiwan, is Mandarin (the dialect of Beijing, China's historic capital city). Cantonese, the language of Canton, is the second most common Chinese dialect; it differs in sound from Mandarin roughly the way French differs from Spanish.

English is the native tongue or official language in several world regions (spoken by one-tenth of humanity) and has become the preferred second language in most of the world.

The largest concentration of Spanish speakers is in Latin America and, of course, Spain. Spanish is also the second most widely spoken language in the United States.

Source: *Peters Atlas of the World* (1990); updated by the author.

tip

Looking at the list of key values of U.S. culture, we are a nation of people who value individualism and achievement (often measured in terms of money and what it will buy). Value 10 is really at odds with the rest of the list, suggesting that our way of life is complex and in some ways inconsistent.

The Australian artist and feminist Sally Swain alters famous artists' paintings to make fun of our culture's tendency to ignore the everyday lives of women. This spoof is titled *Mrs. Chagall Feeds the Baby*.

Mrs. Chagall Feeds the Baby, from *Great Housewives of Art* by Sally Swain, copyright © 1988, 1989 by Sally Swain. Used by permission of Viking Penguin, a division of Penguin Group (USA) Inc.

as broad guidelines for social living. Values are what people who share a culture use to make choices about how to live.

Values are broad principles that support **beliefs,** *specific thoughts or ideas that people hold to be true.* In other words, values are abstract standards of goodness, and beliefs are particular matters that individuals consider true or false. For example, because most U.S. adults share the *value* of providing equal opportunities for all, they believe that a qualified woman could serve as president of the United States (NORC, 2005).

Key Values of U.S. Culture

Because U.S. culture is a mix of ways of life from other countries all around the world, it is highly diverse. In addition, due to the nation's high level of immigration and the creativity of the population, U.S. culture is always changing. Even so, the sociologist Robin Williams (1970) has identified ten values that are widespread in the United States and viewed by many people as central to our way of life:

1. **Equal opportunity.** Most people in the United States favor not *equality of condition* but *equality of opportunity.* We believe that our society should provide everyone with the chance to get ahead according to individual talents and efforts.

2. **Achievement and success.** Our way of life encourages competition so that each person's rewards should reflect personal merit. A successful person is given the respect due a "winner."

3. **Material comfort.** Success in the United States generally means making money and enjoying what it will buy. Although we sometimes say that "money won't buy happiness," most of us pursue wealth all the same.

4. **Activity and work.** Popular U.S. heroes, from golf champion Tiger Woods to the winners of television's *American Idol,* are "doers" who get the job done. Our culture values action over reflection and controlling events over passively accepting fate.

5. **Practicality and efficiency.** We value the practical over the theoretical, "doing" over "dreaming." Activity has value to the extent that it earns money. "Major in something that will help you get a job!" parents say to their college-age children.

6. **Progress.** We are an optimistic people who, despite waves of nostalgia, believe that the present is better than the past. We celebrate progress, viewing "the very latest" as "the very best."

7. **Science.** We expect scientists to solve problems and improve the quality of our lives. We believe we are rational, logical people, which probably explains our cultural tendency (especially among men) to look down on emotion and intuition as sources of knowledge.

8. **Democracy and free enterprise.** Members of our society believe that individuals have rights that governments should not take away. We believe that a just political system is based on free elections in which adults select government leaders and on an economy that responds to the choices of individual consumers.

9. **Freedom.** We favor individual initiative over collective conformity. While we know that everyone has responsibilities to

tip

Think about the messages found in today's popular music, on television, and in films. How well do you think these messages square with the list of key values found in the text?

get it right

Be sure you understand how cultural values in high-income societies differ from those in low-income societies.

others, we believe that people should be free to pursue their personal goals.

10. **Racism and group superiority.** Despite strong ideas about equal opportunity and freedom, most people in the United States judge individuals according to gender, race, ethnicity, and social class. In general, U.S. culture values males above females, whites above people of color, rich above poor, and people with northwestern European backgrounds above those whose ancestors came from other parts of the world. Although we like to describe ourselves as a nation of equals, there is little doubt that some of us are "more equal" than others.

Think about the games you played when you were growing up, like Tag or Capture the Flag, or board games, like Monopoly or Chutes and Ladders. What cultural values do they teach? What about video games like Grand Theft Auto, God of War, or Rainbow Six Vegas?

How does the popularity of the television show *American Idol* illustrate many of the key values of U.S. culture listed here?

Frank Micelotta/Fox Broadcasting/ Photofest

Values: Often in Harmony, Sometimes in Conflict

In many ways, cultural values go together. Williams's list includes examples of *value clusters* in our way of life. For instance, we value activity and work because we expect effort to lead to achievement and success and result in material comfort.

Sometimes, however, one key cultural value contradicts another. Take the first and last items on Williams's list, for example: People in the United States believe in equality of opportunity, yet they may also look down on others because of their sex or race. Value conflict causes strain and often leads to awkward balancing acts in our beliefs. Sometimes people might say they support equal opportunity while at the same time opposing the acceptance of homosexual people in the U.S. military. In such cases, people simply learn to live with the contradictions.

Emerging Values

Like all elements of culture, values change over time. People in the United States have always valued hard work. In recent decades, however, we have placed increasing importance on leisure—having time off from work to do things such as reading, travel, or community service that provide enjoyment and satisfaction. Similarly, although the importance of material comfort remains strong, more people are seeking personal growth through meditation and other spiritual activity.

Values: A Global Perspective

Each of the thousands of cultures in the world has its own values. In general, the values that are important in higher-income countries differ somewhat from those common in lower-income countries.

Lower-income nations have cultures that value survival. This means that people place a great deal of importance on physical safety and economic security. They worry about having enough to eat and a safe place to sleep at night. In addition, lower-income nations tend to be traditional, with values that celebrate the past and emphasize the importance of family and religious beliefs, obedience to authority, and conformity. These nations, in which men have most of the power, typically discourage or forbid practices such as divorce and abortion.

Higher-income countries have cultures that value individualism and self-expression. These countries are rich enough that most of their people take survival for granted, focusing their attention instead on which "lifestyle" they prefer and how to achieve the greatest personal happiness. In addition, these countries tend to be secular-rational, placing less emphasis on family ties and religious beliefs and more on people thinking for themselves and being tolerant of others. In higher-income countries, women have social standing more equal to men, and there is widespread support for practices such as divorce and abortion (World Values Survey, 2004). Figure 2 shows how selected countries of the world compare in terms of their cultural values.

 **get it right**

"Mores" and "folkways" are two types of norms. Neither term is used very much these days, but the point is that some norms involve very serious moral issues (mores) and some involve less serious standards for everyday interactions (folkways).

GLOBAL SNAPSHOT

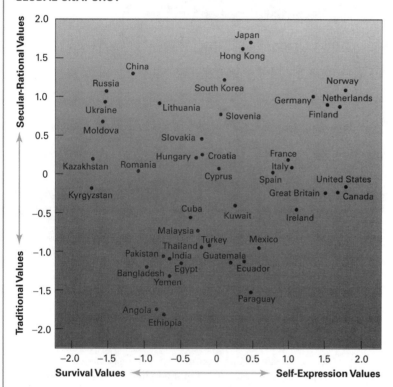

FIGURE 2 Cultural Values of Selected Countries

Higher-income countries are secular-rational and favor self-expression. The cultures of lower-income countries are more traditional and concerned with economic survival.

Source: *Modernization, Cultural Change and Democracy* by Ronald Inglehart and Christian Welzel. New York: Cambridge University Press, 2005.

Figure 3–2 shows that as a rich nation, the United States ranks high in terms of self-expression but is more traditional than many other high-income nations, such as those in Europe. Can you point to specific beliefs or practices that set us apart from Europeans as more traditional?

Norms

Most people in the United States are eager to gossip about "who's hot" and "who's not." Members of American Indian societies, however, typically condemn such behavior as rude and divisive. Both patterns illustrate the operation of **norms**, *rules and expectations by which a society guides the behavior of its members*. Some norms are *proscriptive*, stating

what we *should not* do, as when health officials warn us to avoid casual sex. *Prescriptive* norms, on the other hand, state what we *should* do, as when U.S. schools teach "safe sex" practices.

The most important norms in a culture apply everywhere and at all times. For example, parents expect obedience from young children regardless of the setting. Other norms depend on the situation. In the United States, we expect the audience to applaud after a musical performance; we may applaud (although it is not expected) at the end of a classroom lecture; we do not applaud at the end of a religious sermon.

Mores and Folkways

William Graham Sumner (1959, orig. 1906), an early U.S. sociologist, recognized that some norms are more important to our lives than others. Sumner coined the term **mores** (pronounced "more-ays") to refer to *norms that are widely observed and have great moral significance*. Mores, or *taboos*, include our society's insistence that adults not engage in sexual relations with children.

People pay less attention to **folkways,** *norms for routine or casual interaction*. Examples include ideas about appropriate greetings and proper dress. In short, mores distinguish between right and wrong, and folkways draw a line between right and *rude*. A man who does not wear a tie to a formal dinner party may raise eyebrows for violating folkways. If, however, he were to arrive at the party wearing *only* a tie, he would violate cultural mores and invite a more serious response.

Give two examples of violating campus folkways and two examples of violating campus mores. What are the likely consequences of each type of violation?

Social Control

Mores and folkways are the basic rules of everyday life. Although we sometimes resist pressure to conform, we can see that norms make our dealings with others more orderly and predictable. Observing or breaking the rules of social life prompts a response from others, in the form of reward or punishment. Sanctions—whether an approving smile or a raised eyebrow—operate as a system of **social control,** *attempts by society to regulate people's thoughts and behavior*.

As we learn cultural norms, we gain the capacity to evaluate our own behavior. Doing wrong (say, downloading a term paper from the Internet) can cause both *shame* (the painful sense that others disapprove of our actions) and *guilt* (a negative judgment we make of our-

tip

One way to think of culture is as a system of social control that encourages people to think and act in certain ways.

tip

Technology is one important element of culture. Some sociologists claim that a society's level of technology has a lot to do with its overall way of life.

selves). Of all living things, only cultural creatures can experience shame and guilt. This is probably what Mark Twain had in mind when he remarked that people "are the only animals that blush—or need to."

Ideal and Real Culture

Values and norms do not describe actual behavior so much as they suggest how we *should* behave. We must remember that *ideal* culture always differs from *real* culture, which is what actually occurs in everyday life. For example, most women and men agree on the importance of sexual faithfulness in marriage. Even so, in one study, about 25 percent of married men and 10 percent of married women reported having been sexually unfaithful to their spouses at some point in their marriage (Laumann et al., 1994). But a culture's moral standards are important all the same, calling to mind the old saying "Do as I say, not as I do."

Material Culture and Technology

In addition to symbolic elements such as values and norms, every culture includes a wide range of physical human creations, which sociologists call *artifacts.* The Chinese eat with chopsticks rather than forks, the Japanese put mats rather than rugs on the floor, and many men and women in India prefer flowing robes to the close-fitting clothing common in the United States. The material culture of a people may seem as strange to outsiders as their language, values, and norms.

A society's artifacts partly reflect underlying cultural values. The warlike Yąnomamö carefully craft their weapons and prize the poison tips on their arrows. By contrast, our society's emphasis on individualism and independence goes a long way toward explaining our high regard for the automobile: We own 233 million motor vehicles—more than one for every licensed driver—and in recent years, half of all cars sold in the United States have been the large sports utility vehicles that we might expect rugged, individualistic people to like.

 If archaeologists dig up our civilization 50,000 years from now, based on the artifacts they find, what kind of people will they think we were? Point to specific "artifacts" (such as SUVs, cell phones, and credit cards) and what they say about us.

In addition to reflecting values, material culture also reflects a society's **technology,** *knowledge that people use to make a way of life in their surroundings.* The more com-

plex a society's technology, the more its members are able (for better or worse) to shape the world for themselves. Advanced technology has allowed us to crisscross the country with superhighways and to fill them with automobiles. At the same time, the internal-combustion engines in those cars release carbon dioxide into the atmosphere, which contributes to air pollution and global warming.

Because we attach great importance to science and praise sophisticated technology, people in our society tend to judge cultures with simpler technology as less advanced than our own. Some facts support such an assessment. For example, life expectancy for children born in the United States is more than seventy-seven years; the life span of the Yąnomamö is only about forty years.

However, we must be careful not to make self-serving judgments about other cultures. Although many Yąnomamö are eager to acquire modern technology (such as steel tools and shotguns), they are generally well fed by world standards, and most are very satisfied with their lives (Chagnon, 1992). Remember too that while our powerful and complex technology has produced work-reducing devices and seemingly miraculous medical treatments, it has also contributed to unhealthy levels of stress in the population and created weapons capable of destroying in a blinding flash everything that humankind has achieved.

Standards of beauty—including the color and design of everyday surroundings—vary significantly from one culture to another. These two Ndebele women in South Africa dress in the same bright colors with which they decorate their homes. Members of North American and European societies, by contrast, make far less use of bright colors and intricate detail, so their housing appears much more subdued.

Claudia Adams/DanitaDelimont.com

Finally, technology is not equally distributed within our population. Although many of us cannot imagine life without a personal computer, television, and iPhone, many members of U.S. society cannot afford these luxuries. Others reject them on principle. The Amish, who live in small farming communities in Pennsylvania, Ohio, and Indiana, reject most modern conveniences on religious grounds. With their traditional black clothing and horse-drawn buggies, the Amish may seem like a curious relic of the past. Yet their communities flourish, grounded in strong families that give everyone a sense of identity and purpose. Some researchers who have studied the Amish have concluded that these communities are "islands of sanity in a culture gripped by commercialism and technology run wild" (Hostetler, 1980:4; Kraybill, 1994).

New Information Technology and Culture

Many rich nations, including the United States, have entered a postindustrial phase based on computers and new information technology. Industrial production is centered on factories and machinery that generate material goods. By contrast, postindustrial production is based on computers and other electronic devices that create, process, store, and apply information.

In this new information economy, workers need symbolic skills in place of the mechanical skills of the industrial age. Symbolic skills include the ability to speak, write, compute, design, and create images in fields such as art, advertising, and entertainment. In today's computer-based economy, people with creative jobs are generating new cultural ideas, images, and products all the time.

Cultural Diversity: Many Ways of Life in One World

In the United States, we are aware of our cultural diversity when we hear the distinctive accents of people from New England, the Midwest, or the Deep South. Ours is also a nation of religious pluralism, a land of class differences, and a home to individualists who try to be like no one else. Compared to a country like Japan, whose historic isolation has made it the most *monocultural* of all high-income nations, centuries of immigration have made the United States the most *multicultural* of all high-income countries.

Between 1820 (when the government began keeping track of immigration) and 2007, about 75 million people came to our shores. Our cultural mix continues to increase as more than 1 million people arrive each year. A century ago, almost all immigrants came from Europe; today, most newcomers arrive from Latin America and Asia. To understand the reality of life in the United States, we must move beyond broad cultural patterns and shared values to consider cultural diversity.

High Culture and Popular Culture

Cultural diversity involves not just immigration but also social class. In fact, in everyday talk, we usually use the term "culture" to mean art forms such as classical literature, music, dance, and painting. We describe people who regularly go to the opera or the theater as "cultured," because we think they appreciate the "finer things in life."

We speak less kindly of ordinary people, assuming that everyday culture is somehow less worthy. We are tempted to judge the music of Haydn as "more cultured" than hip-hop, couscous as better than cornbread, and polo as more polished than Ping-Pong.

Many subcultures that develop involve young people. One recent example is the skateboarding subculture that includes not only the sport but also a distinctive style of dress.

Chet Gordon/The Image Works

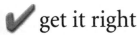
These differences arise because many cultural patterns are readily available to only some members of a society. Sociologists use the term **high culture** to refer to *cultural patterns that distinguish a society's elite* and **popular culture** to designate *cultural patterns that are widespread among a society's population.*

Common sense may suggest that high culture is superior to popular culture, but sociologists are uneasy with such judgments, for two reasons. First, neither elites nor ordinary people share all the same tastes and interests; people in both categories differ in many ways. Second, do we praise high culture because it is inherently better than popular culture or simply because its supporters have more money, power, and prestige? For example, there is no difference between a violin and a fiddle; however, we name the instrument a violin when it is used to produce classical music typically enjoyed by a person of higher position and a fiddle when the musician plays country tunes appreciated by people with lower social standing.

Subculture

The term **subculture** refers to *cultural patterns that set apart some segment of a society's population.* People who ride "chopper" motorcycles, traditional Korean Americans, New England "Yankees," Ohio State football fans, the southern California "beach crowd," Elvis impersonators, and wilderness campers all display subcultural patterns.

 Make a list of five subcultures that are part of your life. Which are the most important?

It is easy but often inaccurate to place people in some subcultural category because almost everyone participates in many subcultures without necessarily having much commitment to any of them. In some cases, however, cultural differences can set people apart from one another with tragic results. Consider the former nation of Yugoslavia in southeastern Europe. The 1990s civil war there was fueled by extreme cultural diversity. This *one* small country used *two* alphabets, embraced *three* religions, spoke *four* languages, was home to *five* major nationalities, was divided into *six* political republics, and absorbed the cultural influences of *seven* surrounding countries. The cultural conflict that plunged this nation into civil war shows that subcultures are a source not only of pleasing variety but also of tension and even violence.

Many people view the United States as a "melting pot" where many nationalities blend into a single "American" culture (Gardyn, 2002). But given so much cultural diversity, how accurate is the "melting pot" image? For one thing, subcultures involve not just *difference* but *hierarchy.* Too often what we view as "dominant" or "mainstream"

A generation ago, most people regarded tattoos as a mark of low social status. Today, this cultural pattern is gaining popularity among people at all social class levels. Kat is a tattoo artist on the nationwide television show *Miami Ink.*

Debbie Van Story/NewsCom

culture are patterns favored by powerful segments of the population, and we view the lives of disadvantaged people as "subculture." But are the cultural patterns of rich skiers in Aspen, Colorado, any less a subculture than the cultural patterns of skateboarders in Los Angeles? Some sociologists therefore prefer to level the playing field of society by emphasizing multiculturalism.

Multiculturalism

Multiculturalism is *a perspective recognizing the cultural diversity of the United States and promoting equal standing for all cultural traditions.* Multiculturalism represents a sharp change from the past, when our society downplayed cultural diversity and defined itself primarily in terms of well-off European and especially English immigrants. Today there is a spirited debate about whether we should continue to focus on historical traditions or highlight contemporary diversity.

E pluribus unum, the Latin phrase that appears on all U.S. coins, means "out of many, one." This motto symbolizes not only our

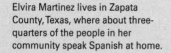

Elvira Martinez lives in Zapata County, Texas, where about three-quarters of the people in her community speak Spanish at home.

Jeffrey Steen lives in Adams County, Ohio, where almost none of his neighbors speaks a language other than English.

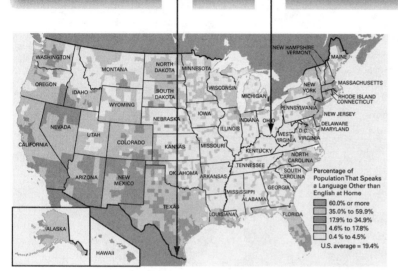

SEEING OURSELVES

NATIONAL MAP 1
Language Diversity across the United States

Of more than 268 million people age five or older in the United States, the Census Bureau reports that 52 million (19 percent) speak a language other than English at home. Of these, 62 percent speak Spanish and 15 percent use an Asian language (the Census Bureau lists 29 languages, each of which is favored by more than 100,000 people). The map shows that non–English speakers are concentrated in certain regions of the country. Which ones? What do you think accounts for this pattern?

Sources: U.S. Census Bureau (2003, 2006).

national political union but also the idea that immigrants from around the world have come together to form a new way of life.

But from the outset, the many cultures did not melt together as much as harden into a hierarchy. At the top were the English, who formed a majority early in U.S. history and established English as the nation's dominant language. Further down, people of other backgrounds were advised to model themselves after "their betters." In practice, then, "melting" was really a process of Anglicization—adoption of English ways. As multiculturalists see it, early in our history, this society set up the English way of life as an ideal that everyone else should imitate and by which everyone should be judged.

Ever since, historians have reported events from the point of view of the English and other people of European ancestry, paying little attention to the perspectives and accomplishments of Native Americans and people of African and Asian descent. Multiculturalists criticize this as **Eurocentrism,** *the dominance of European (especially English) cultural patterns.* Molefi Kete Asante, a supporter of multiculturalism, argues that "like the fifteenth-century Europeans who could not cease believing that the Earth was the center of the universe, many today find it difficult to cease viewing European culture as the center of the social universe" (1988:7).

One controversial issue involves language. Some people believe that English should be the official language of the United States; by 2007, legislatures in twenty-nine states had enacted laws making it the official language. But some 52 million men and women—nearly one in six—speak a language other than English at home. Spanish is the second most commonly spoken language, and across the country we hear several hundred other tongues, including Italian, German,

French, Filipino, Japanese, Korean, and Vietnamese, as well as many Native American languages. National Map 1 shows where in the United States large numbers of people speak a language other than English at home.

Supporters of multiculturalism say it is a way of coming to terms with our country's increasing social diversity. With the Asian and Hispanic populations of this country increasing rapidly, some analysts predict that today's children will live to see people of African, Asian, and Hispanic ancestry become a *majority* of this country's population.

Supporters also claim that multiculturalism is a good way to strengthen the academic achievement of African American children. To counter Eurocentrism, some multicultural educators call for **Afrocentrism,** *emphasizing and promoting African cultural patterns,* which they see as necessary after centuries of minimizing or ignoring the cultural achievements of African societies and African Americans.

Although multiculturalism has found favor in recent years, it has drawn its share of criticism as well. Opponents say it encourages divisiveness rather than unity because it urges people to identify with their own category rather than with the nation as a whole. Instead of recognizing any common standards of truth, say critics, multiculturalism maintains that we should evaluate ideas according to the race (and sex) of those who present them. Our common humanity thus dissolves into an "African experience," an "Asian experience," and so on. In addition, critics say, multiculturalism actually harms minorities themselves. Multicultural policies (from African American studies to all-black dorms) seem to support the same racial segregation that our nation has struggled so long to overcome. Furthermore, in the early grades, an Afrocentric curriculum may deny children a wide range of important knowledge and skills by forcing them to study only certain topics from a single point of view.

Finally, the global war on terror has drawn the issue of multiculturalism into the spotlight. In 2005, British Prime Minister Tony Blair responded to a terrorist attack in London, stating, "It is important that the terrorists realize [that] our determination to defend our values and our way of life is greater than their determination to . . . impose their extremism on the world." He went on to warn that the British government would expel anyone who encouraged hatred and terrorism (Barone, 2005). In a world of cultural difference and conflict, we have much to learn about tolerance and peacemaking.

Counterculture

Cultural diversity also includes outright rejection of conventional ideas or behavior. **Counterculture** refers to *cultural patterns that strongly oppose those widely accepted within a society.*

During the 1960s, for example, a youth-oriented counterculture rejected mainstream culture as overly competitive, self-centered, and materialistic. Instead, hippies and other counterculturalists favored a cooperative lifestyle in which "being" was more important than "doing" and the capacity for personal growth—or "expanded consciousness"— was prized over material possessions like homes and cars. Such differences led some people to "drop out" of the larger society.

Countercultures are still flourishing. At the extreme, small militaristic communities (made up of people born in this country) or bands of religious militants (from other countries) exist in the United States, some of them engaging in violence intended to threaten our way of life.

Cultural Change

Perhaps the most basic human truth of this world is that "all things shall pass." Even the dinosaurs, which thrived on this planet for 160 million years (see the timeline), remain today only as fossils. Will humanity survive for millions of years to come? All we can say with certainty is that given our reliance on culture, for as long as we survive, the human record will show continuous change.

Figure 3 shows changes in attitudes among first-year college students between 1969 (the height of the 1960s' counterculture) and 2006. Some attitudes have changed only slightly: Today, as a generation ago, most men and women look forward to raising a family. But today's students are less concerned with developing a philosophy of life and much more interested in making money.

Change in one part of a culture usually sparks changes in others. For example, today's college women are much more interested in

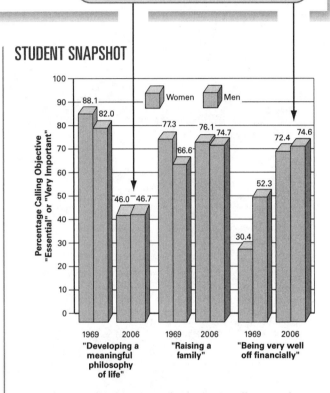

Compared to college students 35 years ago, today's students are less interested in developing a philosophy of life and more interested in making money.

STUDENT SNAPSHOT

FIGURE 3 Life Objectives of First-Year College Students, 1969–2006

Researchers have surveyed first-year college students every year since 1969. While attitudes about some things such as the importance of family have stayed about the same, attitudes about other life goals have changed dramatically.

Sources: Astin et al. (2002) and Pryor et al. (2006).

making money because women are now far more likely to be in the labor force than their mothers or grandmothers were. Working for income may not change their interest in raising a family, but it does increase both the age at first marriage and the divorce rate. Such connections illustrate the principle of **cultural integration,** *the close relationships among various elements of a cultural system.*

Cultural Lag

Some elements of culture change faster than others. William Ogburn (1964) observed that technology moves quickly, generating new elements of material culture (things) faster than nonmaterial culture (ideas) can keep up with them. Ogburn called this inconsistency **cultural lag,** *the fact that some cultural elements change more quickly than others, disrupting a cultural system.* For example, in a world in

 **get it right**

Three sources of social change are mentioned here: *Invention* refers to creating new cultural elements, *discovery* refers to recognizing existing cultural elements, and *diffusion* is the spread of cultural elements from one place to another.

 tip

The timeline inside the front cover of this text provides numerous examples of cultural change.

In the world's low-income countries, most children must work to provide their families with needed income. This seven-year-old boy in eastern Ilam, Nepal, works long hours in a tea field. Is it ethnocentric for people living in high-income nations to condemn the practice of child labor because we think youngsters belong in school? Why or why not?

Alison Wright/Photo Researchers, Inc.

which a woman can give birth to a child by using another woman's egg, which has been fertilized in a laboratory with the sperm of a total stranger, how are we to apply traditional ideas about motherhood and fatherhood?

Causes of Cultural Change

Cultural changes are set in motion in three ways. The first is *invention*, the process of creating new cultural elements. Invention has given us the telephone (1876), the airplane (1903), and the computer (1947); each of these elements of material culture has had a tremendous impact on our way of life. The same is true of the minimum wage (1938), school desegregation (1954), and women's shelters (1975), each an important element of nonmaterial culture.

The process of invention goes on constantly. The timeline on the inside cover of this text shows other inventions that have helped change our way of life.

Discovery, a second cause of cultural change, involves recognizing and understanding more fully something already in existence—perhaps a distant star or the foods of another culture or women's political leadership skills. Some discoveries result from painstaking scientific research, and some result from political struggle. Some even result from luck, as in 1898, when Marie Curie left a rock on a piece of photographic paper, noticed that emissions from the rock had exposed the paper, and thus discovered radium.

The third cause of cultural change is *diffusion*, the spread of cultural traits from one society to another. Because new information technology sends information around the globe in seconds, cultural diffusion has never been greater than it is today.

Certainly our own society has contributed many significant cultural elements to the world, ranging from computers to jazz music. Of course, diffusion works the other way, too, so that much of what we assume to be "American" actually comes from elsewhere. Most of the clothing we wear and the furniture we use, as well as the watch we carry and the money we spend, all had their origin in other cultures (Linton, 1937a).

It is certainly correct to talk about "American culture," especially when we are comparing our way of life to the culture of some other society. But this discussion of cultural change shows us that culture is always complex and always changing. The Thinking About Diversity: Race, Class, & Gender box offers a good example of the diverse and dynamic character of culture with a brief look at the history of rock-and-roll music.

Ethnocentrism and Cultural Relativism

 December 10, a small village in Morocco. Watching many of our fellow travelers browsing through a tiny ceramics factory, we have little doubt that North Americans are among the world's greatest shoppers. We delight in surveying hand-woven carpets in China or India, inspecting finely crafted metals in Turkey, or collecting the beautifully colored porcelain tiles we find here in Morocco. Of course, all these items are wonderful bargains. But one major reason for the low prices is unsettling: Many products from the world's low- and middle-income countries are produced by children—some as young as five or six—who work long days for pennies per hour.

We think of childhood as a time of innocence and freedom from adult burdens like regular work. In poor countries throughout the world, however, families depend on income earned by children. So what people in one society think of as right and natural, people else-where find puzzling and even immoral. Perhaps the Chinese philosopher Confucius had it right when he noted that "all people are the same; it's only their habits that are different."

Just about every imaginable idea or behavior is commonplace somewhere in the world, and this cultural variation causes travelers both excitement and distress. The Australians flip light switches down to turn them on; North Americans flip them up. The Japanese name city blocks; North Americans name streets. Egyptians stand very close to others in conversation; North Americans are used to maintaining several feet of "personal space." Bathrooms lack toilet paper in much of rural Morocco, causing considerable discomfort for North Americans, who recoil at the thought of using the left hand for bathroom hygiene, as the locals do.

Given that a particular culture is the basis for each person's reality, it is no wonder that people everywhere exhibit **ethnocentrism,** *the practice of judging another culture by the standards of one's own culture.* Some degree of ethnocentrism is necessary for people to be emotionally attached to their way of life. But ethnocentrism also generates misunderstanding and sometimes conflict.

Even language is culturally biased. Centuries ago, people in Europe and North America referred to China as the "Far East." But this term, unknown to the Chinese, is an ethnocentric expression for a region that is far to the east *of us.* The Chinese name for their country translates as "Central Kingdom," suggesting that they, like us, see their own society as the center of the world. The map in Figure 4 challenges our own ethnocentrism by presenting a "down under" view of the Western Hemisphere.

The logical alternative to ethnocentrism is **cultural relativism,** *the practice of judging a culture by its own standards.* Cultural relativism can be difficult for travelers to adopt: It requires not only openness to unfamiliar values and norms but also the ability to put aside cultural standards we have known all our lives. Even so, as people of the world come into increasing contact with one another, the importance of understanding other cultures becomes ever greater.

As the opening to this chapter explained, businesses in the United States are learning the value of marketing to a culturally diverse population. Similarly, businesses are learning that success in the global economy depends on awareness of cultural patterns around the world. IBM, for example, now provides technical support for its products using Web sites in more than thirty languages (IBM, 2007).

This trend is a change from the past, when many corporations used marketing strategies that lacked sensitivity to cultural diversity. Coors's phrase "Turn It Loose" startled Spanish-speaking customers by proclaiming that the beer would cause diarrhea. Braniff Airlines translated its slogan "Fly in Leather" so carelessly into Spanish that it read "Fly Naked." Similarly, Eastern Airlines' slogan "We Earn Our

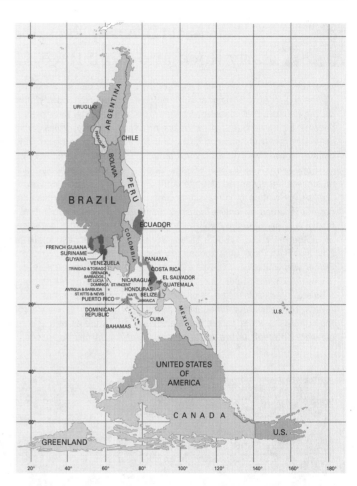

FIGURE 4   The View from "Down Under"

North America should be "up" and South America "down," or so we think. But because we live on a globe, "up" and "down" have no meaning at all. The reason this map of the Western Hemisphere looks wrong to us is not that it is geographically inaccurate; it simply violates our ethnocentric assumption that the United States should be "above" the rest of the Americas.

Wings Every Day" became "We Fly Daily to Heaven." Even poultry giant Frank Purdue fell victim to poor marketing when his pitch "It Takes a Tough Man to Make a Tender Chicken" was transformed into the Spanish words reading "A Sexually Excited Man Will Make a Chicken Affectionate" (Helin, 1992).

But cultural relativism introduces problems of its own. If almost any kind of behavior is the norm *somewhere* in the world, does that mean everything is equally right? Does the fact that some Indian

Thinking About Diversity: Race, Class, & Gender
Early Rock-and-Roll: Race, Class, and Cultural Change

In the 1950s, rock-and-roll emerged as a major part of U.S. popular culture. In the decades that followed, rock grew to become a cultural tide that swept away musical tastes and traditions and changed the country in ways we still experience today.

Early in the 1950s, mainstream "pop" music was largely aimed at white adults. Songs were written by professional composers, recorded by long-established record labels, and performed by well-known artists including Perry Como, Eddie Fisher, Doris Day, and Patti Page. Just about every performer was white.

In the United States, the 1950s was also a time of rigid racial segregation. This racial separation meant social inequality, so that the cultures of white people and black people were different. In the subcultural world of

African Americans, music had different sounds and rhythms, reflecting jazz, gospel singing, and rhythm and blues. All of these musical styles involved African American composers and performers, black-owned record companies and radio stations, and an almost entirely black audience.

Class, too, divided the musical world of the 1950s, even among whites. A second musical subculture was country and western, a musical style popular among poorer whites, especially people living in the South. Like rhythm and blues, country and western music had its own composers and performers, its own record labels, and its own radio stations.

In the early 1950s, just as black and white as well as rich and poor lived in different neighborhoods, there were separate musi-

cal worlds in U.S. society, separated by the walls of race and class. There was little "crossover" music, meaning that almost no performers or songs moved from one world to gain popularity in another.

This musical segregation began to break down about 1955 with the birth of rock-and-roll. Rock was a new mix of many existing musical patterns, drawing on mainstream pop but including country and western and, especially, rhythm and blues.

The new rock-and-roll music drew together musical traditions, but it soon divided society in a new way—by age. Rock-and-roll was the first music linked to the emergence of a youth culture—rock was all the rage among teenagers but was little appreciated or even understood by their parents. One reason for this age split was that

Elvis Presley (*center*) drew together the music of rhythm and blues singers, such as Big Mama Thornton (*left*), and country and western stars, including Carl Perkins (*right*). The development of rock-and-roll illustrates the ever-changing character of U.S. culture.

Carlos Rene Perez/AP Wide World Photos (*left*); © Bettmann/Corbis (*center*); Michael Ochs Archive/Getty Images (*right*)

tip

Youth cultures tend to develop as societies industrialize because young people gain more independence from parents and have more money to spend on their own interests.

in the prosperous 1950s, young people had more and more money to spend, and record companies quickly realized that they could make a fortune selling products to the new "youth market." New, young performers and groups began springing up in suburban garages and on inner-city street corners, and many were signed by new record labels and the music played on new "teenage" radio stations.

Within a few years, the new youth culture presented young people with new musical stars, and many definitely were not people who looked or acted like their parents. The rock-and-roll performers were men (and a few women) who looked young and took a rebellious stand against "adult" culture. The typical rocker was a young man who looked like what parents might have called a "juvenile delinquent" and who claimed to be "cool," an idea that most parents did not even understand.

The first band to make it big in rock-and-roll was Bill Haley and the Comets. These men (Haley lowered his stated age to gain greater acceptance) came out of the country and western tradition (his earlier bands included the Down Homers and the Saddlemen). Haley's first big hits in 1954—"Shake, Rattle, and Roll" and "Rock around the Clock"—were recordings of earlier rhythm and blues songs.

Very quickly, however, young people began to lose interest in older and "straight-looking" performers such as Bill Haley and turned their attention to younger performers who had a stronger juvenile delinquent image—musicians sporting sideburns, turned-up collars, and black leather jackets. By the end of 1955, the unquestioned star of rock-and-roll was a poor white southern boy from Tupelo, Mississippi, named Elvis Aron Presley. From his rural roots, Elvis Presley knew country and western music, and after he moved to his adopted hometown of Memphis, Tennessee, he learned all about black gospel and rhythm and blues.

Before the 1950s ended, Presley had become the first superstar of rock-and-roll not only because he had lots of talent but also because he had great crossover power. With early hits including "Hound Dog" (a rhythm and blues song originally recorded by Big Mama Thornton) and "Blue Suede Shoes" (written by country and western star Carl Perkins), Presley broke down many of the walls of race and class in the music of the United States.

Elvis went on to a twenty-year career as "the King." But during that time, illustrating the expanding and dynamic character of culture, popular music developed in many new and different directions. By the end of the 1950s, popular musical styles included soft rock (Ricky Nelson, Pat Boone), rockabilly (Johnny Cash), and dozens of doo-wop groups, both black and white (often named for birds—the Falcons, the Penguins, the Flamingos—or cars—the Imperials, the Impalas, the Fleetwoods).

By the 1960s, the diversity of rock music was even greater, including folk music (the Kingston Trio; Peter, Paul, and Mary; Bob Dylan), surf music (the Beach Boys, Jan and Dean), and the "British invasion" led by the Beatles, a group that reached an unprecedented level of popularity among young people that was soon dubbed "Beatlemania."

The Beatles were at first very close to the clean-cut, pop side of rock, but they soon shared the spotlight with another British band who was proud of its "delinquent" clothing and street fighter looks—the Rolling Stones. During the 1960s, music became a huge business, including not just the hard rock of the Beatles and Stones but softer "folk rock" performed by the Byrds, Buffalo Springfield, the Mamas and the Papas, Simon and Garfunkel, and Crosby, Stills, and Nash. Mainstream rock continued with bands like the Who, but rhythm and blues gave birth to "Motown" (named after the "Motor

City," Detroit, the automobile-building capital of the United States at the time), as well as "soul" music, creating dozens of African American stars, including Aretha Franklin, James Brown, the Four Tops, the Temptations, and Diana Ross and the Supremes.

On the West Coast, San Francisco developed a different, more political rock music performed by Jefferson Airplane, the Grateful Dead, and Janis Joplin. West Coast spin-off musical styles included "acid rock," influenced by drug use, performed by the Doors and Jimi Hendrix. The jazz influence also returned to the world of rock, creating such "jazz rock" groups as Blood, Sweat, and Tears, and Chicago.

What does this brief look at the early decades of rock-and-roll tell us about culture? It shows the power of race and class to divide and separate people, shaping different subcultural patterns. It also shows us that the production of culture—in terms of music as well as movies and music videos—has become a megabusiness. Most of all, it shows us that culture is not a rigid system that stands still but rather a living process, changing, adapting, and reinventing itself over time.

WHAT DO YOU THINK?

1. Many dimensions of our way of life shaped rock-and-roll. In what ways do you think the emergence of rock-and-roll changed U.S. culture?

2. Throughout this period of musical change, most musical performers were men. What does this tell us about our way of life? Do you think today's popular music is still dominated by men?

3. Can you carry on the story of musical change in the United States to the present (think of disco, heavy metal, punk rock, rap, and hip-hop)?

Source: Based on Stuessy & Lipscomb (2006).

tip
One good piece of evidence supporting the claim that a global culture is emerging is the widespread use of English as a second language almost everywhere in the world (see Global Map 1).

and Moroccan families benefit from having their children work long hours justify child labor? Since we are all members of a single species, surely there must be some universal standards of proper conduct. But what are they? And in trying to develop them, how can we avoid imposing our own standards on others? There are no simple answers. But when confronting an unfamiliar cultural practice, it is best to resist making judgments before grasping what "they" think of the issue. Remember also to think about your own way of life as others might see it. After all, what we gain most from studying others is better insight into ourselves.

A Global Culture?

Today more than ever, we can observe many of the same cultural practices the world over. Walking the streets of Seoul, South Korea; Kuala Lumpur, Malaysia; Chennai, India; Cairo, Egypt; or Casablanca, Morocco, we see people wearing jeans, hear familiar music, and read ads for many of the same products we use at home. Recall, too, from Global Map 1 that English is rapidly emerging as the preferred second language around the world. Are we witnessing the birth of a single global culture?

Societies now have more contact with one another than ever before, thanks to the flow of goods, information, and people:

1. **The global economy: The flow of goods.** International trade has never been greater. The global economy has spread many of the same consumer goods—from cars and TV shows to music and fashions—throughout the world.

2. **Global communications: The flow of information.** Satellite-based communications enable people to experience the sights and sounds of events taking place thousands of miles away, often as they happen.

3. **Global migration: The flow of people.** Knowing about the rest of the world motivates people to move to where they imagine life will be better. In addition, today's transportation technology, especially air travel, makes relocating easier than ever before. As a result, in most countries, significant numbers of people were born elsewhere (including some 35 million people in the United States, 12 percent of the population).

These global links make the cultures of the world more similar. In addition, the spread of computer technology is closely linked to the English language—about 85 percent of the world's Web pages are written in English—which is also making cultures more similar (Drori, 2006). Even so, as people enter an unfamiliar culture, they encounter a number of challenges and problems, as suggested by "In the *Times*."

There are three important limitations to the global culture thesis. First, the global flow of goods, information, and people is uneven. Generally speaking, urban areas (centers of commerce, communication, and people) have stronger ties to one another, while many rural villages remain isolated. In addition, the greater economic and military power of North America and Western Europe means that these regions influence the rest of the world more than the rest of the world influences them.

Second, the global culture thesis assumes that people everywhere are able to *afford* various new goods and services. Desperate poverty in much of the world deprives people of even the basic necessities of a safe and secure life.

Third, although many cultural practices are now found throughout the world, people everywhere do not attach the same meanings to them. Do children in Tokyo draw the same lessons from reading the Harry Potter books as their counterparts in New York or London? Similarly, we enjoy foods from around the world while knowing little about the lives of the people who created them. In short, people everywhere still see the world through their own cultural lenses.

Theoretical Analysis of Culture

Sociologists have the special task of understanding how culture helps us make sense of ourselves and the surrounding world. Here we will examine several macro-level theoretical approaches to understanding culture.

The Functions of Culture: Structural-Functional Analysis

The structural-functional approach explains culture as a complex strategy for meeting human needs. Borrowing from the philosophical doctrine of *idealism,* this approach considers values the core of a culture (Parsons, 1966; R. M. Williams, 1970). In other words, cultural values direct our lives, give meaning to what we do, and bind people together. Countless other cultural traits have various functions that support the operation of society.

Thinking functionally helps us understand an unfamiliar way of life. Consider the Amish farmer plowing hundreds of acres on an Ohio farm with a team of horses. His farming methods may violate our cultural value of efficiency, but from the Amish point of view, hard work functions to develop the discipline necessary for a highly religious way of life. Long days of working together not only make the Amish self-sufficient but also strengthen family ties and unify local communities.

The New York Times

HOME PAGE
MARKET
...ESTATE
AUTOS
ALL CLASSIFIEDS

WORLD
U.S.
Politics
Washington
Education
N.Y./REGION
BUSINESS
TECHNOLOGY
SPORTS
SCIENCE
HEALTH
OPINION
ARTS
Books
Movies
Music
Television
Theater
STYLE
Dining & Wine
Fashion & Style
Home & Garden
Weddings/
Celebrations
TRAVEL

Blogs
Cartoons
Classifieds
Corrections
Crossword/
Games
First Look
Learning
Network
Multimedia
NYC Guide
Obituaries
Podcasts
The Public
Editor
Sunday
Magazine
Weather
Week in Review

NEWSPAPER
Get Home
Delivery
Customer Care
TimesPoints

The Economy May Be Global, But Not Languages or Culture

By DAVID KOEPPEL
July 2, 2006

Precision, skill and a tendency toward perfection are what earned the Swiss watchmaker Vincent Roberts a customer service job at the luxury jeweler Harry Winston in New York.

So it came as . . . a shock to Mr. Roberts, a French-speaking 28-year-old, when his craftsmanship was overshadowed by an inability to communicate effectively with his boss and colleagues.

Before Mr. Roberts moved . . . to New York in 2004, he took English classes. . . . But when he entered the American workplace, he discovered that he was unprepared for the language of work—the industry's technical jargon and lexicon.

"I was thrown in here by myself, . . ." he recalled. "It was not easy to confront someone or defend my decisions. . . . It was frustrating, and I ended up letting people walk all over me."

Many . . . immigrants can sympathize with that sinking feeling. Language barriers and cultural chasms both large and small are more predominant as the workplace becomes increasingly multicultural and a global economy requires increased interaction with foreign-born bosses, subordinates and co-workers.

Culture clashes and language barriers can sometimes result in miscommunication and conflict and, in some cases, formal complaints and lawsuits, workplace experts say. . . .

In 2005, foreign-born workers accounted for about 15 percent of the civilian work force, according to the Bureau of Labor Statistics. Since 2000, the foreign-born have accounted for 46 percent of the total gain in the labor force.

Mr. Roberts, for one, says he was "forced to adjust" or risk losing his job. His command of English improved in the first year, and he admitted to letting go of his "Swiss behavior." To Mr. Roberts, that meant becoming less obsessive about "tiny scratches" while still upholding the company's high standards.

While Mr. Roberts said he felt alone in his job, some new immigrants find comfort by working alongside others from their home country. . . . Maricarmen Lopez, 25, born in Mexico, buses tables alongside her husband, brother-in-law and stepfather. . . .

After working at the restaurant for just over a year, Ms. Lopez has developed a better command of English, but is still easily confounded by customer requests. "I still get confused sometimes," she said. "I'm afraid to make a mistake."

Suzanne Stillenger, the restaurant manager who hired Ms. Lopez, . . . said there had always been enough bilingual workers to maintain functional communications. Still, some things get lost in translation. Two well-regarded Mexican chefs found it difficult to accept Ms. Stillenger as their supervisor, and what they regarded as playful banter she considered verbal harassment.

Some of their banter, she said, translated into sexual innuendo. After years of being warned to stop, the chefs were finally fired.

"I'm not easily offended," she said. ". . . But translated, what they were saying was pretty raunchy. I said, 'I hope someone says that to your daughter someday so you know how it feels,' and the response was, 'I hope so too, she's a beautiful girl.' "

Just such confrontations are what diversity consultants and organizational experts want to avoid. . . .

[Pamela] Leri [of MeridianEaton Global, a consulting company that specializes in diversity training], . . . has discovered that foreign-born executives are often baffled by American expressions like "Let's hit the ground running" or "Let's wing it." Europeans, Latin Americans and Asians, she said, often perceive such phrases as "unnecessarily risk-oriented."

Anita Zanchettin, the company's Chicago-based director of global inclusion, . . . advises American executives to avoid using slang, to slow down the pace of conversation and to check frequently to make sure foreign-born business partners, colleagues and employees comprehend what is being said.

They advise executives to be sensitive to the needs of "face saving" cultures like China and India, where people are taught not to speak out in front of managers.

Benjamin Dattner, the principal of Dattner Consulting, . . . says foreign-born workers who are "culturally reluctant to share" often irritate American employers, who may misinterpret the silence as lack of interest or belligerence.

But even with an apparent increase in diversity training, lawsuits based on national origin are still a staple of labor law, said [labor attorney] Lawrence Z. Lorber. . . . At the Equal Employment Opportunity Commission, private-sector complaints, which include charges of discrimination by national origin, language or accent, rose 8 percent from 1992 to 2005, to 8,035 complaints, from 7,434. . . .

Belen Lopez-Garrido, 32, a Spanish-born television producer, enjoys New York's professional corporate culture but at first was taken aback by the city's fast pace and her blunt-speaking colleagues. "American workers are totally wired, 100 percent of the day," she said. "I don't think wired translates into being more effective. I think Americans see Europeans as being lazier, not taking their work as seriously. Just because there's a different attitude doesn't mean we're not as serious."

WHAT DO YOU THINK?

1. Have you ever lived or worked in a place where most people spoke a language unfamiliar to you? What challenges did you face? How did you cope?

2. How much responsibility do companies have to help workers who may face language difficulties? How much is it up to workers to learn the language of their supervisors?

3. Can you think of other examples of how cultural differences can lead to workplace problems? Explain.

Of course, Amish practices have dysfunctions as well. The hard work and strict religious discipline are too demanding for some, who end up leaving the community. Then, too, strong religious beliefs sometimes prevent compromise; slight differences in religious practices have caused the Amish to divide into different communities (Kraybill, 1989; Kraybill & Olshan, 1994).

If cultures are strategies for meeting human needs, we would expect to find many common patterns around the world. The term **cultural universals** refers to *traits that are part of every known culture.* Comparing hundreds of cultures, George Murdock (1945) identified dozens of cultural universals. One common element is the family, which functions everywhere to control sexual reproduction and to oversee the care of children. Funeral rites, too, are found everywhere, because all human communities cope with the reality of death. Jokes are another cultural universal, serving as a safe means of releasing social tensions.

▶**CRITICAL REVIEW** The strength of the structural-functional approach is that it shows how culture operates to meet human needs. Yet by emphasizing a society's dominant cultural patterns, this approach largely ignores cultural diversity. Also, because this approach emphasizes cultural stability, it downplays the impor-

tance of change. In short, cultural systems are not as stable nor a matter of as much agreement as structural functionalism leads us to believe. The Applying Theory table summarizes this theoretical approach's main lessons about culture.

 YOUR LEARNING In the United States, what are some of the functions of sports, July Fourth celebrations, and Black History month?

Inequality and Culture: Social-Conflict Analysis

The social-conflict approach stresses the link between culture and inequality. Any cultural trait, from this point of view, benefits some members of society at the expense of others.

Why do certain values dominate a society in the first place? Many conflict theorists, especially Marxists, argue that culture is shaped by a society's system of economic production. "It is not the consciousness of men that determines their being," Karl Marx proclaimed; "it is their social being that determines their consciousness" (Marx & Engels, 1978:4, orig. 1859). Social-conflict theory, then, is rooted in the philosophical doctrine of *materialism,* which holds that a society's system of material production (such as our own capitalist economy) has a powerful effect on the rest of a culture. This materialist approach contrasts with the idealist leanings of structural functionalism.

Social-conflict analysis ties our cultural values of competitiveness and material success to our country's capitalist economy, which serves the interests of the nation's wealthy elite. The culture of capitalism further teaches us to think that rich and powerful people work harder or longer than others and therefore deserve their wealth and privileges. It also encourages us to view capitalism as somehow "natural," discouraging us from trying to reduce economic inequality.

Eventually, however, the strains of inequality erupt into movements for social change. Two examples in the United States are the civil rights movement and the women's movement. Both have sought greater equality, and both have encountered opposition from defenders of the status quo.

▶**CRITICAL REVIEW** The social-conflict approach suggests that cultural systems do not address human needs equally, allowing some people to dominate others. This inequity in turn generates pressure toward change.

Following the structural-functional approach, what do you make of the Amish practice of "barn raising," when everyone in a community joins together to raise a family's new barn in a day? Why is such a ritual almost unknown in U.S. society outside of Amish communities?

Paul Solomon/Woodfin Camp & Associates

tip

Because it is concerned with patterns of social inequality, feminism is correctly viewed as a social-conflict theory of culture.

tip

Theories dealing with how biology affects human behavior do not have wide support in sociology. Sociobiology is a theory—supported by some sociologists, not by others—that has one foot in biology and the other in sociology.

Yet by stressing the divisiveness of culture, this approach understates the ways that cultural patterns integrate members of society. We should therefore consider both social-conflict and structural-functional insights for a fuller understanding of culture.

 YOUR LEARNING How might a social-conflict analysis of college fraternities and sororities differ from a structural-functional analysis?

Evolution and Culture: Sociobiology

We know that culture is a human creation, but does human biology influence how this process unfolds? A third theoretical approach, standing with one leg in biology and one in sociology, is **sociobiology,** *a theoretical approach that explores ways in which human biology affects how we create culture.*

Sociobiology rests on the theory of evolution proposed by Charles Darwin in *On the Origin of Species* (1859). Darwin asserted that living organisms change over long periods of time as a result of *natural selection,* a matter of four simple principles. First, all living things live to reproduce themselves. Second, the blueprint for reproduction is in the genes, the basic units of life that carry traits of one generation into the next. Third, some random variation in genes allows a species to "try out" new life patterns in a particular environment. This variation allows some organisms to survive better than others and pass on their advantageous genes to their offspring. Fourth and finally, over thousands of generations, the genetic patterns that promote reproduction survive and become dominant. In this way, as biologists say, a species *adapts* to its environment, and dominant traits emerge as the "nature" of the organism.

Sociobiologists claim that the large number of cultural universals reflects the fact that all humans are members of a single biological species. It is our common biology that underlies, for example, the apparently universal "double standard" of sexual behavior. As the sex researcher Alfred Kinsey put it, "Among all people everywhere in the world, the male is more likely than the female to desire sex with a variety of partners" (quoted in Barash, 1981:49). But why?

We all know that children result from joining a woman's egg with a man's sperm. But the biolog-ical importance of a single sperm and of a single egg is quite different. For healthy men, sperm represent a "renewable resource" produced by the testes throughout most of the life course. A man releases hundreds of millions of sperm in a single ejaculation—technically, enough to fertilize every woman in North America (Barash, 1981:47). A newborn female's ovaries, however, contain her entire lifetime supply of immature eggs. A woman generally releases a single egg cell from her ovaries each month. So although a man is biologically capable of fathering thousands of offspring, a woman is able to bear only a relatively small number of children.

Given this biological difference, men reproduce their genes most efficiently by being promiscuous—readily engaging in sex. This scheme, however, opposes the reproductive interests of women. Each of a woman's relatively few pregnancies demands that she carry the child for nine months, give birth, and provide care for some time afterward. Thus efficient reproduction on the part of the woman depends on carefully selecting a mate whose qualities (beginning with the likelihood that he will simply stay around) will contribute to their child's survival and, later, successful reproduction.

Using an evolutionary perspective, sociobiologists explain that different reproductive strategies give rise to a double standard: Men treat women as sexual objects more than women treat men that way. While this may be so, many sociologists counter that behavior such as that shown in Ruth Orkin's photograph *American Girl in Italy* is more correctly understood as resulting from a culture of male domination.
Copyright 1952, 1980 Ruth Orkin.

tip

The Applying Theory table provides a good summary of the three theoretical approaches discussed in the chapter. Review it to ensure that you understand all three.

APPLYING THEORY

Culture

	Structural-Functional Approach	Social-Conflict Approach	Sociobiology Approach
What is the level of analysis?	Macro-level	Macro-level	Macro-level
What is culture?	Culture is a system of behavior by which members of societies cooperate to meet their needs.	Culture is a system that benefits some people and disadvantages others.	Culture is a system of behavior that is partly shaped by human biology.
What is the foundation of culture?	Cultural patterns are rooted in a society's core values and beliefs.	Cultural patterns are rooted in a society's system of economic production.	Cultural patterns are rooted in humanity's biological evolution.
What core questions does the approach ask?	How does a cultural pattern help society operate?	How does a cultural pattern benefit some people and harm others?	How does a cultural pattern help a species adapt to its environment?
	What cultural patterns are found in all societies?	How does a cultural pattern support social inequality?	

The double standard certainly involves more than biology and is tangled up with the historical domination of women by men. But sociobiology suggests that this cultural pattern, like many others, has an underlying "bio-logic." Simply put, the double standard exists around the world because biological differences lead women and men everywhere to favor distinctive reproductive strategies.

▶**CRITICAL REVIEW** Sociobiology has generated intriguing theories about the biological roots of some cultural patterns. But the approach remains controversial for two main reasons.

First, some critics fear that sociobiology may revive biological arguments, from over a century ago, that claimed the superiority of one race or sex. But defenders counter that sociobiology rejects the past pseudoscience of racial and gender superiority. In fact, they say, sociobiology unites all of humanity because all people share a single evolutionary history. Sociobiology does assert that men and women differ biologically in some ways that culture cannot easily overcome. But far from claiming that males are somehow more important than females,

sociobiology emphasizes that both sexes are vital to human reproduction and survival.

Second, say the critics, sociobiologists have little evidence to support their theories. Research to date suggests that biological forces do not *determine* human behavior in any rigid sense. Rather, humans *learn* behavior within a cultural system. The contribution of sociobiology, then, lies in explaining why some cultural patterns seem easier to learn than others (Barash, 1981).

 YOUR LEARNING Using the sociobiology approach, explain why some cultural patterns such as sibling rivalry (the fact that children in the same family often compete and even fight with each other) are widespread.

Because any analysis of culture requires a broad focus on the workings of society, the three approaches discussed in this chapter are all macro-level in scope. The symbolic-interaction approach has a micro-level focus on behavior in everyday situations.

Thinking Globally
The United States and Canada: Are They Culturally Different?

The United States and Canada are two of the largest high-income countries in the world, and they share a common border of about 4,000 miles. But do the United States and Canada share the same culture?

One important point to make right away is that both nations are *multicultural*. Not only do the two countries have hundreds of Native American societies, but immigration has brought people from all over the world to both the United States and Canada. Most early immigrants to both countries came from Europe, but in recent decades, most have come from Asia and Latin America. The Canadian city of Vancouver, for example, has a Chinese community of about the same size as the Latino community in Los Angeles.

Canada and the United States differ in one important respect—historically, Canada has had *two* dominant cultures: French (about 25 percent of the population) and British (roughly 40 percent). People of French ancestry are a large majority in the province of Quebec (where French is the official language) and a large minority in New Brunswick (which is officially bilingual).

Are the dominant values of Canada much the same as those we have described for the United States? Seymour Martin Lipset (1985) finds that they differ to some degree. The United States declared its independence from Great Britain in 1776, but Canada did not formally separate from Great Britain until 1982 and the British monarch is still Canada's official head of state. Thus, Lipset continues, the dominant culture of Canada lies somewhere between the culture of the United States and that of Great Britain.

The culture of the United States is more individualistic, and Canada's is more collective. In the United States, individualism is seen in the historical importance of the cowboy, a self-sufficient loner, and even outlaws such as Jesse James and Billy the Kid are regarded as

heroes because they challenged authority. In Canada, by contrast, it is the Mountie—Canada's well-known police officer on horseback—who is looked on with great respect.

Politically, people in the United States tend to think individuals ought to do things for themselves. In Canada, however, much as in Great Britain, there is a strong sense that government should look after the interests of everyone. This is one reason, for example, that Canada has a much broader social welfare system (including universal health care) than the United States (the only high-income nation without such a program). It also helps explain the fact that about 40 percent of all households in the United States own one or more guns and the idea that individuals are entitled to own a gun, although controversial,

is strong. In Canada, by contrast, few households have a gun, and the government greatly restricts gun ownership, as in Great Britain.

WHAT DO YOU THINK?

1. Why do you think some Canadians feel that their way of life is overshadowed by that of the United States?

2. Ask your friends to name the capital city of Canada. (The correct answer is Ottawa, in the province of Ontario.) Are you surprised by how many know the answer? Why or why not?

3. Why do many people in the United States not know very much about either Canada or Mexico, countries with which we share long borders?

Who members of a society celebrate as heroic is a good indication of people's cultural values. In the United States, outlaws such as Jesse James (and, later, Bonnie and Clyde) were regarded as heroes because they represented the strength of the individual standing up against authority. In Canada, by contrast, people have always looked up to the Mountie, who symbolizes society's authority over the individual.

© Bettmann/Corbis (*left*); Canadian Government Travel Bureau (*right*)

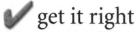

Culture and Human Freedom

This entire chapter leads us to ask an important question: To what extent are human beings, as cultural creatures, free? Does culture bind us to each other and to the past? Or does culture enhance our capacity for individual thought and independent choice?

Culture as Constraint

As symbolic creatures, humans cannot live without culture. But the capacity for culture does have some drawbacks. We may be the only animal to name ourselves, but living in a symbolic world means that we are also the only creature that experiences alienation. In addition, culture is largely a matter of habit, which limits our choices and drives us to repeat troubling patterns, such as racial prejudice and sex discrimination, in each new generation.

Our society's emphasis on competitive achievement urges us toward excellence, yet this same pattern also isolates us from one another. Material things comfort us in some ways but divert us from the security and satisfaction that come from close relationships and spiritual strength.

Culture as Freedom

For better or worse, human beings are cultural creatures, just as ants and bees are prisoners of their biology. But there is a crucial difference. Biological instincts create a ready-made world; culture forces us to choose as we make and remake a world for ourselves. No better evidence of this freedom exists than the cultural diversity of our own society and the even greater human diversity around the world.

Learning more about this cultural diversity is one goal shared by sociologists. The Thinking Globally box on the previous page offers some contrasts between the cultures of the United States and Canada. Wherever we may live, the better we understand the workings of the surrounding culture, the better prepared we are to use the freedom it offers us.

Applying Sociology in Everyday Life

1. New words are created all the time. Describe what was going on in the United States that helps explain the creation of the following new words (Herzog, 2004): *sweatshop* (1892), *motel* (1925), *supermarket* (1933), *teenager* (1938), *workaholic* (1971), *couch potato* (1976), and *soccer mom* (1996).

2. Find someone on campus who has lived in another country, and ask how the culture of that society differs from the way of life here. Look for ways in which the other person sees U.S. culture differently from people who have lived here all their lives.

3. Watch an animated Disney film such as *Finding Nemo, The Lion King, The Little Mermaid, Aladdin,* or *Pocahontas*. One reason for the popularity of these films is that they all share cultural themes. Using the list of key values of U.S. culture on pages 66–67 of this chapter as a guide, what makes the film you selected especially "American"?

MAKING THE GRADE

Culture

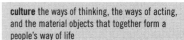

What Is Culture?

Culture is a **WAY OF LIFE**.
- Culture is shared by members of a society.
- Culture shapes how we act, think, and feel.

Culture is a **HUMAN TRAIT**.
- Although several species display limited capacity for culture, only human beings rely on culture for survival.

Culture is a **PRODUCT OF EVOLUTION**.
- As the human brain evolved, culture replaced biological instincts as our species' primary strategy for survival.

culture the ways of thinking, the ways of acting, and the material objects that together form a people's way of life

nonmaterial culture the ideas created by members of a society

material culture the physical things created by members of a society

culture shock personal disorientation when experiencing an unfamiliar way of life

- We experience **CULTURE SHOCK** when we enter an unfamiliar culture and are not able to "read" meaning in our new surroundings.
- We create culture shock for others when we act in ways they do not understand.

✔ Approximately 200 different cultures exist in the United States. Worldwide, there are roughly 7,000 different cultures.

The Elements of Culture

Culture relies on **SYMBOLS** in the form of words, gestures, and actions to express meaning.

- The fact that different meanings can come to be associated with the same symbol (for example, a wink of an eye) shows the human capacity to create and manipulate symbols.
- Societies create new symbols all the time (for example, new computer technology has sparked the creation of new cyber-symbols).

LANGUAGE is the symbolic system by which people in a culture communicate with one another.

- People use language—both spoken and written—to transmit culture from one generation to the next.
- Because every culture is different, each language has words or expressions not found in any other language.

symbol anything that carries a particular meaning recognized by people who share a culture

language a system of symbols that allows people to communicate with one another

cultural transmission the process by which one generation passes culture to the next

Sapir-Whorf thesis the idea that people see and understand the world through the cultural lens of language

values culturally defined standards that people use to decide what is desirable, good, and beautiful and that serve as broad guidelines for social living

beliefs specific thoughts or ideas that people hold to be true

norms rules and expectations by which a society guides the behavior of its members

mores norms that are widely observed and have great moral significance

folkways norms for routine or casual interaction

social control attempts by society to regulate people's thoughts and behavior

technology knowledge that people use to make a way of life in their surroundings

VALUES are abstract standards of what *ought to be* (for example, equality of opportunity).

- Values can sometimes be in conflict with one another.
- Lower-income countries have cultures that value survival; higher-income countries have cultures that value individualism and self-expression.

BELIEFS are specific statements that people who share a culture hold to be true (for example, "A qualified woman could be elected president").

NORMS, rules that guide human behavior, are of two types:

- **mores** (for example, sexual taboos), which have great moral significance
- **folkways** (for example, greetings or dining etiquette), which are matters of everyday politeness

✔ Values and norms (standards for how we should behave) reflect **ideal culture**, which differs from **real culture** (what actually occurs in everyday life).

◉ See this chapter for ten key values of U.S. culture.

TECHNOLOGY AND CULTURE

- A society's **artifacts**—the wide range of physical human creations that together make up a society's material culture—reflect underlying cultural values and technology.
- The more complex a society's technology, the more its members are able to shape the world as they wish.

✔ Members of societies that possess sophisticated technology should be careful not to judge cultures with simpler technology as inferior.

MAKING THE GRADE *continued . . .*

Cultural Diversity

We live in a **CULTURALLY DIVERSE SOCIETY**.

- This diversity is due to our country's history of immigration.
- Diversity reflects regional differences.
- Diversity reflects differences in social class that set off **high culture** (available only to elites) from **popular culture** (available to average people).

A number of values are central to our way of life. But **CULTURAL PATTERNS** are not the same throughout our society.

Subculture is based on differences in interests and life experiences.

- Hip-hop fans and jocks are two examples of youth subcultures in the United States.

Multiculturalism is an effort to enhance appreciation of cultural diversity.

- Multiculturalism developed as a reaction to the earlier "melting pot" idea, which was thought to result in minorities' losing their identity as they adopted mainstream cultural patterns.

Counterculture is strongly at odds with conventional ways of life.

- Militant religious fundamentalist groups in the United States who plot to destroy Western society are examples of a counterculture.

CULTURAL CHANGE results from

- **invention** (examples include the telephone and the computer),
- **discovery** (for example, the recognition that women are capable of political leadership), and
- **diffusion** (for example, the growing popularity of various ethnic foods and musical styles).

CULTURAL LAG results when some parts of a cultural system change faster than others.

How do we understand cultural differences?

- **ETHNOCENTRISM** links people to their society but can cause misunderstanding and conflict between societies.
- **CULTURAL RELATIVISM** is increasingly important as people of the world come into more and more contact with each other.

high culture cultural patterns that distinguish a society's elite

popular culture cultural patterns that are widespread among a society's population

subculture cultural patterns that set apart some segment of a society's population

multiculturalism a perspective recognizing the cultural diversity of the United States and promoting equal standing for all cultural traditions

Eurocentrism the dominance of European (especially English) cultural patterns

Afrocentrism emphasizing and promoting African cultural patterns

counterculture cultural patterns that strongly oppose those widely accepted within a society

cultural integration the close relationships among various elements of a cultural system

cultural lag the fact that some cultural elements change more quickly than others, disrupting a cultural system

ethnocentrism the practice of judging another culture by the standards of one's own culture

cultural relativism the practice of judging a culture by its own standards

✔ *Global cultural patterns result from the worldwide flow of goods, information, and people.*

Theoretical Analysis of Culture

The **STRUCTURAL-FUNCTIONAL APPROACH** views culture as a relatively stable system built on core values. All cultural patterns play some part in the ongoing operation of society.

The **SOCIAL-CONFLICT APPROACH** sees culture as a dynamic arena of inequality and conflict. Cultural patterns benefit some categories of people more than others.

SOCIOBIOLOGY explores how the long history of evolution has shaped patterns of culture in today's world.

cultural universals traits that are part of every known culture

sociobiology a theoretical approach that explores ways in which human biology affects how we create culture

See the Applying Theory table in this chapter.

Culture and Human Freedom

- Culture can limit the choices we make.
- As cultural creatures, we have the capacity to shape and reshape our world to meet our needs and pursue our dreams.

MAKING THE GRADE

Sample Test Questions

These questions are similar to those found in the test bank that accompanies this textbook.

Multiple-Choice Questions

1. Of all the world's countries, the United States is the most
   a. multicultural.
   b. culturally uniform.
   c. slowly changing.
   d. resistant to cultural diversity.

2. Ideas created by members of a society are part of
   a. high culture.
   b. material culture.
   c. norms.
   d. nonmaterial culture.

3. Sociologists define a symbol as
   a. any gesture that insults others.
   b. any element of material culture.
   c. anything that has meaning to people who share a culture.
   d. any pattern that causes culture shock.

4. U.S. culture holds a strong belief in
   a. the traditions of the past.
   b. individuality.
   c. equality of condition for all.
   d. All of the above are correct.

5. Cheating on a final examination is an example of violating campus
   a. folkways.
   b. symbols.
   c. mores.
   d. high culture.

6. *Subculture* refers to
   a. a part of the population lacking culture.
   b. elements of popular culture.
   c. people who embrace high culture.
   d. cultural patterns that set apart a segment of a society's population.

7. Which region of the United States has the largest share of people who speak a language other than English at home?
   a. the Southwest
   b. the Northeast
   c. the Northwest
   d. the South

8. Sociologists use the term "cultural lag" to refer to
   a. the slowing of cultural change in the United States.
   b. the fact that some societies change faster than others do.
   c. that fact that some elements of culture change faster than others.
   d. people who are less cultured than others.

9. Which of the following is a description of ethnocentrism?
   a. taking pride in your ethnicity
   b. judging another culture using the standards of your own culture
   c. seeing another culture as better than your own
   d. judging another culture by its own standards

10. Which theoretical approach focuses on the link between culture and social inequality?
    a. the structural-functional approach
    b. the social-conflict approach
    c. the symbolic-interaction approach
    d. the sociobiology approach

ANSWERS: 1(a); 2(d); 3(c); 4(b); 5(c); 6(d); 7(a); 8(c); 9(b); 10(b).

Essay Questions

1. In the United States, hot dogs, hamburgers, French fries, and ice cream have long been considered national favorites. What cultural patterns help explain the love of these kinds of foods?

2. From what you have learned in this chapter, do you think that a global culture is emerging? Do you regard the prospect of a global culture as positive or negative? Why?

Society

Society

WHAT factors shape society?

WHY do societies change?

HOW have Karl Marx, Max Weber, and Emile Durkheim increased our understanding of modern societies?

All human beings live in societies. But societies around the world differ from one another in many ways just as each society changes over time. This chapter presents classic theories that explain what "society" is all about.

Sididi Ag Inaka has never used instant messaging, logged on to the Internet, or even spoken on a cell phone. Does such a person really exist in today's high-technology world? Well, how about this: Neither Inaka nor anyone in his family has ever been to a movie, watched television, or even read a newspaper.

Are these people visitors from another planet? Prisoners on some remote island? Not at all. They are Tuareg nomads who wander over the vast Sahara in the western African nation of Mali. Known as the "blue men of the desert" for the flowing blue robes worn by both men and women, the Tuareg herd camels, goats, and sheep and live in camps where the sand blows and the daytime temperature often reaches 120 degrees Fahrenheit. Life is hard, but most Tuareg try to hold on to traditional ways. With a stern look, Inaka says, "My father was a nomad. His father was a nomad. I am a nomad. My children will be nomads."

The Tuareg are among the world's poorest people. When the rains fail to come, they and their animals are at risk of losing their lives. Even in good times, Inaka and his people are a society set apart, with little knowledge of the larger world and its advanced technology. But Inaka does not complain: "This is the life of my ancestors. This is the life that we know" (Buckley, 1996; Matloff, 1997; Lovgren, 1998).

©1996, *The Washington Post*. Photo by Carol Guzy. Reprinted with permission

The societies that exist around the world can be quite different from our own. But what is a society? What makes societies different? How and why do they change over time?

Society refers to *people who interact in a defined territory and share a culture.* In this chapter, you will learn more about human societies with the help of four important sociologists. We begin with the approach of **Gerhard Lenski,** who describes how societies have changed over the past 10,000 years. Lenski points to the importance of *technology* in shaping any society. Then we turn to three of sociology's founders. **Karl Marx,** like Lenski, took a long historical view of societies. But Marx's story of society is all about *social conflict* that arises as people work within an economic system to produce material goods. **Max Weber** tells a different tale, showing that the power of *ideas* shapes society. Weber contrasted the traditional thinking of simple societies with the rational thought that dominates complex societies today. Finally, **Emile Durkheim** helps us see the different ways that traditional and modern societies hang together.

All four visions of society answer a number of important questions: What makes the way of life of people such as the Tuareg of the Sahara so different from your life as a college student in the United States? How and why do all societies change? What forces divide a society? What forces hold a society together? This chapter will provide answers to all of these questions as we look at the work of important sociologists.

Gerhard Lenski: Society and Technology

Members of our society, who take instant messaging and television, as well as schools and hospitals, for granted, must wonder at the nomads of the Sahara, who live the same simple life their ancestors did centuries ago. The work of Gerhard Lenski (Nolan & Lenski, 2004) helps us understand the great differences among societies that have existed throughout human history.

Lenski uses the term **sociocultural evolution** to mean *changes that occur as a society gains new technology.* With only simple technology, societies such as the Tuareg have little control over nature, so they can support just a small number of people. Societies with complex technology such as cars and cell phones, while not necessarily "better," support hundreds of millions of people in far more affluent ways of life.

Inventing or adopting new technology sends ripples of change throughout a society. When our ancestors first discovered how to use wind to move a boat using a sail, they created a device that would take them to new lands, greatly expand their economy, and increase their military power. In addition, the more technology a society has, the faster it changes. Technologically simple societies change very slowly; Sididi Ag Inaka says he lives "the life of my ancestors." How many people in U.S. society can say that they live the way their grandparents or great-grandparents did? Modern, high-technology societies such as our own change so fast that people usually experience major social changes during a single lifetime. Imagine how surprised your great-grandmother would be to hear about the Internet and instant messaging, artificial intelligence and iPods, replacement hearts and test-tube babies, space shuttles and screamo music.

 Which of the items just mentioned would most amaze your great-grandmother? Why?

Drawing on Lenski's work, we will describe five types of societies, defined by their technology: hunting and gathering societies, horticultural and pastoral societies, agrarian societies, industrial societies, and postindustrial societies.

Hunting and Gathering Societies

In the simplest of all societies, people live by **hunting and gathering,** *making use of simple tools to hunt animals and gather vegetation for food.* From the time that our species appeared 3 million years ago until

This chapter examines the concept of "society" through the work of one of today's leading sociologists, Gerhard Lenski, and three of sociology's founders, Karl Marx, Max Weber, and Emile Durkheim.

about 12,000 years ago, *all* humans were hunters and gatherers. Even in 1800, many hunting and gathering societies could be found around the world. But today just a few remain, including the Aka and Pygmies of Central Africa, the Bushmen of southwestern Africa, the Aborigines of Australia, the Kaska Indians of northwestern Canada, and the Batek and Semai of Malaysia.

With little ability to control their environment, hunters and gatherers spend most of their time looking for game and collecting plants to eat. Only in lush areas with lots of food do hunters and gatherers have much free time. Because it takes a large amount of land to support even a few people, hunting and gathering societies have just a few dozen members. They must also be nomadic, moving on to find new sources of vegetation or to follow migrating animals. Although they may return to favored sites, they rarely form permanent settlements.

Hunting and gathering societies depend on the family to do many things. The family must get and distribute food, protect its members, and teach the children. Everyone's life is much the same; people spend most of their time getting their next meal. Age and gender have some effect on what individuals do. Healthy adults do most of the work, leaving the very young and the very old to help out as they can. Women gather vegetation—which provides most of the food—while men take on the less certain job of hunting. Although men and women perform different tasks, most hunters and gatherers probably see the sexes as having about the same social importance (Leacock, 1978).

Hunting and gathering societies usually have a *shaman,* or spiritual leader, who enjoys high prestige but has to work to find food like everyone else. In short, people in hunting and gathering societies come close to being socially equal.

Hunters and gatherers use simple weapons—the spear, bow and arrow, and stone knife—but rarely to wage war. Their real enemy is the forces of nature: Storms and droughts can kill off their food supply, and there is little they can do for someone who has a serious accident or illness. Being at risk in this way encourages people to cooperate and share, a strategy that raises everyone's chances of survival. But the truth is that many die in childhood, and no more than half reach the age of twenty (Lenski, Nolan, & Lenski, 1995).

During the past century, societies with more powerful technology have closed in on the few remaining hunters and gatherers, reducing their food supply. As a result, hunting and gathering societies are disappearing. Fortunately, study of this way of life has given us valuable information about human history and our basic ties to the natural world.

What do you think are some of the important lessons we can learn from studying hunting and gathering societies?

In technologically simple societies, successful hunting wins men great praise. However, the gathering of vegetation by women is a more dependable and easily available source of nutrition.

Horticultural and Pastoral Societies

Ten to twelve thousand years ago, as the timeline inside the front cover shows, a new technology began to change the lives of human beings. People discovered **horticulture,** *the use of hand tools to raise crops.* Using a hoe to work the soil and a digging stick to punch holes in the ground to plant seeds may not seem like something that would change the world, but these inventions allowed people to give up gathering in favor of growing their own food. The first humans to plant gardens lived in fertile regions of the Middle East. Soon after, cultural diffusion spread this knowledge to Latin America and Asia and eventually all over the world.

Not all societies were quick to give up hunting and gathering for horticulture. Hunters and gatherers living where food was plentiful probably saw little reason to change their ways. People living in

SOCIETY   101

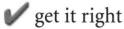

dry regions (such as the deserts of Africa or the Middle East) or mountainous areas found little use for horticulture because they could not grow much anyway. Such people (including the Tuareg) were more likely to adopt **pastoralism,** *the domestication of animals.* Today, societies that mix horticulture and pastoralism can be found throughout South America, Africa, and Asia. "In the *Times*" takes a closer look at some of the problems facing pastoral communities that exist in today's world.

Growing plants and raising animals greatly increased food production, so populations expanded from dozens to hundreds of people. Pastoralists remained nomadic, leading their herds to fresh grazing lands. But horticulturalists formed settlements, moving only when the soil gave out. Joined by trade, these settlements formed societies with populations reaching into the thousands.

Once a society is capable of producing a *material surplus*—more resources than are needed to support the population—not everyone has to work at providing food. Greater specialization results: Some make crafts, while others engage in trade, cut hair, apply tattoos, or serve as priests. Compared to hunting and gathering societies, horticultural and pastoral societies are more socially diverse.

But being more productive does not make a society "better" in every sense. As some families produce more than others, they become richer and more powerful. Horticultural and pastoral societies have greater inequality, with elites using government power—and military force—to serve their own interests. But leaders do not have the ability to communicate or to travel over large distances, so they can control only a small number of people, rather than vast empires.

Religion also differs among types of societies. Hunters and gatherers believe that many spirits inhabit the world. Horticulturalists, however, are more likely to think of one God as the creator of the world. Pastoral societies carry this belief further, seeing God as directly involved in the well-being of the entire world. The pastoral roots of Judaism and Christianity are evident in the term "pastor" and the common view of God as a shepherd ("The Lord is my shepherd," says Psalm 23) who stands watch over us all.

Agrarian Societies

About 5,000 years ago, another revolution in technology was taking place in the Middle East, one that would end up changing life on Earth. This was the discovery of **agriculture,** *large-scale cultivation using plows harnessed to animals or more powerful energy sources.* So important was the invention of the animal-drawn plow, along with other breakthroughs of the period—including irrigation, the wheel, writing, numbers, and the use of various metals—that this moment in history is often called the "dawn of civilization."

Using animal-drawn plows, farmers could cultivate fields far bigger than the garden-sized plots planted by horticulturalists. Plows have the added advantage of turning and aerating the soil, making it more fertile. As a result, farmers could work the same land for generations, encouraging the development of permanent settlements. With the ability to grow a surplus of food and to transport goods using animal-powered wagons, agrarian societies greatly expanded in size and population. About 100 C.E., for example, the agrarian Roman Empire contained some 70 million people spread over 2 million square miles (Nolan & Lenski, 2004).

Greater production meant even more specialization. Now there were dozens of distinct occupations, from farmers to builders to metalworkers. With so many people producing so many different things, people invented money as a common standard of exchange, and the old barter system—by which people traded one thing for another—was abandoned.

Agrarian societies have extreme social inequality, typically more than modern societies such as our own. In most cases, a large number of the people are

What would it be like to live in a society with simple technology? That's the premise of the television show *Survivor*. What advantages do societies with simple technology afford their members? What disadvantages do you see?

Bill Inoshita/CBS/Landov LLC

The New York Times

E★TRADE B...

...KET
...L ESTATE
AUTOS
ALL CLASSIFIEDS

WORLD
U.S.
  Politics
  Washington
  Education
N.Y./REGION
BUSINESS
TECHNOLOGY
SPORTS
SCIENCE
HEALTH
OPINION
ARTS
  Books
  Movies
  Music
  Television
  Theater
STYLE
  Dining & Wine
  Fashion & Style
  Home & Garden
  Weddings/
  Celebrations
TRAVEL

Blogs
Cartoons
Classifieds
Corrections
Crossword/
Games
First Look
Learning
Network
Multimedia
NYC Guide
Obituaries
Podcasts
The Public
Editor
Sunday
Magazine
Weather
Week in Review
NEWSPAPER
Get Home
Delivery
Customer Care
TimesPoints

Animal Herders of 23 Lands Meet and Swap Stories

By MARC LACEY
February 5, 2005

ADDIS ABABA, Ethiopia—Bring together pastoralists from 23 countries around the globe and, not surprisingly, the talk will inevitably shift to the sheep, goats, cows and other more exotic animals that play such a central part in their lives.

The Iranian contingent at an international gathering of nomads held this week in the southernmost reaches of Ethiopia amazed others with their descriptions of two-humped camels, which are not known in these parts.

An Indian delegate to the conference, which was convened in the tiny village of Turmi, several hundred miles south of the Ethiopian capital, near the border with Kenya, said fellow herders could not believe that he raised domesticated buffalo.

The herders, from Mauritius to Mongolia, were united on one overriding issue: their common struggle against encroachment on their grazing land.

"Increasing gaps between poor pastoralists and rich others, increasing frustration at erosion of rights and loss of land and increasing destitution, will lead to conflict and migration," the 120 leaders from herder communities said in a statement at the close of the five-day conference.

Pastoralists have gathered in the past to discuss their woes, but this meeting was deemed the first broad international gathering to be staged in a pastoral community. With the nomads' plane fares picked up by the United Nations, the session drew Mongolian camel owners and Spanish shepherds, as well as herders from such far-flung places as Kazakhstan, Chile, Burkino Faso and Switzerland.

"Imagine you're an isolated tribe in the mountains of Iran, or somewhere in Argentina or Kenya, and all of a sudden you realize you're not alone," said Taghi Farvar, who comes from a pastoral tribe in Iran and works at that country's Center for Sustainable Development.

The attendees stayed in tents in a part of Ethiopia so remote that it is considered too harsh for city dwellers. But it was nothing for this lot, some of whom trek hundreds of miles in search of fresh pasture. Making the group feel at home, livestock ambled by as the nomads discussed their threatened existence.

"Globally, pastoralists are on the whole being marginalized by mainstream societies," said Paul Hebert, head of the United Nations Office for Coordination of Humanitarian Affairs, which organized the conference through its Pastoral Communication Initiative. "We're trying to create some political space for them."

With many translators on hand, the pastoralists discussed how education could be provided in mobile schools so that their children could learn without abandoning their culture. They debated the role of women in their cultures, which varied from political leaders to pawns. They motivated each other to keep fighting for nomad rights.

Cattle rustling also popped up in discussions, as well as the use of cattle as payment for brides, and techniques for making milk last longer before spoiling.

There are more than 50 million pastoralists in sub-Saharan Africa, more than [on] any other continent. Ethiopia alone has eight million people—12 percent of its population—who move from place to place with their animals. Experts say their livelihood contributes about a quarter of the country's gross domestic product.

Each person at the conference came away with a different lesson learned. Mr. Farvar, a white-bearded Iranian, said he had learned from Spanish shepherds that the government there protected their migratory routes by law, even if animals must stroll right through cities. Such nomad-friendly policies, he said, might have helped the 300 sheep that were killed in a traffic accident in the southern Iranian city of Shiraz not long ago.

Dolat Ram Guzzar, who raises buffalo, goats and cows in northwest India, said he had picked up new techniques for preserving milk, which is a major part of his diet. The members of the Iranian delegation offered a presentation on how they boiled sour milk and then dried it in the sun, producing milk balls that are nutritious and can be kept for years. Amazed delegates even got to sample some of the balls.

"We're all different, but we share so much," Mr. Farvar said after the conference, as he watched an Ethiopian sheepherder struggle to get a flock to cross a busy street in the capital. "If you take mobility from pastoralists, we're as good as dead. We feel sorry for those of you who live sedentary lives."

WHAT DO YOU THINK?

1. What are some of the problems with living as a pastoralist in today's world?
2. Do you think societies should support such people in their traditional ways or encourage them to modernize? Why?
3. Would you require young people in pastoral societies to attend school? What if that meant that few young people would continue in the pastoral ways of their parents?

tip

"Sociocultural evolution" refers to the way that new technology changes a society. This process is described in terms of five stages of productive technology: (1) hunting and gathering, (2) horticultural and pastoral, (3) agrarian, (4) industrial, and (5) postindustrial.

 tip

Agrarian societies are so much more productive than earlier types that the spread of agriculture is generally identified in high school world history as the "dawn of civilization."

peasants or slaves, who do most of the work. Elites therefore have time for more "refined" activities, including the study of philosophy, art, and literature. This explains the historical link between "high culture" and social privilege.

Among hunters and gatherers and also among horticulturalists, women provide most of the food, which gives them social importance. Agriculture, however, raises men to a position of social dominance. Using heavy metal plows pulled by large animals, men take charge of food production in agrarian societies. Women are left with the support tasks, such as weeding and carrying water to the fields (Boulding, 1976; Fisher, 1979).

In agrarian societies, religion reinforces the power of elites by defining both loyalty and hard work as moral obligations. Many of the "Wonders of the Ancient World," such as the Great Wall of China and the Great Pyramids of Egypt, were possible only because emperors and pharaohs had almost absolute power and were able to control a large political system and order their people to work for a lifetime without pay.

Of the societies described so far, agrarian societies have the most social inequality. Agrarian technology also gives people a greater range of life choices, which is the reason that agrarian soci-eties differ more from one another than horticultural and pastoral societies do.

Industrial Societies

Industrialism, which first took hold in the rich nations of today's world, is *the production of goods using advanced sources of energy to drive large machinery.* Until the industrial era began, the major source of energy had been the muscles of humans and the animals they tended. Around the year 1750, people turned to water power and then steam boilers to operate mills and factories filled with larger and larger machines.

Industrial technology gave people such power to alter their environment that change took place faster than ever before. It is probably correct to say that the new industrial societies changed more in one century than they had over the course of the previous thousand years. Change was so rapid that it sparked the birth of sociology itself. By 1900, railroads crossed the land, steamships traveled the seas, and steel-framed skyscrapers reached far higher than any of the old cathedrals that symbolized the agrarian age.

But that was only the beginning. Soon automobiles allowed people to move quickly almost anywhere, and electricity powered homes full of modern "conveniences" such as refrigerators, washing machines, air conditioners, and entertainment centers. Electronic communication, beginning with the telegraph and the telephone and followed by radio, television, and computers, gave people the ability to reach others instantly, all over the world.

Work also changed. In agrarian communities, most men and women worked in the home or in the fields nearby. Industrialization drew people away from home to factories situated near energy sources (such as coalfields) that power their machinery. The result was a weakening of close working relationships, strong family ties, and many of the traditional values, beliefs, and customs that guide agrarian life.

Agrarian technology allows societies to produce a surplus—more food than people need to survive. Because not everyone has to produce food, this bounty encourages a greater range of productive work. At the same time, it also increases the extent of social inequality involving class as well as gender.

Paul Nevin/Photolibrary.com

 December 28, Moray, in the Andes high-lands of Peru. We are high in the mountains in a small community of several dozen families, miles from the nearest electric line or paved road. At about 12,000 feet, breathing is hard for people not used to the thin air, so we walk slowly. But hard work is no problem for the man

tip

The beginning of "modernity" is linked to the development of industrial production, first in Europe and soon after in the United States. The industrial era also sparked the development of sociology.

tip

Industrial societies are the first type in which most energy for production no longer comes from muscles.

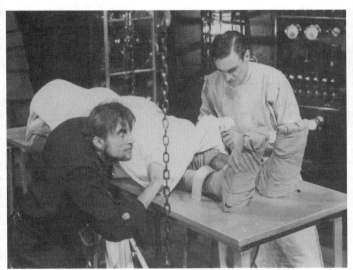

Does advancing technology make society better? In some ways, perhaps. However, many films—as far back as *Frankenstein* (left) in 1931 and as recently as the Will Smith film *I Robot* (right)—have expressed the concern that new technology not only solves old problems but also creates new ones. All the sociological theorists discussed in this chapter shared this ambivalent view of the modern world.

Getty Images Inc.—Hulton Archive Photos (*left*); 20th Century Fox/Picture Desk, Inc./Kobal Collection (*right*)

and his son tilling a field near their home with a horse and plow. Too poor to buy a tractor, these people till the land in the same way that their ancestors did 500 years ago.

With industrialization, occupational specialization became greater than ever. Today, the kind of work you do has a lot to do with your standard of living, so people now often size up one another in terms of their jobs rather than according to their family ties, as agrarian people do. Rapid change and people's tendency to move from place to place also make social life more anonymous, increase cultural diversity, and promote subcultures and countercultures.

Industrial technology changes the family, too, reducing its traditional importance as the center of social life. No longer does the family serve as the main setting for work, learning, and religious worship. Technological change also plays a part in making families more diverse, with a greater share of single people, divorced people, single-parent families, and stepfamilies.

Perhaps the greatest effect of industrialization has been to raise living standards, which increased fivefold in the United States over the past century. Although at first it only benefits the elite few, industrial technology is so productive that incomes rise over time and peo-

ple have longer and more comfortable lives. Even social inequality decreases slightly, because industrial societies provide extended schooling and greater political rights. Around the world, industrialization has had the effect of increasing the demand for a greater political voice, a pattern evident in South Korea, Taiwan, the People's Republic of China, and the nations of Eastern Europe and the former Soviet Union.

Postindustrial Societies

Many industrial societies, including the United States, have now entered a new phase of technological development, and we can extend Lenski's analysis to take account of recent trends. A generation ago, the sociologist Daniel Bell (1973) coined the term **postindustrialism** to refer to *the production of information using computer technology.* Production in industrial societies centers on factories and machinery generating material goods; postindustrial production relies on computers and other electronic devices that create, process, store, and apply information. Just as people in industrial societies learn mechanical skills, people in postindustrial societies such as ours develop information-based skills and carry out their work using computers and other forms of high-technology communication.

SUMMING UP

Sociocultural Evolution

Type of Society	Historical Period	Productive Technology	Population Size
Hunting and Gathering Societies	Only type of society until about 12,000 years ago; still common several centuries ago; the few examples remaining today are threatened with extinction	Primitive weapons	25–40 people
Horticultural and Pastoral Societies	From about 12,000 years ago, with decreasing numbers after about 3000 B.C.E.	Horticultural societies use hand tools for cultivating plants; pastoral societies are based on the domestication of animals	Settlements of several hundred people, connected through trading ties to form societies of several thousand people
Agrarian Societies	From about 5,000 years ago, with large but decreasing numbers today	Animal-drawn plow	Millions of people
Industrial Societies	From about 1750 to the present	Advanced sources of energy; mechanized production	Millions of people
Postindustrial Societies	Emerging in recent decades	Computers that support an information-based economy	Millions of people

A postindustrial society uses less and less of its labor force for industrial production. At the same time, more jobs become available for clerical workers, teachers, writers, sales managers, and marketing representatives, all of whom process information.

The Information Revolution, which is at the heart of postindustrial society, is most evident in rich nations, yet new information technology affects the whole world. A worldwide flow of goods, people, and information now links societies and has advanced a global culture. In this sense, the postindustrial society is at the heart of globalization.

Why do you think many people are quick to see the advantages of advancing technology but slow to see many of its negative consequences?

The Summing Up table reviews how technology shapes societies at different stages of sociocultural evolution.

The Limits of Technology

More complex technology has made life better by raising productivity, reducing infectious disease, and sometimes just relieving boredom. But technology provides no quick fix for social problems. Poverty, for example, remains a reality for tens of millions of women and men in the United States and 1 billion people worldwide.

Technology also creates new problems that our ancestors (and people like Sididi Ag Inaka today) could hardly imagine. Industrial and postindustrial societies give us more personal freedom, but they often lack the sense of community that was part of preindustrial life. Further, although technology can be used for good, the most powerful nations in the world today have stockpiles of nuclear weapons that could send the world back to the Stone Age—if we survive at all.

Advancing technology has also threatened the physical environment. Each stage in sociocultural evolution has introduced more powerful sources of energy and increased our appetite for Earth's

 get it right

The discussion of limits to technology highlights a major point: Lenski believes that technology improves society by raising living standards but does not solve all social problems (such as social inequality) and may actually increase some problems (such as the sense of losing human community, creating dangerous weapons of war, and harming the natural environment).

 tip

Our society is now in the postindustrial stage. Notice that more of today's jobs make use of computer technology to process information and fewer of them involve industrial (factory) work.

Settlement Pattern	Social Organization	Examples
Nomadic	Family-centered; specialization limited to age and sex; little social inequality	Pygmies of Central Africa, Bushmen of southwestern Africa, Aborigines of Australia, Semai of Malaysia, Kaska Indians of Canada
Horticulturalists form small permanent settlements; pastoralists are nomadic	Family-centered; religious system begins to develop; moderate specialization; increased social inequality	Middle Eastern societies about 5000 B.C.E., various societies today in New Guinea and other Pacific islands, Yanomamö today in South America
Cities become common, but they generally contain only a small proportion of the population	Family loses significance as distinct religious, political, and economic systems emerge; extensive specialization; increased social inequality	Egypt during construction of the Great Pyramids, medieval Europe, numerous predominantly agrarian societies of the world today
Cities contain most of the population	Distinct religious, political, economic, educational, and family systems; highly specialized; marked social inequality persists, lessening somewhat over time	Most societies today in Europe and North America, Australia, and Japan, which generate most of the world's industrial production
Population remains concentrated in cities	Similar to industrial societies, with information processing and other service work gradually replacing industrial production	Industrial societies noted above are now entering the postindustrial stage

resources. Ask yourself whether we can continue to pursue material prosperity without permanently damaging our planet.

In some ways, technological advances have improved life and brought the world's people closer. But establishing peace, ensuring justice, and protecting the environment are problems that technology alone cannot solve.

 YOUR LEARNING Identify the five levels of sociocultural evolution discussed in this first part of the chapter. Name the technology that defines each, and describe how this technology shapes human society.

Karl Marx: Society and Conflict

The first of our classic visions of society comes from Karl Marx (1818–1883), an early giant in the field of sociology whose influence continues today. Keenly aware of how the Industrial Revolution had changed Europe, Marx spent most of his adult life in London, the capital of what was then the vast British Empire. He was awed by the size and productive power of the new factories going up all over Britain. Along with other industrial nations, Great Britain was producing more goods than ever before, drawing resources from around the world and churning out products at a dizzying rate.

What astounded Marx even more was that the riches produced by this new technology ended up in the hands of only a few people. As he walked around the city of London, he could see for himself that a handful of aristocrats and industrialists lived in fabulous mansions staffed by servants, where they enjoyed both luxury and privilege. At the same time, most people labored long hours for low wages and lived in slums. Some even slept in the streets, where they were likely to die young from diseases brought on by cold and poor nutrition.

Marx saw his society in terms of a basic contradiction: In a country so rich, how could so many people be so poor? Just as important, he asked, how can this situation be changed? Many people think Marx set out to tear societies apart. But he was motivated by compassion

tip

Take a careful look at Figure 1, which shows Marx's belief that the economy is the foundation of society (the "infrastructure") that affects the operation of the other social institutions as well as cultural ideas and values (the "superstructure"). This approach is called *materialism* because how a society produces material goods is seen as defining the whole social system.

and wanted to help a badly divided society create a new and more just social order.

At the heart of Marx's thinking is the idea of **social conflict,** *the struggle between segments of society over valued resources.* Social conflict can, of course, take many forms: Individuals quarrel, colleges have longstanding sports rivalries, and nations go to war. For Marx, however, the most important type of social conflict was *class conflict* arising from the way a society produces material goods.

Society and Production

Living in the nineteenth century, Marx observed the early decades of industrial capitalism in Europe. This economic system, Marx explained, turned a small part of the population into **capitalists,** *people who own and operate factories and other businesses in pursuit of profits.* A capitalist tries to make a profit by selling a product for more than it costs to produce. Capitalism turns most of the population into industrial workers, whom Marx called **proletarians,** *people who sell their labor for wages.* To Marx, a system of capitalist production always ends up creating conflict between capitalists and workers. To keep

profits high, capitalists keep wages low. But workers want higher wages. Since profits and wages come from the same pool of funds, the result is conflict. As Marx saw it, this conflict could end only with the end of capitalism itself.

All societies are composed of **social institutions,** *the major spheres of social life, or societal subsystems, organized to meet human needs.* Examples of social institutions include the economy, the political system, the family, religion, and education. In his analysis of society, Marx argued that one institution—the economy—dominates all the others and defines the true nature of a society. Drawing on the philosophical approach called *materialism,* which says that how humans produce material goods shapes their experiences, Marx believed that the other social institutions all operate in a way that supports a society's economy. Lenski focused on how technology molds a society, but Marx argued that the economy is a society's "real foundation" (1959:43, orig. 1859).

Marx viewed the economic system as society's *infrastructure* (*infra* is Latin, meaning "below"). Other social institutions, including the family, the political system, and religion, are built on this foundation; they form society's *superstructure* and support the economy. Marx's theory is illustrated in Figure 1. For example, under capitalism, the legal system protects capitalists' wealth, and the family allows capitalists to pass their property from one generation to the next.

Marx was well aware that most people living in industrial-capitalist societies do not recognize how capitalism shapes the entire operation of their society. Most people, in fact, regard the right to own private property or pass it on to their children as "natural." In the same way, many of us tend to see rich people as having "earned" their money through long years of schooling and hard work; we see the poor, on the other hand, as lacking skills and the personal drive to make more of themselves. Marx rejected this type of thinking, calling it **false consciousness,** *explanations of social problems as the shortcomings of individuals rather than as the flaws of society.* Marx was saying, in effect, that it is not "people" who make society so unequal but rather the system of capitalist production. False consciousness, he believed, hurts people by hiding the real cause of their problems.

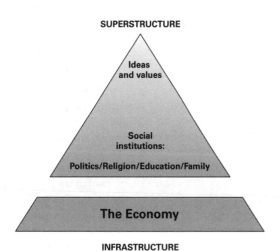

SUPERSTRUCTURE

Ideas and values

Social institutions:

Politics/Religion/Education/Family

The Economy

INFRASTRUCTURE

FIGURE 1 Karl Marx's Model of Society

This diagram illustrates Marx's materialist view that the system of economic production shapes the entire society. Economic production involves both technology (industry, in the case of capitalism) and social relationships (for capitalism, the relationship between the capitalists, who own the factories and businesses, and the workers, who are the source of labor). On this infrastructure, or foundation, rests society's superstructure, which includes its major social institutions as well as core cultural values and ideas. Marx maintained that every part of a society supports the economic system.

Conflict and History

For Marx, conflict is the engine that drives social change. Sometimes societies change at a slow, *evolutionary* rate. But they may erupt in rapid, *revolutionary* change.

To Marx, early hunters and gatherers formed primitive communist societies. *Communism* is a system in which people commonly own and equally share the food and other things they produce. People in hunting and gathering societies do not have much, but they

✔ **get it right**

Marx's analysis of society uses the social-conflict approach. In his eyes, class conflict (rather than gender conflict or racial conflict) is most important.

student 2 student

"I have always heard about Karl Marx as some sort of bad guy. I'm not sure I agree with him, but I'm glad to have some idea of what he was really talking about."

share what they have. In addition, because everyone does the same kind of work, there is little chance of social conflict.

With technological advance comes social inequality. Among horticultural, pastoral, and early agrarian societies—which Marx lumped together as the "ancient world"—warfare was frequent, and the victors made their captives slaves.

Agriculture brings still more wealth to a society's elite but does little for most other people, who labor as serfs and are barely better off than slaves. As Marx saw it, the state supported the feudal system (in which the elite or nobility had all the power), assisted by the church, which claimed that this arrangement was God's will. This is why Marx thought that feudalism was simply "exploitation, veiled by religious and political illusions" (Marx & Engels, 1972:337, orig. 1848).

Gradually, new productive forces started to break down the feudal order. As trade steadily increased, cities grew, and merchants and skilled craftsworkers formed the new capitalist class or *bourgeoisie* (a French word meaning "people of the town"). After 1800, the bourgeoisie also controlled factories, becoming richer and richer so that they soon rivaled the ancient landowning nobility. For their part, the nobles looked down their noses at this upstart "commercial" class, but in time, these capitalists took control of European societies. To Marx's way of thinking, then, new technology was only part of the Industrial Revolution; it also served as a class revolution in which capitalists overthrew the old agrarian elite.

Industrialization also led to the growth of the proletariat. English landowners converted fields once plowed by serfs into grazing land for sheep to produce wool for the textile mills. Forced from the land, millions of people migrated to cities to work in factories. Marx envisioned these workers one day joining together to form a revolutionary class that would overthrow the capitalist system.

Capitalism and Class Conflict

"The history of all hitherto existing society is the history of class struggles." With these words, Marx and his collaborator, Friedrich Engels, began their best-known statement, the *Manifesto of the Communist Party* (1972:335, orig. 1848). Industrial capitalism, like earlier types of society, contains two major social classes—the ruling class, whose members (capitalists or bourgeoisie) own productive property, and the oppressed (proletarians), who sell their labor—reflecting the two basic positions in the productive system. Like masters and slaves in the ancient world and like nobles and serfs in feudal systems, capitalists and proletarians are engaged in class conflict today. Currently, as in the past, one class controls the other as productive property. Marx used the term **class conflict** (and sometimes *class struggle*) to refer to *conflict between entire classes over the distribution of a society's wealth and power.*

Karl Marx was surely the pioneering sociologist with the greatest influence on the world as a whole. Through the second half of the last century, 1 billion people—nearly one-fifth of humanity—lived in societies organized on Marxist principles.

Getty Images/De Agostini Editore Picture Library

Class conflict is nothing new. What distinguishes the conflict in capitalist society, Marx pointed out, is how out in the open it is. Agrarian nobles and serfs, for all their differences, were bound together by traditions and mutual obligations. Industrial capitalism dissolved those ties so that loyalty and honor were replaced by "naked self-interest." Because the proletarians had no personal ties to the capitalists, Marx saw no reason for them to put up with their oppression.

Marx knew that revolution would not come easily. First, workers must *become aware* of their oppression and see capitalism as its true cause. Second, they must *organize and act* to address their problems. This means that false consciousness must be replaced with **class consciousness,** *workers' recognition of themselves as a class unified in opposition to capitalists and ultimately to capitalism itself.* Because the inhumanity of early capitalism was plain for him to see, Marx concluded that industrial workers would soon rise up to destroy this economic system.

How would the capitalists react? Their wealth made them strong. But Marx saw a weakness in the capitalist armor. Motivated by a desire for personal gain, capitalists feared competition with other capitalists. Marx predicted, therefore, that capitalists would be slow to band

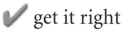

get it right

Pay attention to Marx's concept of alienation, one of his most important contributions to sociology. Later on, we will discuss Max Weber's view of alienation, which has a somewhat different meaning, so try to keep the two clear.

together despite their common interests. In addition, he reasoned, capitalists kept employees' wages low in order to maximize profits, which made the workers' misery grow ever greater. In the long run, Marx believed, capitalists would bring about their own undoing.

Capitalism and Alienation

Marx also condemned capitalist society for producing **alienation,** *the experience of isolation and misery resulting from powerlessness.* To the capitalists, workers are nothing more than a source of labor, to be hired and fired at will. Dehumanized by their jobs (repetitive factory work in the past and processing orders on a computer today), workers find little satisfaction and feel unable to improve their situation. Here we see another contradiction of capitalist society: As people develop technology to gain power over the world, the capitalist economy gains more control over people.

Marx noted four ways in which capitalism alienates workers:

1. **Alienation from the act of working.** Ideally, people work to meet their needs and to develop their personal potential. Capitalism, however, denies workers a say in what they make or how they make it. Further, much of the work is a constant repetition of routine tasks. The fact that today we replace workers with machines whenever possible would not have surprised Marx. As far as he was concerned, capitalism had turned human beings into machines long ago.

The 2004 film *The Motorcycle Diaries* tells the story of the motorcycle journey through South America of Che Guevara. Seeing such desperate poverty inspired Guevara to become a Marxist and fight for revolutionary change. He went on to play an important role in the Cuban Revolution.

2. **Alienation from the products of work.** The product of work belongs not to workers but to capitalists, who sell it for profit. Thus, Marx reasoned, the more of themselves workers invest in their work, the more they lose.

3. **Alienation from other workers.** Through work, Marx claimed, people build bonds of community. Industrial capitalism, however, makes work competitive rather than cooperative, setting each person apart from everyone else and offering little chance for human companionship.

4. **Alienation from human potential.** Industrial capitalism alienates workers from their human potential. Marx argued that a worker "does not fulfill himself in his work but denies himself, has a feeling of misery rather than well-being, does not freely develop his physical and mental energies, but is physically exhausted and mentally debased. The worker, therefore, feels himself to be at home only during his leisure time, whereas at work he feels homeless" (1964:124–25, orig. 1844). In short, industrial capitalism turns an activity that should express the best qualities in human beings into a dull and dehumanizing experience.

 SOCIOLOGY WORK

Marx viewed alienation, in its various forms, as a barrier to social change. But he hoped that industrial workers would overcome their alienation by uniting into a true social class, aware of the cause of their problems and ready to change society.

 Can you think of workplace settings that do not produce alienation? What are they, and what makes them better?

Revolution

The only way out of the trap of capitalism, Marx argued, is to remake society. He imagined a system of production that could provide for the social needs of all. He called this system *socialism.* Although Marx knew that such a dramatic change would not come easily, he must have been disappointed that he did not live to see workers in England rise up. Still, convinced that capitalism was a social evil, he believed that in time the working majority would realize they held the key to a better future. This change would certainly be revolutionary and perhaps even violent. Marx believed a socialist society would bring class conflict to an end.

Marx failed to foresee that the revolution he imagined could take the form of repressive regimes, such as Stalin's gov-

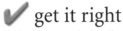

ernment in the Soviet Union, that would end up killing tens of millions of people (R. F. Hamilton, 2001). But in his own time, Marx looked toward the future with hope: "The proletarians have nothing to lose but their chains. They have a world to win" (Marx & Engels, 1972:362, orig. 1848).

YOUR LEARNING: Explain why social conflict is key to Marx's analysis of society.

Max Weber: The Rationalization of Society

With a wide knowledge of law, economics, religion, and history, Max Weber (1864–1920) produced what many experts regard as the greatest individual contribution to sociology. This scholar, born to a prosperous family in Germany, had much to say about how modern society differs from earlier types of social organization.

Weber understood the power of technology, and he shared many of Marx's ideas about social conflict. But he disagreed with Marx's philosophy of materialism. Weber's philosophical approach, called *idealism,* emphasized how human ideas—especially beliefs and values—shape society. He argued that societies differ not in terms of how people produce things but in how people think about the world. In Weber's view, modern society was the product of a new way of thinking.

Sociologists sometimes say that Weber's work is "a debate with the ghost of Karl Marx." Thinking of the basic approach of both of these early sociologists, can you explain why?

YOUR TURN

Weber compared societies in different times and places. To make the comparisons, he relied on the **ideal type,** *an abstract statement of the essential characteristics of any social phenomenon.* Following Weber's approach, for example, we might speak of "preindustrial" and "industrial" societies as ideal types. The use of the word "ideal" does not mean that one or the other is "good" or "the best." Nor does an ideal type refer to any actual society. Rather, think of an ideal type as a way of defining a type of society in its pure form. We have already used ideal types in comparing "hunting and gathering societies" with "industrial societies" and "capitalism" with "socialism."

A common fear among thinkers in the early industrial era was that people, now slaves to the new machines, would be stripped of their humanity. No one captured this idea better than the comic actor Charlie Chaplin, who wrote and starred in the 1936 film *Modern Times.*

Photofest

Two Worldviews: Tradition and Rationality

Rather than categorizing societies according to their technology or productive systems, Weber focused on ways people think about their world. Members of preindustrial societies are bound by *tradition,* and people in industrial-capitalist societies are guided by *rationality.*

By **tradition,** Weber meant *values and beliefs passed from generation to generation.* In other words, traditional people are guided by the past. They consider particular actions right and proper mostly because they have been accepted for so long.

People in modern societies, however, favor **rationality,** *a way of thinking that emphasizes deliberate, matter-of-fact calculation of the most efficient way to accomplish a particular task.* Sentimental ties to the past have no place in a rational worldview, and tradition becomes simply one kind of information. Typically, modern people think and act on the basis of what they see as the present and future consequences of their choices. They evaluate jobs, schooling, and even relationships in terms of what they put into them and what they expect to receive in return.

Weber viewed both the Industrial Revolution and the development of capitalism as evidence of modern rationality. Such changes are all part of the **rationalization of society,** *the historical change from tradition to rationality as the main type of human thought.* Weber went on to describe modern society as "disenchanted" because scientific thinking has swept away most of people's sentimental ties to the past.

The willingness to adopt the latest technology is one strong indicator of how rationalized a society is. To illustrate the global pattern of rationalization, Global Map 1 shows where in the world personal computers are found. In general, the high-income countries of North America and Europe use personal computers the most, but they are rare in low-income nations.

Why are some societies more eager than others to adopt new technology? Those with a more rational worldview might consider new computer or medical technology a breakthrough, but those with a very traditional culture might reject such devices as a threat to their way of life. The Tuareg nomads of northern Mali, described at the beginning of this chapter, shrug off the idea of using telephones: Why would anyone in the desert want a cell phone? Similarly, in the United States, the Amish refuse to have telephones in their homes because it is not part of their traditional way of life.

In Weber's view, the amount of technological innovation depends on how a society's people understand their world. Many people throughout history have had the opportunity to adopt new technol-ogy, but only in the rational cultural climate of Western Europe did people exploit scientific discoveries to spark the Industrial Revolution (Weber, 1958, orig. 1904–05).

Is Capitalism Rational?

Is industrial capitalism a rational economic system? Here again, Weber and Marx came down on different sides. Weber considered industrial capitalism highly rational because capitalists try to make money in any way they can. Marx, however, thought capitalism irrational because it fails to meet the basic needs of most of the people (Gerth & Mills, 1946:49).

Weber's Great Thesis: Protestantism and Capitalism

Weber spent many years considering how and why industrial capitalism developed in the first place. Why did it emerge in parts of Western Europe during the eighteenth and nineteenth centuries?

Weber claimed that the key to the birth of industrial capitalism lay in the Protestant Reformation. Specifically, he saw industrial capitalism as the major outcome of Calvinism, a Christian religious movement founded by John Calvin (1509–1564). Calvinists approached life in a highly disciplined and rational way. One of Calvin's most important ideas was *predestination,* the belief that an all-knowing and all-powerful God had predestined some people for salvation and others for damnation. Believing that everyone's fate was set before birth, early Calvinists thought people could do nothing to change their destiny, and even worse, they did not know what their destiny was. So Calvinists swung between hopeful visions of spiritual salvation and anxious fears of eternal damnation.

Frustrated at not knowing their fate, Calvinists gradually came to a resolution of sorts. Why shouldn't those chosen for glory in the next world, they reasoned, see signs of divine favor in *this* world? In this way, Calvinists came to see worldly prosperity as a sign of God's grace. Eager to gain this reassurance, Calvinists threw themselves into a quest for success, applying rationality, discipline, and hard work to their tasks. They did not pursue wealth for its own sake because spending on themselves would be self-indulgent and sinful. Neither were Calvinists likely to share their wealth with the poor, because they viewed poverty as a sign of God's rejection. Their duty was to press forward in what they saw as their personal *calling* from God, reinvesting profits for still greater success. It is easy to see how such activity—saving money,

To the outside observer, the trading floor of a stock exchange may look like complete craziness. But in such activity Weber saw the essence of modern rationality.

Tim Boyle/Getty Images, Inc—Liaison

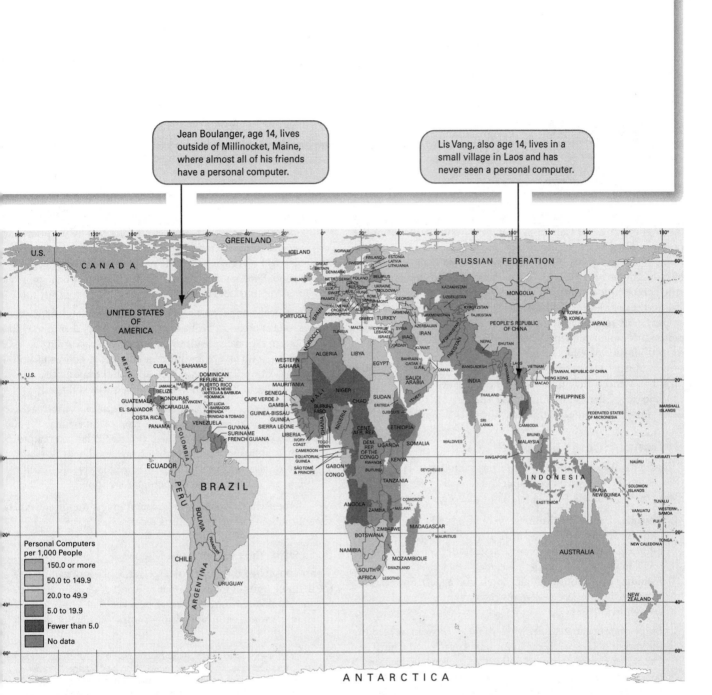

Jean Boulanger, age 14, lives outside of Millinocket, Maine, where almost all of his friends have a personal computer.

Lis Vang, also age 14, lives in a small village in Laos and has never seen a personal computer.

Personal Computers per 1,000 People
- 150.0 or more
- 50.0 to 149.9
- 20.0 to 49.9
- 5.0 to 19.9
- Fewer than 5.0
- No data

WINDOW ON THE WORLD

GLOBAL MAP 1   High Technology in Global Perspective

Countries with traditional cultures cannot afford, choose to ignore, or even intentionally resist new technology that nations with highly rationalized ways of life quickly embrace. Personal computers, central to today's high technology, are commonplace in high-income countries such as the United States. In low-income nations, by contrast, they are unknown to most people.

Source: International Telecommunication Union (2006, 2007).

using wealth to create more wealth, and adopting new technology—became the foundation of capitalism.

Other world religions did not encourage the rational pursuit of wealth the way Calvinism did. Catholicism, the traditional religion in most of Europe, taught a passive, "otherworldly" view: Good deeds performed humbly on Earth would bring rewards in heaven. For Catholics, making money had none of the spiritual significance it had for Calvinists. Weber concluded that this was the reason that industrial capitalism developed primarily in areas of Europe where Calvinism was strong.

tip

It is probably fair to say that Weber viewed modern capitalism as Calvinism minus Christianity: a *religious* ethic evolving into a *work* ethic.

Weber's study of Calvinism provides striking evidence of the power of ideas to shape society. Not one to accept simple explanations, Weber knew that industrial capitalism had many causes. But by stressing the importance of ideas, Weber tried to counter Marx's strictly economic explanation of modern society.

As the decades passed, later generations of Calvinists lost much of their early religious enthusiasm. But their drive for success and personal discipline remained, and slowly a *religious* ethic was transformed into a *work* ethic. In this sense, industrial capitalism can be seen as "disenchanted" religion, with wealth now valued for its own sake. This trend is seen in the fact that the practice of "accounting," which to early Calvinists meant keeping a daily record of moral deeds, before long came to mean simply keeping track of money.

Rational Social Organization

According to Weber, rationality is the basis of modern society, giving rise to both the Industrial Revolution and capitalism. He went on to identify seven characteristics of rational social organization:

1. **Distinctive social institutions.** In hunting and gathering societies, the family is the center of all activity. Gradually, however, religious, political, and economic systems develop as separate social institutions. In modern societies, new institutions—including education and health care—also appear. Specialized social institutions are a rational strategy to meet human needs efficiently.

2. **Large-scale organizations.** Modern rationality can be seen in the spread of large-scale organizations. As early as the horticultural era, small groups of political officials made decisions concerning religious observances, public works, and warfare. By the time Europe developed agrarian societies, the Catholic church had grown into a much larger organization with thousands of officials. In today's modern, rational society, almost everyone works for large formal organizations, and federal and state governments employ tens of millions of workers.

3. **Specialized tasks.** Unlike members of traditional societies, people in modern societies are likely to have very specialized jobs. The Yellow Pages of any city's telephone directory suggest just how many different occupations there are today.

4. **Personal discipline.** Modern societies put a premium on self-discipline. Most business and government organizations expect their workers to be disciplined, and discipline is also encouraged by our cultural values of achievement and success.

5. **Awareness of time.** In traditional societies, people measure time according to the rhythm of sun and seasons. Modern

people, by contrast, schedule events precisely by the hour and even the minute. Clocks began appearing in European cities some 500 years ago, about the same time commerce began to expand. Soon people began to think (to borrow Benjamin Franklin's phrase) that "time is money."

6. **Technical competence.** Members of traditional societies size up one another on the basis of *who* they are—their family ties. Modern rationality leads us to judge people according to *what* they are, with an eye toward their education, skills, and abilities. Most workers have to keep up with the latest skills and knowledge in their field in order to be successful.

7. **Impersonality.** In a rational society, technical competence is the basis for hiring, so the world becomes impersonal. People interact as specialists concerned with particular tasks rather than as individuals concerned with one another as people. Because showing your feelings can threaten personal discipline, modern people tend to devalue emotion.

All these characteristics can be found in one important expression of modern rationality: bureaucracy.

Rationality, Bureaucracy, and Science

Weber considered the growth of large, rational organizations one of the defining traits of modern societies. Another term for this type of organization is *bureaucracy*. Weber believed that bureaucracy has much in common with capitalism—another key factor in modern social life:

> Today, it is primarily the capitalist market economy which demands that the official business of public administration be discharged precisely, unambiguously, continuously, and with as much speed as possible. Normally, the very large capitalist enterprises are themselves unequaled models of strict bureaucratic organization. (1978:974, orig. 1921)

We find aspects of bureaucracy in today's businesses, government agencies, labor unions, and universities. Weber considered bureaucracy highly rational because its elements—offices, duties, and policies—help achieve specific goals as efficiently as possible. Weber saw that capitalism, bureaucracy, and also science—the highly disciplined pursuit of knowledge—are all expressions of the same underlying factor: rationality.

Rationality and Alienation

Max Weber agreed with Karl Marx that industrial capitalism was highly productive. Weber also agreed with Marx that modern society generates widespread alienation, although his reasons were different.

tip

The Tooker painting on this page captures Weber's view of alienation resulting from rationality that puts us all in a "box" in which rigid rules and regulations limit our lives and make everyone's experience much the same. This "horizontal" view of alienation contrasts with Marx's "vertical" approach, which links alienation to social inequality.

Marx thought alienation was caused by economic inequality. Weber blamed alienation on bureaucracy's countless rules and regulations. Bureaucracies, Weber warned, treat a human being as a "number" or a "case" rather than as a unique individual. In addition, working for large organizations demands highly specialized and often tedious routines. In the end, Weber saw modern society as a vast and growing system of rules trying to regulate everything, and he feared that modern society would end up crushing the human spirit.

Like Marx, Weber found it ironic that modern society, meant to serve humanity, turns on its creators and enslaves them. Just as Marx described the dehumanizing effects of industrial capitalism, Weber portrayed the modern individual as "only a small cog in a ceaselessly moving mechanism that prescribes to him an endlessly fixed routine of march" (1978:988, orig. 1921). Although Weber could see the advantages of modern society, he was deeply pessimistic about the future. He feared that in the end, the rationalization of society would reduce human beings to robots.

 Marx saw revolution as the way to overcome the problems of capitalism. Would the creation of a socialist government solve the problem of excessive rationality that worried Weber? Why or why not?

✓ **YOUR LEARNING** What did Weber mean by saying that modern society is defined by a rational worldview?

Max Weber agreed with Karl Marx that modern society is alienating to the individual, but they identified different causes of this problem. For Marx, economic inequality is the reason; for Weber, the issue is widespread and dehumanizing bureaucracy. George Tooker's painting *Landscape with Figures* echoes Weber's sentiments.

George Tooker, *Landscape with Figures*, 1963, egg tempera on gesso panel, 26 × 30 inches Private collection. Reproduction courtesy DC Moore Gallery, NYC.

Emile Durkheim: Society and Function

"To love society is to love something beyond us and something in ourselves." These are the words (1974:55, orig. 1924) of the French sociologist Emile Durkheim (1858–1917), another of the discipline's founders. In Durkheim's ideas we find another important vision of human society.

Structure: Society beyond Ourselves

Emile Durkheim's great insight was recognizing that society exists beyond ourselves. Society is more than the individuals who compose it. Society was here long before we were born, it shapes us while we live, and it will remain long after we are gone. Patterns of human behavior—cultural norms, values, and beliefs—exist as established structures, or *social facts*, that have an objective reality beyond the lives of individuals.

Because society is bigger than any one of us, it has the power to guide our thoughts and actions. This is why studying individuals alone (as psychologists or biologists do) can never capture the heart of the social experience. A classroom of college students taking a math exam, a family gathered around a table sharing a meal, people quietly waiting their turn in a doctor's office—all are examples of the countless situations that have a familiar organization apart from any particular individual who has ever been part of them.

Once created by people, Durkheim claimed, society takes on a life of its own and demands a measure of obedience from its creators. We experience the reality of society in the order of our lives or as we face temptation and feel the tug of morality.

Function: Society as System

Having established that society has structure, Durkheim turned to the concept of *function*. The significance of any social fact, he explained, is more than what individuals see in their immediate lives; social facts help society operate.

tip
Durkheim's view of society most clearly follows
the structural-functional approach.

Consider crime. As victims of crime, individuals experience pain and loss. But taking a broader view, Durkheim saw that crime is vital to the ongoing life of society itself. Only by defining acts as wrong do people construct and defend morality, which gives direction and meaning to our collective life. For this reason, Durkheim rejected the common view of crime as abnormal. On the contrary, he concluded, crime is "normal" for the most basic of reasons: A society could not exist without it (1964a, orig. 1893; 1964b, orig. 1895).

Personality: Society in Ourselves

Durkheim said that society is not only "beyond ourselves" but also "in ourselves," helping form our personalities. How we act, think, and feel is drawn from the society that nurtures us. Society shapes us in another way as well—by providing the moral discipline that guides our behavior and controls our desires. Durkheim believed that human beings need the restraint of society because as creatures who can want more and more, we are in constant danger of being overpowered by our own desires. As he put it, "The more one has, the more one wants, since satisfactions received only stimulate instead of filling needs" (1966:248, orig. 1897).

Nowhere is the need for societal regulation better illustrated than in Durkheim's study of suicide (1966, orig. 1897). Why is it that rock stars—from Janis Joplin and Jim Morrison to Jimi Hendrix and Kurt Cobain—seem so prone to self-destruction? Durkheim had the answer long before the invention of the electric guitar: Now as back then, the *highest* suicide rates are found among categories of people with the *lowest* level of societal integration. In short, the enormous freedom of the young, rich, and famous carries a high price in terms of the risk of suicide.

Modernity and Anomie

Compared to traditional societies, modern societies impose fewer restrictions on everyone. Durkheim acknowledged the advantages of modern-day freedom, but he warned of increased **anomie,** *a condition in which society provides little moral guidance to individuals.* The pattern by which many celebrities are "destroyed by fame" well illustrates the destructive effects of anomie. Sudden fame tears people from their families and familiar routines, disrupts established values and norms, and breaks down society's support and regulation of the individual—sometimes with fatal results. Therefore, Durkheim

Durkheim's observation that people with weak social bonds are prone to self-destructive behavior stands as stark evidence of the power of society to shape individual lives. When rock-and-roll singers become famous, they are wrenched out of familiar life patterns and existing relationships, sometimes with deadly results. The history of rock-and-roll contains many tragic stories of this kind, including (from left) Janis Joplin's and Jimi Hendrix's deaths by drug overdose (both 1970) and Jim Morrison's (1971) and Kurt Cobain's (1994) suicides.

Elliott Landy/Magnum Photos, Inc. (*left, second from left, and third from left*); AP/Wide World Photos (*far right*)

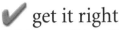

In traditional societies, such as Amish communities in the United States, everyone does much the same work (*left*). These societies are held together by strong moral beliefs. Modern societies, illustrated by urban areas in this country, are held together by a system of production in which people perform specialized work and rely on one another (*right*).

Peter Finger/Corbis/ Bettmann (*left*); Mikael Karlsson/Arresting Images (*right*)

explained, an individual's desires must be balanced by the claims and guidance of society—a balance that is sometimes difficult to achieve in the modern world. Durkheim would not have been surprised to see a rising suicide rate in modern societies such as the United States.

 Compare Durkheim's concept of anomie with the concepts of alienation developed by Marx and Weber. What is an important similarity? What is an important difference?

Evolving Societies: The Division of Labor

Like Marx and Weber, Durkheim lived through rapid social change in Europe during the nineteenth century. But Durkheim offered different reasons for this change.

In preindustrial societies, he explained, tradition operates as the social cement that binds people together. In fact, what he termed the *collective conscience* is so strong that the community moves quickly to punish anyone who dares to challenge conventional ways of life. Durkheim used the term **mechanical solidarity** to refer to *social bonds, based on common sentiments and shared moral values, that are strong among members of preindustrial societies*. In practice, mechanical solidarity is based on *similarity*. Durkheim called these bonds "mechanical" because people are linked together in lockstep, with a more or less automatic sense of belonging together and acting alike.

With industrialization, Durkheim continued, mechanical solidarity becomes weaker and weaker, and people are much less bound by tradition. But this does not mean that society dissolves. Modern life creates a new type of solidarity. Durkheim called this new social integration **organic solidarity**, defined as *social bonds, based on specialization and interdependence, that are strong among members of industrial societies*. The solidarity that was once rooted in likeness is now based on *differences* among people who find that their specialized work—as plumbers, college students, midwives, or sociology instructors—makes them rely on other people for most of their daily needs.

For Durkheim, then, the key to change in a society is an expanding **division of labor**, or *specialized economic activity*. Weber said that modern societies specialize in order to become more efficient, and

tip

Be sure to do all the "✓ Your Learning" exercises to see how well you understand the material.

 tip

Before you read this page, consider how each major theorist would answer the three questions in the "Four Visions of Society's section. This is a great way to review the chapter's material.

Durkheim filled out the picture by showing that members of modern societies count on tens of thousands of others—most of them strangers—for the goods and services needed every day. As members of modern societies, we depend more and more on people we trust less and less. Why do we look to people we hardly know and whose beliefs may well differ from our own? Durkheim's answer was "because we can't live without them."

So modern society rests far less on *moral consensus* and far more on *functional interdependence.* Herein lies what we might call "Durkheim's dilemma": The technological power and greater personal freedom of modern society come at the cost of declining morality and the rising risk of anomie.

Like Marx and Weber, Durkheim worried about the direction society was taking. But of the three, Durkheim was the most optimistic. He saw that large, anonymous societies gave people more freedom and privacy than small towns. Anomie remains a danger, but Durkheim hoped we would be able to create laws and other norms to regulate our behavior.

How can we apply Durkheim's views to the Information Revolution? The Seeing Sociology in Everyday Life box suggests that he and two of the other theorists we have considered in this chapter would have had much to say about today's new computer technology.

How do we understand something as complex as human society? Each of the thinkers profiled in this chapter offers insights about the meaning and importance of modern society. Each has a somewhat different view and provides a partial answer to a very complex issue.

Jeff Greenberg/PhotoEdit Inc.

 YOUR LEARNING What did Durkheim see as key differences between traditional and modern societies?

Critical Review: Four Visions of Society

This chapter opened with several important questions about society. We will conclude by summarizing how each of the four visions of society answers these questions.

What Holds Societies Together?

How is something as complex as society possible? Lenski claims that members of a society are united by a shared culture, although cultural patterns become more diverse as a society gains more complex technology. He also points out that as technology becomes more complex, inequality divides a society more and more, although industrialization reduces inequality somewhat.

Marx saw in society not unity but social division based on class position. From his point of view, elites may force an uneasy peace, but true social unity can occur only if production becomes a cooperative process. To Weber, the members of a society share a worldview. Just as tradition joined people together in the past, so modern societies have created rational, large-scale organizations that connect people's lives. Finally, Durkheim made solidarity the focus of his work. He contrasted the mechanical solidarity of preindustrial societies, which is based on shared morality, with modern society's organic solidarity, which is based on specialization.

How Have Societies Changed?

According to Lenski's model of sociocultural evolution, societies differ mostly in terms of changing technology. Modern society stands out from past societies in terms of its enormous productive power. Marx, too, noted historical differences in productivity yet pointed to continuing social conflict (except perhaps among simple hunters and gatherers). For Marx, modern society is distinctive mostly because it brings that conflict out into the open. Weber considered the question of change from the perspective of how people look at the world. Members of preindustrial societies have a traditional outlook; modern people take a rational worldview. Finally, for Durkheim, traditional societies are characterized by

tip

ll the sociologists discussed in this chapter have
ood and bad things to say about modern society.
Veber was the most pessimistic, and Durkheim
as the most optimistic.

tip

The box below shows how the ideas of sociology's
founders who lived a century ago, can be applied
to our lives today.

Seeing Sociology in Everyday Life

Today's Information Revolution: What Would Durkheim, Weber, and Marx Have Thought?

COLLEEN: Didn't Marx predict there'd be a class revolution?

MASAKO: Well, yes, but in the information age, what are the classes that are supposed to be in conflict?

New technology is changing our society at a dizzying pace. Were they alive today, the founding sociologists discussed in this chapter would be eager observers of the current scene. Imagine for a moment the kinds of questions Emile Durkheim, Max Weber, and Karl Marx might ask about the effects of computer technology on our everyday lives.

Durkheim, who emphasized the increasing division of labor in modern society, would probably wonder if new information technology is pushing work specialization even further. There is good reason to think that it is. Because electronic communication (say, a Web site) gives anyone a vast market (already, several billion people access the Internet), people can specialize far more than if they were trying to make a living in a small geographic area. For example, while most small-town lawyers have a general practice, an information age attorney, living anywhere, can provide specialized guidance on, say, prenuptial agreements or electronic copyright law. As we move into the electronic age, the number of highly specialized small businesses (some of which end up becoming very large) in all fields is increasing rapidly.

Durkheim might also point out that the Internet threatens to increase our experience of anomie. Using computers has a tendency to isolate people from personal relationships with others. In addition, although the Internet offers a flood of information, it provides little in the way of moral guidance about what is wise or good or worth knowing.

Weber believed that modern societies are distinctive because their members share a rational worldview, and nothing illustrates this worldview better than bureaucracy. But will bureaucracy be as important during the twenty-first century? Here is one reason to think it may not: Although organizations will probably continue to regulate workers performing the kinds of routine tasks that were common in the industrial era, much work in the postindustrial era involves imagination. Consider such "new age" work as designing homes, composing music, and writing software. This kind of creative work cannot be regulated in the same way as putting together automobiles as they move down an assembly line. Perhaps this is the reason many high-technology companies have done away with worker dress codes and having employees punch in and out on a time clock.

Finally, what might Marx make of the Information Revolution? Since Marx considered the earlier Industrial Revolution a *class* revolution that allowed the owners of industry to dominate society, he would probably be concerned about the emergence of a new symbolic elite. Some analysts point out that film and television writers, producers, and performers now enjoy vast wealth, international prestige, and enormous power (Lichter, Rothman, & Lichter, 1990). Just as people without industrial skills stayed at the bottom of the class system in past decades, so people without symbolic skills may well become the "underclass" of the twenty-first century.

Durkheim, Weber, and Marx greatly improved our understanding of industrial societies. As we continue into the postindustrial age, there is plenty of room for new generations of sociologists to carry on.

"Lucidio Studio, Inc."/The Stock Connection

WHAT DO YOU THINK?

1. Is computer technology likely to continue to increase specialization? Why or why not?

2. Can you think of examples of "creative" businesses that are less bureaucratic than industrial companies used to be? Why would you expect this to be the case?

3. What effect will the increased importance of symbolic skills have on the "earning power" of a college degree?

tip

The Applying Sociology in Everyday Life items provide additional ways for you to connect the ideas found in this chapter with your own life.

---

mechanical solidarity based on moral likeness. In industrial societies, mechanical solidarity gives way to organic solidarity based on productive specialization.

Why Do Societies Change?

As Lenski sees it, social change comes about through technological innovation that over time transforms an entire society. Marx's materialist approach highlights the struggle between classes as the engine of change, pushing societies toward revolution. Weber, by contrast, pointed out that ideas contribute to social change. He demonstrated how a particular worldview—Calvinism—set in motion the Industrial Revolution, which ended up reshaping all of society. Finally, Durkheim pointed to an expanding division of labor as the key dimension of social change.

The fact that these four approaches are so different does not mean that any one of them is right or wrong in an absolute sense. Society is exceedingly complex, and our understanding of society benefits from applying all four visions.

Applying Sociology in Everyday Life

1. Hunting and gathering people gazed at the stars and named the constellations in terms that reflected their way of life—mostly after animals and hunters. As a way of revealing what is important to everyday life *today*, write a short paper imagining the meanings we would give clusters of stars if people in postindustrial societies were naming them and starting from scratch.

2. Spend a few minutes walking around your apartment, dorm room, or home trying to identify every device that has a computer chip in it. How many did you find? Were you surprised by the number?

3. Over the next few days, be alert for everyday evidence of these concepts: Marx's alienation, Weber's alienation, and Durkheim's anomie. What type of behavior or social pattern qualifies as an example of each in action? How are they different?

MAKING THE GRADE

Society

SOCIETY refers to people who interact in a defined territory and share a culture.

- What forces hold a society together?
- What makes societies different?
- How and why do societies change over time?

FOUR VISIONS OF SOCIETY

Gerhard Lenski: Society and Technology

Gerhard Lenski points to the importance of **TECHNOLOGY** in shaping any society. He uses the term **SOCIOCULTURAL EVOLUTION** to mean changes that occur as a society gains new technology.

In **HUNTING AND GATHERING SOCIETIES**, men use simple tools to hunt animals and women gather vegetation.

Hunting and gathering societies

- are the simplest of all societies and were the earliest type of society on Earth;
- are nomadic;
- have only a few dozen members;
- are built around the family;
- consider men and women roughly equal in social importance.

HORTICULTURAL AND PASTORAL SOCIETIES developed some 12,000 years ago as people began to use hand tools to raise crops and as they shifted to raising animals for food instead of hunting them.

Horticultural and pastoral societies

- are able to produce more food, so populations expand to hundreds;
- show greater specialization of work;
- show increasing levels of social inequality.

sociocultural evolution Lenski's term for the changes that occur as a society gains new technology

hunting and gathering making use of simple tools to hunt animals and gather vegetation for food

horticulture the use of hand tools to raise crops

pastoralism the domestication of animals

agriculture large-scale cultivation using plows harnessed to animals or more powerful energy sources

industrialism the production of goods using advanced sources of energy to drive large machinery

postindustrialism the production of information using computer technology

AGRARIAN SOCIETIES developed 5,000 years ago as the use of plows harnessed to animals or more powerful energy sources enabled large-scale cultivation.

Agrarian societies

- may expand into vast empires;
- show even greater specialization, with dozens of distinct occupations;
- have extreme social inequality;
- reduce the importance of women.

INDUSTRIAL SOCIETIES, which developed first in Europe 250 years ago, use advanced sources of energy to drive large machinery.

Industrialization

- provides many modern conveniences and advanced forms of transportation and communication;
- moves work from the home to the factory;
- reduces the traditional importance of the family;
- raises living standards.

POSTINDUSTRIAL SOCIETIES represent the most recent stage of technological development, namely, technology that supports an information-based economy.

Postindustrialization

- shifts production from heavy machinery making material things to computers and related technology processing information;
- requires a population with information-based skills;
- is the driving force behind the Information Revolution, a worldwide flow of information that now links societies with an emerging global culture.

See the Summing Up table in this chapter.

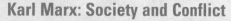

Karl Marx: Society and Conflict

Karl Marx's **MATERIALIST APPROACH** claims that societies are defined by their economic systems: How humans produce material goods shapes their experiences.

CONFLICT AND HISTORY

CLASS CONFLICT is the conflict between entire classes over the distribution of a society's wealth and power.

Marx traced conflict between social classes in societies as the source of social change throughout history:

- In "ancient" societies, masters dominated slaves.
- In agrarian societies, nobles dominated serfs.
- In industrial-capitalist societies, capitalists dominate proletarians.

CAPITALISM

Marx focused on the role of **CAPITALISM** in creating inequality and class conflict in modern societies.

- Under capitalism, the ruling class (capitalists, who own the means of production) oppresses the working class (proletarians, who sell their labor).
- Capitalism alienates workers from the act of working, from the products of work, from other workers, and from their own potential.
- Marx predicted that a workers' revolution would eventually overthrow capitalism and replace it with socialism, a system of production that would provide for the social needs of all.

social conflict the struggle between segments of society over valued resources

capitalists people who own and operate factories and other businesses in pursuit of profits

proletarians people who sell their labor for wages

social institutions the major spheres of social life, or societal subsystems, organized to meet human needs

false consciousness Marx's term for explanations of social problems as the shortcomings of individuals rather than as the flaws of society

class conflict conflict between entire classes over the distribution of a society's wealth and power

class consciousness Marx's term for workers' recognition of themselves as a class unified in opposition to capitalists and ultimately to capitalism itself

alienation the experience of isolation and misery resulting from powerlessness

Max Weber: The Rationalization of Society

Max Weber's **IDEALIST APPROACH** emphasizes the power of ideas to shape society.

IDEAS AND HISTORY

Weber traced the ideas—especially beliefs and values—that have shaped societies throughout history.

- Members of preindustrial societies are bound by **TRADITION**, the beliefs and values passed from generation to generation.
- Members of industrial-capitalist societies are guided by **RATIONALITY**, a way of thinking that emphasizes deliberate, matter-of-fact calculation of the most efficient way to accomplish a particular task.

RATIONALISM

Weber focused on the growth of large, rational organizations as the defining characteristic of modern societies.

- Rationality gave rise to both the Industrial Revolution and capitalism.
- Protestantism (specifically, Calvinism) encouraged the rational pursuit of wealth, laying the groundwork for the rise of industrial-capitalism.
- Weber defined seven characteristics of rational social organization, or **BUREAUCRACY** (see page xxx), and feared that excessive rationality would stifle human creativity.

ideal type an abstract statement of the essential characteristics of any social phenomenon

tradition values and beliefs passed from generation to generation

rationality a way of thinking that emphasizes deliberate, matter-of-fact calculation of the most efficient way to accomplish a particular task

rationalization of society Weber's term for the historical change from tradition to rationality as the main type of human thought

Emile Durkheim: Society and Function

Emile Durkheim claimed that society has an objective existence apart from its individual members.

STRUCTURE AND FUNCTION

Durkheim believed that because society is bigger than any one of us, it dictates how we are expected to act in any given social situation.

- He pointed out that social elements (such as crime) have functions that help society operate.
- Society also shapes our personalities and provides the moral discipline that guides our behavior and controls our desires.

EVOLVING SOCIETIES

Durkheim traced the evolution of social change by describing the different ways societies throughout history have guided the lives of their members.

- In preindustrial societies, **MECHANICAL SOLIDARITY**, or social bonds based on common sentiments and shared moral values, guides the social life of individuals.
- Industrialization and the **DIVISION OF LABOR** weakens traditional bonds, so that social life in modern societies is characterized by **ORGANIC SOLIDARITY**, social bonds based on specialization and interdependence.
- Durkheim warned of increased **ANOMIE** in modern societies, as society provides little moral guidance to individuals.

anomie Durkheim's term for a condition in which society provides little moral guidance to individuals

mechanical solidarity Durkheim's term for social bonds, based on common sentiments and shared moral values, that are strong among members of preindustrial societies

organic solidarity Durkheim's term for social bonds, based on specialization and interdependence, that are strong among members of industrial societies

division of labor specialized economic activity

MAKING THE GRADE

Sample Test Questions

These questions are similar to those found in the test bank that accompanies this textbook.

Multiple-Choice Questions

1. Which of the following would Lenski highlight as a cause of change in society?
   a. new religious movements
   b. conflict between workers and factory owners
   c. the steam engine
   d. the extent to which people share moral values

2. Horticultural societies are those in which
   a. people hunt animals and gather vegetation.
   b. people are nomadic.
   c. people have learned to raise animals.
   d. people use simple hand tools to raise crops.

3. Lenski claims that the development of more complex technology
   a. has both positive and negative effects.
   b. is entirely positive.
   c. is mostly negative.
   d. has little or no effect on society.

4. Marx believed that the industrial-capitalist economic system
   a. was very productive.
   b. concentrated wealth in the hands of a few.
   c. created conflict between two great classes: capitalists and proletarians.
   d. All of the above are correct.

5. Marx considered which of the following to be the "foundation" of society?
   a. technology
   b. the economy
   c. dominant ideas
   d. type of solidarity

6. Unlike Marx, Weber thought alienation was caused by
   a. social change that is too rapid.
   b. extensive social inequality.
   c. the high level of rationality in modern society.
   d. All of the above are correct.

7. What Lenski called the "industrial" society and Marx called the "capitalist" society, Weber called
   a. the "rational" society.
   b. the "ideal" society.
   c. the "traditional" society.
   d. the "technological" society.

8. Marx's "materialist" analysis contrasts with Weber's
   a. "optimistic" analysis.
   b. "idealist" analysis.
   c. "traditional" analysis.
   d. "technological" analysis.

9. Durkheim thought of society as
   a. existing only in people's minds.
   b. constantly changing.
   c. an objective reality.
   d. having no clear existence at all.

10. Which of the following questions might Durkheim ask about the ongoing war on terror?
   a. Would the war on terror unite people across the United States?
   b. Which class benefits most from the war on terror?
   c. How does war lead to new kinds of technology?
   d. How does war increase the scope of bureaucracy?

ANSWERS: 1 (c); 2 (d); 3 (a); 4 (d); 5 (b); 6 (c); 7 (a); 8 (b); 9 (c); 10 (a).

Essay Questions

1. How would Marx, Weber, and Durkheim imagine U.S. society a century from now? What kinds of questions or concerns would each thinker have?

2. Link Marx, Weber, and Durkheim to one of sociology's theoretical approaches, and explain your choices.

Socialization

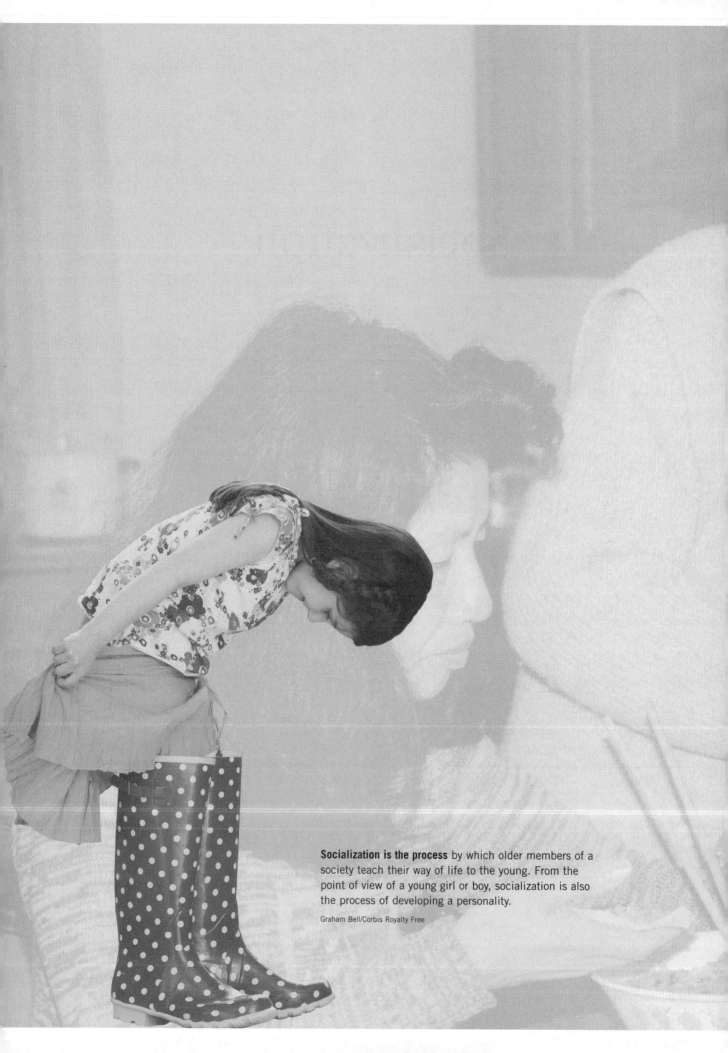

Socialization is the process by which older members of a society teach their way of life to the young. From the point of view of a young girl or boy, socialization is also the process of developing a personality.

Graham Bell/Corbis Royalty Free

Socialization

WHY is social experience the key to human personality?

WHAT familiar social settings have special importance to human development?

HOW do people's experiences change over the life course?

Robert Clay/Robert Clay Photography (*background*)

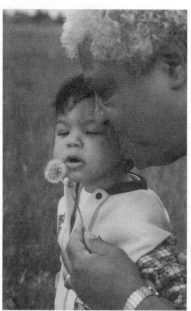
David Falconer/Folio, Inc.

On a cold winter day in 1938, a social worker walked quickly to the door of a rural Pennsylvania farmhouse. Investigating a case of possible child abuse, the social worker entered the home and soon discovered a five-year-old girl hidden in a second-floor storage room. The child, whose name was Anna, was wedged into an old chair with her arms tied above her head so that she couldn't move. She was wearing filthy clothes, and her arms and legs were as thin as matchsticks (K. Davis, 1940).

Anna's situation can only be described as tragic. She had been born in 1932 to an unmarried and mentally impaired woman of twenty-six who lived with her strict father. Angry about his daughter's "illegitimate" motherhood, the grandfather did not even want the child in his house, so for the first six months of her life, Anna was passed among several welfare agencies. But her mother could not afford to pay for her care, and Anna was returned to the hostile home of her grandfather.

To lessen the grandfather's anger, Anna's mother kept Anna in the storage room and gave her just enough milk to keep her alive. There she stayed—day after day, month after month, with almost no human contact—for five long years.

Learning of the discovery of Anna, the sociologist Kingsley Davis immediately went to see her. He found her with local officials at a county home. Davis was stunned by the emaciated child, who could not laugh, speak, or even smile. Anna was completely unresponsive, as if alone in an empty world.

Social Experience: The Key to Our Humanity

Socialization is so basic to human development that we sometimes overlook its importance. But here, in the terrible case of an isolated child, we can see what humans would be like without social contact. Although physically alive, Anna hardly seems to have been human. We can see that without social experience, a child is not able to act or communicate in a meaningful way and seems to be as much an object as a person.

Sociologists use the term **socialization** to refer to *the lifelong social experience by which people develop their human potential and learn culture.* Unlike other living species, whose behavior is mostly or entirely set by biology, humans need social experience to learn their culture and to survive. Social experience is also the foundation of **personality,** *a person's fairly consistent patterns of acting, thinking, and feeling.* We build a personality by internalizing—taking in—our surroundings. But without social experience, as Anna's case shows, personality hardly develops at all.

Human Development: Nature and Nurture

Anna's case makes clear that humans depend on others to provide the care and nurture needed not only for physical growth but also for personality to develop. A century ago, however, people mistakenly believed that humans were born with instincts that determined their personality and behavior.

The Biological Sciences: The Role of Nature

Charles Darwin's groundbreaking 1859 study of evolution, described in Chapter 3 ("Culture"), led people to think that human behavior was instinctive, simply our "nature." Such ideas led to claims that the U.S. economic system reflects "instinctive human competitiveness," that

some people are "born criminals," or that women are "naturally" emotional while men are "naturally" rational.

People trying to understand cultural diversity also misunderstood Darwin's thinking. From centuries of world exploration, Western Europeans knew that people around the world behaved quite differently from one another. But Europeans linked these differences to biology rather than culture. It was an easy, although incorrect and very damaging, step to claim that members of technologically simple societies were biologically less evolved and therefore "less human." This ethnocentric view helped justify colonialism: Why not take advantage of others if they seem not to be human in the same sense that you are?

The Social Sciences: The Role of Nurture

In the twentieth century, biological explanations of human behavior came under fire. The psychologist John B. Watson (1878–1958) developed a theory called *behaviorism,* which holds that behavior is not instinctive but learned. Thus people everywhere are equally human, differing only in their cultural patterns. In short, Watson rooted human behavior not in nature but in *nurture.*

Today, social scientists are cautious about describing *any* human behavior as instinctive. This does not mean that biology plays no part in human behavior. Human life, after all, depends on the functioning of the body. We also know that children often share biological traits (like height and hair color) with their parents and that heredity plays a part in intelligence, musical and artistic talent, and personality (such as how you react to frustration). However, whether you develop your inherited potential depends on how you are raised. For example, unless children use their brain early in life, the brain does not fully develop (Goldsmith, 1983; Begley, 1995).

Without denying the importance of nature, then, we can correctly say that nurture matters more in shaping human behavior. More precisely, *nurture is our nature.*

Chapter Overview

We turn now to a micro-level look at how individuals become members of society through the process of socialization.

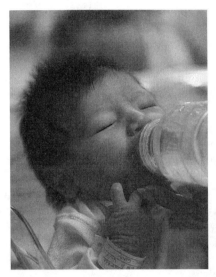 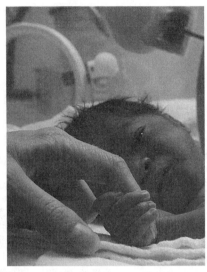 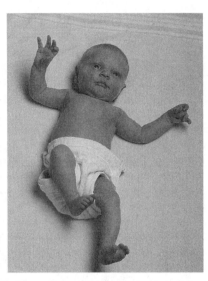

Human infants display various reflexes—biologically based behavior patterns that enhance survival. The sucking reflex, which actually begins before birth, enables the infant to obtain nourishment. The grasping reflex, triggered by placing a finger on the infant's palm causing the hand to close, helps the infant maintain contact with a parent and, later on, grasp objects. The Moro reflex, activated by startling the infant, has the infant swinging both arms outward and then bringing them together across the chest. This action, which disappears after several months of life, probably developed among our evolutionary ancestors so that a falling infant could grasp the body hair of a parent.

Ted Horowitz/Corbis/Stock Market (*left*); Henley & Savage/Corbis/Stock Market (*center*); Tom Pollak (*right*);

 How does the case of Anna confirm that "nurture is our nature"?

Social Isolation

As the story of Anna shows, cutting people off from the social world is very harmful. For ethical reasons, researchers can never place human beings in total isolation to study what happens. But in the past, they have studied the effects of social isolation on nonhuman primates.

Studies of Nonhuman Primates

In a classic study, the psychologists Harry and Margaret Harlow (1962) placed rhesus monkeys—whose behavior is in some ways surprisingly similar to human behavior—in various conditions of social isolation. They found that complete isolation (with adequate nutrition) for even six months seriously disturbed the monkeys' development. When returned to their group, these monkeys were passive, anxious, and fearful.

The Harlows then placed infant rhesus monkeys in cages with an artificial "mother" made of wire mesh with a wooden head and the nipple of a feeding tube where the breast would be. These monkeys also survived but were unable to interact with others when placed in a group.

But monkeys in a third category, isolated with an artificial wire mesh "mother" covered with soft terry cloth, did better. Each of these monkeys would cling to its mother closely. Because these monkeys showed less developmental damage than earlier groups, the Harlows concluded that the monkeys benefited from this closeness. The experiment confirmed how important it is that adults cradle infants affectionately.

Finally, the Harlows discovered that infant monkeys could recover from about three months of isolation. But by about six months, isolation caused irreversible emotional and behavioral damage.

 An ad campaign for strengthening families used the tag line, "Have you hugged your child today?" What new understanding of this line do you gain from the Harlow research?

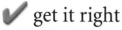

Studies of Isolated Children

Tragic cases of children isolated by abusive family members show the damage caused by depriving human beings of social experience. We will review three such cases.

Anna: The Rest of the Story The rest of Anna's story squares with the Harlows' findings. After her discovery, Anna received extensive medical attention and soon showed improvement. When Kingsley Davis visited her after ten days, he found her more alert and even smiling (perhaps for the first time in her life). Over the next year, Anna made slow but steady progress, showing more interest in other people and gradually learning to walk. After a year and a half, she could feed herself and play with toys.

But as the Harlows might have predicted, five long years of social isolation had caused permanent damage. At age eight, her mental development was less than that of a two-year-old. Not until she was almost ten did she begin to use words. Because Anna's mother was mentally retarded, perhaps Anna was also. The riddle was never solved, because Anna died at age ten from a blood disorder, possibly related to the years of abuse she suffered (K. Davis, 1940, 1947).

Another Case: Isabelle A second case involves another girl found at about the same time as Anna and under similar circumstances. After more than six years of virtual isolation, this girl, named Isabelle, displayed the same lack of responsiveness as Anna. But Isabelle had the benefit of an intensive learning program directed by psychologists. Within a week, Isabelle was trying to speak, and a year and a half later, she knew some 2,000 words. The psychologists concluded that intensive effort had pushed Isabelle through six years of normal development in only two years. By the time she was fourteen, Isabelle was attending sixth-grade classes, damaged by her early ordeal but on her way to a relatively normal life (K. Davis, 1947).

A Third Case: Genie A more recent case of childhood isolation involves a California girl abused by her parents (Curtiss, 1977; Rymer, 1994). From the time she was two, Genie was tied to a potty chair in a dark garage. In 1970, when she was rescued at age thirteen, Genie weighed only fifty-nine pounds and had the mental development of a one-year-old. With intensive treatment, she became physically healthy, but her language ability remains that of a young child. Today, Genie lives in a home for developmentally disabled adults.

▶ **CRITICAL REVIEW** All evidence points to the crucial importance of social experience in personality development. Human beings can recover from abuse and short-term isolation. But there is a point—precisely when is unclear from the small number of cases

studied—at which isolation in childhood causes permanent developmental damage.

 YOUR LEARNING What do studies of isolated children teach us about the importance of social experience?

Understanding Socialization

Socialization is a complex, lifelong process. The following discussions highlight the work of six researchers who have made lasting contributions to our understanding of human development.

Sigmund Freud's Elements of Personality

Sigmund Freud (1856–1939) lived in Vienna at a time when most Europeans considered human behavior to be biologically fixed. Trained as a physician, Freud gradually turned to the study of personality and mental disorders and eventually developed the celebrated theory of psychoanalysis.

Basic Human Needs

Freud claimed that biology plays a major part in human development, although not in terms of specific instincts, as is the case in other species. Rather, he theorized that humans have two basic needs or drives that are present at birth. First is a need for sexual and emotional bonding, which he called the "life instinct," or *eros* (from the Greek god of love). Second, we share an aggressive drive he called the "death instinct," or *thanatos* (from the Greek, meaning "death"). These opposing forces, operating at an unconscious level, create deep inner tension.

Freud's Model of Personality

Freud combined basic needs and the influence of society into a model of personality with three parts: id, ego, and superego. The **id** (the Latin word for "it") represents *the human being's basic drives,* which are unconscious and demand immediate satisfaction. Rooted in biology, the id is present at birth, making a newborn a bundle of demands for attention, touching, and food. But society opposes the self-centered id, which is why one of the first words a child typically learns is "no."

To avoid frustration, a child must learn to approach the world realistically. This is done through the **ego** (Latin for "I"), which is *a person's conscious efforts to balance innate pleasure-seeking drives with the demands of society.* The ego develops as we become aware of ourselves and at the same time realize that we cannot have everything we want.

In the human personality, **superego** (Latin meaning "above" or "beyond" the ego) is *the cultural values and norms internalized by an*

individual. The superego operates as our conscience, telling us *why* we cannot have everything we want. The superego begins to form as a child becomes aware of parental demands, and it matures as the child comes to understand that everyone's behavior should take account of cultural norms.

Personality Development

To the id-centered child, the world is a bewildering assortment of physical sensations that bring either pleasure or pain. As the superego develops, however, the child learns the moral concepts of right and wrong. Initially, in other words, children can feel good only in a physical way (such as by being held and cuddled), but after three or four years, they feel good or bad according to how they judge their behavior against cultural norms (doing "the right thing").

The id and superego remain in conflict, but in a well-adjusted person, the ego manages these two opposing forces. If conflicts are not resolved during childhood, Freud claimed, they may surface as personality disorders later on.

Culture, in the form of the superego, *represses* selfish demands, forcing people to look beyond their own desires. Often the competing demands of self and society result in a compromise that Freud called *sublimation.* Sublimation redirects selfish drives into socially acceptable behavior. For example, marriage makes the satisfaction of sexual urges socially acceptable, and competitive sports are an outlet for aggression.

▶**CRITICAL REVIEW** In Freud's time, few people were ready to accept sex as a basic human drive. More recent critics have charged that Freud's work presents humans in male terms and devalues women (Donovan & Littenberg, 1982). Freud's theories are also difficult to test scientifically. But Freud influenced everyone who later studied human personality. Of special importance to sociology are his ideas that we internalize social norms and that childhood experiences have a lasting impact on our personalities.

✔ **YOUR LEARNING** What are the three elements in Freud's model of personality? What does each one mean?

The personalities we develop depend largely on the environment in which we live. When a child's world is shredded by violence, the damage can be profound and lasting. This drawing was made by thirteen-year-old Rahid in the Darfur region of Sudan, where armed militia have killed more than 150,000 people since 2003. What are the likely effects of such experiences on a young person's self-confidence and capacity to form trusting ties with others?

Courtesy of Dr. Annie Sparrow, Human Rights Watch.

Jean Piaget's Theory of Cognitive Development

The Swiss psychologist Jean Piaget (1896–1980) studied human *cognition,* how people think and understand. As Piaget watched his own three children grow, he wondered not just what they knew but how they made sense of the world. Piaget went on to identify four stages of cognitive development.

The Sensorimotor Stage

Stage one is the **sensorimotor stage,** *the level of human development at which individuals experience the world only through their senses.* For about the first two years of life, the infant knows the world only through the five senses: touching, tasting, smelling, looking, and listening. "Knowing" to young children amounts to what their senses tell them.

tip

Piaget's theory is about cognitive development, how we learn to think and understand the world around us. This is the first of our theories of personality development that identifies clear stages of development, stages that Piaget linked to biological maturation (age) as well as experience.

tip

Be sure to answer all the ✓ Your Learning questions that follow the discussions of the theories of socialization.

The Preoperational Stage

About age two, children enter the **preoperational stage,** *the level of human development at which individuals first use language and other symbols.* Now children begin to think about the world mentally and use imagination. But "pre-op" children between about two and six still attach meaning only to specific experiences and objects. They can identify a toy as their "favorite" but cannot explain what *kinds* of toys they like.

Lacking abstract concepts, a child also cannot judge size, weight, or volume. In one of his best-known experiments, Piaget placed two identical glasses containing equal amounts of water on a table. He asked several children aged five and six if the amount in each glass was the same. They nodded that it was. The children then watched Piaget take one of the glasses and pour its contents into a taller, narrower glass so that the level of the water in the glass was higher. He asked again if each glass held the same amount. The typical five- or six-year-old now insisted that the taller glass held more water. By about age seven, children are able to think abstractly and realize that the amount of water stays the same.

The Concrete Operational Stage

Next comes the **concrete operational stage,** *the level of human development at which individuals first see causal connections in their surroundings.* Between the ages of seven and eleven, children focus on

how and why things happen. In addition, children now attach more than one symbol to a particular event or object. If, for example, you say to a child of five, "Today is Wednesday," she might respond, "No, it's my birthday!" indicating that she can use just one symbol at a time. But a ten-year-old at the concrete operational stage would be able to respond, "Yes, and it's also my birthday!"

The Formal Operational Stage

The last stage in Piaget's model is the **formal operational stage,** *the level of human development at which individuals think abstractly and critically.* At about age twelve, young people begin to reason abstractly rather than thinking only of concrete situations. If, for example, you were to ask a seven-year-old, "What would you like to be when you grow up?" you might receive a concrete response such as "a teacher." But most teenagers can think more abstractly and might reply, "I would like a job that helps others." As they gain the capacity for abstract thought, young people also learn to understand metaphors. Hearing the phrase "A penny for your thoughts" might lead a child to ask for a coin, but a teenager will recognize a gentle invitation to intimacy.

YOUR TURN Using Piaget's concepts, can you explain why young children will reach for a nickel rather than a dime?

▶**CRITICAL REVIEW** Freud saw human beings torn by opposing forces of biology and culture. Piaget saw the mind as active and creative. He saw an ability to engage the world unfolding in stages as the result of both biological maturation and social experience.

But do people in all societies pass through all four of Piaget's stages? Living in a traditional society that changes slowly probably limits a person's capacity for abstract and critical thought. Even in the United States, perhaps 30 percent of people never reach the formal operational stage (Kohlberg & Gilligan, 1971).

✓ **YOUR LEARNING** What are Piaget's four stages of cognitive development? What does his theory teach us about socialization?

Lawrence Kohlberg's Theory of Moral Development

Lawrence Kohlberg (1981) built on Piaget's work to study *moral reasoning,* how individuals judge situations as right or wrong. Here again, development occurs in stages.

Childhood is a time to learn principles of right and wrong. According to Carol Gilligan, however, boys and girls define what is "right" in different ways. After reading about Gilligan's theory, can you suggest what these two might be arguing about?

Corbis Royalty Free

SOCIALIZATION

Thinking About Diversity: Race, Class, & Gender
The Importance of Gender in Research

Carol Gilligan (1990) has shown how gender guides social behavior. Her early work exposed the gender bias in studies by Kohlberg and others who had used only male subjects. But as her research progressed, Gilligan made a major discovery: Boys and girls actually use different standards in making moral decisions. By ignoring gender, we end up with an incomplete view of human behavior.

Gilligan has also looked at the effect of gender on self-esteem. Her research team interviewed more than 2,000 girls, aged six to eighteen, over a five-year period. She found a clear pattern: Young girls start out eager and confident, but their self-esteem slips away as they pass through adolescence.

Why? Gilligan claims that the answer lies in our society's socialization of females. In U.S. society, the ideal woman is calm, controlled, and eager to please. Then too, as girls move from the elementary grades to secondary school, they have fewer women teachers and find that most authority figures are men. As a result, by their late teens, girls struggle to regain the personal strength they had a decade earlier.

When their research was finished, Gilligan and her colleagues returned to a private girls' school where they had interviewed their subjects to share the results of their work. As their conclusions led them to expect, most younger girls who had been interviewed were eager to have their names appear in the forthcoming book. But the older girls were hesitant—many were fearful that they would be talked about.

WHAT DO YOU THINK?

1. How does Gilligan's research show the importance of gender in the socialization process?

2. Do you think boys are subject to some of the same pressures and difficulties as girls? Explain your answer.

3. Can you think of ways in which your gender has shaped the development of your personality?

Young children who experience the world in terms of pain and pleasure (Piaget's sensorimotor stage) are at the *preconventional* level of moral development. At this early stage, in other words, "rightness" amounts to "what feels good to me." For example, a young child may simply reach for something on a table that looks shiny, which is the reason parents of young children have to "childproof" their homes.

The *conventional* level, Kohlberg's second stage, appears by the teen years (corresponding to Piaget's final, formal operational stage). At this point, young people lose some of their selfishness as they learn to define right and wrong in terms of what pleases parents and conforms to cultural norms. Individuals at this stage also begin to assess intention in reaching moral judgments instead of simply looking at what people do. For example, they understand that stealing food to feed one's hungry children is not the same as stealing an iPod to sell for pocket change.

In Kohlberg's final stage of moral development, the *postconventional* level, people move beyond their society's norms to consider abstract ethical principles. Now they think about liberty, freedom, or justice, perhaps arguing that what is legal still may not be right. When the African American activist Rosa Parks refused to give up her seat on a Montgomery, Alabama, bus in 1955, she violated that city's segregation laws in order to call attention to the racial injustice of the law.

▶**CRITICAL REVIEW** Like the work of Piaget, Kohlberg's model explains moral development in terms of distinct stages. But whether this model applies to people in all societies remains unclear. Further, many people in the United States apparently never reach the postconventional level of moral reasoning, although exactly why is still an open question.

Another problem with Kohlberg's research is that his subjects were all boys. He committed a common research error by generalizing the results of male subjects to all people. This problem led a colleague, Carol Gilligan, to investigate how gender affects moral reasoning.

YOUR LEARNING What are Kohlberg's three stages of moral development? What does his theory teach us about socialization?

Carol Gilligan's Theory of Gender and Moral Development

Carol Gilligan, whose approach is highlighted in the Thinking About Diversity: Race, Class, & Gender box, compared the moral development of girls and boys and concluded that the two sexes use different standards of rightness.

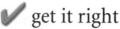
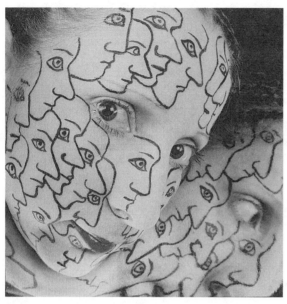

George Herbert Mead wrote, "No hard-and-fast line can be drawn between our own selves and the selves of others." The painting *Manyness* by Rimma Gerlovina and Valeriy Gerlovin conveys this important truth. Although we tend to think of ourselves as unique individuals, each person's characteristics develop in an ongoing process of interaction with others.

Rimma Gerlovina and Valeriy Gerlovin, *Manyness*, 1990. © the artists, New City, N.Y.

Gilligan (1982, 1990) claims that boys have a *justice perspective,* relying on formal rules to define right and wrong. Girls, by contrast, have a *care and responsibility perspective,* judging a situation with an eye toward personal relationships. For example, as boys see it, stealing is wrong because it breaks the law. Girls are more likely to wonder why someone would steal and to be sympathetic toward a poor person who steals, say, to feed her family.

Kohlberg treats rule-based male reasoning as superior to the person-based female approach. Gilligan notes that impersonal rules dominate men's lives in the workplace, but personal relationships are more relevant to women's lives as mothers and caregivers. Why, then, Gilligan asks, should we set up male standards as the norms by which to judge everyone?

▶ **CRITICAL REVIEW** Gilligan's work sharpens our understanding of both human development and gender issues in research. Yet the question remains: Does nature or nurture account for the differences between females and males? In Gilligan's view, cultural conditioning is at work. If so, the moral reasoning of women and men will probably become more similar as more women organize their lives around the workplace.

 YOUR LEARNING According to Gilligan, how do boys and girls differ in their approach to understanding right and wrong?

George Herbert Mead's Theory of the Social Self

George Herbert Mead (1863–1931) developed the theory of *social behaviorism* to explain how social experience develops an individual's personality (1962, orig. 1934).

The Self

Mead's central concept is the **self,** *the part of an individual's personality composed of self-awareness and self-image.* Mead's genius was in seeing the self as the product of social experience.

First, said Mead, *the self develops only with social experience.* The self is not part of the body, and it does not exist at birth. Mead rejected the idea that personality is guided by biological drives (as Freud asserted) or biological maturation (as Piaget claimed). For Mead, self develops only as the individual interacts with others. Without interaction, as we see from cases of isolated children, the body grows, but no self emerges.

Second, Mead explained, *social experience is the exchange of symbols.* Only people use words, a wave of the hand, or a smile to create meaning. We can train a dog using reward and punishment, but the dog attaches no meaning to its actions. Human beings, by contrast, find meaning in action by imagining people's underlying intentions. In short, a dog responds to *what you do;* a human responds to *what you have in mind* as you do it. You can train a dog to go to the hallway and bring back an umbrella. But because it doesn't understand intention, if the dog cannot find the umbrella, it is incapable of the *human* response: to look for a raincoat instead.

Third, Mead continued, *understanding intention requires imagining the situation from the other's point of view.* Using symbols, we imagine ourselves "in another person's shoes" and see ourselves as that person does. We can therefore anticipate how others will respond to us even before we act. A simple toss of a ball requires stepping outside ourselves to imagine how another will catch our throw. All social interaction involves seeing ourselves as others see us—a process that Mead termed *taking the role of the other.*

The Looking-Glass Self

In effect, others are a mirror (which people used to call a "looking glass") in which we can see ourselves. What we think of ourselves, then, depends on how we think others see us. For example, if we think

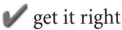
others see us as clever, we will think of ourselves in the same way. But if we feel they think of us as clumsy, then that is how we will see ourselves. Charles Horton Cooley (1864–1929) used the phrase **looking-glass self** to mean *a self-image based on how we think others see us* (1964, orig. 1902).

The I and the Me

Mead's fourth point is that *by taking the role of the other, we become self-aware.* Another way of saying this is that the self has two parts. One part of the self operates as subject, being active and spontaneous. Mead called the active side of the self the "I" (the subjective form of the personal pronoun). The other part of the self works as an object, the way we imagine others see us. Mead called the objective side of the self the "me" (the objective form of the personal pronoun). All social experience has both components: We initiate an action (the I-phase, or subject side, of self), and then we continue the action based on how others respond to us (the me-phase, or object side, of self).

Development of the Self

According to Mead, the key to developing the self is learning to take the role of the other. With limited social experience, infants can do this only through *imitation.* They mimic behavior without understanding underlying intentions, and so at this point, they have no self.

As children learn to use language and other symbols, the self emerges in the form of *play.* Play involves assuming roles modeled on **significant others,** *people, such as parents, who have special importance for socialization.* Playing "mommy and daddy" is an important activity that helps young children imagine the world from a parent's point of view.

Gradually, children learn to take the roles of several others at once. This skill lets them move from simple play (say, playing catch) with one other to complex *games* (like baseball) involving many others. By about age seven, most children have the social experience needed to engage in team sports.

 Have you ever seen young children put on their parents' shoes, literally putting themselves "in the shoes" of another person? How does this action help children learn to "take the role of the other"?

Figure 1 charts the progression from imitation to play to games. But there is a final stage in the development of the self. A game involves taking the role of specific people in just one situation. Everyday life demands that we see ourselves in terms of cultural norms as *any* member of our society might. Mead used the term **generalized other** to refer to *widespread cultural norms and values we use as a reference in evaluating ourselves.*

As life goes on, the self continues to change along with our social experiences. But no matter how much the world shapes us, we always remain creative beings, able to act back toward the world. Thus, Mead concluded, we play a key role in our own socialization.

▶**CRITICAL REVIEW** Mead's work explores the character of social experience itself. In the symbolic interaction of human beings, he believed he had found the root of both self and society.

Mead's view is completely social, allowing no biological element at all. This is a problem for critics who stand with Freud (who said our general drives are rooted in the body) and Piaget (whose stages of development are tied to biological maturity).

Be careful not to confuse Mead's concepts of the I and the me with Freud's id and superego. For Freud, the id originates in our biology, but Mead rejected any biological element of the self (although he never clearly spelled out the origin of the I). In addition, the id and the superego are locked in continual combat, but the I and the me work cooperatively together (Meltzer, 1978).

 YOUR LEARNING Explain the meaning and importance of Mead's concepts of the "I" and the "me." What did Mead mean by "taking the role of the other"? Why is this process so important to socialization?

The self is able simultaneously to take the role of:	*no one* (no ability to take the role of the other)	*one* other in *one* situation	*many* others in *one* situation	*many* others in *many* situations
when:	engaging in imitation	engaging in play	engaging in games	recognizing the generalized other

FIGURE 1 Building on Social Experience

George Herbert Mead described the development of the self as a process of gaining social experience. That is, the self develops as we expand our capacity to take the role of the other.

Erik H. Erikson's Eight Stages of Development

Although some analysts (including Freud) point to childhood as the crucial time when personality takes shape, Erik H. Erikson (1902–1994) took a broader view of socialization. He explained that we face challenges throughout the life course (1963, orig. 1950).

Stage 1: Infancy—the challenge of trust (versus mistrust). Between birth and about eighteen months, infants face the first

Sociological research indicates that wealthy parents tend to encourage creativity in their children while poor parents tend to foster conformity. Although this general difference may be valid, parents at all class levels can and do provide loving support and guidance by simply involving themselves in their children's lives. Henry Ossawa Tanner's painting *The Banjo Lesson* stands as a lasting testament to this process.

Henry Ossawa Tanner, *The Banjo Lesson*, 1893. Oil on canvas. Hampton University Museum, Hampton, Virginia.

of life's challenges: to establish a sense of trust that their world is a safe place. Family members play a key part in how any infant meets this challenge.

Stage 2: Toddlerhood—the challenge of autonomy (versus doubt and shame). The next challenge, up to age three, is to learn skills to cope with the world in a confident way. Failing to gain self-control leads children to doubt their abilities.

Stage 3: Preschool—the challenge of initiative (versus guilt). Four- and five-year-olds must learn to engage their surroundings—including people outside the family—or experience guilt at failing to meet the expectations of parents and others.

Stage 4: Preadolescence—the challenge of industriousness (versus inferiority). Between ages six and thirteen, children enter school, make friends, and strike out on their own more and more. They either feel proud of their accomplishments or fear that they do not measure up.

Stage 5: Adolescence—the challenge of gaining identity (versus confusion). During the teen years, young people struggle to establish their own identity. In part, teenagers identify with others, but they also want to be unique. Almost all teens experience some confusion as they struggle to establish an identity.

Stage 6: Young adulthood—the challenge of intimacy (versus isolation). The challenge for young adults is to form and maintain intimate relationships with others. Falling in love (as well as making close friends) involves balancing the need to bond with the need to have a separate identity.

Stage 7: Middle adulthood—the challenge of making a difference (versus self-absorption). The challenge of middle age is contributing to the lives of others in the family, at work, and in the larger world. Failing at this, people become self-centered, caught up in their own limited concerns.

Stage 8: Old age—the challenge of integrity (versus despair). Near the end of our lives, Erikson explains, people hope to look back on what they have accomplished with a sense of integrity and satisfaction. For those who have been self-absorbed, old age brings only a sense of despair over missed opportunities.

▶ **CRITICAL REVIEW** Erikson's theory views personality formation as a lifelong process, with success at one stage (say, as an infant gaining trust) preparing us to meet the next challenge. However, not everyone faces these challenges in the exact order presented by Erikson. Nor is it clear that failure to meet the challenge of one stage of life means that a person is doomed to fail later on. A

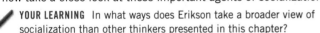
Alejo Gonzalez, a native of Los Angeles, considers himself white, African American, and Latino.

Emily Johnston attends school in Herkimer County in upstate New York, where almost all of her classmates are white.

tip

Here the chapter shifts from a review of theorists to looking at the various "agents" (settings or situations in our everyday lives) where socialization takes place. Discussion begins with the family, which, for most people, has the greatest influence on development.

SEEING OURSELVES

NATIONAL MAP 1
Racially Mixed People across the United States

This map shows the county-by-county distribution of people who described themselves as racially mixed in the 2000 census. How do you think growing up in an area with a high level of racially mixed people (such as Los Angeles or Miami) would be different from growing up in an area with few such people (for example, the Plains States in the middle of the country)?

Source: U.S. Census Bureau (2001).

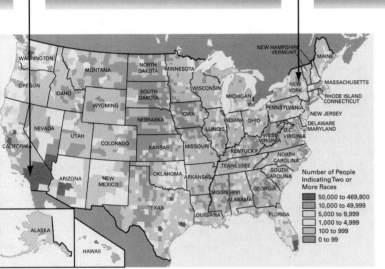

Number of People Indicating Two or More Races

■	50,000 to 469,800
▨	10,000 to 49,999
□	5,000 to 9,999
□	1,000 to 4,999
□	100 to 999
▨	0 to 99

broader question, raised earlier in our discussion of Piaget's ideas, is whether people in other cultures and in other times in history would define a successful life in Erikson's terms.

In sum, Erikson's model points out that many factors—including the family and school—shape our personalities. We now take a close look at these important agents of socialization.

✔ YOUR LEARNING In what ways does Erikson take a broader view of socialization than other thinkers presented in this chapter?

Agents of Socialization

Every social experience we have affects us in at least a small way. However, several familiar settings have special importance in the socialization process.

The Family

There are many ways in which the family affects socialization. For most people, in fact, the family may be the most important socialization agent of all.

Nurture in Early Childhood

Infants are totally dependent on others for care. The responsibility for providing a safe and caring environment typically falls on parents and other family members. For several years—at least until children begin school—the family also has the job of teaching children skills, values, and beliefs. Overall, research suggests, nothing is more likely to produce a happy, well-adjusted child than being in a loving family (Gibbs, 2001).

Not all family learning results from intentional teaching by parents. Children also learn from the type of environment adults create. Whether children learn to see themselves as strong or weak, smart or stupid, loved or simply tolerated—and as Erik Erikson suggests, whether they see the world as trustworthy or dangerous—depends largely on the quality of the surroundings provided by parents and other caregivers.

Race and Class

Through the family, parents give a social identity to children. In part, social identity involves race. Racial identity can be complex because societies define race in various ways. In addition, in the 2000 census, more than 7 million people (about 2.5 percent) said they consider themselves to be of two or more racial categories. This number is rising, and 5 percent of all births in the United States are now recorded as interracial. National Map 1 shows where interracial births are most and least common.

Social class, like race, plays a large part in shaping a child's personality. Whether born into families of high or low social position, children gradually come to realize that their family's social standing affects how others see them and, in time, how they come to see themselves.

In addition, research shows that class position affects not just how much money parents have to spend on their children but also what parents expect of them (Ellison, Bartkowski, & Segal, 1996). When people in the United States were asked to pick from a list of traits that are most desirable in a child, those with lower social standing favored obedience and conformity. Well-to-do people, by contrast, chose good judgment and creativity (NORC, 2005).

tip

We all experience socialization, but this process varies according to class, gender, and race.

Seeing Sociology in Everyday Life
Are We Grown Up Yet? Defining Adulthood

Solly: *(seeing several friends walking down the dorm hallway, just returned from dinner)* Yo, guys! Jeremy's twenty-one today. We're going down to the Box Car to celebrate.

Matt: *(shaking his head)* Dunno, dude. I got a lab to finish up. It's just another birthday.

Solly: Not just any birthday, my friend. He's twenty-one—an ADULT!

Matt: *(sarcastically)* If turning twenty-one would make me an adult, I wouldn't be so clueless about what I want to do with my life!

Are you an adult or still an adolescent? Does turning twenty-one make you a "grown-up"? According to the sociologist Tom Smith (2003), in our society, there is no one factor that announces the onset of adulthood. In fact, the results of his survey—using a representative sample of 1,398 people over the age of eighteen—suggest that many factors play a part in our decision to consider a young person "grown up."

According to the survey, the single most important transition in claiming adult standing in the United States today is the completion of schooling. But other factors are also important: Smith's respondents linked adult standing to taking on a full-time job, gaining the ability to support a family financially, no longer living with parents, and finally, marrying and becoming a parent. In other words, almost everyone in the United States thinks a person who has done *all* of these things is fully "grown up."

When are these transitions likely to be completed? On average, the answer is about age twenty-six. But such an average masks an important difference based on social class. People who do not attend college (more common among people growing up in lower-income families) typically finish school before age twenty, and a full-time job, independent living,

marriage, and parenthood may follow in a year or two. Those from more privileged backgrounds are likely to attend college and may even go on to graduate or professional school, delaying the process of becoming an adult for as long as ten years, past the age of thirty.

WHAT DO YOU THINK?

1. Do you consider yourself an adult? At what age did your adulthood begin?

2. Consider a woman whose children are grown, who has had a recent divorce, and is now going to college getting a degree so that she can find a job. Is she likely to feel that she is suddenly not quite "grown up," now that she's back in school? Why or why not?

3. How does the research described in this box show that adulthood is a socially defined concept rather than a biological stage of life?

What accounts for the difference? Melvin Kohn (1977) explains that people of lower social standing usually have limited education and perform routine jobs under close supervision. Expecting that their children will hold similar positions, they encourage obedience and may even use physical punishment like spanking to get it. Because well-off parents have had more schooling, they usually have jobs that demand imagination and creativity, so they try to inspire the same qualities in their children. Consciously or not, all parents act in ways that encourage their children to follow in their footsteps.

Wealthier parents typically provide their children with an extensive program of leisure activities, including sports, travel, and music lessons. These enrichment activities—far less available to children growing up in low-income families—build *cultural capital*, which advances learning and creates a sense of confidence in these children that they will succeed later in life (Lareau, 2002).

Social class also affects how long the process of growing up takes, as the Seeing Sociology in Everyday Life box explains.

The School

Schooling enlarges children's social world to include people with backgrounds different from their own. It is only as they encounter people who differ from themselves that children come to understand the importance of factors such as race and social position. As they do, they are likely to cluster in playgroups made up of one class, race, and gender.

Gender

Schools join with families in socializing children into gender roles. Studies show that at school, boys engage in more physical activities and spend more time outdoors, and girls are more likely to help teachers with various housekeeping chores. Boys also engage in more aggressive behavior in the classroom, while girls are typically quieter and better behaved (R. Best, 1983; Jordan & Cowan, 1995).

 In what specific ways is life on your campus different for women and men?

tip

Global Snapshots in the text compare the United States to other countries. Here we see that the United States is near the top of the list in terms of the extent of television ownership.

In high-income countries such as the United States, television is an important part of socialization.

In low-income countries such as Nigeria, the mass media play a smaller role in socialization.

What Children Learn

Schooling is not the same for children living in rich and poor communities. Children from well-off families typically have a far better experience in school than those whose families are poor.

For all children, the lessons learned in school include more than the formal lesson plans. Schools informally teach many things, which together might be called the *hidden curriculum*. Activities such as spelling bees teach children not only how to spell but how society divides the population into "winners" and "losers." Sports help students develop their strength and skills and also teach children important lessons in cooperation and competition.

School is also the first experience with bureaucracy for most children. The school day is based on impersonal rules and a strict time schedule. Not surprisingly, these are also the traits of the large organizations that will employ young people later in life.

The Peer Group

By the time they enter school, children have joined a **peer group**, *a social group whose members have interests, social position, and age in common.* Unlike the family and the school, the peer group lets children escape the direct supervision of adults. Among their peers, children learn how to form relationships on their own. Peer groups also offer the chance to discuss interests that adults may not share with their children (such as clothing and popular music) or permit (such as drugs and sex).

It is not surprising, then, that parents express concern about who their children's friends are. In a rapidly changing society, peer groups have great influence, and the attitudes of young and old may differ because of a "generation gap." The importance of peer groups typically peaks during adolescence, when young people begin to break away from their families and think of themselves as adults.

Even during adolescence, however, parental influence on children remains strong. Peers may affect short-term interests such as music or films, but parents have greater influence on long-term goals, such as going to college (Davies & Kandel, 1981).

Finally, any neighborhood or school is made up of many peer groups. Individuals tend to view their own group in positive terms and put down other groups. In addition, people are influenced by peer groups they would like to join, a process sociologists call **anticipatory socialization,** *learning that helps a person achieve a desired position.* In school, for example, young people may copy the styles and slang of a

GLOBAL SNAPSHOT

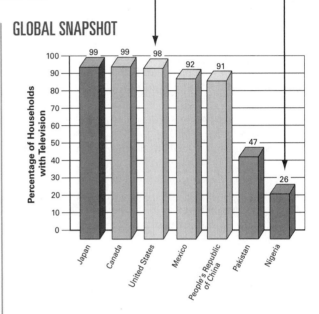

FIGURE 2 Television Ownership in Global Perspective

Television is popular in high- and middle-income countries, where almost every household owns at least one TV set.

Sources: U.S. Census Bureau (2006) and International Telecommunication Union (2007).

group they hope will accept them. Later in life, a young lawyer who hopes to become a partner in the law firm may conform to the attitudes and behavior of the firm's partners in order to be accepted.

The Mass Media

August 30, Isle of Coll, off the west coast of Scotland. The last time we visited this remote island, there was no electricity and most of the people spoke the ancient Gaelic language. Now that a power cable comes from the mainland, homes have lights, appliances, television, and the Internet! Almost with the flip of a switch, this tiny place has been thrust into the modern world. It is no surprise that the island's traditions are fast disappearing, with few performances of its historical dancing or music to be found. A rising share of the population now consists of mainlanders who ferry over with their cars to spend time in their vacation homes. And everyone now speaks English.

tip

Families are as old as humanity; the mass media
are a relatively new agent of socialization.
Electronic media using screens (films, television,
and computer programs) now have major
importance in our culture.

The **mass media** are *the means for delivering impersonal communications to a vast audience.* The term *media* comes from the Latin word for "middle," suggesting that media connect people. *Mass* media arise as communications technology (first newspapers and then radio, television, films, and the Internet) spreads information on a mass scale.

In the United States today, the mass media have an enormous influence on our attitudes and behavior. Television, introduced in the 1930s, became the dominant medium after World War II, and 98 percent of U.S. households now have at least one set (by comparison, just 94 percent have telephones). Two out of three households also have cable or satellite television. As Figure 2 shows, the United States has one of the highest rates of television ownership in the world. In this country, it is people with lower incomes who spend the most time watching TV.

The Extent of Television Viewing

Just how "glued to the tube" are we? Survey data show that the average household has at least one set turned on for seven hours each day and that people spend almost half their free time watching television. One study, by the Kaiser Family Foundation, found that youngsters between the ages of two and eighteen average 5½ hours a day "consuming media," including almost three hours of television and the rest watching video movies and playing video games (Cornell, 2000; Nielsen Media Research, 2005).

Years before children learn to read, television watching is a regular part of their daily routine. As they grow, children spend as many hours in front of a television as they do in school or interacting with their parents. This is the case despite research suggesting that television makes children more passive and less likely to use their imagination (American Psychological Association, 1993; Fellman, 1995).

Television and Politics

The comedian Fred Allen once quipped that we call television a "medium" because it is "rarely well done." For a number of reasons, television (as well as other mass media) provokes plenty of criticism. Some liberal critics argue that for most of television's history, racial and ethnic minorities have not been visible or have been included only in stereotypical roles (such as African Americans playing butlers, Asian Americans playing gardeners, or Hispanics playing new immigrants). In recent years, however, minorities have moved closer to center stage on television. There are ten times as many Hispanic actors on prime-time television as there were a decade or two ago, and they play a far larger range of characters (Lichter & Amundson, 1997; Fetto, 2003b).

On the other side of the fence, conservative critics charge that the television and film industries are dominated by a liberal "cultural elite." In recent years, they claim, "politically correct" media have advanced liberal causes, including feminism and gay rights (Rothman, Powers, & Rothman, 1993; B. Goldberg, 2002). On the other hand, the increasing popularity of the Fox Network—home to Sean Hannity, Bill O'Reilly, Brit Hume, and other conservative commentators—suggests that television programming offers "spin" from both sides of the political spectrum.

Television and Violence

In 1996, the American Medical Association (AMA) issued the startling statement that violence in television and films had reached such a high level that it posed a hazard to our health. More recently, a study found a strong link between aggressive behavior and the amount of time elementary school children spend watching television and playing video games (Robinson et al., 2001). The public is concerned about this issue: Three-fourths of U.S. adults report having walked out of a movie or turned off the television because of too much violence. Almost two-thirds of television programs contain violence, and in most such scenes, violent characters show no remorse and are not punished (B. J. Wilson, 1998).

Concern with violence and the mass media extends to the world of video games, especially those popular with young boys. Among the most controversial games, which include high levels of violence, is *Grand Theft Auto*. Do you think the current rating codes are sufficient to guide parents and children who buy video games, or would you support greater restrictions on game content?

In 1997, the television industry adopted a rating system. But we are left to wonder whether watching sexual or violent programming harms people as much as critics say. More important, why do the mass media contain so much sex and violence in the first place?

Television and the other mass media enrich our lives with entertaining and educational programming. The media also increase our exposure to diverse cultures and provoke discussion of current issues. At the same time, the power of the media—especially television—to shape how we think remains highly controversial.

Other spheres of life beyond family, school, peer group, and the media also play a part in social learning. For most people in the United States, these include the workplace, religious organizations, the military, and social clubs. In the end, socialization proves to be not a simple matter of learning but a complex balancing act as we absorb information from different sources. In the process of sorting and weighing all the information we receive, we form our own distinctive personalities.

Socialization and the Life Course

Although childhood has special importance in the socialization process, learning continues throughout our lives. An overview of the life course reveals that our society organizes human experience according to age—childhood, adolescence, adulthood, and old age.

Childhood

A few years ago, the Nike Corporation, maker of popular athletic shoes, came under attack. Their shoes are made in Taiwan and Indonesia, in many cases by children who work in factories instead of going to school. Some 250 million of the world's children work, half of them full time, earning about 50 cents an hour (Human Rights Watch, 2006). Global Map 1 shows that child labor is most common in Africa and Asia.

Criticism of Nike springs from the fact that most North Americans think of *childhood*—roughly the first twelve years of life—as a carefree time for learning and play. Yet as the historian Philippe Ariès (1965) explains, the whole idea of "childhood" is fairly new. During the Middle Ages, children of four or five were treated like adults and expected to fend for themselves.

We defend our idea of childhood because children are biologically immature. But a look back in time and around the world shows that the concept of childhood is grounded not in biology but in culture (LaRossa & Reitzes, 2001). In rich countries, not everyone has to work, so childhood can be extended to allow time for young people to learn the skills they will need in a high-technology workplace.

Because childhood in the United States lasts such a long time, some people worry when children seem to be growing up too fast. In part, this "hurried child" syndrome results from changes in the family—including high divorce rates and both parents in the labor force—that leave children with less supervision. In addition, "adult" programming on television (not to mention in films and on the Internet) carries grown-up concerns such as sex, drugs, and violence into young people's lives. Today's ten- to twelve-year-olds, says one executive of a children's television channel, have about the same interests and experiences typical of twelve- to fourteen-year-olds a generation ago (K. S. Hymowitz, 1998). Perhaps this is why today's children, compared to kids fifty years ago, have higher levels of stress and anxiety (Gorman, 2000).

In recent decades, some people have become concerned that U.S. society is shortening childhood, pushing children to grow up faster and faster. Do films such as *Mean Girls*, starring Lindsay Lohan, which show young girls dressing and behaving as if they were much older, encourage a "hurried childhood"? Do you see this as a problem or not?

Paramount/Picture Desk, Inc./Kobal Collection

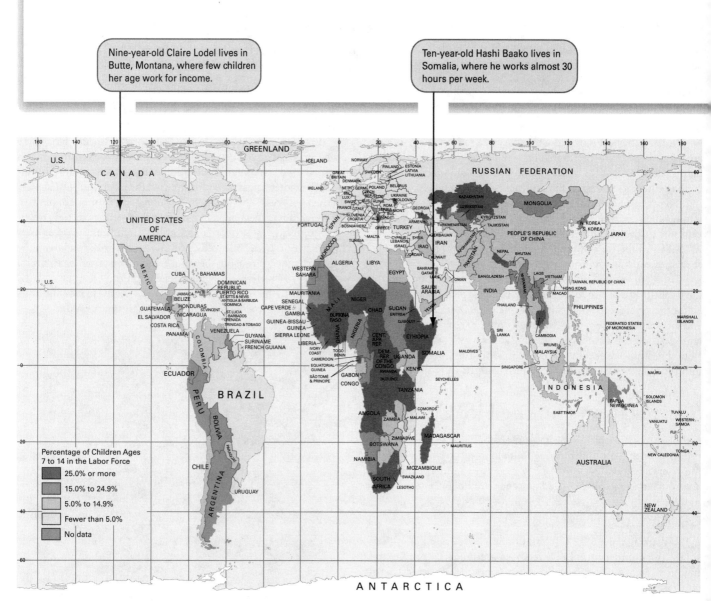

Nine-year-old Claire Lodel lives in Butte, Montana, where few children her age work for income.

Ten-year-old Hashi Baako lives in Somalia, where he works almost 30 hours per week.

Percentage of Children Ages 7 to 14 in the Labor Force

- 25.0% or more
- 15.0% to 24.9%
- 5.0% to 14.9%
- Fewer than 5.0%
- No data

WINDOW ON THE WORLD

GLOBAL MAP 1   Child Labor in Global Perspective

Industrialization extends childhood and discourages children from work and other activities considered suitable only for adults. This is why child labor is uncommon in the United States and other high-income countries. In less economically developed nations of the world, however, children are a vital economic asset, and they typically begin working as soon as they are able. How would childhood in, say, the African nations of Chad or Sudan differ from that in the United States or Canada?

Sources: Global March against Child Labor (2007), UNICEF (2007), and World Bank (2007); map projection from *Peters Atlas of the World* (1990).

In 2005, a thirteen-year-old soccer player named Freddy Adu was offered a $1 million contract by Nike. Can you see any reasons he or his parents should be concerned about accepting this offer?

Adolescence

At the same time that industrialization created childhood as a distinct stage of life, adolescence emerged as a buffer between childhood and adulthood. We generally link *adolescence,* or the teenage years,

SOCIALIZATION

tip

The box five pages back provides insights on the meaning of adulthood.

with emotional and social turmoil as young people struggle to develop their own identities. Again, we are tempted to attribute teenage rebelliousness and confusion to the biological changes of puberty. But it correctly reflects cultural inconsistency. For example, the mass media glorify sex and schools hand out condoms, even as parents urge restraint. Consider, too, that an eighteen-year-old may face the adult duty of going to war but lacks the adult right to drink a beer. In short, adolescence is a time of social contradictions, when people are no longer children but not yet adults.

As is true of all stages of life, adolescence varies according to social background. Most young people from working-class families move directly from high school into the adult world of work and parenting. Wealthier teens, however, have the resources to attend college and perhaps graduate school, stretching adolescence into the late twenties and even the thirties (T. W. Smith, 2003).

Gender, too, affects the process of growing up. "In the *Times*" on the next page looks at the opportunities and challenges faced by girls in a competitive, suburban high school.

Many of our soldiers in Iraq are still teenagers. Why should we not be surprised to learn that most of these young men and women performing adult jobs are from small-town, working-class families?

Adulthood

If stages of the life course were based on biological changes, it would be easy to define *adulthood*. Regardless of exactly when it begins, adulthood is the time when most of life's accomplishments take place, including pursuing a career and raising a family. Personalities are largely formed by then, although marked changes in a person's environment—such as unemployment, divorce, or serious illness—may cause significant changes to the self.

Early Adulthood

During early adulthood—until about age forty—young adults learn to manage day-to-day affairs for themselves, often juggling conflicting priorities: parents, partner, children, schooling, and work. Women are especially likely to try to "do it all" because our culture gives them the major responsibility for child rearing and housework even if they have demanding jobs outside the home.

Middle Adulthood

In middle adulthood—roughly ages forty to sixty—people sense that their life circumstances are pretty well set. They also become more aware of the fragility of health, which the young typically take for

granted. Women who have spent many years raising a family find middle adulthood emotionally trying. Children grow up and require less attention, and husbands become absorbed in their careers, leaving some women with spaces in their lives that are difficult to fill. Many women who divorce also face serious financial problems (Weitzman, 1985, 1996). For all these reasons, an increasing number of women in middle adulthood return to school and seek new careers.

For everyone, growing older means facing physical decline, a prospect our culture makes especially painful for women. Because good looks are considered more important for women, wrinkles and graying hair can be traumatic. Men have their own particular difficulties as they get older. Some must admit that they are never going to reach earlier career goals. Others realize that the price of career success has been neglect of family or personal health.

Old Age

Old age—the later years of adulthood and the final stage of life itself—begins about the mid-sixties. In the United States, about one in eight people is at least age sixty-five, and the elderly now outnumber teenagers (U.S. Census Bureau, 2006).

Once again, societies attach different meanings to this stage of life. It is older members of traditional societies who typically control most of the land and other wealth. Also, since traditional societies change slowly, older people possess useful wisdom gained over their lifetime, which earns them much respect.

In industrial societies, however, most younger people work and live apart from their parents, becoming independent of their elders. Rapid change also gives our society a "youth orientation" that defines what is old as unimportant or even obsolete. To younger people, the elderly may seem out of touch with new trends and fashions, and their knowledge and experience may seem of little value.

Perhaps this anti-elderly bias will decline as the share of older people in the United States steadily increases. The percentage of the U.S. population over age sixty-five has more than tripled in the past hundred years. With life expectancy still increasing, most men and women in their mid-sixties (the "young elderly") can look forward to living decades longer. By 2030, the number of seniors will double to 71 million, and the "average" person in the United States will be almost forty (U.S. Census Bureau, 2006).

Old age differs in an important way from earlier stages in the life course. Growing up typically means entering new roles and taking on new responsibilities, but growing old is the opposite experience—leaving roles that provided both satisfaction and social identity. For

The New York Times

NYT Archive Since 1981 | Search   Get Home Delivery | New York Cloudy 48°F

WORLD
U.S.
Politics
Washington
Education
N.Y./REGION
BUSINESS
TECHNOLOGY
SPORTS
SCIENCE
HEALTH
OPINION
ARTS
Books
Movies
Music
Television
Theater
STYLE
Dining & Wine
Fashion & Style
Home & Garden
Weddings/
Celebrations
TRAVEL

Blogs
Cartoons
Classifieds
Corrections
Crossword/
Games
First Look
Learning
Network
Multimedia
NYC Guide
Obituaries
Podcasts
The Public
Editor
Sunday
Magazine
Weather
Week in Review

NEWSPAPER
Get Home
Delivery
Customer Care
TimesPoints

Amazing +: Driven to Excel, For Girls, It's Be Yourself, and Be Perfect, Too

By SARAH RIMER
April 1, 2007

NEWTON, Mass.—To anyone who knows 17-year-old Esther Mobley, one of the best students at one of the best public high schools in the country, it is absurd to think she doesn't measure up. But Esther herself is quick to set the record straight.

"First of all, I'm a terrible athlete," she said over lunch one day.

"I run, I do, but not very quickly, and always exhaustedly," she continued. "This is one of the things I'm most insecure about. You meet someone, especially on a college tour, adults ask you what you do. They say, 'What sports do you play?' I don't play any sports. It's awkward." . . .

Esther [is one] of the amazing girls at Newton North High School here in this affluent suburb just outside Boston. "Amazing girls" translation: Girls by the dozen who are high achieving, ambitious and confident. . . . Girls who do everything: Varsity sports. Student government. Theater. Community service. Girls who have grown up learning they can do anything a boy can do, which is anything they want to do.

But being an amazing girl often doesn't feel like enough these days when you're competing with all the other amazing girls around the country who are applying to the same elite colleges that you have been encouraged to aspire to practically all your life. . . .

To spend several months in a pressure cooker like Newton North is to see what a girl can be—what any young person can be—when encouraged by committed teachers and by engaged parents who can give them wide-ranging opportunities.

It is also to see these girls struggle to navigate the conflicting messages they have been absorbing, if not from their parents then from the culture, since elementary school. The first message: Bring home A's. Do everything. Get into a top college. . . .

The second message: Be yourself. Have fun. Don't work too hard.

And, for all their accomplishments and ambitions, the amazing girls, as their teachers and classmates call them, are not immune to the third message: While it is now cool to be smart, it is not enough to be smart.

You still have to be pretty, thin and, as one of Esther's classmates, Kat Jiang, a go-to stage manager for student theater who has a perfect 2400 score on her SATs, wrote in an e-mail message, "It's out of style to admit it, but it is more important to be hot than smart."

"Effortlessly hot," Kat added.

If you are free to be everything, you are also expected to be everything. . . .

Balance is out the window when you're a high-achieving senior in the home stretch of the race for which all the years of achieving and the disciplined focusing on the future have been preparing you. These students are aware that because more girls apply to college than boys, amid concerns about gender balance, boys may have an edge at some small selective colleges.

"You're supposed to have all these extracurriculars, to play sports and do theater," said another of Esther's 17-year-old classmates, Julie Mhlaba, who aspires to medical school and juggles three Advanced Placement classes, gospel choir and a part-time job as a waitress. "You're supposed to do well in your classes and still have time to go out."

"You're supposed to do all these things," Julie said, "and not go insane." . . .

This year Esther has been trying life without a boyfriend. It was her mother's idea. "She'd say, 'I think it's time for you to take a break and discover who you are,'" Esther said over lunch with [her friend] Colby Kennedy. "She was right. I feel better." . . .

Boyfriends or not, a deeper question for Esther and Colby is how they negotiate their identities as young women. They have grown up watching their mothers, and their friends' mothers, juggle family and career. They take it for granted that they will be able to carve out similar paths, even if it doesn't look easy from their vantage point.

They say they want to be both feminine and assertive, like their mothers. But Colby made the point at lunch that she would rather be considered too assertive and less conventionally feminine than "be totally passive and a bystander in my life."

Esther agreed. She said she admired Cristina, the spunky resident on "Grey's Anatomy," one of her favorite TV shows.

"She really stands up for herself and knows who she is, which I aspire to," Esther said.

Cristina is also "gorgeous," Esther laughed. "And when she's taking off her scrubs, she's always wearing cute lingerie." . . .

WHAT DO YOU THINK?

1. Girls in Newton North High School strive to (a) be high achievers, (b) be themselves and have fun, and (c) be "hot." Can you relate to any or all of these demands? Explain.

2. Do you think all this direction from adults and the larger culture makes it easier or harder for these girls to grow up? Why?

3. Does the desire on the part of girls to be assertive and successful conflict with the desire to be feminine? Explain.

tip

Each stage of life has its own joys and challenges, but in our society, early stages of life typically involve *adding* roles and responsibilities; old age differs in that it typically involves *losing* roles and responsibilities.

some people, retirement is a period of restful activity, but for others, it can mean losing valued routines and even outright boredom. Like any life transition, retirement demands learning new patterns while at the same time letting go of habits from the past.

Death and Dying

Through most of human history, low living standards and limited medical technology meant that death from accident or disease could come at any stage of life. Today, however, 85 percent of people in the United States die after age fifty-five (Hoyert et al., 2006).

After observing many dying people, the psychiatrist Elisabeth Kübler-Ross (1969) described death as an orderly transition involving five distinct stages. Typically, a person first faces death with *denial*, perhaps out of fear and perhaps because our culture tends to ignore the reality of death. The second phase is *anger*, when a person facing death sees it as a gross injustice. Third, anger gives way to *negotiation* as the person imagines avoiding death by striking a bargain with God. The fourth response, *resignation*, is often accompanied by psychological depression. Finally, a complete adjustment to death requires *acceptance*. At this point, no longer paralyzed by fear and anxiety, the person whose life is ending now finds peace and makes the most of whatever time remains.

As the share of women and men in old age increases, we can expect our culture to become more comfortable with the idea of death. In recent years, people in the United States have started talking about death more openly, and the trend is to view dying as natural and better than painful or prolonged suffering. More married couples now prepare for death with legal and financial planning. This openness may ease somewhat the pain of the surviving spouse, a consideration for women, who, more often than not, outlive their husbands.

The Life Course: Patterns and Variations

This brief look at the life course points to two major conclusions. First, although each stage of life is linked to the biological process of aging, the life course is largely a social construction. For this reason, people in other societies may experience a stage of life quite differently or, for that matter, not at all. Second, in any society, the stages of the life course present certain problems and

transitions that involve learning something new and, in many cases, unlearning familiar routines.

Societies organize the life course according to age, but other forces, such as class, race, ethnicity, and gender, also shape people's lives. This means that the general patterns described in this chapter apply somewhat differently to various categories of people within any society. The Thinking About Diversity: Race, Class, & Gender box provides an example of how race and ethnicity can shape the academic performance of high school students.

People's life experiences also vary, depending on when, in the history of the society, they were born. A **cohort** is *a category of people with something in common, usually their age.* Because age cohorts are generally influenced by the same economic and cultural trends, they tend to have similar attitudes and values. Women and men born in the 1940s and 1950s, for example, grew up during a time of economic expansion that gave them a sense of optimism. Today's college students, who have grown up in an age of economic uncertainty, are less confident about the future.

 What major events or trends have shaped the personalities of people your age?

One effect of the "graying of U.S. society" is that older women and men will play a bigger part in everyday life.

Jeff Greenberg/The Image Works

tip

This chapter has made generalizations about the socialization process. But how each of us experiences society at any age depends partly on social forces such as class, race, ethnicity, and gender. The box below explains how race and ethnicity affect the way young people learn to view themselves.

tip

The final topic of this chapter is resocialization. This is a special type of socialization in which a staff tries to make big changes in people's personalities through controlling their environment in what sociologists call a "total institution."

Thinking About Diversity: Race, Class, & Gender
The Development of Self among High School Students

Adolescence is a time when people ask questions like "Who am I?" and "What do I want to become?" In the end, we all have to answer these questions for ourselves. But race and ethnicity are likely to have an effect on what our answers turn out to be.

Grace Kao (2000) studied the identity and goals of students enrolled in Johnstown High School, a large (3,000-student) school in a Chicago suburb. Johnstown High is considered a good school, with above-average test scores. It is also racially and ethnically diverse: 47 percent of the students are white, 43 percent are African American, 7 percent are Hispanic, and 3 percent are of Asian descent.

Kao interviewed sixty-three Johnstown students—female and male—both individually and in small groups with others of the same race and ethnicity. Talking with them, she learned how important racial and ethnic stereotypes are in young people's developing sense of self.

What are these stereotypes? White students are seen as hardworking in school and

concerned about getting high grades. African American students are thought to study less, either because they are not as smart or because they just don't try as hard. In any case, students see African Americans at high risk of failure in school. Because the stereotype says that Hispanics are headed for manual occupations—as gardeners or laborers—they are seen as not caring very much about doing well. Finally, Asian American students are seen as hardworking high achievers, either because they are smart or because they spend their time on academics rather than, say, sports.

From her interviews, Kao learned that most students think these stereotypes are true and take them personally. They expect people, including themselves, to perform in school more or less the way the stereotype predicts. In addition, young people—whether white, black, Hispanic, or Asian—mostly hang out with others like themselves, which gives them little chance to find out that their beliefs are wrong.

Students of all racial and ethnic categories say they *want* to do well in school. But

not getting to know those who differ from themselves means that they measure success *only in relation to their own category*. To African American students, in other words, "success" means doing as well as other black students and not flunking out. To Hispanics, "success" means avoiding manual labor and ending up with any job in an office. Whites and Asians, by contrast, define "success" as earning high grades and living up to the high-achievement stereotype. For all these young people, then, "self" develops through the lens of how race and ethnicity are defined by our society.

WHAT DO YOU THINK?

1. Were there racial and ethnic stereotypes, similar to those described here, in your high school? What about your college?

2. Do you think that gender stereotypes affect the performance of women and men in school as much as racial and ethnic stereotypes? Explain.

3. What can be done to reduce the damaging effects of racial and ethnic stereotypes?

Resocialization: Total Institutions

A final type of socialization, experienced by more than 2 million people in the United States, involves being confined—usually against their will—in prisons or mental hospitals. This is the world of the **total institution,** *a setting in which people are isolated from the rest of society and manipulated by an administrative staff.*

According to Erving Goffman (1961), total institutions have three important characteristics. First, staff members supervise all aspects of daily life, including where residents (often called "inmates") eat, sleep, and work. Second, life in a total institution is controlled and standardized, with the same food, uniforms, and activities for everyone. Third, formal rules dictate when, where, and how inmates perform their daily routines.

The purpose of such rigid routines is **resocialization,** *radically changing an inmate's personality by carefully controlling the environment.* Prisons and mental hospitals physically isolate inmates behind fences, barred windows, and locked doors and limit their access to the telephone, mail, and visitors. The institution becomes their entire world, making it easier for the staff to bring about personality change—or at least obedience—in the inmate.

Resocialization is a two-part process. First, the staff breaks down the new inmate's existing identity. For example, an inmate must give up personal possessions, including clothing and grooming articles used to maintain a distinctive appearance. Instead, the staff provides standard-issue clothes so that everyone looks alike. The staff subjects new inmates to "mortifications of self," which can include searches, head shaving, medical examinations, fingerprinting, and assignment

✿ tip

Of the theories of human development we have considered in this chapter, Freud's probably points to the least human freedom, because we are all caught between two powerful forces—biology (id) and culture (superego).

✿ tip

Mead's theory of human development points to the most human freedom, because he saw no biological drives as Freud did and saw humans as spontaneous and creative.

Controversy & Debate
Are We Free within Society?

MIKE: Sociology is a good course. Since my professor started telling us how to look at the world with a sociological eye, I'm realizing that a lot of who I am and where I am is because of society.

KIM: *(teasingly)* Oh, so society is responsible for making you so smart and witty and handsome?

MIKE: No, that's all me. But I'm seeing that being at college and playing football is maybe not all me. What do you think? How free are we, really?

This chapter stresses one key theme: Society shapes how we think, feel, and act. If this is so, then in what sense are we free? To answer this important question, consider the Muppets, puppet stars of television and film. Watching the antics of Kermit the Frog, Miss Piggy, and the rest of the troupe, we almost believe they are real rather than objects controlled from backstage or below. As the sociological perspective points out, human beings are like puppets in that we, too, respond to backstage forces. Society, after all, gives us a culture and shapes our lives according to class, race, and gender. If this is so, can we really claim to be free?

Sociologists answer this question with many voices. The politically liberal response is that individuals are *not* free of society—in fact, as social creatures, we never could be. But if we have to live in a society with power over us, it is important to do what we can to

make our home as just as possible, by working to lessen class differences and other barriers to opportunity for minorities, including women. Conservatives answer that we *are* free because society can never dictate our dreams. Our history as a nation, right from the revolutionary acts that led to its founding, is one story after another of people pursuing personal goals despite great odds.

Does understanding more about how society shapes our lives give us greater power to "cut the strings" and choose for ourselves how to live?

James Porto/Getty Images, Inc.—Taxi

Both attitudes are found in George Herbert Mead's analysis of socialization. Mead knew that society makes demands on us, sometimes limiting our options. But he also saw that human beings are spontaneous and creative, capable of continually acting on society and bringing about change. Mead noted the power of society while still affirming the human capacity to evaluate, criticize, and ultimately choose and change.

In the end, then, we may seem like puppets, but only on the surface. A crucial difference is that we can stop, look up at the "strings" that make us move, and even yank on them defiantly (Berger, 1963:176). If our pull is strong enough, we can do more than we might think. As Margaret Mead once remarked, "Never doubt that a small group of thoughtful, committed citizens can change the world. Indeed, it is the only thing that ever has."

WHAT DO YOU THINK?

1. Do you think our society gives more freedom to males than to females? Why or why not?

2. Are people in modern, high-income countries more free than those in traditional, low-income nations? Explain your answer.

3. Has learning about socialization increased or decreased your feeling of freedom? Why?

---

of a serial number. Once inside the walls, individuals also give up their privacy as guards routinely inspect their living quarters.

In the second part of the resocialization process, the staff tries to build a new self in the inmate through a system of rewards and punishments. Having a book to read, watching television, or making a telephone call may seem like minor pleasures to the outsider, but in

the rigid environment of the total institution, gaining such simple privileges as these can be a powerful motivation to conform. The length of confinement typically depends on how well the inmate cooperates with the staff.

Total institutions affect people in different ways. Some inmates may end up "rehabilitated" or "recovered," but others may change

Prisons are one example of a total institution in which inmates dress alike and carry out daily routines under the direct supervision and control of the institutional staff. What do we expect prison to do to young people convicted of crimes? How well do you think prisons do what people expect them to do?

© John Zich/Corbis. All Rights Reserved

little, and still others may become hostile and bitter. Over a long period of time, living in a rigidly controlled environment can leave some *institutionalized*, without the capacity for independent living.

But what about the rest of us? Does socialization crush our individuality or empower us to reach our creative potential? Society does affect our actions, thoughts, and feelings, but we also have the ability to act back on the world around us. The Controversy & Debate box takes a closer look at this important question.

Applying Sociology in Everyday Life

1. Get together with several members of your sociology class, and gather data by asking classmates and friends to name traits they consider part of "human nature." Compare notes, and discuss the extent to which these traits come from nature or nurture.

2. Here is an easy and effective way to understand George Herbert Mead's claim that the self is composed of two parts, the "I" and the "me." Place your left hand, palm down, on a desk or table; then run your right hand softly over the back of your left hand. Focus on how your left hand feels using the sensations provided through the fingertips of your right hand. In this exercise, the right hand (the one that is active) represents the I. The left hand (the object being examined) is the me. Of course, as Mead would quickly add, both hands are part of a single self.

3. Watch several hours of prime-time programming on network or cable television. Keep track of every time any element of violence is shown, and calculate the number of violent scenes per hour. On the basis of observing a small and unrepresentative sample of programs, what are your conclusions?

MAKING THE GRADE

Socialization

What Is Socialization?

Socialization is a **LIFELONG PROCESS**.

- Socialization develops our humanity as well as our particular personalities.
- The importance of socialization is seen in the fact that extended periods of social isolation result in permanent damage (cases of Anna, Isabelle, and Genie).

Socialization is a matter of **NURTURE** rather than **NATURE**.

- A century ago, most people thought human behavior resulted from biological instinct.
- For us as human beings, it is our nature to nurture.

socialization the lifelong social experience by which people develop their human potential and learn culture

personality a person's fairly consistent patterns of acting, thinking, and feeling

Important Contributions to Our Understanding of Socialization

SIGMUND FREUD'S model of the human personality has three parts:

- *id*: innate, pleasure-seeking human drives
- *superego*: the demands of society in the form of internalized values and norms
- *ego*: our efforts to balance innate, pleasure-seeking drives and the demands of society

LAWRENCE KOHLBERG applied Piaget's approach to stages of moral development:

- We first judge rightness in *preconventional* terms, according to our individual needs.
- Next, *conventional* moral reasoning takes account of parental attitudes and cultural norms.
- Finally, *postconventional* reasoning allows us to criticize society itself.

To **GEORGE HERBERT MEAD**,

- the self is part of our personality and includes self-awareness and self-image;
- the self develops only as a result of social experience;
- social experience involves the exchange of symbols;
- social interaction depends on understanding the intention of another, which requires taking the role of the other;
- human action is partly spontaneous (the I) and partly in response to others (the me);
- we gain social experience through imitation, play, games, and understanding the *generalized other*.

JEAN PIAGET believed that human development involves both biological maturation and gaining social experience. He identified four stages of cognitive development:

- First, the *sensorimotor stage* involves knowing the world only through the senses.
- Next, the *preoperational stage* involves starting to use language and other symbols.
- Next, the *concrete operational stage* allows individuals to understand causal connections.
- Finally, the *formal operational stage* involves abstract and critical thought.

CAROL GILLIGAN found that gender plays an important part in moral development, with males relying more on abstract standards of rightness and females relying more on the effects of actions on relationships.

CHARLES HORTON COOLEY used the term *looking-glass self* to explain that we see ourselves as we imagine others see us.

ERIK H. ERIKSON identified challenges that individuals face at each stage of life from infancy to old age.

id Freud's term for the human being's basic drives

ego Freud's term for a person's conscious efforts to balance innate pleasure-seeking drives with the demands of society

superego Freud's term for the cultural values and norms internalized by an individual

sensorimotor stage Piaget's term for the level of human development at which individuals experience the world only through their senses

preoperational stage Piaget's term for the level of human development at which individuals first use language and other symbols

concrete operational stage Piaget's term for the level of human development at which individuals first see causal connections in their surroundings

formal operational stage Piaget's term for the level of human development at which individuals think abstractly and critically

self George Herbert Mead's term for the part of an individual's personality composed of self-awareness and self-image

looking-glass self Cooley's term for a self-image based on how we think others see us

significant others people, such as parents, who have special importance for socialization

generalized other George Herbert Mead's term for widespread cultural norms and values we use as a reference in evaluating ourselves

Agents of Socialization

The **FAMILY** is usually the first setting of socialization.
- Family has the greatest impact on attitudes and behavior.
- A family's social position, including race and social class, shapes a child's personality.
- Ideas about gender are learned first in the family.

SCHOOLS give most children their first experience with bureaucracy and impersonal evaluation.
- Schools teach knowledge and skills needed for later life.
- Schools expose children to greater social diversity.
- Schools reinforce ideas about gender.

peer group a social group whose members have interests, social position, and age in common

anticipatory socialization learning that helps a person achieve a desired position

mass media the means for delivering impersonal communications to a vast audience

The **PEER GROUP** helps shape attitudes and behavior.
- The peer group takes on great importance during adolescence.
- The peer group frees young people from adult supervision.

The **MASS MEDIA** have a huge impact on socialization in modern, high-income societies.
- The average U.S. child spends as much time watching television and videos as attending school and interacting with parents.
- The mass media often reinforce stereotypes about gender and race.
- The mass media expose people to a great deal of violence.

Socialization and the Life Course

The concept of **CHILDHOOD** is grounded not in biology but in culture. In high-income countries, childhood is extended.

The emotional and social turmoil of **ADOLESCENCE** results from cultural inconsistency in defining people who are not children but not yet adults. Adolescence varies by social class position.

cohort a category of people with something in common, usually their age

ADULTHOOD is the stage of life when most accomplishments take place. Although personality is now formed, it continues to change with new life experiences.

OLD AGE is defined as much by culture as biology.
- Traditional societies give power and respect to elders.
- Industrial societies define elders as unimportant and out of touch.

Acceptance of **DEATH AND DYING** is part of socialization for the elderly. This process typically involves five stages: denial, anger, negotiation, resignation, and acceptance.

✔ *Every stage of life is socially constructed in ways that vary from society to society.*

Total Institutions

TOTAL INSTITUTIONS include prisons, mental hospitals, and monasteries.
- Staff members supervise all aspects of life.
- Life is standardized, with all inmates following set rules and routines.

RESOCIALIZATION is a two-part process:
- breaking down inmates' existing identity
- building a new self through a system of rewards and punishments

total institution a setting in which people are isolated from the rest of society and manipulated by an administrative staff

resocialization radically changing an inmate's personality by carefully controlling the environment

MAKING THE GRADE

Sample Test Questions

These questions are similar to those found in the test bank that accompanies this textbook.

Multiple-Choice Questions

1. Kingsley Davis's study of Anna, the girl isolated for five years, shows that
   a. humans have all the same instincts found in other animal species.
   b. without social experience, a child never develops personality.
   c. personality is present in all humans at birth.
   d. many human instincts disappear in the first few years of life.

2. Most sociologists take the position that
   a. humans have instincts that direct behavior.
   b. biological instincts develop in humans at puberty.
   c. it is human nature to nurture.
   d. All of the above are correct.

3. Lawrence Kohlberg explored socialization by studying
   a. cognition.
   b. the importance of gender in socialization.
   c. the development of biological instincts.
   d. moral reasoning.

4. Carol Gilligan added to Kohlberg's findings by showing that
   a. girls and boys typically use different standards in deciding what is right and wrong.
   b. girls are more interested in right and wrong than boys are.
   c. boys are more interested in right and wrong than girls are.
   d. today's children are far less interested in right and wrong than their parents are.

5. The "self," said George Herbert Mead, is
   a. the part of the human personality made up of self-awareness and self-image.
   b. the presence of culture within the individual.
   c. basic drives that are self-centered.
   d. present in infants from birth.

6. Why is the family so important to the socialization process?
   a. Family members provide vital caregiving to infants and children.
   b. Families give children social identity in terms of class, ethnicity, and religion.
   c. Parents greatly affect a child's self-concept.
   d. All of the above are correct.

7. Social class position affects socialization: Lower-class parents tend to stress _____, and well-to-do parents stress _____.
   a. independence; protecting children
   b. independence; dependence
   c. obedience; creativity
   d. creativity; obedience

8. In global perspective, which statement about childhood is correct?
   a. In every society, the first ten years of life are a time of play and learning.
   b. Rich societies extend childhood much longer than poor societies do.
   c. Poor societies extend childhood much longer than rich societies do.
   d. Childhood is defined by being biologically immature.

9. Modern, high-income societies typically define people in old age as
   a. the wisest of all.
   b. the most up-to-date on current fashion and trends.
   c. less socially important than younger adults.
   d. All of the above are correct.

10. According to Erving Goffman, the purpose of a total institution is
    a. to reward someone for achievement in the outside world.
    b. to give a person more choices about how to live.
    c. to encourage lifelong learning in a supervised context.
    d. to change a person's personality or behavior.

ANSWERS: 1 (b); 2 (c); 3 (d); 4 (a); 5 (a); 6 (d); 7 (c); 8 (b); 9 (c); 10 (d).

Essay Questions

1. State the two sides of the "nature-nurture" debate. In what important way are nature and nurture not opposed to each other?

2. What are common themes in the ideas of Freud, Piaget, Kohlberg, Gilligan, Mead, and Erikson? In what ways do their theories differ?

Social Interaction in Everyday Life

Sociology points to the many rules that guide behavior in everyday situations. The more we learn about the rules of social interaction, the better we can play the game.

Barnabas Kindersley © Dorling Kindersley

Social Interaction in Everyday Life

HOW do we create reality in our face-to-face interactions?

WHY do employers try to control their workers' feelings as well as their on-the-job behavior?

WHAT makes something funny?

Harold and Sybil are on their way to another couple's home in an unfamiliar area near Wilkes Barre, Pennsylvania. They have been driving in circles looking for Joseph Camp Road, and now they are late. Harold, gripping the wheel ever more tightly, is doing a slow burn. Sybil, sitting next to him, looks straight ahead, afraid to say a word.

Harold and Sybil are lost in more ways than one: They are unable to understand why they are growing angry at their situation and at each other. Like most men, Harold can't stand getting lost, and the longer he drives around, the more incompetent he feels. Sybil cannot understand why Harold does not pull into a gas station and ask someone where Joseph Camp Road is. If she were driving, she thinks to herself, they would already have arrived and would now be comfortably settled in with their friends.

Why don't men like to ask for directions? Because men value their independence, they don't like to ask for help (and are reluctant to accept it). To ask someone for assistance is the same as saying, "You know something I don't." If it takes Harold a few more minutes to find the street on his own—and keep his self-respect in the process—he thinks that's the way to go.

Women, on the other hand, are more in tune with others and strive for connectedness. From Sybil's point of view, asking for help is right because sharing information builds social bonds and at the same time gets the job done quickly and efficiently. Asking for directions seems as natural to her as searching on his own is to Harold. Obviously, getting lost is sure to result in conflict as long as neither one understands the other's point of view.

Such everyday experiences are the focus of this chapter. The central concept is **social interaction,** *the process by which people act and react in relation to others.* We begin with several important sociological concepts that describe the building blocks of common experience and then explore the almost magical way that face-to-face interaction creates the reality in which we live.

Social Structure: A Guide to Everyday Living

October 21, Ho Chi Minh City, Vietnam. This morning we leave the ship and make our way along the docks toward the center of Ho Chi Minh City, known to an earlier generation as Saigon. The government security officers wave us through the heavy metal gates. Pressed against the fence are dozens of men who operate cyclos (bicycles with small carriages attached to the front), the Vietnamese version of taxicabs. We wave them off and spend the next twenty minutes shaking our heads at several drivers who pedal alongside, pleading for our business. The pressure is uncomfortable. We decide to cross the street but realize suddenly that there are no stop signs or signal lights—and the street is an unbroken stream of bicycles, cyclos, motorbikes,

and small trucks. The locals don't bat an eye; they just walk at a steady pace across the street, parting waves of vehicles that immediately close in again behind them. Walk right into traffic? With our small children on our backs? Yup, we did it; that's the way it works in Vietnam.

Members of every society rely on social structure to make sense of everyday situations. As our family's introduction to the streets of Vietnam suggests, the world can be confusing—even frightening—when society's rules are unclear. Let's take a closer look at the ways in which societies set the rules of everyday life.

Status

In every society, people build their everyday lives using the idea of **status,** *a social position that a person holds.* In everyday use, the word *status* generally means "prestige," as when we say that a college president has more "status" than a newly hired assistant professor. But sociologically speaking, both "president" and "professor" are statuses within the collegiate organization.

Status is part of our social identity and helps define our relationship to others. As Georg Simmel (1950:307, orig. 1902), one of the founders of sociology, once pointed out, before we can deal with anyone, we need to know *who* the person is.

Chapter Overview

This chapter takes a "micro-level" look at society, examining patterns of everyday social interaction. First, the chapter identifies important social structures, including status and role. Then it explains how we construct reality in social interaction. Finally, it applies the lessons learned to three everyday experiences: emotion, gender, and humor.

Status Set

Each of us holds many statuses at once. The term **status set** refers to *all the statuses a person holds at a given time.* A teenage girl is a daughter to her parents, a sister to her brother, a student at her school, and a goalie on her soccer team.

Status sets change over the life course. A child grows up to become a parent, a student graduates to become a lawyer, and a single person marries to become a husband or wife, sometimes becoming single again as a result of death or divorce. Joining an organization or finding a job enlarges our status set; withdrawing from activities makes it smaller. Over a lifetime, people gain and lose dozens of statuses.

Ascribed and Achieved Status

Sociologists classify statuses in terms of how people attain them. An **ascribed status** is *a social position a person receives at birth or takes on involuntarily later in life.* Examples of ascribed statuses include being a daughter, a Cuban, a teenager, or a widower. Ascribed statuses are matters about which we have little or no choice.

By contrast, an **achieved status** refers to *a social position a person takes on voluntarily that reflects personal ability and effort.* Achieved statuses in the United States include honors student, Olympic athlete, nurse, software writer, and thief.

In the real world, of course, most statuses involve a combination of ascription and achievement. That is, people's ascribed statuses influence the statuses they achieve. People who achieve the status of lawyer, for example, are likely to share the ascribed benefit of being born into relatively well-off families. By the same token, many less desirable statuses, such as criminal, drug addict, or unemployed worker, are more easily achieved by people born into poverty.

Make a list of ten important statuses in your own life. Indicate whether each one is ascribed or achieved. Is this sometimes difficult to do? Why?

Master Status

Some statuses matter more than others. A **master status** is *a status that has special importance for social identity, often shaping a person's entire life.* For most people, a job is a master status because it reveals a great deal about social background, education, and income. In a few cases, name is a master status; being in the Bush or Kennedy family attracts attention and creates opportunities.

In any rigidly ranked setting, no interaction can proceed until people assess each other's social standing. For this reason, military personnel wear insignia, clear symbols of their level of authority. Don't we size up one another in much the same way in routine interactions, noting a person's rough age, quality of clothing, and manner for clues about social position?

Gunnery Sgt. Blair A. McClellan, U.S. Marine Corps./US Department of Defense

A master status can be negative as well as positive. Take, for example, serious illness. Sometimes people, even longtime friends, avoid cancer patients or people with AIDS because of their illnesses. As another example, the fact that all societies limit the opportunities of women makes gender a master status.

Sometimes a physical disability serves as a master status to the point where we dehumanize people by seeing them only in terms of their disability. The Thinking About Diversity: Race, Class, & Gender box shows how.

Role

A second important social structure is **role**, *behavior expected of someone who holds a particular status.* A person *holds* a status and *performs* a role (Linton, 1937b). For example, holding the status of student leads you to perform the role of attending classes and completing assignments.

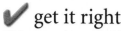 get it right

Statuses can be *ascribed* (meaning "given" or "assigned") or *achieved* (meaning "earned"). Usually, people can easily describe social positions they hold as one type or the other. But most statuses are a combination of the two—partly given and partly earned.

 tip

Remember that *status* refers to a social position and *role* refers to behavior. We *hold* a status and *perform* a role.

 ## Thinking About Diversity: Race, Class, & Gender
Physical Disability as a Master Status

Physical disability works in much the same ways as class, gender, or race in defining people in the eyes of others. In the following interviews, two women explain how a physical disability can become a master status—a trait that overshadows everything else about them. The first voice is that of twenty-nine-year-old Donna Finch, who lives with her husband and son in Muskogee, Oklahoma, and holds a master's degree in social work. She is also blind.

> Most people don't expect handicapped people to grow up; they are always supposed to be children. . . . You aren't supposed to date, you aren't supposed to have a job, somehow you're just supposed to disappear. I'm not saying this is true of anyone else, but in my own case I think I was more intellectually mature than most children, and more emotionally immature. I'd say that not until the last four or five years have I felt really whole.

Rose Helman is an elderly woman who has retired and lives near New York City. She suffers from spinal meningitis and is also blind.

> You ask me if people are really different today than in the '20s and '30s. Not too much. They are still fearful of the handicapped. I don't know if *fearful* is the

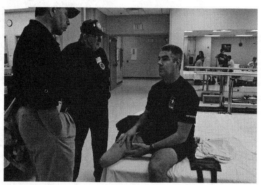
Modern technology means that most soldiers who lose limbs in war now survive. How do you think the loss of an arm or a leg affects a person's social identity and sense of self?

David S. Holloway/Getty Images

right word, but uncomfortable at least. But I can understand it somewhat; it happened to me. I once asked a man to tell me which staircase to use to get from the subway out to the street. He started giving me directions that were confusing, and I said, "Do you mind taking me?" He said, "Not at all." He grabbed me on the side with my dog on it, so I asked him to take my other arm. And he said, "I'm sorry, I have no other arm." And I said, "That's all right, I'll hold onto the jacket." It felt funny hanging onto the sleeve without the arm in it.

WHAT DO YOU THINK?

1. Have you ever had a disease or disability that became a master status? If so, how did others react?

2. How might such a master status affect someone's personality?

3. Can being very fat or very thin serve as a master status? Why or why not?

Source: Orlansky & Heward (1981).

Both statuses and roles vary by culture. In the United States, the status of "uncle" refers to the brother of either your mother or your father. In Vietnam, however, the word for "uncle" is different on the mother's and father's sides of the family, and the two men have different responsibilities. In every society, actual role performance varies according to an individual's unique personality, although some societies permit more individual expression of a role than others.

Role Set

Because we hold many statuses at once—a status set—everyday life is a mix of multiple roles. Robert Merton (1968) introduced the term **role set** to identify *a number of roles attached to a single status.*

Figure 1 shows four statuses of one person, each status linked to a different role set. First, as a professor, this woman interacts with students (the teacher role) and with other academics (the colleague role). Second, in her work as a researcher, she gathers and analyzes data (the fieldwork role) that she uses in her publications (the author role). Third, the woman occupies the status of "wife," with a marital role (such as confidante and sexual partner) toward her husband, with whom she shares household duties (domestic role). Fourth, she holds the status of "mother," with routine responsibilities for her children (the maternal role), as well as toward their school and other organizations in her community (the civic role).

A global perspective shows that the roles people use to define their lives differ from society to society. In low-income countries, people spend fewer years as students, and family roles are often very

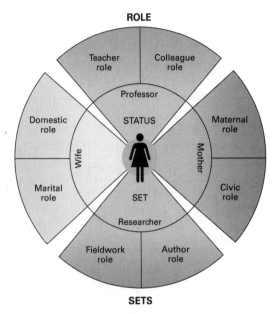

get it right

Role conflict and role strain are easily confused. Think of it this way: It takes two to have conflict—therefore, role conflict is conflict among roles linked to two or more statuses. Role strain is tension arising from a single status.

important to social identity. In high-income nations, people spend more years as students, and family roles are typically less important to social identity. Another dimension of difference involves housework. As Global Map 1 shows, especially in poor countries, housework falls heavily on women.

Role Conflict and Role Strain

People in modern, high-income nations juggle many responsibilities demanded by their various statuses and roles. As most mothers (and more and more fathers) can testify, the combination of parenting and working outside the home is physically and emotionally draining. Sociologists thus recognize **role conflict** as *conflict among the roles connected to two or more statuses.*

We experience role conflict when we find ourselves pulled in various directions as we try to respond to the many statuses we hold. One response to role conflict is deciding that "something has to go." More than one politician, for example, has decided not to run for office because of the conflicting demands of a hectic campaign schedule and family life. In other cases, people put off having children in order to stay on the "fast track" for career success.

Even roles linked to a single status may make competing demands on us. **Role strain** refers to *tension among the roles connected to a single status.* A college professor may enjoy being friendly with students. At the same time, however, the professor must maintain the personal distance needed in order to evaluate students fairly. In short, performing the various roles attached to even one status can be something of a balancing act.

One strategy for minimizing role conflict is separating parts of our lives so that we perform roles for one status at one time and place and carry out roles connected to another status in a completely different setting. A familiar example of this idea is deciding to "leave the job at work" before heading home to the family.

Give one example of role conflict and one example of role strain in your own life.

Role Exit

After she left the life of a Catholic nun to become a university sociologist, Helen Rose Fuchs Ebaugh (1988) began to study her own experience of *role exit,* the process by which people disengage from

FIGURE 1 Status Set and Role Sets

A status set includes all the statuses a person holds at a given time. The status set defines "who we are" in society. The many roles linked to each status define "what we do."

important social roles. Studying a range of "exes," including ex-nuns, ex-doctors, ex-husbands, and ex-alcoholics, Ebaugh identified elements common to the process of becoming an "ex."

According to Ebaugh, the process begins as people come to doubt their ability to continue in a certain role. As they imagine alternative roles, they ultimately reach a tipping point when they decide to pursue a new life. Even as they are moving on, however, a past role can continue to influence their lives. Exes carry with them a self-image shaped by an earlier role, which can interfere with building a new sense of self. For example, an ex-nun may hesitate to wear stylish clothing and makeup.

Exes must also rebuild relationships with people who knew them in their earlier life. Learning new social skills is another challenge. For example, Ebaugh reports, ex-nuns who enter the dating scene after decades in the church are often surprised to learn that sexual norms are very different from those they knew when they were teenagers.

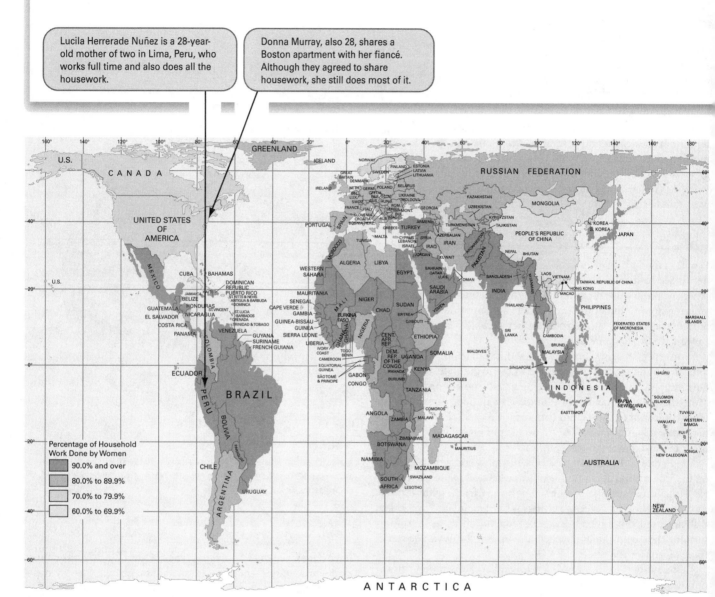

Lucila Herrerade Nuñez is a 28-year-old mother of two in Lima, Peru, who works full time and also does all the housework.

Donna Murray, also 28, shares a Boston apartment with her fiancé. Although they agreed to share housework, she still does most of it.

Percentage of Household Work Done by Women

- 90.0% and over
- 80.0% to 89.9%
- 70.0% to 79.9%
- 60.0% to 69.9%

WINDOW ON THE WORLD

GLOBAL MAP 1 Housework in Global Perspective

Throughout the world, housework is a major part of women's routines and identities. This is especially true in poor nations of Latin America, Africa, and Asia, where the social position of women is far below that of men. But our society also defines housework and child care as "feminine" activities, even though women and men have the same legal rights and most women work outside the home.

Source: *Peters Atlas of the World* (1990); updated by the author.

The Social Construction of Reality

In 1917, the Italian playwright Luigi Pirandello wrote a play called *The Pleasure of Honesty* about a character named Angelo Baldovino—a brilliant man with a checkered past. Baldovino enters the fashionable home of the Renni family and introduces himself in a peculiar way:

Inevitably we construct ourselves. Let me explain. I enter this house and immediately I become what I have to become, what I can become: I construct myself. That is, I present myself to you in a form suitable to the relationship I wish to achieve with you. And, of course, you do the same with me. (1962:157–58)

Baldovino suggests that although behavior is guided by status and role, we have the ability to shape who we are and to guide what

tip

The section "The Social Construction of Reality" shifts the focus from structure to process. The key idea here is that in everyday interaction, we build the reality that we experience.

tip

The Thomas theorem is the useful idea that reality, although created in our interaction, is (or becomes) real in its effects or consequences.

happens from moment to moment. In other words, "reality" is not as fixed as we may think.

The **social construction of reality** is *the process by which people creatively shape reality through social interaction.* This idea is the familiar foundation of the symbolic-interaction approach. As Baldovino's remark suggests, quite a bit of "reality" remains unclear in everyone's mind, especially in unfamiliar situations. So we present ourselves in terms that suit the setting and our purposes, we try to guide what happens next, and as others do the same, reality takes shape.

Social interaction is thus a complex negotiation that builds reality. Most everyday situations involve at least some agreement about what's going on. But how people see events depends on their different backgrounds, interests, and intentions.

"Street Smarts"

What people commonly call "street smarts" is actually a form of constructing reality. In his autobiography *Down These Mean Streets*, Piri Thomas recalls moving to an apartment in Spanish Harlem. Returning home one evening, young Piri found himself cut off by Waneko, the leader of the local street gang, who was flanked by a dozen others.

"Whatta ya say, Mr. Johnny Gringo," drawled Waneko.

Think man, I told myself, *think your way out of a stomping. Make it good.* "I hear you 104th Street coolies are supposed to have heart," I said. "I don't know this for sure. You know there's a lot of streets where a whole 'click' is made out of punks who can't fight one guy unless they all jump him for the stomp." I hoped this would push Waneko into giving me a fair one. His expression didn't change.

"Maybe we don't look at it that way."

Crazy, man, I cheer inwardly, *the cabron is falling into my setup....* "I wasn't talking to you," I said. "Where I come from, the pres is president 'cause he got heart when it comes to dealing."

Waneko was starting to look uneasy. He had bit on my worm and felt like a sucker fish. His boys were now light on me. They were no longer so much interested in stomping me as seeing the outcome between Waneko and me. "Yeah," was his reply....

I knew I'd won. Sure, I'd have to fight; but one guy, not ten or fifteen. If I lost, I might still get stomped, and if I won I might get stomped. I took care of this with my next sentence. "I don't know you or your boys," I said, "but they look cool to me. They don't feature as punks."

I had left him out purposely when I said "they." Now his boys were in a separate class. I had cut him off. He would have to fight me on his own, to prove his heart to himself, to his boys, and most important, to his turf. He got away from the stoop and asked, "Fair one, Gringo?" (1967:56–57)

This situation reveals the drama—sometimes subtle, sometimes savage—by which human beings creatively build reality. But of course, not everyone enters a situation with equal standing. If a police offi-

Flirting is an everyday experience in reality construction. Each person offers information to the other and hints at romantic interest. Yet the interaction proceeds with a tentative and often humorous air so that either individual can withdraw at any time without further obligation.

Ron Chapple/Getty Images, Inc.—Taxi

cer had driven by when Piri and Waneko were fighting, both young men might have ended up in jail.

The Thomas Theorem

By displaying his wits and fighting with Waneko until they both tired, Piri Thomas won acceptance by the gang. What took place that evening in Spanish Harlem is an example of the **Thomas theorem,** named after W. I. Thomas (1966:301, orig. 1931): *Situations that are defined as real are real in their consequences.*

Applied to social interaction, the Thomas theorem means that although reality is initially "soft" as it is being shaped, it can become "hard" in its effects. In the case just described, local gang members saw Piri Thomas act in a worthy way, so in their eyes, he *became* worthy.

Have you used Internet sites such as MySpace.com, Xanga.com, Facebook.com, or YouTube.com to "present" yourself to others? How "real" are these constructed realities?

Ethnomethodology

Most of the time, we take social reality for granted. To become more aware of the world we help create, Harold Garfinkel (1967) devised **ethnomethodology,** *the study of the way people make sense of their everyday surroundings.* This approach begins by pointing out that everyday behavior rests on a number of assumptions. When you ask someone the simple question "How are you?" you usually want to know how the person is doing in general, but you might really be wondering how the person is dealing with a specific physical, mental, spiritual, or financial challenge. However, the person being asked probably assumes that you are not really interested in details about any of these things, that you are just "being polite."

One good way to discover the assumptions we make about reality is to purposely break the rules. For example, the next time someone greets you by saying, "How're you doing?" offer details from your last physical examination or explain all the good and bad things that have happened since you woke up that morning and see how the person reacts.

The results are predictable, because we all have some idea of what the "rules" of everyday interaction are. The person will most likely become confused or irritated by your unexpected behavior—a reaction that helps us see not only what the rules are but also how important they are to everyday reality.

Members of every culture have rules about how close people should stand while talking. To see what the rules are in your social world, during a conversation, slowly move closer and closer to the other person and see what happens.

Reality Building: Class and Culture

People do not build everyday experience out of thin air. In part, how we act or what we see in our surroundings depends on our interests. Gazing at the sky on a starry night, for example, lovers discover romance, and scientists see hydrogen atoms fusing into helium. Social background also affects what we see, which is why residents of Spanish Harlem experience a different world than people living on Manhattan's pricey Upper East Side.

In global perspective, reality construction varies even more. Consider these everyday situations: People waiting for a bus in London typically "queue up" in a straight line; people in New York are rarely so orderly. The law forbids women in Saudi Arabia to drive cars, a ban unthinkable in the United States. In this country, people assume that "a short walk" means a few blocks or a few minutes; in the Andes Mountains of Peru, this same phrase means a few miles.

The point is that people build reality from the surrounding culture. People the world over find different meanings in specific gestures, so inexperienced travelers can find themselves building an unexpected and unwelcome reality. Similarly, in a study of popular culture, JoEllen Shively (1992) screened western films to men of European descent and to Native American men. The men in both categories claimed to enjoy the films, but for very different reasons. White men interpreted the films as praising rugged people striking out for the West and conquering the forces of nature. Native American men saw in the same films a celebration of land and nature. Given their different cultures, it is as if people in the two categories saw two different films.

Films also have an effect on the reality we all experience. The 2004 film *Ray,* about the life of the musician Ray Charles, who overcame the challenge of blindness, is one of a series of films that have changed the public's awareness of disabilities.

People build reality from their surrounding culture. Yet because cultural systems are marked by diversity and even outright conflict, reality construction always involves tensions and choices. Turkey is a nation with a mostly Muslim population, but it is also a country that has embraced Western culture. Here, women confront starkly different definitions of what is "feminine."

Staton R. Winter/*The New York Times.*

SOCIAL INTERACTION IN EVERYDAY LIFE

Dramaturgical Analysis: The "Presentation of Self"

Erving Goffman (1922–1982) was another sociologist who studied social interaction, explaining that people live their lives much like actors performing on a stage. If we imagine ourselves as directors observing what goes on in the theater of everyday life, we are doing what Goffman called **dramaturgical analysis,** *the study of social interaction in terms of theatrical performance.*

Dramaturgical analysis offers a fresh look at the concepts of status and role. A status is like a part in a play, and a role serves as a script, supplying dialogue and action for the characters. Goffman described each individual's "performance" as the **presentation of self,** *a person's efforts to create specific impressions in the minds of others.* This process, sometimes called *impression management,* begins with the idea of personal performance (Goffman, 1959, 1967).

Performances

As we present ourselves in everyday situations, we reveal information—consciously and unconsciously—to others. Our performance includes the way we dress (costume), the objects we carry (props), and our tone of voice and gestures (manner). In addition, we vary our performance according to where we are (the set). We may joke loudly in a restaurant, for example, but lower our voice when entering a church. People design settings, such as homes or offices, to bring about desired reactions in others.

In the computer age, the process of reality construction, including personal performances, now takes place online as well as in real life. The Seeing Sociology in Everyday Life box considers the popular Web site Second Life.

An Application: The Doctor's Office

Consider how a physician uses an office to convey particular information to an audience of patients. The fact that medical doctors enjoy high prestige and power in the United States is clear upon entering a doctor's office. First, the doctor is nowhere to be seen. Instead, in what Goffman describes as the "front region" of the setting, the patient encounters a receptionist, or gatekeeper, who decides whether and when the patient can meet the doctor. A simple glance around the doctor's waiting room, with patients (often impatiently) waiting to be invited into the inner sanctum, leaves little doubt that the doctor and the staff are in charge.

The "back region" is composed of the examination room plus the doctor's private office. Once inside the office, the patient can see

SOCIOLOGY (WORK

© 2002 David Sipress from cartoonbank.com. All Rights Reserved

a wide range of props, such as medical books and framed degrees, that give the impression that the doctor has the specialized knowledge necessary to call the shots. The doctor is usually seated behind a desk—the larger the desk, the greater the statement of power—and the patient is given only a chair.

The doctor's appearance and manner offer still more information. The white lab coat (costume) may have the practical function of keeping clothes from becoming dirty, but its social function is to let others know at a glance the physician's status. A stethoscope around the neck and a medical chart in hand (more props) have the same purpose. A doctor uses highly technical language that is often mystifying to the patient, again emphasizing that the doctor is in charge. Finally, patients use the title "doctor," but they, in turn, are often addressed by their first names, which further shows the doctor's dominant position. The overall message of a doctor's performance is clear: "I will help you, but you must allow me to take charge."

Try doing a similar analysis of the offices of several faculty members on your campus. What differences do you notice? How do you explain the patterns?

student 2 student

"Did you read that the IRS is now trying to tax money people's avatars make in Second Life?"

Seeing Sociology in Everyday Life
Performances Online? Visit "Second Life"!

Ben Folds is a large and carelessly dressed man who is trying to make it as a comedian. Tonight, he has had too much to drink. His comedy act is crashing and the audience has erupted with booing. Suddenly, he becomes alert, glares at the audience, and pulls out a light saber, which he swings menacingly in the direction of the people in the first row. Several women and men near the stage jump out of their seats and quickly move to safety. But Folds knows that enough is enough and staggers off stage (based on Gross, 2006).

This event might have been part of the late-night scene in New York or Los Angeles, but it actually happened nowhere at all—at least nowhere in the real world. This bit of nonreality took place in a comedy club that is part of Second Life, the virtual world accessed through the Web site http://secondlife.com.

Invented in 2003 by Linden Research, Inc., Second Life has become a popular Web destination that has been visited by as many as 10 million people around the world. If there is anything the visitors to Second Life have in common (other than their speedy connections and very good graphics cards), it is that they tend to be creative people looking for something different from their ordinary lives.

Experiencing something new is exactly the point of Second Life, according to its inventors. Residents of this computer universe can turn loose their imagination and creativity in surroundings "teeming with people, entertainment, experiences, and opportunity."

Second Life allows you to put many of the concepts described in this chapter into action. First, to become a "resident" in the world of Second Life, you need to construct an identity. Your character is called an "avatar," which you create as you decide to be female or male (or both) and design every feature of your "body"

from height to hair color, from the contours of your hips to the color of your skin. (That is, assuming you want a "humanoid" appearance at all—anything is possible and the options are limited only by your imagination.) This virtual world contains people who look rich, poor, attractive, even scary. Whatever you can dream up becomes real in this unreal world.

Having constructed your identity, you can interact with the million or so other avatars who inhabit this virtual world at any given time. Select a setting by looking at events that are going on, and walk, skate, ride, or teleport to whatever activity interests you. There are shopping malls, dance halls, classroom lectures, open-air concerts, quiet beaches for walking, and pulsating clubs for dancing. You can choose to go to a strip club or attend church on Sunday morning. Many companies are open for business, and several real-life countries have even set up virtual embassies on the site.

Once you have arrived at an event, walk up to someone (or be ready when someone walks up to you). As the avatars interact, "reality" is constructed. As in any society, rules guide behavior (for example, Second Life has recently banned gambling). Also in real life, you can evaluate your own actions by seeing how others respond to what you say or do. It is

not far from the truth to say that Second Life is a laboratory in which you can study many of the elements of social interaction.

Just like the real world, many of the activities found in Second Life cost money. The currency of this virtual society is Linden dollars, which can be purchased for "real" money (have your credit card ready). You can buy and sell property or services, making money or going broke in the process.

Virtual reality sites such as Second Life are gaining in popularity because they allow us to be or do what we have always dreamed about. Put another way, if you don't find everything you need in your real life (RL, for short), try a second life (SL) online. But the experience may not be quite what you would hope. For one thing, researchers who have begun studying Second Life report that the identities and behavior that people create turn out to be not so very different from those of the real world. In addition, some regular visitors to Second Life report that the experience can be lonely, raising questions about how satisfying virtual interaction is compared to the real thing.

WHAT DO YOU THINK?

1. Have you ever visited Second Life (http://secondlife.com)? If so, what did you like about the experience? What did you not enjoy?

2. Some analysts claim that Web sites like this one are the future of entertainment because, while television turns people into a passive audience, sites such as Second Life make people active participants. Do you agree or not? Why?

3. If you were to create an online identity, in what ways would it be like your real-life identity? How would it be different? Why?

Sources: Gross (2006), Itzkoff (2007), and Lagorio (2007)

Second Life Website

tip

You can apply Goffman's dramaturgical analysis to almost any setting or situation—the more complex and formal it is, the more fun it is to analyze. Try thinking about a church service, a rock concert, a courtroom trial, or a football game.

tip

The discussion of nonverbal communication is important because, as Goffman's work has already explained, we build interaction not just from what we say but from all elements of our performance, including "body language."

Nonverbal Communication

The novelist William Sansom describes a fictional Mr. Preedy, an English vacationer on a beach in Spain:

> He took care to avoid catching anyone's eye. First, he had to make it clear to those potential companions of his holiday that they were of no concern to him whatsoever. He stared through them, round them, over them—eyes lost in space. The beach might have been empty. If by chance a ball was thrown his way, he looked surprised; then let a smile of amusement light his face (Kindly Preedy), looked around dazed to see that there were people on the beach, tossed it back with a smile to himself and not a smile *at* the people. . . .
>
> [He] then gathered together his beach-wrap and bag into a neat sand-resistant pile (Methodical and Sensible Preedy), rose slowly to stretch his huge frame (Big-Cat Preedy), and tossed aside his sandals (Carefree Preedy, after all). (1956:230–31)

Without saying a single word, Mr. Preedy offers a great deal of information about himself to anyone watching him. This is the process of **nonverbal communication,** *communication using body movements, gestures, and facial expressions rather than speech.*

People use many parts of the body to convey information to others through *body language.* Facial expressions are the most important type of body language. Smiling, for instance, shows pleasure, although we distinguish among the deliberate smile of Kindly Preedy on the beach, a spontaneous smile of joy at seeing a friend, a pained smile of embarrassment after spilling a cup of coffee, and the full, unrestrained smile of self-satisfaction we often associate with winning some important contest.

Eye contact is another key element of nonverbal communication. Generally, we use eye contact to invite social interaction. Someone across the room "catches our eye," sparking a conversation. Avoiding another's eyes, by contrast, discourages communication. Hands, too, speak for us. Common hand gestures in our society convey, among other things, an insult, a request for a ride, an invitation for someone to join us, or a demand that others stop in their tracks. Gestures also supplement spoken words. For example, pointing at someone in a threatening way gives greater emphasis to a word of warning, just as shrugging the shoulders adds an air of indifference to the phrase "I don't know" and rapidly waving the arms adds urgency to the single word "Hurry!"

Body Language and Deception

As any actor knows, it is very difficult to pull off a perfect performance. In everyday performances, unintended body language can contradict our planned meaning: A teenage boy offers an explanation for getting home late, for example, but his mother doubts his words because he avoids looking her in the eye. The teenage celebrity on a television talk show claims that her recent musical flop is "no big deal," but the nervous swing of her leg suggests otherwise. Because nonverbal communication is hard to control, it offers clues to deception, in much the same way that changes in breathing, pulse rate, perspiration, and blood pressure recorded on a lie detector indicate that a person is lying.

Detecting phony performances is difficult, because no bodily gesture tells us conclusively that someone is lying. But because any performance involves so much body language, few people can lie without some slip-up, raising the suspicions of a careful observer. The key to detecting lies is to view the whole performance with an eye for inconsistencies.

Gender and Performances

Because women are socialized to respond to others, they tend to be more sensitive than men to nonverbal communication. In fact, gender is a central element in personal performances.

Demeanor

Demeanor—the way we act and carry ourselves—is a clue to social power. Simply put, powerful people enjoy more freedom in how they act. Off-color remarks, swearing, or putting your feet on the desk may be acceptable for the boss but rarely for employees. Similarly, powerful people can interrupt others; less powerful people are expected to show respect through silence (Smith-Lovin & Brody, 1989; Henley, Hamilton, & Thorne, 1992; C. Johnson, 1994).

Because women generally occupy positions of lesser power, demeanor is a gender issue as well. Forty percent of all working women in the United States hold clerical or service jobs under the control of supervisors who are usually men. Women, then, learn to craft their personal performances more carefully than men and to defer to men more often in everyday interaction.

Use of Space

How much space does a personal performance require? Power plays a key role here; the more power you have, the more space you use. Men typically command more space than women, whether pacing back and forth before an audience or casually sitting on a bench. Why? Our culture has traditionally measured femininity by how *little* space women occupy—the standard of "daintiness"—and masculinity by how *much* territory a man controls—the standard of "turf" (Henley, Hamilton, & Thorne, 1992).

tip

Goffman did not have much to say about gender, which is why a discussion of gender and performances is needed here.

tip

The idealization of performances shows us that what matters is not just how we behave but also why we act as we do. We often try to convince others that we are doing the "right" thing in the "right" way for the "right" reason.

For both sexes, the concept of **personal space** refers to *the surrounding area over which a person makes some claim to privacy*. In the United States, people typically position themselves several feet apart when speaking; throughout the Middle East, by contrast, people stand much closer. Just about everywhere, men (with their greater social power) often intrude into women's personal space. If a woman moves into a man's personal space, however, he is likely to take it as a sign of sexual interest.

In recent decades, a great deal of research has looked at how we use space in everyday life. "In the *Times*" provides some examples of when and why people get closer—and farther—from one another.

Staring, Smiling, and Touching

Eye contact encourages interaction. In conversations, women hold eye contact more than men. But men have their own brand of eye contact: staring. When men stare at women, they are claiming social dominance and defining women as sexual objects.

Although it often shows pleasure, smiling can also be a sign of trying to please someone or submission. In a male-dominated world, it is not surprising that women smile more than men (Henley, Hamilton, & Thorne, 1992).

Finally, mutual touching suggests intimacy and caring. Apart from close relationships, touching is generally something men do to women (but rarely, in our culture, to other men). A male physician touches the shoulder of his female nurse as they examine a report, a young man touches the back of his woman friend as he guides her across the street, or a male skiing instructor touches young women as he teaches them to ski. In such examples, the intent of touching may be harmless and may bring little response, but it amounts to a subtle ritual by which men claim dominance over women.

Watch male-female couples holding hands. Which person has the hand to the front and which has the hand to the rear? Can you see a pattern and offer an explanation?

Idealization

People behave the way they do for many often complex reasons. Even so, Goffman suggests, we construct performances to *idealize* our intentions. That is, we try to convince others (and perhaps ourselves) that what we do reflects ideal cultural standards rather than selfish motives.

Idealization is easily illustrated by returning to the world of doctors and patients. In a hospital, doctors engage in a performance commonly described as "making rounds." Entering the room of a patient, the doctor often stops at the foot of the bed and silently reads the patient's chart. Afterward, doctor and patient talk briefly. In ideal terms, this routine involves a doctor making a personal visit to check on a patient's condition.

In reality, the picture is not so perfect. A doctor may see several dozen patients a day and remember little about many of them. Reading the chart is a chance to recall the patient's name and medical problems, but revealing the impersonality of medical care would undermine the cultural ideal of the doctor as deeply concerned about the welfare of others.

 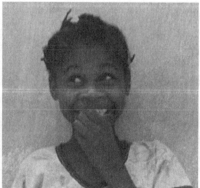 

Hand gestures vary widely from one culture to another. Yet people everywhere chuckle, grin, or smirk to indicate that they don't take another person's performance seriously. Therefore, the world over, people who cannot restrain their mirth tactfully cover their faces.

Paul W. Liebhardt (*left, center, and right*)

The New York Times

NYT Archive Since 1981 | Search

Get Home Delivery | New York Cloudy 48°F

TRADE D...

...RKET
...L ESTATE
...TOS
...L CLASSIFIEDS
...ORLD
S.
...litics
...ashington
...ducation
...Y./REGION
...USINESS
...ECHNOLOGY
...ORTS
...IENCE
...EALTH
...PINION
...RTS
...ooks
...ovies
...usic
...levision
...heater
...YLE
...ning & Wine
...ashion & Style
...me & Garden
...eddings/
...elebrations
...RAVEL
...ogs
...artoons
...lassifieds
...orrections
...rossword/
...ames
...rst Look
...aming
...etwork
...ultimedia
...YC Guide
...bituaries
...odcasts
...e Public
...ditor
...unday
...agazine
...eek in Review
...EWSPAPER
...et Home
...elivery
...ustomer Care
...mesPoints

In Certain Circles, Two Is a Crowd

By STEPHANIE ROSENBLOOM
November 16, 2006

Chances are that in the last week someone has irritated you by standing too close, talking too loud or making eye contact for too long. They have offended you with the high-pitched shrill emanating from the earphones of their iPod or by spreading their legs unnecessarily wide on a packed subway car.

But what makes you feel hostile toward "close talkers," as the show *Seinfeld* dubbed people who get within necking distance of you when they speak? Or toward strangers who stand very near to you in line? Or toward people who take the bathroom stall next to yours when every other one is available?

Communications scholars began studying personal space and people's perception of it decades ago, in a field known as proxemics. But with the population in the United States climbing above 300 million, urban corridors becoming denser and people with wealth searching for new ways to separate themselves from the masses, interest in the issue of personal space—that invisible force field around your body—is intensifying.

Scientists who say Americans share patterns of movement and behaviors to protect their personal space have recently found new evidence in a cyber game.

Researchers who observed the avatars (digital representations of the humans that control them) of participants in Second Life, a virtual reality universe, found that some of the avatars' physical behavior was in keeping with studies about how humans protect their personal space. . . .

Humans tend to avert eye gaze if they feel someone is standing too close. They retreat to corners, put distance between themselves and strangers, and sit or stand equidistant from one another like birds on a wire.

The study . . . found that the unwritten rules of personal space are so powerful, people even impose them on their cyber selves. . . .

While people may crave space, they rarely realize how entrenched proxemics are. Scholars can predict which areas of an elevator are likely to fill up first and which urinal a man will choose. They know people will stare at the lighted floor numbers in elevators, not one another.

"In order to overcome the intimacy, you have to make sure you don't make eye contact," said Dane Archer, a professor of sociology at the University of California, Santa Cruz, who studies proxemics.

"If you videotape people at a library table, it's very clear what seat somebody will take," Dr. Archer said, adding that one of the corner seats will go first, followed by the chair diagonally opposite because that is farthest away. "If you break those rules, it's fascinating," he said. "People will pile up books as if to make a wall."

Edward T. Hall, an anthropologist and the father of proxemics, even put numbers to the unspoken rules. He defined the invisible zones around us and attributed a range of distance to each one: intimate distance (6 to 18 inches); personal distance (18 inches to 4 feet); social distance (4 to 12 feet); and public distance (about 12 feet or more).

But personal space is not merely a numbers game. Preferences differ from culture to culture. Scholars have found that Americans, conquerors of the wild frontier, generally prefer more personal space than people in Mediterranean and Latin American cultures, and more than men in Arab countries.

"In the U.S., it's very closely linked to ideals of individuals," said Kathryn Sorrells, an associate professor of communication studies at California State University, Northridge. . . . "There's an idea that you have the right to this space," she said, noting that it was born of a culture that prizes independence, privacy and capitalism.

Dr. Archer tells of a Brazilian man he interviewed who, when speaking to the American waiters with whom he worked, used to casually touch them for emphasis. The man's overtures of friendship toward his co-workers were always rejected and he wanted to know why. So when business was slow he observed how the Americans interacted. And eventually he arrived at this conclusion: Americans hate to be touched. . . .

The Brazilian man's experience also shows how people are quick to judge those who break the unwritten rules, unless we are attuned to the cultural differences. . . .

Proxemics, however, is not merely about interactions between individuals. On a larger scale, it helps developers, urban planners and executives in various industries understand how people move through public spaces, how they shop, even what type of restaurants they find most comfortable. . . .

And so, what may seem like a minor behavioral tic can help department stores determine how far apart to place racks of clothes, bistro owners figure out how to configure the bar area and college campuses to design residence halls.

WHAT DO YOU THINK?

1. When was the last time you were irritated by someone standing too close to you?

2. Why do you think we feel a need to protect a certain amount of "personal space"? How big is your personal space?

3. What did you read in the article that shows our ideas about personal space are cultural?

tip

Embarrassment and *tact* are two concepts that go together. The first refers to the "loss of face," and the second refers to efforts to help someone "save face."

Doctors, college professors, and other professionals typically idealize their motives for entering their chosen careers. They describe their work as "making a contribution to science," "helping others," "serving the community," and even "answering a calling from God." Rarely do they admit the more common, less honorable, motives: the income, power, prestige, and leisure time that these occupations provide.

We all use idealization to some degree. When was the last time you smiled and spoke politely to someone you do not like? Have you acted interested in a class that was really boring? Such little lies in our performances help us get through everyday life. Even when we suspect others are putting on an act, we are unlikely to challenge their performances, for reasons we shall examine next.

Embarrassment and Tact

The famous speaker keeps mispronouncing the dean's name; the visiting ambassador rises from the table to speak, unaware of the napkin still tucked in his collar; the president becomes ill at a state dinner. As carefully as individuals may craft their performances, slip-ups of all kinds occur. The result is *embarrassment,* discomfort following a spoiled performance. Goffman describes embarrassment as "losing face."

Embarrassment is an ever-present danger because idealized performances usually contain some deception. In addition, most performances involve juggling so many elements that one thoughtless moment can shatter the intended impression.

A curious fact is that an audience often overlooks flaws in a performance, allowing the actor to avoid embarrassment. If we do point out a misstep ("Excuse me, but your fly is open") we do it quietly and only to help someone avoid even greater loss of face. In Hans Christian Andersen's classic fable "The Emperor's New Clothes," the child who blurts out the truth, that the emperor is parading about naked, is scolded for being rude.

Often members of an audience actually help the performer recover from a flawed performance. *Tact* is helping someone "save face." After hearing a supposed expert make an embarrassingly inaccurate remark, for example, people may tactfully ignore the comment, as if it had never been spoken, or with mild laughter treat what was said as a joke. Or they may simply respond, "I'm sure you didn't mean that," hearing the statement but not allowing it to destroy the actor's performance. With such efforts in mind, we can understand Abraham Lincoln's comment that "tact is the ability to describe others the way they see themselves."

Why is tact so common? Because embarrassment creates discomfort not just for the actor but for everyone else as well. Just as a theater audience feels uneasy when an actor forgets a line, people who observe awkward behavior are reminded of how fragile their own performances often are. Socially constructed reality thus functions like a dam holding back a sea of chaos. When one person's performance springs a leak, others tactfully help make repairs. Everyone lends a hand in building reality, and no one wants it suddenly swept away.

In sum, Goffman's research shows that although behavior is spontaneous in some respects, it is more patterned than we often think. Four centuries ago, Shakespeare captured this idea in memorable lines that still ring true:

> All the world's a stage,
> And all the men and women merely players:
> They have their exits and their entrances;
> And one man in his time plays many parts.
>
> (*As You Like It,* act 2, scene 7)

 Using Goffman's approach, explain the importance of performances, nonverbal communication, idealization, and tact, using, as much as you can, examples from your own life.

  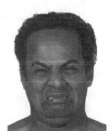   

To most people in the United States, these expressions convey anger, fear, disgust, happiness, surprise, and sadness. But do people elsewhere in the world define them in the same way? Research suggests that all human beings experience the same basic emotions and display them to others in the same basic ways. But culture plays a part by specifying the situations that trigger one emotion or another.

Barbara Penoya/Getty Images, Inc.- Photodisc. (*left*); Alan Weiner/Alan S. Weiner (*second from left*); Andy Crawford © Dorling Kindersley (*third from left*); © Guido Alberto Rossi/TIPS Images (*third from right*); Chris Carroll/Corbis/ Bettmann (*second from right*); Costa Manos/Magnum Photos, Inc. (*right*)

SOCIAL INTERACTION IN EVERYDAY LIFE

Interaction in Everyday Life: Three Applications

The final sections of this chapter illustrate the major elements of social interaction by focusing on three dimensions of everyday life: emotions, language, and humor.

Emotions: The Social Construction of Feeling

Emotions, more commonly called *feelings,* are an important element of human social life. In truth, what we *do* often matters less than how we *feel* about it. Emotions seem very personal because they are "inside." Even so, just as society guides our behavior, it guides our emotional life.

The Biological Side of Emotions

Studying people all over the world, Paul Ekman (1980a, 1980b) reports that people everywhere express six basic emotions: happiness, sadness, anger, fear, disgust, and surprise. In addition, Ekman found that people everywhere use much the same facial expressions to show these emotions. Ekman believes that some emotional responses are "wired" into human beings; that is, they are biologically programmed in our facial features, muscles, and central nervous system.

Why? Over centuries of evolution, emotions developed in the human species because they serve a social purpose: supporting group life. Emotions are powerful forces that allow us to overcome our self-centeredness and build connections with others. Thus the capacity for emotion arose in our ancestors along with the capacity for culture (Turner, 2000).

The Cultural Side of Emotions

But culture does play an important role in guiding human emotions. First, Ekman explains, culture defines *what triggers* an emotion. Whether people define the departure of an old friend as joyous (causing happiness), insulting (arousing anger), a loss (producing sadness), or mystical (provoking surprise and awe) has a lot to do with culture. Second, culture provides rules for the *display* of emotions. For example, most people in the United States express emotions more freely with family members than with colleagues in the workplace. Similarly, we expect children to express emotions to parents, but parents tend to hide their emotions from their children. Third, culture guides how we *value* emotions. Some societies encourage the expression of emotion; others expect members to control their feelings and maintain a "stiff upper lip." Gender also plays a part; traditionally, at least, many cultures expect women to show emotions, but they discourage

Many of us think emotions are simply part of our biological makeup. While there is a biological foundation to human emotion, sociologists have demonstrated that what triggers an emotion—as well as when, where, and to whom the emotion is displayed—is shaped by culture. For example, many jobs not only regulate a worker's behavior but also expect workers to display a particular emotion, as in the case of the always-smiling airline flight attendant. Can you think of other jobs that regulate emotions in this way?

Jack Hollingsworth/Getty Images, Inc.- Photodisc.

emotional expression by men as a sign of weakness. In some cultures, of course, this pattern is less pronounced or even reversed.

Emotions on the Job

In the United States, most people are freer to express their feelings at home than on the job. The reason, as Arlie Russell Hochschild (1979, 1983) explains, is that the typical company tries to regulate not only the behavior of its employees but also their emotions. Take the case of an airline flight attendant who offers passengers a drink and a smile. Although this smile may convey real pleasure at serving the customer, Hochschild's study points to a different conclusion: The smile is an emotional script demanded by the airline as the right way to do the job. Therefore, we see that the "presentation of self" described by Erving Goffman can involve not just surface acting but also the "deep acting" of emotions.

With these patterns in mind, it is easy to see that we socially construct our emotions as part of our everyday reality, a process sociologists call *emotion management.* The Controversy & Debate box links

tip
Raise the questions at the end of the box in class
to see what other students think.

Controversy & Debate
Managing Feelings: Women's Abortion Experiences

Liz: I just *can't* be pregnant! I'm going to see my doctor tomorrow about an abortion. There's no way I can deal with a baby at this point in my life!

Jen: I can't believe you'd do that, Liz! How are you going to feel in two years when you think about what that *baby* would be doing if you'd let it live?

Few issues today generate as much emotion as abortion. In a study of women's abortion experiences, the sociologist Jennifer Keys (2002) discovered emotional scripts or "feeling rules" that guided how women feel about ending a pregnancy.

Keys explains that emotional scripts arise from the political controversy surrounding abortion. The antiabortion movement defines abortion as a personal tragedy, the "killing of an unborn child." Given this definition, women who terminate a pregnancy through abortion are doing something morally wrong and can expect to feel grief, guilt, and regret. So intense are these feelings, according to supporters of this position, that such women often suffer from "postabortion syndrome."

Those who take the pro-choice position have an opposing view of abortion. From this point of view, the woman's problem is the *unwanted pregnancy*; abortion is an acceptable medical solution. Therefore, the emotion common to women who terminate a pregnancy should be not guilt but relief.

In her research, Keys conducted in-depth interviews with forty women who had recently had abortions and found that all of them used such scripts to "frame" their situation in an antiabortion or pro-choice manner. In part, this construction of reality reflected the women's own attitude about abortion.

In addition, however, the women's partners and friends typically encouraged specific feelings about the event. Ivy, one young woman in the study, had a close friend who was also pregnant. "Congratulations!" she exclaimed when she learned of Ivy's condition. "We're going to be having babies together!" Such a statement established one "feeling rule"—having a baby is *good*—which sent the message to Ivy that her planned abortion should trigger guilt. Working in the other direction, Jo's partner was horrified by the news that she was pregnant. Doubting his own ability to be a father, he blurted out, "I would rather put a gun to my head than have this baby!" His panic not only defined having the child as a mistake but alarmed Jo as well. Clearly, her partner's reaction made the decision to end the pregnancy a matter of relief from a terrible problem.

Medical personnel also play a part in this process of reality construction by using specific terms. Nurses and doctors who talk about "the baby" encourage the antiabortion

The words that doctors and nurses use guide whether a woman having an abortion defines the experience in positive or negative terms.

© Furgolle/Image Point FR/Corbis. All Rights Reserved

framing of abortion and provoke grief and guilt. On the other hand, those who use language such as "pregnancy tissue," "fetus," or "the contents of the uterus" encourage the pro-choice framing of abortion as a simple medical procedure leading to relief. Olivia began using the phrase "products of conception," which she picked up from her doctor. Denise spoke of her procedure as "taking the extra cells out of my body. Yeah, I did feel some guilt when I thought that this was the beginning of life, but my body is full of life—you have lots of cells in you."

After the procedure, most women reported actively trying to manage their feelings. Explained Ivy, "I never used the word 'baby.' I kept saying to myself that it was not formed yet. There was nothing there yet. I kept that in my mind." On the other hand, Keys found that all of the women in her study who leaned toward the antiabortion position did use the term "baby." Gina explained, "I do think of it as a baby. The truth is that I ended my baby's life. . . . Thinking that makes me feel guilty. But—considering what I did—maybe I *should* feel guilty." Believing that what she had done was wrong, in other words, Gina actively called out the feeling of guilt—in part, Keys concluded, to punish herself.

WHAT DO YOU THINK?

1. In your own words, what are "emotional scripts" or "feeling rules"?

2. Can you apply the idea of "feeling rules" to the experience of getting married?

3. In light of this discussion, how accurate is it to say that our feelings are not as personal as we may think they are?

tip

The chapter's final topic is humor. The foundation
of humor follows from the earlier discussion of
the social construction of reality—building two
contrasting definitions of reality.

the emotions displayed by women who decide to have an abortion to
politics and their personal view of terminating a pregnancy.

Language: The Social Construction of Gender

Language is the thread that weaves members of a society into the symbolic web we call culture. Language communicates not only a surface reality but also deeper levels of meaning. One such level involves gender. Language defines men and women differently in terms of both power and value (Henley, Hamilton, & Thorne, 1992; Thorne, Kramarae, & Henley, 1983).

Language and Power

A young man proudly rides his new motorcycle up his friend's driveway and boasts, "Isn't she a beauty?" On the surface, the question has little to do with gender. Yet why does he use the pronoun *she* instead of *he* or *it* to refer to his prized possession?

The answer is that men often use language to establish control over their surroundings. A man attaches a female pronoun to a motorcycle (or car, boat, or other object) because it reflects the power of *ownership*. Perhaps this is also why, in the United States and elsewhere, a woman who marries traditionally takes the last name of her husband. Because many of today's married women value their independence, an increasing share (about 15 percent) now keep their own name or combine the two family names.

Language and Value

Typically, the English language treats as masculine whatever has greater value, force, or significance. For instance, the word *virtuous,* meaning "morally worthy" or "excellent," comes from the Latin word *vir,* meaning "man." On the other hand, the adjective *hysterical,* meaning "emotionally out of control," comes from the Greek word *hystera,* meaning "uterus."

In many familiar ways, language also confers different value on the two sexes. Traditional masculine terms such as *king* and *lord* have a positive meaning, and comparable terms, such as *queen, madam,* and *dame,* can have negative meanings. Similarly, use of the suffixes *-ette* and *-ess* to denote femininity usually devalues the words to which they are added. For example, a *major* has higher standing than a *majorette,* as does a *host* in relation to a *hostess* or a *master* in relation to a *mistress.* Language both mirrors social attitudes and helps perpetuate them.

 List words that describe a very sexually active female. Are they positive or negative in meaning? Repeat this exercise for a very sexually active male. What differences do you notice?

Given the importance of gender in everyday life, perhaps we should not be surprised that women and men sometimes have trouble communicating with each other. In the Thinking About Diversity: Race, Class, & Gender box on page 158, Harold and Sybil, whose misadventures in trying to find their friends' home opened this chapter, return to illustrate how the two sexes often seem to be speaking different languages.

Reality Play: The Social Construction of Humor

Humor plays an important part in everyday life. Everyone laughs at a joke, but few people stop to think about what makes something funny. We can apply many of the ideas developed in this chapter to explain how, by using humor, we "play with reality" (Macionis, 1987).

The Foundation of Humor

Humor is produced by the social construction of reality; it arises as people create and contrast two different realities. Generally, one reality is *conventional,* that is, what people expect in a specific situation. The other reality is *unconventional,* an unexpected violation of cultural patterns. Humor therefore arises from contradiction, ambiguity, and double meanings found in differing definitions of the same situation.

There are countless ways to mix realities and generate humor. Contrasting realities are found in statements that contradict themselves, such as "Nostalgia is not what it used to be"; statements that repeat themselves, such as Yogi Berra's line "It's *déjà vu* all over again"; or statements that mix up words, such as Oscar Wilde's line "Work is the curse of the drinking class." Even switching around syllables does the trick, as in the case of the country song "I'd Rather Have a Bottle in Front of Me Than a Frontal Lobotomy."

Of course, a joke can be built the other way around, so that the audience is led to expect an unconventional answer and then receives a very ordinary one. When a reporter asked the famous gangster Willy Sutton why he robbed banks, for example, he replied dryly, "Because that's where the money is." However a joke is constructed, the greater the opposition or difference between the two definitions of reality, the greater the humor.

When telling jokes, the comedian uses various strategies to strengthen this opposition and make the joke funnier. One common technique is to present the first, or conventional, remark in conversation with another actor and then to turn toward the audience (or the camera) to deliver the second, unexpected line. In a Marx Brothers film, Groucho remarks, "Outside of a dog, a book is a man's best friend." Then, raising his voice and turning to the camera, he adds, "And *inside* of a dog, it's too dark to read!" Such "changing channels" emphasizes the difference between the two realities. Following the

student 2 student

"Gender is even in our language! No wonder women are still unequal to men."

Thinking About Diversity: Race, Class, & Gender
Gender and Language: "You Just Don't Understand!"

In the story that opened this chapter, Harold and Sybil faced a situation that rings all too true to many people: When they are lost, men grumble to themselves and perhaps blame their partners but avoid asking for directions. For their part, women can't understand why men refuse help when they need it.

Deborah Tannen (1990) explains that men typically define most everyday encounters as competitive. Therefore, getting lost is bad enough without asking for help, which lets someone else get "one up." By contrast, because women have traditionally had a subordinate position, they find it easy to ask for help. Sometimes, Tannen points out, women ask for assistance even when they don't need it.

A similar gender-linked problem common to couples involves what women consider "trying to be helpful" and men call "nagging." Consider the following exchange (adapted from Adler, 1990:74):

SYBIL: What's wrong, honey?
HAROLD: Nothing.
SYBIL: Something is bothering you. I can tell.
HAROLD: I told you nothing is bothering me. Leave me alone.
SYBIL: But I can see that there is a problem.
HAROLD: OK. Just why do you think there is a problem?
SYBIL: Well, for one thing, you're bleeding all over your shirt.

HAROLD: [now irritated] Yeah, well, it doesn't bother me.
SYBIL: [losing her temper] WELL, IT SURE IS BOTHERING ME!
HAROLD: Fine. I'll go change my shirt.

The problem here is that what one partner *intends* by a comment is not always what the other *hears* in the words. To Sybil, her opening question is an effort at cooperative problem solving. She can see that something is wrong with Harold (who has cut himself

Amy Etra/PhotoEdit Inc.

while doing yard work), and she wants to help him. But Harold interprets her pointing out his problem as belittling him, and he tries to close off the discussion. Sybil, believing that Harold would be more positive if he understood that she just wants to be helpful, repeats her question. This reaction sets in motion a vicious circle in which Harold, who feels his wife is thinking that he cannot take care of himself, responds by digging in his heels. This response, in turn, makes Sybil all the more sure that she needs to get through to him. And around it goes until somebody gets really angry.

In the end, Harold agrees to change his shirt but still refuses to discuss the original problem. Defining his wife's concern as "nagging," Harold just wants Sybil to leave him alone. For her part, Sybil fails to understand her husband's view of the situation and walks away convinced that he is a stubborn grouch.

WHAT DO YOU THINK?

1. Do you agree with Tannen that men and women communicate in different ways? Explain your view.

2. In your opinion, what is the reason for any gender difference in how people use language?

3. Do you think that an understanding of Tannen's work can help female-male couples communicate better? Why or why not?

same logic, stand-up comedians may "reset" the audience to conventional expectations by interjecting the phrase, "But seriously, folks," between jokes. Monty Python comedian John Cleese did this with his trademark line, "And now for something completely different."

Comedians pay careful attention to their performances—the precise words they use and the timing of their delivery. A joke is well told if the comedian creates the sharpest possible opposition between the realities; in a careless performance, the joke falls flat. Because the key to humor lies in the collision of realities, we can see why the climax of a joke is termed the "*punch* line."

The Dynamics of Humor: "Getting It"

After someone tells you a joke, have you ever had to say, "I don't get it"? To "get" humor, you must understand both the conventional and the unconventional realities well enough to appreciate their difference. A comedian may make getting a joke harder by leaving out some important information. In such cases, listeners must pay attention to the stated elements of the joke and then fill in the missing pieces on their own. A simple example is the comment of the movie producer Hal Roach on his one hundredth birthday: "If I had known I would live to

SOCIAL INTERACTION IN EVERYDAY LIFE

tip

Much of this discussion of humor is based on the symbolic-interaction approach. The final two sections provide a short look at what the structural-functional and social-conflict approaches have to say about humor.

be one hundred, I would have taken better care of myself!" Here, getting the joke depends on realizing that Roach must have taken pretty good care of himself because he did make it to one hundred. Or take one of W. C. Fields's lines: "Some weasel took the cork out of my lunch." "What a lunch!" we think to ourselves to "finish" the joke.

Here is an even more complex joke: What do you get if you cross an insomniac, a dyslexic, and an agnostic? Answer: A person who stays up all night wondering if there is a dog. To get this one, you must know that insomnia is an inability to sleep, that dyslexia causes a person to reverse the letters in words, and that an agnostic doubts the existence of God.

Why would a comedian want the audience to make this sort of effort to understand a joke? Our enjoyment of a joke is increased by the pleasure of figuring out all the pieces needed to "get it." In addition, getting the joke makes you an "insider" compared to those who don't get it. We have all experienced the frustration of *not* getting a joke: fear of being judged stupid, along with a sense of being excluded from a pleasure shared by others. Sometimes someone may tactfully explain the joke so that the other person doesn't feel left out. But as the old saying goes, if a joke has to be explained, it isn't very funny.

The Topics of Humor

All over the world, people smile and laugh, making humor a universal element of human culture. But because the world's people live in different cultures, humor rarely travels well.

October 1, Kobe, Japan. Can you share a joke with people who live halfway around the world? At dinner, I ask two Japanese college women to tell me a joke. "You know 'crayon'?" Asako asks. I nod. "How do you ask for a crayon in Japanese?" I respond that I have no idea. She laughs out loud as she says what sounds like "crayon crayon." Her companion Mayumi laughs too. My wife and I sit awkwardly, straight-faced. Asako relieves some of our embarrassment by explaining that the Japanese word for "give me" is <u>kureyo</u>, which sounds like "crayon." I force a smile.

What is humorous to the Japanese may be lost on the Chinese, Brazilians, or people in the United States. Even the social diversity of this country means that different types of people will find humor in different situations. New Englanders, Southerners, and Westerners have their own brands of humor, as do Latinos and Anglos, fifteen- and forty-year-olds, Wall Street bankers and rodeo riders.

But for everyone, topics that lend themselves to double meanings or controversy generate humor. In the United States, the first jokes many of us learned as children concerned bodily functions kids are not

supposed to talk about. The mere mention of "unmentionable acts" or even certain parts of the body can dissolve young faces in laughter.

Are there jokes that do break through the culture barrier? Yes, but they must touch on universal human experiences such as, say, turning on a friend:

I think of a number of jokes, but none seems likely to work. Understanding jokes about the United States is difficult for people who know little of our culture. Is there something more universal? Inspiration: "Two fellows are walking in the woods and come upon a huge bear. One guy leans over and tightens up the laces on his running shoes. 'Jake,' says the other, 'what are you doing? You can't outrun this bear!' 'I don't have to outrun the bear,' responds Jake. 'All I have to do is outrun <u>you</u>!'" Smiles all around.

Humor often walks a fine line between what is funny and what is "sick." During the Middle Ages, people used the word *humors* (derived from the Latin *humidus,* meaning "moist") to mean a balance of bodily fluids that regulated a person's health. Researchers today document the power of humor to reduce stress and improve health. One recent study of cancer patients, for example, found that the greater people's sense of humor, the greater their odds of surviving the disease. Such findings confirm the old saying that "laughter is the best medicine" (Bakalar, 2005; Svebak, cited in M. Elias, 2007). At the extreme, however, people who always take conventional reality lightly risk being defined as deviant or even mentally ill (a common stereotype shows insane people laughing uncontrollably, and for a long time mental hospitals were known as "funny farms").

Then, too, every social group considers certain topics too sensitive for humorous treatment, and joking about them risks criticism for having a "sick" sense of humor (or being labeled "sick" yourself). People's religious beliefs, tragic accidents, or appalling crimes are the stuff of sick jokes or no jokes at all. Even all these years later, no one jokes about the September 11, 2001, terrorist attacks.

The Functions of Humor

Humor is found everywhere because it works as a safety valve for potentially disruptive sentiments. Put another way, humor provides an acceptable way to discuss a sensitive topic without appearing to be serious. Having said something controversial, people can use humor to defuse the situation by simply stating, "I didn't mean anything by what I said—it was just a joke!"

People also use humor to relieve tension in uncomfortable situations. One study of medical examinations found that most patients try to joke with doctors to ease their own nervousness (P. S. Baker et al., 1997).

Because humor involves challenging established conventions, most U.S. comedians—including Carlos Mencia—have been social "outsiders," members of racial and ethnic minorities.

Chris Gordon/Getty Images

Humor and Conflict

Humor may be a source of pleasure, but it can also be used to put down other people. Men who tell jokes about women, for example, typically are expressing some measure of hostility toward them (Powell & Paton, 1988; Benokraitis & Feagin, 1995). Similarly, jokes about gay people reveal tensions about sexual orientation. Real conflict can be masked by humor in situations where one or both parties choose not to bring the conflict out into the open (Primeggia & Varacalli, 1990).

"Put-down" jokes make one category of people feel good at the expense of another. After collecting and analyzing jokes from many societies, Christie Davies (1990) confirmed that ethnic conflict is one driving force behind humor in most of the world. The typical ethnic joke makes fun of some disadvantaged category of people, at the same time making the joke teller feel superior. Given the Anglo-Saxon traditions of U.S. society, Poles and other ethnic and racial minorities have long been the butt of jokes in the United States, as have Newfoundlanders in eastern Canada, the Irish in Scotland, Sikhs in India, Turks in Germany, Hausas in Nigeria, Tasmanians in Australia, and Kurds in Iraq.

 Humor is most common among people with roughly the same social standing. Why is it risky to joke with people who have more power than you do? What about joking with people who have less power?

Disadvantaged people also make fun of the powerful, although usually with some care. Women in the United States joke about men, just as African Americans find humor in white people's ways and poor people poke fun at the rich. Throughout the world, people target their leaders with humor, and officials in some countries take such jokes seriously enough to arrest those who do not show proper respect (Speier, 1998).

In sum, humor is much more important than we may think. It is a means of mental escape from a conventional world that is never entirely to our liking (Flaherty, 1984, 1990; Yoels & Clair, 1995). This fact helps explain why so many of our nation's comedians are from the ranks of historically marginalized peoples, including Jews and African Americans. As long as we maintain a sense of humor, we assert our freedom and are not prisoners of reality. By putting a smile on our faces, we can change ourselves and the world just a little and for the better.

Applying Sociology in Everyday Life

1. Sketch out your own status set and the role set that goes with it. Identify any master statuses and also any sources of role conflict or role strain.

2. During one full day, every time somebody asks, "How are you?" or "How's it goin'?" stop and actually give a complete, truthful answer. What happens when you respond to a polite question in an honest way? Listen to how people respond, and also watch their body language. What can you conclude?

3. Stroll around downtown or at a local mall. Pay attention to how many women and men you find at each location. From your observations, are there stores that are "gendered" so that there are "female spaces" and "male spaces"? How and why are spaces "gendered"?

MAKING THE GRADE

Social Interaction in Everyday Life

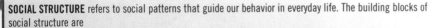

What Is Social Structure?

SOCIAL STRUCTURE refers to social patterns that guide our behavior in everyday life. The building blocks of social structure are

- **STATUS**—a social position that is part of our social identity and that defines our relationships to others
- **ROLE**—the action expected of a person who holds a particular status

✔ *A person holds* a status *and performs* a role.

A status can be either an

- **ASCRIBED STATUS**, which is involuntary (for example, being a teenager, an orphan, or a Mexican American), or an
- **ACHIEVED STATUS**, which is earned (for example, being an honors student, a pilot, or a thief).

A **MASTER STATUS**, which can be either ascribed or achieved, has special importance for a person's identity (for example, being blind, a doctor, or a Kennedy).

ROLE CONFLICT results from tension among roles linked to two or more statuses (for example, a woman who juggles her responsibilities as a mother and a corporate CEO).

ROLE STRAIN results from tension among roles linked to a single status (for example, the college professor who enjoys personal interaction with students but at the same time knows that social distance is necessary in order to evaluate students fairly).

✔ *A person's status set changes over the life course.*

✔ *The role sets attached to a single status vary from society to society around the world.*

social interaction the process by which people act and react in relation to others

status a social position that a person holds

status set all the statuses a person holds at a given time

ascribed status a social position a person receives at birth or takes on involuntarily later in life

achieved status a social position a person takes on voluntarily that reflects personal ability and effort

master status a status that has special importance for social identity, often shaping a person's entire life

role behavior expected of someone who holds a particular status

role set a number of roles attached to a single status

role conflict conflict among the roles connected to two or more statuses

role strain tension among the roles connected to a single status

The Social Construction of Reality

Through **SOCIAL INTERACTION**, we construct the reality we experience.

- For example, two people interacting both try to shape the reality of their situation.

The **THOMAS THEOREM** says that the reality people construct in their interaction has real consequences for the future.

- For example, a teacher who believes a certain student to be intellectually gifted may well encourage exceptional academic performance.

ETHNOMETHODOLOGY is a strategy to reveal the assumptions people have about their social world.

- We can expose these assumptions by intentionally breaking the "rules" of social interaction and observing the reactions of other people.

Both **CULTURE** and **SOCIAL CLASS** shape the reality people construct.

- For example, a "short walk" for a New Yorker is a few city blocks, but for a peasant in Latin America, it could be a few miles.

social construction of reality the process by which people creatively shape reality through social interaction

Thomas theorem W. I. Thomas's statement that situations defined as real are real in their consequences

ethnomethodology Harold Garfinkel's term for the study of the way people make sense of their everyday surroundings

✔ *Through the social construction of reality, people creatively shape their social world.*

MAKING THE GRADE *continued . . .*

Dramaturgical Analysis: The "Presentation of Self"

DRAMATURGICAL ANALYSIS explores social interaction in terms of theatrical performance: A status operates as a part in a play and a role is a script.

PERFORMANCES are the way we present ourselves to others.

- Performances are both conscious (intentional action) and unconscious (nonverbal communication).
- Performances include costume (the way we dress), props (objects we carry), and demeanor (tone of voice and the way we carry ourselves).

GENDER affects performances because men typically have greater social power than women. Gender differences involve *demeanor, use of space,* and *staring, smiling, and touching.*

DEMEANOR—With greater social power, men have more freedom in how they act.

USE OF SPACE—Men typically command more space than women.

STARING and **TOUCHING** are generally done by men to women.

SMILING, as a way to please another, is more commonly done by women.

IDEALIZATION of performances means we try to convince others that our actions reflect ideal culture rather than selfish motives.

EMBARRASSMENT is the "loss of face" in a performance. People use **TACT** to help others "save face."

dramaturgical analysis Erving Goffman's term for the study of social interaction in terms of theatrical performance

presentation of self Erving Goffman's term for a person's efforts to create specific impressions in the minds of others

nonverbal communication communication using body movements, gestures, and facial expressions rather than speech

personal space the surrounding area over which a person makes some claim to privacy

Interaction in Everyday Life: Three Applications

EMOTIONS: The Social Construction of **FEELING**

The same basic emotions are biologically programmed into all human beings, but culture guides what triggers emotions, how people display emotions, and how people value emotions. In everyday life, the presentation of self involves managing emotions as well as behavior.

LANGUAGE: The Social Construction of **GENDER**

Gender is an important element of everyday interaction. Language defines women and men as different types of people, reflecting the fact that society attaches greater power and value to what is viewed as masculine.

REALITY PLAY: The Social Construction of **HUMOR**

Humor results from the difference between conventional and unconventional definitions of a situation. Because humor is a part of culture, people around the world find different situations funny.

MAKING THE GRADE

Social Interaction in Everyday Life

Sample Test Questions

These questions are similar to those found in the test bank that accompanies this textbook.

Multiple-Choice Questions

1. Which term defines who and what we are in relation to others?
   a. role
   b. status
   c. role set
   d. master status

2. In U.S. society, which of the following is often a master status?
   a. occupation
   b. physical or mental disability
   c. race or color
   d. All of the above are correct.

3. "Role set" refers to
   a. a number of roles found in any one society.
   b. a number of roles attached to a single status.
   c. a number of roles that are more or less the same.
   d. a number of roles within any one organization.

4. Frank excels at football at his college, but he doesn't have enough time to study as much as he wants to. This problem is an example of
   a. role set.
   b. role strain.
   c. role conflict.
   d. role exit.

5. The Thomas theorem states that
   a. our statuses and roles are the keys to our personality.
   b. most people rise to their level of incompetence.
   c. people know the world only through their language.
   d. situations defined as real are real in their consequences.

6. Which of the following is the correct meaning of "presentation of self"?
   a. efforts to create impressions in the minds of others
   b. acting out a master status
   c. thinking back over the process of role exit
   d. trying to take attention away from others

7. Paul Ekman points to what as an important clue to deception by another person?
   a. smiling
   b. using tact
   c. inconsistencies in a presentation
   d. All of the above are correct.

8. In terms of dramaturgical analysis, tact is understood as
   a. helping someone take on a new role.
   b. helping another person "save face."
   c. making it hard for someone to perform a role.
   d. negotiating a situation to get your own way.

9. In her study of human emotion, Arlie Hochschild explains that companies typically
   a. try to regulate the emotions of workers.
   b. want workers to be unemotional.
   c. encourage people to express their true emotions.
   d. profit from making customers more emotional.

10. People are likely to "get" a joke when they
    a. know something about more than one culture.
    b. have a different social background than the joke teller.
    c. understand the two different realities being presented.
    d. know why someone wants to tell the joke.

ANSWERS: 1 (b); 2 (d); 3 (b); 4 (c); 5 (d); 6 (a); 7 (c); 8 (b); 9 (a); 10 (c).

Essay Questions

1. Explain Erving Goffman's idea that we engage in a "presentation of self." What are the elements of this presentation? Apply this approach to an analysis of a professor teaching a class.

2. In what ways are human emotions rooted in biology? In what ways are emotions guided by culture?

Groups and Organizations

Groups and Organizations

HOW do groups affect how we behave?

WHY can *who* you know be as important as *what* you know?

In **WHAT** ways have large business organizations changed in recent decades?

We carry out much of our daily lives as members of small groups, such as sports teams, and large organizations, such as the businesses where we work. Both small groups and large organizations operate according to general rules, which this chapter explains.

Susanna Price © Dorling Kindersley

Walter Hodges/Getty Images Inc.—Stone Allstock (*background*)

Historic Site of the Original McDonalds

Back in 1948, people in Pasadena, California, paid little attention to the opening of a new restaurant by brothers Maurice and Richard McDonald. Yet this one small business would not only transform the restaurant industry but also introduce a new organizational model copied by countless businesses of all kinds.

The McDonald brothers' basic concept, which was soon called "fast food," was to serve meals quickly and cheaply to large numbers of people. The brothers trained employees to do highly specialized jobs: One person grilled hamburgers while others "dressed" them, made French fries, whipped up milkshakes, and presented the food to the customers in assembly-line fashion.

As the years went by, the McDonald brothers prospered, and they opened several more restaurants, including one in San Bernardino. It was there, in 1954, that Ray Kroc, a traveling blender and mixer salesman, paid them a visit.

Kroc was fascinated by the efficiency of the brothers' system and saw the potential for a whole chain of fast-food restaurants. The three launched the plan as partners. In 1961, in the face of rapidly increasing sales, Kroc bought out the McDonalds (who went back to running their original restaurant) and went on to become one of the great success stories of all time. Today, McDonald's has become one of the most widely known brand names in the world, with more than 30,000 restaurants that serve 50 million people daily throughout the United States and in 118 other countries around the world.

The success of McDonald's points to more than just the popularity of burgers and fries. The organizational principles that guide this company have come to dominate social life in the United States and elsewhere.

We begin this chapter with an examination of *social groups,* the clusters of people with whom we interact in everyday life. As you will learn, the scope of group life in the United States expanded greatly during the twentieth century. From a world of families, local neighborhoods, and small businesses, our society now turns on the operation of huge corporations and other bureaucracies that sociologists describe as *formal organizations.* Understanding this expanding scale of social life and appreciating what it means for us as individuals are the main objectives of this chapter.

Social Groups

Almost everyone wants a sense of belonging, which is the essence of group life. A **social group** is *two or more people who identify and interact with one another.* Human beings come together in couples, families, circles of friends, churches, clubs, businesses, neighborhoods, and large organizations. Whatever its form, a group is made up of people with shared experiences, loyalties, and interests. In short, while keeping their individuality, members of social groups also think of themselves as a special "we."

List all the groups in your life that you think of in terms of "we."

Not every collection of individuals forms a group. People all over the country with a status in common, such as women, homeowners, soldiers, millionaires, college graduates, and Roman Catholics, are not a group but a *category.* Though they know that others hold the same status, most are strangers to one another. Similarly, students sitting in a large stadium interact to a very limited extent. Such a loosely formed collection of people in one place is a *crowd* rather than a group.

However, the right circumstances can quickly turn a crowd into a group. Unexpected events, from power failures to terrorist attacks, can make people bond quickly with strangers.

Primary and Secondary Groups

Friends often greet one another with a smile and the simple phrase, "Hi! How are you?" The response usually is, "Fine, thanks. How about you?" This answer is often more scripted than truthful. Explaining how you are *really* doing would make most people feel so awkward that they would beat a hasty retreat.

Social groups are of two types, depending on their members' degree of personal concern for one another. According to Charles Horton Cooley (1864–1929), a **primary group** is *a small social group whose members share personal and lasting relationships.* Joined by *primary relationships,* people spend a great deal of time together, engage in a wide range of activities, and feel that they know one another pretty well. In short, they show real concern for one another. The family is every society's most important primary group.

Cooley called personal and tightly integrated groups "primary" because they are among the first groups we experience in life. In

GROUPS AND ORGANIZATIONS

Chapter Overview

This chapter analyzes social groups, both small and large, highlighting the differences between them. Then the focus shifts to formal organizations that carry out various tasks in our modern society.

addition, family and friends have primary importance in the socialization process, shaping our attitudes, behavior, and social identity.

Members of primary groups help one another in many ways, but they generally think of the group as an end in itself rather than as a means to some goal. In other words, we prefer to think that family and friendship link people who "belong together." Members of a primary group also tend to view each other as unique and irreplaceable. Especially in the family, we are bound to others by emotion and loyalty. Brothers and sisters may not always get along, but they always remain "family."

In contrast to the primary group, the **secondary group** is *a large and impersonal social group whose members pursue a specific goal or activity*. In most respects, secondary groups have characteristics opposite to those of primary groups. *Secondary relationships* involve weak emotional ties and little personal knowledge of one another. Most secondary groups are short-term, beginning and ending without particular significance. Students in a college course, who interact but may not see one another after the semester ends, are one example of a secondary group.

Secondary groups include many more people than primary groups. For example, dozens or even hundreds of people may work together in the same company, yet most of them pay only passing attention to one another. In some cases, time may transform a group from secondary to primary, as with co-workers who share an office for many years and develop closer relationships. But generally, members of a secondary group do not think of themselves as "we." Secondary ties need not be hostile or cold, of course. Interactions among students, co-workers, and business associates are often quite pleasant even if they are impersonal.

Unlike members of primary groups, who display a *personal orientation*, people in secondary groups have a *goal orientation*. Primary group members define each other according to *who* they are in terms of family ties or personal qualities, but people in secondary groups look to one another for *what* they are, that is, what they can do for each other. In secondary groups, we tend to "keep score," aware of what we give others and what we receive in return. This goal orientation means that secondary-group members usually remain formal and polite. In a secondary relationship, therefore, we ask the question "How are you?" without expecting a truthful answer.

The Summing Up table reviews the characteristics of primary and secondary groups. Keep in mind that these traits define two types of groups in ideal terms; most real groups contain elements of both. For example, a women's group on a university campus may be quite large (and therefore secondary), but its members may identify strongly with one another and provide lots of mutual support (making it seem primary).

As human beings, we live our lives as members of groups. Such groups may be large or small, temporary or long-lasting, and can be based on kinship, cultural heritage, or some shared interest.

Getty Images, Inc.

Many people think that small towns and rural areas have mostly primary relationships and that large cities are characterized by more secondary ties. This generalization is partly true, but some urban neighborhoods—especially those populated by people of a single ethnic or religious category—are very tightly knit.

 List five social groups on campus that you belong to. In each case, is the group more primary or more secondary?

Group Leadership

How do groups operate? One important element of group dynamics is leadership. Though a small circle of friends may have no leader at all, most large secondary groups place leaders in a formal chain of command.

Two Leadership Roles

Groups typically benefit from two kinds of leadership. **Instrumental leadership** refers to *group leadership that focuses on the completion of tasks*. Members look to instrumental leaders to make plans, give

student 2 student

"I finally figured out why so many of the 'polite' questions we ask people never get a truthful answer!"

✤ tip

The chapter's topics have a historical flow. In the past, small, rural communities were built on primary relationships; today's large, urban areas encourage mostly secondary relationships and large, formal organizations.

SUMMING UP

Primary Groups and Secondary Groups

	Primary Group ⟵——————————⟶	Secondary Group
Quality of relationships	Personal orientation	Goal orientation
Duration of relationships	Usually long-term	Variable; often short-term
Breadth of relationships	Broad; usually involving many activities	Narrow; usually involving few activities
Perception of relationships	Ends in themselves	Means to an end
Examples	Families, circles of friends	Co-workers, political organizations

orders, and get things done. **Expressive leadership,** by contrast, is *group leadership that focuses on the group's well-being.* Expressive leaders take less interest in achieving goals than in raising group morale and minimizing tension and conflict among members.

Because they concentrate on performance, instrumental leaders usually have formal secondary relationships with other members. These leaders give orders and reward or punish members according to how much the members contribute to the group's efforts. Expressive leaders build more personal primary ties. They offer sympathy to a member going through tough times, keep the group united, and lighten serious moments with humor. Typically, successful instrumental leaders enjoy more *respect* from members and expressive leaders generally receive more personal *affection.*

Three Leadership Styles

Sociologists also describe leadership in terms of decision-making style. *Authoritarian leadership* focuses on instrumental concerns, takes personal charge of decision making, and demands that group members obey orders. Although this leadership style may win little affection from the group, a fast-acting authoritarian leader is appreciated in a crisis.

Democratic leadership is more expressive and makes a point of including everyone in the decision-making process. Although less successful in a crisis situation, democratic leaders generally draw on the ideas of all members to develop creative solutions to problems.

Laissez-faire leadership allows the group to function more or less on its own (*laissez-faire* in French means "leave it alone"). This style typically is the least effective in promoting group goals (White & Lippitt, 1953; Ridgeway, 1983).

Group Conformity

Groups influence the behavior of their members by promoting conformity. "Fitting in" provides a secure feeling of belonging, but at the extreme, group pressure can be unpleasant and even dangerous. As experiments by Solomon Asch and Stanley Milgram showed, even strangers can encourage conformity.

Asch's Research

Solomon Asch (1952) recruited students, supposedly to study visual perception. Before the experiment began, he explained to all but one member in a small group that their real purpose was to put pressure on the remaining person. Arranging six to eight students around a table, Asch showed them a "standard" line, as drawn on Card 1 in Figure 1, and asked them to match it to one of three lines on Card 2.

Anyone with normal vision could easily see that the line marked "A" on Card 2 is the correct choice. At the beginning of the experiment, everyone made the matches correctly. But then Asch's secret accomplices began answering incorrectly, leaving the uninformed student (seated at the table so as to answer next to last) bewildered and uncomfortable.

What happened? Asch found that one-third of all subjects chose to conform by answering incorrectly. Apparently, many of us are willing to compromise our own judgment to avoid the discomfort of being different, even from people we do not know.

Milgram's Research

Stanley Milgram, a former student of Solomon Asch's, conducted conformity experiments of his own. In Milgram's controversial study (1963, 1965; A. G. Miller, 1986), a researcher explained to male recruits

tip

Study the Summing Up table to be sure you understand the difference between primary and secondary groups.

tip

How groups affect the behavior of individuals is a key focus of social psychology. Solomon Asch and Stanley Milgram were well-known social psychologists.

that they would be taking part in a study of how punishment affects learning. One by one, he assigned the subjects to the role of teacher and placed another person—actually an accomplice of Milgram's—in a connecting room to pose as a learner.

The teacher watched as the learner was seated in what looked like an electric chair. The researcher applied electrode paste to one of the learner's wrists, explaining that this would "prevent blisters and burns." The researcher then attached an electrode to the wrist and secured the leather straps, explaining that these would "prevent excessive movement while the learner was being shocked." The researcher assured the teacher that although the shocks would be painful, they would cause "no permanent tissue damage."

The researcher then led the teacher back to the next room, explaining that the "electric chair" was connected to a "shock generator," actually a phony but realistic-looking piece of equipment with a label that read "Shock Generator, Type ZLB, Dyson Instrument Company, Waltham, Mass." On the front was a dial that appeared to regulate electric shock from 15 volts (labeled "Slight Shock") to 300 volts (marked "Intense Shock") to 450 volts (marked "Danger: Severe Shock").

Seated in front of the "shock generator," the teacher was told to read aloud pairs of words. Then the teacher was to repeat the first word of each pair and wait for the learner to recall the second word. Whenever the learner failed to answer correctly, the teacher was told to apply an electric shock.

The researcher directed the teacher to begin at the lowest level (15 volts) and to increase the shock by another 15 volts every time the learner made a mistake. And so the teacher did. At 75, 90, and 105 volts, the teacher heard moans from the learner; at 120 volts, shouts of pain; at 270 volts, screams; at 315 volts, pounding on the wall; after that, dead silence. None of forty subjects assigned to the role of teacher during the initial research even questioned the procedure before reaching 300 volts, and twenty-six of the subjects—almost two-thirds—went all the way to 450 volts. Even Milgram was surprised at how readily people obeyed authority figures.

Do you think that sociologists today would consider Milgram's research ethical? Why or why not?

Milgram (1964) then modified his research to see if groups of ordinary people—not authority figures—could pressure people to administer electrical shocks, as Asch's groups had pressured individuals to match lines incorrectly.

This time, Milgram formed a group of three teachers, two of whom were his accomplices. Each of the three teachers was to suggest

a shock level when the learner made an error; the rule was that the group would then administer the *lowest* of the three suggested levels. This arrangement gave the person not "in" on the experiment the power to deliver a lesser shock regardless of what the others said.

The accomplices suggested increasing the shock level with each error, putting pressure on the third member to do the same. The subjects in these groups applied voltages three to four times higher than the levels applied by subjects acting alone. In this way, Milgram showed that people are likely to follow the lead of not only legitimate authority figures but also groups of ordinary individuals, even when it means harming another person.

Janis's "Groupthink"

Experts also cave in to group pressure, says Irving L. Janis (1972, 1989). Janis argues that a number of U.S. foreign policy errors, including the failure to foresee Japan's attack on Pearl Harbor during World War II and our ill-fated involvement in the Vietnam War, resulted from group conformity among our highest-ranking political leaders.

Common sense tells us that group discussion improves decision making. Janis counters that group members often seek agreement that closes off other points of view. Janis called this process **groupthink,** *the tendency of group members to conform, resulting in a narrow view of some issue.*

A classic example of groupthink led to the failed invasion of Cuba at the Bay of Pigs in 1961. Looking back, Arthur Schlesinger Jr., an adviser to President John F. Kennedy, confessed to feeling guilty for

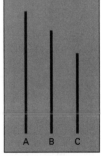

Card 1   Card 2

FIGURE 1 Cards Used in Asch's Experiment in Group Conformity

In Asch's experiment, subjects were asked to match the line on Card 1 to one of the lines on Card 2. Many subjects agreed with the wrong answers given by others in their group.

Source: Asch (1952).

"having kept so quiet during those crucial discussions in the Cabinet Room," adding that the group discouraged anyone from challenging what, in hindsight, Schlesinger considered "nonsense" (quoted in Janis, 1972:30, 40). Groupthink may also have been a factor in 2003 when U.S. leaders went to war on the assumption that Iraq had stockpiles of weapons of mass destruction.

Reference Groups

How do we assess our own attitudes and behavior? Frequently, we use a **reference group,** *a social group that serves as a point of reference in making evaluations and decisions.*

A young man who imagines his family's response to a woman he is dating is using his family as a reference group. A supervisor who tries to predict her employees' reaction to a new vacation policy is using them in the same way. As these examples suggest, reference groups can be primary or secondary. In either case, our need to conform shows how others' attitudes affect us.

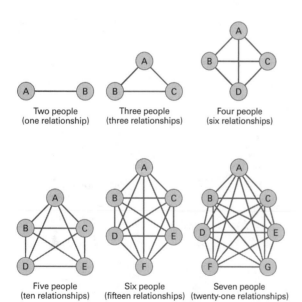

FIGURE 2   Group Size and Relationships

As the number of people in a group increases, the number of relationships that link them increases much faster. By the time six or seven people share a conversation, the group usually divides into two. Why are relationships in smaller groups typically more intense?

Source: Created by the author.

We also use groups that we do *not* belong to for reference. Being well prepared for a job interview means showing up dressed the way people in that company dress for work. Conforming to groups we do not belong to is a strategy to win acceptance and illustrates the process of *anticipatory socialization.*

Stouffer's Research

Samuel A. Stouffer and his colleagues (1949) conducted a classic study of reference group dynamics during World War II. Researchers asked soldiers to rate their own or any competent soldier's chances of promotion in their army unit. You might guess that soldiers serving in outfits with a high promotion rate would be optimistic about advancement. Yet Stouffer's research pointed to the opposite conclusion: Soldiers in army units with low promotion rates were actually more positive about their chances to move ahead.

The key to understanding Stouffer's results lies in the groups against which soldiers measured themselves. Those assigned to units with lower promotion rates looked around them and saw people making no more headway than they were. That is, although they had not been promoted, neither had many others, so they did not feel slighted. However, soldiers in units with a higher promotion rate could easily think of people who had been promoted sooner or more often than they had. With such people in mind, even soldiers who had been promoted were likely to feel shortchanged.

The point is that we do not make judgments about ourselves in isolation, nor do we compare ourselves with just anyone. Regardless of our situation in *absolute* terms, we form a subjective sense of our well-being by looking at ourselves *relative* to specific reference groups.

In-Groups and Out-Groups

Each of us favors some groups over others, based on political outlook, social prestige, or even just manner of dress. On the college campus, for example, left-leaning student activists may look down on fraternity members, whom they consider too conservative; fraternity members, in turn, may snub the computer "nerds," who they feel work too hard. People in every social setting make positive and negative evaluations of members of other groups.

Such judgments illustrate another important element of group dynamics: the opposition of in-groups and out-groups. An **in-group** is *a social group toward which a member feels respect and loyalty.* An in-group exists in relation to an **out-group,** *a social group toward which a person feels a sense of competition or opposition.* In-groups and out-groups are based on the idea that "we" have valued traits that "they" lack.

Tensions between groups sharpen the groups' boundaries and give people a clearer social identity. However, members of in-groups

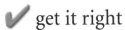

generally hold overly positive views of themselves and unfairly negative views of various out-groups.

Power also plays a part in intergroup relations. A powerful in-group can define others as a lower-status out-group. Historically, in countless U.S. towns and cities, many white people viewed people of color as an out-group and subordinated them socially, politically, and economically. Internalizing these negative attitudes, minorities often struggle to overcome negative self-images. In this way, in-groups and out-groups foster loyalty but also generate conflict (Tajfel, 1982; Bobo & Hutchings, 1996).

 In terms of in-groups and out-groups, explain what happens when people who may not like each other discover that they have a common enemy.

Group Size

The next time you go to a party, try to arrive first. If you do, you will be able to watch some fascinating group dynamics. Until about six people enter the room, every person who arrives shares a single conversation. As more people arrive, the group divides into two clusters, and it divides again and again as the party grows. Size plays an important role in how group members interact.

To understand why, note the mathematical number of relationships among two to seven people. As shown in Figure 2, two people form a single relationship; adding a third person results in three relationships; adding a fourth person yields six. Increasing the number of people one at a time, then, expands the number of relationships much more rapidly since every new individual can interact with everyone already there. Thus by the time seven people join one conversation, twenty-one "channels" connect them. With so many open channels, some people begin to feel left out, and the group usually divides.

The Dyad

The German sociologist Georg Simmel (1858–1918) studied social dynamics in the smallest groups. Simmel (1950, orig. 1902) used the term **dyad** (Greek for "pair") to designate *a social group with two members.*

Simmel explained that social interaction in a dyad is typically more intense than in larger groups because neither member shares the other's attention with anyone else. In the United States, love affairs, marriages, and the closest friendships are dyadic.

But like a stool with only two legs, dyads are unstable. Both members of a dyad must work to keep the relationship going; if either withdraws, the group collapses. Because the stability of marriages is

important to society, the marital dyad is supported by legal, economic, and often religious ties.

The Triad

Simmel also studied the **triad**, *a social group with three members,* which contains three relationships, each uniting two of the three people. A triad is more stable than a dyad because one member can act as a mediator should the relationship between the other two become strained. Such group dynamics help explain why members of a dyad (say, a married couple) often seek out a third person (such as a counselor) to discuss tensions between them.

The triad, illustrated by Jonathan Green's painting *Friends,* includes three people. A triad is more stable than a dyad because conflict between any two persons can be mediated by the third member. Even so, should the relationship between any two become more intense in a positive sense, those two are likely to exclude the third.

Jonathan Green, *Friends,* 1992. Oil on masonite, 14 in. × 11 in. © Jonathan Green, Naples, Florida. Collection of Patric McCoy.

 get it right

Is a network a group? No, because there is no common identification or frequent interaction among members. But fuzzy or not, networks are a valuable resource, which is probably the best reason to understand a little about how they work.

On the other hand, two of the three can pair up to press their views on the third, or two may intensify their relationship, leaving the other feeling left out. For example, when two of the three develop a romantic interest in each other, they will come to understand the old saying, "Two's company, three's a crowd."

As groups grow beyond three people, they become more stable and capable of withstanding the loss of one or more members. At the same time, increases in group size reduce the intense personal interaction possible only in the smallest groups. This is why larger groups are based less on personal attachment and more on formal rules and regulations.

Social Diversity: Race, Class, and Gender

Race, ethnicity, class, and gender each play a part in group dynamics. Peter Blau (1977; Blau, Blum, & Schwartz, 1982; South & Messner, 1986) points out three ways in which social diversity influences intergroup contact:

Today's college campuses value social diversity. One of the challenges of this movement is ensuring that all categories of students are fully integrated into campus life. This is not always easy. Following Blau's theory of group dynamics, as the number of minority students increases, these men and women are able to form a group unto themselves, perhaps interacting less with others.

Spencer Grant/PhotoEdit Inc.

1. **Large groups turn inward.** Blau explains that the larger a group is, the more likely its members are to have relationships just among themselves. To enhance social diversity, a college increases the number of international students. These students may add a dimension of difference, but as their numbers rise, they become more likely to form their own social group. Thus efforts to promote social diversity may have the unintended effect of promoting separatism.

2. **Heterogeneous groups turn outward.** The more internally diverse a group is, the more likely its members are to interact with outsiders. Members of campus groups that recruit people of both sexes and various social backgrounds typically have more intergroup contact than those with members of one social category.

3. **Physical boundaries create social boundaries.** To the extent that a social group is physically segregated from others (by having its own dorm or dining area, for example), its members are less likely to interact with other people.

Networks

A **network** is *a web of weak social ties.* Think of a network as a "fuzzy" group containing people who come into occasional contact but who lack a sense of boundaries and belonging. If a group is a "circle of friends," then a network might be described as a "social web" expanding outward, often reaching great distances and including large numbers of people.

Some networks come close to being groups, as is the case with college classmates who stay in touch after graduation through class newsletters and reunions. More commonly, however, a network includes people we *know of*—or who *know of us*—but with whom we interact rarely, if at all. As one woman with a widespread reputation as a community organizer explains, "I get calls at home, someone says, 'Are you Roseann Navarro? Somebody told me to call you. I have this problem. . . .'" (quoted in Kaminer, 1984:94).

Computer technology has created new networks on the college campus. "In the *Times*" looks at some issues raised by the popularity of facebook.com.

Network ties often give us the sense that we live in a "small world." In a classic experiment, Stanley Milgram (1967; Watts, 1999) gave letters to subjects in Kansas and Nebraska intended for a few specific people in Boston who were unknown to the original subjects. No addresses were supplied, and the subjects in the study were told to send the letters to others they knew personally who might know the target people. Milgram found that the target people received the letters with, on average, six subjects passing them on. This result led Milgram to conclude that just

The New York Times

NYT Archive Since 1981 | Search

 ▸ Get Home Delivery | New York Cloudy 48°F

MARKET
REAL ESTATE
AUTOS
ALL CLASSIFIEDS

WORLD
U.S.
Politics
Washington
Education
N.Y./REGION
BUSINESS
TECHNOLOGY
SPORTS
SCIENCE
HEALTH
OPINION
ARTS
Books
Movies
Music
Television
Theater
STYLE
Dining & Wine
Fashion & Style
Home & Garden
Weddings/
Celebrations
TRAVEL

Blogs
Cartoons
Classifieds
Corrections
Crossword/
Games
First Look
Learning
Network
Multimedia
NYC Guide
Obituaries
Podcasts
The Public
Editor
Sunday
Magazine
Weather
Week in Review

NEWSPAPER
Get Home
Delivery
Customer Care
TimesPoints

In Your Facebook.com

By NANCY HASS
January 8, 2006

As far as Kyle Stoneman is concerned, the campus police were the ones who started the Facebook wars. "We were just being, well, college students, and they used it against us," says Mr. Stoneman, a senior at George Washington University in Washington. He is convinced that the campus security force got wind of a party he and some buddies were planning last year by monitoring Facebook.com, the phenomenally popular college networking site. The officers waited till the shindig was in full swing, Mr. Stoneman grouses, then shut it down on discovering under-age drinking.

Mr. Stoneman and his friends decided to fight back. Their weapon of choice? Facebook, of course.

Once again they used the site, which is visited by more than 80 percent of the student body, to chat up a beer blast. But this time, when the campus police showed up, they found 40 students and a table of cake and cookies, all decorated with the word "beer." "We even set up a cake-pong table," a twist on the beer-pong drinking game, he says. "The look on the faces of the cops was priceless." As the coup de grâce, he posted photographs of the party on Facebook, including a portrait of one nonplussed officer. . . .

The stunt could be read as a sign that Facebook has become more than a way for young people to stay in touch. Started in 2004 by Harvard students who wanted to animate the black-and-white thumbnail photos of freshman directories, the site is the ninth most visited on the Internet, according to Nielsen/Net Ratings, and is used by nearly five million college students. . . .

Because of its popularity, though, the site has become a flashpoint for debates about free speech, privacy and whether the Internet should be a tool for surveillance. It has also raised concerns from parents, administrators and even students about online "addiction." "There are people on this campus who are totally obsessed with it, who check their profile 5, 6, 20 times a day," says Ingrid Gallagher, a sophomore at the University of Michigan. "But I think that more and more people are realizing that it also has a dark side."

Her estimates are not far off. Nearly three-quarters of Facebook users sign on at least once every 24 hours, and the average users sign on six times a day, says Chris Hughes, a spokesman for the site. . . .

One of the most attractive features to many students is that they can track down friends from high school at other colleges. Users can also join or form groups with names that run from the prosaic ("Campus Republicans") to the prurient ("We Need to Have Sex in Widener Before We Graduate") and the dadaesque ("I Am Fond of Biscuits and Scones"). . . .

Facebook's charms are obvious even to administrators. "It's a fantastic tool for building community," says Anita Farrington-Brathwaite, assistant dean for freshmen at New York University. "In a school like ours that doesn't have an enclosed campus, it really gives people a way to find each other and connect." . . .

But concerns have flourished with Facebook's popularity. Despite safeguards placed on access—only those with valid university e-mail addresses, ending in edu, can register as users, and students can bar specific people from viewing their profiles—administrators and parents worry about cyberstalking. . . .

It's not just parents who are uneasy.

"Every girl I know has had some sort of weird experience," says Shanna Andus, a freshman at the University of California, Berkeley. "Someone gets on a 'friend list' of one of your friends and starts to contact you. They met you at a party or checked out your picture online or went to high school with someone you barely know. It's just a little creepy." . . .

But parents and administrators have another worry: that potential employers are wangling themselves e-mail addresses ending with edu . . . so that they can vet job applicants. Administrators at both N.Y.U. and Brandeis say on-campus employers use the site for just that purpose. Aware that many students post pictures and descriptions of their X-rated, booze-soaked exploits, administrators at Tufts and Texas Christian University began offering seminars in Facebook propriety last year.

Students themselves seem split on the issue of Facebook exposure: some are outraged that their youthful indiscretions may be used against them; others seem resigned to privacy being a fantasy in the age of the Internet. . . .

Ms. Farrington-Brathwaite acknowledges that the privacy issues presented by Facebook create challenges for administrators, even at liberal institutions like N.Y.U., which she says has not used the site to patrol student behavior. . . .

But Ms. Farrington-Brathwaite encourages resident advisers to come to her if they spot a Facebook cry for help, like an allusion to suicide. N.Y.U. has experienced a spate of student suicides in recent years. "Still, it's a difficult balancing act, preserving student privacy and freedom, yet not sticking our head in the sand," she says. . . .

WHAT DO YOU THINK?

1. Do you use Facebook.com? How popular is this Web site among students on your campus?

2. How might networking through sites such as Facebook affect your life in years to come?

3. What are the drawbacks and dangers of Web sites like this one?

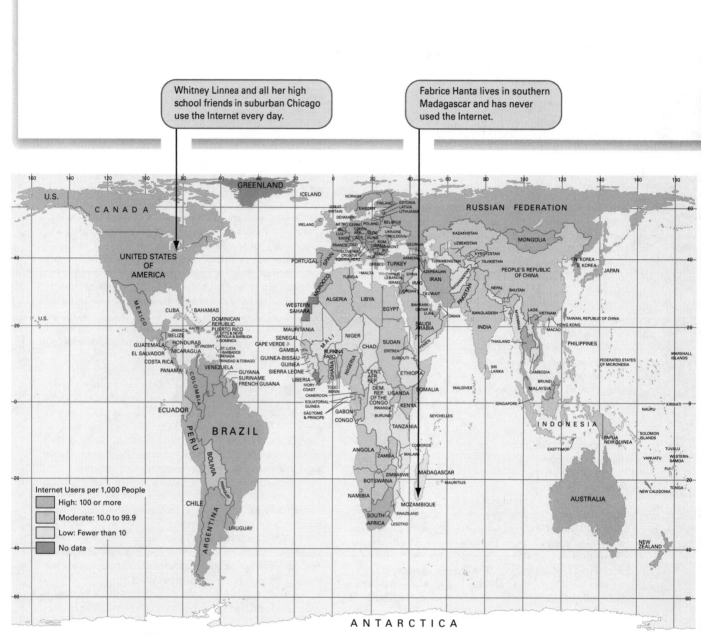

Whitney Linnea and all her high school friends in suburban Chicago use the Internet every day.

Fabrice Hanta lives in southern Madagascar and has never used the Internet.

Internet Users per 1,000 People

- High: 100 or more
- Moderate: 10.0 to 99.9
- Low: Fewer than 10
- No data

WINDOW ON THE WORLD

GLOBAL MAP 1 Internet Users in Global Perspective

This map shows how the Information Revolution has affected countries around the world. In most high-income nations, at least one-third of the population uses the Internet. By contrast, only a small share of people in low-income nations does so. What effect does this have on people's access to information? What does this mean for the future in terms of global inequality?

Sources: United Nations Development Programme (2006) and International Telecommunication Union (2007).

about everyone is connected to everyone else by "six degrees of separation." Later research, however, has cast doubt on Milgram's conclusions. Examining Milgram's original data, Judith Kleinfeld points out that most of Milgram's letters (240 out of 300) never arrived at all (Wildavsky, 2002). Those that did were typically given to people who were wealthy, a fact that led Kleinfeld to conclude that rich people are far better connected across the country than ordinary women and men.

Network ties may be weak, but they can be a powerful resource. For immigrants trying to become established in a new community, businesspeople seeking to expand their operations, or anyone

student **2** student

"My father always told me that the people I meet in college will be just as important as what I learn. Now I see where he was coming from."

 tip

Look at Global Map 1, which shows the share of a country's people using the Internet. What do you think is true about the numbers and importance of formal organizations in low- and high-Internet countries?

looking for a job, *whom* you know is often as important as *what* you know (Hagan, 1998; Petersen, Saporta, & Seidel, 2000).

Networks are based on people's colleges, clubs, neighborhoods, political parties, and personal interests. Obviously, some networks contain people with considerably more wealth, power, and prestige than others; that explains the importance of being "well connected." The networks of more privileged categories of people—such as the members of an expensive country club—are a valuable form of "social capital," which is more likely to lead people to higher-paying jobs (Green, Tigges, & Diaz, 1999; Lin, Cook, & Burt, 2001).

Some people also have denser networks than others; that is, they are connected to more people. Typically, the largest social networks include people who are young, well educated, and living in large cities (Fernandez & Weinberg, 1997; Podolny & Baron, 1997).

Gender also shapes networks. Although the networks of men and women are typically the same size, women include more relatives (and more women) in their networks, and men include more co-workers (and more men). Research suggests that women's ties do not carry quite the same clout as typical "old boy" networks. Even so, research suggests that as gender equality increases in the United States, the networks of women and men are becoming more alike (Reskin & McBrier, 2000; Torres & Huffman, 2002).

Finally, new information technology has generated a global network of unprecedented size in the form of the Internet. But the Internet has not yet linked the entire world. Global Map 1 shows that Internet use is high in rich countries and far less common in poor nations.

Formal Organizations

A century ago, most people lived in small groups of family, friends, and neighbors. Today, our lives revolve more and more around **formal organizations,** *large secondary groups organized to achieve their goals efficiently.* Formal organizations, such as business corporations and government agencies, differ from families and neighborhoods in their impersonality and their formally planned atmosphere.

Today's world has so many large organizations that we identify them just by initials: IRS, FBI, IBM, CIA, NATO, CNN, PTA, WWE, and so on. How many more examples can you think of?

When you think about it, organizing more than 300 million people in this country into a single society is truly remarkable, whether it involves paving roads, collecting taxes, schooling children, or delivering the mail. To carry out most of these tasks, we rely on different types of large formal organizations.

Types of Formal Organizations

Amitai Etzioni (1975) identified three types of formal organizations, distinguished by the reasons people participate in them: utilitarian organizations, normative organizations, and coercive organizations.

Utilitarian Organizations

Just about everyone who works for income belongs to a *utilitarian organization,* one that pays people for their efforts. Large businesses, for example, generate profits for their owners and income for their employees. Joining a utilitarian organization is usually a matter of individual choice, although most people must join one or another such organization to make a living.

Normative Organizations

People join *normative organizations* not for income but to pursue some goal they think is morally worthwhile. Sometimes called *voluntary associations,* these include community service groups (such as the PTA, the Lions Club, the League of Women Voters, and the Red Cross), as well as political parties and religious organizations. In global perspective, people living in the United States and other high-income nations with relatively democratic political systems are likely to join voluntary associations. A recent study found that 82 percent of first-year college students in the United States claimed to have participated in some volunteer activity within the past year (Curtis, Baer, & Grabb, 2001; Schofer & Fourcade-Gourinchas, 2001; Pryor et al., 2006).

Coercive Organizations

Membership in *coercive organizations* is involuntary. People are forced to join these organizations as a form of punishment (prisons) or treatment (some psychiatric hospitals). Coercive organizations have special physical features, such as locked doors and barred windows, and are supervised by security personnel. They isolate people, whom they label "inmates" or "patients," for a period of time in order to radically change their attitudes and behavior.

It is possible for a single organization to fall into all three categories. For example, a mental hospital serves as a coercive organization for a patient, a utilitarian organization for a psychiatrist, and a normative organization for a hospital volunteer.

tip

Bureaucracy was discussed extensively in Chapter 4 ("Society"). Read or review the section headed "Max Weber: The Rationalization of Society" on pages 101–5.

tip

The six traits listed here defined, for Weber, the *ideal* bureaucracy. This means that in its pure form, bureaucracy has all these traits.

Origins of Formal Organizations

Formal organizations date back thousands of years. Elites who controlled early empires relied on government officials to collect taxes, undertake military campaigns, and build monumental structures, from the Great Wall of China to the pyramids of Egypt.

However, early organizations had two limitations. First, they lacked the technology to let people travel over large distances, to communicate quickly, and to gather and store information. Second, the preindustrial societies elites were trying to rule had traditional cultures, so for the most part ruling organizations tried to preserve cultural systems, not to change them. But during the last few centuries, what Max Weber called a "rational worldview" emerged in parts of the world. In Europe and North America, the Industrial Revolution ushered in a new structure for formal organizations concerned with efficiency that Weber called "bureaucracy."

Characteristics of Bureaucracy

Bureaucracy is *an organizational model rationally designed to perform tasks efficiently.* Bureaucratic officials regularly create and revise policy to increase efficiency. To appreciate the power and scope of bureau-

cratic organization, consider that any one of more than 300 million telephones in the United States can connect you within seconds to any other phone in a home, business, automobile, or even a hiker's backpack on a remote trail in the Rocky Mountains. Such instant communication is beyond the imagination of people who lived in the ancient world.

Our telephone system depends on technology such as electricity, fiber optics, and computers. But the system could not exist without the bureaucracy that keeps track of every telephone call—noting which phone calls which other phone, when, and for how long—and then presents the relevant information to more than 100 million telephone users in the form of a monthly bill.

What specific traits promote organizational efficiency? Max Weber (1978, orig. 1921) identified six key elements of the ideal bureaucratic organization:

1. **Specialization.** Our ancestors spent most of their time looking for food and shelter. Bureaucracy, by contrast, assigns individuals highly specialized jobs.

2. **Hierarchy of offices.** Bureaucracies arrange personnel in a vertical ranking of offices. Each person is supervised by "higher-ups" in the organization while in turn supervising others in lower positions. With few people at the top and many at the bottom, bureaucratic organizations take the form of a pyramid.

3. **Rules and regulations.** Cultural tradition counts for little in a bureaucracy. Instead, rationally enacted rules and regulations guide a bureaucracy's operation. Ideally, a bureaucracy operates in a completely predictable way.

4. **Technical competence.** Bureaucratic officials and staff have the technical competence to carry out their duties. Bureaucracies typically hire new members according to set standards and then monitor their job performance. Such impersonal evaluation contrasts with the ancient custom of favoring relatives, whatever their talents, over strangers.

5. **Impersonality.** Bureaucracy puts rules ahead of personal whim so that both clients and workers are treated in the same way. From this impersonal approach comes the idea of the "faceless bureaucrat."

6. **Formal, written communications.** Someone once said that the heart of bureaucracy is not

Weber described the operation of the ideal bureaucracy as rational and highly efficient. In real life, actual large organizations often operate very differently from Weber's model, as shown on the popular television show *The Office.*

Chris Haston/NBCU Photo Bank

tip

Look closely at the Summing Up table to be sure
you understand the differences between small
groups and formal organizations.

SUMMING UP

Small Groups and Formal Organizations

	Small Groups	Formal Organizations
Activities	Much the same for all members	Distinct and highly specialized
Hierarchy	Often informal or nonexistent	Clearly defined, corresponding to offices
Norms	General norms, informally applied	Clearly defined rules and regulations
Membership criteria	Variable; often based on personal affection or kinship	Technical competence to carry out assigned tasks
Relationships	Variable and typically primary	Typically secondary, with selective primary ties
Communications	Typically casual and face to face	Typically formal and in writing
Focus	Person-oriented	Task-oriented

people but paperwork. Rather than casual, face-to-face talk, bureaucracy relies on formal, written memos and reports, which accumulate in vast files.

Give an example of each of the factors listed above in the operation of your college or university bureaucracy.

Bureaucratic organization promotes efficiency by carefully hiring workers and limiting the unpredictable effects of personal taste and opinion. The Summing Up table reviews the differences between small social groups and large bureaucratic organizations.

Organizational Environment

No organization operates in a vacuum. The performance of any organization depends not only on its own goals and policies but also on the **organizational environment,** *factors outside an organization that affect its operation.* These factors include technology, economic and political trends, current events, the available workforce, and other organizations.

Modern organizations are shaped by the *technology* of computers, telephone systems, and personal digital assistants (PDAs). Computers give employees access to more information and people than ever before. At the same time, computer technology allows managers to monitor closely the activities of workers (Markoff, 1991).

Economic and political trends affect organizations. All organizations are helped or hurt by periodic economic growth or recession. Most industries also face competition from abroad as well as changes in laws—such as new environmental standards—at home.

Current events can have significant effects on organizations that are far removed from the location of the events themselves. Events such as the rise in energy prices that followed the 2005 hurricanes that devastated the Gulf states and the 2006 elections that switched control of Congress from Republicans to Democrats affected both government and business organizations.

Population patterns also affect organizations. The average age, typical level of education, social diversity, and size of a local community determine the available workforce and sometimes the market for an organization's products or services.

Other organizations also contribute to the organizational environment. To be competitive, a hospital must be responsive to the insurance industry and to organizations representing doctors, nurses, and other health care workers. It must also be aware of the equipment and procedures available at nearby facilities, as well as their prices.

The Informal Side of Bureaucracy

Weber's ideal bureaucracy deliberately regulates every activity. In actual organizations, however, human beings are creative (and stubborn) enough to resist bureaucratic regulation. Informality may amount to simply cutting corners on your job, but it can also provide the flexibility needed to adapt and prosper.

In part, informality comes from the personalities of organizational leaders. Studies of U.S. corporations document that the qualities and quirks of individuals—including personal charisma, interpersonal skills, and the willingness to recognize problems—can have a great effect on organizational outcomes (Halberstam, 1986; Baron, Hannan, & Burton, 1999).

Authoritarian, democratic, and laissez-faire types of leadership (described earlier in this chapter) reflect individual personality as much as any organizational plan. In the "real world" of organizations, leaders sometimes seek to benefit personally by abusing organizational power. Recent high-profile examples include corporate scandals such as the collapse of Enron and other companies. More commonly, leaders take credit for the efforts of the people who work for them. For example, the authority and responsibilities of many secretaries are far greater than their official job titles and salaries suggest.

Communication offers another example of organizational informality. Memos and other written communications are the formal way to spread information throughout an organization. Typically, however, individuals also create informal networks, or "grapevines," that spread information quickly, if not always accurately. Grapevines, using both word of mouth and e-mail, are particularly important to rank-and-file workers because higher-ups often try to keep important information from them.

The spread of e-mail has "flattened" organizations somewhat, allowing even the lowest-ranking employee to bypass immediate superiors and communicate directly with the organization's leader or with all fellow employees at once. Some organizations object to "open-channel" communication and limit the use of e-mail. Microsoft Corporation (whose founder, Bill Gates, has an unlisted e-mail address that helps him limit his mail to hundreds of messages each day) has developed "screens" that filter out messages from everyone except certain approved people (Gwynne & Dickerson, 1997).

Using new information technology as well as age-old human ingenuity, members of organizations often try to break free of rigid rules in order to personalize procedures and surroundings. Such efforts suggest that we should now take a closer look at some of the problems of bureaucracy.

Problems of Bureaucracy

We rely on bureaucracy to manage everyday life efficiently, but many people are uneasy about large organizations. Bureaucracy can dehumanize and manipulate us, and some say it poses a threat to political democracy.

Bureaucratic Alienation

Max Weber held up bureaucracy as a model of productivity. However, Weber was keenly aware of bureaucracy's ability to *dehumanize* the people it is supposed to serve. The same impersonality that fosters efficiency also keeps officials and clients from responding to one another's unique personal needs. Typically, officials at large government and corporate agencies must treat each client impersonally as a standard "case."

Formal organizations cause *alienation,* according to Weber, by reducing the human being to "a small cog in a ceaselessly moving mechanism" (1978:988, orig. 1921). Although formal organizations are intended to benefit humanity, Weber feared that humanity might well end up serving formal organizations.

Bureaucratic Inefficiency and Ritualism

On Labor Day 2005, as people in New Orleans and other coastal areas were battling to survive in the wake of Hurricane Katrina, 600

George Tooker's painting *Government Bureau* is a powerful statement about the human costs of bureaucracy. The artist paints members of the public in a drab sameness—reduced from human beings to mere "cases" to be disposed of as quickly as possible. Set apart from others by their positions, officials are "faceless bureaucrats" concerned more with numbers than with providing genuine assistance (notice that the artist places the fingers of the officials on calculators).

George Tooker, *Government Bureau*, 1956. Egg tempera on gesso panel, 19⅝ × 29⅝ inches. The Metropolitan Museum of Art, George A. Hearn Fund, 1956 (56.78). Photograph Courtesy of The Metropolitan Museum of Art.

tip

Although Weber claimed that bureaucracy in its ideal form is a rational and efficient type of organization, most of us think of real-life bureaucracy as inefficient. The section outlining the problems of bureaucracy explains why this is often the case.

tip

The discussion of oligarchy suggests that the most serious problem with formal organization may not be inefficiency but weakening democracy and giving power to elites.

firefighters from around the country assembled in a hotel meeting room in Atlanta awaiting deployment. Officials of the Federal Emergency Management Agency (FEMA) explained to the crowd that they were first going to be given a lecture on "equal opportunity, sexual harassment, and customer service." Then, the official continued, they would each be given a stack of FEMA pamphlets with the agency's phone number to distribute to people in the devastated areas. A firefighter stood up and shouted, "This is ridiculous! Our fire departments and mayors sent us down here to save lives, and you've got us doing *this*?" The FEMA official thundered back, "You are now employees of FEMA, and you will follow orders and do what you are told" ("Places," 2005:39).

Criticism of the government response to the hurricane disaster of 2005 was widespread and pointed to the problem of bureaucratic *inefficiency*, the failure of an organization to carry out the work that it exists to perform. People sometimes describe the problem of inefficiency by saying that an organization has too much *red tape*, a term that refers to the red tape used by eighteenth-century English administrators to wrap official parcels and records (Shipley, 1985).

To Robert Merton (1968), red tape amounts to a new twist on the already familiar concept of group conformity. He coined the term **bureaucratic ritualism** to describe *a focus on rules and regulations to the point of undermining an organization's goals*. After the terrorist attacks of September 11, 2001, for example, the U.S. Postal Service continued to help deliver mail addressed to Osama bin Laden at a post office in Afghanistan, despite the objections of the FBI. It took an act of Congress to change the policy (Bedard, 2002).

Do you think FEMA or other large government organizations are inherently inefficient, or do you think their leaders sometimes make bad decisions? Explain your answer.

Bureaucratic Inertia

If bureaucrats sometimes have little reason to work especially hard, they have every reason to protect their jobs. Officials typically work to keep an organization going even after its original goal has been realized. As Weber put it, "Once fully established, bureaucracy is among the social structures which are hardest to destroy" (1978:987, orig. 1921).

Bureaucratic inertia refers to *the tendency of bureaucratic organizations to perpetuate themselves*. Formal organizations tend to take on a life of their own beyond their formal objectives. For example, the U.S. Department of Agriculture has offices in nearly every county in all fifty states, even though only one county in seven has any working farms. Usually, an organization stays in business by redefining its goals. For example, the Agriculture Department now performs a

broad range of work not directly related to farming, including nutritional and environmental research.

Oligarchy

Early in the twentieth century, Robert Michels (1876–1936) pointed out the link between bureaucracy and political **oligarchy**, *the rule of the many by the few* (1949, orig. 1911). According to what Michels called "the iron law of oligarchy," the pyramid shape of bureaucracy places a few leaders in charge of the resources of the entire organization.

Max Weber credited a strict hierarchy of responsibility with high organizational efficiency. But Michels countered that this hierarchical structure also concentrates power and thus threatens democracy because officials can and often do use their access to information, resources, and the media to promote their personal interests.

Furthermore, bureaucracy helps distance officials from the public, as in the case of the corporate president or public official who is "unavailable for comment" to the local press or the U.S. president who withholds documents from Congress claiming "executive privilege." Oligarchy, then, thrives in the hierarchical structure of bureaucracy and reduces the accountability of leaders to the people (Tolson, 1995).

Political competition, term limits, and a system of checks and balances prevent the U.S. government from becoming an out-and-out oligarchy. Even so, incumbents enjoy a significant advantage in U.S. politics. In recent congressional elections, only about 5 percent of officeholders running for reelection were defeated by their challengers.

The Evolution of Formal Organizations

The problems of bureaucracy—especially the alienation it produces and its tendency toward oligarchy—stem from two organizational traits: hierarchy and rigidity. To Weber, bureaucracy was a top-down system: Rules and regulations made at the top guide every facet of people's lives down the chain of command. A century ago in the United States, Weber's ideas took hold in an organizational model called *scientific management*. We take a look at this model and then examine three challenges over the course of the twentieth century that gradually led to a new model: the *flexible organization*.

Scientific Management

Frederick Winslow Taylor (1911) had a simple message: Most businesses in the United States were sadly inefficient. Managers had little idea of how to increase their business's output, and workers relied on the same tired skills of earlier generations. To increase efficiency,

Taylor explained, business should apply the principles of science. **Scientific management,** then, is *the application of scientific principles to the operation of a business or other large organization.*

Scientific management involves three steps. First, managers carefully observe the task performed by each worker, identifying all the operations involved and measuring the time needed for each. Second, managers analyze their data, trying to discover ways for workers to perform each job more efficiently. For example, managers might decide to give the worker different tools or to reposition various work operations within the factory. Third, management provides guidance and incentives for workers to do their jobs more quickly. If a factory worker moves 20 tons of pig iron in one day, for example, management shows the worker how to do the job more efficiently and then provides higher wages as the worker's productivity rises. Taylor concluded that if scientific principles were applied in this way, companies would become more profitable, workers would earn higher wages, and consumers would pay lower prices.

A century ago, the auto pioneer Henry Ford put it this way: "Save ten steps a day for each of 12,000 employees, and you will have saved fifty miles of wasted motion and misspent energy" (Allen & Hyman, 1999:209). In the early 1900s, the Ford Motor Company and many other businesses followed Taylor's lead and made improvements in efficiency.

A century ago, the principles of scientific management were applied to automobile production. Today, human workers stand alongside mechanical robots as cars make their way down the assembly line in a process that, in many respects, has changed little since Henry Ford's day.

Ron Sherman/Creative Eye/MIRA.com

The principles of scientific management suggested that workplace power should reside with owners and executives, who paid little attention to the ideas of their workers. As the decades passed, formal organizations faced important challenges, involving race and gender, rising competition from abroad, and the changing nature of work. We now take a brief look at each of these challenges.

The First Challenge: Race and Gender

In the 1960s, critics pointed out that big businesses and other organizations engaged in unfair hiring practices. Rather than hiring on the basis of competence as Weber had proposed, they had excluded women and other minorities, especially from positions of power. Hiring on the basis of competence is partly a matter of fairness; it is also a matter of increasing the source of talent to promote efficiency.

Patterns of Privilege and Exclusion

Even in the early twenty-first century, as shown in Figure 3, non-Hispanic white men in the United States—34 percent of the working-age population—still held 55 percent of management jobs. Non-Hispanic white women made up 34 percent of the population but held just 29 percent of managerial positions (U.S. Equal Employment Opportunity Commission, 2007). The members of other minorities lagged further behind.

Rosabeth Moss Kanter (1977; Kanter & Stein, 1979) points out that excluding women and minorities from the workplace ignores the talents of more than half the population. Furthermore, underrepresented people in an organization often feel like socially isolated out-groups—uncomfortably visible, taken less seriously, and given fewer chances for promotion.

Opening up an organization so that change and advancement happen more often, Kanter claims, improves everyone's on-the-job performance by motivating employees to become "fast-trackers" who work harder and are more committed to the company. By contrast, an organization with many dead-end jobs turns workers into less productive "zombies" who are never asked for their opinion on anything. An open organization encourages leaders to seek out the input of all employees, which usually improves decision making.

The "Female Advantage"

Some organizational researchers argue that women bring special management skills that strengthen an organization. According to Deborah Tannen (1994), women have a greater "information focus" and more readily ask questions in order to understand an issue. Men, on the other hand, have an "image

GROUPS AND ORGANIZATIONS

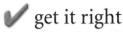

get it right
Be sure you understand the differences researchers have found in male and female behavior in large organizations.

focus" that makes them wonder how asking questions in a particular situation will affect their reputation.

In another study of women executives, Sally Helgesen (1990) found three other gender-linked patterns. First, women place greater value on communication skills than men and share information more than men do. Second, women are more flexible leaders who typically give their employees greater freedom. Third, compared to men, women tend to emphasize the interconnectedness of all organizational operations. Thus women bring a *female advantage* to companies striving to be more flexible and democratic.

In sum, one challenge to conventional bureaucracy is to become more open and flexible in order to take advantage of the experience, ideas, and creativity of everyone, regardless of race or gender. The result goes right to the bottom line: greater profits.

The Second Challenge:
The Japanese Work Organization

In 1980, the U.S. corporate world was shaken to discover that the most popular automobile model sold in this country was not a Chevrolet, Ford, or Plymouth but the Honda Accord, made in Japan. Today, the Japanese corporation Toyota is poised to pass General Motors to become the largest car maker in the world. This is quite a change. As late as the 1950s, U.S. auto makers dominated car production, and the label "Made in Japan" was generally found on products that were cheap and poorly made. The success of the Japanese auto industry, as well as companies making cameras and other products, has drawn attention to the "Japanese work organization." What has made Japanese companies so successful?

Japanese organizations reflect that country's strong collective spirit. In contrast to the U.S. emphasis on rugged individualism, the Japanese value cooperation. In effect, formal organizations in Japan are more like large primary groups. A generation ago, William Ouchi (1981) highlighted five differences between formal organizations in Japan and those in the United States. First, Japanese companies hired new workers in groups, giving everyone the same salary and responsibilities. Second, many Japanese companies hired workers for life, fostering a strong sense of loyalty. Third, with the idea that employees would spend their entire careers there, many Japanese companies trained workers in all phases of their operations. Fourth, although Japanese corporate leaders took final responsibility for their organization's performance, they involved workers in "quality circles" to discuss decisions that affected them. Fifth, Japanese companies played a large role in the lives of workers, providing home mortgages, sponsoring recreational activities, and scheduling social events. Together, such policies encourage much more loyalty among members of Japanese organizations than is typically the case in their U.S. counterparts.

> Compared to their percentage of the total population, white men are overrepresented in management positions.

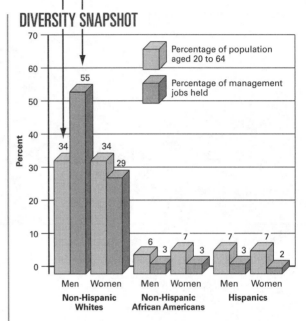

DIVERSITY SNAPSHOT

FIGURE 3   U.S. Managers in Private Industry by Race, Sex, and Ethnicity, 2005

White men are more likely than their population size suggests to be managers in private industry. The opposite is true for white women and other minorities. What factors do you think may account for this pattern?

Sources: U.S. Census Bureau (2006) and U.S. Equal Employment Opportunity Commission (2007).

Not everything has worked well for Japan's corporations. About 1990, the Japanese economy entered a recession that is only now coming to an end. During this downturn, many Japanese companies changed their policies, no longer offering workers jobs for life or many of the other benefits noted by Ouchi. But the long-term outlook for Japan's business organizations is bright.

The Third Challenge:
The Changing Nature of Work

Beyond rising global competition and the need to provide equal opportunity for all, pressure to modify conventional organizations is coming from changes in the nature of work itself. Rather than working in factories using heavy machinery to make *things,* more and more people are using computers and other electronic technology to create or process *information.* The postindustrial society, then, is characterized by information-based organizations.

student 2 student

"I worked at a fast-food restaurant during my sophomore year. I worked hard but I didn't have to think very much"

The best of today's information age jobs—including working at the popular search-engine Web site Google—allow people lots of personal freedom as long as they produce good ideas. At the same time, many other jobs—such as working the counter at McDonald's—involve the same routines and strict supervision found in factories a century ago.

Courtesy: Google Inc. (*left*); Michael Newman/PhotoEdit Inc. (*right*)

Frederick Taylor developed his concept of scientific management at a time when jobs involved tasks that, though often backbreaking, were routine. Workers shoveled coal, poured liquid iron into molds, welded body panels to automobiles on an assembly line, or shot hot rivets into steel girders to build skyscrapers. In addition, many of the industrial workers in Taylor's day were immigrants, most of whom had little schooling and many of whom knew little English. The routine nature of industrial jobs, coupled with the limited skills of the labor force, led Taylor to treat work as a series of fixed tasks, set down by management and followed by employees.

Many of today's information age jobs are very different: The work of designers, artists, writers, composers, programmers, business owners, and others now demands individual creativity and imagination. Here are several ways in which today's organizations differ from those of a century ago:

1. **Creative autonomy.** As one Hewlett-Packard executive put it, "From their first day of work here, people are given important responsibilities and are encouraged to grow" (cited in Brooks, 2000:128). Today's organizations now treat employees with information age skills as a vital resource. Executives can set production goals but cannot dictate how a worker is to accomplish tasks that require imagination and discovery. This gives highly skilled workers *creative freedom,* which means less day-to-day supervision as long as they generate good ideas in the long run.

2. **Competitive work teams.** Organizations typically give several groups of employees the freedom to work on a problem, offering the greatest rewards to those who come up with the best solution. Competitive work teams, a strategy first used by Japanese organizations, draw out the creative contributions of everyone and at the same time reduce the alienation often found in conventional organizations (Maddox, 1994; Yeatts, 1994).

3. **A flatter organization.** By spreading responsibility for creative problem solving throughout the workforce, organizations take on a flatter shape. That is, the pyramid shape of conventional bureaucracy is replaced by an organizational form with fewer levels in the chain of command, as shown in Figure 4.

4. **Greater flexibility.** The typical industrial age organization was a rigid structure guided from the top. Such organizations may accomplish a large amount of work, but they are not especially creative or able to respond quickly to changes in the larger environment. The ideal model in the information age is a more open, *flexible* organization that both generates new ideas and, in a rapidly changing global marketplace, adapts quickly.

What does all this mean for formal organizations? As David Brooks puts it, "The machine is no longer held up as the standard that healthy organizations should emulate. Now it's the ecosystem" (2000:128). Today's "smart" companies seek out intelligent, creative

tip

The Sociology@Work icons mark places in the text that apply sociology's insights to today's world of jobs.

people (America Online's main building is called "Creative Center One") and nurture the growth of their talents.

 Is your college or university a top-down bureaucracy or a flatter, more flexible organization? How might you find out?

Keep in mind, however, that many of today's jobs do not involve creative work at all. More correctly, the postindustrial economy has created two very different types of work: high-skill creative work and low-skill service work. Work in the fast-food industry, for example, is routine and highly supervised and thus has much more in common with the factory work of a century ago than with the creative teamwork typical of today's information organizations. Therefore, at the same time that some organizations have taken on a flexible, flatter form, others continue to use the rigid chain of command.

 Have you ever had a "dead-end" job? A job that demanded creativity? Which would you prefer and why?

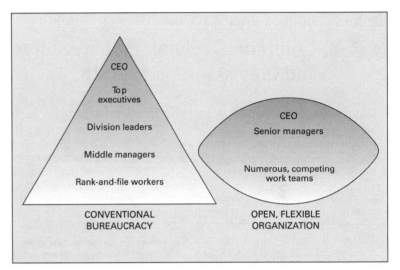

FIGURE 4 Two Organizational Models

The conventional model of bureaucratic organizations has a pyramid shape, with a clear chain of command. Orders flow from the top down, and reports of performance flow from the bottom up. Such organizations have extensive rules and regulations, and their workers have highly specialized jobs. More open and flexible organizations have a flatter shape, more like a football. With fewer levels in the hierarchy, responsibility for generating ideas and making decisions is shared throughout the organization. Many workers do their jobs in teams and have a broad knowledge of the entire organization's operation.

Source: Created by the author.

The "McDonaldization" of Society[1]

As noted in the opening to this chapter, McDonald's has enjoyed enormous success, now operating more than 30,000 restaurants in the United States and around the world. Japan has more than 2,400 Golden Arches, and the world's largest McDonald's is located in China's capital city of Beijing.

McDonald's is far more than a restaurant chain; it is a symbol of U.S. culture. Not only do people around the world associate McDonald's with the United States, but here at home, one poll found that 98 percent of schoolchildren could identify Ronald McDonald, making him as well known as Santa Claus.

Even more important, the organizational principles that underlie McDonald's are coming to dominate our entire society. Our culture is becoming "McDonaldized," an awkward way of saying that we model many aspects of life on this restaurant chain: Parents buy toys at worldwide chain stores like Toys 'Я' Us; we drive to Jiffy Lube for a ten-minute oil change; face-to-face communication is being replaced

more and more by e-mail, voice mail, and instant messaging; more vacations take the form of resorts and tour packages; television presents news in the form of ten-second sound bites; college admissions officers size up students they have never met by their GPA and SAT scores; and professors assign ghost-written textbooks[2] and evaluate students with tests mass-produced for them by publishing companies. The list goes on and on.

McDonaldization: Three Principles

What do all these developments have in common? According to George Ritzer (1993), the McDonaldization of society rests on three organizational principles:

1. **Efficiency.** Ray Kroc, the marketing genius behind the expansion of McDonald's, set out to serve a hamburger, French fries, and a milkshake to a customer in fifty seconds. Today, one of

---

[1]The term "McDonaldization" was coined by Jim Hightower (1975); much of this discussion is based on Ritzer (1993, 1998, 2000) and Schlosser (2002).

[2]A number of popular sociology books were not written by the person whose name appears on the cover. This book is not one of them. Even the test bank that accompanies this text was written by the author.

student 2 student

"Why do so many organizations collect so much personal information about us? I always ask people why they need to know something about me."

Controversy & Debate

Computer Technology, Large Organizations, and the Assault on Privacy

JAKE: I'm doing "MySpace"—It's really cool.
DUNCAN: Why do you want to put your whole life out there for everyone to see?
JAKE: I'm famous, man!
DUNCAN: You mean you're throwing away whatever privacy you have left . . .

Jake completes a page on Myspace.com, which includes his name and college, e-mail, photo, biography, and current personal interests. It can be accessed by billions of people around the world.

Late for a meeting with a new client, Sarah drives her car through a yellow light as it turns red at a main intersection. A computer linked to a pair of cameras notes the violation and takes one picture of her license plate and another of her sitting in the driver's seat. In seven days, she receives a summons to appear in traffic court.

Julio looks through his mail and finds a letter from a Washington, D.C., data services company telling

him that he is one of about 145,000 people whose name, address, Social Security number, and credit file have recently been sold to criminals in California posing as businesspeople. With this information, other people can obtain credit cards or take out loans in his name (A. Hamilton, 2001; O'Harrow, 2005).

These are all cases showing that today's organizations—which know more about us than ever before and more than most of us realize—pose a growing threat to personal privacy. Large organizations are necessary for today's society to operate. In some cases, organizations using information about us may actually be helpful. But cases of identity theft are on the rise, and personal privacy is on the decline.

In the past, small-town life gave people little privacy. But at least if people knew something about you, you were just as likely to know something about them. Today, unknown people "out there" can access information about each of us all the time.

In part, the loss of privacy is a result of more and more complex computer technology. Are you aware that every e-mail you send and every Web site you visit leaves a record in one or more computers? Most of these records can be retrieved by people you don't know, as well as by employers and other public officials.

---

the company's most popular items is the Egg McMuffin, an entire breakfast in a single sandwich. In the restaurant, customers dispose of their trash and stack their own trays as they walk out the door or, better still, drive away from the pickup window taking whatever mess they make with them. Such efficiency is now central to our way of life. We tend to think that anything done quickly is, for that reason alone, good.

2. **Uniformity.** The first McDonald's operating manual set the weight of a regular raw hamburger at 1.6 ounces, its size at 3.875 inches across, and its fat content at 19 percent. A slice of cheese weighs exactly half an ounce. Fries are cut precisely 9/32 of an inch thick.

Think about how many objects around your home, the workplace, and the campus are designed and mass-produced

according to a standard plan. Not just our environment but our life experiences—from traveling the nation's interstates to sitting at home viewing television—are more standardized than ever before.

Almost anywhere in the world, a person can walk into a McDonald's restaurant and purchase the same sandwiches, drinks, and desserts prepared in precisely the same way.[3]

---

[3] As McDonald's has "gone global," a few products have been added or changed according to local tastes. For example, in Uruguay, customers enjoy the McHuevo (hamburger with poached egg on top); Norwegians can buy McLaks (grilled salmon sandwiches); the Dutch favor the Groenteburger (vegetable burger); in Thailand, McDonald's serves Samurai pork burgers (pork burgers with teriyaki sauce); the Japanese can purchase a Chicken Tatsuta Sandwich (chicken seasoned with soy and ginger); Filipinos eat McSpaghetti (spaghetti with tomato sauce and bits of hot dogs); and in India, where Hindus eat no beef, McDonald's sells a vegetarian Maharaja Mac (B. Sullivan, 1995).

Another part of today's loss of privacy reflects the number and size of formal organizations. As explained in this chapter, large organizations tend to treat people impersonally, and they have a huge appetite for information. Mix large organizations with ever more complex computer technology, and it is no wonder that most people in the United States are concerned about who knows what about them and what people are doing with this information.

For decades, the level of personal privacy in the United States has been declining. Early in the twentieth century, when state agencies began issuing driver's licenses, for example, they generated files for every licensed driver. Today, officials can send this information at the touch of a button not only to the police but to other organizations as well. The Internal Revenue Service and the Social Security Administration, as well as government agencies that benefit veterans, students, the unemployed, and the poor, all collect mountains of personal information.

Business organizations now do much the same thing, and many of the choices we make end up in a company's database. Most of us use credit—the U.S. population now has more than 1 billion credit cards, an average of five per adult—but the companies that do "credit checks" collect and distribute information about us to almost anyone who asks, including criminals planning to steal our identity.

Then there are the small cameras found not only at traffic intersections but also in stores, public buildings, and parking garages and across college campuses. The number of surveillance cameras that monitor our movements is rapidly increasing with each passing year. So-called security cameras may increase public safety in some ways—say, by discouraging a mugger or even a terrorist—at the cost of the little privacy we have left.

After the September 11, 2001, terrorist attacks, the federal government took steps (including the USA PATRIOT Act) to strengthen national security. Today, government officials more closely monitor not just who enters the country but the activities of all of us. Increased national security and privacy do not mix.

Some legal protections remain. Each of the fifty states has laws that give citizens the right to examine some records about themselves kept by employers, banks, and credit bureaus. The federal Privacy Act of 1974 also limits the exchange of personal information among government agencies and permits citizens to examine and correct most government files. In response to rising levels of identity theft, Congress is likely to pass more laws to regulate the sale of credit information. But so many organizations, private as well as public, now have information about us—experts estimate that 90 percent of U.S. households are profiled in databases somewhere—that current laws simply cannot effectively address the privacy problem.

WHAT DO YOU THINK?

1. Do you believe that our concern about national security is destroying privacy? How can the loss of privacy threaten our security?

2. Do you use Internet sites such as http://www.myspace.com? Why do you think so many young people are eager to spread personal information in this way?

3. Have you checked your credit history recently? Do you know how to reduce the chances of someone stealing your identity? (If not, one place to start is http://www.stopidentitytheft.org).

Sources: Robert Wright (1998), "Online Privacy" (2000), A. Hamilton (2001), Heymann (2002), and O'Harrow (2005).

Uniformity results from a highly rational system that specifies every action and leaves nothing to chance.

3. **Control.** The most unreliable element in the McDonald's system is human beings. After all, people have good and bad days, sometimes let their minds wander, or simply decide to try something a different way. To minimize the unpredictable human element, McDonald's has automated its equipment to cook food at a fixed temperature for a set length of time. Even the cash register at McDonald's is keyed to pictures of the items so that ringing up a customer's order is as simple as possible.

Similarly, automatic teller machines are replacing bank tellers, highly automated bakeries now produce bread while people stand back and watch, and chickens and eggs (or is it eggs and chickens?) emerge from automated hatcheries. In supermarkets, laser scanners at self-checkouts are phasing out human checkers. We do most of our shopping in malls, where everything from temperature and humidity to the kinds of stores and products is carefully controlled and supervised (Ide & Cordell, 1994).

Can Rationality Be Irrational?

There is no doubt about the popularity or efficiency of McDonald's. But there is another side to the story.

Max Weber was alarmed at the increasing rationalization of the world, fearing that formal organizations would cage our imaginations and crush the human spirit. As Weber saw it, rational systems were efficient but dehumanizing. McDonaldization bears him out.

tip

The Applying Sociology in Everyday Life items provide additional ways for you to connect the ideas found in this chapter with your own life.

Each of the three principles just discussed limits human creativity, choice, and freedom. Echoing Weber, Ritzer states that "the ultimate irrationality of McDonaldization is that people could lose control over the system and it would come to control us" (1993:145). Perhaps even McDonald's understands this—the company has now expanded into more upscale, less McDonaldized restaurants such as Chipotle's and Pret-à-Manger that offer food that is more sophisticated, fresh, and healthful (Philadelphia, 2002).

The Future of Organizations: Opposing Trends

Early in the twentieth century, ever-larger organizations arose in the United States, most taking on the bureaucratic form described by Max Weber. In many respects, these organizations resembled armies led by powerful generals who issued orders to their captains and lieutenants. Foot soldiers, working in the factories, did what they were told.

With the emergence of a postindustrial economy around 1950, as well as rising competition from abroad, many organizations evolved toward a flatter, more flexible model that prizes communication and creativity. Such "intelligent organizations" (Pinchot & Pinchot, 1993; Brooks, 2000) have become more productive than ever. Just as important, for highly skilled people who now enjoy creative freedom, these organizations cause less of the alienation that so worried Weber.

But this is only half the story. Though the postindustrial economy has created many highly skilled jobs, it has created even more routine service jobs, such as those offered by McDonald's. Fast-food companies now represent the largest pool of low-wage labor, aside from migrant workers, in the United States (Schlosser, 2002). Work of this kind, which Ritzer terms "McJobs," offers few of the benefits that today's highly skilled workers enjoy. On the contrary, the automated routines that define work in the fast-food industry, telemarketing, and similar fields are very much the same as those that Frederick Taylor described a century ago.

Today, the organizational flexibility that gives better-off workers more freedom carries, for rank-and-file employees, the ever-present threat of "downsizing" (Sennett, 1998). Organizations facing global competition are eager to have creative employees, but they are also eager to cut costs by eliminating as many routine jobs as possible. The net result is that some people are better off than ever, while others worry about holding their jobs and struggle to make ends meet.

U.S. organizations are the envy of the world for productive efficiency. For example, there are few places on Earth where the mail arrives as quickly and dependably as it does in this country. But we should remember that the future is far brighter for some workers than for others. In addition, as the Controversy & Debate box on pages 184–85 explains, organizations pose an increasing threat to our privacy—something to keep in mind as we envision our organizational future.

Applying Sociology in Everyday Life

1. The next time you are eating at a fast-food restaurant, watch to see how not just employees but also customers are expected to behave in certain ways. For example, many such restaurants expect customers to line up to order, get their own drinks, find their own table, and clean up their own mess. What other norms are at work?

2. Visit any large public building with an elevator. Observe groups of people as they approach the elevator, and enter the elevator with them. Watch their behavior: What happens to conversations as the elevator doors close? Where do people fix their eyes? Can you explain these patterns?

3. Using campus publications or your school's Web page (and some assistance from an instructor), try to draw an organizational pyramid for your college or university. Show the key offices and how they supervise and report to one another.

MAKING THE GRADE

Groups and Organizations

What Are Social Groups?

SOCIAL GROUPS are two or more people who identify and interact with one another.

A **PRIMARY GROUP** is small, personal, and lasting (examples include family and close friends).

A **SECONDARY GROUP** is large, impersonal and goal-oriented, and often of shorter duration (examples include a college class or a corporation).

⊞ See the Summing Up table in this chapter.

ELEMENTS OF GROUP DYNAMICS

GROUP LEADERSHIP

- *Instrumental leadership* focuses on completing tasks.
- *Expressive leadership* focuses on a group's well-being.
- *Authoritarian leadership* is a "take charge" style that demands obedience; *democratic leadership* includes everyone in decision making; *laissez-faire leadership* lets the group function mostly on its own.

GROUP CONFORMITY

- The Asch, Milgram, and Janis research shows that group members often seek agreement and may pressure one another toward conformity.
- Individuals use *reference groups*—including both *in-groups* and *out-groups*—to form attitudes and make evaluations.

GROUP SIZE and DIVERSITY

- Georg Simmel described the *dyad* as intense but unstable; the *triad*, he said, is more stable but can dissolve into a dyad by excluding one member.
- Peter Blau claimed larger groups turn inward, socially diverse groups turn outward, and physically segregated groups turn inward.

NETWORKS are relational webs that link people with little common identity and limited interaction. Being "well connected" in networks is a valuable type of social capital.

social group two or more people who identify and interact with one another

primary group a small social group whose members share personal and lasting relationships

secondary group a large and impersonal social group whose members pursue a specific goal or activity

instrumental leadership group leadership that focuses on the completion of tasks

expressive leadership group leadership that focuses on the group's well-being

groupthink the tendency of group members to conform, resulting in a narrow view of some issue

reference group a social group that serves as a point of reference in making evaluations and decisions

in-group a social group toward which a member feels respect and loyalty

out-group a social group toward which a person feels a sense of competition or opposition

dyad a social group with two members

triad a social group with three members

network a web of weak social ties

What Are Formal Organizations?

FORMAL ORGANIZATIONS are large secondary groups organized to achieve their goals efficiently.

UTILITARIAN ORGANIZATIONS pay people for their efforts (examples include a business or government agency).

NORMATIVE ORGANIZATIONS have goals people consider worthwhile (examples include voluntary associations such as the PTA).

COERCIVE ORGANIZATIONS are organizations people are forced to join (examples include prisons and mental hospitals).

formal organization a large secondary group organized to achieve its goals efficiently

MAKING THE GRADE *continued . . .*

What Are Formal Organizations? *(continued)*

All formal organizations operate in an **ORGANIZATIONAL ENVIRONMENT** which is influenced by

- technology
- political and economic trends
- current events
- population patterns
- other organizations

organizational environment factors outside an organization that affect its operation

⊞ See the Summing Up table in this chapter.

Modern Formal Organizations: Bureaucracy

BUREAUCRACY, which Max Weber saw as the dominant type of organization in modern societies, is based on

- specialization
- hierarchy of offices
- rules and regulations
- technical competence
- impersonality
- formal, written communications

PROBLEMS OF BUREAUCRACY include

- bureaucratic alienation
- bureaucratic inefficiency and ritualism
- bureaucratic inertia
- oligarchy

bureaucracy an organizational model rationally designed to perform tasks efficiently

bureaucratic ritualism a focus on rules and regulations to the point of undermining an organization's goals

bureaucratic inertia the tendency of bureaucratic organizations to perpetuate themselves

oligarchy the rule of the many by the few

The Evolution of Formal Organizations

CONVENTIONAL BUREAUCRACY

In the early 1900s, Frederick Taylor's **SCIENTIFIC MANAGEMENT** applied scientific principles to increase productivity.

MORE OPEN, FLEXIBLE ORGANIZATIONS

In the 1960s, Rosabeth Moss Kanter proposed that opening up organizations for all employees, especially women and other minorities, increased organizational efficiency.

In the 1980s, global competition drew attention to the Japanese work organization's collective orientation.

scientific management Frederick Taylor's term for the application of scientific principles to the operation of a business or other large organization

THE CHANGING NATURE OF WORK

Recently, the rise of a postindustrial economy has created two very different types of work:

- highly skilled and creative work (examples include designers, consultants, programmers, and executives)
- low-skilled service work associated with the "McDonaldization" of society, based on efficiency, uniformity, and control (examples include jobs in fast-food restaurants and telemarketing)

MAKING THE GRADE

Sample Test Questions

These questions are similar to those found in the test bank that accompanies this textbook.

Multiple-Choice Questions

1. What term did Charles Cooley give to a small social group whose members share personal and lasting relationships?
   a. expressive group
   b. in-group
   c. primary group
   d. secondary group

2. Which type of group leadership is concerned with getting the job done?
   a. laissez-faire leadership
   b. secondary group leadership
   c. expressive leadership
   d. instrumental leadership

3. The research done by Solomon Asch, in which subjects were asked to pick lines of the same length, showed that
   a. groups encourage their members to conform.
   b. most people are stubborn and refuse to change their minds.
   c. groups often generate conflict.
   d. group members rarely agree on everything.

4. What term refers to a social group that someone uses as a point of reference in making an evaluation or decision?
   a. out-group
   b. reference group
   c. in-group
   d. primary group

5. A network is correctly thought of as
   a. the most close-knit social group.
   b. a category of people with something in common.
   c. a social group in which most people know one another.
   d. a web of weak social ties.

6. From the point of view of a nurse, a hospital is a
   a. normative organization.
   b. coercive organization.
   c. utilitarian organization.
   d. All of the above are correct.

7. Bureaucracy is a type of social organization characterized by
   a. specialized jobs.
   b. offices arranged in a hierarchy.
   c. lots of rules and regulations.
   d. All of the above are correct.

8. According to Robert Michels, bureaucracy always means
   a. inefficiency.
   b. oligarchy.
   c. alienation.
   d. specialization.

9. Rosabeth Moss Kanter claims that large business organizations
   a. need to "open up" opportunity to encourage workers to perform well.
   b. must have clear and stable rules to survive in a changing world.
   c. do well or badly depending on how talented the leader is.
   d. suffer if they do not adopt the latest technology.

10. The "McDonaldization of society" means that
    a. organizations can provide food for people more efficiently than families can.
    b. impersonal organizations concerned with efficiency, uniformity, and control are becoming more and more common.
    c. it is possible for organizations to both do their job and meet human needs.
    d. society today is one vast social network.

ANSWERS: 1 (c); 2 (d); 3 (a); 4 (b); 5 (d); 6 (c); 7 (d); 8 (b); 9 (a); 10 (b).

Essay Questions

1. How do primary groups differ from secondary groups? Give examples of each in your own life.

2. According to Max Weber, what are the six traits that define bureaucracy? What is the advantage of this organizational form? What are several problems that often go along with it?

Sexuality
and Society

If you think that sexuality is simply a matter of biology, think again. Sexually is constructed by society and is an important part of our everyday lives.

Doug Menuez/Getty Images, Inc.- Photodisc.

Sexuality and Society

WHAT is the sexual revolution, and how did it change U.S. society?

WHY do societies control people's sexual behavior?

HOW does sexuality play a part in social inequality?

Matt Sayles/AP Wide World Photos (*background*)

Blend Images/Alamy Images

Pam Goodman walks along the hallway with her friends Jen Delosier and Cindy Thomas. The three young women are sophomores at Jefferson High School, in Jefferson City, a small town in the Midwest.

"What's happening after school?" Pam asks.

"Dunno," replies Jennifer. "Maybe Todd is coming over."

"Got the picture," adds Cindy. "We're so gone."

"Shut up!" Pam stammers, smiling. "I hardly know Todd."

"OK, but . . ." The three girls break into laughter.

It is no surprise that young people spend a lot of time thinking and talking about sex. And as the sociologist Peter Bearman (Bearman, Moody, & Stovel, 2004) discovered, sex involves more than just talk. Bearman conducted confidential interviews with 832 students at the high school in a Midwestern town he called Jefferson City, learning that 573 (69 percent of the students) had had at least one "sexual and romantic relationship" during the previous eighteen months. So most, but certainly not all, of these students are sexually active.

Bearman wanted to learn about sexual activity in order to understand the problem of sexually transmitted diseases (STDs) among young people. Why are the rates of STDs so high? And why can there be sudden "outbreaks" of disease that involve dozens of young people in the community?

To find the answers to these questions, Bearman asked the students to identify their sexual partners (promising, of course, not to reveal any confidential information). This allowed him to trace connections between individual students in terms of sexual activity, which revealed a surprising pattern: Sexually active students were linked to each other through networks of common partners much more than anyone might have expected. In all, common partners linked half of the sexually active students, as shown in the diagram below.

Awareness of the connections among people can help us understand how STDs spread from one infected person to many others in a short period of time. Bearman's study also shows that research can teach us a great deal about human sexuality, which is an important dimension of social life. You will also see that sexual attitudes and behavior have changed dramatically over the past century in the United States.

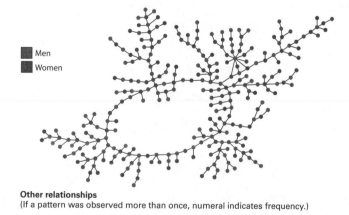

■ Men
■ Women

Other relationships
(If a pattern was observed more than once, numeral indicates frequency.)

2   2   9   12   63

Bearman et al. (2004).

Understanding Sexuality

How much of your thoughts and actions every day involve sexuality? If you are like most people, your answer would have to be "quite a lot," because sexuality is about much more than just having sex. Sexuality is a theme found almost everywhere—in sports, on campus, in the workplace, and especially in the mass media. There is also a sex industry that includes pornography and prostitution, both of which are multibillion-dollar businesses in this country. The bottom line is that sexuality is an important part of how we think about ourselves as well as how others think about us. For this reason, there are few areas of everyday life in which sexuality does not play some part.

Nevertheless, U.S. culture has long treated sex as taboo; even today, many people avoid talking about it. As a result, although sex can produce much pleasure, it also causes confusion, anxiety, and sometimes outright fear. Even scientists long considered sex off limits as a topic of research. Not until the middle of the twentieth century did researchers turn their attention to this vital dimension of social life. Since then, as this chapter explains, we have discovered a great deal about human sexuality.

Sex: A Biological Issue

Sex refers to *the biological distinction between females and males.* From a biological point of view, sex is the way humans reproduce. A female ovum and a male sperm, each containing twenty-three matching chromosomes (biological codes that guide physical development),

Chapter Overview

This chapter explains how society shapes human sexuality and also how sexuality figures into our everyday lives. Although sexuality is biological, society (including culture and patterns of inequality) shapes how we experience sexuality.

We claim that beauty is in the eye of the beholder, which suggests the importance of culture in setting standards of attractiveness. All of the people pictured here—from Morocco, South Africa, Nigeria, Myanmar, Japan, and Ecuador—are considered beautiful by members of their own society. At the same time, sociobiologists point out that in every society on Earth, people are attracted to youthfulness. The reason, as sociobiologists see it, is that attractiveness underlies our choices about reproduction, which is most readily accomplished in early adulthood.

Andre Gallant (*top left*); Pete Turner Studio (*top center*); Brun/Photo Researchers, Inc. (*top right*); Bruno Hadjih (*bottom left*); Elliot Erwitt/Magnum Photos, Inc. (bottom center); George Holton/Photo Researchers, Inc. (*bottom right*)

combine to form an embryo. To one of these pairs of chromosomes, which determines the child's sex, the mother contributes an X chromosome and the father contributes either an X or a Y. A second X from the father produces a female (XX) embryo; a Y from the father produces a male (XY) embryo. A child's sex is determined biologically at the moment of conception.

The sex of an embryo guides its development. If the embryo is male, the growth of testicular tissue starts to produce large amounts of testosterone, a hormone that triggers the development of male genitals (sex organs). If little testosterone is present, the embryo develops female genitals.

Look at the six photos on this page. Do you think that what people in a society consider beautiful is more a matter of biology or of culture? Explain your answer.

Sex and the Body

Some differences in the body set males and females apart. Right from birth, the two sexes have different **primary sex characteristics,** namely, *the genitals, organs used for reproduction.* At puberty, as people reach sexual maturity, additional sex differentiation takes place.

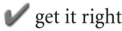
At this point, people develop **secondary sex characteristics,** *bodily development, apart from the genitals, that distinguishes biologically mature females and males.* Mature females have wider hips for giving birth, milk-producing breasts for nurturing infants, and deposits of soft, fatty tissue that provide a reserve supply of nutrition during pregnancy and breast feeding. Mature males typically develop more muscle in the upper body, more extensive body hair, and deeper voices. Of course, these are general differences; some males are smaller and have less body hair and higher voices than some females.

Keep in mind that sex is not the same thing as gender. *Gender* is an aspect of culture that refers to the personal traits and patterns of behavior (including responsibilities, opportunities, and privileges) that a culture attaches to being female or male.

Intersexual People

Sex is not always as clear-cut as has just been described. The term **intersexual people** refers to *people whose bodies (including genitals) have both female and male characteristics.* Another term for intersexual people is *hermaphrodites* (derived from Hermaphroditus, the child of the mythological Greek gods Hermes and Aphrodite, who embodied both sexes). A true hermaphrodite has both a female ovary and a male testis.

However, our culture demands that sex be clear-cut, a fact evident in the requirement that parents record the sex of their new child at birth as either female or male. In the United States, some people respond to hermaphrodites with confusion or even disgust. But attitudes in other cultures are quite different: The Pokot of eastern Africa, for example, pay little attention to what they consider a simple biological error, and the Navajo look on intersexual people with awe, seeing in them the full potential of both the female and the male (Geertz, 1975).

Transsexuals

Transsexuals are *people who feel they are one sex even though biologically they are the other.* Tens of thousands of people in the United States have experienced the feeling of being trapped in a body of the wrong sex and a desire to be the other sex. Most become *transgendered,* meaning that they begin to disregard conventional ideas about how females and males should look and behave. Many go one step further and undergo *gender reassignment,* surgical alteration of their genitals, usually accompanied by hormone treatments. This medical procedure is complex and takes months or even years, but it helps many people gain a joyful sense of finally becoming on the outside who they feel they are on the inside (Gagné, Tewksbury, & McGaughey, 1997).

 In 2001, San Francisco became the first city with a health plan for city employees that includes paying the cost of gender reassignment surgery (which can cost $50,000 or more). Would you support enacting similar policies in other places? Why or why not?

Sex: A Cultural Issue

Sexuality has a biological foundation. But like all aspects of human behavior, sexuality is also very much a cultural issue. Biology may explain some animals' mating rituals, but humans have no similar biological program. Although there is a biological "sex drive" in the sense that people find sex pleasurable and may want to engage in

The film *Transamerica* was the first widely seen Hollywood production about transsexuality. This story of a man who wishes to become a woman (played by Felicity Huffman) demonstrates that such a transformation involves much more than surgery. Imagine for a moment all the "complications" you would have to deal with if you were planning to change your sex.

IFC Films/Picture Desk, Inc./Kobal Collection

SEXUALITY AND SOCIETY

In Montana, marriage between first cousins is against the law.

In Indiana, first cousins Shawn and Delia Dawson were able to marry only because they are both 70 years old.

 tip

So much about sexuality varies from society to society. The incest taboo is one sexual element of culture that is found everywhere.

SEEING OURSELVES

NATIONAL MAP 1

First-Cousin Marriage Laws across the United States

There is no single view on first-cousin marriages in the United States: Twenty-four states forbid such unions, nineteen allow them, and seven allow them with restrictions.* In general, states that permit first-cousin marriages are found in New England, the Southeast, and the Southwest.

*Of the seven states that allow first-cousin marriages with restrictions, six states permit them only when couples are past childbearing age.

Source: "State Laws regarding Marriages" (2007).

---

sexual activity, our biology does not dictate any specific ways of being sexual any more than our desire to eat dictates any particular foods or table manners.

Cultural Variation

Almost every sexual practice shows considerable variation from one society to another. In his pioneering study of sexuality in the United States, Alfred Kinsey and his colleagues (1948) found that most heterosexual couples reported having intercourse in a single position—face to face, with the woman on the bottom and the man on top. Halfway around the world, in the South Seas, most couples *never* have sex in this way. In fact, when the people of the South Seas learned of this practice from Western missionaries, they poked fun at it as the strange "missionary position."

Even the simple practice of showing affection varies from society to society. Most people in the United States kiss in public, but the Chinese kiss only in private. The French kiss publicly, often twice (once on each cheek), and the Belgians kiss three times (starting on either cheek). The Maoris of New Zealand rub noses, and most people in Nigeria don't kiss at all.

Modesty, too, is culturally variable. If a woman stepping into a bath is disturbed, what body parts do you think she would cover? Helen Colton (1983) reports that an Islamic woman covers her face, a Laotian woman covers her breasts, a Samoan woman covers her navel, a Sumatran woman covers her knees, and a European woman covers her breasts with one hand and her genital area with the other.

Around the world, some societies restrict sexuality, and others are more permissive. In China, for example, norms closely regulate sexuality so that few people have sexual intercourse before they marry. In the United States, at least in recent decades, intercourse prior to marriage has become the norm, and some people choose to have sex even without a strong emotional commitment.

Cultural variation in standards for sexual expression means that moving from one society to another raises the risk of offending people whose beliefs may differ from your own. "In the *Times*" on page 196 describes one recent case in point.

The Incest Taboo

When it comes to sex, do all societies agree on anything? The answer is yes. One cultural universal—an element found in every society the world over—is the **incest taboo,** *a norm forbidding sexual relations or marriage between certain relatives.* In the United States, both law and cultural mores prohibit close relatives (including brothers and sisters, parents and children) from having sex or marrying. But in another example of cultural variation, exactly which family members are included in a society's incest taboo varies from state to state. National Map 1 shows that twenty-four U.S. states outlaw marriage between first cousins; twenty-six states do not.

Some societies (such as the North American Navajo) apply incest taboos only to the mother and others on her side of the family. There are also societies on record (including ancient Peru and Egypt) that have approved brother-sister marriages among the nobility to keep power within a single family (Murdock, 1965, orig. 1949).

Why does some form of incest taboo exist everywhere? Part of the reason is biology: Reproduction between close relatives of any species raises the odds of producing offspring with mental or physical problems.

The New York Times

MARKET
...ESTATE
AUTOS
ALL CLASSIFIEDS

WORLD
U.S.
Politics
Washington
Education
N.Y./REGION
BUSINESS
TECHNOLOGY
SPORTS
SCIENCE
HEALTH
OPINION
ARTS
Books
Movies
Music
Television
Theater
STYLE
Dining & Wine
Fashion & Style
Home & Garden
Weddings/
Celebrations
TRAVEL

Blogs
Cartoons
Classifieds
Corrections
Crossword/
Games
First Look
Learning
Network
Multimedia
NYC Guide
Obituaries
Podcasts
The Public
Editor
Sunday
Magazine
Weather
Week in Review

NEWSPAPER
Get Home
Delivery
Customer Care
TimesPoints

When a Kiss Is More than a Kiss

By PAUL VITELLO
May 6, 2007

Richard Gere, while not the first person you'd think most likely to invoke the wrath of a conservative religious mob by kissing somebody in public, was at least a passably recognizable symbolic target for Hindu demonstrators last week, when they burned his figure in effigy in cities across India.

If not a wavy-haired, pretty-faced, prostitute-patronizer-portraying American actor, then who are religious firebrands supposed to burn in effigy when a man violates a cultural taboo by kissing a woman in public, as Mr. Gere did? (He planted several lingering kisses on the neck of an Indian actress, Shilpa Shetty, at a televised charity event in Mumbai.)

Surely not Mahmoud Ahmadinejad.

But think again. When Mr. Ahmadinejad, the ultraconservative president of Iran, kissed the gloved hand last week of an elderly woman who had once been his school teacher, at a ceremony for a national teachers' day, he, too, received sharp rebukes from clerics.

Islamic religious leaders accused him of "indecency." Islamic newspapers noted that under Shariah law contact with a woman with whom one is not related is a crime sometimes punishable by death. . . .

Anthropologists and philematologists (people who study kissing) say the harsh reactions to Mr. Ahmadinejad's and Mr. Gere's kisses underline a certain cultural and political mystery about the seemingly simple act of kissing.

Kissing in public (private kissing exists in a different universe of discourse, and for the most part will remain there for the duration of this discussion) is quite often a public statement, they say: Witness the use of the public kiss in the lore of organized crime (to mean soon dead). Or in the political world, the moment in the 2000 campaign when Al Gore passionately kissed his wife, Tipper (to signify his Alpha-Maleness). Or the mostly forgotten but once infamous kiss Hillary Rodham Clinton planted on the cheek of Yasir Arafat's wife (signifying many things, not least of which that she would spend a good deal of time repairing relations with Jewish voters).

Vaughn M. Bryant Jr., an anthropologist at Texas A&M University, said that contrary to the lyrics of "As Time Goes By," a kiss is almost never just a kiss. It is a language with a grammar all its own, which is as strict as the syntax of international diplomacy.

"When people kiss, there are all kinds of hidden rules in play," he said. "Where they are; who they are to each other; what the relationship between the sexes is in a country; all that gets considered."

Robert Albro, a professor of anthropology at George Washington University, in Washington, D.C., who specializes in the role that culture plays in international relations, said Mr. Gere's

faux pas was an example of a cultural "border clash" that is increasingly common in the era of globalization.

To plant a kiss on the face of an Indian woman in public, he said, would be seen by conservative Indians as a trespass on "the cultural space" of their country.

"Women, in particular conspicuous women such as the actress, bear the burden of cultural identity in many parts of the world," he said. "They are like the social skin of society itself."

Kissing is more or less universal. People in all but a few, tiny cultures do it. And wherever people kiss, they practice the same categories of kissing that the Romans first identified: the "basium," for the standard romantic kiss; the "osculum," for the friendship kiss; and the "savium," the most passionate kind, sometimes referred to as a French kiss. (Mr. Ahmadinejad's was a classic osculum. Mr. Gere's was probably an osculum playfully masquerading as a basium that, unfortunately for Mr. Gere, may have looked a little too much like a savium on TV.)

Monkeys do not kiss. Apes do, but usually only on the arm or the chest, to show respect. "Except among the bonobos, there is nothing like sexual kissing among the apes," said Frans B. M. de Waal, a professor of primate behavior at Emory University. "Apes do not practice foreplay."

The earliest written record of humans' kissing appears in Vedic Sanskrit texts—in India—from around 1500 B.C., where certain passages refer to lovers "setting mouth to mouth," according to Mr. Bryant.

There is debate among scientists over whether the kiss is an innately human practice, or one that we fortuitously acquired along the way. Some trace it to the mother who made the first mouth-to-mouth transfer of pre-chewed food to her child; others to prettier biological Eureka-moments. But in general it is agreed that people kiss in private mainly because it is nice.

So what does it mean when people, especially public people, . . . commit kisses in public places? . . .

Robin Hicks, a cultural anthropologist, . . . said that when the kissing involves people of different ethnicities—especially a Western man and a local woman, as in the case of Mr. Gere's kiss in India—the cultural sensitivity of conservative-minded people is often greatly heightened.

WHAT DO YOU THINK?

1. Do you think the reaction to Richard Gere's public kissing of actress Shilpa Shetty was justified or not? Why?

2. What are some of our cultural rules for kissing?

3. Why does our more global way of life make it important to understand the rules for sexual expression elsewhere?

student 2 student

"Isn't sex supposed to be about biology? The birds and the bees? Here's another case where sociology delivers an unexpected—and very interesting—lesson."

tip

The following pages describe our society's increasing openness to sexuality, what we call the "sexual revolution." This did not happen all at once: It began in the 1920s and accelerated in the 1960s. The "sexual counterrevolution," a conservative response to these changes, began around 1980.

But why, of all living species, do only humans observe an incest taboo? This fact suggests that controlling sexuality among close relatives is a necessary element of *social* organization. For one thing, the incest taboo limits sexual competition in families by restricting sex to spouses (ruling out, for example, sex between parent and child). Second, because family ties define people's rights and obligations toward one another, reproduction between close relatives would hopelessly confuse kinship; if a mother and son had a daughter, would the child consider the male a father or a brother? Third, by requiring people to marry outside their immediate families, the incest taboo integrates the larger society as people look beyond their close kin when seeking to form new families.

The incest taboo has long been a sexual norm in the United States and throughout the world. But in this country, many other sexual norms have changed over time. In the twentieth century, as the next section explains, our society experienced both a sexual revolution and a sexual counterrevolution.

Sexual Attitudes in the United States

What do people in the United States think about sex? Our cultural attitudes about sexuality have always been somewhat contradictory. Most European immigrants arrived with rigid ideas about "correct" sexuality, typically limiting sex to reproduction within marriage. The early Puritan settlers of New England demanded strict conformity in attitudes and behavior, and they imposed severe penalties for any sexual "misconduct," even if it took place in the privacy of the home. Some regulation of sexuality has continued ever since. As late as the 1960s, several states legally prohibited the sale of condoms in stores. Until 2003, when the Supreme Court struck them down, laws in thirteen states banned sexual acts between partners of the same sex. Even today, "fornication" laws, which forbid intercourse by unmarried couples, are still on the books in eleven states.

But this is just one side of the story. As Chapter 3 ("Culture") explains, because U.S. culture is individualistic, many of us believe that people should be free to do pretty much as they wish as long as they cause no direct harm to others. The idea that what people do in the privacy of their own home is no one else's business makes sex a matter of individual freedom and personal choice.

When it comes to sexuality, is the United States restrictive or permissive? The answer is both. On one hand, many people in the United States still view sexual conduct as an important indicator of personal morality. On the other, sex is more and more a part of the mass media—one recent report concluded that the number of scenes in television shows with sexual content doubled in a mere ten years (Kunkel et al., 2005). Within this complex framework, we turn to

Over the course of the past century, social attitudes in the United States have become more accepting of human sexuality. What do you see as some of the benefits of this greater openness? What are some of the negative consequences?

Brand X Pictures/Alamy Images Royalty Free (*left*); Thomas Schweizer/Corbis/Bettmann (*right*)

Nancy Houck, now 73 years old, has lived most of her life in a social world where men have had much more sexual freedom than women.

Sarah Roholt, 47, is a baby boomer who feels that she and her women friends have pretty much the same sexual freedom as men.

DIVERSITY SNAPSHOT

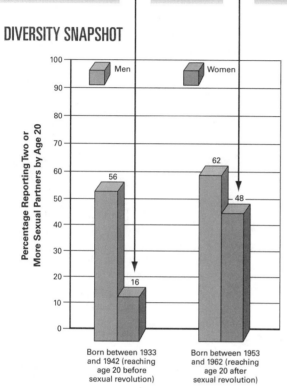

FIGURE 1   The Sexual Revolution: Closing the Double Standard

A larger share of men than women report having had two or more sexual partners by age twenty. But the sexual revolution greatly reduced this gender difference.

Source: Laumann et al. (1994:198).

changes in sexual attitudes and behavior that have taken place in the United States over the past century.

The Sexual Revolution

Over the course of the twentieth century, people witnessed major changes in sexual attitudes and practices. The first indications of this change came in the 1920s as millions of women and men migrated from farms and small towns to rapidly growing cities. There, living apart from their families and meeting new people in the workplace, young people enjoyed considerable sexual freedom, one reason the decade became known as the "Roaring Twenties."

In the 1930s and 1940s, the Great Depression and World War II slowed the rate of change. But in the postwar period, after 1945, Alfred Kinsey set the stage for what later came to be known as the *sexual revolution.* In 1948, Kinsey and his colleagues published their first study of sexuality in the United States, and it raised eyebrows everywhere. The national uproar resulted not so much from what he said as from the fact that scientists were actually studying sex, a topic many people were uneasy talking about even in the privacy of their homes.

Kinsey also had some interesting things to say. His two books (Kinsey, Pomeroy, & Martin, 1948; Kinsey et al., 1953) became best-sellers partly because they revealed that people in the United States, on average, were far less conventional in sexual matters than most had thought. These books encouraged a new openness toward sexuality, which helped set the sexual revolution in motion.

The revolution truly came of age in the late 1960s. Youth culture dominated public life, and expressions like "sex, drugs, and rock-and-roll" and "if it feels good, do it" summed up a new, freer attitude toward sex. The baby boom generation, born between 1946 and 1964, became the first cohort in U.S. history to grow up with the idea that sex was part of people's lives, whether they were married or not.

New technology also played a part in the sexual revolution. The birth control pill, introduced in 1960, not only prevented pregnancy but also made sex more convenient. Unlike a condom or a diaphragm, which must be applied at the time of intercourse, the pill could be taken anytime during the day. Now women and men could engage in sex spontaneously without any special preparation.

Because women were historically subject to greater sexual regulation than men, the sexual revolution had special significance for them. Society's "double standard" allows (and even encourages) men to be sexually active but expects women to be virgins until marriage and faithful to their husbands afterward. The survey data in Figure 1 show the narrowing of the double standard. Among people born between 1933 and 1942 (that is, people who are in their sixties and seventies today), 56 percent of men but just 16 percent of women report having had two or more sexual partners by the time they reached age twenty. Compare this wide gap to the pattern among the baby boomers born between 1953 and 1962 (people now in their forties and fifties), who came of age after the sexual revolution. In this category, 62 percent of men and 48 percent of women say they had two or more sexual partners by age twenty (Laumann et al., 1994:198). The sexual revolution increased sexual activity overall, but it changed women's behavior more than men's.

Greater openness about sexuality develops as societies become richer and the opportunities for women increase. With these facts in mind, look for a pattern in the global use of birth control shown in Global Map 1.

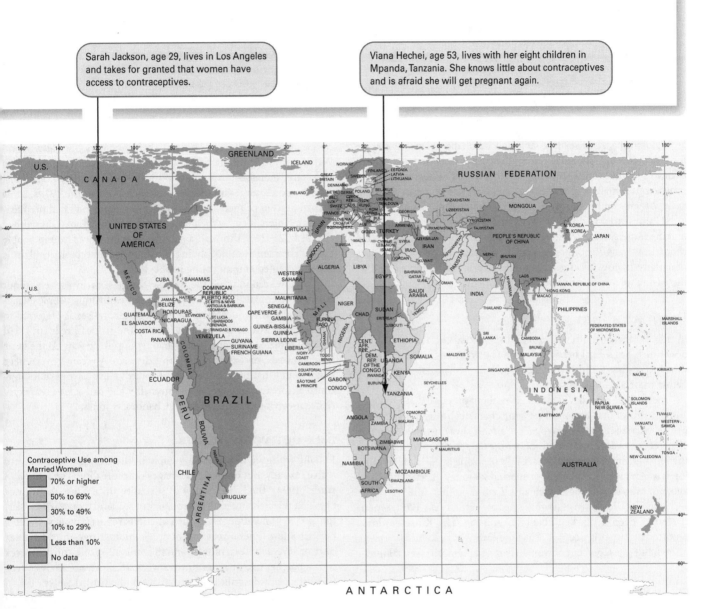

Sarah Jackson, age 29, lives in Los Angeles and takes for granted that women have access to contraceptives.

Viana Hechei, age 53, lives with her eight children in Mpanda, Tanzania. She knows little about contraceptives and is afraid she will get pregnant again.

Contraceptive Use among Married Women

- 70% or higher
- 50% to 69%
- 30% to 49%
- 10% to 29%
- Less than 10%
- No data

WINDOW ON THE WORLD

GLOBAL MAP 1   Contraceptive Use in Global Perspective

The map shows the percentage of married women using modern contraception methods (such as barrier methods, contraceptive pill, implants, injectables, intrauterine contraceptive devices [IUDs], or sterilization). In general, how do high-income nations differ from low-income nations? Can you explain this difference?

Sources: Data from United Nations Development Programme (2005, 2006), Population Reference Bureau (2006), and World Bank (2006, 2007).

The Sexual Counterrevolution

The sexual revolution made sex a topic of everyday discussion and sexual activity more a matter of individual choice. However, by 1980, the climate of sexual freedom that had marked the late 1960s and 1970s was criticized by some as evidence of our country's moral decline, and the *sexual counterrevolution* began.

Politically speaking, the sexual counterrevolution was a conservative call for a return to "family values" and a change from sexual freedom back toward what critics saw as the sexual responsibility valued by earlier generations. Critics of the sexual revolution objected not just to the idea of "free love" but to trends such as cohabitation (living together) and unmarried couples having children.

tip

Notice that on almost all the global maps, high-income countries tend to differ from lower-income countries. In lower-income nations, both cultural beliefs and political policies can encourage (Cuba) or discourage (Sudan) contraceptive use.

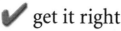**get it right**

Notice from the discussion below that no single stereotype accurately describes the sexual activity of the U.S. adult population.

Looking back, the sexual counterrevolution did not greatly change the idea that people should decide for themselves when and with whom to have a sexual relationship. But whether for moral reasons or concerns about sexually transmitted diseases, more people began choosing to limit their number of sexual partners or not to have sex at all.

Is the sexual revolution over? It is true that many people are making more careful decisions about sexuality. But as the rest of this chapter explains, the ongoing sexual revolution is evident in the fact that there is now greater acceptance of premarital sex as well as increasing tolerance for various sexual orientations.

Premarital Sex

In light of the sexual revolution and the sexual counterrevolution, how much has sexual behavior in the United States really changed? One interesting trend involves premarital sex—sexual intercourse before marriage—among young people.

Consider, first, what U.S. adults *say* about premarital intercourse. Table 1 shows that about 35 percent characterize sexual relations before marriage as "always wrong" or "almost always wrong." Another 17 percent consider premarital sex "wrong only sometimes," and more than 45 percent say premarital sex is "not wrong at all." Public opinion is much more accepting of premarital sex today than a generation ago, but even so, our society remains divided on this issue.

Now let's look at what young people actually *do*. For women, there has been a marked change over time. The Kinsey studies reported that among people born in the early 1900s, about 50 percent of men but just 6 percent of women had had premarital sexual inter-

course before age nineteen. Studies of baby boomers, born after World War II, show a slight increase in premarital intercourse among men and a large increase—to about one-third—among women. The most recent studies, targeting men and women born in the 1970s, show that 76 percent of men and 66 percent of women had had premarital sexual intercourse by their senior year in high school (Laumann et al., 1994:323–24). Although a significant minority of young people choose abstinence, or not having sexual intercourse, premarital sex is largely accepted among young people today.

Finally, keep in mind that people can be sexually active without having intercourse. In recent years, the share of young people engaging in oral sex has increased. In many cases, oral sex is preferred to intercourse because it does not involve the risk of pregnancy and because some people see it as less than "going all the way." At the same time, however, oral sex can transmit diseases. A recent government study found that only 20 percent of today's teens have sexual intercourse before reaching the age of fifteen, but half had at least one experience involving oral sex (Mosher, Chandra, & Jones, 2005).

Sex between Adults

Judging from the mass media, people in the United States are very active sexually. But do popular images reflect reality? The Laumann study (1994), the largest study of sexuality since Kinsey's groundbreaking research, found that frequency of sexual activity varies widely in the U.S. population. One-third of adults report having sex with a partner a few times a year or not at all, another one-third have sex once or several times a month, and the remaining one-third have sex with a partner two or more times a week. In short, no single stereotype accurately describes sexual activity in the United States.

Despite the widespread image of "swinging singles" seen on television shows such as *Sex and the City,* it is married people who have sex with partners the most. Married people also report the highest level of satisfaction—both emotional and physical—with their partners (Laumann et al., 1994).

Extramarital Sex

What about married people having sex outside of marriage? This practice, commonly called "adultery" (sociologists prefer the more neutral term *extramarital sex*), is widely condemned. Table 1 shows that more than 90 percent of U.S. adults consider a married person having sex with someone other than the marital partner "always wrong" or "almost always wrong." The norm of sexual fidelity within marriage has been and remains a strong element of U.S. culture.

But actual behavior falls short of the cultural ideal. The Laumann study reports that about 25 percent of married men and 10

Table 1 How We View Premarital and Extramarital Sex

Survey Question: "There's been a lot of discussion about the way morals and attitudes about sex are changing in this country. If a man and a woman have sexual relations before marriage, do you think it is always wrong, almost always wrong, wrong only sometimes, or not wrong at all? What about a married person having sexual relations with someone other than the marriage partner?"

	Premarital Sex	Extramarital Sex
"Always wrong"	26.3%	79.9%
"Almost always wrong"	8.8	11.9
"Wrong only sometimes"	17.3	4.9
"Not wrong at all"	45.1	2.1
"Don't know"/No answer	2.5	1.2

Source: *General Social Surveys, 1972–2004: Cumulative Codebook* (Chicago: National Opinion Research Center, 2005), p. 291.

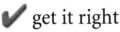 **get it right**
Be sure you clearly understand the four sexual orientations described below.

 get it right
Study Figure 2 closely. Sometimes we are quick to think that people are either heterosexual or homosexual. But there are four sexual orientations, and individuals may fall anywhere within the area of the figure.

percent of married women have had at least one extramarital sexual experience. Or stating this the other way around, 75 percent of men and 90 percent of women remain sexually faithful to their partners throughout their married lives (Laumann et al., 1994:214; NORC, 2005:1702).

 Why do you think U.S. society has become more accepting of premarital sex but not of extramarital sex?

Sex over the Life Course

Patterns of sexual activity change with age. In the United States, most young men become sexually active by the time they reach sixteen and women by the age of seventeen. By the time they reach their mid-twenties, more than 90 percent of both women and men reported being sexually active with a partner at least once during the past year.

The picture begins to change by about age fifty, after which advancing age is linked to a decline in the share of people who are sexually active. By age sixty, about 85 percent of men and 60 percent of women say they have been sexually active in the past year. By age seventy, only half of women claim to be sexually active; by age eighty, half of men say the same (Laumann et al., 1994). Contrary to popular stereotypes, these data show that sexual activity is a normal part of life for most older adults.

Sexual Orientation

In recent decades, public opinion about sexual orientation has shown a remarkable change. **Sexual orientation** is *a person's romantic and emotional attraction to another person.* The norm in all human societies is **heterosexuality** (*hetero* is Greek for "the other of two"), meaning *sexual attraction to someone of the other sex.* Yet in every society, a significant share of people experience **homosexuality** (*homo* is Greek for "the same"), *sexual attraction to someone of the same sex.* Keep in mind that people do not necessarily fall into just one of these categories; they may have varying degrees of attraction to both sexes.

The idea that sexual orientation is not always clear-cut is confirmed by the existence of **bisexuality**, *sexual attraction to people of both sexes.* Some bisexual people are equally attracted to males and females; many others are more attracted to one sex than the other. Finally, **asexuality** refers to *a lack of sexual attraction to people of either sex.* Figure 2 shows each of these sexual orientations in relation to the others.

It is important to remember that sexual *attraction* is not the same thing as sexual *behavior.* Many people, perhaps even most people, have

DIVERSITY SNAPSHOT

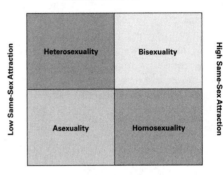

FIGURE 2 Four Sexual Orientations

A person's level of same-sex attraction and opposite-sex attraction are two distinct dimensions that combine in various ways to produce four major sexual orientations.

Source: Adapted from Storms (1980).

experienced attraction to someone of the same sex, but far fewer ever engage in same-sex behavior. This is in large part because our culture discourages such actions.

In the United States and around the world, heterosexuality is the norm because, biologically speaking, heterosexual relations permit human reproduction. Even so, most societies tolerate homosexuality, and some have even celebrated it. Among the ancient Greeks, for example, upper-class men considered homosexuality the highest form of relationship, partly because they looked down on women as intellectually inferior. As men saw it, heterosexuality was necessary only so they could have children, and "real" men preferred homosexual relations (Kluckhohn, 1948; Ford & Beach, 1951; Greenberg, 1988).

What Gives Us a Sexual Orientation?

The question of how people come to have a particular sexual orientation is strongly debated. The arguments cluster into two general positions: sexual orientation as a product of society and sexual orientation as a product of biology.

Sexual Orientation: A Product of Society

This approach argues that people in any society attach meanings to sexual activity, and these meanings differ from place to place and over time. As Michel Foucault (1990, orig. 1978) points out, for example,

there was no distinct category of people called "homosexuals" until a century ago, when scientists and eventually the public as a whole began defining people that way. Throughout history, many people no doubt had homosexual experiences, but neither they nor others saw in this behavior the basis for any special identity.

Anthropological studies show that patterns of homosexuality differ from one society to another. In Siberia, for example, the Chukchee Eskimo have a practice in which one man dresses as a female and does a woman's work. The Sambia, who dwell in the Eastern Highlands of New Guinea, have a ritual in which young boys perform oral sex on older men in the belief that eating semen will make them more masculine. The existence of such diverse patterns in societies around the world seems to indicate that human sexual expression is socially constructed (Murray & Roscoe, 1998; Blackwood & Wieringa, 1999).

Sexual Orientation: A Product of Biology

A growing body of evidence suggests that sexual orientation is innate, or rooted in human biology in much the same way that people are born right-handed or left-handed. Arguing this position, Simon LeVay (1993) links sexual orientation to the structure of a person's brain. LeVay studied the brains of both homosexual and heterosexual men

and found a small but important difference in the size of the hypothalamus, a part of the brain that regulates hormones. Such an anatomical difference, he claims, plays a part in shaping sexual orientation.

Genetics may also influence sexual orientation. One study of forty-four pairs of brothers—all homosexual—found that thirty-three pairs had a distinctive genetic pattern involving the X chromosome. The gay brothers also had an unusually high number of gay male relatives—but only on their mother's side. Such evidence leads some researchers to think there may be a "gay gene" located on the X chromosome (Hamer & Copeland, 1994).

▶**CRITICAL REVIEW**   Mounting evidence supports the conclusion that sexual orientation is rooted in biology, although the best guess at present is that both nature and nurture play a part. Remember that sexual orientation is not a matter of neat categories. Most people who think of themselves as homosexual have had some heterosexual experiences, just as many people who think of themselves as heterosexual have had some homosexual experiences. Explaining sexual orientation, then, is not easy.

There is also a political issue here with great importance for gay men and lesbians. To the extent that sexual orientation is based in biology, homosexuals have no more choice about their sexual orientation than they do about their skin color. If this is so, shouldn't gay men and lesbians expect the same legal protection from discrimination as African Americans?

 YOUR LEARNING   What evidence supports the position that sexual behavior is constructed by society? What evidence supports the position that sexual orientation is rooted in biology?

It was only about thirty years ago (1977) that the first gay character appeared in a television program in the United States (*Soap*). Gay people now have a larger place in our society's popular culture as suggested by the success of shows including *The L Word*.

Showtime/Picture Desk, Inc./Kobal Collection

How Many Gay People Are There?

What share of our population is gay? This is a difficult question to answer because, as noted earlier, sexual orientation is not a matter of neat categories. In addition, not all people are willing to reveal their sexuality to strangers or even to family members. Kinsey estimated that about 4 percent of males and 2 percent of females have an exclusively same-sex orientation, although he pointed out that most people experience same-sex attraction at some point in their lives.

Some social scientists put the gay share of the population at 10 percent. But the Laumann (1994) research shows that how homosexuality is defined makes a big difference in the results. As part (a) of Figure 3 shows, about

9 percent of U.S. men and about 4 percent of U.S. women between the ages of eighteen and fifty-nine reported homosexual activity *at some time in their lives.* The second set of numbers in the bar graph shows that fewer men (and even fewer women) had a homosexual experience in childhood but not after puberty. Finally, only 2.8 percent of men and 1.4 percent of women defined themselves as "partly" or "entirely" homosexual.

In the Laumann survey, less than 1 percent of adults described themselves as bisexual. But bisexual experiences appear to be fairly common (at least for a time) among younger people, especially on college and university campuses (Laumann et al., 1994; Leland, 1995). Many bisexuals do not think of themselves as either gay or straight, and their behavior reflects aspects of both gay and straight living.

The Gay Rights Movement

The public's attitude toward homosexuality has been moving toward greater acceptance. Back in 1973, as shown in part (b) of Figure 3, about three-fourths of adults in the United States claimed that homosexual relations were "always wrong" or "almost always wrong." Although that percentage changed little during the 1970s and 1980s, by 2002 it had dropped to 57 percent, rising slightly since then to its current level of 60 percent (NORC, 2005:292). Among college students, who are generally more tolerant of homosexuality than the general population, we see a similar trend. In 1980, about half of college students supported laws prohibiting homosexual relationships; by 2006, as Figure 4 shows, less than one-third felt this way (Astin et al., 2002; Pryor et al., 2006).

In large measure, this change was brought about by the gay rights movement, which began in the middle of the twentieth century. Up to that time, most people in this country did not discuss homosexuality, and it was common for companies (including the federal government and the armed forces) to fire anyone who was accused of being gay. Mental health professionals, too, took a hard line, describing homosexuals as "sick," sometimes placing them in mental hospitals where, it was hoped, they might be "cured." It is no surprise that most lesbians and gay men remained "in the closet," closely guarding the secret of their sexual orientation. But the gay rights movement gained strength during the 1960s. One early milestone occurred in 1973, when the American Psychiatric Association declared that homosexuality was not an illness but simply "a form of sexual behavior."

The gay rights movement also began using the term **homophobia** to describe *discomfort over close personal interaction with people thought to be gay, lesbian, or bisexual* (Weinberg, 1973). The concept of homo-

FIGURE 3 Sexual Orientation in the United States: Survey Data

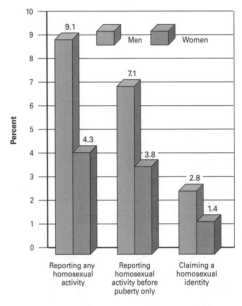

(a) How Many Gay People?

The percentage of people who are classified as having a homosexual orientation depends on how this concept is operationalized. Research suggests that 2.8 percent of adult men and 1.4 percent of adult women claim a homosexual identity.
Source: Adapted from Laumann et al. (1994).

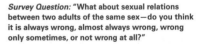
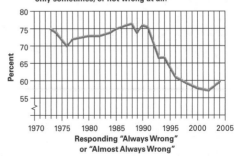

(b) Attitudes toward Homosexual Relations, 1973–2004

Between 1990 and 2002, the percentage of U.S. adults who disapprove of homosexual relations went down. Between 2002 and 2004, however, it rose slightly and now stands at about 60 percent.
Source: NORC (2005).

SEXUALITY AND SOCIETY

tip

Notice from Figure 4 that a larger share of college men than college women oppose homosexuality, even though more men than women claim a homosexual identity.

STUDENT SNAPSHOT

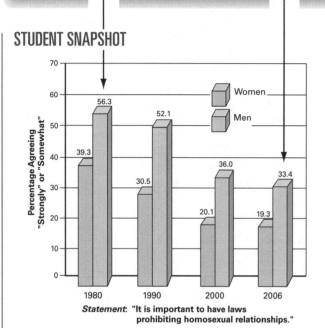

FIGURE 4 Opposition to Homosexual Relationships: Attitudes of First-Year College Students, 1980–2006

The historical trend among college students is toward greater tolerance of homosexual relatinships, a view held by a large majority.

Sources: Astin et al. (2002) and Pryor et al. (2006).

Sexual Issues and Controversies

Sexuality lies at the heart of a number of controversies in the United States today. Here we take a look at four key issues: teen pregnancy, pornography, prostitution, and sexual violence.

Teen Pregnancy

Because it carries the risk of pregnancy, being sexually active—especially having intercourse—demands a high level of responsibility. Teenagers may be biologically mature enough to conceive, but many are not emotionally secure enough to appreciate the consequences of their actions. Surveys show that there are about 750,000 teen pregnancies in the United States each year, most of them unplanned. This country's rate of births to teens is higher than that of all other high-income countries and is twice the rate in Canada (Darroch et al., 2001).

For young women of all racial and ethnic categories, weak families and low income sharply raise the risk of becoming sexually active and having an unplanned child. To make matters worse, having unplanned children raises the risk that young women (as well as young fathers-to-be) will not finish school and will end up poor (Alan Guttmacher Institute, 2002).

Did the sexual revolution raise the level of teenage pregnancy? Perhaps surprisingly, the answer is no. The rate of pregnancy among U.S. teens in 1950 was higher than it is today, partly because people back then married at a younger age. Because abortion was against the law, many pregnancies led to quick marriages. As a result, there were many pregnant teenagers, but almost 90 percent were married. Today, the number of pregnant teens is lower, but in about 80 percent of cases, the women are unmarried. In a slight majority (57 percent) of such cases, these women keep their babies; in the remainder, they have abortions (29 percent) or miscarriages (14 percent) (Alan Guttmacher Institute, 2006). National Map 2 shows the pregnancy rates for women between the ages of fifteen and nineteen throughout the United States.

 In light of the fact that 80 percent of today's pregnant teens are unmarried, what responsibilities should teen fathers-to-be have toward their children?

Pornography

Pornography is *sexually explicit material intended to cause sexual arousal.* But what is or is not pornographic has long been a matter of debate. Recognizing that different people view portrayals of sexuality differently, the U.S. Supreme Court gives local communities the power to decide for themselves what violates "community standards" of decency and lacks "redeeming social value."

phobia turns the tables on society: Instead of asking "What's wrong with gay people?" the question becomes "What's wrong with people who can't accept a different sexual orientation?"

In 2004, a number of cities and towns began to allow gay couples to marry, although these unions were later declared illegal. But gay marriage is now legal in the state of Massachusetts, and gay civil unions (marriage by another name) are legal in Vermont, Connecticut, and New Jersey. A number of other states, including California and Washington, recognize "domestic partnerships" that provide most of the benefits of marriage. At the same time, seventeen states have enacted laws that forbid gay marriage and prohibit recognizing gay marriages performed elsewhere.

 What changes in laws regarding gay marriage do you expect over the next ten years? Why?

In Tucson, Arizona, 18-year-old Ramona Ramirez was just given a baby shower by her high school classmates, many of whom are already married and have children.

In Bangor, Maine, Sandy Johnson, also 18, reports that only "one or two" girls in her high school have become pregnant.

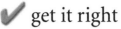

get it right

You might guess that because of the sexual revolution, teenage pregnancy rates have gone up. The opposite is the case: Teenage pregnancy rates have gone down—mostly because young women now typically marry not as teenagers but in their mid-twenties.

SEEING OURSELVES

NATIONAL MAP 2
Teenage Pregnancy Rates across the United States

The map shows pregnancy rates for 2000 for women aged fifteen to nineteen. In what regions of the country are rates high? Where are they low? What explanation can you offer for these patterns?
Source: Alan Guttmacher Institute (2006).

Definitions aside, pornography is very popular in the United States: X-rated videos, telephone "sex lines," a host of sexually explicit movies and magazines, and thousands of Internet Web sites make up a thriving industry that takes in more than $10 billion each year. The vast majority of consumers of pornography are men.

Traditionally, people have criticized pornography on *moral* grounds. As national surveys confirm, 60 percent of U.S. adults are concerned that "sexual materials lead to a breakdown of morals" (NORC, 2005:293). Today, however, pornography is also seen as a *power* issue because most of it degrades women, portraying them as the sexual playthings of men.

Some critics also claim that pornography is a cause of violence against women. Although it is difficult to prove a scientific cause-and-effect relationship between what people view and how they act, the public shares a concern about pornography and violence, with almost half of adults holding the opinion that pornography encourages people to commit rape (NORC, 2005:293).

Although people everywhere object to sexual material they find offensive, many also value the principle of free speech and the protection of artistic expression. Nevertheless, pressure to restrict pornography is building from an unlikely coalition of conservatives (who oppose pornography on moral grounds) and liberals (who condemn it for political reasons).

Prostitution

Prostitution is *the selling of sexual services.* Often called "the world's oldest profession," prostitution has been widespread throughout recorded history. In the United States today, about one in five adult

men reports having paid for sex at some time (NORC, 2005:1701). Because most people think of sex as an expression of intimacy between two people, they find the idea of sex for money disturbing. As a result, prostitution is against the law everywhere in the United States except for parts of rural Nevada.

Around the world, prostitution is most common in poor countries, where patriarchy is strong and traditional cultural norms limit women's ability to earn a living. Global Map 2 shows where in the world prostitution is most widespread.

Types of Prostitution

Most prostitutes (many prefer the morally neutral term "sex workers") are women, and they fall into different categories. *Call girls* are elite prostitutes, typically young, attractive, and well-educated women who arrange their own "dates" with clients by telephone. The classified pages of any large city newspaper contain numerous ads for "escort services," by which women (and sometimes men) offer both companionship and sex for a fee.

In the middle category are prostitutes employed in "massage parlors" or brothels under the control of managers. These sex workers have less choice about their clients, receive less money for their services, and get to keep no more than half of what they make.

At the bottom of the sex worker hierarchy are *streetwalkers*, women and men who "work the streets" of large cities. Some female streetwalkers are under the control of male pimps who take most of their earnings. Many others are addicts who sell sex in order to buy the drugs they need. Both types of people are at high risk of becoming the victims of violence (Davidson, 1998; Estes, 2001).

tip

Social class affects almost every social pattern discussed in this book. In this case, you can see that there are several types of prostitution, which correspond to the income levels of the women and their clients.

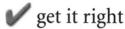**get it right**

The legal term is "rape," and "date rape" is a type of rape. The term "date rape" is used to indicate common situations in which the victim knows her attacker.

Most prostitutes offer heterosexual services. However, gay male prostitutes also trade sex for money. Researchers report that many gay prostitutes end up selling sex after having suffered rejection by family and friends because of their sexual orientation (Weisberg, 1985; Boyer, 1989; Kruks, 1991).

A Victimless Crime?

Prostitution is against the law almost everywhere in the United States, but many people consider it a victimless crime (defined in Chapter 9, "Deviance," as a crime in which there is no obvious victim). As a result, instead of enforcing prostitution laws all the time, police stage only occasional crackdowns. This policy reflects a desire to control prostitution while recognizing that it is impossible to eliminate it entirely.

Many people take a "live and let live" attitude about prostitution and say that adults ought to be able to do as they please so long as no one is forced to do anything. But is prostitution really victimless? The sex trade subjects many women to abuse and outright violence and also plays a part in spreading sexually transmitted diseases, including AIDS. In addition, many poor women—especially in low-income nations—become trapped in a life of selling sex. Thailand, in South-east Asia, has 2 million prostitutes, representing about 10 percent of all women in the labor force. Many of these women begin working before they are teenagers, suffer physical abuse, and become infected with HIV (Wonders & Michalowski, 2001).

In the past, the focus of attention has been on the women who earn money as sex workers. But prostitution would not exist at all if it were not for demand on the part of men. For this reason, law enforcement is now more likely to target "Johns" when they attempt to buy sex.

 Do you consider prostitution a victimless crime or not? Explain your position.

Sexual Violence: Rape and Date Rape

Ideally, sexual activity occurs within a loving relationship between consenting adults. In reality, however, sex can be twisted by hate and violence. Here we consider two types of sexual violence: rape and date rape.

Rape

Although some people think rape is motivated only by a desire for sex, it is actually an expression of power—a violent act that uses sex to hurt, humiliate, or control another person. According to the Federal Bureau of Investigation (2006), about 94,000 women report being raped to the police each year. This number reflects only the reported cases, and the actual number of rapes is almost certainly several times higher.

The official government definition of rape is "the carnal knowledge of a female forcibly and against her will." Thus official rape statistics include only victims who are women. But men, too, are raped—in perhaps 10 percent of all cases. Most men who rape men are not homosexual; they are heterosexuals who are motivated by a desire not for sex but to dominate another person.

Date Rape

A common myth is that rape involves strangers. In reality, however, only about one-third of rapes fit this pattern. About two-thirds of rapes involve people who know one another—more often than not, pretty well—and these crimes usually take place in familiar surroundings,

Brothels like this one are found in rural counties of Nevada. Some people claim that legalizing prostitution permits the government to protect the health and safety of "sex workers," who have the opportunity to earn a good income. Others claim that selling sex is degrading to women as well as men and that women's economic opportunities should not depend on selling themselves in this way. Where do you stand on the issue of legalized prostitution? Why?

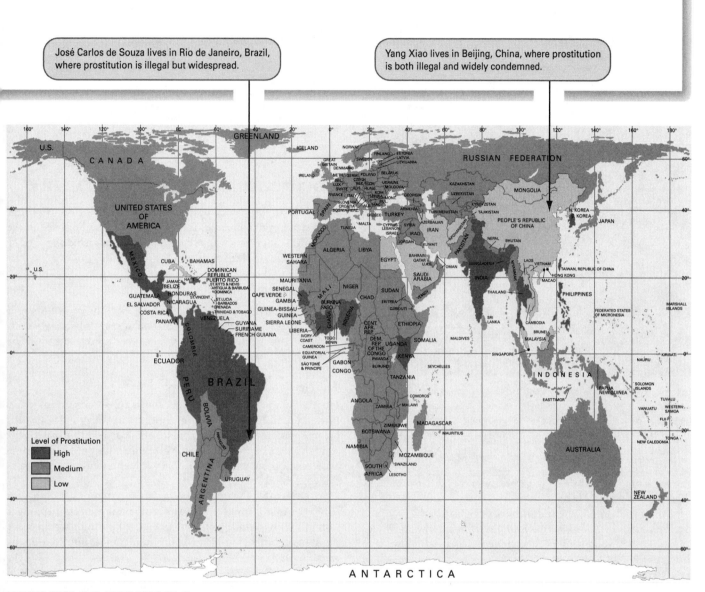

José Carlos de Souza lives in Rio de Janeiro, Brazil, where prostitution is illegal but widespread.

Yang Xiao lives in Beijing, China, where prostitution is both illegal and widely condemned.

Level of Prostitution
- High
- Medium
- Low

WINDOW ON THE WORLD

GLOBAL MAP 2 Prostitution in Global Perspective

Generally speaking, prostitution is widespread in societies where women have low standing. Officially, at least, the People's Republic of China boasts of gender equality, including the elimination of "vice" such as prostitution, which oppresses women. By contrast, in much of Latin America, where patriarchy is strong, prostitution is common. In many Islamic societies, patriarchy is also strong, but religion is a counterbalance, so prostitution is limited. Western, high-income nations have a moderate amount of prostitution.

Sources: *Peters Atlas of the World* (1990) and Mackay (2000).

especially the home and the campus. For this reason, the term "date rape" or "acquaintance rape" is used to refer to forcible sexual violence against women by men they know (Laumann et al., 1994; U.S. Bureau of Justice Statistics, 2006).

A second myth, often linked to date rape, is that the victim of rape must have done something to encourage the man and make him think she wanted to have sex. Perhaps the victim agreed to go out with the offender. Maybe she even invited him into her room. But of

tip

Here sociology's three major theoretical approaches
are applied to sexuality. Each provides different
insights, and all are helpful in getting a full
understanding of the issue.

Experts agree that one factor that contributes to the problem of sexual
violence on the college campus is the widespread use of alcoholic
beverages. What policies are in force on your campus to discourage the
kind of drinking that leads to one person imposing sex on another?

AP Photo/Victor R. Caivano

course, acting in this way no more justifies rape than it would any
other type of physical assault.

Although rape is a physical attack, it often leaves emotional and
psychological scars. Beyond the brutality of being physically violated, rape by an acquaintance also undermines a victim's sense of
trust. Psychological scars are especially serious among the half of
rape victims who are under eighteen; one-third of these young victims are attacked by their own fathers or stepfathers (Greenfield,
1996).

How common is date rape? One study found that about 20 percent of a sample of high school girls in the United States reported
being the victim of sexual or physical violence inflicted by boys they
were dating (Dickinson, 2001).

Nowhere has the issue of date rape been more widely discussed
than on college campuses, where the danger of date rape is high. The
collegiate environment promotes easy friendships and encourages
trust among young people who still have much to learn about relationships and about themselves. As the Seeing Sociology in Everyday
Life box explains, the same college environment that encourages communication provides few social norms to help guide young people's
sexual experiences. To counter the problem, many schools now
actively address myths about rape. In addition, greater attention is

now focused on the abuse of alcohol, which increases the likelihood
of sexual violence.

Theoretical Analysis of Sexuality

Applying sociology's various theoretical approaches gives us a better
understanding of human sexuality. The following sections discuss the
three major approaches, and the Applying Theory table on page 211
highlights the key insights of each approach.

Structural-Functional Analysis

The structural-functional approach highlights the contribution of
any social pattern to the overall operation of society. Because sexuality can have such important consequences, society regulates this type
of behavior.

The Need to Regulate Sexuality

From a biological point of view, sex allows our species to reproduce.
But culture and social institutions regulate *with whom* and *when* people reproduce. For example, most societies condemn a married person for having sex with someone other than his or her spouse. To
allow sexual passion to go unchecked would threaten family life, especially the raising of children.

The fact that the incest taboo exists everywhere shows that no
society permits completely free choice in sexual partners. Reproduction by family members other than married partners would break
down the system of kinship and hopelessly confuse human relationships.

Historically, the social control of sexuality was strong, mostly
because sex often led to childbirth. We see these controls at work in
the traditional distinction between "legitimate" reproduction (within
marriage) and "illegitimate" reproduction (outside marriage). But
once a society develops the technology to control births, its sexual
norms become more permissive. This occurred in the United States,
where over the course of the twentieth century, sex moved beyond its
basic reproductive function and became accepted as a form of intimacy and even recreation (Giddens, 1992).

Latent Functions: The Case of Prostitution

It is easy to see that prostitution is harmful because it spreads disease
and exploits women. But are there latent functions that help explain
why prostitution is so widespread? According to Kingsley Davis (1971),
prostitution performs several useful functions. It is one way to meet the
sexual needs of a large number of people who may not have ready

tip

How do your friends feel about hooking up? Use the questions at the end of the box to talk with them about sexuality on campus.

Seeing Sociology in Everyday Life

When Sex Is Only Sex: The Campus Culture of "Hooking Up"

BRYNNE: My mom told me once that she didn't have sex with my dad until after they were engaged.

KATY: I guess times have really changed!

Have you ever been in a sexual situation and not been sure of the right thing to do? Most colleges and universities highlight two important rules. First, sexual activity must take place only when both participants have given clear statements of consent. The consent principle is what makes "having sex" different from date rape. Second, no one should knowingly expose another person to a sexually transmitted disease, especially when the partner is unaware of the danger.

These rules are very important, but they say little about the larger issue of what sex *means.* For example, when is it "right" to have a sexual relationship? How well do you have to know the other person? If you do have sex, are you obligated to see the person again?

Two generations ago, there were informal rules for campus sex. Dating was considered part of the courtship process. That is, "going out" was the way in which women and men evaluated each other as possible marriage partners while they sharpened their own sense of what they wanted in a mate. Because, on average, marriage took place in the early twenties, many college students became engaged and married while they were still in school. In this cultural climate, sex was viewed by college students as part of a relationship that carried a commitment—a serious interest in the other person as a possible marriage partner.

Today, the sexual culture of the campus is very different. Partly because people now marry much later, the culture of courtship has declined dramatically. About three-fourths of women in a recent national survey point to a new campus pattern, the culture of "hooking up." What exactly is "hooking up"? Most describe it in words like these: "When a girl and a guy get together for a physical encounter—anything from kissing to having sex—and don't necessarily expect anything further."

Student responses to the survey suggest that hookups have three characteristics. First, most couples who hook up know little about each other. Second, a typical hookup involves people who have been drinking alcohol, usually at a campus party. Third, most women

Michelle Joyce / Index Stock/NewsCom

are critical of the culture of hooking up and express little satisfaction with these encounters. Certainly, some women (and men) who hook up simply walk away, happy to have enjoyed a sexual experience free of further obligation. But given the powerful emotions that sex can unleash, hooking up often leaves someone wondering what to expect next: "Will you call me tomorrow?" "Will I see you again?"

The survey asked women who had experienced a recent hookup to report how they felt about the experience a day later. A majority of respondents said they felt "awkward," about half felt "disappointed" and "confused," and one in four felt "exploited." Clearly, for many people, sex is more than a physical encounter. In addition, because today's campus climate is very sensitive to charges of sexual exploitation, there is a need for clearer standards of fair play.

WHAT DO YOU THINK?

1. How extensive is the pattern of hooking up on your campus? Are you aware of differences in these types of encounters between heterosexuals and homosexuals?

2. What do you see as the advantages of sex without commitment? What are the disadvantages of this kind of relationship? Are men and women likely to answer this question differently? Explain.

3. Do you think college students need more guidance about sexual issues? If so, who should provide this guidance?

Source: Based in part on Marquardt & Glenn (2001).

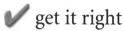

get it right

Answer all the "✓ Your Learning" questions in the theory section of the chapter to be sure you understand the material.

tip

Making global comparisons shows us that sexuality is an element of culture, not just biology.

access to sex, including soldiers, travelers, people who are not physically attractive, or people too poor to attract a marriage partner. Some people favor prostitution because they want sex without the "trouble" of a relationship. As one analyst put it, "Men don't pay for sex; they pay so they can leave" (Miracle, Miracle, & Baumeister, 2003:421).

▶ **CRITICAL REVIEW** The structural-functional approach helps us see the important part sexuality plays in the organization of society. The incest taboo and other cultural norms also suggest that society has always paid attention to who has sex with whom and, especially, who reproduces with whom.

Functionalist analysis sometimes ignores gender; when Kingsley Davis wrote of the benefits of prostitution for society, he was really talking about the benefits to *men*. In addition, the fact that sexual patterns change over time, just as they differ in remarkable ways around the world, is ignored by this perspective. To appreciate the varied and changeable character of sexuality, we now turn to the symbolic-interaction approach.

The control of women's sexuality is a common theme in human history. During the Middle Ages, Europeans devised the "chastity belt"—a metal device locked about a woman's groin that prevented sexual intercourse (and probably interfered with other bodily functions as well). While such devices are all but unknown today, the social control of sexuality continues. Can you point to examples?

AKG-Images

 YOUR LEARNING Compared to traditional societies, why do modern societies give people more choice about matters involving sexuality?

Symbolic-Interaction Analysis

The symbolic-interaction approach highlights how, as people interact, they construct everyday reality. People sometimes construct very different realities, so the views of one group or society may well differ from those of another. In the same way, our understanding of sexuality can and does change over time.

The Social Construction of Sexuality

Almost all social patterns involving sexuality saw considerable change over the course of the twentieth century. One good illustration is the changing importance of virginity. A century ago, our society's norm—for women, at least—was virginity before marriage. This norm was strong because there was no effective means of birth control, and virginity was the only guarantee a man had that his bride-to-be was not carrying another man's child.

Today, because birth control has separated sex from reproduction, the virginity norm has weakened considerably. In the United States, among people born between 1963 and 1974, just 16.3 percent of men and 20.1 percent of women reported being virgins at first marriage (Laumann et al., 1994:503).

Another example of our society's construction of sexuality involves young people. A century ago, childhood was a time of innocence in sexual matters. In recent decades, however, thinking has changed. Although few people encourage sexual activity between children, most people believe that children should be educated about sex by the time they are teenagers so that they can make intelligent choices about their behavior as they grow older.

Global Comparisons

Around the world, different societies attach different meanings to sexuality. For example, the anthropologist Ruth Benedict (1938), who spent years learning the ways of life of the Melanesian people of southeastern New Guinea, reported that adults paid little attention when young children engaged in sexual experimentation with one another. Parents in Melanesia shrugged off such activity because, before puberty, sex cannot lead to reproduction. Is it likely that most parents in the United States would respond the same way?

Sexual practices also vary from culture to culture. Male circumcision of infant boys (the practice of removing all or part of the foreskin of the penis) is common in the United States but rare in most

tip

Carefully study the Applying Theory table to be sure you understand what the three theoretical approaches tell you about sexuality.

APPLYING THEORY

Sexuality

	Structural-Functional Approach	Symbolic-Interaction Approach	Social-Conflict Approach
What is the level of analysis?	Macro-level	Micro-level	Macro-level
What is the importance of sexuality for society?	Society depends on sexuality for reproduction. Society uses the incest taboo and other norms to control sexuality in order to maintain social order.	Sexual practices vary among the many cultures of the world. Some societies allow individuals more freedom than others in matters of sexual behavior.	Sexuality is linked to social inequality. U.S. society regulates women's sexuality more than men's, which is part of the larger pattern of men dominating women.
Has sexuality changed over time? How?	Yes. As advances in birth control technology separate sex from reproduction, societies relax some controls on sexuality.	Yes. The meanings people attach to virginity and other sexual matters are all socially constructed and subject to change.	Yes and no. Some sexual standards have relaxed, but society still defines women in sexual terms, just as homosexual people are harmed by society's heterosexual bias.

other parts of the world. A practice sometimes referred to incorrectly as female circumcision (the removal of the clitoris) is rare in the United States and much of the world but common in parts of Africa and the Middle East (Crossette, 1995; Huffman, 2000).

▶**CRITICAL REVIEW** The strength of the symbolic-interaction approach lies in revealing the constructed character of familiar social patterns. Understanding that people "construct" sexuality, we can better appreciate the variety of sexual practices found over the course of history and around the world.

One limitation of this approach, however, is that not all sexual practices are so variable. Throughout our own history—and around the world—men are more likely to see women in sexual terms than the other way around. Some broader social structure must be at work in a pattern that is this widespread, as we shall see in the next section on the social-conflict approach.

 YOUR LEARNING What evidence can you provide that human sexuality is socially constructed?

Social-Conflict Analysis

As you have seen in earlier chapters, the social-conflict approach (particularly the gender-conflict or feminist approach) highlights dimensions of inequality. This approach shows how sexuality both reflects patterns of social inequality and helps perpetuate them.

Sexuality: Reflecting Social Inequality

Recall our discussion of prostitution, a practice outlawed almost everywhere in the United States. Enforcement of prostitution laws is uneven at best, especially when it comes to who is and is not likely to be arrested. Although two people are involved, the record shows that police are far more likely to arrest (less powerful) female prostitutes than (more powerful) male clients. Similarly, of all women engaged in prostitution, it is streetwalkers—women with the least income and those most likely to be minorities—who face the highest risk of arrest

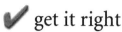 get it right

Be sure you understand how sexuality can be an element of social inequality.

 tip

In general, the political right tends to view pornography as a moral issue, and the political left tends to see it as a power issue. The social-conflict approach, being left of center, highlights power.

Controversy & Debate
The Abortion Controversy

FRANK: The abortion people are marching again across campus.

MARVIN: For or against?

FRANK: Both. I'm not sure which came first, but somebody said there were already some fights. . . .

A black van pulls up in front of the storefront in a busy section of the city. Two women get out of the front seat and cautiously look up and down the street. After a moment, one nods to the other and they open the rear door to let a third woman out of the van. Standing to the right and left of the woman, the two quickly escort her inside the building.

This scene might describe two federal marshals taking a convict to a police station, but it is actually an account of two clinic workers helping a woman who has decided to have an abortion. Why are they so cautious? Anyone who has read the papers in recent years knows about the angry confrontations at abortion clinics across North America. Some opponents have even targeted and killed doctors who carried out abortions,

some 1.3 million of which are performed in the United States each year. It is one of the most hotly debated issues of our day.

Abortion has not always been so controversial. In colonial times, midwives and other healers performed abortions with little community opposition and with full approval of the law. But controversy arose about 1850, when early medical doctors wanted to eliminate the competition they faced from midwives and other traditional health providers, whose income came largely from ending pregnancies. By 1900, medical doctors had succeeded in getting every state to pass a law banning abortion.

Such laws greatly reduced the number of abortions. Those that did occur were performed "underground," as secretly as possible. Many women who wanted abortions—especially those who were poor—had little choice but to seek help from unlicensed "back alley" abortionists, sometimes with tragic results due to unsanitary conditions and the use of medically dangerous techniques.

By the 1960s, opposition to antiabortion laws was rising. In 1973, the U.S. Supreme

Court made a landmark decision (in the cases of *Roe* v. *Wade* and *Doe* v. *Bolton*), striking down all state laws banning abortion. In effect, this action established a woman's legal access to abortion nationwide.

Even so, the abortion controversy continues. On one side of the issue are people who describe themselves as "pro-choice," supporting a woman's right to choose abortion. On the other side are those who call themselves "pro-life," opposing abortion as morally wrong; these people would like to see the Supreme Court reverse its 1973 decision.

How strong is the support for each side of the abortion controversy? A recent national survey asked a sample of adults the question "Should it be possible for a pregnant woman to obtain a legal abortion if the woman wants it for any reason?" In response, 38.5 percent said yes (placing them in the pro-choice camp) and 56.5 percent said no (expressing the pro-life position); the remaining 5 percent offered no opinion (NORC, 2005:282).

A closer look shows that circumstances make a big difference in how people see this issue. The figure shows that large majorities

(COYOTE Los Angeles, 2004). We might also wonder whether so many women would be involved in prostitution in the first place if they had the economic opportunities equal to those of men.

More generally, which categories of people in U.S. society are most likely to be defined in terms of sexuality? The answer, once again, is those with less power: women compared to men and people of color compared to whites. In this way, sexuality—which is a natural part of human life—is used by society to define some categories of people as less worthy.

Sexuality: Creating Social Inequality

Social-conflict theorists, especially feminists, point to sexuality as the root of inequality between women and men. Defining women in sexual terms amounts to devaluing them from full human beings into

objects of men's interest and attention. Is it any wonder that the word *pornography* comes from the Greek word *porne*, meaning "harlot" or "prostitute"?

If men define women in sexual terms, it is easy to see pornography—almost all of which is consumed by males—as a power issue. Because pornography typically shows women focused on pleasing men, it supports the idea that men have power over women.

Some radical critics doubt that this element of power can ever be removed from heterosexual relations (A. Dworkin, 1987). Most social-conflict theorists do not reject heterosexuality, but they do agree that sexuality can and does degrade women. Our culture often describes sexuality in terms of sport (men "scoring" with women) and violence ("slamming," "banging," and "hitting on," for example, are verbs used for both fighting and sex).

tip

Looking at the box on the abortion controversy, notice from the figure that the level of support for abortion depends on exactly how a researcher asks the question.

of U.S. adults favor legal abortion if a pregnancy seriously threatens a woman's health, if the pregnancy is a result of rape, or if a fetus is likely to have a serious defect. The bottom line is that about 38 percent support access to abortion under *any* circumstances, but nearly 83 percent support access to abortion under *some* circumstances.

Many of those who take the pro-life position feel strongly that abortion amounts to killing unborn children—some 42 million since *Roe* v. *Wade* was passed in 1973. To them, people never have the right to end innocent life in this way. But pro-choice advocates are no less committed to the position that women must have control over their own bodies. If pregnancy decides the course of women's lives, women will never be able to compete with men on equal terms, whether it is on campus or in the workplace. Therefore, access to legal, safe abortion is a necessary condition to women's full participation in society.

*Survey Question: "It should be possible for a pregnant woman to obtain a **legal abortion** . . ."*

A bar chart titled "Percentage Answering Yes" showing the following values:
- "... if the woman's own health is seriously endangered by the pregnancy.": 82.6
- "... if she became pregnant as a result of rape.": 72.5
- "... if there is a strong chance of serious defect in the baby.": 69.5
- "... if she is married and does not want any more children.": 40.1
- "... if she is not married and does not want to marry the man.": 39.4
- "... if the family has a very low income and cannot afford any more children.": 39.2
- "... for any reason.": 38.5

When Should the Law Allow a Woman to Choose Abortion?

The extent of public support for legal abortion depends on exactly how the issue is presented.
Source: NORC (2005).

WHAT DO YOU THINK?

1. The more conservative, pro-life position sees abortion as a moral issue, and the more liberal, pro-choice position views abortion as a power issue. Compare these positions to how conservatives and liberals view the issue of pornography.

2. Surveys show that men and women have almost the same opinions about abortion. Does this surprise you? Why or why not?

3. Why do you think the abortion controversy is often so bitter? Do you think our nation can find a middle ground on this issue?

Queer Theory

Finally, social-conflict theory has taken aim not only at the domination of women by men but also at heterosexuals dominating homosexuals. In recent years, as many lesbians and gay men have sought public acceptance, a gay voice has arisen in sociology. The term **queer theory** refers to *a body of research findings that challenges the heterosexual bias in U.S. society.*

Queer theory begins with the claim that our society is characterized by **heterosexism,** *a view that labels anyone who is not heterosexual as "queer."* Our heterosexual culture victimizes a wide range of people, including gay men, lesbians, bisexuals, intersexuals, transsexuals, and even asexual people. Although most people agree that bias against women (sexism) and people of color (racism) is

wrong, heterosexism is widely tolerated and sometimes well within the law. For example, U.S. military forces cannot legally discharge a female soldier simply for "acting like a woman" because this would be a clear case of gender discrimination. But the military forces can discharge her for homosexuality if she is a sexually active lesbian.

Heterosexism is also part of everyday culture. When we describe something as "sexy," for example, don't we really mean attractive to *heterosexuals?*

 Can you think of three attitudes or social patterns (like the one just mentioned) that are examples of heterosexism?

From a social-conflict point of view, sexuality is not so much a "natural" part of our humanity as it is a socially constructed pattern of behavior. Sexuality plays an important part in social inequality: By defining women in sexual terms, men devalue them as objects. Would you consider the behavior shown here to be "natural" or socially directed? Why?

Richard Lord/The Image Works

CRITICAL REVIEW The social-conflict approach shows that sexuality is both a cause and an effect of inequality. In particular, it helps us understand men's power over women and heterosexual people's domination of homosexual people.

At the same time, this approach overlooks the fact that many people do not see sexuality as a power issue. On the contrary, many couples enjoy a vital sexual relationship that deepens their commitment to one another. In addition, the social-conflict approach pays little attention to steps U.S. society has taken toward reducing inequality. Today's men are less likely to describe women as sex objects than they were a few decades ago. One of the most important issues in the workplace today is ensuring that all employees remain free from sexual harassment. Rising public concern has reduced the abuse of sexuality in the workplace. Likewise, there is ample evidence that the gay rights movement has secured greater opportunities and social acceptance for gay people.

 YOUR LEARNING How does sexuality play a part in creating social inequality?

This chapter closes with a look at what is perhaps the most divisive issue involving sexuality: **abortion,** *the deliberate termination of a pregnancy.* There seems to be no middle ground in the debate over this controversial issue. The Controversy & Debate box helps explain why.

Applying Sociology in Everyday Life

1. The most complete study of sexual patterns in the United States to date is *The Social Organization of Sexuality: Sexual Practices in the United States* by Edward Laumann and others. Get a copy from your campus or community library, and read a chapter or two. See if what you read surprises you, and explain why.

2. Contact your school's student services office, and ask for information about the extent of sexual violence on your campus. Do people typically report such crimes? What policies and procedures does your school have to respond to sexual violence?

3. Use the campus library and Internet sources to learn more about the experiences of women and men involved in prostitution. As you learn more, decide whether you think prostitution should be considered a "victimless crime."

MAKING THE GRADE

Sexuality

What Is Sexuality?

SEX is biological, referring to bodily differences between females and males.

GENDER is cultural, referring to behavior, power, and privileges a society attaches to being female or male.

Sexuality is a **BIOLOGICAL ISSUE**.
- Sex is determined at conception as a male sperm joins a female ovum.
- Males and females have different genitals (*primary sex characteristics*) and bodily development (*secondary sex characteristics*).
- *Intersexual people* (*hermaphrodites*) have some combination of male and female genitalia.
- *Transsexual people* feel they are one sex although biologically they are the other.

Sexuality is a **CULTURAL ISSUE**.
- For humans, sex is a matter of cultural meaning and personal choice rather than biological programming.
- Sexual practices vary considerably from one society to another (examples include kissing, ideas about modesty, and standards of beauty).
- The *incest taboo* exists in all societies because regulating sexuality, especially reproduction, is a necessary element of social organization. Specific taboos vary from one society to another.

sex the biological distinction between females and males

primary sex characteristics the genitals, organs used for reproduction

secondary sex characteristics bodily development, apart from the genitals, that distinguishes biologically mature females and males

intersexual people people whose bodies (including genitals) have both female and male characteristics

transsexuals people who feel they are one sex even though biologically they are the other

incest taboo a norm forbidding sexual relations or marriage between certain relatives

 Sexuality is a theme found throughout most areas of social life in the United States.

Sexual Attitudes in the United States

The **SEXUAL REVOLUTION**, which peaked in the 1960s and 1970s, drew sexuality out into the open. Baby boomers were the first generation to grow up with the idea that sex was a normal part of social life.

The **SEXUAL COUNTERREVOLUTION**, which was evident by 1980, aimed criticism at "permissiveness" and urged a return to more traditional "family values."

Beginning with the work of Alfred Kinsey, researchers have studied sexual behavior in the United States and reached many interesting conclusions:
- Premarital sexual intercourse became more common during the twentieth century.
- About three-fourths of young men and two-thirds of young women have intercourse by their senior year in high school.
- Among all U.S. adults, sexual activity varies: One-third report having sex with a partner a few times a year or not at all; another one-third have sex once to several times a month; the remaining one-third have sex two or more times a week.
- Extramarital sex is widely condemned, and just 25 percent of married men and 10 percent of married women report being sexually unfaithful to their spouses at some time.

Sexual Orientation

SEXUAL ORIENTATION is a person's romantic or emotional attraction to another person. Four sexual orientations are
- heterosexuality
- homosexuality
- bisexuality
- asexuality

Most research supports the claim that sexual orientation is rooted in biology in much the same way as being right-handed or left-handed.

Sexual orientation is not a matter of neat categories because many people who think of themselves as heterosexual have homosexual experiences; the reverse is also true.

- The share of the U.S. population that is homosexual depends on how you define "homosexuality."
- About 9% of adult men and 4% of adult women report engaging in some homosexual activity; 2.8% of men and 1.4% of women consider themselves homosexual.

The gay rights movement helped change public attitudes toward greater acceptance of homosexuality. Still, 60 percent of U.S. adults say homosexuality is wrong.

sexual orientation a person's romantic and emotional attraction to another person

heterosexuality sexual attraction to someone of the other sex

homosexuality sexual attraction to someone of the same sex

bisexuality sexual attraction to people of both sexes

asexuality a lack of sexual attraction to people of either sex

homophobia discomfort over close personal interaction with people thought to be gay, lesbian, or bisexual

Sexual Issues and Controversies

TEEN PREGNANCY About 750,000 U.S. teenagers become pregnant each year. The rate of teenage pregnancy has dropped since 1950, when many teens married and had children. Today, most pregnant teens are not married and are at high risk of dropping out of school and being poor.

PORNOGRAPHY The law allows local communities to set standards of decency. Conservatives condemn pornography on moral grounds; liberals view pornography as a power issue, condemning it as demeaning to women.

pornography sexually explicit material intended to cause sexual arousal

prostitution the selling of sexual services

abortion the deliberate termination of a pregnancy

PROSTITUTION The selling of sexual services is illegal almost everywhere in the United States. Many people view prostitution as a victimless crime, but it victimizes women and spreads sexually transmitted diseases.

SEXUAL VIOLENCE Some 94,000 rapes are reported each year in the United States, but the actual number is probably several times higher. Rapes are violent crimes in which victims and offenders typically know one another.

ABORTION Laws banned abortion in all states by 1900. Opposition to these laws rose during the 1960s, and in 1973, the U.S. Supreme Court declared these laws unconstitutional. Today, some 1.3 million abortions are performed each year. People who describe themselves as "pro-choice" support a woman's right to choose abortion; people who call themselves "pro-life" oppose abortion on moral grounds.

Theoretical Analysis of Sexuality

The **STRUCTURAL-FUNCTIONAL APPROACH** highlights society's need to regulate sexual activity and especially reproduction. One universal norm is the incest taboo, which keeps family relations clear.

The **SYMBOLIC-INTERACTION APPROACH** emphasizes the various meanings people attach to sexuality. The social construction of sexuality can be seen in sexual differences between societies and in changing sexual patterns over time.

The **SOCIAL-CONFLICT APPROACH** links sexuality to social inequality. Feminist theory claims that men dominate women by devaluing them to the level of sexual objects. Queer theory claims our society has a heterosexual bias, defining anything different as "queer."

queer theory a body of research findings that challenges the heterosexual bias in U.S. society

heterosexism a view that labels anyone who is not heterosexual as "queer"

⊞   See the Applying Theory table in this chapter.

MAKING THE GRADE

Sexuality and Society

Sample Test Questions

These questions are similar to those found in the test bank that accompanies this textbook.

Multiple-Choice Questions

1. **What is the term for humans who have some combination of female and male genitalia?**
   a. asexual people
   b. bisexual people
   c. transsexual people
   d. intersexual people

2. **A global perspective on human sexuality shows us that**
   a. although sex involves our biology, it is also a cultural trait that varies from place to place.
   b. people everywhere in the world have the same sexual practices.
   c. people in all societies are uncomfortable talking about sex.
   d. All of the above are correct.

3. **Why is the incest taboo found in every society?**
   a. It limits sexual competition between members of families.
   b. It helps define people's rights and obligations toward one another.
   c. It integrates members of a family within the larger society.
   d. All of the above are correct.

4. **The sexual revolution came of age during the**
   a. 1890s.
   b. 1920s.
   c. 1960s.
   d. 1980s.

5. **Survey data show that the largest share of U.S. adults reject which of the following?**
   a. extramarital sex
   b. homosexuality
   c. premarital sex
   d. sex simply for pleasure

6. **According to the Laumann study of sexuality in the United States,**
   a. only one-third of the adult population is sexually active.
   b. there is great diversity in levels of sexual activity, so no one stereotype is correct.
   c. single people have more sex than married people.
   d. most married men admit to cheating on their wives at some point in their marriage.

7. **What is the term meaning "sexual attraction to people of both sexes"?**
   a. heterosexuality
   b. homosexuality
   c. bisexuality
   d. asexuality

8. **Compared to 1950, the U.S. rate of teenage pregnancy today is**
   a. higher.
   b. the same, but more teens become pregnant by choice.
   c. the same, but more pregnant teens are married.
   d. lower.

9. **By what point in their lives do most young people in the United States today become sexually active?**
   a. when they marry
   b. by the middle of college
   c. by the end of high school
   d. by age thirteen

10. **If we look back in history, we see that once a society develops birth control technology,**
    a. social control of sexuality becomes more strict.
    b. the birth rate actually goes up.
    c. attitudes about sexuality become more permissive.
    d. people no longer care about incest.

ANSWERS: 1 (d); 2 (a); 3 (d); 4 (c); 5 (a); 6 (b); 7 (c); 8 (d); 9 (c); 10 (c).

Essay Questions

1. What was the "sexual revolution"? What changed? Can you point to reasons for the change?

2. Of the issues discussed in this chapter (prostitution, teen pregnancy, pornography, sexual violence, and abortion), which do you think is the most important for U.S. society today? Why?

Deviance

We are all familiar with the experience of being "different." Deviance—or standing out from what is normal—is not just a matter of individual choice but has much to do with the operation of society.

Peter Frischmuth/ argus

Deviance

WHY is deviance found in all societies?

HOW does *who* and *what* are defined as deviant reflect social inequality?

WHAT effect has punishment had in reducing crime in the United States?

AP Wide World Photos

The black SUV rolled through the gates of the federal women's prison in Alderson, West Virginia, threading its way among the sea of news reporters, many of whom leaned toward the vehicle to catch a glimpse of the famous woman sitting in back. Martha Stewart had just been released from jail. Stewart was sent to prison in 2004 after being convicted of lying about an improper stock deal. After five months behind bars, she was eager to get home. Soon after leaving the prison, the woman who made a fortune explaining how to live well boarded a private jet that whisked her away to her 153-acre ranch in Katonah, New York. Within three days, she reported to her probation officer, who placed an electronic monitor on her ankle and explained that she would have to spend the next five months at home under house arrest.

The day after her release, Wes Smith, a postal carrier in Katonah, smiled at reporters as he delivered mail to Stewart's home. "She's served her time. She's probably a changed person. Maybe she learned her lesson" (Fitzgerald, 2005).

This chapter explores crime, criminals, and punishment, showing that individuals convicted of wrongdoing do not always fit the common stereotype of the "street" criminal. The chapter also tackles the larger question of why societies develop standards of right and wrong in the first place. As we shall see, law is simply one part of a complex system of social control: Society teaches us all to conform, at least most of the time, to countless rules. We begin our investigation by defining several basic concepts.

What Is Deviance?

Deviance is *the recognized violation of cultural norms.* Norms guide almost all human activities, so the concept of deviance is quite broad. One category of deviance is **crime,** *the violation of a society's formally enacted criminal law.* Even criminal deviance spans a wide range, from minor traffic violations to sexual assault to murder.

Most familiar examples of nonconformity are negative instances of rule breaking, such as stealing from a campus bookstore, assaulting a fellow student, or driving while intoxicated. But we also define especially righteous people—students who speak up too much in class or people who are overly enthusiastic about new computer technology—as deviant, even if we give them a measure of respect. What deviant actions or attitudes, whether negative or positive, have in common is some element of *difference* that causes us to think of another person as an "outsider" (H. S. Becker, 1966).

Not all deviance involves action or even choice. The very *existence* of some categories of people can be troublesome to others. To the young, elderly people may seem hopelessly "out of it," and to some whites, the mere presence of people of color may cause discomfort. Able-bodied people often view people with disabilities as an out-group, just as rich people may shun the poor for falling short of their standards.

Social Control

All of us are subject to **social control,** *attempts by society to regulate people's thoughts and behavior.* Often this process is informal, as when parents praise or scold their children or when friends make fun of a

classmate's choice of music. Cases of serious deviance, however, may involve the **criminal justice system,** *a formal response by police, courts, and prison officials to alleged violations of the law.*

How a society defines deviance, *who* is branded as deviant, and *what* people decide to do about deviance all have to do with the way society is organized. Only gradually, however, have people recognized that deviance is much more than a matter of individual choice, as this chapter now explains.

The Biological Context

Chapter 5 ("Socialization") explained that a century ago, most people understood—or more correctly, misunderstood—human behavior to be the result of biological instincts. Early interest in criminality thus focused on biological causes. In 1876, Cesare Lombroso (1835–1909), an Italian physician who worked in prisons, theorized that criminals stand out physically, with low foreheads, prominent jaws and cheekbones, hairiness, and unusually long arms. All in all, Lombroso claimed that criminals look like our apelike ancestors.

Had Lombroso looked more carefully, he would have found the physical features he linked to criminality throughout the entire population. We now know that no physical traits distinguish criminals from noncriminals.

In the middle of the twentieth century, William Sheldon took a different approach, suggesting that general body structure might predict criminality (Sheldon, Hartl, & McDermott, 1949). He cross-checked hundreds of young men for body type and criminal history and concluded that criminality was most likely among boys with muscular, athletic builds. Sheldon Glueck and Eleanor Glueck (1950) confirmed Sheldon's conclusion but cautioned that a powerful build does not necessarily *cause* criminality. Parents, they suggested, tend to be somewhat distant from powerfully built sons, who in turn grow up to show less sensitivity toward others. Moreover, in a self-fulfilling prophecy, people who expect muscular boys to be bullies may act in ways that bring about the aggressive behavior they expect.

Today, genetics research seeks possible links between biology and crime. In 2003, scientists at the University of Wisconsin reported results of a twenty-five-year study of crime among 400 boys. The researchers collected DNA samples from each boy and noted any trouble they had with the law. The researchers concluded that genetic factors (especially defective genes that, say, make too much of an enzyme) together with environmental factors (especially abuse early in life) were strong predictors of adult crime and violence. They noted, too, that these factors together were a better predictor of crime than either one alone (Lemonick, 2003; Pinker, 2003).

▶**CRITICAL REVIEW**   Biological theories offer a limited explanation of crime. The best guess at present is that biological traits in combination with environmental factors explain some serious crime. But most of the actions we define as deviant are carried out by people who are physically quite normal.

In addition, because a biological approach looks at the individual, it offers no insight into how some kinds of behaviors come to be defined as deviant in the first place. Therefore, although there is much to be learned about how human biology may affect behavior, research currently puts far greater emphasis on social influences.

Personality Factors

Like biological theories, psychological explanations of deviance focus on abnormality in the individual personality. Some personality traits are inherited, but most psychologists think that personality is shaped primarily by social experience. Deviance, then, is viewed as the result of "unsuccessful" socialization.

Classic research by Walter Reckless and Simon Dinitz (1967) illustrates the psychological approach. Reckless and Dinitz began by asking a number of teachers to categorize twelve-year-old male students as either likely or unlikely to get into trouble with the law. They then interviewed both the boys and their mothers to assess each boy's self-concept and how he related to others. Analyzing their results, Reckless and Dinitz found that the "good boys" displayed a strong conscience (what Freud called superego), could handle frustration, and identified with cultural norms and values. The "bad boys," by contrast, had a weaker conscience, displayed little tolerance of frustration, and felt out of step with conventional culture.

As we might expect, the "good boys" went on to have fewer run-ins with the police than the "bad boys." Because all the boys lived in an area where delinquency was widespread, the investigators attributed staying out of trouble to a personality that controlled deviant impulses. Based on this conclusion, Reckless and Dinitz called their analysis *containment theory*.

Deviance is always a matter of difference. Deviance emerges in everyday life as we encounter people whose appearance or behavior differs from what we consider to be "normal." Who is the "deviant" in this photograph? From whose point of view?

Melissa Moore/The Image Works

▶**CRITICAL REVIEW**   Psychologists have shown that personality patterns have some connection to deviance. Some serious criminals are psychopaths who do not feel guilt or shame, have no fear of punishment, and have little or no sympathy for the people they harm (Herpertz & Sass, 2000). However, as noted in the case of biological factors, most serious crimes are committed by people whose psychological profiles are normal.

Both the biological and psychological approaches view deviance as a trait of individuals. The reason that these approaches have had limited value in explaining deviance is that wrongdoing has more to do with the organization of society. We now turn to a sociological approach, which explores where ideas of right and wrong come from, why people define some

rule breakers but not others as deviant, and what role power
plays in this process.

YOUR LEARNING Why does a biological or psychological analysis
not explain deviance very well?

The Social Foundations of Deviance

Although we tend to view deviance as the free choice or personal failings of individuals, all behavior—deviance as well as conformity—is
shaped by society. Three social foundations of deviance identified
here will be detailed later in this chapter:

1. **Deviance varies according to cultural norms.** No thought or
   action is inherently deviant; it becomes deviant only in relation
   to particular norms. Because norms vary from place to place,
   deviance also varies. For instance, New Jersey law does not permit people to pump their own gas at gas stations. Nevada state
   law permits prostitution in rural areas of the state, although
   the practice is outlawed in the rest of the United States. Eleven
   states have gambling casinos, and twenty-eight have casinos on
   Indian reservations; in all other states, however, casino gambling is illegal.

Further, most cities and towns have at least one unique
law. For example, Bangor, Maine, does not permit smoking in
a car carrying a young child; Mobile, Alabama, outlaws the
wearing of stiletto-heeled shoes; in Juneau, Alaska, it is illegal
to bring a flamingo into a barbershop; South Padre Island,
Texas, bans the wearing of neckties; Mount Prospect, Illinois,
has a law against keeping pigeons or bees; Topeka, Kansas,
bans snowball fights; Hoover, South Dakota, does not allow
fishing with a kerosene lantern; and Beverly Hills, California,
regulates the number of tennis balls allowed on the court at
one time (R. Steele, 2000; "Notebook," 2006).

Around the world, deviance is even more diverse. Albania
outlaws any public display of religious faith, such as "crossing"
oneself; Cuba bans citizens from owning personal computers;
Vietnam can prosecute citizens for meeting with foreigners;
Malaysia does not allow women to wear tight-fitting jeans; police
in Iran can arrest a woman simply for wearing makeup; and
Saudi Arabia bans the sale of red flowers on Valentine's Day.

2. **People become deviant as others define them that way.**
   Everyone violates cultural norms at one time or another. Have
   you ever walked around talking to yourself or "borrowed" a
   pen from your workplace? Whether such behavior defines us
   as mentally ill or criminal depends on how others perceive,
   define, and respond to it.

3. **Both norms and the way people define rule-breaking involve
   social power.** The law, declared Karl Marx, is the means by
   which powerful people protect their interests. A homeless person who stands on a street corner speaking out against the
   government risks arrest for disturbing the peace; a mayoral
   candidate during an election campaign does exactly the same
   thing and gets police protection. In short, norms and how we
   apply them reflect social inequality.

The Functions of Deviance: Structural-Functional Analysis

The key insight of the structural-functional approach is that deviance
is a necessary part of social organization. This point was made a century ago by Emile Durkheim.

Durkheim's Basic Insight

In his pioneering study of deviance, Emile Durkheim (1964a, orig.
1893; 1964b, orig. 1895) made the surprising claim that there is nothing abnormal about deviance. In fact, it performs four essential
functions:

Why is it that street-corner gambling like this is usually against the law but
playing the same games in a fancy casino is not?
© Shepard Sherbell / Corbis SABA

tip

Notice that Durkheim considered deviance to be a natural and necessary part of all social organization.

student 2 student

"Wow! Today's class was really great! I never thought about the possibility that deviance is actually very normal. Okay, sociology really is not just common sense."

1. **Deviance affirms cultural values and norms.** As moral creatures, people must prefer some attitudes and behaviors to others. But any definition of virtue rests on an opposing idea of vice: There can be no good without evil and no justice without crime. Deviance is needed to define and support morality.

2. **Responding to deviance clarifies moral boundaries.** By defining some individuals as deviant, people draw a boundary between right and wrong. For example, a college marks the line between academic honesty and cheating by punishing students who cheat on exams.

3. **Responding to deviance brings people together.** People typically react to serious deviance with shared outrage. In doing so, Durkheim explained, they reaffirm the moral ties that bind them. For example, after the September 11, 2001, terrorist attacks, people across the United States were joined by a common desire to protect the country and bring those responsible to justice.

4. **Deviance encourages social change.** Deviant people push a society's moral boundaries, suggesting alternatives to the status quo and encouraging change. Today's deviance, declared Durkheim, can become tomorrow's morality (1964b:71, orig. 1895). For example, rock-and-roll, condemned as immoral in the 1950s, became a multibillion-dollar industry just a few years later; in recent years, hip-hop music has followed the same path.

 Keeping in mind Durkheim's claim that society creates deviance to mark moral boundaries, why do we often define people only in terms of their deviance by calling someone an "addict" or a "thief"?

An Illustration: The Puritans of Massachusetts Bay

Kai Erikson's classic study of the Puritans of Massachusetts Bay brings Durkheim's theory to life. Erikson (2005b, orig. 1966) shows that even the Puritans, a disciplined and highly religious group, created deviance to clarify their moral boundaries. In fact, Durkheim might well have had the Puritans in mind when he wrote:

> Imagine a society of saints, a perfect cloister of exemplary individuals. Crimes, properly so called, will there be unknown; but faults which appear [insignificant] to the layman will create there the same scandal that the ordinary offense does in ordinary consciousness.... For the same reason, the perfect and upright man judges his smallest failings with a severity that the majority reserve for acts more truly in the nature of an offense. (1964b:68–69, orig. 1895)

Durkheim claimed that deviance is a necessary element of social organization, serving several important functions. In the wake of a double homicide and suicide in 2006, residents of Laramie, Wyoming, came together to affirm their community ties as well as their understanding of right and wrong. Has any event on your campus caused a similar reaction?

Barbara J. Perenic/The Laramie Boomerang/AP Wide World Photos

Deviance is not a matter of a few "bad apples" but a necessary condition of "good" social living.

Deviance may be found in every society, but the *kind* of deviance people generate depends on the moral issues they seek to clarify. The Puritans, for example, experienced a number of "crime waves," including the well-known outbreak of witchcraft in 1692. With each response, the Puritans answered questions about the range of proper beliefs by celebrating some of their members and condemning others as deviant.

Erikson discovered that even though the offenses changed, the proportion of people the Puritans defined as deviant remained steady over time. This stability, he concluded, confirms Durkheim's claim that society creates deviants to mark its changing moral boundaries. In other words, by constantly defining a small number of people as deviant, the Puritans maintained the moral shape of their society.

Merton's Strain Theory

Some deviance may be necessary for a society to function, but Robert Merton (1938, 1968) argued that society can be set up in a way that encourages too much deviance. In addition, he explained, the type of deviance people engage in depends on whether a society provides

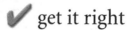
them the *means* (such as schooling and job opportunities) to achieve cultural *goals* (such as financial success).

Conformity lies in pursuing cultural goals through approved means. Thus the U.S. "success story" is someone who gains wealth and prestige through talent, schooling, and hard work. But not everyone who wants conventional success has the opportunity to attain it. For example, people raised in poverty may have little hope of becoming successful if they play by the rules. According to Merton, the strain between our culture's emphasis on wealth and the lack of opportunities to get rich may encourage some people, especially the poor, to engage in stealing, drug dealing, or other forms of street crime. Merton called this type of deviance *innovation*—using unconventional means (street crime) to achieve a culturally approved goal (wealth). Figure 1 shows that innovation involves accepting a cultural goal (financial success) but rejecting the conventional means (hard work at a "straight" job) in favor of unconventional means (street crime).

The inability to reach a cultural goal may also prompt another type of deviance that Merton calls *ritualism* (see Figure 1). For example, many people may not care much about becoming rich, but they rigidly stick to the rules (the conventional means) in order to at least feel respectable.

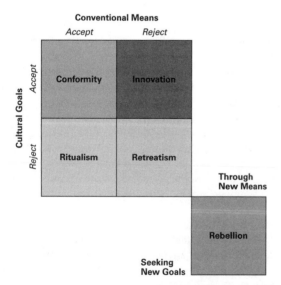

FIGURE 1 Merton's Strain Theory of Deviance

Combining a person's view of cultural goals and the conventional means to obtain them allowed Robert Merton to identify various types of deviance.
Source: Merton (1968).

A third response to the inability to succeed is *retreatism*: rejecting both cultural goals and conventional means, so that a person in effect "drops out." Some alcoholics, drug addicts, and street people can be described as retreatists. The deviance of retreatists lies in their unconventional lifestyle and also in what seems to be their willingness to live this way.

The fourth response to failure is *rebellion*. Like retreatists, rebels such as radical "survivalists" reject both the cultural definition of success and the conventional means of achieving it, but they go one step further by forming a counterculture supporting alternatives to the existing social order.

Deviant Subcultures

Richard Cloward and Lloyd Ohlin (1966) extended Merton's theory, proposing that crime results not simply from limited legitimate (legal) opportunity but also from readily accessible illegitimate (illegal) opportunity. In short, deviance or conformity arises from the *relative opportunity structure* that frames a person's life.

The life of Al Capone, a notorious gangster, illustrates Cloward and Ohlin's theory. As the son of poor immigrants, Capone faced barriers of poverty and ethnic prejudice, which lowered his odds of achieving success in conventional terms. Yet as a young man during Prohibition (when alcoholic beverages were banned in the United States between 1920 and 1933), Capone found in his neighborhood people who could teach him how to sell alcohol illegally—a source of illegitimate opportunity. Where the structure of opportunity favors criminal activity, Cloward and Ohlin predict the development of *criminal subcultures*, such as street gangs.

But what happens when people cannot identify *any* kind of opportunity, legal or illegal? Then deviance may take the form of *conflict subcultures* (armed street gangs), where violence is ignited by frustration and a desire for respect, or *retreatist subcultures*, in which deviants drop out and may abuse alcohol or other drugs.

Albert Cohen (1971, orig. 1955) suggests that delinquency is most common among lower-class youths because they have the least opportunity to achieve conventional success. Neglected by society, they seek self-respect by creating a delinquent subculture that defines as worthy the traits these youths do have. Being feared on the street may not win many points with society as a whole, but it may satisfy a young person's desire to "be somebody" in the local neighborhood.

Walter Miller (1970, orig. 1958) adds that delinquent subcultures are characterized by (1) *trouble,* arising from frequent conflict with teachers and police; (2) *toughness,* the value placed on physical size and strength, especially among males; (3) *smartness,* the ability to

tip

In this section, we return to the concept of subculture. The point here is that subculture can encourage crime or other deviance.

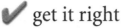

get it right

Study the definition of labeling theory, which is the key idea of the symbolic-interaction approach. Be sure you understand this statement: Deviance results not so much from what people do as from how others respond to what they do.

succeed on the streets, to outsmart or "con" others, and to avoid being similarly taken advantage of; (4) *a need for excitement,* the search for thrills, risk, or danger; (5) *a belief in fate,* a sense that people lack control over their own lives; and (6) *a desire for freedom,* often expressed as anger toward authority figures.

Finally, Elijah Anderson (1994, 2002; Kubrin, 2005) explains that in poor urban neighborhoods, most people manage to conform to conventional or "decent" values. Yet faced with neighborhood crime and violence, indifference or even hostility from police, and sometimes even neglect by their own parents, some young men decide to live by the "street code." To show that they can survive on the street, a young man displays "nerve," a willingness to stand up to any threat. Following this street code, which is also evident in much recent rap music, the young man believes that a violent death is better than being "dissed" (disrespected) by others. Some manage to escape the dangers, but the risk of ending up in jail—or worse—is very high for these young men, who have been pushed to the margins of our society.

▶**CRITICAL REVIEW** Durkheim made an important contribution by pointing out the functions of deviance. However, there is evidence that a community does not always come together in reaction to crime; sometimes fear of crime causes people to withdraw from public life (Liska & Warner, 1991; Warr & Ellison, 2000).

Merton's strain theory has been criticized for explaining some kinds of deviance (stealing, for example) better than others (such as crimes of passion or mental illness). In addition, not everyone seeks success in the conventional terms of wealth, as strain theory suggests.

The general argument of Cloward and Ohlin, Cohen, Miller, and Anderson—that deviance reflects the opportunity structure of society—has been confirmed by subsequent research (Allan & Steffensmeier, 1989; Uggen, 1999). However, these theories fall short by assuming that everyone shares the same cultural standards for judging right and wrong. If we define crime as not just burglary and auto theft but the type of illegal stock deals that sent Martha Stewart to prison, then more high-income people will be counted among criminals. There is evidence that people of all social backgrounds are becoming more casual about breaking the rules, as the Seeing Sociology in Everyday Life box explains.

Finally, all structural-functional theories suggest that everyone who breaks important rules will be labeled deviant. However, becoming deviant is actually a highly complex process, as the next section explains.

Young people cut off from legitimate opportunity often form subcultures that many people view as deviant. Gang subcultures are one way young people gain the sense of belonging and respect denied to them by the larger culture.

Hector Mata/ Getty Images, Inc.—Agence France Presse

 YOUR LEARNING: Why do you think many of the theories just discussed seem to say that crime is more common among people with lower social standing?

Labeling Deviance: Symbolic-Interaction Analysis

The symbolic-interaction approach explains how people define deviance in everyday situations. From this point of view, definitions of deviance and conformity are surprisingly flexible.

Labeling Theory

The main contribution of symbolic-interaction analysis is **labeling theory,** *the idea that deviance and conformity result not so much from what people do as from how others respond to those actions.* Labeling theory stresses the relativity of deviance, the idea that people may define the same behavior in any number of ways.

Consider these situations: A college student takes a sweater off the back of a roommate's chair and wears it without asking, a married woman at a convention in a distant city has sex with an old boyfriend, and a city mayor gives a big contract to a major campaign

tip

Once you understand labeling theory, it is easy to apply this approach to everyday life, which is the goal of all the remaining sections in this part of the chapter.

Seeing Sociology in Everyday Life
Deviant Subculture: Has It Become OK to Break the Rules?

It's been a bad couple of years for the idea of playing by the rules. First, we learn that the executives of not just one but many U.S. corporations are guilty of fraud and outright stealing on a scale most of us cannot even imagine. Then Martha Stewart, the country's lifestyle guru, is sent to jail for trading stocks illegally and lying about it. Perhaps worst of all, the Catholic church, which we hold up as a model of moral behavior, has been stunned by charges that thousands of priests have sexually abused parishioners (most of them children) while church officials busied themselves covering up the crimes. By 2005, more than 300 priests in the United States had been removed from their duties pending investigations of abuse. Finally, in 2006, a number of members of Congress—the people we elected as our leaders—were found to have accepted money illegally in influence peddling scandals by lobbyists.

There are plenty of ideas about what is causing this widespread wrongdoing. Some people suggest that the pressure to win—by whatever means necessary—in today's highly competitive corporate world can be overwhelming. As one analyst put it, "You can get away with your embezzle-

ments and your lies—but you can never get away with *failing*."

Such thinking helps explain the wrongdoing among many CEOs in the corporate world and taking money by some members of Congress, but it offers little insight into the problem of abusive priests. In some ways at least, wrongdoing seems to have become a way of life for just about everybody. For example, the Internal Revenue Service reports that many U.S. taxpayers cheat on their taxes, failing to pay an estimated $200 billion each year (an average of about $1,600 per taxpayer). The

Do you consider cheating in school wrong? Would you turn in someone you saw cheating? Why or why not?

SW Production/Photolibrary.com

music industry claims that it has lost a vast amount of money because of illegal piracy of recordings, a practice especially common among young people. Perhaps most disturbing of all, surveys of high school and college students show that at least half say they cheated on a test at least once during the past year.

Emile Durkheim viewed society as a moral system built on a set of rules about what people should and should not do. Years earlier, another French thinker named Blaise Pascal made the contrasting claim that "cheating is the foundation of society."

Today, which of the two statements is closer to the truth?

WHAT DO YOU THINK?

1. In your opinion, how widespread is wrongdoing in U.S. society today? Have you downloaded music illegally? What about cheating on your college assignments or tests?

2. Do you think people who break the rules usually consider what they are doing as wrong? Why or why not?

3. What do you think are the reasons for the apparent increase in dishonesty?

Sources: "Our Cheating Hearts" (2002) and Bono (2006).

---

contributor. We might define the first situation as carelessness, borrowing, or theft. The consequences of the second case depend largely on whether the woman's behavior becomes known back home. In the third situation, is the official choosing the best contractor or paying off a political debt? The social construction of reality is a highly variable process of detection, definition, and response.

Explain in your own words sociologist Howard Becker's (1966) statement that deviance is nothing more than behavior that people define as deviant.

Primary and Secondary Deviance

Edwin Lemert (1951, 1972) observed that some norm violations—say, skipping school or underage drinking—provoke slight reaction from others and have little effect on a person's self-concept. Lemert calls such passing episodes *primary deviance.*

But what happens if other people notice someone's deviance and make something of it? For example, if people begin to describe a young man as an "alcohol abuser" and exclude him from their friendship group, he may become bitter, drink even more, and seek the company of others who approve of his behavior. The response to primary

　　　　　　　　　　　DEVIANCE

tip

Here's a helpful idea: "Deviance is a difference that people think makes a difference." In other words, we all differ from one another in lots of ways without anyone taking special note of it. But when people do make something of a difference, the possibility of becoming deviant is very high.

student 2 student

"Labeling theory seems to be saying that deviance lies not in the person doing it but in the people responding to it."

deviance sets in motion *secondary deviance*, by which a person repeatedly violates a norm and begins to take on a deviant identity.

Can you see how the development of secondary deviance is one application of the Thomas theorem (discussed in Chapter 6, "Social Interaction in Everyday Life"), which states that situations defined as real become real in their consequences?

Stigma

Secondary deviance marks the start of what Erving Goffman (1963) calls a *deviant career*. As people develop a stronger commitment to deviant behavior, they typically acquire a **stigma,** *a powerfully negative label that greatly changes a person's self-concept and social identity.*

A stigma operates as a master status, overpowering other aspects of social identity so that a person is discredited in the minds of others and becomes socially isolated. Sometimes an entire community formally stigmatizes an individual through what Harold Garfinkel (1956) calls a *degradation ceremony.* A criminal trial is one example, operating much the way a high school graduation does but in reverse: A person stands before the community to be labeled in a negative rather than a positive way.

Retrospective and Projective Labeling

Once people stigmatize an individual, they may engage in *retrospective labeling,* interpreting someone's past in light of some present deviance (Scheff, 1984). For example, after discovering that a priest has sexually molested a child, others rethink his past, perhaps musing, "He always seemed to like being around young children." Retrospective labeling, which distorts a person's biography by being highly selective, typically deepens a deviant identity.

Similarly, people may engage in *projective labeling* of a stigmatized person. That is, they use a deviant identity to predict future action. Regarding the priest, people might say, "He's going to keep at it until he gets caught." The more people in someone's social world think such things, the greater is the chance that they will come true.

Labeling Difference as Deviance

Is a homeless man who refuses to allow police to take him to a city shelter on a cold night simply trying to live independently, or is he "crazy"? People have a tendency to treat behavior that irritates or threatens them not simply as "different" but as deviance or even mental illness.

The psychiatrist Thomas Szasz (1961, 1970, 2003, 2004) charges that people are too quick to apply the label of mental ill-

ness to conditions that simply amount to a difference we don't like. The only way to avoid this troubling practice, Szasz continues, is to abandon the idea of mental illness entirely. The world is full of people whose "differences" in thought or action may irritate us, but such differences are not grounds for defining someone as mentally ill. Such labeling, Szasz claims, simply enforces conformity to the standards of people powerful enough to impose their will on others.

Most mental health care professionals reject the idea that mental illness does not exist. But they agree that it is important to think critically about how we define "difference." First, people who are mentally ill are no more to blame for their condition than people who suffer from cancer or some other physical problem. Therefore, having a mental or physical illness is not grounds for being labeled "deviant." Second, ordinary people without the medical knowledge to diagnose mental illness should avoid using such labels in an effort to make people conform to certain standards of behavior.

The Medicalization of Deviance

Labeling theory, particularly the ideas of Szasz and Goffman, helps explain an important shift in the way our society understands deviance. Over the past fifty years, the growing influence of

The nation was stunned by the 2007 rampage on the Virginia Tech campus that left thirty-one people dead to become the deadliest mass shooting in U.S. history. In your opinion, was the man responsible, senior English major Cho Heung Hui, "crazy," "evil," "sick," or simply very misguided?

© Courtesy NBC

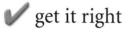
psychiatry and medicine in the United States has led to the **medicalization of deviance,** *the transformation of moral and legal deviance into a medical condition.*

Medicalization amounts to swapping one set of labels for another. In moral terms, we evaluate people or their behavior as "bad" or "good." However, the scientific objectivity of medicine passes no moral judgment, instead using clinical diagnoses such as "sick" or "well."

To illustrate, until the mid-twentieth century, people generally viewed alcoholics as morally weak people easily tempted by the pleasure of drink. Gradually, however, medical specialists redefined alcoholism so that most people now consider it a disease, rendering people "sick" rather than "bad." In the same way, obesity, drug addiction, child abuse, sexual promiscuity, and other behaviors that used to be strictly moral matters are widely defined today as illnesses for which people need help rather than punishment.

 Why do you think that politicians and other well-known people who get into trouble with the law often claim they have a problem with alcohol or other drugs and check into "rehab"?

The Difference Labels Make

Whether we define deviance as a moral or a medical issue has three consequences. First, it affects *who responds* to deviance. An offense against common morality usually brings about a reaction from members of the community or the police. A medical label, however, places the situation under the control of clinical specialists, including counselors, psychiatrists, and physicians.

A second difference is *how people respond* to deviance. A moral approach defines deviants as offenders subject to punishment. Medically, however, they are patients who need treatment. Punishment is designed to fit the crime, but treatment programs are tailored to fit the patient and may involve virtually any therapy that a specialist thinks might prevent future illness.

Third, and most important, the two labels differ on *the personal competence of the deviant person.* From a moral standpoint, whether we are right or wrong, at least we take responsibility for our own behavior. Once we are defined as sick, however, we are seen as unable to control (or, if "mentally ill," even understand) our actions. People who are labeled incompetent are in turn subjected to treatment, often against their will. For this reason alone, attempts to define deviance in medical terms should be made with extreme caution.

 An old saying goes, "Sticks and stones can break my bones, but names can never hurt me." What might labeling theory have to say about this idea?

Sutherland's Differential Association Theory

Learning any behavioral pattern, whether conventional or deviant, is a process that takes place in groups. According to Edwin Sutherland (1940), a person's tendency toward conformity or deviance depends on the amount of contact with others who encourage or reject conventional behavior. This is Sutherland's theory of *differential association.*

A number of studies confirm the idea that young people are more likely to engage in delinquency if they believe members of their peer groups encourage such activity (Akers et al., 1979; Miller & Mathews, 2001). One recent investigation focused on sexual activity among eighth-grade students. Two strong predictors of such behavior for young girls was having a boyfriend who encouraged sexual relations and having girlfriends they believed would approve of such activity. Similarly, boys were encouraged to become sexually active by friends who rewarded them with high status in the peer group (Little & Rankin, 2001).

Hirschi's Control Theory

The sociologist Travis Hirschi (1969; Gottfredson & Hirschi, 1995) developed *control theory,* which states that social control depends on people anticipating the consequences of their behavior. Hirschi assumes that everyone finds at least some deviance tempting. But the thought of a ruined career keeps most people from breaking the rules; for some, just imagining the reactions of family and friends is enough. On the other hand, individuals who feel they have little to lose by deviance are likely to become rule breakers.

Specifically, Hirschi links conformity to four different types of social control:

1. **Attachment.** Strong social attachments encourage conformity. Weak family, peer, and school relationships leave people freer to engage in deviance.

2. **Opportunity.** The greater a person's access to legitimate opportunity, the greater the advantages of conformity. By contrast, someone with little confidence in future success is more likely to drift toward deviance.

3. **Involvement.** Extensive involvement in legitimate activities—such as holding a job, going to school, or playing sports—

tip

Most sociologists consider Hirschi's control theory one of the most important explanations of deviant behavior.

inhibits deviance (Langbein & Bess, 2002). By contrast, people who simply "hang out" waiting for something to happen have time and energy to engage in deviant activity.

4. **Belief.** Strong belief in conventional morality and respect for authority figures restrain tendencies toward deviance. People who have a weak conscience (and who are left unsupervised) are more open to temptation (Stack, Wasserman, & Kern, 2004).

Hirschi's analysis combines a number of earlier ideas about the causes of deviant behavior. Note that a person's relative social privilege as well as family and community environment are likely to affect the risk of deviant behavior (Hope, Grasmick, & Pointon, 2003).

▶**CRITICAL REVIEW** The various symbolic-interaction theories all see deviance as a process. Labeling theory links deviance not to action but to the *reaction* of others. Thus some people are defined as deviant and others who think or behave in the same way are not. The concepts of secondary deviance, deviant career, and stigma show how being labeled deviant can become a lasting self-concept.

Yet labeling theory has several limitations. First, because it takes a highly relative view of deviance, labeling theory ignores the fact that some kinds of behavior—such as murder—are condemned just about everywhere. Therefore, labeling theory is most usefully applied to less serious issues, such as sexual promiscuity or mental illness. Second, research on the consequences of deviant labeling does not clearly show whether deviant labeling produces further deviance or discourages it (Smith & Gartin, 1989; Sherman & Smith, 1992). Third, not everyone resists being labeled deviant; some people actively seek it out (Vold & Bernard, 1986). For example, people take part in civil disobedience and willingly subject themselves to arrest in order to call attention to social injustice.

Sociologists consider Sutherland's differential association theory and Hirschi's control theory important contributions to our understanding of deviance. But why do society's norms and laws define certain kinds of activities as deviant in the first place? This question is addressed by social-conflict analysis, the focus of the next section.

All social groups teach their members skills and attitudes that encourage certain behavior. In recent years, discussion on college campuses has focused on the dangers of binge drinking, which results in about 300 deaths each year in the United States. How much of a problem is binge drinking on your campus?

AP Wide World Photos

 YOUR LEARNING Clearly define primary deviance, secondary deviance, deviant career, and stigma.

Deviance and Inequality: Social-Conflict Analysis

The social-conflict approach links deviance to social inequality. That is, *who* or *what* is labeled "deviant" depends on which categories of people hold power in a society.

Deviance and Power

Alexander Liazos (1972) points out that the people we tend to define as deviants—those we dismiss as "nuts" and "sluts"—are typically those who share the trait of powerlessness. Or, as Russell Simmons (2007:8) asks, "We talk about gangsta rappers, but why do we never talk about gangsta government?" Bag ladies, not corporate polluters, and unemployed men on street corners, not international arms dealers, carry the greatest stigma of deviance.

tip

As always, the social-conflict approach links deviance to power and social inequality. The ideas of Liazos and Spitzer are inspired by the thinking of Karl Marx.

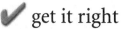

get it right

White-collar crime and corporate crime are similar concepts, and there is not always a clear line separating the two. White-collar criminals are *individuals* of high social position who commit crimes while doing their jobs. Corporate crime occurs when a *company* acts in violation of the law.

Social-conflict theory explains this pattern in three ways. First, all norms and especially the laws of any society generally reflect the interests of the rich and powerful. People who threaten the wealthy, either by taking their property or by advocating a more egalitarian society, are defined as "common thieves" or "political radicals." Karl Marx argued that the law and all other social institutions support the interests of the rich. Or as Richard Quinney puts it, "Capitalist justice is by the capitalist class, for the capitalist class, and against the working class" (1977:3).

Second, even if their behavior is called into question, the powerful have the resources to resist deviant labels. The majority of the executives involved in recent corporate scandals have yet to be arrested; only a few have gone to jail.

Third, the widespread belief that norms and laws are natural and good masks their political character. For this reason, although we may condemn the unequal application of the law, we give little thought to whether the laws themselves are really fair or not.

Deviance and Capitalism

In the Marxist tradition, Steven Spitzer (1980) argues that deviant labels are applied to people who interfere with the operation of capitalism. First, because capitalism is based on private control of wealth, people who threaten the property of others—especially the poor who steal from the rich—are prime candidates for being labeled deviant. On the other hand, the rich who take advantage of the poor are less likely to be labeled deviant. For example, landlords who charge poor tenants high rents and evict anyone who cannot pay are not considered criminals; they are simply "doing business."

Second, because capitalism depends on productive labor, people who cannot or will not work risk being labeled deviant. Many members of our society think people who are out of work, even through no fault of their own, are somehow deviant.

Third, capitalism depends on respect for authority figures, causing people who resist authority to be labeled deviant. Examples are children who skip school or talk back to parents and teachers and adults who do not cooperate with employers or police.

Fourth, anyone who directly challenges the capitalist status quo is likely to be defined as deviant. Such has been the case with labor organizers, radical environmentalists, and antiwar activists.

On the other side of the coin, society positively labels whatever supports the operation of capitalism. For example, winning athletes enjoy celebrity status because they express the values of individual achievement and competition, both vital to capitalism. Also, Spitzer notes, we condemn using drugs of escape (marijuana, psychedelics, heroin, and crack) as deviant but encourage drugs (such as alcohol and caffeine) that promote adjustment to the status quo.

The capitalist system also tries to control people who are not economically productive. The elderly, people with mental or physical disabilities, and Robert Merton's retreatists (people addicted to alcohol or other drugs) are a "costly yet relatively harmless burden" on society. Such people, claims Spitzer, are subject to control by social welfare agencies. But people who openly challenge the capitalist system, including the inner-city underclass and revolutionaries—Merton's innovators and rebels—are controlled by the criminal justice system and, in times of crisis, military forces such as the National Guard.

Note that both the social welfare and criminal justice systems blame individuals, not the system, for social problems. Welfare recipients are considered unworthy freeloaders, poor people who express rage at their plight are labeled rioters, anyone who challenges the government is branded a radical or a communist, and those who try to gain illegally what they will never get legally are rounded up as common criminals.

How would a Marxist analysis explain the fact that hundreds of miners have died in coal mines in West Virginia and other states in recent decades without anyone being charged with any crime?

White-Collar Crime

In a sign of things to come, a Wall Street stockbroker named Michael Milken made headlines back in 1987 when he was jailed for business fraud. Milken attracted attention because not since the days of Al Capone had anyone made so much money in one year: $550 million—about $1.5 million a day (Swartz, 1989).

Milken engaged in **white-collar crime,** defined by Edwin Sutherland (1940) as *crime committed by people of high social position in the course of their occupations.* White-collar crimes do not involve violence and rarely attract police to the scene with guns drawn. Rather, white-collar criminals use their powerful offices to illegally enrich themselves and others, often causing significant public harm in the process. For this reason, sociologists sometimes call white-collar offenses that occur in government offices and corporate boardrooms "crime in the suites" as opposed to "crime in the streets."

The most common white-collar crimes are bank embezzlement, business fraud, bribery, and antitrust violations. Sutherland (1940) explains that such white-collar offenses typically end up in a civil hearing rather than a criminal courtroom. *Civil law* regulates business dealings between private parties, and *criminal law* defines the individual's moral responsibilities to society. In practice, then, someone who

tip

The discussion of organized crime brings to mind the ideas of Merton and also of Cloward and Ohlin, discussed earlier. In this case, we understand organized crime as one way that immigrants who are denied legitimate opportunity find success through illegitimate means.

loses a civil case pays for damage or injury but is not labeled a criminal. Corporate officials are also protected by the fact that most charges of white-collar crime target the organization rather than individuals.

When white-collar criminals are charged and convicted, they usually escape punishment. A government study found that those convicted of fraud and punished with a fine ended up paying less than 10 percent of what they owed; most managed to hide or transfer their assets to avoid paying up. Among white-collar criminals convicted of the more serious crime of embezzlement, only about half ever served a day in jail. One accounting found that just 52 percent of the embezzlers convicted in the U.S. federal courts served prison sentences; the rest were put on probation or issued a fine (Willing, 2005; U.S. Bureau of Justice Statistics, 2007). "In the *Times*" on page 232 looks at another way the rich are treated more favorably by our criminal justice system.

Corporate Crime

Sometimes whole companies, not just individuals, break the law. **Corporate crime** is *the illegal actions of a corporation or people acting on its behalf.*

Corporate crime ranges from knowingly selling faulty or dangerous products to deliberately polluting the environment (Derber, 2004). The collapse of Enron, Global Crossing, and other corporations in recent years has cost tens of thousands of people their jobs and their pensions. Even more serious, forty-seven people died in underground coal mines in 2006, and hundreds more died from "black lung" disease caused by years of inhaling coal dust. The death toll for all job-related hazards in the United States is close to 50,000 each year (J. Jones, 1999; U.S. Census Bureau, 2006; Frank, 2007).

Organized Crime

Organized crime is *a business supplying illegal goods or services.* Sometimes criminal organizations force people to do business with them, as when a gang extorts money from shopkeepers for "protection." In most cases, however, organized crime involves the sale of illegal goods and services—including sex, drugs, and gambling—to willing buyers.

Organized crime has flourished in the United States for more than a century. The scope of its operations expanded among immigrants, who found that this society was not willing to share its opportunities with them. Some ambitious individuals (such as Al Capone, described earlier) made their own success, especially during Prohibition, when the government banned the production and sale of alcohol.

Not since the popular *Godfather* films has one show so influenced the public view of organized crime. That show, of course, is the HBO series, *The Sopranos.* How accurately do you think the mass media portray organized crime? Explain.

HBO/Photofest

The Italian Mafia is a well-known example of organized crime. But other criminal organizations involve African Americans, Chinese, Colombians, Cubans, Haitians, Nigerians, and Russians, as well as others of almost every racial and ethnic category. Today, organized crime involves a wide range of activities, from selling illegal drugs to prostitution to credit-card fraud to selling false identification papers to illegal immigrants (Valdez, 1997).

▶**CRITICAL REVIEW** According to social-conflict theory, a capitalist society's inequality in wealth and power shapes its laws and how they are applied. The criminal justice and social welfare systems thus act as political agents, controlling categories of people who are a threat to the capitalist system.

Like other approaches to deviance, social-conflict theory has its critics. First, this approach implies that laws and other cultural norms are created directly by the rich and powerful. At the very least, this is an oversimplification, as laws also protect workers, consumers, and the environment, sometimes opposing the interests of corporations and the rich.

Second, social-conflict analysis argues that criminality springs up only to the extent that a society treats its members unequally. However, as Durkheim noted, deviance exists in all societies, whatever their economic system and their degree of inequality.

The New York Times

HOME PAGE / MY TIMES / TODA... / VIDEO / MOST POPULAR / TIMES TOPICS

MARKET
REAL ESTATE
AUTOS
ALL CLASSIFIEDS

WORLD
U.S.
Politics
Washington
Education
N.Y./REGION
BUSINESS
TECHNOLOGY
SPORTS
SCIENCE
HEALTH
OPINION
ARTS
Books
Movies
Music
Television
Theater
STYLE
Dining & Wine
Fashion & Style
Home & Garden
Weddings/
Celebrations
TRAVEL

Blogs
Cartoons
Classifieds
Corrections
Crossword/
Games
First Look
Learning
Network
Multimedia
NYC Guide
Obituaries
Podcasts
The Public
Editor
Sunday
Magazine
Weather
Week in Review

NEWSPAPER
Get Home
Delivery
Customer Care
TimesPoints

For $82 a Day, Booking a Cell in a 5-Star Jail

By JENNIFER STEINHAUER
April 29, 2007

Anyone convicted of a crime knows a debt to society often must be paid in jail. But a slice of Californians willing to supplement that debt with cash (no personal checks, please) are finding that the time can be almost bearable.

For offenders whose crimes are usually relatively minor (car-jackers should not bother) and whose bank accounts remain lofty, a dozen or so city jails across the state offer pay-to-stay upgrades. Theirs are a clean, quiet ... alternative to the standard county jails, where the walls are bars, the fellow inmates are hardened and privileges are few.

Many of the self-pay jails operate like secret velvet-roped nightclubs of the corrections world. You have to be in the know to even apply for entry, and even if the court approves your sentence there, jail administrators can operate like bouncers, rejecting anyone they wish.

"I am aware that this is considered to be a five-star Hilton," said Nicole Brockett, 22, who was recently booked into one of the jails, here in Orange County about 30 miles southeast of Los Angeles, and paid $82 a day to complete a 21-day sentence for a drunken driving conviction.

Ms. Brockett, who in her oversize orange T-shirt and flip-flops looked more like a contestant on *The Real World* than an inmate, shopped around for the best accommodations, travelocity.com-style.

"It's clean here," she said, perched in a jail day room on the sort of couch found in a hospital emergency room. "It's safe and everyone here is really nice. I haven't had a problem with any of the other girls. They give me shampoo."

For roughly $75 to $127 a day, these convicts—who are known in the self-pay parlance as "clients"—get a small cell behind a regular door, distance of some amplitude from violent offenders and, in some cases, the right to bring an iPod or computer on which to compose a novel, or perhaps a song.

Many of the overnighters are granted work furlough, enabling them to do most of their time on the job, returning to the jail simply to go to bed (often following a strip search, which granted is not so five-star).

The clients usually share a cell, but otherwise mix little with the ordinary nonpaying inmates, who tend to be people arrested and awaiting arraignment, or federal prisoners on trial or awaiting deportation and simply passing through. ...

The California prison system, severely overcrowded, teeming with violence and infectious diseases and so dysfunctional that much of it is under court supervision, is one that anyone with the slightest means would most likely pay to avoid.

"The benefits are that you are isolated and you don't have to expose yourself to the traditional county system," said Christine Parker, a spokeswoman for CSI, a national provider of jails that runs three in Orange County with pay-to-stay programs. "You can avoid gang issues. You are restricted in terms of the number of people you are encountering and they are a similar persuasion such as you." ...

The typical pay-to-stay client, jail representatives agreed, is a man in his late 30s who has been convicted of driving while intoxicated and sentenced to a month or two in jail.

But there are single-night guests, and those who linger well over a year.

"One individual wanted to do four years here," said Christina Holland, a correctional manager of the Santa Ana jail.

Inmates in Santa Ana who have been approved for pay to stay by the courts and have coughed up a hefty deposit for their stay, enter the jail through a lobby and not the driveway reserved for the arrival of other prisoners. They are strip searched when they return from work each day because the biggest problem they pose is the smuggling of contraband, generally cigarettes, for nonpaying inmates.

Most of the jailers require the inmates to do chores around the jails, even if they work elsewhere during the day.

"I try real hard to keep them in custody for 12 hours," Ms. Holland said. "Because I think that's fair."

Critics argue that the systems create inherent injustices, offering cleaner, safer alternatives to those who can pay.

"It seems to be a little unfair," said Mike Jackson, the training manager of the National Sheriff's Association. "Two people come in, have the same offense, and the guy who has money gets to pay to stay and the other doesn't. The system is supposed to be equitable."

But cities argue that the paying inmates generate cash, often hundreds of thousands of dollars a year—enabling them to better afford their other taxpayer-financed operations. ...

WHAT DO YOU THINK?

1. Do you support or oppose the pay-to-stay policy of letting people pay for safer and more comfortable jail cells? Why?

2. Should people in jail be permitted to use cell phones? What about computers and Internet access? Why or why not?

3. Should punishment be equal for everyone, regardless of social standing? If so, is it fair to set fines unequally according to people's ability to pay?

tip

Carefully study the Applying Theory table. It provides a clear and brief statement of how all of sociology's theoretical approaches understand deviance.

tip

The section "Deviance, Race, and Gender" is an extension of the social-conflict approach, which shows how inequality based on race and gender can affect the way we understand deviance.

APPLYING THEORY

Deviance

	Structural-Functional Approach	Symbolic-Interaction Approach	Social-Conflict Approach
What is the level of analysis?	Macro-level	Micro-level	Macro-level
What is deviance? What part does it play in society?	Deviance is a basic part of social organization. By defining deviance, society sets its moral boundaries.	Deviance is part of socially constructed reality that emerges in interaction. Deviance comes into being as individuals label something deviant.	Deviance results from social inequality. Norms, including laws, reflect the interests of powerful members of society.
What is important about deviance?	Deviance is universal: It exists in all societies.	Deviance is variable: Any act or person may or may not be labeled deviant.	Deviance is political: People with little power are at high risk of being labeled deviant.

The sociological explanations for crime and other types of deviance that we have discussed are summarized in the Applying Theory table.

 YOUR LEARNING Define white-collar crime, corporate crime, and organized crime.

Deviance, Race, and Gender

What people consider deviant reflects the relative power and privilege of different categories of people. The following sections offer two examples: how racial and ethnic hostility motivates hate crimes and how gender is linked to deviance.

Hate Crimes

A **hate crime** is *a criminal act against a person or a person's property by an offender motivated by racial or other bias.* A hate crime may express hostility toward someone's race, religion, ancestry, sexual orientation, or physical disability. The federal government recorded about 7,200 hate crimes in 2005.

In 1998, people across the country were stunned by the brutal killing of Matthew Shepard, a gay student at the University of

Wyoming, by two men filled with hatred toward homosexuals. The National Gay and Lesbian Task Force reports that one in five lesbians and gay men is physically assaulted and more than 90 percent are verbally abused because of sexual orientation (cited in Berrill, 1992:19–20). People who contend with multiple stigmas, such as gay men of color, are especially likely to be victims. Yet it can happen to anyone: A recent study found that about 25 percent of the hate crimes based on race targeted white people (Jenness & Grattet, 2001).

By 2007, forty-nine states and the federal government had enacted legislation that increased penalties for crimes motivated by hatred. Supporters are gratified, but opponents charge that such laws, which increase penalties based on the attitudes of the offender, punish "politically incorrect" thoughts. The Thinking About Diversity: Race, Class, & Gender box takes a closer look at the issue of hate crime laws.

The Feminist Perspective: Deviance and Gender

Virtually every society in the world places stricter controls on women than on men. Historically, our own society has centered the lives of women on the home. In the United States even today, women's

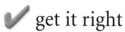

Thinking About Diversity: Race, Class, & Gender
Hate Crime Laws: Should We Punish Attitudes as Well as Actions?

On a cool October evening, nineteen-year-old Todd Mitchell, an African American, was standing with some friends in front of their apartment complex in Kenosha, Wisconsin. They had just seen the film *Mississippi Burning* and were fuming over a scene that showed a white man beating a young black boy while he knelt in prayer.

"Do you feel hyped up to move on some white people?" asked Mitchell. Minutes later, they saw a young white boy walking toward them on the other side of the street. Mitchell commanded, "There goes a white boy; go get him!" The group swarmed around the youngster, beating him bloody and leaving him on the ground in a coma. The attackers took the boy's tennis shoes as a trophy.

Police soon arrested the teenagers and charged them with the beating. Mitchell went to trial as the ringleader, and the jury found him guilty of aggravated battery *motivated by racial hatred*. Instead of the usual two-year sentence, Mitchell went to jail for four years.

As this case illustrates, hate crime laws punish a crime more severely if the offender is motivated by bias against some category of people. Supporters make three arguments in favor of hate crime legislation. First, as noted in the text discussion of crime, the offender's intentions are always important in weighing criminal responsibility, so considering hatred an intention is nothing new. Second, a crime motivated by racial or other bias inflames the

public mood more than a crime carried out, say, for money. Third, victims of hate crimes typically suffer greater injury than victims of crimes with other motives.

Critics counter that while some hate crime cases involve hard-core racism, most are impulsive acts by young people. Even more important, critics maintain, hate crime

Do you think this example of vandalism should be prosecuted as a hate crime? In other words, should the punishment be more severe than if the spray painting were just "normal" graffiti? Why or why not?

Reuters/Corbis/Reuters America LLC

laws are a threat to First Amendment guarantees of free speech. Hate crime laws allow courts to sentence offenders not just for their actions but for their attitudes. As the Harvard University law professor Alan Dershowitz cautions, "As much as I hate bigotry, I fear much more the Court attempting to control the minds of its citizens." In short, according to critics, hate crime statutes open the door to punishing beliefs rather than behavior.

In 1993, the U.S. Supreme Court upheld the sentence handed down to Todd Mitchell. In a unanimous decision, the justices stated that the government should not punish an individual's beliefs. But, they reasoned, a belief is no longer protected when it becomes the motive for a crime.

WHAT DO YOU THINK?

1. Do you think crimes motivated by hate are more harmful than those motivated by greed? Why or why not?

2. Do you think minorities such as African Americans should be subject to the same hate crime laws as white people? Why or why not?

3. Do you favor or oppose hate crime laws? Why?

Sources: Terry (1993), A. Sullivan (2002), and Hartocollis (2007).

opportunities in the workplace, in politics, in athletics, and in the military are more limited than men's. Elsewhere in the world, the constraints on women are greater still. In Saudi Arabia, women cannot vote or legally operate motor vehicles; in Iran, women who dare to expose their hair or wear makeup in public can be whipped; and not long ago, a Nigerian court convicted a divorced woman of bearing a child out of wedlock and sentenced her to death by stoning; her life was later spared out of concern for her child (Eboh, 2002).

Gender also figures in the theories of deviance you read about earlier in the chapter. Robert Merton's strain theory, for example, defines cultural goals in terms of financial success. Traditionally, at least, this goal has had more to do with the lives of men because women have been taught to define success in terms of relationships, particularly marriage and motherhood (Leonard, 1982). A more woman-focused theory might recognize the "strain" that results from the cultural ideal of equality clashing with the reality of gender-based inequality.

Sam Pearson, who lives in Renville County, North Dakota, rarely locks his doors when he leaves the house.

Serge Shuman, who lives in Robeson County, North Carolina, knows many people who have been victims of crime and avoids going out at night.

tip

At this point, the chapter turns from deviance in general terms to the more specific violations of law we call crime.

SEEING OURSELVES

NATIONAL MAP 1
The Risk of Violent Crime across the United States

This map shows the risk of becoming a victim of violent crime. In general, the risk is highest in low-income, rural counties that have a large population of men between the ages of fifteen and twenty-four. After reading this section of the text, see whether you can explain this pattern.

Source: *American Demographics* magazine, December 2000 issue. Copyright © 2004 by Crain Communications, Inc.

Risk of Violent Crime
■ Above average
□ Average
■ Below average

According to labeling theory, gender influences how we define deviance because people commonly use different standards to judge the behavior of females and males. Further, because society puts men in positions of power over women, men often escape direct responsibility for actions that victimize women. In the past, at least, men who sexually harassed or assaulted women were labeled only mildly deviant and sometimes escaped punishment entirely.

By contrast, women who are victimized may have to convince others—even members of a jury—that they were not to blame for their own sexual harassment or assault. Research confirms an important truth: Whether people define a situation as deviance—and, if so, who the deviant is—depends on the sex of both the audience and the actors (King & Clayson, 1988).

Finally, despite its focus on social inequality, much social-conflict analysis does not address the issue of gender. If economic disadvantage is a primary cause of crime, as conflict theory suggests, why do women (whose economic position is much worse than men's) commit far *fewer* crimes than men?

Why do you think that women commit fewer crimes than men?

Crime

Crime is the violation of criminal laws enacted by a locality, a state, or the federal government. All crimes are composed of two elements: the *act* itself (or in some cases, the failure to do what the law requires)

and *criminal intent* (in legal terminology, *mens rea*, or "guilty mind"). Intent is a matter of degree, ranging from willful conduct to negligence. Someone who is negligent does not deliberately set out to hurt anyone but acts (or fails to act) in a way that results in harm. Prosecutors weigh the degree of intent in deciding whether, for example, to charge someone with first-degree murder, second-degree murder, or negligent manslaughter. Alternatively, they may consider a killing justifiable, as in self-defense.

Types of Crime

In the United States, the Federal Bureau of Investigation gathers information on criminal offenses and regularly reports the results in a publication called *Crime in the United States.* Two major types of crime make up the FBI "crime index."

Crimes against the person, also called *violent crimes*, are *crimes that direct violence or the threat of violence against others.* Violent crimes include murder and manslaughter (legally defined as "the willful killing of one human being by another"), aggravated assault ("an unlawful attack by one person upon another for the purpose of inflicting severe or aggravated bodily injury"), forcible rape ("the carnal knowledge of a female forcibly and against her will"), and robbery ("taking or attempting to take anything of value from the care, custody, or control of a person or persons by force or threat of force or violence and/or putting the victim in fear"). National Map 1 shows the risk of violent crime in counties all across the United States.

Crimes against property, also called *property crimes*, are *crimes that involve theft of property belonging to others.* Property crimes

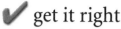 get it right

The profile of the street criminal is based on arrest data and not on convictions in a court of law. This is because the data made available by the FBI are based on arrests.

include burglary ("the unlawful entry of a structure to commit a [serious crime] or a theft"), larceny-theft ("the unlawful taking, carrying, leading, or riding away of property from the possession of another"), auto theft ("the theft or attempted theft of a motor vehicle"), and arson ("any willful or malicious burning or attempt to burn the personal property of another").

A third category of offenses, not included in major crime indexes, is **victimless crimes,** *violations of law in which there are no obvious victims.* Also called *crimes without complaint,* they include illegal drug use, prostitution, and gambling. The term "victimless crime" is misleading, however. How victimless is a crime when young people steal to support a drug habit? What about a young pregnant woman who, by smoking crack, permanently harms her baby? Perhaps it is more correct to say that people who commit such crimes are both offenders and victims.

Because public views of victimless crimes vary greatly, laws differ from place to place. In the United States, although gambling and prostitution are legal in very limited areas, both activities are common across the country.

 Do you think a student who downloads music in violation of the law is guilty of theft? Why or why not?

Criminal Statistics

Statistics gathered by the Federal Bureau of Investigation show crime rates rising from 1960 to 1990 and then declining through 2005. Even so, police count nearly 12 million serious crimes each year. Figure 2 shows the trends for various serious crimes.

Always read crime statistics with caution, because they include only crimes known to the police. Almost all homicides are reported, but assaults—especially among people who know one another—often are not. Police records include an even smaller share of property crimes, especially when the losses are small.

Researchers check official crime statistics using *victimization surveys,* in which they ask a representative sample of people if they have had any experience with crime. According to such surveys, the overall crime rate is about three times higher than official reports indicate (Russell, 1995b).

The Street Criminal: A Profile

Using government crime reports, we can gain a general description of the categories of people most likely to be arrested for violent and property crimes.

Age

Official crime rates rise sharply during adolescence, peak in the late teens, and then fall as people get older. People between the ages of fifteen and twenty-four represent just 14 percent of the U.S. population, but in 2005, they accounted for 39.7 percent of all arrests for violent crimes and 45.1 percent of arrests for property crimes.

Gender

Although each sex makes up roughly half the population, police collared males in 67.4 percent of all property crime arrests in 2005; the other 32.6 percent of arrests involved women. In other words, men are arrested more than twice as often as women for property crimes. In the case of violent crimes, the difference is even greater, with 82.0 percent of arrests involving males and just 18.0 percent females (almost a five-to-one ratio).

It may be that law enforcement officials are reluctant to define women as criminals. In fact, all over the world, the greatest gender differences in crime rates occur in societies that most severely limit the opportunities of women. In the United States, however, the difference in arrest rates for women and men is narrowing, which probably indicates increasing sexual equality in our society. Between 1996 and 2005, there was a 7.4 percent *increase* in arrests of women and a 7.6 percent *drop* in arrests of men (Federal Bureau of Investigation, 2006).

Social Class

The FBI does not assess the social class of arrested persons, so no statistical data of the kind given for age and gender are available. But research has long indicated that street crime is more widespread among people of lower social position (Thornberry & Farnsworth, 1982; Wolfgang, Thornberry, & Figlio, 1987).

Yet the link between class and crime is more complicated than it appears on the surface. For one thing, many people look on the poor as less worthy than the rich, whose wealth and power confer "respectability" (Tittle, Villemez, & Smith, 1978; Elias, 1986). And although crime—especially violent crime—is a serious problem in the poorest inner-city communities, most of these crimes are committed by a few hard-core offenders. The majority of the people who live in poor communities have no criminal record at all (Wolfgang, Figlio, & Sellin, 1972; Elliott & Ageton, 1980; Harries, 1990).

The connection between social standing and criminality also depends on the type of crime. If we expand our definition of crime beyond street offenses to include white-collar crime and corporate crime, the "common criminal" suddenly looks much more affluent and may live in a $100 million home.

DEVIANCE

tip

Take a good look at Figure 2, which shows that crime rates rose between 1960 and the early 1990s and have generally fallen since then.

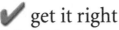get it right

Notice that the rate of property crime is much higher than the rate of violent crime.

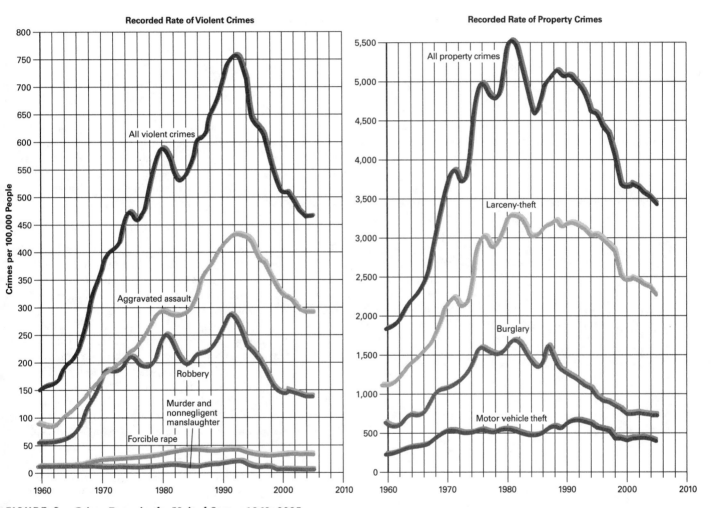

FIGURE 2   Crime Rates in the United States, 1960–2005

The graphs show the rates for various violent crimes and property crimes during recent decades.
Since about 1990, the trend has been downward.

Source: Federal Bureau of Investigation (2006).

Race and Ethnicity

Both race and ethnicity are strongly linked to crime rates, although the reasons are many and complex. Official statistics show that 69.8 percent of arrests for FBI index crimes in 2005 involved white people. However, the African American arrest rate was higher than the rate for whites in proportion to their representation in the general population. African Americans account for 12.3 percent of the population but 28.6 percent of arrests for property crimes (versus 68.8

percent for whites) and 38.8 percent of arrests for violent crimes (versus 59.0 percent for whites) (Federal Bureau of Investigation, 2006).

There are several reasons for the disproportionate number of arrests among African Americans. First, race in the United States closely relates to social standing, which, as already explained, affects the likelihood of engaging in street crimes. Many poor people living in the midst of wealth come to perceive society as unjust and are

get it right

Remember that the profile of a criminal depends on the type of crime. Street crime involves a larger share of lower-income people; corporate crime involves mostly high-income people. With regard to race, most street crime is committed by whites.

therefore more likely to turn to crime to get their share (Blau & Blau, 1982; E. Anderson, 1994; Martinez, 1996).

Second, black and white family patterns differ: Two-thirds of non-Hispanic black children (compared to one-fourth of non-Hispanic white children) are born to single mothers. Single parenting carries two risks: Children receive less supervision and are at greater risk of poverty. Knowing that one of every three African American children is growing up poor (compared to one in seven white children), no one should be surprised at the proportionately higher crime rates for African Americans (Courtwright, 1996; Jacobs & Helms, 1996; Martin et al., 2006; U.S. Census Bureau, 2006).

Third, prejudice prompts white police to arrest black people more readily and leads citizens to report African Americans more willingly, so people of color are overly criminalized (Chiricos, McEntire, & Gertz, 2001; Quillian & Pager, 2001; Demuth & Steffensmeier, 2004).

Fourth, remember that the official crime index does not include arrests for offenses ranging from drunk driving to white-collar violations. This omission contributes to the view of the typical criminal as a person of color. If we broaden our definition of crime to include drunk driving, business fraud, embezzlement, stock swindles, and cheating on income tax returns, the proportion of white criminals rises dramatically.

Keep in mind, too, that categories of people with high arrest rates are also at higher risk of being victims of crime. In the United States, for example, African Americans are almost six times as likely as white people to die as a result of homicide (Rogers et al., 2001; Hoyert et al., 2006).

Finally, some categories of the population have unusually low rates of arrest. People of Asian descent, who account for about 4 percent of the population, figure in only 1.0 percent of all arrests. Asian Americans enjoy higher than average educational achievement and income. Also, Asian American culture emphasizes family solidarity and discipline, both of which keep criminality down.

Crime in Global Perspective

By world standards, the crime rate in the United States is high. Although recent crime trends are downward, there were 16,692 murders in the United States in 2005, which amounts to one every half hour around the clock. In large cities such as New York, rarely does a day pass without someone being killed.

The rate of violent crime (but not property crime) in the United States is several times higher than in Europe. The contrast is even greater between our country and the nations of Asia, including India and Japan, where rates of violent and property crime are among the lowest in the world.

Elliott Currie (1985) suggests that crime stems from our culture's emphasis on individual economic success, frequently at the expense of strong families and neighborhoods. The United States also has extraordinary cultural diversity, a result of centuries of immigration. In addition, economic inequality is higher in this country than in most other high-income nations. Thus our society's relatively weak social fabric, combined with considerable frustration among the poor, generates widespread criminal behavior.

Another factor contributing to violence in the United States is extensive private ownership of guns. About two-thirds of murder victims in the United States die from shootings. Since the early 1990s, the number of shooting deaths in Texas and several other southern states has exceeded the number of automobile-related fatalities. The U.S. rate of handgun deaths is about seven times higher than the rate in Canada, a country that strictly limits handgun ownership.

Surveys suggest that up to 40 percent of U.S. households have at least one gun. In fact, there are more guns

"You look like this sketch of someone who's thinking about committing a crime."

DEVIANCE

tip

In global perspective, the United States has a high crime rate. There are many reasons for this, including our materialistic culture, the great importance we give to independence and individuality, a high level of social inequality, our relatively weak social fabric, and the extensive private ownership of guns.

tip

Students with an interest in the criminal justice system should pay special attention to the pages that follow.

than adults in this country, and one-third of these weapons are handguns, commonly used in violent crimes. In large part, gun ownership reflects people's fear of crime, yet the easy availability of guns in this country also makes crime more deadly (NORC, 2005; Brady Campaign, 2007).

But as critics of gun control point out, waiting periods and background checks at retail gun stores do not keep guns out of the hands of criminals, who almost always obtain guns illegally (J. D. Wright, 1995). And gun control is not a magic bullet in the war on crime. Elliott Currie (1985) notes, for example, that the number of Californians killed each year by knives exceeds the number of Canadians killed by weapons of all kinds. However, most experts do think that stricter gun control would lower the level of deadly violence.

 December 24–25, traveling through Peru. In Lima, Peru's capital city, the concern with crime is obvious. Almost every house is fortified with gates, barbed wire, or broken glass embedded in cement at the top of a wall. Private security forces are everywhere in the rich areas along the coast, where we find the embassies, expensive hotels, and the international airport.

The picture is very different as we pass through small villages high in the Andes to the east. The same families have lived in these communities for generations, and people know one another. No gates and fences here. And we've seen only one police car all afternoon.

Crime rates are high in some of the largest cities of the world, including Lima, Peru, São Paulo, Brazil, and Manila in the Philippines, all of which have rapid population growth and millions of desperately poor people. Outside of big cities, however, the traditional character of low-income societies and their strong families allow local communities to control crime informally.

Some types of crime have always been multinational, such as terrorism, espionage, and arms dealing (Martin & Romano, 1992). But today, the globalization we are experiencing on many fronts also extends to crime. A recent case in point is the illegal drug trade. In part, the problem of illegal drugs in the United States is a *demand* issue. That is, the demand for cocaine and other drugs in this country is high, and many people risk arrest or even a violent death for a chance to get rich in the drug trade. But the *supply* side of the issue is just as important. In the South American nation of Colombia, at least 20 percent of the people depend on cocaine production for their liveli-

The recent film *Crash* shows how much ideas about race and class color our thinking about crime in the United States. For example, looking at this scene, what do you assume is going on? If the three men were white, would your assumption be the same? What if they were wearing button-down shirts and khakis? Why?

hood. Not only is cocaine Colombia's most profitable export, but it outsells all other exports combined—and that includes coffee. Clearly, drug dealing and many other crimes are closely related to social and economic conditions both in the United States and elsewhere.

Different countries have different strategies for dealing with crime. The use of the death penalty provides a case in point. According to Amnesty International (2007b), six nations (China, Iran, Pakistan, Iraq, Sudan, and the United States) account for 91 percent of the world's executions carried out by governments. Global Map 1 shows which countries currently use capital punishment. The global trend is toward abolishing the death penalty: Amnesty International (2007b) reports that since 1985, more than fifty nations have ended this practice.

The U.S. Criminal Justice System

The criminal justice system is a society's formal system of social control. We shall briefly examine the key elements of the U.S. criminal

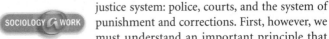 justice system: police, courts, and the system of punishment and corrections. First, however, we must understand an important principle that underlies the entire system, the idea of due process.

Due Process

Due process is a simple but very important idea: The criminal justice system must operate according to law. This principle is grounded in the first ten amendments to the U.S. Constitution—known as the Bill of Rights—adopted by Congress in 1791. The Constitution offers various protections to any person charged with a crime, including the right to counsel, the right to refuse to testify against oneself, the right to confront all accusers, freedom from being tried twice for the same crime, and freedom from being "deprived of life, liberty, or property without due process of law." Furthermore, the Constitution gives all

Police must be allowed discretion if they are to handle effectively the many different situations they face every day. At the same time, it is important that the police treat people fairly. Here we see a police officer deciding whether or not to charge a young woman with driving while intoxicated. What factors do you think enter into this decision?

Kayte M. Deioma/PhotoEdit Inc.

people the right to a speedy and public trial by jury, and freedom from excessive bail as well as cruel and unusual punishment.

In general terms, the concept of due process means that anyone charged with a crime must receive (1) fair notice of the proceedings, (2) a hearing on the charges conducted according to law and with the ability to present a defense, and (3) a judge or jury that weighs evidence impartially (Inciardi, 2000).

Due process limits the power of government, with an eye toward this nation's cultural support of individual rights and freedoms. Deciding exactly how far government can go is an ongoing process that makes up much of the work of the judicial system, especially the U.S. Supreme Court.

Police

The police generally serve as the primary point of contact between a society's population and the criminal justice system. In principle, the police maintain public order by enforcing the law. Of course, there is only so much that the 673,146 full-time police officers in the United States can do to monitor the activities of 300 million people. As a result, the police use a great deal of personal judgment in deciding which situations warrant their attention and how to handle them.

How do police officers carry out their duties? In a study of police behavior in five cities, Douglas Smith and Christy Visher (1981; D. A. Smith, 1987) concluded that because they must act swiftly, police officers quickly size up situations in terms of six factors. First, the more serious they think the situation is, the more likely they are to make an arrest. Second, officers take account of the victim's wishes in deciding whether or not to make an arrest. Third, the odds of arrest go up the more uncooperative a suspect is. Fourth, officers are more likely to take into custody someone they have arrested before, presumably because this suggests guilt. Fifth, the presence of observers increases the chances of arrest. According to Smith and Visher, the presence of observers prompts police to take stronger control of a situation, if only to move the encounter from the street (the suspect's turf) to the police department (where law officers have the edge). Sixth, all else being equal, police officers are more likely to arrest people of color than whites, perceiving suspects of African or Latino descent as either more dangerous or more likely to be guilty.

Courts

After arrest, a court determines a suspect's guilt or innocence. In principle, U.S. courts rely on an adversarial process involving attorneys—one representing the defendant and another the state—in the presence of a judge, who monitors legal procedures.

In practice, however, about 90 percent of criminal cases are resolved prior to court appearance through **plea bargaining,** *a legal*

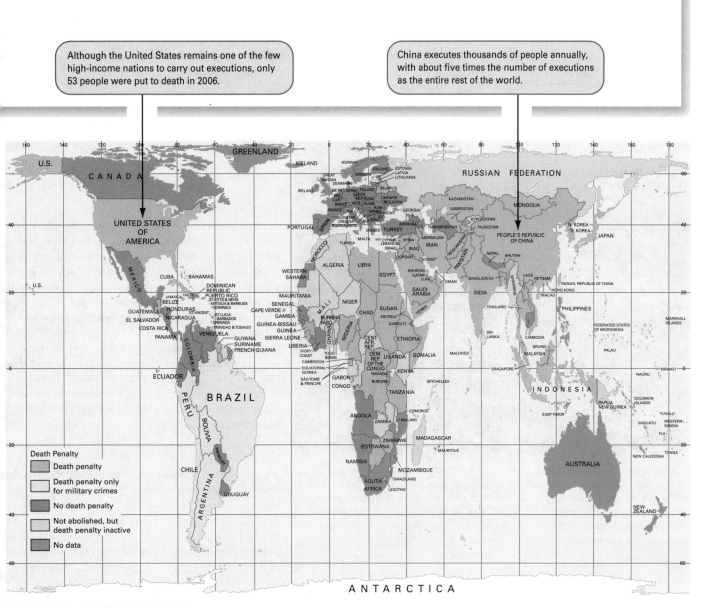

Although the United States remains one of the few high-income nations to carry out executions, only 53 people were put to death in 2006.

China executes thousands of people annually, with about five times the number of executions as the entire rest of the world.

Death Penalty

- Death penalty
- Death penalty only for military crimes
- No death penalty
- Not abolished, but death penalty inactive
- No data

WINDOW ON THE WORLD

GLOBAL MAP 1 Capital Punishment in Global Perspective

The map identifies sixty-eight countries and territories in which the law allows the death penalty for ordinary crimes; in ten more, the death penalty is reserved for exceptional crimes under military law or during times of war. The death penalty does not exist in eighty-nine countries and territories; in thirty more, although the death penalty remains in law, no execution has taken place in more than ten years. Compare rich and poor nations: What general pattern do you see? In what way are the United States and Japan exceptions to this pattern?

Source: Amnesty International (2007a).

negotiation in which a prosecutor reduces a charge in exchange for a defendant's guilty plea. For example, the state may offer a defendant charged with burglary a lesser charge, perhaps possession of burglary tools, in exchange for a guilty plea.

Plea bargaining is widespread because it spares the system the time and expense of trials. A trial is usually unnecessary if there is little disagreement over the facts of the case. In addition, because the number of cases entering the system annually has doubled over the past decade,

tip

Notice that each of the first three justifications for punishment arose at a particular time in history.

To increase the power of punishment to deter crime, capital punishment was long carried out in public. Here is a photograph from the last public execution in the United States, with twenty-two-year-old Rainey Bethea standing on the scaffold moments from death in Owensboro, Kentucky, on August 16, 1937. Children as well as adults were in the crowd. Now that the mass media report the story of executions across the country, states carry out capital punishment behind closed doors.

US Information Agency

prosecutors could not bring every case to trial even if they wanted to. By quickly resolving most of their work, the courts channel their resources into the most important cases.

But plea bargaining pressures defendants (who are presumed innocent) to plead guilty. A person can exercise the right to a trial, but only at the risk of receiving a more severe sentence if found guilty. Furthermore, low-income defendants enter the process with the guidance of a public defender—typically an overworked and underpaid attorney who may devote little time to even the most serious cases (Novak, 1999). Plea bargaining may be efficient, but it undercuts both the adversarial process and the rights of defendants.

Punishment

When a young man is shot dead on the street after leaving a restaurant, some people may wonder why it happened, but almost everyone believes that someone should have to pay for the crime. Sometimes the desire to punish is so great that in the end, justice may not be done.

Why should a society punish wrongdoers? Scholars answer with four basic reasons: retribution, deterrence, rehabilitation, and societal protection.

Retribution

The oldest justification for punishment is to satisfy people's need for **retribution,** *an act of moral vengeance by which society makes the offender suffer as much as the suffering caused by the crime.* Retribution rests on a view of society as a moral balance. When criminality upsets this balance, punishment in equal measure restores the moral order, as suggested in the ancient code calling for "an eye for an eye, a tooth for a tooth."

In the Middle Ages, most people viewed crime as sin—an offense against God as well as society that required a harsh response. Today, although critics point out that retribution does little to reform the offender, many people consider vengeance reason enough for punishment.

Deterrence

A second justification for punishment is **deterrence,** *the attempt to discourage criminality through the use of punishment.* Deterrence is based on the eighteenth-century Enlightenment idea that humans, as calculating and rational creatures, will not break the law if they think that the pain of punishment will outweigh the pleasure of the crime.

Deterrence emerged as a reform measure in response to the harsh punishments based on retribution. Why put someone to death for stealing if theft can be discouraged with a prison sentence? As the concept of deterrence gained acceptance in industrial nations, the execution and physical mutilation of criminals in most high-income societies were replaced by milder forms of punishment such as imprisonment.

Punishment can deter crime in two ways. *Specific deterrence* is used to convince an individual offender that crime does not pay. Through *general deterrence,* the punishment of one person serves as an example to others.

Rehabilitation

The third justification for punishment is **rehabilitation,** *a program for reforming the offender to prevent later offenses.* Rehabilitation arose along with the social sciences in the nineteenth century. Since then, sociologists have claimed that crime and other deviance spring from

tip

Take a close look at the Summing Up table to be sure you understand the four justifications for punishment.

SUMMING UP

Four Justifications for Punishment

Retribution	The oldest justification for punishment. Punishment is society's revenge for a moral wrong. In principle, punishment should be equal in severity to the crime itself.
Deterrence	An early modern approach. Crime is considered social disruption, which society acts to control. People are viewed as rational and self-interested; deterrence works because the pain of punishment outweighs the pleasure of crime.
Rehabilitation	A modern strategy linked to the development of social sciences. Crime and other deviance are viewed as the result of social problems (such as poverty) or personal problems (such as mental illness). Social conditions are improved; treatment is tailored to the offender's condition.
Societal protection	A modern approach easier to carry out than rehabilitation. Even if society is unable or unwilling to rehabilitate offenders or reform social conditions, people are protected by the imprisonment or execution of the offender.

a social environment marked by poverty or a lack of parental supervision. Logically, then, if offenders learn to be deviant, they can also learn to obey the rules; the key is controlling their environment. *Reformatories* or *houses of correction* provided controlled settings where people could learn proper behavior.

Like deterrence, rehabilitation motivates the offender to conform. In contrast to deterrence and retribution, which simply make the offender suffer, rehabilitation encourages constructive improvement. Unlike retribution, which demands that the punishment fit the crime, rehabilitation tailors treatment to each offender. Thus identical crimes would prompt similar acts of retribution but different rehabilitation programs.

Societal Protection

A final justification for punishment is **societal protection,** *rendering an offender incapable of further offenses temporarily through imprisonment or permanently by execution.* Like deterrence, societal protection is a rational approach to punishment intended to protect society from crime.

Currently, about 2.2 million people are jailed in the United States. Although the crime rate has gone down in recent years, the number of offenders locked up across the country has gone up, tripling since 1980. This rise in the prison population reflects both tougher public

attitudes toward crime and punishing offenders and an increasing number of drug-related arrests. As a result, the United States now incarcerates a larger share of its population than any other country in the world (Sentencing Project, 2006; U.S. Bureau of Justice Statistics, 2006).

 Which of the four reasons for punishment do you think is most important in U.S. society? Why? Do you think most other people would agree with you? Explain.

▶ **CRITICAL REVIEW** The Summing Up table reviews the four justifications for punishment. However, an accurate assessment of the consequences of punishment is no simple task.

The value of retribution lies in Durkheim's claim that punishing the deviant person increases society's moral awareness. For this reason, punishment was traditionally a public event. Although the last public execution in the United States took place in Kentucky seventy years ago, today's mass media ensure public awareness of executions carried out inside prison walls (Kittrie, 1971).

Does punishment deter crime? Despite our extensive use of punishment, our society has a high rate of **criminal recidivism,** *later offenses by people previously convicted of crimes.* About

DEVIANCE 263

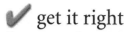 **get it right**

Be sure you understand the differences between probation, shock probation, and parole.

 tip

"Community-based corrections" refers to ways of dealing with offenders without sending them to prison.

three-fourths of prisoners in state penitentiaries have been jailed before, and about half will be back in prison within a few years after release (Petersilia, 1997; DeFina & Arvanites, 2002). So does punishment really deter crime? Only about one-third of all crimes are known to police, and of these, only about one in five results in an arrest. Most crimes, therefore, go unpunished, so the old saying "Crime doesn't pay" rings hollow.

General deterrence is even more difficult to investigate scientifically, since we have no way of knowing how people might act if they were unaware of the punishments handed down to others. Opponents of capital punishment point to research suggesting that the death penalty has limited value as a general deterrent and note that the United States is the only high-income Western nation that routinely executes serious offenders. Half of the 3,254 prisoners currently on death row are in just four states: California, Texas, Florida, and Pennsylvania.

It is also true that some death sentences have been pronounced against innocent people. Between 1973 and 2005, almost 100 people were released from death row after new evidence established their innocence. How many did not get that chance? Before leaving office in January 2003, Illinois Governor George Ryan claimed that his state's judicial system was seriously flawed and commuted the sentences of all 167 of the state's death row inmates to life in prison (S. Levine, 2003). In 2005, the U.S. Supreme Court limited the scope of capital punishment, ruling that offenders who were younger than eighteen when they committed their crimes cannot be put to death.

Despite growing controversy over the death penalty, a majority of U.S. adults (64 percent) say they support capital punishment for people convicted of murder (NORC, 2005:156). Among first-year college students, support for the death penalty rose between 1970 and 1990 but has declined since then (Pryor et al., 2006).

Prisons provide short-term societal protection by keeping offenders off the streets, but they do little to reshape attitudes or behavior in the long term (Carlson, 1976; R. A. Wright, 1994). Perhaps rehabilitation is an unrealistic expectation, because according to Sutherland's theory of differential association, locking up criminals together for years probably strengthens criminal attitudes and skills. Incarceration also stigmatizes prisoners, making jobs hard to find later on (Pager, 2003). Finally, prison breaks the social ties inmates may have in the outside world, which, following Hirschi's control theory, leaves these individuals more likely to commit new crimes upon release.

 YOUR LEARNING What are society's four justifications for punishment? Does sending offenders to prison accomplish each of them? Why?

Community-Based Corrections

Prisons keep convicted criminals off the streets. But the evidence suggests that they do little to rehabilitate most offenders. Furthermore, prisons are expensive, costing approximately $25,000 per year to support each inmate, in addition to the initial costs of building the facilities.

One alternative to the traditional prison that has been adopted by cities and states across the country is **community-based corrections,** *correctional programs operating within society at large rather than behind prison walls.* Community-based corrections have three main advantages: They reduce costs, reduce overcrowding in prisons, and allow for supervision of convicts while eliminating the hardships of prison life and the stigma that accompanies going to jail. In general, the idea of community-based corrections is not so much to punish as to reform; such programs are therefore usually offered to individuals who have committed less serious offenses and appear to be good prospects for avoiding future criminal violations (Inciardi, 2000).

Probation

One form of community-based corrections is *probation,* a policy permitting a convicted offender to remain in the community under conditions imposed by a court, including regular supervision. Courts may require that a probationer receive counseling, attend a drug treatment program, hold a job, avoid associating with "known criminals," or anything else a judge thinks is appropriate. Typically, a probationer must check in with an officer of the court (the *probation officer*) on a regular schedule to make sure the guidelines are being followed. Should the probationer fail to live up to the conditions set by the court or commit a new offense, the court may revoke probation and send the offender to jail.

Shock Probation

A related strategy is *shock probation,* a policy by which a judge orders a convicted offender to prison for a short time but then suspends the remainder of the sentence in favor of probation. Shock probation is thus a mix of prison and probation, used to impress on the offender the seriousness of the situation without resorting to full-scale imprisonment. In some cases, shock probation takes place in a special "boot camp" facility where offenders might spend one to three months in a military-style setting intended to teach discipline and respect for authority (Cole & Smith, 2002).

tip

Notice that changes in crime rates, like all trends, have many causes.

Controversy & Debate
Violent Crime Is Down—but Why?

DUANE: I'm a criminal justice major and I want to be a police officer. Crime is a huge problem in America, and police are what keep the crime rate low.

SANDY: I'm a sociology major. As for the crime rate, I'm not sure it's quite that simple. . . .

During the 1980s, crime rates shot upward. Just about everyone lived in fear of violent crime, and in many larger cities, the numbers killed and wounded made whole neighborhoods seem like war zones. There seemed to be no solution to the problem.

In the 1990s, something good and unexpected happened: Serious crime rates began to fall, until by 2000 they were at levels not seen in more than a generation. Why? Researchers point to several reasons:

1. **A reduction in the youth population.** The text noted that young people (particularly males) are responsible for much violent crime. During the 1990s, the population aged fifteen to twenty-four dropped by 5 percent (in part because of the legalization of abortion in 1973).

2. **Changes in policing.** Much of the drop in crime (as well as the earlier rise in crime) took place in large cities. New York City, where the number of murders fell from 2,245 in 1990 to just 539 in 2005, has adopted a policy of *community policing,* which means that police are concerned not just with making arrests but with preventing crime before it happens. Officers get to know the areas they patrol and stop young men for jaywalking or other minor infractions so they can check them for concealed weapons (the word has got-

ten around that you can be arrested for carrying a gun). There are also *more* police at work in large cities. Los Angeles added more than 2,000 police officers in the 1990s, which contributed to its drop in violent crime during that period.

3. **More prisoners.** From 1985 to 2006, the number of inmates in U.S. jails and prisons soared from 750,000 to more than 2 million. The main reason for this increase is tough laws that demand prison time for many crimes, especially drug offenses. As one analyst put it, "When you lock up an extra million people, it's got to have some effect on the crime rate" (Franklin Zimring, quoted in Witkin, 1998:31).

4. **A better economy.** The U.S. economy boomed during the 1990s. With unemployment down, more people were working, reducing the likelihood that some would turn to crime out of economic desperation. The logic here is simple: More jobs, fewer crimes. By the same token,

One reason that crime has gone down is that there are more than 2 million people incarcerated in this country. This has caused severe overcrowding of facilities such as this Maricopa County, Arizona, prison.
A. Ramey/PhotoEdit Inc.

the economic downturn of the early 2000s slowed the downward crime trend.

5. **The declining drug trade.** Many analysts agree that the most important factor in reducing rates of violent crime was the decline of crack cocaine. Crack came on the scene about 1985, and violence spread as young people—especially in the inner cities and increasingly armed with guns—became part of a booming drug trade. Facing few legitimate job opportunities but with increasing opportunity to make money illegally, a generation of young people became part of a wave of violence. By the early 1990s, the popularity of crack began to fall as people saw the damage it was causing to entire communities. This realization, coupled with steady economic improvement and stiffer sentences for drug offenses, helped bring about the turnaround in violent crime.

The current picture looks better relative to what it was a decade or two ago. But one researcher cautions, "It looks better . . . only because the early 1990s were so bad. So let's not fool ourselves into thinking everything is resolved. It's not."

WHAT DO YOU THINK?

1. Do you support the policy of community policing? Why or why not?

2. What do you see as the pros and cons of building more prisons?

3. Of all the factors mentioned here, which do you think is the most important in crime control? Which is least important? Why?

Sources: Winship & Berrien (1999), Donahue & Leavitt (2000), Rosenfeld (2002), Federal Bureau of Investigation (2006), and U.S. Bureau of Justice Statistics (2006).

Parole

Parole is a policy of releasing inmates from prison to serve the remainder of their sentences in the local community under the supervision of a parole officer. Although some sentences specifically deny the possibility of parole, most inmates become eligible for parole after serving a certain portion of their sentences. At that time, a parole board evaluates the risks and benefits of the inmate's early release from prison. If parole is granted, the parole board monitors the offender's conduct until the sentence is completed. Should the offender not comply with the conditions of parole or be arrested for another crime, the board can revoke parole and return the offender to prison to complete the sentence.

▶ **CRITICAL REVIEW** Evaluations of probation and parole are mixed. There is little question that probation and parole programs are much less expensive than conventional imprisonment; they also

free up room in prisons for people who commit more serious crimes. Yet research suggests that although probation and shock probation do seem to work for some people, they do not significantly reduce recidivism. Parole is also useful to prison officials as a means to encourage good behavior among inmates. But levels of crime among those released on parole are so high that a number of states have ended their parole programs entirely (Inciardi, 2000).

Such evaluations point to a sobering truth: The criminal justice system cannot eliminate crime. As the Controversy & Debate box explains, although police, courts, and prisons do affect crime rates, crime and other forms of deviance are not just the acts of "bad people" but reflect the operation of society itself.

✔ **YOUR LEARNING** What are three types of community-based corrections? What are their advantages?

Applying Sociology in Everyday Life

1. Identity theft is a new type of crime that victimizes as many as 10 million people each year in the United States. Research this phenomenon, and explain how this offense differs from property crime that takes place "on the street." (Consider differences in the crime, the offenders, and the victims.)

2. Rent a wheelchair for a day or two (check with a local pharmacy or medical supply store), and use it as much as possible. Not only will you gain a firsthand understanding of the

physical barriers to getting around, but you will also discover that people respond to you in many new ways. (If you cannot actually get your hands on a wheelchair, at least think about how being disabled would affect what you do during a typical day.)

3. Watch an episode of the real-action police show *Cops*. Based on what you see, how would you profile the people who commit crimes?

MAKING THE GRADE

Deviance

What Is Deviance?

DEVIANCE refers to norm violations ranging from minor infractions, such as bad manners, to major infractions, such as serious violence.

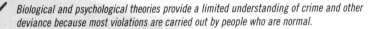

THEORIES OF DEVIANCE

BIOLOGICAL THEORIES
- focus on individual abnormality
- explain human behavior as the result of biological instincts

Lombroso claimed criminals have ape-like physical traits; later research links criminal behavior to certain body types and genetics.

PSYCHOLOGICAL THEORIES
- focus on individual abnormality
- see deviance as the result of "unsuccessful socialization"

Reckless and Dinitz's *containment theory* links delinquency to weak conscience.

deviance the recognized violation of cultural norms

crime the violation of a society's formally enacted criminal law

social control attempts by society to regulate people's thoughts and behavior

criminal justice system a formal response by police, courts, and prison officials to alleged violations of the law

✔ *Biological and psychological theories provide a limited understanding of crime and other deviance because most violations are carried out by people who are normal.*

SOCIOLOGICAL THEORIES view all behavior—deviance as well as conformity—as products of society. Sociologists point out that
- what is deviant varies from place to place according to cultural norms
- behavior and individuals become deviant as others define them that way
- what and who a society defines as deviant reflect who has and who does not have social power

Theoretical Analysis of Deviance

THE FUNCTIONS OF DEVIANCE: STRUCTURAL-FUNCTIONAL ANALYSIS

Durkheim claimed deviance is a normal element of society that
- affirms cultural norms and values
- clarifies moral boundaries
- brings people together
- encourages social change

Merton's **strain theory** explains deviance in terms of a society's cultural goals and the means available to achieve them.

Deviant subcultures are discussed by Cloward and Ohlin, Cohen, Miller, and Anderson.

labeling theory the idea that deviance and conformity result not so much from what people do as from how others respond to those actions

stigma a powerfully negative label that greatly changes a person's self-concept and social identity

medicalization of deviance the transformation of moral and legal deviance into a medical condition

LABELING DEVIANCE: SYMBOLIC-INTERACTION ANALYSIS

Labeling theory claims that deviance depends less on what someone does than on how others react to that behavior. If people respond to primary deviance by stigmatizing a person, secondary deviance and a deviant career may result.

The **medicalization of deviance** is the transformation of moral and legal deviance into a medical condition. In practice, this means a change in labels, replacing "good" and "bad" with "sick" and "well."

white-collar crime crime committed by people of high social position in the course of their occupations

corporate crime the illegal actions of a corporation or people acting on its behalf

organized crime a business supplying illegal goods or services

Sutherland's **differential association theory** links deviance to how much others encourage or discourage such behavior.

Hirschi's **control theory** states that imagining the possible consequences of deviance often discourages such behavior. People who are well integrated into society are less likely to engage in deviant behavior.

hate crime a criminal act against a person or a person's property by an offender motivated by racial or other bias

⊞ See the Applying Theory table in this chapter.

MAKING THE GRADE *continued . . .*

Theoretical Analysis of Deviance *(continued)*

DEVIANCE AND INEQUALITY: SOCIAL-CONFLICT ANALYSIS

Based on Karl Marx's ideas, social-conflict theory holds that laws and other norms operate to protect the interests of powerful members of any society.

- **White-collar offenses** are committed by people of high social position as part of their jobs. Sutherland claimed such offenses are rarely prosecuted and are most likely to end up in civil rather than criminal court.
- **Corporate crime** refers to illegal actions by a corporation or people acting on its behalf. Although corporate crimes cause considerable public harm, most cases of corporate crime go unpunished.
- **Organized crime** has a long history in the United States, especially among categories of people with few legitimate opportunities.

DEVIANCE, RACE, AND GENDER

- What people consider deviant reflects the relative power and privilege of different categories of people.
- **Hate crimes** are crimes motivated by racial or other bias; they target people with disadvantages based on race, gender, or sexual orientation.
- In the United States and elsewhere, societies control the behavior of women more closely than that of men.

What Is Crime?

CRIME is the violation of criminal laws enacted by local, state, or federal governments. There are two major categories of serious crime:

- crimes against the person (violent crime), including murder, aggravated assault, forcible rape, and robbery
- crimes against property (property crime), including burglary, larceny-theft, auto theft, and arson

crimes against the person crimes that direct violence or the threat of violence against others; also known as *violent crimes*

crimes against property crimes that involve theft of property belonging to others; also known as *property crimes*

victimless crimes violations of law in which there are no obvious victims

PATTERNS OF CRIME IN THE UNITED STATES

- Official statistics show that arrest rates peak in late adolescence and drop steadily with advancing age.
- About 67% of people arrested for property crimes and 82% of people arrested for violent crimes are male.
- Street crime is more common among people of lower social position. Including white-collar and corporate crime makes class differences in criminality smaller.
- More whites than African Americans are arrested for street crimes. However, African Americans are arrested more often than whites in relation to their population size. Asian Americans have a lower-than-average rate of arrest.
- By world standards, the U.S. crime rate is high.

The U.S. Criminal Justice System

plea bargaining a legal negotiation in which a prosecutor reduces a charge in exchange for a defendant's guilty plea

retribution an act of moral vengeance by which society makes the offender suffer as much as the suffering caused by the crime

deterrence the attempt to discourage criminality through the use of punishment

rehabilitation a program for reforming the offender to prevent later offenses

societal protection rendering an offender incapable of further offenses temporarily through imprisonment or permanently by execution

criminal recidivism later offenses by people previously convicted of crimes

community-based corrections correctional programs operating within society at large rather than behind prison walls

POLICE

The police maintain public order by enforcing the law.

- Police use personal discretion in deciding whether and how to handle a situation.
- Research suggests that police are more likely to make an arrest if the offense is serious, if bystanders are present, or if the suspect is African American or Latino.

COURTS

Courts rely on an adversarial process in which attorneys—one representing the defendant and one representing the state—present their cases in the presence of a judge who monitors legal procedures.

- In practice, U.S. courts resolve most cases through plea bargaining. Though efficient, this method puts less powerful people at a disadvantage.

PUNISHMENT

There are four justifications for punishment:

- retribution
- deterrence
- rehabilitation
- societal protection

Community-based corrections include probation and parole. These programs lower the cost of supervising people convicted of crimes and reduce prison overcrowding but have not been shown to reduce recidivism.

⊞ See the Summing Up table in this chapter.

MAKING THE GRADE

Sample Test Questions

These questions are similar to those found in the test bank that accompanies this textbook.

Multiple-Choice Questions

1. Crime is a special type of deviance that
   a. refers to violations of law.
   b. involves punishment.
   c. refers to any violation of a society's norms.
   d. always involves a particular person as the offender.

2. Emile Durkheim explains that deviance is
   a. defined by the rich and used against the poor.
   b. harmful not just to victims but to society as a whole.
   c. often at odds with public morality.
   d. found in every society.

3. Applying Robert Merton's strain theory, a person selling illegal drugs for a living would be an example of which of the following categories?
   a. conformist
   b. innovator
   c. retreatist
   d. ritualist

4. Labeling theory states that deviance
   a. is a normal part of social life.
   b. always changes people's social identity.
   c. arises not from what people do as much as how others respond.
   d. All of the above are correct.

5. When Jake's friends began calling him a "dope-head," he left the group and spent more time smoking marijuana. He also began hanging out with others who used drugs, and by the end of the term, he had dropped out of college. Edwin Lemert would call this situation an example of
   a. primary deviance.
   b. the development of secondary deviance.
   c. the formation of a deviant subculture.
   d. the beginning of retreatism.

6. A social-conflict approach claims that who a society calls deviant depends on
   a. who has and does not have power.
   b. a society's moral values.
   c. how often the behavior occurs.
   d. how harmful the behavior is.

7. Stealing a laptop computer from the study lounge in a college dorm is an example of which criminal offense?
   a. burglary
   b. motor vehicle theft
   c. robbery
   d. larceny-theft

8. The FBI's criminal statistics used in this chapter to create a profile of the street criminal reflect
   a. all crimes that occur.
   b. offenses known to the police.
   c. offenses that involve violence.
   d. offenses resulting in a criminal conviction.

9. Most people arrested for a violent crime in the United States are
   a. white.
   b. African American.
   c. Hispanic.
   d. Asian.

10. Which of the following is the oldest justification for punishing an offender?
    a. deterrence
    b. retribution
    c. societal protection
    d. rehabilitation

ANSWERS: 1 (a); 2 (d); 3 (b); 4 (c); 5 (b); 6 (a); 7 (d); 8 (b); 9 (a); 10 (b).

Essay Questions

1. How does a sociological view of deviance differ from the commonsense idea that bad people do bad things?

2. Research (Mauer, 1999) shows that one in three black men between the ages of twenty and twenty-nine is in jail, on probation, or on parole. What factors, noted in this chapter, help explain this pattern?

Social Stratification

FROM CHAPTER 10 OF *SOCIOLOGY*, 12/E. JOHN J. MACIONIS. COPYRIGHT © 2008 BY PEARSON EDUCATION. ALL RIGHTS RESERVED.

All societies rank people so that some have far greater opportunities and resources than others. What the specific inequalities are and how great they are vary from place to place and over time.

Rafiqur Rahman/Corbis/Reuters America LLC

Social Stratification

WHAT is social stratification?

WHY does social inequality exist?

HOW does social stratification differ in societies around the world?

Zack Seckler/CORBIS (*background*)

On April 10, 1912, the ocean liner *Titanic* slipped away from the docks of Southampton, England, on its maiden voyage across the North Atlantic to New York. A proud symbol of the new industrial age, the towering ship carried 2,300 men, women, and children, some enjoying more luxury than most travelers today could imagine. Poor passengers crowded the lower decks, journeying to what they hoped would be a better life in the United States.

Two days out, the crew received radio warnings of icebergs in the area but paid little notice. Then, near midnight, as the ship steamed swiftly westward, a lookout was stunned to see a massive shape rising out of the dark ocean directly ahead. Moments later, the *Titanic* collided with a huge iceberg, as tall as the ship itself, which split open its side as if the grand vessel were a giant tin can.

Seawater flooded into the ship's lower levels. Within twenty-five minutes of impact, people were rushing for the lifeboats. By 2:00 A.M., the bow was completely submerged, and the stern rose high above the water. Minutes later, all the lights went out. Clinging to the deck, quietly observed by those huddled in lifeboats, hundreds of helpless passengers and crew solemnly passed their final minutes before the ship disappeared into the frigid Atlantic (W. Lord, 1976).

Illustration by Ken Marschall ©1992 from *Titanic: An Illustrated History*, a Hyperion/Madison Press Book

The tragic loss of more than 1,600 lives when the *Titanic* sank made news around the world. Looking back at this terrible accident with a sociological eye, we note that some categories of passengers had much better odds of survival than others. Reflecting that era's traditional ideas about gender, women and children were allowed to board the lifeboats first, with the result that 80 percent of the people who died were men. Class, too, was at work. More than 60 percent of people holding first-class tickets were saved because they were on the upper decks, where warnings were sounded first and lifeboats were accessible. Only 36 percent of the second-class passengers survived, and of the third-class passengers on the lower decks, only 24 percent escaped drowning. On board the *Titanic,* class turned out to mean much more than the quality of accommodations—it was a matter of life or death.

The fate of the passengers on the *Titanic* dramatically illustrates how social inequality affects the way people live and sometimes whether they live at all. This chapter explores the important concept of social stratification.

What Is Social Stratification?

For tens of thousands of years, humans the world over lived in small hunting and gathering societies. Although members of these bands might single out one person as swifter, stronger, or more skillful in collecting food, everyone had roughly the same social standing. As societies became more complex, a major change came about. Societies began to elevate specific categories of people above others, giving some parts of the population more wealth, power, and prestige than others.

Social stratification, *a system by which a society ranks categories of people in a hierarchy,* is based on four basic principles:

1. **Social stratification is a trait of society, not simply a reflection of individual differences.** Many of us think of social standing in terms of personal talent and effort, and as a result, we often exaggerate the extent to which we control our own fate. Did a higher percentage of the first-class passengers on the *Titanic* survive because they were better swimmers than second- and third-class passengers? Hardly. They did better because of their privileged position on the ship, which gave them first access to the lifeboats. Similarly, children born into wealthy families are more likely than children born into poverty to enjoy good health, do well in school, succeed in a career, and live a long life. Neither the rich nor the poor created social stratification, yet this system shapes the lives of us all.

2. **Social stratification carries over from generation to generation.** We have only to look at how parents pass their social position on to their children to see that stratification is a trait of societies rather than individuals. Some individuals, especially in high-income societies, do experience **social mobility,** *a change in position within the social hierarchy.* Social mobility may be upward or downward. We celebrate the achievements of rare individuals such as Christina Aguilera and Michael Jordan, both of whom rose from modest beginnings to fame and fortune. Some people move downward because of business failures, unemployment, or illness. More often people move *horizontally;* they switch from one job to another at about the same social level. The social standing of most people remains much the same over their lifetime.

3. **Social stratification is universal but variable.** Social stratification is found everywhere. Yet *what* is unequal and *how* unequal it is varies from one society to another. In some

Chapter Overview

This chapter introduces the central concept of social stratification, the focus of the next six chapters of the text. Social stratification is important because our social standing affects almost everything about our lives.

societies, inequality is mostly a matter of prestige; in others, wealth or power is the key element of difference. In addition, some societies contain more inequality than others.

4. **Social stratification involves not just inequality but beliefs as well.** Any system of inequality not only gives some people more than others but also defines these arrangements as fair. Just as the details of inequality vary, the explanations of *why* people should be unequal differ from society to society.

Caste and Class Systems

Sociologists distinguish between *closed systems*, which allow for little change in social position, and *open systems*, which permit much more social mobility. Closed systems are called *caste systems*, and more open systems are called *class systems*.

The Caste System

A **caste system** is *social stratification based on ascription, or birth*. A pure caste system is closed because birth alone determines a person's entire future, allowing little or no social mobility based on individual effort. People live out their lives in the rigid categories assigned to them, without the possibility of change for the better or worse.

An Illustration: India

Many of the world's societies, most of them agrarian, are caste systems. In India, for example, much of the population still lives in traditional villages where the caste system persists. The Indian system identifies four major castes (or *varna*, a Sanskrit word that means "color"): Brahman, Kshatriya, Vaishya, and Sudra. On the local level, each of these is composed of hundreds of subcaste groups (*jati*).

From birth, a caste system determines the direction of a person's life. First, with the exception of farming, which is open to everyone, families in each caste perform one type of work, as priests, soldiers, barbers, leather workers, sweepers, and so on.

Second, a caste system demands that people marry others of the same ranking. If people were to have "mixed" marriages with members of other castes, what rank would their children hold? Sociologists call this pattern of marrying within a social category *endogamous* marriage (*endo* stems from the Greek, meaning "within"). According to tradition—this practice is now rare and found only in remote rural areas—Indian parents select their children's marriage partners, often before the children reach their teens.

Third, caste guides everyday life by keeping people in the company of "their own kind." Norms reinforce this practice by teaching, for example, that a "purer" person of a higher caste is "polluted" by contact with someone of lower standing.

The personal experience of poverty is clear in this photograph of a homeless couple spending the night in a low-cost rooming house. The main sociological insight is that although we feel the effects of social stratification personally, our social standing is largely the result of the way society (or a world of societies) structures opportunity and reward. To the core of our being, we are all products of social stratification.

Mary Ellen Mark

Fourth, caste systems rest on powerful cultural beliefs. Indian culture is built on the Hindu tradition that doing the caste's life work and accepting an arranged marriage are moral duties.

Caste and Agrarian Life

Caste systems are typical of agrarian societies because agriculture demands a lifelong routine of hard work. By teaching a sense of moral duty, a caste system ensures that people are disciplined for a lifetime of work and are willing to perform the same jobs as their parents. Thus the caste system has hung on in rural areas of India more than sixty years after being formally outlawed.

People living in the industrial cities of India have many more choices about work and marriage partners than people in rural areas.

The New York Times

In Today's India, Status Comes with Four Wheels

By AMY WALDMAN
December 5, 2005

On the dark highway, the car showroom glowed in the night like an American drive-in. Inside, it looked more like a game-show set: bright lights, white floors, huge windows, high ceilings and ad posters of beaming consumers far paler than most Indians. For 36-year-old Ram Reddy, the price was right enough to make a down payment on his fifth family car.

He and his brother already had one car "for the children," two "for the ladies," and so on. Now they were buying the Toyota Innova, a big-as-a-boat luxury van that retails for a minimum of $23,000, seven times India's per capita income of about $3,000.

The Innova is a new plaything of the moneyed here. . . . It is yet another symbol of the kid-in-a-candy-store psyche that has seized India's growing consuming class, once denied capitalism's choices and now flooded with them.

Fifteen years after India began its transition from a state-run to a free-market economy, a new culture of money—making it, and even more, spending it—is afoot. . . .

So intense is the advertising onslaught, so giddy the media coverage of the new affluence, that it is almost easy to forget that India remains home to the world's largest number of poor people, according to the World Bank.

Still, India's middle class has grown to an estimated 250 million in the past decade, and the number of super-rich has grown sharply as well.

And, after more decades of socialist deprivation, when consumer goods were so limited that refrigerators were given pride of place in living rooms, they have ever more wares to spend it on: cellphones, air-conditioners and washing machines; Botox, sushi and Louis Vuitton bags; and, perhaps the biggest status symbol of all, cars.

India has become one of the world's fastest-growing car markets, with about a million being sold each year. It once had only two kinds, Fiats and Ambassadors. Now, dozens of models ride the roads. . . .

Indians are discovering in cars everything Americans did: control and freedom, privacy and privilege, speed and status. Car showrooms, the bigger the better, are the new temples here, and cars the icons of a new individualism taking root. . . .

In a historical blink, capitalism, which postcolonial analysis once labeled poverty's cause, is now seen as its solution. Debt, once anathema for the middle class, is now an acceptable means to an end.

For a sliver of Indians, the go-go years are here. . . . Young men drive bright yellow motorbikes with names like Ambition and dream of becoming crorepatis, or multimillionaires.

America, of course, went through a similar evolution: the making of a postwar consumerist economy; the introduction of credit cards and growing comfort with, and dependence on, debt; the rise of an advertising culture. . . .

"Now the people want to spend and enjoy," said [Sasty V. Prakky, the Toyota dealership's senior sales and marketing manager]. "Everyone wants upgradation: the scooter owner wants a motorbike, the motorbike owner a car, the car owner a more expensive one." . . .

India's state-run rail network may have been built by the British, but it came to represent a certain egalitarianism. Powerful and voiceless, rich and poor—all navigated the same chaotic, crowded stations and rode the same jam-packed trains, if not in the same class.

Cars, in contrast, reflect the atomization prosperity brings.

This is a far bigger change for Indian society than it was for America, which in many ways was founded around the notion of the individual. Indian society has always been more about duty, or dharma, than drive, more about responsibility to others than the realization of individual desire.

That ethos is changing. . . .

Spreading affluence also has brought new competitive anxiety. Where once everyone in a neighborhood had an Ambassador or a Fiat, the hierarchy of livelihoods, of success, now can be parsed easily through cars.

P. V. J. Mohanrao, 48, an assistant college professor, who came to the Toyota showroom to look at the Innova, could afford only cheaper cars: the Indian-made Maruti and Tata Sumo.

A neighbor who was with him, P. Srinivas, 41, a businessman, . . . could afford . . . the more luxurious Chevrolet Tavera.

Another neighbor, a software entrepreneur, . . . outclassed them both: at any given time, he had three or four cars, none of them cheap.

"He has booked this car, I heard," Mr. Mohanrao said of his neighbor and the Innova.

WHAT DO YOU THINK?

1. Why does the emergence of an industrial class system raise the social importance of owning things like cars?

2. The manifest function of cars is to get people from one place to another. What are some of the latent functions of cars involving social standing?

3. Why does owning automobiles go hand in hand with a society becoming more individualistic?

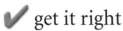

student 2 student

"Loyalties in a pure meritocracy? Forget it. As they say in the music business, 'You're only as hot as your last CD.'"

In addition, as "In the *Times*" explains, social standing in richer, more modern Indian society has much to do with how much people earn and what they can buy with their money.

 Are there elements of caste in U.S. society? To what extent do parents pass on their social position to children? What about the idea that there are "women's jobs" and "men's jobs"?

Another country dominated by caste is South Africa, although the system of *apartheid,* or separation of the races, is no longer legal and is now in decline. The Thinking Globally box on page 256 takes a closer look.

The Class System

Because a modern economy must attract people to work in many occupations other than farming, it depends on developing people's talents in diverse fields. This gives rise to a **class system,** *social stratification based on both birth and individual achievement.*

Class systems are more open than caste systems, so people who gain schooling and skills may experience social mobility. As a result, class distinctions become blurred, and even blood relatives may have different social standings. Categorizing people according to their color, sex, or social background comes to be seen as wrong in modern societies as all people gain political rights and, in principle, equal standing before the law. In addition, work is no longer fixed at birth but involves some personal choice. Greater individuality also translates into more freedom in selecting a marriage partner.

Meritocracy

The concept of **meritocracy** refers to *social stratification based on personal merit.* Because industrial societies need to develop a broad range of abilities beyond farming, stratification is based not just on the accident of birth but also on *merit* (from a Latin word meaning "earned"), which includes a person's knowledge, abilities, and effort. A rough measure of merit is a person's job and how well it is done. To increase meritocracy, industrial societies expand equality of opportunity and teach people to expect unequal rewards based on individual performance.

In rural India, the traditional caste system still shapes people's lives. This girl is a member of the "untouchables," a category below the four basic castes. She and her family are clothes washers, people who clean material "polluted" by blood or human waste. Such work is defined as unclean for people of higher caste position.

William Albert Allard/ National Geographic Image Collection

In a pure meritocracy, social position would depend entirely on a person's ability and effort. Such a system would have ongoing social mobility, blurring social categories as individuals continuously move up or down in the system, depending on their latest performance.

Caste societies define merit in terms of loyalty to the system—that is, dutifully performing whatever job comes with a person's birth. Caste systems waste human potential, but they are very orderly. A need for order is the reason industrial societies keep some elements of caste—such as letting wealth pass from generation to generation—rather than becoming complete meritocracies. A pure meritocracy would weaken families and other social groupings. After all, economic performance is not everything: Would we want to evaluate our family members solely on how successful they are in their jobs outside the home? Probably not. Class systems in industrial societies move toward meritocracy to promote productivity and efficiency but keep caste elements, such as family, to maintain order and social unity.

 How much of your social position is due to merit (personal ability and effort), and how much is due to caste (passed on from your parents)?

tip
A pure meritocracy would have extreme social mobility, with people moving up and down according to their own performance against the competition.

student 2 student
"Reading about the history of racial apartheid in South Africa made me think about the history of racial caste in the United States."

Thinking Globally
Race as Caste: A Report from South Africa

JEROME: It's good that racial caste is no longer the law in South Africa.
REGGIE: But racial inequality is far from over. . . .

At the southern tip of the African continent lies South Africa, a country about the size of Alaska with a population of about 47 million. For 300 years, the native Africans who lived there were ruled by white people, first by the Dutch traders and farmers who settled there in the mid-seventeenth century and then by the British, who colonized the area early in the nineteenth century. By the early 1900s, the British had taken over the entire country, naming it the Union of South Africa.

In 1961, the nation declared its independence from Britain, calling itself the Republic of South Africa, but freedom for the black majority was still decades away. To ensure their political control over the black population, whites instituted the policy of *apartheid*, or racial separation. Apartheid, written into law in 1948, denied blacks national citizenship, ownership of land, and any voice in the nation's government. As a lower caste, blacks received little schooling and performed menial, low-paying jobs. White people with even average wealth had at least one black household servant.

The members of the white minority claimed that apartheid protected their cultural traditions from the influence of people they considered inferior. When blacks resisted apartheid, whites used brutal military repression to maintain their power.

Even so, steady resistance—especially from younger blacks, who demanded a political voice and economic opportunity—gradually forced the country to change. Criticism from other industrial nations added to the pressure. By the mid-1980s, the tide began to turn as the South African government granted limited political rights to people of mixed race and Asian ancestry. Next came the right of all people to form labor unions, to enter occupations once limited to whites, and to own property. Officials also repealed apartheid laws that separated the races in public places.

The pace of change increased in 1990 with the release from prison of Nelson Mandela, who led the fight against apartheid. In 1994, the first national election open to all races made Mandela president, ending centuries of white minority rule.

Despite this dramatic political change, social stratification in South Africa is still based on race. Even with the right to own property, one-third of black South Africans have no work, and the majority remain dirt poor. The worst off are some 7 million *ukuhleleleka,* which means "marginal people" in the Xhosa language. Soweto-by-the-Sea may sound like a summer getaway, but it is home to thousands of people who live crammed into shacks made of packing cases, corrugated metal, cardboard, and other discarded materials. There is no electricity for lights or refrigeration. Without plumbing, people use buckets to haul sewerage. The community's women line up to take a turn at a single water tap that serves more than 1,000 people. Jobs are hard to come by, and those who do find work are lucky to earn $250 a month.

South Africa's current president, Thabo Mbeki, who was elected in 1999, leads a nation still crippled by its history of racial caste. Tourism is up and holds the promise of an economic boom in years to come, but the country can break from the past only by providing real opportunity to all its people.

WHAT DO YOU THINK?

1. How has race been a form of caste in South Africa?

2. Although apartheid is no longer law, why does racial inequality continue to shape South African society?

3. Does race operate as an element of caste in the United States? Explain your answer.

Sources: Fredrickson (1981), Wren (1991), Hawthorne (1999), and Mabry & Masland (1999).

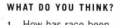
Abbas/Magnum Photos, Inc.

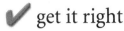
Status Consistency

Status consistency is *the degree of uniformity in a person's social standing across various dimensions of social inequality.* A caste system has limited social mobility and high status consistency, so the typical person has the same relative ranking with regard to wealth, power, and prestige. The greater mobility of class systems produces less status consistency, so people are ranked higher on some dimensions of social standing and lower on others. In the United States, for example, most college professors with advanced academic degrees enjoy high social prestige but earn only modest incomes. Low status consistency means that it is harder to define people's social position. Therefore, *classes* are much harder to define than *castes.*

Caste and Class: The United Kingdom

The mix of caste and meritocracy in class systems is well illustrated by the United Kingdom (Great Britain—consisting of England, Wales, and Scotland—and Northern Ireland), an industrial nation with a long agrarian history.

Aristocratic England

In the Middle Ages, England had a castelike system of aristocracy. The aristocracy included the leading members of the church, who were thought to speak with the authority of God. Some clergy were local priests, who were not members of the aristocracy and who lived simple lives. But the highest church officials lived in palaces and presided over an organization that owned much land, which was the major source of wealth. Church leaders, typically referred to as the *first estate* in France and other European countries, also had a great deal of power to shape the political events of the day.

The rest of the aristocracy, which in France and other European countries was known as the *second estate*, was a hereditary nobility that made up barely 5 percent of the population. The royal family—the king and queen at the top of the power structure—as well as lesser nobles (including several hundred families headed by men titled as dukes, earls, and barons) together owned most of the nation's land. Most of the men and women within the aristocracy were wealthy due to their holdings of land, and they had many servants for their homes as well as ordinary farmers to work their fields. With all their work done for them by others, members of the aristocracy had no occupation and came to believe that engaging in a trade or any other work for income was beneath them. Aristocrats used their leisure time to develop skills in horseback riding and warfare and to cultivate refined tastes in art, music, and literature.

To prevent their vast landholdings from being divided by heirs when they died, aristocrats devised the law of *primogeniture* (from the Latin meaning "firstborn"), which required that all property pass to the old-

In U.S. society, everyone's social position reflects both birth and personal achievement. Dave Chappell, popular television comedian and actor, was born to a middle-class family (his parents are both college professors) and rose to become one of the highest-paid people in the country. Such upward social mobility is common in the entertainment business, which is open to new talent. Do you think this upward mobility is as common in the medical profession or the world of finance? Explain.

CBS/ Monty Brinton/Landov LLC

est son or other male relation. Younger sons had to find other means of support. Some of these men became leaders in the church—where they would live as well as they were used to—and helped tie together the church and the state by having members of the same families running both. Other younger sons within the aristocracy became military officers or judges or took up other professions considered honorable for gentlemen. In an age when no woman could inherit her father's property and few women had the opportunity to earn a living on their own, a noble daughter depended for her security on marrying well.

Below the high clergy and the rest of the aristocracy, the vast majority of men and women were simply called *commoners* or, in France and other European countries, the *third estate*. Most commoners were serfs working land owned by nobles or the church. Unlike

Following the centuries-old practice among aristocratic men in England, Prince Harry completed military training as part of his studies at Eton. He is part of a royal family that traces its ancestry back for more than a thousand years—an element of caste that remains in the British class system.

Tim Graham Picture Library/Getty Images

members of the aristocracy, most commoners had little schooling and were illiterate.

As the Industrial Revolution expanded England's economy, some commoners living in cities made enough money to challenge the nobility. More emphasis on meritocracy, the growing importance of money, and the expansion of schooling and legal rights eventually blurred the difference between aristocrats and commoners and gave rise to a class system.

Perhaps it is a sign of the times that these days, traditional titles are put up for sale by aristocrats who need money. In 1996, for example, Earl Spencer—the brother of Princess Diana—sold one of his titles, Lord of Wimbledon, to raise the $300,000 he needed to redo the plumbing in one of his large homes (McKee, 1996).

The United Kingdom Today

The United Kingdom has a class system, but caste elements from England's aristocratic past are still evident. A small number of British families still holds considerable inherited wealth and enjoys high prestige, schooling at excellent universities, and substantial political influence. A traditional monarch, Queen Elizabeth II, is the United

Kingdom's head of state, and Parliament's House of Lords is composed of "peers," about half of whom are aristocrats of noble birth. However, control of government now rests with commoners—specifically, members of Parliament's House of Commons—where the prime minister and other leaders reach their positions by achievement—winning an election—rather than by birth.

Lower in the class hierarchy, roughly one-fourth of the British people form the middle class. Many earn comfortable incomes from professions and business and are likely to have investments in the form of stocks and bonds. Below the middle class, perhaps half of all Britons think of themselves as "working-class," earning modest incomes through manual labor. The remaining one-fourth of the British people make up the lower class, the poor who lack steady work or who work full time but are paid too little to live comfortably. Most lower-class Britons live in the nation's northern and western regions, which have been further impoverished by the closings of mines and factories.

Today's British class system has a mix of caste elements and meritocracy, producing a highly stratified society with some opportunity to move upward or downward. One result of centuries of aristocracy is that social mobility occurs less often in the United Kingdom than it does in the United States (Kerckhoff, Campbell, & Winfield-Laird, 1985). This more rigid system of inequality in the United Kingdom is reflected in the importance attached to accent. Distinctive patterns of speech develop in any society when people are set off from one another over many generations. People in the United States treat accent as a clue to where a person lives or grew up (we can easily identify a midwestern "twang" or a southern "drawl"). In the United Kingdom, however, accent is a mark of social class, with upper-class people speaking "the King's English" but most people speaking "like commoners." So different are these two accents that the British seem to be, as the saying goes, "a single people divided by a common language."

 What do the distinctive accents of people living in poor rural areas or poor inner cities in the United States say about their social history?

Another Example: Japan

Social stratification in Japan also mixes caste and meritocracy. Japan is both the world's oldest continuously operating monarchy and a modern society where wealth follows individual achievement.

tip

In modern Japan, notice how elements of meritocracy (such as people going to school in order to get a better job) mix with elements of caste (such as the continuing importance of people's social background and differences in opportunities for women and men).

Aristocratic Japan

By the fifth century C.E., Japan was an agrarian society with a rigid caste system, ruled by an imperial family, containing both aristocrats and commoners. The emperor ruled by divine right (meaning that he claimed that God intended him to rule), and his military leader (or *shogun*) enforced the emperor's rule with the help of regional nobles or warlords.

Below the nobility were the *samurai,* a warrior caste whose name means "to serve." This second rank of Japanese society was made up of soldiers who learned martial arts and who lived by a code of honor based on absolute loyalty to their leaders.

As in Great Britain, most people in Japan at this time in history were commoners who worked very hard to live from day to day. Unlike their European counterparts, however, Japanese commoners were not lowest in rank. At the bottom were the *burakumin,* or "outcasts," looked down on by both lord and commoner. Like the lowest-caste groups in India, these outcasts lived apart from others, performed the most distasteful work, and could not change their social standing.

Modern Japan

By the 1860s (the time of the Civil War in the United States), the nobles realized that Japan's traditional caste system would prevent the country from entering the modern industrial era. Besides, as in Britain, some nobles were happy to have their children marry wealthy commoners who had more money than they did. As Japan opened up to the larger world, the traditional caste system weakened. In 1871, the Japanese legally banned the social category of "outcast," although some people still look down on those whose ancestors held this rank. After Japan's defeat in World War II, the nobility lost their privileges, so only the emperor remains as a symbol of Japan's traditions, but he has little real power.

Social stratification in Japan is very different from the rigid caste system of centuries ago. Today, Japanese society consists of "upper," "upper-middle," "lower-middle," and "lower" classes. The exact lines between these classes are unclear to most Japanese, and many people do move between classes over time. But because Japanese culture tends to respect tradition, family background is never far from the surface when sizing up someone's social standing. Officially, everyone is equal before the law, but in reality, many people still look at one another through the centuries-old lens of caste.

Finally, traditional ideas about gender continue to shape Japanese society. Legally, the two sexes are equal, but men dominate women in many ways. Because Japanese parents are more likely to send sons than daughters to college, there is a significant gender gap in educa-tion. With the recent economic downturn in Japan, many more women have entered the labor force. But most working women fill lower-level support positions in the corporate world, only rarely assuming leadership roles. In short, individual achievement in Japan's modern class system operates in the shadow of centuries of traditional male privilege (Norbeck, 1983; Brinton, 1988; H. W. French, 2002).

Classless Societies?
The Former Soviet Union

Nowhere in the world do we find a society without some degree of social inequality. Yet some nations have claimed to be classless.

The Russian Revolution

The Union of Soviet Socialist Republics (USSR), which rivaled the United States as a military superpower in the mid- to late twentieth century, was born out of a revolution in Russia in 1917. The Russian Revolution ended the feudal aristocracy in which a nobility ruled the country and transferred farms, factories, and other productive property from private ownership to a new, centralized state government.

The Russian Revolution was guided by the ideas of Karl Marx, who wrote that private ownership of productive property is the basis of social classes. When the state took control of the economy, Soviet officials boasted that they had created the first modern classless society.

Critics, however, pointed out that based on their jobs, the Soviet people were actually stratified into four unequal categories. At the top were high government officials, or *apparatchiks.* Next came the Soviet intelligentsia, including lower government officials, college professors, scientists, physicians, and engineers. Below them were manual workers and, at the lowest level, the rural peasantry.

In reality, the Soviet Union was not classless at all. But putting factories, farms, colleges, and hospitals under state control did create more economic equality (although with sharp differences in power) than in capitalist societies such as the United States.

The Modern Russian Federation

In 1985, Mikhail Gorbachev came to power in the Soviet Union with a new economic program known as *perestroika,* meaning "restructuring." Gorbachev saw that although the Soviet system had reduced economic inequality, living standards were far behind those of other industrial nations. Gorbachev tried to generate economic growth by reducing the inefficient centralized control of the economy.

Gorbachev's economic reforms turned into one of the most dramatic social movements in history. People in the Soviet Union and in other socialist countries of Eastern Europe blamed their poverty and

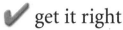
Structural social mobility is caused not by individual effort but by changes in the structure of society. For example, when a society industrializes, people change jobs from farm work to factory work and typically earn higher wages.

After the collapse of the Soviet Union in 1991, Russia began a transition toward a market economy. Since then, some people have become quite rich, but others have lost their jobs as old, inefficient factories closed. As a result, the problem of poverty has become widespread, affecting perhaps one-third of the Russian people. Scenes like this one are all too common.

Peter Turnley/ Corbis

their lack of basic freedoms on the repressive ruling class of Communist party officials. Beginning in 1989, people throughout Eastern Europe toppled their socialist governments, and at the end of 1991, the Soviet Union itself collapsed, with its largest republic remaking itself as the Russian Federation.

The Soviet Union's story shows that social inequality involves more than economic resources. Soviet society did not have the extremes of wealth and poverty found in the United Kingdom, Japan, and the United States. But an elite class existed all the same, one based on political power rather than wealth.

What about social mobility in so-called classless societies? During the twentieth century, there was as much upward social mobility in the Soviet Union as in the United States. Rapidly expanding industry and government drew many poor rural peasants into factories and offices. This trend illustrates what sociologists call **structural social mobility,** *a shift in the social position of large numbers of people due more to changes in society itself than to individual efforts.*

 November 24, Odessa, Ukraine. The first snow of our voyage flies over the decks as our ship docks at Odessa, the former Soviet Union's southernmost

port on the Black Sea. A short distance away, we gaze up the Potemkin Steps, the steep stairway up to the city, where the first shots of the Russian Revolution rang out. It has been several years since our last visit, and much has changed; in fact, the Soviet Union itself has collapsed. Has life improved? For some people, certainly: There are now chic boutiques where well-dressed shoppers buy fine wines, designer clothes, and imported perfumes. But for most people, life seems much worse. Flea markets line the curbs as families sell their home furnishings. When meat costs $4 a pound and the average person earns about $30 a month, people become desperate. Even the city has to save money by turning off street lights after 8:00 P.M. The spirits of most people seem as dim as Odessa's streets.

During the 1990s, the forces of structural social mobility in the new Russian Federation turned downward. One indicator is that the average life span for Russian men dropped by eight years and for women by two years. Many factors are involved in this decline, including Russia's poor health care system, but the Russian people clearly have suffered in the turbulent period of economic change that began in 1991 (Bohlen, 1998; Gerber & Hout, 1998).

The hope was that in the long run, closing inefficient state industries would improve the nation's economic performance. The economy has expanded, but living standards have fallen, and although a few people have made huge fortunes, most citizens have faced hard times. In recent years, President Vladimir Putin has begun to restore centralized state power. As a result, economic inequality has declined. At the same time, however, many people wonder what a return to a more socialist society will mean for their living standards and political freedoms (Zuckerman, 2006).

China: Emerging Social Classes

Sweeping political and economic change has affected not just the Russian Federation but also the People's Republic of China. After the Communist revolution in 1949, the state took control of all farms, factories, and other productive property. Communist party leader Mao Zedong declared all types of work to be equally important, so officially, social classes no longer existed.

The new program greatly reduced economic inequality. But as in the Soviet Union, social differences remained. The country was ruled by a political elite with enormous power and considerable privilege; below them were managers of large factories as well as skilled

Stratification systems produce ideas and beliefs
that define their operation as just. In short,
stratification involves not just who has what but
also beliefs about justice—why people should
have what they have.

In recent decades, the government of China has permitted a market
economy to operate in limited areas of the country. The result has been
increased production and the emergence of a new business class with a
lifestyle similar to that of wealthy people in the United States.

Julia Calfee/Polaris Images

professionals; next came industrial workers; at the bottom were rural
peasants, who were not even allowed to leave their villages and migrate
to cities.

Further economic change came in 1978 when Mao died and
Deng Xiaoping became China's leader. The state gradually loosened
its hold on the economy, allowing a new class of business owners to
emerge. Communist party leaders remain in control of the country,
and some have prospered as they have joined the ranks of the small
but wealthy elite who control new privately run industries. Much of
this new economic growth has been concentrated in coastal areas,
where living standards have soared far above those in China's rural
interior.

Today, the booming cities along China's coast contain many people made rich by the expanding economy. In addition, these cities
have attracted tens of millions of migrants in search of better jobs, but
most are poor, and many are being cheated by employers (Atlas, 2007).

In sum, China displays a new and emerging class system that is
a mix of the old political hierarchy and a new business hierarchy.
Economic inequality in China has increased, and as Figure 1 shows,
it is now as great as in the United States. At this early stage, scholars
point to the new system's complexity and debate its likely future. But
one lesson is clear: With new patterns of inequality emerging over
time, social stratification in China is becoming dynamic (Bian, 2002).

Ideology: The Power behind Stratification

How do societies persist without sharing resources more equally? The
highly stratified British aristocracy and the caste system in Japan each
survived for centuries, and for 2,000 years people in India accepted the
idea that they should be privileged or poor based on the accident of
birth.

A major reason that social hierarchies endure is **ideology,** *cultural
beliefs that justify particular social arrangements, including patterns of
inequality.* A belief—for example, the idea that rich people are smart
and poor people are lazy—is ideological to the extent that it supports
inequality by defining it as fair.

Plato and Marx on Ideology

According to the ancient Greek philosopher Plato (427–347 B.C.E.),
every culture considers some type of inequality just. Although Karl
Marx understood this, he was far more critical of inequality than
Plato. Marx criticized capitalist societies for defending wealth and
power in the hands of a few as "a law of the marketplace." Capitalist
law, he continued, defines the right to own property and ensures that
money stays within the same families from one generation to the next.
In short, Marx concluded, culture and institutions combine to support a society's elite, which is why established hierarchies last a long
time.

Historical Patterns of Ideology

Ideology changes along with a society's economy and technology.
Because agrarian societies depend on most people's lifelong labor,
they develop caste systems that view performing the duties of a person's social position a moral responsibility. With the rise of industrial capitalism, an ideology of meritocracy arises, defining wealth
and power as prizes to be won by those individuals who perform
the best. This change means that the poor—often given charity
under feudalism—come to be looked down on as personally undeserving. This harsh view is found in the ideas of the early sociologist

tip

Figure 1 shows that lower-income countries (such as Brazil, Ecuador, and Mexico) have more social inequality than high-income countries (such as the United Kingdom, Canada, and Sweden). This pattern is explained at the end of this chapter in the discussion of the Kuznets curve.

Driving to work in São Paulo, Brazil, Fabio Campos passes both gated mansions of the very rich and run-down shacks of the very poor.

On her way to work in Stockholm, Sweden, Sylvia Arnbjörg passes through mostly middle-class neighborhoods.

GLOBAL SNAPSHOT

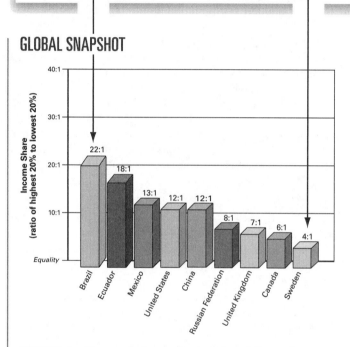

FIGURE 1   Economic Inequality in Selected Countries

Many low- and middle-income countries have greater economic inequality than the United States. But this country has more economic inequality than most high-income nations.

These data are the most recent available, representing income share for various years between 1999 and 2005.

Sources: U.S. Census Bureau (2006) and World Bank (2007).

Herbert Spencer, as explained in the Seeing Sociology in Everyday Life box.

History shows how difficult it is to change social stratification. However, challenges to the status quo always arise. The traditional idea that "a woman's place is in the home," for example, has given way to increased economic opportunities for women in many societies today. The continuing progress toward racial equality in South Africa reflects widespread rejection of the ideology of apartheid.

The Functions of Social Stratification

Why does social stratification exist at all? One answer, consistent with the structural-functional approach, is that social inequality plays a vital part in the operation of society. This argument was set forth more than sixty years ago by Kingsley Davis and Wilbert Moore (1945).

The Davis-Moore Thesis

The **Davis-Moore thesis** states that *social stratification has beneficial consequences for the operation of a society.* How else, ask Davis and Moore, can we explain the fact that some form of social stratification has been found in every society?

Davis and Moore note that modern societies have hundreds of occupational positions of varying importance. Certain jobs—say,

washing windows, cutting grass, or answering a telephone—are fairly easy and can be performed by almost anyone. Other jobs—such as designing new generations of computers or transplanting human organs—are difficult and demand the scarce talents of people with extensive (and expensive) training.

Therefore, Davis and Moore explain, the greater the functional importance of a position, the more rewards a society attaches to it. This strategy promotes productivity and efficiency because rewarding important work with income, prestige, power, and leisure encourages people to do these jobs and to work better, longer, and harder. In short, unequal rewards (which is what social stratification is) benefit society as a whole.

Davis and Moore claim that any society could be egalitarian, but only to the extent that people are willing to let *anyone* perform *any* job. Equality would also demand that someone who carries out a job poorly be rewarded the same as someone who performs it well. Such a system would clearly offer little incentive for people to try their best, reducing the society's productive efficiency.

The Davis-Moore thesis suggests the reason stratification exists; it does not state what rewards a society should give to any occupational position or how unequal rewards should be. It merely points out that positions a society considers more important must offer enough rewards to draw talented people away from less important work.

Following Davis and Moore's thinking, why do professors give grades from A to F? What would happen if they gave every student the same grade? Explain.

▶ **CRITICAL REVIEW**   Although the Davis-Moore thesis is an important contribution to understanding social stratification, it has provoked criticism. Melvin Tumin (1953) wondered, first, how we assess the importance of a particular occupation. Perhaps the high rewards our society gives to physicians results partly from deliberate efforts by the medical profession to limit the supply of physicians and thereby increase the demand for their services.

student 2 student

"Our market economy doesn't reward people for doing 'good' for society; it rewards activity that creates market value."

Seeing Sociology in Everyday Life
The Meaning of Class: Is Getting Rich "the Survival of the Fittest"?

"The survival of the fittest"—we have all heard these words used to describe society as a competitive jungle. The phrase was coined by one of sociology's pioneers, Herbert Spencer (1820–1903), whose ideas about social inequality are still widespread today.

Spencer, who lived in England, eagerly followed the work of the natural scientist Charles Darwin (1809–1882). Darwin's theory of biological evolution holds that a species changes physically over thousands of generations as it adapts to the natural environment. Spencer distorted Darwin's theory, applying it to the operation of society: Society became the "jungle," with the "fittest" people rising to wealth and the "failures" sinking into miserable poverty.

It is no surprise that Spencer's views were popular among the rising U.S. industrialists of the day. John D. Rockefeller (1839–1937), who made a fortune building the oil industry, recited Spencer's "social gospel" to young children in Sunday school. As Rockefeller saw it, the growth of giant corporations—and the astounding wealth of their owners—was merely a result of "the survival of the fittest," a basic fact of nature. Neither Spencer nor Rockefeller had much sympathy for the poor, seeing poverty as evidence of not measuring up in a competitive world. Spencer opposed social welfare programs, saying that they penalized society's "best" members (through taxes) and rewarded society's "worst" members (through welfare benefits).

Today's sociologists are quick to point out that society is far from a meritocracy, as Spencer claimed. And it is not the case that companies or individuals who generate lots of money necessarily benefit society. Yet Spencer's view that people get what they deserve in life remains part of our individualistic culture.

WHAT DO YOU THINK?

1. What did Herbert Spencer mean when he said society encourages "the survival of the fittest"?

2. Why do you think that Spencer's ideas are still popular in the United States today?

3. Do you think that how much you earn reflects your importance to society? Why or why not?

Furthermore, do rewards actually reflect the contribution someone makes to society? With income of $230 million per year, Oprah Winfrey earns more in one day than the U.S. president earns all year. Would anyone argue that hosting a talk show is more important than leading a country? And what about members of the U.S. military in Iraq? Facing the risks of combat, they earn only about $12,000 a year. Then there are many cases like that of Larry Ellison, the chief executive officer of Oracle, who even as the value of his company slid downward still earned $700 million, an amount that would take a typical U.S. soldier almost 60,000 years to earn (M. Benjamin, 2002; Broder, 2002; Dunn, 2003). Do corporate executives deserve such megasalaries for their contributions to society?

Second, Tumin claimed that Davis and Moore ignore how caste elements of social stratification can prevent the development of individual talent. Born to privilege, rich children have opportunities to develop their abilities that many gifted poor children never have.

Third, living in a society that places so much emphasis on money, we tend to overestimate the importance of high-paying work; how do stockbrokers or people who trade international currencies really contribute to society? For the same reason, it is difficult for us to see the value of work that is not oriented toward making money, such as parenting, creative writing, playing music in a symphony, or just being a good friend to someone in need (Packard, 2002).

Finally, by suggesting that social stratification benefits all of society, the Davis-Moore thesis ignores how social inequality promotes conflict and even outright revolution. This criticism leads us to the social-conflict approach, which provides a very different explanation for social inequality.

 YOUR LEARNING State the Davis-Moore thesis in your own words. What are Tumin's criticisms of this thesis?

Stratification and Conflict

Social-conflict analysis argues that rather than benefiting society as a whole, social stratification benefits some people and disadvantages others. This analysis draws heavily on the ideas of Karl Marx, with contributions from Max Weber.

Karl Marx: Class Conflict

Karl Marx explained that most people have one of two basic relationships to the means of production: They either own productive property or labor for others. Different productive roles arise from different million in today's dollars), when the average worker earned roughly $500 a year (Baltzell, 1964; Pessen, 1990).

Marx explained that capitalist society *reproduces the class structure in each new generation.* This happens as families gain wealth and pass it down from generation to generation. But, he predicted, oppression and misery would eventually drive the working majority to come together to overthrow capitalism in favor of a socialist system that would end class differences.

▶ **CRITICAL REVIEW** Marx has had enormous influence on sociological thinking. But his revolutionary ideas—calling for the overthrow of capitalist society—also make his work highly controversial.

One of the strongest criticisms of Marxism is that it denies a central idea of the Davis-Moore thesis: that a system of unequal rewards is necessary to place talented people in the right jobs and to motivate them to work hard. Marx separated reward from performance; his egalitarian ideal was based on the principle "from each according to his ability; to each according to his needs" (Marx & Engels, 1972:388, orig. 1848). However, failure to reward individual performance may be precisely what caused the low productivity of the former Soviet Union and other socialist economies around the world. Defenders of Marxism respond to such criticism by asking why we assume that humanity is inherently selfish rather than social, noting that individual rewards are not the only way to motivate people to perform their social roles (M. S. Clark, 1991).

A second problem is that the revolutionary change Marx predicted has failed to happen, at least in advanced capitalist societies. The next section explains why.

Why No Marxist Revolution?

Despite Marx's prediction, capitalism is still thriving. Why have industrial workers not overthrown capitalism? Ralf Dahrendorf (1959) suggested four reasons:

1. **The fragmentation of the capitalist class.** Today, millions of stockholders, rather than single families, own most large companies. Day-to-day corporate operations are in the hands of a large class of managers, who may or may not be major stockholders. With stock widely held—about 40 percent of U.S. adults own stocks—more and more people have a direct stake in the capitalist system.

2. **A higher standard of living.** A century ago, most workers were in factories or on farms employed in **blue-collar occupa-**

Oprah Winfey reported income of $230 million in 2006 and enjoys fame to match her fortune. Guided by the Davis-Moore thesis, why would societies reward some people so much more than others? How would Karl Marx answer this question differently?

AP Wide World Photos

social classes. In medieval Europe, aristocratic families, including high church officials and titled nobles, owned the land on which peasants labored as farmers. In industrial class systems, the capitalists (or the bourgeoisie) own the factories, which use the labor of workers (the proletarians).

Marx lived during the nineteenth century, a time when a small number of industrialists in the United States were amassing great fortunes. Andrew Carnegie, J. P. Morgan, John D. Rockefeller, and John Jacob Astor (one of the few very rich passengers to die on the *Titanic*) lived in fabulous mansions staffed by dozens of servants. Even by today's standards, their incomes were staggering. For example, Andrew Carnegie earned about $20 million a year in 1900 (more than $100

get it right

Marx viewed social stratification in terms of
classes. Weber viewed inequality in terms of a
socioeconomic status hierarchy with multiple
dimensions. Individuals stand higher on some
dimensions and lower on others, so there are
no clear-cut classes.

tions, *lower-prestige jobs that involve mostly manual labor.*
Today, most workers are engaged in **white-collar occupations,**
higher-prestige jobs that involve mostly mental activity. These
jobs are in sales, management, and other service fields. Most of
today's white-collar workers do not think of themselves as an
"industrial proletariat." Just as important, the average income
in the United States rose almost tenfold over the course of the
twentieth century, even allowing for inflation, and the number
of hours in the workweek decreased. In short, whether the
times are good or bad, most of today's workers are far better
off than workers were a century ago, an example of structural
social mobility. One result of this rising standard of living is
that people are more willing to accept the status quo.

3. **More worker organizations.** Workers today have the right to
form labor unions, to make demands of management, and to
back up their demands with threats of work slowdowns and
strikes. As a result, labor disputes are settled without threatening the capitalist system.

4. **Greater legal protections.** Over the past century, the government passed laws to make workplaces safer. In
addition, unemployment insurance, disability
protection, and Social Security now provide
workers with greater financial security.

A Counterpoint

These developments suggest that U.S. society has
smoothed many of capitalism's rough edges. Yet many
observers claim that Marx's analysis of capitalism is
still largely valid (Domhoff, 1983; Stephens, 1986;
Boswell & Dixon, 1993; Hout, Brooks & Manza, 1993).
First, wealth remains highly concentrated, with 40 percent of all privately owned property in the hands of
just 1 percent of the U.S. population (Keister, 2000).
Second, many of today's white-collar jobs offer no
more income, security, or satisfaction than factory
work did a century ago. Third, many benefits enjoyed
by today's workers came about through the class conflict Marx described. Workers still struggle to hold on
to what they have, and in recent years, many workers
have actually lost pensions and other benefits. Fourth,
although workers have gained some legal protections,
ordinary people still face disadvantages that the law
cannot overcome. Therefore, social-conflict theorists

conclude, the absence of a socialist revolution in the United States
does not mean that Marx was wrong about capitalism.

 Using what you have learned so far about social inequality in
the United States, how correct do you think Marx was about
capitalism? Explain your answer.

Max Weber: Class, Status, and Power

Max Weber agreed with Karl Marx that social stratification causes
social conflict, but he viewed Marx's economics-based model as simplistic. Instead, he claimed that social stratification involves three distinct dimensions of inequality.

The first dimension is economic inequality—the issue so important to Marx—which Weber termed *class* position. Weber did not
think of classes as well-defined categories but as a continuum ranging from high to low. Weber's second dimension is *status,* or social
prestige, and the third is *power.*

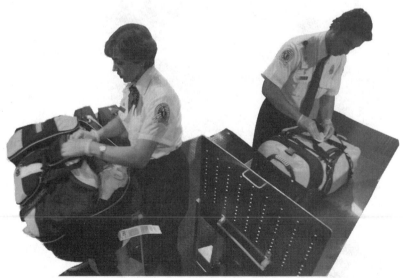

Most workers in the United States today have service jobs; instead of farming or working in a
factory, they work with other people. Some analysts say that the spread of service work has
made many people feel that they are "getting ahead" and reduced class conflict in U.S. society;
others claim that many service jobs actually provide lower pay, fewer benefits, and less job
security than many factory jobs of the past. Which argument do you think is more correct? Why?

AP Wide World Photos

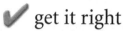
Weber's Socioeconomic Status Hierarchy

Marx viewed social prestige and power as simple reflections of economic position and did not treat them as distinct dimensions of inequality. But Weber noted that status consistency in modern societies is often quite low: A local official might exercise great power yet have little wealth or social prestige.

Weber, then, portrays social stratification in industrial societies as a multidimensional ranking rather than a hierarchy of clearly defined classes. In line with Weber's thinking, sociologists use the term **socioeconomic status (SES)** to refer to *a composite ranking based on various dimensions of social inequality.*

Inequality in History

Weber claimed that each of his three dimensions of social inequality stands out at different points in the evolution of human societies. Status or social prestige is the main difference in agrarian societies, taking the form of honor. Members of these societies (whether nobles or servants) gain status by conforming to cultural norms that apply to their particular rank.

Industrialization and the development of capitalism eliminate traditional rankings based on birth but create striking financial inequality. Thus in an industrial society, the crucial difference between people is the economic dimension of class.

Over time, industrial societies witness the growth of a bureaucratic state. Bigger government and the spread of all sorts of other organizations make power more important in the stratification system. Especially in socialist societies, where government regulates many aspects of life, high-ranking officials become the new ruling elite.

This historical analysis points to a final difference between Weber and Marx. Marx thought societies could eliminate social stratification by abolishing the private ownership of productive property that is the basis of capitalism. Weber doubted that overthrowing capitalism would significantly lessen social stratification. It might reduce economic differences, he reasoned, but socialism would increase inequality by expanding government and concentrating power in the hands of a political elite. Popular uprisings against socialist bureaucracies in Eastern Europe and the former Soviet Union show the discontent that can be generated by socialist political elites and support Weber's position.

▶ **CRITICAL REVIEW**   Max Weber's multidimensional view of social stratification has influenced sociological thinking greatly. But critics (particularly those who favor Marx's ideas) argue that although social class boundaries may have blurred, industrial and postindustrial societies still show striking patterns of social inequality.

Income inequality has been increasing in the United States. Although some people still favor Weber's multidimensional hierarchy, in light of this trend, others think that Marx's view of the rich versus the poor is closer to the truth.

The extent of social inequality in agrarian systems is greater than that found in industrial societies. One indication of the unchallenged power of rulers is the monumental structures built over years with the unpaid labor of common people. Although the Taj Mahal in India is among the world's most beautiful buildings, it is merely a tomb for a single individual.

© Doranne Jacobson/International Images

student **2** student

"Conspicuous consumption depends on advertising convincing us that owning some product will make others think more of us."

Seeing Sociology in Everyday Life
When Class Gets Personal: Picking (with) Your Friends

The sound of banjo music drifted across the field late one summer afternoon. I lay down my brush, climbed over the fence I had been painting, and walked toward the sound of the music to see what was going on. That's how I met my neighbor Max, a retired factory worker who lived just up the road. Max was a pretty good "picker," and within an hour, I was back on his porch with my guitar. I called Howard, a friend who teaches at the college, and he showed up a little while later, six-string in hand. The three of us jammed for a couple of hours, smiling all the while.

The next morning, I was mowing the grass in front of the house when Max came walking down the road. I turned off the mower as he got closer. "Hi, Max," I said. "Thanks for having us over last night. I really had fun."

"Don't mention it," Max responded with a wave. Then he stopped and shook his head a little and added, "Ya know, I was thinkin' after you guys left. I mean, it was really somethin' how you guys looked like you

Getty Images, Inc.

were having a great time. With somebody like *me!*"

"Well, yeah," I replied, not sure of what he meant. "You sure played better than we did."

Max looked down at the ground, embarrassed by the compliment. Then he added, "What I mean is that you guys were having a good time with somebody like *me*. You're both professors, right? *Doctors,* even . . ."

WHAT DO YOU THINK?

1. Why did Max assume that two college teachers would not enjoy spending time with him?

2. How does his reaction suggest that people take social position personally?

3. Can you think of a similar experience you have had with someone of a different social position?

 YOUR LEARNING What are Weber's three dimensions of social inequality? According to Weber, which of them would you expect to be most important in the United States? Why?

Stratification and Interaction

Because social stratification has to do with the way an entire society is organized, sociologists (Marx and Weber included) typically treat it as a macro-level issue. But a micro-level analysis of social stratification is also important because people's social standing affects their everyday interactions.

In most communities, people interact primarily with others of about the same social standing. To some extent, this is because we tend to live with others like ourselves. As we observe people during the course of our everyday activities, such as walking in a downtown shopping area, we see that couples or groups tend to be made up of individuals whose appearance and shopping habits are similar. People with

very different social standing commonly keep their distance from one another. Well-dressed people walking down the street on their way to an expensive restaurant, for example, might move across the sidewalk or even cross the street to avoid getting close to others they think are homeless people. The Seeing Sociology in Everyday Life box gives another example of how differences in social class position can affect interaction.

Finally, just about everyone realizes that the way we dress, the car we drive (or the bus we ride), and even the food and drink we order at the campus snack bar say something about our budget and personal tastes. Sociologists use the term **conspicuous consumption** to refer to *buying and using products because of the "statement" they make about social position*. Ignoring the water fountain in favor of paying for bottled water tells people you have extra money to spend. And no one needs a $100,000 automobile to get around, of course, but being seen in such a vehicle says "I have arrived" in more ways than one.

tip

Study the Applying Theory table to be sure you understand the three theoretical approaches to social stratification.

APPLYING THEORY

Social Stratification

	Structural-Functional Approach	Social-Conflict Approach	Symbolic-Interaction Approach
What is the level of analysis?	Macro-level	Macro-level	Micro-level
What is social stratification?	Stratification is a system of unequal rewards that benefits society as a whole.	Stratification is a division of a society's resources that benefits some people and harms others.	Stratification is a factor that guides people's interactions in everyday life.
What is the reason for our social position?	Social position reflects personal talents and abilities in a competitive economy.	Social position reflects the way society divides resources.	The products we consume all say something about social position.
Are unequal rewards fair?	Yes. Unequal rewards boost economic production by encouraging people to work harder and try new ideas. Linking greater rewards to more important work is widely accepted.	No. Unequal rewards only serve to divide society, creating "haves" and "have-nots." There is widespread opposition to social inequality.	Maybe. People may or may not define inequality as fair. People may view their social position as a measure of self-worth, justifying inequality in terms of personal differences.

The Applying Theory table summarizes the contributions of the three theoretical approaches to social stratification.

Stratification and Technology: A Global Perspective

We can weave together a number of observations made in this chapter to show that a society's technology affects its type of social stratification. This analysis draws on Gerhard Lenski's model of sociocultural evolution.

Hunting and Gathering Societies

With simple technology, hunters and gatherers produce only what is necessary for day-to-day living. Some people may produce more than others, but the group's survival depends on all sharing what they have. Thus no categories of people are better off than others.

Horticultural, Pastoral, and Agrarian Societies

As technological advances create a surplus, social inequality increases. In horticultural and pastoral societies, a small elite controls most of the surplus. Large-scale agriculture is more productive still, and striking inequality—as great as at any time in history—places the nobility in an almost godlike position over the masses.

Industrial Societies

Industrialization turns the tide, pushing inequality downward. Prompted by the need to develop individual talents, meritocracy takes hold and weakens the power of traditional aristocracy. Industrial productivity also raises the standard of living of the historically poor majority. Specialized work demands schooling for all, sharply reducing illiteracy. A literate population, in turn, presses for a greater voice in political decision making, reducing social inequality and lessening men's domination of women.

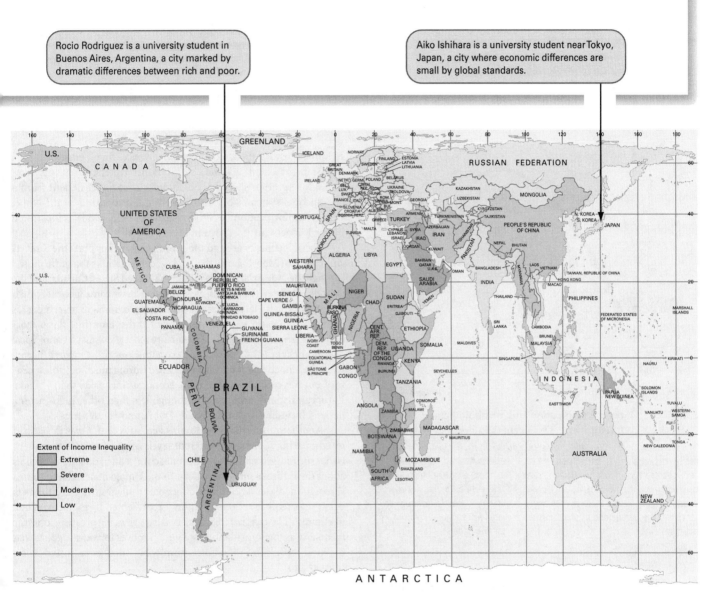

Rocio Rodriguez is a university student in Buenos Aires, Argentina, a city marked by dramatic differences between rich and poor.

Aiko Ishihara is a university student near Tokyo, Japan, a city where economic differences are small by global standards.

Extent of Income Inequality
- Extreme
- Severe
- Moderate
- Low

WINDOW ON THE WORLD

GLOBAL MAP 1   Income Inequality in Global Perspective

Societies throughout the world differ in the rigidity and extent of their social stratification and their overall standard of living. This map highlights income inequality. Generally speaking, the United States stands out among high-income nations, such as Great Britain, Sweden, Japan, and Australia, as having greater income inequality. The less economically developed countries of Latin America and Africa, including Colombia, Brazil, and the Central African Republic, as well as much of the Arab world, exhibit the most pronounced inequality of income. Is this pattern consistent with the Kuznets curve?

Source: Based on Gini coefficients obtained from World Bank (2007).

SOCIAL STRATIFICATION   291

tip

The Kuznets curve, shown in Figure 10–2, helps explain why most socialist revolutions have taken place in agrarian societies rather than in advanced capitalist societies.

tip

A great story to read is Kurt Vonnegut's "Harrison Bergeron" in his book *Welcome to the Monkey House*. It's very short but has important insights about the dangers of government efforts to eliminate all social inequality.

The Kuznets Curve

In human history, then, technological advances first increase but then moderate the extent of social stratification. Greater inequality is functional for agrarian societies, but industrial societies benefit from a less unequal system. This historical trend, recognized by the Nobel Prize–winning economist Simon Kuznets (1955, 1966), is illustrated by the Kuznets curve, shown in Figure 2.

Social inequality around the world generally supports the Kuznets curve. Global Map 1 shows that high-income nations that have passed through the industrial era (including the United States, Canada, and the nations of Western Europe) have somewhat less income inequality than nations in which a larger share of the labor force remains in farming (as is common in Latin America and Africa). At the same time, it is important to remember that income inequality reflects not just technological development but also political and economic priorities. Income disparity in the United States may have declined during much of the last century, but this country still has more economic inequality than Canada, European nations, and Japan (although less than other high-income nations, including Argentina, Saudi Arabia, and South Africa).

Another criticism of the Kuznets curve is that it was developed by comparing societies at different levels of economic development (what sociologists call "cross-sectional data"). Such data do not tell us about the future of any one society. In the United States, recent trends showing increases in economic inequality suggest that the Kuznets curve may require serious revision—represented by the broken line in Figure 2. The fact that U.S. society is experiencing greater economic inequality as the Information Revolution moves forward suggests that the long-term trend may differ from what Kuznets projected half a century ago.

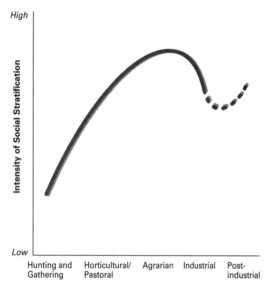

FIGURE 2 Social Stratification and Technological Development: The Kuznets Curve

The Kuznets curve shows that greater technological sophistication is generally accompanied by more pronounced social stratification. The trend reverses itself as industrial societies relax rigid, castelike distinctions in favor of greater opportunity and equality under the law. Political rights are more widely extended, and there is even some leveling of economic differences. However, the emergence of postindustrial society has brought an upturn in economic inequality, as indicated by the broken line added by the author.

Source: Created by the author, based on Kuznets (1955) and Lenski (1966).

Social Stratification: Facts and Values

> The year was 2081 and everybody was finally equal. They weren't only equal before God and the law. They were equal every which way. Nobody was smarter than anybody else. Nobody was better looking than anybody else. Nobody was stronger or quicker than anybody else. All this equality was due to the 211th, 212th, and 213th Amendments to the Constitution and the unceasing vigilance of agents of the Handicapper General.

With these words, the novelist Kurt Vonnegut Jr. (1968:7) begins the story of "Harrison Bergeron," an imaginary account of a future United States in which all social inequality has been abolished. Vonnegut warns that although attractive in principle, equality can be a

Over time, even wealth becomes somewhat less concentrated (contradicting Marx's prediction). In the 1920s, the richest 1 percent of the U.S. population owned about 40 percent of all wealth, a figure that fell to 30 percent by the 1980s as higher taxes on the rich paid for new government programs benefiting the poor (Williamson & Lindert, 1980; Beeghley, 1989; U.S House of Representatives, 1991). Such trends help explain why Marxist revolutions occurred in *agrarian* societies—such as Russia (1917), Cuba (1959), and Nicaragua (1979)—where social inequality is most pronounced, rather than in industrial societies as Marx had predicted. However, U.S. wealth inequality increased after 1990 and is once again about the same as it was in the 1920s (Keister, 2000).

Can you identify aspects of everyday life that seem to suggest that economic inequality is increasing? Explain.

✿ tip

Raise the questions found at the end of the box in class to see what other students think.

Controversy & Debate
The Bell Curve Debate: Are Rich People Really Smarter?

ELENA: [*with a smile*] Do you think that going out with me is giving you upward social mobility?

JOE: Give me a break. Your family is richer than mine. That doesn't mean you're better or smarter. . . .

Are rich people smarter than the rest of us? Few books in sociology have taken on this question as directly as *The Bell Curve: Intelligence and Class Structure in American Life* (1994) by Richard J. Herrnstein and Charles Murray. The book ignited a firestorm of controversy over why social stratification divides our society and, just as important, what should be done about it.

The Bell Curve is a long book that addresses many complex issues, but it makes eight major claims:

1. Something we can describe as "general intelligence" exists; people with more of it tend to be more successful in their careers than those with less.

2. At least half the variation in human intelligence is transmitted genetically from parents to children; the remaining variability is due to environmental factors that affect socialization.

3. During the past century—and especially since the Information Revolution began several decades ago—intelligence has become more necessary to perform our society's most important jobs.

4. At the same time, the most selective U.S. colleges and universities have shifted their admissions policies away from favoring children of inherited wealth to admitting young people with high grades and the highest scores on standardized tests such as the Scholastic Assessment Test (SAT), American College Testing Program (ACT), and Graduate Record Examination (GRE).

5. As a result of these changes in the workplace and on campus, our society is now dominated by a "cognitive elite," people who are not only better educated but actually more intelligent.

6. As very intelligent people interact with others like themselves, both on the campus and in the workplace, the odds are high that they will pair up, marry, and have intelligent children, extending the "cognitive elite" into another generation.

7. A similar process is at work at the other end of the social ladder: Poor people who, on average, have lower intelligence have become socially segregated and tend to marry others like themselves, thus passing along their more modest abilities to their children.

8. Herrnstein and Murray therefore conclude that because membership in the affluent elite or the impoverished underclass is at least partly rooted in genetically inherited intelligence, we should not be surprised that the poor are more likely to have higher rates of crime and drug abuse. Further, we should expect that programs such as Head Start and affirmative action will do little to help the poor.

Evaluating the claims made in *The Bell Curve* must begin with a hard look at the concept of intelligence. Critics of the book argue that most of what we call "intelligence" is the result not of genetic inheritance but of socialization. Intelligence tests, in other words, do not measure cognitive *ability* as much as they measure cognitive *performance*. Average IQ scores have been rising as the U.S. population becomes more educated. If schooling is so important to intelligence, then educational advantages alone would explain why rich children perform better on such tests.

Most researchers who study intelligence agree that genetics plays a part in children's intelligence, but most conclude that only 25 to 40 percent of intelligence is inherited—less than Herrnstein and Murray claim. *The Bell Curve* therefore misleads readers when it states that social stratification is a natural product of differences in inherited intelligence. Critics claim that this book echoes the social Darwinism popular a century ago, which justified the great wealth of industrial tycoons as "the survival of the fittest."

Could it be that the more today's competitive society seems like a jungle, the more people think of stratification as a matter of nature rather than nurture? But even if it is flawed, *The Bell Curve* raises important issues. If some people are smarter than others, shouldn't we expect them to end up in higher social positions? Shouldn't we expect the people who rise to the top in most fields to be at least a little smarter than the rest of us? If this is true, is it fair? Finally, what can our society do to ensure that all people will have the opportunity to develop their abilities as fully as possible?

WHAT DO YOU THINK?

1. Do you think there is such a thing as "general intelligence"? Why or why not?

2. Do you think that well-off people, on average, are more intelligent than people of low social position? If so, how do you know which factor is the cause and which the effect?

3. Do you think social scientists should study issues such as differences in human intelligence if their results could justify social inequality? Why or why not?

Sources: Herrnstein & Murray (1994), Jacoby & Glauberman (1995), Kohn (1996), and Arrow, Bowles, & Durlauf (2000).

tip

The Applying Sociology in Everyday Life items
provide additional ways for you to connect the
ideas found in this chapter with your own life.

dangerous concept in practice. His story describes a nightmare of social engineering in which every individual talent that makes one person different from another is systematically neutralized by the government.

To eliminate differences that make one person "better" than another, Vonnegut's state requires that physically attractive people wear masks that make them average-looking, that intelligent people wear earphones that generate distracting noise, and that the best athletes and dancers be fitted with weights to make them as clumsy as everyone else. In short, although we may imagine that social equality would liberate people to make the most of their talents, Vonnegut concludes that an egalitarian society could exist only if everyone is reduced to the lowest common denominator.

Like Vonnegut's story, all of this chapter's explanations of social stratification involve value judgments. The Davis-Moore thesis states not only that social stratification is universal but also that it is neces-

sary to make society highly productive. Class differences in U.S. society, from this point of view, reflect both variation in human abilities and the relative importance of different jobs. This makes complete equality undesirable because it could be achieved only in an inefficient society that cared little for developing individual talent and rewarding excellence.

Social-conflict analysis, advocated by Karl Marx, takes a much more positive view of equality. Marx thought that inequality is harmful because it causes both human suffering and conflict between haves and have-nots. As he saw it, social stratification springs from injustice and greed. As a result, Marx wanted people to share resources equally.

The Controversy & Debate box addresses the connection between intelligence and social class. This issue is among the most troublesome in social science, partly because of the difficulty in defining and measuring "intelligence" but also because the idea that elites are somehow "better" than others challenges our democratic culture.

Applying Sociology in Everyday Life

1. Write down three examples of the effects of social stratification on your college campus, and indicate in what ways the people represented are unequal. Does family background or individual talent seem to be more important in creating these social differences?

2. Sit down with parents, grandparents, or other relatives, and talk about how your family's social position has changed over the last three generations. Has social mobility taken

place? If so, describe the change. Was it caused by the effort of individuals or changes in society itself?

3. The "seven deadly sins," the human failings recognized by the Catholic church during the Middle Ages, were pride, greed, envy, anger, lust, gluttony, and sloth. Why are these traits dangerous to an agrarian caste system? Are they a threat to a modern, capitalist class system? Why or why not?

MAKING THE GRADE
Social Stratification

What Is Social Stratification?

SOCIAL STRATIFICATION is a system by which a society ranks categories of people in a hierarchy, so that some people have more money, power, and prestige than others.

Social stratification

- is a trait of society, not simply a reflection of individual differences
- is found in all societies but varies according to *what* is unequal and *how* unequal it is
- carries over from one generation to the next
- is supported by a system of cultural beliefs that defines certain kinds of inequality as just
- takes two general forms: caste systems and class systems

social stratification a system by which a society ranks categories of people in a hierarchy

social mobility a change in position within the social hierarchy

✔ *Although some people, especially in high-income countries, may experience **social mobility**, the social standing of most people remains pretty much the same over their lifetime.*

Caste and Class Systems

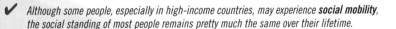

CASTE SYSTEMS

- are based on birth (ascription)
- permit little or no social mobility
- shape a person's entire life, including occupation and marriage
- are common in traditional, agrarian societies

CLASS SYSTEMS

- are based on both birth (ascription) and **meritocracy** (individual achievement)
- permit some social mobility based on individual achievement
- are common in modern industrial and postindustrial societies

caste system social stratification based on ascription, or birth

class system social stratification based on both birth and individual achievement

meritocracy social stratification based on personal merit

status consistency the degree of uniformity in a person's social standing across various dimensions of social inequality

structural social mobility a shift in the social position of large numbers of people due more to changes in society itself than to individual efforts

ideology cultural beliefs that justify particular social arrangements, including patterns of inequality

AN ILLUSTRATION: INDIA

Although the caste system is formally outlawed in India, it is still observed in rural areas, where agriculture demands a lifetime of hard work and discipline.

- In traditional villages, people's caste determines the type of work they perform.
- People must interact with and marry others of the same ranking.
- Powerful cultural beliefs make observing caste rules a moral duty.

- Class systems include elements of both caste and meritocracy.
- Class systems advance meritocracy to promote specialization, productivity, and efficiency.
- Class systems keep caste elements, such as family, to maintain order and social unity.
- **Status consistency** in class systems is low due to increased social mobility.

CASTE AND CLASS: THE UNITED KINGDOM

- In the Middle Ages, England had a castelike aristocracy, including the leading clergy and a hereditary nobility. The vast majority of people were considered commoners.
- Today's British class system mixes caste and meritocracy, producing a highly stratified society with some social mobility.

CASTE AND CLASS: JAPAN

- In the Middle Ages, Japan had a rigid caste system in which an imperial family ruled over nobles and commoners.
- Today's Japanese class system still places great importance on family background and traditional gender roles.

MAKING THE GRADE *continued . . .*

Caste and Class Systems *(continued)*

CLASSLESS SOCIETIES? THE FORMER SOVIET UNION

- Although the Russian Revolution in 1917 attempted to abolish social classes, the new Soviet Union was still stratified based on unequal job categories and the concentration of power in the new political elite. Economic development created new types of jobs, which resulted in **structural social mobility**.
- Since the collapse of the Soviet Union in the early 1990s, the forces of structural social mobility have turned downward and the gap between rich and poor has increased.

CHINA: EMERGING SOCIAL CLASSES

- Economic reforms introduced after the Communist revolution in 1949—including state control of factories and productive property— greatly reduced economic inequality, although social differences remained.
- In the last thirty years, China's government has loosened control of the economy, causing the emergence of a new class of business owners and an increase in economic inequality.

✔ *Both caste and class systems are supported by **ideology**—cultural values and beliefs—that defines certain kinds of inequality as just.*

Theoretical Analysis of Social Stratification

The **STRUCTURAL-FUNCTIONAL APPROACH** points to ways social stratification helps society to operate.

- The Davis-Moore thesis states that social stratification is universal because of its functional consequences.
- In caste systems, people are rewarded for performing the duties of their position at birth.
- In class systems, unequal rewards attract the ablest people to the most important jobs and encourage effort.

The **SOCIAL-CONFLICT APPROACH** claims that stratification divides societies in classes, benefiting some categories of people at the expense of others and causing social conflict.

- Karl Marx claimed that capitalism places economic production under the ownership of capitalists, who exploit the proletarians who sell their labor for wages.
- Max Weber identified three distinct dimensions of social stratification: economic class, social status or prestige, and power. Conflict exists between people at various positions on a multidimensional hierarchy of **socioeconomic status (SES)**.

Davis-Moore thesis the assertion that social stratification has beneficial consequences for the operation of society

blue-collar occupations lower-prestige jobs that involve mostly manual labor

white-collar occupations higher-prestige jobs that involve mostly mental activity

socioeconomic status (SES) a composite ranking based on various dimensions of social inequality

conspicuous consumption buying and using products because of the "statement" they make about social position

The **SYMBOLIC-INTERACTION APPROACH**, a micro-level analysis, explains that we size up people by looking for clues to their social standing. **Conspicuous consumption** refers to buying and displaying products that make a "statement" about social class. Most people tend to socialize with others whose social standing is similar to their own.

⊞ See the Applying Theory table in this chapter.

Social Stratification and Technology: A Global Perspective

Hunting and Gathering → Horticultural and Pastoral → Agrarian ——— Industrial ——————— Postindustrial

- Gerhard Lenski explains that advancing technology initially increases social stratification, which is most intense in agrarian societies.

- Industrialization reverses the trend, reducing social stratification.

- In postindustrial societies, social stratification again increases.

⬤ See the Kuznets curve (Figure 2).

Stratification: Facts and Values

People's beliefs about social inequality reflect not just facts but also politics and values concerning how a society should be organized.

MAKING THE GRADE

Social Stratification

Sample Test Questions

These questions are similar to those found in the test bank that accompanies this textbook.

Multiple-Choice Questions

1. *Social stratification* refers to
   a. job specialization.
   b. ranking categories of people in a hierarchy.
   c. the fact that some people work harder than others.
   d. inequality of personal talent and individual effort.

2. Looking back in history and around the world today, we see that social stratification may involve differences in
   a. how unequal people are.
   b. what resources are unequally distributed.
   c. why a society claims people should be unequal.
   d. All of the above are correct.

3. A caste system is social stratification
   a. based on individual achievement.
   b. based on meritocracy.
   c. based on birth.
   d. in which a person's social position is likely to change over time.

4. Sally has two advanced degrees, earns an average salary, and is working at a low-prestige job. Which concept best describes her situation?
   a. low status consistency
   b. horizontal social mobility
   c. upward social mobility
   d. high status consistency

5. According to the Davis-Moore thesis,
   a. equality is functional for society.
   b. the more inequality a society has, the more productive it is.
   c. more important jobs must offer enough rewards to draw talent from less important work.
   d. societies with more meritocracy are less productive than those with caste systems.

6. Karl Marx claimed that society "reproduces the class structure." By this, he meant that
   a. society benefits from inequality.
   b. class differences are passed on from one generation to the next.
   c. class differences are the same everywhere.
   d. a society without classes is impossible.

7. Max Weber claimed that social stratification is based on
   a. economic class.
   b. social status or prestige.
   c. power.
   d. All of the above are correct.

8. A society with which type of productive technology has the least amount of social stratification?
   a. hunting and gathering
   b. horticultural/pastoral
   c. industrial
   d. postindustrial

9. Keeping the Kuznets curve in mind, which type of society has the most social stratification?
   a. hunting and gathering
   b. horticultural/pastoral
   c. agrarian
   d. industrial

10. The "bell curve" thesis suggests that which of the following is more important than ever to social position in the United States?
    a. family background
    b. intelligence
    c. hard work
    d. whom you know

Answers: 1 (b); 2 (d); 3 (c); 4 (a); 5 (c); 6 (b); 7 (d); 8 (a); 9 (c); 10 (b).

Essay Questions

1. Explain why social stratification is a creation of society, not just a reflection of individual differences.

2. How do caste and class systems differ? How are they the same? Why does industrialization introduce a measure of meritocracy into social stratification?

Social Class in
the United States

Many people think of the United States as a "middle-class society." But social inequality in our society is greater than in most other high-income nations, and it is increasing.

David Young-Wolff/PhotoEdit Inc.

Social Class in the United States

HOW are income and wealth divided within the U.S. population?

WHAT factors place people in different social classes?

WHY is the poverty rate higher among some categories of people in the United States than others?

Mary Kate Denny/PhotoEdit Inc.

Rosa Urias leans forward, pushing and pulling the vacuum cleaner across the hardwood floors, a motion she has repeated hundreds of times to the point that her right wrist and elbow are sore. It is now almost five o'clock in the afternoon, and this forty-five-year-old single mother of two is on her third cleaning job of the day. She works with her cousin Melitsa Sermiento, thirty-six, cleaning nine apartments and five houses each week. The two women, who both came to the United States from El Salvador, divide the money they earn, giving each one an annual income of about $28,000, barely enough to pay the bills in New York City.

But there is no shortage of work cleaning homes. Hundreds of thousands of New Yorkers make more than enough money to hire people like Rosa and Melitsa to dust their tables, mop their floors, and scrub their sinks and toilets while they are out doing their high-paying jobs, working out at the health club, or having lunch with friends.

Rosa reaches up over the bathroom sink to turn on a light so she can see better. She pulls the silver chain, but it breaks and she stands there with part of the chain hanging from her hand. She looks over at Melitsa, and both do their best to laugh it off. Then Rosa turns serious and says softly, in Spanish, "My daughter tells me I need some new dreams" (Eisenstadt, 2004).

New York may be a single large city, but the social world in which Rosa and Melitsa live is not the same as the social world of the people who hire these women. How different are the lives of the richest people in the United States and the lives of those who work hard all day just to get by? What about the lives of those who do not even have the security of work? This chapter answers all these questions, explaining some of the different "worlds" found in U.S. society, how different we are, and why the differences are getting bigger.

Dimensions of Social Inequality

The United States differs from most European nations and Japan in never having had a titled nobility. With the significant exception of our racial history, we have never known a caste system that rigidly ranks categories of people.

Even so, U.S. society is highly stratified. Not only do the rich have most of the money, but they also receive the most schooling, enjoy the best health, and consume the most goods and services. Such privilege contrasts sharply with the poverty of millions of women and men who worry about paying next month's rent or a doctor's bill when a child becomes ill. Many people think of the United States as a middle-class society, but is this really the case?

 Why do you think so many people view the United States as a middle-class society in which most people have more or less equal social standing?

Income

One important dimension of inequality is **income**, *earnings from work or investments*. The Census Bureau reports that the median U.S. family income in 2005 was $56,194. The first part of Figure 1 illustrates the distribution of income among all U.S. families.[1] The richest 20 percent of families (earning at least $103,000 annually, with a mean of about $176,000) received 48.1 percent of all income, while the bottom 20 percent (earning less than $26,000, with a mean of about $14,700) received only 4.0 percent.

Table 1 provides a closer look at income distribution. In 2005, the highest-paid 5 percent of U.S. families earned at least $185,000 (averaging almost $310,000), or 21.1 percent of all income, more than the total earnings of the lowest-paid 40 percent. At the very top of

Table 1   U.S. Family Income, 2005

Highest-Paid . . .	Annually Earns at Least . . .
0.5% of the population	$1,750,000
1	400,000
5	185,000
10	125,000
20	103,000
30	80,000
40	68,000
50	58,000
60	45,000
70	34,000
80	26,000
90	10,500

Source: U.S. Census Bureau (2006) and author calculations.

[1]The Census Bureau reports both mean and median incomes for families ("two or more persons related by blood, marriage, or adoption") and households ("two or more persons sharing a living unit"). In 2005, mean family income was $73,304, higher than the median ($56,194) because high-income families pull up the mean but not the median. For households, these figures are somewhat lower—a mean of $63,344 and a median of $46,326—largely because families average 3.1 people and households average 2.6.

Chapter Overview

This chapter surveys social stratification in the United States, beginning with a look at important measures of inequality. Many dimensions of inequality exist in our society, and inequality is greater than many people imagine.

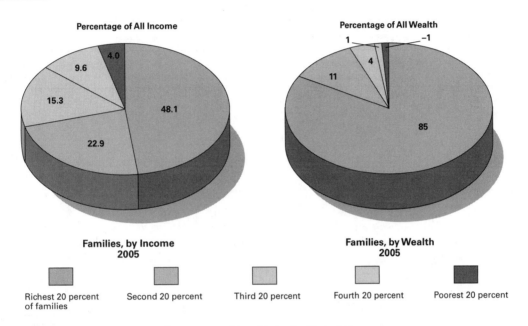

Percentage of All Income

48.1

22.9

15.3

9.6

4.0

**Families, by Income
2005**

Percentage of All Wealth

1

−1

4

11

85

**Families, by Wealth
2005**

- Richest 20 percent of families
- Second 20 percent
- Third 20 percent
- Fourth 20 percent
- Poorest 20 percent

FIGURE 1 Distribution of Income and Wealth in the United States

Income, and especially wealth, is divided unequally in U.S. society.

Sources: Income data from U.S. Census Bureau (2006); wealth data based on Keister (2000), Wolff (2004), Bucks, Kennickell, & Moore (2006), and author estimates.

the income pyramid, the richest half of 1 percent earned at least $1.75 million. In short, while a small number of people earn very high incomes, the majority make do with far less.

Wealth

Income is only a part of a person's or family's **wealth,** *the total value of money and other assets, minus outstanding debts.* Wealth—including stocks, bonds, and real estate—is distributed more unequally than income. Recent reductions in taxes on income earned by individuals and on wealth passed from one generation to the next are likely to make this inequality even greater (Wahl, 2003).

The right side of Figure 1 shows the distribution of wealth. The richest 20 percent of U.S. families own roughly 85 percent of the country's wealth. High up in this privileged category are the wealthiest 5 percent of families—the "very rich," who own 60 percent of all private property. Richer still, with wealth in the tens of millions of dollars, are the 1 percent of families that qualify as "super-rich" and possess about 40 percent of this nation's privately held resources (Keister, 2000; Keis-

ter & Moller, 2000; Wolff, 2004; Bucks, Kennickell, & Moore, 2006). At the top of the wealth pyramid, the ten richest U.S. families have a combined net worth of more than $232 billion (Miller & Serafin, 2006). This amount equals the total property of 2.5 million average families, including enough people to fill the cities of Chicago, Illinois; Houston, Texas; Philadelphia, Pennsylvania; and Phoenix, Arizona.

The wealth of the average U.S. family is currently about $93,100 (Bucks, Kennickell, & Moore, 2006). Family wealth reflects the value of homes, cars, investments, insurance policies, retirement pensions, furniture, clothing, and all other personal property, minus a home mortgage and other debts. The wealth of average people is not only less than that of the rich, however, but also different in kind. Most people's wealth centers on a home and a car—that is, property that generates no income—but the wealth of the rich is mostly in the form of stocks and other income-producing investments.

When financial assets are balanced against debts, the lowest-ranking 40 percent of U.S. families have virtually no wealth at all. The negative percentage shown in Figure 1 for the poorest 20 percent of the population means that these families actually live in debt.

student 2 student

"Whoa! The wealth figure sure doesn't make our country look like 'middle-class America.'"

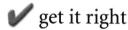

get it right

Income and wealth are both about money, but the first refers to what you earn and the second to what you own. Notice in Figure 1 that wealth inequality is greater than income inequality.

Table 2   The Relative Social Prestige of Selected Occupations in the United States

White-Collar Occupations	Prestige Score	Blue-Collar Occupations	White-Collar Occupations	Prestige Score	Blue-Collar Occupations
Physician	86		Funeral director	49	
Lawyer	75		Real estate agent	49	
College/university professor	74		Bookkeeper	47	
Architect	73			47	Machinist
Chemist	73			47	Mail carrier
Physicist/astronomer	73		Musician/composer	47	
Aerospace engineer	72			46	Secretary
Dentist	72		Photographer	45	
Member of the clergy	69		Bank teller	43	
Psychologist	69			42	Tailor
Pharmacist	68			42	Welder
Optometrist	67			40	Farmer
Registered nurse	66			40	Telephone operator
Secondary school teacher	66			39	Carpenter
Accountant	65			36	Bricklayer/stonemason
Athlete	65			36	Child care worker
Electrical engineer	64		File clerk	36	
Elementary school teacher	64			36	Hairdresser
Economist	63			35	Baker
Veterinarian	62			34	Bulldozer operator
Airplane pilot	61			31	Auto body repairer
Computer programmer	61		Retail apparel salesperson	30	
Sociologist	61			30	Truck driver
Editor/reporter	60		Cashier	29	
	60	Police officer		28	Elevator operator
Actor	58			28	Garbage collector
Radio/TV announcer	55			28	Taxi driver
Librarian	54			28	Waiter/waitress
	53	Aircraft mechanic		27	Bellhop
	53	Firefighter		25	Bartender
Dental hygienist	52			23	Farm laborer
Painter/sculptor	52			23	Household laborer
Social worker	52			22	Door-to-door salesperson
	51	Electrician		22	Janitor
Computer operator	50			09	Shoe shiner

Source: Adapted from *General Social Surveys, 1972–2004: Cumulative Codebook* (Chicago: National Opinion Research Center, 2005), pp. 2031–49.

Power

In the United States, wealth is an important source of power. The small proportion of families that controls most of the nation's wealth also shapes the agenda of the entire society. Some sociologists argue that such concentrated wealth weakens democracy because the political system serves the interests of the super-rich.

 People of all social classes have the same right to vote. But can you think of ways in which the rich have more power to shape U.S. society than the rest of us?

Occupational Prestige

In addition to generating income, work is also an important source of social prestige. We commonly evaluate each other according to the kind of work we do, giving greater respect to those who do what we consider important work and less respect to others with more modest jobs.

Sociologists measure the relative prestige of various occupations (NORC, 2005). Table 2 shows that people give high prestige to occupations such as physician, lawyer, and engineer that require extensive training and generate high income. By contrast, less prestigious work—as a waitress or janitor, for example—pays less and requires less schooling. Occupational prestige rankings are much the same in all high-income nations (Lin & Xie, 1988).

In any society, high-prestige occupations go to privileged categories of people. In Table 2, for example, the highest-ranking occupations are dominated by men. We have to go more than a dozen jobs down the list to find "registered nurse" and "secondary school teacher," careers chosen mostly by women.

 Identify the jobs in Table 2 that have traditionally been performed by people of color. What pattern do you discover?

Schooling

Industrial societies have expanded opportunities for schooling, but some people still receive much more education than others. Table 3 shows the levels of schooling achieved by U.S. women and men aged twenty-five and older. In 2006, although 85 percent completed high school, only about 28 percent were college graduates.

Schooling affects both occupation and income, since most (but not all) of the better-paying white-collar jobs shown in Table 2 require a college degree or other advanced study. Most blue-collar jobs, which bring lower income and social prestige, require less schooling.

U.S. Stratification: Merit and Caste

The U.S. class system is partly a meritocracy in that social position reflects individual talent and effort. But it also has caste elements, because birth plays a part in what we become later in life.

Ancestry

Nothing affects social standing in the United States as much as being born into a particular family, which has a strong bearing on schooling, occupation, and income. Research suggests that more than one-third of our country's richest individuals—those with hundreds of millions of dollars in wealth—acquired some of their fortunes from inheritance (Miller & Newcomb, 2005). Inherited poverty shapes the future of tens of millions of others.

Race and Ethnicity

Race is closely linked to social position in the United States. White people receive more schooling than African Americans and have higher overall occupational standing. The median African American family's income was $35,464 in 2005, just 56 percent of the $63,156 earned by non-Hispanic white families. This inequality in income makes a real difference in people's lives. For example, non-Hispanic white families are more likely to own their homes (76 percent do) than black families (48 percent) (U.S. Census Bureau, 2007).

Table 3   Schooling of U.S. Adults, 2006
(aged 25 and over)

	Women	Men
Not a high school graduate	**14.1%**	**15.0%**
8 years or less	5.9	6.4
9–11 years	8.2	8.6
High school graduate	**85.8**	**85.1**
High school only	31.6	31.9
1–3 years of college	27.3	24.0
College graduate or more	26.9	29.2

Source: U.S. Census Bureau (2007).

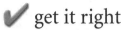

Thinking About Diversity: Race, Class, & Gender
The Color of Money: Being Rich in Black and White

African American families earn 56 cents for every dollar a non-Hispanic white family earns, which helps explain why black families are three times as likely to be poor. But there is another side to black America—an affluent side—that has grown dramatically in recent decades.

The number of affluent families—those with incomes over $75,000 a year—is increasing faster among African Americans than among whites. According to Census Bureau statistics for 2005, 1.8 million African American families (19 percent) were financially well-off, nearly ten times the number in 1970 (taking inflation into account). About 18 percent of Latino families were well-off, along with 40 percent of non-Hispanic white families.

The color of money is the same for everyone, but black and white affluence differs in several ways. First, well-off people of African descent are *not as rich* as their white counterparts. Sixty-three percent of affluent non-Hispanic white families (26 percent of all non-Hispanic white families) earn more than $100,000 a year, compared to 53 percent of affluent African American families (10 percent of all black families).

Second, African Americans are more likely than white people to achieve affluence through multiple incomes. Among non-Hispanic white people, 15.8 percent of men

and 4.9 percent of women earn more than $75,000; among African Americans, the same is true of just 4.9 percent of men and 2.9 percent of women. Rich black families

Will Smith and Jada Pinkett Smith are among the best-known and most affluent African Americans. But race still has a lot to do with which families are wealthy.

Charley Gallay/Getty Images

are more likely to contain two or more working people.

Third, affluent African Americans are more likely to get their income from salaries rather than investments. More than 80 percent of wealthy white families have investment income, compared to two-thirds of affluent African American families.

Beyond differences in income, affluent people of color must deal with social barriers that do not limit whites. Even African Americans with the money to purchase a home, for example, may find they are unwelcome as neighbors. This is one reason that a smaller share of well-off African American families (59 percent) live in the suburbs (the richest areas of the country) than affluent white families (72 percent).

Affluent Americans come in all colors. But having money does not completely overcome the racial barriers in the United States.

WHAT DO YOU THINK?

1. What do you think are some of the reasons for the rising number of well-off African American families?

2. In what ways are affluent African Americans still disadvantaged by their race?

3. Do you think affluent African Americans feel less secure about their social position than affluent whites? Why or why not?

Some of the racial difference in income results from the larger share of single-parent families among African Americans. Comparing only families headed by married couples, African Americans earned 80 percent as much as non-Hispanic white families.

Over time, the income difference builds into a huge wealth gap (Altonji, Doraszelski, & Segal, 2000). A recent survey of families by the Federal Reserve found that median wealth for minority families, including African Americans, Hispanics, and Asian Americans ($27,100) is just 19 percent of the median ($142,700) for non-Hispanic white families (Bucks, Kennickell, & Moore, 2006). Even

among families who do have a lot of money, race makes a difference, as the Thinking About Diversity: Race, Class, & Gender box explains.

Social ranking involves ethnicity as well. People of English ancestry have always enjoyed the most wealth and the greatest power in U.S. society. The Latino population—the largest U.S. racial or ethnic minority—has long been disadvantaged. In 2005, the median income among Hispanic families was $37,867, which is 60 percent of the median income for non-Hispanic white families.

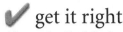

People often distinguish between the "new rich" and families with "old money." Men and women who suddenly begin to earn high incomes tend to spend their money on status symbols because they enjoy the new thrill of high-roller living and they want others to know of their success. Those who grow up surrounded by wealth, on the other hand, are used to a privileged way of life and are more quiet about it. Thus the conspicuous consumption of the lower-upper class (*left*) can differ dramatically from the more private pursuits and understatement of the upper-upper class (*right*).

Patrick Wallet/Corbis/Bettmann (*left*); Burt Glinn/Magnum Photos, Inc. (*right*)

Gender

Of course, both men and women are found in families at every class level. Yet on average, women have less income, wealth, and occupational prestige than men. Among single-parent families, those headed by a woman are almost three times more likely to be poor than those headed by a man.

Social Classes in the United States

Rankings in a caste system are rigid and obvious to all. Defining social categories in a more fluid class system such as ours, however, is not so easy.

There is an old joke about a couple who orders a pizza, asking that it be cut into six slices because they aren't hungry enough to eat eight. Sociologists do the same thing with social class; some divide the population into more classes than others. At one extreme, people find as many as six or even seven social classes; at the other, some follow Karl Marx and see two major classes: capitalists and proletarians. Still others side with Max Weber, claiming that people form not classes but a multidimensional status hierarchy.

Defining classes in U.S. society is difficult because of our relatively low level of status consistency. Especially toward the middle of

the hierarchy, people's standing in one dimension may not be the same as their standing in another. For example, a government official may have the power to administer a multimillion-dollar budget yet may earn only a modest personal income. Similarly, many members of the clergy enjoy great prestige but moderate power and low pay. Or consider a lucky day trader on the stock market who wins no special respect but makes a lot of money.

Finally, the social mobility characteristic of class systems—again, most pronounced around the middle—means that social position may change during a person's lifetime, further blurring class boundaries. With these issues in mind, we will examine four general rankings: the upper class, the middle class, the working class, and the lower class.

The Upper Class

Families in the upper class—5 percent of the U.S. population—earn at least $185,000 a year, and some earn ten times that much or more. As a general rule, the more a family's income comes from inherited wealth in the form of stocks and bonds, real estate, and other investments, the stronger a family's claim to being upper-class.

In 2006, *Forbes* magazine profiled the richest 400 people in the United States who were worth at least $1 billion (and as much as $53 billion) (Miller & Serafin, 2006). These people form the core of the

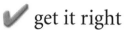
upper class, or Karl Marx's "capitalists"—the owners of the means of production or most of the nation's private wealth. Many upper-class people are business owners, top executives in large corporations, or senior government officials. Historically, the upper class has been composed mostly of white Anglo-Saxon Protestants, but this is less true today (Pyle & Koch, 2001).

Upper-Uppers

The *upper-upper class,* sometimes called "blue bloods" or simply "society," includes less than 1 percent of the U.S. population (Coleman & Neugarten, 1971; Baltzell, 1995). Membership is almost always the result of birth, as suggested by the joke that the easiest way to become an upper-upper is to be born one. Most of these families possess enormous wealth, which is primarily inherited. For this reason, members of the upper-upper class are said to have "old money."

For decades, U.S. farm families who worked hard could expect to end up in the middle class. But the trend toward large-scale agribusiness has put the future of the small family farm in doubt. Although many young people in rural areas are turning away from farming toward other careers, some carry on, incorporating high technology into their farm management in their determined efforts to succeed.

Set apart by their wealth, upper-uppers live in old, exclusive neighborhoods, such as Beacon Hill in Boston, Rittenhouse Square in Philadelphia, the Gold Coast of Chicago, and Nob Hill in San Francisco. Their children typically attend private schools with others of similar background and complete their schooling at high-prestige colleges and universities. In the tradition of European aristocrats, they study liberal arts rather than vocational skills.

Women of the upper-upper class do volunteer work for charitable organizations. Such activities serve a dual purpose: They help the larger community, and they build networks that broaden this elite's power (Ostrander, 1980, 1984).

Lower-Uppers

Most upper-class people actually fall into the *lower-upper class.* The queen of England is in the upper-upper class based not on her fortune of $500 million but on her family tree. J. K. Rowling, author of the Harry Potter books, is richer still—with more than $1 billion—but this woman (who was once on welfare) is a member of the lower-upper class. The major difference, in other words, is that lower-uppers are the "working rich" who get their money mostly by earning it rather than inheritance. These well-to-do families—who make up 3 or 4 percent of the U.S. population—generally live in large homes in expensive neighborhoods, own vacation homes near the water or in the mountains, and send their children to private schools and good colleges. Yet most of the "new rich" do not gain entry into the clubs and associations of "old money" families.

In the United States, what we often call the "American dream" has been to earn enough to join the ranks of the lower-upper class. The athlete who signs a multimillion-dollar contract, the actress who lands a starring role in a Hollywood film, the computer whiz who starts a successful Internet company, and even the person who hits it big by winning the lottery are the talented achievers and lucky people who reach the lower-upper class.

The Middle Class

Made up of 40 to 45 percent of the U.S. population, the large middle class has a tremendous influence on our culture. Television programs and movies usually show middle-class people, and most commercial advertising is directed at these average consumers. The middle class contains far more racial and ethnic diversity than the upper class.

Upper-Middles

People in the top half of this category are called the *upper-middle class,* based on above-average income in the range of $100,000 to $185,000 a year. Such income allows upper-middle-class families to

Joe Waehner lives in Marin County, California, one of the highest income communities in the United States, where annual family income averages $100,000.

Mitakuye Oyasin lives on the Pine Ridge Indian Reservation, one of the poorest communities in the United States, where annual family income averages less than $4,000.

♣ tip

In terms used later in the chapter, the lower class would include the poor and the "near-poor."

SEEING OURSELVES

NATIONAL MAP 1
Per Capita Income across the United States, 2003

This map shows the median per-person income (that is, how much money, on average, a person has to spend) in the more than 3,000 counties that make up the United States, for the year 2003. The richest counties, shown in dark green, are not spread randomly across the country. Nor are the poorest U.S. counties, which are shown in dark red. Looking at the map, what patterns do you see in the distribution of wealth and poverty across the United States? What can you say about wealth and poverty in urban and rural areas?

Source: *National Atlas of the United States* (2007).

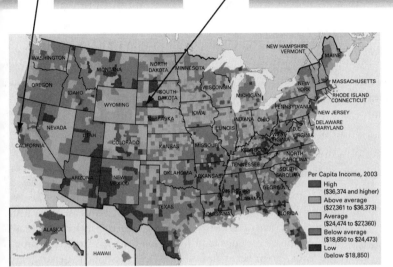

Per Capita Income, 2003

- High ($36,374 and higher)
- Above average ($27,361 to $36,373)
- Average ($24,474 to $27,360)
- Below average ($18,850 to $24,473)
- Low (below $18,850)

live in comfortable homes in fairly expensive areas, own several automobiles, and build investments. Two-thirds of upper-middle-class children graduate from college, and postgraduate degrees are common. Many go on to high-prestige careers as physicians, engineers, lawyers, accountants, and business executives. Lacking the power of the richest people to influence national or international events, upper-middles often play an important role in local political affairs.

Average-Middles

The rest of the middle class falls close to the center of the U.S. class structure. *Average-middles* typically work at less prestigious white-collar jobs as bank branch managers, high school teachers, and government office workers, or in highly skilled blue-collar jobs such as electrical work and carpentry. Family income is between $45,000 and $100,000 a year, which is roughly the national average.[2] Middle-class people typically build up a small amount of wealth over the course of their working lives, mostly in the form of a house and a retirement account. Middle-class men and women are likely to be high school graduates, but the odds are just fifty-fifty that they will complete a college degree, usually at a less expensive, state-supported school.

[2]In some parts of the United States where the cost of living is very high (say, San Francisco), a family might need $150,000 or more in annual income to reach the middle class.

The Working Class

About one-third of the population falls within the working class (sometimes called the *lower-middle class*). In Marxist terms, the working class forms the core of the industrial proletariat. Their blue-collar jobs usually yield a family income of between $25,000 and $45,000 a year, somewhat below the national average. Most working-class families have little or no wealth and all are vulnerable to financial problems caused by unemployment or illness.

Many working-class jobs provide little personal satisfaction, require discipline but rarely imagination, and subject workers to continual supervision. These jobs also offer fewer benefits, such as medical insurance and pension plans. About half of working-class families own their own homes, usually in lower-cost neighborhoods. College becomes a reality for only about one-third of working-class children.

The Lower Class

The remaining 20 percent of our population make up the lower class. Low income makes their lives insecure and difficult. In 2005, the federal government classified 37 million people (12.6 percent of the population) as poor. Millions more—called the "working poor"—are slightly better off, holding low-prestige jobs that provide little satisfaction and minimal income. Barely half manage to complete high school, and only one in four ever reaches college.

Society segregates the lower class, especially when the poor are racial or ethnic minorities. About 40 percent of lower-class families own their own homes, typically in the least desirable neighborhoods.

tip

Social class is linked to health, values and attitudes, politics, and family life. In truth, there are very few personal traits that are *not* linked to social class.

 tip

The idea of "cultural capital" is important because it shows that, at any social position, families pass on to their children not only material things such as wealth but also nonmaterial things such as attitudes and particular experiences.

Although poor neighborhoods are usually found in our inner cities, lower-class families also live in rural communities, especially across the South.

Most communities contain people of various class levels. In the country as a whole, however, some areas are wealthier than others. National Map 1 shows one measure of social class—per capita income—for all the counties in the United States.

If you wanted to assess someone's social class position and could ask only one question, what would it be? Explain your decision.

Compared to high-income people, low-income people are half as likely to report good health and, on average, live about seven fewer years. The toll of low income—played out in inadequate nutrition, little medical care, and high stress—is easy to see on the faces of the poor, who look old before their time.

Russell Lee/Corbis/Bettmann

The Difference Class Makes

Social stratification affects nearly every dimension of our lives. We will briefly examine some of the ways social standing is linked to our health, values, politics, and family life.

Health

Health is closely related to social standing. Children born into poor families are three times more likely to die from disease, neglect, accidents, or violence during their first years of life than children born into privileged families. Among adults, people with above-average incomes are almost twice as likely as low-income people to describe their health as excellent. In addition, richer people live, on average, seven years longer because they eat more nutritious food, live in safer and less stressful environments, and receive better medical care (Pleis & Lethbridge-Çejku, 2006).

Values and Attitudes

Some cultural values vary from class to class. The "old rich" have an unusually strong sense of family history because their social position is based on wealth passed down from generation to generation. Secure in their birthright privileges, upper-uppers also favor understated manners and tastes; many "new rich" engage in conspicuous consumption, using homes, cars, and even airplanes as status symbols to make a statement about their social position.

Affluent people with greater education and financial security are also more tolerant of controversial behavior such as homosexuality. Working-class people, who grow up in an atmosphere of greater supervision and discipline and are less likely to attend college, tend to be less tolerant (Lareau, 2002; NORC, 2005).

Politics

Do political attitudes follow class lines? The answer is yes, but the pattern is complex. A desire to protect their wealth prompts well-off people to be more conservative on *economic* issues, favoring, for example, lower taxes. But on *social* issues such as abortion and gay rights, highly educated, more affluent people are more liberal. People of lower social standing, by contrast, tend to be economic liberals, favoring government social programs that benefit them, but typically hold more conservative views on social issues (NORC, 2005).

A clearer pattern emerges when it comes to political involvement. Higher-income people, who are better served by the system, are more likely to vote and to join political organizations than people with low incomes. In presidential elections, three-fourths of adults with

student 2 student

"Wasn't it Ernest Hemingway who said that 'the rich are not like the rest of us'? Is this what 'cultural capital' is all about?"

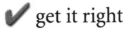

get it right

Be sure you understand the differences between intergenerational mobility and intragenerational mobility. Both types can be upward, downward, or horizontal.

---

family incomes of $75,000 vote, compared to about half of those with family incomes of $35,000 (Samuelson, 2003).

Family and Gender

Social class also shapes family life. Generally, lower-class families are somewhat larger than middle-class families because of earlier marriage and less use of birth control. Another family pattern is that working-class parents encourage children to conform to conventional norms and to respect authority figures. Parents of higher social standing pass on different "cultural capital" to their children, teaching them to express their individuality and use their imagination more freely. In both cases, parents are looking to the future: The odds are that less privileged children will have jobs that require them to follow rules and that more privileged children will have careers that require more creativity (Kohn, 1977; McLeod, 1995; Lareau, 2002).

The more money a family has, the more parents can develop their children's talents and abilities. An affluent family earning an average of $112,200 a year will spend $289,380 raising a child born in 2006 to the age of eighteen. Middle-class people, with an average annual income of $59,300, will spend $197,700, and a lower-income family, earning less than $44,500, will spend $143,790 (Lino, 2007). Privilege leads to privilege as family life reproduces the class structure in each generation.

Class also shapes our world of relationships. In a classic study of married life, Elizabeth Bott (1971, orig. 1957) found that most working-class couples divide their responsibilities according to gender roles; middle-class couples, by contrast, are more egalitarian, sharing more activities and expressing greater intimacy. More recently, Karen Walker (1995) discovered that working-class friendships typically serve as sources of material assistance; middle-class friendships are likely to involve shared interests and leisure pursuits.

In short, social class shapes just about all our everyday experiences. "In the *Times*" on page 288 takes a closer look.

Social Mobility

Ours is a dynamic society marked by quite a bit of social movement. Earning a college degree, landing a higher-paying job, or marrying someone who earns a good income contributes to *upward social mobility;* dropping out of school, losing a job, or becoming divorced (especially for women) may result in *downward social mobility.*

Over the long term, social mobility is not so much a matter of changes in individuals as changes in society itself. In the first half of the twentieth century, for example, industrialization expanded the

U.S. economy, pushing up living standards. Even people who were not good swimmers rode the rising tide of prosperity. More recently, the closing of U.S. factories has pushed *structural social mobility* in a downward direction, dealing economic setbacks to many people.

Sociologists distinguish between shorter- and longer-term changes in social position. **Intragenerational social mobility** is *a change in social position occurring during a person's lifetime* (*intra* is Latin for "within"). **Intergenerational social mobility,** *upward or downward social mobility of children in relation to their parents,* is important because it usually reveals long-term changes in society, such as industrialization, that affect everyone (*inter* is Latin for "between").

Myth versus Reality

In few societies do people think about "getting ahead" as much as in the United States. Moving up, after all, is the American dream. But is there as much social mobility as we like to think?

Studies of intergenerational mobility (most of which have focused only on men) show that nearly 40 percent of the sons of blue-collar workers take white-collar jobs and about 30 percent of sons born into white-collar families end up doing blue-collar work. *Horizontal social mobility*—changing jobs at the same class level—is even more common; overall, about 80 percent of sons show at least some type of social mobility in relation to their fathers (Blau & Duncan, 1967; Featherman & Hauser, 1978; Hout, 1998).

Research points to four general conclusions about social mobility in the United States:

1. **Social mobility over the past century has been fairly high.** A high level of mobility is what we would expect in an industrial class system.

2. **The long-term trend in social mobility has been upward.** Industrialization, which greatly expanded the U.S. economy, and the growth of white-collar work over the course of the twentieth century have raised living standards.

3. **Within a single generation, social mobility is usually small.** Most young families increase their income over time as they gain education and skills. For example, a typical family headed by a thirty-year-old earned about $53,000 in 2005; a typical family headed by a fifty-year-old earned $73,000 (U.S. Census Bureau, 2006). Yet only a few people move "from rags to riches" (the way J. K. Rowling did) or lose a lot of money (a number of rock stars who made it big had little money a few years later). Most social mobility involves limited movement

The New York Times

Money Changes Everything

By JENNIE YABROFF
May 7, 2006

Greta Gilbertson was caught off guard recently when her 9-year-old daughter, who attends a private school on the Upper West Side, requested a cellphone.

"I sort of snapped at her," recalled Ms. Gilbertson, an assistant professor at Fordham University in the Bronx. "I said, 'Don't think that you're one of the rich kids, because you're not.' " . . .

Carol Paik, a former lawyer who is married to a partner at a prominent New York law firm, found herself on the other side of that money equation. When she returned to school in 2002 to get her M.F.A. in creative writing at Columbia, her diamond engagement ring attracted particular attention from her new group of friends. "When I was working," she said, "I never thought about the ring, it seemed unremarkable."

But at school, she said, "People said things like, 'That's a really big diamond,' and not necessarily in a complimentary way." So she began taking off the ring before class.

If, as Samuel Butler said, friendships are like money, easier made than kept, economic differences can add yet another obstacle to maintaining them. More friends and acquaintances are now finding themselves at different points on the financial spectrum, scholars and sociologists say, thanks to broad social changes like meritocracy-based higher education, diversity in the workplace and a disparity of incomes among professions.

As people with various-sized bank accounts brush up against each other, there is ample cause for social awkwardness, which can strain relationships. . . .

"The real issue is not money itself, but the power money gives you," said Dalton Conley, a professor of sociology and the director of the Center for Advanced Social Science Research at New York University, who studies issues of wealth and class. "Money makes explicit the inequalities in a relationship, so we work hard to minimize it as a form of tact."

For Ms. Gilbertson, that means not having her daughter's friends over to play because, she said, her apartment in Washington Heights is small and in what some parents might consider a marginal neighborhood. . . .

For Ms. Paik, that meant avoiding inviting her classmates to her prewar, three-bedroom co-op on the Upper West Side, because many of them lived in student housing and she feared they would think she was showing off. . . .

Money's discomfiting effects are explored in the recent film *Friends with Money,* in which three of four female friends are well-off while one is barely getting by. In an early scene the friends are gathered for dinner when Olivia, a former schoolteacher played by Jennifer Aniston, announces that she has started working as a maid. A few moments later Franny, played

by Joan Cusack, says she and her husband will be making a $2 million donation to their child's elementary school. When another friend asks why Franny doesn't just give the money to Olivia, everyone laughs uncomfortably and the subject is changed. . . .

Economic barriers to friendship have come about in part because other barriers have been broken down, sociologists say. College, where people form some of the most intense friendships of their lives, is a melting pot of economic differences. Students from country-club families and those on scholarships are thrown together as roommates, on athletic teams and in classes.

"There has been an incredible expansion of higher education," Professor Conley said. "More people from more varied backgrounds are going to college." . . .

According to data compiled by Thomas Mortenson, a senior scholar at the Pell Institute in Washington, 42 percent of young adults (age 18 to 24) from the bottom quarter of family income were enrolled in college in 2003, compared with 28 percent in 1970. Enrollment for students from the two middle income quarters also increased. Participation of students from the highest-income families changed the least, with 80 percent attending college in 2003, compared with 74 percent in 1970.

Once college friends leave campus, their economic status can diverge widely depending on their careers. While 20 years ago a young lawyer and a new college instructor might have commiserated about their jobs over coffee and doughnuts, today the lawyer would be able to invite the assistant professor out for a meal at a restaurant with two sommeliers and a cheese expert. . . .

"We are allegedly a classless society, and that's obviously completely untrue, but people don't want to acknowledge that those differences exist," said Jamie Johnson, a 26-year-old heir to the Johnson & Johnson fortune. . . .

Mr. Johnson said that some of his moneyed friends act like they have fewer resources than they do, making a show of taking the subway and saying they can't afford a cab. "It's to avoid that awkwardness of seeing the distinction of social class," he said.

WHAT DO YOU THINK?

1. Have you ever felt uncomfortable in the company of people who were either richer or poorer than you? Explain.

2. Do you think money has a lot to do with who our friends are? Why or why not?

3. Why do you think differences in social class make people feel uncomfortable?

tip

Reminder from the last chapter: Caste systems have low social mobility, with people remaining in the social position into which they were born; class systems have fairly high levels of social mobility, especially near the middle of the distribution.

within one class level rather than striking moves between classes.

4. **Social mobility since the 1970s has been uneven.** Real income (adjusted for inflation) rose steadily during the twentieth century until the 1970s. Between 1975 and 1985, gains were far smaller. During the 1980s, real income changed little for many people, rising slowly during the 1990s, then falling slightly after 2000. But general trends do not show the experiences of different categories of people, as the next section explains.

Mobility by Income Level

Figure 2 shows how U.S. families at different income levels made out between 1980 and 2005. Well-to-do families (the highest 20 percent, but not all the same families over the entire period) saw their incomes jump 60 percent, from an average $110,507 in 1980 to $176,292 in 2005. People in the middle of the population also had gains, but more modest ones. The lowest-income 20 percent saw only a 2.6 percent increase in earnings.

For families at the top of the income scale (the highest 5 percent), recent decades have brought a windfall. These families, with an average income of almost $150,000 in 1980, were making $308,636 in 2005—more than twice as much (U.S. Census Bureau, 2006).

Mobility: Race, Ethnicity, and Gender

White people in the United States have always been in a more privileged position than people of African or Hispanic descent. Through the economic expansion of the 1980s and 1990s, many more African Americans entered the ranks of the wealthy. But overall, the real income of African Americans has changed little in three decades. African American family income as a percentage of white family income was the same in 2005 as it was in 1970 (60 percent). Compared with white families, Latino families in the United States lost ground between 1975 (when their average income was 67 percent as much as that of white families) and 2005 (when it had slipped to 64 percent) (Pomer, 1986; U.S. Census Bureau, 2006).

Feminists point out that historically, women in U.S. society have had less opportunity for upward mobility than men because most working women hold clerical jobs (such as secretary) and service positions (such as food server) that offer few opportunities for advancement. Over time, however, the earnings gap between women and men has been narrowing. Women working full time in 1980 earned 60 percent as much as men working full time; by 2005, women were earning 77 percent as much (U.S. Census Bureau, 2006).

How easy is it to move up in social position? The mass media generally convey the message that talent and effort (and often luck) are the keys to success. The recent movie *Friends with Money* describes the life of one young woman (played by Jennifer Aniston) who works as a maid and hangs out with old friends who are now quite rich. The gap between the lives of the "haves" and "have-nots" often leaves Aniston's character feeling that she lives in a different world.

Sony Pictures Classics/Photofest

Mobility and Marriage

Research points to the conclusion that marriage has an important effect on social standing. In a study of women and men in their forties, Jay Zagorsky (2006) found that people who marry and stay married accumulate about twice as much wealth as people who remain single or who divorce. Reasons for this difference include the fact that couples who live together typically enjoy double incomes and also pay only half the bills they would have if they were single and living in separate households.

It is also likely that, compared to single people, married men and women work harder in their jobs and save more money. Why? Primarily because they are working not just for themselves but to support others who are counting on them (Popenoe, 2006).

Just as marriage pushes social standing upward, divorce usually makes social position go down. Couples who divorce take on the financial burden of supporting two households. After divorce, women are hurt more than men because it is typically the man who earns more. Many women who divorce lose not only most of their income but they may also lose benefits, including health care and insurance coverage (Weitzman, 1996).

tip

One reason for the increasing gap between high- and low-paid workers is the increasing value of a college degree in our postindustrial society.

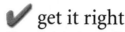
get it right

Figure 3 shows how median family income has changed over time. Figure 2 shows that it has changed differently for different categories of families.

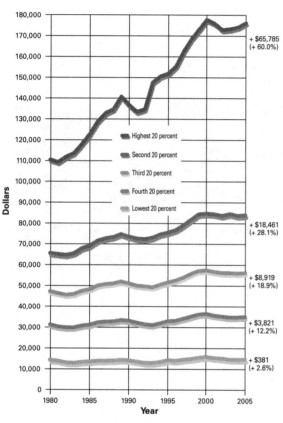

FIGURE 2   Mean Annual Income, U.S. Families, 1980–2005 (in 2005 dollars, adjusted for inflation)

The gap between high-income and low-income families is wider today than it was in 1980.

Source: U.S. Census Bureau (2006).

The American Dream: Still a Reality?

The expectation of upward social mobility is deeply rooted in U.S. culture. Through most of our history, the economy has grown steadily, raising living standards. Even today, for some people at least, the American dream is alive and well. In 2005, fully 22 percent of U.S. families earned $100,000 or more, compared with just 3 percent back in 1967 (in dollars controlled for inflation). There are now at least 5 million millionaires in the United States, four times the number a decade ago (Rank & Hirschl, 2001; U.S. Census Bureau, 2006).

Yet not all indicators are positive. Note these disturbing trends:

1. **For many workers, earnings have stalled.** The annual income of a fifty-year-old man working full time climbed 49 percent between 1958 and 1974 (from $25,671 to $38,190 in constant 2001 dollars). Between 1974 and 2005, however, this worker's income rose by barely 30 percent, even as the number of hours worked increased and the cost of necessities like housing, education, and medical care went way up (Russell, 1995a; U.S. Census Bureau, 2006).

2. **More jobs offer little income.** The expanding global economy has moved many industrial jobs overseas, reducing the number of high-paying factory jobs here in the United States. At the same time, the expansion of our service economy means that more of today's jobs—in fast-food restaurants or large discount stores—offer relatively low wages.

3. **Young people are remaining at home.** For the first time in history, nearly half of young people aged eighteen to twenty-four are living with their parents. Since 1975, the average age at marriage has moved upward four years (to 25.5 years for women and 27.5 years for men).

Over the past generation, more people have become rich, and the rich have become richer. At the very top of the pile, as the Seeing Sociology in Everyday Life box explains, the highest-paid corporate executives have enjoyed a runaway rise in their earnings. Yet the increasing share of low-paying jobs has also brought downward mobility for millions of families, feeding the fear that the chance to enjoy a middle-class lifestyle is slipping away. As Figure 3 shows, although median income doubled between 1950 and 1973, it has grown by only 23 percent since then (U.S. Census Bureau, 2006).

Do you feel that you are likely to end up with a higher social position than your parents? The same? Lower? Why? How much of the mobility you expect is due to changes in U.S. society?

The Global Economy and the U.S. Class Structure

Underlying the shifts in U.S. class structure is global economic change. Much of the industrial production that gave U.S. workers high-paying jobs a generation ago has moved overseas. With less industry at home, the United States now serves as a vast market for industrial goods such as cars and popular items like stereos, cameras, and computers made in China, Japan, Korea, and elsewhere.

tip
This discussion explains how changes in the
global economy affect social class patterns here
at home.

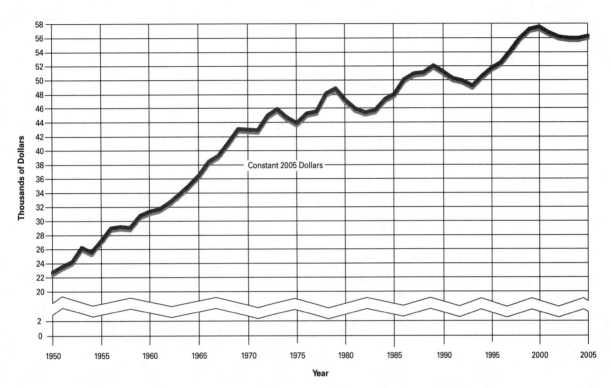

FIGURE 3 Median Annual Income, U.S. Families, 1950–2005

Average family income in the United States grew rapidly between 1950 and 1970. Since then,
however, the increase has been smaller.

Source: U.S. Census Bureau (2006).

High-paying jobs in manufacturing, held by 26 percent of the U.S. labor force in 1960, support only 11 percent of workers today. In their place, the economy now offers service work, which often pays far less. A traditionally high-paying corporation like USX (formerly United States Steel) now employs fewer people than the expanding McDonald's chain, and fast-food clerks make only a fraction of what steelworkers earn.

The global reorganization of work has not been bad news for everyone. On the contrary, the global economy is driving upward social mobility for educated people who specialize in law, finance, marketing, and computer technology. Global economic expansion has also helped push up the stock market more than tenfold between 1980 and 2007, reaping profits for families with money to invest.

But the same trend has hurt many average workers, who have lost their factory jobs and now perform low-wage service work. In addition, many companies (General Motors and Ford are recent examples) have downsized, cutting the ranks of their workforce, to stay competitive in world markets. As a result, even though more than 50 percent of all families contain two or more workers—more than twice the share in 1950—many families are working harder simply to hold on to what they have (A. L. Nelson, 1998; Sennett, 1998; U.S. Census Bureau, 2006).

Poverty in the United States

Social stratification creates both "haves" and "have-nots." All systems of social inequality create poverty, or at least **relative poverty,** *the lack of resources of some people in relation to those who have more.* A more

tip
Big houses are one example of conspicuous consumption.

Seeing Sociology in Everyday Life
As CEOs Get Richer, the Great Mansions Return

I grew up in Elkins Park, Pennsylvania, an older suburban community just north of Philadelphia. Elkins Park was at that time and still is a mostly middle-class community, although, like most of suburbia, some neighborhoods boast bigger houses than others.

What made Elkins Park special was that scattered over the area were a handful of great mansions, built a century ago by early Philadelphia industrialists. At that time, just about all there was to the town was these great "estates," along with fields and meadows. By about 1940, however, most of the land was split off into lots for the homes of newer middle-class suburbanites. The great mansions suddenly seemed out of place, with heirs trying to figure out how to pay the rising property taxes. As a result, many of the great mansions were sold, the buildings were torn down, and the land was subdivided.

In the 1960s, when I was a teenager, a short ride on my bicycle could take me past what was left of the Breyer estate (built by the founder of the ice-cream company, now the township police building), the Curtis estate (built by a magazine publisher, now transformed into a community park), and the Wanamaker estate (built by the founder of a large Philadelphia department store, now the site of high-rise apartments). Probably the grandest of them all was the Wiedner estate, modeled after a French château, complete with doorknobs and window pulls covered in gold; it now stands empty.

In their day, these structures were not just homes to families with many servants; they also served as monuments to a time when the rich were, well, *really* rich. By contrast, the community that emerged on the grounds once owned by these wealthy families is middle-class, with homes built on small lots.

But did the so-called Gilded Age of great wealth disappear forever? Hardly. By the 1980s, a new wave of great mansions was being built in the United States. Take the architect Thierry Despont, who designs huge houses for the super-rich. One of Despont's smaller homes might be 20,000 square feet (about ten times the size of the average U.S. house), and the larger ones go all the way up to 60,000 square feet (as big as any of the Elkins Park mansions built a century ago and almost the size of the White House). These megahomes have kitchens as large as college classrooms, exercise rooms, indoor swimming pools, and even indoor tennis courts (Krugman, 2002).

Megahouses are being built by newly rich chief executive officers (CEOs) of large corporations. CEOs have always made more money than most people, but recent years have seen executive pay soar. Between 1970 and 2005, the average U.S. family saw only a modest increase in income (about 20 percent after inflation is taken into account). Yet according to *Fortune* magazine, during the same period, the average annual compensation for the 100 highest-paid CEOs skyrocketed from $1.3 million (about 40 times the earnings of an average worker of that time) to $37.5 million (roughly a 2,800 percent increase and equal to 1,000 times as much as the earnings of today's average worker). Some CEOs, of course, earn far more: In the year before Enron collapsed, for example, Kenneth Lay earned about $150 million. In 2006, the highest-paid CEO was Ray Irani, chairman of Occidental Petroleum Corporation, who earned more than $400 million, mostly from stock options. That amounts to more than $1 million every day of the year. Assuming that Irani worked forty hours per week and fifty weeks that year, his pay amounts to about $200,000 *per hour*.

Some analysts argue that in today's competitive global economy, many CEOs are true "superstars" who build company profits and deserve every penny they earn. Others take a less generous view, suggesting that CEOs have stacked their corporate boards of directors with friends, who then paid them back by approving enormous paychecks and bonuses. In any case, executive pay has become a national scandal. In light of this situation (not to mention the many cases of outright fraud and theft that led to convictions for executives like Kenneth Lay), it appears that we have been living in an era of uncontrolled greed.

AP Wide World Photos

WHAT DO YOU THINK?

1. Do you consider increasing economic inequality a problem? Why or why not?

2. How many times more than an average worker should a CEO earn? Explain your answer.

3. Do you think that very high CEO pay hurts stockholders? What about the general public? Why or why not?

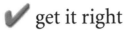
serious but preventable problem is **absolute poverty,** *a lack of resources that is life-threatening.*

About 1 billion human beings—one person in six—are at risk of absolute poverty. Even in the affluent United States, families go hungry, live in inadequate housing, and suffer poor health because of a serious lack of resources.

The Extent of U.S. Poverty

In 2005, the government classified 37 million men, women, and children—12.6 percent of the population—as poor. This count of relative poverty refers to families with incomes below an official poverty line, which for a family of four in that year was set at $19,971. The poverty line is about three times what the government estimates people must spend for food. But the income of the average poor family was just 60 percent of this amount. This means that the typical poor family had to get by on less than $12,000 in 2005 (U.S. Census Bureau, 2006). Figure 4 shows that the official poverty rate fell during the 1960s and has stayed about the same since then.

Who Are the Poor?

Although no single description fits all poor people, poverty is pronounced among certain categories of our population. Where these categories overlap, the problem is especially serious.

Age

A generation ago, the elderly were at greatest risk for poverty. But thanks to better retirement programs offered today by private employers and the government, the poverty rate for people over age sixty-five fell from 30 percent in 1967 to 10.1 percent—well below the national average—in 2005. Looking at it from another angle, 10 percent (3.6 million) of the poor are elderly.

Today the burden of poverty falls more heavily on children. In 2005, 17.6 percent of people under age eighteen (12.9 million children) were poor. Put another way, 35 percent of the U.S. poor are children. The poverty rate for young adults between the ages of eighteen and twenty-four was even higher—18.2 percent.

Race and Ethnicity

Two-thirds of all poor people are white; 25 percent are African Americans. But in relation to their overall numbers, African Americans are about three times as likely as non-Hispanic whites to be poor. In 2005, 24.9 percent of African Americans (9.2 million people) lived in

FIGURE 4   The Poverty Rate in the United States, 1960–2005

The share of our population in poverty fell dramatically between 1960 and 1970. Since then, the poverty rate has remained between 10 and 15 percent of the population.

Source: U.S. Census Bureau (2006).

poverty, compared to 21.8 percent of Hispanics (9.4 million), 11.1 percent of Asians and Pacific Islanders (1.4 million), and 8.3 percent of non-Hispanic whites (16.2 million). The poverty gap between whites and minorities has changed little since 1975.

People of color have especially high rates of child poverty. Among African American children, 34.5 percent are poor; the comparable figures are 28.3 percent among Hispanic children and 10.0 percent among non-Hispanic white children (U.S. Census Bureau, 2006).

Gender and Family Patterns

Of all poor people age eighteen or older, 61 percent are women and 39 percent are men. This difference reflects the fact that women who head households are at high risk of poverty. Of all poor families, 53 percent are headed by women with no husband present; just 9 percent of poor families are headed by single men.

The United States has experienced the **feminization of poverty,** *the trend of women making up an increasing proportion of the poor.* In 1960, 25 percent of all poor households were headed by women; the

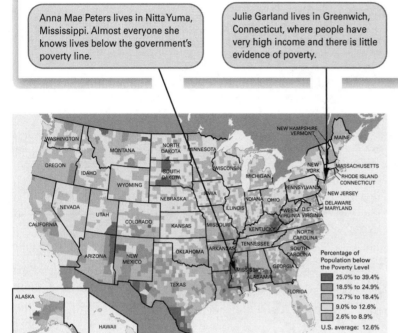

Anna Mae Peters lives in Nitta Yuma, Mississippi. Almost everyone she knows lives below the government's poverty line.

Julie Garland lives in Greenwich, Connecticut, where people have very high income and there is little evidence of poverty.

SEEING OURSELVES

NATIONAL MAP 2
Poverty across the United States

This map shows that the poorest counties in the United States—where the poverty rate is more than twice the national average—are in Appalachia, spread across the Deep South, along the border with Mexico, near the Four Corners region of the Southwest, and in the Dakotas. Can you suggest some reasons for this pattern?

Source: U.S. Census Bureau (2006).

Percentage of Population below the Poverty Level

- 25.0% to 39.4%
- 18.5% to 24.9%
- 12.7% to 18.4%
- 9.0% to 12.6%
- 2.6% to 8.9%

U.S. average: 12.6%

---

majority of poor families had both wives and husbands in the home. By 2005, however, the share of poor households headed by a single woman had more than doubled to 53 percent.

The feminization of poverty is one result of a larger change: the rapidly increasing number of households at all class levels headed by single women. This trend, coupled with the fact that households headed by women are at high risk of poverty, helps explain why women and their children make up an increasing share of the U.S. poor.

Urban and Rural Poverty

The greatest concentration of poverty is found in central cities, where the 2005 poverty rate stood at 17.0 percent. The poverty rate in suburbs is 9.3 percent. Thus the poverty rate for urban areas as a whole is 12.2 percent—somewhat lower than the 14.5 percent found in rural areas. National Map 2 shows that most of the counties with the highest poverty rate in the United States are rural.

Explaining Poverty

The richest nation on Earth contains tens of millions of poor people, a fact that raises serious questions. It is true, as some analysts remind us, that most poor people in the United States are far better off than the poor in other countries: 41 percent of U.S. poor families own a home, 70 percent own a car, and only a few percent report often going without food (Rector, 1998; M. Gallagher, 1999). But there is little doubt that poverty harms the overall well-being of millions of people in this country.

Why is there poverty in the first place? We will examine two opposing explanations for poverty that lead to a lively and important political debate.

One View: Blame the Poor

One approach holds that *the poor are mostly responsible for their own poverty.* Throughout the nation's history, people have placed a high value on self-reliance, convinced that social standing is mostly a matter of individual talent and effort. According to this view, society offers plenty of opportunities to anyone able and willing to take advantage of them, and the poor are people who cannot or will not work due to a lack of skills, schooling, or motivation.

In his study of poverty in Latin American cities, the anthropologist Oscar Lewis (1961) noted that many poor become trapped in a *culture of poverty,* a lower-class subculture that can destroy people's ambition to improve their lives. Raised in poor families, children become resigned to their situation, producing a self-perpetuating cycle of poverty.

In 1996, hoping to break the cycle of poverty in the United States, Congress changed the welfare system, which had provided federal funds to assist poor people since 1935. The federal government continues to send money to the states to distribute to needy people, but benefits carry strict time limits—in most cases, no more than two years at a stretch and a total of five years as an individual moves in and out of the welfare system. The stated purpose of this reform was to force people to be self-supporting and move them away from dependency on government.

Seeing Sociology in Everyday Life
When Work Disappears, the Result Is Poverty

The U.S. economy has created tens of millions of new jobs in recent decades. Yet African Americans who live in inner cities have faced a catastrophic loss of work. William Julius Wilson points out that although people continue to talk about welfare reform, neither major political party (Democrats or Republicans) has said anything about the lack of work in central cities.

With the loss of inner-city jobs, Wilson continues, for the first time in U.S. history a large majority of the adults in our inner cities are not working. Studying the Washington Park area of Chicago, Wilson found a troubling trend. Back in 1950, most adults in this African American community had jobs, but by the mid-1990s, two-thirds did not. As one elderly woman who moved to the neighborhood in 1953 explained:

> When I moved in, the neighborhood was intact. It was intact with homes, beautiful homes, mini-mansions, with stores, laundromats, with Chinese cleaners. We had drugstores. We had hotels. We had doctors over on 39th Street. We had doctors' offices in the neighborhood. We had the middle class and the upper-middle class. It has gone from affluent to where it is today. (Wilson, 1996b:28)

Why has this neighborhood declined? Wilson's eight years of research point to one answer: There are barely any jobs. It is the loss of work that has pushed people into desperate poverty, weakened families, and made people turn to welfare. In nearby Woodlawn, Wilson identified more than 800 businesses that had operated in

1950; today, just 100 remain. In addition, a number of major employers in the past—including Western Electric and International Harvester—closed their plant doors in the late 1960s. The inner cities have fallen victim to economic change, including downsizing and the loss of industrial jobs that have moved overseas.

Wilson paints a grim picture. But he also believes the answer lies in creating new jobs. Wilson proposes attacking the problem in stages. First, the government could hire people to do all kinds of work, from clearing slums to putting up new housing. Such a program, modeled on the Works Progress Administration (WPA) created in 1935 during the Great Depression, would move people from welfare to work and in the process create much-needed hope. In addition, federal and state governments must improve schools by enacting performance standards and pro-

William Julius Wilson spent years studying neighborhoods like this one in Chicago. He now teaches at Harvard University in Cambridge, Massachusetts.

Carl Wagner/Chicago Tribune/NewsCom

viding more funding. Of special importance is teaching children language skills and computer skills to prepare them for the jobs being created by the Information Revolution. Improved regional public transportation would connect cities (where people need work) and suburbs (where most jobs now are). In addition, more affordable child care would help single mothers and fathers balance the responsibilities of employment and parenting.

Wilson claims that his proposals are well grounded in research. But he knows that politics revolves around other considerations as well. For one thing, because the public *thinks* there are plenty of jobs, it is hard to change the perception that the poor are simply avoiding work. He also concedes that his proposals, at least in the short term, are more expensive than continuing to funnel welfare assistance to jobless communities.

But what are the long-term costs of allowing our cities to decay while suburbs prosper? On the other hand, what would be the benefits of giving everyone the hope and satisfaction that are supposed to define our way of life?

WHAT DO YOU THINK?

1. If Wilson were running for public office, do you think he would be elected? Why or why not?

2. In your opinion, why are people so reluctant to see inner-city poverty as a problem?

3. Where do you agree with Wilson's analysis of poverty? Where do you disagree?

tip

Many people feel differently toward the working poor than the nonworking poor. Do you? Do you think there are jobs for all people who want to work?

The African American artist Henry Ossawa Tanner captured the humility and humanity of impoverished people in his painting *The Thankful Poor*. This insight is important in a society that tends to define poor people as morally unworthy and deserving of their bitter plight.

Henry Ossawa Tanner (1859–1937), *The Thankful Poor*. Private collection. Art Resource, New York.

Another View: Blame Society

A different position, argued by William Julius Wilson (1996a, 1996b; Mouw, 2000), holds that *society is mostly responsible for poverty*. Wilson points to the loss of jobs in the inner cities as the main cause of poverty, claiming that there is simply not enough work to support families. Wilson sees any apparent lack of trying on the part of poor people as a result of little opportunity rather than a cause of poverty. From Wilson's point of view, Lewis's analysis amounts to blaming the victims for their own suffering. The Seeing Sociology in Everyday Life box provides a closer look at Wilson's argument and how it would shape public policy.

▶ **CRITICAL REVIEW** The U.S. public is evenly divided over whether the government or people themselves should take responsibility for reducing poverty (NORC, 2005). And here's what we know about poverty and work: Government statistics show that 52 percent of the heads of poor households did not work at all during 2005, and an additional 30 percent worked only part time (U.S. Census Bureau, 2006). Such facts seem to support the "blame

the poor" side of the argument, because one major cause of poverty is not holding a job.

But the *reasons* that people do not work seem more in step with the "blame society" position. Middle-class women may be able to combine working and child rearing, but this is much harder for poor women who cannot afford child care, and few employers provide child care programs. As Wilson explains, many people are idle not because they are avoiding work but because there are not enough jobs to go around. In short, the most effective way to reduce poverty is to ensure a greater supply of jobs as well as child care for parents who work (W. J. Wilson, 1996a; Pease & Martin, 1997; Duncan, 1999; Bainbridge, Meyers, & Waldfogel, 2003).

 YOUR LEARNING: Explain the view that the poor should take responsibility for poverty and the view that society is responsible for poverty. Which is closer to your own view?

The Working Poor

Not all poor people are jobless. The *working poor* command the sympathy and support of people on both sides of the poverty debate. In 2005, 18 percent of heads of poor families (1.4 million women and men) worked at least fifty weeks of the year and yet could not escape poverty. Another 30 percent of these heads of families (2.3 million people) remained poor despite part-time employment. Put differently, 3.4 percent of full-time workers earn so little that they remain poor (U.S. Census Bureau, 2006). Congress plans to raise the minimum wage (which was $5.15 early in 2007) to about $7.25 by 2009. But even this increase will not end working poverty—even earning $8.00 an hour, a full-time worker still cannot lift an urban family of four above the poverty line.

Another category we might call the "working near-poor" includes another 5 or 6 million families that are only slightly better off, earning more than those officially counted as poor but less than 150 percent of the poverty line. Among these families, more than half include at least one full-time worker. With only low-wage jobs available, people who work hard can boost incomes above the poverty line, but not by much (O'Hare, 2002).

Individual ability and personal effort do play a part in shaping social position. However, the weight of sociological evidence points to society—not individual character traits—as the primary cause of poverty because more and more available jobs offer only low wages. In addition, the poor are *categories* of people—female heads of families, people of color, people isolated from the larger society in inner-city areas—who face special barriers and limited opportunities.

tip

In the Controversy & Debate box, notice that welfare reform had two goals. One was getting people off welfare, and to a substantial degree, the recent reforms have done that. Second was reducing poverty, and the recent reforms have not done that.

Controversy & Debate
The Welfare Dilemma

MARCO: My father says welfare reform was a huge success—millions of people on welfare got jobs.

SERGI: But many of them are still poor. . . .

In 1996, Congress ended federal public assistance, which guaranteed some income to all poor people. New state-run programs were enacted that require people who receive aid to get job training or find work—or have their benefits cut off.

What, exactly, is welfare? The term "welfare" refers to an assortment of policies and programs designed to improve the well-being of some low-income people. Until the welfare reform of 1996, most people used the term to refer to just one part of the overall system: Aid for Families with Dependent Children (AFDC), a program of monthly financial support for parents (mostly single women) to care for themselves and their children. In 1996, about 5 million households received AFDC for some part of the year.

Conservatives opposed AFDC, claiming that rather than reducing child poverty, AFDC made the problem worse, in two ways. First, they claimed that AFDC weakened families, because for years after the program began, it paid benefits to poor mothers only if no husband lived in the home. As a result, AFDC operated as an economic incentive to women to have children outside of marriage, and they blame it for the rapid rise of out-of-wedlock births among poor people. To conservatives, marriage is one key to reducing poverty: Fewer than one in ten married-couple families are poor; more than nine in ten AFDC families were headed by an unmarried woman.

Second, conservatives believe that welfare encouraged poor people to become dependent on government handouts, the main reason that eight out of ten poor heads of households did not have full-time jobs. Furthermore, only 5 percent of single mothers receiving AFDC worked full time, com-

pared to more than half of nonpoor single mothers. Conservatives say that welfare strayed from its original purpose of short-term help to nonworking women with children (say, after divorce or death of a husband) and became a way of life. Once trapped in dependency, poor women would raise children who were themselves likely to be poor as adults.

Liberals have a different view. Why, they ask, do people object to government money going to poor mothers and children when most "welfare" actually goes to richer people? The AFDC budget was about $25 billion annually—no small sum, to be sure, but just half of the $50 billion in home mortgage deductions that homeowners pocket each year. And it pales in comparison to the $300 billion in annual Social Security benefits Uncle Sam provides to senior citizens, most of whom are not poor. And what about "corporate welfare" to big companies? Their tax write-offs and other benefits run into hundreds of billions of dollars per year.

Liberals add that the stereotype of do-nothing "welfare queens" masks the fact that most poor families who turn to public assistance are truly needy. The typical AFDC household received barely $400 per month, hardly enough to attract people to a life of welfare dependency. In constant dollars, AFDC payments actually declined over the years. Liberals fault public assistance as a "Band-Aid approach" to the serious social problems of too few jobs and too much income inequality in the United States.

As for the charge that public assistance weakens families, liberals agree that the proportion of single-parent families has risen, but they do not see AFDC as the reason. Rather, they see single parenting as a broad cultural trend found at all class levels in many countries.

Given our individualistic culture, people in the United States are much more likely

than people in other industrial nations to see poverty as a mark of laziness and personal failure (Inglehart et al., 2000). It should not be surprising, then, that in 1996, Congress replaced the federal AFDC program with state-run programs called Temporary Assistance for Needy Families (TANF). The federal government provides funding, and states set their own qualifications and benefits, but they must limit assistance to two consecutive years with a lifetime limit of five years.

By 2006, TANF had moved more than half of single parents on welfare into jobs or job training. In addition, the rate of out-of-wedlock births has fallen. Supporters of welfare reform see the new program as a success. But critics point out that many of the people who are now working earn so little pay that they are hardly better off than before, and half of these workers have no health insurance. In other words, the reform has greatly reduced the number of people receiving welfare, but it has done little to reduce poverty. In addition, say the critics, many of these working women now spend less time with their children. And so the welfare debate goes on.

WHAT DO YOU THINK?

1. How does our cultural emphasis on self-reliance help explain the controversy surrounding public assistance? Why do people not criticize benefits (such as home mortgage deductions) for people who are better off?

2. Do you approve of the time limits on benefits built into the TANF program? Why or why not?

3. Why do you think the welfare reforms have done little to reduce poverty?

Sources: Corcoran et al. (2000), U.S. Department of Health and Human Services (2000), Rogers-Dillon (2001), Hofferth (2002), Lichter & Crowley (2002), and Lichter & Jayakody (2002).

get it right

Most homeless people lack education and sometimes even social skills. But there is a debate about how much of such personal deficiency is a *cause* of homelessness and how much is an *effect* of living on the street.

tip

The Applying Sociology in Everyday Life items provide additional ways for you to connect the ideas found in this chapter with your own life.

The Controversy & Debate box takes a closer look at current welfare policy. Understanding this important social issue can help us decide how our society should respond to the problem of poverty, as well as the problem of homelessness discussed next.

Homelessness

In 2005, the government's Department of Housing and Urban Development conducted a national survey of cities and towns to find out how many people in the United States were homeless at some time during 2005. The answer was about 754,000, including people living in shelters, in transitional housing, and on the street (Ohlemacher, 2007). As with earlier estimates of the homeless population, critics claimed that the HUD survey undercounted the homeless, who may well number several million people. In addition, they add, evidence suggests that the number of homeless people in the United States is increasing (Wickham, 2000; Marks, 2001; L. Kaufman, 2004).

The familiar stereotypes of homeless people—men sleeping in doorways and women carrying everything they own in a shopping bag—have been replaced by the "new homeless": people thrown out of work because of plant closings, women who take their children and leave home to escape domestic violence, women and men forced out of apartments by rent increases, and others unable to meet mortgage or rent payments because of low wages or no work at all. Today, no stereotype paints a complete picture of the homeless.

The majority of homeless people report that they do not work, but 44 percent say they work at least part time (U.S. Department of Housing and Urban Development, 1999). Working or not, all homeless people have one thing in common: *poverty*. For that reason, the explanations of poverty just presented also apply to homelessness. Some people blame the *personal traits* of the homeless themselves.

One-third of homeless people are substance abusers, and one-fourth are mentally ill. More broadly, a fraction of 1 percent of our population, for one reason or another, seems unable to cope with our complex and highly competitive society (Bassuk, 1984; Whitman, 1989).

Other people see homelessness as resulting from *societal factors*, including low wages and a lack of low-income housing (Kozol, 1988; Bohannan, 1991; L. Kaufman, 2004). Supporters of this position note that one-third of the homeless consists of entire families, and they point to children as the fastest-growing category of the homeless.

Our society has been more generous with the "worthy" poor (such as elderly people) than with the "unworthy" poor (such as able-bodied people who, we assume, should take care of themselves). Why do you think we have not done more to reduce poverty among children, who surely fall into the "worthy" category?

No one disputes that a large proportion of homeless people are personally impaired to some degree, but cause and effect are difficult to untangle. Structural changes in the U.S. economy, coupled with reduced aid to low-income people and a real estate market that puts housing out of the reach of the poorest members of U.S. society, all contribute to homelessness.

Finally, social stratification extends far beyond the borders of the United States. In fact, the most striking social inequality is found not within any one nation but in the different living standards from nation to nation around the world.

Applying Sociology in Everyday Life

1. Develop several questions that together will let you measure social class position. The trick is to decide what you think social class really means. Then try your questions on several adults, refining the questions as you proceed.

2. During an evening of television viewing, assess the social class level of the characters you see on various shows. In each case, explain why you assign someone a particular social position. Do you find many clearly upper-class people? Middle-class people? Working-class people? Poor people? Describe the patterns you find.

3. Governor Arnold Schwarzenegger of California said, "In this country, it doesn't make any difference where you were born. It doesn't make any difference who your parents were. It doesn't make any difference if, like me, you couldn't even speak English until you were in your twenties. America gave me opportunities, and my immigrant dreams came true. I want other people to get the same chances I did, the same opportunities. And I believe they can." Ask a number of people who came to the United States from another country the extent to which they agree or disagree with this statement.

MAKING THE GRADE

Social Class in the United States

Dimensions of Social Inequality

SOCIAL STRATIFICATION involves many dimensions:

- *Income*—Earnings from work and investments are unequal, with the richest 20% of families earning twelve times as much as the poorest 20% of families.

- *Wealth*—The total value of all assets minus debts, wealth is distributed more unequally than income, with the richest 20% of families holding 84% of all wealth.

- *Power*—Income and wealth are important sources of power.

- *Schooling*—Schooling affects both occupation and income. Some categories of people have greater opportunities for schooling than others.

- *Occupational Prestige*—Work generates not only income but prestige. White-collar jobs generally offer more income and prestige than blue-collar jobs. Many lower-prestige jobs are performed by women and people of color.

income earnings from work or investments

wealth the total value of money and other assets, minus outstanding debts

U.S. Stratification: Merit and Caste

Although the United States is a meritocracy, social position in this country involves some caste elements.

ANCESTRY

Being born into a particular family affects a person's opportunities for schooling, occupation, and income.

RACE AND ETHNICITY

Non-Hispanic white families enjoy high social standing based on income and wealth. By contrast, African American and Hispanic families remain disadvantaged.

GENDER

On average, women have less income, wealth, and occupational prestige than men.

Social Classes in the United States

Defining **SOCIAL CLASSES** in the United States is difficult because of low status consistency and relatively high social mobility. But we can describe four general rankings:

- the upper class
- the middle class
- the working class
- the lower class

$185,000

$185,000

UPPER CLASS—5% of the population. Most members of the *upper-upper class*, or "old rich," inherited their wealth; the *lower-upper class*, or "new rich," work at high-paying jobs.

MIDDLE CLASS—40 to 45% of the population. People in the *upper-middle class* have significant wealth; *average-middles* have less prestige, do white-collar work, and most attend college.

$45,000

$45,000

WORKING CLASS—30 to 35% of the population. People in the *lower-middle class* do blue-collar work; only about one-third of children attend college.

$25,000

$25,000

LOWER CLASS—20% of the population. Most people in the lower class lack financial security due to low income; many live below the poverty line; half do not complete high school.

MAKING THE GRADE *continued . . .*

The Difference Class Makes

HEALTH

- Rich people, on average, live longer and receive better health care than poor people.

VALUES AND ATTITUDES

- Affluent people, with greater education and financial security, display greater tolerance than working-class people.

POLITICS

- Affluent people tend to be more conservative on economic issues and more liberal on social issues than poor people.
- Affluent people, who are better served by the political system, are more likely to vote than poor people.

FAMILY AND GENDER

- Affluent families pass on advantages in the form of "cultural capital" to their children.
- Class also shapes the division of family responsibilities, with lower-class people maintaining more traditional gender roles.

Social Mobility

- Social mobility is common in the United States, as it is in other high-income countries, but typically only small changes occur from one generation to the next.
- In the last twenty-five years, the richest 20% of U.S. families have enjoyed a 60% jump in annual income, while the 20% of families with the lowest income saw only a 2.6% increase.
- Historically, African Americans, Hispanic Americans, and women have had less opportunity for upward mobility in U.S. society than white men.
- The American Dream—the expectation of upward social mobility—is deeply rooted in our culture. Although high-income families are earning more and more, many average families are struggling to hold on to what they have.
- Marriage encourages upward social mobility. Divorce lowers social standing.
- The global reorganization of work has created upward social mobility for educated people in the United States but has hurt average workers, whose factory jobs have moved overseas and who are forced to take low-wage service work.

intragenerational social mobility a change in social position occurring during a person's lifetime

intergenerational social mobility upward or downward social mobility of children in relation to their parents

Poverty in the United States

POVERTY PROFILE

- The government classifies 37 million people, 12.6% of the population, as poor.
- About 35% of the poor are children under age 18.
- Two-thirds of the poor are white, but in relation to their population, African Americans and Hispanics are more likely to be poor.
- The **feminization of poverty** means that more poor families are headed by women.
- About 48% of the heads of poor families are among the "working poor" who work at least part-time but do not earn enough to lift a family of four above the poverty line.
- An estimated 750,000 people are homeless at some time during the course of a year.

EXPLANATIONS OF POVERTY

- Blame individuals: The *culture of poverty* thesis states that poverty is caused by shortcomings in the poor themselves (Oscar Lewis).
- Blame society: Poverty is caused by society's unequal distribution of wealth and lack of good jobs (William Julius Wilson).

relative poverty the lack of resources of some people in relation to those who have more

absolute poverty a lack of resources that is life-threatening

feminization of poverty the trend of women making up an increasing proportion of the poor

MAKING THE GRADE

Social Class in the United States

Sample Test Questions

These questions are similar to those found in the test bank that accompanies this textbook.

Multiple-Choice Questions

1. Which of the following terms refers to earnings from work or investments?
   a. income
   b. assets
   c. wealth
   d. power

2. The wealthiest 20 percent of people in the United States own about how much of the country's privately owned wealth?
   a. 35 percent
   b. 55 percent
   c. 85 percent
   d. 95 percent

3. About what share of U.S. adults over the age of twenty-five are college graduates?
   a. 10 percent
   b. 28 percent
   c. 40 percent
   d. 68 percent

4. In the United States, average income for African American families is what share of average income for non-Hispanic white families?
   a. 86 percent
   b. 76 percent
   c. 66 percent
   d. 56 percent

5. Which of the following is another term for the "working class"?
   a. upper-middle class
   b. average-middle class
   c. lower-middle class
   d. lower class

6. In terms of health, people living in high-income families
   a. live in safer and less stressful environments.
   b. are more likely to describe their own health as "excellent."
   c. live longer lives.
   d. All of the above are correct.

7. Which quintile (20 percent) of the U.S. population has seen the greatest change in income over the last generation?
   a. the top quintile
   b. the middle quintile
   c. the lowest quintile
   d. All quintiles have seen the same change.

8. Change in social position during a person's own lifetime is called
   a. intergenerational social mobility.
   b. intragenerational social mobility.
   c. structural social mobility.
   d. horizontal social mobility.

9. In 2005, about what share of the U.S. population was officially counted as poor?
   a. 42.6 percent
   b. 22.6 percent
   c. 12.6 percent
   d. 2.6 percent

10. Which age category of the U.S. population has the highest percentage of people in poverty?
    a. seniors over age sixty-five
    b. middle-aged people
    c. young people aged eighteen to twenty-four
    d. children under age eighteen

ANSWERS: 1 (a); 2 (c); 3 (b); 4 (d); 5 (c); 6 (d); 7 (a); 8 (b); 9 (c); 10 (c).

Essay Questions

1. We often hear people say that the United States is a "middle-class society." Where does this idea come from? Based on what you have read in this chapter, how true do you think this claim is? Why?

2. What is the extent of poverty in the United States? Who are the poor in terms of age, race and ethnicity, and gender?

Global Stratification

FROM CHAPTER 12 OF *SOCIOLOGY*, 12/E. JOHN J. MACIONIS. COPYRIGHT © 2008 BY PEARSON EDUCATION. ALL RIGHTS RESERVED.

Around the world, social inequality is dramatic, with some people in some countries earning far more than people living elsewhere. Low wage levels is one reason many corporations that once produced their products in the United States now operate factories in China and other countries.

Masterfile Royalty Free

Global Stratification

WHAT share of the world's people live in absolute poverty?

WHY are some of the world's countries so rich and others so poor?

HOW do rich nations affect global poverty?

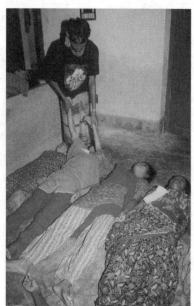

Getty Images, Inc.—
Agence France Presse

More than 1,000 workers were busily sewing together polo shirts on the fourth floor of the garment factory in Narsingdi, a small town about 30 miles northeast of Bangladesh's capital city of Dhaka. The thumping of hundreds of sewing machines combined to produce a steady roar that never stopped throughout the long working day.

But in an instant everything changed. An electric gun a worker used to shoot spot remover gave off a spark, which ignited the flammable liquid. Suddenly, a worktable burst into flames. People rushed to smother the fire with shirts, but there was no stopping the blaze: In a room filled with combustible materials, the flames spread quickly.

The workers scrambled toward the narrow staircase that led to the street. At the bottom, however, the human wave pouring down the steep steps collided with a folding metal gate across the doorway that was kept locked to prevent workers from leaving during working hours. Panicked, the people turned, only to be pushed back by the hundreds behind them. In a single terrifying minute of screaming voices, thrusting legs, and pounding hearts, dozens were crushed and trampled. By the time the gates were opened and the fire put out, fifty-two garment workers lay dead.

Garment factories like this one are big business in Bangladesh, where clothing accounts for 75 percent of the country's total economic exports. Half of these garments end up in stores in the United States. The reason so much of the clothing we buy is made in poor countries like Bangladesh is simple economics—Bangladeshi garment workers labor for close to twelve hours a day, typically seven days a week, and yet earn only about $500 a year, which is just a few percent of what a garment worker makes in the United States.

Tanveer Chowdhury manages the garment factory owned by his family. Speaking to reporters, he complained bitterly about the tragedy. "This fire has cost me $586,373, and that does not include $70,000 for machinery and $20,000 for furniture. I made commitments to meet deadlines, and I still have the deadlines. I am now paying for air freight at $10 a dozen when I should be shipping by sea at 87 cents a dozen."

There was one other cost Chowdhury did not mention. To compensate families for the loss of their loved ones in the fire, he eventually agreed to pay $1,952 per person. In Bangladesh, life—like labor—is cheap (based on Bearak, 2001).

Garment workers in Bangladesh are among the roughly 1 billion of the world's people who work hard every day and yet remain poor. As this chapter explains, although poverty is a reality in the United States and other nations, the greatest social inequality is not *within* nations but *between* them (Goesling, 2001). We can understand the full dimensions of poverty only by exploring **global stratification,** *patterns of social inequality in the world as a whole.*

Global Stratification: An Overview

In global perspective, however, social stratification is far greater. Figure 1 divides the world's total income by fifths of the population. The richest 20 percent of the U.S. population earn about 48 percent of the national income. The richest 20 percent of global population, however, receive about 80 percent of world income. At the other extreme, the poorest 20 percent of the U.S. population earn 4 percent of our national income; the poorest fifth of the world's people struggles to survive on just 1 percent of global income.

Because some countries are so much richer than others, even people in the United States with income below the government's poverty line live far better than the majority of people on the planet. The average person living in a rich nation such as the United States is extremely well off by world standards. At the very top of the pyramid, the wealth of the world's richest person (Bill Gates in the United States, who was worth about $53 billion in 2006) equals the total economic output of the world's forty-three poorest *countries* (Miller & Serafin, 2006; United Nations Development Programme, 2006).

A Word about Terminology

Classifying the 193 nations on Earth into categories ignores many striking differences. These nations have rich and varied histories, speak different languages, and take pride in distinctive cultures. However, various models have been developed that help distinguish countries on the basis of global stratification.

One such model, developed after World War II, labeled the rich, industrial countries the "First World"; the less industrialized, socialist countries the "Second World"; and nonindustrialized, poor countries the "Third World." But the "three worlds" model is now less

Chapter Overview

This chapter shifts the focus from inequality within the United States to inequality in the world as a whole. The chapter begins by describing global inequality and then provides two theoretical models that explain global stratification.

useful. For one thing, it was a product of Cold War politics by which the capitalist West (the First World) faced off against the socialist East (the Second World) while other nations (the Third World) remained more or less on the sidelines. But the sweeping changes in Eastern Europe and the collapse of the former Soviet Union in the early 1990s mean that a distinctive Second World no longer exists.

Another problem is that the "three worlds" model lumped together more than 100 countries as the Third World. In reality, some relatively better-off nations of the Third World (such as Chile in South America) have industrialized enough that they have more than ten times the per-person productivity of the poorest countries of the world (such as Ethiopia in East Africa).

These facts call for a modestly revised system of classification. The sixty *high-income countries* are defined as the richest nations with the highest overall standards of living. The world's seventy-six *middle-income countries* are not as rich; they are nations with a standard of living about average for the world as a whole. The remaining fifty-seven *low-income countries* are nations with a low standard of living in which most people are poor.

This model has two advantages over the older "three worlds" system. First, it focuses on economic development rather than political structure (capitalist or socialist). Second, it gives a better picture of the relative economic development of various countries because it does not lump together all less developed nations into a single "Third World."

When ranking countries, keep in mind that there is social stratification within every nation. In Bangladesh, for example, members of the Chowdhury family, who own the garment factory in the chapter-opening story, earn as much as $1 million per year, which is several thousand times more than their workers earn. Of course, the full extent of global inequality is even greater, because the wealthiest people in rich countries such as the United States live worlds apart from the poorest people in low-income nations such as Bangladesh, Haiti, or Sudan.

High-Income Countries

In nations where the Industrial Revolution first took place more than two centuries ago, productivity increased more than 100-fold. To understand the power of industrial and computer technology, consider that the Netherlands, one small European nation, is more productive than the whole continent of Africa south of the Sahara.

Global Map 1 shows that the high-income nations of the world include the United States and Canada, Argentina and Chile, the nations of Western Europe, Israel, Saudi Arabia, South Africa, Singapore, Hong Kong (part of the People's Republic of China), Japan, South Korea, Malaysia, Australia, and New Zealand.

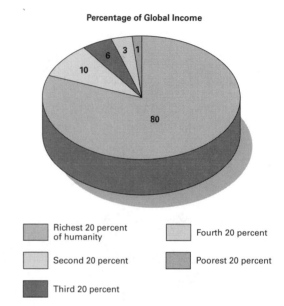

Percentage of Global Income

Richest 20 percent of humanity

Second 20 percent

Third 20 percent

Fourth 20 percent

Poorest 20 percent

FIGURE 1 Distribution of World Income

Global income is very unequal, with the richest 20 percent of the world's people earning eighty times as much as the poorest 20 percent.

Sources: Calculated by the author based on United Nations Development Programme (2000) and World Bank (2001).

These countries cover roughly 25 percent of Earth's land area, including parts of five continents, and they lie mostly in the Northern Hemisphere. In 2007, the total population of these nations was about 1.1 billion, or about 18 percent of the world's people. About three-fourths of the people in high-income countries live in or near cities.

Significant cultural differences exist among high-income countries; for example, the nations of Europe recognize more than thirty official languages. But these societies all produce enough economic goods and services to enable their people to lead comfortable lives. Per capita income (that is, average income per person per year) ranges from about $10,000 annually (in Malaysia and Chile) to more than $38,000 annually (in the United States and Norway). In fact, people in high-income countries enjoy 79 percent of the world's total income.

Keep in mind that high-income countries have many low-income people. The Thinking About Diversity: Race, Class, & Gender box profiles the striking poverty that exists along the southern border of the United States.

Production in rich nations is capital-intensive; it is based on factories, big machinery, and advanced technology. Most of the largest

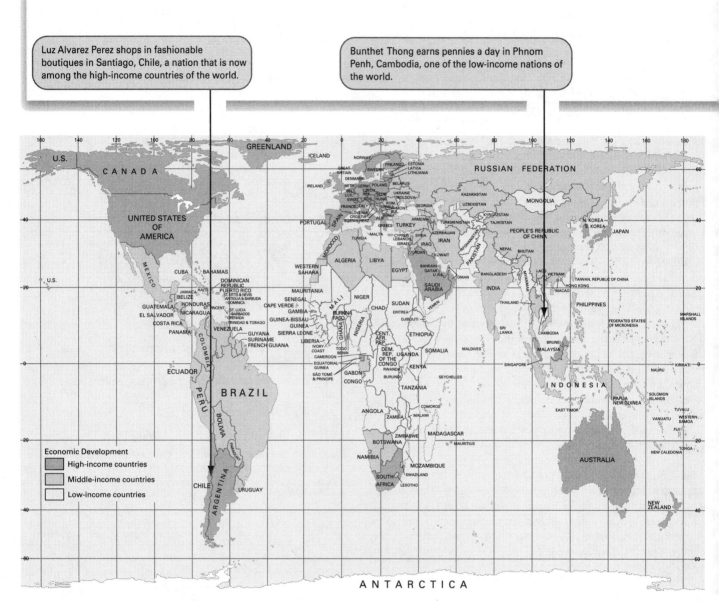

Luz Alvarez Perez shops in fashionable boutiques in Santiago, Chile, a nation that is now among the high-income countries of the world.

Bunthet Thong earns pennies a day in Phnom Penh, Cambodia, one of the low-income nations of the world.

Economic Development
High-income countries
Middle-income countries
Low-income countries

WINDOW ON THE WORLD

GLOBAL MAP 1   Economic Development in Global Perspective

In high-income countries—including the United States, Canada, Chile, Argentina, the nations of Western Europe, South Africa, Israel, Saudi Arabia, Malaysia, Australia, and Japan—a highly productive economy provides people, on average, with material plenty. Middle-income countries—including most of Latin America and Asia—are less economically productive, with a standard of living about average for the world as a whole but far below that of the United States. These nations also have a significant share of poor people who are barely able to feed and house themselves. In the low-income countries of the world, poverty is severe and widespread. Although small numbers of elites live very well in the poorest nations, most people struggle to survive on a small fraction of the income common in the United States.

Note: Data for this map are provided by the United Nations. Each country's economic productivity is measured in terms of its gross domestic product (GDP), which is the total value of all the goods and services produced by a country's economy within its borders in a given year. Dividing each country's GDP by the country's population gives us the per capita (per-person) GDP and allows us to compare the economic performance of countries of different population sizes. High-income countries have a per capita GDP of more than $10,000. Many are far richer than this, however; the figure for the United States exceeds $39,000. Middle-income countries have a per capita GDP ranging from $2,500 to $10,000. Low-income countries have a per capita GDP of less than $2,500. Figures used here reflect the United Nations "purchasing power parities" system, which is an estimate of what people can buy using their income in the local economy.

Source: Data from United Nations Development Programme (2006). Map projection from *Peters Atlas of the World* (1990).

get it right

Remember from Chapter 11 ("Social Class in the United States") that here at home, inequality of wealth is much greater than inequality of income. Notice in Figure 1 that the distribution of income for the world as a whole is similar to our national inequality of wealth.

 tip

Although most people think of severe poverty as something that exists only in some other nation, the box explains that the United States, too, has extremely poor communities.

 Thinking About Diversity: Race, Class, & Gender
Las Colonias: "America's Third World"

"We wanted to have something for ourselves," explains Olga Ruiz, who has lived in the border community of College Park, Texas, for eleven years. There is no college in College Park, nor does this dusty stretch of rural land have sewer lines or even running water. Yet this town is one of some 1,800 settlements that have sprouted up in southern Texas along the 1,200-mile border from El Paso down to Brownsville. Together, they are home to perhaps 700,000 people, a number expected to pass 1 million by 2010.

Many people speak of *las colonias* (Spanish for "the colonies") as "America's Third World" because these desperately poor communities look much like their counterparts in Mexico or many other middle- or low-income nations. But this is the United States, and almost all of the people living in the *colonias* are Hispanic Americans, 85 percent of them legal residents and more than half U.S. citizens.

Anastacia Ledsema, now seventy-two years old, moved to a *colonia* called Sparks more than forty years ago. Born in Mexico, Ledsema married a Texas man, and together they paid $200 for a quarter-acre lot in a

new border community. For months, they camped out on their land. Step by step, they invested their labor and their money to build a modest house. Not until 1995 did their small community get running water—a service that had been promised by developers years before. When the water line finally did arrive, however, things changed more than they expected. "When we got water," recalls Ledsema, "that's when so many people came in." The population of Sparks quickly doubled to about 3,000, overwhelming the water supply so that sometimes the faucet does not run at all.

The residents of all the *colonias* know that they are poor. Indeed, the Census Bureau

© Peter Turnley/Corbis. All rights reserved

declared the county surrounding one border community the poorest in the United States. Concerned over the lack of basic services in so many of these communities, Texas officials have banned new settlements. But most of the people who move here—even those who start off sleeping in their cars or trucks—see these communities as the first step on the path to the American dream. Oscar Solis, a neighborhood leader in Panorama Village, a community with a population of about 150, is proud to show visitors around the small but growing town. "All of this work we have done ourselves," he says with a smile, "to make our dreams come true."

WHAT DO YOU THINK?

1. Are you surprised that such poverty exists in the United States? Why or why not?

2. Why do you think such communities get little attention from the U.S. mass media?

3. To what extent do you think people living in these communities will have their "dreams come true"? Explain.

Source: Based on Schaffer (2002).

corporations that design and market computers, as well as most computer users, are located in high-income countries. High-income countries control the world's financial markets, so daily events in the financial exchanges of New York, London, and Tokyo affect people throughout the world.

Middle-Income Countries

Middle-income countries have a per capita income of between $2,500 and $10,000, roughly the median for the world's nations. Two-thirds of the people in middle-income countries live in cities, and industrial jobs are common. The remaining one-third of people live in rural

areas, where most are poor and lack access to schools, medical care, adequate housing, and even safe drinking water.

Looking at Global Map 1, we see that seventy-six of the world's nations fall into the middle-income category. At the high end are Mexico (Latin America) and Botswana (Africa), where annual income is about $9,800. At the low end are Bolivia (Latin America), Lesotho (Africa), and Vietnam (Asia), with roughly $3,000 annually in per capita income.

One cluster of middle-income countries consists of what used to be known as the Second World, including the countries that once made up the Soviet Union and the nations of Eastern Europe. These countries had mostly socialist economies until popular revolts between

tip
Looking at the three photographs on this page,
you begin to see how a country's level of
economic development is evident in everyday
life.

student 2 student
"It seems to me that until we figure out a way to
get economic inequality way down, our world is
unlikely to ever know peace."

Japan is among the world's high-income countries, in which industrial technology and economic expansion have produced material prosperity. The presence of market forces is evident in this view of downtown Tokyo (above, left). The Russian Federation is one of the middle-income countries of the world. Industrial development and economic performance were sluggish under socialism; as a result, Moscow residents had to wait in long lines for their daily needs (above, right). The hope is that the introduction of a market system will raise living standards, although in the short run, Russian citizens must adjust to increasing economic inequality. Bangladesh (left) is among the world's low-income countries. As the photograph suggests, these nations have limited economic development and rapidly increasing populations. The result is widespread poverty.

Martin Benjamin/The Image Works (*top left*); Peter Turnley/Corbis/Bettmann (*top right*); Pablo Bartholomew (*bottom left*)

1989 and 1991 swept their governments aside. Since then, these nations have begun to introduce market systems, but so far the results have been uneven. Some (including Poland) have improving economies, but living standards in others (including Russia) have fallen.

Other middle-income nations include Peru and Brazil in South America and Namibia and Gabon in Africa. Recently, both India and the People's Republic of China have entered the middle-income category, which now includes most of Asia.

Taken together, middle-income countries span roughly 55 percent of Earth's land area and are home to about 4.5 billion people, or about 70 percent of humanity. Some countries (such as Russia) are far less crowded than others (such as El Salvador), but compared to high-income countries, these societies are densely populated.

Why do you think most people from high-income countries who travel to middle- or low-income nations do so as tourists, but most who travel from middle- or low-income nations to high-income countries do so as immigrants?

Low-Income Countries

Low-income countries, where most people are very poor, are mostly agrarian societies with some industry. Fifty-seven low-income countries, identified in Global Map 1, are spread across Central and East Africa and Asia. Low-income countries cover 20 percent of the planet's land area and are home to 12 percent of its people. Population density is generally high, although it is greater in Asian countries (such as Bangladesh and Pakistan) than in Central African nations (such as Chad and the Democratic Republic of the Congo).

In poor countries, one-third of the people live in cities; most inhabit villages and farms as their ancestors have done for centuries. In fact, half the world's people are farmers, most of whom follow cultural traditions. With limited industrial technology, they cannot be very productive, one reason that many suffer severe poverty. Hunger, disease, and unsafe housing shape the lives of the world's poorest people.

People living in affluent nations such as the United States find it hard to understand the scope of human need in much of the world. From time to time, televised pictures of famine in very poor countries

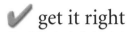
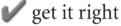
such as Ethiopia and Bangladesh give us shocking glimpses of the poverty that makes every day a life-and-death struggle for many people in low-income nations. Behind these images lie cultural, historical, and economic forces that we shall explore in the remainder of this chapter.

Global Wealth and Poverty

 October 14, Manila, Philippines. What caught my eye was how clean she was—a girl no more than seven or eight years old. She was wearing a freshly laundered dress, and her hair was carefully combed. She stopped to watch us, following us with her eyes: Camera-toting Americans stand out here, one of the poorest neighborhoods in the world.

Fed by methane from decomposing garbage, the fires never go out on Smokey Mountain, the vast garbage dump on the north side of Manila. Smoke covers the hills of refuse like a thick fog. But Smokey Mountain is more than a dump; it is a neighborhood that is home to thousands of people. It is hard to imagine a setting more hostile to human life. Amid the smoke and the squalor, men and women do what they can to survive. They pick plastic bags from the garbage and wash them in the river, and they collect cardboard boxes or anything else they can sell. What chance do their children have, coming from families that earn only a few hundred dollars a year, with hardly any opportunity for schooling, year after year breathing this foul air? Against this backdrop of human tragedy, one lovely little girl has put on a fresh dress and gone out to play.

Now our taxi driver threads his way through heavy traffic as we head for the other side of Manila. The change is amazing: The smoke and smell of the dump give way to neighborhoods that could be in Miami or Los Angeles. A cluster of yachts floats on the bay in the distance. No more rutted streets; now we glide quietly along wide boulevards lined with trees and filled with expensive Japanese cars. We pass shopping plazas, upscale hotels, and high-rise office buildings. Every block or so we see the gated entrance to yet another exclusive residential community with security guards standing watch. Here, in large, air-conditioned homes, the rich of Manila live—and many of the poor work.

Low-income nations are home to some rich and many poor people. The fact that most people live with incomes of just a few hundred dollars a year means that the burden of poverty is far greater than among the poor of the United States. This is not to suggest that U.S. poverty is a minor problem. In so rich a country, too little food, sub-

standard housing, and no medical care for tens of millions of people—almost half of them children—amount to a national tragedy.

The Severity of Poverty

Poverty in poor countries is more severe than it is in rich countries. A key reason that the quality of life differs so much around the world is that economic productivity is lowest in precisely the regions where population growth is highest. Figure 2 shows the proportion of world population and global income for countries at each level of economic development. High-income countries are by far the most advantaged, with 79 percent of global income supporting just 18 percent of humanity. In middle-income nations, 70 percent of the world's people earn 20 percent of global income. This leaves 12 percent of the planet's population with just 1 percent of global income. In short, for every dollar received by individuals in a low-income country, someone in a high-income country takes home $53.

Table 1 shows the extent of wealth and well-being in specific countries around the world. The first column of figures gives gross domestic product (GDP) for a number of high-, middle-, and low-

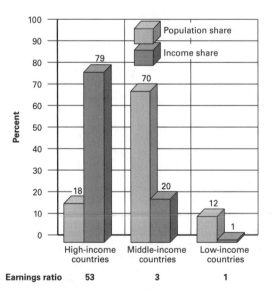

FIGURE 2 The Relative Share of Income and Population by Level of Economic Development

For every dollar earned by people in low-income countries, people in high-income countries earn $53.

Sources: Calculated by the author based on United Nations Development Programme (2000) and World Bank (2001).

tip

As you look at Table 1, remember that GDP depends on both level of economic development and the country's population size; per capita GDP is a good measure of average living standards; the UN quality of life index reflects not only income levels but also a society's health and levels of inequality.

tip

Look carefully at Global Map 2. There is probably no more dramatic indication of the effects of poverty than its effects on life span.

Table 1 Wealth and Well-Being in Global Perspective, 2004

Country	Gross Domestic Product (US$ billions)	GDP per Capita (PPP US$)*	Quality of Life Index
High-Income			
Norway	250	38,454	.965
Australia	637	30,331	.957
Sweden	346	29,541	.951
Canada	978	31,263	.950
Japan	4,623	29,251	.949
United States	11,712	39,676	.948
United Kingdom	2,124	30,821	.940
South Korea	680	20,499	.912
Middle-Income			
Eastern Europe			
Romania	73	8,480	.805
Russian Federation	581	9,902	.797
Ukraine	65	6,394	.774
Latin America			
Mexico	677	9,803	.821
Brazil	604	8,195	.792
Venezuela	110	6,043	.784
Asia			
Thailand	162	8,090	.784
People's Republic of China	1,932	5,896	.768
India	691	3,139	.611
Middle East			
Iran	163	7,525	.746
Syria	24	3,610	.716
Africa			
Algeria	85	6,603	.728
Botswana	9	9,945	.570
Low-Income			
Latin America			
Haiti	4	1,892	.482
Asia			
Cambodia	5	2,423	.583
Pakistan	96	2,225	.539
Bangladesh	57	1,870	.530
Africa			
Guinea	4	2,180	.445
Ethiopia	8	756	.371
Niger	3	779	.311

*These data are the United Nations' purchasing power parity (PPP) calculations, which avoid currency rate distortion by showing the local purchasing power of each domestic currency.

Source: United Nations Development Programme, *Human Development Report 2006* (New York: Palgrave Macmillan, 2006).

income countries.[1] The United States, a large and highly productive nation, had a 2004 GDP of more than $11 trillion; Japan's GDP was more than $4 trillion. A comparison of GDP figures shows that the world's richest nations are thousands of times more productive than the poorest countries.

The second column of figures in Table 1 divides GDP by the entire population size to give an estimate of what people can buy with their income in the local economy. The per capita GDP for rich countries like the United States, Sweden, and Canada is very high, exceeding $29,000. For middle-income countries, such as Mexico and the Russian Federation, the figures are in the $9,000 range. In the world's low-income countries, per capita GDP is just a few hundred dollars. In Niger or in Ethiopia, for example, a typical person labors all year to make what the average worker in the United States earns in a week.

The last column of Table 1 measures quality of life in the various nations. This index, calculated by the United Nations, is based on income, education (extent of adult literacy and average years of schooling), and longevity (how long people typically live). Index values are decimals that fall between extremes of one (highest) and zero (lowest). By this calculation, Norwegians enjoy the highest quality of life (.965), with residents of the United States close behind (.948). At the other extreme, people in the African nation of Niger have the lowest quality of life (.311).

Relative versus Absolute Poverty

The distinction between relative and absolute poverty has an important application to global inequality. People living in rich countries generally focus on *relative poverty,* meaning that some people lack resources that are taken for granted by others. By definition, relative poverty exists in every society, rich or poor.

More important in global perspective, however, is *absolute poverty,* a lack of resources that is life-threatening. Human beings in absolute poverty lack the nutrition necessary for health and long-term survival. To be sure, some absolute poverty exists in the United States. But such immediately life-threatening poverty strikes only a very small proportion of the U.S. population; in low-income countries, by contrast, one-third or more of the people are in desperate need.

Because absolute poverty is deadly, one global indicator of this problem is median age at death. Global Map 2 identifies the age by which half of all people born in a nation die. In rich societies, most people die after the age of seventy-five; in poor countries, half of all deaths occur among children under the age of ten.

---

[1]Gross domestic product is the value of all the goods and services produced by a country's economy within its borders in a given year.

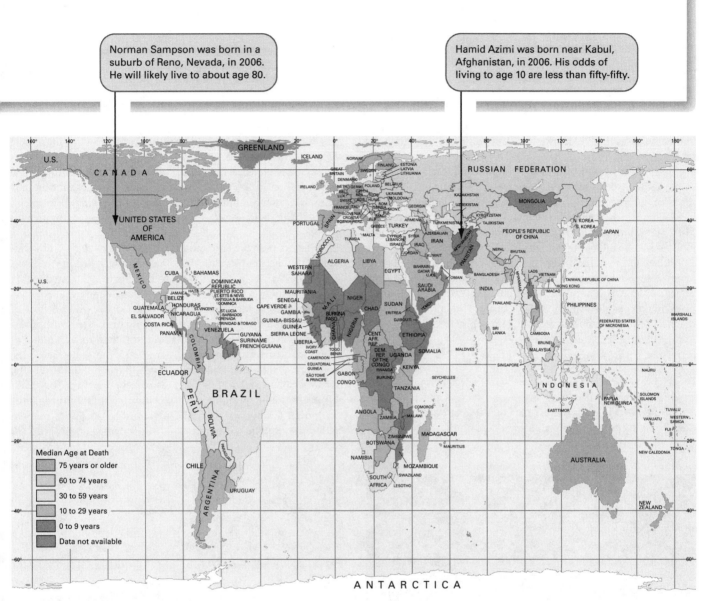

Norman Sampson was born in a suburb of Reno, Nevada, in 2006. He will likely live to about age 80.

Hamid Azimi was born near Kabul, Afghanistan, in 2006. His odds of living to age 10 are less than fifty-fifty.

Median Age at Death
- 75 years or older
- 60 to 74 years
- 30 to 59 years
- 10 to 29 years
- 0 to 9 years
- Data not available

WINDOW ON THE WORLD

GLOBAL MAP 2   Median Age at Death in Global Perspective

This map identifies the age below which half of all deaths occur in any year. In the high-income countries of the world, including the United States, it is mostly the elderly who face death, that is, people aged seventy-five or older. In middle-income countries, including most of Latin America, most people die years or even decades earlier. In low-income countries, especially in Africa and parts of Asia, it is children who die, half of them never reaching their tenth birthday.

Sources: World Bank (1993), with updates by the author; map projection from *Peters Atlas of the World* (1990).

The Extent of Poverty

Poverty in poor countries is more widespread than it is in rich nations such as the United States. The U.S. government officially classifies almost 13 percent of the population as poor. In low-income coun- tries, however, most people live no better than the poor in the United States, and many are far worse off. As Global Map 2 shows, the high death rates among children in Africa indicate that absolute poverty is greatest there, where half the population is malnourished. In the world as a whole, at any given time, 15 percent of the people—about 1 bil- lion—suffer from chronic hunger, which leaves them less able to work

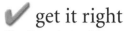 **get it right**

The discussion on this page includes the stunning fact that 15 million people on the planet die each year from various causes related to poverty and hunger.

 tip

The description of the lives of poor children is very different from what most people in this country think of as an ideal childhood.

and puts them at high risk of disease (United Nations Development Programme, 2001; Chen & Ravallion, 2004).

The typical adult in a rich nation such as the United States consumes about 3,500 calories a day, an excess that contributes to widespread obesity and related health problems. The typical adult in a low-income country not only does more physical labor but consumes just 2,000 calories a day. The result is undernourishment: too little food or not enough of the right kinds of food.

In the ten minutes it takes to read this section of the chapter, about 300 people in the world who are sick and weakened from hunger will die. This number amounts to about 40,000 people a day, or 15 million people each year. Clearly, easing world hunger is one of the most serious responsibilities facing humanity today.

Poverty and Children

Death comes early in poor societies, where families lack adequate food, safe water, secure housing, and access to medical care. Organizations fighting child poverty estimate that at least 100 million children living in cities in poor countries beg, steal, sell sex, or work for drug gangs to provide income for their families. Such a life almost always means dropping out of school and puts children at high risk of disease and violence. Many girls, with little or no access to medical assistance, become pregnant, a case of children who cannot support themselves having children of their own. "In the *Times*" takes a look at how living in a poor country limits children's opportunities for schooling.

Analysts estimate that another 100 million of the world's children leave their families altogether, sleeping and living on the streets as best they can or perhaps trying to migrate to the United States. Roughly 50 million of these street children are found in Latin American cities such as Mexico City and Rio de Janeiro, where half of all children grow up in poverty. Many people in the United States know these cities as exotic travel destinations, but they are also home to thousands of street children living in makeshift huts, under bridges, or in alleyways. In Africa, according to recent reports, children in the Darfur region of Sudan are subject to not just poverty but "unspeakable abuse," being forced to join armed rebel or militia groups, provide physical labor without pay, and work as sex slaves (United Nations Development Programme, 2000; Collymore, 2002; Leopold, 2007).

 How do you think the experience of childhood as a stage of the life course differs in high- and low-income countries?

Poverty and Women

In rich societies, much of the work women do is undervalued, underpaid, or overlooked entirely. In poor societies, women face even greater disadvantages. Most of the people who work in sweatshops like the one described in the opening to this chapter are women.

To make matters worse, tradition keeps women out of many jobs in low-income nations; in Bangladesh, for example, women work in garment factories because that society's conservative Muslim religious norms bar them from most other paid work and limit their opportunity for advanced schooling (Bearak, 2001). At the same time, traditional norms in poor societies give women primary responsibility for child rearing and maintaining the household. The United Nations estimates that in poor countries, men own 90 percent of the land, a far greater gender disparity in wealth than is found in high-income nations. It is no surprise, then, that about 70 percent of the world's 1 billion people living near absolute poverty are women (C. Hymowitz, 1995).

Tens of millions of children fend for themselves every day on the streets of Latin America, where many fall victim to disease, drug abuse, and violence. What do you think must be done to put an end to scenes like this one in Kathmandu, Nepal?

The New York Times

Crowds of Pupils but Little Else in African Schools

By SHARON LAFRANIERE
December 30, 2006

Even before workers hung the last wooden shutter on the new classrooms here, School H was overcrowded.

Makamba Keito, the school's director, was expecting no more than 420 first through sixth graders. But as he opened registration on a sizzling Saturday in September, twice that number were already on the list—and those were only the students who had transferred from other jam-packed schools nearby.

Mr. Keito registered a few dozen more, then halted with a whopping 887 pupils, an average of 126 per teacher. "That's it," he recalled telling parents who had been turned away. "You must go find some other place."

Finding places for millions of new students is one of sub-Saharan Africa's most overwhelming and gratifying missions. After two decades of sluggish growth in enrollment rates, the region's 45 countries find themselves with an embarrassment of eager schoolchildren.

Nearly 22 million more students flooded classrooms between 1999 and 2004, increasing the enrollment rate by 18 percent, more than any other region of the world, according to Unesco. More than 6 out of 10 primary school-age children are now enrolled. . . .

"The whole climate has changed," said Nicholas Burnett, who produces an annual global report on schooling for Unesco. "Resources are becoming available. You can definitely see the attitudes of African parents changing. Africa is starting to move in such a positive direction."

Two trends have converged to produce such change: One is a new willingness by international donors and African governments to spend hundreds of millions of dollars more on basic education. That has fed a rising demand for education by the region's parents, who for perhaps the first time see a chance to give their children a future that they were denied.

The challenges, however, remain staggering. Foremost is a flood tide of school-age children in a region whose birth rate is nearly twice the world's average. Forty-four in 100 sub-Saharan residents are under age 15, the highest proportion on Earth. By some estimates, the next decade could raise the school-age population by another 28 million.

The region must absorb those newcomers while trying to lift itself from the subbasement of global education. Sub-Saharan Africa is home to barely one-sixth of the world's children under 15, but fully half the world's uneducated children—the legacy of poverty, colonialism and historically inadequate schools. . . .

The pupil-teacher ratio, averaging 44 to 1, is the world's highest; the percentage of trained teachers is among the lowest.

Mali is a template for those challenges. One of Earth's poorest nations, it also has the world's second-highest birth rate,

behind only neighboring Niger. It lags even most African nations in the share of children in primary school.

Yet a crusade is under way to get Malian children out of thatched huts and arid fields and into classrooms. . . .

School H, in the dusty suburbs of Mali's fast-growing capital, exemplifies how far the region has come—and how far it still must go.

The latest newcomer to H's staff is Miriam Coulibaly, whose delicate features hide a ferocious teaching style. Just 25, she graduated in June from one of Mali's revived teacher training institutes. All but three institutes were closed during the budget-slashing of the 1980s; today, about a dozen churn out new teachers.

One recent Friday, a gaggle of second graders, crammed five to a desk, clamored for Mrs. Coulibaly's attention as she whipped through her classroom's narrow aisles. She teaches half of her 195 pupils in the morning, runs home for lunch, then races back to teach the other half.

Perhaps three of them have textbooks. . . . Mrs. Coulibaly said she had to borrow textbooks herself, just to create her lessons. "Textbooks would make my job so much easier," she said as pandemonium reigned in the dirt schoolyard during recess. "They have nothing—no reading, no language, no math books, nothing. They may not even have a simple piece of chalk." . . .

The sixth grade is School H's second smallest, with one class of 105 students, some as old as 17. Fewer than half of Mali's primary school students finish sixth grade. One in five repeats a grade. . . .

Such discouraging figures do not diminish Kadia Keita's sense that she is part of a historic shift. One morning in December, she asked her 125 third graders how many were first-generation learners whose parents could neither read nor write.

A third of the hands shot up.

"This is why I am here," she said, before reading a few sentences in French off the blackboard, tapping out each word with a broken twig in lieu of a pointer. "It is not the numbers I look at. It is the kids." . . .

WHAT DO YOU THINK?

1. Why do you think parents in traditional societies may not encourage their children to attend school?

2. Why are schooling and literacy important factors that help a society's economic development?

3. What strategies would you suggest to lift educational achievement in a low-income country such as Mali?

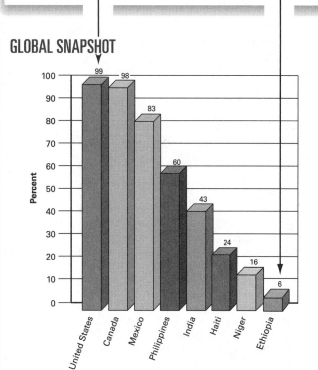

Compared to a woman in the United States, an Ethiopian woman is far less likely to give birth with the help of medical professionals and is much more likely to die in childbirth.

GLOBAL SNAPSHOT

FIGURE 3 Percentage of Births Attended by Skilled Health Staff

In the United States, most women give birth with the help of medical professionals, but this is usually not the case in low-income nations.
Source: World Bank (2007).

 tip

Many people living in this country think of slavery as something that existed way back in our history. But slavery is a reality in some of the world today, one serious consequence of global poverty.

Finally, most women in poor countries receive little or no reproductive health care. Limited access to birth control keeps women at home with their children, keeps the birth rate high, and limits the economic production of the country. In addition, the world's poorest women typically give birth without help from trained health care personnel. Figure 3 draws a stark difference between low- and high-income countries in this regard.

Slavery

Poor societies have many problems in addition to hunger, including illiteracy, warfare, and even slavery. The British Empire banned slavery in 1833, followed by the United States in 1865. But according to Anti-Slavery International (ASI), as many as 200 million men, women, and children (about 3 percent of humanity) still live in conditions that amount to slavery.

ASI distinguishes four types of slavery. The first is *chattel slavery,* in which one person owns another. The number of chattel slaves is difficult to estimate because this practice is against the law almost everywhere. But the buying and selling of slaves still takes place in many countries in Asia, the Middle East, and especially Africa. The Thinking Globally box describes the reality of one slave's life in the African nation of Mauritania.

A second, more common form of bondage is *child slavery,* in which desperately poor families send their children out into the streets to beg or steal or do whatever they can to survive. Perhaps 100 million children—many in the poorest countries of Latin America and Africa—fall into this category.

Third, *debt bondage* is the practice by which an employer pays workers wages that are not enough to cover the food and housing provided by the employer. Unable to settle their ever-increasing debts, workers cannot leave and are therefore slaves. Many sweatshop workers in low-income nations fall into this category.

Fourth, *servile forms of marriage* may also amount to slavery. In India, Thailand, and some African nations, families marry off women against their will. Many end up as slaves working for their husband's family; some are forced into prostitution.

An additional form of slavery is *human trafficking,* the moving of men, women, and children from one place to another for the purpose of performing forced labor. Women or men are brought to a new country with the promise of a job and then forced to become prostitutes or farm laborers, or people adopt children from another country and then force them to work in sweatshops. Such activity is big business: Next to trading in guns and drugs, trading in people brings the greatest profit to organized crime around the world (Orhant, 2002).

In 1948, the United Nations issued its Universal Declaration of Human Rights, which states, "No one shall be held in slavery or servitude; slavery and the slave trade shall be prohibited in all their forms." Unfortunately, six decades later, this social evil persists.

Explanations of Global Poverty

What accounts for the severe and extensive poverty throughout much of the world? The rest of this chapter provides answers using the following facts about poor societies:

1. **Technology.** About one-quarter of people in low-income countries farm the land using human muscle or animal power. With limited energy sources, economic production is modest.

2. **Population growth.** The poorest countries have the world's highest birth rates. Despite the death toll from poverty, the

tip

In many respects, women are disadvantaged in relation to men. In poor societies, this inequality is typically greater than in the United States.

 tip

The list beginning on the previous page identifies six factors that play a part in explaining global poverty. As you read on, you will see that the first three are closer to modernization theory and the next three are closer to dependency theory.

Thinking Globally
"God Made Me to Be a Slave"

Fatma Mint Mamadou is a young woman living in North Africa's Islamic Republic of Mauritania. Asked her age, she pauses, smiles, and shakes her head. She has no idea when she was born. Nor can she read or write. What she knows is tending camels, herding sheep, hauling bags of water, sweeping, and serving tea to her owners. This young woman is one of perhaps 90,000 slaves in Mauritania.

In the central region of this nation, having dark brown skin almost always means being a slave to an Arab owner. Fatma accepts her situation; she has known nothing else. She explains in a matter-of-fact voice that she is a slave like her mother before her and her grandmother before that. "Just as God created a camel to be a camel," she shrugs, "he created me to be a slave."

Fatma, her mother, and her brothers and sisters live in a squatter settlement on the edge of Nouakchott, Mauritania's capital city. Their home is a 9-by-12-foot hut that they built from wood scraps and other mate-rials found at construction sites. The roof is nothing more than a piece of cloth; there is no plumbing or furniture. The nearest water comes from a well a mile down the road.

In this region, slavery began 500 years ago, about the time Columbus sailed west toward the Americas. As Arab and Berber tribes raided local villages, they made slaves of the people, and so it has been for dozens

Human slavery continues to exist in the twenty-first century.

Malcolm Linton/Getty Images, Inc—Liaison

of generations ever since. In 1905, the French colonial rulers of Mauritania banned slavery. After the nation gained independence in 1961, the new government reaffirmed the ban. But such proclamations have done little to change strong traditions. Indeed, people like Fatma have no idea what "freedom to choose" means.

The next question is more personal: "Are you and other girls ever raped?" Again, Fatma hesitates. With no hint of emotion, she responds, "Of course, in the night the men come to breed us. Is that what you mean by rape?"

WHAT DO YOU THINK?

1. How does tradition play a part in keeping people in slavery?

2. Why do you think the world still tolerates slavery?

3. Explain the connection between slavery and poverty.

Source: Based on Burkett (1997).

populations of many poor countries in Africa, for example, double every twenty-five years. In these countries, half the people are teenagers or younger. With so many people entering their childbearing years, a wave of population growth will roll into the future. In recent years, for example, the population of Chad has swelled by 2.8 percent annually, so even with economic development, living standards have fallen.

3. **Cultural patterns.** Poor societies are usually traditional. Holding on to long-established ways of life means resisting change—even change that promises a richer material life. The Seeing Sociology in Everyday Life box explains why traditional people in India respond to their poverty differently than poor people in the United States.

4. **Social stratification.** Low-income societies distribute their wealth very unequally. Social inequality is greater in agrarian societies than in industrial societies. In Brazil, for example, half of all farmland is owned by just 1 percent of the people (Bergamo & Camarotti, 1996).

5. **Gender inequality.** Gender inequality in poor societies keeps women from holding jobs, which typically means they have many children. An expanding population, in turn, slows economic development. Many analysts conclude that raising living standards in much of the world depends on improving the social standing of women.

6. **Global power relationships.** A final cause of global poverty lies in the relationships between the nations of the world.

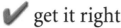
Seeing Sociology in Everyday Life
"Happy Poverty" in India: Making Sense of a Strange Idea

Although India has become a middle-income nation, its per capita GDP is just $3,139, less than one-tenth that in the United States. For this reason, India is home to one-fourth of the world's hungry people.

But most North Americans do not readily understand the reality of poverty in India. Many of the country's 1.1 billion people live in conditions far worse than those our society labels "poor." A traveler's first experience of Indian life can be shocking. Chennai (formerly known as Madras), for example, one of India's largest cities with 7 million inhabitants, seems chaotic to an outsider—streets choked with motorbikes, trucks, carts pulled by oxen, and waves of people. Along the roadway, vendors sit on burlap cloths selling fruits, vegetables, and cooked food while people nearby talk, bathe, and sleep.

Although some people live well, Chennai is dotted with more than 1,000 shanty settlements, home to half a million people from rural villages who have come in search of a better life. Shantytowns are clusters of huts built with branches, leaves, and pieces of discarded cardboard and tin. These dwellings offer little privacy and have no refrigeration, running water, or bathrooms. A visitor from the United States may feel uneasy in such an area, knowing that the poorest sections of our own inner cities seethe with frustration and sometimes explode with violence.

But India's people understand poverty differently than we do. No restless young men hang out at the corner, no drug dealers work the streets, and there is little danger of violence. In the United States, poverty often means anger and isolation; in India, even shantytowns are organized around strong families—children, parents, and often grand-parents—who offer a smile of welcome to a stranger.

For traditional people in India, life is shaped by *dharma,* the Hindu concept of duty and destiny that teaches people to accept their fate, whatever it may be. Mother Teresa, who worked among the poorest of India's people, went to the heart of the cultural differences: "Americans have angry poverty," she explained. "In India, there is worse poverty, but it is a happy poverty."

Perhaps we should not describe anyone who clings to the edge of survival as happy. But poverty in India is eased by the strength and support of families and communities, a sense that life has a purpose, and a world-view that encourages each person to accept whatever life offers. As a result, a visitor may well come away from a first encounter with Indian poverty in confusion: "How can people be so poor and yet apparently content, active, and *joyful?*"

WHAT DO YOU THINK?

1. What did Mother Teresa mean when she said that in India there is "happy poverty"?

2. How might an experience like this in a very poor community change the way you think of being "rich"?

3. Do you know of any poor people in the United States who have attitudes toward poverty similar to these people in India? What would make people seem to accept being poor?

Steve Maines/Stock Boston

Historically, wealth flowed from poor societies to rich nations through **colonialism,** *the process by which some nations enrich themselves through political and economic control of other nations.* The countries of Western Europe colonized much of Latin America beginning roughly 500 years ago. Such global exploitation allowed some nations to develop economically at the expense of other nations.

Although 130 former colonies gained their independence during the twentieth century, exploitation continues today through **neocolonialism** (*neo* is Greek for "new"), *a new form of global power relationships that involves not direct political control but economic exploitation by multinational corporations.* A **multinational corporation** is *a large business that operates in many countries.* Corporate leaders often impose their will on countries in which they do business to create favorable economic conditions for the operation of their corporations, just as colonizers did in the past (Bonanno, Constance, & Lorenz, 2000).

In rich nations such as the United States, most parents expect their children to enjoy years of childhood, largely free from the responsibilities of adult life. This is not the case in poor nations across Latin America, Africa, and Asia. Poor families depend on whatever income their children can earn, and many children as young as six or seven work full days weaving or performing other kinds of manual labor. Child labor lies behind the low prices of many products imported for sale in this country.

Joe McDonald/Corbis/Bettmann (*left*); Robert van der Hilst/Corbis/Bettmann (*center*); Wolfgang Kaehler/Corbis/Bettmann (*right*)

Global Stratification: Theoretical Analysis

There are two major explanations for the unequal distribution of the world's wealth and power: *modernization theory* and *dependency theory*. Each theory suggests a different solution to the suffering of hungry people in much of the world.

Modernization Theory

Modernization theory is *a model of economic and social development that explains global inequality in terms of technological and cultural differences between nations.* Modernization theory emerged in the 1950s, a time when U.S. society was fascinated by new developments in technology. To showcase the power of productive technology and also to counter the growing influence of the Soviet Union, U.S. policymakers drafted a market-based foreign policy that has been with us ever since (Rostow, 1960, 1978; Bauer, 1981; Berger, 1986; Firebaugh, 1996; Firebaugh & Sandhu, 1998).

Historical Perspective

Until a few centuries ago, the entire world was poor. Because poverty is the norm throughout human history, modernization theory claims that it is *affluence* that demands an explanation.

Affluence came within reach of a growing share of people in Western Europe during the late Middle Ages as world exploration and trade expanded. Soon after, the Industrial Revolution transformed first Western Europe and then North America. Industrial technology and the spirit of capitalism created new wealth as never before. At first, this wealth benefited only a few. But industrial technology was so productive that gradually the living standards of even the poorest people began to improve. Absolute poverty, which had plagued humanity throughout history, was finally in decline.

In high-income countries, where the Industrial Revolution began in the late 1700s or early 1800s, the standard of living jumped at least fourfold during the twentieth century. As middle-income nations in Asia and Latin America have industrialized, they too have become richer. But with limited industrial technology, low-income countries have changed much less.

The Importance of Culture

Why didn't the Industrial Revolution sweep away poverty the world over? Modernization theory points out that not every society wants to adopt new technology. Doing so takes a cultural environment that emphasizes the benefits of material wealth and new ideas.

Modernization theory identifies *tradition* as the greatest barrier to economic development. In some societies, strong family systems and a reverence for the past discourage people from adopting new technologies that would raise their living standards. Even today, many people—from the Amish in North America to Islamic people in the Middle East to the Semai of Malaysia—oppose new technology as a threat to their families, customs, and religious beliefs.

Max Weber (1958, orig. 1904–05) found that at the end of the Middle Ages, Western Europe's cultural environment favored change. The Protestant Reformation reshaped traditional Christian beliefs to generate a progress-oriented way of life. Wealth—looked on with suspicion by the Catholic church—became a sign of personal virtue, and the growing importance of individualism steadily replaced the traditional emphasis on family and community. Taken together, these new cultural patterns nurtured the Industrial Revolution.

Rostow's Stages of Modernization

Modernization theory holds that the door to affluence is open to all. As technological advances spread around the world, all societies should gradually industrialize. According to Walt W. Rostow (1960, 1978), modernization occurs in four stages:

1. **Traditional stage.** Socialized to honor the past, people in traditional societies cannot easily imagine that life could or should be any different. They therefore build their lives around families and local communities, following well-worn paths that allow little individual freedom or change. Life is often spiritually rich but lacking in material goods.

   A century ago, much of the world was in this initial stage of economic development. Nations such as Bangladesh, Niger, and Somalia are still at the traditional stage and remain poor.

2. **Take-off stage.** As a society shakes off the grip of tradition, people start to use their talents and imagination, sparking economic growth. A market emerges as people produce goods not just for their own use but to trade with others for profit. Greater individualism, a willingness to take risks, and a desire for material goods also take hold, often at the expense of family ties and time-honored norms and values.

   Great Britain reached take-off by about 1800, the United States by 1820. Thailand, a middle-income country in eastern Asia, is now in this stage. Such development is typically speeded by help from rich nations, including foreign aid, the availability of advanced technology and investment capital, and opportunities for schooling abroad.

3. **Drive to technological maturity.** In this stage, "growth" is a widely accepted idea that fuels a society's pursuit of higher living standards. A diversified economy drives a population eager to enjoy the benefits of industrial technology. At the same time, however, people begin to realize (and sometimes regret) that industrialization is eroding traditional family and local community life. Great Britain reached this point by about 1840, the United States by 1860. Today, Mexico, the U.S. territory of Puerto Rico, and South Korea are among the nations driving to technological maturity.

   Absolute poverty is greatly reduced in nations in this stage of development. Cities swell with people who leave rural villages in search of economic opportunity. Specialization creates the wide range of jobs that we find in our economy today. An increasing focus on work makes relationships less personal. Growing individualism generates social movements demanding greater political rights. Societies approaching technological maturity also provide basic schooling for all their people and advanced training for some. The newly educated consider tradition "backward" and push for further change. The social position of women steadily approaches that of men.

   SOCIOLOGY @ WORK

4. **High mass consumption.** Economic development steadily raises living standards as mass production stimulates mass consumption. Simply put, people soon learn to "need" the expanding array of goods that their society produces. The United States, Japan, and other rich nations moved into this stage by 1900. Now entering this level of economic development are two former British colonies that are prosperous small societies of eastern Asia: Hong Kong (part of the People's Republic of China since 1997) and Singapore (independent since 1965).

The Role of Rich Nations

Modernization theory claims that high-income countries play four important roles in global economic development:

1. **Controlling population.** Because population growth is greatest in the poorest societies, rising population can overtake economic advances. Rich nations can help limit population growth by exporting birth control technology and promoting its use. Once economic development is under way, birth rates should decline, as they have in industrialized nations, because children are no longer an economic asset.

2. **Increasing food production.** Rich nations can export high-tech farming methods to poor nations to increase agricultural yields. Such techniques, collectively referred to as the Green Revolution, include new hybrid seeds, modern irrigation methods, chemical fertilizers, and pesticides for insect control.

3. **Introducing industrial technology.** Rich nations can encourage economic growth in poor societies by introducing machinery and information technology, which raise productivity. Industrialization also shifts the labor force from farming to skilled industrial and service jobs.

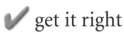
4. **Providing foreign aid.** Investment capital from rich nations can boost the prospects of poor societies trying to reach Rostow's take-off stage. Foreign aid can raise farm output by helping poor countries buy more fertilizer and build irrigation projects. In the same way, financial and technical assistance can help build power plants and factories to improve industrial output. Each year, the United States provides about $12 billion in foreign aid to developing countries.

▶**CRITICAL REVIEW** Modernization theory has many influential supporters among social scientists (Parsons, 1966; W. E. Moore, 1977, 1979; Bauer, 1981; Berger, 1986; Firebaugh & Beck, 1994; Firebaugh, 1996, 1999; Firebaugh & Sandu, 1998). For decades, it has shaped the foreign policy of the United States and other rich nations. Supporters point to rapid economic development in Asia—including South Korea, Taiwan, Singapore, and Hong Kong—as proof that the affluence that accompanied industrialization in Western Europe and North America is within reach of all countries.

But modernization theory comes under fire from socialist countries (and left-leaning analysts in the West) as little more than a defense of capitalism. Its most serious flaw, according to critics, is that modernization simply has not occurred in many poor countries. The United Nations reported that living standards in a number of nations, including Haiti and Nicaragua in Latin America and Sudan, Ghana, and Rwanda in Africa, are actually lower today than in 1960 (United Nations Development Programme, 1996).

A second criticism of modernization theory is that it fails to recognize how rich nations, which benefit from the status quo, often block the path to development for poor countries. Centuries ago, critics charge, rich countries industrialized from a position of global strength. Can we expect poor countries today to do so from a position of global weakness?

Third, modernization theory treats rich and poor societies as separate worlds, ignoring the ways in which international relations have affected all nations. Many countries in Latin America and Asia are still struggling to overcome the harm caused by colonialism, which boosted the fortunes of Europe.

Fourth, modernization theory holds up the world's most developed countries as the standard for judging the rest of humanity, revealing an ethnocentric bias. We should remember that our Western idea of "progress" has caused us to rush headlong into a competitive, materialistic way of life, which uses up the world's scarce resources and pollutes the natural environment.

Fifth and finally, modernization theory suggests that the causes of global poverty lie almost entirely in the poor societies themselves. Critics see this analysis as little more than blaming the victims for their own problems. Instead, these critics argue, an analysis of global inequality should focus just as much on the behavior of rich nations as it does on the behavior of poor ones.

Concerns such as these reflect a second major approach to understanding global inequality: dependency theory.

✔ **YOUR LEARNING** State the important ideas of modernization theory, including Rostow's four stages of economic development. Point to several strengths and weaknesses of this theory.

Dependency Theory

Dependency theory is *a model of economic and social development that explains global inequality in terms of the historical exploitation of poor nations by rich ones.* This analysis puts the main responsibility for global poverty on rich nations, which for centuries have systematically impoverished low-income countries and made them dependent on rich ones. This destructive process continues today.

Modernization theory claims that corporations that build factories in low-income nations help people by providing them with jobs and higher wages than they had before; dependency theory views these factories as "sweatshops" that exploit workers. In response to the Olympic Games selling sports clothing produced by sweatshops, these women staged a protest in Athens, Greece; they are wearing white masks to symbolize the "faceless" workers who make much of what we wear. Is any of the clothing you wear made in sweatshop factories?

Andrea Comas/Corbis/Reuters America LLC

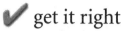
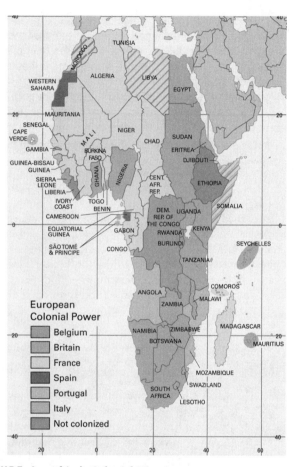

FIGURE 4 **Africa's Colonial History**

For more than a century, most of Africa was colonized by European nations,
with France dominating in the northwest region of the continent and Great
Britain dominating in the east and south.

Historical Perspective

Everyone agrees that before the Industrial Revolution, there was little
affluence in the world. Dependency theory asserts, however, that people living in poor countries were actually better off economically in the
past than their descendants are now. André Gunder Frank (1975), a
noted supporter of this theory, argues that the colonial process that
helped develop rich nations also *underdeveloped* poor societies.

Dependency theory is based on the idea that the economic positions of rich and poor nations of the world are linked and cannot be
understood apart from each other. Poor nations are not simply lagging behind rich ones on the "path of progress"; rather, the prosper-

ity of the most developed countries came largely at the expense of
less developed ones. In short, some nations became rich only because
others became poor. Both are products of the global commerce that
began five centuries ago.

The Importance of Colonialism

Late in the fifteenth century, Europeans began exploring the Americas
to the west, Africa to the south, and Asia to the east in order to establish colonies. They were so successful that a century ago, Great Britain
controlled about one-fourth of the world's land, boasting that "the
sun never sets on the British Empire." The United States, itself originally a collection of small British colonies on the eastern seaboard of
North America, soon pushed across the continent, purchased Alaska,
and gained control of Haiti, Puerto Rico, Guam, the Philippines, the
Hawaiian Islands, part of Panama, and Guantanamo Bay in Cuba.

As colonialism spread, there emerged a brutal form of human
exploitation—the international slave trade—beginning about 1500 and
continuing until 1850. Even as the world was turning away from slavery, Europeans took control of most of the African continent, as Figure
4 shows, and dominated most of the continent until the early 1960s.

Formal colonialism has almost disappeared from the world.
However, according to dependency theory, political liberation has not
translated into economic independence. Far from it—the economic
relationship between poor and rich nations continues the colonial
pattern of domination. This neocolonialism is the heart of the capitalist world economy.

Wallerstein's Capitalist World Economy

Immanuel Wallerstein (1974, 1979, 1983, 1984) explains global stratification using a model of the "capitalist world economy." Wallerstein's
term *world economy* suggests that the prosperity of some nations and the
poverty and dependency of other countries result from a global economic system. He traces the roots of the global economy to the beginning of colonization more than 500 years ago, when Europeans began
gathering wealth from the rest of the world. Because the world economy is based in the high-income countries, it is capitalist in character.[2]

Wallerstein calls the rich nations the *core* of the world economy.
Colonialism enriched this core by funneling raw materials from
around the world to Western Europe, where they fueled the Industrial
Revolution. Today, multinational corporations operate profitably
worldwide, channeling wealth to North America, Western Europe,
Australia, and Japan.

Low-income countries represent the *periphery* of the world economy. Drawn into the world economy by colonial exploitation, poor

[2]This section also draws on Frank (1980, 1981), Delacroix & Ragin (1981), Bergesen
(1983), Dixon & Boswell (1996), and Kentor (1998).

tip

The list below identifies three ways in which poor countries become dependent on rich countries. This argument implies that poor countries would be better off without any contact with rich nations.

nations continue to support rich ones by providing inexpensive labor and a vast market for industrial products. The remaining countries are considered the *semiperiphery* of the world economy. They include middle-income countries like Mexico and Brazil that have closer ties to the global economic core.

According to Wallerstein, the world economy benefits rich societies (by generating profits) and harms the rest of the world (by causing poverty). The world economy thus makes poor nations dependent on rich ones. This dependency involves three factors:

1. **Narrow, export-oriented economies.** Poor nations produce only a few crops for export to rich countries. Examples include coffee and fruit from Latin American nations, oil from Nigeria, hardwoods from the Philippines, and palm oil from Malaysia. Today's multinational corporations purchase raw materials cheaply in poor societies and transport them to core nations, where factories process them for profitable sale. Thus poor nations develop few industries of their own.

2. **Lack of industrial capacity.** Without an industrial base, poor societies face a double bind: They count on rich nations to buy their inexpensive raw materials and try to buy from them whatever expensive manufactured goods they can afford. In a classic example of this dependency, British colonialists encouraged the people of India to raise cotton but prevented them from weaving their own cloth. Instead, the British shipped Indian cotton to their own textile mills in Birmingham and Manchester, manufactured the cloth, and shipped finished goods back to India, where the very people who harvested the cotton bought the garments.

   Dependency theorists claim that the Green Revolution—widely praised by modernization theorists—works the same way. Poor countries sell cheap raw materials to rich nations and then try to buy expensive fertilizers, pesticides, and machinery in return. Rich countries profit from this exchange more than poor nations.

3. **Foreign debt.** Unequal trade patterns have plunged poor countries into debt to the core nations. Collectively, the poor nations of the world owe rich countries some $2.7 trillion; hundreds of billions of dollars are owed to the United States. Such staggering debt paralyzes a country, causing high unemployment and rampant inflation (World Bank, 2007).

The Role of Rich Nations

Modernization theory and dependency theory assign very different roles to rich nations. Modernization theory holds that rich countries *produce wealth* through capital investment and new technology.

Although the world continues to grow richer, billions of people are being left behind. The shantytown of Cité Soleil ("Sun City") near Port-au-Prince, the capital of Haiti, is built around an open sewer. What would you estimate life expectancy to be in such a place?

Mark Edwards/Still Pictures/Peter Arnold, Inc.

Dependency theory views global inequality in terms of how countries *distribute wealth*, arguing that rich nations have *overdeveloped* themselves as they have *underdeveloped* the rest of the world.

Dependency theorists dismiss the idea that programs developed by rich countries to control population and boost agricultural and industrial output raise living standards in poor countries. Instead, they claim, such programs actually benefit rich nations and the ruling elites, not the poor majority, in low-income countries (Kentor, 2001).

The hunger activists Frances Moore Lappé and Joseph Collins (1986; Lappé, Collins, & Rosset, 1998) maintain that the capitalist culture of the United States encourages people to think of poverty as somehow inevitable. In this line of reasoning, poverty results from "natural" processes, including having too many children, and natural disasters such as droughts. But global poverty is far from inevitable; in their view, it results from deliberate policies. Lappé and Collins point out that the world already produces enough food to allow every person on the planet to become quite fat. Moreover, India and most of Africa actually *export* food, even though many people in African nations go hungry.

According to Lappé and Collins, the contradiction of poverty amid plenty stems from the rich-nation policy of producing food for profit, not people. That is, corporations in rich nations cooperate with elites in poor countries to grow and export profitable crops such

 **get it right**

Be sure you understand the main points of dependency theory as well as criticisms of this theory.

 tip

One key difference between modernization theory and dependency theory is their view of rich nations. The first approach sees rich nations as a solution to the problem of poverty; the second sees them as a cause of the problem.

---

as coffee, which means using land that could otherwise produce basics such as beans and corn for local families. Governments of poor countries support the practice of growing for export because they need food profits to repay foreign debt. According to Lappé and Collins, the capitalist corporate structure of the global economy is at the core of this vicious cycle.

▶ **CRITICAL REVIEW** The main idea of dependency theory is that no nation becomes rich or poor in isolation because a single global economy shapes the destiny of all nations. Pointing to continuing poverty in Latin America, Africa, and Asia, dependency theorists claim that development simply cannot proceed under the constraints now imposed by rich countries. Rather, they call for radical reform of the entire world economy so that it operates in the interests of the majority of people.

Critics charge that dependency theory wrongly treats wealth as if no one gets richer without someone else getting poorer. Corporations, small business owners, and farmers can and do create new wealth through hard work and imaginative use of new technology. After all, they point out, the entire world's wealth has increased sixfold since 1950.

Second, dependency theory is wrong in blaming rich nations for global poverty because many of the world's poorest countries (like Ethiopia) have had little contact with rich nations. On the contrary, a long history of trade with rich countries has dramatically improved the economies of many nations, including Sri Lanka, Singapore, and Hong Kong (all former British colonies), as well as South Korea and Japan. In short, say the critics, most evidence shows that foreign investment by rich nations encourages economic growth, as modernization theory claims, not economic decline, as dependency theorists claim (E. F. Vogel, 1991; Firebaugh, 1992).

Third, critics call dependency theory simplistic for pointing the finger at a single factor—the capitalist market system—as the cause of global inequality (Worsley, 1990). Dependency theory views poor societies as passive victims and ignores factors inside these countries that contribute to their economic problems. Sociologists have long recognized the vital role of culture in shaping people's willingness to embrace or resist change. Under the rule of the ultratraditional Muslim Taliban, for example, Afghanistan became economically isolated, and its living standards sank to among the lowest in the world. Is it reasonable to blame capitalist nations for that country's stagnation?

Nor can rich societies be held responsible for the reckless behavior of foreign leaders whose corruption and militaristic campaigns impoverish their countries. Examples include the regimes of Ferdinand Marcos in the Philippines, François Duvalier in Haiti, Manuel Noriega in Panama, Mobutu Sese Seko in Zaire (today's Democratic Republic of the Congo), and Saddam Hussein in Iraq. Some leaders even use food supplies as weapons in internal political struggles, leaving the masses starving, as in the African nations of Ethiopia, Sudan, and Somalia. Likewise, many countries throughout the world have done little to improve the status of women or control population growth.

Fourth, critics say that dependency theory is wrong to claim that global trade always makes rich nations richer and poor nations poorer. For example, in 2005, the United States had a trade deficit of $716 billion, meaning that this nation imports two-thirds of a trillion dollars more than it sells abroad. The single greatest debt was to China, whose profitable trade has now pushed that country into the ranks of middle-income countries (Crutsinger, 2005).

Fifth, critics fault dependency theory for offering only vague solutions to global poverty. Most dependency theorists urge poor nations to end all contact with rich countries, and some call for nationalizing foreign-owned industries. In other words, dependency theory is really an argument for some sort of world socialism. In light of the difficulties that socialist societies (even better-off socialist countries such as the former Soviet Union) have had in meeting the needs of their own people, critics ask, should we really expect such a system to rescue the entire world from poverty?

The Applying Theory table summarizes the main arguments of modernization theory and dependency theory.

✔ **YOUR LEARNING** State the main ideas of dependency theory. What are several of its strengths and weaknesses?

Global Stratification: Looking Ahead

Among the most important trends in recent decades is the development of a global economy. In the United States, rising production and sales abroad bring profits to many corporations and their stockholders, especially those who already have substantial wealth. At the same time, the global economy has moved manufacturing jobs abroad, closing factories in this country and hurting many average workers. The net result: economic polarization in the United States.

People who support the global economy claim that the expansion of trade results in benefits for all countries involved. For this reason, they endorse policies like the North American Free Trade Agreement (NAFTA) signed by the United States, Canada, and Mexico. Critics

tip

The Applying Theory table provides a summary
of modernization theory and dependency theory.
Look closely at this table to be sure you
understand both approaches to global poverty.

APPLYING THEORY

Global Poverty

	Modernization Theory	Dependency Theory
Which theoretical approach is applied?	Structural-functional approach	Social-conflict approach
How did global poverty come about?	The whole world was poor until some countries developed industrial technology, which allowed mass production and created affluence.	Colonialism moved wealth from some countries to others, making some nations poor as it made other nations rich.
What are the main causes of global poverty today?	Traditional culture and a lack of productive technology.	Neocolonialism—the operation of multinational corporations in the global, capitalist economy.
Are rich countries part of the problem or part of the solution?	Rich countries are part of the solution, contributing new technology, advanced schooling, and foreign aid.	Rich countries are part of the problem, making poor countries economically dependent and in debt.

of expanding globalization make other claims: Manufacturing jobs are being lost in the United States, and more manufacturing now takes place abroad in factories where workers are paid little and few laws ensure workplace safety. In addition, other critics of expanding globalization point to the ever-greater stress that our economy places on the natural environment.

But perhaps the greatest concern is the vast economic inequality that exists between the world's countries. The concentration of wealth in high-income countries, coupled with the grinding poverty in low-income nations, may well be the biggest problem facing humanity in the twenty-first century.

Both modernization theory and dependency theory offer some understanding of this urgent problem. In evaluating these theories, we must consider empirical evidence. Over the course of the twentieth century, living standards rose in most of the world. Even the economic output of the poorest 25 percent of the world's people almost tripled over the course of the twentieth century. However, the economic output of the other 75 percent of the world's people increased about sixfold. By this measure, although all people are better off in *absolute* terms, there was almost twice as much *relative* economic inequality in the world in 2000 as there was in 1900. As Figure 5 suggests, the poorest of the world's people are being left behind.

Most of this economic polarization took place between 1900 and 1970. Since 1970, the degree of economic inequality worldwide has

declined. In addition, the numbers of the world's poorest people—those living on less than $1 per day—fell from about 1.5 billion in 1980 to 1 billion in 2001 (Firebaugh, 1999, 2000; Sala-i-Martin, 2002; Chen & Ravallion, 2004).

The greatest reduction in poverty has taken place in Asia, a region generally regarded as an economic success story. Back in 1980, 85 percent of global $1-per-day poverty was found in Asia; by 2001, that figure had fallen to 64 percent. Since then, two countries—India and China—have joined the ranks of the middle-income nations (Sala-i-Martin, 2002; Chen & Ravallion, 2004; United Nations Development Programme, 2004).

Latin America represents a mixed case. During the 1970s, this region enjoyed significant economic growth; during the 1980s and 1990s, however, there was little overall improvement. The share of the global $1-per-day poverty was the same in 2001 (4 percent) as it was in 1970 (Sala-i-Martin, 2002; Chen & Ravallion, 2004).

 An increasingly popular idea is "fair trade," paying people in poor nations a fair price for their products. Would you pay more for a cup of coffee to ensure that it was made using beans for which a farmer in a low-income country was paid a higher price? Why or why not?

In Africa, about half of the nations are showing increasing economic growth. In many countries, however, especially those south of

GLOBAL SNAPSHOT

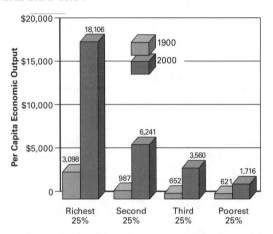

FIGURE 5   **The World's Increasing Economic Inequality**

The gap between the richest and poorest people in the world is twice as
big as it was a century ago.

Source: International Monetary Fund (2000).

the Sahara, extreme poverty is getting worse. In 1980, sub-Saharan
Africa accounted for 11 percent of $1-per-day poverty; by 2001, this
share had risen to 29 percent (Sala-i-Martin, 2002; Chen & Ravillion,
2004; Dunphy, 2006).

These trends in economic performance have caused both modernization and dependency theorists to revise their views. Governments have played a large role in the economic growth that has
occurred in Asia and elsewhere; this fact challenges modernization
theory and its free-market approach to development. On the other
hand, since the upheavals in the former Soviet Union and Eastern

Europe, a global reevaluation of socialism has been taking place.
Because socialist nations have a record of decades of poor economic
performance and political repression, many low-income nations are
unwilling to follow the advice of dependency theory and place economic development entirely under government control.

Although the world's future is uncertain, we have learned a great
deal about global stratification. One insight offered by modernization theory is that poverty is partly a *problem of technology*. A higher
standard of living for a surging world population depends on the ability of poor nations to raise their agricultural and industrial productivity. A second insight, derived from dependency theory, is that global
inequality is also a *political issue*. Even with higher productivity, the
human community must address crucial questions concerning how
resources are distributed, both within societies and around the globe.

Although economic development raises living standards, it also
places greater strains on the natural environment. As nations such as
India and China—with a combined population of 2.5 billion—
become more affluent, their people will consume more energy and
other resources (China has recently passed Japan to become the second largest consumer of oil, behind the United States, which is one
reason that oil prices have been rising). Richer nations also produce
more solid waste and create more pollution.

Finally, the vast gulf that separates the world's richest and poorest people puts everyone at greater risk of war and terrorism as the
poorest people challenge the social arrangements that threaten their
existence (Lindauer & Weerapana, 2002). In the long run, we can
achieve peace on this planet only by ensuring that all people enjoy a
significant measure of dignity and security.

Based on what you have read here and elsewhere, do you think
that global hunger fifty years from now will be more or less
serious? Explain your answer.

Applying Sociology in Everyday Life

1. Page through several issues of any current newsmagazine or
   travel magazine, and notice any stories or advertising men-
   tioning low-income countries (selling, say, coffee from
   Colombia or exotic vacations to India). What picture of life
   in low-income countries does the advertising present? In
   light of what you have learned in this chapter, how accurate
   does this image seem to you?

2. Millions of students from abroad study on U.S. campuses.
   Find a woman and a man on your campus who were raised
   in a low-income country. After explaining that you have

been studying global inequality, ask if they are willing to
share information about what life is like back home. If they
are, ask about stratification as well as their social position in
their home country.

3. Pick five of the global maps in this text (the full list is found
   in the Table of Contents), and identify social traits of high-
   income countries and those of low-income countries. Try to
   use both modernization theory and dependency theory to
   explain the patterns you find.

MAKING THE GRADE
Global Stratification

Global Stratification: An Overview

HIGH-INCOME COUNTRIES
- contain 18% of the world's people
- generate 79% of global income
- have a high standard of living based on advanced technology
- produce enough economic goods to enable their people to lead comfortable lives
- include about 60 nations, among them the United States, Canada, Argentina, Chile, the nations of Western Europe, Israel, Saudi Arabia, South Africa, Japan, South Korea, Malaysia, and Australia

global stratification patterns of social inequality in the world as a whole

MIDDLE-INCOME COUNTRIES
- contain 70% of the world's people
- generate 20% of global income
- have a standard of living about average for the world as a whole
- include about 76 nations, among them Russia, the nations of Eastern Europe, Mexico, Peru, Brazil, Botswana, Namibia, Egypt, Indonesia, India, and the People's Republic of China

LOW-INCOME COUNTRIES
- contain 12% of the world's people
- generate 1% of global income
- have a low standard of living due to limited industrial technology
- include about 57 nations, generally in Central and East Africa and Asia, among them Chad, the Democratic Republic of the Congo, Ethiopia, Bangladesh, and Pakistan

See Global Map 1.

✔ *Although poverty is a reality in the United States and other nations, the greatest social inequality is not within nations but between them.*

Global Wealth and Poverty

All societies contain **RELATIVE POVERTY**, but low-income nations face widespread **ABSOLUTE POVERTY** that is life-threatening.
- Worldwide, about 1 billion people are at risk due to poor nutrition.
- About 15 million people, most of them children, die each year from diseases caused by poverty.
- Throughout the world, women are more likely than men to be poor. Gender bias is strongest in poor societies.
- As many as 200 million men, women, and children (about 3% of humanity) live in conditions that can be described as slavery.

FACTORS CAUSING POVERTY
- Lack of technology limits production.
- High birth rates produce rapid population increase.
- Traditional cultural patterns make people resist change.
- Extreme social inequality distributes wealth very unequally.
- Extreme gender inequality limits the opportunities of women.
- Colonialism allowed some nations to exploit other nations; neocolonialism continues today.

colonialism the process by which some nations enrich themselves through political and economic control of other nations

neocolonialism a new form of global power relationships that involves not direct political control but economic exploitation by multinational corporations

multinational corporation a large business that operates in many countries

MAKING THE GRADE *continued . . .*

Global Stratification: Theoretical Analysis

MODERNIZATION THEORY maintains that nations achieve affluence by developing advanced technology. This process depends on a culture that encourages innovation and change toward higher living standards.

W.W. Rostow identified four stages of development:

- *Traditional stage*—People's lives are built around families and local communities. (Example: Bangladesh)
- *Take-off stage*—A market emerges as people produce goods not just for their own use but to trade with others for profit. (Example: Thailand)
- *Drive to technological maturity*—The ideas of economic growth and higher living standards gain widespread support; schooling is widely available; the social standing of women improves. (Example: Mexico)
- *High mass consumption*—Advanced technology fuels mass production and mass consumption as people now "need" countless goods. (Example: the United States)

modernization theory a model of economic and social development that explains global inequality in terms of technological and cultural differences between nations

dependency theory a model of economic and social development that explains global inequality in terms of the historical exploitation of poor nations by rich ones

Modernization theory claims

- Rich nations can help poor nations by providing technology to control population size, increase food production, and expand industrial and information economy output, and by providing foreign aid to pay for new economic development.
- Rapid economic development in Asia shows that affluence is within reach of other nations of the world.

Critics claim

- Rich nations do little to help poor countries and benefit from the status quo. Low living standards in much of Africa and South America result from the policies of rich nations.
- Because rich nations, including the United States, control the global economy, many poor nations struggle to support their people and cannot follow the path to development taken by rich countries centuries ago.

DEPENDENCY THEORY maintains that global wealth and poverty were created by the colonial process beginning 500 years ago that developed rich nations and underdeveloped poor nations. This capitalist process continues today in the form of neocolonialism—economic exploitation of poor nations by multinational corporations.

Immanuel Wallerstein's model of the capitalist world economy identified three categories of nations:

- *Core*—the world's high-income countries, which are home to multinational corporations
- *Semiperiphery*—the world's middle-income countries, with ties to core nations
- *Periphery*—the world's low-income countries, which provide low-cost labor and a vast market for industrial products

Dependency theory claims

- Three key factors—export-oriented economies, a lack of industrial capacity, and foreign debt— make poor countries dependent on rich nations and prevent their economic development.
- Radical reform of the entire world economy is needed so that it operates in the interests of the majority of people.

Critics claim

- Dependency theory overlooks the sixfold increase in global wealth since 1950 and the fact that the world's poorest countries have had weak, not strong, ties to rich countries.
- Rich nations are not responsible for cultural patterns or political corruption that block economic development in many poor nations.

See the Applying Theory table in this chapter.

MAKING THE GRADE

Sample Test Questions

These questions are similar to those found in the test bank that accompanies this textbook.

Multiple-Choice Questions

1. In global perspective, the richest 20 percent of all people earn about what share of the entire world's income?
   a. 20 percent
   b. 40 percent
   c. 60 percent
   d. 80 percent

2. The United States, Canada, and Japan are all
   a. high-income countries.
   b. middle-income countries.
   c. low-income countries.
   d. in different income categories.

3. Low-income nations
   a. are evenly spread in all world regions.
   b. are found mostly in Africa and Asia.
   c. are all in Latin America.
   d. contain a majority of the world's people.

4. China and India are now
   a. the world's poorest countries.
   b. counted among the world's low-income nations.
   c. counted among the world's middle-income nations.
   d. counted among the world's high-income nations.

5. Which of the following is the range of annual personal income for people living in middle-income nations?
   a. $250 to $1,000
   b. $1,000 to $2,500
   c. $2,500 to $10,000
   d. $10,000 to $25,000

6. How does poverty in poor nations compare to poverty in the United States?
   a. In poor nations, poverty is more likely to involve men.
   b. In most poor nations, the problem of poverty has been all but solved.
   c. In poor nations, most people do not consider poverty a problem.
   d. In poor nations, there is far more absolute poverty.

7. *Neocolonialism* refers to the process by which
   a. rich countries gain new colonies to replace older ones.
   b. multinational corporations dominate the economy of a poor country.
   c. rich countries grant independence to their former colonies.
   d. more and more large corporations do business in many countries at once.

8. Which of the following statements is the basis of modernization theory?
   a. The main cause of poverty in the world is low productivity due to simple technology and traditional culture.
   b. Poor nations can never become rich if they remain part of the global capitalist economy.
   c. The main cause of poverty in the world is the operation of multinational corporations.
   d. Most poor nations were richer in the past than they are today.

9. According to Walt Rostow, which is the final stage of economic development?
   a. drive to technological maturity
   b. traditional
   c. high mass consumption
   d. take-off

10. Dependency theory differs from modernization theory by saying that
    a. poor nations are responsible for their own poverty.
    b. capitalism is the best way to produce economic development.
    c. economic development is not a good idea for poor countries.
    d. global stratification results from the exploitation of poor countries by rich countries.

ANSWERS: 1 (d); 2 (a); 3 (b); 4 (c); 5 (c); 6 (d); 7 (b); 8 (a); 9 (c); 10 (d).

Essay Questions

1. What are the differences between relative poverty and absolute poverty? Describe global social stratification using both concepts.
2. Why do many analysts believe that economic development in low-income countries depends on raising the social standing of women?

Gender Stratification

Gender is more than differences in the ways society expects women and men to behave. It is also a matter of social stratification placing men in positions of power over women.
Photodisc/ Getty Images

Gender Stratification

HOW is gender a creation of society?

WHAT difference does gender make in people's lives?

WHY is gender an important dimension of social stratification?

Corbis/Bettmann

At first we traveled quite alone . . . but before we had gone many miles, we came on other wagon-loads of women, bound in the same direction. As we reached different cross-roads, we saw wagons coming from every part of the country and, long before we reached Seneca Falls, we were a procession.

So wrote Charlotte Woodward in her journal as she made her way along the rutted dirt roads leading to Seneca Falls, a small town in upstate New York. The year was 1848, a time when slavery was legal in much of the United States and the social standing of all women, regardless of color, was far below that of men. Back then, in much of the country, women could not own property, keep their wages if they were married, draft a will, file lawsuits in a court (including lawsuits seeking custody of their children), or attend college, and husbands were widely viewed as having unquestioned authority over their wives and children.

Some 300 women gathered at Wesleyan Chapel in Seneca Falls to challenge this second-class citizenship. They listened as their leader, Elizabeth Cady Stanton, called for expanding women's rights and opportunities, including the right to vote. At that time, most people considered such a proposal absurd and outrageous. Even many attending the conference were shocked by the idea: Stanton's husband, Henry, rode out of town in protest (Gurnett, 1998).

Much has changed since the Seneca Falls convention, and many of Stanton's proposals are now widely accepted as matters of basic fairness. But as this chapter explains, women and men still lead different lives, in the United States and elsewhere in the world; in most respects, men are still in charge. This chapter explores the importance of gender and explains how, like class position, gender is a major dimension of social stratification.

Gender and Inequality

Chapter 8 ("Sexuality and Society") explained the biological differences based on sex that divide the human population into categories of female and male. **Gender** refers to *the personal traits and social positions that members of a society attach to being female or male.* Gender operates as a dimension of social organization, shaping how we interact with others and how we think about ourselves. More important, gender also involves *hierarchy,* ranking men and women differently in terms of power, wealth, and other resources. This is why sociologists speak of **gender stratification,** *the unequal distribution of wealth, power, and privilege between men and women.* In short, gender affects the opportunities and constraints we face throughout our lives.

Male-Female Differences

Many people think there is something "natural" about gender distinctions because biology does make one sex different from the other. But we must be careful not to think of social differences in biological terms. In 1848, for example, women were denied the vote because many people assumed that women did not have enough intelligence or interest in politics. Such attitudes had nothing to do with biology; they reflected the *cultural* patterns of that time and place.

Another example is athletic performance. In 1925, most people—women and men—believed that the best women runners could never

compete with men in a marathon. Today, as Figure 1 shows, the gender gap has greatly narrowed, and the fastest women routinely post better times than the fastest men of decades past. Even here, most of the differences between men and women turn out to be socially created.

Do you think female and male athletes should compete on the same teams? Why or why not? Do you think men and women see this issue differently?

There are some differences in physical ability between the sexes. On average, males are 10 percent taller, 20 percent heavier, and 30 percent stronger, especially in their upper bodies (Ehrenreich, 1999). On the other hand, women outperform men in the ultimate game of life itself: Life expectancy for men in the United States is 75.2 years, and women can expect to live 80.4 years (Miniño, Heron, & Smith, 2006).

In adolescence, males do a bit better in mathematics, and females show stronger verbal skills, a difference that reflects both biology and socialization (Maccoby & Jacklin, 1974; Baker, Gugin, & Segal, 1980; Lengermann & Wallace, 1985; Tavris & Wade, 2001). However, research does not point to any difference in overall intelligence between males and females.

Biologically, then, men and women differ in limited ways; neither one is naturally superior. But culture can define the two sexes very differently, as the global study of gender described in the next section shows.

Gender in Global Perspective

The best way to see the cultural foundation of gender is by comparing one society to another. Three important studies highlight just how different "masculine" and "feminine" can be.

Chapter Overview

This chapter examines gender, the meaning societies attach to being female or male, and explains how gender is an important dimension of social stratification.

The Israeli Kibbutz

In Israel, collective settlements are called *kibbutzim*. The *kibbutz* (the singular form of the word) is an important setting for research because gender equality is one of its stated goals; men and women share in both work and decision making.

In kibbutzim, both sexes share most everyday jobs. Both men and women take care of children, cook and clean, repair buildings, and make day-to-day decisions concerning life in the kibbutz. Girls and boys are raised in the same way, and from the first weeks of life, children live together in dormitories. Women and men in kibbutzim have achieved remarkable (although not complete) social equality, evidence that cultures define what is feminine and what is masculine.

Margaret Mead's Research

The anthropologist Margaret Mead carried out groundbreaking research on gender. If gender is based on the biological differences between men and women, she reasoned, people everywhere should define "feminine" and "masculine" in the same way; if gender is cultural, these conceptions should vary.

Mead studied three societies in New Guinea (1963, orig. 1935). In the mountainous home of the Arapesh, Mead observed men and women with remarkably similar attitudes and behavior. Both sexes, she reported, were cooperative and sensitive to others—in short, what our culture would label "feminine."

Moving south, Mead then studied the Mundugumor, whose headhunting and cannibalism stood in striking contrast to the gentle ways of the Arapesh. In this culture, both sexes were typically selfish and aggressive, traits we define as more "masculine."

Finally, traveling west to the Tchambuli, Mead discovered a culture that, like our own, defined females and males differently. But, Mead reported, the Tchambuli *reversed* many of our notions of gender: Females were dominant and rational, and males were submissive, emotional, and nurturing toward children. Based on her observations, Mead concluded that culture is the key to gender differences, because what one society defines as masculine another may see as feminine.

Some critics view Mead's findings as "too neat," as if she saw in these three societies just the patterns she was looking for. Deborah Gewertz (1981) challenged what she called Mead's "reversal hypothesis," pointing out that Tchambuli males are really the more aggressive sex. Gewertz explains that Mead visited the Tchambuli (who themselves spell their name Chambri) during the 1930s, after they had lost much of their property in tribal wars, and observed men rebuilding their homes, a temporary role for Chambri men.

> The women's movement of the 1960s helped women show their true abilities.

DIVERSITY SNAPSHOT

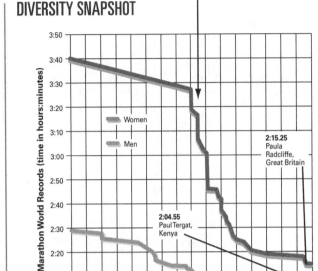

FIGURE 1   Men's and Women's Athletic Performance

Do men naturally outperform women in athletic competition? The answer is not obvious. Early in the twentieth century, men outpaced women by more than an hour in marathon races. But as opportunities for women in athletics have increased, women have been closing the performance gap. Only ten minutes separate the current world marathon records for women and for men (both set in 2003).

Sources: *Christian Science Monitor*, © 1995 Christian Science Monitor, and Marathonguide.com (2007). Adapted with permission of the *Christian Science Monitor*.

George Murdock's Research

In a broader study of more than 200 preindustrial societies, George Murdock (1937) found some global agreement about which tasks are feminine and which masculine. Hunting and warfare, Murdock concluded, generally fall to men, and home-centered tasks such as cooking and child care tend to be women's work. With their simple technology, preindustrial societies apparently assign roles reflecting men's and women's physical characteristics. With greater size and strength, men hunt game and protect the group; because women bear children, they do most of the work in the home.

But beyond this general pattern, Murdock found much variety. Consider agriculture: Women did the farming in about the same

Sex is a biological distinction that develops prior to birth. Gender is the meaning that a society attaches to being female or male. Gender differences are a matter of power, because what is defined as masculine typically has more importance than what is feminine. Infants begin to learn the importance of gender by the way parents treat them. Do you think this child is a girl or a boy? Why?

CDC/Photo Researchers, Inc.

number of societies as men; in most, the two sexes shared this work. When it came to many other tasks, from building shelters to tattooing the body, Murdock found that societies of the world were as likely to turn to one sex as the other.

 Did you grow up in a home in which females and males had different jobs and responsibilities? How did this affect your view of gender?

▶ **CRITICAL REVIEW** Global comparisons show that overall, societies do not consistently define tasks as either feminine or masculine. With industrialization, the importance of muscle power declines, further reducing gender differences (Nolan & Lenski, 2004). In sum, gender is too variable across cultures to be a simple expression of biology; what it means to be female and male is mostly a creation of society.

 YOUR LEARNING By comparing many cultures, what do we learn about the origin of gender differences?

Patriarchy and Sexism

Conceptions of gender vary, and there is evidence of societies in which women have greater power than men. One example is the Musuo, a very small society in China's Yunnan province, in which women control most property, select their sexual partners, and make most decisions about everyday life. The Musuo appear to be a case of **matriarchy** ("rule of mothers"), *a form of social organization in which females dominate males*, which has only rarely been documented in human history. Near-matriarchy existed among the Seneca of North America during the 1700s and 1800s, when women did the farming and controlled the food supply. Seneca men had to obtain women's support for their objectives (such as a military campaign), or women could simply withhold the necessary food (Freedman, 2002).

The pattern found almost everywhere in the world is **patriarchy** ("rule of fathers"), *a form of social organization in which males dominate females*. Global Map 1 shows the great variation in the relative power and privilege of females and males that exists from country to country. According to the United Nations, Norway, Iceland, and Australia give women the highest social standing; by contrast, women in the African nations of Niger, Sierra Leone, Mali, and Burkina Faso have the lowest social standing compared to men. Of the world's nations, the United States was ranked eighth in terms of gender equality (United Nations Development Programme, 2006).

The justification for patriarchy is **sexism,** *the belief that one sex is innately superior to the other.* Sexism is not just a matter of individual attitudes; it is built into the institutions of society. *Institutional sexism* is found throughout the economy, with women concentrated in low-paying jobs. Similarly, the legal system has long excused violence against women, especially on the part of boyfriends, husbands, and fathers.

The Costs of Sexism

Sexism limits the talents and ambitions of the half of the human population who are women. Although men benefit in some respects from sexism, their privilege comes at a high price. Masculinity in our culture encourages men to engage in many high-risk behaviors: using tobacco and alcohol, playing dangerous sports, and even driving recklessly. As Marilyn French (1985) argues, patriarchy leads men to seek control, not only of women but also of themselves and their world.

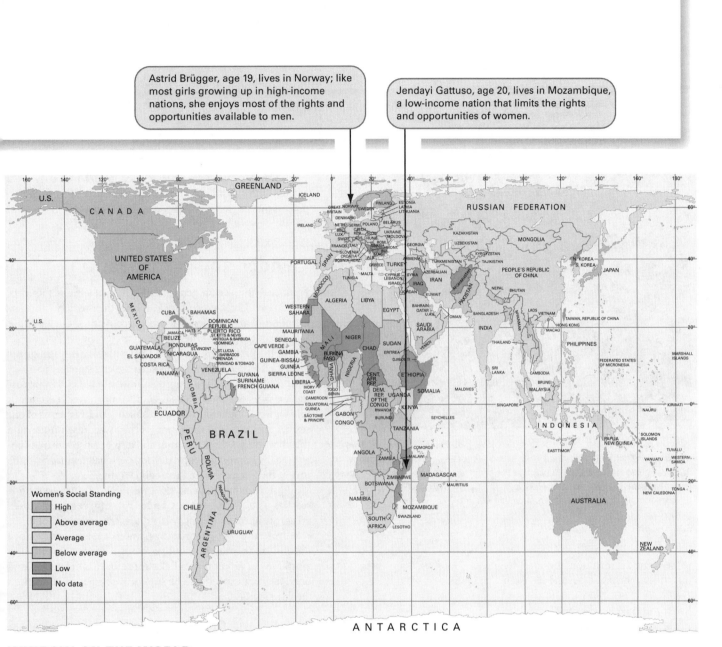

Astrid Brügger, age 19, lives in Norway; like most girls growing up in high-income nations, she enjoys most of the rights and opportunities available to men.

Jendayi Gattuso, age 20, lives in Mozambique, a low-income nation that limits the rights and opportunities of women.

Women's Social Standing
- High
- Above average
- Average
- Below average
- Low
- No data

WINDOW ON THE WORLD

GLOBAL MAP 1   Women's Power in Global Perspective

Women's social standing in relation to men's varies around the world. In general, women live better in rich countries than in poor countries. Even so, some nations stand out: In Norway, Iceland, and Australia, women come closest to social equality with men.

Source: Data from Seager (2003).

This is why masculinity is closely linked not only to accidents but also to suicide, violence, and stress-related diseases. The *Type A personality*—marked by chronic impatience, driving ambition, competitiveness, and free-floating hostility—is a recipe for heart disease

and almost perfectly matches the behavior that our culture considers masculine (Ehrenreich, 1983).

Finally, as men seek control over others, they lose opportunities for intimacy and trust. As one analyst put it, competition is supposed

tip

The concept of sexism parallels the concept of racism, which is discussed in the next chapter.

In every society, people assume that certain jobs, patterns of behavior, and ways of dressing are "naturally" feminine while others are just as obviously masculine. But in global perspective, we see remarkable variety in such social definitions. These men, Wodaabe pastoral nomads who live in the African nation of Niger, are proud to engage in a display of beauty most people in our society would consider feminine.

Carol Beckwith/Robert Estall Photo Agency

to "separate the men from the boys." In practice, however, it separates men from men and everyone else (Raphael, 1988).

Must Patriarchy Go On?

In preindustrial societies, women have little control over pregnancy and childbirth, which limits the scope of their lives. In those same societies, men's greater height and physical strength are highly valued resources. But industrialization, including birth control technology, gives people choices about how to live. In societies like our own, biological differences offer little justification for patriarchy.

But males are dominant in the United States and elsewhere. Does this mean that patriarchy is inevitable? Some researchers claim that biological factors such as differences in hormones and slight differences in brain structure "wire" the two sexes with different motivations and behaviors—especially aggressiveness in males—making patriarchy difficult or perhaps even impossible to eliminate (S. Goldberg, 1974; Rossi, 1985; Popenoe, 1993b; Udry, 2000). However, most sociologists believe that gender is socially constructed and *can* be changed. Just because no society has yet eliminated patriarchy does not mean that we must remain prisoners of the past.

To understand why patriarchy continues today, we must examine how gender is rooted and reproduced in society, a process that begins in childhood and continues throughout our lives.

Gender and Socialization

From birth until death, gender shapes human feelings, thoughts, and actions. Children quickly learn that their society considers females and males different kinds of people; by about age three, they begin to think of themselves in these terms.

In the past, many people in the United States traditionally described women using terms such as "emotional," "passive," and "cooperative." By contrast, men were described in opposing terms, as "rational," "active," and "competitive." It is curious that we were taught for so long to think of gender in terms of one sex being opposite to the other, especially because women and men have so much in common and also because research suggests that most young people develop personalities that are some mix of these feminine and masculine traits (Bem, 1993).

Just as gender affects how we think of ourselves, so it teaches us how to behave. **Gender roles** (also known as **sex roles**) are *attitudes and activities that a society links to each sex.* A culture that defines males as ambitious and competitive encourages them to seek out positions of leadership and play team sports. To the extent that females are defined as deferential and emotional, they are expected to be supportive helpers and quick to show their feelings.

Gender and the Family

The first question people usually ask about a newborn—"Is it a boy or a girl?"—has great importance because the answer involves not just sex but the likely direction of the child's life. In fact, gender is at work even before the birth of a child, because especially in lower-income nations, parents hope their firstborn will be a boy rather than a girl.

Soon after birth, family members welcome infants into the "pink world" of girls or the "blue world" of boys (Bernard, 1981). Parents even send gender messages in the way they handle infants. One researcher at an English university presented an infant dressed as either a boy or a girl to a number of women; her subjects handled the "female" child tenderly, with frequent hugs and caresses, and treated the "male" child more roughly, often lifting him up high in the air or bouncing him on a knee (Bonner, 1984; Tavris & Wade, 2001). The lesson to children is clear: The female world revolves around cooperation and emotion, and the male world puts a premium on independence and action.

tip

This part of the chapter looks at how social institutions transmit messages about gender to each new generation.

 Did you grow up in a home in which females and males had different jobs and responsibilities? How did this affect your view of gender?

 What is your declared or likely major? Based on the classes you have taken, what share of students in this major are female and what share are male? Does the pattern agree with those described here?

Gender and the Peer Group

About the time they enter school, children begin to move outside the family and make friends with others of the same age. Considerable research shows that young children tend to form single-sex play groups (Martin & Fabes, 2001).

Peer groups teach additional lessons about gender. After spending a year observing children at play, Janet Lever (1978) concluded that boys favor team sports that have complex rules and clear objectives such as scoring runs or making touchdowns. Such games nearly always have winners and losers, reinforcing masculine traits of aggression and control.

Girls, too, play team sports. But, Lever explains, girls also play hopscotch, jump rope, or simply talk, sing, or dance. These activities have few rules, and rarely is "victory" the ultimate goal. Instead of teaching girls to be competitive, Lever explains, female peer groups promote the interpersonal skills of communication and cooperation, presumably the basis for girls' future roles as wives and mothers.

The games we play offer important lessons for our later lives. Lever's observations recall Carol Gilligan's gender-based theory of moral reasoning. Boys, Gilligan (1982) claims, reason according to abstract principles. For them, "rightness" amounts to "playing by the rules." Girls, on the other hand, consider morality a matter of responsibility to others.

Gender and Schooling

Gender shapes our interests and beliefs about our own abilities, guiding areas of study and, eventually, career choices (Correll, 2001). In high school, more girls than boys learn secretarial skills and take vocational classes such as cosmetology and food services. Classes in woodworking and auto mechanics attract mostly young men.

Women have now become a majority (57 percent) of the students on college campuses across the United States. As their numbers have increased, women have become well represented in many fields of study that once excluded them, including mathematics, chemistry, and biology. But men still predominate in many fields, including engineering, physics, and philosophy, and women cluster in the fine arts (including music, dance, and drama) as well as the social sciences (including anthropology and sociology). New areas of study are also gender-typed: More men than women take computer science, and courses in gender studies enroll mostly women.

Gender and the Mass Media

Since television first captured the public imagination in the 1950s, white males have held center stage; racial and ethnic minorities were all but absent from television until the early 1970s. Even when both sexes appeared on camera, men generally played the brilliant detectives, fearless explorers, and skilled surgeons. Women played the less capable characters and were often important only for the sexual interest they added to the story.

Historically, advertisements have shown women in the home, cheerfully using cleaning products, serving food, and modeling clothes. Men predominate in ads for cars, travel, banking services, and alcoholic beverages. The authoritative voiceover—the faceless

Movies such as *Superman 3* have male lead characters with women in supporting roles largely to provide romantic interest. Can you think of other movies or television shows that display this pattern?

Warner Bros./DC Comics/Picture Desk, Inc./Kobal Collection

Seeing Sociology in Everyday Life
The Beauty Myth

The Duchess of Windsor once remarked, "A woman cannot be too rich or too thin." The first half of her observation might apply to men as well, but certainly not the second. The answer lies in the fact that the vast majority of ads placed by the $30-billion-a-year cosmetics industry and the $50-billion diet industry target women.

According to Naomi Wolf (1990), certain cultural patterns create a "beauty myth" that is damaging to women. The beauty myth arises, first, because society teaches women to measure their worth in terms of physical appearance. Yet the standards of beauty embodied in the *Playboy* centerfold or the 100-pound New York fashion model are out of reach for most women.

The way society teaches women to prize relationships with men, whom they presumably attract with their beauty, also contributes to the beauty myth. Striving for beauty drives women to be extremely disciplined but also forces them to be highly attuned and responsive to men. In short, beauty-minded women try to please men and avoid challenging male power.

Belief in the beauty myth is one reason that so many young women are focused on body image, particularly being as thin as possi-

ble, often to the point of endangering their health. During the past several decades, the

Many young women in our society are concerned with being as thin as possible—one result of the beauty myth.
AP Wide World Photos

share of young women who develop an eating disorder such as anorexia nervosa (dieting to the point of starvation) or bulimia (binge eating followed by vomiting) has risen dramatically.

The beauty myth affects males as well: Men are told repeatedly that they should want to possess beautiful women. Such ideas about beauty reduce women to objects and motivate thinking about women as if they were dolls or pets rather than human beings.

There can be little doubt that the idea of beauty is important in everyday life. The question, according to Wolf, is whether beauty is about how we look or how we act.

WHAT DO YOU THINK?

1. Is there a "money myth" that states that people's income is a reflection of their worth? Does it apply more to one sex than to the other?

2. Can you see a connection between the beauty myth and the rise of eating disorders among young women in the United States? Explain the link.

3. Among people with physical disabilities, do you think that issues of "looking different" are more serious for women or for men? Why?

voice that describes a product on television and radio—is almost always male (D. M. Davis, 1993).

A closer look at gender in advertising reveals that men usually appear taller than women, implying male superiority. Women, by contrast, are more frequently presented lying down (on sofas and beds) or, like children, seated on the floor. Men's facial expressions and behavior give off an air of competence and imply dominance; women often appear childlike, submissive, and sexual. Men focus on the products being advertised; women often focus on the men (Goffman, 1979; Cortese, 1999).

Advertising also actively perpetuates what Naomi Wolf calls the "beauty myth." The Seeing Sociology in Everyday Life box takes a closer look.

Gender and Social Stratification

Gender affects more than how people think and act. It is also about social hierarchy. The reality of gender stratification can be seen, first, in the world of work.

tip

As you look at Table 1, think about which jobs have a high concentration of men (some are noted in the text below). How do they differ from the jobs in Table 1?

Working Women and Men

Back in 1900, just 20 percent of U.S. women were in the labor force. Today, the figure has tripled to 59 percent, and 72 percent of these working women work full time. The traditional view that earning an income is a man's role no longer holds true.

Factors that have changed the U.S. labor force include the decline of farming, the growth of cities, shrinking family size, and a rising divorce rate. The United States, along with most other nations of the world, considers women working for income the rule rather than the exception. Women make up almost half the U.S. paid labor force, and more than half of U.S. married couples depend on two incomes.

In the past, many women in the U.S. labor force were childless. But today, 60 percent of married women with children under age six are in the labor force, as are 75 percent of married women with children between six and seventeen years of age. For widowed, divorced, or separated women with children, the comparable figures are 74 percent of women with younger children and 82 percent of women with older children (U.S. Census Bureau, 2006).

Gender and Occupation

Although women are closing the gap with men as far as working for income is concerned, the work done by the two sexes remains very different. The U.S. Department of Labor (2007) reports a high concentration of women in two job types. Administrative support work draws 21 percent of working women, most of whom are secretaries or other office workers. These are often called "pink-collar jobs" because 75 percent are filled by women. Another 19 percent of employed women do service work. Most of these jobs are in food service industries, child care, and health care.

Table 1 shows the ten occupations with the highest concentrations of women. These jobs tend to be at the low end of the pay scale, with limited opportunities for advancement and with men as supervisors (U.S. Department of Labor, 2007).

Men dominate most other job categories, including the building trades, where 99 percent of heavy equipment mechanics and 98 percent of bricklayers and stonemasons are men. Likewise, men make up 87 percent of police officers, 85 percent of engineers, 68 percent of physicians and surgeons, 67 percent of lawyers, and 63 percent of corporate managers. According to a recent survey, the top earners in *Fortune* 500 corporations were 1,973 men (93 percent of the total) and 142 women (7 percent). Just 25 of the 1,000 largest U.S. corporations have a woman chief executive officer (Catalyst, 2007b; U.S. Department of Labor, 2007).

Table 1 Jobs with the Highest Concentrations of Women, 2006

Occupation	Number of Women Employed	Percentage in Occupation Who Are Women
1. Dental hygienist	142,000	98.6%
2. Preschool or kindergarten teacher	674,000	97.7
3. Secretary or administrative assistant	3,348,000	96.9
4. Dental assistant	261,000	95.4
5. Speech-language pathologist	109,000	95.3
6. Child care worker	1,320,000	94.2
7. Licensed practical or licensed vocational nurse	524,000	94.2
8. Hairdresser, hairstylist, or cosmetologist	716,000	93.4
9. Receptionist or information clerk	1,301,000	92.7
10. Payroll or timekeeping clerk	146,000	92.4

Source: U.S. Department of Labor (2007).

Gender stratification in everyday life is easy to see: Female nurses assist male physicians, female secretaries serve male executives, and female flight attendants are under the command of male airplane pilots. In any field, the greater the income and prestige associated with a job, the more likely it is to be held by a man. For example, women represent 98 percent of kindergarten teachers, 82 percent of elementary school teachers, 56 percent of secondary school educators, 39 percent of college and university professors, and 18 percent of college and university presidents (*Chronicle of Higher Education*, 2006; U.S. Department of Labor, 2007).

How are women kept out of certain jobs? By defining some kinds of work as "men's work," companies define women as less competent than men. In a study of coal mining in southern West Virginia, Suzanne Tallichet (2000) found that most men considered it "unnatural" for women to join them working in the mines. Women who did so were defined as deviant and subject to labeling as "sexually loose" or as lesbians. Such labeling made these women outcasts, presented a challenge to holding the job, and made career advancement all but impossible.

In the corporate world, as already noted, the higher in the company we look, the fewer women we find. You hardly ever hear anyone say that women don't belong at the top levels of a company. But many people seem to feel this way, which can prevent women from being promoted. Sociologists describe this barrier as a *glass ceiling* that is

tip

An example of gender as a dimension of social
stratification: Women working full time earn 77
cents for every dollar earned by men.

not easy to see but blocks women's careers all the same (Benokraitis & Feagin, 1995).

One challenge to male domination in the workplace comes from women who are entrepreneurs. Between 1997 and 2002, women-owned businesses in the United States increased in number from 5.4 million to 6.5 million. In 2002, these businesses made up 28 percent of the national total and employed 7 percent of the labor force. Through starting their own businesses, women have shown that they can make opportunities for themselves outside larger, male-dominated companies (U.S. Small Business Administration, 2006).

Gender, Income, and Wealth

In 2005, the median earnings of women working full time were $31,858; for men, the figure was $41,386. This means that for every dollar earned by men, women earned about 77 cents. This difference is greater among older workers because older working women typically have less education and seniority than older working men. Earning differences are smaller among younger workers because younger men and women tend to have similar schooling and work experience.

Among all full-time workers of all ages, 33 percent of women earned less than $25,000 in 2005, compared with 22 percent of men.

At the upper end of the income scale, men were nearly 2½ times more likely than women (19.3 percent versus 8.3 percent) to earn more than $75,000 (U.S. Census Bureau, 2006).

The main reason women earn less is the *type* of work they do, largely clerical and service jobs. In effect, jobs and gender interact. People still perceive jobs with less clout as "women's work," just as people devalue certain work simply because it is performed by women (England, Hermsen, & Cotter, 2000; Cohen & Huffman, 2003).

In recent decades, supporters of gender equality have proposed a policy of "comparable worth," paying people not according to the historical double standard but according to the level of skill and responsibility involved in the work. Several nations, including Great Britain and Australia, have adopted comparable worth policies, but such policies have found limited acceptance in the United States. As a result, critics claim, women in this country lose as much as $1 billion in income annually.

A second cause of gender-based income disparity has to do with the family. Both men and women have children, of course, but our culture gives more responsibility for parenting to women. Pregnancy and raising small children keep many young women out of the labor force at a time when their male peers are making significant career advancements. When women workers return to the labor force, they have less job seniority than their male counterparts (Stier, 1996; Waldfogel, 1997). "In the *Times*" looks more closely at the challenges faced by women trying to succeed in today's business corporations.

In addition, women who choose to have children may be unable or unwilling to take on demanding jobs that tie up their evenings and weekends. To avoid role strain, they may take jobs that offer shorter commuting distances, more flexible hours, and employer-provided child care services.

SOCIOLOGY WORK   Women pursuing both a career and a family are often torn between their dual responsibilities in ways that men are not. Consider this: At age forty, 90 percent of men but only 35 percent of women in executive positions have at least one child (F. N. Schwartz, 1989). This pattern is also found on campus, where one recent study concluded that young female professors with at least one child were at least 20 percent less likely to have tenure than male professors in the same field (Shea, 2002).

Over the last few generations, women have moved into the paid labor force. But men have not taken on their share of housework, so running the home becomes a "second shift" for women. Why do you think women still do most of the housework?

Consider the statements "He fathered the child" and "She mothered the child." How do you think gender shapes the meaning of parenting?

Tony Freeman/PhotoEdit Inc.

The New York Times

IN THE TIMES

How Suite It Isn't: A Dearth of Female Bosses

By JULIE CRESSWELL
December 17, 2006

Like so many other women who entered corporate America in the 1970s, Carol Bartz simply wanted to make a little money. She did not harbor secret desires to run her own company or become chief executive of a large corporation. She just wanted to do a good job.

After working her way through college at the University of Wisconsin in Madison as a cocktail waitress (required uniform: red miniskirt, black fishnets and red feather in hair), Ms. Bartz graduated with a computer science degree in 1971. . . . She entered the work force at a time when the promise of new professional opportunities for women was in the air.

What Ms. Bartz says she discovered, however, was that male counterparts and supervisors shook the corporate ladder ever more fiercely with each rung that she and other pioneering women of her generation ascended. But by combining a first-rate mind with hard work and decisive career moves, she managed to duck, bob and weave her way through Silicon Valley's male-dominated technology industry in the 1980s. . . .

Despite her hard-won reputation as an astute businesswoman, Ms. Bartz found herself repeatedly skipped over during a recent meeting of business and political leaders in Washington. The reason was that the men at the table assumed that she was an office assistant, not a fellow executive. "Happens all the time," Ms. Bartz said drily, recalling the incident. "Sometimes I stand up. Sometimes I just ignore it." . . .

While top business schools are churning out an increasing number of female M.B.A.'s, only about 16 percent of corporate officers at *Fortune* 500 companies are women, according to Catalyst, an organization that studies women in the workplace. The numbers are even sparer at the top of the pyramid: Women fill only nine, or less than 2 percent, of the chief executive jobs at *Fortune* 500 companies. . . .

The complex question of why women remain so underrepresented in the corporate suite yields a variety of possible answers. A number of women leave their careers—sometimes by choice, sometimes not—to focus on rearing families. . . .

Many other women end up in dead-end staff positions, says Ilene H. Lang, president of Catalyst. "Women are almost two and one half times as likely to be channeled into staff jobs like H.R. and communications than into operating roles where they would be generating revenue and managing profit and loss," Ms. Lang says. . . .

Analysts and executive women also say that one of the biggest roadblocks between women and the c-suite is the thick layer of men who dominate boardrooms and corner offices across the country. . . .

Corporate boards remain, for the most part, clubby and male-dominated worlds where members have attended many of the same schools, dress the same and represent a single social class, says Douglas M. Branson, a professor of corporate governance at the University of Pittsburgh School of Law. In his new book, *No Seat at the Table: How Corporate Governance and Law Keep Women Out of the Boardroom,* he argues that boards can minimize their isolation from larger social issues by adding women. Others agree. . . .

"Women on boards are the ones who pay attention to the pool of employees and succession planning and whether there are women and people of color coming up in those succession plans," says Vicki W. Kramer, a management consultant and co-author of a study, "Critical Mass on Corporate Boards: Why Three or More Women Enhance Governance," that was released this fall by the Wellesley Centers for Women.

Through interviews with 12 C.E.O.'s and 50 women who served on a combined 175 boards of *Fortune* 1000 companies, the study examined how the dynamics and issues discussed in the boardroom changed as more women were added to the mix. A single woman on a board is typically viewed as a "token woman" and is unlikely to drive female-related issues because she does not want to be seen as a one-issue director, Ms. Kramer says.

The addition of a second woman to the board only slightly changes the environment. The women sometimes feel the need to stay away from each other, worried that it will appear as if they are conspiring against the men on the board.

The tipping point is the presence of three women on a board. "Somehow, at three, gender goes away and they are much less concerned about being seen together," Ms. Kramer says.

Ms. Bartz says she believes that a lot of women take themselves out of the race to the c-suite before it ever begins. "There is a whole lot of hand-wringing going on with women," she says. "They get the high-power degrees and then they drop back because they tell themselves they're not going to get very far anyway. I think they look around and wonder whether the struggle is worth it or not." . . .

WHAT DO YOU THINK?

1. Are you (or do you know) a woman who has had some of the same experiences as Carol Bartz in the article? Explain.

2. What are examples of the "glass ceiling" in this article?

3. Why do you think some women "take themselves out of the race" in the corporate world? What can be done to change this pattern?

tip
Gender stratification involves not just income and type of job but also responsibility for housework. For all categories of people, women do more work in and around the home than men.

DIVERSITY SNAPSHOT

On average, women spend almost twice as much time doing housework as men.

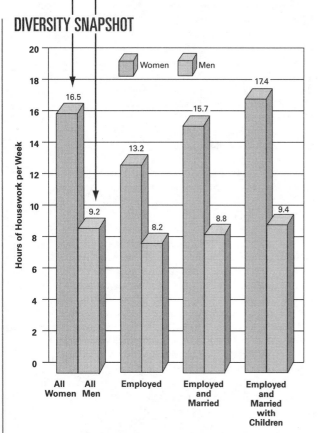

FIGURE 2 Housework: Who Does How Much?

Regardless of employment or family status, women do more housework than men. What effect do you think the added burden of housework has on women's ability to advance in the workplace?

Source: Adapted from Stapinski (1998).

The two factors noted so far—type of work and family responsibilities—account for about two-thirds of the earnings difference between women and men. A third factor—discrimination against women—accounts for most of the remainder (Fuller & Schoenberger, 1991). Because overt discrimination is illegal, it is practiced in subtle ways. Women on their way up the corporate ladder often run into the glass ceiling described earlier; company officials may deny its existence, but it effectively prevents many women from rising above middle management.

For all these reasons, women earn less than men in all major occupational categories. Even so, many people think that women own most of this country's wealth, perhaps because women typically out-

live men. Government statistics tell a different story: Fifty-five percent of individuals with $1 million or more in assets are men, although widows are highly represented in this elite club (Johnson & Raub, 2006). Just 11 percent of the individuals identified in 2005 by *Forbes* magazine as the richest people in the United States were women (Miller & Serafin, 2006).

Housework: Women's "Second Shift"

In the United States, we have always been of two minds about housework: We claim that it is essential to family life, but people get little reward for doing it (Bernard, 1981). Here, as around the world, taking care of the home and children has always been considered "women's work." As women have entered the labor force, the amount of housework women do has gone down, but the *share* done by women has stayed the same. Figure 2 shows that overall, women average 16.5 hours a week of housework, compared to 9.2 hours for men. As the figure shows, women in all categories do significantly more housework than men (Stapinski, 1998).

Men do support the idea of women entering the paid labor force, and most husbands count on the money their wives earn. But many men resist taking on a more equal share of household duties (Heath & Bourne, 1995; Harpster & Monk-Turner, 1998; Stratton, 2001).

Gender and Education

In the past, our society considered schooling more necessary for men, who worked outside the home, than for women, who worked in the home. But times have changed. By 1980, women earned a majority of all associate's and bachelor's degrees; in 2005, that share was 60 percent (National Center for Education Statistics, 2006).

College doors have opened to women, and the differences in men's and women's majors are becoming smaller. In 1970, for example, women earned just 17 percent of bachelor's degrees in the natural sciences, computer science, and engineering; by 2004, their proportion had doubled to 34 percent.

In 1992, for the first time, women also earned a majority of postgraduate degrees, which often serve as a springboard to high-prestige jobs. In all areas of study in 2004, women earned 59 percent of master's degrees and 48 percent of doctorates (including 60 percent of all Ph.D.s in sociology). Women have also broken into many graduate fields that used to be almost all male. For example, in 1970, only a few hundred women earned a master's of business administration (M.B.A.) degree, compared to more than 58,000 in 2004 (42 percent of all such degrees) (National Center for Education Statistics, 2006).

Despite this progress, men still predominate in some professional fields. In 2004, men received 51 percent of law degrees (LL.B. and

tip

Worth remembering is that our nation extended the right to vote to African American men (1870) fifty years before it extended this right to women (1920).

student **2** student

"I'm glad to see a woman making a serious run for president of the United States!"

J.D.), 54 percent of medical degrees (M.D.), and 58 percent of dental degrees (D.D.S. and D.M.D.) (National Center for Education Statistics, 2006). Our society still defines high-paying professions (and the drive and competitiveness needed to succeed in them) as masculine. But the share of women in all these professions is rising steadily. For example, the American Bar Association (2007) reports that women are 47 percent of law school students across the United States.

Gender and Politics

A century ago, men held virtually every elected office in the United States. By law, women could not even vote in national elections until the passage of the Nineteenth Amendment to the Constitution in 1920. However, a few women were candidates for political office even before they could vote. The Equal Rights party supported Victoria Woodhull for the U.S. presidency in 1872; perhaps it was a sign of the times that she spent election day in a New York City jail. Table 2 identifies later milestones in women's gradual movement into political life.

Today, thousands of women serve as mayors of cities and towns across the United States, and tens of thousands hold responsible administrative posts in the federal government. At the state level, 24 percent of legislators in 2007 were women (up from just 6 percent in 1970). National Map 1 shows where in the United States women have made the greatest political gains.

Change is coming more slowly at the highest levels of politics, although a majority of U.S. adults claim they would support a qualified woman for any office, including the presidency. In 2007, nine of the fifty state governors were women (18 percent), and in Congress, women held 70 of 435 seats (16 percent) in the House of Representatives and 16 of 100 seats (16 percent) in the Senate.

Women make up half the world's population, but they hold just 17 percent of seats in the world's 189 parliaments. Although this percentage represents a rise from 3 percent fifty years ago, in only a dozen countries, among them Sweden and Norway, do women represent more than one-third of the members of parliament (Paxton, Hughes, & Green, 2006; Inter-Parliamentary Union, 2007).

Sweden, Norway, Finland, and Denmark have laws that require at least 25 percent of candidates for elected office to be women. Do you think the United States should enact such a law? Why or why not?

Gender and the Military

Since colonial times, women have served in the U.S. armed forces. Yet in 1940, at the outset of World War II, just 2 percent of armed forces personnel were women. By the time of the war in Iraq, women

Table 2 Significant "Firsts" for Women in U.S. Politics

1869	Law allows women to vote in Wyoming territory.
1872	First woman to run for the presidency (Victoria Woodhull) represents the Equal Rights party.
1917	First woman elected to the House of Representatives (Jeannette Rankin of Montana).
1924	First women elected state governors (Nellie Taylor Ross of Wyoming and Miriam "Ma" Ferguson of Texas); both followed their husbands into office. First woman to have her name placed in nomination for the vice-presidency at the convention of a major political party (Lena Jones Springs, a Democrat).
1931	First woman to serve in the Senate (Hattie Caraway of Arkansas); completed the term of her husband upon his death and won reelection in 1932.
1932	First woman appointed to the presidential cabinet (Frances Perkins, secretary of labor in the cabinet of President Franklin D. Roosevelt).
1964	First woman to have her name placed in nomination for the presidency at the convention of a major political party (Margaret Chase Smith, a Republican).
1972	First African American woman to have her name placed in nomination for the presidency at the convention of a major political party (Shirley Chisholm, a Democrat).
1981	First woman appointed to the U.S. Supreme Court (Sandra Day O'Connor).
1984	First woman to be successfully nominated for the vice-presidency (Geraldine Ferraro, a Democrat).
1988	First woman chief executive to be elected to a consecutive third term (Madeleine Kunin, governor of Vermont).
1992	Political "Year of the Woman" yields record number of women in the Senate (six) and the House (forty-eight), as well as (1) first African American woman to win election to U.S. Senate (Carol Moseley-Braun of Illinois), (2) first state (California) to be served by two women senators (Barbara Boxer and Dianne Feinstein), and (3) first woman of Puerto Rican descent elected to the House (Nydia Velazquez of New York).
1996	First woman appointed secretary of state (Madeleine Albright).
2000	First First Lady to win elected political office (Hillary Rodham Clinton, senator from New York).
2001	First woman to serve as national security adviser (Condoleezza Rice); first Asian American woman to serve in a presidential cabinet (Elaine Chao).
2005	First African American woman appointed secretary of state (Condoleezza Rice).
2007	First woman elected as Speaker of the House (Nancy Pelosi). Record number of women in the Senate (sixteen) and the House (seventy).

Source: Compiled by the author.

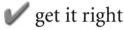
get it right

We can answer the question of whether or not women are a minority in two ways: Subjectively, most women do not think of themselves that way; objectively, women are a distinctive category of people who are disadvantaged.

In general, the western states have a higher percentage of legislators who are women than the midwestern and southern states.

SEEING OURSELVES

NATIONAL MAP 1
Women in State Government across the United States

Although women make up half of U.S. adults, just 24 percent of the seats in state legislatures are held by women. Look at the state-by-state variation in the map. In which regions of the country have women gained the greatest political power? What do you think accounts for this pattern?

Source: Center for American Women and Politics (2007).

Share of State Legislative Seats Held by Women

- High: 34.0% and over
- Above average: 27.0% to 33.9%
- Average: 20.0% to 26.9%
- Below average: 13.0% to 19.9%
- Low: 12.9% and under

U.S. average: 23.5%

represented about 15 percent of the U.S. military and 15 percent of all deployed U.S. troops.

Clearly, women make up a growing share of the U.S. military, and almost all military assignments are now open to both women and men. But law prevents women from engaging in offensive warfare. Even so, the line between troop support and outright combat is easily crossed, as the women serving in Iraq have learned. In fact, between 2003 and March 2007, the war in Iraq has claimed the lives of 71 women soldiers.

Debate on women's role in the military has been going on for centuries. Some people object to opening doors in this way, claiming that women lack the physical strength of men. Others reply that military women are better educated and score higher on intelligence tests than military men. But the heart of the issue is our society's deeply held view of women as *nurturers*—people who give life and help others—which clashes with the image of women trained to kill.

Whatever our views of women and men, the reality is that military women are in harm's way. In part, this fact reflects the strains experienced by a military short of personnel. In addition, the type of insurgency that surrounds our troops in Iraq can bring violent combat to any soldier at any time. Finally, modern warfare technology now blurs the distinction between combat and noncombat personnel. A combat pilot can fire missiles by radar at a target miles away; by contrast, noncombat medical evacuation teams routinely travel directly into the line of fire in their efforts to rescue the wounded and to save lives (Segal & Hansen, 1992; Wilcox, 1992; Kaminer, 1997; McGirk, 2006).

Are Women a Minority?

A **minority** is *any category of people distinguished by physical or cultural difference that a society sets apart and subordinates.* Given the economic disadvantage of being a woman in our society, it seems reasonable to say that U.S. women are a minority even though they outnumber men.[1]

Even so, most white women do not think of themselves in this way (Lengermann & Wallace, 1985). This is partly because, unlike racial minorities (including African Americans) and ethnic minorities (say, Hispanics), white women are well represented at all levels of the class structure, including the very top.

Bear in mind, however, that at every class level, women typically have less income, wealth, education, and power than men. Patriarchy makes women dependent on men—first their fathers and later their husbands—for their social standing (Bernard, 1981).

Minority Women: Intersection Theory

If women are defined as a minority, what about minority women? Are they doubly handicapped? This question lies at the heart of **intersection theory,** *analysis of the interplay of race, class, and gender, often resulting in multiple dimensions of disadvantage.* Research shows

---

[1]Sociologists use the term "minority" instead of "minority group" because, as explained in Chapter 7 ("Groups and Organizations"), women make up a *category,* not a group. People in a category share a status or identity but generally do not know one another or interact.

that disadvantages linked to gender and race often combine to produce especially low social standing (Ovadia, 2001).

Income data illustrate the validity of this theory. Looking first at race and ethnicity, the median income in 2005 for African American women working full time was $30,363, which is 85 percent as much as the $35,797 earned by non-Hispanic white women; Hispanic women earned $25,022—just 70 percent as much as their white counterparts. Looking at gender, African American women earned 89 percent as much as African American men, and Hispanic women earned 93 percent as much as Hispanic men.

Combining these disadvantages, African American women earned 63 percent as much as non-Hispanic white men, and Hispanic women earned 52 percent as much (U.S. Census Bureau, 2006). These differences reflect minority women's lower positions in the occupational and educational hierarchies. These data confirm that although gender has a powerful effect on our lives, it does not operate alone. Class position, race and ethnicity, and gender form a multilayered system of disadvantage for some and privilege for others (Saint Jean & Feagin, 1998).

Violence against Women

In the nineteenth century, men claimed the right to rule their households, even to the point of using physical discipline against their wives, and a great deal of "manly" violence is still directed at women. A government report estimates 387,000 aggravated assaults against women annually. To this number can be added 177,000 rapes or sexual assaults and perhaps 1.4 million simple assaults (U.S. Bureau of Justice Statistics, 2006).

Gender violence is also an issue on college and university campuses. A report from the U.S. Department of Justice (2000) states that 1.7 percent of female college students have been victims of rape and another 1.1 percent have been victims of attempted rape. In 90 percent of all cases, the victim knew the offender, and most of the assaults took place in the woman's living quarters.

Off campus, most gender-linked violence also occurs where men and women interact most: in the home. Richard Gelles (cited in Roesch, 1984) argues that with the exception of the police and the military, the family is the most violent organization in the United States, and women suffer most of the injuries (Gelles & Cornell, 1990; Smolowe, 1994).

Violence against women also occurs in casual relationships. Most rapes involve men known, and often trusted, by the victims. Dianne Herman (2001) claims that abuse of women is built into our way of life. All forms of violence against women—from the catcalls that intimidate women on city streets to a pinch in a crowded subway to

physical assaults that occur at home—express what she calls a "rape culture" of men trying to dominate women. Sexual violence is fundamentally about *power,* not sex, and therefore should be understood as a dimension of gender stratification.

In global perspective, violence against women is built into different cultures in different ways. One case in point is the practice of female genital mutilation, a painful and often dangerous surgical procedure performed in more than forty countries and known to occur in the United States, as shown in Global Map 2. The Thinking About Diversity: Race, Class, & Gender box highlights a case of genital mutilation that took place in California.

The basic insight of intersection theory is that various dimensions of social stratification—including race and gender—can add up to great disadvantages for some categories of people. Just as African Americans earn less than whites, women earn less than men. Thus African American women confront a "double disadvantage," earning just 63 cents for every dollar earned by non-Hispanic white men. How would you explain the fact that some categories of people are much more likely to end up in low-paying jobs like this one?

David Grossman/The Image Works

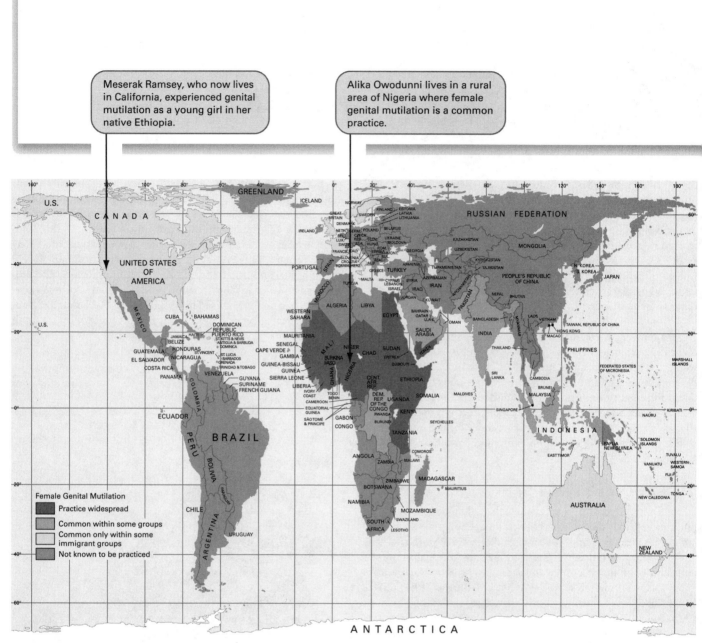

Meserak Ramsey, who now lives in California, experienced genital mutilation as a young girl in her native Ethiopia.

Alika Owodunni lives in a rural area of Nigeria where female genital mutilation is a common practice.

Female Genital Mutilation

- Practice widespread
- Common within some groups
- Common only within some immigrant groups
- Not known to be practiced

WINDOW ON THE WORLD

GLOBAL MAP 2   Female Genital Mutilation in Global Perspective

Female genital mutilation is known to be performed in more than forty countries around the world. Across Africa, the practice is common and affects a majority of girls in the eastern African nations of Sudan, Ethiopia, and Somalia. In several Asian nations, including India, the practice is limited to a few ethnic minorities. In the United States, Canada, several European nations, and Australia, there are reports of the practice among some immigrants.

Source: Data from Seager (2003).

Violence against Men

If our way of life encourages violence against women, it may encourage even more violence against men. In more than 80 percent of cases in which police make an arrest for a violent crime, including mur-

der, robbery, and assault, the offender is a male. In addition, 59 percent of all victims of violent crime are also men (Federal Bureau of Investigation, 2006; U.S. Bureau of Justice Statistics, 2006).

Our culture tends to define masculinity in terms of aggression and violence. "Real men" work and play hard, speed on the highways,

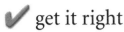

get it right

Feminists argue that rape is not about sex but about power. It is this claim that makes sexual violence against women a matter of gender stratification rather than just crime.

Thinking About Diversity: Race, Class, & Gender
Female Genital Mutilation: Violence in the Name of Morality

Meserak Ramsey, a woman born in Ethiopia and now working as a nurse in California, paid a visit to an old friend's home. Soon after arriving, she noticed her friend's eighteen-month-old daughter huddled in the corner of a room in obvious distress. "What's wrong with her?" she asked.

Ramsey was shocked when the woman said her daughter had recently had a clitoridectomy, the surgical removal of the clitoris. This type of female genital mutilation—performed by a midwife, a tribal practitioner, or a doctor, and typically without anesthesia—is common in Nigeria, Sierra Leone, Senegal, Sudan, Ethiopia, Somalia, and Egypt and is known to exist in certain cultural groups in other nations around the world. It is illegal in the United States.

Among members of highly patriarchal societies, husbands demand that their wives be virgins at marriage and remain sexually faithful thereafter. The point of female genital mutilation is to eliminate sexual feeling, which, people assume, makes the girl less likely to violate sexual norms and thus be more desirable to men. In about one-fifth of all cases, an even more severe procedure, called infibulation, is performed, in which the entire external genital area is removed and the surfaces are stitched together, leaving only a small hole for urination and menstruation. Before marriage, a husband retains

the right to open the wound and ensure himself of his bride's virginity.

How many women have undergone genital mutilation? Worldwide, estimates place the number at 135 million. In the United States, hundreds or even thousands of such procedures are performed every year. In most cases, immigrant mothers and grandmothers who have themselves been mutilated insist that young girls in their family follow their example. Indeed, many immigrant women demand the procedure *because* their daughters now live in the United States, where sexual mores are more lax. "I don't have to worry about her now," the girl's mother explained to Meserak Ramsey. "She'll be a good girl."

Medically, the consequences of genital mutilation include more than the loss of sexual pleasure. Pain is intense and can persist for years. There is also danger of infection, infertility, and even death. Ramsey knows this all too well: She herself underwent genital mutilation as a young girl. She is one of the lucky ones who has had few medical problems since. But the extent of her suffering is suggested by this story: She invited a young U.S. couple to stay at her home. Late at night, she heard the woman cry out and burst into their room to investigate, only to learn that the couple was making love and the woman had just had an orgasm. "I didn't understand," Ramsey recalls. "I thought that there must be something wrong with American girls. But now I know that there is something wrong with me." Or with a system that inflicts such injury in the name of traditional morality.

WHAT DO YOU THINK?

1. Is female genital mutilation a medical procedure or a means of social control? Explain your answer.

2. Can you think of other examples of physical mutilation imposed on women? What are they?

3. What do you think should be done about female genital mutilation in places where it is widespread? Do you think respect for human rights should override respect for cultural differences in this case? Explain your answer.

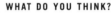

Sources: Crossette (1995) and Boyle, Songora, & Foss (2001).

These young women have just undergone female genital mutilation. What do you think should be done about this practice?

Kuenzig/laif/Aurora & Quanta Productions Inc

---

and let nothing stand in their way. A higher crime rate is one result. But even when no laws are broken, men's lives involve more stress and isolation than women's lives, which is one reason that the suicide rate for men is four times higher than for women. In addition,

as noted earlier, men live, on average, about five fewer years than women.

Violence is not simply a matter of choices made by individuals. It is built into our way of life, with resulting harm to both men and

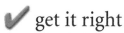

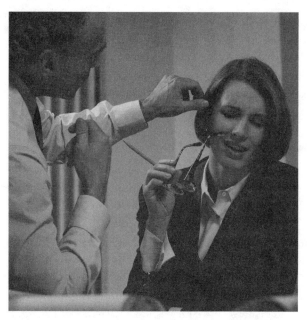

In the last twenty years, our society has defined sexual harassment as an important problem. As a result, at least officially, unwelcome sexual attention is no longer tolerated in the workplace. To what extent do you think sexual comments, off-color jokes, and unnecessary touching still take place on the job?

Keith Brofsky/Getty Images, Inc.—PhotoDisc

women. In short, the way any culture constructs gender plays an important part in how violent or peaceful a society will be.

Sexual Harassment

Sexual harassment refers to *comments, gestures, or physical contacts of a sexual nature that are deliberate, repeated, and unwelcome.* During the 1990s, sexual harassment became an issue of national importance that rewrote the rules for workplace interaction between women and men.

Most (but not all) victims of sexual harassment are women. The reason is that, first, our culture encourages men to be sexually assertive and to see women in sexual terms. As a result, social interaction in the workplace, on campus, and elsewhere can easily take on sexual overtones. Second, most people in positions of power—including business executives, doctors, bureau chiefs, assembly-line supervisors, professors, and military officers—are men who oversee the work of women. Surveys carried out in widely different work settings show that half of the women respondents receive unwanted sexual attention (NORC, 2005).

Sexual harassment is sometimes obvious and direct: A supervisor may ask for sexual favors from an employee and make threats if

the advances are refused. Courts have declared such *quid pro quo* sexual harassment (the Latin phrase means "one thing in return for another") to be a violation of civil rights.

More often, however, sexual harassment is a matter of subtle behavior—suggestive teasing, off-color jokes, comments about someone's looks—that may not even be intended to harass anyone. But based on the *effect* standard favored by many feminists, such actions add up to creating a *hostile environment.* Incidents of this kind are far more complex because they involve different perceptions of the same behavior. For example, a man may think that repeatedly complimenting a co-worker on her appearance is simply being friendly. The co-worker may believe that the man is thinking of her in sexual terms and is not taking her work seriously, an attitude that could harm her job performance and prospects for advancement.

Pornography

Pornography is sexually explicit material that causes sexual arousal. Keep in mind, however, that people take different views of what is and what is not pornographic. The law gives local communities the power to define what sexually explicit materials violate "community standards of decency" and "lack any redeeming social value."

Traditionally, people have raised concerns about pornography as a *moral* issue. But pornography also plays a part in gender stratification. From this point of view, pornography is really a *power* issue because most pornography dehumanizes women, depicting them as the playthings of men.

In addition, there is widespread concern that pornography promotes violence against women by portraying them as weak and undeserving of respect. Men may show contempt for women defined this way by striking out against them. Surveys show that about half of U.S. adults think that pornography encourages men to commit rape (NORC, 2005:293).

Like sexual harassment, pornography raises complex and conflicting issues. Despite the fact that some material may offend just about everybody, many people defend the rights of free speech and artistic expression. Pressure to restrict pornography has increased in recent decades, reflecting both the long-standing concern that pornography weakens morality and more recent concerns that it is demeaning and threatening to women.

 The Internet has made pornography more accessible; do you think it has become more acceptable as well? Why or why not?

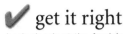 get it right

Look closely at the Applying Theory table to be sure you understand the two theoretical approaches to gender.

 tip

The structural-functional approach emphasizes how gender helps integrate men and women into families by giving instrumental work to males and expressive activity to females. Parsons's thinking appealed to people back in the 1950s when ideas about gender were more traditional.

APPLYING THEORY

Gender

	Structural-Functional Approach	Social-Conflict Approach
What is the level of analysis?	Macro-level	Macro-level
What does gender mean?	Parsons described gender in terms of two complementary patterns of behavior: masculine and feminine.	Engels described gender in terms of the power of one sex over the other.
Is gender helpful or harmful?	Helpful. Gender gives men and women distinctive roles and responsibilities that help society operate smoothly. Gender builds social unity as men and women come together to form families.	Harmful. Gender limits people's personal development. Gender divides society by giving power to men to control the lives of women. Capitalism makes patriarchy stronger.

Theoretical Analysis of Gender

Why does gender exist in the first place? Sociology's macro-level approaches offer insights about the importance of gender in social organization. The Applying Theory table summarizes the important insights offered by the structural-functional and social-conflict approaches.

Structural-Functional Analysis

The structural-functional approach views society as a complex system of many separate but integrated parts. From this point of view, gender serves as a means to organize social life.

Members of hunting and gathering societies had little power over the forces of biology. Lacking effective birth control, women were frequently pregnant, and the responsibilities of child care kept them close to home. At the same time, men's greater strength made them more suited for warfare and hunting game. Over the centuries, this sexual division of labor became institutionalized and largely taken for granted (Lengermann & Wallace, 1985; Freedman, 2002).

Industrial technology opens up a much greater range of cultural possibilities. With human muscles no longer the main energy source, the physical strength of men becomes less important. In addition, the ability to control reproduction gives women greater choices about how to live. Modern societies relax traditional gender roles as they become more meritocratic because such rigid roles waste an enormous amount of human talent. Yet change comes slowly because gender is deeply rooted in culture.

Talcott Parsons: Gender and Complementarity

Talcott Parsons (1942, 1951, 1954) argued that keeping some gender differences helps integrate society, at least in its traditional form. Gender establishes a *complementary* set of roles that links men and women into family units and gives each sex responsibility for important tasks. Women take the lead in managing the household and raising children. Men connect the family to the larger world as they participate in the labor force.

Thus gender plays an important part in socialization. Society teaches boys—presumably destined for the labor force—to be rational, self-assured, and competitive. Parsons called this complex of traits *instrumental* qualities. To prepare girls for child rearing, their socialization stresses *expressive* qualities, such as emotional responsiveness and sensitivity to others.

Society encourages gender conformity by instilling in men and women a fear that straying too far from accepted standards of masculinity or femininity will cause rejection by the other sex. In simple terms, women learn to reject nonmasculine men as sexually unattractive, and men learn to reject unfeminine women. In sum, gender integrates society both structurally (in terms of what we do) and morally (in terms of what we believe).

 get it right

The structural-functional approach is a more "horizontal" view of gender that emphasizes complementarity. The social-conflict approach is a more "vertical" view of gender that emphasizes inequality.

 tip

Engels was, of course, Marx's friend and colleague. Marx, however, writes very little about gender.

In the 1950s, Talcott Parsons proposed that sociologists interpret gender as a matter of *differences*. As he saw it, masculine men and feminine women formed strong families and made for an orderly society. In recent decades, however, social-conflict theory has reinterpreted gender as a matter of *inequality*. From this point of view, U.S. society places men in a position of dominance over women.

FPG/Getty Images, Inc.—Taxi

CRITICAL REVIEW Influential in the 1950s, this approach has lost much of its standing today. First, functionalism assumes a singular vision of society that is not shared by everyone. Historically, many women have worked outside the home because of economic need, a fact not reflected in Parsons's conventional, middle-class view of family life. Second, Parsons's analysis ignores the personal strains and social costs of rigid, traditional gender roles. Third, in the eyes of those seeking sexual equality, Parsons's gender "complementarity" amounts to little more than women submitting to male domination.

 YOUR LEARNING In Parsons's analysis, what functions does gender perform for society?

Social-Conflict Analysis

From a social-conflict point of view, gender involves differences not just in behavior but in power as well. Consider the striking similarity between the way ideas about gender benefit men and the way oppression of racial and ethnic minorities benefits white people. Conventional ideas about gender do not make society operate smoothly;

they create division and tension, with men seeking to protect their privileges as women challenge the status quo.

As earlier chapters explain, the social-conflict approach draws heavily on the ideas of Karl Marx. Yet as far as gender is concerned, Marx was a product of his time, and his writings focused almost entirely on men. However, his friend and collaborator Friedrich Engels did develop a theory of gender stratification.

Friedrich Engels: Gender and Class

Looking back through history, Engels saw that in hunting and gathering societies, the activities of women and men, although different, had equal importance. A successful hunt brought men great prestige, but the vegetation gathered by women provided most of a group's food supply. As technological advances led to a productive surplus, however, social equality and communal sharing gave way to private property and ultimately a class hierarchy, and men gained significant power over women. With surplus wealth to pass on to heirs, upper-class men needed to be sure their sons were their own, which led them to control the sexuality of women. The desire to control property brought about monogamous marriage and the family. Women were taught to remain virgins until marriage, to remain faithful to their husbands thereafter, and to build their lives around bearing and raising one man's children.

According to Engels (1902, orig. 1884), capitalism makes male domination even stronger. First, capitalism creates more wealth, which gives greater power to men as income earners and owners of property. Second, an expanding capitalist economy depends on turning people, especially women, into consumers who seek personal fulfillment through buying and using products. Third, society assigns women the task of maintaining the home to free men to work in factories. The double exploitation of capitalism, as Engels saw it, lies in paying men low wages for their labor and paying women no wages at all.

CRITICAL REVIEW Social-conflict analysis is critical of conventional ideas about gender, claiming that society would be better off if we minimized or even did away with this dimension of social structure. One problem with this approach is that it regards conventional families, supported by traditionalists as morally positive, as a social evil. Second, social-conflict analysis minimizes the extent to which women and men live together cooperatively, and often happily, in families. A third problem lies in the assertion that capitalism is the basis of gender stratification. In fact, agrarian societies are typically more patriarchal than industrial-capitalist

GENDER STRATIFICATION

societies. Although socialist nations, including the People's Republic of China and the former Soviet Union, did move women into the workforce, by and large they provided women with very low pay in sex-segregated jobs (Rosendahl, 1997; Haney, 2002).

 YOUR LEARNING According to Engels, how does gender support social inequality in a capitalist class system?

Feminism

Feminism is *support of social equality for women and men, in opposition to patriarchy and sexism.* The first wave of feminism in the United States began in the 1840s as women opposed to slavery, including Elizabeth Cady Stanton and Lucretia Mott, drew parallels between the oppression of African Americans and the oppression of women. Their main objective was obtaining the right to vote, which was finally achieved in 1920. But other disadvantages persisted, causing a second wave of feminism to arise in the 1960s that continues today.

Basic Feminist Ideas

Feminism views the personal experiences of women and men through the lens of gender. How we think of ourselves (gender identity), how we act (gender roles), and our sex's social standing (gender stratification) are all rooted in the operation of society.

Although feminists disagree about many things, most support five general principles:

1. **Working to increase equality.** Feminist thinking is strongly political; it links ideas to action. Feminism is critical of the status quo, pushing for change toward social equality for women and men.

2. **Expanding human choice.** Feminists argue that cultural conceptions of gender divide the full range of human qualities into two opposing and limiting spheres: the female world of emotions and cooperation and the male world of rationality and competition. As an alternative, feminists propose a "reintegration of humanity" by which all individuals can develop all human traits (French, 1985).

3. **Eliminating gender stratification.** Feminism opposes laws and cultural norms that limit the education, income, and job opportunities of women. For this reason, feminists have long supported passage of the Equal Rights Amendment (ERA) to the U.S. Constitution, which states, in its entirety, "Equality of

Tennis star Maria Sharapova is not the top-ranking player in the world, but she has consistently earned the most money from the endorsement of various products. How much of her financial success can be attributed to talent on the courts and how much is due to her good looks? Do you think, for women, "beauty is power" or not? Why?

Henry Romero/Corbis/Reuters America LLC

rights under the law shall not be denied or abridged by the United States or any State on account of sex." The ERA was first proposed in Congress in 1923. Although surveys show widespread public support, it has yet to become law.

4. **Ending sexual violence.** Today's women's movement seeks to eliminate sexual violence. Feminists argue that patriarchy distorts the relationships between women and men, encouraging violence against women in the form of rape, domestic abuse, sexual harassment, and pornography (A. Dworkin, 1987; Freedman, 2002).

5. **Promoting sexual freedom.** Finally, feminism supports women's control over their sexuality and reproduction. Feminists support the free availability of birth control information. As Figure 3 shows, about three-fourths of married U.S. women of childbearing age use contraception; the use of contraceptives is far less common in many lower-income nations. Most feminists also support a woman's right to choose whether to bear children or end a pregnancy, rather than allowing men—husbands, physicians, and legislators—to control their reproduction. Many feminists also support gay people's efforts to

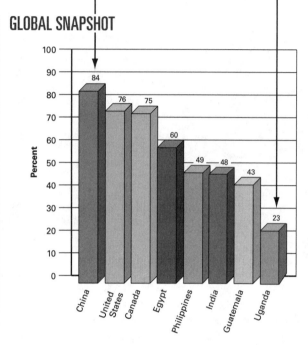

Achen Eke, age 24 and mother of three, lives in Uganda, where many women do not have access to contraception.

Chen-chi Bai, age 31 and the mother of one boy, lives in China, where contraception is encouraged and widely practiced.

GLOBAL SNAPSHOT

FIGURE 3 Use of Contraception by Married Women of Childbearing Age

In the United States, most married women of childbearing age use contraception. In many lower-income countries, however, most women do not have the opportunity to make this choice.

Source: United Nations Development Programme (2006).

end prejudice and discrimination in a mostly heterosexual culture (Ferree & Hess, 1995; Armstrong, 2002).

 On your campus, do men's organizations (such as fraternities and athletic teams) enjoy any special privileges? What about women's organizations?

Types of Feminism

Although feminists agree on the importance of gender equality, they disagree on how to achieve it: through liberal feminism, socialist feminism, or radical feminism (Stacey, 1983; L. Vogel, 1983; Ferree & Hess, 1995; Armstrong, 2002; Freedman, 2002). The Applying Theory table highlights the key arguments made by each type of feminist thinking.

Liberal Feminism

Liberal feminism is rooted in the classic liberal thinking that individuals should be free to develop their own talents and pursue their own interests. Liberal feminism accepts the basic organization of our society but seeks to expand the rights and opportunities of women, in part by passage of the Equal Rights Amendment. Liberal feminists also support reproductive freedom for all women. They respect the family as a social institution but seek changes, including more widely available maternity and paternity leave and child care for parents who work.

Given their belief in the rights of individuals, liberal feminists think that women should advance according to their own efforts, rather than working collectively for change. Both women and men, through their individual achievement, are capable of improving their lives, as long as society removes legal and cultural barriers.

Socialist Feminism

Socialist feminism evolved from the ideas of Karl Marx and Friedrich Engels. From this point of view, capitalism strengthens patriarchy by concentrating wealth and power in the hands of a small number of men. Socialist feminists do not think the reforms supported by liberal feminism go far enough. The family form created by capitalism must change if we are to replace "domestic slavery" with some collective means of carrying out housework and community-run child care. Replacing the traditional family can come about only through a socialist revolution that creates a state-centered economy to meet the needs of all.

Radical Feminism

Like socialist feminism, *radical feminism* finds liberal feminism inadequate. Radical feminists believe that patriarchy is so deeply rooted in society that even a socialist revolution would not end it. Instead, reaching the goal of gender equality means that society must eliminate gender itself.

One possible way to achieve this goal is to use new reproductive technology to separate women's bodies from the process of childbearing. With an end to motherhood, radical feminists reason, society could leave behind the entire family system, liberating women, men, and children from the oppression of family, gender, and sex itself (A. Dworkin, 1987). Radical feminism seeks an egalitarian and gender-free society, a revolution more sweeping than that sought by Marx.

Opposition to Feminism

Because feminism calls for significant change, it has always been controversial. But today, just 20 percent of U.S. adults say they oppose feminism, a share that has declined over time (NORC, 2005). Figure

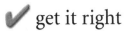 get it right

The three types of feminism all agree on the importance of gender and the need to make women and men more socially equal. They disagree on the way to do that, with liberal feminism involving the least societal change and radical feminism involving the most.

 tip

Look closely at the Applying Theory table to be sure you understand the three types of feminism and their differences.

APPLYING THEORY

Feminism

	Liberal Feminism	Socialist Feminism	Radical Feminism
Does it accept the basic order of society?	Yes. Liberal feminism seeks change only to ensure equality of opportunity.	No. Socialist feminism supports an end to social classes and to family gender roles that encourage "domestic slavery."	No. Radical feminism supports an end to the family system.
How do women improve their social standing?	Individually, according to personal ability and effort.	Collectively, through socialist revolution.	Collectively, by working to eliminate gender itself.

4 shows a similar downward trend in opposition to feminism among college students after 1970. Note, however, that there has been little change in attitudes in recent years and that more men than women express antifeminist attitudes.

Feminism provokes criticism and resistance from both men and women who hold conventional ideas about gender. Some men oppose sexual equality for the same reason that many white people have historically opposed social equality for people of color: They do not want to give up their privileges. Other men and women, including those who are neither rich nor powerful, distrust a social movement (especially its radical expressions) that attacks the traditional family and rejects patterns that have guided male-female relations for centuries.

Men who have been socialized to value strength and dominance feel uneasy about feminist ideas of men as gentle and warm (Doyle, 1983). Similarly, some women whose lives center on their husbands and children may think feminism does not value the social roles that give meaning to their lives. In general, resistance to feminism is strongest among women who have the least education and those who do not work outside the home (Marshall, 1985; Ferree & Hess, 1995).

Race and ethnicity play some part in shaping people's attitudes toward feminism. In general, African Americans (especially African American women) express the greatest support of feminist goals, followed by whites, with Hispanic Americans holding somewhat more traditional attitudes when it comes to gender (Kane, 2000).

Resistance to feminism is also found in academic circles. Some sociologists charge that feminism ignores a growing body of evidence that men and women do think and act in somewhat different ways,

which may make complete gender equality impossible. Furthermore, say critics, with its drive to increase women's presence in the workplace, feminism undervalues the crucial and unique contribution women make to the development of children, especially in the first years of life (Baydar & Brooks-Gunn, 1991; Popenoe, 1993b; Gibbs, 2001).

Finally, there is the question of *how* women should go about improving their social standing. A large majority of U.S. adults believe that women should have equal rights, but 70 percent also say that women should advance individually, according to their abilities; only 10 percent favor women's rights groups or collective action (NORC, 2005:426).

For these reasons, most opposition to feminism is directed toward its socialist and radical forms, while support for liberal feminism is widespread. In addition, there is an unmistakable trend toward greater gender equality. In 1977, some 65 percent of all adults endorsed the statement "It is much better for everyone involved if the man is the achiever outside the home and the woman takes care of the home and family." By 2004, the share supporting this statement had dropped sharply, to 38 percent (NORC, 2005:314).

Gender: Looking Ahead

Predictions about the future are no more than educated guesses. Just as economists disagree about what the inflation rate will be a year from now, sociologists can offer only general observations about the likely future of gender and society.

tip

The Applying Sociology in Everyday Life items provide additional ways for you to connect the ideas found in this chapter with your own life.

STUDENT SNAPSHOT

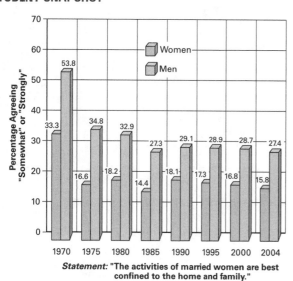

FIGURE 4   Opposition to Feminism among First-Year College Students, 1970–2005

The share of college students expressing antifeminist views declined after 1970. Men are still more likely than women to hold such attitudes.

Sources: Astin et al. (2002) and Pryor et al. (2005).

Change so far has been remarkable. A century ago, women were second-class citizens, without access to many jobs, barred from political office, and with no right to vote. Although women remain socially disadvantaged, the movement toward equality has surged ahead. Two-thirds of people entering the workforce during the 1990s were women, and in 2000, for the first time, a majority of U.S. families had both husband and wife in the paid labor force. Today's economy depends a great deal on the earnings of women.

Many factors have contributed to this transformation. Perhaps most important, industrialization and recent advances in computer technology have shifted the nature of work from physically demanding tasks that favor male strength to jobs that require thought and imagination. This change puts women and men on an even footing. Also, because birth control technology has given us greater control over reproduction, women's lives are less constrained by unwanted pregnancies.

Many women and men have also deliberately pursued social equality. For example, complaints of sexual harassment in the workplace are now taken much more seriously than they were a generation ago. As more women assume positions of power in the corporate and political worlds, social changes in the twenty-first century may be as great as those that have already taken place.

Applying Sociology in Everyday Life

1. Take a walk through a business area of your local community. Which businesses are frequented almost entirely by women? By men? By both men and women? Try to explain the patterns you find.

2. Watch several hours of children's television programming on a Saturday morning. Notice the advertising, which mostly sells toys and breakfast cereal. Keep track of what share of toys are "gendered," that is, aimed at one sex or the other. What traits do you associate with toys intended for boys and those intended for girls?

3. Do some research on the history of women's issues in your state. When was the first woman sent to Congress? What laws once existed that restricted the work women could do? Do any such laws exist today? Did your state support the passage of the Equal Rights Amendment or not? What share of political officials today are women?

MAKING THE GRADE

Gender Stratification

Gender and Inequality

GENDER refers to the meaning a culture attaches to being female or male.

- Evidence that gender is rooted in culture includes global comparisons by Margaret Mead and others showing how societies define what is feminine and masculine in various ways.
- Gender is not only about difference: Because societies give more power and other resources to men than to women, gender is an important dimension of social stratification. **Sexism** is built into the operation of social institutions.
- Although some degree of **patriarchy** is found almost everywhere, it varies throughout history and from society to society.

gender the personal traits and social positions that members of a society attach to being female or male

gender stratification the unequal distribution of wealth, power, and privilege between men and women

matriarchy a form of social organization in which females dominate males

patriarchy a form of social organization in which males dominate females

sexism the belief that one sex is innately superior to the other

Gender and Socialization

Through the socialization process, gender becomes part of our personalities (**gender identity**) and our actions (**gender roles**). All the major agents of socialization—family, peer groups, schools, and the mass media—reinforce cultural definitions of what is feminine and masculine.

gender roles (sex roles) attitudes and activities that a society links to each sex

Gender and Social Stratification

Gender stratification shapes **THE WORKPLACE**:

- A majority of women are now in the paid labor force, but 40% hold clerical or service jobs.
- Comparing full-time U.S. workers, women earn 77% as much as men.
- This gender difference in earnings results from differences in jobs, differences in family responsibilities, and discrimination.

Gender stratification shapes **FAMILY LIFE**:

- Most unpaid housework is performed by women, whether or not they hold jobs outside the home.
- Pregnancy and raising small children keep many women out of the labor force at a time when their male peers are making important career gains.

Gender stratification shapes **POLITICS**:

- Until a century ago, almost no women held any elected office in the United States.
- In recent decades, the number of women in politics has increased significantly.
- Even so, the vast majority of elected officials, especially at the national level, are men.
- Women make up only about 15% of U.S. military personnel.

minority any category of people distinguished by physical or cultural difference that a society sets apart and subordinates

intersection theory analysis of the interplay of race, class, and gender, often resulting in multiple dimensions of disadvantage

sexual harassment comments, gestures, or physical contacts of a sexual nature that are deliberate, repeated, and unwelcome

INTERSECTION THEORY investigates the intersection of race, class, and gender, factors that combine to cause special disadvantages to some categories of people.

- Women of color encounter greater social disadvantages than white women and earn much less than white men.
- Because all women have a distinctive social identity and are disadvantaged, they are a minority, although most white women do not think of themselves this way.

VIOLENCE AGAINST WOMEN AND MEN is a widespread problem that is linked to how a society defines gender. Related issues include

- **sexual harassment**, which mostly victimizes women because our culture encourages men to be assertive and to see women in sexual terms.
- **pornography**, which portrays women as sexual objects. Many see pornography as a moral issue; because pornography dehumanizes women, it is also a power issue.

Gender stratification shapes **EDUCATION**:

- Women now earn 60% of all associate's and bachelor's degrees.
- Women make up 47% of law school students and are an increasing share of graduates in professions traditionally dominated by men, including medicine and business administration.

MAKING THE GRADE *continued . . .*

Theoretical Analysis of Gender

The **STRUCTURAL-FUNCTIONAL APPROACH** suggests that

- in preindustrial societies, distinctive roles for males and females reflect biological differences between the sexes.
- in industrial societies, marked gender inequality becomes dysfunctional and gradually decreases.

Talcott Parsons described gender differences in terms of complementary roles that promote the social integration of families and society as a whole.

The **SOCIAL-CONFLICT APPROACH** suggests that

- gender is an important dimension of social inequality and social conflict.
- gender inequality benefits men and disadvantages women.

Friedrich Engels tied gender stratification to the rise of private property and a class hierarchy. Marriage and the family are strategies by which men control their property through control of the sexuality of women. Capitalism exploits everyone by paying men low wages and assigning women the task of maintaining the home.

See the Applying Theory table in this chapter.

Feminism

FEMINISM

- endorses the social equality of women and men and opposes patriarchy and sexism.
- seeks to eliminate violence against women.
- advocates giving women control over their reproduction.

There are three types of feminism:

- Liberal feminism seeks equal opportunity for both sexes within the existing society.
- Socialist feminism claims that gender equality will come about by replacing capitalism with socialism.
- Radical feminism seeks to eliminate the concept of gender itself and to create an egalitarian and gender-free society.

Today, only 20% of U.S. adults say they oppose feminism. Most opposition is directed toward socialist and radical feminism. Support for liberal feminism is widespread.

feminism support of social equality for women and men, in opposition to patriarchy and sexism

See the Applying Theory table in this chapter.

Sample Test Questions

These questions are similar to those found in the test bank that accompanies this textbook.

Multiple-Choice Questions

1. Gender is not just a matter of difference but also a matter of
   a. power.
   b. wealth.
   c. prestige.
   d. All of the above are correct.

2. The anthropologist Margaret Mead studied gender in three societies in New Guinea and found that
   a. all societies define femininity in much the same way.
   b. all societies define masculinity in much the same way.
   c. what is feminine in one society may be masculine in another.
   d. the meaning of gender is changing everywhere toward greater equality.

3. For all of us raised in U.S. society, gender shapes our
   a. feelings.
   b. thoughts.
   c. actions.
   d. All of the above are correct.

4. There is a "beauty myth" in U.S. society that encourages
   a. women to believe that their personal importance depends on their looks.
   b. beautiful women to think that they do not need men.
   c. men to improve their physical appearance to get the attention of women.
   d. women to think they are as physically attractive as today's men are.

5. In the United States, what share of women work for income?
   a. 79 percent
   b. 59 percent
   c. 49 percent
   d. 29 percent

6. In the U.S. labor force,
   a. men and women have the same types of jobs.
   b. men and women have the same pay.
   c. women are still concentrated in several types of jobs.
   d. almost all working women hold "pink-collar jobs."

7. For which of the following categories of people in the United States is it true that women do more housework than men?
   a. people who work for income
   b. people who are married
   c. people who have children
   d. All of the above are correct.

8. In the United States, women in the labor force working full time earn how much for every dollar earned by men working full time?
   a. 77 cents
   b. 86 cents
   c. 97 cents
   d. 99 cents

9. After the 2006 elections, women held about what percentage of seats in Congress?
   a. 6 percent
   b. 16 percent
   c. 36 percent
   d. 56 percent

10. Which type of feminism accepts U.S. society as it is but wants to give women the same rights and opportunities as men?
    a. socialist feminism
    b. liberal feminism
    c. radical feminism
    d. All of the above are correct.

ANSWERS: 1 (d); 2 (c); 3 (d); 4 (a); 5 (b); 6 (c); 7 (d); 8 (a); 9 (b); 10 (b).

Essay Questions

1. How do the concepts "sex" and "gender" differ? In what ways are they related?

2. Why is gender considered a dimension of social stratification? How does gender intersect with other dimensions of inequality such as class, race, and ethnicity?

Race and Ethnicity

Ours is among the most racially and ethnically diverse of all societies. Racial and ethnic differences reflect people's traditional heritage and are a source of pride. At the same time, they are also an important foundation of social stratification.

Dean Conger/ NGS Image Collection

Race and Ethnicity

WHAT are race and ethnicity, and how are they created by society?

WHY does the United States have so much racial and ethnic diversity?

HOW are race and ethnicity important dimensions of social inequality today?

Bryant Mason

In a sociology class at Bronx Community College in New York, the instructor is leading a small-group discussion of race and ethnicity. He explains that there has been a lot of change in how people think about these concepts. He suggests that the students find some examples in books published over the last few decades. Then he asks them, "How do you describe yourself?"

Eva Rodriguez is quick to respond. "This is hard for me to answer. Most people think of race as black and white. But it's not. I have both black and white ancestry in me, but you know what? I don't think of myself in that way. I don't think of myself in terms of race at all. You can call me Puerto Rican or call me Hispanic. I prefer the term 'Latina.' Calling myself Latina says I have a mixed racial heritage, and that's what I am. I wish more people understood that race is not clear-cut."

This chapter examines the meaning of race and ethnicity. There are now millions of people in the United States who, like Eva Rodriguez, do not think of themselves in terms of a single category but as having a mix of ancestry.

The Social Meaning of Race and Ethnicity

As the opening to this chapter suggests, people frequently confuse race and ethnicity. For this reason, we begin with some definitions.

Race

A **race** is *a socially constructed category of people who share biologically transmitted traits that members of a society consider important.* People may classify one another racially based on physical characteristics such as skin color, facial features, hair texture, and body shape.

Physical diversity appeared among our human ancestors as the result of living in different geographic regions of the world. In regions of intense heat, for example, humans developed darker skin (from the natural pigment melanin) as protection from the sun; in regions with moderate climates, people have lighter skin. Such differences are literally only skin deep because human beings the world over are members of a single biological species.

The striking variety of physical traits found today is also the product of migration; genetic characteristics once common to a single place (such as light skin or curly hair) are now found in many lands. Especially pronounced is the racial mix in the Middle East (western Asia), historically a crossroads of migration. Greater physical uniformity characterizes more isolated people, such as the island-dwelling Japanese. But every population has some genetic mixture, and increasing contact among the world's people ensures even more blending of physical characteristics in the future.

Although we think of race in terms of biological elements, race is a socially constructed concept. It is true that human beings differ in any number of ways involving physical traits, but a "race" comes into being only when the members of a society decide that some physical trait (such as skin color or eye shape) actually *matters*.

Because race is a matter of social definitions, it is a highly variable concept. For example, the members of U.S. society consider racial differences more important than people of many other countries. We also tend to "see" three racial categories—typically, black, white, and Asian—while people in other societies identify many more categories. People in Brazil, for example, distinguish between *branca* (white), *parda* (brown), *morena* (brunette), *mulata* (mulatto), *preta* (black), and *amarela* (yellow) (Inciardi, Surratt, & Telles, 2000).

In addition, race may be defined differently by various categories of people within a society. In the United States, for example, research shows that white people "see" black people as having darker skin than black people do (Hill, 2002).

The meanings and importance of race not only differ from place to place but also change over time. For example, in 1900, it was common in the United States to consider people of Irish, Italian, or Jewish ancestry as "nonwhite." By 1950, however, this was no longer the case, and such people today are considered part of the "white" category (Loveman, 1999; Brodkin, 2007).

Today, the Census Bureau allows people to describe themselves using more than one racial category (offering a total of sixty-three racial options). Our society officially recognizes a wide range of multiracial people (Porter, 2001).

Researchers have found that biracial and multiracial people choose different racial identities in different settings, depending on the people they are with (Harris & Sim, 2002). Have you ever experienced such a "racial shift"? Explain.

Racial Types

Scientists invented the concept of "race" more than a century ago as they tried to organize the world's physical diversity into three racial types. They called people with relatively light skin and fine hair *Caucasoid,* people with darker skin and coarse hair *Negroid,* and people with yellow or brown skin and distinctive folds on the eyelids *Mongoloid.*

Sociologists consider such terms misleading at best and harmful at worst. For one thing, no society contains biologically "pure" people. The skin color of people we might call "Caucasoid" (or

Chapter Overview

This chapter explains how race and ethnicity are created by society. Both race and ethnicity are not only matters of difference but also dimensions of social inequality.

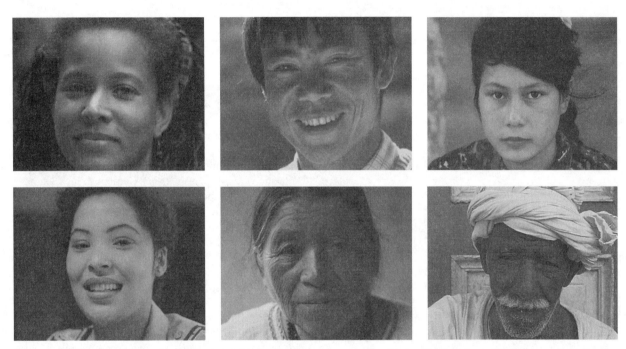

The range of biological variation in human beings is far greater than any system of racial classification allows. This fact is made obvious by trying to place all of the people pictured here into simple racial categories.

Joel Gordon/Joel Gordon Photography/Design Conceptions (*top left*); Leong Ka Tai (*top center*); Owen Franken/Corbis/Bettmann (*top right*); Charles O'Rear/Corbis/Bettmann (*bottom left*); Paul W. Liebhardt (*bottom center*); Lisi Dennis/Lisl Dennis (*bottom right*)

"Indo-European," "Caucasian," or more commonly, "white") ranges from very light (typical in Scandinavia) to very dark (in southern India). The same variation exists among so-called "Negroids" ("Africans" or more commonly, "black" people) and "Mongoloids" ("Asians"). In fact, many "white" people (say, in southern India) actually have darker skin than many "black" people (the Negroid Aborigines of Australia). Overall, the three racial categories differ in only 6 percent of their genes, and there is actually more genetic variation *within* each category than *between* categories. This means that two people in the European nation of Sweden, randomly selected, are likely to have at least as much genetic difference as a Swede and a person in the African nation of Senegal (Harris & Sim, 2002; American Sociological Association, 2003; California Newsreel, 2003).

So how important is race? From a biological point of view, knowing people's racial category allows us to predict almost nothing about them. Why, then, do societies make so much of race? Such categories allow societies to rank people in a hierarchy, giving some people more money, power, and prestige than others and allowing some people to feel that they are inherently "better" than others. Because race may matter so much, societies may construct racial categories in extreme

ways. Throughout much of the twentieth century, for example, many southern states labeled as "colored" anyone with as little as one thirty-second African ancestry (that is, one African American great-great-great-grandparent). Today, the law allows parents to declare the race of a child (or not) as they wish. Even so, most members of U.S. society are still very sensitive to people's racial backgrounds.

 How much dating is there between people of different racial categories on your campus? Is the pattern changing over time?

A Trend toward Mixture

Over many generations and throughout the Americas, the genetic traits from around the world have become mixed. Many "black" people have a significant Caucasoid ancestry, just as many "white" people have some Negroid genes. Whatever people may think, race is not a black-and-white issue.

Today, people are more willing to define themselves as multiracial. When completing their 2000 census forms, almost 7 million

student 2 student

"When I started reading about race, I realized that a lot of what I thought was true is not."

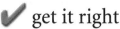 get it right

Keep in mind that race is based on biological factors and ethnicity is based on cultural factors. Both racial and ethnic identities are socially created, meaning that racial or ethnic differences come into existence only when people take note of some factor and decide that it "matters."

Table 1 Racial and Ethnic Categories in the United States, 2000

Racial or Ethnic Classification*	Approximate U.S. Population	Percentage of Total Population
Hispanic descent	**35,305,818**	**12.5%**
Mexican	20,640,711	7.3
Puerto Rican	3,406,178	1.2
Cuban	1,241,685	0.4
Other Hispanic	10,017,244	3.6
African descent	**34,658,190**	**12.3**
Nigerian	165,481	0.1
Ethiopian	86,918	<
Cape Verdean	77,103	<
Other African	34,328,688	12.1
Native American descent	**2,475,956**	**0.9**
American Indian	1,815,653	0.6
Eskimo	45,919	<
Other Native American	614,384	0.2
Asian or Pacific Island descent	**10,641,833**	**3.8**
Chinese	2,432,585	0.9
Filipino	1,850,314	0.7
Asian Indian	1,678,765	0.6
Vietnamese	1,122,528	0.4
Korean	1,076,872	0.4
Japanese	796,700	0.3
Cambodian	171,937	<
Other Asian or Pacific Islander	1,512,132	0.5
West Indian descent	**1,869,504**	**0.7**
Arab descent	**1,202,871**	**0.4**
Non-Hispanic European descent	**194,552,774**	**70.9**
German	42,885,162	15.2
Irish	30,528,492	10.8
English	24,515,138	8.7
Italian	15,723,555	5.6
Polish	8,977,444	3.2
French	8,309,908	3.0
Scottish	4,890,581	1.7
Dutch	4,542,494	1.6
Other Non-Hispanic European	54,180,000	21.1
Two or more races	**6,826,228**	**2.4**

*People of Hispanic descent may be of any race. Many people also identify with more than one ethnic category. Therefore, figures total more than 100 percent.

<indicates less than 1/10 of 1 percent.

Sources: U.S. Census Bureau (2001, 2002, 2004).

people described themselves by checking two or more racial categories. In addition, the official number of interracial births tripled over the past twenty years to 185,000 annually, about 5 percent of all births.

Ethnicity

Ethnicity is *a shared cultural heritage*. People define themselves—or others—as members of an *ethnic category* based on common ancestry, language, or religion that gives them a distinctive social identity. The United States is a multiethnic society. Even though we favor the English language, more than 52 million people (19 percent of the U.S. population) speak Spanish, Italian, German, French, Chinese, or some other language in their homes. In California, more than one-third of the population does so. With regard to religion, the United States is a predominantly Protestant nation, but most people of Spanish, Italian, and Polish descent are Roman Catholic, and many of Greek, Ukrainian, and Russian descent belong to the Eastern Orthodox church. More than 6 million Jewish Americans have ancestral ties to various nations around the world. The population of Muslim men and women is rapidly increasing and is variously estimated at between 2 and 8 million.

Like the reality of race, the meaning of ethnicity is socially constructed, becoming important only because society defines it that way. For example, U.S. society defines people of Spanish descent as "Latin," even though Italy probably has a more "Latin" culture than Spain. People of Italian descent are not viewed as Latin but as "European" and therefore less different (Camara, 2000; Brodkin, 2007). Like racial differences, the importance of ethnic differences can change over time. A century ago, Catholics and Jews were considered "different" in the mostly Protestant United States. This is much less true today.

Keep in mind that *race* is constructed from *biological* traits and *ethnicity* is constructed from *cultural* traits. However, the two often go hand in hand. For example, Japanese Americans have distinctive physical traits and, for those who hold to a traditional way of life, a distinctive culture as well. Table 1 presents the broad sweep of racial and ethnic diversity in the United States, as recorded by the 2000 census.

On an individual level, people play up or play down cultural traits, depending on whether they want to fit in or stand apart from the surrounding society. Immigrants may drop their cultural traditions or, like many people of Native American descent in recent years, try to revive their heritage. For most people, ethnicity is more complex than race because they identify with several ethnic backgrounds. The golf star Tiger Woods describes himself as one-eighth American Indian, one-fourth Thai, and one-fourth Chinese, as well as one-eighth white and one-fourth black (J. E. White, 1997).

Marcos Chapa attends college in San Diego and lives in a community where most people are in some minority category.

Marianne Blumquist attends a community college in a small town an hour west of Minneapolis, where there are few racial or ethnic minorities.

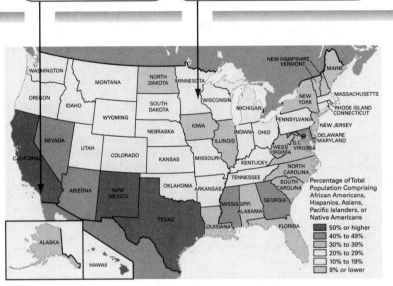

SEEING OURSELVES

NATIONAL MAP 1
Where the Minority Majority Already Exists

By 2004, minorities had become a majority in four states—Hawaii, California, New Mexico, and Texas—and the District of Columbia. At the other extreme, Vermont and Maine have the lowest share of racial and ethnic minorities (about 4 percent each). Why are states with high minority populations located in the South and Southwest?

Source: U.S. Census Bureau (2006).

Percentage of Total Population Comprising African Americans, Hispanics, Asians, Pacific Islanders, or Native Americans

- 50% or higher
- 40% to 49%
- 30% to 39%
- 20% to 29%
- 10% to 19%
- 9% or lower

Minorities

March 3, Dallas, Texas. Sitting in the lobby of just about any hotel in a major U.S. city presents a lesson in contrasts: The majority of the guests checking in and out are white; the majority of hotel employees who carry luggage, serve the food, and clean the rooms are people of color.

A **minority** is *any category of people distinguished by physical or cultural difference that a society sets apart and subordinates.* Minority standing can be based on race, ethnicity, or both. As shown in Table 1, non-Hispanic white people (71 percent of the total) are still a majority of the U.S. population. But the share of minorities is increasing. Today, minorities are a majority in four states (California, New Mexico, Texas, and Hawaii) and in half the country's 100 largest cities. By about 2050, minorities are likely to form a majority of the entire U.S. population. National Map 1 shows where a minority majority already exists.

Minorities have two important characteristics. First, they share a *distinctive identity,* which may be based on physical or cultural traits. Second, minorities experience *subordination.* As the rest of this chapter shows, U.S. minorities typically have lower income, lower occupational prestige, and limited schooling. These facts mean that class, race, and ethnicity, as well as gender, are overlapping and reinforcing dimensions of social stratification. The Thinking About Diversity: Race, Class, & Gender box on the next page profiles the struggles of recent Latin American immigrants.

Of course, not all members of any minority category are disadvantaged. Some Latinos are quite wealthy, certain Chinese Americans are celebrated business leaders, and African Americans are among our nation's leading scholars. But even job success rarely allows individuals to escape their minority standing. Race or ethnicity often serves as a *master status* that overshadows personal accomplishments.

Minorities usually make up a small proportion of a society's population, but this is not always the case. Black South Africans are disadvantaged even though they are a numerical majority in their country. In the United States, women represent slightly more than half the population but still lack many of the opportunities and privileges enjoyed by men.

Do you think all U.S. people of color, rich and poor alike, should be considered minorities? Why or why not?

Prejudice and Stereotypes

November 19, Jerusalem, Israel. We are driving along the outskirts of this historic city—a holy place to Jews, Christians, and Muslims—when Razi, our taxi driver, spots a small group of Falasha—Ethiopian Jews—on a street corner. "Those people over there," he points as he speaks, "they are different. They don't drive cars. They don't want to improve themselves. Even when our country offers them schooling, they don't take it." He shakes his head at the Ethiopians and drives on.

get it right

As you read ahead, be sure you understand the differences between racism, prejudice, and discrimination.

 Thinking About Diversity: Race, Class, & Gender

Hard Work: The Immigrant Life in the United States

Early in the morning, it is already hot in Houston as a line of pickup trucks snakes slowly into a dusty yard, where 200 laborers have been gathering since dawn, hoping for a day's work. The driver of the first truck opens his window and tells the foreman that he is looking for a crew to spread boiling tar on a roof. Abdonel Cespedes, the foreman, turns to the crowd, and after a few minutes, three workers step forward and climb into the back of the truck. The next driver is looking for two experienced house-painters. The scene is repeated over and over as men and a few women leave to dig ditches, spread cement, hang drywall, open clogged septic tanks, or crawl under houses to poison rats.

SOCIOLOGY @ WORK

As each driver pulls into the yard, the foreman asks, "How much?" Most offer $5 an hour. Cespedes automatically responds, "$6.50; the going rate is $6.50 for an hour's hard work." Sometimes he convinces them to pay that much, but usually not. The workers, who come from Mexico, El Salvador, and Guatemala, know that dozens of them will end up with no work at all this day. Most accept $5 an hour because they know that when the day is over, $50 is better than nothing.

Labor markets like this one are common in large cities, especially across the southwestern United States.

The surge in immigration in recent years has brought millions of people to this country in search of work, and most have little schooling and speak little English.

Manuel Barrera has taken a day's work moving the entire contents of a store to a storage site. He arrives at the boarded-up store and gazes at the mountains of heavy furniture that he must carry out to a moving van, drive across town, and then carry again. He sighs when he realizes how hot it is outside and that it is even hotter inside the building. He will have no break for lunch. No one says anything about toilets. Barrera shakes his head: "I will do this kind of work

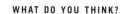

These immigrants gather on a New York City street corner every morning hoping to be hired for construction work that pays about $60 a day with no benefits.

Shannon Stapleton/*The New York Times*

because it puts food on the table. But I did not foresee it would turn out like this."

The hard truth is that immigrants to the United States do the jobs that no one else wants. At the bottom level of the national economy, they perform low-skill jobs in restaurants and hotels and on construction crews, and they work in private homes cooking, cleaning, and caring for children. Across the United States, about half of all housekeepers, household cooks, tailors, and restaurant waiters are men or women born abroad. Few immigrants make much more than the official minimum wage ($5.15 per hour in 2007), and it is rare that immigrant workers receive any health or pension benefits. Many well-off families take the labor of immigrants as much for granted as their sport utility vehicles and cell phones.

WHAT DO YOU THINK?

1. In what ways do you or members of your family depend on the low-paid labor of immigrants?

2. Do you favor allowing the 12 million who entered this country illegally to earn citizenship? What should be done?

3. Should the U.S. government act to reduce the number of immigrants entering this country in the future? Why or why not?

Sources: Booth (1998) and Tumulty (2006).

Prejudice is *a rigid and unfair generalization about an entire category of people.* Prejudice is unfair because all people in some category are rigidly described as the same based on little or no direct evidence. Prejudice may target people of a particular social class, sex, sexual orientation, age, political affiliation, physical disability, race, or ethnicity.

Prejudices are *prejudgments* that can be either positive or negative. Our positive prejudices tend to exaggerate the virtues of people like ourselves, and our negative prejudices condemn those who differ from us. Negative prejudice can be expressed as anything from mild dislike to outright hostility. Because such attitudes are rooted in culture, everyone has at least some prejudice.

The New York Times

WORLD
U.S.
Politics
Washington
Education
N.Y./REGION
BUSINESS
TECHNOLOGY
SPORTS
SCIENCE
HEALTH
OPINION
ARTS
Books
Movies
Music
Television
Theater
STYLE
Dining & Wine
Fashion & Style
Home & Garden
Weddings/
Celebrations
TRAVEL

Blogs
Cartoons
Classifieds
Corrections
Crossword/
Games
First Look
Learning
Network
Multimedia
NYC Guide
Obituaries
Podcasts
The Public
Editor
Sunday
Magazine
Weather
Week in Review

NEWSPAPER
Get Home
Delivery
Customer Care
TimesPoints

The Price of a Word and the Pain It Causes

By KEVIN COYNE
March 25, 2007

The two friends had ridden together everywhere in the back of her car since they first met in kindergarten a decade earlier—school, football practice, their jobs at a Subway. But when Leslie Wilborn picked them up from work one summer evening, she heard them use a word she didn't allow in her own home, a word that nobody, she believed, should ever use.

"I was like, 'What are you talking about?'" Ms. Wilborn said.

Then her son Rob and his best friend, Bayshawn Wells, finally told her about the slur they had been hearing from their manager at work for weeks—and so began a case that put a price on a word that has been the subject of much debate in New Jersey lately.

"I was shocked," Bayshawn said, recounting the first time he heard it directed at him. "After that, he said it every day, just about."

The word is a knife, so sharp and vicious that it is generally sheathed by coy phraseology, "the n-word," so hateful and degrading that it is the target of a wave of local protests that feel as if they may be adding up to a movement. Irvington, East Orange, Paterson, even New York City, have passed resolutions against its use. From the Subway, though, came something more than symbolism.

"We were making subs and he said it in front of everybody," Rob Wilborn, now 17, said of the manager just a few years older than himself. . . . "People were looking at us and I felt kind of humiliated, and I said, 'Could you please not say that.' That's when he said, 'You work for me, I own you.'"

Growing up black in this racially mixed township between Trenton and Princeton, Rob and Bayshawn had heard the word mainly in rap videos and movies. No one had ever wielded it against them before.

"I didn't know how my family would react to it," said Bayshawn, 18, who had told nobody before that evening in Ms. Wilborn's car. "I wanted the job, and I didn't want them to take that away from me."

Rob's silence had similar roots. "That was my first job, and I was excited when I saw the paycheck," he said. They made $6.50 an hour, working evenings until closing and all day on weekends. "The money wasn't much," Rob said, "but it was mine."

Ms. Wilborn made the boys quit, then took them to the state attorney general's office in Trenton, where the law, she told them, was on their side. In August 2005 they walked in and filed a complaint with the State Division on Civil Rights. For more than a year the case was stalled, awaiting a response, which never came, from either the owner or the manager of the Subway.

Two football seasons passed for Rob and Bayshawn, and two Colonial Valley Conference championships for the Lawrence Cardinals. Just as they had stood together behind the Subway counter, Rob and Bayshawn stood side by side on the field as the punt return team.

Rob was also the team's star cornerback, assigned to cover each opponent's best receiver; he had six interceptions in the Cardinals' 9-1 season last fall. Bayshawn was the star running back, scoring 17 touchdowns. In 2005 he set a school record with a 92-yard punt return.

"This year not many people punted to him, but when they did, they paid the price," said the Lawrence head coach, Rob Radice, who described Rob and Bayshawn as "the kind of kids you want your own kids to be like and be around."

Subway was ordered to pay a price, too. After a hearing at which nobody from Subway appeared to testify, an administrative law judge recently found that Rob and Bayshawn had been subjected to "extremely egregious" harassment that was "designed to inflict lasting harm," and awarded each of them $60,000, plus $2,433 in back wages. . . .

A spokesman for Subway, Les Winograd, said by e-mail that the Lawrence Township location, like all the chain's restaurants, is individually owned and operated. "We are clearly upset by and do not condone the actions alleged to have taken place," he said.

Rob and Bayshawn aren't sure when, or even if, they will see the money the judge awarded them, but they have earmarked it for college. They were both recruited to play football at Hudson Valley Community College near Albany next fall, and they hope to continue from there to a four-year school.

"I told them I was proud of them," said Mr. Radice, who teaches American Civilization II to juniors. "I teach a civil rights unit, and you talk about civil rights activists in our country who used passive ways to resist, and they certainly practiced that."

He will have to replace Rob and Bayshawn on his roster, but their story may linger in his classroom. "It hasn't come up yet, but I'm close," he said. "I'm just in my second lesson."

WHAT DO YOU THINK?

1. Have you ever experienced prejudice like the one described here involving Rob Wilborn and Bayshawn Wells? Explain.

2. What is the harm that behavior of this kind causes to people and their careers? Consider both personal harm and damage to earnings and careers.

3. Do you support the court judgment against the Subway store? Should more or less have been done?

tip

Stereotypes, as a type of prejudice, are not necessarily all wrong. But they are typically unfair because they are *largely* wrong and also because they are applied to all people in some category.

The efforts of Barack Obama to become the first African American president of the United States reflect both his personal abilities and the increasing acceptance, by the public as a whole, of minorities in the highest positions of leadership.

Prejudice not only degrades the person who expresses hateful language but also harms the person who is targeted. "In the *Times*" on page 363 describes one recent case in point.

Prejudice often takes the form of a **stereotype** (*stereo* is derived from a Greek word meaning "solid"), *a simplified description applied to every person in some category.* Many white people hold stereotypical views of minorities. Stereotyping is especially harmful to minorities in the workplace. If company officials see workers only in terms of a stereotype, they will make assumptions about their abilities, steering them toward certain jobs and limiting their access to better opportunities (R. L. Kaufman, 2002).

Minorities, too, stereotype whites and other minorities (T. W. Smith, 1996; Cummings & Lambert, 1997). Surveys show, for example, that more African Americans than whites express the belief that Asians engage in unfair business practices and that more Asians than whites criticize Hispanics for having too many children (Perlmutter, 2002).

Do you see stereotypes in common phrases such as "French kiss," "Dutch treat," "Indian giver," or being "gypped" (a reference to Gypsies)? Explain.

Measuring Prejudice: The Social Distance Scale

A good measure of prejudice is *social distance,* how closely people are willing to interact with members of some category. In the 1920s, Emory Bogardus developed the *social distance scale* shown in Figure 1. Bogardus (1925) asked students at U.S. colleges and universities to look at this scale and indicate how closely they were willing to interact with people in thirty racial and ethnic categories. At one extreme, students could express the greatest social distance (most negative prejudice) by declaring that a particular category of people should be barred from the country entirely (point 7); at the other extreme, students could express the least social distance (most social acceptance) by saying they would accept members of a particular category into their family through marriage (point 1).

Bogardus (1925, 1967; Owen, Elsner, & McFaul, 1977) found that people felt much more social distance from some categories than from others. In general, students in his surveys expressed the most social distance from Hispanics, African Americans, Asians, and Turks, indicating that they would be willing to tolerate such people as co-workers but not as neighbors, friends, or family members. Students expressed the least social distance from those from northern and western Europe, including English and Scottish people, and also Canadians, indicating that they were willing to include them in their families by marriage.

What patterns of social distance do we find among college students today? A recent study using the same social distance scale reported three major findings (Parrillo & Donoghue, 2005):[1]

1. **Student opinion shows a trend toward greater social acceptance.** Today's students appear to have fewer prejudices toward minorities than students several decades ago. Figure 14–1 shows that the mean (average) score on the social distance scale declined from 2.14 in 1925 to 1.93 in 1977 to 1.44 in 2001. Respondents (81 percent of whom were white) showed notably greater acceptance of African Americans, a category that moved up from near the bottom in 1925 to the top one-third in 2001.

2. **People see less difference between various minorities.** The earliest studies found the difference between the highest- and lowest-ranked minorities (the range of averages) equal to

---

[1]Parrillo and Donoghue dropped seven of the categories used by Bogardus (Armenians, Czechs, Finns, Norwegians, Scots, Swedes, and Turks), claiming they were no longer visible minorities. They added nine new categories (Africans, Arabs, Cubans, Dominicans, Haitians, Jamaicans, Muslims, Puerto Ricans, and Vietnamese), claiming these are visible minorities today. This change probably encouraged higher social distance scores, making the trend toward decreasing social distance all the more significant.

RACE AND ETHNICITY

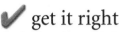

get it right

On the Bogardus social distance scale, the greater the social distance, the greater the intensity of negative prejudice.

student ❷ student

"I was glad to see that research using the social distance scale showed that racial and ethnic prejudice among U.S. students is getting steadily weaker."

STUDENT SNAPSHOT

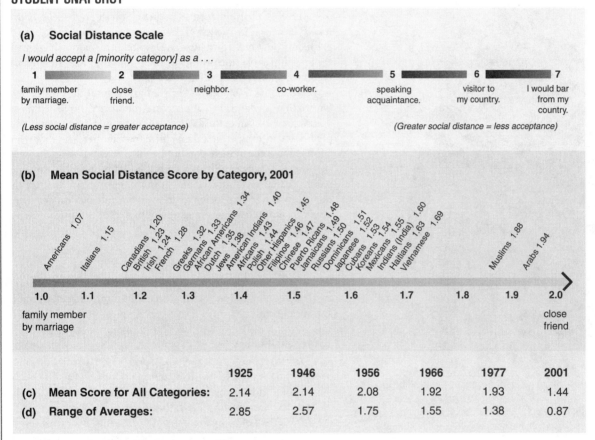

(a) Social Distance Scale

I would accept a [minority category] as a . . .

1	2	3	4	5	6	7
family member by marriage.	close friend.	neighbor.	co-worker.	speaking acquaintance.	visitor to my country.	I would bar from my country.

(Less social distance = greater acceptance)   *(Greater social distance = less acceptance)*

(b) Mean Social Distance Score by Category, 2001

Americans 1.07, Italians 1.15, Canadians 1.20, British 1.23, Irish 1.24, French 1.28, Greeks 1.32, Germans 1.33, African Americans 1.34, Dutch 1.35, Jews 1.38, American Indians 1.40, Africans 1.43, Polish 1.44, Other Hispanics 1.45, Filipinos 1.46, Chinese 1.47, Puerto Ricans 1.48, Jamaicans 1.49, Russians 1.50, Dominicans 1.51, Japanese 1.52, Cubans 1.53, Koreans 1.54, Mexicans 1.55, Indians (India) 1.60, Haitians 1.63, Vietnamese 1.69, Muslims 1.88, Arabs 1.94

1.0	1.1	1.2	1.3	1.4	1.5	1.6	1.7	1.8	1.9	2.0
family member by marriage										close friend

		1925	1946	1956	1966	1977	2001
(c)	**Mean Score for All Categories:**	2.14	2.14	2.08	1.92	1.93	1.44
(d)	**Range of Averages:**	2.85	2.57	1.75	1.55	1.38	0.87

FIGURE 1 Bogardus Social Distance Research

The social distance scale is a good way to measure prejudice. Part (a) illustrates the complete social distance scale, from least social distance at the far left to greatest social distance at the far right. Part (b) shows the mean (average) social distance score received by each category of people in 2001. Part (c) presents the overall mean score (the average of the scores received by all racial and ethnic categories) in specific years. These scores have fallen from 2.14 in 1925 to 1.44 in 2001, showing that students express less social distance toward minorities today than they did in the past. Part (d) shows the range of averages, the difference between the highest and lowest scores in given years (in 2001, for instance, it was 0.87, the difference between the high score of 1.94 for Arabs and the low score of 1.07 for Americans). This figure has also become smaller since 1925, indicating that today's students tend to see fewer differences between various categories of people.

Source: Parrillo & Donoghue (2005).

almost three points on the scale. As the figure shows, the most recent research produced a range of averages of less than one point, indicating that today's students see fewer differences between various categories of people.

3. **The terrorist attacks of September 11, 2001, may have reduced social acceptance of Arabs and Muslims.** The most recent study was conducted just a few weeks after September 11, 2001. Perhaps the fact that the nineteen men who

tip

The text presents four theories of prejudice. After reading them all, check your understanding of each by completing this sentence: "This theory explains that prejudice is caused by . . ."

Recent research measuring student attitudes confirms the trend of declining prejudice toward all racial and ethnic categories. On your campus, does race and ethnicity guide people's choice in romantic attachments? Do some racial and ethnic categories mix more often than others? Explain.

David Young-Wolff/PhotoEdit Inc.

attacked the World Trade Center and the Pentagon were Arabs and Muslims is part of the reason that students ranked these categories last on the social distance scale. However, not a single student gave Arabs or Muslims a 7, indicating that they should be barred from the country. On the contrary, the 2001 mean scores (1.94 for Arabs and 1.88 for Muslims) show higher social acceptance than students in 1977 expressed toward eighteen of the thirty categories of people studied.

Do you think students on your campus have become more accepting of social diversity? Explain why or why not.

Racism

A powerful and harmful form of prejudice, **racism** is *the belief that one racial category is innately superior or inferior to another*. Racism has existed throughout world history. Despite their many achievements, the ancient Greeks, the peoples of India, and the Chinese all considered people unlike themselves inferior.

Racism has also been widespread throughout the history of the United States, where ideas about racial inferiority supported slavery. Today, overt racism in this country has decreased because more people believe in evaluating others, in Martin Luther King Jr.'s words, "not by the color of their skin but by the content of their character."

Even so, racism remains a serious social problem, as some people think that certain racial and ethnic categories are smarter than others. As the Seeing Sociology in Everyday Life box explains, however, racial differences in mental abilities result from environment rather than biology.

Theories of Prejudice

Where does prejudice come from? Social scientists provide several answers to this question, focusing on frustration, personality, culture, and social conflict.

Scapegoat Theory

Scapegoat theory holds that prejudice springs from frustration among people who are themselves disadvantaged (Dollard et al., 1939). Take the case of a white woman frustrated by her low-paying job in a textile factory. Directing hostility at the powerful factory owners carries the obvious risk of being fired; therefore, she may blame her low pay on the presence of minority co-workers. Her prejudice does not improve her situation, but it is a relatively safe way to express anger, and it may give her the comforting feeling that at least she is superior to someone.

A **scapegoat,** then, is *a person or category of people, typically with little power, whom people unfairly blame for their own troubles*. Because they have little power and thus are usually "safe targets," minorities often are used as scapegoats.

Authoritarian Personality Theory

Theodor Adorno and colleagues (1950) considered extreme prejudice a personality trait of certain individuals. This conclusion is supported by research showing that people who express strong prejudice toward one minority typically do so toward all minorities. These *authoritarian personalities* rigidly conform to conventional cultural values and see moral issues as clear-cut matters of right and wrong. People with authoritarian personalities also view society as naturally

Seeing Sociology in Everyday Life
Does Race Affect Intelligence?

As we go through an average day, we encounter people of various racial and ethnic categories. We also deal with people who are very intelligent as well as those whose abilities are more modest. But is there a connection between race and ethnicity and intelligence?

Common stereotypes say that Asian Americans are smarter than white people and that the typical white person is more intelligent than the average African American. These stereotypes are not new. Throughout the history of the United States, many people have assumed that some categories of people are smarter than others. Just as important, people have used this thinking to justify privileges for the allegedly superior category and even to bar supposedly inferior people from entering this country.

So what do we know about intelligence? We know that people, as individuals, differ in mental abilities. The distribution of human intelligence forms a "bell curve," as shown in the figure. A person's *intelligence quotient* (IQ) is calculated as the person's mental age in years, as measured by a test, divided by the person's actual age in years, with the result multiplied by 100. An eight-year-old who performs like a ten-year-old has an IQ of $10 \div 8 = 1.25 \times 100 = 125$. Average performance yields an IQ of 100.

In a controversial study of intelligence and social inequality, Richard Herrnstein and Charles Murray (1994) claim that race is related to measures of intelligence. They say that the average IQ for people with European ancestry is 100, for people with East Asian ancestry is 103, and for people with African ancestry is 90.

Such assertions go against our democratic and egalitarian beliefs that no racial type is naturally better than another. Because these findings can increase prejudice, critics

charge that intelligence tests are not valid and even that the concept of intelligence has little real meaning.

Most social scientists believe that IQ tests do measure something important that we think of as intelligence, and they agree that *individuals* vary in intellectual aptitude. But they reject the idea that any *category* of people, on average, is naturally or biologically smarter than any other. So how do we explain the overall differences in IQ scores by race?

Thomas Sowell (1994, 1995) explains that most of this difference results not from biology but from environment. In some skillful sociological detective work, Sowell traced IQ scores for various racial and ethnic categories throughout the twentieth century. He found that on average, early-twentieth-century immigrants from European nations such as Poland, Lithuania, Italy, and Greece, as well as from Asian countries including China and Japan, scored 10 to 15 points below the U.S. average. But by the end of the twentieth century, people in these same categories had IQ scores that were average or above average. Among Italian Americans, for example, average IQ jumped almost 10 points; among Polish and Chinese Americans, the increase was almost 20 points.

Because genetic changes occur over thousands of years and most people in these categories marry others like themselves, biological factors cannot explain such a rapid rise in IQ scores. The only reasonable explanation is changing cultural patterns. The descendants of early immigrants improved their intellectual performance as their standard of living rose and their opportunity for schooling increased.

Sowell found that much the same was true of African Americans. Historically, the average IQ score of African Americans living in the North has been about 10 points higher than the average score of those living in the South. Among the descendants of African Americans who migrated from the South to the North after 1940, IQ scores went up, just as they did with descendants of European and Asian immigrants. Thus environmental factors appear to be critical in explaining differences in IQ among various categories of people.

According to Sowell, these test score differences tell us that *cultural patterns matter.* Asians who score high on tests are no smarter than other people, but they have been raised to value learning and pursue excellence. African Americans are no less intelligent than anyone else, but they carry a legacy of disadvantage that can undermine self-confidence and discourage achievement.

WHAT DO YOU THINK?

1. If IQ scores reflect people's environment, are they valid measures of intelligence? Could they be harmful?

2. According to Thomas Sowell, why do some racial and ethnic categories show dramatic short-term gains in average IQ scores?

3. Do you think parents and schools influence a child's IQ score? If so, how?

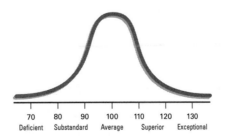

IQ: The Distribution of Intelligence

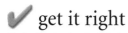 **get it right**

Prejudice is about attitudes; discrimination is about action.

 tip

The importance of institutional prejudice and discrimination can be summed up like this: Prejudice and discrimination are found in individuals but are rooted in society itself.

competitive and hierarchical, with "better" people (like themselves) inevitably dominating those who are weaker (all minorities).

Adorno and his colleagues also found the opposite pattern to be true: People who express tolerance toward one minority are likely to be accepting of all. They tend to be more flexible in their moral judgments and treat all people as equals.

Adorno thought that people with little schooling and those raised by cold and demanding parents tend to develop authoritarian personalities. Filled with anger and anxiety as children, they grow into hostile, aggressive adults who seek out scapegoats.

Culture Theory

A third theory claims that although extreme prejudice may be found in some people, some prejudice is found in everyone. Why? Because prejudice is part of the culture in which we all live and learn. The Bogardus social distance studies help prove the point. Bogardus found that students across the country had much the same attitudes toward specific racial and ethnic categories, feeling closer to some and more distant from others.

More evidence that prejudice is rooted in culture is the fact that minorities express the same attitudes as white people toward categories other than their own. Such patterns suggest that individuals hold prejudices because we live in a "culture of prejudice" that has taught us all to view certain categories of people as "better" or "worse" than others.

Conflict Theory

A fourth explanation proposes that prejudice is used as a tool by powerful people to oppress others. Anglos who look down on Latino immigrants in the Southwest, for example, can get away with paying the immigrants low wages for hard work. Similarly, all elites benefit when prejudice divides workers along racial and ethnic lines and discourages them from working together to advance their common interests (Geschwender, 1978; Olzak, 1989).

According to another conflict-based argument, made by Shelby Steele (1990), minorities themselves encourage *race consciousness* to win greater power and privileges. Because of their historical disadvantage, minorities claim that they are victims entitled to special consideration based on their race. This strategy may bring short-term gains, but Steele cautions that such thinking often sparks a backlash from whites or others who oppose "special treatment" on the basis of race or ethnicity.

 YOUR LEARNING State the basic idea of scapegoat theory, authoritarian personality theory, culture theory, and conflict theory. How do they each explain prejudice?

Discrimination

Closely related to prejudice is **discrimination,** *unequal treatment of various categories of people. Prejudice* refers to *attitudes,* but *discrimination* is a matter of *action.* Like prejudice, discrimination can be either positive (providing special advantages) or negative (creating obstacles) and ranges from subtle to extreme.

Institutional Prejudice and Discrimination

We typically think of prejudice and discrimination as the hateful ideas or actions of specific people. But Stokely Carmichael and Charles Hamilton (1967) pointed out that far greater harm results from **institutional prejudice and discrimination,** *bias built into the operation of society's institutions,* including schools, hospitals, the police, and the workplace. For example, researchers have found that banks reject home mortgage applications from minorities at a higher rate than those from white people, even when income and quality of neighborhood are held constant (Gotham, 1998).

According to Carmichael and Hamilton, people are slow to condemn or even recognize institutional prejudice and discrimination because it often involves respected public officials and long-established practices. A case in point is *Brown* v. *Board of Education of Topeka,* the 1954 Supreme Court decision that ended the legal segregation of schools. The principle of "separate but equal" schooling had been the law of the land, supporting racial inequality by allowing school segregation. Despite this change in the law, half a century later, most U.S. students still attend schools that are overwhelmingly of one race (Barnes, 2004). In 1991, the courts declared that neighborhood schools will never provide equal education as long as our population is segregated, with most African Americans living in central cities and most white people and Asian Americans living in suburbs.

Prejudice and Discrimination: The Vicious Circle

Prejudice and discrimination reinforce each other. The Thomas theorem, discussed in Chapter 6 ("Social Interaction in Everyday Life"), offers a simple explanation of this fact: *Situations that are defined as real become real in their consequences* (W. I. Thomas, 1966:301, orig. 1931).

As Thomas recognized, stereotypes become real to people who believe them and sometimes even to those who are victimized by them. Prejudice on the part of white people toward people of color does not produce *innate* inferiority, but it can produce *social* inferiority, pushing minorities into low-paying jobs, inferior schools, and racially segregated housing. Then, as white people see social disadvantage as evidence that minorities do not measure up, they unleash a new round of prejudice and discrimination, giving rise to a vicious circle in which each perpetuates the other, as shown in Figure 2.

Majority and Minority: Patterns of Interaction

Sociologists describe patterns of interaction among racial and ethnic categories in a society in terms of four models: pluralism, assimilation, segregation, and genocide.

Pluralism

Pluralism is *a state in which people of all races and ethnicities are distinct but have equal social standing.* In other words, people who differ in appearance or social heritage all share resources roughly equally.

The United States is pluralistic to the extent that all people have equal standing under the law. In addition, large cities contain countless "ethnic villages," where people proudly display the traditions of their immigrant ancestors. These include New York's Spanish Harlem, Little Italy, and Chinatown; Philadelphia's Italian "South Philly"; Chicago's Little Saigon; and Latino East Los Angeles. New York City alone has 189 different ethnic newspapers (Paul, 2001; Logan, Alba, & Zhang, 2002).

But the United States is not truly pluralistic for three reasons. First, although most people value their cultural heritage, few want to live just with others exactly like themselves (NORC, 2005). Second, our tolerance of social diversity goes only so far. One reaction to the rising number of U.S. minorities is a social movement to make English the nation's official language. Third, as you will see later in this chapter, people of various colors and cultures do *not* have equal social standing.

Assimilation

Many people think of the United States as a "melting pot" in which different nationalities blend together. But rather than everyone "melting" into some new cultural pattern, most minorities have adopted the dominant culture established by our earliest settlers. Why? Because doing so is both the path to upward social mobility and a way to escape the prejudice and discrimination directed at more visible foreigners. Sociologists use the term **assimilation** to describe *the process by which minorities gradually adopt patterns of the dominant culture.* Assimilation can involve changing modes of dress, values, religion, language, and friends.

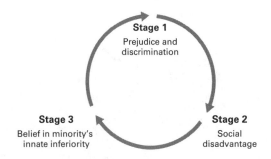

Stage 1: Prejudice and discrimination begin, often as an expression of ethnocentrism or an attempt to justify economic exploitation.

Stage 2: As a result of prejudice and discrimination, a minority is socially disadvantaged, occupying a low position in the system of social stratification.

Stage 3: This social disadvantage is then interpreted not as the result of earlier prejudice and discrimination but as evidence that the minority is innately inferior, unleashing renewed prejudice and discrimination by which the cycle repeats itself.

FIGURE 2 Prejudice and Discrimination: The Vicious Circle

Prejudice and discrimination can form a vicious circle, perpetuating themselves.

The amount of assimilation varies by category. For example, Canadians have "melted" more than Cubans, the Dutch more than Dominicans, Germans more than the Japanese. Multiculturalists oppose making assimilation a goal because it suggests that minorities are "the problem" and defines them (rather than majority people) as the ones who need to do all the changing.

Note that assimilation involves changes in ethnicity but not in race. For example, many descendants of Japanese immigrants discard their ethnic traditions but retain their racial identity. In order for racial traits to diminish over generations, **miscegenation**, or *biological reproduction by partners of different racial categories,* must occur. Although interracial marriage is becoming more common, it still amounts to only 4 percent of all U.S. marriages (U.S. Census Bureau, 2006).

Segregation

Segregation is *the physical and social separation of categories of people.* Some minorities, especially religious orders like the Amish, voluntarily segregate themselves. However, majorities usually segregate minorities by excluding them. Residential neighborhoods, schools, occupations, hospitals, and even cemeteries may be segregated.

student 2 student

"I was shocked to realize how common genocide has been in human history. And it is still going on today!"

In an effort to force assimilation, the U.S. Bureau of Indian Affairs took American Indian children from their families and placed them in boarding schools like this one, Oklahoma's Riverside Indian School. There they were taught to speak English by non-Indian teachers with the goal of making them into "Americans."

Western History Collections, University of Oklahoma Libraries. Phillips Collection (357)

Pluralism encourages distinctiveness without disadvantage, but segregation enforces separation that harms a minority.

Racial segregation has a long history in the United States, beginning with slavery and evolving into racially separated housing, schools, buses, and trains. Court decisions such as the 1954 *Brown* case have reduced *de jure* (Latin, meaning "by law") discrimination in this country. However, *de facto* ("in actual fact") segregation continues to this day in the form of countless neighborhoods that are home to people of a single race.

Despite some recent decline, segregation persists in the United States. For example, Livonia, Michigan, is 96 percent white, and neighboring Detroit is 83 percent African American. Kurt Metzger (2001) explains, "Livonia was pretty much created by white flight [from Detroit]." Further, research shows that across the country, whites (especially those with young children) avoid neighborhoods where African Americans live (Emerson, Yancey, & Chai, 2001; Krysan, 2002). At the extreme, Douglas Massey and Nancy Denton (1989) document the *hypersegregation* of poor African Americans in some

inner cities. Hypersegregation means having little contact of any kind with people outside the local community. Hypersegregation is the daily experience of about 20 percent of poor African Americans.

In your city or town, are there minority neighborhoods? Which categories of people live there? To what degree is your community racially or ethnically segregated?

Genocide

Genocide is *the systematic killing of one category of people by another.* This deadly form of racism and ethnocentrism violates nearly every recognized moral standard, yet it has occurred time and again in human history.

Genocide was common in the history of contact between Europeans and the original inhabitants of the Americas. From the sixteenth century on, the Spanish, Portuguese, English, French, and Dutch forcibly colonized vast empires. Although most native people died from diseases brought by Europeans, against which they had no natural defenses, many who opposed the colonizers were killed deliberately (Matthiessen, 1984; Sale, 1990).

Genocide also occurred during the twentieth century. Unimaginable horror befell European Jews during Adolf Hitler's reign of terror, known as the Holocaust. From about 1935 to 1945, the Nazis murdered more than 6 million Jewish men, women, and children, along with gay people, Gypsies, and people with handicaps. The Soviet dictator Josef Stalin murdered on an even greater scale, killing perhaps 30 million real and imagined enemies during decades of violent rule. Between 1975 and 1980, Pol Pot's communist regime in Cambodia butchered all "capitalists," a category that included anyone able to speak a Western language. In all, some 2 million people (one-fourth of the population) perished in the Cambodian "killing fields" (Shawcross, 1979).

Tragically, genocide continues today. Recent examples include Hutus killing Tutsis in the African nation of Rwanda, Serbs killing Bosnians in the Balkans of Eastern Europe, and the killing of hundreds of thousands of people in the Darfur region of Sudan in Africa.

These four patterns of minority-majority interaction have all been played out in the United States. Although many people proudly point to patterns of pluralism and assimilation, it is also important to recognize the degree to which U.S. society has been built on segregation (of African Americans) and genocide (of Native Americans). The

tip

The final sections of the chapter survey the history and social standing of various racial and ethnic categories of the U.S. population.

tip

Think about the four patterns of minority-majority interaction—pluralism, assimilation, segregation, and genocide—when reading the sections on the different racial and ethnic categories.

SEEING OURSELVES

NATIONAL MAP 2
Land Controlled by Native Americans, 1790 to Today

In 1790, Native Americans controlled three-fourths of the land (blue-shaded areas) that eventually became the United States. Today, Native Americans control 314 reservations, scattered across the United States, that account for just 2 percent of the country's land area. How would you characterize these locations?

Source: Copyright © 1998 by The New York Times Co. Reprinted by permission. All rights reserved.

remainder of this chapter examines how these four patterns have shaped the history and present social standing of major racial and ethnic categories in the United States.

Race and Ethnicity in the United States

> Give me your tired, your poor,
> Your huddled masses yearning to breathe free,
> The wretched refuse of your teeming shore,
> Send these, the homeless, tempest-tossed to me:
> I lift my lamp beside the golden door.

These words by Emma Lazarus, inscribed on the Statue of Liberty, express cultural ideals of human dignity, personal freedom, and economic opportunity. The United States has provided more of the "good life" to more immigrants than any other nation. About 1.5 million immigrants come to this country every year, and their many ways of life create a social mosaic that is especially evident in large cities.

However, as a survey of this country's racial and ethnic minorities will show, our country's golden door has opened more widely for some than for others. We turn next to the history and current social standing of the major categories of the U.S. population.

Native Americans

The term "Native Americans" refers to many different societies—including the Aztec, Inca, Aleut, Eskimo, Cherokee, Zuni, Sioux, and Mohawk—that first settled the Western Hemisphere. Some 30,000

years before Christopher Columbus landed in the Americas in 1492, migrating peoples crossed a land bridge from Asia to North America where the Bering Strait (off the coast of Alaska) lies today. Gradually, they made their way throughout North and South America.

When the first Europeans arrived late in the fifteenth century, Native Americans numbered in the millions. But by 1900, after centuries of conflict and even acts of genocide, the "vanishing Americans" numbered just 250,000 (Dobyns, 1966; Tyler, 1973). The land they controlled also shrank dramatically, as shown in National Map 2.

Columbus first referred to Native Americans that he encountered (on the Bahama Islands) as "Indians" because unaware of the existence of the Americas, he mistakenly thought he had reached his destination of India. Columbus found the native people passive and peaceful, in stark contrast to the materialistic and competitive Europeans. Yet Europeans justified the seizure of Native American land by calling their victims thieves and murderers (Josephy, 1982; Matthiessen, 1984; Sale, 1990).

After the Revolutionary War, the new U.S. government took a pluralistic approach to Native American societies, seeking to gain more land through treaties. Payment for the land was far from fair, however, and when Native Americans resisted the surrender of their homelands, the U.S. government simply used its superior military power to evict them. By the early 1800s, few Native Americans remained east of the Mississippi River.

In 1871, the United States declared Native Americans wards of the government and adopted a strategy of forced assimilation. Relocated to specific territories designated as "reservations," Native Americans

tip

People tend to think about race and ethnicity when they deal with categories of people whom they think of as "other." WASPs have race and ethnicity, too, of course, but U.S. society does not construct these into a racial or ethnic identity.

Table 2   The Social Standing of Native Americans, 2000

	Native Americans	Entire U.S. Population
Median family income	$33,144*	$50,891
Percentage in poverty	25.7%*	11.3%
Completion of four or more years of college (age 25 and over)	11.5%	24.4%

*Data are for 1999.

Sources: U.S. Census Bureau (2004, 2006).

continued to lose their land and were well on their way to losing their culture as well. Reservation life encouraged dependency, replacing ancestral languages with English and traditional religion with Christianity. Officials of the Bureau of Indian Affairs took children from their parents and put them in boarding schools, where they were resocialized as "Americans." Authorities gave local control of reservation life to the few Native Americans who supported government policies, and they distributed reservation land, traditionally held collectively, as private property to individual families (Tyler, 1973).

Not until 1924 were Native Americans entitled to U.S. citizenship. After that, many migrated from reservations, adopting mainstream cultural patterns and marrying non–Native Americans. Today, four out of ten Native Americans consider themselves biracial or multiracial (Raymond, 2001; Wellner, 2001), and many large cities now contain sizable Native American populations. However, as Table 2 shows, Native American income is far below the U.S. average, and relatively few Native Americans earn a college degree.[2]

From in-depth interviews with Native Americans in a western city, Joan Albon (1971) linked low Native American social standing to a range of cultural factors, including a noncompetitive view of life and a reluctance to pursue higher education. In addition, she noted, many Native Americans have dark skin, which makes them targets of prejudice and discrimination.

Members of more than 500 American Indian nations today are reclaiming pride in their cultural heritage. Traditional cultural organ-

izations report a surge in new membership applications, and many children can speak native languages better than their parents. The legal right of Native Americans to govern their reservations has enabled some tribes to build profitable gaming casinos. But the wealth produced from gambling has enriched relatively few Native peoples, and most profits go to non-Indian investors (Bartlett & Steele, 2002). While some prosper, most Native Americans remain severely disadvantaged and share a profound sense of the injustice they have suffered at the hands of white people.

White Anglo-Saxon Protestants

White Anglo-Saxon Protestants (WASPs) were not the first people to inhabit the United States, but they soon dominated this nation after European settlement began. Most WASPs are of English ancestry, but the category also includes people from Scotland and Wales. With some 31 million people of English ancestry, 11 percent of our society claims some WASP background, and WASPs are found at all class levels.

Many people associate WASPs with elite communities along the East and West Coasts. But the highest concentrations of WASPs are in Utah (because of migrations of Mormons with English ancestry), Appalachia, and northern New England (because of historical immigration).

Looking back in time, WASP immigrants were highly skilled and motivated to achieve by what we now call the Protestant work ethic. Because of their high social standing, WASPs were not subject to the prejudice and discrimination experienced by other categories of immigrants. In fact, the historical dominance of WASPs has led others to want to become more like them (K. W. Jones, 2001).

WASPs were never one single group; especially in colonial times, considerable hostility separated English Anglicans and Scottish Presbyterians (Parrillo, 1994). But in the nineteenth century, most WASPs joined together to oppose the arrival of "undesirables" such as Germans in the 1840s and Italians in the 1880s. Those who could afford it sheltered themselves in exclusive suburbs and restrictive clubs. Thus the 1880s—the decade when the Statue of Liberty first welcomed immigrants to the United States—also saw the founding of the first country club with exclusively WASP members (Baltzell, 1964).

By about 1950, however, WASP wealth and power had peaked, as indicated by the 1960 election of John Fitzgerald Kennedy, the first Irish Catholic president. Yet the WASP cultural legacy remains. English is this country's dominant language, and Protestantism its majority religion. Our legal system also reflects our English origins. But the historical dominance of WASPs is most evident in the widespread use of the terms *race* and *ethnicity* to refer to everyone but them.

[2]In making comparisons of education and especially income, keep in mind that various categories of the U.S. population have different median ages. In 2000, the median age for all U.S. people was 35.4 years. Non-Hispanic white people have a median age of 38.6 years; for Native Americans, the figure is 28.5 years. Because people's schooling and income increase over time, this age difference accounts for some of the disparities seen in Table 2.

The efforts of these four women greatly advanced the social standing of African Americans in the United States. Pictured above, from left to right: Sojourner Truth (1797–1883), born a slave, became an influential preacher and outspoken abolitionist who was honored by President Lincoln at the White House. Harriet Tubman (1820–1913), after escaping from slavery herself, masterminded the flight from bondage of hundreds of African American men and women via the "Underground Railroad." Ida Wells-Barnett (1862–1931), born to slave parents, became a partner in a Memphis newspaper and served as a tireless crusader against the terror of lynching. Marian Anderson (1902–1993), an exceptional singer whose early career was restrained by racial prejudice, broke symbolic "color lines" by singing in the White House (1936) and on the steps of the Lincoln Memorial to a crowd of almost 100,000 people (1939).

Corbis/Bettmann (*left*); Culver Pictures, Inc. (*second from left*); Photographs and Prints Division, Schomburg Center for Research in Black Culture/The New York Public Library/Astor, Lenox and Tilden Foundations (*second from right*); UPI/Corbis/Bettmann (*right*)

African Americans

Africans accompanied European explorers to the New World in the fifteenth century. But most accounts mark the beginning of black history in the United States as 1619, when a Dutch trading ship brought twenty Africans to Jamestown, Virginia. Whether these people arrived as slaves or indentured servants who paid their passage by agreeing to work for a period of time, being of African descent on these shores soon became virtually the same as being a slave. In 1661, Virginia enacted the first law recognizing slavery (Sowell, 1981).

Slavery was the foundation of the southern colonies' plantation system. White people ran plantations using slave labor, and until 1808, some were also slave traders. Traders—including Europeans, Africans, and North Americans—forcibly transported some 10 million Africans to various countries in the Americas, including 400,000 to the United States. On small sailing ships, hundreds of slaves were chained together for the several weeks it took to cross the Atlantic Ocean. Filth and disease killed many and drove others to suicide. Overall, perhaps half died en route (Franklin, 1967; Sowell, 1981).

Surviving the miserable crossing was a mixed blessing, as the journey's end brought with it a life of servitude. Although some slaves worked in cities at various trades, most labored in the fields, often from daybreak until sunset and even longer during the harvest. The law allowed owners to use whatever disciplinary measures they deemed necessary to ensure that slaves were obedient and hardworking. Even killing a slave rarely prompted legal action. Owners also divided slave families at public auctions, where human beings were bought and sold as property. Unschooled and dependent on their owners for all their basic needs, slaves had little control over their lives (Franklin, 1967; Sowell, 1981).

Some free persons of color lived in both the North and the South, laboring as small-scale farmers, skilled workers, and small business owners. But the lives of most African Americans stood in glaring contradiction to the principles of equality and freedom on which the United States was founded. The Declaration of Independence states:

> We hold these Truths to be self-evident, that all Men are created equal, that they are endowed by their Creator with certain unalienable Rights, that among these are Life, Liberty, and the Pursuit of Happiness.

However, most white people did not apply these ideals to black people. In the *Dred Scott* case of 1857, the U.S. Supreme Court addressed the question "Are blacks citizens?" by writing, "We think they are not, and that they are not included, and were not intended to be included, under the word 'citizens' in the Constitution, and can therefore claim

tip

As you read this section, note ways in which the social standing of African Americans has improved and ways in which racial inequality remains significant.

Table 3 The Social Standing of African Americans, 2005

	African Americans*	Entire U.S. Population
Median family income	$35,464	$56,194
Percentage in poverty	24.9%	12.6%
Completion of four or more years of college (age 25 and over)	17.6%	27.7%

*For comparison with other tables in this chapter, 2000 data are as follows: median family income, $34,204; percentage in poverty, 22.1%; completion of four or more years of college, 16.6%.

Sources: U.S. Census Bureau (2000, 2001, 2006).

none of the rights and privileges which that instrument provides for and secures for citizens of the United States" (quoted in Blaustein & Zangrando, 1968:160). Thus arose what the Swedish sociologist Gunnar Myrdal (1944) called the "American dilemma": a democratic society's denial of basic rights and freedoms to an entire category of people. People would speak of equality, in other words, but do little to make all categories of people equal. Many white people resolved this dilemma by defining black people as naturally inferior and undeserving of equality (Leach, 2002).

In 1865, the Thirteenth Amendment to the Constitution outlawed slavery. Three years later, the Fourteenth Amendment reversed the *Dred Scott* ruling, giving citizenship to all people born in the United States. The Fifteenth Amendment, ratified in 1870, stated that neither race nor previous condition of servitude could deprive anyone of the right to vote. However, so-called *Jim Crow laws*—classic cases of institutional discrimination—segregated U.S. society into two racial castes. Especially in the South, white people beat and lynched black people (and some white people) who challenged the racial hierarchy.

The twentieth century brought dramatic changes for African Americans. After World War I, tens of thousands of men, women, and children left the rural South for jobs in northern factories. Although most did find economic opportunities, few escaped racial prejudice and discrimination, which placed them lower in the social hierarchy than white immigrants arriving from Europe.

In the 1950s and 1960s, a national civil rights movement led to landmark judicial decisions outlawing segregated schools and overt discrimination in employment and public accommodations. The Black Power movement gave African Americans a renewed sense of pride and purpose.

Despite these gains, people of African descent continue to occupy a lower social position in the United States, as shown in Table 14–3. The median income of African American families in 2005 ($35,464) was only 56 percent of non-Hispanic white family income ($63,156), a ratio that has changed little in thirty years.[3] Black families remain three times as likely as white families to be poor.

The number of African Americans securely in the middle class rose by more than half between 1980 and 2005; 36 percent earn $50,000 or more. But most African Americans are still working-class or poor, and in recent years, many have seen earnings slip as urban factory jobs, vital to residents of central cities, have been lost to other countries where labor costs are lower. This is one reason that black unemployment is more than twice as high as white unemployment; among African American teenagers in many cities, the figure exceeds 40 percent (R. A. Smith, 2002; U.S. Department of Labor, 2007).

Since 1980, African Americans have made remarkable educational progress. The share of adults completing high school rose from half to more than three-fourths, nearly closing the gap between whites and blacks. Between 1980 and 2005, the share of African American adults with at least a college degree rose from 8 to more than 17 percent. But as Table 3 shows, African Americans are still at just over half the national standard when it comes to completing four years of college.

The political clout of African Americans has also increased. As a result of black migration to the cities and white flight to the suburbs, African Americans have gained greater political power in urban places, and half of this country's ten largest cities have elected African American mayors (Marshall & Ruhil, 2006). At the national level, the candidacy of Senator Barack Obama has attracted national attention, raising the prospect of an African American becoming president. Yet in 2007, African Americans accounted for just 40 members of the House of Representatives (9.2 percent of 435); one member, Obama, in the Senate (out of 100); and one state governor.

In sum, for nearly 400 years, African Americans have struggled for social equality. As a nation, the United States has come far in this pursuit. Overt discrimination is now illegal, and research documents a long-term decline in prejudice against African Americans (Firebaugh & Davis, 1988; J. Q. Wilson, 1992; NORC, 2005).

In 1913, nearly fifty years after the abolition of slavery, W. E. B. Du Bois pointed to the extent of black achievement but cautioned

[3]Here again, a median age difference (non-Hispanic white people, 38.6; black people, 30.2) accounts for some of the income and educational disparities. More important is a higher proportion of one-parent families among blacks than whites. If we compare only married-couple families, African Americans (median income $56,054 in 2005) earned 80 percent as much as non-Hispanic whites ($70,307).

♣ tip

Many minority categories formed their own residential communities, partly as a result of prejudice and discrimination and partly to maintain their culture and assist one another.

that racial caste remained strong in the United States. Almost a century later, this racial hierarchy persists.

In your opinion, how much change has there been in racial prejudice and discrimination against African Americans during your lifetime? Explain your position.

Asian Americans

Although Asian Americans share some physical traits, enormous cultural diversity characterizes this category of people with ancestors from dozens of nations. In 2000, the total number of Asian Americans exceeded 10 million, approaching 4 percent of the U.S. population. The largest category of Asian Americans is people of Chinese ancestry (2.4 million), followed by those of Filipino (1.8 million), Asian Indian (1.7 million), Vietnamese (1.1 million), Korean (1 million), and Japanese (800,000) descent. More than one-third of Asian Americans live in California.

Young Asian Americans command attention and respect as high achievers and are disproportionately represented at our country's best colleges and universities. Many of their elders, too, have made economic and social gains; most Asian Americans now live in middle-class suburbs. Yet despite (and sometimes because of) this achievement, Asian Americans often find that others are aloof or outright hostile toward them (O'Hare, Frey, & Fost, 1994; Chua-Eoan, 2000).

The achievement of some Asian Americans has given rise to a "model minority" stereotype that is misleading because it hides the differences in class standing and the outright poverty that are found among their ranks. We will focus first on the history and current standing of Chinese Americans and Japanese Americans—the longest-established Asian American minorities—and conclude with a brief look at the most recent arrivals.

Chinese Americans

Chinese immigration to the United States began in 1849 with the economic boom of California's Gold Rush. New towns and businesses sprang up overnight, and the demand for cheap labor attracted some 100,000 Chinese immigrants. Most Chinese workers were young men willing to take tough, low-status jobs that whites did not want. But the economy soured in the 1870s, and desperate whites began to compete with the Chinese for whatever work could be found. Suddenly, the hardworking Chinese were seen as a threat. Economic hard times led to prejudice and discrimination (Ling, 1971; Boswell, 1986). Soon laws were passed barring Chinese people from many occupations, and public opinion turned strongly against the "Yellow Peril."

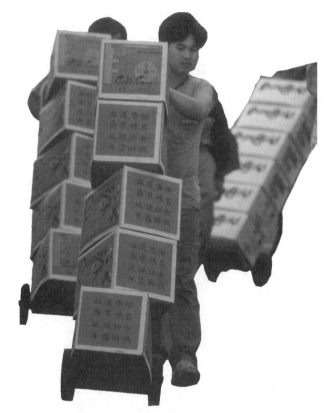

On average, Asian Americans have income above the national median. At the same time, however, the poverty rate in many Asian American communities—including San Francisco's Chinatown—is well above average.

In 1882, the U.S. government passed the first of several laws limiting Chinese immigration. This action caused domestic hardship because in the United States, Chinese men outnumbered Chinese women by twenty to one. This sex imbalance drove the Chinese population down to only 60,000 by 1920. Because Chinese women already in the United States were in high demand, they soon lost much of their traditional submissiveness to men (Hsu, 1971; Lai, 1980; Sowell, 1981).

Responding to racial hostility, some Chinese moved east; many more sought the relative safety of urban Chinatowns. There Chinese traditions flourished, and kinship networks, called *clans*, provided financial assistance to individuals and represented the interests of all. At the same time, however, living in an all-Chinese community

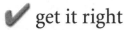

get it right

Don't assume all Asian Americans (or Hispanics, or members of any other minority category) are the same. The tables in this chapter highlight important differences among members of each minority category.

Table 4 The Social Standing of Asian Americans, 2005

	All Asian Americans**	Chinese Americans*	Japanese Americans*	Korean Americans*	Filipino Americans*	Entire U.S. Population
Median family income	$68,957	$60,058	$70,849	$47,624	$65,189	$56,194
Percentage in poverty	11.1%	13.2%	9.5%	14.4%	6.2%	12.6%
Completion of four or more years of college (age 25 and over)	49.4%	48.1%	41.9%	43.8%	43.8%	27.7%

*Income data are for 1999; poverty and college completion data are for 2000.
**For comparison with other tables in this chapter, 2000 data for all Asians are as follows: median family income, $62,617; percentage in poverty, 10.8%; completion of four or more years of college, 43.9%.

Sources: U.S. Census Bureau (2000, 2001, 2006).

discouraged residents from learning English, which limited their job opportunities (Wong, 1971).

A renewed need for labor during World War II prompted President Franklin Roosevelt to end the ban on Chinese immigration in 1943 and to extend the rights of citizenship to Chinese Americans born abroad. Many responded by moving out of Chinatowns and pursuing cultural assimilation. In Honolulu in 1900, for example, 70 percent of Chinese people lived in Chinatown; today, the figure is below 20 percent.

By 1950, many Chinese Americans had experienced upward social mobility. Today, people of Chinese ancestry are no longer limited to self-employment in laundries and restaurants; many hold high-prestige positions, especially in fields related to science and new information technology.

As shown in Table 4, the median family income of Chinese Americans is $60,058, which is above the national average of $56,194. However, the higher income of all Asian Americans reflects a larger number of family members in the labor force.[4] Chinese Americans also have a record of educational achievement, with almost twice the national average of college graduates.

Despite their successes, many Chinese Americans still grapple with subtle (and sometimes blatant) prejudice and discrimination. Such hostility is one reason that poverty remains a problem for many Chinese Americans. The problem of poverty is most common among people who remain in the socially isolated Chinatowns working in restaurants or other low-paying jobs, raising the question of whether racial and ethnic enclaves help their residents or exploit them (Portes & Jensen, 1989; Kinkead, 1992; Gilbertson & Gurak, 1993).

Japanese Americans

Japanese immigration to the United States began slowly in the 1860s, reaching only 3,000 by 1890. Most were men who came to the Hawaiian Islands (annexed by the United States in 1898 and made a state in 1959) as a source of cheap labor. After 1900, however, as the number of Japanese immigrants to California rose (reaching 140,000 by 1915), white hostility increased (Takaki, 1998). In 1907, the United States signed an agreement with Japan curbing the entry of men—the chief economic threat—while allowing women to enter this country to ease the Japanese sex ratio imbalance. In the 1920s, state laws in California and elsewhere segregated the Japanese and banned interracial marriage, just about ending further Japanese immigration. Not until 1952 did the United States extend citizenship to foreign-born Japanese.

Immigrants from Japan and China differed in three important ways. First, there were fewer Japanese immigrants, so they escaped some of the hostility directed toward the more numerous Chinese. Second, the Japanese knew more about the United States than the Chinese did, which helped them assimilate (Sowell, 1981). Third, Japanese immigrants preferred rural farming to clustering in cities, which made them less visible. But many white people objected to Japanese ownership of farmland, so in 1913, California barred further purchases. Many foreign-born Japanese (called *Issei*) responded by placing farmland in the names of their U.S.-born children (*Nisei*), who were constitutionally entitled to citizenship.

Japanese Americans faced their greatest crisis after Japan bombed the U.S. naval fleet at Hawaii's Pearl Harbor on December 7, 1941.

---

[4]Median age for all Asian Americans in 2000 was 32.7 years, somewhat below the national median of 35.4 and the non-Hispanic white median of 38.6. But specific categories vary widely in median age: Japanese, 42; Chinese, 35; Filipino, 35; Korean, 32; Asian Indian, 30; Cambodian, 23; Hmong, 16 (U.S. Census Bureau, 2002, 2006).

tip

Watch for ways in which recent immigrants differ
from those whose families have been in the
United States for a longer period.

Rage was directed at the Japanese living in the United States. Some people feared that Japanese Americans would spy for Japan or commit acts of sabotage. Within a year, President Franklin Roosevelt signed Executive Order 9066, an unprecedented action designed to ensure national security by detaining people of Japanese ancestry in military camps. Authorities soon relocated 110,000 people of Japanese descent (90 percent of the total in this country) to remote inland reservations (Sun, 1998).

Concern about national security always rises in times of war, but Japanese internment was sharply criticized. First, it targeted an entire category of people, not a single one of whom was known to have committed a disloyal act. Second, most of those imprisoned were *Nisei*, U.S. citizens by birth. Third, the United States was also at war with Germany and Italy, but no comparable action was taken against people of German or Italian ancestry.

Relocation meant selling homes, furnishings, and businesses on short notice for pennies on the dollar. As a result, almost the entire Japanese American population was economically devastated. In military prisons—surrounded by barbed wire and guarded by armed soldiers—families crowded into single rooms, often in buildings that had previously sheltered livestock. The internment ended in 1944 when the Supreme Court declared it unconstitutional. In 1988, Congress awarded $20,000 to each victim as token compensation for the hardships they endured.

After World War II, Japanese Americans staged a dramatic recovery. Having lost their traditional businesses, many entered new occupations; driven by cultural values stressing the importance of education and hard work, Japanese Americans have enjoyed remarkable success. In 2005, the median income of Japanese American families was almost 50 percent higher than the national average. The rate of poverty among Japanese Americans was well below the national figure.

Upward social mobility has encouraged cultural assimilation and intermarriage. Younger generations of Japanese Americans rarely live in residential enclaves, as many Chinese Americans do, and most marry non-Japanese partners. In the process, some have abandoned their traditions, including the Japanese language. A high proportion of Japanese Americans, however, belong to cultural associations as a way of maintaining their ethnic identity. Still, some appear to be caught between two worlds: no longer culturally Japanese yet, because of racial differences, not completely accepted in the larger society.

Recent Asian Immigrants

More recent immigrants from Asia include Filipinos, Indians, Koreans, Vietnamese, Guamanians, and Samoans. The Asian American population increased by 48 percent between 1990 and 2000 and currently

In the film *The Namesake*, members of an Indian American family wrestle with their desire to both honor their cultural traditions and to be accepted in their new home. What challenges do you think immigrants face in the workplace? On your campus?

Mira Nair/Fox Searchlight Pictures/Picture Desk, Inc./Kobal Collection

accounts for one-third of all immigration to the United States (U.S. Department of Homeland Security, 2007). A brief look at Koreans and Filipinos—both from countries that have had special ties to the United States—shows the social diversity of people arriving from Asia.

Koreans Korean immigration to the United States followed the U.S. involvement in the Korean War (1950–53). U.S. troops in South Korea experienced Korean culture firsthand, and some soldiers found Korean spouses. For South Koreans, contact with the troops raised interest in the United States.

The entrepreneurial spirit is strong among Asian immigrants. Asians are slightly more likely than Latinos, three times more likely than African Americans, and eight times more likely than Native Americans to own and operate small businesses (U.S. Small Business Administration, 2001). Among all Asian Americans, Koreans are the most likely to own small businesses. For example, residents of New York City know that most small grocery stores there are Korean-owned; in Los Angeles, Koreans operate a large share of liquor stores.

Although many Koreans work long hours in businesses such as these, Korean American families earn slightly below-average incomes, as shown in Table 4. In addition, Korean Americans face limited social acceptance, even among other categories of Asian Americans.

Filipinos The large number of immigrants from the Philippines is explained partly by the fact that the United States controlled the Philippine Islands between 1898, when Spain ceded it to this country in partial settlement of the Spanish-American War, and 1946, when the Philippines became an independent republic.

The data in Table 4 show that Filipinos have generally fared well. But a closer look reveals a mixed pattern, with some Filipinos highly successful in the professions (especially in medicine) and others struggling to get by in low-skilled jobs (Parrillo, 1994).

For many Filipino families, the key to high income is working women. Almost three-fourths of Filipino American women are in the labor force, compared to just half of Korean American women. In addition, many of these women are professionals, reflecting the fact that 42 percent of Filipino American women have a four-year college degree, compared with 26 percent of Korean American women.

In sum, a survey of Asian Americans presents a complex picture. The Japanese come closest to gaining social acceptance, but surveys reveal greater prejudice against Asian Americans than against African Americans (Parrillo, 2003a). Median income data suggest that many Asian Americans have prospered. But these numbers reflect the fact that many Asian Americans live in Hawaii, California, and New York, where incomes are high but so are living costs (Takaki, 1998). Then too, many Asian Americans remain poor. One thing is clear—their high immigration rate means that people of Asian ancestry are sure to play a central role in U.S. society in the decades to come.

Hispanic Americans/Latinos

In 2000, the number of people of Hispanic descent in the United States topped 35 million (12.5 percent of the population), surpassing the number of African Americans (12.3 percent) and making Hispanics the largest racial or ethnic minority. However, keep in mind that few people who fall into this category describe themselves as "Hispanic" or "Latino." Like Asian Americans, Hispanics are really a cluster of distinct populations, each of which identifies with a particular ancestral nation (Marín & Marín, 1991). About two out of three Hispanics (some 20 million) are Mexican Americans, or "Chicanos." Puerto Ricans are next in population size (3.4 million), followed by Cuban Americans (1.2 million). Many other nations of Latin America are represented by smaller numbers.

Although the Hispanic population is increasing all over the country, most Hispanic Americans still live in the Southwest. One of four Californians is a Latino (in greater Los Angeles, almost half the people are Latino). National Map 3 shows the distribution of the Hispanic, African American, Asian American, and Arab American populations across the United States.

Median family income for all Hispanics—$37,867 in 2005, as shown in Table 5 on page 380—is well below the national average.[5] As the following sections explain, however, some categories of Hispanics have fared better than others.

Mexican Americans

Some Mexican Americans are descendants of people who lived in a part of Mexico annexed by the United States after the Mexican American War (1846–48). Most, however, are more recent immigrants. Indeed, more immigrants now come to the United States from Mexico than from any other country.

The strength of family bonds and neighborhood ties is evident in Carmen Lomas Garza's painting *Barbacoa para Cumpleaños* (Birthday Party Barbecue).

Carmen Lomas Garza, *Barbacoa para Cumpleaños* (Birthday Party Barbecue). Alkyds on canvas, 38 × 48 inches. © 1993 Carmen Lomas Garza (reg. 1994). Photo credit: M. Lee Fatherree. Collection of Federal Reserve Bank of Dallas.

---

[5]The 2000 median age of the U.S. Hispanic population was 25.8 years, well below the national median of 35.4 years. This difference accounts for some of the disparity in income and education.

tip

Look closely at the maps. Can you explain why various categories of people tend to be concentrated in certain regions of the United States?

tip

Wherever you may live in the United States, you are likely to encounter people of certain racial and ethnic categories.

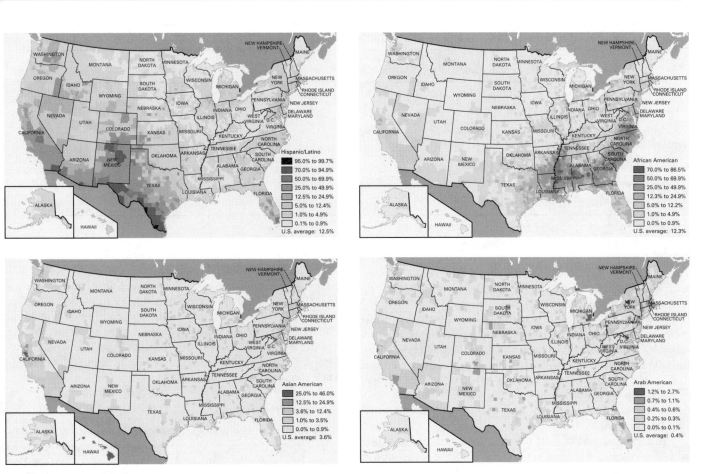

SEEING OURSELVES

NATIONAL MAP 3

The Concentration of Hispanics or Latinos, African Americans, Asian Americans, and Arab Americans, by County, 2000

In 2000, people of Hispanic or Latino descent represented 12.5 percent of the U.S. population, compared with 12.3 percent African Americans, 3.6 percent Asian Americans, and 0.4 percent Arab Americans. These maps show the geographic distribution of these categories of people in 2000. Comparing them, we see that the southern half of the United States is home to far more minorities than the northern half. But do they all concentrate in the same areas? What patterns do the maps reveal?

Sources: U.S. Census Bureau (2001, 2003).

Like many other immigrants, many Mexican Americans have worked as low-wage laborers, on farms and in factories. Table 5 shows that the 2003 median family income for Mexican Americans was $32,263, little more than half the national average. Almost one-fourth of Chicano families are poor—nearly twice the national average. Finally, despite gains since 1980, Mexican Americans still have a high dropout rate and receive much less schooling, on average, than the U.S. population as a whole.

Table 5   The Social Standing of Hispanic Americans, 2005

	All Hispanics**	Mexican Americans*	Puerto Ricans*	Cuban Americans*	Entire U.S. Population
Median family income	$37,867	$32,263	$34,519	$44,847	$56,194
Percentage in poverty	21.8%	23.8%	22.9%	14.5%	12.6%
Completion of four or more years of college (age 25 and over)	12.1%	7.9%	14.1%	24.0%	27.7%

*Income data are for 2003; poverty data are for 2004; college completion data are for 2005.
**For comparison with other tables in this chapter, 2000 data for all Hispanics are as follows: median family income, $35,050; percentage in poverty, 21.2%; completion of four or more years of college, 10.6%.
Sources: U.S. Census Bureau (2000, 2001, 2005, 2006).

Puerto Ricans

The island of Puerto Rico, like the Philippines, became a U.S. possession when the Spanish-American War ended in 1898. In 1917, Puerto Ricans (but not Filipinos) became U.S. citizens.

New York City is home to nearly 1 million Puerto Ricans. However, about one-third of this community is severely disadvantaged. Adjusting to cultural patterns on the mainland—including, for many, learning English—is one major challenge; also, Puerto Ricans with dark skin encounter prejudice and discrimination. As a result, more people return to Puerto Rico each year than arrive. During the 1990s, the Puerto Rican population of New York actually fell by about 100,000 (Navarro, 2000).

This "revolving door" pattern limits assimilation. About 70 percent of Puerto Rican families in the United States speak Spanish at home. Speaking Spanish keeps ethnic identity strong but limits economic opportunity. Puerto Ricans also have a higher incidence of woman-headed households than most other Hispanics, a pattern that puts families at greater risk of poverty (U.S. Census Bureau, 2007).

Table 5 shows that the 2003 median family income for Puerto Ricans was $34,519, a little more than 60 percent of the national average. Although long-term mainland residents have made economic gains, more recent immigrants from Puerto Rico continue to struggle to find work. Overall, Puerto Ricans remain the most socially disadvantaged Hispanic minority.

Cuban Americans

Within a decade after the 1959 Marxist revolution led by Fidel Castro, 400,000 Cubans had fled to the United States. Most settled with other Cuban Americans in Miami. Many were highly educated business and professional people who wasted little time becoming as successful in the United States as they had been in their homeland.

Table 5 shows that the 2003 median household income for Cuban Americans was $44,847, above that of other Hispanics yet still well below the national average. The 1.2 million Cuban Americans living in the United States today have managed a delicate balancing act, achieving in the larger society while holding on to much of their traditional culture. Of all Hispanics, Cubans are the most likely to speak Spanish in their homes: Eight out of ten families do so. However, cultural distinctiveness and highly visible communities, such as Miami's Little Havana, provoke hostility from some people.

Arab Americans

Arab Americans are another U.S. minority that is increasing in size. Like Hispanic Americans, these are people whose ancestors lived in one or more different countries. What is sometimes called "the Arab world" includes twenty-two nations and stretches across northern Africa, from Mauritania and Morocco on Africa's west coast to Egypt and Sudan on Africa's east coast, and extends into the Middle East (western Asia), including Iraq and Saudi Arabia. Not all the people who live in these nations are Arabs, however; for example, the Berber people in Morocco and the Kurds of Iraq are not Arab.

Arab cultures differ from society to society, but they share widespread use of the Arabic alphabet and language and have Islam as their dominant religion. But keep in mind that "Arab" (an ethnic category) is not the same as "Muslim" (a follower of Islam). A majority of the people living in most Arab countries are Muslims, but some Arabs are Christians or followers of other religions. In addition, most of the world's Muslims do not live in Africa or the Middle East and are not Arabs.

Because many of the world's nations have large Arab populations, immigration to the United States has created a culturally diverse population of Arab Americans. Some Arab Americans are Muslims,

tip

Arab Americans are highly diverse, with many
different national and religious backgrounds.

and some are not; some speak Arabic, and some do not; some maintain the traditions of their homeland, and some do not. As is the case with Hispanic Americans and Asian Americans, some are recent immigrants, and some have lived in this country for decades or even for generations.

As noted in Table 1, the government gives the official number of Arab Americans as 1.2 million, but because people may not declare their ethnic background, it is likely that the actual number is at least twice as high.[6] The largest populations of Arab Americans have ancestral ties to Lebanon (29 percent of all Arab Americans), Syria (15 percent), and Egypt (9 percent). Most Arab Americans (71 percent) report ancestral ties to one nation, but 28 percent report both Arab and non-Arab ancestry (U.S. Census Bureau, 2003). A look at National Map 3 shows the distribution of the Arab American population throughout the United States.

Included in the Arab American population are people of all social classes. Some are highly educated professionals who work as physicians, engineers, and professors; others are working-class people who perform various skilled jobs in factories or on construction sites; still others do service work in restaurants, hospitals, or other settings or work in small family businesses. As shown in Table 6, median family income for Arab Americans is slightly above the national average ($52,318 compared to the national median of $50,046 in 1999), but Arab Americans have a higher than average poverty rate (16.7 percent versus 12.4 percent for the population as a whole in 1999) (U.S. Census Bureau, 2005).

 Do you know of any highly educated immigrants who worked as professionals in their birth nations and who are now performing working-class jobs here in the United States? How would you explain this pattern?

Arab American communities can be found in many large cities on the East and West coasts of the United States, but the heaviest concentrations are found across the upper Midwest. This mosque rises above the cornfields in a rural area near Toledo, Ohio.

Peter Yates/Corbis/Bettmann

Table 6   The Social Standing of Arab Americans, 1999

	Arab Americans	Entire U.S. Population
Median family income	$52,318	$50,046
Percentage in poverty	16.7%	12.4%
Completion of four or more years of college (age 25 and over)	41.2%*	24.4%*

*Data are for 2000.
Source: U.S. Census Bureau (2005).

[6]The 2000 median age for Arab Americans was 33.1 years, only slightly below the national median of 35.4 years.

There are large, visible Arab American communities in a number of U.S. cities, including New York, Chicago, Los Angeles, Houston, and Dearborn (Michigan). Even so, Arab Americans may choose to downplay their ethnicity as a way to avoid prejudice and discrimination. The fact that many terrorist attacks against the United States and other nations have been carried out by Arabs has fueled a stereotype that links being Arab (or Muslim) with being a terrorist. This stereotype is unfair because it blames an entire category of people for actions by a few individuals. But it is probably the reason that the social distance research discussed earlier in this chapter shows students expressing more negative attitudes toward Arabs than toward any other racial or ethnic category. Its also helps explain why Arab Americans have been targets of an increasing number of hate crimes and why many Arab Americans feel that they are subject to "ethnic profiling" that threatens their privacy and freedom (Ali & Juarez, 2003; Ali, Lipper, & Mack, 2004; Hagopian, 2004).

get it right

After reading the box below, be sure you can state
arguments for and against affirmative action.
(Then decide what you think.)

 Controversy & Debate

Affirmative Action: Solution or Problem?

STEPHANIE: I think Ms. Gruttner got, well, messed over. She should have been admitted.

GINA: Maybe. But diversity is important. I believe in affirmative action.

MARCO: Maybe some people do get into college more easily. But that includes guys like me whose father went here.

Barbara Gruttner, who is white, claimed that she was the victim of racial discrimination. She maintained that the University of Michigan Law School had unfairly denied her application for admission while admitting many less qualified African American applicants. The basis of her claim was the fact that Michigan, a state university, admitted just 9 percent of white students with her grade point average and law school aptitude test scores while admitting 100 percent of African American applicants with comparable scores.

In 2003, the U.S. Supreme Court heard Gruttner's complaint in a review of the admissions policies of both the law school and the undergraduate program at the University of Michigan. In a 6–3 decision, the Court ruled against Gruttner, claiming that the University of Michigan Law School could use a policy of affirmative action that takes account of the race of applicants in the interest of creating a socially diverse student body. At the same time, however, the Court struck down the university's undergraduate admissions policy, which awarded points not only for grades and college board scores but also for being a member of an underrepresented minority. A point system of this kind, the Court ruled, is too close to the rigid quota systems rejected by the Court in the past.

Carl D. Walsh/Aurora & Quanta Productions Inc

With this ruling, the Supreme Court continued to oppose any quotalike systems while at the same time reaffirming the importance of racial diversity on campus. Thus colleges and universities can take account of race in order to increase the number of traditionally underrepresented students as long as race is treated as one variable in a process that evaluates each applicant as an individual (Stout, 2003).

How did the controversial policy of affirmative action begin? The answer takes us back to the end of World War II, when the U.S. government funded higher education for veterans of all races. The so-called G.I. Bill held special promise for African Americans, most of whom needed financial assistance to enroll in college. The program was so successful that by 1960, some 350,000 black men and women were on college campuses with government funding.

There was just one problem: These individuals were not finding the kinds of jobs for which they were qualified. In short, educational opportunity was not producing economic opportunity.

So in the early 1960s, the Kennedy administration devised a program of "affirmative action" to provide broader opportunities to qualified minorities. Employers were instructed to monitor hiring, promotion, and admissions policies to eliminate discrimination—even if unintended—against minorities.

White Ethnic Americans

The term "white ethnics" recognizes the ethnic heritage and social disadvantages of many white people. White ethnics are non-WASPs whose ancestors lived in Ireland, Poland, Germany, Italy, or other European countries. More than half the U.S. population falls into one or more white ethnic categories.

High rates of emigration from Europe during the nineteenth century first brought Germans and Irish and then Italians and Jews to our shores. Despite cultural differences, all shared the hope that the United States would offer greater political freedom and economic opportunity than their homelands. Most did live better in this country, but the belief that "the streets of America were paved with gold" turned out to

tip

Use the questions at the end of the box to start a discussion about affirmative action with your classmates.

Defenders of affirmative action see it, first, as a sensible response to our nation's racial and ethnic history, especially for African Americans, who suffered through two centuries of slavery and a century of segregation under Jim Crow laws. Throughout our history, they claim, being white gave people a big advantage. They see minority preference today as a step toward fair compensation for unfair majority preference in the past.

Second, given our racial history, many analysts doubt that the United States will ever become a color-blind society. They claim that because prejudice and discrimination are rooted deep in the fabric of U.S. society, simply claiming that we are color-blind does not mean everyone will compete fairly.

Third, supporters maintain that affirmative action has worked. Where would minorities be if the government had not enacted this policy four decades ago? Major employers, such as fire and police departments in large cities, began hiring minorities and women for the first time only because of affirmative action. This program has played an important part in expanding the African American middle class. Affirmative action has also increased racial diversity on campus, which benefits everyone, and has advanced the careers of an entire generation of black students.

About 80 percent of African Americans claim that affirmative action is needed to secure equal opportunity. But affirmative action draws criticism from others. A 2003 poll shows that 73 percent of white people and 56 percent of Hispanics oppose preferences for African Americans (NORC, 2005). As this opposition to affirmative action was building during the 1990s, courts began to trim back such policies. Critics argue, first, that affirmative action started out as a temporary remedy to ensure fair competition but became a system of "group preferences" and quotas. In other words, the policy did not remain true to the goal of promoting color blindness as set out in the 1964 Civil Rights Act. By the 1970s, it had become "reverse discrimination," favoring people not because of performance but because of race, ethnicity, or sex.

Second, critics argue that affirmative action divides society. If racial preferences were wrong in the past, they are wrong now. Why should whites today, many of whom are far from privileged, be penalized for past discrimination that was in no way their fault? Our society has undone most of the institutional prejudice and discrimination of earlier times, opponents continue, so that minorities can and do enjoy success according to personal merit. Giving entire categories of people special treatment compromises standards of excellence, calls into question the real accomplishments of minorities, and offends public opinion.

A third argument against affirmative action is that it benefits those who need it least. Favoring minority-owned corporations or holding places in law school helps already privileged people. Affirmative action has done little for the African American underclass that needs the most help.

In sum, there are good arguments for and against affirmative action, and people who want our society to have more racial or ethnic equality fall on both sides of the debate. The disagreement is not whether people of all colors should have equal opportunity but whether the current policy of affirmative action is part of the solution or part of the problem.

WHAT DO YOU THINK?

1. In view of the fact that society has historically favored males over females and whites over people of color, would you agree that white males have received more "affirmative action" than anyone? Why or why not?

2. Should affirmative action include only disadvantaged categories of minorities (say, African Americans and Native Americans) and exclude more affluent categories (such as Japanese Americans)? Why or why not?

3. Should state universities admit applicants with an eye toward advancing minorities in order to lessen racial inequality? Do you think that goal is more or less important than the goal of admitting the most qualified individuals? Explain your answer.

Sources: Bowen & Bok (1999), Kantrowitz & Wingert (2003), and NORC (2005).

be a far cry from reality. Many immigrants found only hard labor for low wages.

White ethnics also endured their share of prejudice and discrimination. Many employers shut their doors to immigrants, posting signs that warned "None need apply but Americans" (Handlin, 1941:67). By 1921, the federal government had passed a quota system greatly limiting immigration, especially by southern and eastern Europeans, who were likely to have darker skin and different cultural backgrounds than the dominant WASPs. This system continued until 1968.

In response to this hostility, many white ethnics formed supportive residential enclaves. Some also established footholds in certain businesses and trades: Italian Americans entered the construction

tip
The Applying Sociology in Everyday Life items provide additional ways for you to connect the ideas found in this chapter with your own life.

industry; the Irish worked in construction and in civil service jobs; Jews predominated in the garment industry; many Greeks (like the Chinese) worked in the retail food business (W. M. Newman, 1973).

Many working-class people still live in traditional neighborhoods, although those who prospered have gradually assimilated. Most descendants of immigrants who labored in sweatshops and lived in crowded tenements now lead more comfortable lives. As a result, their ethnic heritage has become a source of pride.

Race and Ethnicity: Looking Ahead

The United States has been and will remain a land of immigrants. Immigration has brought striking cultural diversity and tales of hope, struggle, and success told in hundreds of languages.

Most immigrants arrived in a great wave that peaked about 1910. The next two generations saw gradual economic gains and at least some assimilation. The government also extended citizenship to Native Americans (1924), foreign-born Filipinos (1942), Chinese Americans (1943), and Japanese Americans (1952).

Another wave of immigration began after World War II and swelled as the government relaxed immigration laws in the 1960s. Today, about 1.5 million people come to the United States each year (about 1 million who enter legally and perhaps 500,000 people who enter illegally). This is twice the number that arrived during the "Great Immigration" a century ago (although newcomers now enter a coun-

try that has five times as many people). Today's immigrants come not from Europe but from Latin America and Asia, with Mexicans, Asian Indians, and Filipinos arriving in the largest numbers.

Many new arrivals face the same kind of prejudice and discrimination experienced by those who came before them. In fact, recent years have witnessed rising hostility toward foreigners (sometimes termed *xenophobia,* with Greek roots meaning "fear of what is strange"). In 1994, California voters passed Proposition 187, which cut off social services (including schooling) for illegal immigrants. More recently, voters there mandated that all children learn English in school. Since 2000, some landowners in the Southwest have taken up arms to discourage the large number of illegal immigrants crossing the border from Mexico, and some political candidates have called for drastic action to cut off further immigration.

Even minorities who have been in the United States for generations feel the sting of prejudice and discrimination. Affirmative action, a policy meant to provide opportunities for members of racial and ethnic minorities, continues to be hotly debated in this country, as the Controversy & Debate box two pages back describes.

Like other minorities, today's immigrants hope to gain acceptance and to blend into U.S. society without completely giving up their traditional culture. Some still build racial and ethnic enclaves so that in many cities across the country, the Little Havanas and Koreatowns of today stand alongside the Little Italys and Chinatowns of the past. In addition, new arrivals still carry the traditional hope that their racial and ethnic identities can be a source of pride and strength rather than a badge of inferiority.

Applying Sociology in Everyday Life

1. Does your college or university take account of race and ethnicity in its admissions policies? Ask to speak with an admissions officer to see what you can learn about your school's policies and the reasons for them. Ask whether there is a "legacy" policy that favors applicants with a parent who attended the school.

2. Give several of your friends or family members a quick quiz, asking them what share of the U.S. population is white, Hispanic, African American, and Asian (see Table 1

for the correct figures). Most white people think that minority shares of the population are much higher than they really are (C. A. Gallagher, 2003). Why do you think that is?

3. Interview immigrants on your campus or in your local community about their homelands and their experiences since arriving in the United States. Were they surprised by their experiences in this country? If so, why?

MAKING THE GRADE
Race and Ethnicity

The Social Meaning of Race and Ethnicity

RACE refers to socially constructed categories based on biological traits a society defines as important.

- The meaning and importance of race vary from place to place and over time.
- Societies use racial categories to rank people in a hierarchy, giving some people more money, power, and prestige than others.
- In the past, scientists created three broad categories—Caucasoids, Mongoloids, and Negroids—but there are no biologically pure races.

ETHNICITY refers to socially constructed categories based on cultural traits a society defines as important.

- Ethnicity reflects common ancestors, language, and religion.
- The importance of ethnicity varies from place to place and over time.
- People choose to play up or play down their ethnicity.
- Societies may or may not set categories of people apart based on differences in ethnicity.

race a socially constructed category of people who share biologically transmitted traits that members of a society consider important

ethnicity a shared cultural heritage

minority any category of people distinguished by physical or cultural difference that a society sets apart and subordinates

✔ *Minorities are people of various racial and ethnic categories who are visually distinctive and disadvantaged by a society.*

Prejudice and Stereotypes

PREJUDICE is a rigid and unfair generalization about a category of people.

- The social distance scale is one measure of prejudice.
- One type of prejudice is the **STEREOTYPE**, an exaggerated description applied to every person in some category.
- **RACISM**, a very destructive type of prejudice, asserts that one race is innately superior or inferior to another.

There are four **THEORIES OF PREJUDICE**:

- **Scapegoat theory** claims that prejudice results from frustration among people who are disadvantaged.
- **Authoritarian personality theory** (Adorno) claims prejudice is a personality trait of certain individuals, especially those with little education and those raised by cold and demanding parents.
- **Culture theory** (Bogardus) claims that prejudice is rooted in culture; we learn to feel greater social distance from some categories of people.
- **Conflict theory** claims that prejudice is a tool used by powerful people to divide and control the population.

prejudice a rigid and unfair generalization about an entire category of people

stereotype a simplified description applied to every person in some category

racism the belief that one racial category is innately superior or inferior to another

scapegoat a person or category of people, typically with little power, whom people unfairly blame for their own troubles

Discrimination

DISCRIMINATION refers to actions by which a person treats various categories of people unequally.

- Prejudice refers to *attitudes*; discrimination involves *actions*.
- Institutional prejudice and discrimination is bias built into the operation of society's institutions, including schools, hospitals, the police, and the workplace.
- Prejudice and discrimination perpetuate themselves in a vicious circle, resulting in social disadvantage that fuels additional prejudice and discrimination.

discrimination unequal treatment of various categories of people

institutional prejudice and discrimination bias built into the operation of society's institutions

Majority and Minority: Patterns of Interaction

PLURALISM means that racial and ethnic categories, although distinct, have roughly equal social standing.

- U.S. society is pluralistic in that all people in the United States, regardless of race or ethnicity, have equal standing under the law.
- U.S. society is not pluralistic in that all racial and ethnic categories do not have equal social standing.

ASSIMILATION is a process by which minorities gradually adopt the patterns of the dominant culture.

- Assimilation involves changes in dress, language, religion, values, and friends.
- Assimilation is a strategy to escape prejudice and discrimination and to achieve upward social mobility.
- Some categories of people have assimilated more than others.

pluralism a state in which people of all races and ethnicities are distinct but have equal social standing

assimilation the process by which minorities gradually adopt patterns of the dominant culture

miscegenation biological reproduction by partners of different racial categories

segregation the physical and social separation of categories of people

genocide the systematic killing of one category of people by another

SEGREGATION is the physical and social separation of categories of people.

- Although some segregation is voluntary (for example, the Amish), majorities usually segregate minorities by excluding them from neighborhoods, schools, and occupations.
- *De jure* segregation is segregation by law; *de facto* segregation describes settings that contain only people of one category.
- Hypersegregation means having little social contact with people beyond the local community.

GENOCIDE is the systematic killing of one category of people by another.

- Historical examples of genocide include the extermination of Jews by the Nazis and the killing of Western-leaning people in Cambodia by Pol Pot.
- Recent examples of genocide include Hutus killing Tutsis in the African nation of Rwanda, Serbs killing Bosnians in the Balkans of Eastern Europe, and the systematic killing in the Darfur region of Sudan.

Race and Ethnicity in the United States

NATIVE AMERICANS, the earliest human inhabitants of the Americas, have endured genocide, segregation, and forced assimilation. Today, the social standing of Native Americans is well below the national average.

WHITE ANGLO-SAXON PROTESTANTS (WASPS) were most of the original European settlers of the United States, and many continue to enjoy high social position today.

AFRICAN AMERICANS experienced two centuries of slavery. Emancipation in 1865 gave way to segregation by law (the so-called Jim Crow laws). In the 1950s and 1960s, a national civil rights movement resulted in legislation that outlawed segregated schools and overt discrimination in employment and public accommodations. Today, despite legal equality, African Americans are still disadvantaged.

ASIAN AMERICANS have suffered both racial and ethnic hostility. Although some prejudice and discrimination continue, both Chinese and Japanese Americans now have above-average income and schooling. Asian immigrants, especially Koreans and Filipinos, now account for one-third of all immigration to the United States.

HISPANIC AMERICANS/LATINOS, the largest U.S. minority, include many ethnicities sharing a Spanish heritage. Mexican Americans, the largest Hispanic minority, are concentrated in the southwest region of the country and are the poorest Hispanic category. Cubans, concentrated in Miami, are the most affluent Hispanic category.

ARAB AMERICANS are a growing U.S. minority. Because they come to the United States from so many different nations, Arab Americans are a culturally diverse population, and they are represented in all social classes. They have been a target of prejudice and hate crimes in recent years as a result of a stereotype that links all Arab Americans with terrorism.

WHITE ETHNIC AMERICANS are non-WASPs whose ancestors emigrated from Europe in the nineteenth and twentieth centuries. In response to prejudice and discrimination, many white ethnics formed supportive residential enclaves.

MAKING THE GRADE

Race and Ethnicity

Sample Test Questions

These questions are similar to those found in the test bank that accompanies this textbook.

Multiple-Choice Questions

1. Race refers to _____ considered important by a society, and ethnicity refers to _____.
   a. biological traits; cultural traits
   b. cultural traits; biological traits
   c. differences; what we have in common
   d. what we have in common; differences

2. What share of the U.S. population consists of people of Hispanic ancestry?
   a. 42.5 percent
   b. 32.5 percent
   c. 22.5 percent
   d. 12.5 percent

3. A minority is defined as a category of people who
   a. have physical traits that make them different.
   b. are less than half the society's population.
   c. are defined as both different and disadvantaged.
   d. are below average in terms of income.

4. In this country, four states now have a "minority majority." Which of the following is not one of them?
   a. California
   b. Florida
   c. Hawaii
   d. New Mexico

5. Research using the Bogardus social distance scale shows that U.S. college students
   a. are less prejudiced than students fifty years ago.
   b. believe that Arabs and Muslims should be kept out of the country.
   c. have the strongest prejudice against African Americans.
   d. All of the above are correct.

6. Prejudice is a matter of _____, and discrimination is a matter of _____.
   a. biology; culture
   b. attitudes; behavior
   c. choice; social structure
   d. what rich people think; what rich people do

7. The United States is not truly pluralistic because
   a. part of our population lives in "ethnic enclaves."
   b. this country has a history of slavery.
   c. different racial and ethnic categories are unequal in social standing.
   d. All of the above are correct.

8. Which term is illustrated by immigrants from Ecuador learning to speak the English language?
   a. genocide
   b. segregation
   c. assimilation
   d. pluralism

9. During the late 1400s, the first Europeans came to the Americas; Native Americans
   a. followed shortly thereafter.
   b. had just migrated from Asia.
   c. came with them from Europe.
   d. had inhabited this land for 30,000 years.

10. Which of the following is the largest category of Asian Americans in the United States?
    a. Chinese American
    b. Japanese American
    c. Korean American
    d. Vietnamese American

ANSWERS: 1 (a); 2 (d); 3 (c); 4 (b); 5 (a); 6 (b); 7 (c); 8 (c); 9 (d); 10 (a).

Essay Questions

1. What is the difference between race and ethnicity? What does it mean to say that race and ethnicity are socially constructed?

2. What is a minority? Support the claim that African Americans and Arab Americans are both minorities in the United States using specific facts from the chapter.

Families

Families

WHAT is a family?

HOW are families in the United States changing?

WHY is there a debate over the future of the family?

Families are an important social institution in every society, guiding the behavior of both young and old as well as playing a part in continuing social inequality. Many debates surround today's families, including exactly what relationships should be considered families.

Bob Daemmrich/The Image Works

Michael Newman/PhotoEdit Inc.

Rosa Yniguez is one of seven children who grew up in Jalisco, Mexico, in a world in which families worked hard, went to church regularly, and were proud of having many children. Rosa remembers visiting the home of friends of her parents who had a clock in their living room with a picture of each of their twelve children where the numbers on the clock face would be.

Now thirty-five years old, Rosa is living in San Francisco and working as a cashier in a department store. In some respects, she has carried on her parents' traditions—but not in every way. Recalling her childhood, she says, "In Mexico, many of the families I knew had six, eight, ten children. Sometimes more. But I came to this country to get ahead. That is simply impossible with too many kids." As a result of her desire to keep her job and make a better life for her family, Yniguez has decided to have no more than the three children she has now.

A tradition of having large families has helped make Hispanics the largest ethnic minority in the United States. But today more and more Latinas are making the same decision as Rosa Yniguez and opting to have fewer children. Studies show that the birth rate for all immigrant women has dropped by 30 percent during the past decade (Navarro, 2004).

Families have been with us for a very long time. But as this story indicates, U.S. families are changing in response to a number of factors, including the desire of women to have more career options and to provide better lives for their children. In fact, the family is changing faster than any other social institution (Bianchi & Spain, 1996). This chapter explores the changes in family life, as well as the diversity of families both around the world and here in the United States.

Families: Basic Concepts

The **family** is *a social institution found in all societies that unites people in cooperative groups to care for one another, including any children.* Family ties are also called **kinship**, *a social bond based on common ancestry, marriage, or adoption.* All societies contain families, but exactly whom people call their kin has varied through history and varies today from one culture to another. From the point of view of any individual, families change as we grow up, leaving the family into which we were born to form a family of our own.

Here as in other countries, families form around **marriage**, *a legal relationship, usually involving economic cooperation, sexual activity, and childbearing.* The traditional belief in the United States is that people should marry before having children; this expectation is found in the word *matrimony,* which in Latin means "the condition of motherhood." Today two-thirds of children are born to married couples, but one-third are born to single women who may or may not live with a partner.

Families, then, have become more diverse. Which relationships are and are not considered a family can have important consequences, because companies typically extend benefits such as health care only to family members. The U.S. Census Bureau, which collects data used by sociologists, counts as families only people living together who are linked by "blood, marriage, or adoption."[1] All Census Bureau data on families in this chapter are based on that definition. However, the trend in the United States is toward a broader definition of families to include both homosexual and heterosexual partners and unmarried as well as married couples who live together. These *families of affinity* are made up of people who think of themselves as a family and wish others to see them that way.

Families: Global Variations

How closely related do people have to be to consider themselves a "family"? In preindustrial societies, people commonly recognize the **extended family**, *a family consisting of parents and children as well as other kin.* This group is sometimes called the *consanguine family* because it includes everyone with "shared blood." With industrialization, however, increased social mobility and geographic migration give rise to the **nuclear family**, *a family composed of one or two parents and their children.* The nuclear family is also called the *conjugal family* (*conjugal* means "based on marriage"). Although many people in our society think of kinship in terms of extended families, most people carry out their everyday routines within a nuclear family.

The family is changing most quickly in nations that have a large welfare state. In the Thinking Globally box two pages ahead, the sociologist David Popenoe takes a look at Sweden, which, he claims, is home to the weakest families in the world.

Marriage Patterns

Cultural norms, and often laws, identify people as suitable or unsuitable marriage partners. Some marital norms promote **endogamy**, *marriage between people of the same social category.* Endogamy

---

[1]According to the U.S. Census Bureau, there were 114 million U.S. households in 2005. Of these, 77.4 million (68 percent) met the bureau's definition of "family." The remaining living units contained single people or unrelated individuals living together. In 1950, 90 percent of all households were families.

Chapter Overview

This chapter explores the family, a major social institution. The chapter begins by introducing a number of important concepts that sociologists use to describe and analyze families.

limits potential partners to people of the same age, race, religion, or social class. By contrast, **exogamy** is *marriage between people of different social categories.* In rural areas of India, for example, people are expected to marry someone of the same caste (endogamy) but from a different village (exogamy). The reason for endogamy is that people of similar position pass along their standing to their offspring, maintaining the traditional social hierarchy. Exogamy, on the other hand, links communities and encourages the spread of culture.

In high-income nations, laws permit only **monogamy** (from the Greek, meaning "one union"), *marriage that unites two partners.* Global Map 1 shows that monogamy is the rule throughout North and South America as well as Europe, although many countries in Africa and southern Asia permit **polygamy** (from the Greek, meaning "many unions"), *marriage that unites a person with two or more spouses.* Polygamy has two forms. By far the more common form is **polygyny** (from the Greek, meaning "many women"), *marriage that unites one man and two or more women.* For example, Islamic nations in the Middle East and Africa permit men up to four wives. Even so, most Islamic families are monogamous because few men can afford to support several wives and even more children.

Polyandry (from the Greek, meaning "many men" or "many husbands") is *marriage that unites one woman and two or more men.* This extremely rare pattern exists in Tibet, a mountainous land where agriculture is difficult. There, polyandry discourages the division of land into parcels too small to support a family and divides the hard work of farming among many men.

Most of the world's societies have at some time permitted more than one marital pattern. Even so, most marriages have been monogamous (Murdock, 1965, orig. 1949). This historical preference for monogamy reflects two facts of life: Supporting several spouses is very expensive, and the number of men and women in most societies is roughly equal.

Given the high level of divorce in the United States, do you think it would be more accurate to call our marriage system "serial monogamy" (one partner after another)? Explain.

Families in the United States have diverse forms, and celebrity couples represent them all. Although same-sex couples can marry only in Massachusetts, they are becoming more common across the United States; comedian Ellen DeGeneres lives with her partner Portia de Rossi. Cohabitation without marriage is also becoming more common in our society; Brad Pitt and Angelina Jolie live together and have three adopted children and one biological child.

Residential Patterns

Just as societies regulate mate selection, they also designate where a couple lives. In preindustrial societies, most newlyweds live with one set of parents who offer them protection, support, and assistance. Most common is the norm of **patrilocality** (Greek for "place of the father"), *a residential pattern in which a married couple lives with or near the husband's family.* But some societies (such as the North American Iroquois) favor **matrilocality** (meaning "place of the mother"), *a residential pattern in which a married couple lives with or near the wife's family.* Societies that engage in frequent local warfare tend toward patrilocality, so sons are close to home to offer protection. On the other hand, societies that engage only in distant warfare may be either patrilocal or matrilocal, depending on whether its sons or daughters have greater economic value (Ember & Ember, 1971, 1991).

Industrial societies show yet another pattern. Finances permitting, they favor **neolocality** (from the Greek, meaning "new place"), *a residential pattern in which a married couple lives apart from both sets of parents.*

FAMILIES

423

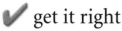 **get it right**

There are several similar concepts—extended family and nuclear family; endogamy and exogamy; monogamy and polygamy; polygyny and polyandry; patrilocality and matrilocality; patrilineal descent and matrilineal descent—that have specific meanings. Be sure you understand and can clearly define all these concepts.

student 2 student

"Government should be 'family friendly.' But what policy is good for families? The box on Sweden says that government doing more for people tends to mean that families get weaker. It makes you stop and think."

Thinking Globally
The Weakest Families on Earth? A Report from Sweden

INGE: In Sweden, we have a government that takes care of every person!
SAM: In the United States, we have families to do that. . . .

We in the United States can envy the Swedes for avoiding many of our worst social problems, including violent crime, drug abuse, and savage poverty. Instead, this Scandinavian nation seems to fulfill the promise of the modern welfare state, with a large and professional government bureaucracy that sees to virtually all human needs.

But one drawback of such a large welfare state, according to David Popenoe (1991, 1994), is that Sweden has the weakest families on Earth. Because people look to the government, not spouses, for economic assistance, Swedes are less likely to marry than members of any other high-income society. For the same reason, Sweden also has a high share of adults living alone (36 percent, compared to 24 percent in the United States). In addition, a large proportion of couples live together outside marriage (28 percent, versus 8 percent in the United States), and more than half of all Swedish children (compared to one-third in the United States) are born to unmarried parents. Average household size in Sweden is also the smallest in the world (2.0 persons, versus 2.6 in the United States). Finally, Swedish couples, whether married or not, are more likely to break up than partners in the United States or any other high-income nation.

Popenoe claims that a growing culture of individualism and self-

fulfillment, along with the declining influence of religion, began eroding Swedish families in the 1960s. The movement of women into the labor force also played a part. Today, Sweden has the lowest proportion of women who are homemakers (10 percent, versus 22 percent in the United States) and the highest percentage of women in the labor force (77 percent, versus 59 percent in the United States).

But most important, according to Popenoe, is the expansion of the welfare state. The Swedish government offers its citizens a lifetime of services. Swedes can count on the government to deliver and school their children, provide comprehensive health care, support them when they are out of work, and pay for their funerals.

Many Swedes supported this welfare state, thinking it would strengthen families. But as Popenoe sees it, government is really *replacing* families. Take the case of child care: The Swedish government operates child

John Terence Turner/Getty Images, Inc.—Taxi

care centers that are staffed by professionals and available regardless of parents' income. However, the government gives nothing to parents who wish to care for their children in their own home. In effect, government benefits encourage people to let the state do what family members used to do for themselves.

But if Sweden's system has solved so many social problems, why should anyone care about the family getting weaker? For two reasons, says Popenoe. First, it is very expensive for government to provide many "family" services; this is the main reason that Sweden has one of the highest rates of taxation in the world. Second, at any price, Popenoe says that government employees in large child care centers cannot provide children with the same love and emotional security given by two parents living as a family. When it comes to taking care of people—especially young children—small, intimate groups do the job better than large, impersonal organizations.

WHAT DO YOU THINK?

1. Do you agree with Popenoe that government should not replace families? Explain your answer.

2. In the United States, we have a much smaller welfare state than Sweden has. Should our government do more for its people? Why or why not?

3. With regard to children, list two specific things that government can do better than parents and two things that parents do better than government.

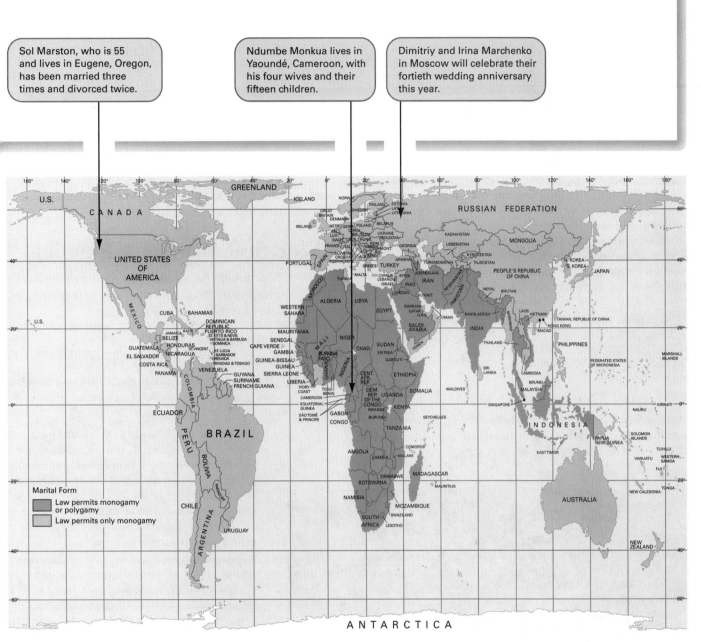

Sol Marston, who is 55 and lives in Eugene, Oregon, has been married three times and divorced twice.

Ndumbe Monkua lives in Yaoundé, Cameroon, with his four wives and their fifteen children.

Dimitriy and Irina Marchenko in Moscow will celebrate their fortieth wedding anniversary this year.

WINDOW ON THE WORLD

GLOBAL MAP 1   Marital Form in Global Perspective

Monogamy is the only legal form of marriage throughout the Western Hemisphere and in much of the rest of the world. In most African nations and in southern Asia, however, polygamy is permitted by law. In many cases, this practice reflects the influence of Islam, a religion that allows a man to have up to four wives. Even so, most marriages in these countries are monogamous, primarily for financial reasons.

Source: *Peters Atlas of the World* (1990) with updates by the author.

Patterns of Descent

Descent refers to *the system by which members of a society trace kinship over generations*. Most preindustrial societies trace kinship through either the father's side or the mother's side of the family.

Patrilineal descent, the more common pattern, is *a system tracing kinship through men*. In this pattern, children are related to others only through their fathers, so that fathers pass property on to their sons. Patrilineal descent characterizes most pastoral and agrarian societies, in which men produce the most valued resources. Less

tip

To analyze family life, this chapter uses the major theoretical approaches—structural-functional, social-conflict, and micro-level—that you have seen in earlier chapters.

common is **matrilineal descent**, *a system tracing kinship through women.* Matrilineal descent, in which mothers pass property to their daughters, is found more frequently in horticultural societies, where women are the main food producers.

Industrial societies with greater gender equality recognize **bilateral descent** ("two-sided descent"), *a system tracing kinship through both men and women.* In this pattern, children include people on both the father's side and the mother's side among their relatives.

In terms of patterns of descent, how would you describe the common practice in the United States of a woman adopting her husband's last name after marriage?

Patterns of Authority

Worldwide, polygyny, patrilocality, and patrilineal descent are dominant and reflect the common global pattern of patriarchy. In industrial societies like the United States, men are still typically heads of

households, and most U.S. parents give children their father's last name. However, more egalitarian family patterns have evolved as the share of women in the labor force has gone up.

Theoretical Analysis of Families

As in earlier chapters, the three major theoretical approaches offer a range of insights about the family. We can use all three to gain a deeper understanding of family life.

Functions of the Family: Structural-Functional Analysis

According to the structural-functional approach, the family performs many vital tasks. For this reason, the family is often called the backbone of society.

1. **Socialization.** The family is the first and most important setting for child rearing. Ideally, parents help children become well-integrated, contributing members of society. Of course, family socialization continues throughout the life cycle. Adults change within marriage, and as any parent knows, mothers and fathers learn as much from their children as their children learn from them.

2. **Regulation of sexual activity.** Every culture regulates sexual activity in the interest of maintaining kinship organization and property rights. The **incest taboo** is *a norm forbidding sexual relations or marriage between certain relatives.* Although the incest taboo exists in every society, exactly which relatives cannot marry varies from one culture to another. The matrilineal Navajo, for example, forbid marrying any relative of one's mother. Our bilateral society applies the incest taboo to both sides of the family but limits it to close relatives, including parents, grandparents, siblings, aunts, and uncles. But even brother-sister (but not parent-child) marriages existed among the ancient Egyptian, Incan, and Hawaiian nobility (Murdock, 1965, orig. 1949).

Reproduction between close relatives of any species can result in mental and physical damage to

The family is a basic building block of society because it performs important functions, such as conferring social position and regulating sexual activity. To most family members, however, the family (at least in ideal terms) is a "haven in a heartless world" in which individuals enjoy the feeling of belonging and find emotional support. Marc Chagall conveyed the promise of marriage in his painting *To My Wife.* Looking at the painting, how does the artist characterize marriage?

Marc Chagall (1887–1985), painting, *To My Wife,* 1933–44. Centre Georges Pompidou, Paris. The Bridgeman Art Library, London. © 2003 Artists Rights Society (ARS), New York/ADAGP, Paris.

FAMILIES

tip

Generally speaking, feminists have been critical
of traditional families because they support the
power of men over women. Liberal feminists typically argue for more egalitarian marriages; many
socialist and radical feminists argue for the abolition of the family.

offspring. Yet only human beings observe an incest taboo, a fact
suggesting that the key reason for controlling incest is social.
Why? First, the incest taboo limits sexual competition in families
by restricting sex to spouses. Second, because kinship defines
people's rights and obligations toward one another, reproduction among close relatives would hopelessly confuse kinship
ties and threaten social order. Third, forcing people to marry
outside their immediate families ties together the larger society.

3. **Social placement.** Families are not needed for people to
reproduce, but they do help maintain social organization. Parents pass on their own social identity—in terms of race, ethnicity, religion, and social class—to their children at birth.

4. **Material and emotional security.** Many people view the family as a "haven in a heartless world," offering physical protection, emotional support, and financial assistance. Perhaps this
is why people living in families tend to be happier, healthier,
and wealthier than people living alone (Goldstein & Kenney,
2001; U.S. Census Bureau, 2006).

▶**CRITICAL REVIEW** Structural-functional analysis explains why
society, at least as we know it, is built on families. But this
approach glosses over the diversity of U.S. family life and ignores
how other social institutions (such as government) could
meet some of the same human needs. Finally, structural-
functionalism overlooks negative aspects of family life, including
patriarchy and family violence.

✔ **YOUR LEARNING** Identify four important functions of the family for
society.

Inequality and the Family:
Social-Conflict and Feminist Analysis

Like the structural-functional approach, the social-conflict approach,
including feminist analysis, considers the family central to our way of
life. But rather than focusing on ways that kinship benefits society,
this approach points out how the family perpetuates social inequality.

1. **Property and inheritance.** Friedrich Engels (1902, orig. 1884)
traced the origin of the family to men's need (especially in the
upper classes) to identify heirs so that they could hand down
property to their sons. Families thus concentrate wealth and
reproduce the class structure in each new generation.

2. **Patriarchy.** Feminists link the family to patriarchy. To know
their heirs, men must control the sexuality of women. Families
therefore transform women into the sexual and economic

Women have long been taught to see marriage as the key to a happy life.
Social-conflict theory, however, points to the fact that marriage often means
a lifetime sentence of unpaid domestic labor. Susan Pyzow's painting *Bridal
Bouquet* makes the point.
© Susan Pyzow, *Bridal Bouquet*, watercolor on paper, 10 × 13.5 in. Studio SPM Inc.

property of men. A century ago in the United States, most
wives' earnings belonged to their husbands. Today, women still
bear most of the responsibility for child rearing and housework (Benokraitis & Feagin, 1995; Stapinski, 1998; England,
2001).

3. **Race and ethnicity.** Racial and ethnic categories persist over
generations because most people marry others like themselves.
Endogamous marriage supports racial and ethnic hierarchies.

▶**CRITICAL REVIEW** Social-conflict and feminist analysis shows
another side of family life: its role in social stratification. Engels criticized the family for its support of capitalism. But noncapitalist

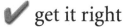
APPLYING THEORY

Family

	Structural-Functional Approach	Social-Conflict and Feminist Approaches	Symbolic-Interaction and Social-Exchange Approaches
What is the level of analysis?	Macro-level	Macro-level	Micro-level
What is the importance of family for society?	The family performs vital tasks, including socializing the young and providing emotional and financial support for members. The family helps regulate sexual activity.	The family perpetuates social inequality by handing down wealth from one generation to the next. The family supports patriarchy as well as racial and ethnic inequality.	The symbolic-interaction approach explains that the reality of family life is constructed by members in their interaction. The social-exchange approach shows that courtship typically brings together people who offer the same level of advantages.

societies also have families (and family problems). The family may be linked to social inequality, as Engels argued, but the family carries out societal functions not easily accomplished by other means.

 YOUR LEARNING Point to ways in which families support social inequality.

Constructing Family Life: Micro-Level Analysis

Both structural-functional and social-conflict analyses view the family as a structural system. By contrast, micro-level analysis explores how individuals shape and experience family life.

The Symbolic-Interaction Approach

Ideally, family living offers an opportunity for intimacy, a word with Latin roots meaning "sharing fear." As family members share many activities over time, they build emotional bonds. Of course, the fact that parents act as authority figures often limits their closeness with younger children. Only as children approach adulthood do kinship ties open up to include sharing confidences with greater intimacy (Macionis, 1978).

The Social-Exchange Approach

Social-exchange analysis, another micro-level approach, describes courtship and marriage as forms of negotiation (Blau, 1964). Dating allows each person to assess the advantages and disadvantages of a potential spouse. In essence, exchange analysts suggest, people "shop around" for partners to make the best "deal" they can.

In patriarchal societies, gender roles dictate the elements of exchange: Men bring wealth and power to the marriage marketplace, and women bring beauty. The importance of beauty explains women's traditional concern with their appearance. But as women have joined the labor force, they are less dependent on men to support them, and so the terms of exchange are converging for men and women.

 Thinking about the "marriage marketplace," why do you think women have traditionally been less willing than men to reveal their age?

▶ **CRITICAL REVIEW** Micro-level analysis balances structural-functional and social-conflict visions of the family as an institutional system. Both the interaction and exchange viewpoints focus on the individual experience of family life. However, micro-level

tip

This part of the chapter uses what sociologists call a "life course" approach—looking at the way people typically experience family life over time.

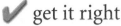

get it right

Although our society links marriage to romantic love, notice from the discussion below that love may not be a stable foundation for marriage.

analysis misses the bigger picture: Family life is similar for people in the same social and economic categories. The Applying Theory table summarizes what we can learn by applying each of the theoretical approaches to family life.

 YOUR LEARNING How does a micro-level approach to understanding family differ from a macro-level approach? State the main ideas of the symbolic-interaction approach and the social-exchange approach.

Stages of Family Life

The family is a dynamic institution, with marked changes across the life course. New families begin with courtship and evolve as the new partners settle into the realities of married life. Next, for most couples at least, come the years spent developing careers and raising children, leading to the later years of marriage after the children have left home to form families of their own. We will look briefly at each of these four stages.

Courtship

November 2, Kandy, Sri Lanka. Winding through the rain forest of this beautiful island, our van driver, Harry, recounts how he met his wife. Actually, he explains, it was more of an arrangement: The two families were both Buddhist and of the same caste. "We got along well, right from the start," recalls Harry. "We had the same background. I suppose she or I could have said no. But love marriages happen in the city, not in the village where I grew up."

In rural Sri Lanka, as in rural areas of low- and middle-income countries throughout the world, most people consider courtship too important to be left to the young (L. Stone, 1977). *Arranged marriages* are alliances between extended families of similar social standing and usually involve an exchange not just of children but also of wealth and favors. Romantic love has little to do with marriage, and parents may make such arrangements when their children are very young. A century ago in Sri Lanka and India, for example, half of all girls married before reaching age fifteen (Mayo, 1927; Mace & Mace, 1960). As the Thinking Globally box on page 472 explains, child marriage is still found in some parts of the world today.

Because traditional societies are more culturally homogeneous, almost all young men and women have been well socialized to be good spouses. Therefore, parents can arrange marriages with little thought about whether or not the two individuals involved are

Actor Michael Douglas married Catherine Zeta-Jones, a woman twenty-five years younger than he is. Guided by social-exchange analysis, what do you think each of these individuals offers to the other?

Paul Skipper

personally compatible because they know that the partners will be *culturally* compatible.

Industrialization both erodes the importance of extended families and weakens tradition. As young people begin the process of choosing their own mate, dating sharpens courtship skills and allows sexual experimentation. Marriage is delayed until young people complete their schooling, build the financial security needed to live apart from their parents, and gain the experience needed to select a suitable partner.

Romantic Love

Our culture celebrates *romantic love*—affection and sexual passion for another person—as the basis for marriage. We find it hard to imagine marriage without love, and popular culture—from fairy tales like "Cinderella" to today's television sitcoms and dramas—portrays love as the key to a successful marriage.

Our society's emphasis on romance motivates young people to "leave the nest" to form new families of their own, and physical passion can help a new couple through the difficult adjustments of living together (W. J. Goode, 1959). On the other hand, because feelings change over time, romantic love is a less stable foundation for marriage than social and economic considerations, which is one reason

tip

Arranged marriage is a pattern associated with caste systems. A greater emphasis on love and personal choice in mate selection arises in class systems.

tip

The odds of someone marrying a person of a different age, class position, race, and ethnicity are much higher than they used to be. Our society is becoming more tolerant of "mixed" marriages; in addition, first marriages now occur at a later age, when parents have less influence over their children's choice of partner.

Thinking Globally
Early to Wed: A Report from Rural India

Sumitra Jogi cries as her wedding is about to begin. Are they tears of joy? Not exactly. This "bride" is an eighteen-month-old squirming in the arms of her mother. The groom? A boy of seven.

In a remote, rural village in India's western state of Rajasthan, two families gather at midnight to celebrate a traditional wedding ritual. It is May 2, in Hindu tradition an especially good day to marry. Sumitra's father smiles as the ceremony begins; her mother cradles the infant, who has fallen asleep. The groom, dressed in a special costume with a red and gold turban on his head, gently reaches up and grasps the baby's hand. Then, as the ceremony reaches its conclusion, the young boy leads the child and mother around the wedding fire three-and-one-half times as the audience beams at the couple's first steps together as husband and wife.

Child weddings are illegal in India, but in the rural regions, traditions are strong and marriage laws are hard to enforce. As a result, thousands of children marry each year. "In rural Rajasthan," explains one social welfare worker, "all the girls are married by age fourteen. These are poor, illiterate families, and they don't want to keep girls past their first menstrual cycle."

For the immediate future, Sumitra Jogi will remain with her parents. But in eight or ten years, a second ceremony will send her to

The eighteen-month-old girl on the left is breastfeeding during her wedding ceremony in a small village in the state of Rajasthan, India; her new husband is seven years old. Although outlawed, such arranged marriages involving children are still known to take place in traditional, remote areas of India.

AP Wide World Photos

live with her husband's family, and her married life will begin.

If the responsibilities of marriage lie years in the future, why do families push their children to marry at such an early age? Parents of girls know that the younger the bride, the smaller the dowry offered to the groom's family. Then, too, when girls marry this young, there is no question about their virginity, which raises their value on the marriage market. Arranged marriages are an alliance between families. No one thinks about love or the fact that the children are too young to understand what is taking place (J. W. Anderson, 1995).

WHAT DO YOU THINK?

1. Why are arranged marriages common in very traditional regions?

2. List several advantages and disadvantages of arranged marriages from the point of view of the families involved.

3. Can you point to ways in which mate selection in the United States is "arranged" by society?

---

that the divorce rate is much higher in the United States than in nations in which culture is a stronger guide in the choice of a partner.

But even in our country, sociologists point out, society aims Cupid's arrow more than we like to think. Most people fall in love with others of the same race, of comparable age, and of similar social class. Our society "arranges" marriages by encouraging **homogamy** (literally, "like marrying like"), *marriage between people with the same social characteristics.*

How similar are your parents (or you and your spouse) in terms of age, social class, race, ethnicity, and education?

Settling In: Ideal and Real Marriage

Our culture gives the young an idealized, "happily ever after" picture of marriage. Such optimism can lead to disappointment, especially for women, who are taught to view marriage as the key to personal happiness. Also, romantic love involves a good deal of fantasy: We fall in love with others not always as they are but as we want them to be.

Sexuality, too, can be a source of disappointment. In the romantic haze of falling in love, people may see marriage as an endless sexual honeymoon, only to face the sobering realization that sex becomes a less-than-all-consuming passion. Although the frequency of marital sex does decline over time, about two in three married people report that they are satisfied with the sexual dimension of their relationship. In general, couples with the best sexual relationships experience the

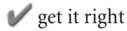
most satisfaction in their marriages. Sex may not be the key to marital bliss, but more often than not, good sex and good relationships usually go together (Blumstein & Schwartz, 1983; Laumann et al., 1994).

Infidelity—*sexual activity outside one's marriage*—is another area where the reality of marriage does not match our cultural ideal. In a recent survey, 92 percent of U.S. adults said sex outside of marriage is "always wrong" or "almost always wrong." Even so, 21 percent of men and 13 percent of women indicated on a private, written questionnaire that they had been sexually unfaithful to their partners at least once (NORC, 2005:291, 1702).

Child Rearing

Despite the demands children make on us, adults in this country overwhelmingly identify raising children as one of life's greatest joys. Today, about half of U.S. adults say that two children is the ideal number, and few people want more than three (NORC, 2005:1478-79, 287). This is a change from two centuries ago, when *eight* children was the U.S. average.

Big families pay off in preindustrial societies because children supply needed labor. People therefore regard having children as a wife's duty, and without effective birth control, childbearing is a regular event. Of course, a high death rate in preindustrial societies prevents many children from reaching adulthood; as late as 1900, one-third of children born in the United States died by age ten.

Economically speaking, industrialization transforms children from an asset to a liability. It now costs more than $200,000 to raise one child, including college tuition (Lino, 2007). No wonder the average size of the U.S. family dropped steadily during the twentieth century to one child per family![2]

The trend toward smaller families is most pronounced in high-income nations. The picture differs in low-income countries in Latin America, Asia, and especially Africa, where many women have few alternatives to bearing children. In such societies, between four and six children is still the norm.

Parenting is a very expensive, lifelong commitment. As our society has given people greater choices about family life, more U.S. adults have decided to delay childbirth or to remain childless. In 1960, almost 90 percent of women between twenty-five and twenty-nine who had ever married had at least one child; today, this proportion is just 70 percent (U.S. Census Bureau, 2005).

Although the trend is toward less and less homogamy, it is still true that people who get married are likely to have many factors in common, including age, class, race and ethnicity, and level of education.

LWA-Dann Tardif/Corbis/Bettmann

No one doubts that almost all parents care deeply about their children, but about two-thirds of parents in the United States say they don't have enough time to spend with their kids (Snell, 1990; K. Clark 2002). But unless we accept a lower standard of living, economic realities demand that most parents pursue careers outside the home, even if that means devoting less time to their children. For many families, including the Yniguez family described in the opening to this chapter, having fewer children is an important step toward resolving the tension between work and parenting (Gilbert, 2005).

Children of working parents spend most of the day at school. But after school, some 3.3 million children (15 percent of six- to twelve-year-olds) are *latchkey kids* who are left to fend for themselves (Vandivere et al., 2003). Traditionalists in the "family values" debate charge that many mothers work at the expense of their children, who receive less parenting. Progressives counter that such criticism targets women for wanting the same opportunities men have long enjoyed.

Congress took a step toward easing the conflict between family and job responsibilities by passing the Family and Medical Leave Act in 1993. This law allows up to ninety days of unpaid leave from work to care for a new child or to deal with a serious family emergency. Still,

---

[2]According to the U.S. Census Bureau, the median number of children per family was 0.86 in 2005. Among all families, the medians were 0.83 for whites, 1.04 for African Americans, and 1.21 for Hispanics.

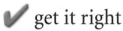 get it right

Based on the discussion on the previous page,
what can you say about the social class position
of the people in the cartoon below?

*"Son, you're all grown up now. You owe me two
hundred and fourteen thousand dollars."*

most adults in this country have to juggle parental and job responsibilities. When parents work, who cares for the kids? The Seeing Sociology in Everyday Life box provides the answer.

The Family in Later Life

Increasing life expectancy in the United States means that couples who remain married will stay together for a long time. By about age sixty, most have finished the task of raising children. At this point, marriage brings a return to living with only a spouse.

Like the birth of children, their departure—creating the "empty nest"—requires adjustments, although a marriage often becomes closer and more satisfying. Years of living together may have lessened a couple's sexual passion, but understanding and commitment often increase.

Personal contact with children usually continues because most older adults live a short distance from at least one of their children. One-third of all U.S. adults (56 million) are grandparents. Most grandparents help with child care and other responsibilities. Among African Americans, who have a high rate of single parenting, grandmothers have an especially important position in family life (Clemetson, 2000; U.S. Census Bureau, 2006).

The other side of the coin is that more adults in midlife now care for aging parents. The "empty nest" may not be filled by a parent coming to live in the home, but many adults find that caring for parents, who now live to eighty, ninety, and beyond, can be as taxing as raising young children. The oldest of the "baby boomers"—now passing sixty—are called the "sandwich generation" because many (especially women) will spend as many years caring for their aging parents as they did caring for their children (Lund, 1993).

The final and surely the most difficult transition in married life comes with the death of a spouse. Wives typically outlive their husbands because of their greater life expectancy and the fact that women usually marry men several years older than themselves. Wives can thus expect to spend some years as widows. The challenge of living alone following the death of a spouse is especially great for men, who usually have fewer friends than widows and may lack housekeeping skills.

U.S. Families: Class, Race, and Gender

Dimensions of inequality—social class, ethnicity and race, and gender—are powerful forces that shape marriage and family life. This discussion addresses each factor in turn, but bear in mind that they overlap in our lives.

Social Class

Social class determines both a family's financial security and its range of opportunities. Interviewing working-class women, Lillian Rubin (1976) found that wives thought a good husband was one who held a steady job, did not drink too much, and was not violent. Rubin's middle-class respondents, by contrast, never mentioned such things; these women simply *assumed* that a husband would provide a safe and secure home. Their ideal husband was someone they could talk to easily, sharing feelings and experiences.

Clearly, what women (and men) think they can hope for in marriage—and what they end up with—is linked to their social class. Much the same holds for children; boys and girls lucky enough to be born into more affluent families enjoy better mental and physical

Seeing Sociology in Everyday Life
Who's Minding the Kids?

Traditionally, the task of providing daily care for young children fell to stay-at-home mothers. But with a majority of mothers and fathers now in the labor force, finding quality, affordable child care is a high priority for parents.

The figure shows the various arrangements reported by working mothers to care for children under the age of five. The majority of these children, 53 percent, receive care at home from a parent (27 percent) or a relative (26 percent). The remaining 47 percent are cared for by a nonrelative: 29 percent attend preschool or a day care program, 13 percent go to the home of a nonrelative, and only 5 percent of children are cared for in their own home by a nanny or babysitter (Urban Institute, 2004).

The use of day care programs has doubled over the past decade because many parents cannot find affordable in-home care for their children. Some day

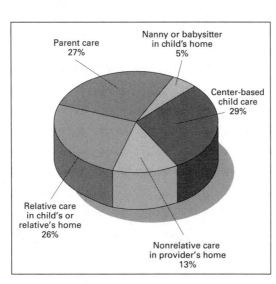

Working mothers report that a majority of their young children receive care in the home.

care centers are so big that they amount to "tot lots" where parents "park" their children for the day. The impersonality of such settings and the rapid turnover in staff prevent the warm and consistent nurturing that young children need to develop a sense of trust. But other child care centers offer a secure and healthful environment. Research suggests that *good* care centers are good for children; *bad* facilities are not.

WHAT DO YOU THINK?

1. Why do so many parents have trouble finding affordable child care? Should employers do more?

2. As parents, would you and your partner be willing to limit your working hours to allow child care at home? Why or why not?

3. How can parents assess the quality of a child care center? What should they look for?

---

health, develop more self-confidence, and go on to greater achievement than children born to poor parents (McLeod & Shanahan, 1993; Duncan et al., 1998).

Ethnicity and Race

Ethnicity and race are powerful social forces that can affect family life. Keep in mind, however, that American Indian, Latino, and African American families (like all families) do not fit any single generalization or stereotype (Allen, 1995).

American Indian Families

American Indians display a wide variety of family types. Some patterns emerge, however, among people who migrate from tribal reservations to cities. Women and men who arrive in cities often seek out others—especially kin and members of the same tribe—for help getting settled. One study, for example, tells the story of two women migrants to the San Francisco area who met at a meeting of an Indian organization and realized that they were of the same tribe. The women and their children decided to share an apartment, and soon after, the children began to refer to one another as brothers, sisters, and cousins. As the months passed, the two mothers came to think of themselves as sisters (Lobo, 2002).

Migration also creates many "fluid households" with changing membership. In another case from the same research, a large apartment in San Francisco was rented by a woman, her aunt, and their children. Over the course of the next month, however, they welcomed into their home more than thirty other urban migrants, who stayed for a short time until they found housing of their own. Such patterns of mutual assistance, often involving real and fictional kinship, are common among all low-income people.

American Indians who leave tribal reservations for the cities are typically better off than those who stay behind. Because people on

tip

Remember that family patterns for American Indians, Latinos, or any other racial or ethnic category vary by social class, and the experiences of family life may also differ for women and men.

student 2 student

"After reading about how family is different for each sex, for each social class, and for various racial and ethnic populations, you can understand why this chapter is titled 'Families' rather than 'The Family.'"

DIVERSITY SNAPSHOT

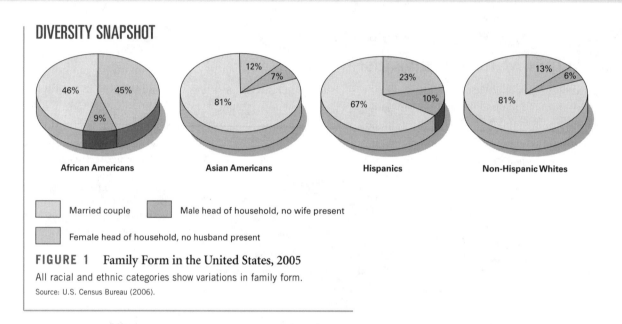

African Americans — 46%, 45%, 9%

Asian Americans — 81%, 12%, 7%

Hispanics — 67%, 23%, 10%

Non-Hispanic Whites — 81%, 13%, 6%

☐ Married couple   ☐ Male head of household, no wife present

☐ Female head of household, no husband present

FIGURE 1   Family Form in the United States, 2005

All racial and ethnic categories show variations in family form.

Source: U.S. Census Bureau (2006).

reservations have a hard time finding work, they cannot easily form stable marriages, and problems such as alcoholism and drug abuse can shatter the ties between parent and child.

Latino Families

Many Latinos enjoy the loyalty and support of extended families. Traditionally, too, Latino parents exercise considerable control over children's courtship, considering marriage an alliance of families, not just a union based on romantic love. Some Latino families also follow conventional gender roles, encouraging *machismo*—strength, daring, and sexual conquest—among men and treating women with respect but also close supervision.

However, assimilation into the larger society is changing these traditional patterns. As the story opening this chapter explained, many women who come to California from Mexico favor smaller families. Similarly, many Puerto Ricans who migrate to New York do not maintain the strong extended family ties they knew in Puerto Rico. Traditional male authority over women has also lessened, especially among affluent Latino families, whose number has tripled in the past twenty years (Lach, 1999; Navarro, 2004; Raley et al., 2004).

Overall, however, the typical Hispanic family had an income of $37,867 in 2005, or 67 percent of the national average (U.S. Census Bureau, 2006). Many Hispanic families suffer the stress of unemployment and other poverty-related problems.

African American Families

African American families face economic disadvantages: The typical African American family earned $35,464 in 2005, which was 63 percent of the national average. People of African ancestry are three times as likely as non-Hispanic whites to be poor, and poverty means that both parents and children are likely to experience unemployment, substandard housing, and poor health.

Under these circumstances, maintaining a stable marriage is difficult. Consider that 28 percent of African American women in their forties have never married, compared to about 10 percent of white women of the same age. This means that African American women—often with children—are more likely to be single heads of households. Figure 1 shows that women headed 45 percent of all African American families in 2005, compared to 23 percent of Hispanic families, 13 percent of non-Hispanic white families, and 12 percent of Asian or Pacific Islander families (U.S. Census Bureau, 2006).

Regardless of race, single-mother families are always at high risk of poverty. Twenty-two percent of single families headed by non-Hispanic white women are poor. Higher yet, the poverty rate among families headed by African American women (36 percent) and Hispanic women (39 percent) is strong evidence of how the intersection of class, race, and gender can put women at a disadvantage. African American families with both wife and husband in the home, which represent 46 percent of the total, are much stronger economically, earning 80 percent as much as comparable non-Hispanic white families. But 68 percent of African American children are born to single women, and 35 percent of African American boys and girls are growing up poor today, meaning that these families carry much of the burden of child poverty in the United States (Martin et al., 2005; U.S. Census Bureau, 2006).

Ethnically and Racially Mixed Marriages

Most spouses have similar social backgrounds with regard to class and race. But over the course of the twentieth century, ethnicity came to matter less and less. In recent decades, for example, a woman of German and French ancestry might readily marry a man of Irish and English background without inviting disapproval from their families or from society in general. As the age of first marriage has gone up (to an average of 27.5 for men and 25.5 for women), young people are more likely to make choices about whom to marry without much input from parents. One consequence of this increasing freedom of choice is more ethnically and racially mixed marriages (Rosenfeld & Kim, 2005).

Even so, race remains a powerful barrier in mate selection. Before a 1967 Supreme Court decision (*Loving* v. *Virginia*), interracial marriage was actually illegal in sixteen states. Today, African, Asian, and Native Americans represent 17 percent of the U.S. population; if people ignored race in choosing spouses, we would expect about the same share of marriages to be mixed. The actual proportion of mixed marriages is 4 percent, showing that race still matters in social relations. But the number of racially mixed marriages is rising steadily.

The most common type of interracial married couple is a white husband and an Asian wife, which accounts for about 14 percent of all interracial married couples. About one-fourth of all interracial married couples contain at least one partner who claimed a multiple-race identity in the 2000 census. Interracial married couples are likely to live in the West; in five states—Hawaii, Alaska, California, Nevada, and Oklahoma—more than 10 percent of all married couples are interracial (Lee & Edmonston, 2005).

 Surveys report that most U.S. teens now claim they have dated someone of another race. Do you think the proportion of mixed-race marriages will rise in the next twenty years? Why or why not?

Gender

The sociologist Jessie Bernard (1982) claimed that every marriage is actually two different relationships: the woman's marriage and the man's marriage. The reason is that few marriages have two equal part-

ners. Although patriarchy has weakened, most people still expect husbands to be older and taller than their wives and to have more important, better-paid jobs.

Why, then, do many people think that marriage benefits women more than men? The positive stereotype of the carefree bachelor contrasts sharply with the negative image of the lonely spinster, suggesting that women are fulfilled only through being wives and mothers.

However, Bernard continued, married women actually have poorer mental health, less happiness, and more passive attitudes toward life than single women. Married men, on the other hand, generally live longer, are mentally better off, and report being happier overall than single men. These differences suggest why, after divorce, men are more eager than women to find a new partner.

Bernard concluded that there is no better assurance of long life, health, and happiness for a man than a woman well socialized to devote her life to taking care of him and providing the security of a well-ordered home. She is quick to add that marriage *could* be healthful for women if husbands did not dominate wives and expect them to do almost all the housework.

For most of our nation's history, interracial marriage was illegal. Although the last of these laws was struck down forty years ago, race and ethnicity continue to guide the process of courtship and marriage. Even so, interracial relationships are becoming more and more common.

Getty Images—Stockbyte

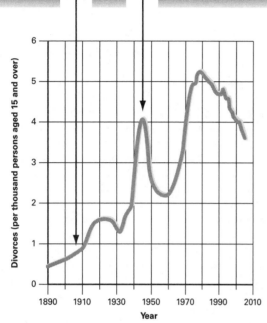

A century ago, many people looked upon divorce as a mark of personal failure.

The divorce rate rose during World War II, when many couples were separated for long periods of time.

FIGURE 2 Divorce Rate for the United States, 1890–2005

Over the long term, the U.S. divorce rate has gone up. Since about 1980, however, the trend has been downward.

Source: Munson & Sutton (2006).

Transitions and Problems in Family Life

The newspaper columnist Ann Landers once remarked that one marriage in twenty is wonderful, five in twenty are good, ten in twenty are tolerable, and the remaining four are "pure hell." Families can be a source of joy, but for some, the reality falls far short of the ideal.

Divorce

U.S. society strongly supports marriage, and about nine out of ten people at some point "tie the knot." But many of today's marriages unravel. Figure 2 shows the tenfold increase in the U.S. divorce rate over the past century. In 2005, almost four in ten marriages were ending in divorce (for African Americans, the rate was about six in ten). Ours is the highest divorce rate in the world, about half again as high as in Canada and Japan and five times higher than in Italy (U.S. Census Bureau, 2006).

The high U.S. divorce rate has many causes (Furstenberg & Cherlin, 1991; Etzioni, 1993; Popenoe, 1999; Greenspan, 2001):

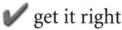 **get it right**

As the discussion below makes clear, our society's divorce rate has no single cause.

1. **Individualism is on the rise.** Today's family members spend less time together. We have become more individualistic and more concerned about personal happiness and earning income than about the well-being of our partners and children.

2. **Romantic love fades.** Because our culture bases marriage on romantic love, relationships may fail as sexual passion fades. Many people end a marriage in favor of a new relationship that promises renewed excitement and romance.

3. **Women are less dependent on men.** Women's increasing participation in the labor force has reduced wives' financial dependence on husbands. Therefore, women find it easier to leave unhappy marriages.

4. **Many of today's marriages are stressful.** With both partners working outside the home in most cases, jobs leave less time and energy for family life. This makes raising children harder than ever. Children do stabilize some marriages, but divorce is most common during the early years of marriage, when many couples have young children.

5. **Divorce is socially acceptable.** Divorce no longer carries the powerful stigma it did several generations ago. Family and friends are now less likely to discourage couples in conflict from divorcing.

6. **Legally, a divorce is easier to get.** In the past, courts required divorcing couples to show that one or both were guilty of behavior such as adultery or physical abuse. Today, all states allow divorce if a couple simply declares that the marriage has failed. Concern about easy divorces, shared by more than half of U.S. adults, has led some states to consider rewriting their marriage laws (Phillips, 2001; NORC, 2005).

Who Divorces?

At greatest risk of divorce are young spouses—especially those who marry after a brief courtship—who lack money and emotional maturity. The chance of divorce also rises if the couple marries after an unexpected pregnancy or if one or both partners have substance abuse problems. People whose parents divorced also have a higher divorce rate themselves. Researchers suggest that a role-modeling effect is at work: Children who see parents go through divorce are more likely to consider divorce themselves (Amato, 2001). Finally, people who are not religious are more likely to divorce than those who have strong religious beliefs.

Divorce is also more common when both partners have successful careers, perhaps because of the strains of a two-career marriage but also because financially secure people do not feel that they have to remain

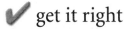 **get it right**

We tend to think of divorce as something involving spouses. As this discussion shows, however, the most lasting effects of divorce may be experienced by children.

 tip

Any society that has a high rate of divorce is likely to have a high rate of remarriage. Half of all marriages in the United States are now remarriages for at least one partner.

in an unhappy home. Finally, men and women who divorce once are more likely to divorce again, probably because high-risk factors follow them from one marriage to another (Glenn & Shelton, 1985).

Divorce and Children

Because mothers usually gain custody of children but fathers typically earn more income, the well-being of children often depends on fathers' making court-ordered child support payments. As Figure 3 indicates, courts award child support in 60 percent of all divorces involving children. Yet in any given year, almost half the children legally entitled to support receive only partial payments (which can be as little as $1) or no payments at all. Some 3.5 million "deadbeat dads" fail to support their youngsters. In response, federal legislation now mandates that employers withhold money from the earnings of fathers or mothers who fail to pay up; it is a serious crime to refuse to make child support payments or to move to another state to avoid making them (U.S. Census Bureau, 2006).

The effects of divorce on children go beyond financial support. Divorce can tear young people from familiar surroundings, entangle them in bitter feuding, and distance them from a parent they love. Most serious of all, many children blame themselves for their parents' breakup. Divorce changes the course of many children's lives, causing emotional and behavioral problems and raising the risk of dropping out of school and getting into trouble with the law. Many experts counter that divorce is better for children than their staying in a family torn by tension and violence. In any case, parents should remember that if they consider divorce, more than their own well-being is at stake (Wallerstein & Blakeslee, 1989; Amato & Sobolewski, 2001).

Divorce may be a solution for a couple in an unhappy marriage, but it can be a problem for children who experience the withdrawal of a parent from their social world. In what ways can divorce be harmful to children? Is there a positive side to divorce? How might separating parents better prepare their children for the transition of parental divorce?

Mark J. Barrett/Creative Eye/MIRA.com

Remarriage

Four out of five people who divorce remarry, most within five years. Nationwide, almost half of all marriages are now remarriages for at least one partner. Men, who benefit more from wedlock, are more likely than women to remarry.

Remarriage often creates *blended families,* composed of children and some combination of biological parents and stepparents. With brothers, sisters, half siblings, a stepparent—not to mention a biological parent who might live elsewhere and be married to someone else with other children—young people in blended families face the challenge of defining many new relationships and deciding just who is part of the nuclear family. Parents often have trouble defining responsibility for household work among people unsure of their relationships to each other. When the custody of children is an issue, ex-spouses can be an unwelcome presence for people in a new marriage. Although blended families require that members adjust to their new

circumstances, they offer both young and old the chance to relax rigid family roles (Furstenberg & Cherlin, 2001; McLanahan, 2002).

 A girl who has been an only child becomes part of a "blended family" and suddenly has two older brothers. What adjustments might she have to make?

Family Violence

The ideal family is a source of pleasure and support. However, the disturbing reality of many homes is **family violence,** *emotional, physical, or sexual abuse of one family member by another.* With the exception of the police and the military, says the sociologist Richard J. Gelles, the family is "the most violent group in society" (quoted in Roesch, 1984:75).

tip

All the alternative family forms discussed on the
following pages are increasing in popularity. In
general, conservatives see these trends as
harmful to society and liberals see them as
good for society.

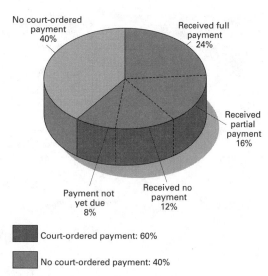

Court-ordered payment: 60%

No court-ordered payment: 40%

FIGURE 3 Payment of Child Support after Divorce

In almost half of all cases of court-ordered child support, the full payment
is never received.

Source: U.S. Census Bureau (2006).

Violence against Women

Family brutality often goes unreported to police. Even so, the U.S.
Bureau of Justice Statistics (2006) estimates that about 700,000 people are victims of domestic violence each year. Of this total, 73 percent
of cases involve violence against women, and the remaining 27 percent
involve violence against men. Fully 33 percent of women who are victims of homicide (but just 3 percent of men) are killed by spouses or,
more often, ex-spouses. Nationwide, the death toll from family violence is about 1,250 women each year. Overall, women are more likely
to be injured by a family member than to be mugged or raped by a
stranger or hurt in an automobile accident (Shupe, Stacey, & Hazlewood, 1987; Blankenhorn, 1995; Federal Bureau of Investigation,
2006).

Historically, the law defined wives as the property of their husbands, so no man could be charged with raping his wife. Today,
however, all states have enacted *marital rape laws.* The law no longer
regards domestic violence as a private family matter; it gives victims
more options. Now, even without a formal separation or divorce, a
woman can obtain court protection from an abusive spouse, and all
states have "stalking laws" that forbid one ex-partner from following

or otherwise threatening the other. Communities across the United
States have established shelters to provide counseling and temporary
housing for women and children driven from their homes by domestic violence.

Finally, the harm caused by domestic violence goes beyond the
physical injuries. Victims often lose their ability to trust others. One
study found that women who had been physically or sexually abused
were much less likely than nonvictims to form stable relationships
later on (Cherlin et al., 2004).

Violence against Children

Family violence also victimizes children. Each year, there are more
than 3 million reports of alleged child abuse or neglect, about 1,500
of them involving a child's death. Child abuse entails more than physical injury; abusive adults misuse power and trust to damage a child's
emotional well-being. Child abuse and neglect are most common
among the youngest and most vulnerable children (Besharov & Laumann, 1996).

Although child abusers conform to no simple stereotype, they
are more likely to be women (58 percent) than men (42 percent). But
almost all abusers share one trait—having been abused themselves
as children. Research shows that violent behavior in close relationships is learned; in families, violence begets violence (S. Levine, 2001;
U.S. Department of Health and Human Services, 2007).

Alternative Family Forms

Most families in the United States are composed of a married couple
who raise children. But in recent decades, our society has displayed
increasing diversity in family life.

One-Parent Families

Thirty-one percent of U.S. families with children under eighteen have
only one parent in the household, a proportion that more than doubled during the last generation. Put another way, more than one-
fourth of U.S. children now live with only one parent, and about half
will do so before reaching eighteen. One-parent families, 73 percent
of which are headed by a single mother, result from divorce, death, or
an unmarried woman's decision to have a child.

Single parenthood increases a woman's risk of poverty because
it limits her ability to work and to further her education. The opposite is also true: Poverty raises the odds that a young woman will
become a single mother. But single parenthood goes well beyond the

✦ tip

As shown in Figure 4, marriage affects children's lives as much as their parents'.

poor: One-third of women in the United States become pregnant as teenagers, and many decide to raise their children whether they marry or not. Looking back at Figure 1, note that 54 percent of African American families are headed by a single parent. Single parenting is less common among Hispanics (33 percent), Asian Americans (19 percent), and non-Hispanic whites (19 percent). In many single-parent families, mothers turn to their own mothers for support. In the United States, then, the rise in single parenting is tied to a declining role for fathers and the growing importance of grandparenting.

Research shows that growing up in a one-parent family usually puts children at a disadvantage. Some studies claim that because a father and a mother each make distinctive contributions to a child's social development, one parent has a hard time doing as good a job alone. But the most serious problem for one-parent families, especially if that parent is a woman, is poverty. On average, children growing up in a single-parent family start out poorer, get less schooling, and end up with lower incomes as adults. Such children are also more likely to be single parents themselves (Popenoe, 1993a; Blankenhorn, 1995; Wu, 1996; Duncan et al., 1998; Kantrowitz & Wingert, 2001; McLanahan, 2002).

Cohabitation

Cohabitation is *the sharing of a household by an unmarried couple.* In global perspective, cohabitation as a long-term form of family life, with or without children, is especially common in Sweden and other Scandinavian countries and gaining popularity in other European nations. In the United States, the number of cohabiting couples increased from about 500,000 in 1970 to about 5.6 million today (4.9 million heterosexual couples and 700,000 homosexual couples), or about 9 percent of all couples. Almost half of all people between twenty-five and forty-four years of age have cohabited at some point (U.S. Census Bureau, 2006).

Cohabiting tends to appeal to more independent-minded individuals as well as those who favor gender equality (Brines & Joyner, 1999). Most couples cohabit for no more than a few years; at that point, about half decide to marry and half split up. Mounting evidence suggests that living together may actually discourage marriage because partners (especially men) become used to low-commitment relationships. For this reason, cohabiting couples who have children—currently representing about one in eight births in the United States—may not always be long-term parents. Figure 4 shows that just 5 percent of children born to cohabiting couples will live until age eighteen with both biological parents if the parents remain unmarried.

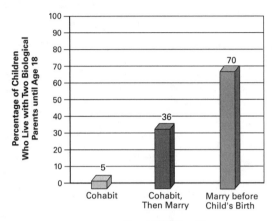

FIGURE 4   Parental Involvement in Children's Lives: Cohabiting and Married Parents

Marriage increases the odds that parents will share the same household with their child.

Source: Phillips (2001).

The share rises to 36 percent among children whose parents marry at some point, but even this is half of the 70 percent figure among children whose parents married before they were born. When cohabiting couples with children separate, the involvement of both parents, including financial support, is highly uncertain (Popenoe & Whitehead, 1999; Booth & Crouter, 2002; Scommegna, 2002).

Gay and Lesbian Couples

In 1989, Denmark became the first country to permit registered partnerships with the benefits of marriage for same-sex couples. This change extended social legitimacy to gay and lesbian couples and equalized advantages in inheritance, taxation, and joint property ownership. Since then, Norway (1993), Sweden (1994), Iceland (1996), Finland (2001), and the United Kingdom (2004) have followed suit. However, only five countries have extended marriage—in name as well as practice—to same-sex couples: the Netherlands (2001), Belgium (2003), Canada (2005), Spain (2005), and South Africa (2006).

In the United States, Vermont, Connecticut, New Jersey, and California have enacted laws recognizing same-sex civil unions, and a number of major cities, including San Francisco and New York, have passed laws giving limited marital benefits to gay and lesbian

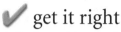 get it right

As the box explains, people may see "traditional families" as good or bad; in any case, such families are becoming less common.

 Controversy & Debate

Should We Save the Traditional Family?

Aaron: My parents were really goin' at each other last night. Man, I don't know whether they are going to stay together.

Abdul: I hope they do, my friend. Families are what ties society together.

Tawneesha: Listen to you guys! The important thing is for each person to be happy. If being married does it for you, great. But there's lots of different ways for people to find happiness.

What are "traditional families"? Are they vital to our way of life or a barrier to progress? People use the term *traditional family* to mean a married couple who at some point in their lives raise children. Statistically speaking, traditional families are less common than they used to be. In 1950, as the figure shows, 90 percent of U.S. households were families—using the Census Bureau's definition of two or more persons related by blood, marriage, or adoption. By 2005, just 68 percent of households were families, due to rising levels of divorce, cohabitation, and singlehood.

"Traditional family" is more than just a handy expression; it is also a moral statement. Belief in the traditional family implies giving high value to becoming and staying married, putting children ahead of careers, and favoring two-parent families over various alternatives.

On one side of the debate, David Popenoe (1993a) warns that there has been a serious erosion of the traditional family since 1960. At that time, married couples with young children accounted for almost half of all households; today, the figure is 24 percent. Singlehood is up, from 10 percent of households in 1960 to 26 percent today. And the divorce rate has risen by 60 percent since 1960, so that nearly four in ten of today's marriages end in permanent separation. Because of both divorce and the

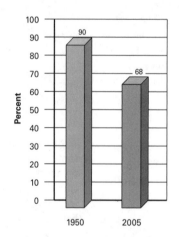

Share of U.S. Households That the Census Bureau Classifies as Families, 1950 and 2005

Families were a smaller share of all U.S. households in 2005 compared to 1950.

increasing number of children born to single women, the share of youngsters who will live with just one parent before age eighteen has quadrupled since 1960 to 50 percent. In other words, just one in four of today's children will grow up with two parents and go on to maintain a stable marriage as an adult.

In light of such data, Popenoe concludes, it may not be an exaggeration to say that the family is falling apart. He sees a fundamental shift from a "culture of marriage" to a "culture of divorce," where traditional vows of marital commitment—"till death do us part"—now amount to little more than "as long as I am happy." Daniel Yankelovich (1994:20) summed it up this way:

> The quest for greater individual choice clashed directly with the obligations and social norms that held families and communities together in earlier years. People came to feel that questions of how to live and with whom to live were a matter of individual choice not to be governed by restrictive norms. As a nation, we came to experience the bonds of marriage, family, children, job, community, and country as constraints that were no longer necessary. Commitments have loosened.

The negative consequences of the cultural trend toward weaker families, Popenoe continues, are obvious and can be found every-

couples. Although the U.S. Congress passed a law in 1996 defining marriage as joining one man and one woman, in 2004, Massachusetts became the first state to provide for lawful same-sex marriage. The Massachusetts court decision prompted officials in San Francisco and a number of other U.S. cities to perform thousands of marriages for gay and lesbian couples, despite state laws banning such unions. Courts later declared those marriages to be illegal. By the beginning of 2007, nineteen states had amended their state constitutions to permit marriage only between one man and one woman.

The trend in public opinion is toward greater support for committed homosexual relationships. Currently, about one-third of U.S. adults support gay marriage, and half support civil unions providing the rights enjoyed by married couples (Gallup, 2002; NORC, 2005:1477).

Most gay couples with children in the United States are raising the offspring of previous heterosexual unions; others have adopted

FAMILIES

tip

One cause of the rising number of single people in the United States is the later age of first marriage for both women and men.

tip

Raise the questions at the end of the box in class to see what other students think.

where: As we pay less and less attention to children, the crime rate among young people goes up, along with a host of other problem behaviors including underage smoking and drinking, premarital sex, and teen suicide.

As Popenoe sees it, we must work hard and act quickly to reverse current trends. Government cannot be the solution and may even be part of the problem: Since 1960, as families have weakened, government spending on social programs has soared fivefold. To save the traditional family, says Popenoe, we need a cultural turnaround similar to what happened with regard to cigarette smoking. In this case, we must replace our "me first" attitudes with commitment to our spouse and children and publicly endorse the two-parent family as best for the well-being of children.

Judith Stacey (1993) provides a feminist viewpoint, saying "good riddance" to the traditional family. In her view, the traditional family is more problem than solution: "The family is not here to stay. Nor should we wish it were. On the contrary, I believe that all democratic people, whatever their kinship preferences, should work to hasten its demise" (Stacey, 1990:269).

The main reason for rejecting the traditional family, Stacey explains, is that it perpetuates social inequality. Families play a key role in maintaining the class hierarchy by transferring wealth as well as "cultural capital" from one generation to another. Feminists criticize the traditional family's patriarchal form, which subjects women to their husbands' authority and gives them most of the responsibility for housework and child care. From a gay rights perspective, she adds, a society that values traditional families also denies homosexual men and women equal participation in social life.

Stacey thus applauds the breakdown of the family as social progress. She does not view the family as a necessary social institution but as a political construction that elevates one category of people—affluent white males—above others, including women, homosexuals, and poor people.

Stacey also claims that the concept of the "traditional family" is increasingly irrelevant in a diverse society in which both men and women work for income. What our society needs, Stacey concludes, is not a return to some golden age of the family but political and economic change, including income parity for women, universal health care and child care, programs to reduce unemployment, and expanded sex education in the schools. Such measures not only help families but also ensure that people in diverse family forms receive the respect and dignity they deserve.

Whether the traditional family is a positive force in U.S. society or a negative one depends on your point of view.

Dan Bosler

WHAT DO YOU THINK?

1. To strengthen families, David Popenoe suggests that parents put children ahead of their own careers by limiting their joint workweek to sixty hours. Do you agree? Why or why not?

2. Judith Stacey thinks that marriage is weaker today because women are rejecting patriarchal relationships. What do you think about this argument?

3. Do we need to change family patterns for the well-being of our children? As you see it, what specific changes are called for?

children. But many gay parents are quiet about their sexual orientation, not wishing to draw unwelcome attention to their children or to themselves. In several widely publicized cases, courts have removed children from the custody of homosexual couples, citing the "best interests" of the children.

Gay parenting challenges many traditional ideas. But it also shows that many gay people value family life as highly as heterosexuals do.

Singlehood

Because nine out of ten people in the United States marry, we tend to view singlehood as a temporary stage of life. However, increasing numbers of people are choosing to live alone. In 1950, only one household in ten contained a single person. By 2006, this share had risen to one in four, a total of 30 million single adults (U.S. Census Bureau, 2006).

The New York Times

Girl or Boy? As Fertility Technology Advances, So Does an Ethical Debate

By DENISE GRADY
February 6, 2007

If people want to choose their baby's sex before pregnancy, should doctors help?

Some parents would love the chance to decide, while others wouldn't dream of meddling with nature. The medical world is also divided. Professional groups say sex selection is allowable in certain situations, but differ as to which ones. Meanwhile, it's not illegal, and some doctors are already cashing in on the demand.

There are several ways to pick a baby's sex before a woman becomes pregnant, or at least to shift the odds. Most of the procedures were originally developed to treat infertility or prevent genetic diseases.

The most reliable method is not easy or cheap. It requires in vitro fertilization, in which doctors prescribe drugs to stimulate the mother's ovaries, perform surgery to collect her eggs, fertilize them in the laboratory and then insert the embryos into her uterus.

Before the embryos are placed in the womb, some doctors will test for sex and, if there are enough embryos, let the parents decide whether to insert exclusively male or female ones. Pregnancy is not guaranteed, and the combined procedures can cost $20,000 or more, often not covered by insurance. Many doctors refuse to perform these invasive procedures just for sex selection, and some people are troubled by what eventually becomes of the embryos of the unwanted sex, which may be frozen or discarded.

Another method, used before the eggs are fertilized, involves sorting sperm, because it is the sperm and not the egg that determines a baby's sex. Semen normally has equal numbers of male- and female-producing sperm cells, but a technology called MicroSort can shift the ratio to either 88 percent female or 73 percent male. The "enriched" specimen can then be used for insemination or in vitro fertilization. It can cost $4,000 to $6,000, not including in vitro fertilization. . . .

The technique has been used in more than 1,000 pregnancies, with more than 900 births so far, a spokesman for the clinic said. As of January 2006 (the most recent figures released), the success rate among parents who wanted girls was 91 percent, and for those who wanted boys, it was 76 percent.

Regardless of the method, the American College of Obstetricians and Gynecologists opposes sex selection except in people who carry a genetic disease that primarily affects one sex. But allowing sex selection just because the parents want it, with no medical reason, may support "sexist practices," the college said in an opinion paper published this month in its journal, *Obstetrics and Gynecology.*

Some people say sex selection is ethical if parents already have one or more boys and now want a girl, or vice versa. In that case, it's "family balancing," not sex discrimination. . . .

Much of the worry about this issue derives from what has happened in China and India, where preferences for boys led to widespread aborting of female fetuses when ultrasound and other tests made it possible to identify them. China's one-child policy is thought to have made matters worse. Last month, Chinese officials said that 118 boys were born for every 100 girls in 2005, and some reports have projected an excess of 30 million males in less than 15 years. The United Nations opposes sex selection for nonmedical reasons, and a number of countries have outlawed it, including Australia, Canada and Britain, and other nations in Asia, South America and Europe. Left unanswered is the question of whether societies, and families, that favor boys should just be allowed to have them, since attitudes are hard to change, and girls born into such environments may be abused. . . .

Dr. Jeffrey M. Steinberg, from Encino, Calif., who has three clinics that offer sex selection, . . . said: "We prefer to do it for family balancing, but we've never turned away someone who came in and said, 'I want my first to be a boy or a girl.' If they all said a boy first, we'd probably shy away, but it's 50-50."

"Reproductive choice, as far as I'm concerned, is a very personal issue," Dr. Steinberg said. "If it's not going to hurt anyone, we go ahead and give them what they want." . . .

John A. Robertson, a professor of law and bioethics at the University of Texas, said: "The distinction between doing it for so-called family balancing or gender variety would be a useful line to draw at this stage of the debate, just as maybe a practice guideline, and let's just see how it works out."

In the long run, Mr. Robertson said, he doubted that enough Americans would use genetic tests to skew the sex balance in the population, and he pointed out that so far, sperm sorting was more successful at producing girls than boys.

He concluded, "I think this will slowly get clarified, and people will see it's not as big a deal as they think."

WHAT DO YOU THINK?

1. Do you support or oppose parents selecting the sex of their children? Why?

2. Is reproduction a personal issue for parents to decide or should the government create laws to control how reproductive technology is used? Explain your view.

3. In your mind, what other ethical issues does new reproductive technology raise?

Most striking is the rising number of single young women. In 1960, 28 percent of U.S. women aged twenty to twenty-four were single; by 2006, the proportion had soared to about 78 percent. Underlying this trend is women's greater participation in the labor force. Although most of these women will marry later on, women who are economically secure view a husband as a matter of choice rather than a financial necessity and marry later or, in some cases, not at all (Edwards, 2000).

By midlife, many unmarried women sense a lack of available men. Because we expect a woman to "marry up," the older a woman is, the more education she has, and the better her job, the more difficulty she has finding a suitable husband.

New Reproductive Technologies and Families

Medical advances involving new reproductive technologies are also changing families. In 1978, England's Louise Brown became the world's first "test-tube baby"; since then, tens of thousands of children have been conceived outside the womb.

Test-tube babies are the product of *in vitro fertilization*, in which doctors unite a woman's egg and a man's sperm "in glass" (usually not a test tube but a shallow dish) rather than in a woman's body. Doctors then either implant the resulting embryo in the womb of the woman who is to bear the child or freeze it for implantation at a later time.

Modern reproductive technologies allow some couples who cannot conceive by conventional means to have children. These techniques may also eventually help reduce the incidence of birth defects. Genetic screening of sperm and eggs allows medical specialists to increase the odds of having a healthy baby. But new reproductive technologies also raise difficult and troubling questions: When one woman carries an embryo developed from the egg of another, who is the mother? When a couple divorces, which spouse is entitled to use, or destroy, their frozen embryos? Should parents use genetic screening to select the traits of their child? Such questions remind us that technology changes faster than our ability to understand the consequences of its use (Adam Cohen, 1998; Nock, Wright, & Sanchez, 1999). "In the *Times*" takes a closer look at the reproductive technologies debate.

Families: Looking Ahead

Family life in the United States will continue to change in years to come, and with change comes controversy. Advocates of "traditional family values" line up against those who support greater personal

In 2007, New Jersey joined the increasing number of states that permit civil unions for same-sex couples. Some people oppose any same-sex relationships; others support civil unions; still others believe same-sex marriage should become lawful across the United States. Where do you stand on this issue? Why?

Colin Archer/Getty Images

choice; the Controversy & Debate box two pages back outlines some of the issues. Sociologists cannot predict the outcome of this debate, but we can suggest five likely future trends.

First, the divorce rate is likely to remain high, even in the face of evidence that marital breakups harm children. Today's marriages are about as durable as they were a century ago, when many were cut short by death. The difference is that now more couples *choose* to end marriages that fail to live up to their expectations. So even though the divorce rate has declined since 1980, it is unlikely to return to the low rates that marked the early decades of the twentieth century.

Second, family life in the twenty-first century will be more diverse than ever. Cohabiting couples, one-parent families, gay and lesbian families, and blended families are all on the rise. Most families are still based on marriage, and most married couples still have children. But the diversity of family forms implies a trend toward more personal choice.

Third, men will play a limited role in child rearing. In the 1950s, a decade that many people view as the "golden age" of families, men began to withdraw from active parenting (Snell, 1990; Stacey, 1990). In recent years, a countertrend has become evident, with some older, highly educated men staying at home with young children, many using computer technology to continue their work. But the stay-at-home dad represents no more than 10 percent of fathers with young children (U.S. Census Bureau, 2006). The bigger picture is that the high U.S. divorce rate and the increase in single motherhood are weakening children's ties to fathers and increasing children's risk of poverty.

Fourth, families will continue to feel the effects of economic changes. In many homes, both household partners work, reducing marriage and family to the interaction of weary men and women who try to fit a little "quality time" with their children into an already full schedule. The long-term effects of the two-career couple on families as we have known them are likely to be mixed.

Fifth and finally, the importance of new reproductive technologies will increase. Ethical concerns about whether what *can* be done *should* be done will slow these developments, but new approaches to reproduction will continue to alter the traditional experience of parenthood.

Despite the changes and controversies that have shaken the family in the United States, most people still report being happy as partners and parents. Marriage and family life are likely to remain foundations of our society for generations to come.

Applying Sociology in Everyday Life

1. Parents and grandparents can be a wonderful source of information about changes in marriage and the family. Ask them at what ages they married, what their married lives have been like, and what changes in family life today stand out for them. Compare the answers of two or more relatives. Are they very different?

2. Relationships with various family members differ. With which family member—mother, father, brother, sister—do you most readily share confidences? Who in your family would be the last to know? Why? Which family member would you turn to first in a crisis, and why?

3. Nowadays, just one-third of families eat dinner together often (D. G. Myers, 2000:179). Are family meals part of your routine? What other regular family rituals do you participate in? Do members of your family feel that they spend enough time together?

MAKING THE GRADE

Families

Families: Basic Concepts

All societies are built on *kinship*. The **FAMILY** varies across cultures and over time:

- In industrialized societies such as the United States, *marriage* is monogamous.
- Preindustrial societies recognize the *extended family*; industrialization gives rise to the *nuclear family*.
- Many preindustrial societies permit *polygamy*, of which there are two types: *polygyny* and *polyandry*.
- In global perspective, *patrilocality* is most common, but industrial societies favor *neolocality* and a few societies have *matrilocal residence*.
- Industrial societies use bilateral *descent*; preindustrial societies are either patrilineal or matrilineal.

Theoretical Analysis of Families

 macro-level

The **STRUCTURAL-FUNCTIONAL APPROACH** identifies major family functions that help society operate smoothly:

- socialization of children to help them become well-integrated members of society
- regulation of sexual activity in order to maintain kinship organization and property rights
- giving children a social identity within society in terms of race, ethnicity, religion, and social class
- providing material and emotional support to family members

The **SOCIAL-CONFLICT APPROACH** and **FEMINIST APPROACH** point to ways in which families perpetuate social inequality:

- Families ensure the continuation of the class structure by passing on wealth to their children.
- Families perpetuate gender roles by establishing men as the heads of the household and by assigning the responsibility for child rearing and housework to women.
- The tendency of people to marry others like themselves supports racial and ethnic hierarchies.

The **incest taboo**, which restricts sexual relations between certain relatives, exists in all societies.

 micro-level

- The **SYMBOLIC-INTERACTION APPROACH** explores how family members build emotional bonds in the course of everyday family life.
- The **SOCIAL-EXCHANGE APPROACH** sees courtship and marriage as a process of negotiation in which each person weighs the advantages and disadvantages of a potential partner.

See the Applying Theory table in this chapter.

Stages of Family Life

COURTSHIP AND ROMANTIC LOVE

- Arranged marriages are common in preindustrial societies.
- Courtship based on romantic love is central to mate selection in the United States and leads to the formation of new families.
- The contrast between our culture's idealized vision of marriage and the everyday realities of married life can lead to disappointment and failed marriages.

CHILD REARING

- Large families are necessary in preindustrial societies because children are a source of needed labor.
- Family size has decreased over time as industrialization increases the costs of raising children.
- As more women choose to go to school or join the labor force, fewer children are born.
- The "family values" debate revolves around who cares for children when both parents work outside the home.

THE FAMILY IN LATER LIFE

- The departure of children, known as the "empty nest," requires adjustments to family life.
- Many middle-aged couples care for aging parents, and many older couples are active grandparents.
- The final transition in marriage begins with the death of a spouse.

family a social institution found in all societies that unites people in cooperative groups to care for one another, including any children

kinship a social bond based on common ancestry, marriage, or adoption

marriage a legal relationship, usually involving economic cooperation, sexual activity, and childbearing

extended family a family consisting of parents and children as well as other kin; also known as a *consanguine family*

nuclear family a family composed of one or two parents and their children; also known as a *conjugal family*

endogamy marriage between people of the same social category

exogamy marriage between people of different social categories

monogamy marriage that unites two partners

polygamy marriage that unites a person with two or more spouses

polygyny marriage that unites one man and two or more women

polyandry marriage that unites one woman and two or more men

patrilocality a residential pattern in which a married couple lives with or near the husband's familiy

matrilocality a residential pattern in which a married couple lives with or near the wife's familiy

neolocality a residential pattern in which a married couple lives apart from both sets of parents

descent the system by which members of a society trace kinship over generations

patrilineal descent a system tracing kinship through men

matrilineal descent a system tracing kinship through women

bilateral descent a system tracing kinship through both men and women

incest taboo a norm forbidding sexual relations or marriage between certain relatives

homogamy marriage between people with the same social characteristics

infidelity sexual activity outside one's marriage

MAKING THE GRADE *continued . . .*

U.S. Families: Class, Gender, and Race

SOCIAL CLASS is a powerful force that shapes family life.
- Social class determines a family's financial security and opportunities available to family members.
- Children born into rich families typically have better mental and physical health and go on to achieve more in life than children born into poor families.

GENDER affects family dynamics because husbands dominate in most marriages.
- Research suggests that marriage provides more benefits for men than for women.
- After divorce, men remarry more quickly than women.

ETHNICITY AND RACE can affect a person's experience of family life, although no single generalization fits all families within a particular category.
- Migration of American Indians from reservations to cities creates many "fluid households" with changing membership.
- The traditional pattern of extended families common to Latinos is changing as Latinos assimilate into the larger U.S. society.
- African American families face severe economic disadvantages, and more than one-third of African American children are growing up poor.

Most married couples have similar social background with regard to class and race, but over the past century, ethnicity has mattered less and less.

Transitions and Problems in Family Life

DIVORCE

The divorce rate is ten times what it was a century ago; four in ten of today's marriages will end in divorce. Researchers point to six causes:
- Individualism is on the rise.
- Romantic love fades.
- Women are less dependent on men.
- Many of today's marriages are stressful.
- Divorce is socially acceptable.
- Legally, a divorce is easier to get.

REMARRIAGE
- Four out of five people who divorce eventually remarry.
- Remarriage creates blended families that include children from previous marriages.

family violence emotional, physical, or sexual abuse of one family member by another

cohabitation the sharing of a household by an unmarried couple

FAMILY VIOLENCE
- Family violence, which victimizes mostly women and children, is far more common than official records indicate.
- Most adults who abuse family members were themselves abused as children.

Alternative Family Forms

ONE-PARENT FAMILIES
- The proportion of one-parent families—now 31% of all families in the United States—more than doubled during the last generation.
- Single parenthood increases a woman's risk of poverty, which puts children at a disadvantage.

COHABITATION
- Almost half of all people 25 to 44 years of age have cohabited at some point.
- Research shows that children born to cohabiting couples are less likely to live with both biological parents until age 18 than children born to married parents.

GAY AND LESBIAN COUPLES
- Although only Massachusetts has lawful same-sex marriage, many gay men and lesbians form long-lasting relationships and, increasingly, are becoming parents.

SINGLEHOOD
- One in four households today—up from one in ten households in 1950—contains a single person.
- The number of young women who are single is rising dramatically, a result of women's greater participation in the workforce and lessened dependence on men for material supoort.

New Reproductive Technologies

- Although ethically controversial, new reproductive technologies are changing conventional ideas of parenthood.

MAKING THE GRADE

Sample Test Questions

These questions are similar to those found in the test bank that accompanies this textbook.

Multiple-Choice Questions

1. **The family is a social institution that is found in**
   a. most but not all societies.
   b. low-income nations but typically not in high-income nations.
   c. high-income nations but typically not in low-income nations.
   d. every society.

2. **What is the term sociologists use for a family containing parents, children, and other kin?**
   a. a nuclear family
   b. an extended family
   c. a family of affinity
   d. a conjugal family

3. **A system of marriage that unites one woman with two or more men is called**
   a. polygamy.
   b. polygyny.
   c. polyandry.
   d. bilateral marriage.

4. **Sociologists claim that marriage in the United States follows the principle of homogamy, which means that partners are**
   a. people of the same sex.
   b. people who are socially alike in terms of class, age, and race.
   c. people who marry due to social pressure.
   d. selected based on love rather than by parents.

5. **Which of the following are included among the functions of the family?**
   a. socialization of children
   b. regulation of sexual activity
   c. social placement of children
   d. All of the above are correct.

6. **Which theoretical approach states that people select partners who have about the same to offer as they do?**
   a. the structural-functional approach
   b. the social-exchange approach
   c. the social-conflict approach
   d. the feminist approach

7. **Which of the following transitions in married life is usually the hardest for people?**
   a. the birth of the second child
   b. the last child leaving home
   c. the death of a spouse
   d. retiring from the labor force

8. **In the United States, many Latino families are characterized by**
   a. strong extended kinship.
   b. parents exerting a great deal of control over their children's courtship.
   c. traditional gender roles.
   d. All of the above are correct.

9. **For which category of the U.S. population is the highest proportion of children born to single women?**
   a. African Americans
   b. Asian Americans
   c. Hispanic Americans
   d. non-Hispanic white Americans

10. **Which category of people in the United States is at the highest risk of divorce?**
    a. gay and lesbian couples
    b. young people who marry after a short courtship
    c. a couple whose parents never experienced divorce
    d. a couple facing a wanted and expected pregnancy

ANSWERS: 1 (d); 2 (b); 3 (c); 4 (b); 5 (d); 6 (b); 7 (c); 8 (d); 9 (a); 10 (b).

Essay Questions

1. Sociologists point to ways in which family life reflects not just individual choices but the structure of society as well. Provide three examples of how society shapes family life.

2. Overall, do you think families in the United States are becoming weaker or simply more diverse? Support your position.

Religion

FROM CHAPTER 19 OF *SOCIOLOGY*, 12/E. JOHN J. MACIONIS. COPYRIGHT © 2008 BY PEARSON EDUCATION. ALL RIGHTS RESERVED.

Religion

WHY is the United States more religious than other high-income nations?

WHAT effects does being religious have on social behavior?

HOW do religions in the East and the West differ?

Religion is the social institution involving beliefs and practices based on recognizing what is sacred. There are many world religions, just as there are many different religious organizations within U.S. society.

Mashkov Yuri/ITAR-TASS/Corbis

A. Ramey/PhotoEdit, Inc. (*background*)

Getty Images, Inc.

With its many churches, synagogues, temples, and mosques (a recent study put the figure at one house of worship for every 865 people), one country stands out as among the most religious countries on Earth. For its entire history, its leaders have proclaimed that God is responsible for its prosperity and liberty; today, four out of five of this nation's people say they have "experienced God's presence or a spiritual force." Together, they give more than $55 billion each year to religious organizations—more than the total economic output of most low-income countries. In schools, their children stand before the national flag and pledge their allegiance to "one nation under God" (Sheler, 2002).

You have already guessed that the country described is the United States. But although the United States is a religious nation, it is also a country of immigrants, and as a result, its people have many different images of God. In countless places of worship—from soaring Gothic cathedrals in New York City to small storefront tabernacles in Los Angeles—Christians, Muslims, Jews, Buddhists, Hindus, Sikhs, Jains, Zoroastrians, and followers of dozens of other religions can be found (Yang & Ebaugh, 2001; Sheler, 2002). One scholar described the United States as the world's most religiously diverse nation, a country in which Hindu and Jewish children go to school together and Muslims, Buddhists, and Sikhs work in the same factories and offices as Protestants and Catholics (Eck, 2001). And as you will see, many people in the United States today are spiritual without being part of any organized religion.

This chapter begins by explaining what religion is from a sociological point of view. We then explore the changing face of religious belief throughout history and around the world and examine the vital and sometimes controversial place of religion in today's society.

Religion: Basic Concepts

The French sociologist Emile Durkheim stated that religion involves "things that surpass the limits of our knowledge" (1965:62, orig. 1915). We define most objects, events, or experiences as **profane** (from Latin, meaning "outside the temple"), *included as an ordinary element of everyday life.* But we also consider some things **sacred**, *set apart as extraordinary, inspiring awe and reverence.* Setting the sacred apart from the profane is the essence of all religious belief. **Religion**, then, is *a social institution involving beliefs and practices based on recognizing the sacred.*

There is great diversity in matters of faith, and nothing is sacred to everyone on Earth. Although people regard most books as profane, Jews believe that the Torah (the first five books of the Hebrew Bible or Old Testament) is sacred, in the same way that Christians revere the Old and New Testaments of the Bible and Muslims exalt the Qur'an (Koran).

But no matter how a community of believers draws religious lines, Durkheim (1965, orig. 1915) explained, people understand profane things in terms of their everyday usefulness: We log on to the Internet with our computer or turn a key to start our car. What is sacred we reverently set apart from daily life, giving it a "forbidden" or "holy" aura. Marking the boundary between the sacred and the profane, for example, Muslims remove their shoes before entering a mosque, to avoid defiling a sacred place with soles that have touched the profane ground outside.

The sacred is embodied in **ritual**, or *formal, ceremonial behavior.* Holy communion is the central ritual of Christianity; to the Christian faithful, the wafer and wine consumed during communion are never treated in a profane way as food but as the sacred symbols of the body and blood of Jesus Christ.

Religion and Sociology

Because religion deals with ideas that transcend everyday experience, neither common sense nor sociology can prove or disprove religious doctrine. Religion is a matter of **faith**, *belief based on conviction rather than on scientific evidence.* The New Testament of the Bible defines faith as "the conviction of things not seen" (Hebrews 11:1) and urges Christians to "walk by faith, not by sight" (2 Corinthians 5:7).

Some people with strong faith may be disturbed by the thought of sociologists turning a scientific eye on what they hold sacred. However, a sociological study of religion is no threat to anyone's faith. Sociologists study religion just as they study the family, to understand religious experiences around the world and how religion is tied to other social institutions. They make no judgments that a specific religion is right or wrong. Rather, scientific sociology takes a more worldly approach, asking why religions take a particular form in one society or another and how religious activity affects society as a whole.

Theoretical Analysis of Religion

Sociologists apply the major theoretical approaches to the study of religion just as they do to any other topic. Each approach provides distinctive insights into the way religion shapes social life.

This chapter explores the meaning and importance of religion, a major social institution, which is based on the concept of the sacred.

Functions of Religion: Structural-Functional Analysis

According to Durkheim (1965, orig. 1915), society has a life and power of its own beyond the life of any individual. In other words, society itself is godlike, shaping the lives of its members and living on beyond them. Practicing religion, people celebrate the awesome power of their society.

No wonder people around the world transform certain everyday objects into sacred symbols of their collective life. Members of technologically simple societies do this with a **totem**, *an object in the natural world collectively defined as sacred.* The totem—perhaps an animal or an elaborate work of art—becomes the centerpiece of ritual, symbolizing the power of society over the individual. In our society, the flag is treated with respect and is not used in a profane way (say, as clothing) or allowed to touch the ground.

Similarly, putting the words "In God We Trust" on all currency (a practice started in the 1860s at the time of the Civil War) or adding the words "under God" to the Pledge of Allegiance (in 1954) symbolizes some widespread beliefs that tie society together. Across the United States, local communities also gain a sense of unity by linking totems to sports teams, from the New England Patriots to the Iowa State University Cyclones to the San Francisco 49ers.

Durkheim identified three major functions of religion that contribute to the operation of society:

1. **Social cohesion.** Religion unites people through shared symbolism, values, and norms. Religious thought and ritual establish rules of fair play, organizing our social life.

2. **Social control.** Every society uses religious ideas to promote conformity. By defining God as a "judge," many religions encourage people to obey cultural norms. Religion can also be used to back up the power of political systems. In medieval Europe, for example, monarchs claimed to rule by "divine right," so that obedience was seen as doing God's will. Even today, our leaders ask for God's blessing, implying that their efforts are right and just.

3. **Providing meaning and purpose.** Religious belief offers the comforting sense that our brief lives serve some greater purpose. Strengthened by such beliefs, people are less likely to despair in the face of change or even tragedy. For this reason, we mark major life course transitions—including birth, marriage, and death—with religious observances.

Religion is founded on the concept of the sacred—that which is set apart as extraordinary and demands our submission. Bowing, kneeling, or prostrating oneself are all ways of symbolically surrendering to a higher power. These Buddhist pilgrims are making their way to a holy place on Mount Kallas in western Tibet.

Galen Rowell/Peter Arnold, Inc.

When immigrants move from a familiar world to a new society, religion can help answer countless questions that arise in everyday life. "In the *Times*" on the next page takes a closer look.

Sports culture often has a semireligious character. What is the function for communities of supporting teams, such as the Ohio State Buckeyes, the University of Michigan Wolverines, or the Miami Dolphins?

The New York Times

HOME PAGE
...RKET
...L ESTATE
AUTOS
ALL CLASSIFIEDS

WORLD
U.S.
Politics
Washington
Education
N.Y./REGION
BUSINESS
TECHNOLOGY
SPORTS
SCIENCE
HEALTH
OPINION
ARTS
Books
Movies
Music
Television
Theater
STYLE
Dining & Wine
Fashion & Style
Home & Garden
Weddings/
Celebrations
TRAVEL

Blogs
Cartoons
Classifieds
Corrections
Crossword/
Games
First Look
Learning
Network
Multimedia
NYC Guide
Obituaries
Podcasts
The Public
Editor
Sunday
Magazine
Weather
Week in Review

NEWSPAPER
Get Home
Delivery
Customer Care
TimesPoints

A Muslim Leader in Brooklyn, Reconciling Two Worlds

By ANDREA ELLIOTT
March 5, 2006

The imam begins his trek before dawn, his long robe billowing like a ghost through empty streets. In this dark, quiet hour, his thoughts sometimes drift back to the Egyptian farming village where he was born.

But as the sun rises over Bay Ridge, Brooklyn, Sheik Reda Shata's new world comes to life. The R train rattles beneath a littered stretch of sidewalk, where Mexican workers huddle in the cold. An electric Santa dances in a doughnut shop window. Neon signs beckon. Gypsy cabs blare their horns.

The imam slips into a plain brick building, nothing like the golden-domed mosque of his youth. He stops to pray, and then climbs the cracked linoleum steps to his cluttered office. The answering machine blinks frantically, a portent of the endless questions to come.

A teenage girl wants to know: Is it halal, or lawful, to eat a Big Mac? Can alcohol be served, a waiter wonders, if it is prohibited by the Koran? Is it wrong to take out a mortgage, young Muslim professionals ask, when Islam frowns upon monetary interest?

The questions are only a piece of the daily puzzle Mr. Shata must solve as the imam of the Islamic Society of Bay Ridge, a thriving New York mosque where several thousand Muslims worship.

To his congregants, Mr. Shata is far more than the leader of daily prayers and giver of the Friday sermon. Many of them now live in a land without their parents, who typically assist with finding a spouse. There are fewer uncles and cousins to help resolve personal disputes. There is no local House of Fatwa to issue rulings on ethical questions.

Sheik Reda, as he is called, arrived in Brooklyn one year after Sept. 11. Virtually overnight, he became an Islamic judge and nursery school principal, a matchmaker and marriage counselor, a 24-hour hot line on all things Islamic.

Day after day, he must find ways to reconcile Muslim tradition with American life. Little in his rural Egyptian upbringing or years of Islamic scholarship prepared him for the challenge of leading a mosque in America. . . .

"America transformed me from a person of rigidity to flexibility," said Mr. Shata, speaking through an Arabic translator. "I went from a country where a sheik would speak and the people listened to one where the sheik talks and the people talk back."

This is the story of Mr. Shata's journey west: the making of an American imam.

Over the last half-century, the Muslim population in the United States has risen significantly. Immigrants from the Middle East, South Asia and Africa have settled across the country, establishing mosques from Boston to Los Angeles, and turning Islam into one of the nation's fastest growing religions. By some estimates, as many as six million Muslims now live in America.

Leading this flock calls for improvisation. Imams must unify diverse congregations with often-clashing Islamic traditions. They must grapple with the threat of terrorism, answering to law enforcement agents without losing the trust of their fellow Muslims. Sometimes they must set aside conservative beliefs that prevail in the Middle East, the birthplace of Islam.

Islam is a legalistic faith: Muslims believe in a divine law that guides their daily lives, including what they should eat, drink and wear. In countries where the religion reigns, this is largely the accepted way. . . .

The religion's fiqh, or jurisprudence, is built on 14 centuries of scholarship, but imams in Europe and America often find this body of law insufficient to address life in the West. The quandaries of America were foreign to Mr. Shata.

Pornography was rampant, prompting a question Mr. Shata had never heard in Egypt: Is oral sex lawful? Pork and alcohol are forbidden in Islam, raising questions about whether Muslims could sell beer or bacon. Tired of the menacing stares in the subway, women wanted to know if they could remove their headscarves. Muslims were navigating their way through problems Mr. Shata had never fathomed.

For a while, the imam called his fellow sheiks in Egypt with requests for fatwas, or nonbinding legal rulings. But their views carried little relevance to life in America. Some issues, like oral sex, he dared not raise. Over time, he began to find his own answers and became, as he put it, flexible.

Is a Big Mac permissible? Yes, the imam says, but not a bacon cheeseburger.

It is a woman's right, Mr. Shata believes, to remove her hijab if she feels threatened. Muslims can take jobs serving alcohol and pork, he says, but only if other work cannot be found. Oral sex is acceptable, but only between married couples. Mortgages, he says, are necessary to move forward in America.

"Islam is supposed to make a person's life easier, not harder," Mr. Shata explained. . . .

WHAT DO YOU THINK?

1. In your own words, how would you describe Sheik Rada Shata's function as imam in his Brooklyn congregation?

2. In what ways do Muslim traditions blend well with U.S. cultural traditions? In what ways do they conflict? How does Sheik Rata deal with these conflicts?

3. Has religion helped guide your own everyday life behavior and decisions? If so, give some examples.

tip

Our modern society encourages rational thinking guided by the evidence we gather using our senses. Faith is nonrational (but not irrational), meaning that it is based on belief rather than scientific evidence.

tip

Here we apply sociology's three major theoretical approaches, familiar to you from earlier chapters, to religion. Durkheim's structural-functional analysis cites the functions of religion as providing cohesion, control, and meaning.

CRITICAL REVIEW In Durkheim's structural-functional analysis, religion represents the collective life of society. The major weakness of this approach is that it downplays religion's dysfunctions, especially the fact that strongly held beliefs can generate social conflict. Terrorists have claimed that God supports their actions, and many nations march to war under the banner of their God. A study of conflict in the world would probably show that religious beliefs have provoked more violence than differences of social class.

YOUR LEARNING What are Durkheim's three functions of religion for society?

Constructing the Sacred: Symbolic-Interaction Analysis

From a symbolic-interaction point of view, religion (like all of society) is socially constructed (although perhaps with divine inspiration). Through various rituals—from daily prayers to annual religious observances such as Easter, Passover, or Ramadan—people sharpen the distinction between the sacred and the profane. Peter Berger (1967:35–36) claims that placing our small, brief lives within some "cosmic frame of reference" gives us the appearance of "ultimate security and permanence."

Marriage is a good example. If two people look on marriage as merely a contract, they can walk away whenever they want. Their bond makes far stronger claims on them when it is defined as holy matrimony, which is surely one reason that the divorce rate is lower among people with strong religious beliefs. More generally, whenever human beings face uncertainty or life-threatening situations—such as illness, natural disaster, terrorist attack, or war—we turn to our sacred symbols.

Do you recall examples of people turning to sacred symbols after tragic events such as the 2007 Virginia Tech shootings? Explain what happened.

CRITICAL REVIEW Using the symbolic-interaction approach, people use religion to give everyday life sacred meaning. Berger adds that the sacred's ability to give special meaning to society depends on ignoring the fact that it is socially constructed. After all, how much strength could we gain from beliefs if we saw them merely as strategies for coping with tragedy? Also, this micro-level analysis ignores religion's link to social inequality, to which we turn next.

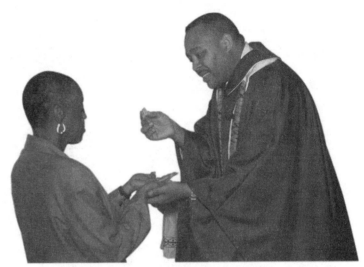

Regularly taking part in religious rituals sharpens the distinction between the sacred and the profane. The wafer used in the Christian ritual of holy communion is never thought of in the everyday sense of food; rather, it is a sacred symbol of the body of Christ.

Michael Newman/PhotoEdit Inc.

YOUR LEARNING How would Peter Berger explain the fact that deeply religious people have a low divorce rate?

Inequality and Religion: Social-Conflict Analysis

The social-conflict approach highlights religion's support of social inequality. Religion, proclaimed Karl Marx, serves ruling elites by legitimizing the status quo and diverting people's attention from social inequities.

Today, the British monarch is the formal head of the Church of England, illustrating the close ties between religious and political elites. In practical terms, working for political change would mean opposing the church and, by implication, God. Religion also encourages people to accept the social problems of this world while they look hopefully to a "better world to come." In a well-known statement, Marx dismissed religion as "the sigh of the oppressed creature, the sentiment of a heartless world, and the soul of soulless conditions. It is the opium of the people" (1964:27, orig. 1848).

Religion and social inequality are also linked through gender. Virtually all the world's major religions are patriarchal, as the Thinking About Diversity: Race, Class, & Gender box on page 496 explains.

student 2 student

"After reading this chapter, I saw new meaning in everyday rituals like saying grace at dinner. And I never really thought about why so many weddings take place in a church."

Thinking About Diversity: Race, Class, & Gender
Religion and Patriarchy: Does God Favor Males?

Why do two-thirds of adults in the United States say they think of God as "father" rather than "mother" (NORC, 2005:185)? It is probably because we link godly traits such as wisdom and power to men. Just about all the world's religions tend to favor males, a fact evident in passages from their sacred writings.

The Qur'an (Koran), the sacred text of Islam, declares that men are to dominate women: "Men are in charge of women. . . . Hence good women are obedient. . . . As for those whose rebelliousness you fear, admonish them, banish them from your bed, and scourge them" (quoted in W. Kaufman, 1976:163).

Christianity, the major religion of the Western world, also supports patriarchy. Many Christians revere Mary, the mother of Jesus, but the New Testament also includes the following passages:

A man . . . is the image and glory of God; but woman is the glory of man. For man was not made from woman, but woman from man. Neither was man created for woman, but woman for man. (1 Corinthians 11:7–9)

As in all the churches of the saints, the women should keep silence in the churches. For they are not permitted to speak, but should be subordinate, as even the law says. If there is anything they desire to know, let them ask their husbands at home. For it is shameful for a woman to speak in church. (1 Corinthians 14:33–35)

Wives, be subject to your husbands, as to the Lord. For the husband is the head of the wife as Christ is the head of the church. . . . As the church is subject to Christ,

so let wives also be subject in everything to their husbands. (Ephesians 5:22–24)

Let a woman learn in silence with all submissiveness. I permit no woman to teach or to have authority over men; she is to keep silent. For Adam was formed first, then Eve; and Adam was not deceived, but the woman was deceived and became a transgressor. Yet woman will be saved through bearing children, if she continues in faith and love and holiness, with modesty. (1 Timothy 2:11–15)

Judaism has also traditionally supported patriarchy. Male Orthodox Jews say the following words in daily prayer:

Blessed art thou, O Lord our God, King of the Universe, that I was not born a gentile.
Blessed art thou, O Lord our God, King of the Universe, that I was not born a slave.

Patriarchy is found in all the world's major religions, including Christianity, Judaism, and Islam. Male dominance can be seen in restrictions that limit religious leadership to men and also in regulations that prohibit women from worshiping alongside men.

David H. Wells/ Corbis Digital Stock

Blessed art thou, O Lord our God, King of the Universe, that I was not born a woman.

Many patriarchal religions also exclude women from the clergy. Today, Islam and the Roman Catholic Church ban women from the priesthood, as do about half of Protestant denominations. But a growing number of Protestant religious organizations, including the Church of England, ordain women, who now represent 18 percent of U.S. clergy. Orthodox Judaism upholds the traditional prohibition against women serving as rabbis, but Reform and Conservative Judaism look to both men and women as spiritual leaders. Across the United States, the proportion of women in seminaries has never been higher (now roughly one-third), which is more evidence of a trend toward greater equality (Chaves, 1997; Nesbitt, 1997).

SOCIOLOGY ✷ WORK

Feminists argue that unless traditional ideas of gender are removed from our understanding of God, women will never be equal to men in the church. The theologian Mary Daly puts the matter bluntly: "If God is male, then male is God" (quoted in Woodward, 1989:58).

WHAT DO YOU THINK?

1. Are you or other members of your family affiliated with a religious organization? If so, what evidence of patriarchy do you see in this religion?

2. Why do you think many religions encourage people to think of God as male?

3. Can you think of God in terms that do not include gender? Explain your answer.

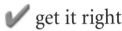
Look closely at the Applying Theory table to be
sure you understand what each of the three major
theoretical approaches is saying about religion.

APPLYING THEORY

Religion

	Structural-Functional Approach	Symbolic-Interaction Approach	Social-Conflict Approach
What is the level of analysis?	Macro-level	Micro-level	Macro-level
What is the importance of religion for society?	Religion performs vital tasks, including uniting people and controlling behavior.	Religion strengthens marriage by giving it (and family life) sacred meaning.	Religion supports social inequality by claiming that the social order is just.
	Religion gives life meaning and purpose.	People often turn to sacred symbols for comfort when facing danger and uncertainty.	Religion turns attention from problems in this world to a "better world to come."

▶**CRITICAL REVIEW**   Social-conflict analysis emphasizes the power of religion to support social inequality. Yet religion also promotes change toward equality. For example, nineteenth-century religious groups in the United States played an important part in the movement to abolish slavery. In the 1950s and 1960s, religious organizations and their leaders were the core of the civil rights movement. In the 1960s and 1970s, many clergy opposed the Vietnam War, and today many support any number of progressive causes such as feminism and gay rights.

✔ **YOUR LEARNING**   How does religion help maintain class inequality and gender stratification?

The Applying Theory table summarizes the three theoretical approaches to understanding religion.

 Can you think of an example of one society using the idea of "converting heathens" to justify controlling another society? Explain.

Religion and Social Change

Religion can be the conservative force portrayed by Karl Marx. But at some points in history, as Max Weber (1958, orig. 1904–05) explained, religion has promoted dramatic social change.

Max Weber: Protestantism and Capitalism

Max Weber argued that particular religious ideas set into motion a wave of change that brought about the Industrial Revolution in Western Europe. The rise of industrial capitalism was encouraged by Calvinism, a movement within the Protestant Reformation.

John Calvin (1509–1564) was a leader in the Protestant Reformation who preached the doctrine of predestination. According to Calvin, an all-powerful and all-knowing God had selected some people for salvation but condemned most to eternal damnation. Each individual's fate, sealed before birth and known only to God, was either eternal glory or endless hellfire.

Driven by anxiety over their fate, Calvinists understandably looked for signs of God's favor in this world and came to see prosperity as a sign of divine blessing. Religious conviction and a rigid devotion to duty led Calvinists to work hard, and many amassed great wealth. But money was not for selfish spending or even for sharing with the poor, whose plight they saw as a mark of God's rejection. As agents of God's work on Earth, Calvinists believed that they best fulfilled their "calling" by reinvesting profits and achieving ever-greater success in the process.

All the while, Calvinists lived thrifty lives and adopted technological advances, which laid the groundwork for the rise of industrial capitalism. In time, the religious fervor that motivated early Calvinists weakened, leaving a profane "Protestant work ethic." To Max Weber, industrial capitalism itself arose as a "disenchanted" religion, further showing the power of religion to alter the shape of society.

tip

Because liberation theology is an activist approach
focusing on how religion can reduce social
inequality, it is one example of social-conflict
analysis.

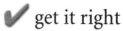 **get it right**

As you read the discussion below, be sure you
understand the specific definitions of church,
sect, and cult, as well as why some churches are
correctly called a state church or a denomination.

Liberation Theology

Historically, Christianity has reached out to oppressed people, urging all to a stronger faith in a better life to come. In recent decades, however, some church leaders and theologians have taken a decidedly political approach and endorsed **liberation theology,** *the combining of Christian principles with political activism, often Marxist in character.*

This social movement started in the 1960s in Latin America's Roman Catholic Church. Today, Christian activists continue to help people in poor nations liberate themselves from abysmal poverty. Their message is simple: Social oppression runs counter to Christian morality, so as a matter of faith and justice, Christians must promote greater social equality.

Pope Benedictine XVI, like Pope John Paul II before him, condemns liberation theology for distorting traditional church doctrine with left-wing politics. Nevertheless, the liberation theology movement has gained strength in the poorest countries of Latin America, where many people's Christian faith drives them to improve conditions for the poor and oppressed (Neuhouser, 1989; J. E. Williams, 2002).

Types of Religious Organizations

Sociologists categorize the hundreds of different religious organizations found in the United States along a continuum, with *churches* at one end and *sects* at the other. We can describe any actual religious organization in relation to these two ideal types by locating it on the church-sect continuum.

Church

Drawing on the ideas of his teacher Max Weber, Ernst Troeltsch (1931) defined a **church** as *a type of religious organization that is well integrated into the larger society.* Churchlike organizations usually persist for centuries and include generations of the same families. Churches have well-established rules and regulations and expect leaders to be formally trained and ordained.

Though concerned with the sacred, a church accepts the ways of the profane world. Church members think of God in intellectual terms (say, as a force for good) and favor abstract moral standards ("Do unto others as you would have them do unto you") over specific rules for day-to-day living. By teaching morality in safely abstract terms, church leaders avoid social controversy. For example, many congregations celebrate the unity of all peoples but say little about their own lack of racial diversity. By downplaying this type of conflict, a church makes peace with the status quo (Troeltsch, 1931).

A church may operate with or apart from the state. As its name implies, a **state church** is *a church formally allied with the state.* State churches have existed throughout human history. For centuries, Roman Catholicism was the official religion of the Roman Empire, and Confucianism was the official religion of China until early in the twentieth century. Today, the Anglican church is the official church of England, and Islam is the official religion of Pakistan and Iran. State churches count everyone in the society as a member, which sharply limits tolerance of religious differences.

A **denomination,** by contrast, is *a church, independent of the state, that recognizes religious pluralism.* Denominations exist in nations, including the United States, that formally separate church and state. This country has dozens of Christian denominations—including Catholics, Baptists, Episcopalians, Presbyterians, and Lutherans—as well as various categories of Judaism, Islam, and other traditions. Although members of any denomination hold to their own doctrine, they recognize the right of others to have other beliefs.

Sect

The second general religious form is the **sect,** *a type of religious organization that stands apart from the larger society.* Sect members have rigid religious convictions and deny the beliefs of others. Compared to churches, which try to appeal to everyone (the term *catholic* also means "universal"), a sect forms an exclusive group. To members of a sect, religion is not just one aspect of life but a firm plan for living. In extreme cases, members of a sect withdraw completely from society in order to practice their religion without interference. The Amish community is one example of a North American sect that isolates itself. Because our culture generally considers religious tolerance a virtue, members of sects are sometimes accused of being narrow-minded in insisting that they alone follow the true religion (Kraybill, 1994; P. W. Williams, 2002).

In organizational terms, sects are less formal than churches. Sect members may be highly spontaneous and emotional in worship, compared to members of churches, who tend to listen passively to their leaders. Sects also reject the intellectualized religion of churches, stressing instead the personal experience of divine power. Rodney Stark (1985:314) contrasts a church's vision of a distant God ("Our Father, who art in Heaven") with a sect's more immediate God ("Lord, bless this poor sinner kneeling before you now").

Churches and sects also have different patterns of leadership. The more churchlike an organization, the more likely that its leaders are formally trained and ordained. Sectlike organizations, which celebrate the personal presence of God, expect their leaders to exhibit divine inspiration in the form of **charisma** (from Greek, meaning

 tip

In general, the importance of charisma is greatest in cults, less so in sects, and least in churches.

"divine favor"), *extraordinary personal qualities that can infuse people with emotion and turn them into followers.*

Sects generally form as breakaway groups from established religious organizations (Stark & Bainbridge, 1979). Their psychic intensity and informal structure make them less stable than churches, and many sects blossom only to disappear soon after. The sects that do endure typically become more like churches, with declining emphasis on charismatic leadership as they become more bureaucratic.

To sustain their membership, many sects actively recruit, or *proselytize,* new members. Sects highly value the experience of *conversion,* a personal transformation or religious rebirth. For example, members of Jehovah's Witnesses go door to door to share their faith with others in the hope of attracting new members.

Finally, churches and sects differ in their social composition. Because they are more closely tied to the world, well-established churches tend to include people of high social standing. Sects attract more disadvantaged people. A sect's openness to new members and its promise of salvation and personal fulfillment appeal to people who feel they are social outsiders.

Cult

A **cult** is *a religious organization that is largely outside a society's cultural traditions.* Most sects spin off from conventional religious organizations. However, a cult typically forms around a highly charismatic leader who offers a compelling message about a new and very different way of life. As many as 5,000 cults exist in the United States (Marquand & Wood, 1997).

Because some cult principles or practices are unconventional, the popular view is that they are deviant or even evil. The suicides of thirty-nine members of California's Heaven's Gate cult in 1997—people who claimed that dying was a doorway to a higher existence, perhaps in the company of aliens from outer space—confirmed the negative image the public holds of most cults. In short, calling any religious community a "cult" amounts to dismissing its members as crazy (Shupe, 1995; Gleick, 1997).

This charge is unfair because there is nothing basically wrong with this kind of religious organization. Many longstanding religions—Christianity, Islam, and Judaism included—began as cults. Of course, few cults exist for very long. One reason is that they are even more at odds with the larger society than sects. Many cults demand that members not only accept their doctrine but also adopt a radically new lifestyle. This is why people sometimes accuse cults of brainwashing their members, although research suggests that most people who join cults experience no psychological harm (Kilbourne, 1983; P. W. Williams, 2002).

In global perspective, the range of religious activity is truly astonishing. Members of this Southeast Asian cult show their devotion to God by suspending themselves in the air using ropes and sharp hooks that pierce their skin. What religious practices that are common in the United States might seem astonishing to people living in other countries?

© Doranne Jacobson/International Images

 Can you think of ways in which a religious organization that began as a cult becomes a church? What has to change?

Religion in History

Like other social institutions, religion shows marked variation according to time and place. Let us look at several ways in which religion has changed over the course of history.

Animism is widespread among Native Americans, who live respectfully within the natural world on which they depend for their survival. These Aleuts live in Eklutna, a village north of Anchorage, Alaska, which has been inhabited by people with much the same way of life for almost 500 years. Animists see a divine force present not only in themselves but in everything around them.

Ian Berry/Magnum Photos, Inc.

Religion in Preindustrial Societies

Early hunters and gatherers practiced **animism** (from a Latin word meaning "breath of life"), *the belief that elements of the natural world are conscious life forms that affect humanity.* Animists view forests, oceans, mountains, and even the wind as spiritual forces. Many Native American societies are animistic, which explains their reverence for the natural environment.

Belief in a single divine power responsible for creating the world began with pastoral and horticultural societies, which first appeared 10,000 to 12,000 years ago. The conception of God as a "shepherd" arose because Christianity, Judaism, and Islam had their beginnings among pastoral peoples.

Religion becomes more important in agrarian societies, which develop a specialized priesthood in charge of religious organizations. The central role of religion is seen in the huge cathedrals that dominated the towns of medieval Europe.

Religion in Industrial Societies

The Industrial Revolution introduced a growing emphasis on science. More and more, people looked to doctors and scientists for the knowledge and comfort they used to get from priests. But religion persists in industrial societies because science is powerless to address issues of ultimate meaning in human life. In other words, learning *how* the world works is a matter for scientists, but *why* we and the rest of the universe exist at all is a question of faith.

World Religions

The diversity of religions in the world is almost as wide-ranging as the diversity of culture itself. Many of the thousands of different religions are found in just one place and have few followers. But there are a number of *world religions,* which are widely known and have millions of adherents. We shall briefly examine six world religions, which together claim at least 4 billion believers—two-thirds of humanity.

Christianity

Christianity is the most widespread religion, with 2 billion followers, almost one-third of the world's people. Most Christians live in Europe or the Americas; more than 85 percent of the people in the United States and Canada identify with Christianity. As shown in Global Map 1, people who think of themselves as Christian represent a large share of the population in many world regions, with the notable exceptions of northern Africa and Asia. European colonization spread Christianity throughout much of the world over the past 500 years. Its dominance in the West is shown by the fact that our calendar numbers years from the birth of Jesus Christ.

As noted earlier, Christianity began as a cult, drawing elements from Judaism, a much older religion. Like many cults, Christianity was built on the personal charisma of a leader, Jesus of Nazareth, who preached a message of personal salvation. Jesus did not directly challenge the political power of his day, the Roman Empire, telling his followers to "render therefore to Caesar things that are Caesar's" (Matthew 22:21). But his message was revolutionary all the same, promising that faith and love would triumph over sin and death.

Christianity is one example of **monotheism,** *belief in a single divine power.* This new religion was quite different from the Roman Empire's traditional **polytheism,** *belief in many gods.* Yet Christianity views the Supreme Being as a sacred Trinity: God the Creator; Jesus Christ, Son of God and Redeemer; and the Holy Spirit, a Christian's personal experience of God's presence.

The claim that Jesus was divine rests on accounts of his final days on Earth. Brought to trial as a threat to established political leaders, Jesus was tried in Jerusalem and sentenced to death by crucifixion, a

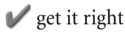 get it right

Make sure you understand the difference between monotheism and polytheism.

 tip

The global maps in this chapter show that specific religions tend be dominant in particular world regions.

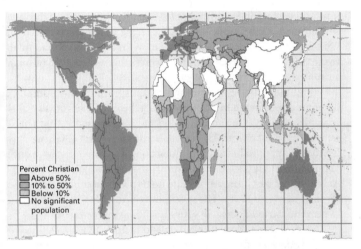

WINDOW ON THE WORLD

GLOBAL MAP 1

Christianity in Global Perspective

Christianity is the dominant religion of Western Europe and became the dominant religion of the Americas. Can you explain this pattern?

Source: *Peters Atlas of the World* (1990).

Percent Christian
- Above 50%
- 10% to 50%
- Below 10%
- No significant population

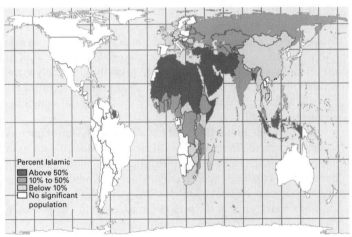

WINDOW ON THE WORLD

GLOBAL MAP 2

Islam in Global Perspective

Islam is the dominant religion of the Middle East, but most of the world's Muslims live in North Africa and Southeast Asia.

Source: *Peters Atlas of the World* (1990).

Percent Islamic
- Above 50%
- 10% to 50%
- Below 10%
- No significant population

common means of execution at the time. This explains why the cross became a sacred Christian symbol. According to Christian belief, three days after his execution, Jesus rose from the dead, revealing that he was the Son of God.

Jesus' followers, especially his twelve closest associates, known as the apostles, spread Christianity throughout the Mediterranean region. At first, the Roman Empire persecuted Christians. But by the fourth century, the empire had adopted Christianity as a state church, the official religion of what became known as the Holy Roman Empire.

Christianity took various forms, including the Roman Catholic Church and the Eastern Orthodox Church, based in Constantinople (now Istanbul, Turkey). Toward the end of the Middle Ages, the

Protestant Reformation in Europe gave rise to hundreds of new denominations. In the United States, dozens of these denominations—the Baptists and Methodists are the two largest—command sizable followings (W. Kaufman, 1976; Jacquet & Jones, 1991).

Islam

Islam has about 1.2 billion followers, which is almost one-fifth of humanity. Followers of Islam are called Muslims. A majority of people in the Middle East are Muslims, so we tend to associate Islam with Arabs in that region of the world. But most of the world's Muslims live elsewhere: Global Map 2 shows that most people in northern Africa

student 2 student

"I'm glad to know more about Islam. I think the more we learn, the better we will understand other people."

and Indonesia are Muslims. In addition, large concentrations of Muslims are found in western Asia in Pakistan, India, Bangladesh, and the southern republics of the former Soviet Union. Because Muslims have a higher birth rate than followers of any other major religion, it is possible that Islam could become the world's dominant religion by the end of this century.

Estimates of the Muslim population of the United States range from 2 to 8 million, making Islam a significant part of our country's religious life. The Muslim population is not only large but quite diverse. It includes Arab Americans and others with Middle Eastern ancestry, Asian Americans, and African Americans (Blank, 1998; Eck, 2001; *Society,* 2004).

Islam is the word of God as revealed to Muhammad, who was born in the city of Mecca (now in Saudi Arabia) about the year 570. To Muslims, Muhammad is a prophet, not a divine being as Jesus is to Christians. The text of the Qur'an (Koran), which is sacred to Muslims, is the word of Allah (Arabic for "God") as transmitted through Muhammad, Allah's messenger. In Arabic, the word *islam* means both "submission" and "peace," and the Qur'an urges submission to Allah as the path to inner peace. Muslims express this personal devotion in a ritual of prayers five times each day.

After the death of Muhammad, Islam spread rapidly. Although divisions arose among Muslims, all accept the Five Pillars of Islam: (1) recognizing Allah as the one, true God and Muhammad as God's messenger; (2) ritual prayer; (3) giving alms to the poor; (4) fasting during the month of Ramadan; and (5) making a pilgrimage at least once in one's life to the Sacred House of Allah in Mecca (Weeks, 1988; El-Attar, 1991). Like Christianity, Islam holds people accountable to God for their deeds on Earth. Those who live obediently will be rewarded in heaven, and evildoers will suffer unending punishment.

Muslims are also required to defend their faith, which has led to calls for holy wars against unbelievers (in roughly the same way that medieval Christians fought in the Crusades). Recent decades have witnessed a rise in militancy and anti-Western feeling in much of the Muslim world, where many people see the United States as both militarily threatening and representing a way of life that they view as materialistic and immoral. Many Westerners—who typically know little about Islam and often stereotype all Muslims in terms of the terrorist actions of a few—respond with confusion and sometimes hostility (Eck, 2001; Ryan, 2001).

Many people in the United States also view Muslim women as socially oppressed. There are differences among Muslim nations in terms of rights given to women: Tunisia allows women far more opportunities than, say, Saudi Arabia, which does not allow women to vote or even drive a car (Ganley, 1998). It is true that many Muslim women lack some of the personal freedoms enjoyed by Muslim men. Yet many—perhaps even most—accept the mandates of their religion and find security in a system that guides the behavior of both women and men (Peterson, 1996). Defenders of Islam also point out that patriarchy was well established in the Middle East long before the birth of Muhammad and that Islam actually improved the social position of women by requiring husbands to deal justly with their wives. For example, Islam permits a man to have up to four wives, but it requires men to have only one wife if having more would cause him to treat any woman unjustly (Qur'an, "The Women," v. 3).

Judaism

In terms of numbers, Judaism's 15 million followers worldwide make it something less than a world religion. Jews make up a majority of the population in only one country—Israel. But Judaism has special

Many religions promote literacy because they demand that followers study sacred texts. As part of their upbringing, most Muslim parents teach their children lessons from the Qur'an; later, the children will do the same for a new generation of believers.

Annie Griffiths Belt/NGS Image Collection

tip

Notice how many world religions contain
denominations.

tip

Hinduism and Buddhism have influenced New
Age spirituality in the United States, as explained
later in this chapter.

importance to the United States because the largest concentration of Jews (6 million people) is found in North America.

Jews look to the past as a source of guidance in the present and for the future. Judaism has deep historical roots that extend 4,000 years before the birth of Christ to the ancient societies of Mesopotamia. At this time, Jews were animistic, but this belief changed after Jacob—grandson of Abraham, the earliest great ancestor—led his people to Egypt.

Jews survived centuries of slavery in Egypt. In the thirteenth century B.C.E., Moses, the adopted son of an Egyptian princess, was called by God to lead the Jews from bondage. This exodus (a word with Latin and Greek roots mean "marching out") from Egypt is remembered by Jews today in the annual ritual of Passover. Once liberated, the Jews became monotheistic, recognizing a single, all-powerful God.

A distinctive concept of Judaism is the *covenant*, a special relationship with God by which the Jews became God's "chosen people." The covenant implies a duty to observe God's law, especially the Ten Commandments as revealed to Moses on Mount Sinai. Jews regard the Old Testament of the Bible as both a record of their history and a statement of the obligations of Jewish life. Of special importance are the Bible's first five books (Genesis, Exodus, Leviticus, Numbers, and Deuteronomy), called the *Torah* (a word meaning "teaching" and "law"). In contrast to Christianity's central concern with personal salvation, Judaism emphasizes moral behavior in this world.

Judaism has three main denominations. Orthodox Jews (including more than 1 million people in the United States) strictly observe traditional beliefs and practices, wear traditional dress, segregate men and women at religious services, and eat only kosher foods (prepared precisely as prescribed in the Torah). Such traditional practices set off Orthodox Jews in the United States from the larger society, making them the most sectlike. In the mid-nineteenth century, many Jews wanted to join in with the larger society, which led to the formation of more churchlike Reform Judaism (now including more than 1.3 million people in this country). A third segment, Conservative Judaism (with about 2 million U.S. adherents), has established a middle ground between the other two denominations.

Whatever the denomination, Jews share a cultural history of oppression as a result of prejudice and discrimination. A collective memory of centuries of slavery in Egypt, conquest by Rome, and persecution in Europe has shaped the Jewish identity. It was Jews in Italy who first lived in an urban ghetto (this word comes from the Italian *borghetto*, meaning "settlement outside of the city walls"), and this residential segregation soon spread to other parts of Europe.

Jewish immigration to the United States began in the mid-1600s. The early immigrants who prospered were assimilated into largely Christian communities. But as great numbers entered the country at the end of the nineteenth century, prejudice and discrimination against Jews—commonly termed *anti-Semitism*—increased. Before and during World War II, anti-Semitism reached a vicious peak as the Nazi regime in Germany systematically annihilated 6 million Jews.

Today, the social standing of Jews is well above average. Still, many Jews are concerned about the future of their religion because in the United States, only half the children growing up in Jewish households are learning Jewish culture and ritual, and more than half marry non-Jews. Others are more optimistic, suggesting that a rising number of "mixed marriages" may attract new people to Judaism (Dershowitz, 1997; Keister, 2003; Goldscheider, 2004).

Hinduism

Hinduism is the oldest of all the world religions, originating in the Indus River valley about 4,500 years ago. Today, there are about 800 million Hindus, which is 12 percent of the world's people. Global Map 3 shows that Hinduism remains an Eastern religion, mostly practiced in India and Pakistan but with a significant presence in southern Africa and Indonesia.

Over the centuries, Hinduism and the culture of India have blended so that now one is not easily described apart from the other (although India also has a sizable Muslim population). This connection also explains why Hinduism, unlike Christianity, Islam, and Judaism, has not diffused widely to other nations. But with 1.5 million followers in the United States, Hinduism is an important part of our country's cultural diversity.

Hinduism differs from most other religions in that it is not linked to the life of any single person. In addition, Hinduism envisions God as a universal moral force rather than a specific entity. For this reason, Hinduism—like other Eastern religions, as you will see shortly—is sometimes described as an "ethical religion." Hindu beliefs and practices vary widely, but all Hindus believe that they have moral responsibilities, called *dharma*. Dharma, for example, calls people to observe the traditional caste system.

Another Hindu principle, *karma*, involves a belief in the spiritual progress of the human soul. To a Hindu, each action has spiritual consequences, and proper living results in moral development. Karma works through *reincarnation*, a cycle of death and rebirth by which a person is born into a spiritual state corresponding to the moral quality of a previous life. Unlike Christianity and Islam, Hinduism recognizes no ultimate judgment at the hands of a supreme god. But in the ongoing cycle of rebirth, it may be said that people get what they

tip
Because of our society's history of immigration, all world religions are found to varying degrees in the United States.

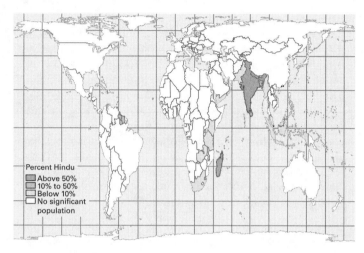

WINDOW ON THE WORLD

GLOBAL MAP 3
Hinduism in Global Perspective

Hinduism is closely linked to the culture of India.
Source: *Peters Atlas of the World* (1990).

Percent Hindu
- Above 50%
- 10% to 50%
- Below 10%
- No significant population

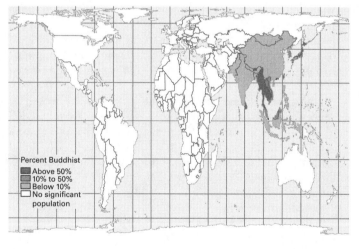

WINDOW ON THE WORLD

GLOBAL MAP 4
Buddhism in Global Perspective

Buddhists represent a large part of the populations of most Asian nations.
Source: *Peters Atlas of the World* (1990).

Percent Buddhist
- Above 50%
- 10% to 50%
- Below 10%
- No significant population

deserve. For those who reach *moksha,* the state of spiritual perfection, the soul has no further need to be reborn.

The case of Hinduism shows that not all religions can be neatly labeled as monotheistic or polytheistic. Hinduism is monotheistic insofar as it views the universe as a single moral system; yet Hindus see this moral force at work in every element of nature. Hindus connect to this moral force through their private meditation and rituals, which vary from village to village across the vast nation of India. Many also participate in public events, such as the *Kumbh Mela,* which every twelve years brings some 20 million pilgrims to bathe in the purifying waters of the sacred Ganges River.

Hinduism is not well understood by most people in the United States, although elements of Hindu thought have entered the New

Age movement discussed later in this chapter. But almost 2 million people in this country claim Asian Indian ancestry, and the number of immigrants from India is rising, which is making Hinduism more and more important in the United States (W. Kaufman, 1976; Larson, 2000; Eck, 2001).

Buddhism

Twenty-five hundred years ago, the rich culture of India gave rise to Buddhism. Today, some 350 million people, or 5 percent of humanity, are Buddhists, and almost all live in Asia. As shown in Global Map 4, Buddhists are a majority of the population in Myanmar (Burma), Thailand, Cambodia, and Japan. Buddhism is also widespread in India and

tip

There is no global map for Confucianism; this religion is in China as well as in communities of Chinese immigrants in other nations.

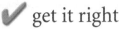 **get it right**

Pay attention to the two main differences between Eastern and Western religions.

the People's Republic of China. Buddhism has much in common with Hinduism: It recognizes no god of judgment, sees each daily action as having spiritual consequences, and believes in reincarnation. But like Christianity, Buddhism has origins in the life of one person.

Siddhartha Gautama was born to a high-caste family in Nepal in 563 B.C.E. Even as a young man, he was deeply spiritual. At the age of twenty-nine, he experienced a personal transformation, which led him to years of travel and meditation. By the end of this journey, he achieved what Buddhists describe as *bodhi,* or enlightenment. By gaining an understanding of the essence of life, Gautama became the Buddha.

Drawn by his personal charisma, followers spread the Buddha's teachings—the *dhamma*—across India. In the third century B.C.E., India's ruler became a Buddhist and sent missionaries throughout Asia, transforming Buddhism into a world religion.

Buddhists believe that much of life in this world involves suffering. This idea is rooted in the Buddha's own travels in a very poor society. But, the Buddha claimed, the solution to suffering is not worldly wealth and power. On the contrary, a concern with worldly things holds back spiritual development. Instead, the Buddha taught that we must use meditation to move beyond selfish concerns and material desires. Only by quieting the mind can people connect with the power of the larger universe—the goal described as *nirvana,* a state of enlightenment and peace (E. J. Thomas, 1975; Van Biema, 1997; Eck, 2001).

The Dalai Lama is the religious and political leader of the Tibetan people and is the best-known Buddhist teacher in the world. He received the Nobel Peace Prize in 1989 for his efforts to liberate his people from Chinese control through nonviolent means.

Geert Vanden Wijngaert/AP Wide World Photos

Confucianism

From about 200 B.C.E. until the beginning of the twentieth century, Confucianism was a state church—the official religion of China. After the 1949 revolution, the communist government of the new People's Republic of China repressed all religious expression. But even today, hundreds of millions of Chinese are still influenced by Confucianism. China is still home to Confucian thought, although Chinese immigration has spread this religion to other nations in Southeast Asia. Perhaps 100,000 followers of Confucius live in North America.

Confucius, whose Chinese name was K'ung-Fu-tzu, lived between 551 and 479 B.C.E. Like the Buddha, Confucius was deeply moved by people's suffering. The Buddha's response was sectlike—a spiritual withdrawal from the world. Confucius took a more churchlike approach, instructing his followers to engage the world according to a code of moral conduct. In the same way that Hinduism became part of the Indian way of life, Confucianism became linked to the traditional culture of China.

A central idea of Confucianism is *jen,* meaning "humaneness." In practice, this means that we must always place moral principle above our self-interest, looking to tradition for guidance in how to live. In the family, Confucius taught, each of us must be loyal and considerate. For their part, families must remember their duties toward the larger community. In this model, layers of moral obligation unite society as a whole.

Of all world religions, Confucianism stands out as lacking a clear sense of the sacred. Perhaps Durkheim would have said that Confucianism is the celebration of the sacred character of society itself. Others might call Confucianism less a religion than a model of disciplined living. However you look at it, Confucianism shares with religion a body of beliefs and practices that seek moral goodness and social harmony (Schmidt, 1980; McGuire, 1987; Ellwood, 2000).

Religion: East and West

You may already have noticed two general differences between the belief systems of Eastern and Western societies. First, religions that arose in the West (Christianity, Islam, Judaism) have a clear focus on

GLOBAL SNAPSHOT

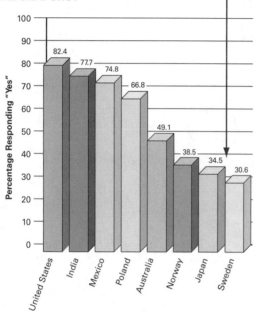

Percentage Responding "Yes"

- United States 82.4
- India 77.7
- Mexico 74.8
- Poland 66.8
- Australia 49.1
- Norway 38.5
- Japan 34.5
- Sweden 30.6

Survey Question: **"Do you gain comfort and strength from religion?"**

FIGURE 1   Religiosity in Global Perspective

Religion is stronger in the United States than in many other nations.
Source: Inglehart et al. (2000).

Religion in the United States

As noted in the opening to this chapter, the United States is one of the most religious of the high-income nations of the world. As Figure 1 shows, eight in ten members of our society say they gain "comfort and strength from religion," a higher share than in most other countries.

That said, scholars debate exactly how religious we are. Some claim that religion remains central to our way of life, but others conclude that a decline of the traditional family and the growing importance of science are weakening religious faith (Greeley, 1989; Woodward, 1992a; Hadaway, Marler, & Chaves, 1993).

Religious Affiliation

National surveys show that about 85 percent of U.S. adults identify with a religion (NORC, 2005:169). Table 1 shows that more than 52 percent of U.S. adults consider themselves Protestants, 23 percent are Catholics, and 2 percent say they are Jewish. Large numbers of people follow dozens of other religions, from animism to Zen Buddhism, making our society the most religiously diverse on Earth (Eck, 2001).

About 90 percent of U.S. adults report that they had at least some formal religious instruction when growing up, and 60 percent say they belong to a religious organization (NORC, 2005:4405). National Map 1 shows the share of people who claim to belong to any church across the United States.

National Map 2 goes a step further, showing that the religion most people identify with varies by region. New England and the Southwest are mostly Catholic, the South is mostly Baptist, and in the northern Plains states, Lutherans predominate. In and around Utah, most people belong to the Church of Jesus Christ of Latter-Day Saints, whose followers are more commonly known as Mormons.

Religiosity

Religiosity is *the importance of religion in a person's life.* However, exactly how religious we are depends on how we operationalize this concept. For example, 86 percent of U.S. adults claim to believe in a divine power, although just 60 percent claim that they "know that God exists and have no doubts about it" (NORC, 2005:442). Fifty-six percent of adults say they pray at least once a day, but just 30 percent report attending religious services on a weekly or almost weekly basis (NORC, 2005:171, 179).

Clearly, the question "How religious are we?" has no easy answer, and it is likely that many people in the United States claim to be more religious than they really are. Although most people in the United States say they are at least somewhat religious, probably no more than about one-third actually are. Religiosity also varies among denominations. Members of sects are the most religious of all, followed by

God as a distinct entity. Eastern religions (Hinduism, Buddhism, Confucianism), however, see divine power in everything, so that these religions make little distinction between the sacred and the profane and seem more like ethical codes for living.

Second, followers of Western religions form congregations, worshiping together in a special place at a regular time. Followers of Eastern religions, by contrast, express their religion anywhere and everywhere in their daily lives. Religious temples do exist, but they are used by individuals as part of their daily routines rather than by groups according to a rigid schedule. This is why visitors to a country like Japan are as likely to find temples there filled with tourists as with worshipers.

Despite these two differences, however, all religions have a common element: a call to move beyond selfish, everyday concerns in pursuit of a higher moral purpose. Religions may take different paths to this goal, but they all encourage a spiritual sense that there is more to life than what we see around us.

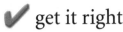

get it right

Class, ethnicity, and race affect religion as they affect many other social patterns.

Catholics and then "mainstream" Protestant denominations such as Episcopalians, Methodists, and Presbyterians. In general, older people are more religious than younger people, and women are more religious than men (Hadaway, Marler, & Chaves, 1993; Sherkat & Ellison, 1999; Miller & Stark, 2002).

What difference does being more religious make? Researchers have linked a number of social patterns to strong religious beliefs, including low rates of delinquency among young people and low rates of divorce among adults. According to one study, religiosity helps unite children, parents, and local communities in ways that benefit young people, enhancing their educational achievement (Muller & Ellison, 2001).

 Do you think our society would be better off if more people were religious? Or would it be worse off? Explain your answer.

Religion: Class, Ethnicity, and Race

Religious affiliation is related to a number of other factors, including social class, ethnicity, and race.

Social Class

A study of *Who's Who in America*, which profiles U.S. high achievers, showed that 33 percent of the people who gave a religious affiliation were Episcopalians, Presbyterians, and United Church of Christ members, denominations that together account for less than 10 percent of the population. Jews, too, enjoy high social position, with this 2 percent of the population accounting for 12 percent of the listings in *Who's Who*.

Research shows that other denominations, including Congregationalists, Methodists, and Catholics, have moderate social standing. Lower social standing is typical of Baptists, Lutherans, and members of sects. Of course, there is considerable variation within all denominations (Davidson, Pyle, & Reyes, 1995; Waters, Heath, & Watson, 1995; Keister, 2003).

Ethnicity

Throughout the world, religion is tied to ethnicity, mostly because one religion stands out in a single nation or geographic region. Islam predominates in the Arab societies of the Middle East, Hinduism is fused with the culture of India, and Confucianism runs deep in Chinese society. Christianity and Judaism do not follow this pattern; although these religions are mostly Western, Christians and Jews are found all over the world.

Religion and national identity are joined in the United States as well. For example, we have Anglo-Saxon Protestants, Irish Catholics,

Table 1	Religious Identification in the United States, 2004
Religion	**Percentage of Respondents Indicating a Preference**
Protestant denominations	**52.7%**
Baptist	17.7
Methodist	6.8
Lutheran	4.5
Presbyterian	2.4
Episcopalian	2.1
All others or no denomination	19.2
Catholic	**23.3**
Jewish	**2.0**
Other or no answer	**7.6**
No religious preference	**14.3**

Source: *General Social Surveys, 1972–2004: Cumulative Codebook* (Chicago: National Opinion Research Center, 2005), pp. 169–70.

Russian Jews, and people of Greek Orthodox heritage. This linking of nation and creed results from the influx of immigrants from nations with a single major religion. Still, nearly every ethnic category displays some religious diversity. For example, people of English ancestry may be Protestants, Roman Catholics, Jews, Hindus, Muslims, or followers of other religions.

Race

Scholars claim that the church is both the oldest and the most important social institution in the African American community. Transported to the Western Hemisphere in slave ships, most Africans became Christians, the dominant religion in the Americas, but they blended Christian belief with elements of African religions. Guided by this religious mix, African American Christians have developed rituals that seem, by European standards, far more spontaneous and emotional (Frazier, 1965; Paris, 2000; McRoberts, 2003).

When African Americans started moving from the rural South to the industrial cities of the North around 1940, the church played a major role in addressing the problems of dislocation, poverty, and prejudice (Pattillo-McCoy, 1998). Black churches have also provided an important avenue of achievement for talented men and women. Ralph Abernathy, Martin Luther King Jr., and Jesse Jackson have all achieved world recognition for their work as religious leaders.

Recent years have witnessed an increasing number of non-Christian African Americans, especially in large U.S. cities. Among

tip

The United States is religiously diverse, but because certain religions predominate in particular regions of the country, most people do not experience the full range of this diversity in their everyday lives.

 tip

Secularization is one example of Weber's historical process of rationalization.

SEEING OURSELVES

NATIONAL MAP 1
Religious Membership across the United States

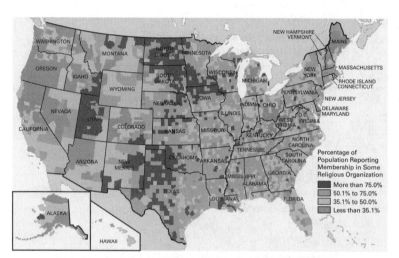

In general, people in the United States are more religious than people in other high-income nations. Yet membership in a religious organization is more common in some parts of the country than in others. What pattern do you see in the map? Can you explain the pattern?

Source: Glenmary Research Center (2002).

NATIONAL MAP 2
Religious Diversity across the United States

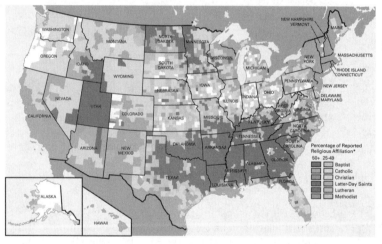

In most counties, at least 25 percent of people who report having an affiliation are members of the same religious organization. So although the United States is religiously diverse at the national level, most people live in communities where one denomination predominates. What historical facts might account for this pattern?

*When two or more churches have 25 to 49 percent of the membership in a county, the largest is shown. When no church has 25 percent of the membership, that county is left blank.

Source: Glenmary Research Center (2002).

them, the most common non-Christian religion is Islam, with an estimated 1 million African American followers (Paris, 2000).

Religion in a Changing Society

June 4, Ticonderoga, New York. Our summer church is small—maybe forty people attend on a typical Sunday. These days, Ed Keller says, it's tough for churches to survive with kids' sports teams scheduling practices and games on Sunday morning, Wal-Mart and the other discount stores open for shopping, and many dog-tired people taking advantage of the chance to sleep a little later. Ed thinks that our modern world sometimes seems less than "church-friendly."

All social institutions evolve over time. Just as the economy, politics, and the family have changed over the course of the past century, so has our society's religious life.

Secularization

Secularization is *the historical decline in the importance of the supernatural and the sacred.* Secularization (from a Latin word for "worldly," meaning literally "of the present age") is commonly associated with modern, technologically advanced societies in which science is the major way of understanding.

468   RELIGION

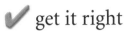 get it right

Be sure you understand why some people support, and other people oppose, secularization.

Today, we are more likely to experience the transitions of birth, illness, and death in the presence of physicians (people with scientific knowledge) than in the company of religious leaders (whose knowledge is based on faith). This shift alone suggests that religion's relevance to our everyday lives has declined. Harvey Cox explains:

> The world looks less and less to religious rules and rituals for its morality or its meanings. For some, religion provides a hobby, for others a mark of national or ethnic identification, for still others an aesthetic delight. For fewer and fewer does it provide an inclusive and commanding system of personal and cosmic values and explanations. (1971:3)

If Cox is right, should we expect religion to disappear someday? Most sociologists say no. The vast majority of people in the United States still say they believe in God, and more people claim to pray each day than vote in national elections. In addition, religious affiliation today is actually proportionately higher than it was in 1850. And one of the most watched movies in recent years was Mel Gibson's *Passion of the Christ*, which portrayed the final days leading up to the crucifixion of Jesus.

Our society does not seem to be on the road to secularization. It is true that some dimensions of religiosity (such as belief in life after death) have declined, but others (such as religious affiliation) have increased. Similarly, some religious organizations have lost members, but others find their membership increasing. Among college students, as Figure 2 shows, the share of first-year students saying they have no religious preference has gone up, more than doubling between 1980 and 2006 (a trend mirrored in the larger adult population). But this share is still just a minority. Putting all this together, the claim that religion is declining in this country may be off the mark (Gorski, 2000; Stark & Finke, 2000; Hout & Fischer, 2002; Marwell & Demerath, 2003; Pryor et al., 2006).

Few doubt that religious patterns are changing, but people disagree about what is good or bad. Conservatives tend to see any weakening of religion as a mark of moral decline. Progressives view secularization as liberation from the all-encompassing beliefs of the past, giving people more choice about what to believe. Secularization has also helped bring some practices of many religious organizations, such as ordaining only men, into line with widespread social attitudes that support greater gender equality.

An important event that helped spark the secularization debate took place in 1963, when the U.S. Supreme Court banned prayer in public schools as a violation of the constitutional separation of church and state. In recent years, however, religion has returned to many public schools—the Seeing Sociology in Everyday Life box takes a closer look at this trend.

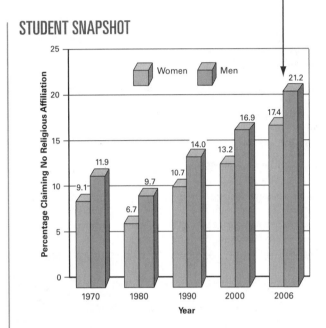

Fewer than one-quarter of women and men on U.S. campuses claim no religious affiliation.

STUDENT SNAPSHOT

FIGURE 2 Religious Nonaffiliation among First-Year College Students, 1970–2006

The share of students claiming no religious affiliation has risen in recent decades.

Sources: Astin et al. (2002) and Pryor et al. (2006).

According to the secularization thesis, religion should weaken in high-income nations as people enjoy higher living standards and greater security. A global perspective shows that this thesis holds for the countries of Western Europe, where most measures of religiosity have declined and are now low. But the United States—the richest country of all—is an exception; religion remains quite strong in our country and perhaps is even getting stronger.

 Do you think the rise of fundamentalist Islam in some of the world challenges the secularization thesis? Why or why not?

Civil Religion

One expression of secularization in the world is the rise of what the sociologist Robert Bellah (1975) calls **civil religion**, *a quasi-religious loyalty binding individuals in a basically secular society*. In other words,

Seeing Sociology in Everyday Life
Should Students Pray in School?

It is late afternoon on a cloudy spring day in Minneapolis, and two dozen teenagers have come together to pray. They share warm smiles as they enter the room. As soon as everyone is seated, the prayers begin, with one voice following another. One girl prays for her brother; a boy prays for the success of an upcoming food drive; another asks God to comfort a favorite teacher who is having a hard time. Then they join their voices to pray for all the teachers at their school who are not Christians. Following the prayers, the young people sing Christian songs, discuss a Scripture lesson, and bring their meeting to a close with a group hug (Van Biema, 1998, 1999).

What is so unusual about this prayer meeting is that it is taking place in Room 133 of Patrick Henry High School, a public institution. In public schools from coast to coast, something of a religious revival is taking place as more and more students hold meetings like this one.

You would have to be at least fifty years old to remember when it was routine for public school students to start the day with Bible reading and prayer. In 1963, the Supreme Court ruled that religion in the schools violated the separation of church and state set by the U.S. Constitution, making any religious activity in a public school illegal. But from the

moment the ruling was announced, critics charged that by supporting a wide range of other activities and clubs while banning any religious activity, schools were really being *antireligious*. In 1990, the Supreme Court handed down a new ruling, stating that religious groups can meet on school property as long as group membership is voluntary, the meetings are held outside regular class hours, and students rather than adults run them.

Although some U.S. colleges and universities are operated by religious organizations, most offer a secular education. At secular schools, do you think religious groups should be treated the same in terms of funding as any other groups? Why or why not?

In recent years, student religious groups have formed in perhaps one-fourth of all public schools. Evangelical Christian organizations such as First Priority and National Network of Youth are using the Internet as well as word of mouth in an effort to expand the place of religion in every public school across the country. However, opponents of school prayer worry that religious enthusiasm may lead some students to pressure others to join their groups. Such disagreements ensure that the debate over prayer in school will continue.

WHAT DO YOU THINK?

1. Do you think that religious clubs should have the same freedom to operate on school grounds as other organizations? Why or why not?

2. The writers of our Constitution stated in the First Amendment that Congress should not establish any official religion and should also pass no law that would interfere with the free practice of religion. How do you think this amendment applies to the issue of prayer in school?

3. Schools support mental and physical development of students, but should they support spiritual development? If you were a member of the local school board, what would be your position on the place of religion in public schools?

formal religion may lose power, but citizenship takes on religious qualities. Most people in the United States consider our way of life a force for moral good in the world. Many people also find religious qualities in political movements, whether liberal or conservative (Williams & Demerath, 1991).

Civil religion also involves a range of rituals, from singing the national anthem at sporting events to waving the flag at public parades. At all such events, the U.S. flag serves as a sacred symbol of our national identity, and we expect people to treat it with respect.

"New Age" Seekers: Spirituality Without Formal Religion

December 29, Machu Picchu, Peru. We are ending the first day exploring this magnificent city built by the Inca people high in the Andes Mountains. Lucas, a local shaman, or religious leader, is leading a group of twelve travelers in a ceremony of thanks. He kneels on the dirt floor of the small stone building and places

offerings—corn and beans, sugar, plants of all colors, and even bits of gold and silver—in front of him as gifts to Mother Earth as he prays for harmony, joy, and the will to do good for one another. His words and the magical setting make the ceremony a very powerful experience.

In recent decades, an increasing number of people are seeking spiritual development outside of established religious organizations. This trend has led some analysts to conclude that the United States is becoming a *postdenomination society.* In simple terms, more people seem to be spiritual seekers, believing in a vital spiritual dimension to human existence that they pursue more or less separately from membership in any formal denomination.

What exactly is the difference between this so-called New Age focus on spirituality and a traditional concern with religion? As one analysis (Cimino & Lattin, 1999:62) puts it:

> [Spirituality] is the search for . . . a religion of the heart, not the head. It's a religious expression that downplays doctrine and dogma, and revels in direct experience of the divine—whether it's called the "holy spirit" or "divine consciousness" or "true self." It's practical and personal, more about stress reduction than salvation, more therapeutic than theological. It's about feeling good rather than being good. It's as much about the body as the soul.

Millions of people in the United States take part in New Age spirituality. Hank Wesselman (2001:39–42), an anthropologist and spiritual teacher, identifies five core values that define this approach:

1. **Seekers believe in a higher power.** There exists a higher power, a vital force that is within all things and all people. Humans, then, are partly divine.

2. **Seekers believe we're all connected.** Everything and everyone is interconnected as part of a universal divine pattern.

3. **Seekers believe in a spirit world.** The physical world is not all there is; a more important spiritual reality (or "spirit world") also exists.

4. **Seekers want to experience the spirit world.** Spiritual development means gaining the ability to experience the spirit world. Many seekers come to understand that helpers and teachers who dwell in the spirit world can and do touch their lives.

5. **Seekers pursue transcendence.** Various techniques (such as yoga, meditation, and prayer) give people an increasing ability to rise above the immediate physical world (the experience of "transcendence"), which is seen as the larger purpose of life.

New Age "seekers" are people in pursuit of spiritual growth, often using the age-old technique of meditation. The goal of this activity is to quiet the mind so that by moving away from everyday concerns, one can hear an inner, divine voice. Countless people attest to the spiritual value of meditation; it has also been linked to improved physical health.

Philip North-Coombes/Getty Images Inc.—Stone Allstock

From a traditional point of view, this New Age spirituality may seem more like psychology than religion. Yet it is an important new form of religious expression in the modern world, one that is increasing the religious involvement of many highly educated people (Tucker, 2002; Wuthnow, 2003).

Can you see elements of both Western and Eastern religions in New Age spirituality? Explain.

Religious Revival: "Good Old-Time Religion"

At the same time as New Age spirituality is becoming more popular, a great deal of change has been going on in the world of organized religion. In the United States, membership in liberal mainstream denominations such as Episcopalian and Presbyterian has dropped by almost 50 percent since 1960. During the same period, affiliation with more conservative religious organizations (including the Mormons, the Seventh-Day Adventists, and especially Christian sects) has risen just as fast.

tip
Fundamentalism tends to oppose secularization.

tip
Fundamentalism is more likely to be found in
Western religions than in Eastern religions.

In this outstanding example of U.S. folk art, Anna Bell Lee Washington's
Baptism 3 (1924) depicts the life-changing experience by which many people
enter the Christian faith.

Anna Belle Lee Washington/SuperStock, Inc.

These opposing trends suggest that secularization may be self-
limiting: As many churchlike organizations become more worldly,
many people leave them in favor of more sectlike communities offering a more intense religious experience (Stark & Bainbridge, 1981;
Jacquet & Jones, 1991; Iannaccone, 1994; Hout, Greeley, & Wilde,
2001).

Religious Fundamentalism

Fundamentalism is *a conservative religious doctrine that opposes intellectualism and worldly accommodation in favor of restoring traditional,
otherworldly religion.* In the United States, fundamentalism has made
the greatest gains among Protestants. Southern Baptists, for example, are the largest religious community in the country. But fundamentalist groups have also grown among Roman Catholics, Jews, and
Muslims.

In response to what they see as the growing influence of science
and the weakening of the conventional family, religious fundamentalists defend what they call "traditional values." As they see it, liberal
churches are simply too open to compromise and change. Religious
fundamentalism is distinctive in five ways (Hunter, 1983, 1985, 1987):

1. **Fundamentalists take the words of sacred texts literally.**
   Fundamentalists insist on a literal reading of sacred texts such

as the Bible to counter what they see as excessive intellectualism among more liberal religious organizations. For example,
fundamentalist Christians believe that God created the world
in seven days precisely as described in the biblical book of
Genesis.

2. **Fundamentalists reject religious pluralism.** Fundamentalists
   believe that tolerance and relativism water down personal
   faith. Therefore, they maintain that their religious beliefs are
   true and other beliefs are not.

3. **Fundamentalists pursue the personal experience of God's
   presence.** In contrast to the worldliness and intellectualism of
   other religious organizations, fundamentalism seeks a return
   to "good old-time religion" and spiritual revival. To fundamentalist Christians, being "born again" and having a personal
   relationship with Jesus Christ should be evident in a person's
   everyday life.

4. **Fundamentalists oppose "secular humanism."** Fundamentalists think accommodation to the changing world weakens
   religious faith. They reject "secular humanism," our society's
   tendency to look to scientific experts rather than God for
   guidance about how to live. There is nothing new in this
   tension between science and religion; it has existed for
   several centuries, as the Controversy & Debate box explains.

5. **Many fundamentalists endorse conservative political goals.**
   Although fundamentalism tends to back away from worldly
   concerns, some fundamentalist leaders (including Ralph Reed,
   Pat Robertson, and Gary Bauer) have entered politics to
   oppose what they call the "liberal agenda," including feminism
   and gay rights. Fundamentalists oppose abortion and gay marriage; they support the traditional two-parent family, seek a
   return of prayer in schools, and criticize the mass media for
   coloring stories with a liberal bias (Manza & Brooks, 1997;
   Thomma, 1997; Rozell, Wilcox, & Green, 1998).

Opponents regard fundamentalism as rigid and self-righteous.
But many find in fundamentalism, with its greater religious certainty
and emphasis on the emotional experience of God's presence, an
appealing alternative to the more intellectual, tolerant, and worldly
"mainstream" denominations (Marquand, 1997).

Which religions are fundamentalist? In recent years, the world
has become familiar with an extreme form of fundamentalist Islam
that supports violence directed against Western culture. In the United
States, the term is most correctly applied to conservative Christian
organizations in the evangelical tradition, including Pentecostals,
Southern Baptists, Seventh-Day Adventists, and Assemblies of God.

✔ get it right

The debate over science and religion arises in part from not realizing that the two approaches look at different levels of existence. Science is focused on the profane and concerned with patterns of everyday life. Religion is focused on the sacred and concerned with questions of ultimate meaning and purpose.

 tip

Reading the box below, notice how the tension between religion and science has existed for centuries.

Controversy & Debate
Does Science Threaten Religion?

CIHAN: I think someday science will prove religion to be false.

RASHEED: I don't think science and religion are talking about the same thing at all.

About 400 years ago, the Italian physicist and astronomer Galileo (1564–1642) helped launch the Scientific Revolution with a series of startling discoveries. Dropping objects from the Leaning Tower of Pisa, he discovered some of the laws of gravity; making his own telescope, he observed the stars and found that Earth orbited the sun, not the other way around.

For his trouble, Galileo was challenged by the Roman Catholic Church, which had preached for centuries that Earth stood motionless at the center of the universe. Galileo only made matters worse by responding that religious leaders had no business talking about matters of science. Before long, he found his work banned and himself under house arrest.

As Galileo's treatment shows, right from the start, science has had an uneasy relationship with religion. In the twentieth century, the two clashed again over the issue of creation. Charles Darwin's masterwork, *On the Origin of Species,* states that humanity evolved from lower forms of life over a billion years. Yet this theory seems to fly in the face of the biblical account of creation found in Genesis, which states that "God created the heavens and the earth," introducing life on the third day and, on the fifth and sixth days, animal life, including human beings fashioned in God's own image.

Galileo would certainly have been an eager observer of the famous "Scopes monkey trial." In 1925, the state of Tennessee put a small-town science teacher named John Thomas Scopes on trial for teaching Darwinian evolution in the local high school. State law forbade teaching

"any theory that denies the story of the Divine Creation of man as taught in the Bible" and especially the idea that "man descended from a lower order of animals." Scopes was found guilty and fined $100. His conviction was reversed on appeal, so the case never reached the U.S. Supreme Court, and the Tennessee law stayed on the books until 1967. A year later, the Supreme Court, in *Epperson* v. *Arkansas*, struck down all such laws as unconstitutional government support of religion.

Today—almost four centuries after Galileo was silenced—many people still debate the apparently conflicting claims of science and religion. A third of U.S. adults believe that the Bible is the literal word of God, and many of them reject any scientific findings that run counter to it (NORC, 2005:198). In 2005, all eight members of the school board in Dover, Pennsylvania, were voted out of office after they took a stand that many townspeople saw as weakening the teaching of evolution; at the same time, the Kansas state school board ordered the teaching of evolution to include its weaknesses and limitations from a religious point of view ("Much Ado about Evolution," 2005).

But a middle ground is emerging: Half of U.S. adults (and also many church leaders) say the Bible is a book of truths inspired by God without being correct in a literal, scientific sense. That is, science and religion are two different ways of understanding that

answer different questions. Both Galileo and Darwin devoted their lives to investigating *how* the natural world works. Yet only religion can address *why* we and the natural world exist in the first place.

This basic difference between science and religion helps explain why our nation is both the most scientific and the most religious in the world. As one scientist noted, the mathematical odds that a cosmic "big bang" 12 billion years ago created the universe and led to the formation of life as we know it are even smaller than the chance of winning a state lottery twenty weeks in a row. Doesn't such a scientific fact suggest an intelligent and purposeful power in our creation? Can't a person be a religious believer and at the same time a scientific investigator?

In 1992, a Vatican commission concluded that the church's silencing of Galileo was wrong. Today, most scientific and religious leaders agree that science and religion represent important but different truths. Many also believe that in today's rush to scientific discovery, our world has never been more in need of the moral guidance provided by religion.

WHAT DO YOU THINK?

1. Why do you think some scientific people reject religious accounts of human creation? Why do some religious people reject scientific accounts?

2. Does the sociological study of religion challenge anyone's faith? Why or why not?

3. About half of U.S. adults think science is changing our way of life too fast. Do you agree? Why or why not?

Sources: Gould (1981), Huchingson (1994), and Applebome (1996).

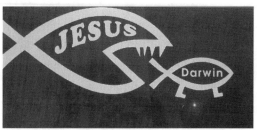 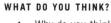 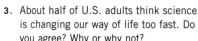

tip

The Applying Sociology in Everyday Life items provide additional ways for you to connect the ideas found in this chapter with your own life.

Several national religious movements, including Promise Keepers (a men's organization) and Chosen Women, have a fundamentalist orientation. In national surveys, 30 percent of U.S. adults describe their religious upbringing as "fundamentalist," 42 percent claim a "moderate" upbringing, and 25 percent, a "liberal" background (NORC, 2005:190).

The Electronic Church

In contrast to local congregations of years past, some religious organizations, especially fundamentalist ones, have become electronic churches featuring "prime-time preachers" (Hadden & Swain, 1981). Electronic religion is found only in the United States. It has made Billy Graham, Robert Schuller, and others more famous than all but a few clergy of the past. About 5 percent of the national television audience (some 10 million people) regularly view religious television, and 20 percent (about 40 million) watch or listen to some religious program every week (NORC, 2005:441).

Religion: Looking Ahead

The popularity of media ministries, the growth of fundamentalism, new forms of spiritualism, and the connection of millions of people to mainstream churches show that religion will remain a major part of modern society for decades to come. High levels of immigration from many religious countries (in Latin America and elsewhere) should intensify as well as diversify the religious character of U.S. society in the twenty-first century (Yang & Ebaugh, 2001).

The world is becoming more complex, and change seems to move more rapidly than our ability to make sense of it all. But rather than weakening religion, this process fires the religious imagination. As new technology gives us the power to change, extend, and even create life, we are faced with increasingly difficult moral questions. Against this backdrop of uncertainty, it is little wonder that many people look to their faith for guidance and hope.

Applying Sociology in Everyday Life

1. Some colleges are very religious; others are very secular. Investigate the place of religion on your campus. Is your school affiliated with a religious organization? Was it ever? Is there a chaplain or other religious official? See if you can learn from campus sources what share of students regularly attend a religious service.

2. Develop five questions that might be used on a questionnaire or in an interview to measure how religious people are. Present them to several people. Use the results to show that how religious people appear to be depends on exactly what questions you ask them.

3. Is religion getting weaker? To evaluate the claim that our society is undergoing secularization, go to the library or local newspaper office and obtain an issue of your local newspaper published fifty years ago and, if possible, one published 100 years ago. Compare the amount of attention given to religious issues then and now. What pattern do you see?

MAKING THE GRADE

Religion

Religion: Basic Concepts

- **RELIGION** is a major social institution based on setting the *sacred* apart from the *profane*.
- Religion is grounded in *faith* rather than scientific evidence, and people express their religious beliefs through various rituals.

 Sociologists study how religion is linked to other social patterns but make no claims about the truth of any religious belief.

profane included as an ordinary element of everyday life

sacred set apart as extraordinary, inspiring awe and reverence

religion a social institution involving beliefs and practices based on recognizing the sacred

ritual formal, ceremonial behavior

faith belief based on conviction rather than on scientific evidence

Theoretical Analysis of Religion

The **STRUCTURAL-FUNCTIONAL APPROACH** desribes how people celebrate the power of society through religion. Emile Durkheim identified three major functions of religion:

- Religion unites people, promoting social cohesion.
- Religion encourages people to obey cultural norms, promoting conformity.
- Religion gives meaning and purpose to life.

The **SYMBOLIC-INTERACTION APPROACH** explains that people use religion to give everyday life sacred meaning.

- People create rituals that separate the sacred from the profane.
- Peter Berger claimed that people are especially likely to seek religious meaning when faced with life's uncertainties and disruptions.

The **SOCIAL-CONFLICT APPROACH** highlights religion's support of social inequality.

- Karl Marx claimed that religion justifies the status quo and diverts people's attention from social injustice.
- In this way, religion discourages change toward a more just and equal society.
- Religion is also linked to gender inequality: The world's major religions are all patriarchal.

totem an object in the natural world collectively defined as sacred

⊞ See the Applying Theory table in this chapter.

Religion and Social Change

- Max Weber argued, in opposition to Marx, that religion can encourage social change. He showed how Calvinism became "disenchanted," leading to a profane "Protestant work ethic" that contributed to the rise of industrial capitalism.
- **LIBERATION THEOLOGY**, a fusion of Christian principles and political activism, tries to encourage social change.

liberation theology the combining of Christian principles with political activism, often Marxist in character

Types of Religious Organizations

CHURCHES are religious organizations well integrated into their society. Churches fall into two categories: state churches (examples: the Anglican Church in England and Islam in Morocco), and denominations (examples: Christian denominations such as Baptists and Lutherans, as well as various categories of Judaism, Islam, and other traditions).

SECTS are the result of religious division. They are marked by charismatic leadership and members' suspicion of the larger society.

CULTS are religious organizations based on new and unconventional beliefs and practices.

church a type of religious organization that is well integrated into the larger society

state church a church formally allied with the state

denomination a church, independent of the state, that recognizes religious pluralism

sect a type of religious organization that stands apart from the larger society

charisma extraordinary personal qualities that can infuse people with emotion and turn them into followers

cult a religious organization that is largely outside a society's cultural traditions

Sociologists categorize religious organizations in the United States along a continuum, with churches at one end and sects at the other.

Churches ⟵	⟶ Sects
try to appeal to everyone	hold rigid religious convictions
have a highly formal style of worship	have a spontaneous and emotional style of worship
formally train and ordain leaders	follow highly charismatic leaders
are long-established and organizationally stable	form as breakaway groups and are less stable
attract members of high social standing	attract members who are social outsiders

RELIGION

MAKING THE GRADE *continued . . .*

Religion in History

- Hunting and gathering societies practiced *animism*, viewing elements of the natural world as spiritual forces.
- Belief in a single divine power began in pastoral and horticultural societies.
- Organized religion gained importance in agrarian societies.
- In industrial societies, scientific knowledge explains *how* the world works, but people look to religion to answer questions about *why* the world exists.

animism the belief that elements of the natural world are conscious life forms that affect humanity

World Religions

WESTERN RELIGIONS

CHRISTIANITY
- Christianity is the most widespread religion, with 2 billion followers—almost one-third of the world's people.
- Christianity began as a cult built on the personal charisma of Jesus of Nazareth; Christians believe Jesus is the Son of God and follow his teachings.

ISLAM
- Islam has about 1.2 billion followers, who are known as Muslims—almost one-fifth of the world's people.
- Muslims follow the word of God as revealed to the prophet Muhammad and written in the Qur'an, the sacred text of Islam.

JUDAISM
- Judaism's 15 million followers are mainly in Israel and the United States.
- Jewish belief rests on the covenant between God and his chosen people, embodied in the Ten Commandments and the Old Testament of the Bible.

EASTERN RELIGIONS

HINDUISM
- Hinduism is the oldest world religion and today counts about 800 million members.
- Hindus see God as a universal moral force rather than a specific being and believe in the principles of *dharma* (moral responsibilities) and *karma* (the spiritual progress of the human soul).

BUDDHISM
- Buddhists number about 350 million people.
- Buddhist teachings are similar to Hindu beliefs, but Buddhism is based on the life of one person, Siddhartha Gautama, who taught the use of meditation as a way to move beyond selfish desires to achieve *nirvana*, a state of enlightenment and peace.

CONFUCIANISM
- Confucianism was the state church of China until the 1949 communist revolution repressed religious expression. It is still strongly linked to Chinese culture.
- Confucianism teaches *jen*, or "humaneness," meaning that people must place moral principles above self-interest. Layers of moral obligations unite society as a whole.

✔ *Western religions share a focus on God and have well-defined congregations. Eastern religions tend to be ethical codes largely fused with the broader culture.*

Religion in the United States

The United States is one of the most religious and religiously diverse nations. How researchers operationalize "religiosity" affects how "religious" our people seem to be:
- 85% of adults identify with a religion
- 60% profess a firm belief in God and belong to a religious organization
- 56% of adults say they pray at least once a day
- just 30% say they attend religious services weekly

Religious affiliation is tied to *social class*, *ethnicity*, and *race*:
- On average, Episcopalians, Presbyterians, and Jews enjoy high standing; lower social standing is typical of Baptists, Lutherans, and members of sects.
- Religion is often linked to ethnic background because people came to the United States from countries that have a major religion (e.g., most Irish Americans are Catholics).
- Transported to this country in slave ships, most Africans became Christians, but they blended Christian beliefs with elements of African religions they brought with them.

monotheism belief in a single divine power
polytheism belief in many gods

religiosity the importance of religion in a person's life

Religion in a Changing Society

- **SECULARIZATION** is a decline in the importance of the supernatural and sacred.
- In the United States, while some indicators of religiosity (like membership in mainstream churches) have declined, others (such as membership in sects) have increased.
- Today, **CIVIL RELIGION** takes the form of a quasi-religious patriotism that ties people to their society.

- *Spiritual seekers* are part of the "New Age" movement, which pursues spiritual development outside conventional religious organizations.
- **FUNDAMENTALISM** opposes religious accommodation to the world, interprets religious texts literally, and rejects religious diversity.

secularization the historical decline in the importance of the supernatural and the sacred
civil religion a quasi-religious loyalty binding individuals in a basically secular society
fundamentalism a conservative religious doctrine that opposes intellectualism and worldly accommodation in favor of restoring traditional, otherworldly religion

MAKING THE GRADE

Sample Test Questions

These questions are similar to those found in the test bank that accompanies this textbook.

Multiple-Choice Questions

1. What term did Emile Durkheim use to refer to the everyday elements of our lives?
   a. religion
   b. profane
   c. sacred
   d. ritual

2. Faith, or belief in religious matters, is best described as
   a. what we learn from science.
   b. what our senses tell us.
   c. our cultural traditions.
   d. conviction in things unseen.

3. The reason sociologists study religion is to learn
   a. the meaning of life.
   b. whether a particular religion is true or not.
   c. how patterns of religious activity affect society.
   d. which religious organization they wish to join.

4. Which of the following is *not* one of the important functions of religion, according to Durkheim?
   a. generating social conflict
   b. generating social cohesion
   c. providing social control
   d. providing meaning and purpose

5. Peter Berger claims that we are most likely to turn to religion when we experience
   a. social conflict.
   b. the best of times.
   c. familiar, everyday routines.
   d. important events that are out of our control.

6. Which sociologist explained how religion helps support social inequality?
   a. Emile Durkheim
   b. Karl Marx
   c. Max Weber
   d. Ernst Troeltsch

7. Which type of religious organization is most integrated into the larger society?
   a. cult
   b. church
   c. sect
   d. New Age spirituality

8. A sect is a type of religious organization that
   a. has formally trained leaders.
   b. is well integrated into the larger society.
   c. rejects the importance of charisma.
   d. stands apart from the larger society.

9. Which of the following religions is found in the United States?
   a. Islam
   b. Judaism
   c. Christianity
   d. All of the above are correct.

10. The term "secularization" refers to which of the following?
    a. religion becoming more important in people's lives
    b. increasing popularity of fundamentalism
    c. the decline in the importance of religion and the sacred
    d. churches resisting social change

Answers: 1 (b); 2 (d); 3 (c); 4 (a); 5 (d); 6 (b); 7 (b); 8 (d); 9 (d); 10 (c).

Essay Questions

1. What is the basic distinction between the sacred and the profane that underlies all religious belief?
2. In what ways do churches, sects, and cults differ?

Population,
Urbanization,
and Environment

An increasing share of our planet's population lives in cities. Researchers study the differences between rural and urban life, and they also track global population increase and the ways in which human societies are altering the natural environment.

Clark J. Mishler/Mira.com

Population, Urbanization, and Environment

WHY should we worry about the rapid rate of global population increase?

WHAT makes city and rural living different?

HOW is the state of the natural environment a social issue?

Looking for a new place to live after you finish college?
Crosby, North Dakota, would really like you to call it home. The town's officials will do more than welcome you—they will give you a free piece of land on which to build a house. As a bonus, they will throw in a free membership in the local country club.

Ellsworth, Kansas, also wants you. The town leaders will match Crosby's offer of free land and go one better, paying you $1,000 cash toward a down payment on your new home.

Perhaps the best deal of all is found in Plainville, Kansas. In addition to free land, you can forget about property taxes for the next ten years!

Why are these towns so eager to attract new residents? The answer is that they are all in the Great Plains, the central region of the United States extending from North Dakota all the way down to Texas, which has lost much of its population in recent decades. People in Crosby (current population 1,100), Ellsworth (2,500), and Plainville (2,000) are offering these fantastic deals because they are worried that unless there is a turnaround, their towns may disappear like hundreds of other nearby communities already have (Greene, 2005).

All across the Great Plains, towns are hanging on by a thread. This chapter investigates population patterns, explaining why people move from place to place, why some cities get so large, and why small towns sometimes die. It also looks at how population change and our entire way of life affect the physical environment.

Demography: The Study of Population

When humans first began to cultivate plants some 12,000 years ago, Earth's entire *Homo sapiens* population was around 5 million, about the number living in Minnesota today. Very slow growth pushed the global total in 1 C.E. to perhaps 300 million, or about the population of the United States today.

Starting around 1750, world population began to spike upward. We now add more than 74 million people to the planet each year; today, the world holds 6.6 billion people.

The causes and consequences of this drama are the basis of **demography,** *the study of human population.* Demography (from the Greek, meaning "description of people") is a cousin of sociology that analyzes the size and composition of a population and studies how and why people move from place to place. Demographers not only collect statistics but also raise important questions about the effects of population growth and suggest how it might be controlled. The following sections present basic demographic concepts.

Fertility

The study of human population begins with how many people are born. **Fertility** is *the incidence of childbearing in a country's population.* During her childbearing years, from the onset of menstruation (typically in the early teens) to menopause (usually in the late forties), a woman is capable of bearing more than twenty children. But *fecundity,* or maximum possible childbearing, is sharply reduced by cultural norms, finances, and personal choice.

Demographers describe fertility using the **crude birth rate,** *the number of live births in a given year for every 1,000 people in a population.* To calculate a crude birth rate, divide the number of live births in a year by the society's total population, and multiply the result by 1,000. In the United States in 2005, there were 4.1 million live births in a population of 297 million, yielding a crude birth rate of 13.8 (Munson & Sutton, 2006).

January 18, Coshocton County, Ohio. Having just finished the mountains of meat and potatoes that make up a typical Amish meal, we have gathered in the living room of Jacob Raber, a member of this rural Amish community. Mrs. Raber, a mother of four, is telling us about Amish life. "Most of the women I know have five or six children," she says with a smile, "but certainly not everybody—some have eleven or twelve!"

A country's birth rate is described as "crude" because it is based on the entire population, not just women in their childbearing years. In addition, this measure ignores differences between various categories of the population: Fertility among the Amish, for example, is quite high, and fertility among Asian Americans is low. But the crude measure is easy to calculate and allows rough comparisons of the fertility of one country or region in relation to others. Part (a) of Figure 1 shows that on a global scale, the crude birth rate of North America is low.

How do you think low-fertility societies differ from high-fertility societies with respect to (1) age at first marriage, (2) opportunities available to women, and (3) attitudes toward homosexuality? Explain your responses.

Mortality

Population size also reflects **mortality,** *the incidence of death in a country's population.* To measure mortality, demographers use a **crude death rate,** *the number of deaths in a given year for every 1,000 people*

Chapter Overview

This chapter explores three related dimensions of social change—population dynamics, urbanization, and increasing threats to the natural environment.

GLOBAL SNAPSHOT

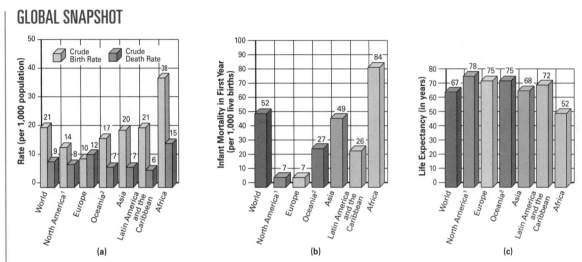

FIGURE 1 (a) Crude Birth Rates and Crude Death Rates, (b) Infant Mortality Rates, and (c) Life Expectancy around the World, 2005

By world standards, North America has low birth and death rates, very low infant mortality rates, and high life expectancy.

[1]United States and Canada.
[2]Australia, New Zealand, and South Pacific Islands.

Source: Population Reference Bureau (2006).

---

in a population. This time, we take the number of deaths in a year, divide by the total population, and multiply the result by 1,000. In 2005, there were 2.4 million deaths in the U.S. population of 297 million, yielding a crude death rate of 8.1 (Munson & Sutton, 2006). Part (a) of Figure 1 shows that this rate is about average.

A third useful demographic measure is the **infant mortality rate,** *the number of deaths among infants under one year of age for each 1,000 live births in a given year.* To compute infant mortality, divide the number of deaths of children under one year of age by the number of live births during the same year, and multiply the result by 1,000. In 2005, there were 28,000 infant deaths and 4.1 million live births in the United States. Dividing the first number by the second and multiplying the result by 1,000 yields an infant mortality rate of 6.8. Part (b) of Figure 22–1 indicates that by world standards, North American infant mortality is low.

But remember differences exist among various categories of people. For example, African Americans, with nearly three times the burden of poverty as whites, have an infant mortality rate of 14.4—more than twice the white rate of 5.8.

Low infant mortality greatly raises **life expectancy,** *the average life span of a country's population.* U.S. males born in 2004 can expect to live 75.2 years, and females can look forward to 80.4 years. As part (c) of Figure 1 shows, life expectancy in North America is 26 years greater than is typical of low-income countries of Africa.

Migration

Population size is also affected by **migration,** *the movement of people into and out of a specified territory.* Movement into a territory, or *immigration,* is measured as an *in-migration rate,* calculated as the number of people entering an area for every 1,000 people in the population. Movement out of a territory, or *emigration,* is measured in terms of an *out-migration rate,* the number leaving for every 1,000 people. Both types of migration usually occur at the same time; the difference between them is the *net migration rate.*

All nations experience internal migration, that is, movement within their borders from one region to another. National Map 1 shows where the U.S. population is moving and the places left behind

Cheryl Richardson, 36, has just moved to Las Vegas to work in the expanding tourism industry, which has boosted the region's population.

Tom and Ellen Posten, in their sixties, live in Wichita County, Kansas; like many other families in the area, their four children have all moved out of the county in search of better jobs.

 get it right

This chapter begins with a number of important terms; be sure you understand *fertility*, typically measured as the crude birth rate, and *mortality*, measured as the crude death rate.

SEEING OURSELVES

NATIONAL MAP 1
Population Change across the United States

This map shows that, since 2000, population has been moving from the heartland of the United States toward the coasts. What do you think is causing this internal migration? What types of people do you think remain in counties that are losing population?

Source: U.S. Census Bureau (2006).

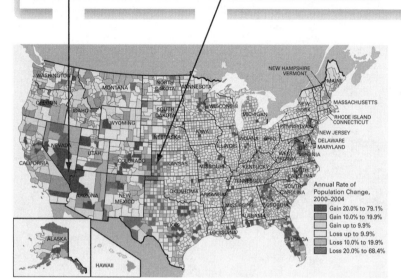

Annual Rate of Population Change, 2000–2004
- Gain 20.0% to 79.1%
- Gain 10.0% to 19.9%
- Gain up to 9.9%
- Loss up to 9.9%
- Loss 10.0% to 19.9%
- Loss 20.0% to 68.4%

(as suggested by the chapter opening, notice the heavy losses in the Plains States in the middle of the country).

Migration is sometimes voluntary, as when people leave a small town and move to a larger city. In such cases, "push-pull" factors are typically at work; a lack of jobs "pushes" people to move, and more opportunity elsewhere "pulls" them to a larger city. Migration can also be involuntary, such as when millions of people fled New Orleans after Hurricane Katrina.

Population Growth

Fertility, mortality, and migration all affect the size of a society's population. In general, rich nations (such as the United States) grow as much from immigration as from natural increase; poorer nations (such as Pakistan) grow almost entirely from natural increase.

To calculate a population's natural growth rate, demographers subtract the crude death rate from the crude birth rate. The natural growth rate of the U.S. population in 2005 was 5.7 per 1,000 (the crude birth rate of 13.8 minus the crude death rate of 8.1), or about 0.6 percent annual growth.

Global Map 1 shows that population growth in the United States and other high-income nations is well below the world average of 1.2 percent. Earth's low-growth continents are Europe (currently posting a slight decline, expressed as a *negative* 0.1 percent annual rate), North America (0.6 percent), and Oceania (1.0 percent). Close to the global average are Asia (1.2 percent) and Latin America (1.5 percent). The highest growth region in the world is Africa (2.3 percent).

A handy rule of thumb for estimating a nation or region's growth is to divide the number 70 by the population growth rate; this yields the *doubling time* in years. Thus an annual growth rate of 2 percent (found in parts of Latin America) doubles a population in thirty-five years, and a 3 percent growth rate (found in some countries in Africa) drops the doubling time to just twenty-three years. The rapid population growth of the poorest countries is deeply troubling because these countries can barely support the populations they have now.

 Saudi Arabia's current population growth rate is 2.7 percent. At this rate, how long will it take the Saudi population to double?

Population Composition

Demographers also study the makeup of a society's population at a given point in time. One variable is the **sex ratio,** *the number of males for every 100 females in a nation's population.* In 2005, the sex ratio in the United States was 96, or 96 males for every 100 females. Sex ratios are usually below 100 because, on average, women outlive men. In India, however, the sex ratio is 106 because many parents value sons more than daughters and may either abort a female fetus or, after birth, give more care to their male children, lowering the female child's chances of survival.

A more complex measure is the **age-sex pyramid,** *a graphic representation of the age and sex of a population.* Figure 2 presents the age-sex pyramids for the populations of the United States and Mexico. Higher mortality with advancing age gives these figures a rough pyramid shape. In the U.S. pyramid, the bulge in the middle reflects high birth rates during the *baby boom* from the mid-1940s to the mid-1960s. The contraction for people in their twenties and thirties reflects

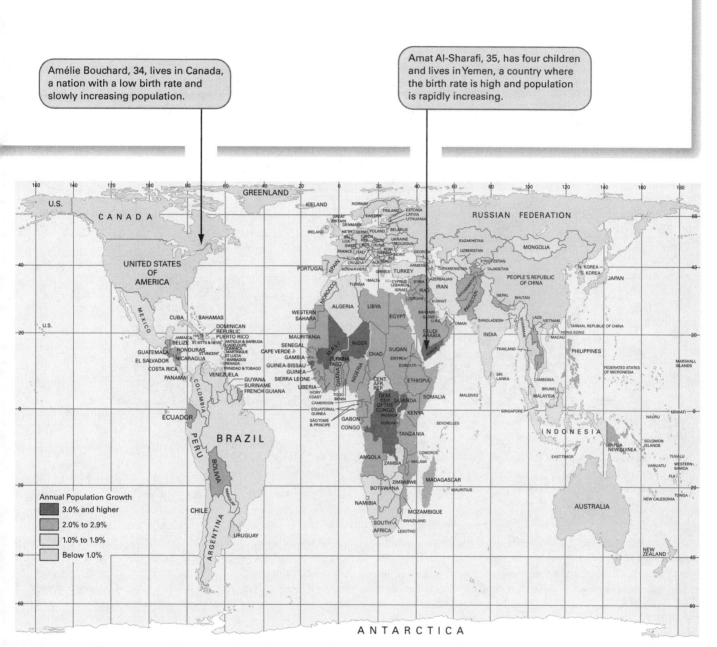

Amélie Bouchard, 34, lives in Canada, a nation with a low birth rate and slowly increasing population.

Amat Al-Sharafi, 35, has four children and lives in Yemen, a country where the birth rate is high and population is rapidly increasing.

Annual Population Growth
- 3.0% and higher
- 2.0% to 2.9%
- 1.0% to 1.9%
- Below 1.0%

WINDOW ON THE WORLD

GLOBAL MAP 1   Population Growth in Global Perspective

The richest countries of the world—including the United States, Canada, and the nations of Europe—have growth rates below 1 percent. The nations of Latin America and Asia typically have growth rates around 1.5 percent, a rate that doubles a population in forty-seven years. Africa has an overall growth rate of 2.3 percent (despite only small increases in countries with a high rate of AIDS), which cuts the doubling time to thirty years. In global perspective, we see that a society's standard of living is closely related to its rate of population growth: Population is rising fastest in the world regions that can least afford to support more people.

Source: Population Reference Bureau (2006); map projection from *Peters Atlas of the World* (1990).

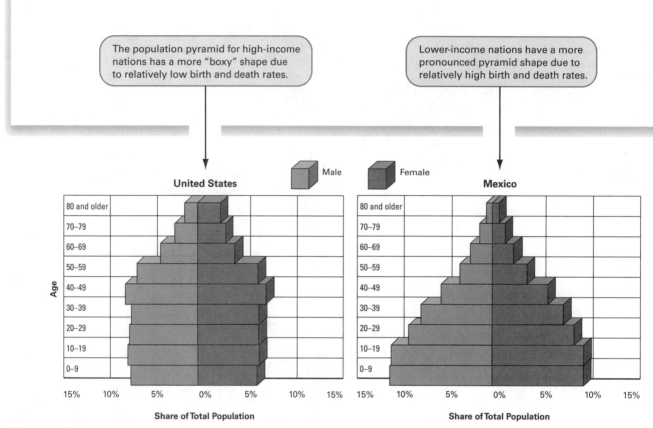

The population pyramid for high-income nations has a more "boxy" shape due to relatively low birth and death rates.

Lower-income nations have a more pronounced pyramid shape due to relatively high birth and death rates.

United States

Male   Female

Mexico

FIGURE 2   Age-Sex Population Pyramids for the United States and Mexico, 2005

By looking at the shape of a country's population pyramid, you can tell its level of economic development and predict future levels of population increase.

Source: U.S. Census Bureau (2007).

the subsequent *baby bust.* The birth rate has continued to decline from its high of 25.3 in 1957 to 13.8 in 2005.

Comparing the U.S. and Mexican age-sex pyramids shows different demographic trends. The age-sex pyramid for Mexico, like that of other lower-income nations, is wide at the bottom (reflecting higher birth rates) and narrows quickly by what we would term middle age (due to higher mortality). In short, Mexico is a much younger society, with a median age of twenty-five, compared to thirty-five in the United States. With a larger share of females still in their childbearing years, Mexico's crude birth rate (22) is nearly twice our own (13.8), and its annual rate of population growth (1.7 percent) is almost three times the U.S. rate (0.6 percent).

History and Theory of Population Growth

In the past, people wanted large families because human labor was the key to productivity. In addition, until rubber condoms were invented 150 years ago, the prevention of pregnancy was uncertain at best. But high death rates from infectious diseases put a constant brake on population growth.

A major demographic shift began about 1750 as the world's population turned upward, reaching the 1 billion mark by 1800. This milestone (which took all of human history to reach) was repeated barely a century later in 1930, when a second billion people were added to the planet. In other words, not only was population increasing, but the *rate* of growth was accelerating. Global population reached 3 billion by 1962 (just thirty-two years later) and 4 billion by 1974 (only twelve years after that). The rate of world population increase has stabilized recently, but our planet passed the 5 billion mark in 1987, the 6 billion mark in 1999, and the 6.5 billion mark in 2006. In no previous century did the world's population even double; in the twentieth century, it *quadrupled.*

Currently, the world is gaining 74 million people each year; 96 percent of this increase is in poor countries. Experts predict that Earth's population will reach between 8 billion and 9 billion by 2050 (O'Neill & Balk, 2001). Given the world's troubles feeding the present population, such an increase is a matter of urgent concern.

Malthusian Theory

The sudden population growth 250 years ago sparked the development of demography. Thomas Robert Malthus (1766–1834), an English economist and clergyman, warned that population increase would soon lead to social chaos. Malthus (1926, orig. 1798) calculated that population would increase in what mathematicians call a *geometric progression,* illustrated by the series of numbers 2, 4, 8, 16, 32, and so on. At such a rate, Malthus concluded, world population would soon soar out of control.

Food production would also increase, Malthus explained, but only in *arithmetic progression* (as in the series 2, 3, 4, 5, 6, and so on) because even with new agricultural technology, farmland is limited. Thus Malthus presented a distressing vision of the future: people reproducing beyond what the planet could feed, leading ultimately to widespread starvation and war over what resources were left.

Malthus recognized that artificial birth control or abstinence might change his prediction. But he considered one morally wrong and the other impractical. Famine and war therefore stalked humanity in Malthus's mind, and he was justly known as "the dismal parson."

▶**CRITICAL REVIEW** Fortunately, Malthus's prediction was flawed. First, by 1850, the European birth rate began to drop, partly because children were becoming an economic liability rather than an asset and partly because people began using artificial birth control. Second, Malthus underestimated human ingenuity: Modern irrigation techniques, fertilizers, and pesticides increased farm production far more than he could have imagined.

Some people criticized Malthus for ignoring the role of social inequality in world abundance and famine. For example, Karl Marx (1967, orig. 1867) objected to viewing suffering as a "law of nature" rather than the curse of capitalism. More recently, "critical demographers" have claimed that saying poverty is caused by high birth rates in low-income countries amounts to blaming the victims. On the contrary, they see global inequality as the real issue (Horton, 1999; Kuumba, 1999).

Still, Malthus offers an important lesson. Habitable land, clean water, and fresh air are limited resources, and greater economic productivity has taken a heavy toll on the natural environment. In addition, medical advances have lowered death rates, pushing up world population. Common sense tells us that no level of population growth can go on forever. People everywhere must become aware of the dangers of population increase.

✓ **YOUR LEARNING** What did Malthus predict about human population increase? About food production? What was his overall conclusion?

Demographic Transition Theory

A more complex analysis of population change is **demographic transition theory,** *a thesis that links population patterns to a society's*

level of technological development. Figure 3 shows the demographic consequences at four levels of technological development.

Preindustrial, agrarian societies (Stage 1) have high birth rates because of the economic value of children and the absence of birth control. Death rates are also high because of low living standards and limited medical technology. Deaths from outbreaks of disease cancel out births, so population rises and falls only slightly over time. This was the case for thousands of years in Europe before the Industrial Revolution.

This street scene in Kolkata (Calcutta), India, conveys the vision of the future found in the work of Thomas Robert Malthus, who feared that population increase would overwhelm the world's resources. Can you explain why Malthus had such a serious concern about population? How is demographic transition theory a more hopeful analysis?

AP Wide World Photos

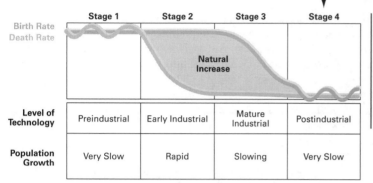

The United States is in this stage with both a low birth rate and a low death rate.

	Stage 1	Stage 2	Stage 3	Stage 4
Birth Rate Death Rate		Natural Increase		
Level of Technology	Preindustrial	Early Industrial	Mature Industrial	Postindustrial
Population Growth	Very Slow	Rapid	Slowing	Very Slow

FIGURE 3 Demographic Transition Theory

Demographic transition theory links population change to a society's level of technological development.

Stage 2, the onset of industrialization, brings a demographic transition as death rates fall due to greater food supplies and scientific medicine. But birth rates remain high, resulting in rapid population growth. It was during Europe's Stage 2 that Malthus formulated his ideas, which accounts for his pessimistic view of the future. The world's poorest countries today are in this high-growth stage.

In Stage 3, a mature industrial economy, the birth rate drops, curbing population growth once again. Fertility falls because most children survive to adulthood and because high living standards make raising children expensive. In short, affluence transforms children from economic assets into economic liabilities. Smaller families, made possible by effective birth control, are also favored by women working outside the home. As birth rates follow death rates downward, population growth slows further.

Stage 4 corresponds to a postindustrial economy in which the demographic transition is complete. The birth rate keeps falling, partly because dual-income couples gradually become the norm and partly because the cost of raising children continues to increase. This trend, linked to steady death rates, means that population grows only very slowly or even decreases. This is the case today in Japan, Europe, and the United States.

▶ **CRITICAL REVIEW** Demographic transition theory suggests that the key to population control lies in technology. Instead of the runaway population increase feared by Malthus, this theory sees technology slowing growth and spreading material plenty.

Demographic transition theory is linked to modernization theory, one approach to global development discussed. Modern-

ization theorists are optimistic that poor countries will solve their population problems as they industrialize. But critics, notably dependency theorists, strongly disagree. Unless there is a redistribution of global resources, they maintain, our planet will become increasingly divided into industrialized "haves," enjoying low population growth, and nonindustrialized "have-nots," struggling in vain to feed more and more people.

 YOUR LEARNING Explain the four stages of demographic transition theory.

Global Population Today: A Brief Survey

What can we say about population in today's world? Drawing on the discussion so far, we can identify important patterns and reach several conclusions.

The Low-Growth North

When the Industrial Revolution began in the Northern Hemisphere, the population increase in Western Europe and North America was a high 3 percent annually. But in the centuries since, the growth rate has steadily declined, and in 1970, it fell below 1 percent. As our postindustrial society settles into Stage 4, the U.S. birth rate is less than the replacement level of 2.1 children per woman, a point demographers term **zero population growth**, *the rate of reproduction that maintains population at a steady level.* More than sixty nations, almost all of them rich, are at or below the point of zero population growth.

Among the factors that serve to hold down population in these postindustrial societies include a high proportion of men and women in the labor force, rising costs of raising children, trends toward later marriage and singlehood, and widespread use of contraceptives and abortion.

In high-income nations, then, population increase is not the pressing problem that it is in poor countries. On the contrary, many governments in high-income countries are concerned about a future problem of *underpopulation* because declining population may be difficult to reverse and because the swelling ranks of the elderly can look to fewer and fewer young people for support (P. McDonald, 2001; Kent & Mather, 2002).

 Typically, immigrants are younger than most people in their new country. What is the likely effect of high immigration on a country's ability to support more and more older people?

The High-Growth South

Population is a critical problem in poor nations of the Southern Hemisphere. No nation of the world lacks industrial technology entirely; demographic transition theory's Stage 1 applies today to remote rural areas of low-income nations. But much of Latin America, Africa, and Asia is at Stage 2, with a mix of agrarian and industrial economies. Advanced medical technology, supplied by rich countries, has sharply reduced death rates, but birth rates remain high. This is why poor countries now account for two-thirds of Earth's people and 96 percent of global population increase.

In poor countries throughout the world, birth rates have fallen from an average of about six children per woman in 1950 to about three today. But fertility this high will only intensify global poverty. At a 1994 global population conference in Cairo, delegates from 180 nations agreed that a key element in controlling world population growth was improving the status of women. The Thinking About Diversity: Race, Class, & Gender box on page 582 takes a closer look.

In much of the world, mortality is falling. To limit population growth, the world—especially poor countries—must control births as successfully as it is fending off deaths.

Fertility in the United States has fallen during the past century and is now quite low. But some categories of the U.S. population have much higher fertility rates. One example is the Amish, a religious society living in rural areas of Ohio, Pennsylvania, and other states. It is common for Amish couples to have five, six, or more children. Why do you think the Amish favor large families?

David and Peter Turnley/Corbis/Bettmann

Urbanization: The Growth of Cities

October 8, Hong Kong. The cable train grinds to the top of Victoria Peak, where we behold one of the world's most spectacular vistas: the city of Hong Kong at night! A million bright, colorful lights ring the harbor as ships, ferries, and traditional Chinese junks slowly slip by. Day or night, few places match Hong Kong for sheer energy: This small city is as economically productive as the state of Wisconsin or the nation of Finland. We could sit here for hours entranced by the spectacle of Hong Kong.

For most of human history, the sights and sounds of great cities such as Hong Kong, Paris, and New York were simply unimaginable. Our distant ancestors lived in small, nomadic groups, moving as they depleted vegetation or hunted migratory game. The tiny settlements that marked the emergence of civilization in the Middle East some

12,000 years ago held only a small fraction of Earth's people. Today, the largest three or four cities of the world hold as many people as the entire planet did back then.

Urbanization is *the concentration of population into cities.* Urbanization redistributes population within a society and transforms many patterns of social life. We will trace these changes in terms of three urban revolutions: the emergence of cities 10,000 years ago, the development of industrial cities after 1750, and the explosive growth of cities in poor countries today.

The Evolution of Cities

Cities are a relatively new development in human history. Only about 12,000 years ago did our ancestors begin founding permanent settlements, which paved the way for the *first urban revolution.*

The First Cities

Hunting and gathering forced people to move all the time; however, once our ancestors discovered how to domesticate animals and cultivate crops, they were able to stay in one place. Raising their own food also created a material surplus, which freed some people from food production and allowed them to build shelters, make tools, weave

student 2 student

"I was surprised to learn that cities existed for such a small part of human history."

 tip

As the sections describing preindustrial and industrial cities explain, the size and shape of a city provide clues to a society's technology and culture.

Thinking About Diversity: Race, Class, & Gender
Empowering Women: The Key to Controlling Population Growth

Sohad Ahmad lives with her husband in a farming village 50 miles south of Cairo, Egypt's capital. Ahmad lives a poor life, like hundreds of millions of other women in the world. Yet her situation differs in an important respect: She has had only two children and will have no more.

Why do Ahmad and her husband reject the conventional wisdom that children are an economic asset? One part of the answer is that Egypt's growing population has already created such a demand for land that Ahmad's family could not afford more even if they had the children to farm it. But the main reason is that she does not want her life defined only by childbearing.

Like Ahmad, more women in Egypt are taking control of their fertility and seeking educational and economic opportunities. For this reason, Egypt has made great progress in reducing its annual population growth from 3 percent in the 1990s to 2 percent today.

With its focus on raising the standing of women, the 1994 Cairo conference broke new ground. Past population control programs have simply tried to make birth control technology available to women. This effort is vital, since only half the

world's married women use effective birth control. But even with birth control available, the population continues to expand in societies that define women's primary responsibility as raising children.

Nafis Sadik, the female Egyptian physician who leads the United Nations' efforts at population control, sums up the new

A simple truth: Women who have more opportunity for schooling and paid work have fewer children. As more women attend school in traditional societies, the fertility rate in these countries is falling.

Lauren Goodsmith/The Image Works

approach to lowering birth rates this way: *Give women more life choices, and they will have fewer children.* In other words, women who have access to schooling and jobs, who can decide when and whether to marry, and who bear children as a matter of choice will limit their own fertility. Schooling must be available to older women, too, Dr. Sadik adds, because elders exercise great influence in local communities.

Evidence from countries around the world is that controlling population and raising the social standing of women go hand in hand.

WHAT DO YOU THINK?

1. Why do many analysts claim that controlling population depends on expanding women's choices?

2. What specific laws or programs can you suggest that might reduce women's childbearing?

3. Is population control an issue for people in rich countries as well as those in poor countries? Why or why not?

Sources: Ashford (1995), Axinn & Barber (2001), and Population Reference Bureau (2006).

---

cloth, and take part in religious rituals. The emergence of cities led to both higher living standards and job specialization.

The first city that we know of was Jericho, which lies to the north of the Dead Sea in what is now the West Bank. When first settled some 10,000 years ago, it was home to only 600 people. But as the centuries passed, cities grew to tens of thousands of people and became the centers of vast empires. By 3000 B.C.E., Egyptian cities flourished, as did cities in China about 2000 B.C.E. and in Central and South America about 1500 B.C.E. In North America, however, only a few Native American societies formed settlements; widespread

urbanization had to await the arrival of European settlers in the seventeenth century.

Preindustrial European Cities

European cities date back some 5,000 years to the Greeks and later the Romans, both of whom created great empires and founded cities across Europe, including Vienna, Paris, and London. With the fall of the Roman Empire, the so-called Dark Ages began as people withdrew into defensive walled settlements and warlords battled for territory. Only in the eleventh century did Europe become more peaceful; trade flourished once again, allowing cities to grow.

Medieval cities were quite different from those familiar to us today. Beneath towering cathedrals, the narrow and winding streets of London, Brussels, and Florence teemed with merchants, artisans, priests, peddlers, jugglers, nobles, and servants. Occupational groups such as bakers, carpenters, and metalworkers clustered together in distinct sections or "quarters." Ethnicity also defined communities as residents tried to keep out people who differed from themselves. The term "ghetto" (from the Italian *borghetto,* meaning "outside the city walls") was first used to describe the neighborhood in which the Jews of Venice were segregated.

Industrial European Cities

As the Middle Ages came to a close, steadily increasing commerce enriched a new urban middle class, or *bourgeoisie* (French, meaning "townspeople"). With more and more money, the bourgeoisie soon rivaled the hereditary aristocracy.

By about 1750, the Industrial Revolution triggered a *second urban revolution,* first in Europe and then in North America. Factories unleashed tremendous productive power, causing cities to grow bigger than ever before. London, the largest European city, reached 550,000 people by 1700 and exploded to 6.5 million by 1900 (A. F. Weber, 1963, orig. 1899; Chandler & Fox, 1974).

Cities not only grew but changed shape as well. Older winding streets gave way to broad, straight boulevards to handle the increasing flow of commercial traffic. Steam and electric trolleys soon crisscrossed the expanding cities. Because land was now a commodity to be bought and sold, developers divided cities into regular-sized lots (Mumford, 1961). The center of the city was no longer the cathedral but a bustling central business district filled with banks, retail stores, and tall office buildings.

With a new focus on business, cities became more crowded and impersonal. Crime rates rose. Especially at the outset, a few industrialists lived in grand style, but most men, women, and children barely survived by working in factories.

Organized efforts by workers to improve their lives eventually brought changes to the workplace, better housing, and the right to vote. Public services such as water, sewer systems, and electricity further improved urban living. Today, some urbanites still live in poverty, but a rising standard of living has partly fulfilled the city's historical promise of a better life.

The Growth of U.S. Cities

Most of the Native Americans who inhabited North America for thousands of years before the arrival of Europeans were migratory people who formed few permanent settlements. The spread of villages and towns came after European colonization.

Colonial Settlement, 1565–1800

In 1565, the Spanish built a settlement at Saint Augustine, Florida, and in 1607, the English founded Jamestown, Virginia. The first lasting settlement came in 1624, when the Dutch established New Amsterdam, later renamed New York.

New York and Boston (founded by the English in 1630) started out as tiny villages in a vast wilderness. They resembled medieval towns in Europe, with narrow, winding streets that still curve through lower Manhattan and downtown Boston. When the first census was completed in 1790, as Table 1 shows, just 5 percent of the nation's people lived in cities.

Urban Expansion, 1800–1860

Early in the nineteenth century, as cities along the East Coast grew bigger, towns sprang up along the transportation routes that opened the American West. By 1860, Buffalo, Cleveland, Detroit, and Chicago were changing the face of the Midwest, and about one-fifth of the U.S. population lived in cities.

Urban expansion was greatest in the northern states; New York City, for example, had ten times the population of Charleston, South Carolina. The division of the United States into the industrial-urban North and the agrarian-rural South was one major cause of the Civil War (A. M. Schlesinger, 1969).

Table 1 Urban Population of the United States, 1790–2000

Year	Population (in millions)	Percentage Urban
1790	3.9	5.1%
1800	5.3	6.1
1820	9.6	7.3
1840	17.1	10.5
1860	31.4	19.7
1880	50.2	28.1
1900	76.0	39.7
1920	105.7	51.3
1940	131.7	56.5
1960	179.3	69.9
1980	226.5	73.7
2000	281.4	79.0

Source: U.S. Census Bureau (2006).

tip

Most large U.S. cities (at least in the eastern United States) were founded before the Civil War, grew to metropolitan size by 1950, and decentralized after that.

The Metropolitan Era, 1860–1950

The Civil War (1861–65) gave an enormous boost to urbanization as factories strained to produce weapons. Waves of people deserted the countryside for cities in hopes of finding better jobs. Joining them were tens of millions of immigrants, mostly from Europe, forming a culturally diverse urban mix.

In 1900, New York's population soared past the 4 million mark, and Chicago, a city of only 100,000 people in 1860, was closing in on 2 million. Such growth marked the era of the **metropolis** (from the Greek, meaning "mother city"), *a large city that socially and economically dominates an urban area.* Metropolises became the economic centers of the United States. By 1920, urban areas were home to a majority of the U.S. population.

Industrial technology pushed the urban skyline ever higher. In the 1880s, steel girders and mechanical elevators permitted buildings to rise more than ten stories high. In 1930, New York's Empire State Building was hailed as an urban wonder, reaching 102 stories into the clouds.

Urban Decentralization, 1950–Present

The industrial metropolis reached its peak about 1950. Since then, something of a turnaround—termed *urban decentralization*—has occurred as people have left downtown areas for outlying **suburbs,** *urban areas beyond the political boundaries of a city.* The old industrial

cities of the Northeast and Midwest stopped growing, and some lost considerable population in the decades after 1950. At the same time, suburban populations increased rapidly. The urban landscape of densely packed central cities evolved into sprawling suburban regions.

Suburbs and Urban Decline

Imitating the European aristocracy, some of the rich had town houses in the city as well as large country homes beyond the city limits. But not until after World War II did ordinary people find a suburban home within their reach. With more and more cars in circulation, new four-lane highways, government-backed mortgages, and inexpensive tract homes, the suburbs grew rapidly. By 1999, most of the U.S. population lived in the suburbs and shopped at nearby malls rather than in the older and more distant downtown shopping districts (Pederson, Smith, & Adler, 1999; Macionis & Parrillo, 2007).

As many older cities of the Snowbelt—the Northeast and Midwest—lost higher-income taxpayers to the suburbs, they struggled to pay for expensive social programs for the poor who remained. Many cities fell into financial crisis, and urban decay became severe. Soon the inner city came to be synonymous with slums, crime, drugs, unemployment, poverty, and minorities.

The urban critic Paul Goldberger (2002) points out that the decline of central cities also has led to a decline in the importance of public space. Historically, the heart of city life was played out on the streets. The French word for a sophisticated person is *boulevardier*, which literally means "street person." However, this term has a negative meaning in the United States today. The active life that once took place on public streets and in public squares now takes place in shopping malls, the lobbies of cineplex theaters, and gated residential communities—all privately owned spaces. Further reducing the vitality of today's urban places is the spread of television, the Internet, and other media that people use without leaving home.

Is there a class difference in people's use of the streets as a place to meet and greet others? For example, do you think working-class people are more likely to use the streets in this way than middle-class suburbanites?

In recent decades, many U.S. cities in the Sunbelt have spread outward in a process called urban sprawl. Los Angeles, for example, now covers about 500 square miles so that, even with a vast system of freeways, people moving around the city often find themselves stuck in slow-moving traffic. What are other disadvantages of urban sprawl?

AP Wide World Photos

Postindustrial Sunbelt Cities

As older Snowbelt cities fell into decline, Sunbelt cities in the South and the West began to grow rapidly. The soaring populations of cities such as Los Angeles and

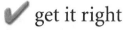
Houston reflect a population shift to the Sunbelt, where 60 percent of U.S. people now live. In addition, most of today's immigrants enter the country in the Sunbelt region. In 1950, nine of the ten biggest U.S. cities were in the Snowbelt; in 2005, seven of the top ten were in the Sunbelt (U.S. Census Bureau, 2006).

Unlike their colder counterparts, Sunbelt cities came of age *after* urban decentralization began. So although cities like Chicago have long been enclosed by a ring of politically independent suburbs, cities like Houston have pushed their boundaries outward to include suburban communities. Chicago covers 227 square miles, Houston is more than twice that size, and the greater Houston urban area covers almost 9,000 square miles—an area the size of the state of New Jersey.

The great sprawl of Sunbelt cities has drawbacks. Many people in cities such as Atlanta, Dallas, Phoenix, and Los Angeles complain that unplanned growth results in traffic-clogged roads leading to poorly planned housing developments and schools that cannot keep up with the inflow of children. Not surprisingly, voters in many communities across the United States have passed ballot initiatives seeking to limit urban sprawl (Lacayo, 1999; Romero & Liserio, 2002; Sullivan, 2007).

The rural rebound has been most pronounced in towns that offer spectacular natural beauty. There are times when people living in the scenic town of Park City, Utah, cannot even find a parking space.

Steve C. Wilson/Online USA, Inc./Steven C. Wilson

Megalopolis: The Regional City

Another result of urban decentralization is urban regions or regional cities. The U.S. Census Bureau (2005) recognizes 362 *metropolitan statistical areas* (MSAs). These areas include at least one city with 50,000 or more people. The bureau also recognizes 560 *micropolitan statistical areas,* urban areas with at least one city of 10,000 to 50,000 people. *Core based statistical areas* (CBSAs) include both metropolitan and micropolitan statistical areas.

The biggest CBSAs contain millions of people and cover large areas that extend into several states. In 2005, the largest MSA was New York and its adjacent urban areas in Long Island, western Connecticut, northern New Jersey, and eastern Pennsylvania, with a total population of more than 18 million. Next in size is the CBSA in southern California that includes Los Angeles, Riverside, and Long Beach, with a population of more than 13 million.

As regional cities grow, they begin to overlap. In the early 1960s, the French geographer Jean Gottmann (1961) coined the term **megalopolis** to designate *a vast urban region containing a number of cities and their surrounding suburbs.* Along the East Coast, a 400-mile megalopolis stretches all the way from New England to Virginia. Other supercities cover the eastern coast of Florida and stretch from Cleveland west to Chicago.

Edge Cities

Urban decentralization has also created *edge cities,* business centers some distance from the old downtowns. Edge cities—a mix of corporate office buildings, shopping malls, hotels, and entertainment complexes—differ from suburbs, which contain mostly homes. The population of suburbs peaks at night, but the population of edge cities peaks during the workday.

As part of expanding urban regions, most edge cities have no clear physical boundaries. Some do have names, including Las Colinas (near the Dallas–Fort Worth airport), Tyson's Corner (in Virginia, near Washington, D.C.), and King of Prussia (northwest of Philadelphia). Other edge cities are known only by the major highways that flow through them, including Route 1 in Princeton, New Jersey, and Route 128 near Boston (Garreau, 1991; Macionis & Parrillo, 2007).

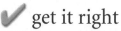 get it right

Tönnies's concept of *Gemeinschaft* corresponds
to Durkheim's mechanical solidarity; *Gesellschaft*
corresponds to organic solidarity.

Peasant Dance (above, c. 1565), by Pieter Breughel the Elder, conveys the
essential unity of rural life forged by generations of kinship and neighborhood. By contrast, Ernest Fiene's *Nocturne* (left) communicates the
impersonality common to urban areas. Taken together, these paintings
capture Tönnies's distinction between *Gemeinschaft* and *Gesellschaft*.

Pieter Breughel the Elder (c. 1525/30–1569), *Peasant Dance*, c. 1565, Kunsthistorisches Museum,
Vienna/Superstock. Ernest Fiene (1894–1965), *Nocturne*. Photograph © Christie's Images.

The Rural Rebound

Over the course of U.S. history, as shown by the data in Table 1, the
urban population of the nation has increased steadily. Immigration
has played a part in this increase because most newcomers settle in
cities. At the same time, there has been considerable migration from
rural areas to urban places, typically by people seeking greater social,
educational, and economic opportunity.

However, since about 1990, three-fourths of the rural counties
across the United States gained population, a trend analysts have called
the "rural rebound." Most of this gain resulted from the migration of
people from urban areas. This trend has not affected all rural places:
As the opening to this chapter explains, many small towns in rural
areas (especially in the Plains States) are struggling simply to stay
alive. But even there, losses slowed during the 1990s (K. M. Johnson,
1999; D. Johnson, 2001).

The greatest gains have come to rural communities that offer
scenic and recreational attractions, such as lakes, mountains, and
ski areas. People are drawn to rural communities not only by their
natural beauty but also by their slower pace: less traffic, a lower
crime rate, and cleaner air. A number of companies have relocated

to rural counties, which has increased economic opportunity for
the rural population (K. M. Johnson, 1999; Johnson & Fuguitt,
2000).

Urbanism as a Way of Life

Early sociologists in Europe and the United States focused their attention on the rise of cities and how urban life differed from rural life.
We briefly examine their accounts of urbanism as a way of life.

Ferdinand Tönnies: *Gemeinschaft* and *Gesellschaft*

In the late nineteenth century, the German sociologist Ferdinand Tönnies (1855–1937) studied how life in the new industrial metropolis
differed from life in rural villages. From this contrast, he developed two concepts that have become a lasting part of sociology's
terminology.

Tönnies (1963, orig. 1887) used the German word ***Gemeinschaft***
(meaning roughly "community") to refer to *a type of social organiza-*

tip

The early European sociologists were more theoretical in their approach; the early U.S. sociologists did more research in actual cities.

tion in which people are closely tied by kinship and tradition. The *Gemeinschaft* of the rural village joins people in what amounts to a single primary group.

By and large, argued Tönnies, *Gemeinschaft* is absent in the modern city. On the contrary, urbanization creates **Gesellschaft** (a German word meaning roughly "association"), *a type of social organization in which people come together only on the basis of individual self-interest.* In the *Gesellschaft* way of life, individuals are motivated by their own needs rather than by a desire to help improve the well-being of everyone. By and large, city dwellers have little sense of community or common identity and look to others mainly when they need something. Tönnies saw in urbanization a weakening of close, long-lasting social relations in favor of the brief and impersonal ties or secondary relationships typical of business.

 How might Tönnies explain social patterns such as our high rate of divorce, widespread fear of crime, and incidents of "road rage" on the highways?

Emile Durkheim: Mechanical and Organic Solidarity

The French sociologist Emile Durkheim agreed with much of Tönnies's thinking about cities. However, Durkheim countered that urbanites do not lack social bonds; they simply organize social life differently than rural people.

Durkheim described traditional, rural life as *mechanical solidarity,* social bonds based on common sentiments and shared moral values. With its emphasis on tradition, Durkheim's concept of mechanical solidarity bears a striking similarity to Tönnies's *Gemeinschaft.* Urbanization erodes mechanical solidarity, Durkheim explained, but it also generates a new type of bonding, which he called *organic solidarity,* social bonds based on specialization and interdependence. This concept, which parallels Tönnies's *Gesellschaft,* reveals an important difference between the two thinkers. Both thought the growth of industrial cities weakened tradition, but Durkheim optimistically pointed to a new kind of solidarity. Whereas people had been joined by *likeness* (mechanical solidarity), Durkheim now saw them joined by *difference* (organic solidarity).

For Durkheim, urban society offered more individual choice, moral tolerance, and personal privacy than people find in rural villages. In sum, Durkheim acknowledged that something is lost in the process of urbanization, but much else is gained.

Georg Simmel: The Blasé Urbanite

The German sociologist Georg Simmel (1858–1918) offered a microanalysis of cities, studying how urban life shapes the everyday experience of individuals. According to Simmel, individuals perceive the city as a crush of people, objects, and events. To prevent being overwhelmed by all this stimulation, urbanites develop a *blasé attitude,* tuning out much of what goes on around them. Such detachment does not mean that city dwellers lack compassion for others; they simply keep their distance as a survival strategy so that they can focus their time and energy on the people and things that really matter to them.

 How would Simmel explain cases of people turning away from others in need on the grounds that they simply "don't want to get involved"?

The Chicago School: Robert Park and Louis Wirth

Sociologists in the United States soon joined the study of rapidly growing cities. Robert Park, a leader of the first U.S. sociology program at the University of Chicago, sought to add a street-level perspective by getting out and studying real cities. As he said of himself, "I suspect that I have actually covered more ground, tramping about in cities in different parts of the world, than any other living man" (1950:viii). Walking the streets, Park found the city to be an organized mosaic of distinctive ethnic communities, commercial centers, and industrial districts. Over time, he observed, these "natural areas" develop and change in relation to one another. To Park, the city was a living organism—a human kaleidoscope.

Another major figure in the Chicago School of urban sociology was Louis Wirth (1897–1952). Wirth (1938) is best known for blending the ideas of Tönnies, Durkheim, Simmel, and Park into a comprehensive theory of urban life.

Wirth began by defining the city as a setting with a large, dense, and socially diverse population. These traits result in an impersonal, superficial, and transitory way of life. Living among millions of others, urbanites come into contact with many more people than residents of rural areas. So when city people notice others at all, they usually know them not in terms of *who they are* but *what they do*—as, for instance, the bus driver, the florist, or the grocery store clerk. Specialized urban relationships are pleasant for all concerned, but self-interest rather than friendship is usually the main reason for the interaction.

tip

A minority majority also exists in four states: Hawaii, California, New Mexico, and Texas.

Thinking About Diversity: Race, Class, & Gender
Minorities Now a Majority in the Largest U.S. Cities

According to the results of the 2000 census, minorities—Hispanics, African Americans, and Asians—are now a majority of the population in 48 of the 100 largest U.S. cities, up from 30 in 1990.

What accounts for the change? One reason is that large cities have been losing their non-Hispanic white population. Santa Ana, California, for example, lost 38 percent of its 1990 white population; the drop was 40 percent in Birmingham, Alabama, and a whopping 53 percent in Detroit, Michigan. The white share of the population of all 100 of the largest cities fell from 52.1 percent in 1990 to 43.8 percent in 2000, as the figure shows.

But an even bigger reason for the minority-majority trend is the increase in immigration. Immigration, coupled with higher birth rates among new immigrants, resulted in a 43 percent gain in the Hispanic population (almost 4 million people) of the largest 100 cities between 1990 and 2000. The Asian population also surged by 40 percent (more than

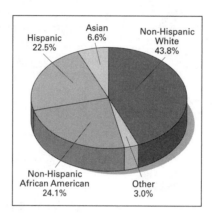

Population Profile for the 100 Largest U.S. Cities, 2000

Racial and ethnic minorities make up a majority of the population of this country's 100 largest cities.

Source: U.S. Census Bureau (2001).

1.1 million people). The African American population was steady over the course of the 1990s. Political officials and other policy-makers have been watching these figures closely, for the future vitality of the largest U.S. cities depends on meeting the needs and welcoming the contributions of the swelling minority populations.

WHAT DO YOU THINK?

1. Why are the minority populations of large U.S. cities increasing?

2. What positive changes and what challenges does a minority-majority bring to a city?

3. Before Hurricane Katrina, African Americans represented 60 percent of the population of New Orleans; afterward, the share was about 40 percent. What difference might this change make in the city's immediate future?

Sources: Schmitt (2001) and U.S. Census Bureau (2005).

The impersonal nature of urban relationships, together with the great social diversity found in cities today, makes city dwellers more tolerant than rural villagers. Rural communities often jealously enforce their narrow traditions, but the heterogeneous population of a city rarely shares any single code of moral conduct (T. C. Wilson, 1985, 1995).

▶ **CRITICAL REVIEW** In both Europe and the United States, early sociologists presented a mixed view of urban living. Rapid urbanization troubled Tönnies, and Wirth saw personal ties and traditional morality lost in the anonymous rush of the city. Durkheim and Park emphasized urbanism's positive face, pointing to more personal freedom and greater personal choice.

One problem with all these views is that they paint urbanism in broad strokes that overlook the effects of class, race, and gender. There are many kinds of urbanites—rich and poor, black and white, Anglo and Latino, women and men—all leading dis-

tinctive lives (Gans, 1968). As the Thinking About Diversity: Race, Class, & Gender box explains, the share of minorities in the largest U.S. cities increased sharply during the 1990s. We see social diversity most clearly in cities, where various categories of people are large enough to form distinct, visible communities (Macionis & Parrillo, 2007).

 YOUR LEARNING Of these urban sociologists—Tönnies, Durkheim, Park, and Wirth—which were more positive about urban life? Which were more negative? In each case, explain why.

Urban Ecology

Sociologists (especially members of the Chicago School) developed **urban ecology,** *the study of the link between the physical and social dimensions of cities.* One issue of interest to urban ecologists is why cities are located where they are. Broadly speaking, the first cities

tip

Read the Critical Review sections carefully to better understand the strengths and weaknesses of each theoretical analysis.

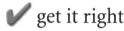 get it right

Answer all the "✓ Your Learning" questions to be sure you understand each of the theoretical discussions.

emerged in fertile regions where the ecology favored raising crops. In addition, preindustrial people were concerned with defense, so they built their cities on mountains (ancient Athens was perched on an outcropping of rock) or surrounded by water (Paris and Mexico City were founded on islands). With the coming of the Industrial Revolution, economic considerations gained importance, which explains why all the major U.S. cities were situated near rivers and natural harbors that facilitated trade.

Urban ecologists also study the physical design of cities. In 1925, Ernest W. Burgess, a student and colleague of Robert Park's, described land use in Chicago in terms of *concentric zones*. City centers, Burgess observed, are business districts bordered by a ring of factories, followed by residential rings with housing that becomes more expensive the farther it is from the noise and pollution of the city's center.

Homer Hoyt (1939) refined Burgess's observations, noting that distinctive districts sometimes form *wedge-shaped sectors*. For example, one fashionable area may develop next to another, or an industrial district may extend outward from a city's center along a train or trolley line.

Chauncy Harris and Edward Ullman (1945) added yet another insight: As cities decentralize, they lose their single-center form in favor of a *multicentered model*. As cities grow, residential areas, industrial parks, and shopping districts typically push away from one another. Few people wish to live close to industrial areas, for example, so the city becomes a mosaic of distinct districts.

Social area analysis investigates what people in particular neighborhoods have in common. Three factors seem to explain most of the variation: family patterns, social class, and race and ethnicity (Shevky & Bell, 1955; R. J. Johnston, 1976). Families with children look for areas with single-family homes or large apartments and good schools. The rich seek high-prestige neighborhoods, often in the central city near cultural attractions. People with a common race or ethnic heritage cluster in distinctive communities.

Finally, Brian Berry and Philip Rees (1969) tie together many of these insights. They explain that distinct family types tend to settle in the concentric zones described by Burgess. Specifically, households with many children tend to live in the outer areas of a city, while "young singles" cluster toward the city's center. This is especially true, as "In the Times" on page 590 explains, where cities make efforts to attract young people into their labor force. Social class differences are primarily responsible for the sector-shaped districts described by Hoyt—for instance, the rich occupy one "side of the tracks" and the poor the other. And racial and ethnic neighborhoods are found at various points throughout the city, consistent with Harris and Ullman's multicentered model.

Urban Political Economy

In the late 1960s, many large U.S. cities were rocked by major riots. In the wake of this unrest, some analysts turned away from the ecological approach to a social-conflict understanding of city life. The *urban political economy* model applies Karl Marx's analysis of conflict in the workplace to conflict in the city (Lindstrom, 1995).

Political economists reject the ecological approach's view of the city as a natural organism with particular districts and neighborhoods developing according to an internal logic. They claim that city life is defined by larger institutional structures, especially the economy. Capitalism, which transforms the city into real estate traded for profit and concentrates wealth and power in the hands of the few, is the key to understanding city life. From this point of view, for example, the decline in industrial Snowbelt cities after 1950 was the result of deliberate decisions by the corporate elite to move their production facilities to the Sunbelt (where labor is cheaper and less likely to be unionized) or to move them out of the country entirely to low-income nations (Molotch, 1976; Castells, 1977, 1983; Feagin, 1983; Lefebvre, 1991; Jones & Wilson, 1999).

 CRITICAL REVIEW   The fact that many U.S. cities are in crisis, with widespread poverty, high crime, and barely functioning schools, seems to favor the political economy model over the urban ecology approach. But one criticism applies to both: They focus on U.S. cities during a limited period of history. Much of what we know about industrial cities does not apply to preindustrial U.S. towns in our own past or to the rapidly growing cities in many poor nations today. It is unlikely that any single model of cities can account for the full range of urban diversity.

✓ **YOUR LEARNING**   In your own words, explain what the urban ecology theories and the urban political economy theory teach us about cities.

Urbanization in Poor Nations

November 16, Cairo, Egypt. People call the vast Muslim cemetery in Old Cairo the City of the Dead. In truth, it is very much alive: Tens of thousands of squatters have moved into the mausoleums, making this place an eerie mix of life and death. Children run across the stone floors, clotheslines stretch between the monuments, and an occasional television antenna protrudes from a tomb roof. With Cairo's population increasing at the rate of 1,000 people a day, families live where they can.

The New York Times

MARKET
REAL ESTATE
AUTOS
ALL CLASSIFIEDS

WORLD
U.S.
Politics
Washington
Education
N.Y./REGION
BUSINESS
TECHNOLOGY
SPORTS
SCIENCE
HEALTH
OPINION
ARTS
Books
Movies
Music
Television
Theater
STYLE
Dining & Wine
Fashion & Style
Home & Garden
Weddings/
Celebrations
TRAVEL

Blogs
Cartoons
Classifieds
Corrections
Crossword/
Games
First Look
Learning
Network
Multimedia
NYC Guide
Obituaries
Podcasts
The Public
Editor
Sunday
Magazine
Weather
Week in Review

NEWSPAPER
Get Home
Delivery
Customer Care
TimesPoints

Cities Compete in Hipness Battle to Attract Young

By SHAILA DEWAN; BRENDA GOODMAN CONTRIBUTED REPORTING
November 25, 2006

Some cities will do anything they can think of to keep young people from fleeing to a hipper town.

In Lansing, Mich., partiers can ease from bar to bar on the new Entertainment Express trolley, part of the state's Cool Cities Initiative. In Portland, Ore., employees at an advertising firm can watch indie rock concerts at lunch and play "bump," an abbreviated form of basketball, every afternoon.

And in Memphis, employers pay for recruits to be matched with hip young professionals in a sort of corporate Big Brothers program. A new biosciences research park is under construction—not in the suburbs, but downtown, just blocks from the nightlife of Beale Street.

These measures reflect a hard demographic reality: Baby boomers are retiring and the number of young adults is declining. By 2012, the work force will be losing more than two workers for every one it gains.

Cities have long competed over job growth, struggling to revive their downtowns and improve their image. But the latest population trends have forced them to fight for college-educated 25- to 34-year-olds, a demographic group increasingly viewed as the key to an economic future.

Mobile but not flighty, fresh but technologically savvy, "the young and restless," as demographers call them, are at their most desirable age, particularly because their chances of relocating drop precipitously when they turn 35. Cities that do not attract them now will be hurting in a decade

"It's a zero-sum game," said William H. Frey, a demographer with the Brookings Institution, noting that one city's gain can only be another's loss. "These are rare and desirable people."

They are people who, demographers say, are likely to choose a location before finding a job. They like downtown living, public transportation and plenty of entertainment options. They view diversity and tolerance as marks of sophistication.

The problem for cities, says Richard Florida, a public policy professor at George Mason University who has written about what he calls "the creative class," is that those cities that already have a significant share of the young and restless are in the best position to attract more.

"There are a dozen places, at best, that are becoming magnets for these people," Mr. Florida said.

That disparity was evident in a report released this week by the Metropolitan Atlanta Chamber of Commerce, which showed Atlanta leading the pack among big cities, while other metro areas, like Philadelphia, hemorrhaged young people from 1990 to 2000. . . .

In that decade, the Atlanta study said, the number of 25- to 34-year-olds with four-year college degrees in the city increased by 46 percent, placing Atlanta in the top five metropolitan areas in terms of growth rate, and a close second to San Francisco in terms of overall numbers. Charlotte, N.C., also outperformed Atlanta, with a growth rate of 57 percent, the second highest in the country after Las Vegas.

(Demographers point out that Las Vegas started with very small numbers and still ranks last among major cities when it comes to the percentage of its 25- to 34-year-olds with a college degree.)

Atlanta did particularly well with young, educated blacks—a boon for employers seeking to diversify their ranks. The city's report zeroed in on people like Tiffany Patterson, 27, who on a recent Thursday night was hanging out at Verve, the sleek new Midtown bar and restaurant that is one of her marketing clients.

The place was thrumming with young African Americans in leather jackets, stilettos or pinstripe suits—the kind of vibe, said Ms. Patterson, who is from Dallas, that made her stay in Atlanta after college.

"If I go home, women my age are looking for a husband," she said. "They have a cubicle job."

In Atlanta, Ms. Patterson said, she can afford a new town house. A few years ago, she decided to leave her financial sector job and start her own business as a marketing consultant.

"I thought, I can break out and do it myself," she said. "It really is the city of the fearless." . . .

In addition to Atlanta, the biggest gainers in market share of the young and restless were San Francisco; Denver; Portland; and Austin, Tex. The biggest losers included Washington, Philadelphia, New York and Los Angeles. . . .

Studies like Atlanta's are common these days. From Milwaukee to Tampa Bay, consultants have been hired to score such nebulous indexes as "social capital," "after hours" and "vitality." Relocation videos have begun to feature dreadlocks and mosh pits instead of sunsets and duck ponds. In the governor's race in Michigan this fall, the candidates repeatedly sparred over how best to combat "brain drain." . . .

WHAT DO YOU THINK?

1. Why should cities be concerned about the number of young people who live there?

2. Did you select a city in which to live based on a job or other considerations? What factors might attract you to a particular city when you finish college?

3. What policies can cities use to attract more young, highly educated people?

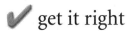 **get it right**
Be sure you understand the three urban
revolutions in terms of when and where they
occurred.

student 2 student
"Sociology shows us that environmental issues
are really about how society operates."

As noted earlier, twice in its history, the world has experienced a revolutionary expansion of cities. The first urban revolution began about 8000 B.C.E. with the first urban settlements and continued until permanent settlements were in place on several continents. About 1750, the second urban revolution took off; it lasted for two centuries as the Industrial Revolution spurred rapid growth of cities in Europe and North America.

A third urban revolution is now under way. Today, approximately 75 percent of people in industrial societies are already city dwellers. But extreme urban growth is occurring in low-income nations. In 1950, about 25 percent of the people in poor countries lived in cities; in 2005, the figure was close to 50 percent. In 1950, only seven cities in the world had populations over 5 million, and only two of these were in low-income countries. By 2005, forty-nine cities had passed this mark, and thirty-two of them were in less developed nations (Brockerhoff, 2000; GeoHive, 2005).

This third urban revolution is taking place because many poor nations have entered the high-growth Stage 2 of demographic transition theory. Falling death rates have fueled population increases in Latin America, Asia, and especially Africa. For urban areas, the rate of increase is *twice* as high because in addition to natural increase, millions of people leave the countryside each year in search of jobs, health care, education, and conveniences such as running water and electricity.

Cities do offer more opportunities than rural areas, but they provide no quick fix for the massive problems of escalating population and grinding poverty. Many cities in less economically developed nations—including Mexico City, Egypt's Cairo, India's Kolkata (formerly Calcutta), and Manila in the Philippines—are simply unable to meet the basic needs of much of their populations. All these cities are surrounded by wretched shantytowns—settlements of makeshift homes built from discarded materials. Even city dumps are home to thousands of poor people, who pick through the piles of waste hoping to find enough to eat or sell to make it through another day.

Environment and Society

The human species has prospered, rapidly expanding over the entire planet. An increasing share of the global population now lives in cities, complex settlements that offer the promise of a better life than that found in rural villages.

But these advances have come at a high price. Never before in history have human beings placed such demands on the planet. This disturbing development brings us to the final section of this chapter: the interplay between the natural environment and society. Like

The most important insight sociology offers about our physical world is that environmental problems do not simply "happen." Rather, the state of the natural environment reflects the ways in which social life is organized—how people live and what they think is important. The greater the technological power of a society, the greater that society's ability to threaten the natural environment.

Wilfried Krecichwost/Zefa/Corbis Zefa Collection

demography, **ecology** is another cousin of sociology, formally defined as *the study of the interaction of living organisms and the natural environment*. Ecology rests on the research of natural scientists as well as social scientists. This text focuses on the aspects of ecology that involve familiar sociological concepts and issues.

The **natural environment** is *Earth's surface and atmosphere, including living organisms, air, water, soil, and other resources necessary to sustain life*. Like every other species, humans depend on the natural environment to survive. Yet with our capacity for culture, humans stand apart from other species; we alone take deliberate action to remake the world according to our own interests and desires, for better and for worse.

Why is the environment of interest to sociologists? Simply because environmental problems—from pollution to acid rain to global warming—do not arise from the natural world operating on its own. Such problems result from the specific actions of human beings, so they are *social* problems (L. Marx, 1994).

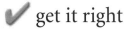

✔ get it right

I = PAT is an important environmental idea; be sure you understand its meaning.

The Global Dimension

The study of the natural environment requires a global perspective. The reason is simple: Regardless of political divisions among nations, the planet is a single **ecosystem,** *a system composed of the interaction of all living organisms and their natural environment.*

The Greek meaning of *eco* is "house," reminding us that this planet is our home and that all living things and their natural environment are interrelated. A change in any part of the natural environment ripples throughout the entire global ecosystem.

Consider, from an ecological point of view, our national love of eating hamburgers. People in North America (and, increasingly, around the world) have created a huge demand for beef, which has greatly expanded the ranching industry in Brazil, Costa Rica, and other Latin American nations. To produce the lean meat sought by fast-food corporations, cattle in Latin America feed on grass, which requires a great deal of land. Latin American ranchers get the land for grazing by clearing thousands of square miles of forests each year. These tropical forests are vital to maintaining Earth's atmosphere. Deforestation ends up threatening everyone, including people in the United States enjoying their hamburgers (N. Myers, 1984a).

Technology and the Environmental Deficit

Sociologists point to a simple formula: $I = PAT$, where environmental impact (I) reflects a society's population (P), its level of affluence (A), and its level of technology (T). Members of societies with simple technology hardly affect the environment because they are small in number, are poor, and have only simple technology. On the contrary, nature affects their lives as they follow the migration of game, watch the rhythm of the seasons, and suffer from natural catastrophes such as fires, floods, droughts, and storms.

Societies at intermediate stages of technological development have a somewhat greater capacity to affect the environment. Such societies are both larger and richer. But the environmental impact of horticulture (small-scale farming), pastoralism (the herding of animals), and even agriculture (the use of animal-drawn plows) is limited because people still rely on muscle power for producing food and other goods.

Humans' ability to control the natural environment increased dramatically with the Industrial Revolution. Muscle power gave way to engines that burn fossil fuels: coal at first and then oil. Such machinery affects the environment in two ways: We consume more natural resources, and we release more pollutants into the atmosphere. Even more important, armed with industrial technology, we are able to bend nature to our will, tunneling through mountains, damming rivers, irrigating deserts, and drilling for oil in the arctic wilderness and on the ocean floor. This explains why people in rich nations, who represent just 18 percent of humanity, now use 80 percent of the world's energy (G. T. Miller, 1992; York, Rosa, & Deitz, 2002).

The environmental impact of industrial technology goes beyond energy consumption. Just as important is the fact that members of industrial societies produce 100 times more goods than people in agrarian societies do. Higher living standards in turn increase the problem of solid waste (since people ultimately throw away most of what they produce) and pollution (since industrial production generates smoke and other toxic substances).

From the start, people recognized the material benefits of industrial technology. But only a century later did they begin to see the long-term effects on the natural environment. Today, we realize that the technological power to make our lives better can also put the lives of future generations at risk, and there is a national debate about how to address this issue.

Evidence is mounting that we are running up an **environmental deficit,** *profound long-term harm to the natural environment caused by humanity's focus on short-term material affluence* (Bormann, 1990). The concept of environmental deficit is important for three reasons. First, it reminds us that environmental concerns are *sociological,* reflecting societies' priorities about how people should live. Second, it suggests that much environmental damage—to the air, land, and water—is *unintended.* By focusing on the short-term benefits of, say, cutting down forests, strip mining, or using throwaway packaging, we fail to see their long-term environmental effects. Third, in some respects, the environmental deficit is *reversible.* Societies have created environmental problems but can also undo many of them.

Culture: Growth and Limits

Whether we recognize environmental dangers and decide to do something about them is a cultural matter. Thus along with technology, culture has powerful environmental consequences.

The Logic of Growth

When you turn on the television news, you might hear a story like this: "The government reported good economic news today, with the economy growing by 3.2 percent during the first quarter of the year." If you stop to think about it, our culture almost always defines growth as good. An economy that isn't growing is "stagnant" (which is bad); one that is getting smaller is in a "depression" (which is *very* bad). More cars, more and bigger homes, more income, more spending—

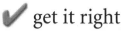
the idea of *more* is at the heart of our cultural definition of living well (McKibben, 2007).

One of the reasons we define growth in positive terms is that we value *material comfort,* believing that money and the things it buys improve our lives. We also believe in the idea of *progress,* thinking the future will be better than the present. In addition, we look to *science* to make our lives easier and more rewarding. In simple terms, "having things is good," "life gets better," and "people are clever." Taken together, such cultural values form the *logic of growth.*

 Can you identify ways in which the mass media and our popular culture (music, films, and television) encourage people to support the logic of growth? How?

An optimistic view of the world, the logic of growth holds that more powerful technology has improved our lives and new discoveries will continue to do so in the future. Throughout the history of the United States and other high-income nations, the logic of growth has been the driving force behind settling the wilderness, building towns and roads, and pursuing material affluence.

However, "progress" can lead to unexpected problems, including strain on the environment. The logic of growth responds by arguing that people (especially scientists and other technology experts) will find a way out of any problem that growth places in our path. For example, before the world runs short of oil, we will come up with hydrogen, solar, or nuclear engines or some other as yet unknown technology to meet the world's energy needs.

Environmentalists counter that the logic of growth is flawed because it assumes that natural resources such as oil, clean air, fresh water, and topsoil will always be plentiful. We can and will exhaust these *finite* resources if we continue to pursue growth at any cost. Echoing Malthus, environmentalists warn that if we call on Earth to support increasing numbers of people, we will surely deplete finite resources, destroying the environment—and ourselves—in the process.

The Limits to Growth

If we cannot invent our way out of the problems created by the logic of growth, perhaps we need another way of thinking about the world. Environmentalists therefore counter that growth must have limits. Stated simply, the *limits-to-growth thesis* is that humanity must put in place policies to control the growth of population, production, and use of resources in order to avoid environmental collapse.

In *The Limits to Growth,* a controversial book that was influential in launching the environmental movement, Donella Meadows and

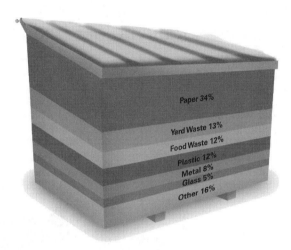

FIGURE 4 **Composition of Community Trash**

We throw away a wide range of material, with paper the single largest part of our trash.

Source: U.S. Environmental Protection Agency (2007).

her colleagues (1972) used a computer model to calculate the planet's available resources, rates of population growth, amount of land available for cultivation, levels of industrial and food production, and amount of pollutants released into the atmosphere. The authors concede that any long-range predictions are speculative, and some critics think they are plain wrong (Simon, 1981). But right or wrong, the conclusions of the study call for serious consideration. First, the authors claim that we are quickly consuming Earth's finite resources. Supplies of oil, natural gas, and other energy sources are already falling sharply and will continue to drop, a little faster or slower depending on the conservation policies of rich nations and the speed with which other nations such as India and China continue to industrialize. Within the next 100 years, resources will run out and cripple industrial output, which will also cause a decline in food production.

This limits-to-growth theory shares Malthus's pessimism about the future. People who accept it doubt that current patterns of life are sustainable for even another century. Perhaps we all can learn to live with less. This may not be as hard as you might think: Research shows, for example, that as material consumption has gone up in recent decades, there has been no increase in levels of personal happiness (D. G. Myers, 2000). In the end, environmentalists warn, either

student**2**student

"I love Grandma Macionis! If more people lived like her, we'd have fewer environmental problems."

 tip

Think about how specific ways we live put more or less strain on the natural environment.

 Seeing Sociology in Everyday Life
Why Grandmother Had No Trash

Grandma Macionis never threw anything away. She was born and raised in Lithuania—the "old country"—where life in a poor village shaped her in ways that never changed, even after she emigrated to the United States as a young woman and settled in Philadelphia.

In her later years, when I knew her, I can remember the family traveling together to her house to celebrate her birthday. We never knew what to get Grandma, because she never seemed to need anything. She lived a simple life and had simple clothes and showed little interest in "fancy things." She used everything until it wore out. Her kitchen knives, for example, were worn narrow from decades of sharpening. And she hardly ever threw anything away—she recycled all her garbage as compost for her vegetable garden.

After opening a birthday present, she would carefully save the box, wrapping paper, and ribbon, which meant as much to her as whatever gift they surrounded. We all expected her to save every bit of whatever she was given, smiling to each other as we

watched her put everything away, knowing she would find a way to use it all again and again.

As strange as Grandma sometimes seemed to her grandchildren, she was a product of her culture. A century ago, in fact, there was little "trash." If a pair of socks wore thin, people mended them, probably more than once. When they were beyond repair, they were used as rags for cleaning or

Culver Pictures, Inc.

sewn with other old clothing into a quilt. Everything had value—if not in one way, then in another.

During the twentieth century, as women joined men in working outside the home, income went up, and families began buying more and more "time-saving" products. Before long, few people cared about the kind of recycling that Grandma practiced. Soon cities sent crews from block to block to pick up truckloads of discarded material. The era of "trash" had begun.

WHAT DO YOU THINK?

1. Just as Grandma Macionis was a product of her culture, so are we. What cultural values make people today demand time-saving products and "convenience" packaging?

2. Do you recycle drink containers, paper, or other materials? Why or why not?

3. In what ways does this box demonstrate that the state of the natural environment is a social issue?

make fundamental changes in how we live, placing less strain on the natural environment, or widespread hunger and conflict will force change on us.

 Do you think that having more, in a materialistic sense, is the path to personal happiness? Why or why not?

Solid Waste: The Disposable Society

Across the United States, people generate a massive amount of solid waste—about 1.4 billion pounds *every day.* Figure 4 shows the average composition of a typical community's trash.

As a rich nation of people who value convenience, the United States has become a *disposable society.* We consume more products than virtually any other nation, and many of these products have

throwaway packaging. For example, fast food is served with cardboard, plastic, and Styrofoam containers that we throw away within minutes. Countless other products, from film to fishhooks, are elaborately packaged to make the products more attractive to the customer and to discourage tampering and theft.

Manufacturers market soft drinks, beer, and fruit juices in aluminum cans, glass jars, and plastic containers, which not only consume finite resources but also generate mountains of solid waste. Then there are countless items intentionally designed to be disposable: pens, razors, flashlights, batteries, even cameras. Other products, from light bulbs to automobiles, are designed to have a limited useful life and then become unwanted junk. As Paul Connett (1991) points out, even the words we use to describe what we throw away—*waste, litter, trash, refuse, garbage, rubbish*—show how little we value what we cannot immediately use. But this was not always the case, as the Seeing Sociology in Everyday Life box explains.

tip
Almost all the environmental problems discussed
in this part of the chapter can be expected to
get much worse as other countries gain more
powerful technology and become more affluent.

tip
Some analysts suggest that in the centuries to
come, water will be as valuable as oil is today.

Living in a rich society, the average person in the United States consumes hundreds of times more energy, plastics, lumber, water, and other resources than someone living in a low-income country such as Bangladesh or Tanzania and nearly twice as much as people in some other high-income countries such as Sweden and Japan. This high level of consumption means not only that we in the United States use a disproportionate share of the planet's natural resources but also that we generate most of the world's refuse.

We like to say that we throw things "away." But 80 percent of our solid waste never goes away. Rather, it ends up in landfills, which are, literally, filling up. Material in landfills can pollute underground water supplies. Although in most places, laws now regulate what can be discarded in a landfill, the Environmental Protection Agency has identified 30,000 dump sites across the United States containing hazardous materials that are polluting water both above and below the ground. In addition, what goes into landfills all too often stays there, sometimes for centuries. Tens of millions of tires, diapers, and other items we bury in landfills each year do not decompose but will remain as an unwelcome legacy for future generations.

Water is vital to life, and it is also in short supply. The state of Gujarat, in western India, has experienced a long drought. In the village of Natwarghad, people crowd together, lowering pots into the local well, taking what little water is left.

Dave Amit/Reuters/Landov LLC

Environmentalists argue that we should address the problem of solid waste by doing what many of our grandparents did: Use less and turn "waste" into a resource. Part of the solution is *recycling*, reusing resources we would otherwise discard. Recycling is an accepted practice in Japan and many other nations, and it is becoming more common in the United States, where we now reuse about 30 percent of waste materials. The share is increasing as laws require the recovery and reuse of certain materials such as glass bottles and aluminum cans. But recycling is expanding slowly because our nation's market-based economy encourages any activity only to the extent that it is profitable, and the recycling process is still quite costly.

Water and Air

Oceans, lakes, and streams are the lifeblood of the global ecosystem. Humans depend on water for drinking, bathing, cooking, cleaning, recreation, and a host of other activities.

According to what scientists call the *hydrologic cycle,* Earth naturally recycles water and refreshes the land. The process begins as heat from the sun causes Earth's water, 97 percent of which is in the oceans, to evaporate and form clouds. Because water evaporates at lower temperatures than most pollutants, the water vapor that rises from the seas is relatively pure, leaving various contaminants behind. Water then falls to the Earth as rain, which drains into streams and rivers and finally returns to the sea. Two major concerns about water, then, are supply and pollution.

Water Supply

Only about 1 percent of Earth's water is suitable for drinking. It is not surprising, then, that for thousands of years, water rights have figured prominently in laws around the world. Today, some regions of the world, especially the tropics, enjoy plentiful fresh water, using a small share of the available supply. However, high demand, coupled with modest reserves, makes water supply a matter of concern in much of North America and Asia, where people look to rivers rather than rainfall for their water. In China, deep aquifers are dropping rapidly. In the Middle East, water supply is reaching a critical level. Iran is rationing water in its capital city. In Egypt, the Nile River provides just one-sixth as much water per person as it did in 1900. Across northern Africa and the Middle East, as many as 1 billion people may lack the water they need for irrigation and drinking by 2025 ("China Faces Water Shortage," 2001; International Development Research Center, 2006).

student 2 student

"These are some serious environmental problems! What can I do to help solve them?"

Rising population and the development of more complex technology have greatly increased the world's appetite for water. The global consumption of water (now estimated at 4 billion cubic feet per year) has tripled since 1950 and is rising steadily. As a result, even in those parts of the world that receive plenty of rainfall, people are using groundwater faster than it can be replenished naturally. In the Tamil Nadu region of southern India, for example, so much groundwater is being used that the water table has fallen 100 feet over the last several decades. Mexico City—which has sprawled to some 1,400 square miles—has pumped so much water from its underground aquifer that the city has sunk 30 feet during the past century and continues to drop about 2 inches per year. Farther north in the United States, the Ogallala aquifer, which lies below seven states from South Dakota to Texas, is now being pumped so rapidly that some experts fear it could run dry in just a few decades.

In light of such developments, we must face the reality that water is a valuable and finite resource. Greater conservation of water by individuals (the average person consumes 10 million gallons in a lifetime) is part of the answer. However, households around the world account for just 10 percent of water use. It is even more crucial that we curb water consumption by industry, which uses 20 percent of the global total, and farming, which consumes 70 percent of the total for irrigation.

Perhaps new irrigation technology will reduce the future demand for water. But here again, we see how population increase, as well as economic growth, strains our ecosystem (Postel, 1993; Population Action International, 2000).

 Las Vegas is one of the fastest-growing U.S. cities—and it is located in a desert. Do you think the future water needs of this city's people (and those of the entire Southwest) can be met? What will we do if the answer turns out to be no?

Water Pollution

In large cities from Mexico City to Cairo to Shanghai, many people have no choice but to drink contaminated water. Infectious diseases like typhoid, cholera, and dysentery, all caused by waterborne microorganisms, spread rapidly through these populations. Besides ensuring ample *supplies* of water, then, we must also protect the *quality* of water.

Water quality in the United States is generally good by global standards. However, even here the problem of water pollution is steadily growing. According to the Sierra Club, an environmental activist organization, rivers and streams across the United States absorb some 500 million pounds of toxic waste each year. This pollution results not just from intentional dumping but also from the runoff of agricultural fertilizers and lawn chemicals.

A special problem is *acid rain*—rain made acidic by air pollution—which destroys plant and animal life. Acid rain (or snow) begins with power plants burning fossil fuels (oil and coal) to generate electricity; this burning releases sulfuric and nitrous oxides into the air. As the wind sweeps these gases into the atmosphere, they react with the air to form sulfuric and nitric acids, which turns atmospheric moisture acidic.

This is a clear case of one type of pollution causing another: Air pollution (from smokestacks) ends up contaminating water (in lakes and streams that collect acid rain). Acid rain is truly a global phenomenon because the regions that suffer the harmful effects may be thousands of miles from the original pollution. For instance, British power plants have caused acid rain that has devastated forests and fish in Norway and Sweden, up to 1,000 miles to the northeast. In the United States, we see a similar pattern as midwestern smokestacks have harmed the natural environment of upstate New York and New England.

Air Pollution

Because we are surrounded by air, most people in the United States are more aware of air pollution than contaminated water. One of the unexpected consequences of industrial technology, especially the factory and the motor vehicle, has been a decline in air quality. In London in the mid-twentieth century, factory smokestacks, automobiles, and coal fires used to heat homes all added to what was probably the worst urban air quality the world has ever known. The fog that some British jokingly called "pea soup" was in reality a deadly mix of pollution: Over five days in 1952, an especially thick haze that hung over London killed 4,000 people.

Air quality improved in the final decades of the twentieth century. Rich nations passed laws that banned high-pollution heating, including the coal fires that choked London fifty years ago. In addition, scientists devised ways to make factories as well as automobiles and trucks operate more cleanly so that today's vehicles produce only a fraction of the pollution that spewed from models of the 1950s and 1960s.

If high-income countries can breathe a bit more easily than they once did, the problem of air pollution in poor societies is becoming more serious. One reason is that people in low-income countries still rely on wood, coal, peat, and other "dirty" fuels for cooking fires and to heat their homes. In addition, nations eager to encourage short-term industrial development may pay little attention to the longer-term dangers of air pollution. As a result, many cities in Latin America, Eastern Europe, and Asia are plagued by air pollution as bad as London's "pea soup" back in the 1950s.

tip

Evidence of global warming includes not only rising average temperatures but also receding glaciers at the poles and on high mountains.

 tip

The last several years have brought a remarkable rise in the public's awareness of global warming, thanks in large measure to the efforts of former vice president Al Gore.

The Rain Forests

Rain forests are *regions of dense forestation, most of which circle the globe close to the equator.* The largest tropical rain forests are in South America (notably Brazil), west-central Africa, and Southeast Asia. In all, the world's rain forests cover some 2 billion acres, or 7 percent of Earth's total land surface.

Like other global resources, rain forests are falling victim to the needs and appetites of the surging world population. As noted earlier, to meet the demand for beef, ranchers in Latin America burn forested areas to increase their supply of grazing land. We are also losing rain forests to the hardwood trade. People in rich nations pay high prices for mahogany and other woods because, as the environmentalist Norman Myers (1984b:88) puts it, they have "a penchant for parquet floors, fine furniture, fancy paneling, weekend yachts, and high-grade coffins." Under such economic pressure, the world's rain forests are now just half their original size, and they continue to shrink by about 1 percent (65,000 square miles) annually, which amounts to about an acre every second. Unless we stop this loss, the rain forests will vanish before the end of this century, and with them will go protection for Earth's biodiversity and climate.

Global Warming

Why are rain forests so important? One reason is that they cleanse the atmosphere of carbon dioxide (CO_2). Since the beginning of the Industrial Revolution, the amount of carbon dioxide produced by humans, mostly from factories and automobiles, has risen sharply. Much of this carbon dioxide is absorbed by the oceans. But plants also take in carbon dioxide and expel oxygen. This is why rain forests are vital to maintaining the chemical balance of the atmosphere.

The problem is that production of carbon dioxide is rising while the amount of plant life on Earth is shrinking. To make matters worse, rain forests are being destroyed mostly by burning, which releases even more carbon dioxide into the atmosphere. Experts estimate that the atmospheric concentration of carbon dioxide is now 20 to 30 percent higher than it was 150 years ago and rising rapidly (Revkin, 2002; Gore, 2006).

High above Earth, carbon dioxide acts like the glass roof of a greenhouse, letting heat from the sun pass through to the surface while preventing much of it from radiating away from the planet. The result of this *greenhouse effect,* say ecologists, is **global warming,** *a rise in Earth's average temperature due to an increasing concentration of carbon dioxide in the atmosphere.* Over the past century, the global temperature has risen about 1 degree Fahrenheit (to an average of 58° Fahrenheit). Scientists warn that it could rise by 5° to 10° during this century. Already, the polar ice caps are melting, and scientists predict that increasing average temperatures could melt so much ice

Members of small, simple societies, such as the Tan't Batu in the Philippines, live in harmony with nature; they do not have the technological means to greatly affect the natural world. Although we in complex societies like to think of ourselves as superior to such people, the truth is that there is much we can—indeed, must—learn from them.

TCS The Cover Story

that the sea level would rise to cover low-lying land all around the world. Were this to happen, water would cover all of Bangladesh, for example, and much of the coastal United States, including Washington, D.C., right up to the steps of the White House. On the other hand, the U.S. Midwest, currently one of the most productive agricultural regions in the world, probably would become arid.

Some scientists point out that we cannot be sure of the consequences of global warming. Others point to the fact that global temperature changes have been taking place throughout history, apparently having little or nothing to do with rain forests. A few are optimistic, suggesting that higher concentrations of carbon dioxide in the atmosphere might speed up plant growth (since plants thrive on this gas), and this increase would correct the imbalance and push Earth's temperature downward once again. But the consensus of scientists is now clear: Global warming is a serious problem that threatens the future of all of us (Kerr, 2005; Gore, 2006; International Panel on Climate Change, 2007).

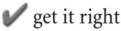

get it right

Be sure you understand the various reasons that declining biodiversity is a threat to our collective future.

tip

Raise the questions found at the end of the box in class to see what other students think.

Controversy & Debate
Apocalypse: Will People Overwhelm the Planet?

NUSHAWN: I'm telling you—there are too many people already! Where is everyone going to live?

TABITHA: Have you ever been to Kansas? Or Wyoming? There's plenty of empty space out there.

MARCO: Maybe now. But I'm not so sure about our children—or their children. . . .

Are you worried about the world's increasing population? Think about this: By the time you finish reading this box, more than 1,000 people will have been added to our planet. By this time tomorrow, global population will have risen by more than 200,000. Currently, as the table shows, there are four births for every two deaths on the planet, pushing the world's population upward by more than 74 million annually. Put another way, global population growth amounts to adding another Ethiopia to the world each year.

It is no wonder that many demographers and environmentalists are deeply concerned about the future. Earth has an unprecedented population: The 2 billion people we have added since 1974 alone exceed the planet's total in 1900. Might Thomas Robert Malthus—who predicted that overpopulation would push the world into war and suffering—be right after all? Lester Brown and other *neo-Malthusians* predict a coming apocalypse if we do not change our ways. Brown (1995) admits that Malthus failed to imagine how much technology (especially fertilizers and altering plant genetics) could boost the planet's agricultural output. But he maintains that Earth's rising population is rapidly outstripping its finite resources. Families in many poor countries can find little firewood, members of rich countries are depleting the oil reserves, and everyone is draining our supply of clean water and poi-

soning the planet with waste. Some analysts argue that we have already passed Earth's "carrying capacity" for population and we need to hold the line or even reduce global population to ensure our long-term survival.

But other analysts, the *anti-Malthusians*, sharply disagree. Julian Simon (1995) points out that two centuries after Malthus predicted catastrophe, Earth supports almost six times as many people who, on average, live longer, healthier lives than ever before. With more advanced technology, people have devised ways to increase productivity and limit population increase. As Simon sees it, this is cause for celebration. Human ingenuity has consistently proved the doomsayers wrong, and Simon is betting it will continue to do so.

WHAT DO YOU THINK?

1. Where do you place your bet? Do you think Earth can support 8 or 10 billion people? Explain your reasoning.

2. Ninety-six percent of current population growth is in poor countries. What does this mean for the future of rich nations? For the future of poor ones?

3. What should people in rich countries do to ensure the future of children everywhere?

Sources: Brown (1995), Simon (1995), Scanlon (2001), and Smail (2007).

Global Population Increase

	Births	Deaths	Net Increase
Per year	130,860,569	56,579,396	74,281,173
Per month	10,905,047	4,714,950	6,190,098
Per day	358,522	155,012	203,510
Per hour	14,938	6,459	8,480
Per minute	249	108	141
Per second	4.1	1.8	2.3

 Do you worry much about global warming? Why or why not? Do you think global warming could affect you personally? How?

Declining Biodiversity

Clearing rain forests also reduces Earth's *biodiversity* because rain forests are home to almost half the planet's living species.

On Earth, there are as many as 30 million species of animals, plants, and microorganisms. Several dozen unique species of plants

and animals cease to exist every day. Given the vast numbers of living species, why should we be concerned by the loss of a few? Environmentalists give four reasons. First, our planet's biodiversity provides a varied source of human food. Using agricultural high technology, scientists can "splice" familiar crops with more exotic plant life, making food more bountiful as well as more resistant to insects and disease. Thus biodiversity helps feed our planet's rapidly increasing population.

Second, Earth's biodiversity is a vital genetic resource used by medical and pharmaceutical researchers to produce hundreds of new

tip

With its focus on inequality, environmental racism
is linked to the social-conflict approach.

compounds each year that cure disease and improve our lives. For example, children in the United States now have a good chance of surviving leukemia, a disease that was almost a sure killer two generations ago, because of a compound derived from a tropical flower called the rosy periwinkle. The oral birth control pill, used by tens of millions of women in this country, is another product of plant research involving the Mexican forest yam.

Third, with the loss of any species of life—whether it is the magnificent California condor, the famed Chinese panda, the spotted owl, or even a single species of ant—the beauty and complexity of our natural environment are diminished. And there are clear warning signs of such loss: Three-fourths of the world's 10,000 species of birds are declining in number.

Finally, unlike pollution, the extinction of any species is irreversible and final. An important ethical question, then, is whether we who live today have the right to impoverish the world for those who live tomorrow (N. Myers, 1991; E. O. Wilson, 1991; Brown et al., 1993).

Environmental Racism

Conflict theory has given rise to the concept of **environmental racism**, *patterns of development that expose poor people, especially minorities, to environmental hazards.* Historically, factories that spew pollution have stood near neighborhoods of the poor and people of color. Why? In part, the poor themselves were drawn to factories in search of work, and their low incomes often meant they could afford housing only in undesirable neighborhoods. Sometimes the only housing that fit their budgets stood in the very shadow of the plants and mills where they worked.

Nobody wants a factory or dump nearby, but the poor have little power to resist. Through the years, the most serious environmental hazards have been located near Newark, New Jersey (not in upscale Bergen County), in southside Chicago (not wealthy Lake Forest), or on Native American reservations in the West (not in affluent suburbs of Denver or Phoenix) (Commission for Racial Justice, 1994; Bohon & Humphrey, 2000).

Looking Ahead: Toward a Sustainable Society and World

The demographic analysis presented in this chapter points to some disturbing trends. We see, first, that Earth's population has reached record levels because birth rates remain high in poor nations and death rates have fallen just about everywhere. Reducing fertility will remain a pressing need throughout this century. Even with some

Virtually no part of Earth has escaped the harm caused by human societies to the natural environment. The trash in this room was carried down from the peak of Mt. Everest by these mountain climbers. The larger question is, can humanity ever really undo the harm it has caused?

Devendra M. Singh/Agence France Presse/Getty Images

recent decline in the rate of population increase, the nightmare Thomas Malthus described is still a real possibility, as the Controversy & Debate box explains.

Further, population growth remains greatest in the poorest countries of the world, those without the means to support their present populations, much less their future ones. Supporting 74 million additional people on our planet each year, 70 million of whom are in low-income countries, will require a global commitment to provide not only food but housing, schools, and employment as well. The well-being of the entire world may ultimately depend on resolving the economic and social problems of poor, overly populated countries and bridging the widening gulf between "have" and "have-not" nations.

Urbanization is continuing, especially in poor countries. Throughout human history, people have sought out cities in the hope of finding a better life. But the sheer numbers of people who live in the emerging global supercities—Mexico City, São Paulo (Brazil), Kinshasa (Democratic Republic of the Congo), Mumbai (India), Manila (Philippines)—have created urban problems on a massive scale.

Around the world, humanity is facing a serious environmental challenge. Part of this problem is population increase, which is

tip

The Applying Sociology in Everyday Life items provide additional ways for you to connect the ideas found in this chapter with your own life.

greatest in poor countries. But part of the problem is the high levels of consumption in rich nations such as our own. By increasing the planet's environmental deficit, our present way of life is borrowing against the well-being of our children and their children. Globally, members of rich societies, who currently consume so much of Earth's resources, are mortgaging the future security of the poor countries of the world.

The answer, in principle, is to create an **ecologically sustainable culture,** *a way of life that meets the needs of the present generation without threatening the environmental legacy of future generations.* Sustainable living depends on three strategies.

First, the world needs to *bring population growth under control.* The current population of 6.6 billion is already straining the natural environment. Clearly, the higher the world's population climbs, the more difficult environmental problems will become. Even if the recent slowing of population growth continues, the world will have 8 billion people by 2050. Few analysts think that the planet can support this many people; most argue that we must hold the line at about 7 billion, and some argue that we must *decrease* population in the coming decades (Smail, 2007).

A second strategy is to *conserve finite resources.* This means meeting our needs with a responsible eye toward the future by using resources efficiently, seeking alternative sources of energy, and in some cases, learning to live with less.

A third strategy is to *reduce waste.* Whenever possible, simply using less is the best solution. Learning to live with less is not likely to come easily, but keep in mind the research that suggests that as our

society has consumed more and more, people have not become any happier. Recycling programs, too, are part of the answer, and recycling can make everyone part of the solution to our environmental problems.

In the end, making all these strategies work depends on a basic change in the way we think about ourselves and our world. Our *egocentric* outlook sets our own interests as standards for how to live, but a sustainable environment demands an *ecocentric* outlook that helps us see how the present is tied to the future and why everyone must work together. Most nations in the southern half of the world are *underdeveloped,* unable to meet the basic needs of their people. At the same time, most countries in the northern half of the world are *overdeveloped,* using more resources than the planet can sustain over time. The changes needed to create a sustainable ecosystem will not come easily, and they will be costly. But the price of not responding to the growing environmental deficit will certainly be greater (Kellert & Bormann, 1991; Brown et al., 1993; Population Action International, 2000; Gore, 2006).

Finally, consider that the great dinosaurs dominated this planet for some 160 million years and then perished forever. Humanity is far younger, having existed for a mere 250,000 years. Compared to the rather dimwitted dinosaurs, our species has the gift of great intelligence. But how will we use this ability? What are the chances that our species will continue to flourish 160 million years—or even 160 years—from now? The answer depends on the choices that will be made by one of the 30 million species living on Earth: human beings.

Applying Sociology in Everyday Life

1. Here is an illustration of the problem of runaway growth (Milbrath, 1989:10): "A pond has a single water lily growing on it. The lily doubles in size each day. In thirty days, it covers the entire pond. On which day does it cover half the pond?" When you realize the answer, discuss the implications of this example for population increase.

2. Draw a mental map of a city familiar to you with as much detail of specific places, districts, roads, and transportation facilities as you can. Compare your map to a real one or,

better yet, a map drawn by someone else. Try to account for the differences.

3. As an interesting exercise, carry a trash bag around for a single day, and collect everything you throw away. Most people are surprised to find that the average person in the United States discards close to 5 pounds of paper, metal, plastic, and other materials daily (over a lifetime, that's about 50 tons).

MAKING THE GRADE
Population, Urbanization, and Environment

Demography: The Study of Population

✔ *Demography analyzes the size and composition of a population and how and why people move from place to place. Demographers collect data and study several factors that affect population.*

FERTILITY
- Fertility is the incidence of childbearing in a country's population.
- Demographers describe fertility using the **crude birth rate**.

MORTALITY
- Mortality is the incidence of death in a country's population.
- Demographers measure mortality using both the **crude death rate** and the **infant mortality rate**.

MIGRATION
The **net migration rate** is the difference between the in-migration rate and the out-migration rate.

POPULATION GROWTH
In general, rich nations grow almost as much from immigration as from natural increase; poorer nations grow almost entirely from natural increase.

POPULATION COMPOSITION
Demographers use **age-sex pyramids** to show graphically the composition of a population and to project population trends.

demography the study of human population

fertility the incidence of childbearing in a country's population

crude birth rate the number of live births in a given year for every 1,000 people in a population

mortality the incidence of death in a country's population

crude death rate the number of deaths in a given year for every 1,000 people in a population

infant mortality rate the number of deaths among infants under one year of age for each 1,000 live births in a given year

life expectancy the average life span of a country's population

migration the movement of people into and out of a specified territory

sex ratio the number of males for every 100 females in a nation's population

age-sex pyramid a graphic representation of the age and sex of a population

History and Theory of Population Growth

- Historically, world population grew slowly because high birth rates were offset by high death rates.
- About 1750, a demographic transition began as world population rose sharply, mostly due to falling death rates.
- In the late 1700s, Thomas Robert Malthus warned that population growth would outpace food production, resulting in social calamity.
- **Demographic transition theory** contends that technological advances gradually slow population increase.
- World population is expected to reach between 8 billion and 9 billion by 2050.

✔ *Currently, the world is gaining 74 million people each year, with 96% of this increase taking place in poor countries.*

demographic transition theory a thesis that links population patterns to a society's level of technological development

zero population growth the rate of reproduction that maintains population at a steady level

Urbanization: The Growth of Cities

The **FIRST URBAN REVOLUTION** began with the appearance of cities about 10,000 years ago.
- By about 2,000 years ago, cities had emerged in most regions of the world except North America and Antarctica.
- Preindustrial cities have low-rise buildings; narrow, winding streets; and personal social ties.

A **SECOND URBAN REVOLUTION** began about 1750 as the Industrial Revolution propelled rapid urban growth in Europe.
- The physical form of cities changed as planners created wide, regular streets to allow for more trade.
- The emphasis on commerce, as well as the increasing size of cities, made urban life more impersonal.

urbanization the concentration of population into cities

metropolis a large city that socially and economically dominates an urban area

suburbs urban areas beyond the political boundaries of a city

megalopolis a vast urban region containing a number of cities and their surrounding suburbs

IN THE UNITED STATES, urbanization has been going on for more than 400 years and continues today.
- Urbanization came to North America with European colonists.
- By 1850, hundreds of new cities had been founded from coast to coast.
- By 1920, a majority of the U.S. population lived in urban areas.
- Since 1950, the decentralization of cities has resulted in the growth of suburbs and edge cities and a "rebound" in rural population.
- Nationally, Sunbelt cities—but not the older Snowbelt cities—are increasing in size and population.

MAKING THE GRADE *continued . . .*

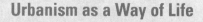

Urbanism as a Way of Life

✔ *Rapid urbanization during the nineteenth century led early sociologists to study the differences between rural and urban life. These early sociologists included, in Europe, Tönnies, Durkheim, and Simmel, and in the United States, Park and Wirth.*

FERDINAND TÖNNIES built his analysis on the concepts of *Gemeinschaft* and *Gesellschaft*.

- *Gemeinschaft*, typical of the rural village, joins people in what amounts to a single primary group.
- *Gesellschaft*, typical of the modern city, describes individuals motivated by their own needs rather than by a desire to help improve the well-being of the community.

EMILE DURKHEIM agreed with much of Tönnies's thinking but claimed that urbanites do not lack social bonds; the basis of social soldarity simply differs in the two settings. He described

- **mechanical solidarity**—social bonds based on common sentiments and shared moral values. This type of social solidarity is typical of traditional, rural life.
- **organic solidarity**—social bonds based on specialization and interdependence. This type of social solidarity is typical of modern, urban life.

Gemeinschaft a type of social organization in which people are closely tied by kinship and tradition

Gesellschaft a type of social organization in which people come together only on the basis of individual self-interest

urban ecology the study of the link between the physical and social dimensions of cities

GEORG SIMMEL claimed that the overstimulation of city life produced a blasé attitude in urbanites.

ROBERT PARK, at the University of Chicago, claimed that cities permit greater social freedom.

LOUIS WIRTH saw large, dense, heterogeneous populations creating an impersonal and self-interested, though tolerant, way of life.

Urbanization in Poor Nations

- The world's first urban revolution took place about 8,000 B.C.E. with the first urban settlements.
- The second urban revolution took place after 1750 in Europe and North America with the Industrial Revolution.
- A third urban revolution is now occurring in poor countries. Today, most of the world's largest cities are found in less developed nations.

ecology the study of the interaction of living organisms and the natural environment

natural environment Earth's surface and atmosphere, including living organisms, air, water, soil, and other resources necessary to sustain life

ecosystem a system composed of the interaction of all living organisms and their natural environment

Environment and Society

The state of the **ENVIRONMENT** is a social issue because it reflects how human beings organize social life.

- Societies increase the **environmental deficit** by focusing on short-term benefits and ignoring the long-term consequences brought on by their way of life.
- The more complex a society's technology, the greater its capacity to alter the natural environment.

- The *logic-of-growth thesis* supports economic development, claiming that people can solve environmental problems as they arise.
- The *limits-to-growth thesis* states that societies must curb development to prevent eventual environmental collapse.

environmental deficit profound long-term harm to the natural environment caused by humanity's focus on short-term material affluence

rain forests regions of dense forestation, most of which circle the globe close to the equator

global warming a rise in Earth's average temperature due to an increasing concentration of carbon dioxide in the atmosphere

ENVIRONMENTAL ISSUES include

- **Disposing of solid waste**—80% of what we throw away ends up in landfills, which are filling up and which can pollute groundwater under Earth's surface.
- **Protecting the quality of water and air**—The supply of clean water is already low in some parts of the world. Industrial technology has caused a decline in air quality.
- **Protecting the rain forests**—Rain forests help remove carbon dioxide from the atmosphere and are home to a large share of this planet's living species. Under pressure from development, the world's rain forests are now half their original size and are shrinking by about 1% annually.
- **Environmental racism**—Conflict theory has drawn attention to the pattern by which the poor, especially minorities, suffer most from environmental hazards.

environmental racism patterns of development that expose poor people, especially minorities, to environmental hazards

ecologically sustainable culture a way of life that meets the needs of the present generation without threatening the environmental legacy of future generations

MAKING THE GRADE

Population, Urbanization, and Environment

Sample Test Questions

These questions are similar to those found in the test bank that accompanies this textbook.

Multiple-Choice Questions

1. *Demography* is defined as the study of
   a. democratic political systems.
   b. human culture.
   c. human population.
   d. the natural environment.

2. Which region of the world has *both* the lowest birth rate and the lowest infant mortality rate?
   a. Latin America
   b. Europe
   c. Africa
   d. Asia

3. Typically, high-income nations grow mostly from _____, and low-income nations grow from _____.
   a. immigration; natural increase
   b. emigration; natural increase
   c. natural increase; immigration
   d. internal migration; natural increase

4. In general, the higher the average income of a country,
   a. the faster the population increases.
   b. the slower the population increases.
   c. the lower the level of immigration.
   d. the lower the level of urbanization.

5. In the United States, urban decentralization has caused
   a. the expansion of suburbs.
   b. the development of vast urban regions.
   c. the growth of edge cities.
   d. All of the above are correct.

6. Which term was used by Ferdinand Tönnies to refer to a type of social organization in which people come together on the basis of individual self-interest?
   a. mechanical solidarity
   b. organic solidarity
   c. *Gesellschaft*
   d. *Gemeinschaft*

7. The world's third urban revolution is now taking place in
   a. the United States.
   b. Europe and Japan.
   c. middle-income nations.
   d. low-income nations.

8. The *environmental deficit* refers to
   a. long-term harm to the environment caused by a shortsighted focus on material affluence.
   b. the public's lack of interest in the natural environment.
   c. the fact that natural scientists ignore the social dimensions of environmental problems.
   d. the lack of funding for important environmental programs.

9. Which of the following statements reflects the "limits to growth" thesis?
   a. People are rapidly consuming Earth's finite resources.
   b. Whatever problems technology creates, technology can solve.
   c. The quality of life on Earth is getting better.
   d. Higher living standards today will benefit future generations.

10. *Environmental racism* is the idea that
    a. few minorities are found within the environmental movement.
    b. prejudice is the major cause of pollution and other environmental problems.
    c. environmental dangers are greatest for the poor and minorities.
    d. All of the above are correct.

ANSWERS: 1 (c); 2 (b); 3 (a); 4 (b); 5 (d); 6 (c); 7 (d); 8 (a); 9 (a); 10 (c).

Essay Questions

1. According to demographic transition theory, how does economic development affect population patterns?

2. According to Ferdinand Tönnies, Emile Durkheim, Georg Simmel, and Louis Wirth, what characterizes urbanism as a way of life? Note several differences in the ideas of these thinkers.

Glossary

Glossary

abortion the deliberate termination of a pregnancy

absolute poverty a lack of resources that is life-threatening

achieved status a social position a person assumes voluntarily that reflects personal ability and effort

activity theory the idea that a high level of activity increases personal satisfaction in old age

Afrocentrism emphasizing and promoting African cultural patterns

ageism prejudice and discrimination against older people

age-sex pyramid a graphic representation of the age and sex of a population

age stratification the unequal distribution of wealth, power, and privilege among people at different stages of the life course

agriculture large-scale cultivation using plows harnessed to animals or more powerful energy sources

alienation the experience of isolation and misery resulting from powerlessness

animism the belief that elements of the natural world are conscious life forms that affect humanity

anomie Durkheim's designation of a condition in which society provides little moral guidance to individuals

anticipatory socialization learning that helps a person achieve a desired position

ascribed status a social position a person receives at birth or takes on involuntarily later in life

asexuality a lack of sexual attraction to people of either sex

assimilation the process by which minorities gradually adopt patterns of the dominant culture

authoritarianism a political system that denies people participation in government

authority power that people perceive as legitimate rather than coercive

beliefs specific thoughts or ideas that people hold to be true

bilateral descent a system tracing kinship through both men and women

bisexuality sexual attraction to people of both sexes

blue-collar occupations lower-prestige jobs that involve mostly manual labor

bureaucracy an organizational model rationally designed to perform tasks efficiently

bureaucratic inertia the tendency of bureaucratic organizations to perpetuate themselves

bureaucratic ritualism a focus on rules and regulations to the point of undermining an organization's goals

capitalism an economic system in which natural resources and the means of producing goods and services are privately owned

capitalists people who own and operate factories and other businesses in pursuit of profits

caregiving informal and unpaid care provided to a dependent person by family members, other relatives, or friends

caste system social stratification based on ascription, or birth

cause and effect a relationship in which change in one variable (the independent variable) causes change in another (the dependent variable)

charisma extraordinary personal qualities that can infuse people with emotion and turn them into followers

charismatic authority power legitimized through extraordinary personal abilities that inspire devotion and obedience

church a type of religious organization that is well integrated into the larger society

civil religion a quasi-religious loyalty binding individuals in a basically secular society

claims making the process of trying to convince the public and public officials of the importance of joining a social movement to address a particular issue

class conflict conflict between entire classes over the distribution of a society's wealth and power

class consciousness Marx's term for workers' recognition of themselves as a class unified in opposition to capitalists and ultimately to capitalism itself

class society a capitalist society with pronounced social stratification

class system social stratification based on both birth and individual achievement

cohabitation the sharing of a household by an unmarried couple

cohort a category of people with something in common, usually their age

collective behavior activity involving a large number of people that is unplanned, often controversial, and sometimes dangerous

collectivity a large number of people whose minimal interaction occurs in the absence of well-defined and conventional norms

colonialism the process by which some nations enrich themselves through political and economic control of other nations

communism a hypothetical economic and political system in which all members of a society are socially equal

community-based corrections correctional programs operating within society at large rather than behind prison walls

concept a mental construct that represents some part of the world in a simplified form

concrete operational stage Piaget's term for the level of human development at which individuals first see causal connections in their surroundings

conglomerate a giant corporation composed of many smaller corporations

conspicuous consumption buying and using products because of the "statement" they make about social position

control holding constant all variables except one in order to see clearly the effect of that variable

corporate crime the illegal actions of a corporation or people acting on its behalf

corporation an organization with a legal existence, including rights and liabilities, separate from that of its members

correlation a relationship in which two (or more) variables change together

counterculture cultural patterns that strongly oppose those widely accepted within a society

crime the violation of a society's formally enacted criminal law

crimes against the person crimes that direct violence or the threat of violence against others; also known as *violent crimes*

crimes against property crimes that involve theft of property belonging to others; also known as *property crimes*

criminal justice system a formal response by police, courts, and prison officials to alleged violations of the law

criminal recidivism later offenses by people previously convicted of crimes

critical sociology the study of society that focuses on the need for social change

crowd a temporary gathering of people who share a common focus of attention and who influence one another

514

crude birth rate the number of live births in a given year for every 1,000 people in a population

crude death rate the number of deaths in a given year for every 1,000 people in a population

cult a religious organization that is largely outside a society's cultural traditions

cultural integration the close relationships among various elements of a cultural system

cultural lag the fact that some cultural elements change more quickly than others, disrupting a cultural system

cultural relativism the practice of judging a culture by its own standards

cultural transmission the process by which one generation passes culture to the next

cultural universals traits that are part of every known culture

culture the ways of thinking, the ways of acting, and the material objects that together form a people's way of life

culture shock personal disorientation when experiencing an unfamiliar way of life

Davis-Moore thesis the assertion that social stratification has beneficial consequences for the operation of a society

deductive logical thought reasoning that transforms general theory into specific hypotheses suitable for testing

democracy a political system that gives power to the people as a whole

demographic transition theory a thesis that links population patterns to a society's level of technological development

demography the study of human population

denomination a church, independent of the state, that recognizes religious pluralism

dependency theory a model of economic and social development that explains global inequality in terms of the historical exploitation of poor nations by rich ones

dependent variable a variable that is changed by another variable (the independent variable)

descent the system by which members of a society trace kinship over generations

deterrence the attempt to discourage criminality through the use of punishment

deviance the recognized violation of cultural norms

direct-fee system a medical care system in which patients pay directly for the services of physicians and hospitals

disaster an event, generally unexpected, that causes extensive harm to people and damage to property

discrimination unequal treatment of various categories of people

disengagement theory the idea that society enhances its orderly operation by removing people from positions of responsibility as they reach old age

division of labor specialized economic activity

dramaturgical analysis Erving Goffman's term for the study of social interaction in terms of theatrical performance

dyad a social group with two members

eating disorder an intense form of dieting or other unhealthy method of weight control driven by the desire to be very thin

ecologically sustainable culture a way of life that meets the needs of the present generation without threatening the environmental legacy of future generations

ecology the study of the interaction of living organisms and the natural environment

economy the social institution that organizes a society's production, distribution, and consumption of goods and services

ecosystem a system composed of the interaction of all living organisms and their natural environment

education the social institution through which society provides its members with important knowledge, including basic facts, job skills, and cultural norms and values

ego Freud's term for a person's conscious efforts to balance innate pleasure-seeking drives with the demands of society

empirical evidence information we can verify with our senses

endogamy marriage between people of the same social category

environmental deficit profound long-term harm to the natural environment caused by humanity's focus on short-term material affluence

environmental racism patterns of development that expose poor people, especially minorities, to environmental hazards

ethnicity a shared cultural heritage

ethnocentrism the practice of judging another culture by the standards of one's own culture

ethnomethodology Harold Garfinkel's term for the study of the way people make sense of their everyday surroundings

Eurocentrism the dominance of European (especially English) cultural patterns

euthanasia assisting in the death of a person suffering from an incurable disease; also known as *mercy killing*

exogamy marriage between people of different social categories

experiment a research method for investigating cause and effect under highly controlled conditions

expressive leadership group leadership that focuses on the group's well-being

extended family a family consisting of parents and children as well as other kin; also known as a *consanguine family*

fad an unconventional social pattern that people embrace briefly but enthusiastically

faith belief based on conviction rather than on scientific evidence

false consciousness Marx's term for explanations of social problems as the shortcomings of individuals rather than as the flaws of society

family a social institution found in all societies that unites people in cooperative groups to care for one another, including any children

family violence emotional, physical, or sexual abuse of one family member by another

fashion a social pattern favored by a large number of people

feminism support of social equality for men and women, in opposition to patriarchy and sexism

feminization of poverty the trend of women making up an increasing proportion of the poor

fertility the incidence of childbearing in a country's population

folkways norms for routine or casual interaction

formal operational stage Piaget's term for the level of human development at which individuals think abstractly and critically

formal organization a large secondary group organized to achieve its goals efficiently

functional illiteracy a lack of the reading and writing skills needed for everyday living

fundamentalism a conservative religious doctrine that opposes intellectualism and worldly accommodation in favor of restoring traditional, otherworldly religion

Gemeinschaft a type of social organization in which people are closely tied by kinship and tradition

gender the personal traits and social positions that members of a society attach to being female or male

gender-conflict approach a point of view that focuses on inequality and conflict between women and men

gender roles (sex roles) attitudes and activities that a society links to each sex

gender stratification the unequal distribution of wealth, power, and privilege between men and women

generalized other George Herbert Mead's term for widespread cultural norms and values we use as a reference in evaluating ourselves

genocide the systematic killing of one category of people by another

gerontocracy a form of social organization in which the elderly have the most wealth, power, and prestige

gerontology the study of aging and the elderly

Gesellschaft a type of social organization in which people come together only on the basis of individual self-interest

global economy economic activity that crosses national borders

global perspective the study of the larger world and our society's place in it

global stratification patterns of social inequality in the world as a whole

global warming a rise in Earth's average temperature due to an increasing concentration of carbon dioxide in the atmosphere

gossip rumor about people's personal affairs

government a formal organization that directs the political life of a society

groupthink the tendency of group members to conform, resulting in a narrow view of some issue

hate crime a criminal act against a person or a person's property by an offender motivated by racial or other bias

Hawthorne effect a change in a subject's behavior caused simply by the awareness of being studied

health a state of complete physical, mental, and social well-being

health maintenance organization (HMO) an organization that provides comprehensive medical care to subscribers for a fixed fee

heterosexism a view that labels anyone who is not heterosexual as "queer"

heterosexuality sexual attraction to someone of the other sex

high culture cultural patterns that distinguish a society's elite

high-income countries nations with the highest overall standards of living

holistic medicine an approach to health care that emphasizes the prevention of illness and takes into account a person's entire physical and social environment

homogamy marriage between people with the same social characteristics

homophobia discomfort over close personal interaction with people thought to be gay, lesbian, or bisexual

homosexuality sexual attraction to someone of the same sex

horticulture the use of hand tools to raise crops

hunting and gathering making use of simple tools to hunt animals and gather vegetation for food

hypothesis a statement of a possible relationship between two (or more) variables

id Freud's term for the human being's basic drives

ideal type an abstract statement of the essential characteristics of any social phenomenon

ideology cultural beliefs that justify particular social arrangements, including patterns of inequality

incest taboo a norm forbidding sexual relations or marriage between certain relatives

income earnings from work or investments

independent variable a variable that causes change in another variable (the dependent variable)

inductive logical thought reasoning that transforms specific observations into general theory

industrialism the production of goods using advanced sources of energy to drive large machinery

infant mortality rate the number of deaths among infants under one year of age for each 1,000 live births in a given year

infidelity sexual activity outside one's marriage

in-group a social group toward which a member feels respect and loyalty

institutional prejudice and discrimination bias built into the operation of society's institutions

instrumental leadership group leadership that focuses on the completion of tasks

intergenerational social mobility upward or downward social mobility of children in relation to their parents

interpretive sociology the study of society that focuses on the meanings people attach to their social world

intersection theory analysis of the interplay of race, class, and gender, often resulting in multiple dimensions of disadvantage

intersexual people people whose bodies (including genitals) have both female and male characteristics

interview a series of questions a researcher asks respondents in person

intragenerational social mobility a change in social position occurring during a person's lifetime

kinship a social bond based on common ancestry, marriage, or adoption

labeling theory the idea that deviance and conformity result not so much from what people do as from how others respond to those actions

labor unions organizations of workers that seek to improve wages and working conditions through various strategies, including negotiations and strikes

language a system of symbols that allows people to communicate with one another

latent functions the unrecognized and unintended consequences of any social pattern

liberation theology the combining of Christian principles with political activism, often Marxist in character

life expectancy the average life span of a country's population

looking-glass self Cooley's term for a self-image based on how we think others see us

low-income countries nations with a low standard of living in which most people are poor

macro-level orientation a broad focus on social structures that shape society as a whole

mainstreaming integrating students with disabilities or special needs into the overall educational program

manifest functions the recognized and intended consequences of any social pattern

marriage a legal relationship, usually involving economic cooperation, sexual activity, and childbearing

Marxist political-economy model an analysis that explains politics in terms of the operation of a society's economic system

mass behavior collective behavior among people spread over a wide geographic area

mass hysteria (moral panic) a form of dispersed collective behavior in which people react to a real or imagined event with irrational and even frantic fear

mass media the means for delivering impersonal communications to a vast audience

mass society a society in which prosperity and bureaucracy have weakened traditional social ties

master status a status that has special importance for social identity, often shaping a person's entire life

material culture the physical things created by members of a society

matriarchy a form of social organization in which females dominate males

matrilineal descent a system tracing kinship through women

matrilocality a residential pattern in which a married couple lives with or near the wife's family

measurement a procedure for determining the value of a variable in a specific case

mechanical solidarity Durkheim's term for social bonds, based on common sentiments and shared moral values, that are strong among members of preindustrial societies

medicalization of deviance the transformation of moral and legal deviance into a medical condition

medicine the social institution that focuses on fighting disease and improving health

megalopolis a vast urban region containing a number of cities and their surrounding suburbs

meritocracy social stratification based on personal merit

metropolis a large city that socially and economically dominates an urban area

micro-level orientation a close-up focus on social interaction in specific situations

middle-income countries nations with a standard of living about average for the world as a whole

migration the movement of people into and out of a specified territory

military-industrial complex the close association of the federal government, the military, and defense industries

minority any category of people distinguished by physical or cultural difference that a society sets apart and subordinates

miscegenation biological reproduction by partners of different racial categories

mob a highly emotional crowd that pursues a violent or destructive goal

modernity social patterns resulting from industrialization

modernization the process of social change begun by industrialization

modernization theory a model of economic and social development that explains global inequality in terms of technological and cultural differences between nations

monarchy a political system in which a single family rules from generation to generation

monogamy marriage that unites two partners

monopoly the domination of a market by a single producer

monotheism belief in a single divine power

moral panic see *mass hysteria*

mores norms that are widely observed and have great moral significance

mortality the incidence of death in a country's population

multiculturalism a perspective recognizing the cultural diversity of the United States and promoting equal standing for all cultural traditions

multinational corporation a large business that operates in many countries

natural environment Earth's surface and atmosphere, including living organisms, air, water, soil, and other resources necessary to sustain life

neocolonialism a new form of global power relationships that involves no direct political control but economic exploitation by multinational corporations

neolocality a residential pattern in which a married couple lives apart from both sets of parents

network a web of weak social ties

nonmaterial culture the ideas created by members of a society

nonverbal communication communication using body movements, gestures, and facial expressions rather than speech

norms rules and expectations by which a society guides the behavior of its members

nuclear family a family composed of one or two parents and their children; also known as a *conjugal family*

nuclear proliferation the acquisition of nuclear weapons technology by more and more nations

objectivity personal neutrality in conducting research

oligarchy the rule of the many by the few

oligopoly the domination of a market by a few producers

operationalize a variable specify exactly what is to be measured before assigning a value to a variable

organic solidarity Durkheim's term for social bonds, based on specialization and interdependence, that are strong among members of industrial societies

organizational environment factors outside an organization that affect its operation

organized crime a business supplying illegal goods or services

other-directedness openness to the latest trends and fashions, often expressed by imitating others

out-group a social group toward which a person feels a sense of competition or opposition

panic a form of collective behavior in which people in one place react to a threat or other stimulus with irrational, frantic, and often self-destructive behavior

participant observation a research method in which investigators systematically observe people while joining them in their routine activities

pastoralism the domestication of animals

patriarchy a form of social organization in which males dominate females

patrilineal descent a system tracing kinship through men

patrilocality a residential pattern in which a married couple lives with or near the husband's family

peer group a social group whose members have interests, social position, and age in common

personality a person's fairly consistent patterns of acting, thinking, and feeling

personal space the surrounding area over which a person makes some claim to privacy

plea bargaining a legal negotiation in which a prosecutor reduces a charge in exchange for a defendant's guilty plea

pluralism a state in which people of all races and ethnicities are distinct but have equal social standing

pluralist model an analysis of politics that sees power as spread among many competing interest groups

political action committee (PAC) an organization formed by a special-interest group, independent of political parties, to raise and spend money in support of political goals

political revolution the overthrow of one political system in order to establish another

politics the social institution that distributes power, sets a society's goals, and makes decisions

polyandry marriage that unites one woman and two or more men

polygamy marriage that unites a person with two or more spouses

polygyny marriage that unites one man and two or more women

polytheism belief in many gods

popular culture cultural patterns that are widespread among a society's population

population the people who are the focus of research

pornography sexually explicit material intended to cause sexual arousal

positivism a way of understanding based on science

postindustrial economy a productive system based on service work and high technology

postindustrialism the production of information using computer technology

postmodernity social patterns characteristic of postindustrial societies

power the ability to achieve desired ends despite opposition from others

power-elite model an analysis of politics that sees power as concentrated among the rich

prejudice a rigid and unfair generalization about an entire category of people

preoperational stage Piaget's term for the level of human development at which individuals first use language and other symbols

presentation of self Erving Goffman's term for a person's efforts to create specific impressions in the minds of others

primary group a small social group whose members share personal and lasting relationships

primary labor market jobs that provide extensive benefits to workers

primary sector the part of the economy that draws raw materials from the natural environment

primary sex characteristics the genitals, organs used for reproduction

profane included as an ordinary element of everyday life

profession a prestigious white-collar occupation that requires extensive formal education

proletarians people who sell their labor for wages

propaganda information presented with the intention of shaping public opinion

prostitution the selling of sexual services

public opinion widespread attitudes about controversial issues

queer theory a body of research findings that challenges the heterosexual bias in U.S. society

questionnaire a series of written questions a researcher presents to subjects

race a socially constructed category of people who share biologically transmitted traits that members of a society consider important

race-conflict approach a point of view that focuses on inequality and conflict between people of different racial and ethnic categories

racism the belief that one racial category is innately superior or inferior to another

rain forests regions of dense forestation, most of which circle the globe close to the equator

rationality a way of thinking that emphasizes deliberate, matter-of-fact calculation of the most efficient way to accomplish a particular task

rationalization of society Weber's term for the historical change from tradition to rationality as the main type of human thought

rational-legal authority power legitimized by legally enacted rules and regulations; also known as *bureaucratic authority*

reference group a social group that serves as a point of reference in making evaluations and decisions

rehabilitation a program for reforming the offender to prevent later offenses

relative deprivation a perceived disadvantage arising from some specific comparison

relative poverty the lack of resources of some people in relation to those who have more

reliability consistency in measurement

religion a social institution involving beliefs and practices based on recognizing the sacred

religiosity the importance of religion in a person's life

replication repetition of research by other investigators

research method a systematic plan for doing research

resocialization radically changing an inmate's personality by carefully controlling the environment

retribution an act of moral vengeance by which society makes the offender suffer as much as the suffering caused by the crime

riot a social eruption that is highly emotional, violent, and undirected

ritual formal, ceremonial behavior

role behavior expected of someone who holds a particular status

role conflict conflict among the roles connected to two or more statuses

role set a number of roles attached to a single status

role strain tension among the roles connected to a single status

routinization of charisma the transformation of charismatic authority into some combination of traditional and bureaucratic authority

rumor unconfirmed information that people spread informally, often by word of mouth

sacred set apart as extraordinary, inspiring awe and reverence

sample a part of a population that represents the whole

Sapir-Whorf thesis the idea that people see and understand the world through the cultural lens of language

scapegoat a person or category of people, typically with little power, whom people unfairly blame for their own troubles

schooling formal instruction under the direction of specially trained teachers

science a logical system that bases knowledge on direct, systematic observation

scientific management Frederick Taylor's term for the application of scientific principles to the operation of a business or other large organization

scientific sociology the study of society based on systematic observation of social behavior

secondary group a large and impersonal social group whose members pursue a specific goal or activity

secondary labor market jobs that provide minimal benefits to workers

secondary sector   the part of the economy that transforms raw materials into manufactured goods

secondary sex characteristics   bodily development, apart from the genitals, that distinguishes biologically mature females and males

sect   a type of religious organization that stands apart from the larger society

secularization   the historical decline in the importance of the supernatural and the sacred

segregation   the physical and social separation of categories of people

self   George Herbert Mead's term for the part of an individual's personality composed of self-awareness and self-image

sensorimotor stage   Piaget's term for the level of human development at which individuals experience the world only through their senses

sex   the biological distinction between females and males

sexism   the belief that one sex is innately superior to the other

sex ratio   the number of males for every 100 females in a nation's population

sexual harassment   comments, gestures, or physical contacts of a sexual nature that are deliberate, repeated, and unwelcome

sexual orientation   a person's romantic and emotional attraction to another person

sick role   patterns of behavior defined as appropriate for people who are ill

significant others   people, such as parents, who have special importance for socialization

social change   the transformation of culture and social institutions over time

social character   personality patterns common to members of a particular society

social conflict   the struggle between segments of society over valued resources

social-conflict approach   a framework for building theory that sees society as an arena of inequality that generates conflict and change

social construction of reality   the process by which people creatively shape reality through social interaction

social control   attempts by society to regulate people's thoughts and behavior

social dysfunction   any social pattern that may disrupt the operation of society

social epidemiology   the study of how health and disease are distributed throughout a society's population

social functions   the consequences of any social pattern for the operation of society as a whole

social group   two or more people who identify and interact with one another

social institutions   the major spheres of social life, or societal subsystems, organized to meet human needs

social interaction   the process by which people act and react in relation to others

socialism   an economic system in which natural resources and the means of producing goods and services are collectively owned

socialization   the lifelong social experience by which people develop their human potential and learn culture

socialized medicine   a medical care system in which the government owns and operates most medical facilities and employs most physicians

social mobility   a change in position within the social hierarchy

social movement   an organized activity that encourages or discourages social change

social stratification   a system by which a society ranks categories of people in a hierarchy

social structure   any relatively stable pattern of social behavior

societal protection   rendering an offender incapable of further offenses temporarily through imprisonment or permanently by execution

society   people who interact in a defined territory and share a culture

sociobiology   a theoretical approach that explores ways in which human biology affects how we create culture

sociocultural evolution   Lenski's term for the changes that occur as a society gains new technology

socioeconomic status (SES)   a composite ranking based on various dimensions of social inequality

sociological perspective   the special point of view of sociology that sees general patterns of society in the lives of particular people

sociology   the systematic study of human society

special-interest group   people organized to address some economic or social issue

spurious correlation   an apparent but false relationship between two (or more) variables that is caused by some other variable

state capitalism   an economic and political system in which companies are privately owned but cooperate closely with the government

state church   a church formally allied with the state

status   a social position that a person holds

status consistency   the degree of uniformity in a person's social standing across various dimensions of social inequality

status set   all the statuses a person holds at a given time

stereotype   a simplified description applied to every person in some category

stigma   a powerfully negative label that greatly changes a person's self-concept and social identity

structural-functional approach   a framework for building theory that sees society as a complex system whose parts work together to promote solidarity and stability

structural social mobility   a shift in the social position of large numbers of people due more to changes in society itself than to individual efforts

subculture   cultural patterns that set apart some segment of a society's population

suburbs   urban areas beyond the political boundaries of a city

superego   Freud's term for the cultural values and norms internalized by an individual

survey   a research method in which subjects respond to a series of statements or questions in a questionnaire or an interview

symbol   anything that carries a particular meaning recognized by people who share a culture

symbolic-interaction approach   a framework for building theory that sees society as the product of the everyday interactions of individuals

technology   knowledge that people use to make a way of life in their surroundings

terrorism   acts of violence or the threat of violence used as a political strategy by an individual or a group

tertiary sector   the part of the economy that involves services rather than goods

theoretical approach   a basic image of society that guides thinking and research

theory   a statement of how and why specific facts are related

Thomas theorem W. I. Thomas's statement that situations that are defined as real are real in their consequences

total institution a setting in which people are isolated from the rest of society and manipulated by an administrative staff

totalitarianism a highly centralized political system that extensively regulates people's lives

totem an object in the natural world collectively defined as sacred

tracking assigning students to different types of educational programs

tradition values and beliefs passed from generation to generation

traditional authority power legitimized by respect for long-established cultural patterns

tradition-directedness rigid conformity to time-honored ways of living

transsexuals people who feel they are one sex even though biologically they are the other

triad a social group with three members

underground economy economic activity involving income not reported to the government as required by law

urban ecology the study of the link between the physical and social dimensions of cities

urbanization the concentration of population into cities

validity actually measuring exactly what you intend to measure

values culturally defined standards that people use to decide what is desirable, good, and beautiful and that serve as broad guidelines for social living

variable a concept whose value changes from case to case

victimless crimes violations of law in which there are no obvious victims

war organized, armed conflict among the people of two or more nations, directed by their governments

wealth the total value of money and other assets, minus outstanding debts

welfare capitalism an economic and political system that combines a mostly market-based economy with extensive social welfare programs

welfare state government agencies and programs that provide benefits to the population

white-collar crime crime committed by people of high social position in the course of their occupations

white-collar occupations higher-prestige jobs that involve mostly mental activity

zero population growth the rate of reproduction that maintains population at a steady level

References

ABERLE, DAVID F. *The Peyote Religion among the Navaho.* Chicago: Aldine, 1966.

"Abramoff Effect: Leaping out of Bed with the Lobbyists." *New York Times* (January 16, 2006). [Online] Available June 3, 2006, at http://www.researchnavigator.com

ADLER, JERRY. "When Harry Called Sally . . ." *Newsweek* (October 1, 1990):74.

ADORNO, THEODORE W., ELSE FRENKEL-BRUNSWIK, DANIEL J. LEVINSON, and R. NEVITT SANFORD. *The Authoritarian Personality.* New York: Harper & Brothers, 1950.

AGUIRRE, BENIGNO E., and E. L. QUARANTELLI. "Methodological, Ideological, and Conceptual-Theoretical Criticisms of Collective Behavior: A Critical Evaluation and Implications for Future Study." *Sociological Focus.* Vol. 16, No. 3 (August 1983):195–216.

AGUIRRE, BENIGNO E., E. L. QUARANTELLI, and JORGE L. MENDOZA. "The Collective Behavior of Fads: Characteristics, Effects, and Career of Streaking." *American Sociological Review.* Vol. 53, No. 4 (August 1988):569–84.

AKERS, RONALD L., MARVIN D. KROHN, LONN LANZA-KADUCE, and MARCIA RADOSEVICH. "Social Learning and Deviant Behavior." *American Sociological Review.* Vol. 44, No. 4 (August 1979):636–55.

ALAN GUTTMACHER INSTITUTE. "Teen Pregnancy: Trends and Lessons Learned." *Issues in Brief.* 2002 Series, No. 1. 2002. [Online] Available May 30, 2005, at http://www.agi-usa.org/pubs/ib_1-02.pdf

———. "U.S. Teenage Pregnancy Statistics: National and State Trends and Trends by Race and Ethnicity." Rev. September 2006. [Online] Available May 8, 2007, at http://www.guttmacher.org/pubs/2006/09/12/USTPstats.pdf

ALBON, JOAN. "Retention of Cultural Values and Differential Urban Adaptation: Samoans and American Indians in a West Coast City." *Social Forces.* Vol. 49, No. 3 (March 1971):385–93.

ALI, LORRAINE, and VANESSA JUAREZ. "We Love This Country." *Newsweek.* April 7, 2003.

ALI, LORRAINE, TAMARA LIPPER, and MOHAMMED MACK. "Voters: A Demographic Shift." *Newsweek.* October 25, 2004.

ALLAN, EMILIE ANDERSEN, and DARRELL J. STEFFENSMEIER. "Youth, Underemployment, and Property Crime: Differential Effects of Job Availability and Job Quality on Juvenile and Young Adult Arrest Rates." *American Sociological Review.* Vol. 54, No. 1 (February 1989):107–23.

ALLEN, THOMAS B., and CHARLES O. HYMAN. *We Americans: Celebrating a Nation, Its People, and Its Past.* Washington, D.C.: National Geographic Society, 1999.

ALLEN, WALTER R. "African American Family Life in Social Context: Crisis and Hope." *Sociological Forum.* Vol. 10, No. 4 (December 1995):569–92.

ALSTER, NORM. "When Gray Heads Roll, Is Age Bias at Work?" *New York Times* (January 30, 2005). [Online] Available April 15, 2005, at http://www.researchnavigator.com

ALTONJI, JOSEPH G., ULRICH DORASZELSKI, and LEWIS SEGAL. "Black/White Differences in Wealth." *Economic Perspectives.* Vol. 24, No. 1 (First Quarter 2000):38–50.

AMATO, PAUL R. "What Children Learn from Divorce." *Population Today.* Vol. 29, No. 1 (January 2001):1, 4.

AMATO, PAUL R., and JULIANA M. SOBOLEWSKI. "The Effects of Divorce and Marital Discord on Adult Children's Psychological Well-Being." *American Sociological Review.* Vol. 66, No. 6 (December 2001):900–21.

AMBLER, JOHN S., and JODY NEATHERY. "Education Policy and Equality: Some Evidence from Europe." *Social Science Quarterly.* Vol. 80, No. 3 (September 1999):437–56.

AMERICAN BAR ASSOCIATION. "First-Year and Total J.D. Enrollment by Gender, 1947–2005." 2006. [Online] Available May 30, 2007, at http://www.abanet.org/legaled/statistics/charts/stats%20-%206.pdf

AMERICAN PSYCHOLOGICAL ASSOCIATION. *Violence and Youth: Psychology's Response.* Washington, D.C.: American Psychological Association, 1993.

AMERICAN SOCIOLOGICAL ASSOCIATION. "Code of Ethics." Washington, D.C.: American Sociological Association, 1997.

———. *Careers in Sociology.* 6th ed. Washington, D.C.: American Sociological Association, 2002.

AMNESTY INTERNATIONAL. "Abolitionist and Retentionist Countries." [Online] Available May 10, 2007a, at http://web.amnesty.org/pages/deathpenalty-countries-eng

———. "Facts and Figures on the Death Penalty." [Online] Available May 20, 2007b, at http://web.amnesty.org/pages/deathpenalty-facts-eng

ANDERSON, ELIJAH. "The Code of the Streets." *Atlantic Monthly.* Vol. 273 (May 1994):81–94.

———. "The Ideologically Driven Critique." *American Journal of Sociology.* Vol. 197, No. 6 (May 2002):1533–50.

ANDERSON, JOHN WARD. "Early to Wed: The Child Brides of India." *Washington Post* (May 24, 1995):A27, A30.

ANNAN, KOFI. "Astonishing Facts." *New York Times* (September 27, 1998):16.

APPLEBOME, PETER. "70 Years after Scopes Trial, Creation Debate Lives." *New York Times* (March 10, 1996):1, 10.

APUZZO, ALAN. "R.I. Official: Club Owners Not Helpful." [Online] Available February 24, 2003, at http://news.yahoo.com

ARENDT, HANNAH. *Between Past and Future: Six Exercises in Political Thought.* Cleveland, Ohio: Meridian Books, 1963.

ARIAS, ELIZABETH. "United States Life Tables, 2003." *National Vital Statistics Report.* Vol. 54, No. 14 (April 19, 2006). Hyattsville, Md.: National Center for Health Statistics, 2006.

ARIÈS, PHILIPPE. *Centuries of Childhood: A Social History of Family Life.* New York: Vintage Books, 1965.

———. *Western Attitudes toward Death: From the Middle Ages to the Present.* Baltimore: Johns Hopkins University Press, 1974.

ARMSTRONG, ELISABETH. *The Retreat from Organization: U.S. Feminism Reconceptualized.* Albany: State University of New York Press, 2002.

ARONOWITZ, STANLEY. *The Politics of Identity: Class, Culture, and Social Movements.* New York: Routledge, 1992.

ARROW, KENNETH, SAMUEL BOWLES, and STEVEN DURLAUF. *Meritocracy and Economic Inequality.* Princeton, N.J.: Princeton University Press, 2000.

ASANTE, MOLEFI KETE. *Afrocentricity.* Trenton, N.J.: Africa World Press, 1988.

ASCH, SOLOMON. *Social Psychology.* Englewood Cliffs, N.J.: Prentice Hall, 1952.

ASHFORD, LORI S. "New Perspectives on Population: Lessons from Cairo." *Population Bulletin.* Vol. 50, No. 1 (March 1995).

———. "Young Women in Sub-Saharan Africa Face a High Risk of HIV Infection." *Population Today.* Vol. 30, No. 2 (February/March 2002):3, 6.

ASTIN, ALEXANDER W., LETICIA OSEGUERA, LINDA J. SAX, and WILLIAM S. KORN. *The American Freshman: Thirty-Five Year Trends.* Los Angeles: UCLA Higher Education Research Institute, 2002.

ATCHLEY, ROBERT C. *Aging: Continuity and Change.* Belmont, Calif.: Wadsworth, 1983.

ATLAS, TERRY. "The Human Cost of China's Boom Times." *U.S. News & World Report* (March 12, 2007):21.

AUSTER, CAROL J., and MINDY MACRONE. "The Classroom as a Negotiated Social Setting: An Empirical Study of the Effects of Faculty Members' Behavior on Students' Participation." *Teaching Sociology.* Vol. 22, No. 4 (October 1994):289–300.

AXINN, WILLIAM G., and JENNIFER S. BARBER. "Mass Education and Fertility Transition." *American Sociological Review.* Vol. 66, No. 4 (August 2001):481–505.

BAINBRIDGE, JAY, MARCIA K. MEYERS, and JANE WALDFOGEL. "Childcare Reform and the Employment of Single Mothers." *Social Science Quarterly.* Vol. 84, No. 4 (December 2003):771–91.

BAKALAR, NICHOLAS. "Reactions: Go On, Laugh Your Heart Out." *New York Times* (March 8, 2005). [Online] Available March 11, 2005, at http://www.nytimes.com/2005/03/08/health/08reac.html

BAKER, MARY ANNE, LINDA GUGIN, and MARCIA SEGAL. *Women Today: A Multidisciplinary Approach to Women's Studies.* Monterey, Calif.: Brooks/Cole, 1980.

BAKER, PATRICIA S., WILLIAM C. YOELS, JEFFREY M. CLAIR, and RICHARD M. ALLMAN. "Laughter in the Triadic Geriatric Encounters: A Transcript-Based Analysis." In REBECCA J. ERIKSON and BEVERLY CUTHBERTSON-JOHNSON, eds., *Social Perspectives on Emotion.* Vol. 4. Greenwich, Conn.: JAI Press, 1997:179–207.

BAKER, ROSS. "Business as Usual." *American Demographics.* Vol. 19, No. 4 (April 1997):28.

BALTES, PAUL B., and K. WARNER SCHAIE. "The Myth of the Twilight Years." *Psychology Today.* Vol. 7, No. 10 (March 1974):35–39.

BALTZELL, E. DIGBY. *The Protestant Establishment: Aristocracy and Caste in America.* New York: Vintage Books, 1964.

———. "Introduction to the 1967 Edition." In W.E.B. DU BOIS, *The Philadelphia Negro: A Social Study.* New York: Schocken Books, 1967; orig. 1899.

———. *Puritan Boston and Quaker Philadelphia.* New York: Free Press, 1979.

———. *Sporting Gentlemen: From the Age of Honor to the Cult of the Superstar.* New York: Free Press, 1995.

BANFIELD, EDWARD C. *The Unheavenly City Revisited.* Boston: Little, Brown, 1974.

BARASH, DAVID P. *The Whisperings Within.* New York: Penguin Books, 1981.

BARNES, JULIAN E. "Wanted: Readers." *U.S. News & World Report* (September 9, 2002a):44–45.

———. "War Profiteering." *U.S. News & World Report* (May 13, 2002b):20–24.

———. "Unequal Education." *U.S. News & World Report* (March 22, 2004):66–75.

BARON, JAMES N., MICHAEL T. HANNAN, and M. DIANE BURTON. "Building the Iron Cage: Determinants of Managerial Intensity in the Early Years of Organizations." *American Sociological Review.* Vol. 64, No. 4 (August 1999):527–47.

BARONE, MICHAEL. "Lessons of History." *U.S. News & World Report* (May 20, 2002):24.

———. "Cultures Aren't Equal." *U.S. News & World Report.* Vol. 139, No. 6 (August 22, 2005):26.

BAROVICK, HARRIET. "Tongues That Go Out of Style." *Time* (June 10, 2002):22.

BARR, BOB. "Euthanasia . . . or a 'Dutch Treat'?" *Washington Times* (December 26, 2004). [Online] Available July 29, 2007, at http://www.bobbarr.org/default.asp?pt=newsdescr&RI=585

BARR, ROBERT. "Archbishop of Canterbury Is Enthroned." [Online] Available February 27, 2003, at http://news.yahoo.com

BARSTOW, DAVID, and C. J. CHIVERS. "A Volatile Mixture Exploded into Rampage in Central Park." *New York Times* (June 17, 2000):A1, B7.

BARTLETT, DONALD L., and JAMES B. STEELE. "Corporate Welfare." *Time* (November 9, 1998):36–54.

———. "How the Little Guy Gets Crunched." *Time* (February 7, 2000):38–41.

———. "Wheel of Misfortune." *Time* (December 16, 2002):44–58.

BASSUK, ELLEN J. "The Homelessness Problem." *Scientific American*. Vol. 251, No. 1 (July 1984):40–45.

BAUER, P. T. *Equality, the Third World, and Economic Delusion*. Cambridge, Mass.: Harvard University Press, 1981.

BAUMGARTNER, M. P. "Introduction: The Moral Voice of the Community." *Sociological Focus*. Vol. 31, No. 2 (May 1998):105–17.

BAYDAR, NAZLI, and JEANNE BROOKS-GUNN. "Effect of Maternal Employment and Child-Care Arrangements on Preschoolers' Cognitive and Behavioral Outcomes: Evidence from Children from the National Longitudinal Survey of Youth." *Developmental Psychology*. Vol. 27, No. 6 (November 1991):932–35.

BEARAK, BARRY. "Lives Held Cheap in Bangladesh Sweatshops." *New York Times* (April 15, 2001):A1, A12.

BEARMAN, PETER S., JAMES MOODY, and KATHERINE STOVEL. "Chains of Affection." *American Journal of Sociology*. Vol. 110, No. 1 (July 2004):44–91.

BECKER, ANNE E. "The Association of Television Exposure with Disordered Eating Among Ethnic Fijian Adolescent Girls." Paper presented at the annual meeting of the American Psychiatric Association, Washington, D.C., May 19, 1999.

———. "New Global Perspectives on Eating Disorders." *Culture, Medicine, and Psychiatry*. Vol. 28, No. 4 (December 2004):434-37.

BECKER, HOWARD S. *Outside: Studies in the Sociology of Deviance*. New York: Free Press, 1966.

BEDARD, PAUL. "Washington Whispers." *U.S. News & World Report* (March 25, 2002):2.

BEEGHLEY, LEONARD. *The Structure of Social Stratification in the United States*. Needham Heights, Mass.: Allyn & Bacon, 1989.

BEGLEY, SHARON. "Gray Matters." *Newsweek* (March 7, 1995):48–54.

———. "How to Beat the Heat." *Newsweek* (December 8, 1997):34–38.

BELLAH, ROBERT N. *The Broken Covenant*. New York: Seabury Press, 1975.

BELLAH, ROBERT N., RICHARD MADSEN, WILLIAM M. SULLIVAN, ANN SWIDLER, and STEVEN M. TIPTON. *Habits of the Heart: Individualism and Commitment in American Life*. New York: Harper & Row, 1985.

BELLANDI, DEANNA. "Study Finds Meal Portion Sizes Growing." [Online] Available January 3, 2003, at http://www.yahoo.com

BEM, SANDRA LIPSITZ. *The Lenses of Gender: Transforming the Debate on Sexual Inequality*. New Haven, Conn.: Yale University Press, 1993.

BENEDICT, RUTH. "Continuities and Discontinuities in Cultural Conditioning." *Psychiatry*. Vol. 1, No. 2 (May 1938):161–67.

BENJAMIN, LOIS. *The Black Elite: Facing the Color Line in the Twilight of the Twentieth Century*. Chicago: Nelson-Hall, 1991.

BENJAMIN, MATTHEW. "Suite Deals." *U.S. News & World Report* (April 29, 2002):32–34.

BENNETT, JESSICA. "No More Junk." *Newsweek* (April 18, 2006). [Online] Available April 25, 2007, at http://www.msnbc.msn.com/id/12359367/site/newsweek

BENOKRAITIS, NIJOLE, and JOE R. FEAGIN. *Modern Sexism: Blatant, Subtle, and Overt Discrimination*. 2nd ed. Englewood Cliffs, N.J.: Prentice Hall, 1995.

BERGAMO, MONICA, and GERSON CAMAROTTI. "Brazil's Landless Millions." *World Press Review*. Vol. 43, No. 7 (July 1996):46–47.

BERGEN, RAQUEL KENNEDY. "Interviewing Survivors of Marital Rape: Doing Feminist Research on Sensitive Topics." In CLAIRE M. RENZETTI and RAYMOND M. LEE, eds., *Researching Sensitive Topics*. Thousand Oaks, Calif.: Sage, 1993.

BERGER, PETER L. *Invitation to Sociology*. New York: Anchor Books, 1963.

———. *The Sacred Canopy: Elements of a Sociological Theory of Religion*. Garden City, N.Y.: Doubleday, 1967.

———. *Facing Up to Modernity: Excursions in Society, Politics, and Religion*. New York: Basic Books, 1977.

———. *The Capitalist Revolution: Fifty Propositions about Prosperity, Equality, and Liberty*. New York: Basic Books, 1986.

BERGER, PETER L., BRIGITTE BERGER, and HANSFRIED KELLNER. *The Homeless Mind: Modernization and Consciousness*. New York: Vintage Books, 1974.

BERGESEN, ALBERT, ed. *Crises in the World-System*. Beverly Hills, Calif.: Sage, 1983.

BERNARD, JESSIE. *The Female World*. New York: Free Press, 1981.

———. *The Future of Marriage*, 2nd ed. New Haven, Conn.: Yale University Press, 1982.

BERRILL, KEVIN T. "Anti-Gay Violence and Victimization in the United States: An Overview." In GREGORY M. HEREK and KEVIN T. BERRILL, *Hate Crimes: Confronting Violence against Lesbians and Gay Men*. Newbury Park, Calif.: Sage, 1992:19–45.

BERRY, BRIAN L., and PHILIP H. REES. "The Factorial Ecology of Calcutta." *American Journal of Sociology*. Vol. 74, No. 5 (March 1969):445–91.

BERTEAU, CELESTE. "Disconnected Intimacy: AOL Instant Messenger Use among Kenyon College Students." Senior thesis. Kenyon College, 2005.

BESHAROV, DOUGLAS J., and LISA A. LAUMANN. "Child Abuse Reporting." *Society*. Vol. 34, No. 4 (May/June 1996):40–46.

BESHAROV, DOUGLAS J., and PETER GERMANIS. "Welfare Reform: Four Years Later." *Public Interest*. No. 140 (Summer 2000):17–35.

BEST, RAPHAELA. *We've All Got Scars: What Boys and Girls Learn in Elementary School*. Bloomington: Indiana University Press, 1983.

BIAN, YANJIE. "Chinese Social Stratification and Social Mobility." *Annual Review of Sociology*. Vol. 28 (2002):91–116.

BIANCHI, SUZANNE M., and LYNNE M. CASPER. "American Families." *Population Bulletin*. Vol. 55, No. 4 (December 2000).

BIANCHI, SUZANNE M., and DAPHNE SPAIN. "Women, Work, and Family in America." *Population Bulletin*. Vol. 51, No. 3 (December 1996).

BLACKWOOD, EVELYN, and SASKIA WIERINGA, eds. *Female Desires: Same-Sex Relations and Transgender Practices across Cultures*. New York: Columbia University Press, 1999.

BLANK, JONAH. "The Muslim Mainstream." *U.S. News & World Report* (July 20, 1998):22–25.

BLANKENHORN, DAVID. *Fatherless America: Confronting Our Most Urgent Social Problem*. New York: HarperCollins, 1995.

BLAU, JUDITH R., and PETER M. BLAU. "The Cost of Inequality: Metropolitan Structure and Violent Crime." *American Sociological Review*. Vol. 47, No. 1 (February 1982):114–29.

BLAU, PETER M. *Exchange and Power in Social Life*. New York: Wiley, 1964.

———. *Inequality and Heterogeneity: A Primitive Theory of Social Structure*. New York: Free Press, 1977.

BLAU, PETER M., TERRY C. BLUM, and JOSEPH E. SCHWARTZ. "Heterogeneity and Intermarriage." *American Sociological Review*. Vol. 47, No. 1 (February 1982):45–62.

BLAU, PETER M., and OTIS DUDLEY DUNCAN. *The American Occupational Structure*. New York: Wiley, 1967.

BLAUSTEIN, ALBERT P., and ROBERT L. ZANGRANDO. *Civil Rights and the Black American*. New York: Washington Square Press, 1968.

BLUMER, HERBERT G. "Collective Behavior." In ALFRED McCLUNG LEE, ed., *Principles of Sociology*. 3rd ed. New York: Barnes & Noble Books, 1969:65–121.

BLUMSTEIN, PHILIP, and PEPPER SCHWARTZ. *American Couples*. New York: Morrow, 1983.

BOBO, LAWRENCE, and VINCENT L. HUTCHINGS. "Perceptions of Racial Group Competition: Extending Blumer's Theory of Group Position to a Multiracial Social Context." *American Sociological Review*. Vol. 61, No. 6 (December 1996):951–72.

BOERNER, CHRISTOPHER, and THOMAS LAMBERT. "Environmental Injustice." *Public Interest*. No. 124 (Winter 1995):61–82.

BOGARDUS, EMORY S. "Social Distance and Its Origins." *Sociology and Social Research*. Vol. 9 (July/August 1925):216–25.

———. *A Forty-Year Racial Distance Study*. Los Angeles: University of Southern California Press, 1967.

BOHANNAN, CECIL. "The Economic Correlates of Homelessness in Sixty Cities." *Social Science Quarterly*. Vol. 72, No. 4 (December 1991):817–25.

BOHLEN, CELESTINE. "Facing Oblivion, Rust-Belt Giants Top Russian List of Vexing Crises." *New York Times* (November 8, 1998):1, 6.

BOHON, STEPHANIE A., and CRAIG R. HUMPHREY. "Courting LULUs: Characteristic of Suitor and Objector Communities." *Rural Sociology*. Vol. 65, No. 3 (September 2000):376–95.

BONANNO, ALESSANDRO, DOUGLAS H. CONSTANCE, and HEATHER LORENZ. "Powers and Limits of Transnational Corporations: The Case of ADM." *Rural Sociology*. Vol. 65, No. 3 (September 2000):440–60.

BONNER, JANE. Research presented in the Public Broadcast System telecast *The Brain #6: The Two Brains*. Videocassette VHS 339. Newark, N.J.: WNET-13 Films, 1984.

BONO, AGOSTINO. "John Jay Study Reveals the Extent of Abuse Problem." [Online] Available September 13, 2006, at http://www.americancatholic.org/news/clergysexabuse/johnjaycns.asp

BOOTH, ALAN, and ANN C. CROUTER, eds. *Just Living Together: Implications of Cohabitation on Families, Children, and Policy*. Mahwah, N.J.: Erlbaum, 2002.

BOOTH, ALAN, and JAMES DABBS. "Male Hormone Is Linked to Marital Problems." *Wall Street Journal* (August 19, 1992):B1.

BOOTH, WILLIAM. "By the Sweat of Their Brows: A New Economy." *Washington Post* (July 13, 1998):A1, A10–A11.

BORMANN, F. HERBERT. "The Global Environmental Deficit." *BioScience*. Vol. 40, No. 2 (1990):74.

BOSTON WOMEN'S HEALTH BOOK COLLECTIVE. *Our Bodies, Ourselves: A Book by and for Women*. New York: Simon & Schuster, 1973.

BOSWELL, TERRY E. "A Split Labor Market Analysis of Discrimination against Chinese Immigrants, 1850–1882." *American Sociological Review*. Vol. 51, No. 3 (June 1986):352–71.

BOSWELL, TERRY E., and WILLIAM J. DIXON. "Marx's Theory of Rebellion: A Cross-National Analysis of Class Exploitation, Economic Development, and Violent Revolt." *American Sociological Review*. Vol. 58, No. 5 (October 1993):681–702.

BOTT, ELIZABETH. *Family and Social Network*. New York: Free Press, 1971; orig. 1957.

BOULDING, ELISE. *The Underside of History.* Boulder, Colo.: Westview Press, 1976.

BOWEN, WILLIAM G., and DEREK K. BOK. *The Shape of the River: Long-Term Consequences of Considering Race in College and University Admissions.* Princeton, N.J.: Princeton University Press, 1999.

BOWLES, SAMUEL, and HERBERT GINTIS. *Schooling in Capitalist America: Educational Reform and the Contradictions of Economic Life.* New York: Basic Books, 1976.

BOYER, DEBRA. "Male Prostitution and Homosexual Identity." *Journal of Homosexuality.* Vol. 17, Nos. 1–2 (1989):151–84.

BOYLE, ELIZABETH HEGER, FORTUNATA SONGORA, and GAIL FOSS. "International Discourse and Local Politics: Anti-Female-Genital-Cutting Laws in Egypt, Tanzania, and the United States." *Social Problems.* Vol. 48, No. 4 (November 2001):524–44.

BOZA, TANYA GOLASH. "Proposed American Sociological Association Statement on Race." [Online] Available October 24, 2002, at http://www.unc.edu/~tatiana

BRADY CAMPAIGN. "Firearm Facts." April 2007. [Online] Available May 20, 2007, at http://www.bradycampaign.org/facts/factsheets/pdf/firearm_facts.pdf

BRAGA, JOSEPH L., and LAURIE D. BRAGA. "Foreword." In ELISABETH KÜBLER-ROSS, *Death: The Final Stage of Growth.* New York: Simon & Schuster, 1975.

BRECHIN, STEVEN R., and WILLETT KEMPTON. "Global Environmentalism: A Challenge to the Postmaterialism Thesis." *Social Science Quarterly.* Vol. 75, No. 2 (June 1994):245–69.

BRIANS, CRAIG LEONARD, and BERNARD GROFMAN. "Election Day Registration's Effect on U.S. Voter Turnout." *Social Science Quarterly.* Vol. 82, No. 1 (March 2001):170–83.

BRIGGS, TRACEY WONG. "Two Years, Changed Lives." *USA Today* (April 22, 2002):D1–D2.

BRINES, JULIE, and KARA JOYNER. "The Ties That Bind: Principles of Cohesion in Cohabitation and Marriage." *American Sociological Review.* Vol. 64, No. 3 (June 1999):333–55.

BRINK, SUSAN. "Living on the Edge." *U.S. News & World Report* (October 14, 2002):58–64.

BRINTON, MARY C. "The Social-Institutional Bases of Gender Stratification: Japan as an Illustrative Case." *American Journal of Sociology.* Vol. 94, No. 2 (September 1988):300–34.

BROCKERHOFF, MARTIN P. "An Urbanizing World." *Population Bulletin.* Vol. 55, No. 3 (September 2000):1–44.

BRODER, DAVID S. "Stock Options Belong in the Line of Fire." *Columbus Dispatch* (April 21, 2002):G3.

BRODKIN, KAREN B. "How Did Jews Become White Folks?" In JOHN J. MACIONIS and NIJOLE V. BENOKRAITIS, eds. *Seeing Ourselves: Classic, Contemporary, and Cross-Cultural Readings in Sociology.* 7th ed. Upper Saddle River, N.J.: Prentice Hall, 2007.

BROOKS, DAVID. *Bobos in Paradise: The New Upper Class and How They Got There.* New York: Simon & Schuster, 2000.

BROWN, LESTER R. "Reassessing the Earth's Population." *Society.* Vol. 32, No. 4 (May/June 1995):7–10.

BROWN, LESTER R., ET AL., eds. *State of the World 1993: A Worldwatch Institute Report on Progress toward a Sustainable Society.* New York: Norton, 1993.

BUCKLEY, STEPHEN. "A Spare and Separate Way of Life." *Washington Post* (December 18, 1996):A1, A32–A33

BUCKS, BRIAN K., ARTHUR B. KENNICKELL, and KEVIN B. MOORE. "Recent Change in U.S. Family Finances: Evidence from the 2001 and 2004 Survey of Consumer Finances." *Federal Reserve Bulletin.* 2006. [Online] Available May 11, 2006, at http://www.federalreserve.gov/pubs/bulletin/2006/financesurvey.pdf

BUECHLER, STEVEN M. *Social Movements in Advanced Capitalism: The Political Economy and Cultural Construction of Social Activism.* New York: Oxford University Press, 2000.

BULLETIN ONLINE. "5 Minutes to Midnight." [Online] Available August 26, 2007, at http://www.thebulletin.org/minutes-to-midnight

BURAWAY, MICHAEL. "Review Essay: The Soviet Descent into Capitalism." *American Journal of Sociology.* Vol. 102, No. 5 (March 1997):1430–44.

BURKETT, ELINOR. "God Created Me to Be a Slave." *New York Times Magazine* (October 12, 1997):56–60.

BUTLER, ROBERT N. *Why Survive? Being Old in America.* New York: Harper & Row, 1975.

CALIFORNIA NEWSREEL. "Race: The Power of an Illusion: Genetic Diversity Quiz." 2003. [Online] Available February 9, 2006, at http://www.pbs.org/race/000_About/002_04_a-godeeper.html

CALLAHAN, DANIEL. *Setting Limits: Medical Goals in an Aging Society.* New York: Simon & Schuster, 1987.

CAMARA, EVANDRO. Personal communication, 2000.

CAMERON, WILLIAM BRUCE. *Modern Social Movements: A Sociological Outline.* New York: Random House, 1966.

CAMPOLO, ANTHONY. *Partly Right: Learning from the Critics of Christianity.* Dallas: Word, 1985.

CAPEK, STELLA A. "The 'Environmental Justice' Frame: A Conceptual Discussion and an Application." *Social Problems.* Vol. 40, No. 1 (February 1993):5–24.

CAPLOW, THEODORE, HOWARD M. BAHR, JOHN MODELL, and BRUCE A. CHADWICK. *Recent Social Trends in the United States, 1960–1990.* Montreal: McGill-Queen's University Press, 1991.

CARLSON, NORMAN A. "Corrections in the United States Today: A Balance Has Been Struck." *American Criminal Law Review.* Vol. 13, No. 4 (Spring 1976):615–47.

CARMICHAEL, STOKELY, and CHARLES V. HAMILTON. *Black Power: The Politics of Liberation in America.* New York: Vintage Books, 1967.

CARMONA, RICHARD H. "The Obesity Crisis in America." Testimony before the Subcommittee on Education Reform, Committee on Education and the Workforce, United States House of Representatives. July 16, 2003. [Online] Available September 25, 2005, at http://www.surgeongeneral.gov/news/testimony/obesity07162003.htm

CASTELLS, MANUEL. *The Urban Question.* Cambridge, Mass.: MIT Press, 1977.

CATALYST. "Catalyst Releases *2006 Census of Women in* Fortune 500 *Corporate Officer and Board Positions.*" Press release. February 21, 2007a. [Online] Available May 30, 2007, at http://www.catalyst.org/pressroom/press_releases/2006_Census_Release.pdf

———. "Corporate Officers and Top Earners." 2007b. [Online] Available May 30, 2007, at http://www.catalyst.org/knowledge/files/COTE.pdf

CDC (CENTERS FOR DISEASE CONTROL AND PREVENTION). "Annual Smoking-Attributable Mortality." *Morbidity and Mortality Weekly Report.* Vol. 54, No. 25 (July 1, 2005):625–28.

———. *Sexually Transmitted Disease Surveillance, 2005.* Atlanta: U.S. Department of Health and Human Services, 2006a.

———. "Tobacco Use among Adults—United States, 2005." *Morbidity and Mortality Weekly Report.* Vol. 55, No. 42 (October 27, 2006b):1145–48.

———. "Youth Risk Behavior Surveillance—United States, 2005." *Morbidity and Mortality Weekly Report.* Vol. 55, No. 5 (June 9, 2006c).

———. *HIV/AIDS Surveillance Report, 2005.* Vol. 17, rev. ed. Atlanta: U.S. Department of Health and Human Services, 2007.

CENTER FOR AMERICAN WOMEN AND POLITICS. "Women in State Legislatures, 2005." Eagleton Institute of Politics, Rutgers University. June 2005. [Online] Available June 23, 2005, at http://www.cawp.rutgers.edu/Facts/Officeholders/stleg.pdf

———. "Women in Elected Office: Fact Sheets and Summaries." Eagleton Institute of Politics, Rutgers University. May 2006. [Online] Available May 24, 2006, at http://www.cawp.rutgers.edu/Facts.html

———. "Women in State Legislatures, 2007." Eagleton Institute of Politics, Rutgers University. April 2007. [Online] Available May 30, 2007, at http://www.cawp.rutgers.edu/Facts/Officeholders/stleg.pdf

CENTER FOR RESPONSIVE POLITICS. "2006 Election Overview." 2007a. [Online] Available June 25, 2007, at http://www.opensecrets.org/overview/stats.asp?cycle=2006

———. "Lobbying Overview: Ranked Sectors." 2007b. [Online] Available September 16, 2007 at http://www.opensecrets.org/lobbyists/index.asp?showyear=2006&txtindextype=c

CENTER ON EDUCATION POLICY. "The Good News about American Education." Reported in BRIGETTE GREENBERG, "Report Finds America's Public Schools Showing Improvement." *Naples* (Fla.) *Daily News* (January 8, 2000):4a.

CERE, DANIEL. "Courtship Today: The View from Academia." *Public Interest.* No. 143 (Spring 2001):53–71.

CHAGNON, NAPOLEON A. *Yanomamö: The Fierce People.* 4th ed. Austin, Tex.: Holt, Rinehart and Winston, 1992.

CHANDLER, TERTIUS, and GERALD FOX. *3000 Years of Urban History.* New York: Academic Press, 1974.

CHAVES, MARK. *Ordaining Women: Culture and Conflict in Religious Organizations.* Cambridge, Mass.: Harvard University Press, 1997.

CHAVEZ, LINDA. "Promoting Racial Harmony." In GEORGE E. CURRY, ed., *The Affirmative Action Debate.* Reading, Mass.: Addison-Wesley, 1996.

"China Faces Water Shortage." *Popline* (December 2001):1–4.

CHEN, SHAOHUA, and MARTIN RAVALLION. "How Have the World's Poorest Fared since the Early 1980s?" World Bank Policy Research Working Paper 3341, June 2004. [Online] Available May 22, 2006, at http://www.worldbank.org

CHERLIN, ANDREW J., LINDA M. BURTON, TERA R. HART, and DIANE M. PURVIN. "The Influence of Physical and Sexual Abuse on Marriage and Cohabitation." *American Sociological Review.* Vol. 69, No. 6 (December 2004):768–89.

CHIRICOS, TED, RANEE McENTIRE, and MARC GERTZ. "Perceived Racial and Ethnic Composition of Neighborhood and Perceived Risk of Crime." *Social Problems.* Vol. 48, No. 3 (August 2001):322–40.

CHRONICLE OF HIGHER EDUCATION. *Almanac 2006-07.* 2006. [Online] Available May 30, 2007, at http://chronicle.com/free/almanac/2006/nation/nation_index.htm#faculty

CHUA-EOAN, HOWARD. "Profiles in Outrage." *Time* (September 25, 2000):38–39.

CIMINO, RICHARD, and DON LATTIN. "Choosing My Religion." *American Demographics.* Vol. 21, No. 4 (April 1999):60–65.

CLARK, J. R., and DWIGHT R. LEE. "Sentencing Laffer Curves, Political Myopia, and Prison Space." *Social Science Quarterly.* Vol. 77, No. 2 (June 1996):245–72.

CLARK, KIM. "Bankrupt Lives." *U.S. News & World Report* (September 16, 2002):52–54.

CLARK, MARGARET S., ed. *Prosocial Behavior.* Newbury Park, Calif.: Sage, 1991.

CLAWSON, DAN, and MARY ANN CLAWSON. "What Has Happened to the U.S. Labor Movement? Union Decline and Renewal." *Annual Review of Sociology.* Vol. 25 (1999):95–119.

CLEMETSON, LYNETTE. "Grandma Knows Best." *Newsweek* (June 12, 2000):60–61.

CLOUD, JOHN. "What Can the Schools Do?" *Time* (May 3, 1999):38–40.

CLOUD, JOHN, and JODIE MORSE. "Home Sweet School." *Time* (August 27, 2001):46–54.

CLOWARD, RICHARD A., and LLOYD E. OHLIN. *Delinquency and Opportunity: A Theory of Delinquent Gangs.* New York: Free Press, 1966.

COHEN, ADAM. "Test-Tube Tug-of-War." *Time* (April 6, 1998):65.

———. "A First Report Card on Vouchers." *Time* (April 26, 1999):36–38.

COHEN, ALBERT K. *Delinquent Boys: The Culture of the Gang.* New York: Free Press, 1971; orig. 1955.

COHEN, ELIAS. "The Complex Nature of Ageism: What Is It? Who Does It? Who Perceives It?" *Gerontologist.* Vol. 41, No. 5 (October 2001):576–78.

COHEN, PHILIP N., and MATT L. HUFFMAN. "Individuals, Jobs, and Labor Markets: The Devaluation of Women's Work." *American Sociological Review.* Vol. 68, No. 3 (June 2003):443–63.

COLE, GEORGE F., and CHRISTOPHER E. SMITH. *Criminal Justice in America.* 3rd ed. Belmont, Calif.: Wadsworth, 2002.

COLEMAN, JAMES S. "The Design of Organizations and the Right to Act." *Sociological Forum.* Vol. 8, No. 4 (December 1993):527–46.

COLEMAN, JAMES S., and THOMAS HOFFER. *Public and Private High Schools: The Impact of Communities.* New York: Basic Books, 1987.

COLEMAN, JAMES S., THOMAS HOFFER, and SALLY KILGORE. *Public and Private Schools: An Analysis of Public Schools and Beyond.* Washington, D.C.: National Center for Education Statistics, 1981.

COLEMAN, JAMES S., ET AL. *Equality of Educational Opportunity.* Washington, D.C.: U.S. Government Printing Office, 1966.

COLEMAN, RICHARD P., and BERNICE L. NEUGARTEN. *Social Status in the City.* San Francisco: Jossey-Bass, 1971.

COLLEGE BOARD. "2006 College-Bound Seniors Tables and Related Items." [Online] Available July 3, 2007, at http://www.collegeboard.com/about/news_info/cbsenior/yr2006/links.html

COLLEGE TOBACCO PREVENTION RESOURCE. "College Tobacco Resources, 1990–2005." 2006. [Online] Available July 9, 2007, at http://www.ttac.org/college/pdfs/TTACFINALLit-Review.pdf

COLLINS, RANDALL. *The Credential Society: A Historical Sociology of Education and Stratification.* New York: Academic Press, 1979.

COLLYMORE, YVETTE. "Migrant Street Children on the Rise in Central America." *Population Today.* Vol. 30, No. 2 (February/March 2002):1, 4.

COLTON, HELEN. *The Gift of Touch: How Physical Contact Improves Communication, Pleasure, and Health.* New York: Seaview/Putnam, 1983.

COMMISSION FOR RACIAL JUSTICE. *CRJ Reporter.* New York: United Church of Christ, 1994.

COMTE, AUGUSTE. *Auguste Comte and Positivism: The Essential Writings.* GERTRUD LENZER, ed. New York: Harper Torchbooks, 1975, orig. 1851–54.

CONNETT, PAUL H. "The Disposable Society." In F. HERBERT BORMANN and STEPHEN R. KELLERT, eds., *Ecology, Economics, and Ethics: The Broken Circle.* New Haven, Conn.: Yale University Press, 1991:99–122.

COOLEY, CHARLES HORTON. *Social Organization.* New York: Schocken Books, 1962; orig. 1909.

———. *Human Nature and the Social Order.* New York: Schocken Books, 1964; orig. 1902.

CORCORAN, MARY, SANDRA K. DANZIGER, ARIEL KALIL, and KRISTIN S. SEEFELDT. "How Welfare Reform Is Affecting Women's Work." *Annual Review of Sociology.* Vol. 26 (2000):241–69.

CORNELL, BARBARA. "Pulling the Plug on TV." *Time* (October 16, 2000):F16.

CORRELL, SHELLEY J. "Gender and the Career Choice Process: The Role of Biased Self-Assessment." *American Journal of Sociology.* Vol. 106, No. 6 (May 2001):1691–1730.

CORTESE, ANTHONY J. *Provocateur: Images of Women and Minorities in Advertising.* Lanham, Md.: Rowman & Littlefield, 1999.

COURTWRIGHT, DAVID T. *Violent Land: Single Men and Social Disorder from the Frontier to the Inner City.* Cambridge, Mass.: Harvard University Press, 1996.

COWLEY, GEOFFREY. "The Prescription That Kills." *Newsweek* (July 17, 1995):54.

COX, HARVEY. *The Secular City.* Rev. ed. New York: Macmillan, 1971.

COYOTE (Call Off Your Old Tired Ethics). "What Is COYOTE?" 2004. [Online] Available May 18, 2007, at http://www.coyotela/what-is.html

CRANE, DIANA. *Fashion and Its Social Agenda: Class, Gender, and Identity in Clothing.* Chicago: University of Chicago Press, 2000.

CRISPELL, DIANE. "Lucky to Be Alive." *American Demographics.* Vol. 19, No. 4 (April 1997):25.

CROOK, STEPHEN, JAN PAKULSKI, and MALCOLM WATERS. *Postmodernization: Change in Advanced Societies.* Thousand Oaks, Calif.: Sage, 1992.

CROSSETTE, BARBARA. "Female Genital Mutilation by Immigrants Is Becoming Cause for Concern in the U.S." *New York Times International* (December 10, 1995):11.

CROUSE, JAMES, and DALE TRUSHEIM. *The Case against the SAT.* Chicago: University of Chicago Press, 1988.

CRUTSINGER, MARTIN. "Trade Deficit Hits $665.9 Billion in 2004." [Online] Available March 16, 2005, at http://news.yahoo.com

CULLEN, LISA TAKEUCHI. "Will Manage for Food." *Time* (October 14, 2002):52–56.

———. "A New Battle of the Bulge." *Time* (February 24, 2003):14.

CUMMING, ELAINE, and WILLIAM E. HENRY. *Growing Old: The Process of Disengagement.* New York: Basic Books, 1961.

CUMMINGS, SCOTT, and THOMAS LAMBERT. "Anti-Hispanic and Anti-Asian Sentiments among African Americans." *Social Science Quarterly.* Vol. 78, No. 2 (June 1997):338–53.

CURRIE, ELLIOTT. *Confronting Crime: An American Challenge.* New York: Pantheon Books, 1985.

CURRY, ANDREW. "The Gullahs' Last Stand?" *U.S. News & World Report* (June 18, 2001):40–41.

CURTIS, JAMES E., DOUGLAS E. BAER, and EDWARD G. GRABB. "Nations of Joiners: Explaining Voluntary Association Membership in Democratic Societies." *American Sociological Review.* Vol. 66, No. 6 (December 2001):783–805.

CURTISS, SUSAN. *Genie: A Psycholinguistic Study of a Modern-Day "Wild Child."* New York: Academic Press, 1977.

CUTCLIFFE, JOHN R. "Hope, Counseling, and Complicated Bereavement Reactions." *Journal of Advanced Nursing.* Vol. 28, No. 4 (October 1998):754–62.

DAHL, ROBERT A. *Who Governs?* New Haven, Conn.: Yale University Press, 1961.

———. *Dilemmas of Pluralist Democracy: Autonomy vs. Control.* New Haven, Conn.: Yale University Press, 1982.

DAHRENDORF, RALF. *Class and Class Conflict in Industrial Society.* Stanford, Calif.: Stanford University Press, 1959.

DANFORTH, MARION M., and J. CONRAD GLASS JR. "Listen to My Words, Give Meaning to My Sorrow: A Study in Cognitive Constructs in Middle-Aged Bereaved Widows." *Death Studies.* Vol. 25, No. 6 (September 2001):413–30.

DARROCH, JACQUELINE E., ET AL. "Teenage Sexual and Reproductive Behavior in Developed Countries: Can More Progress Be Made?" 2001. [Online] Available May 30, 2005, at http://www.guttmacher.org/pubs/eurosynth_rpt.pdf

DAVIDSON, JAMES D., RALPH E. PYLE, and DAVID V. REYES. "Persistence and Change in the Protestant Establishment, 1930–1992." *Social Forces.* Vol. 74, No. 1 (September 1995):157–75.

DAVIDSON, JULIA O'CONNELL. *Prostitution, Power, and Freedom.* Ann Arbor: University of Michigan Press, 1998.

DAVIES, CHRISTIE. *Ethnic Humor around the World: A Comparative Analysis.* Bloomington: Indiana University Press, 1990.

DAVIES, MARK, and DENISE B. KANDEL. "Parental and Peer Influences on Adolescents' Educational Plans: Some Further Evidence." *American Journal of Sociology.* Vol. 87, No. 2 (September 1981):363–87.

DAVIS, BYRON BRADLEY. "Sports World." *Christian Science Monitor* (September 9, 1997):11.

DAVIS, DONALD M., cited in "TV Is a Blonde, Blonde World." *American Demographics,* special issue: *Women Change Places.* 1993.

DAVIS, KINGSLEY. "Extreme Social Isolation of a Child." *American Journal of Sociology.* Vol. 45, No. 4 (January 1940):554–65.

———. "Final Note on a Case of Extreme Isolation." *American Journal of Sociology.* Vol. 52, No. 5 (March 1947):432–37.

———. "Sexual Behavior." In ROBERT K. MERTON and ROBERT NISBET, eds., *Contemporary Social Problems.* 3rd ed. New York: Harcourt Brace Jovanovich, 1971:313–60.

DAVIS, KINGSLEY, and WILBERT MOORE. "Some Principles of Stratification." *American Sociological Review.* Vol. 10, No. 2 (April 1945):242–49.

DEDRICK, DENNIS K., and RICHARD E. YINGER. "MAD, SDI, and the Nuclear Arms Race." Unpublished manuscript. Georgetown, Ky.: Georgetown College, 1990.

DEFINA, ROBERT H., and THOMAS M. ARVANITES. "The Weak Effect of Imprisonment on Crime, 1971–1998." *Social Science Quarterly.* Vol. 83, No. 3 (September 2002):635–53.

DEFRANCIS, MARC. "A Spiraling Shortage of Nurses." *Population Today.* Vol. 30, No. 2 (February/March 2002a):8–9.

———. "U.S. Elder Care Is in a Fragile State." *Population Today.* Vol. 30, No. 1 (January 2002b):1–3.

DELACROIX, JACQUES, and CHARLES C. RAGIN. "Structural Blockage: A Cross-National Study of Economic Dependency, State Efficacy, and Underdevelopment." *American Journal of Sociology.* Vol. 86, No. 6 (May 1981):1311–47.

DELLA CAVA, MARCO R. "For Dutch, It's as Easy as Asking a Doctor." *USA Today* (January 7, 1997):4A.

DEMENTE, BOYE. *Japanese Etiquette and Ethics in Business.* 5th ed. Lincolnwood, Ill.: NTC Business Books, 1987.

DEMUTH, STEPHEN, and DARRELL STEFFENSMEIER. "The Impact of Gender and Race-Ethnicity in the Pretrial Release Process." *Social Problems.* Vol. 51, No. 2 (May 2004):222-42.

DENT, DAVID J. "African-Americans Turning to Christian Academies." *New York Times,* Education Life supplement (August 4, 1996):26–29.

DERBER, CHARLES. *The Wilding of America: Money, Mayhem, and the New American Dream.* 3rd ed. New York: Worth, 2004.

DERSHOWITZ, ALAN. *The Vanishing American Jew.* Boston: Little, Brown, 1997.

DEUTSCHER, IRWIN. *Making a Difference: The Practice of Sociology.* New Brunswick, N.J.: Transaction, 1999.

DICKINSON, AMY. "When Dating Is Dangerous." *Time* (August 27, 2001):76.

DIXON, WILLIAM J., and TERRY BOSWELL. "Dependency, Disarticulation, and Denominator Effects: Another Look at Foreign Capital Penetration." *American Journal of Sociology.* Vol. 102, No. 2 (September 1996):543–62.

DOBYNS, HENRY F. "An Appraisal of Techniques with a New Hemispheric Estimate." *Current Anthropology.* Vol. 7, No. 4 (October 1966):395–446.

DOLLARD, JOHN, ET AL. *Frustration and Aggression.* New Haven, Conn.: Yale University Press, 1939.

DOMHOFF, G. WILLIAM. *Who Rules America Now? A View of the '80s.* Englewood Cliffs, N.J.: Prentice Hall, 1983.

DONAHUE, JOHN J., III, and STEVEN D. LEAVITT. Research cited in "New Study Claims Abortion Is Behind Decrease in Crime." *Population Today.* Vol. 28, No. 1 (January 2000):1, 4.

DONNELLY, PATRICK G., and THEO J. MAJKA. "Residents' Efforts at Neighborhood Stabilization: Facing the Challenges of Inner-City Neighborhoods." *Sociological Forum.* Vol. 13, No. 2 (June 1998):189–213.

DONOVAN, VIRGINIA K., and RONNIE LITTENBERG. "Psychology of Women: Feminist Therapy." In BARBARA HABER, ed., *The Women's Annual, 1981: The Year in Review.* Boston: Hall, 1982:211–35.

DOWNEY, DOUGLAS B., BECKETT A. BROH, and PAUL T. VON HIPPEL. "Are Schools the Great Equalizer? Cognitive Inequality during the Summer Months and School Year." *American Sociological Review.* Vol. 59, No. 5 (October 2004):613–35.

DOYLE, JAMES A. *The Male Experience.* Dubuque, Iowa: Brown, 1983.

DRORI, GILI S. *Global E-litism: Digital Technology, Social Inequality, and Transnationality.* New York: Worth, 2006.

DU BOIS, W.E.B. *The Philadelphia Negro: A Social Study.* New York: Schocken Books, 1967; orig. 1899.

DUBOS, RENÉ. *Man Adapting.* Enlarged ed. New Haven, Conn.: Yale University Press, 1980.

DUDLEY, KATHRYN MARIE. *Debt and Dispossession: Farm Loss in America's Heartland.* Chicago: University of Chicago Press, 2000.

DUNBAR, LESLIE. *The Common Interest: How Our Social Welfare Policies Don't Work and What We Can Do about Them.* New York: Pantheon, 1988.

DUNCAN, CYNTHIA M. *Worlds Apart: Why Poverty Persists in Rural America.* New Haven, Conn.: Yale University Press, 1999.

DUNCAN, GREG J., W. JEAN YEUNG, JEANNE BROOKS-GUNN, and JUDITH R. SMITH. "How Much Does Childhood Poverty Affect the Life Chances of Children?" *American Sociological Review.* Vol. 63, No. 3 (June 1998):406–23.

DUNN, LUCIA F. "Is Combat Pay Effective: Evidence from Operation Desert Storm." *Social Science Quarterly.* Vol. 84, No. 2 (June 2003):344–58.

DUNPHY, HARRY. "World Bank: Sub-Saharan Africa Sees Growth." 2006. [Online] Available April 24, 2006, at http://news.yahoo.com

DUREX GLOBAL SEX SURVEY. Reported in *Time* (October 30, 2000):31.

DURKHEIM, EMILE. *Moral Education: A Study in the Theory and Application of the Sociology of Education.* New York: Free Press, 1961.

———. *The Division of Labor in Society.* New York: Free Press, 1964a; orig. 1893.

———. *The Rules of Sociological Method.* New York: Free Press, 1964b; orig. 1895.

———. *The Elementary Forms of Religious Life.* New York: Free Press, 1965; orig. 1915.

———. *Suicide.* New York: Free Press, 1966; orig. 1897.

———. *Sociology and Philosophy.* New York: Free Press, 1974; orig. 1924.

DWORKIN, ANDREA. *Intercourse.* New York: Free Press, 1987.

DWORKIN, RONALD W. "Where Have All the Nurses Gone?" *Public Interest.* No. 148 (Summer 2002):23–36.

EBAUGH, HELEN ROSE FUCHS. *Becoming an Ex: The Process of Role Exit.* Chicago: University of Chicago Press, 1988.

EBOH, CAMILLUS. "Nigerian Woman Loses Appeal against Stoning Death." [Online] Available August 19, 2002, at http://dailynews.yahoo.com

ECK, DIANA L. *A New Religious America: How a "Christian Country" Has Become the World's Most Religiously Diverse Nation.* San Francisco: HarperSanFrancisco, 2001.

EDWARDS, TAMALA M. "Revolt of the Gentry." *Time* (June 15, 1998):34–35.

———. "Flying Solo." *Time* (August 28, 2000):47–55.

EHRENREICH, BARBARA. *The Hearts of Men: American Dreams and the Flight from Commitment.* Garden City, N.Y.: Anchor Books, 1983.

———. "The Real Truth about the Female Body." *Time* (March 15, 1999):56–65.

———. *Nickel and Dimed: On (Not) Getting By in America.* New York: Henry Holt, 2001.

EICHLER, MARGRIT. *Nonsexist Research Methods: A Practical Guide.* Winchester, Mass.: Unwin Hyman, 1988.

EISENBERG, DANIEL. "Paying to Keep Your Job." *Time* (October 15, 2001):80–3.

EISENSTADT, JILL. "The Maid's Tale." *New York Times* (July 25, 2004). [Online] Available March 22, 2005, at http://www.researchnavigator.com

EISLER, BENITA. *The Lowell Offering: Writings by New England Mill Women, 1840–1845.* Philadelphia: Lippincott, 1977.

EKMAN, PAUL. "Biological and Cultural Contributions to Body and Facial Movements in the Expression of Emotions." In A. RORTY, ed., *Explaining Emotions.* Berkeley: University of California Press, 1980a:73–101.

———. *Face of Man: Universal Expression in a New Guinea Village.* New York: Garland Press, 1980b.

———. *Telling Lies: Clues to Deceit in the Marketplace, Politics, and Marriage.* New York: Norton, 1985.

EL-ATTAR, MOHAMED. Personal communication, 1991.

ELIAS, ROBERT. *The Politics of Victimization: Victims, Victimology, and Human Rights.* New York: Oxford University Press, 1986.

ELLIOT, DELBERT S., and SUZANNE S. AGETON. "Reconciling Race and Class Differences in Self-Reported and Official Estimates of Delinquency." *American Sociological Review.* Vol. 45, No. 1 (February 1980):95–110.

ELLISON, CHRISTOPHER G., JOHN P. BARTKOWSKI, and MICHELLE L. SEGAL. "Do Conservative Protestant Parents Spank More Often? Further Evidence from the National Survey of Families and Households." *Social Science Quarterly.* Vol. 77, No. 3 (September 1996):663–73.

ELLWOOD, ROBERT S. "East Asian Religions in Today's America." In JACOB NEUSNER, ed. *World Religions in America: An Introduction.* Louisville, Ky.: Westminster John Knox Press, 2000:154–71.

ELMER-DEWITT, PHILIP. "Now for the Truth about Americans and Sex." *Time* (October 17, 1994):62–70.

ELSON, JEAN. *Am I Still a Woman? Hysterectomy and Gender Identity.* Philadelphia: Temple University Press, 2004.

EMBER, MELVIN, and CAROL R. EMBER. "The Conditions Favoring Matrilocal versus Patrilocal Residence." *American Anthropologist.* Vol. 73, No. 3 (June 1971):571–94.

———. *Anthropology.* 6th ed. Englewood Cliffs, N.J.: Prentice Hall, 1991.

EMERSON, JOAN P. "Behavior in Private Places: Sustaining Definitions of Reality in Gynecological Examinations." In H. P. DREITZEL, ed., *Recent Sociology.* Vol. 2. New York: Collier, 1970:74–97.

EMERSON, MICHAEL O., GEORGE YANCEY, and KAREN J. CHAI. "Does Race Matter in Residential Segregation? Exploring the Preferences of White Americans." *American Sociological Review.* Vol. 66, No. 6 (December 2001):922–35.

ENGELS, FRIEDRICH. *The Origin of the Family.* Chicago: Kerr, 1902; orig. 1884.

ENGLAND, PAULA. "Three Reviews on Marriage." *Contemporary Sociology.* Vol. 30, No. 6 (November 2001):564–65.

ENGLAND, PAULA, JOAN M. HERMSEN, and DAVID A. COTTER. "The Devaluation of Women's Work: A Comment on Tam." *American Journal of Sociology.* Vol. 105, No. 6 (May 2000):1741–60.

ERIKSON, ERIK H. *Childhood and Society.* New York: Norton, 1963; orig. 1950.

———. *Identity and the Life Cycle.* New York: Norton, 1980.

ERIKSON, KAI T. *Everything in Its Path: Destruction of Community in the Buffalo Creek Flood.* New York: Simon & Schuster, 1976.

———. *A New Species of Trouble: Explorations in Disaster, Trauma, and Community.* New York: Norton, 1994.

———. Lecture at Kenyon College, February 7, 2005a.

———. *Wayward Puritans: A Study in the Sociology of Deviance.* New York: Wiley, 2005b; orig. 1966.

ERIKSON, ROBERT S., NORMAN R. LUTTBEG, and KENT L. TEDIN. *American Public Opinion: Its Origins, Content, and Impact.* 2nd ed. New York: Wiley, 1980.

ESTES, RICHARD J. "The Commercial Sexual Exploitation of Children in the U.S., Canada, and Mexico." Reported in "Study Explores Sexual Exploitation." [Online] Available September 10, 2001, at http://dailynews.yahoo.com

ETZIONI, AMITAI. *A Comparative Analysis of Complex Organization: On Power, Involvement, and Their Correlates.* Revised and enlarged ed. New York: Free Press, 1975.

———. "How to Make Marriage Matter." *Time* (September 6, 1993):76.

———. "The Responsive Community: A Communitarian Perspective." *American Sociological Review.* Vol. 61, No. 1 (February 1996):1–11.

———. *My Brother's Keeper: A Memoir and a Message.* Lanham, Md.: Rowman & Littlefield, 2003.

EVELYN, JAMILAH. "Community Colleges Play Too Small a Role in Teacher Education, Report Concludes." *Chronicle of Higher Education Online.* [Online] Available October 24, 2002, at http://chronicle.com/daily/2002/10/2002102403n.htm

FALLON, A. E., and P. ROZIN. "Sex Differences in Perception of Desirable Body Shape." *Journal of Abnormal Psychology.* Vol. 94, No. 1 (1985):100–105.

FARLEY, CHRISTOPHER JOHN. "Winning the Right to Fly." *Time* (August 28, 1995):62–64.

FATTAH, HASSAN. "A More Diverse Community." *American Demographics.* Vol. 24, No. 7 (July/August 2002):39–43.

FEAGIN, JOE R. *The Urban Real Estate Game.* Englewood Cliffs, N.J.: Prentice Hall, 1983.

———. "Death by Discrimination?" *Newsletter of the Society for the Study of Social Problems.* Vol. 28, No. 1 (Winter 1997):15–16.

FEAGIN, JOE R., and HERNÁN VERA. *Liberation Sociology.* Boulder, Colo.: Westview Press, 2001.

FEATHERMAN, DAVID L., and ROBERT M. HAUSER. *Opportunity and Change.* New York: Academic Press, 1978.

FEDARKO, KEVIN. "Land Mines: Cheap, Deadly, and Cruel." *Time* (May 13, 1996):54–55.

FEDERAL BUREAU OF INVESTIGATION. *Crime in the United States, 2005.* 2006. [Online] Available May 30, 2007, at http://www.fbi.gov/ucr/05cius

FEDERAL ELECTION COMMISSION. Number of Federal PACs Decreases." Press release, July 20, 2007. [Online] Available September 9, 2007, at http://www.fec.gov/press/press2007/20070710paccount.shtml

FEDERAL INTERAGENCY FORUM. *Older Americans Update 2006: Key Indicators of Well-Being.* May 2006. [Online] Available August 22, 2007, at http://www.agingstats.gov

FELLMAN, BRUCE. "Taking the Measure of Children's TV." *Yale Alumni Magazine* (April 1995):46–51.

"Female Opinion and Defense since September 11th." *Society.* Vol. 39, No. 3 (March/April 2002):2.

FENYVESI, CHARLES. "Walled Streets." *U.S. News & World Report* (March 25, 2002):57.

FERNANDEZ, ROBERTO M., and NANCY WEINBERG. "Sifting and Sorting: Personal Contacts and Hiring in a Retail Bank." *American Sociological Review.* Vol. 62, No. 6 (December 1997):883–902.

FERRARO, KENNETH F., and JESSICA A. KELLEY-MOORE. "Cumulative Disadvantage and Health: Long-Term Consequences of Obesity?" *American Sociological Review.* Vol. 68, No. 5 (October 2003):707–29.

FERREE, MYRA MARX, and BETH B. HESS. *Controversy and Coalition: The New Feminist Movement across Four Decades of Change.* 3rd ed. New York: Routledge, 1995.

FETTO, JOHN. "Lean on Me." *American Demographics.* Vol. 22, No. 12 (December 2000):16–17.

———. "Gay Friendly?" *American Demographics.* Vol. 24, No. 5 (May 2002a):16.

———. "Roomier Rentals" *American Demographics.* Vol. 24, No. 5 (May 2002b):17.

———. "A View from the Top?" *American Demographics.* Vol. 24, No. 7 (July/August 2002c):14.

———. "Drug Money." *American Demographics.* Vol. 25, No. 2 (March 2003a):48.

———. "Me Gusta TV." *American Demographics.* Vol. 24, No. 11 (January 2003b):14–15.

FINE, GARY ALAN. "Nature and the Taming of the Wild: The Problem of 'Overpick' in the Culture of Mushrooms." *Social Problems.* Vol. 44, No. 1 (February 1997):68–88.

FINKELSTEIN, NEAL W., and RON HASKINS. "Kindergarten Children Prefer Same-Color Peers." *Child Development.* Vol. 54, No. 2 (April 1983):502–8.

FIREBAUGH, GLENN. "Growth Effects of Foreign and Domestic Investment." *American Journal of Sociology.* Vol. 98, No. 1 (July 1992):105–30.

———. "Does Foreign Capital Harm Poor Nations? New Estimates Based on Dixon and Boswell's Measures of Capital Penetration." *American Journal of Sociology.* Vol. 102, No. 2 (September 1996):563–75.

———. "Empirics of World Income Inequality." *American Journal of Sociology.* Vol. 104, No. 6 (May 1999):1597–1630.

———. "The Trend in Between-Nation Income Inequality." *Annual Review of Sociology.* Vol. 26 (2000):323–39.

FIREBAUGH, GLENN, and FRANK D. BECK. "Does Economic Growth Benefit the Masses? Growth, Dependence, and Welfare in the Third World." *American Sociological Review.* Vol. 59, No. 5 (October 1994):631–53.

FIREBAUGH, GLENN, and KENNETH E. DAVIS. "Trends in Antiblack Prejudice, 1972–1984: Region and Cohort Effects." *American Journal of Sociology.* Vol. 94, No. 2 (September 1988):251–72.

FIREBAUGH, GLENN, and DUMITRU SANDU. "Who Supports Marketization and Democratization in Post-Communist Romania?" *Sociological Forum.* Vol. 13, No. 3 (September 1998):521–41.

FISCHER, CLAUDE W. *The Urban Experience.* 2nd ed. New York: Harcourt Brace Jovanovich, 1984.

FISHER, ELIZABETH. *Woman's Creation: Sexual Evolution and the Shaping of Society.* Garden City, N.Y.: Anchor/Doubleday, 1979.

FISHER, ROGER, and WILLIAM URY. "Getting to Yes." In WILLIAM M. EVAN and STEPHEN HILGARTNER, eds., *The Arms Race and Nuclear War.* Englewood Cliffs, N.J.: Prentice Hall, 1988:261–68.

FITZGERALD, JIM. "Martha Stewart Enjoys Comforts of Home." [Online] Available March 6, 2005, at http://news.yahoo.com

FITZGERALD, JOAN, and LOUISE SIMMONS. "From Consumption to Production: Labor Participation in Grass-Roots Movements in Pittsburgh and Hartford." *Urban Affairs Quarterly.* Vol. 26, No. 4 (June 1991):512–31.

FLAHERTY, MICHAEL G. "A Formal Approach to the Study of Amusement in Social Interaction." *Studies in Symbolic Interaction.* Vol. 5. New York: JAI Press, 1984:71–82.

———. "Two Conceptions of the Social Situation: Some Implications of Humor." *Sociological Quarterly.* Vol. 31, No. 1 (Spring 1990).

FLEXNER, ABRAHAM. *Prostitution in Europe.* New York: Century, 1920.

FOLIART, DONNE E., and MARGARET CLAUSEN. "Bereavement Practices among California Hospices: Results of a Statewide Survey." *Death Studies.* Vol. 25, No. 5 (July 2001):461–68.

FONDA, DAREN. "The Male Minority." *Time* (December 11, 2000):58–60.

FORD, CLELLAN S., and FRANK A. BEACH. *Patterns of Sexual Behavior.* New York: Harper Bros., 1951.

FORLITI, AMY. "R.I. Nightclub Fire Kills at Least 39." [Online] Available February 21, 2003, at http://www.yahoo.com

FOUCAULT, MICHEL. *The History of Sexuality: An Introduction.* Vol. 1. ROBERT HURLEY, trans. New York: Vintage, 1990; orig. 1978.

FRANK, ANDRÉ GUNDER. *On Capitalist Underdevelopment.* Bombay: Oxford University Press, 1975.

———. *Crisis: In the World Economy.* New York: Holmes & Meier, 1980.

———. *Reflections on the World Economic Crisis.* New York: Monthly Review Press, 1981.

FRANK, THOMAS. "Coal Mine Deaths Spike Upward." *USA Today* (January 1, 2007). [Online] Available March 4, 2007, at http://www.usatoday.com

FRANKLIN, JOHN HOPE. *From Slavery to Freedom: A History of Negro Americans.* 3rd ed. New York: Vintage Books, 1967.

FRAZIER, E. FRANKLIN. *Black Bourgeoisie: The Rise of a New Middle Class.* New York: Free Press, 1965.

FREDRICKSON, GEORGE M. *White Supremacy: A Comparative Study in American and South African History.* New York: Oxford University Press, 1981.

FREEDMAN, ESTELLE B. *No Turning Back: The History of Feminism and the Future of Women.* New York: Ballantine Books, 2002.

FREEDOM HOUSE. *Freedom in the World, 2005.* [Online] Available July 11, 2005, at http://www.freedomhouse.org

———. *Freedom in the World, 2007.* [Online] Available June 25, 2007, at http://www.freedomhouse.org

FRENCH, HOWARD W. "Teaching Japan's Salarymen to Be Their Own Men." *New York Times* (November 27, 2002):A4.

FRENCH, MARILYN. *Beyond Power: On Women, Men, and Morals.* New York: Summit Books, 1985.

FRIEDAN, BETTY. *The Fountain of Age.* New York: Simon & Schuster, 1993.

FRIEDMAN, MEYER, and RAY H. ROSENMAN. *Type A Behavior and Your Heart.* New York: Fawcett Crest, 1974.

FRIEDMAN, MILTON, and ROSE FRIEDMAN. *Free to Choose: A Personal Statement.* New York: Harcourt Brace Jovanovich, 1980.

FUGITA, STEPHEN S., and DAVID J. O'BRIEN. "Structural Assimilation, Ethnic Group Membership, and Political Participation among Japanese Americans: A Research Note." *Social Forces.* Vol. 63, No. 4 (June 1985):986–95.

FULLER, REX, and RICHARD SCHOENBERGER. "The Gender Salary Gap: Do Academic Achievement, Intern Experience, and College Major Make a Difference?" *Social Science Quarterly.* Vol. 72, No. 4 (December 1991):715–26.

FURSTENBERG, FRANK F., JR., and ANDREW J. CHERLIN. *Divided Families: What Happens to Children When Parents Part.* Cambridge, Mass.: Harvard University Press, 1991.

———. "Children's Adjustment to Divorce." In BONNIE J. FOX, ed. *Family Patterns, Gender Relations.* 2nd ed. New York: Oxford University Press, 2001.

GAGNÉ, PATRICIA, and RICHARD TEWKSBURY. "Conformity Pressures and Gender Resistance among Transgendered Individuals." *Social Problems.* Vol. 45, No. 1 (February 1998):81–101.

GAGNÉ, PATRICIA, RICHARD TEWKSBURY, and DEANNA MCGAUGHEY. "Coming Out and Crossing Over: Identity Formation and Proclamation in a Transgender Community." *Gender and Society.* Vol. 11, No. 4 (August 1997):478–508.

GALLAGHER, CHARLES A. "Miscounting Race: Explaining Whites' Misperceptions of Racial Group Size." *Sociological Perspectives.* Vol. 46, No. 3 (2003):381–96.

GALLAGHER, MAGGIE. "Does Bradley Know What Poverty Is?" *New York Post* (October 28, 1999):37.

GALLUP ORGANIZATION. Data reported in "Americans and Homosexual Civil Unions." *Society.* Vol. 40, No. 1 (December 2002):2.

GAMSON, WILLIAM A. "Beyond the Science-versus-Advocacy Distinction." *Contemporary Sociology.* Vol. 28, No. 1 (January 1999):23–26.

GANLEY, ELAINE. "Among Islamic Countries, Women's Roles Vary Greatly." *Washington Times* (April 15, 1998):A13.

GANS, HERBERT J. *People and Plans: Essays on Urban Problems and Solutions.* New York: Basic Books, 1968.

GARDYN, REBECCA. "Retirement Redefined." *American Demographics.* Vol. 22, No. 11 (November 2000):52–57.

———. "The Mating Game." *American Demographics.* Vol. 24, No. 7 (July/August 2002):33–37.

GARFINKEL, HAROLD. "Conditions of Successful Degradation Ceremonies." *American Journal of Sociology.* Vol. 61, No. 2 (March 1956):420–24.

REFERENCES

———. *Studies in Ethnomethodology.* Cambridge, Mass.: Polity Press, 1967.

GARREAU, JOEL. *Edge City.* New York: Doubleday, 1991.

GEERTZ, CLIFFORD. "Common Sense as a Cultural System." *Antioch Review.* Vol. 33, No. 1 (Spring 1975):5–26.

GELLES, RICHARD J., and CLAIRE PEDRICK CORNELL. *Intimate Violence in Families.* 2nd ed. Newbury Park, Calif.: Sage, 1990.

GEOHIVE. "Agglomerations." [Online] Available October 3, 2005, at http://www.geohive.com/charts/city_million.php

GERBER, THEODORE P., and MICHAEL HOUT. "More Shock Than Therapy: Market Transition, Employment, and Income in Russia, 1991–1995." *American Journal of Sociology.* Vol. 104, No. 1 (July 1998):1–50.

GERGEN, DAVID. "King of the World." *U.S. News & World Report* (February 25, 2002):84.

GERLACH, MICHAEL L. *The Social Organization of Japanese Business.* Berkeley: University of California Press, 1992.

GERTH, H. H., and C. WRIGHT MILLS, eds. "Marx and Weber." In *From Max Weber: Essays in Sociology.* New York: Oxford University Press, 1946.

GESCHWENDER, JAMES A. *Racial Stratification in America.* Dubuque, Iowa: Brown, 1978.

GEWERTZ, DEBORAH. "A Historical Reconsideration of Female Dominance among the Chambri of Papua New Guinea." *American Ethnologist.* Vol. 8, No. 1 (1981):94–106.

GIBBS, NANCY. "The Pulse of America along the River." *Time* (July 10, 2000):42–46.

———. "What Kids (Really) Need." *Time* (April 30, 2001):48–49.

———. "Darkness Falls." *Time* (April 30, 2007):36–52.

GIBSON, JAMES WILLIAMS. *The Perfect War: Technowar in Vietnam.* Boston: Atlantic Monthly Press, 1986.

GIDDENS, ANTHONY. *The Transformation of Intimacy.* Cambridge: Polity Press, 1992.

GILBERT, NEIL. "Family Life: Sold on Work." *Society.* Vol. 42, No, 3 (2005):12–17.

GILBERTSON, GRETA A., and DOUGLAS T. GURAK. "Broadening the Enclave Debate: The Dual Labor Market Experiences of Dominican and Colombian Men in New York City." *Sociological Forum.* Vol. 8, No. 2 (June 1993):205–20.

GILL, RICHARD T. "What Happened to the American Way of Death?" *Public Interest.* No. 127 (Spring 1996):105–17.

GILLEPSIE, MARK. "Trends Show Bathing and Exercise Up, TV Watching Down." January 2000. [Online] Available April 9, 2006, at http://www.gallup.com

GILLIGAN, CAROL. *In a Different Voice: Psychological Theory and Women's Development.* Cambridge, Mass.: Harvard University Press, 1982.

———. *Making Connections: The Relational Worlds of Adolescent Girls at Emma Willard School.* Cambridge, Mass.: Harvard University Press, 1990.

GILLON, RAANAN. "Euthanasia in the Netherlands: Down the Slippery Slope?" *Journal of Medical Ethics.* Vol. 25, No. 1 (February 1999):3–4.

GIOVANNINI, MAUREEN. "Female Anthropologist and Male Informant: Gender Conflict in a Sicilian Town." In JOHN J. MACIONIS and NIJOLE V. BENOKRAITIS, eds., *Seeing Ourselves: Classic, Contemporary, and Cross-Cultural Readings in Sociology.* 2nd ed. Englewood Cliffs, N.J.: Prentice Hall, 1992:27–32.

GLEICK, ELIZABETH. "The Marker We've Been Waiting For." *Time* (April 7, 1997):28–42.

GLENMARY RESEARCH CENTER. *Religious Congregations and Membership in the United States, 2000.* Nashville, Tenn.: Glenmary Research Center, 2002.

GLENN, NORVAL D., and BETH ANN SHELTON. "Regional Differences in Divorce in the United States." *Journal of Marriage and the Family.* Vol. 47, No. 3 (August 1985):641–52.

GLOBAL MARCH AGAINST CHILD LABOUR. *Country Reports.* [Online] Available August 1, 2007, at http://www.globalmarch.org/child_labour/index.php

GLUECK, SHELDON, and ELEANOR GLUECK. *Unraveling Juvenile Delinquency.* New York: Commonwealth Fund, 1950.

GOESLING, BRIAN. "Changing Income Inequalities within and between Nations: New Evidence." *American Sociological Review.* Vol. 66, No. 5 (October 2001):745–61.

GOFFMAN, ERVING. *The Presentation of Self in Everyday Life.* Garden City, N.Y.: Anchor Books, 1959.

———. *Asylums: Essays on the Social Situation of Mental Patients and Other Inmates.* Garden City, N.Y.: Anchor Books, 1961.

———. *Stigma: Notes on the Management of Spoiled Identity.* Englewood Cliffs, N.J.: Prentice Hall, 1963.

———. *Interactional Ritual: Essays on Face to Face Behavior.* Garden City, N.Y.: Anchor Books, 1967.

———. *Gender Advertisements.* New York: Harper Colophon, 1979.

GOLDBERG, BERNARD. *Bias: A CBS Insider Exposes How the Media Distort the News.* Washington, D.C.: Regnery, 2002.

GOLDBERG, STEVEN. *The Inevitability of Patriarchy.* New York: Morrow, 1974.

———. "Reaffirming the Obvious." *Society.* Vol. 23, No. 6 (September-October 1986a):4–7.

———. "Utopian Yearning versus Scientific Curiosity." *Society.* Vol. 23, No. 6 (September-October 1986b):29–39.

GOLDBERGER, PAUL. Lecture delivered at Kenyon College, Gambier, Ohio, September 22, 2002.

GOLDEN, DANIEL. "Some Community Colleges Fudge the Facts to Attract Foreign Students." *Wall Street Journal* (April 2, 2002):B1, B4.

GOLDEN, FREDERIC. "Lying Faces Unmasked." *Time* (April 5, 1999):52.

GOLDEN, FREDERIC, and MICHAEL D. LEMONICK. "The Race Is Over." *Time* (July 3, 2000):18–23.

GOLDFIELD, MICHAEL. "Rebounding Unions Target Service Sector." *Population Today.* Vol. 28, No. 7 (October 2000):3, 10.

GOLDSCHEIDER, CALVIN. *Studying the Jewish Future.* Seattle: University of Washington Press, 2004.

GOLDSMITH, H. H. "Genetic Influences on Personality from Infancy." *Child Development.* Vol. 54, No. 2 (April 1983):331–35.

GOLDSTEIN, JOSHUA R., and CATHERINE T. KENNEY. "Marriage Delayed or Marriage Forgone? New Cohort Forecasts of First Marriage for U.S. Women." *American Sociological Review.* Vol. 66, No. 4 (August 2001):506–19.

GOODE, ERICH. "No Need to Panic? A Bumper Crop of Books on Moral Panics." *Sociological Forum.* Vol. 15, No. 3 (September 2000):543–52.

GOODE, WILLIAM J. "The Theoretical Importance of Love." *American Sociological Review.* Vol. 24, No. 1 (February 1959):38–47.

———. "Encroachment, Charlatanism, and the Emerging Profession: Psychology, Sociology, and Medicine." *American Sociological Review.* Vol. 25, No. 6 (December 1960):902–14.

GORDON, JAMES S. "The Paradigm of Holistic Medicine." In ARTHUR C. HASTINGS ET AL., eds., *Health for the Whole Person: The Complete Guide to Holistic Medicine.* Boulder, Colo.: Westview Press, 1980:3–27.

GORE, AL. *An Inconvenient Truth: The Crisis of Global Warming.* Emmaus, Pa.: Rodale Books, 2006.

GORMAN, CHRISTINE. "Stressed-Out Kids." *Time* (December 25, 2000):168.

GORSKI, PHILIP S. "Historicizing the Secularization Debate: Church, State, and Society in Late Medieval and Early Modern Europe, ca. 1300 to 1700." *American Sociological Review.* Vol. 65, No. 1 (February 2000):138–67.

GOTHAM, KEVIN FOX. "Race, Mortgage Lending, and Loan Rejections in a U.S. City." *Sociological Focus.* Vol. 31, No. 4 (October 1998):391–405.

GOTTFREDSON, MICHAEL R., and TRAVIS HIRSCHI. "National Crime Control Policies." *Society.* Vol. 32, No. 2 (January/February 1995):30–36.

GOTTMANN, JEAN. *Megalopolis.* New York: Twentieth Century Fund, 1961.

GOUGH, KATHLEEN. "The Origin of the Family." In JOHN J. MACIONIS and NIJOLE V. BENOKRAITIS, eds., *Seeing Ourselves: Classic, Contemporary, and Cross-Cultural Readings in Sociology.* Englewood Cliffs, N.J.: Prentice Hall, 1989.

GOULD, STEPHEN J. "Evolution as Fact and Theory." *Discover* (May 1981):35–37.

———. "Curveball." *New Yorker* (November 28, 1994):139–49.

GRANT, DON SHERMAN, II, and MICHAEL WALLACE. "Why Do Strikes Turn Violent?" *American Journal of Sociology.* Vol. 96, No. 5 (March 1991):1117–50.

GRANT, DONALD L. *The Anti-Lynching Movement.* San Francisco: R&E Research Associates, 1975.

GRATTET, RYKEN. "Hate Crimes: Better Data or Increasing Frequency?" *Population Today.* Vol. 28, No. 5 (July 2000):1, 4.

GREELEY, ANDREW M. *Religious Change in America.* Cambridge, Mass.: Harvard University Press, 1989.

———. "Religious Revival in Eastern Europe." *Society.* Vol. 39, No. 2 (January/February 2002):76–77.

GREEN, GARY PAUL, LEANN M. TIGGES, and DANIEL DIAZ. "Racial and Ethnic Differences in Job-Search Strategies in Atlanta, Boston, and Los Angeles." *Social Science Quarterly.* Vol. 80, No. 2 (June 1999):263–90.

GREENBERG, DAVID F. *The Construction of Homosexuality.* Chicago: University of Chicago Press, 1988.

GREENE, BOB. "Empty House on the Prairie." *New York Times* (March 2, 2005). [Online] Available May 24, 2005, at http://www.researchnavigator.com

GREENFIELD, LAWRENCE A. *Child Victimizers: Violent Offenders and Their Victims.* Washington, D.C.: U.S. Bureau of Justice Statistics, 1996.

GREENHOUSE, STEVEN. "Despite Defeat on China Bill, Labor Is on the Rise." *New York Times* (May 20, 2000):A1, A18.

GREENSPAN, STANLEY I. *The Four-Thirds Solution: Solving the Child-Care Crisis in America.* Cambridge, Mass.: Perseus, 2001.

GRIER, PETER. "How to Slow the Spread of the Bomb." *Christian Science Monitor* (June 5, 2006). [Online] Accessed July 29, 2006, at http://news.yahoo.com/s/csm/20060605

GROSS, MATT. "It's My (Virtual) World." *New York Times Online.* November 3, 2006. Available November 7, 2006, at http://www.nytimes.com.

GURAK, DOUGLAS T., and JOSEPH P. FITZPATRICK. "Intermarriage among Hispanic Ethnic Groups in New York City." *American Journal of Sociology.* Vol. 87, No. 4 (January 1982):921–34.

GURNETT, KATE. "On the Forefront of Feminism." *Albany Times Union* (July 5, 1998):G-1, G-6.

GWYNNE, S. C., and JOHN F. DICKERSON. "Lost in the E-Mail." *Time* (April 21, 1997):88–90.

HABERMAS, JÜRGEN. *Toward a Rational Society: Student Protest, Science, and Politics.* JEREMY J. SHAPIRO, trans. Boston: Beacon Press, 1970.

HADAWAY, C. KIRK, PENNY LONG MARLER, and MARK CHAVES. "What the Polls Don't Show: A Closer Look at U.S. Church Attendance." *American Sociological Review*. Vol. 58, No. 6 (December 1993):741–52.

HADDEN, JEFFREY K., and CHARLES E. SWAIN. *Prime-Time Preachers: The Rising Power of Televangelism*. Reading, Mass.: Addison-Wesley, 1981.

HAFNER, KATIE. "Making Sense of the Internet." *Newsweek* (October 24, 1994):46–48.

HAGAN, JACQUELINE MARIA. "Social Networks, Gender, and Immigrant Incorporation: Resources and Restraints." *American Sociological Review*. Vol. 63, No. 1 (February 1998):55–67.

HAGOPIAN, ELAINE C. *Civil Rights in Peril: The Targeting of Arabs and Muslims*. London: Photo Press, 2004.

HALBERSTAM, DAVID. *The Reckoning*. New York: Avon Books, 1986.

HALBFINGER, DAVID M., and STEVEN A. HOLMES. "Military Mirrors Working-Class America." *New York Times* (March 20, 2003). [Online] Available April 28, 2005, at http://www.researchnavigator.com

HALEDJIAN, DEAN. *How to Tell a Businessman from a Businesswoman*. Annandale: Northern Virginia Community College, 1997.

HALL, JOHN R., and MARY JO NEITZ. *Culture: Sociological Perspectives*. Englewood Cliffs, N.J.: Prentice Hall, 1993.

HALL, KELLEY J., and BETSY LUCAL. "Tapping in Parallel Universes: Using Superhero Comic Books in Sociology Courses." *Teaching Sociology*. Vol. 27, No. 1 (January 1999):60–66.

HALLINAN, MAUREEN T. "The Sociological Study of Social Change." *American Sociological Review*. Vol. 62, No. 1 (February 1997):1–11.

HAMER, DEAN, and PETER COPELAND. *The Science of Desire: The Search for the Gay Gene and the Biology of Behavior*. New York: Simon & Schuster, 1994.

HAMILTON, ANITA. "Speeders, Say Cheese." *Time* (September 17, 2001):32.

HAMILTON, BRADY E., JOYCE A. MARTIN, and STEPHANIE J. VENTURA. "Births: Preliminary Data for 2005." *National Vital Statistics Reports*. Vol. 55, No. 11 (December 28, 2006).

HAMILTON, RICHARD F. "*The Communist Manifesto* at 150." *Society*. Vol. 38, No. 2 (January/February 2001):75–80.

HAMRICK, MICHAEL H., DAVID J. ANSPAUGH, and GENE EZELL. *Health*. Columbus, Ohio: Merrill, 1986.

HAN, WENJUI, and JANE WALDFOGEL. "Child Care Costs and Women's Employment: A Comparison of Single and Married Mothers with Preschool-Aged Children." *Social Science Quarterly*. Vol. 83, No. 5 (September 2001):552–68.

HANDLIN, OSCAR. *Boston's Immigrants, 1790–1865: A Study in Acculturation*. Cambridge, Mass.: Harvard University Press, 1941.

HANEY, CRAIG, W. CURTIS BANKS, and PHILIP G. ZIMBARDO. "Interpersonal Dynamics in a Simulated Prison." *International Journal of Criminology and Penology*. Vol. 1 (1973):69–97.

HANEY, LYNNE. "After the Fall: East European Women since the Collapse of State Socialism." *Contexts*. Vol. 1, No. 3 (Fall 2002):27–36.

HARLOW, HARRY F., and MARGARET KUENNE HARLOW. "Social Deprivation in Monkeys." *Scientific American* (November 1962):137–46.

HARPSTER, PAULA, and ELIZABETH MONK-TURNER. "Why Men Do Housework: A Test of Gender Production and the Relative Resources Model." *Sociological Focus*. Vol. 31, No. 1 (February 1998):45–59.

HARRIES, KEITH D. *Serious Violence: Patterns of Homicide and Assault in America*. Springfield, Ill.: Thomas, 1990.

HARRINGTON, MICHAEL. *The New American Poverty*. New York: Penguin Books, 1984.

HARRIS, CHAUNCY D., and EDWARD L. ULLMAN. "The Nature of Cities." *Annals of the American Academy of Political and Social Sciences*. Vol. 242, No. 1 (November 1945):7–17.

HARRIS, DAVID R., and JEREMIAH JOSEPH SIM. "Who Is Multiracial? Assessing the Complexity of Lived Race." Vol. 67, No. 4 (August 2002):614–27.

HARRIS, MARVIN. *Cultural Anthropology*. 2nd ed. New York: Harper & Row, 1987.

HARRISON, C. KEITH. "Black Athletes at the Millennium." *Society*. Vol. 37, No. 3 (March/April 2000):35–39.

HARTOCOLLIS, ANEMONA. "Man Is Convicted of Attempted Murder as Hate Crime in Village Rampage." *New York Times* (March 2, 2007):B6.

HAUB, CARL. "How Many People Have Ever Lived on Earth?" *Population Today*. Vol. 30, No. 8 (November/December 2002):3–4.

HAWTHORNE, PETER. "South Africa's Makeover." *Time* (July 12, 1999).

HAYDEN, THOMAS. "Losing Our Voices." *U.S. News & World Report* (May 26, 2003):42.

HAYWARD, MARK D., EILEEN M. CRIMMINS, TONI P. MILES, and YU YANG. "The Significance of Socioeconomic Status in Explaining the Racial Gap in Chronic Health Conditions." *American Sociological Review*. Vol. 65, No. 6 (December 2000):910–30.

HEATH, JULIA A., and W. DAVID BOURNE. "Husbands and Housework: Parity or Parody?" *Social Science Quarterly*. Vol. 76, No. 1 (March 1995):195–202.

HELGESEN, SALLY. *The Female Advantage: Women's Ways of Leadership*. New York: Doubleday, 1990.

HELIN, DAVID W. "When Slogans Go Wrong." *American Demographics*. Vol. 14, No. 2 (February 1992):14.

HELLMICH, NANCI. "Environment, Economics Partly to Blame." *USA Today* (October 9, 2002):9D.

HENLEY, NANCY, MYKOL HAMILTON, and BARRIE THORNE. "Womanspeak and Manspeak: Sex Differences in Communication, Verbal and Nonverbal." In JOHN J. MACIONIS and NIJOLE V. BENOKRAITIS, eds., *Seeing Ourselves: Classic, Contemporary, and Cross-Cultural Readings in Sociology*. 2nd ed. Englewood Cliffs, N.J.: Prentice Hall, 1992:10–15.

HERDA-RAPP, ANN. "The Power of Informal Leadership: Women Leaders in the Civil Rights Movement." *Sociological Focus*. Vol. 31, No. 4 (October 1998):341–55.

HERMAN, DIANNE. "The Rape Culture." In JOHN J. MACIONIS and NIJOLE V. BENOKRAITIS, eds., *Seeing Ourselves: Classic, Contemporary, and Cross-Cultural Readings in Sociology*. 5th ed. Upper Saddle River, N.J.: Prentice Hall, 2001.

HERON, MELONIE P., and BETTY L. SMITH. "Deaths: Leading Causes for 2003." *National Vital Statistics Reports*. Vol. 55, No. 10 (March 15, 2007).

HERPERTZ, SABINE C., and HENNING SASS. "Emotional Deficiency and Psychopathy." *Behavioral Sciences and the Law*. Vol. 18, No. 5 (September/October 2000):567–80.

HERRING, HUBERT B. "An Aging Nation Is Choosing Younger Bosses." *New York Times* (February 20, 2005). [Online] Available April 12, 2005, at http://www.researchnavigator.com

HERRNSTEIN, RICHARD J., and CHARLES MURRAY. *The Bell Curve: Intelligence and Class Structure in American Life*. New York: Free Press, 1994.

HERZOG, BRAD. "A Man of His Words." *Cornell Alumni Magazine*. Vol. 106, No. 4 (January/February 2004):58–63.

HESS, BETH B. "Breaking and Entering the Establishment: Committing Social Change and Confronting the Backlash." *Social Problems*. Vol. 46, No. 1 (February 1999):1–12.

HEYMANN, PHILIP B. "Civil Liberties and Human Rights in the Aftermath of September 11." *Harvard Journal of Law and Public Policy*. Vol. 25, No. 2 (Spring 2002):441–57.

HIGHTOWER, JIM. *Eat Your Heart Out: Food Profiteering in America*. New York: Crown, 1975.

HILL, MARK E. "Race of the Interviewer and Perception of Skin Color: Evidence from the Multi-City Study of Urban Inequality." *American Sociological Review*. Vol. 67, No. 1 (February 2002):99–108.

HIMES, CHRISTINE L. "Elderly Americans." *Population Bulletin*. Vol. 56, No. 4 (December 2001):3–40.

HIRSCHI, TRAVIS. *Causes of Delinquency*. Berkeley: University of California Press, 1969.

HOBERMAN, JOHN. *Darwin's Athletes: How Sport Has Damaged Black America and Preserved the Myth of Race*. Boston: Houghton Mifflin, 1997.

———. "Response to Three Reviews of *Darwin's Athletes*." *Social Science Quarterly*. Vol. 79, No. 4 (December 1998):898–903.

HOBSON, KATHERINE. "Kissing Cousins." *U.S. News & World Report* (April 15, 2002):77.

HOCHSCHILD, ARLIE RUSSELL. "Emotion Work, Feeling Rules, and Social Structure." *American Journal of Sociology*. Vol. 85, No. 3 (November 1979):551–75.

———. *The Managed Heart*. Berkeley: University of California Press, 1983.

HOFFERTH, SANDRA. "Did Welfare Reform Work? Implications for 2002 and Beyond." *Contexts*. Vol. 1, No. 1 (Spring 2002):45–51.

HOGAN, RICHARD, and CAROLYN C. PERRUCCI. "Producing and Reproducing the Class and Status Differences: Racial and Gender Gaps in U.S. Employment and Retirement Income." *Social Problems*. Vol. 45, No. 4 (November 1998):528–49.

HOLMSTROM, DAVID. "Abuse of Elderly, Even by Adult Children, Gets More Attention and Official Concern." *Christian Science Monitor* (July 28, 1994):1.

HONEYWELL, ROY J. *The Educational Work of Thomas Jefferson*. Cambridge, Mass.: Harvard University Press, 1931.

HOPE, TRINA L., HAROLD G. GRASMICK, and LAURA J. POINTON. "The Family in Gottfredson and Hrischi's General Theory of Crime: Structure, Parenting, and Self-Control." *Sociological Focus*. Vol. 36, No. 4 (November 2003):291–311.

HORN, WADE F., and DOUGLAS TYNAN. "Revamping Special Education." *Public Interest*. No. 144 (Summer 2001):36–53.

HORTON, HAYWARD DERRICK. "Critical Demography: The Paradigm of the Future?" *Sociological Forum*. Vol. 14, No. 3 (September 1999):363–67.

HOSTETLER, JOHN A. *Amish Society*. 3rd ed. Baltimore: Johns Hopkins University Press, 1980.

HOUT, MICHAEL. "More Universalism, Less Structural Mobility: The American Occupational Structure in the 1980s." *American Journal of Sociology*. Vol. 95, No. 6 (May 1998):1358–1400.

HOUT, MICHAEL, CLEM BROOKS, and JEFF MANZA. "The Persistence of Classes in Post-Industrial Societies." *International Sociology*. Vol. 8, No. 3 (September 1993):259–77.

HOUT, MICHAEL, and CLAUDE S. FISHER. "Why More Americans Have No Religious Preference: Politics and Generations." *American Sociological Review*. Vol. 67, No. 2 (April 2002):165–90.

HOUT, MICHAEL, ANDREW M. GREELEY, and MELISSA J. WILDE. "The Demographic Imperative in Religious Change in the United States." *American Journal of Sociology*. Vol. 107, No. 2 (September 2001):468–500.

HOWDEN, DANIEL. "Latin America's New Socialist Revolution." *New Zealand Herald* (December 20, 2005). [Online] Available February 13, 2006, at http://www.nzherald.co.nz

HOYERT, DONNA L., MELONIE P. HERON, SHERRY L. MURPHY, and HSIANG-CHING KUNG. "Deaths: Final Data for 2003." *National Vital Statistics Reports*. Vol. 54, No. 13 (April 19, 2006).

HOYERT, DONNA L., HSIANG-CHING KUNG, and BETTY L. SMITH. "Deaths: Preliminary Data for 2003." *National Vital Statistics Report*. Vol. 53, No. 15 (February 28, 2005).

HOYT, HOMER. *The Structure and Growth of Residential Neighborhoods in American Cities.* Washington, D.C.: Federal Housing Administration, 1939.

HSU, FRANCIS L. K. *The Challenge of the American Dream: The Chinese in the United States.* Belmont, Calif.: Wadsworth, 1971.

HUCHINGSON, JAMES E. "Science and Religion." *Miami* (Fla.) *Herald* (December 25, 1994):1M, 6M.

HUFFMAN, KAREN. *Psychology in Action.* New York: Wiley, 2000.

HUMAN RIGHTS WATCH. "Children's Rights: Child Labor." 2006. [Online] Available April 9, 2006, at http://www.hrw.org/children/labor.htm

HUMMER, ROBERT A., RICHARD G. ROGERS, CHARLES B. NAM, and FELICIA B. LE CLERE. "Race/Ethnicity, Nativity, and U.S. Adult Mortality." *Social Science Quarterly*. Vol. 80, No. 1 (March 1999):136–53.

HUNTER, JAMES DAVISON. *American Evangelicalism: Conservative Religion and the Quandary of Modernity.* New Brunswick, N.J.: Rutgers University Press, 1983.

———. "Conservative Protestantism." In PHILIP E. HAMMOND, ed., *The Sacred in a Secular Age.* Berkeley: University of California Press, 1985:50–66.

———. *Evangelicalism: The Coming Generation.* Chicago: University of Chicago Press, 1987.

HYMOWITZ, CAROL. "World's Poorest Women Advance by Entrepreneurship." *Wall Street Journal* (September 9, 1995):B1.

HYMOWITZ, KAY S. "Kids Today Are Growing Up Way Too Fast." *Wall Street Journal* (October 28, 1998):A22.

IANNACCONE, LAURENCE R. "Why Strict Churches Are Strong." *American Journal of Sociology.* Vol. 99, No. 5 (March 1994):1180–1211.

IDE, THOMAS R., and ARTHUR J. CORDELL. "Automating Work." *Society.* Vol. 31, No. 6 (September/October 1994):65–71.

INCIARDI, JAMES A. *Elements of Criminal Justice.* 2nd ed. New York: Oxford University Press, 2000.

INCIARDI, JAMES A., HILARY L. SURRATT, and PAULO R. TELLES. *Sex, Drugs, and HIV/AIDS in Brazil.* Boulder, Colo.: Westview Press, 2000.

INGLEHART, RONALD. *Modernization and Postmodernization: Cultural, Economic, and Political Change in 43 Societies.* Princeton, N.J.: Princeton University Press, 1997.

INGLEHART, RONALD, and CHRISTIAN WELZEL. *Modernization, Culture Change, and Democracy.* (New York: Cambridge University Press, 2005).

INGLEHART, RONALD, ET AL. *World Values Surveys and European Values Surveys, 1981–1984, 1990–1993, and 1995–1997.* Computer file. Ann Arbor, Mich.: Interuniversity Consortium for Political and Social Research, 2000.

INGLEHART, RONALD, and WAYNE E. BAKER. "Modernization, Cultural Change, and the Persistence of Traditional Values." *American Sociological Review.* Vol. 65, No. 1 (February 2000):19–51.

INTERNAL REVENUE SERVICE. "Corporation Income Tax Returns, 2002." *Statistics of Income Bulletin.* Summer 2005. [Online] Available June 2, 2006, at http://www.irs.gov/pub/irs-soi/02corart.pdf

INTERNATIONAL BUSINESS MACHINES. "Select a Country/Region and Language." [Online] Available May 7, 2007, at http://www.ibm.com/planetwide/select/selector.html

INTERNATIONAL MONETARY FUND. *World Economic Outlook.* April 2000. [Online] Available http://www.imf.org/external/pubs/ft/weo/2000/01/index.htm

INTERNATIONAL PANEL ON CLIMATE CHANGE. *Climate Change, 2007.* New York: United Nations, 2007.

INTERNATIONAL TELECOMMUNICATION UNION. *World Telecommunication Development Report.* Data cited in WORLD BANK, *2006 World Development Indicators.* Washington, D.C.: World Bank, 2006.

———. *World Telecommunication Development Report.* Data cited in WORLD BANK, *2007 World Development Indicators.* Washington, D.C.: World Bank, 2007.

INTER-PARLIAMENTARY UNION. "Women in National Parliaments." 2005. [Online] Available June 25, 2005, at http://www.ipu.org/wmn-e/classif.htm and http://www.ipu.org/wmn-e/world.htm

———. "Women in National Parliaments." 2007. [Online] Available May 30, 2007, at http://www.ipu.org/wmn-e/classif.htm and http://www.ipu.org/wmn-e/world.htm

ISRAEL, GLENN D., LIONEL J. BEAULIEU, and GLEN HARTLESS. "The Influence of Family and Community Social Capital on Educational Achievement." *Rural Sociology.* Vol. 66, No. 1 (March 2001):43–68.

ISRAELY, JEFF. "Something in the Air." *Time* (December 9, 2002):16.

ITZKOFF, DAVE. "Television: A Brave New World for TV? Virtually." *New York Times Online.* June 24, 2007. Available July 7, 2007, at http://www.nytimes.com

JACOBS, DAVID, and JASON T. CARMICHAEL. "The Political Sociology of the Death Penalty: A Pooled Time-Series Analysis." *American Sociological Review.* Vol. 67, No. 1 (February 2002):109–31.

JACOBS, DAVID, and RONALD E. HELMS. "Toward a Political Model of Incarceration: A Time-Series Examination of Multiple Explanations for Prison Admission Rates." *American Journal of Sociology.* Vol. 102, No. 2 (September 1996):323–57.

JACOBSON, JENNIFER. "Professors Are Finding Better Pay and More Freedom at Community Colleges." *Chronicle of Higher Education Online.* 2003. [Online] Available March 7, 2003, at http://www.chronicle.com

JACOBY, RUSSELL, and NAOMI GLAUBERMAN, eds. *The Bell Curve Debate.* New York: Random House, 1995.

JACQUET, CONSTANT H., and ALICE M. JONES. *Yearbook of American and Canadian Churches, 1991.* Nashville, Tenn.: Abingdon Press, 1991.

JAMES, DAVID R. "City Limits on Racial Equality: The Effects of City-Suburb Boundaries on Public School Desegregation, 1968–1976." *American Sociological Review.* Vol. 54, No. 6 (December 1989):963–85.

JANIS, IRVING L. *Victims of Groupthink.* Boston: Houghton Mifflin, 1972.

———. *Crucial Decisions: Leadership in Policymaking and Crisis Management.* New York: Free Press, 1989.

JASPER, JAMES M. "The Emotions of Protest: Affective and Reactive Emotions in and around Social Movements." *Sociological Forum.* Vol. 13, No. 3 (September 1998):397–424.

JENKINS, J. CRAIG. *Images of Terror: What We Can and Can't Know about Terrorism.* Hawthorne, N.Y.: Aldine de Gruyter, 2003.

JENKINS, J. CRAIG, and CHARLES PERROW. "Insurgency of the Powerless: Farm Worker Movements, 1946–1972." *American Sociological Review.* Vol. 42, No. 2 (April 1977):249–68.

JENKINS, J. CRAIG, DAVID JACOBS, and JON AGONE. "Political Opportunities and African-American Protest, 1948–1997." *American Journal of Sociology.* Vol. 109, No. 2 (September 2003):277–303.

JENKINS, J. CRAIG, and MICHAEL WALLACE. "The Generalized Action Potential of Protest Movements: The New Class, Social Trends, and Political Exclusion Explanations." *Sociological Forum.* Vol. 11, No. 2 (June 1996):183–207.

JENNESS, VALERIE, and RYKEN GRATTET. *Making a Hate Crime: From Movement to Law Enforcement.* New York: Russell Sage Foundation, 2001.

JOHNSON, BARRY W., and BRIAN G. RAUB. "Personal Wealth, 2001." *Statistics of Income Bulletin* (Winter 2005–06). 2006. [Online] Available September 20, 2006, at http://www.irs.gov/pub/irs-soi/01pwart.pdf

JOHNSON, CATHRYN. "Gender, Legitimate Authority, and Leader-Subordinate Conversations." *American Sociological Review.* Vol. 59, No. 1 (February 1994):122–35.

JOHNSON, DIRK. "Death of a Small Town." *Newsweek* (September 10, 2001):30–31.

JOHNSON, KENNETH M. "The Rural Rebound." *Population Reference Bureau Reports on America.* Vol. 1, No. 3 (September 1999). [Online] Available October 9, 2004, at http://www.prb.org/Content/NavigationMenu/PRB/AboutPRB/Reports_on_America/ReportonAmericaRuralRebound.pdf

JOHNSON, KENNETH M., and GLENN V. FUGUITT. "Continuity and Change in Rural Migration Patterns, 1950–1995." *Rural Sociology.* Vol. 65, No. 1 (March 2000):27–49.

JOHNSON, PAUL. "The Seven Deadly Sins of Terrorism." In BENJAMIN NETANYAHU, ed., *International Terrorism.* New Brunswick, N.J.: Transaction Books, 1981:12–22.

JOHNSTON, DAVID CAY. "Voting, America's Not Keen On. Coffee Is Another Matter." *New York Times* (November 10, 1996):sec. 4, p. 2.

JOHNSTON, R. J. "Residential Area Characteristics." In D. T. HERBERT and R. J. JOHNSTON, eds., *Social Areas in Cities. Vol. 1: Spatial Processes and Form.* New York: Wiley, 1976:193–235.

JONES, ANDREW E. G., and DAVID WILSON. *The Urban Growth Machine: Critical Perspectives.* Albany: State University of New York Press, 1999.

JONES, D. GARETH. "Brain Death." *Journal of Medical Ethics.* Vol. 24, No. 4 (August 1998):237–43.

JONES, JUDY. "More Miners Will Be Offered Free X-Rays; Federal Agency Wants to Monitor Black-Lung Cases." *Louisville Courier Journal* (May 13, 1999):1A.

JONES, KATHARINE W. *Accent on Privilege: English Identities and Anglophilia in the U.S.* Philadelphia: Temple University Press, 2001.

JORDAN, ELLEN, and ANGELA COWAN. "Warrior Narratives in the Kindergarten Classroom: Renegotiating the Social Contract?" *Gender and Society.* Vol. 9, No. 6 (December 1995):727–43.

JOSEPHY, ALVIN M., JR. *Now That the Buffalo's Gone: A Study of Today's American Indians.* New York: Knopf, 1982.

JOYNSON, ROBERT B. "Fallible Judgments." *Society.* Vol. 31, No. 3 (March/April 1994):45–52.

KADLEC, DANIEL. "Everyone, Back in the (Labor) Pool." *Time* (July 29, 2002):22–31.

KAIN, EDWARD L. "A Note on the Integration of AIDS into the Sociology of Human Sexuality." *Teaching Sociology.* Vol. 15, No. 4 (July 1987):320–23.

———. *The Myth of Family Decline: Understanding Families in a World of Rapid Social Change.* Lexington, Mass.: Lexington Books, 1990.

KALLEBERG, ARNE L., BARBARA F. RESKIN, and KEN HUDSON. "Bad Jobs in America: Standard and Nonstandard Employment Relations and Job Quality in the United States." *American Sociological Review.* Vol. 65, No 2 (April 2000):256–78.

KALLEBERG, ARNE L., and MARK E. VAN BUREN. "Is Bigger Better? Explaining the Relationship between Organization Size and Job Rewards." *American Sociological Review.* Vol. 61, No. 1 (February 1996):47–66.

KAMINER, WENDY. "Volunteers: Who Knows What's in It for Them?" *Ms.* (December 1984):93–96, 126–28.

———. "Demasculinizing the Army." *New York Times Review of Books* (June 15, 1997):7.

KANE, EMILY W. "Racial and Ethnic Variations in Gender-Related Attitudes." *Annual Review of Sociology.* Vol. 26 (2000):419–39.

KANTER, ROSABETH MOSS. *Men and Women of the Corporation.* New York: Basic Books, 1977.

KANTER, ROSABETH MOSS, and BARRY A. STEIN. "The Gender Pioneers: Women in an Industrial Sales Force." In ROSABETH MOSS KANTER and BARRY A. STEIN, eds., *Life in Organizations.* New York: Basic Books, 1979:134–60.

KANTROWITZ, BARBARA, and PAT WINGERT. "Unmarried with Children." *Newsweek* (May 28, 2001):46–52.

———. "What's at Stake." *Newsweek* (January 27, 2003):30–37.

KAO, GRACE. "Group Images and Possible Selves among Adolescents: Linking Stereotypes to Expectations by Race and Ethnicity." *Sociological Forum.* Vol. 15, No. 3 (September 2000):407–30.

KAPFERER, JEAN-NOEL. "How Rumors Are Born." *Society.* Vol. 29, No. 5 (July/August 1992):53–60.

KAPLAN, DAVID E., and MICHAEL SCHAFFER. "Losing the Psywar." *U.S. News & World Report* (October 8, 2001):46.

KAPTCHUK, TED. "The Holistic Logic of Chinese Medicine." In BERKELEY HOLISTIC HEALTH CENTER, *The New Holistic Health Handbook: Living Well in a New Age.* SHEPARD BLISS ET AL., eds. Lexington, Mass.: Steven Greene Press, 1985:41.

KARATNYCKY, ADRIAN. "The 2001–2002 Freedom House Survey of Freedom: The Democracy Gap." In *Freedom in the World: The Annual Survey of Political Rights and Civil Liberties, 2001–2002.* New York: Freedom House, 2002:7–18.

KARP, DAVID A., and WILLIAM C. YOELS. "The College Classroom: Some Observations on the Meaning of Student Participation." *Sociology and Social Research.* Vol. 60, No. 4 (July 1976):421–39.

KARRFALT, WAYNE. "A Multicultural Mecca." *"American Demographics.* Vol. 25, No. 4 (May 2003):54–55.

KAUFMAN, LESLIE. "Surge in Homeless Families Sets Off Debate on Cause." *New York Times* (July 29, 2004). [Online] Available March 24, 2005, at http://www.researchnavigator.com

KAUFMAN, ROBERT L. "Assessing Alternative Perspectives on Race and Sex Employment Segregation." *American Sociological Review.* Vol. 67, No. 4 (August 2002):547–72.

KAUFMAN, WALTER. *Religions in Four Dimensions: Existential, Aesthetic, Historical, and Comparative.* New York: Reader's Digest Press, 1976.

KAY, PAUL, and WILLETT KEMPTON. "What Is the Sapir-Whorf Hypothesis?" *American Anthropologist.* Vol. 86, No. 1 (March 1984):65–79.

KEISTER, LISA A. *Wealth in America: Trends in Wealth Inequality.* Cambridge: Cambridge University Press, 2000.

———. "Religion and Wealth: The Role of Religious Affiliation and Participation in Early Adult Asset Accumulation." *Social Forces.* Vol. 82, No. 1 (September 2003):175–207.

KEISTER, LISA A., and STEPHANIE MOLLER. "Wealth Inequality in the United States." *Annual Review of Sociology.* Vol. 26 (2000):63–81.

KELLER, HELEN. *The Story of My Life.* New York: Doubleday Page, 1903.

KELLERT, STEPHEN R., and F. HERBERT BORMANN. "Closing the Circle: Weaving Strands among Ecology, Economics, and Ethics." In F. HERBERT BORMANN and STEPHEN R. KELLERT, eds., *Ecology, Economics, and Ethics: The Broken Circle.* New Haven, Conn.: Yale University Press, 1991:205–10.

KENT, MARY M., and MARK MATHER. "What Drives U.S. Population Growth?" *Population Bulletin.* Vol. 57, No. 4 (December 2002):3–40.

KENTOR, JEFFREY. "The Long-Term Effects of Foreign Investment Dependence on Economic Growth, 1940–1990." *American Journal of Sociology.* Vol. 103, No. 4 (January 1998):1024–46.

———. "The Long-Term Effects of Globalization on Income Inequality, Population Growth, and Economic Development." *Social Problems.* Vol. 48, No. 4 (November 2001):435–55.

KERCKHOFF, ALAN C., RICHARD T. CAMPBELL, and IDEE WINFIELD-LAIRD. "Social Mobility in Great Britain and the United States." *American Journal of Sociology.* Vol. 91, No. 2 (September 1985):281–308.

KERR, RICHARD A. "Climate Models Heat Up." *Science Now* (January 26, 2005):1–3.

KEYS, JENNIFER. "Feeling Rules That Script the Abortion Experience." Paper presented at the annual meeting of the American Sociological Association, Chicago, August 2002.

KIDRON, MICHAEL, and RONALD SEGAL. *The New State of the World Atlas.* New York: Simon & Schuster, 1991.

KILBOURNE, BROCK K. "The Conway and Siegelman Claims against Religious Cults: An Assessment of Their Data." *Journal for the Scientific Study of Religion.* Vol. 22, No. 4 (December 1983):380–85.

KILGORE, SALLY B. "The Organizational Context of Tracking in Schools." *American Sociological Review.* Vol. 56, No. 2 (April 1991):189–203.

KING, KATHLEEN PIKER, and DENNIS E. CLAYSON. "The Differential Perceptions of Male and Female Deviants." *Sociological Focus.* Vol. 21, No. 2 (April 1988):153–64.

KINGSBURY, ALEX. "Did Bush Do the Math?" *U.S. News & World Report.* Vol. 140, No. 5 (February 13, 2006):28.

KINKEAD, GWEN. *Chinatown: A Portrait of a Closed Society.* New York: HarperCollins, 1992.

KINSEY, ALFRED, WARDELL BAXTER POMEROY, and CLYDE E. MARTIN. *Sexual Behavior in the Human Male.* Philadelphia: Saunders, 1948.

KINSEY, ALFRED, WARDELL BAXTER POMEROY, CLYDE E. MARTIN, and PAUL H. GEBHARD. *Sexual Behavior in the Human Female.* Philadelphia: Saunders, 1953.

KITTRIE, NICHOLAS N. *The Right to Be Different: Deviance and Enforced Therapy.* Baltimore: Johns Hopkins University Press, 1971.

KLEIN, DANIEL B., and CHARLOTTA STERN. "How Politically Diverse Are the Social Sciences and Humanities? Survey Evidence from Six Fields." National Association of Scholars. 2004. [Online] Available January 13, 2005, at http://www.nas.org/aa/klein_launch.htm

KLUCKHOHN, CLYDE. "As an Anthropologist Views It." In ALBERT DEUTH, ed., *Sex Habits of American Men.* New York: Prentice Hall, 1948.

KOCHANEK, KENNETH D., SHERRY L. MURPHY, ROBERT N. ANDERSON, and CHESTER SCOTT. "Deaths: Final Data for 2002." *National Vital Statistics Report.* Vol. 53, No. 5 (October 12, 2004).

KOELLN, KENNETH, ROSE M. RUBIN, and MARION SMITH PICARD. "Vulnerable Elderly Households: Expenditures on Necessities by Older Americans." *Social Science Quarterly.* Vol. 76, No. 3 (September 1995):619–33.

KOHLBERG, LAWRENCE. *The Psychology of Moral Development: The Nature and Validity of Moral Stages.* New York: Harper & Row, 1981.

KOHLBERG, LAWRENCE, and CAROL GILLIGAN. "The Adolescent as Philosopher: The Discovery of Self in a Postconventional World." *Daedalus.* No. 100 (Fall 1971):1051–86.

KOHN, MELVIN L. *Class and Conformity: A Study in Values.* 2nd ed. Homewood, Ill.: Dorsey Press, 1977.

———. "The 'Bell Curve' from the Perspective of Research on Social Structure and Personality." *Sociological Forum.* Vol. 11, No. 2 (1996):395.

KOLATA, GINA. "When Grandmother Is the Mother, Until Birth." *New York Times* (August 5, 1991):1, 11.

KONO, CLIFFORD, DONALD PALMER, ROGER FRIEDLAND, and MATTHEW ZAFONTE. "Lost in Space: The Geography of Corporate Interlocking Directorates." *American Journal of Sociology.* Vol. 103, No. 4 (January 1998):863–911.

KOONTZ, STEPHANIE. *The Way We Never Were: American Families and the Nostalgia Trap.* New York: Basic Books, 1992.

KORNHAUSER, WILLIAM. *The Politics of Mass Society.* New York: Free Press, 1959.

KORZENIEWICZ, ROBERTO P., and KIMBERLY AWBREY. "Democratic Transitions and the Semiperiphery of the World Economy." *Sociological Forum.* Vol. 7, No. 4 (December 1992):609–40.

KOSTERS, MARVIN. "Looking for Jobs in All the Wrong Places." *Public Interest.* No. 125 (Fall 1996):125–31.

KOZOL, JONATHAN. *Rachel and Her Children: Homeless Families in America.* New York: Crown, 1988.

———. *Savage Inequalities: Children in America's Schools.* New York: Harper Perennial, 1992.

KRAL, BRIGITTA. "The Eyes of Jane Elliott." *Horizon Magazine.* 2000. [Online] Available June 8, 2005, at http://www.horizonmag.com/4/jane-elliott.asp

KRAYBILL, DONALD B. *The Riddle of Amish Culture.* Baltimore: Johns Hopkins University Press, 1989.

———. "The Amish Encounter with Modernity." In DONALD B. KRAYBILL and MARC A. OLSHAN, eds., *The Amish Struggle with Modernity.* Hanover, N.H.: University Press of New England, 1994:21–33.

KRAYBILL, DONALD B., and MARC A. OLSHAN, eds. *The Amish Struggle with Modernity.* Hanover, N.H.: University Press of New England, 1994.

KROLL, LUISA, and LEA GOLDMAN, eds. "Billionaires." *Forbes* (March 15, 2004):91–154.

———, eds. "The World's Billionaires." March 10, 2005. [Online] Available September 15, 2005, at http://www.forbes.com/billionaires

KRUGMAN, PAUL. "For Richer: How the Permissive Capitalism of the Boom Destroyed American Equality." *New York Times Magazine* (September 20, 2002):62–67, 76–77, 141–42.

KRUKS, GABRIEL N. "Gay and Lesbian Homeless/Street Youth: Special Issues and Concerns." *Journal of Adolescent Health.* Special Issue. No. 12 (1991):515–18.

KRYSAN, MARIA. "Community Undesirability in Black and White: Examining Racial Residential Preferences through Community Perceptions." *Social Problems.* Vol. 49, No. 4 (November 2002):521–43.

KÜBLER-ROSS, ELISABETH. *On Death and Dying.* New York: Macmillan, 1969.

KUBRIN, CHARLES E. "Gangstas, Thugs, and Hustlas: Identity and the Code of the Street in Rap Music." *Social Problems.* Vol. 52, No. 3 (2005):360–78.

KUNKEL, DALE, ET AL. *Sex on TV, 2005.* Menlo Park, Calif.: Henry J. Kaiser Family Foundation, 2005. [Online] Available September 13, 2006, at http://www.kff.org/entmedia/upload/Sex-on-TV-4-Full-Report.pdf

KUTTNER, ROBERT. "Targeting Cheats." *American Prospect Online* (March 26, 2004). [Online] Available April 23, 2005, at http://www.prospect.org/webfeatures/2004

KUUMBA, M. BAHATI. "A Cross-Cultural Race/Class/Gender Critique of Contemporary Population Policy: The Impact of Globalization." *Sociological Forum.* Vol. 14, No. 3 (March 1999):447–63.

KUZNETS, SIMON. "Economic Growth and Income Inequality." *American Economic Review.* Vol. 14, No. 1 (March 1955):1–28.

———. *Modern Economic Growth: Rate, Structure, and Spread.* New Haven, Conn.: Yale University Press, 1966.

LACAYO, RICHARD. "The Brawl over Sprawl." *Time* (March 22, 1999):44–48.

———. "Blood at the Root." *Time* (April 10, 2000):122–23.

LACH, JENNIFER. "The Color of Money." *American Demographics.* Vol. 21, No. 2 (February 1999):59–60.

LADD, JOHN. "The Definition of Death and the Right to Die." In JOHN LADD, ed., *Ethical Issues Relating to Life and Death.* New York: Oxford University Press, 1979:118–45.

LAGORIO, CHRISTINE. "Pepperdine in a Treehouse." *New York Times Online.* January 7, 2007. Available January 30, 2007, at http://www.nytimes.com

LAI, H. M. "Chinese." In *Harvard Encyclopedia of American Ethnic Groups.* Cambridge, Mass.: Harvard University Press, 1980:217–33.

LANDSBERG, MITCHELL. "Health Disaster Brings Early Death in Russia." *Washington Times* (March 15, 1998):A8.

LANGBEIN, LAURA I., and ROSEANA BESS. "Sports in School: Source of Amity or Antipathy?" *Social Science Quarterly.* Vol. 83, No. 2 (June 2002):436–54.

LAPCHICK, RICHARD. "The 2005 Racial and Gender Report Cards." Institute for Diversity and Ethics in Sport, University of Central Florida. 2006. [Online] Available October 1, 2006, at http://www.bus.ucf.edu/sport/cgi-bin/site/sitew.cgi?page=/ides/index.htx

LAPPÉ, FRANCES MOORE, and JOSEPH COLLINS. *World Hunger: Twelve Myths.* New York: Grove Press/Food First Books, 1986.

LAPPÉ, FRANCES MOORE, JOSEPH COLLINS, and PETER ROSSET. *World Hunger: Twelve Myths.* 2nd ed. New York: Grove Press, 1998.

LAREAU, ANNETTE. "Invisible Inequality: Social Class and Childrearing in Black Families and White Families." *American Sociological Review.* Vol. 67, No. 5 (October 2002):747–76.

LAROSSA, RALPH, and DONALD C. REITZES. "Two? Two and One-Half? Thirty Months? Chronometrical Childhood in Early Twentieth-Century America." *Sociological Forum.* Vol. 166, No. 3 (September 2001):385–407.

LARSON, GERALD JAMES. "Hinduism in India and in America." In JACOB NEUSNER, ed., *World Religions in America: An Introduction.* Louisville, Ky.: Westminster John Knox Press, 2000:124–41.

LASLETT, BARBARA. "Family Membership, Past and Present." *Social Problems.* Vol. 25, No. 5 (June 1978):476–90.

LASLETT, PETER. *The World We Have Lost: England before the Industrial Age.* 3rd ed. New York: Scribner, 1984.

LASSWELL, MARK. "A Tribe at War: Not the Yanomami, the Anthropologists." *Wall Street Journal* (November 17, 2000):A17.

LAUMANN, EDWARD O., JOHN H. GAGNON, ROBERT T. MICHAEL, and STUART MICHAELS. *The Social Organization of Sexuality: Sexual Practices in the United States.* Chicago: University of Chicago Press, 1994.

LAVIN, DANIELLE, and DOUGLAS W. MAYNARD. "Standardization vs. Rapport: Respondent Laughter and Interviewer Reaction during Telephone Surveys." *American Sociological Review.* Vol. 66, No. 3 (June 2001):453–79.

LEACH, COLIN WAYNE. "Democracy's Dilemma: Explaining Racial Inequality in Egalitarian Societies." *Sociological Forum.* Vol. 17, No. 4 (December 2002):681–96.

LEACOCK, ELEANOR. "Women's Status in Egalitarian Societies: Implications for Social Evolution." *Current Anthropology.* Vol. 19, No. 2 (June 1978):247–75.

LEAVITT, JUDITH WALZER. "Women and Health in America: An Overview." In JUDITH WALZER LEAVITT, ed., *Women and Health in America.* Madison: University of Wisconsin Press, 1984:3–7.

LEBON, GUSTAVE. *The Crowd: A Study of the Popular Mind.* New York: Viking Press, 1960; orig. 1895.

LEE, FELICIA R. "Long Buried, Death Goes Public Again." *New York Times* (2002). [Online] Available November 2, 2002, at http://www.researchnavigator.com

LEE, SHARON M., and BARRY EDMONSTON. "New Marriages, New Families: U.S. Racial and Hispanic Intermarriage." *Population Bulletin.* Vol. 60, No. 2 (June 2005):3–36

LEFEBVRE, HENRI. *The Production of Space.* Oxford: Blackwell, 1991.

LELAND, JOHN. "Bisexuality." *Newsweek* (July 17, 1995):44–49.

LEMERT, EDWIN M. *Social Pathology.* New York: McGraw-Hill, 1951.

———. *Human Deviance, Social Problems, and Social Control.* 2nd ed. Englewood Cliffs, N.J.: Prentice Hall, 1972.

LEMONICK, MICHAEL D. "The Search for a Murder Gene." *Time* (January 20, 2003):100.

———. "Are We Losing Our Edge?" *Time.* Vol. 167, No. 7 (February 13, 2006):22–33.

LENGERMANN, PATRICIA MADOO, and JILL NIEBRUGGE-BRANTLEY. *The Women Founders: Sociology and Social Theory, 1830–1930.* New York: McGraw-Hill, 1998.

LENGERMANN, PATRICIA MADOO, and RUTH A. WALLACE. *Gender in America: Social Control and Social Change.* Englewood Cliffs, N.J.: Prentice Hall, 1985.

LENSKI, GERHARD E. *Power and Privilege: A Theory of Social Stratification.* New York: McGraw-Hill, 1966.

LENSKI, GERHARD E., PATRICK NOLAN, and JEAN LENSKI. *Human Societies: An Introduction to Macrosociology.* 7th ed. New York: McGraw-Hill, 1995.

LEONARD, EILEEN B. *Women, Crime, and Society: A Critique of Theoretical Criminology.* White Plains, N.Y.: Longman, 1982.

LEOPOLD, EVELYN. "Sudan's Young Endure 'Unspeakable' Abuse: Report." [Online] Available April 19, 2007, at http://www.news.yahoo.com

LERNER, DANIEL. *The Passing of Traditional Society: Modernizing in the Middle East.* Glencoe, N.Y.: Free Press, 1958.

LETHBRIDGE-ÇEJKU, MARGARET, DEBORAH ROSE, and JACKLINE VICKERIE. *Summary Health Statistics for U.S. Adults: National Health Interview Survey, 2004.* Vital and Health Statistics, Series 10, No. 228. Hyattsville, Md.: National Center for Health Statistics, 2006.

LETSCHER, MARTIN. "Tell Fads from Trends." *American Demographics.* Vol. 16, No. 12 (December 1994):38–45.

LeVAY, SIMON. *The Sexual Brain.* Cambridge, Mass.: MIT Press, 1993.

LEVER, JANET. "Sex Differences in the Complexity of Children's Play and Games." *American Sociological Review.* Vol. 43, No. 4 (August 1978):471–83.

LEVIN, JACK, and ARNOLD ARLUKE. *Gossip: The Inside Scoop.* New York: Plenum, 1987.

LEVINE, MICHAEL P. *Student Eating Disorders: Anorexia Nervosa and Bulimia.* Washington, D.C.: National Educational Association, 1987.

———. "Reducing Hostility Can Prevent Heart Disease." *Mount Vernon* (Ohio) *News* (August 7, 1990):4A.

LEVINE, SAMANTHA. "The Price of Child Abuse." *U.S. News & World Report* (April 9, 2001):58.

———. "Playing God in Illinois." *U.S. News & World Report* (January 13, 2003):13.

LEWIS, OSCAR. *The Children of Sachez.* New York: Random House, 1961.

LIAZOS, ALEXANDER. "The Poverty of the Sociology of Deviance: Nuts, Sluts, and Perverts." *Social Problems.* Vol. 20, No. 1 (Summer 1972):103–20.

———. *People First: An Introduction to Social Problems.* Needham Heights, Mass.: Allyn & Bacon, 1982.

LICHTER, DANIEL T., and MARTHA L. CROWLEY. "Poverty in America: Beyond Welfare Reform." *Population Bulletin.* Vol. 57, No. 2 (June 2002):3–34.

LICHTER, DANIEL T., and RUKMALIE JAYAKODY. "Welfare Reform: How Do We Measure Success?" *Annual Review of Sociology.* Vol. 28 (2002):117–41.

LICHTER, S. ROBERT, and DANIEL R. AMUNDSON. "Distorted Reality: Hispanic Characters in TV Entertainment." In CLARA E. RODRIGUEZ, ed., *Latin Looks: Images of Latinas and Latinos in the U.S. Media.* Boulder, Colo.: Westview Press, 1997:57–79.

LICHTER, S. ROBERT, STANLEY ROTHMAN, and LINDA S. LICHTER. *The Media Elite: America's New Powerbrokers.* New York: Hastings House, 1990.

LIN, GE, and PETER ROGERSON. Research reported in DIANE CRISPELL, "Sons and Daughters Who Keep in Touch." *American Demographics.* Vol. 16, No. 8 (August 1994):15–16.

LIN, NAN, KAREN COOK, and RONALD S. BURT, eds. *Social Capital: Theory and Research.* Hawthorne, N.Y.: Aldine de Gruyter, 2001.

LIN, NAN, and WEN XIE. "Occupational Prestige in Urban China." *American Journal of Sociology.* Vol. 93, No. 4 (January 1988):793–832.

LINDAUER, DAVID L., and AKILA WEERAPANA. "Relief for Poor Nations." *Society.* Vol. 39, No. 3 (March/April 2002):54–58.

LINDLAW, SCOTT. "President Signs Education Bill." 2002. [Online] Available January 8, 2002, at http://news.yahoo.com

LINDSTROM, BONNIE. "Chicago's Post-Industrial Suburbs." *Sociological Focus.* Vol. 28, No. 4 (October 1995):399–412.

LING, PYAU. "Causes of Chinese Emigration." In AMY TACHIKI ET AL., eds., *Roots: An Asian American Reader.* Los Angeles: UCLA Asian American Studies Center, 1971:134–38.

LINN, MICHAEL. "Class Notes 1970." *Cornell Alumni News.* Vol. 99, No. 2 (September 1996):25.

LINO, MARK. *Expenditures on Children by Families, 2006.* U.S. Department of Agriculture, Center for Nutrition Policy and Promotion. Miscellaneous Publication No. 1528-2006. Washington, D.C.: U.S. Government Printing Office, 2007.

LINTON, RALPH. "One Hundred Percent American." *American Mercury.* Vol. 40, No. 160 (April 1937a):427–29.

———. *The Study of Man.* New York: Appleton-Century, 1937b.

LIPSET, SEYMOUR MARTIN. *Political Man: The Social Bases of Politics.* Garden City, N.Y.: Anchor/Doubleday, 1963.

———. "Canada and the United States." CHARLES F. DONAN and JOHN H. SIGLER, eds. Englewood Cliffs, N.J.: Prentice Hall, 1985.

LISKA, ALLEN E., and BARBARA D. WARNER. "Functions of Crime: A Paradoxical Process." *American Journal of Sociology.* Vol. 96, No. 6 (May 1991):1441–63.

LITTLE, CRAIG, and ANDREA RANKIN. "Why Do They Start It? Explaining Reported Early-Teen Sexual Activity." *Sociological Forum.* Vol. 16, No. 4 (December 2001):703–29.

LIVINGSTON, KEN. "Politics and Mental Illness." *Public Interest.* No. 143 (Winter, 1999):105–9.

LOBO, SUSAN. "Census-Taking and the Invisibility of Urban American Indians." *Population Today.* Vol. 30, No. 4 (May/June 2002):3–4.

LOFLAND, LYN. *A World of Strangers.* New York: Basic Books, 1973.

LOGAN, JOHN R., RICHARD D. ALBA, and WENQUAN ZHANG. "Immigrant Enclaves and Ethnic Communities in New York and Los Angeles." *American Sociological Review.* Vol. 67, No. 2 (April 2002):299–322.

LONGINO, CHARLES F., JR. "Myths of an Aging America." *American Demographics.* Vol. 16, No. 8 (August 1994):36–42.

LORD, MARY. "Good Teachers the Newest Imports." *U.S. News & World Report* (April 9, 2001):54.

———. "A Battle for Children's Futures." *U.S. News & World Report* (March 4, 2002):35–36.

LORD, WALTER. *A Night to Remember.* Rev. ed. New York: Holt, Rinehart and Winston, 1976.

LORENZ, FREDERICK O., and BRENT T. BRUTON. "Experiments in Surveys: Linking Mass Class Questionnaires to Introductory Research Methods." *Teaching Sociology.* Vol. 24, No. 3 (July 1996):264–71.

LOVEMAN, MARA. "Is 'Race' Essential?" *American Sociological Review.* Vol. 64, No. 6 (December 1999):890–98.

LOVGREN, STEFEN. "Will All the Blue Men End Up in Timbuktu?" *U.S. News & World Report* (December 7, 1998):40.

LUND, DALE A. "Conclusions about Bereavement in Later Life and Implications for Interventions and Future Research." In DALE A. LUND, ed., *Older Bereaved Spouses: Research with Practical Applications.* London: Taylor-Francis-Hemisphere, 1989:217–31.

———. "Caregiving." *Encyclopedia of Adult Development.* Phoenix, Ariz.: Oryx Press, 1993:57–63.

LUND, DALE A., MICHAEL S. CASERTA, and MARGARET F. DIMOND. "Gender Differences through Two Years of Bereavement among the Elderly." *Gerontologist.* Vol. 26, No. 3 (1986):314–20.

LUNDMAN, RICHARD L. Personal communication, 1999.

LYND, ROBERT S., and HELEN MERRELL LYND. *Middletown in Transition.* New York: Harcourt, Brace & World, 1937.

LYNOTT, PATRICIA PASSUTH, and BARBARA J. LOGUE. "The 'Hurried Child': The Myth of Lost Childhood on Contemporary American Society." *Sociological Forum.* Vol. 8, No. 3 (September 1993):471–91.

MABRY, MARCUS, and TOM MASLAND. "The Man after Mandela." *Newsweek* (June 7, 1999):54–55.

MACE, DAVID, and VERA MACE. *Marriage East and West.* Garden City, N.Y.: Doubleday/Dolphin, 1960.

MACCOBY, ELEANOR EMMONS, and CAROL NAGY JACKLIN. *The Psychology of Sex Differences.* Stanford, Calif.: Stanford University Press, 1974.

MACIONIS, JOHN J. "Intimacy: Structure and Process in Interpersonal Relationships." *Alternative Lifestyles.* Vol. 1, No. 1 (February 1978):113–30.

———. "A Sociological Analysis of Humor." Presentation to the Texas Junior College Teachers Association, Houston, 1987.

———. *Social Problems.* 3rd ed. Upper Saddle River, N.J.: Prentice Hall, 2008.

MACIONIS, JOHN J., and LINDA GERBER. *Sociology* (6th Canadian ed.). Scarborough, Ontario: Prentice Hall Allyn & Bacon Canada, 2008.

MACIONIS, JOHN J., and VINCENT R. PARRILLO. *Cities and Urban Life.* 4th ed. Upper Saddle River, N.J.: Prentice Hall, 2007.

MACKAY, JUDITH. *The Penguin Atlas of Human Sexual Behavior.* New York: Penguin, 2000.

MADDOX, SETMA. "Organizational Culture and Leadership Style: Factors Affecting Self-Managed Work Team Performance." Paper presented at the annual meeting of the Southwest Social Science Association, Dallas, February 1994.

MALTHUS, THOMAS ROBERT. *First Essay on Population 1798.* London: Macmillan, 1926; orig. 1798.

MANZA, JEFF, and CLEM BROOKS. "The Religious Factor in U.S. Presidential Elections, 1960–1992." *American Journal of Sociology.* Vol. 103, No. 1 (July 1997):38–81.

MARATHONGUIDE.COM. "Marathon Records." 2007. [Online] Available May 30, 2007, at http://www.marathonguide.com/#Records

MARCUSE, HERBERT. *One-Dimensional Man.* Boston: Beacon Press, 1964.

MARÍN, GERARDO, and BARBARA VAN OSS MARÍN. *Research with Hispanic Populations.* Newbury Park, Calif.: Sage, 1991.

MARKLEIN, MARY BETH. "Optimism Rises as SAT Math Scores Hit 30-Year High." *USA Today* (August 30, 2000):1A.

MARKOFF, JOHN. "Remember Big Brother? Now He's a Company Man." *New York Times* (March 31, 1991):7.

MARKS, ALEXANDRA. "U.S. Shelters Swell—with Families." *Christian Science Monitor* (2001). [Online] Available December 4, 2001, at http://www.csmonitor.com

MARQUAND, ROBERT. "Worship Shift: Americans Seek Feeling of 'Awe.'" *Christian Science Monitor* (May 28, 1997):1, 8.

MARQUAND, ROBERT, and DANIEL B. WOOD. "Rise in Cults as Millennium Approaches." *Christian Science Monitor* (March 28, 1997):1, 18.

MARQUARDT, ELIZABETH, and NORVAL GLENN. *Hooking Up, Hanging Out, and Hoping for Mr. Right.* New York: Institute for American Values, 2001.

MARSHALL, MELISSA J., and ANIRUDH V. S. RUHIL. "The Pomp of Power: Black Mayoralties in Urban America." *Social Science Quarterly.* Vol. 87, No. 4 (2006):828–50.

MARSHALL, SUSAN E. "Ladies against Women: Mobilization Dilemmas of Antifeminist Movements." *Social Problems.* Vol. 32, No. 4 (April 1985):348–62.

MARTIN, CAROL LYNN, and RICHARD A. FABES. Research cited in MARIANNE SZEGEDY-MARWELL, GERALD, and N. J. DEMERATH III. "'Secularization' by Any Other Name." *American Sociological Review.* Vol. 68, No. 2 (2003):314–15.

MARTIN, JOHN M., and ANNE T. ROMANO. *Multinational Crime: Terrorism, Espionage, Drug and Arms Trafficking.* Newbury Park, Calif.: Sage, 1992.

MARTIN, JOYCE A., ET AL. "Births: Final Data for 2004." *National Vital Statistics Report.* Vol. 55, No. 1 (September 29, 2006).

MARTINEZ, RAMIRO, JR. "Latinos and Lethal Violence: The Impact of Poverty and Inequality." *Social Problems.* Vol. 43, No. 2 (May 1996):131–46.

MARULLO, SAM. "The Functions and Dysfunctions of Preparations for Fighting Nuclear War." *Sociological Focus.* Vol. 20, No. 2 (April 1987):135–53.

MARX, KARL. Excerpt from "A Contribution to the Critique of Political Economy" (1859). In KARL MARX and FRIEDRICH ENGELS, *Marx and Engels: Basic Writings on Politics and Philosophy.* LEWIS S. FEURER, ed. Garden City, N.Y.: Anchor Books, 1959:42–46.

———. *Karl Marx: Early Writings.* T. B. BOTTOMORE, ed. New York: McGraw-Hill, 1964; orig. 1848.

———. *Capital.* FRIEDRICH ENGELS, ed. New York: International Publishers, 1967; orig. 1867.

MARX, KARL, and FRIEDRICH ENGELS. "Manifesto of the Communist Party." In ROBERT C. TUCKER, ed., *The Marx-Engels Reader.* New York: Norton, 1972:331–62; orig. 1848.

———. *The Marx-Engels Reader.* 2nd ed. ROBERT C. TUCKER, ed. New York: Norton, 1978; orig. 1859.

MARX, LEO. "The Environment and the 'Two Cultures' Divide." In JAMES RODGER FLEMING and HENRY A. GEMERY, eds., *Science, Technology, and the Environment: Multidisciplinary Perspectives.* Akron, Ohio: University of Akron Press, 1994:3–21.

MASSEY, DOUGLAS S. "Housing Discrimination 101." *Population Today.* Vol. 28, No. 6 (August/September 2000):1, 4.

MASSEY, DOUGLAS S., and NANCY A. DENTON. "Hypersegregation in U.S. Metropolitan Areas: Black and Hispanic Segregation along Five Dimensions." *Demography.* Vol. 26, No. 3 (August 1989):373–91.

MATLOFF, JUDITH. "Nomadic 'Blue Men' of the Desert Try to Go Roam Again." *Christian Science Monitor* (September 9, 1997):7.

MATTHIESSEN, PETER. *Indian Country.* New York: Viking Press, 1984.

MAUER, MARC. *The Crisis of the Young African American Male and the Criminal Justice System.* Report prepared for U.S. Commission on Civil Rights. Washington, D.C., April 15–16, 1999. [Online] Available June 5, 2005, at http://www.sentencingproject.org/pdfs/5022.pdf

MAURO, TONY. "Ruling Likely Will Add Fuel to Already Divisive Debate." *USA Today* (January 7, 1997):1A, 2A.

MAUSS, ARMAND L. *Social Problems of Social Movements.* Philadelphia: Lippincott, 1975.

MAYO, KATHERINE. *Mother India.* New York: Harcourt, Brace, 1927.

MCADAM, DOUG. *Political Process and the Development of Black Insurgency, 1930–1970.* Chicago: University of Chicago Press, 1982.

———. "Tactical Innovation and the Pace of Insurgency." *American Sociological Review.* Vol. 48, No. 6 (December 1983):735–54.

———. *Freedom Summer.* New York: Oxford University Press, 1988.

———. "The Biographical Consequences of Activism." *American Sociological Review.* Vol. 54, No. 5 (October 1989):744–60.

———. "Gender as a Mediator of the Activist Experience: The Case of Freedom Summer." *American Journal of Sociology.* Vol. 97, No. 5 (March 1992):1211–40.

MCADAM, DOUG, JOHN D. MCCARTHY, and MAYER N. ZALD. "Social Movements." In NEIL J. SMELSER, ed., *Handbook of Sociology.* Newbury Park, Calif.: Sage, 1988:695–737.

———. "Introduction: Opportunities, Mobilizing Structures, and Framing Processes—Toward a Synthetic, Comparative Perspective on Social Movements." In DOUG MCADAM, JOHN D. MCCARTHY, and MAYER N. ZALD, eds., *Comparative Perspectives on Social Movements: Political Opportunities, Mobilizing Structures, and Cultural Framings.* New York: Cambridge University Press, 1996:1–19.

McBroom, William H., and Fred W. Reed. "Recent Trends in Conservatism: Evidence of Non-Unitary Patterns." *Sociological Focus.* Vol. 23, No. 4 (October 1990):355–65.

McCaffrey, Dawn, and Jennifer Keys. "Competitive Framing Processes in the Abortion Debate: Polarization-Vilification, Frame Saving, and Frame Debunking." *Sociological Quarterly.* Vol. 41, No. 1 (Winter 2000):41–61.

McCall, William. "Oregon Suicides More Than Double." [Online] Available March 4, 2003, at http://dailynews.yahoo.com

McCarthy, John D., and Mayer N. Zald. "Resource Mobilization and Social Movements: A Partial Theory." *American Journal of Sociology.* Vol. 82, No. 6 (May 1977):1212–41.

McCartney, Scott. "U.S. Mulls Raising Pilot Retirement Age." *Baltimore Sun* (February 28, 2005). [Online] Available April 16, 2005, at http://www.Baltimoresun.com

McDonald, Peter. "Low Fertility Not Politically Sustainable." *Population Today.* Vol. 29, No. 6 (August/September 2001):3, 8.

McGirk, Tim. "Crossing the Lines." *Time* (February 27, 2006):36–43.

McGuire, Meredith B. *Religion: The Social Context.* 2nd ed. Belmont, Calif.: Wadsworth, 1987.

McGurn, William. "Philadelphia Dims Edison's Light." *Wall Street Journal* (March 20, 2002):A22.

McKee, Victoria. "Blue Blood and the Color of Money." *New York Times* (June 9, 1996):49–50.

McKibben, Bill. *Deep Economy: The Wealth of Communities and the Durable Future.* New York: Times Books, 2007.

McLanahan, Sara. "Life without Father: What Happens to the Children?" *Contexts.* Vol. 1, No. 1 (Spring 2002):35–44.

McLeod, Jane D., and Michael J. Shanahan. "Poverty, Parenting, and Children's Mental Health." *American Sociological Review.* Vol. 58, No. 3 (June 1993):351–66.

McLeod, Jay. *Ain't No Makin' It: Aspirations and Attainment in a Low-Income Neighborhood.* Boulder, Colo.: Westview Press, 1995.

McPhail, Clark. *The Myth of the Maddening Crowd.* New York: Aldine, 1991.

McPhail, Clark, and Ronald T. Wohlstein. "Individual and Collective Behaviors within Gatherings, Demonstrations, and Riots." *Annual Review of Sociology.* Vol. 9. Palo Alto, Calif.: Annual Reviews, 1983:579–600.

McRoberts, Omar M. *Streets of Glory: Church and Community in a Black Urban Neighborhood.* Chicago: University of Chicago Press, 2003.

Mead, George Herbert. "The Teaching of Science in College." *Science.* Vol. 24 (1906):390–97.

———. "The Psychology of Social Consciousness Implied in Instruction." *Science.* Vol. 31 (1910):688–93.

———. *Mind, Self, and Society.* Charles W. Morris, ed. Chicago: University of Chicago Press, 1962; orig. 1934.

Mead, Margaret. *Sex and Temperament in Three Primitive Societies.* New York: Morrow, 1963; orig. 1935.

Meadows, Donella H., Dennis L. Meadows, Jorgan Randers, and William W. Behrens III. *The Limits to Growth: A Report on the Club of Rome's Project on the Predicament of Mankind.* New York: Universe, 1972.

Meltzer, Bernard N. "Mead's Social Psychology." In Jerome G. Manis and Bernard N. Meltzer, eds., *Symbolic Interaction: A Reader in Social Psychology.* 3rd ed. Needham Heights, Mass.: Allyn & Bacon, 1978.

Melucci, Alberto. *Nomads of the Present: Social Movements and Individual Needs in Contemporary Society.* Philadelphia: Temple University Press, 1989.

Menjivar, Cecilia. "Immigrant Kinship Networks and the Impact of the Receiving Context: Salvadorans in San Francisco in the Early 1990s." *Social Problems.* Vol. 44, No. 1 (February 1997):104–23.

Merton, Robert K. "Social Structure and Anomie." *American Sociological Review.* Vol. 3, No. 6 (October 1938):672–82.

———. *Social Theory and Social Structure.* New York: Free Press, 1968.

Metz, Michael E., and Michael H. Miner. "Psychosexual and Psychosocial Aspects of Male Aging and Sexual Health." *Canadian Journal of Human Sexuality.* Vol. 7, No. 3 (Summer 1998):245–60.

Metzger, Kurt. "Cities and Race." *Society.* Vol. 39, No. 1 (December 2001):2.

Michels, Robert. *Political Parties.* Glencoe, Ill.: Free Press, 1949; orig. 1911.

Milbrath, Lester W. *Envisioning a Sustainable Society: Learning Our Way Out.* Albany: State University of New York Press, 1989.

Milgram, Stanley. "Behavioral Study of Obedience." *Journal of Abnormal and Social Psychology.* Vol. 67, No. 4 (1963):371–78.

———. "Group Pressure and Action against a Person." *Journal of Abnormal and Social Psychology.* Vol. 69, No. 2 (August 1964):137–43.

———. "Some Conditions of Obedience and Disobedience to Authority." *Human Relations.* Vol. 18, No. 1 (February 1965):57–76.

———. "The Small World Problem." *Psychology Today* (May 1967):60–67.

Miller, Alan S., and Rodney Stark. "Gender and Religiousness: Can Socialization Explanations Be Saved?" *American Journal of Sociology.* Vol. 107, No. 6 (May 2002):1399–1423.

Miller, Arthur G. *The Obedience Experiments: A Case of Controversy in Social Science.* New York: Praeger, 1986.

Miller, David L. *Introduction to Collective Behavior.* Belmont, Calif.: Wadsworth, 1985.

Miller, Delbert. *American Sociological Review.* Vol. 10 (1945):691–94.

Miller, Frederick D. "The End of SDS and the Emergence of Weatherman: Demise through Success." In Jo Freeman, ed., *Social Movements of the Sixties and Seventies.* White Plains, N.Y.: Longman, 1983:279–97.

Miller, G. Tyler Jr. *Living in the Environment: An Introduction to Environmental Science.* Belmont, Calif.: Wadsworth, 1992.

Miller, Matthew, and Tatiana Serafin, eds. "The Forbes 400." *Forbes* (Special issue, September 21, 2006).

Miller, Walter B. "Lower-Class Culture as a Generating Milieu of Gang Delinquency" (1958). In Marvin E. Wolfgang, Leonard Savitz, and Norman Johnston, eds., *The Sociology of Crime and Delinquency.* 2nd ed. New York: Wiley, 1970:351–63.

Miller, William J., and Rick A. Matthews. "Youth Employment, Differential Association, and Juvenile Delinquency." *Sociological Focus.* Vol. 34, No. 3 (August 2001):251–68.

Mills, C. Wright. *The Power Elite.* New York: Oxford University Press, 1956.

———. *The Sociological Imagination.* New York: Oxford University Press, 1959.

Miniño, Arialdi M., Melonie P. Heron, and Betty L. Smith. "Deaths: Preliminary Data for 2004." *National Vital Statistics Reports.* Vol. 54, No. 19 (June 28, 2006).

Miracle, Tina S., Andrew W. Miracle, and Roy F. Baumeister. *Human Sexuality: Meeting Your Basic Needs.* Upper Saddle River, N.J.: Prentice Hall, 2003.

Miringoff, Marc, and Marque-Luisa Miringoff. "The Social Health of the Nation." *Economist.* Vol. 352, No. 8128 (July 17, 1999):suppl. 6–7.

Mitchell, Alison. "Give Me a Home Where the Buffalo Roam Less." *New York Times* (January 20, 2002):sec. 4, p. 5.

Moen, Phyllis, Donna Dempster-McClain, and Robin M. Williams. "Successful Aging: A Life-Course Perspective on Women's Multiple Roles and Health." *American Journal of Sociology.* Vol. 97, No. 6 (May 1992):1612–38.

Molotch, Harvey. "The City as a Growth Machine." *American Journal of Sociology.* Vol. 82, No. 2 (September 1976):309–33.

Montaigne, Fen. "Russia Rising." *National Geographic.* Vol. 200, No. 5 (September 2001):2–31.

Moore, Gwen, et al. "Elite Interlocks in Three U.S. Sectors: Nonprofit, Corporate, and Government." *Social Science Quarterly.* Vol. 83, No. 3 (September 2002):726–44.

Moore, Wilbert E. "Modernization as Rationalization: Processes and Restraints." In Manning Nash, ed., *Essays on Economic Development and Cultural Change in Honor of Bert F. Hoselitz.* Chicago: University of Chicago Press, 1977:29–42.

———. *World Modernization: The Limits of Convergence.* New York: Elsevier, 1979.

Morris, Aldon. "Black Southern Sit-In Movement: An Analysis of Internal Organization." *American Sociological Review.* Vol. 46, No. 6 (December 1981):744–67.

Morrison, Denton E. "Some Notes toward Theory on Relative Deprivation, Social Movements, and Social Change." In Louis E. Genevie, ed., *Collective Behavior and Social Movements.* Itasca, Ill.: Peacock, 1978:202–9.

Morse, Jodie. "A Victory for Vouchers." *Time* (July 8, 2002):32–34.

Mosher, William D., Anjani Chandra, and Jo Jones. *Sexual Behavior and Selected Health Measures: Men and Women 15–44 Years of Age, United States, 2002.* [Online] Available August 13, 2007, at http://www.cdc.gov/nchs/products/pubs/pubd/ad/361-370/ad362.htm

Mouw, Ted. "Job Relocation and the Racial Gap in Unemployment in Detroit and Chicago, 1980 to 1990." *American Sociological Review.* Vol. 65, No. 5 (October 2000):730–53.

"Much Ado about Evolution." *Time* (November 21, 2005):23.

Muller, Chandra, and Christopher G. Ellison. "Religious Involvement, Social Capital, and Adolescents' Academic Progress: Evidence from the National Education Longitudinal Study of 1988." *Sociological Focus.* Vol. 34, No. 2 (May 2001):155–83.

Mumford, Lewis. *The City in History: Its Origins, Its Transformations, and Its Prospects.* New York: Harcourt, Brace & World, 1961.

Munson, Martha L., and Paul D. Sutton. "Births, Marriages, Divorces, and Deaths: Provisional Data for 2005." *National Vital Statistics Reports.* Vol. 54, No. 20 (July 21, 2006).

Murdock, George Peter. "Comparative Data on the Division of Labor by Sex." *Social Forces.* Vol. 15, No. 4 (May 1937):551–53.

———. "The Common Denominator of Cultures." In Ralph Linton, ed., *The Science of Man in World Crisis.* New York: Columbia University Press, 1945:123–42.

———. *Social Structure.* New York: Free Press, 1965; orig. 1949.

Murphy, Sherry L. "Death: Final Data for 1998." *National Vital Statistics Report.* Vol. 48, No. 11 (November 2000):1–105.

Murray, Charles A. *Losing Ground: American Social Policy, 1950–1980.* New York: Basic Books, 1984.

Murray, Stephen O., and Will Roscoe, eds. *Boy-Wives and Female-Husbands: Studies of African Homosexualities.* New York: St. Martin's Press, 1998.

Myers, David G. *The American Paradox: Spiritual Hunger in an Age of Plenty.* New Haven, Conn.: Yale University Press, 2000.

MYERS, NORMAN. "Humanity's Growth." In SIR EDMUND HILLARY, ed., *Ecology 2000: The Changing Face of the Earth*. New York: Beaufort Books, 1984a:16–35.
———. "The Mega-Extinction of Animals and Plants." In SIR EDMUND HILLARY, ed., *Ecology 2000: The Changing Face of the Earth*. New York: Beaufort Books, 1984b:82–107.
———. "Biological Diversity and Global Security." In F. HERBERT BORMANN and STEPHEN R. KELLERT, eds., *Ecology, Economics, and Ethics: The Broken Circle*. New Haven, Conn.: Yale University Press, 1991:11–25.
MYERS, SHEILA, and HAROLD G. GRASMICK. "The Social Rights and Responsibilities of Pregnant Women: An Application of Parsons' Sick Role Model." Paper presented to the Southwestern Sociological Association, Little Rock, Ark., March 1989.
MYRDAL, GUNNAR. *An American Dilemma: The Negro Problem and Modern Democracy*. New York: Harper Bros., 1944.
NATIONAL ATLAS OF THE UNITED STATES. Map Maker—Per Capita Personal Income: 2003. July 2007. [Online] Available September 14, 2007, at http://www.nationalatlas.gov/natlas/Natlasstart.asp.
NATIONAL CENTER FOR EDUCATION STATISTICS. *Digest of Education Statistics*. 2005 Tables. [Online] Available July 3, 2007, at http://nces.ed.gov/programs/digest
———. *Dropout Rates in the United States, 2005*. Washington, D.C.: U.S. Government Printing Office. 2007.
NATIONAL CENTER ON ELDER ABUSE. *Elder Abuse Prevalence and Incidence*. Washington, D.C.: U.S. Government Printing Office, 2005. [Online] Available August 23, 2007, at http://www.elderabusecenter.org/pdf/publication/FinalStatistics050331.pdf
NATIONAL COMMISSION ON EXCELLENCE IN EDUCATION. *A Nation at Risk*. Washington, D.C.: U.S. Government Printing Office, 1983.
NAVARRO, MIREYA. "Puerto Rican Presence Wanes in New York." *New York Times* (February 28, 2000):A1, A20.
———. "For Younger Latinas, a Shift to Smaller Families." *New York Times* (December 5, 2004). [Online] Available April 30, 2005, at http://www.researchnavigator.com
NEERGAARD, LAURAN. "Tobacco Devastating Women's Health." [Online] Available March 28, 2001, at http://www.yahoo.com
NELSON, AMY L. "The Effect of Economic Restructuring on Family Poverty in the Industrial Heartland, 1970–1990." *Sociological Focus*. Vol. 31, No. 2 (May 1998):201–16.
NELSON, JOEL I. "Work and Benefits: The Multiple Problems of Service Sector Employment." *Social Problems*. Vol. 42, No. 2 (May 1994):240–55.
NESBITT, PAULA D. *Feminization of the Clergy in America: Occupational and Organizational Perspectives*. New York: Oxford University Press, 1997.
NESSMAN, RAVI. "Stampede at Soccer Match Kills 47." [Online]. Available April 11, 2001, at http://www.dailynews.yahoo.com
NEUGARTEN, BERNICE L. "Grow Old with Me. The Best Is Yet to Be." *Psychology Today* (December 1971):45–48, 79, 81.
———. "Personality and Aging." In JAMES E. BIRREN and K. WARNER SCHAIE, eds., *Handbook of the Psychology of Aging*. New York: Van Nostrand Reinhold, 1977:626–49.
NEUHOUSER, KEVIN. "The Radicalization of the Brazilian Catholic Church in Comparative Perspective." *American Sociological Review*. Vol. 54, No. 2 (April 1989):233–44.
NEWMAN, KATHERINE S. *Declining Fortunes: The Withering of the American Dream*. New York: Basic Books, 1993.
NEWMAN, WILLIAM M. *American Pluralism: A Study of Minority Groups and Social Theory*. New York: Harper & Row, 1973.
NICHOLSON, NIGEL. "Evolved to Chat: The New Word on Gossip." *Psychology Today* (May/June 2001):41–45.
NIELSEN MEDIA RESEARCH. "Nielsen Reports Americans Watch TV at Record Levels." News release. September 29, 2005. [Online] Available August 27, 2006, at http://www.nielsenmedia.com/newsreleases/2005/AvgHoursMinutes92905.pdf
NIESSE, MARK. "Some Bars Pan Hawaii's Tough Smoking Ban." [Online] Available February 19, 2007, at yahoonews.com
NISBET, ROBERT A. *The Sociological Tradition*. New York: Basic Books, 1966.
———. *The Quest for Community*. New York: Oxford University Press, 1969.
NOCK, STEVEN L., JAMES D. WRIGHT, and LAURA SANCHEZ. "America's Divorce Problem." *Society*. Vol. 36, No. 4 (May/June 1999):43–52.
NOLAN, PATRICK, and GERHARD E. LENSKI. *Human Societies: An Introduction to Macrosociology*. 10th ed. Boulder, Colo.: Paradigm, 2007.
NORBECK, EDWARD. "Class Structure." In *Kodansha Encyclopedia of Japan*. Tokyo: Kodansha, 1983:322–25.
NORC. *General Social Surveys, 1972–1991: Cumulative Codebook*. Chicago: National Opinion Research Center, 1991.
———. *General Social Surveys, 1972–2002: Cumulative Codebook*. Chicago: National Opinion Research Center, 2003.
———. *General Social Surveys, 1972–2004: Cumulative Codebook*. Chicago: National Opinion Research Center, 2005.

NORD, MARK. "Does It Cost Less to Live in Rural Areas? Evidence from New Data on Food Scarcity and Hunger." *Rural Sociology*. Vol. 65, No. 1 (March 2000):104–25.
"Notebook." *Time* (September 4, 2006):16.
NOVAK, VIVECA. "The Cost of Poor Advice." *Time* (July 5, 1999):38.
NULAND, SHERWIN B. "The Hazards of Hospitalization." *Wall Street Journal* (December 2, 1999):A22.
OAKES, JEANNIE. "Classroom Social Relationships: Exploring the Bowles and Gintis Hypothesis." *Sociology of Education*. Vol. 55, No. 4 (October 1982):197–212.
———. *Keeping Track: How High Schools Structure Inequality*. New Haven, Conn.: Yale University Press, 1985.
OBERSCHALL, ANTHONY. *Social Conflict and Social Movements*. Englewood Cliffs, N.J.: Prentice Hall, 1973.
O'CONNOR, RORY J. "Internet Declared Protected Speech." *Glens Falls* (N.Y.) *Post-Star* (June 27, 1997):A1–A2.
OGAWA, NAOHIRO, and ROBERT D. RETHERFORD. "Shifting Costs of Caring for the Elderly Back to Families in Japan: Will It Work?" *Population and Development Review*. Vol. 23, No. 1 (March 1997):59–95.
OGBURN, WILLIAM F. *On Culture and Social Change*. Chicago: University of Chicago Press, 1964.
OGDEN, RUSSEL D. "Nonphysician-Assisted Suicide: The Technological Imperative of the Deathing Counterculture." *Death Studies*. Vol. 25, No. 5 (July 2001):387–402.
O'HARE, WILLIAM P. "The Rise of Hispanic Affluence." *American Demographics*. Vol. 12, No. 8 (August 1990):40–43.
———. "Tracking the Trends in Low-Income Working Families." *Population Today*. Vol. 30, No. 6 (August/September 2002):1–3.
O'HARE, WILLIAM P., WILLIAM H. FREY, and DAN FOST. "Asians in the Suburbs." *American Demographics*. Vol. 16, No. 9 (May 1994):32–38.
O'HARROW, ROBERT, JR. "ID Theft Scam Hits D.C. Area Residents." [Online] Available February 21, 2005, at http://news.yahoo.com
OHLEMACHER, STEPHEN. "Official Count: 754,000 People Believed Homeless in U.S." *Seattle Times* (February 28, 2007). [Online] Available March 9, 2007, at http://seattletimes.nwsource.com/html/nationworld/2003592874_homeless28.html
OLSEN, GREGG M. "Remodeling Sweden: The Rise and Demise of the Compromise in a Global Economy." *Social Problems*. Vol. 43, No. 1 (February 1996):1–20.
OLSON, ELIZABETH. "Community Colleges Want You." *New York Times* (October 24, 2006):E2.
OLZAK, SUSAN. "Labor Unrest, Immigration, and Ethnic Conflict in Urban America, 1880–1914." *American Journal of Sociology*. Vol. 94, No. 6 (May 1989):1303–33.
OLZAK, SUSAN, and ELIZABETH WEST. "Ethnic Conflict and the Rise and Fall of Ethnic Newspapers." *American Sociological Review*. Vol. 56, No. 4 (August 1991):458–74.
OMESTAD, THOMAS. "A Balance of Terror." *U.S. News & World Report* (February 3, 2003):33–5.
O'NEILL, BRIAN, and DEBORAH BALK. "World Population Futures." *Population Bulletin*. Vol. 56, No. 3 (September 2001):3–40.
ONISHI, NORMIMITSU. "In a Graying Japan, Lower Shelves and Wider Aisles." *New York Times* (September 4, 2006): A4.
"Online Privacy: It's Time for Rules in Wonderland." *Business Week* (March 20, 2000):82–96.
ORECKLIN, MICHELLE. "Earnings Report: J.K. and Judy." *Time* (January 13, 2003):72.
ORLANSKY, MICHAEL D., and WILLIAM L. HEWARD. *Voices: Interviews with Handicapped People*. Columbus, Ohio: Merrill, 1981.
ORHANT, MELANIE. "Human Trafficking Exposed." *Population Today*. Vol. 30, No. 1 (January 2002):1, 4.
ORWIN, CLIFFORD. "All Quiet on the Western Front?" *Public Interest*. No. 123 (Spring 1996): 3–9.
OSTRANDER, SUSAN A. "Upper-Class Women: The Feminine Side of Privilege." *Qualitative Sociology*. Vol. 3, No. 1 (Spring 1980):23–44.
———. *Women of the Upper Class*. Philadelphia: Temple University Press, 1984.
OUCHI, WILLIAM. *Theory Z: How American Business Can Meet the Japanese Challenge*. Reading, Mass.: Addison-Wesley, 1981.
"Our Cheating Hearts." Editorial. *U.S. News & World Report* (May 6, 2002):4.
OVADIA, SETH. "Race, Class, and Gender Differences in High School Seniors' Values: Applying Intersection Theory in Empirical Analysis." *Social Science Quarterly*. Vol. 82, No. 2 (June 2001):341–56.
OWEN, CAROLYN A., HOWARD C. ELSNER, and THOMAS R. MCFAUL. "A Half-Century of Social Distance Research: National Replication of the Bogardus Studies." *Sociology and Social Research*. Vol. 66, No. 1 (1977):80–98.
PACKARD, MARK. Personal communication (2002).
PACKER, GEORGE. "Smart-Mobbing the War." *New York Times Magazine* (March 9, 2003):46–49.
PAGER, DEVAH. "The Mark of a Criminal Record." *American Journal of Sociology*. Vol. 108, No. 5 (March 2003):937–75.
PAKULSKI, JAN. "Mass Social Movements and Social Class." *International Sociology*. Vol. 8, No. 2 (June 1993):131–58.

534   REFERENCES

PALMORE, ERDMAN. "Predictors of Successful Aging." *Gerontologist.* Vol. 19, No. 5 (October 1979):427–31.

PAMPEL, FRED C. "Socioeconomic Distinction, Cultural Tastes, and Cigarette Smoking." *Social Science Quarterly.* Vol. 87, No. 1 (March 2006):19–35.

PARINI, JAY. "The Meaning of Emeritus." *Dartmouth Alumni Magazine* (July/August 2001):40–43.

PARIS, PETER J. "The Religious World of African Americans." In JACOB NEUSNER, ed. *World Religions in America: An Introduction.* Revised and expanded ed. Louisville, Ky.: Westminster John Knox Press, 2000:48–65.

PARK, ROBERT E. *Race and Culture.* Glencoe, Ill.: Free Press, 1950.

PARRILLO, VINCENT N. "Diversity in America: A Sociohistorical Analysis." *Sociological Forum.* Vol. 9, No. 4 (December 1994):42–45.

———. *Strangers to These Shores.* 7th ed. Boston: Allyn & Bacon, 2003.

PARRILLO, VINCENT, and CHRISTOPHER DONOGHUE. "Updating the Bogardus Social Distance Studies: A New National Survey." *Social Science Journal.* Vol. 42, No. 2 (April 2005):257–71.

PARSONS, TALCOTT. "Age and Sex in the Social Structure of the United States." *American Sociological Review.* Vol. 7, No. 4 (August 1942):604–16.

———. *The Social System.* New York: Free Press, 1951.

———. *Essays in Sociological Theory.* New York: Free Press, 1954.

———. "Definitions of Health and Illness in the Light of American Values and Social Structure." In E. G. Jaco, ed., *Patients, Physicians, and Illness: Sourcebook in Behavioral Science and Medicine.* Glencoe, Ill.: Free Press, 1958:165–87.

———. *Societies: Evolutionary and Comparative Perspectives.* Englewood Cliffs, N.J.: Prentice Hall, 1966.

PASSY, FLORENCE, and MARCO GIUGNI. "Social Networks and Individual Perceptions: Explaining Differential Participation in Social Movements." *Sociological Forum.* Vol. 16, No. 1 (March 2001):123–53.

PATTERSON, ELISSA F. "The Philosophy and Physics of Holistic Health Care: Spiritual Healing as a Workable Interpretation." *Journal of Advanced Nursing.* Vol. 27, No. 2 (February 1998):287–93.

PATTILLO-MCCOY, MARY. "Church Culture as a Strategy of Action in the Black Community." *American Sociological Review.* Vol. 63, No. 6 (December 1998):767–84.

PAUL, PAMELA. "News, Noticias, Nouvelles." *American Demographics.* Vol. 23, No. 11 (November, 2001):26–31.

PAXTON, PAMELA, MELANIE M. HUGHES, and JENNIFER L. GREEN. "The International Women's Movement and Women's Political Participation, 1893–2003." *American Sociological Review.* Vol. 71, No. 6 (December 2006):898–920.

PEAR, ROBERT, and ERIK ECKHOLM. "When Healers Are Entrepreneurs: A Debate over Costs and Ethics." *New York Times* (June 2, 1991):1, 17.

PEARSON, DAVID E. "Post-Mass Culture." *Society.* Vol. 30, No. 5 (July/August 1993):17–22.

———. "Community and Sociology." *Society.* Vol. 32, No. 5 (July/August 1995):44–50.

PEASE, JOHN, and LEE MARTIN. "Want Ads and Jobs for the Poor: A Glaring Mismatch." *Sociological Forum.* Vol. 12, No. 4 (December 1997):545–64.

PEDERSON, DANIEL, VERN E. SMITH, and JERRY ADLER. "Sprawling, Sprawling . . ." *Newsweek* (July 19, 1999):23–27.

PERLMUTTER, PHILIP. "Minority Group Prejudice." *Society.* Vol. 39, No. 3 (March/April 2002):59–65.

PERRUCCI, ROBERT. "Inventing Social Justice: SSSP and the Twenty-First Century." *Social Problems.* Vol. 48, No. 2 (May 2001):159–67.

PESSEN, EDWARD. *Riches, Class, and Power: America before the Civil War.* New Brunswick, N.J.: Transaction, 1990.

Peters Atlas of the World. New York: Harper & Row, 1990.

PETERSEN, TROND, ISHAK SAPORTA, and MARC-DAVID L. SEIDEL. "Offering a Job: Meritocracy and Social Networks." *American Journal of Sociology.* Vol. 106, No. 3 (November 2000):763–816.

PETERSILIA, JOAN. "Probation in the United States: Practices and Challenges." *National Institute of Justice Journal.* No. 233 (September 1997):4.

PETERSON, SCOTT. "Women Live on Own Terms behind the Veil." *Christian Science Monitor* (July 31, 1996):1, 10.

PHILADELPHIA, DESA. "Rookie Teacher, Age 50." *Time* (April 9, 2001):66–68.

———. "Tastier, Plusher—and Fast." *Time* (September 30, 2002):57.

PHILLIPS, MELANIE. "What about the Overclass?" *Public Interest.* No. 145 (Fall 2001):38–43.

PICHARDO, NELSON A. "The Power Elite and Elite-Driven Countermovements: The Associated Farmers of California during the 1930s." *Sociological Forum.* Vol. 10, No. 1 (March 1995):21–49.

PINCHOT, GIFFORD, and ELIZABETH PINCHOT. *The End of Bureaucracy and the Rise of the Intelligent Organization.* San Francisco: Berrett-Koehler, 1993.

PINHEY, THOMAS K., DONALD H. RUBINSTEIN, and RICHARD S. COLFAX. "Overweight and Happiness: The Reflected Self-Appraisal Hypothesis Reconsidered." *Social Science Quarterly.* Vol. 78, No. 3 (September 1997):747–55.

PINKER, STEVEN. *The Language Instinct.* New York: Morrow, 1994.

———. "Are Your Genes to Blame?" *Time* (January 20, 2003):98–100.

PIRANDELLO, LUIGI. "The Pleasure of Honesty" (1917). In *To Clothe the Naked and Two Other Plays.* New York: Dutton, 1962:143–98.

PITTS, LEONARD, JR. "When a Win Sparks a Riot." *Philadelphia Inquirer* (June 26, 2000):A11.

PIVEN, FRANCES FOX, and RICHARD A. CLOWARD. *Poor People's Movements: Why They Succeed, How They Fail.* New York: Pantheon Books, 1977.

"Places Where the System Broke Down." *Time* (September 19, 2005):34–41.

PLEIS, JOHN R., and MARGARET LETHBRIDGE-ÇEJKU. *Summary Health Statistics for U.S. Adults: National Health Interview Survey, 2005.* Vital and Health Statistics, Series 10, No. 232. Hyattsville, Md.: National Center for Health Statistics, 2006.

PODOLNY, JOEL M., and JAMES N. BARON. "Resources and Relationships: Social Networks and Mobility in the Workplace." *American Sociological Review.* Vol. 62, No. 5 (October 1997):673–93.

POLSBY, NELSON W. "Three Problems in the Analysis of Community Power." *American Sociological Review.* Vol. 24, No. 6 (December 1959):796–803.

POMER, MARSHALL I. "Labor Market Structure, Intragenerational Mobility, and Discrimination: Black Male Advancement out of Low-Paying Occupations, 1962–1973." *American Sociological Review.* Vol. 51, No. 5 (October 1986):650–59.

POPENOE, DAVID. "Family Decline in the Swedish Welfare State." *Public Interest.* No. 102 (Winter 1991):65–77.

———. "American Family Decline, 1960–1990: A Review and Appraisal." *Journal of Marriage and the Family.* Vol. 55, No. 3 (August 1993a):527–55.

———. "Parental Androgyny." *Society.* Vol. 30, No. 6 (September/October 1993b):5–11.

———. "Scandinavian Welfare." *Society.* Vol. 31, No. 6 (September/October, 1994):78–81.

———. "Can the Nuclear Family Be Revived?" *Society.* Vol. 36, No. 5 (July/August 1999):28–30.

POPENOE, DAVID, and BARBARA DAFOE WHITEHEAD. *Should We Live Together? What Young Adults Need to Know about Cohabitation before Marriage.* New Brunswick, N.J.: National Marriage Project, 1999.

POPULATION ACTION INTERNATIONAL. *People in the Balance: Population and Resources at the Turn of the Millennium.* Washington, D.C.: Population Action International, 2000.

POPULATION REFERENCE BUREAU. *2003 World Population Data Sheet.* Washington, D.C.: Population Reference Bureau, 2003.

———. *2005 World Population Data Sheet.* Washington, D.C.: Population Reference Bureau, 2005.

———. *2006 World Population Data Sheet.* Washington, D.C.: Population Reference Bureau, 2006.

PORTER, EDUARDO. "Even 126 Sizes Do Not Fit All." *Wall Street Journal* (March 2, 2001):B1.

———. "Old, in the Way, and Hard at Work." *New York Times* (August 29, 2004). [Online] Available April 15, 2005, at http://www.researchnavigator.com

PORTES, ALEJANDRO, and LEIF JENSEN. "The Enclave and the Entrants: Patterns of Ethnic Enterprise in Miami before and after Mariel." *American Sociological Review.* Vol. 54, No. 6 (December 1989):929–49.

POSTEL, SANDRA. "Facing Water Scarcity." In LESTER R. BROWN ET AL., eds., *State of the World, 1993: A Worldwatch Institute Report on Progress toward a Sustainable Society.* New York: Norton, 1993:22–41.

POWELL, CHRIS, and GEORGE E. C. PATON, eds. *Humor in Society: Resistance and Control.* New York: St. Martin's Press, 1988.

PRIMEGGIA, SALVATORE, and JOSEPH A. VARACALLI. "Southern Italian Comedy: Old to New World." In JOSEPH V. SCELSA, SALVATORE J. LA GUMINA, and LYDIO TOMASI, eds., *Italian Americans in Transition.* New York: American Italian Historical Association, 1990:241–52.

PRYOR, JOHN H., ET AL. *The American Freshman: National Norms for Fall 2005.* Los Angeles: UCLA Higher Education Research Institute, 2005.

———. *The American Freshman: National Norms for Fall 2006.* Los Angeles: UCLA Higher Education Research Institute, 2006.

PUTKA, GARY. "SAT to Become a Better Gauge." *Wall Street Journal* (November 1, 1990):B1.

PYLE, RALPH E., and JEROME R. KOCH. "The Religious Affiliation of American Elites, 1930s to 1990s: A Note on the Pace of Disestablishment." *Sociological Focus.* Vol. 34, No. 2 (May 2001):125–37.

QUILLIAN, LINCOLN, and DEVAH PAGER. "Black Neighbors, Higher Crime? The Role of Racial Stereotypes in Evaluations of Neighborhood Crime." *American Journal of Sociology.* Vol. 107, No. 3 (November 2001):717–67.

QUINNEY, RICHARD. *Class, State and Crime: On the Theory and Practice of Criminal Justice.* New York: McKay, 1977.

RADCLIFFE-BROWN, A. R. "On the Concept of Function in Social Science." *American Anthropologist.* Vol. 37, No. 4 (1935):394–402.

RALEY, R. KELLY, T. ELIZABETH DURDEN, and ELIZABETH WILDSMITH. "Understanding Mexican-American Marriage Patterns using a Life Course Approach." *Social Science Quarterly.* Vol. 85, No. 4 (December 2004):872–90.

RANK, MARK R., and THOMAS A. HIRSCHL. "Rags or Riches? Estimating the Probabilities of Poverty and Affluence across the Adult American Life Span." *Social Science Quarterly.* Vol. 82, No. 4 (December 2001):651–69.

RAPHAEL, RAY. *The Men from the Boys: Rites of Passage in Male America.* Lincoln: University of Nebraska Press, 1988.

RATNESAR, ROMESH. "Not Gone, but Forgotten?" *Time* (February 8, 1999):30–31.

RAYMOND, JOAN. "The Multicultural Report." *American Demographics.* Vol. 23, No. 11 (November 2001):S1–S6.

RECKLESS, WALTER C., and SIMON DINITZ. "Pioneering with Self-Concept as a Vulnerability Factor in Delinquency." *Journal of Criminal Law, Criminology, and Police Science.* Vol. 58, No. 4 (December 1967):515–23.

RECTOR, ROBERT. "America Has the World's Richest Poor People." *Wall Street Journal* (September 24, 1998):A18.

REMOFF, HEATHER TREXLER. *Sexual Choice: A Woman's Decision.* New York: Dutton/Lewis, 1984.

RESKIN, BARBARA F., and DEBRA BRANCH MCBRIER. "Why Not Ascription? Organizations' Employment of Male and Female Managers." *American Sociological Review.* Vol. 65, No. 2 (April 2000):210–33.

REVKIN, ANDREW C. "Can Global Warming Be Studied Too Much?" *New York Times* (December 3, 2002):D1, D4.

RIDDLE, JOHN M., J. WORTH ESTES, and JOSIAH C. RUSSELL. "Ever since Eve: Birth Control in the Ancient World." *Archaeology.* Vol. 47, No. 2 (March/April 1994):29–35.

RIDGEWAY, CECILIA L. *The Dynamics of Small Groups.* New York: St. Martin's Press, 1983.

RIEFF, PHILIP. *Freud: The Mind of the Moralist.* New York: Doubleday, 1961.

RIESMAN, DAVID. *The Lonely Crowd: A Study of the Changing American Character.* New Haven, Conn.: Yale University Press, 1970; orig. 1950.

RIMER, SARA. "Blacks Carry Load of Care for Their Elderly." *New York Times* (March 15, 1998):1, 22.

RITZER, GEORGE. *The McDonaldization of Society: An Investigation into the Changing Character of Contemporary Social Life.* Thousand Oaks, Calif.: Pine Forge Press, 1993.

———. *The McDonaldization Thesis: Explorations and Extensions.* Thousand Oaks, Calif.: Sage, 1998.

———. "The Globalization of McDonaldization." *Spark* (February 2000):8–9.

RITZER, GEORGE, and DAVID WALCZAK. *Working: Conflict and Change.* 4th ed. Englewood Cliffs, N.J.: Prentice Hall, 1990.

ROBINSON, LINDA. "A Timeworn Terrorism List." *U.S. News & World Report* (May 20, 2002):18, 21.

ROBINSON, THOMAS N., ET AL. "Effects of Reducing Children's Television and Video Game Use on Aggressive Behavior." *Archives of Pediatrics and Adolescent Medicine.* Vol. 155, No. 1 (January 2001):17–23.

ROESCH, ROBERTA. "Violent Families." *Parents.* Vol. 59, No. 9 (September 1984):74–76, 150–52.

ROETHLISBERGER, F. J., and WILLIAM J. DICKSON. *Management and the Worker.* Cambridge, Mass.: Harvard University Press, 1939.

ROGERS, RICHARD G., REBECCA ROSENBLATT, ROBERT A. HUMMER, and PATRICK M. KRUEGER. "Black-White Differentials in Adult Homicide Mortality in the United States." *Social Science Quarterly.* Vol. 82, No. 3 (September 2001):435–52.

ROGERS-DILLON, ROBIN H. "What Do We Really Know about Welfare Reform?" *Society.* Vol. 38, No. 2 (January/February 2001):7–15.

ROMERO, FRANCINE SANDERS, and ADRIAN LISERIO. "Saving Open Spaces: Determinants of 1998 and 1999 'Antisprawl' Ballot Measures." *Social Science Quarterly.* Vol. 83, No. 1 (March 2002):341–52.

ROSE, FRED. "Toward a Class-Cultural Theory of Social Movements: Reinterpreting New Social Movements." *Sociological Forum.* Vol. 12, No. 3 (September 1997):461–94.

ROSE, JERRY D. *Outbreaks.* New York: Free Press, 1982.

ROSE, LOWELL C., and ALEC M. GALLUP. *The 38th Annual Phi Delta Kappa/Gallup Poll of the Public's Attitudes toward the Public Schools.* 2006. [Online] Available September 26, 2006, at http://www.pdkintl.org/kappan/k0609pol.pdf

ROSEN, ELLEN ISRAEL. *Bitter Choices: Blue-Collar Women in and out of Work.* Chicago: University of Chicago Press, 1987.

ROSENBAUM, DAVID E. "Americans Want a Right to Die. Or So They Think." *New York Times* (June 8, 1997):E3.

ROSENBAUM, MARC. "Americans' Views on Taxes." Report of an NPR/Kaiser Family Foundation/Kennedy School of Government poll. Lecture delivered at Kenyon College, Gambier, Ohio, April 23, 2003.

ROSENDAHL, MONA. *Inside the Revolution: Everyday Life in Socialist Cuba.* Ithaca, N.Y.: Cornell University Press, 1997.

ROSENFELD, MICHAEL J., and BYONG-SOO KIM. "The Independence of Young Adults and the Rise of Interracial and Same-Sex Unions." *American Sociological Review.* Vol. 70, No. 4 (August 2005):541–62.

ROSENFELD, RICHARD. "Crime Decline in Context." *Contexts.* Vol. 1, No. 1 (Spring 2002):20–34.

ROSENTHAL, ELIZABETH. "Canada's National Health Plan Gives Care to All, with Limits." *New York Times* (April 30, 1991):A1, A16.

ROSNOW, RALPH L., and GARY ALAN FINE. *Rumor and Gossip: The Social Psychology of Hearsay.* New York: Elsevier, 1976.

ROSSI, ALICE S. "Gender and Parenthood." In ALICE S. ROSSI, ed., *Gender and the Life Course.* New York: Aldine, 1985:161–91.

ROSTOW, WALT W. *The Stages of Economic Growth: A Non-Communist Manifesto.* Cambridge: Cambridge University Press, 1960.

———. *The World Economy: History and Prospect.* Austin: University of Texas Press, 1978.

ROTHMAN, BARBARA KATZ. "Of Maps and Imaginations: Sociology Confronts the Genome." *Social Problems.* Vol. 42, No. 1 (February 1995):1–10.

ROTHMAN, STANLEY, and AMY E. BLACK. "Who Rules Now? American Elites in the 1990s." *Society.* Vol. 35, No. 6 (September/October 1998):17–20.

ROTHMAN, STANLEY, STEPHEN POWERS, and DAVID ROTHMAN. "Feminism in Films." *Society.* Vol. 30, No. 3 (March/April 1993):66–72.

ROUSSEAU, CARYN. "Unions Rally at Wal-Mart Stores." [Online] Available November 22, 2002, at http://dailynews.yahoo.com

ROZELL, MARK J., CLYDE WILCOX, and JOHN C. GREEN. "Religious Constituencies and Support for the Christian Right in the 1990s." *Social Science Quarterly.* Vol. 79, No. 4 (December 1998):815–27.

RUBENSTEIN, ELI A. "The Not So Golden Years." *Newsweek* (October 7, 1991):13.

RUBIN, JOEL. "E-Mail Too Formal? Try a Text Message." Columbia News Service, March 7, 2003. [Online] Available April 25, 2005, at http://www.jrn.columbia.edu/studentwork/cns/2003-03-07/85.asp

RUBIN, LILLIAN BRESLOW. *Worlds of Pain: Life in the Working-Class Family.* New York: Basic Books, 1976.

RUDEL, THOMAS K., and JUDITH M. GERSON. "Postmodernism, Institutional Change, and Academic Workers: A Sociology of Knowledge." *Social Science Quarterly.* Vol. 80, No. 2 (June 1999):213–28.

RUDOLPH, ELLEN. "Women's Talk: Japanese Women." *New York Times Magazine* (September 1, 1991).

RULE, JAMES, and PETER BRANTLEY. "Computerized Surveillance in the Workplace: Forms and Delusions." *Sociological Forum.* Vol. 7, No. 3 (September 1992):405–23.

RUSSELL, CHERYL. "Are We in the Dumps?" *American Demographics.* Vol. 17, No. 1 (January 1995a):6.

———. "True Crime." *American Demographics.* Vol. 17, No. 8 (August 1995b):22–31.

RUTHERFORD, MEGAN. "Women Run the World." *Time* (June 28, 1999):72.

RYAN, PATRICK J. "The Roots of Muslim Anger." *America* (November 26, 2001):8–16.

RYMER, RUSS. *Genie.* New York: HarperPerennial, 1994.

RYTINA, JOAN HUBER, WILLIAM H. FORM, and JOHN PEASE. "Income and Stratification Ideology: Beliefs about the American Opportunity Structure." *American Journal of Sociology.* Vol. 75, No. 4 (January 1970):703–16.

SACHS, JEFFREY. "The Real Causes of Famine." *Time* (October 26, 1998):69.

SAINT JEAN, YANICK, and JOE R. FEAGIN. *Double Burden: Black Women and Everyday Racism.* Armonk, N.Y.: Sharpe, 1998.

SALA-I-MARTIN, XAVIER. "The World Distribution of Income." Working Paper No. 8933. Cambridge, Mass.: National Bureau of Economic Research, 2002.

SALE, KIRKPATRICK. *The Conquest of Paradise: Christopher Columbus and the Columbian Legacy.* New York: Knopf, 1990.

SAMUELSON, ROBERT J. "The Rich and Everyone Else." *Newsweek* (January 27, 2003):57.

SANSOM, WILLIAM. *A Contest of Ladies.* London: Hogarth, 1956.

SAPIR, EDWARD. "The Status of Linguistics as a Science." *Language.* Vol. 5, No. 4 (1929):207–14.

———. *Selected Writings of Edward Sapir in Language, Culture, and Personality.* DAVID G. MANDELBAUM, ed. Berkeley: University of California Press, 1949.

SAPORITO, BILL. "Can Wal-Mart Get Any Bigger?" *Time* (January 13, 2003):38–43.

SAVISHINSKY, JOEL S. *Breaking the Watch: The Meanings of Retirement in America.* Ithaca, N.Y.: Cornell University Press, 2000.

SAX, LINDA J., ET AL. *The American Freshman: National Norms for Fall 2004.* Los Angeles: UCLA Higher Education Research Institute, 2004.

SCANLON, STEPHAN J. "Food Availability and Access in Less Industrialized Societies: A Test and Interpretation of Neo-Malthusian and Technoecological Theories." *Sociological Forum.* Vol. 16, No. 2 (June 2001):231–62.

SCHAFFER, MICHAEL. "American Dreamers." *U.S. News & World Report* (August 26, 2002):12–16.

SCHAUB, DIANA. "From Boys to Men." *Public Interest.* No. 127 (Spring 1997):108–14.

SCHEFF, THOMAS J. *Being Mentally Ill: A Sociological Theory.* 2nd ed. New York: Aldine, 1984.

SCHLESINGER, ARTHUR M., JR. "The City in American Civilization." In A. B. CALLOW JR., ed., *American Urban History.* New York: Oxford University Press, 1969:25–41.

SCHLOSSER, ERIC. *Fast-Food Nation: The Dark Side of the All-American Meal.* New York: Perennial, 2002.

SCHMIDT, ROGER. *Exploring Religion.* Belmont, Calif.: Wadsworth, 1980.

SCHMITT, ERIC. "Whites in Minority in Largest Cities, the Census Shows." *New York Times* (April 30, 2001):A1, A12.

SCHNAIBERG, ALLAN, and KENNETH ALAN GOULD. *Environment and Society: The Enduring Conflict.* New York: St. Martin's Press, 1994.

SCHNEIDER, MARK, MELISSA MARSCHALL, PAUL TESKE, and CHRISTINE ROCH. "School Choice and Culture Wars in the Classroom: What Different Parents Seek from Education." *Social Science Quarterly.* Vol. 79, No. 3 (September 1998):489–501.

SCHNITTKER, JASON, BERNICE A. PESCOSOLIDO, and THOMAS W. CROGHAN. "Are African Americans Really Less Willing to Use Health Care?" *Social Problems.* Vol. 52, No. 2 (May 2005):255–71.

SCHOFER, EVAN, and MARION FOURCADE-GOURINCHAS. "The Structural Contexts of Civil Engagement: Voluntary Association Membership in Comparative Perspective." *American Sociological Review.* Vol. 66, No. 6 (December 2001):806–28.

SCHULTZ, R., and J. HECKHAUSEN. "A Lifespan Model of Successful Aging." *American Psychologist.* Vol. 7, No. 7 (July 1996): 702–14.

SCHUMAN, HOWARD, and MARIA KRYSAN. "A Historical Note on Whites' Beliefs about Racial Inequality." *American Sociological Review.* Vol. 64, No. 6 (December 1999):847–55.

SCHUR, LISA A., and DOUGLAS L. KRUSE. "What Determines Voter Turnout? Lessons from Citizens with Disabilities." *Social Science Quarterly.* Vol. 81, No. 2 (June 2000): 571–87.

SCHWARTZ, FELICE N. "Management, Women, and the New Facts of Life." *Harvard Business Review.* Vol. 89, No. 1 (January/February 1989):65–76.

SCOMMEGNA, PAOLA. "Increased Cohabitation Changing Children's Family Settings." *Population Today.* Vol. 30, No. 7 (July 2002):3, 6.

SEAGER, JONI. *The Penguin Atlas of Women in the World.* 3rd ed. New York: Penguin Putnam, 2003.

SEARS, DAVID O., and JOHN B. MCCONAHAY. *The Politics of Violence: The New Urban Blacks and the Watts Riot.* Boston: Houghton Mifflin, 1973.

SEGAL, MADY WECHSLER, and AMANDA FAITH HANSEN. "Value Rationales in Policy Debates on Women in the Military: A Content Analysis of Congressional Testimony, 1941–1985." *Social Science Quarterly.* Vol. 73, No. 2 (June 1992):296–309.

SEIDMAN, STEVEN, ed. *Queer Theory/Sociology.* Cambridge, Mass.: Blackwell, 1996.

SENNETT, RICHARD. *The Corrosion of Character: The Personal Consequences of Work in the New Capitalism.* New York: Norton, 1998.

SENNETT, RICHARD, and JONATHAN COBB. *The Hidden Injuries of Class.* New York: Vintage Books, 1973.

SENTENCING PROJECT. "Facts about Prisons and Prisoners." December 2006. [Online] Available July 30, 2007, at http://www.sentencingproject.org/Admin/Documents/publications/inc_factsaboutprison.pdf

SHALIN, DMITRI N. "G. H. Mead, Socialism, and the Progressive Agenda." *American Journal of Sociology.* Vol. 93, No. 4 (January 1988):913–51.

SHAPIRO, JOSEPH P. "Back to Work, on Mission." *U.S. News & World Report* (June 4, 2001).

SHARPE, ANITA. "The Rich Aren't So Different After All." *Wall Street Journal* (November 12, 1996):B1, B10.

SHAWCROSS, WILLIAM. *Sideshow: Kissinger, Nixon and the Destruction of Cambodia.* New York: Pocket Books, 1979.

SHEA, RACHEL HARTIGAN. "The New Insecurity." *U.S. News & World Report* (March 25, 2002):40.

SHEEHAN, TOM. "Senior Esteem as a Factor in Socioeconomic Complexity." *Gerontologist.* Vol. 16, No. 5 (October 1976):433–40.

SHELDON, WILLIAM H., EMIL M. HARTL, and EUGENE MCDERMOTT. *Varieties of Delinquent Youth.* New York: Harper Bros., 1949.

SHELER, JEFFREY L. "Faith in America." *U.S. News & World Report* (May 6, 2002):40–44.

SHERKAT, DARREN E., and CHRISTOPHER G. ELLISON. "Recent Developments and Current Controversies in the Sociology of Religion." *Annual Review of Sociology.* Vol. 25 (1999): 363–94.

SHERMAN, LAWRENCE W., and DOUGLAS A. SMITH. "Crime, Punishment, and Stake in Conformity: Legal and Informal Control of Domestic Violence." *American Sociological Review.* Vol. 57, No. 5 (October 1992):680–90.

SHEVKY, ESHREF, and WENDELL BELL. *Social Area Analysis.* Stanford, Calif.: Stanford University Press, 1955.

SHIPLEY, JOSEPH T. *Dictionary of Word Origins.* Totowa, N.J.: Roman & Allanheld, 1985.

SHIVELY, JOELLEN. "Cowboys and Indians: Perceptions of Western Films among American Indians and Anglos." *American Sociological Review.* Vol. 57, No. 6 (December 1992):725–34.

SHUPE, ANSON. *In the Name of All That's Holy: A Theory of Clergy Malfeasance.* Westport, Conn.: Praeger, 1995.

SHUPE, ANSON, WILLIAM A. STACEY, and LONNIE R. HAZLEWOOD. *Violent Men, Violent Couples: The Dynamics of Domestic Violence.* Lexington, Mass.: Lexington Books, 1987.

SIMMEL, GEORG. *The Sociology of Georg Simmel.* KURT WOLFF, ed. New York: Free Press, 1950; orig. 1902.

———. "Fashion." In DONALD N. LEVINE, ed., *Georg Simmel: On Individuality and Social Forms.* Chicago: University of Chicago Press, 1971; orig. 1904.

SIMMONS, RUSSELL. "10 Questions." *Time.* Vol. 169, No. 20 (May 14, 2007):8.

SIMON, JULIAN. *The Ultimate Resource.* Princeton, N.J.: Princeton University Press, 1981.

———. "More People, Greater Wealth, More Resources, Healthier Environment." In THEODORE D. GOLDFARB, ed., *Taking Sides: Clashing Views on Controversial Environmental Issues.* 6th ed. Guilford, Conn.: Dushkin, 1995.

SIMON, ROGER, and ANGIE CANNON. "An Amazing Journey." *U.S. News & World Report* (August 6, 2001):10–19.

SIMONS, MARLISE. "The Price of Modernization: The Case of Brazil's Kaiapo Indians." In JOHN J. MACIONIS and NIJOLE V. BENOKRAITIS, eds., *Seeing Ourselves: Classic, Contemporary, and Cross-Cultural Readings in Sociology.* 7th ed. Upper Saddle River, N.J.: Prentice Hall, 2007.

SIMPSON, GEORGE EATON, and J. MILTON YINGER. *Racial and Cultural Minorities: An Analysis of Prejudice and Discrimination.* 4th ed. New York: Harper & Row, 1972.

SIVARD, RUTH LEGER. *World Military and Social Expenditures, 1987–88.* 12th ed. Washington, D.C.: World Priorities, 1988.

———. *World Military and Social Expenditures, 1992–93.* 17th ed. Washington, D.C.: World Priorities, 1993.

SIZER, THEODORE R. *Horace's Compromise: The Dilemma of the American High School.* Boston: Houghton Mifflin, 1984.

———. "Private Profit, Public Good?" *Frontline* interview. July 3, 2003. [Online] Available May 20, 2006, at http://www.pbs.org/wgbh/pages/frontline/shows/edison/etc/private.html

SKOCPOL, THEDA. *States and Social Revolutions: A Comparative Analysis of France, Russia, and China.* Cambridge: Cambridge University Press, 1979.

SMAIL, J. KENNETH. "Let's *Reduce* Global Population!" In JOHN J. MACIONIS and NIJOLE V. BENOKRAITIS, eds., *Seeing Ourselves: Classic, Contemporary, and Cross-Cultural Readings in Sociology.* 7th ed. Upper Saddle River, N.J.: Prentice Hall, 2007.

SMART, TIM. "Not Acting Their Age." *U.S. News & World Report.* (June 4, 2001):54–60.

SMELSER, NEIL J. *Theory of Collective Behavior.* New York: Free Press, 1962.

SMITH, ADAM. *An Inquiry into the Nature and Causes of the Wealth of Nations.* New York: Modern Library, 1937; orig. 1776.

SMITH, CRAIG S. "Authorities Took Victim's Organs, His Brother Says." *Columbus* (Ohio) *Dispatch* (March 11, 2001):A3.

SMITH, DOUGLAS A. "Police Response to Interpersonal Violence: Defining the Parameters of Legal Control." *Social Forces.* Vol. 65, No. 3 (March 1987):767–82.

SMITH, DOUGLAS A., and PATRICK R. GARTIN. "Specifying Specific Deterrence: The Influence of Arrest on Future Criminal Activity." *American Sociological Review.* Vol. 54, No. 1 (February 1989):94–105.

SMITH, DOUGLAS A., and CHRISTY A. VISHER. "Street-Level Justice: Situational Determinants of Police Arrest Decisions." *Social Problems.* Vol. 29, No. 2 (December 1981):167–77.

SMITH, RYAN A. "Race, Gender, and Authority in the Workplace: Theory and Research." *Annual Review of Sociology.* Vol. 28 (2002):509–42.

SMITH, TOM W. "Anti-Semitism Decreases but Persists." *Society.* Vol. 33, No. 3 (March/April 1996):2.

———. "Are We Grown Up Yet? U.S. Study Says Not 'til 26." [Online] Available May 23, 2003, at http://news.yahoo.com

SMITH-LOVIN, LYNN, and CHARLES BRODY. "Interruptions in Group Discussions: The Effects of Gender and Group Composition." *American Journal of Sociology.* Vol. 54, No. 3 (June 1989):424–35.

SMOLOWE, JILL. "When Violence Hits Home." *Time* (July 4, 1994):18–25.

SNELL, MARILYN BERLIN. "The Purge of Nurture." *New Perspectives Quarterly.* Vol. 7, No. 1 (Winter 1990):1–2.

SOBEL, RACHEL K. "Herpes Tests Give Answers You Might Need to Know." *U.S. News & World Report* (June 18, 2001):53.

SOUTH, SCOTT J., and KIM L. LLOYD. "Spousal Alternatives and Marital Dissolution." *American Sociological Review.* Vol. 60, No. 1 (February 1995):21–35.

SOUTH, SCOTT J., and STEVEN F. MESSNER. "Structural Determinants of Intergroup Association: Interracial Marriage and Crime." *American Journal of Sociology.* Vol. 91, No. 6 (May 1986):1409–30.

SOWELL, THOMAS. *Ethnic America.* New York: Basic Books, 1981.

———. *Compassion versus Guilt, and Other Essays.* New York: Morrow, 1987.

———. *Race and Culture.* New York: Basic Books, 1994.

———. "Ethnicity and IQ." In STEVEN FRASER, ed., *The Bell Curve Wars: Race, Intelligence, and the Future of America.* New York: Basic Books, 1995:70–79.

SPECTER, MICHAEL. "Plunging Life Expectancy Puzzles Russia." *New York Times* (August 2, 1995):A1, A2.

SPEIER, HANS. "Wit and Politics: An Essay on Laughter and Power." ROBERT JACKALL, ed. and trans. *American Journal of Sociology.* Vol. 103, No. 5 (March 1998):1352–1401.

SPITZER, STEVEN. "Toward a Marxian Theory of Deviance." In DELOS H. KELLY, ed., *Criminal Behavior: Readings in Criminology*. New York: St. Martin's Press, 1980:175–91.

STACEY, JUDITH. *Patriarchy and Socialist Revolution in China*. Berkeley: University of California Press, 1983.

———. *Brave New Families: Stories of Domestic Upheaval in Late Twentieth-Century America*. New York: Basic Books, 1990.

———. "Good Riddance to 'The Family': A Response to David Popenoe." *Journal of Marriage and the Family*. Vol. 55, No. 3 (August 1993):545–47.

STACK, CAROL B. *All Our Kin: Strategies for Survival in a Black Community*. New York: Harper & Row, 1975.

STACK, STEVEN, IRA WASSERMAN, and ROGER KERN. "Adult Social Bonds and the Use of Internet Pornography." *Social Science Quarterly*. Vol. 85, No. 1 (March 2004):75–88.

STAPINSKI, HELENE. "Let's Talk Dirty." *American Demographics*. Vol. 20, No. 11 (November 1998):50–56.

STARK, RODNEY. *Sociology*. Belmont, Calif.: Wadsworth, 1985.

STARK, RODNEY, and WILLIAM SIMS BAINBRIDGE. "Of Churches, Sects, and Cults: Preliminary Concepts for a Theory of Religious Movements." *Journal for the Scientific Study of Religion*. Vol. 18, No. 2 (June 1979):117–31.

———. "Secularization and Cult Formation in the Jazz Age." *Journal for the Scientific Study of Religion*. Vol. 20, No. 4 (December 1981):360–73.

STARK, RODNEY, and ROGER FINKE. *Acts of Faith: Explaining the Human Side of Religion*. Berkeley: University of California Press, 2000.

STARR, PAUL. *The Social Transformation of American Medicine*. New York: Basic Books, 1982.

"State Laws Regarding Marriages between First Cousins." National Conference on State Legislatures. 2007. [Online] Available May 8, 2007, at http://www.ncsl.org/programs/cyf/cousins.htm

STEELE, RANDY. "Awful but Lawful." *Boating* (June 2000):36.

STEELE, SHELBY. *The Content of Our Character: A New Vision of Race in America*. New York: St. Martin's Press, 1990.

STEINBERG, LAURENCE. "Failure outside the Classroom." *Wall Street Journal* (July 11, 1996):A14.

STEPHENS, JOHN D. *The Transition from Capitalism to Socialism*. Urbana: University of Illinois Press, 1986.

STERKE, CLAIRE E. *Tricking and Tripping: Prostitution in the Era of AIDS*. Putnam Valley, N.Y.: Social Change Press, 2000.

STEVENS, GILLIAN, and GRAY SWICEGOOD. "The Linguistic Context of Ethnic Endogamy." *American Sociological Review*. Vol. 52, No. 1 (February 1987):73–82.

STIER, HAYA. "Continuity and Change in Women's Occupations Following First Childbirth." *Social Science Quarterly*. Vol. 77, No. 1 (March 1996):60–75.

STOCKHOLM INTERNATIONAL PEACE RESEARCH INSTITUTE. "SIPRI Data on Military Expenditures." [Online] Available June 25, 2007, at http://www.sipri.org/contents/milap/milex/mex_data_index.html

STOFFERAHN, CURTIS W. "Underemployment: Social Fact or Socially Constructed Reality?" *Rural Sociology*. Vol. 65, No. 2 (June 2000):311–30.

STONE, LAWRENCE. *The Family, Sex, and Marriage in England, 1500–1800*. New York: Harper & Row, 1977.

STONE, PAMELA. "Ghettoized and Marginalized: The Coverage of Racial and Ethnic Groups in Introductory Sociology Texts." *Teaching Sociology*. Vol. 24, No. 4 (October 1996):356–63.

STORMS, MICHAEL D. "Theories of Sexual Orientation." *Journal of Personality and Social Psychology*. Vol. 38, No. 5 (May 1980):783–92.

STOUFFER, SAMUEL A., ET AL. *The American Soldier: Adjustment during Army Life*. Princeton, N.J.: Princeton University Press, 1949.

STOUT, DAVID. "Supreme Court Splits on Diversity Efforts at University of Michigan." [Online] Available June 23, 2003, at http://news.yahoo.com

STRATTON, LESLIE S. "Why Does More Housework Lower Women's Wages? Testing Hypotheses Involving Job Effort and Hours Flexibility." *Social Sciences Quarterly*. Vol. 82, No. 1 (March 2001):67–76.

STREIB, GORDON F. "Are the Aged a Minority Group?" In BERNICE L. NEUGARTEN, ed., *Middle Age and Aging: A Reader in Social Psychology*. Chicago: University of Chicago Press, 1968:35–46.

STROSS, RANDALL E. "The McPeace Dividend." *U.S. News & World Report* (April 1, 2002):36.

SULLIVAN, ANDREW. Lecture delivered at Kenyon College, Gambier, Ohio, April 4, 2002.

SULLIVAN, BARBARA. "McDonald's Sees India as Golden Opportunity." *Chicago Tribune* (April 5, 1995):B1.

SULLIVAN, WILL. "Road Warriors." *U.S. News & World Report*. Vol. 142, No. 16 (May 7, 2007):42–49.

SUMNER, WILLIAM GRAHAM. *Folkways*. New York: Dover, 1959; orig. 1906.

SUN, LENA H. "WWII's Forgotten Internees Await Apology." *Washington Post* (March 9, 1998):A1, A5, A6.

SUTHERLAND, EDWIN H. "White Collar Criminality." *American Sociological Review*. Vol. 5, No. 1 (February 1940):1–12.

SVEBAK, SVEN. Cited in MARILYN ELIAS, "Study Links Sense of Humor, Survival." [Online] Available March 14, 2007, at http://www.usatoday.com

SWARTZ, STEVE. "Why Michael Milken Stands to Qualify for Guinness Book." *Wall Street Journal* (March 31, 1989):1, 4.

SZASZ, THOMAS S. *The Myth of Mental Illness: Foundations of a Theory of Personal Conduct*. New York: Dell, 1961.

———. *The Manufacturer of Madness: A Comparative Study of the Inquisition and the Mental Health Movement*. New York: Harper & Row, 1970.

———. "Idleness and Lawlessness in the Therapeutic State." *Society*. Vol. 32, No. 4 (May/June 1995):30–35.

———. "Cleansing the Modern Heart." *Society*. Vol. 40, No. 4 (May/June 2003):52-59.

———. "Protecting Patients against Psychiatric Intervention." *Society*. Vol. 41, No. 3 (March/April 2004):7–10.

SZEGEDY-MASZAK MARIANNE, "The Power of Gender." *U.S. News & World Report* (June 4, 2001):52.

TAJFEL, HENRI. "Social Psychology of Intergroup Relations." *Annual Review of Psychology*. Palo Alto, Calif.: Annual Reviews, 1982:1–39.

TAKAKI, RONALD. *Strangers from a Different Shore*. Boston: Back Bay Books, 1998.

TALLICHET, SUZANNE E. "Barriers to Women's Advancement in Underground Coal Mining." *Rural Sociology*. Vol. 65, No. 2 (June 2000):234–52.

TANNEN, DEBORAH. *You Just Don't Understand: Women and Men in Conversation*. New York: Morrow, 1990.

———. *Talking from 9 to 5: How Women's and Men's Conversational Styles Affect Who Gets Heard, Who Gets Credit, and What Gets Done at Work*. New York: Morrow, 1994.

TANNENBAUM, FRANK. *Crime and the Community*. New York: Columbia University Press, 1938.

TAVRIS, CAROL, and CAROL WADE. *Psychology in Perspective*. 3rd ed. Upper Saddle River, N.J.: Prentice Hall, 2001.

TAX FOUNDATION. [Online] Available June 15, 2000, at http://www.taxfoundation.org

———. "America Celebrates Tax Freedom Day." Special Report No. 152 (March 2007). [Online] Available September 16, 2007, at http://www.taxfoundation.org/publications/show/93.html

TAYLOR, FREDERICK WINSLOW. *The Principles of Scientific Management*. New York. Harper Bros., 1911.

TERRY, DON. "In Crackdown on Bias, a New Tool." *New York Times* (June 12, 1993):8.

THERNSTROM, ABIGAIL, and STEPHAN THERNSTROM. "American Apartheid? Don't Believe It." *Wall Street Journal* (March 2, 1998):A18.

THOMAS, EDWARD J. *The Life of Buddha as Legend and History*. London: Routledge & Kegan Paul, 1975.

THOMAS, PAULETTE. "Success at a Huge Personal Cost." *Wall Street Journal* (July 26, 1995):B1, B6.

THOMAS, PIRI. *Down These Mean Streets*. New York: Signet, 1967.

THOMAS, W. I. "The Relation of Research to the Social Process." In MORRIS JANOWITZ, ed., *W. I. Thomas on Social Organization and Social Personality*. Chicago: University of Chicago Press, 1966:289–305; orig. 1931.

THOMMA, STEVEN. "Christian Coalition Demands Action from GOP." *Philadelphia Inquirer* (September 14, 1997):A2.

THOMPSON, DICK. "Gene Maverick." *Time* (January 11, 1999):54–55.

THOMPSON, MARK. "Fatal Neglect." *Time* (October 27, 1997):34–38.

———. "Shining a Light on Abuse." *Time* (August 3, 1998):42–43.

THOMPSON, MARK, and DOUGLAS WALLER. "Shield of Dreams." *Time* (May 8, 2001):45–47.

THORLINDSSON, THOROLFUR, and THORODDUR BJARNASON. "Modeling Durkheim on the Micro Level: A Study of Youth Suicidality." *American Sociological Review*. Vol. 63, No. 1 (February 1998):94–110.

THORNBERRY, TERRANCE, and MARGARET FARNSWORTH. "Social Correlates of Criminal Involvement: Further Evidence on the Relationship between Social Status and Criminal Behavior." *American Sociological Review*. Vol. 47, No. 4 (August 1982):505–18.

THORNBURGH, NATHAN. "Dropout Nation." *Time* (April 17, 2006):30–40.

THORNE, BARRIE, CHERIS KRAMARAE, and NANCY HENLEY, eds. *Language, Gender, and Society*. Rowley, Mass.: Newbury House, 1983.

TILLY, CHARLES. *From Mobilization to Revolution*. Reading, Mass.: Addison-Wesley, 1978.

———. "Does Modernization Breed Revolution?" In JACK A. GOLDSTONE, ed., *Revolutions: Theoretical, Comparative, and Historical Studies*. New York: Harcourt Brace Jovanovich, 1986:47–57.

TIRYAKIAN, EDWARD A. "Revisiting Sociology's First Classic: The Division of Labor in Society and Its Actuality." *Sociological Forum*. Vol. 9, No. 1 (March 1994):3–16.

TITTLE, CHARLES R., WAYNE J. VILLEMEZ, and DOUGLAS A. SMITH. "The Myth of Social Class and Criminality: An Empirical Assessment of the Empirical Evidence." *American Sociological Review*. Vol. 43, No. 5 (October 1978):643–56.

TOCQUEVILLE, ALEXIS DE. *The Old Regime and the French Revolution*. STUART GILBERT, trans. Garden City, N.Y.: Anchor/Doubleday, 1955; orig. 1856.

Toffler, Alvin. *Future Shock.* New York: Random House, 1970.

Tolson, Jay. "The Trouble with Elites." *Wilson Quarterly.* Vol. 19, No. 1 (Winter 1995):6–8.

Tönnies, Ferdinand. *Community and Society (Gemeinschaft und Gesellschaft).* New York: Harper & Row, 1963; orig. 1887.

Toossi, Mitra. "Labor Force Projections to 2014: Retiring Boomers." *Monthly Labor Review* (November 2005):25–44. [Online] Available June 2, 2006, at http://www.bls.gov/opub/mlr/2005/11/art3full.pdf

Toppo, Greg, and Anthony DeBarros. "Reality Weighs Down Dreams of College." *USA Today* (February 2, 2005):A1.

Torres, Lisa, and Matt L. Huffman. "Social Networks and Job Search Outcomes among Male and Female Professional, Technical, and Managerial Workers." *Sociological Focus.* Vol. 35, No. 1 (February 2002):25–42.

Treas, Judith. "Older Americans in the 1990s and Beyond." *Population Bulletin.* Vol. 50, No. 2 (May 1995).

Troeltsch, Ernst. *The Social Teaching of the Christian Churches.* New York: Macmillan, 1931.

Tucker, James. "New Age Religion and the Cult of the Self." *Society.* Vol. 39, No. 2 (February 2002):46–51.

Tumin, Melvin M. "Some Principles of Stratification: A Critical Analysis." *American Sociological Review.* Vol. 18, No. 4 (August 1953):387–94.

———. *Social Stratification: The Forms and Functions of Inequality.* 2nd ed. Englewood Cliffs, N.J.: Prentice Hall, 1985.

Turner, Jonathan. *On the Origins of Human Emotions: A Sociological Inquiry into the Evolution of Human Emotions.* Stanford, Calif.: Stanford University Press, 2000.

Turner, Ralph H. "Introduction." In Robert E. Park, *On Social Control and Collective Behavior.* Chicago: University of Chicago, Press, 1967.

Turner, Ralph H., and Lewis M. Killian. *Collective Behavior.* 3rd ed. Englewood Cliffs, N.J.: Prentice Hall, 1987.

Tyler, S. Lyman. *A History of Indian Policy.* Washington, D.C.: U.S. Department of the Interior, Bureau of Indian Affairs, 1973.

Udry, J. Richard. "Biological Limitations of Gender Construction." *American Sociological Review.* Vol. 65, No. 3 (June 2000):443–57.

Uggen, Christopher. "Ex-Offenders and the Conformist Alternative: A Job-Quality Model of Work and Crime." *Social Problems.* Vol. 46, No. 1 (February 1999):127–51.

Uggen, Christopher, and Jeff Manza. "Democratic Contraction? Political Consequences of Felon Disenfranchisement in the United States." *American Sociological Review.* Vol. 67, No. 6 (December 2002):777–803.

UNESCO. Data reported in "Tower of Babel Is Tumbling Down—Slowly." *U.S. News & World Report* (July 2, 2001):9.

UNICEF. *The State of the World's Children, 2007.* 2006. [Online] Available July 2, 2007, at http:www.unicef.org/sowc07/report/report.php

———. "Understanding Children's Work." *Country Statistics.* [Online] Available August 1, 2007, at http://www.childwork-project.org/cgi-bin/ucw/Survey/Main.sql?come=Ucw_Tables.sql

United Nations. "Executive Summary." *World Population Ageing, 1950–2050.* New York: United Nations, 2002. [Online] Available October 20, 2005, at http://www.un.org/esa/population/publications/worldageing19502050/index/htm

———. *2006 Report on the Global AIDS Epidemic.* 2006a. [Online] Available September 27, 2006, at http://www.unaids.org/en/HIV_data/2006GlobalReport/default.asp

———. *UNAIDS.WHO AIDS Epidemic Update, December 2006.* 2006b. [Online] Available July 9, 2007, at http://www.unaids.org/en/HIV_data/epi2006/default.asp

———. *The World's Women, 2005: Progress in Statistics.* New York: United Nations, 2006c.

United Nations Development Programme. *Human Development Report 1990.* New York: Oxford University Press, 1990.

———. *Human Development Report 1996.* New York: Oxford University Press, 1996.

———. *Human Development Report 2000.* New York: Oxford University Press, 2000.

———. *Human Development Report 2001.* New York: Oxford University Press, 2001.

———. *Human Development Report 2002.* New York: Oxford University Press, 2002.

———. *Human Development Report 2005.* New York: Oxford University Press, 2005.

———. *Human Development Report 2006.* New York: Palgrave Macmillan, 2006.

United Nations Population Division. *Population Aging, 1999.* New York: United Nations, 1999.

U.S. Bureau of Economic Analysis. "Foreign Direct Investment in the United States: Selected Items by Detailed Country, 2002–2005." [Online] Available June 22, 2007, at http://www.bea.gov/bea/di/FDI16_0205.pdf

U.S. Bureau of Justice Statistics. *Family Violence Statistics: Including Statistics on Strangers and Acquaintances.* Washington, D.C.: U.S. Government Printing Office, 2005.

———. *Criminal Victimization, 2005.* Washington, D.C.: U.S. Government Printing Office, 2006. [Online] Available May 15, 2007, at http://www.ojp.usdoj.gov/bjs/pub/pdf/cv05.pdf

———. *Prison and Jail Inmates at Midyear 2005.* Washington, D.C.: U.S. Government Printing Office, 2006. [Online] Available May 20, 2007, at http://www.ojp.usdoj.gov/bjs/pub/pdf/pjim05.pdf

———. "Sentences Imposed in Cases Terminated in U.S. District Courts." *Sourcebook of Criminal Justice Statistics Online.* [Online] Available May 20, 2007, at http://www.albany.edu/sourcebook

U.S. Census Bureau. *65+ in the United States.* Washington, D.C.: U.S. Government Printing Office, 1996.

———. *Educational Attainment in the United States, March 2000* (Update). Current Population Reports, P20-536. Washington, D.C.: U.S. Government Printing Office, 2000.

———. *Age: 2000.* Census 2000 Brief, C2KBR/01-12. Washington, D.C.: U.S. Government Printing Office, 2001.

———. *The Black Population, 2000.* Census 2000 Brief, C2KBR/01-5. Washington, D.C.: U.S. Government Printing Office, 2001. [Online] Available August 28, 2007, at http://www.census.gov/population/www/cen2000/briefs.html

———. *The Hispanic Population, 2000.* Census 2000 Brief, C2KBR/01-3. Washington, D.C.: U.S. Government Printing Office, 2001. [Online] Available August 28, 2007, at http://www.census.gov/population/www/cen2000/briefs.html

———. *Mapping Census 2000: The Geography of U.S. Diversity.* Census Special Reports, Series CENSR/01-1. Washington, D.C.: U.S. Government Printing Office, 2001.

———. *Money Income in the United States, 2000.* Current Population Reports, P60-213. Washington, D.C.: U.S. Government Printing Office, 2001.

———. *The Native Hawaiian and Other Pacific Islander Population, 2000.* Census 2000 Brief, C2KBR/01-14. Washington, D.C.: U.S. Government Printing Office, 2001. [Online] Available August 28, 2007, at http://www.census.gov/population/www/cen2000/briefs.html

———. *Population Change and Distribution, 1990 to 2000.* Census 2000 Brief, C2KBR/01-2. Washington, D.C.: U.S. Government Printing Office, 2001.

———. *Poverty in the United States, 2000.* Current Population Reports, P60-214. Washington, D.C.: U.S. Government Printing Office, 2001.

———. *The Two or More Races Population, 2000.* Census 2000 Brief, C2KBR/01-6. Washington, D.C.: U.S. Government Printing Office, 2001. [Online] Available August 28, 2007, at http://www.census.gov/population/www/cen2000/briefs.html

———. *The White Population, 2000.* Census 2000 Brief, C2KBR/01-4. Washington, D.C.: U.S. Government Printing Office, 2001. [Online] Available August 28, 2007, at http://www.census.gov/population/www/cen2000/briefs.html

———. *The American Indian and Alaska Native Population, 2000.* Census 2000 Brief, C2KBR/01-15. Washington, D.C.: U.S. Government Printing Office, 2002. [Online] Available August 28, 2007, at http://www.census.gov/population/www/cen2000/briefs.html

———. *The Asian Population, 2000.* Census 2000 Brief, C2KBR/01-16. Washington, D.C.: U.S. Government Printing Office, 2002. [Online] Available August 28, 2007, at http://www.census.gov/population/www/cen2000/briefs.html

———. *The Arab Population, 2000.* Census 2000 Brief, C2KBR-23. Washington, D.C.: U.S. Government Printing Office, 2003.

———. *Language Use and English-Speaking Ability, 2000.* Census 2000 Brief, C2KBR-29. Washington, D.C.: U.S. Government Printing Office, 2003.

———. *Ancestry, 2000.* Census 2000 Brief, C2KBR-35. Washington, D.C.: U.S. Government Printing Office, 2004.

———. *Statistical Abstract of the United States, 2004–2005.* Washington, D.C.: U.S. Government Printing Office, 2004.

———. "About Metropolitan and Micropolitan Statistical Areas." Rev. June 7, 2005 [Online] Available September 17, 2007, at http://www.census.gov/population/www/estimates/aboutmetro.html.

———. "About Metropolitan and Micropolitan Statistical Areas." Rev. June 7, 2005. [Online] Available September 17, 2007, at http://www.census.gov/population/www.estimates/aboutmetro.html

———. *Fertility of American Women, June 2004.* Current Population Reports (P20-555). Washington, D.C.: U.S. Government Printing Office, 2005.

———. *The Hispanic Population of the United States, 2004.* Detailed tables. Rev. December 14, 2005. [Online] Available August 28, 2007, at http://www.census.gov/population/www/socdemo/hispanic/cps2004.html

———. "Port St. Lucie, Florida, Is Fastest-Growing City, Census Bureau Says." Press release, June 30, 2005. [Online] Available August 28, 2007, at http://www.census.gov/Press-Release/www/releases/archives/population/005268.html

———. Voting and Registration in the Election of November 2004. "(Tables) 1, 2, 8." Rev. May 25, 2005. [Online] Available June 24, 2007, at http://www.census.gov/population/www/socdemo/voting/cps2004.html

———. *We the People of Arab Ancestry in the United States.* Census 2000 Special Reports, CENSR-21. Washington, D.C.: U.S. Government Printing Office, 2005.

———. "Census 2000 Demographic Profile Highlights." [Online] Available September 22, 2006, at http://factfinder.census.gov

———. Current Population Survey, 2006 Annual Social and Economic Supplement. "(Tables) FINC-01, FINC-02, FINC-07." Rev. August 29, 2006. [Online] Available May 28, 2007, at http://pubdb3.census.gov/macro/032006/faminc/toc.htm

————. Current Population Survey, 2006 Annual Social and Economic Supplement. "(Table) HINC-01." Rev. August 29, 2006. [Online] Available May 28, 2007, at http://pubdb3 .census.gov/macro/032006/hhinc/toc.htm

————. Current Population Survey, 2006 Annual Social and Economic Supplement. "(Tables) PINC-01, PINC-03, PINC-05." Rev. August 29, 2006. [Online] Available May 30, 2007, at http://pubdb3.census.gov/macro/032006/perinc/toc.htm

————. Current Population Survey, 2006 Annual Social and Economic Supplement. "(Tables) POV01, POV04, POV06, POV14, POV41." Rev. August 29, 2006. [Online] Available May 28, 2007, at http://pubdb3.census.gov/macro/032006/pov/toc.htm

————. *Custodial Mothers and Fathers and Their Child Support, 2003.* Current Population Reports (P60-230). Washington, D.C.: U.S. Government Printing Office, 2006.

————. *Domestic Net Migration in the United States: 2000 to 2004.* Current Population Reports (P25-1135). April 2006. [Online] Available September 1, 2007, at http://www.census.gov/ prod/2006pubs/p25-1135.pdf

————. *Educational Attainment in the United States: 2005.* Detailed tables. Rev. October 26, 2006. [Online] Available August 22, 2007, at http://www.census.gov/population/www/ socdemo/education/cps2005.html

————. "Facts for Features: Grandparents Day 2006: Sept. 10." Press release, July 10, 2006. [Online] Available September 12, 2007, at http://www.census.gov/Press-Release/www/ releases/archives/fact_for_features_special_editions/007130.html

————. Historical Income Tables—Families. "(Tables) F-1, F-2, F-3, F-7." Rev. September 15, 2006. [Online] Available May 28, 2007, at http://www.census.gov/hhes/www/income/ histinc/incfamdet.html

————. *Income, Poverty, and Health Insurance Coverage in the United States, 2005.* Current Population Reports (P60-231). Washington, D.C.: U.S. Government Printing Office, 2006.

————. "Percent Total Population in Poverty, 2004" (map). Small Area Income and Poverty Estimates. Rev. December 20, 2006. [Online] Available May 28, 2007, at http://www .census.gov/hhes/www/saipe/maps/maps.html

————. *School Enrollment: Social and Economic Characteristics of Students, 2005.* Detailed tables. Rev. December 18, 2006. [Online] Available July 3, 2007, at http://www.census.gov/ population/www/socdemo/school/cps2005.html

————. *Statistical Abstract of the United States, 2007.* Washington, D.C.: U.S. Government Printing Office, 2006.

————. "(Table) S1601. Language Spoken at Home." 2005 American Community Survey. Rev. August 15, 2006. [Online] Available September 22, 2006, at http://factfinder.census.gov

————. *We the People: American Indians and Alaska Natives in the United States.* Census 2000 Special Reports, CENSR-28. Washington, D.C.: U.S. Government Printing Office, 2006.

————. *The American Community: Hispanics, 2004.* February 2007. [Online] Available August 22, 2007, at http://www.census.gov/prod/2007pubs/acs-03.pdf

————. *America's Families and Living Arrangements: 2006.* Detailed tables. Rev. March 30, 2007. [Online] Available September 9, 2007, at http://www.census.gov/population/www/ socdemo/hh-fam/cps2006.html

————. *Educational Attainment in the United States, 2006.* Detailed tables. Rev. March 20, 2007. [Online] Available May 27, 2007, at http://www.census.gov/population/www/ socdemo/education/cps2006.html

————. *Housing Vacancies and Homeownership.* (CPS/HVS). Annual Statistics, 2006. Table 20. Rev. February 12, 2007. [Online] Available May 27, 2007, at http://www.census.gov/hhes/ www/housing/hvs/annual06/ann06ind.html

————. "International Database (IDB): Pyramids." Rev. July 16, 2007. [Online] Available August 28, 2007, at http://www.census.gov/ipc/www/idb/pyramids.html

U.S. CENSUS OFFICE. *Census of the United States, 1900: Vol. 2, Population.* Washington, D.C.: U.S. Census Office, 1902.

U.S. CHARTER SCHOOLS. "New Research and Reports." [Online] Available July 3, 2007, at http://www.uscharterschools.org/pub/uscs_docs/r/index.htm

U.S. CITIZENSHIP AND IMMIGRATION SERVICES. *2002 Yearbook of Immigration Statistics.* [Online] Available December 24, 2003, at http://uscis.gov/graphics/shared/aboutus/statistics/ IMM02yrbk/IMM2002list.htm

U.S. DEPARTMENT OF COMMERCE. *Statistical Abstract of the United States, 1930.* Washington, D.C.: U.S. Government Printing Office, 1930.

U.S. DEPARTMENT OF HEALTH AND HUMAN SERVICES. *Administration for Children and Families. Temporary Assistance for Needy Families (TANF) Program;* Third Annual Report to Congress, August 2000. Washington, D.C.: The Administration, 2000.

————, ADMINISTRATION ON CHILDREN, YOUTH, AND FAMILIES. *Child Maltreatment, 2005.* Washington, D.C.: U.S. Government Printing Office, 2007.

U.S. DEPARTMENT OF HOMELAND SECURITY. *2006 Yearbook of Immigration Statistics.* [Online] Available August 28, 2007, at http://www.dhs.gov/ximgtn/statistics/publications/ yearbook.shtm

U.S. DEPARTMENT OF JUSTICE. "Nearly Three Percent of College Women Experienced a Completed Rape or Attempted Rape During the College Year, According to a New Justice

Department Report." [Online]. Accessed February 15, 2001, at http://www.ojp.usdoj.gov/ bjs/pub/press/svcw.pr

U.S. DEPARTMENT OF LABOR, BUREAU OF LABOR STATISTICS. *Employment and Earnings.* 2007. [Online] Available May 20, 2007, at http://www.bls.gov/cps/#annual

U.S. DEPARTMENT OF STATE. *Country Reports on Terrorism, 2006.* April 2007. [Online] Available June 25, 2007, at http://www.state.gov/s/ct/rls/crt

U.S. ENVIRONMENTAL PROTECTION AGENCY. "Basic Facts: Municipal Solid Waste." June 1, 2007. [Online] Available August 28, 2007, at http://www.epa.gov/msw/facts.htm

U.S. EQUAL EMPLOYMENT OPPORTUNITY COMMISSION. "Occupational Employment in Private Industry by Race/Ethnic Group/Sex and by Industry, United States, 2005." Rev. January 26, 2007. [Online] Available May 15, 2007, at http://www.eeoc.gov/stats/jobpat/2005/ national.html

U.S. HOUSE OF REPRESENTATIVES. *1991 Green Book.* Washington, D.C.: U.S. Government Printing Office, 1991.

————. "Street Children: A Global Disgrace." Hearing on November 7, 1991. Washington, D.C.: U.S. Government Printing Office, 1992.

U.S. SMALL BUSINESS ADMINISTRATION. *Minorities in Business, 2001.* November 2001. [Online] Available September 22, 2006, at http://www.sba.gov/advo/stats/min01/pdf.

————. U.S. SMALL BUSINESS ADMINISTRATION. *Women in Business: A Demographic Review of Women's Business Ownership,* August 2006. [Online] Available May 30, 2007, at http:// www.sba.gov/advo/research/rs280tot.pdf

————. *Minorities in Business: A Demographic Review of Minority Business Ownership.* April 2007. [Online] Available August 28, 2007, at http://www.sba.gov/advo/research/rs298tot .pdf

U.S. SURGEON GENERAL. Cited in "Notebook." *Time* (July 10, 2006):19.

UPTHEGROVE, TAYNA R., VINCENT J. ROSCIGNO, and CAMILLE ZUBRINSKY CHARLES. "Big Money Collegiate Sports: Racial Concentration, Contradictory Pressures, and Academic Performance." *Social Science Quarterly.* Vol. 80, No. 4 (December 1999):718–37.

URBAN INSTITUTE. "Nearly 3 out of 4 Young Children with Employed Mothers Are Regularly in Child Care." Fast Facts on Welfare Policy. April 28, 2004. [Online] Available July 18, 2005, at http://www.urban.org/UploadedPDF/900706.pdf

VALDEZ, A. "In the Hood: Street Gangs Discover White-Collar Crime." *Police.* Vol. 21, No. 5 (May 1997):49–50, 56.

VALLAS, STEPHEN P., and JOHN P. BECK. "The Transformation of Work Revisited: The Limits of Flexibility in American Manufacturing." *Social Problems.* Vol. 43, No. 3 (August 1996):339–61.

VALOCCHI, STEVE. "The Emergence of the Integrationist Ideology in the Civil Rights Movement." *Social Problems.* Vol. 43, No. 1 (February 1996):116–30.

VAN BIEMA, DAVID. "Buddhism in America." *Time* (October 13, 1997):71–81.

————. "Spiriting Prayer into School." *Time* (April 27, 1998):38–41.

————. "A Surge of Teen Spirit." *Time* (May 31, 1999):58–59.

VANDIVERE, SHARON, ET AL. *Unsupervised Time: Family and Child Factors Associated with Self-Care.* Washington, D.C.:Urban Institute, 2003. [Online] Available June 26, 2007, at http:// www.urban.org/UploadedPDF/310894_OP71.pdf

VAN DYKE, NELLA, and SARAH A. SOULE. "Structural Social Change and the Mobilizing Effect of Threat: Explaining Levels of Patriot and Militia Organizing in the United States." *Social Problems.* Vol. 49, No. 4 (November 2002):497–520.

VEBLEN, THORSTEIN. *The Theory of the Leisure Class.* New York: New American Library, 1953; orig. 1899.

VEDDER, RICHARD, and LOWELL GALLAWAY. "Declining Black Employment." *Society.* Vol. 30, No. 5 (July/August 1993):56–63.

VINOVSKIS, MARIS A. "Have Social Historians Lost the Civil War? Some Preliminary Demographic Speculations." *Journal of American History.* Vol. 76, No. 1 (June 1989):34–58.

VIOLENCE POLICY CENTER. "An Analysis of the Decline in Gun Dealers, 1994 to 2005." March 2006. [Online] Available July 30, 2007, at http://www.vpc.org/studies/dealers.pdf

VISSER, JELLE. "Union Membership Statistics in 24 Countries." *Monthly Labor Review* (January 2006):38–49. [Online] Available June 2, 2006, at http://www.bls.gov/opub/mlr/2006/01/ art3full.pdf

VOGEL, EZRA F. *The Four Little Dragons: The Spread of Industrialization in East Asia.* Cambridge, Mass.: Harvard University Press, 1991.

VOGEL, LISE. *Marxism and the Oppression of Women: Toward a Unitary Theory.* New Brunswick, N.J.: Rutgers University Press, 1983.

VOLD, GEORGE B., and THOMAS J. BERNARD. *Theoretical Criminology.* 3d ed. New York: Oxford University Press, 1986.

VONNEGUT, KURT, JR. "Harrison Bergeron." In *Welcome to the Monkey House.* New York: Delacorte Press, 1968:7–13.

WAHL, JENNY B. "From Riches to Riches: Intergenerational Transfers and the Evidence from Estate Tax Returns." *Social Science Quarterly.* Vol. 84, No. 2 (June 2003):278–96.

WALDER, ANDREW G. "Career Mobility and the Communist Political Order." *American Sociological Review.* Vol. 60, No. 3 (June 1995):309–28.

WALDFOGEL, JANE. "The Effect of Children on Women's Wages." *American Sociological Review.* Vol. 62, No. 2 (April 1997):209–17.

WALDROP, JUDITH. "Live Long and Prosper." *American Demographics.* Vol. 14, No. 10 (October 1992):40–45.

WALKER, KAREN. "'Always There for Me': Friendship Patterns and Expectations among Middle- and Working-Class Men and Women." *Sociological Forum.* Vol. 10, No. 2 (June 1995):273–96.

WALL, THOMAS F. *Medical Ethics: Basic Moral Issues.* Washington, D.C.: University Press of America, 1980.

WALLERSTEIN, IMMANUEL. *The Modern World-System: Capitalist Agriculture and the Origins of the European World-Economy in the Sixteenth Century.* New York: Academic Press, 1974.

———. *The Capitalist World-Economy.* New York: Cambridge University Press, 1979.

———. "Crises: The World Economy, the Movements, and the Ideologies." In ALBERT BERGESEN, ed., *Crises in the World-System.* Beverly Hills, Calif.: Sage, 1983:21–36.

———. *The Politics of the World Economy: The States, the Movements, and the Civilizations.* Cambridge: Cambridge University Press, 1984.

WALLERSTEIN, JUDITH S., and SANDRA BLAKESLEE. *Second Chances: Men, Women, and Children a Decade after Divorce.* New York: Ticknor & Fields, 1989.

WALLIS, CLAUDIA, and SONJA STEPTOE. "How to Fix No Child Left Behind." *Time.* Vol. 169, No. 23 (June 4, 2007): 34–41.

WALSH, BRYAN. "How Business Saw the Light." *Time* (January 15, 2007):56–57.

WALSH, MARY WILLIAMS. "No Time to Put Your Feet Up as Retirement Comes in Stages." *New York Times* (April 15, 2001):1, 18.

WALTON, JOHN, and CHARLES RAGIN. "Global and National Sources of Political Protest: Third World Responses to the Debt Crisis." *American Sociological Review.* Vol. 55, No. 6 (December 1990):876–90.

WARR, MARK, and CHRISTOPHER G. ELLISON. "Rethinking Social Reactions to Crime: Personal and Altruistic Fear in Family Households." *American Journal of Sociology.* Vol. 106, No. 3 (November 2000):551–78.

WATERS, MELISSA S., WILL CARRINGTON HEATH, and JOHN KEITH WATSON. "A Positive Model of the Determination of Religious Affiliation." *Social Science Quarterly.* Vol. 76, No. 1 (March 1995):105–23.

WATTS, DUNCAN J. "Networks, Dynamics, and the Small-World Phenomenon." *American Journal of Sociology.* Vol. 105, No. 2 (September 1999):493–527.

WEBER, ADNA FERRIN. *The Growth of Cities.* New York: Columbia University Press, 1963; orig. 1899.

WEBER, MAX. *The Protestant Ethic and the Spirit of Capitalism.* New York: Scribner, 1958; orig. 1904–05.

———. *Economy and Society: An Outline of Interpretive Sociology.* GUENTHER ROTH and CLAUS WITTICH, eds. Berkeley: University of California Press, 1978; orig. 1921.

WEBSTER, ANDREW. *Introduction to the Sociology of Development.* London: Macmillan, 1984.

WEEKS, JOHN R. "The Demography of Islamic Nations." *Population Bulletin.* Vol. 43, No. 4 (December 1988).

WEIDENBAUM, MURRAY. "The Evolving Corporate Board." *Society.* Vol. 32, No. 3 (March/April 1995):9–20.

WEINBERG, GEORGE. *Society and the Healthy Homosexual.* Garden City, N.Y.: Anchor Books, 1973.

WEISBERG, D. KELLY. *Children of the Night: A Study of Adolescent Prostitution.* Lexington, Mass.: Heath, 1985.

WEITZMAN, LENORE J. *The Divorce Revolution: The Unexpected Social and Economic Consequences for Women and Children in America.* New York: Free Press, 1985.

———. "The Economic Consequences of Divorce Are Still Unequal: Comment on Peterson." *American Sociological Review.* Vol. 61, No. 3 (June 1996):537–38.

WELLER, JACK M., and E. L. QUARANTELLI. "Neglected Characteristics of Collective Behavior." *American Journal of Sociology.* Vol. 79, No. 3 (November 1973):665–85.

WELLNER, ALISON STEIN. "Discovering Native America." *American Demographics.* Vol. 23, No. 8 (August 2001):21.

———. "The Power of the Purse." *American Demographics.* Vol. 24, No. 7 (January/February 2002):S3–S10.

WERTHEIMER, BARBARA MAYER. "The Factory Bell." In Linda K. Kerber and JANE DE HART MATHEWS, eds., *Women's America: Refocusing the Past.* New York: Oxford University Press, 1982:130–40.

WESSELMAN, HANK. *Visionseeker: Shared Wisdom from the Place of Refuge.* Carlsbad, Calif.: Hay House, 2001.

WESTERN, BRUCE. "The Impact of Incarceration on Wage Mobility and Inequality." *American Sociological Review.* Vol. 67, No. 4 (August 2002):526–46.

WHALEN, JACK, and RICHARD FLACKS. *Beyond the Barricades: The Sixties Generation Grows Up.* Philadelphia: Temple University Press, 1989.

WHEELIS, ALLEN. *The Quest for Identity.* New York: Norton, 1958.

WHITAKER, MARK. "Ten Ways to Fight Terrorism." *Newsweek* (July 1, 1985):26–29.

WHITE, JACK E. "I'm Just Who I Am." *Time* (May 5, 1997):32–36.

WHITE, KEVIN M., and SAMUEL H. PRESTON. "How Many Americans Are Alive Because of Twentieth-Century Improvements in Mortality?" *Population and Development Review.* Vol. 22, No. 3 (September 1996):405–19.

WHITE, RALPH, and RONALD LIPPITT. "Leader Behavior and Member Reaction in Three 'Social Climates.'" In DORWIN CARTWRIGHT and ALVIN ZANDER, eds., *Group Dynamics.* Evanston, Ill.: Row & Peterson, 1953:586–611.

WHITE, WALTER. *Rope and Faggot.* New York: Arno Press/New York Times, 1969; orig. 1929.

WHITMAN, DAVID. "Shattering Myths about the Homeless." *U.S. News & World Report* (March 20, 1989):26, 28.

WHORF, BENJAMIN LEE. "The Relation of Habitual Thought and Behavior to Language." In *Language, Thought, and Reality.* Cambridge, Mass.: Technology Press of MIT; New York: Wiley, 1956:134–59; orig. 1941.

WHYTE, WILLIAM FOOTE. *Street Corner Society.* 3rd ed. Chicago: University of Chicago Press, 1981; orig. 1943.

WICKHAM, DeWAYNE. "Homeless Receive Little Attention from Candidates." [Online] Available October 24, 2000, at http://www.usatoday.com

WILCOX, CLYDE. "Race, Gender, and Support for Women in the Military." *Social Science Quarterly.* Vol. 73, No. 2 (June 1992):310–23.

WILDAVSKY, BEN. "Small World, Isn't It?" *U.S. News & World Report* (April 1, 2002):68.

WILES, P. J. D. *Economic Institutions Compared.* New York: Halsted Press, 1977.

WILKINSON, DORIS. "Transforming the Social Order: The Role of the University in Social Change." *Sociological Forum.* Vol. 9, No. 3 (September 1994):325–41.

WILLIAMS, JOHNNY E. "Linking Beliefs to Collective Action: Politicized Religious Beliefs and the Civil Rights Movement." *Sociological Forum.* Vol. 17, No. 2 (June 2002):203–22.

WILLIAMS, PETER W. *America's Religions: From Their Origins to the Twenty-First Century.* Urbana: University of Illinois Press, 2002.

WILLIAMS, RHYS H., and N. J. DEMERATH III. "Religion and Political Process in an American City." *American Sociological Review.* Vol. 56, No. 4 (August 1991):417–31.

WILLIAMS, ROBIN M., JR. *American Society: A Sociological Interpretation.* 3rd ed. New York: Knopf, 1970.

WILLIAMSON, JEFFREY G., and PETER H. LINDERT. *American Inequality: A Macroeconomic History.* New York: Academic Press, 1980.

WILSON, BARBARA J. "National Television Violence Study." Reported in JULIA DUIN, "Study Finds Cartoon Heroes Initiate Too Much Violence." *Washington Times* (April 17, 1998):A4.

WILSON, EDWARD O. "Biodiversity, Prosperity, and Value." In F. HERBERT BORMANN and STEPHEN R. KELLERT, eds., *Ecology, Economics, and Ethics: The Broken Circle.* New Haven, Conn.: Yale University Press, 1991:3–10.

WILSON, JAMES Q. "Crime, Race, and Values." *Society.* Vol. 30, No. 1 (November/December 1992):90–93.

WILSON, THOMAS C. "Urbanism and Tolerance: A Test of Some Hypotheses Drawn from Wirth and Stouffer." *American Sociological Review.* Vol. 50, No. 1 (February 1985):117–23.

———. "Urbanism and Unconventionality: The Case of Sexual Behavior." *Social Science Quarterly.* Vol. 76, No. 2 (June 1995):346–63.

WILSON, WILLIAM JULIUS. *The Declining Significance of Race.* Chicago: University of Chicago Press, 1978.

———. *When Work Disappears: The World of the New Urban Poor.* New York: Knopf, 1996a.

———. "Work." *New York Times Magazine* (August 18, 1996b):26 ff.

WINNICK, LOUIS. "America's 'Model Minority.'" *Commentary.* Vol. 90, No. 2 (August 1990):22–29.

WINSHIP, CHRISTOPHER, and JENNY BERRIEN. "Boston Cops and Black Churches." *Public Interest.* No. 136 (Summer 1999):52–68.

WINTER, GREG. "Wider Gap Found between Wealthy and Poor Schools." *New York Times* (October 6, 2004). [Online] Available June 8, 2005, at http://www.researchnavigator.com

WINTERS, REBECCA. "Trouble for School Inc." *Time* (May 27, 2002):53.

WIRTH, LOUIS. "Urbanism as a Way of Life." *American Journal of Sociology.* Vol. 44, No. 1 (July 1938):1–24.

WITKIN, GORDON. "The Crime Bust." *U.S. News & World Report* (May 25, 1998):28–40.

WITT, LOUISE. "Why We're Losing the War against Obesity." *American Demographics.* Vol. 25, No. 10 (January 2004):27–31.

WOLF, NAOMI. *The Beauty Myth: How Images of Beauty Are Used against Women.* New York: Morrow, 1990.

WOLFE, DAVID B. "Targeting the Mature Mind." *American Demographics.* Vol. 16, No. 3 (March 1994):32–36.

WOLFF, EDWARD N. "Changes in Household Wealth in the 1980s and 1990s in the U.S." Working Paper No. 407. Levy Economics Institute of Bard College. May 2004. [Online] Available July 30, 2007, at http://www.levy.org/pubs/wp407.pdf

WOLFF, EDWARD N., and AJIT ZACHARIAS. "Wealth and Economic Inequality: Who's at the Top of the Economic Ladder?" Levy Institute Measure of Economic Well-Being. December 2006. [Online] Available May 27, 2007, at http://www.levy.org/pubs/limew1206.pdf

WOLFGANG, MARVIN E., ROBERT M. FIGLIO, and THORSTEN SELLIN. *Delinquency in a Birth Cohort.* Chicago: University of Chicago Press, 1972.

WOLFGANG, MARVIN E., TERRENCE P. THORNBERRY, and ROBERT M. FIGLIO. *From Boy to Man, from Delinquency to Crime.* Chicago: University of Chicago Press, 1987.

WONDERS, NANCY A., and RAYMOND MICHALOWSKI. "Bodies, Borders, and Sex Tourism in a Globalized World: A Tale of Two Cities—Amsterdam and Havana." *Social Problems.* Vol. 48, No. 4 (November 2001):545–71.

WONG, BUCK. "Need for Awareness: An Essay on Chinatown, San Francisco." In AMY TACHIKI ET AL., eds., *Roots: An Asian American Reader.* Los Angeles: UCLA Asian American Studies Center, 1971:265–73.

WOODWARD, KENNETH L. "Feminism and the Churches." *Newsweek* (February 13, 1989):58–61.
———. "Talking to God." *Newsweek* (January 6, 1992a):38–44.
———. "The Elite, and How to Avoid It." *Newsweek* (July 20, 1992b):55.

WORLD BANK. *World Development Report 1993.* New York: Oxford University Press, 1993.
———. *1999 World Development Indicators.* Washington, D.C.: World Bank, 1999.
———. *World Development Report 2000/2001.* Washington, D.C.: World Bank, 2001.
———. *2004 World Development Indicators.* Washington, D.C.: World Bank, 2004.
———. *2006 World Development Indicators.* Washington, D.C.: World Bank, 2006.
———. *2007 World Development Indicators.* Washington, D.C.: World Bank, 2007.

WORLD HEALTH ORGANIZATION. *Constitution of the World Health Organization.* New York: World Health Organization Interim Commission, 1946.
———. "Russian Federation." [Online] Available July 9, 2007, at http://www.who.int/countries/rus/en

WORLD VALUES SURVEY. "Predict 2005—Figure." 2004. [Online] Available May 7, 2007, at http://www.worldvaluessurvey.com/library/index.html

WREN, CHRISTOPHER S. "In Soweto-by-the-Sea, Misery Lives on as Apartheid Fades." *New York Times* (June 9, 1991):1, 7.

WRIGHT, JAMES D. "Ten Essential Observations on Guns in America." *Society.* Vol. 32, No. 3 (March/April 1995):63–68.

WRIGHT, QUINCY. "Causes of War in the Atomic Age." In WILLIAM M. EVAN and STEPHEN HILGARTNER, eds., *The Arms Race and Nuclear War.* Englewood Cliffs, N.J.: Prentice Hall, 1987:7–10.

WRIGHT, RICHARD A. *In Defense of Prisons.* Westport, Conn.: Greenwood Press, 1994.

WRIGHT, ROBERT. "Sin in the Global Village." *Time* (October 19, 1998):130.

WRIGHT, STUART A., and ELIZABETH S. PIPER. "Families and Cults: Familial Factors Related to Youth Leaving or Remaining in Deviant Religious Groups." *Journal of Marriage and the Family.* Vol. 48, No. 1 (February 1986):15–25.

WU, LAWRENCE L. "Effects of Family Instability, Income, and Income Instability on the Risk of a Premarital Birth." *American Sociological Review.* Vol. 61, No. 3 (June 1996):386–406.

WUTHNOW, ROBERT. *All in Synch: How Music and Art Are Revitalizing American Religion.* Berkeley: University ofCalifornia Press, 2003.

YANG, FENGGANG, and HELEN ROSE FUCHS EBAUGH. "Transformations in New Immigrant Religions and Their Global Implications." *American Sociological Review.* Vol. 66, No. 2 (April 2001):269–88.

YANKELOVICH, DANIEL. "How Changes in the Economy Are Reshaping American Values." In HENRY J. AARON, THOMAS E. MANN, and TIMOTHY TAYLOR, eds., *Values and Public Policy.* Washington, D.C.: Brookings Institution, 1994:20.

YATES, RONALD E. "Growing Old in Japan: They Ask Gods for a Way Out." *Philadelphia Inquirer* (August 14, 1986):3A.

YEATTS, DALE E. "Creating the High Performance Self-Managed Work Team: A Review of Theoretical Perspectives." Paper presented at the annual meeting of the Southwest Social Science Association, Dallas, February 1994.

YIN, SANDRA. "Wanted: One Million Nurses." *American Demographics.* Vol. 24, No. 8 (September 2002):63–65.

YOELS, WILLIAM C., and JEFFREY MICHAEL CLAIR. "Laughter in the Clinic: Humor in Social Organization." *Symbolic Interaction.* Vol. 18, No. 1 (1995):39–58.

YORK, RICHARD, EUGENE A. ROSA, and THOMAS DEITZ. "Bridging Environmental Science with Environmental Policy: Plasticity of Population, Affluence, and Technology." *Social Science Quarterly.* Vol. 83, No. 1 (March 2002):18–34.

YOUNG, MICHAEL. *The Rise of the Meritocracy.* London: Thames & Hudson, 1958.
———. *Society.* Vol. 31, No. 6 (September-October 1994):84–89.

YUDELMAN, MONTAGUE, and LAURA J. M. KEALY. "The Graying of Farmers." *Population Today.* Vol. 28, No. 4 (May/June, 2000):6.

ZAGORSKY, JAY. 2006. "Divorce Drops a Person's Wealth by 77 Percent." Press release (January 18). [Online] Available January 19, 2006, at http://www.eurekalert.org/pub_releases/2006-01/osu-dda011806.php

ZAKARIA, FAREED. "How to Wage the Peace." *Newsweek* (April 21, 2003):38, 48.

ZALMAN, MARVIN, and STEVEN STACK. "The Relationship between Euthanasia and Suicide in the Netherlands: A Time-Series Analysis, 1950–1990." *Social Science Quarterly.* Vol. 77, No. 3 (September 1996):576–93.

"Zandi Group Survey." *American Demographics.* Vol. 20 (March 3, 1998):38.

ZHAO, DINGXIN. "Ecologies of Social Movements: Student Mobilization during the 1989 Prodemocracy Movement in Beijing." *American Journal of Sociology.* Vol. 103, No. 6 (May 1998):1493–1529.

ZHOU, XUEGUANG, and LIREN HOU. "Children of the Cultural Revolution: The State and the Life Course in the People's Republic of China." *American Sociological Review.* Vol. 64, No. 1 (February 1999):12–36.

ZICKLIN, G. "Rebiologizing Sexual Orientation: A Critique." Paper presented at the annual meeting of the Society for the Study of Social Problems, Pittsburgh, 1992.

ZIMBARDO, PHILIP G. "Pathology of Imprisonment." *Society.* Vol. 9, No. 1 (April 1972):4–8.

ZIPP, JOHN F. "The Impact of Social Structure on Mate Selection: An Empirical Evaluation of an Active-Learning Exercise." *Teaching Sociology.* Vol. 30, No. 2 (April 2002):174–84.

ZOGBY INTERNATIONAL. Poll reported in SANDRA YIN, "Race and Politics." *American Demographics.* Vol. 23, No. 8 (August 2001):11–13.

ZUKERMAN, MORTIMER B. "The Russian Conundrum." *U.S. News & World Report* (March 13, 2006):64.

ZURCHER, LOUIS A., and DAVID A. SNOW. "Collective Behavior and Social Movements." In MORRIS ROSENBERG and RALPH H. TURNER, eds., *Social Psychology: Sociological Perspectives.* New York: Basic Books, 1981:447–82.

Invitation to Sociology

PETER L. BERGER

*In this classic essay, Peter Berger gives us a peek at the kinds
of people who become sociologists and the things that interest
them. He argues that the "fascination of sociology lies in the
fact that its perspective makes us see in a new light the very
world in which we have lived all our lives." While looking at
familiar things in an unfamiliar way is exciting, it can also
make us uncomfortable, because it calls into question our previous understandings of the world. Berger's "Invitation to
Sociology" reflects a well-known sociologist's passion for the
discipline.*

. . . The sociologist . . . is a person intensively, endlessly, shamelessly interested in the doings of men. His natural habitat is
all the human gathering places of the world, wherever men come
together. The sociologist may be interested in many other things. But
his consuming interest remains in the world of men, their institutions,
their history, their passions. And since he is interested in men, nothing
that men do can be altogether tedious for him. He will naturally be
interested in the events that engage men's ultimate beliefs, their
moments of tragedy and grandeur and ecstasy. But he will also be fascinated by the commonplace, the everyday. He will know reverence,
but this reverence will not prevent him from wanting to see and to
understand. He may sometimes feel revulsion or contempt. But this also
will not deter him from wanting to have his questions answered. The
sociologist, in his quest for understanding, moves through the world of
men without respect for the usual lines of demarcation. Nobility and

degradation, power and obscurity, intelligence and folly—these are equally *interesting* to him, however unequal they may be in his personal values or tastes. Thus his questions may lead him to all possible levels of society, the best and the least known places, the most respected and the most despised. And, if he is a good sociologist, he will find himself in all these places because his own questions have so taken possession of him that he has little choice but to seek for answers.

. . . We could say that the sociologist, but for the grace of his academic title, is the man who must listen to gossip despite himself, who is tempted to look through keyholes, to read other people's mail, to open closed cabinets. Before some otherwise unoccupied psychologist sets out now to construct an aptitude test for sociologists on the basis of sublimated voyeurism, let us quickly say that we are speaking merely by way of analogy. Perhaps some little boys consumed with curiosity to watch their maiden aunts in the bathroom later become inveterate sociologists. This is quite uninteresting. What interests us is the curiosity that grips any sociologist in front of a closed door behind which there are human voices. If he is a good sociologist, he will want to open that door, to understand these voices. Behind each closed door he will anticipate some new facet of human life not yet perceived and understood.

The sociologist will occupy himself with matters that others regard as too sacred or as too distasteful for dispassionate investigation. He will find rewarding the company of priests or of prostitutes, depending not on his personal preferences but on the questions he happens to be asking at the moment. He will also concern himself with matters that others may find much too boring. He will be interested in the human interaction that goes with warfare or with great intellectual discoveries, but also in the relations between people employed in a restaurant or between a group of little girls playing with their dolls. His main focus of attention is not the ultimate significance of what men do, but the action in itself, as another example of the infinite richness of human conduct. . . .

In these journeys through the world of men the sociologist will inevitably encounter other professional Peeping Toms. Sometimes these will resent his presence, feeling that he is poaching on their pre-serves. In some places the sociologist will meet up with the econo-mist, in others with the political scientist, in yet others with the psy-chologist or the ethnologist. Yet chances are that the questions that have brought him to these same places are different from the ones that propelled his fellow-trespassers. The sociologist's questions always remain essentially the same: "What are people doing with each other here?" "What are their relationships to each other?" "How are these relationships organized in institutions?" "What are the collective ideas that move men and institutions?" In trying to answer these questions in specific instances, the sociologist will, of course, have to deal with economic or political matters, but he will do so in a way rather different from that of the economist or the political scientist. The scene that he contemplates is the same human scene that these other scientists concern themselves with. But the sociologist's angle of vision is different. When this is understood, it becomes clear that it makes little sense to try to stake out a special enclave within which the sociologist will carry on business in his own right. . . . There is, however, one traveler whose path the sociologist will cross more often than anyone else's on his journeys. This is the historian. Indeed, as soon as the sociologist turns from the present to the past, his preoc-cupations are very hard indeed to distinguish from those of the his-torian. However, we shall leave this relationship to the later part of our considerations. Suffice it to say here that the sociological journey will be much impoverished unless it is punctuated frequently by con-versation with that other particular traveler.

Any intellectual activity derives excitement from the moment it becomes a trail of discovery. In some fields of learning this is the dis-covery of worlds previously unthought and unthinkable. . . . The excitement of sociology is usually of a different sort. Sometimes, it is true, the sociologist penetrates into worlds that had previously been quite unknown to him—for instance, the world of crime, or the world of some bizarre religious sect, or the world fashioned by the exclusive concerns of some group such as medical specialists or mil-itary leaders or advertising executives. However, much of the time the

545

sociologist moves in sectors of experience that are familiar to him and to most people in his society. He investigates communities, institutions and activities that one can read about every day in the newspapers. Yet there is another excitement of discovery beckoning in his investigations. It is not the excitement of coming upon the totally unfamiliar, but rather the excitement of finding the familiar becoming transformed in its meaning. The fascination of sociology lies in the fact that its perspective makes us see in a new light the very world in which we have lived all our lives. This also constitutes a transformation of consciousness. Moreover, this transformation is more relevant existentially than that of many other intellectual disciplines, because it is more difficult to segregate in some special compartment of the mind. The astronomer does not live in the remote galaxies, and the nuclear physicist can, outside his laboratory, eat and laugh and marry and vote without thinking about the insides of the atom. The geologist looks at rocks only at appropriate times, and the linguist speaks English with his wife. The sociologist lives in society, on the job and off it. His own life, inevitably, is part of his subject matter. Men being what they are, sociologists too manage to segregate their professional insights from their everyday affairs. But it is a rather difficult feat to perform in good faith.

The sociologist moves in the common world of men, close to what most of them would call real. The categories he employs in his analyses are only refinements of the categories by which other men live—power, class, status, race, ethnicity. As a result, there is a deceptive simplicity and obviousness about some sociological investigations. One reads them, nods at the familiar scene, remarks that one has heard all this before and don't people have better things to do than to waste their time on truisms—until one is suddenly brought up against an insight that radically questions everything one had previously assumed about this familiar scene. This is the point at which one begins to sense the excitement of sociology.

Let us take a specific example. Imagine a sociology class in a Southern college where almost all the students are white Southerners. Imagine a lecture on the subject of the racial system of the South. The lecturer is talking here of matters that have been familiar to his students from the time of their infancy. Indeed, it may be that they are much more familiar with the minutiae of this system than he is. They are quite bored as a result. It seems to them that he is only using more pretentious words to describe what they already know. Thus he may use the term "caste," only commonly used now by American sociologists to describe the Southern racial system. But in explaining the term he shifts to traditional Hindu society, to make it clearer. He then goes on to analyze the magical beliefs inherent in caste tabus, the social dynamics of commensalism and connubium, the economic interests concealed within the system, the way in which religious beliefs relate to the tabus, the effects of the caste system upon the industrial development of the society and vice versa—all in India. But suddenly India is not very far away at all. The lecture then goes back to its Southern theme. The familiar now seems not quite so familiar any more. Questions are raised that are new, perhaps raised angrily, but raised all the same. And at least some of the students have begun to understand that there are functions involved in this business of race that they have not read about in the newspapers (at least not those in their hometowns) and that their parents have not told them—partly, at least, because neither the newspapers nor the parents knew about them.

It can be said that the first wisdom of sociology is this—things are not what they seem. This too is a deceptively simple statement. It ceases to be simple after a while. Social reality turns out to have many layers of meaning. The discovery of each new layer changes the perception of the whole.

Anthropologists use the term "culture shock" to describe the impact of a totally new culture upon a newcomer. In an extreme instance such shock will be experienced by the Western explorer who is told, halfway through dinner, that he is eating the nice old lady he had been chatting with the previous day—a shock with predictable physiological if not moral consequences. Most explorers no longer encounter cannibalism in their travels today. However, the first encounters with polygamy or with puberty rites or even with the way some nations drive their automobiles can be quite a shock to an American visitor. With the shock may go not only disapproval or disgust but a sense of excitement that things can *really* be that different from what they are at home. To some extent, at least, this is the excitement of any first travel abroad. The experience of sociological discovery could be described as "culture shock" minus geographical displacement. In other words, the sociologist travels at home—with shocking results. He is unlikely to find that he is eating a nice old lady for dinner. But the discovery, for instance, that his own church has considerable money invested in the missile industry or that a few blocks from his home there are people who engage in cultic orgies may not be drastically different in emotional impact. Yet we would not want to imply that sociological discoveries are always or even usually outrageous to moral sentiment. Not at all. What they have in common with exploration in distant lands, however, is the sudden illumination of new and unsuspected facets of human existence in society. . . .

People who like to avoid shocking discoveries, who prefer to believe that society is just what they were taught in Sunday School, who like the safety of the rules and the maxims of what Alfred Schuetz has called the "world-taken-for-granted," should stay away from sociology. People who feel no temptation before closed doors, who have no curiosity about human beings, who are content to admire scenery without wondering about the people who live in those houses on the other side of that river, should probably also stay away from sociology. They will find it unpleasant or, at any rate, unrewarding. People who are interested in human beings only if they can change, convert or reform them should also be warned, for they will find sociology much less useful than they hoped. And people whose interest is mainly in their own conceptual constructions will do just as well to turn to the study of little white mice. Sociology will be satisfying, in the long run, only to those who can think of nothing more entrancing than to watch men and to understand things human.

. . . To be sure, sociology is an individual pastime in the sense that it interests some men and bores others. Some like to observe human beings, others to experiment with mice. The world is big enough to hold all kinds and there is no logical priority for one interest as against another. But the word "pastime" is weak in describing what we mean. Sociology is more like a passion. The sociological perspective is more like a demon that possesses one, that drives one compellingly, again and again, to the questions that are its own. An introduction to sociology is, therefore, an invitation to a very special kind of passion. . . .

◉ ◉ ◉

Questions

1. According to Berger, what is the role of curiosity in sociological studies?

2. What do sociologists study?

3. Why did Berger argue that sociology can be dangerous? If sociology can be viewed as dangerous, to what extent might sociologists also be viewed as dangerous?

4. What does Berger mean when he says that "things are not what they seem. . . . Social reality turns out to have many layers of meaning. The discovery of each new layer changes the perception of the whole." Provide an example to illustrate Berger's statement.

Teenage Wasteland

DONNA GAINES

The power of the sociological imagination lies in showing that even the most personal decision people might make have social causes. In this article, Donna Gaines explains how the 1987 suicide of four teenagers in Bergenfield, New Jersey, is the result of a society that provides many working-class young men and women with little meaning and little opportunity.

. . .

In Bergenfield, New Jersey, on the morning of March 11, 1987, the bodies of four teenagers were discovered inside a 1977 rust-colored Chevrolet Camaro. The car, which belonged to Thomas Olton, was parked in an unused garage in the Foster Village garden apartment complex, behind the Foster Village Shopping Center. Two sisters, Lisa and Cheryl Burress, and their friends, Thomas Rizzo and Thomas Olton, had died of carbon monoxide poisoning.

Lisa was sixteen, Cheryl was seventeen, and the boys were nineteen—they were suburban teens, turnpike kids like the ones in the town I live in. And thinking about them made me remember how it felt being a teenager too. I was horrified that it had come to this. I believed I understood why they did it, although it wasn't a feeling I could have put into words.

You could tell from the newspapers that they were rock and roll kids. The police had found a cassette tape cover of AC/DC's *If You Want Blood, You've Got It* near the bodies. Their friends were described as kids who listened to thrash metal, had shaggy haircuts, wore lots of black and leather. "Dropouts," "druggies," the papers called them. Teenage suburban rockers whose lives revolved around their favorite

---

bands and their friends. Youths who barely got by in school and at home and who did not impress authority figures in any remarkable way. Except as fuck-ups.

My friends, most of whom were born in the 1950s, felt the same way about the kids everyone called "burnouts." On the weekend following the suicides, a friend's band, the Grinders, were playing at My Father's Place, a Long Island club. That night the guys dedicated a song, "The Kids in the Basement," to the four teens from Bergenfield—"This is for the suicide kids." In the weeks following the suicide pact, a number of bands in the tri-state area also dedicated songs to them. Their deaths had hit close to home. . . .

By the beginning of the 1980s, . . . I went back to school. I spent the next few years working on a doctorate in sociology, commuting a few days a week from my neighborhood to the State University of New York at Stony Brook, teaching, doing consulting work, and freelancing as a journalist. In my free time I stayed involved with the Grinders, but was now also interested in the West Coast–based hardcore bands like Black Flag, MDC, and Flipper. By 1987, the young people in my life were either my students, my neighbors, or people I met at shows.

A week or two after the suicide pact, *The Village* Voice assigned me to go to Bergenfield. . . . [My editor] knew my background—that I knew suburbia, that I could talk to kids. By now I fully embraced the sociologist's ethical commitment to the "rights of the researched," and the social worker's vow of client confidentiality. As far as suicidal teenagers were concerned, I felt that if I couldn't help them, I didn't want to bother them.

But I was really pissed off at what I kept reading. How people in Bergenfield openly referred to the four kids as "troubled losers." Even after they were dead, nobody cut them any slack. "Burnouts," "druggies," "dropouts." Something was wrong. So I took the opportunity.

From the beginning, I believed that the Bergenfield suicides symbolized a tragic defeat for young people. Something was happening in the larger society that was not yet comprehended. Scholars spoke ominously of "the postmodern condition," "societal upheaval," "decay," "anomie." Meanwhile, American kids kept losing ground, showing all the symptoms of societal neglect. Many were left to fend for themselves, often with little success. The news got worse. Teenage suicides continued, and still nobody seemed to be getting the point.

Now, in trying to understand this event, I might have continued working within the established discourse on teenage suicide. I might have carried on the tradition of obscuring the bigger picture, psychologizing the Bergenfield suicide pact, interviewing the parents of the four youths, hounding their friends for the gory details. I might have spent my time probing school records, tracking down their teachers and shrinks for insights, focusing on their personal histories and intimate relationships. I might have searched out the individual motivations behind the words left in the note written and signed by each youth on the brown paper bag found with their bodies on March 11. But I did not.

Because the world has changed for today's kids. We also engaged in activities that adults called self-destructive. But for my generation, "doing it" meant having sex; for them, it means committing suicide.

"Teenage suicide" was a virtually nonexistent category prior to 1960. But between 1950 and 1980 it nearly tripled, and at the time of the Bergenfield suicide pact it was the second leading cause of death among America's young people; "accidents" were the first. The actual suicide rate among people aged fifteen to twenty-four—the statistical category for teenage suicide—is estimated to be even higher, underreported because of social stigma. Then there are the murky numbers derived from drug overdoses and car crashes, recorded as accidents. To date, there are more than 5,000 teen suicides annually, accounting for 12 percent of youth mortalities. An estimated 400,000 adolescents attempt suicide each year. While youth suicide rates leveled off by 1980, by mid-decade they began to increase again. Although they remained lower than adult suicide rates, the acceleration at which youth suicide rates increased was alarming. By 1987, we had books and articles detailing "copycat" and "cluster" suicides. Teenage suicide was now described as an epidemic.

Authors, experts, and scholars compiled the lists of kids' names, ages, dates, and possible motives. They generated predictive models: Rural and suburban white kids do it more often. Black kids in

America's urban teenage wastelands are more likely to kill each other. Increasingly, alcohol and drugs are involved. In some cases adults have tried to identify the instigating factor as a lyric or a song—Judas Priest, Ozzy Osbourne. Or else a popular film about the subject—the suicide of a celebrity; too much media attention or not enough.

Some kids do it violently: drowning, hanging, slashing, jumping, or crashing. Firearms are still the most popular. Others prefer to go out more peacefully, by gas or drug overdose. Boys do it more than girls, though girls try it more often than boys. And it does not seem to matter if kids are rich or poor.

Throughout the 1980s, teenage suicide clusters appeared across the country—six or seven deaths, sometimes more, in a short period of time in a single community. In the boomtown of Plano, Texas. The fading factory town of Leominster, Massachusetts. At Bryan High School in a white, working-class suburb of Omaha, Nebraska. A series of domino suicides among Arapaho Indian youths at the Wind River Reservation in Wyoming. Six youth suicides in the county of Westchester, New York, in 1984; five in 1985 and seven in 1986.

Sometimes they were close friends who died together in pacts of two. In other cases, one followed shortly after the other, unable to survive apart. Then there were strangers who died alone, in separate incidents timed closely together.

The Bergenfield suicide pact of March 11 was alternately termed a "multiple-death pact," a "quadruple suicide," or simply a "pact," depending on where you read about it. Some people actually called it a *mass* suicide because the Bergenfield case reminded them of Jonestown, Guyana, in 1978, where over nine hundred followers of Jim Jones poisoned themselves, fearing their community would be destroyed.

As experts speculated over the deaths in Bergenfield, none could recall a teenage suicide pact involving four people dying together; *it was historically unique.*

I wondered, did the "burnouts" see themselves as a community under siege? . . . Were the "burnouts" of Bergenfield choosing death over surrender? Surrender to what? Were they martyrs? If so, what was their common cause?

553

Because the suicide pact was a *collective* act, it warrants a social explanation—a portrait of the "burnouts" in Bergenfield as actors within a particular social landscape.

For a long time now, the discourse of teenage suicide has been dominated by atomizing psychological and medical models. And so the larger picture of American youth as members of a distinctive generation with a unique collective biography, emerging at a particular moment in history, has been lost.

The starting-off point for this [analysis] then, is a teenage suicide pact in an "upper-poor" white ethnic suburb in northern New Jersey. But, of course, the story did not begin and will not end in Bergenfield. . . .

This was a suicide pact that involved close friends who were by no accounts obsessed, star-crossed lovers. What would make four people want to die together? Why would they ask, in their collective suicide note, to be waked and buried together? Were they part of a suicide cult?

If not, what was the nature of the *social* bond that tied them so closely? What could be so intimately binding that in the early morning hours of March 11 not one of them could stop, step back from the pact they had made to say, "Wait, I can't do this"? Who were these kids that everybody called "burnouts"? . . .

From the beginning, I decided I didn't want to dwell too much on the negatives. I wanted to understand how alienated kids survived, as well as how they were defeated. How did they maintain their humanity against what I now felt were impossible odds? I wondered. What keeps young people together when the world they are told to trust no longer seems to work? What motivates them to be decent human beings when nobody seems to respect them or take them seriously? . . .

Somewhat like a nervous breakdown, burnout involves a change in your ability to function, to "perform." You numb out, hoping to lower anxiety by shutting down, denying access to your feelings. The body, the organism, is overwhelmed. Burnout is a way of slipping out the back door with your body still present. You can still go through the motions of living, but you feel dead.

The burned-out individual protects the self for the moment, but in the long run the self is estranged. The ability to relate in any way at all is compromised. You are living at half speed in a world you cannot handle—shut down, tuned out; you're gone.

This estrangement from feeling, this disowning and disengaging from feeling, is a form of *alienation*. According to Marx, in the process of laboring, human beings enjoy the creative activity of transforming the world. If the product of this pleasure is taken from you, alienated (as in the process of capitalist production), you experience deep loss. You become detached from your world because your connection to that world, your power to create and transform in that world *through your own efforts*, has been taken from you. So you are living in the world in a state of detachedness; you no longer feel viable.

Powerless, useless, ineffectual, you are only remotely connected to life around you. The most you can hope for is to get through the day—at home, at work, in school. Drugs and alcohol will help to kill the pain, protect you from things that would, if fully perceived, drive you crazy. But then you have to deal with the secondary effects of your anodyne solution. Either way, you know you're not well.

It is not surprising that the Alcoholics Anonymous doctrine advises never to let yourself get too hungry, too tired, or too lonely. Being emotionally strung out often leads to desperate self-medicating. The active alcoholic, overworked professional, and emotionally overwhelmed kid all appear to be wasted. Often, they are. Whether stressful life experiences or excessive drug taking has wasted you is unimportant—a burned-out soul feels empty, the spirit seems depleted.

For a bored, ignored, lonely kid, drug oblivion may offer immediate comfort; purpose and adventure in the place of everyday ennui. But soon it has a life of its own—at a psychic and a social level, the focus of your life becomes *getting high* (or *well* as some people describe it). Ironically, the whole miserable process often begins as a positive act of self-preservation. . . .

So they end up stranded in teenage wasteland. They devote their lives to their bands, to their friends, to partying; they live in the moment. They're going down in flames, taking literally the notion that "rust never sleeps," that it is "better to burn out than fade away."

Such wasted suburban kids are typically not politically "correct," nor do they constitute an identifiable segment of the industrial working class. They are not members of a specific racial or ethnic minority.

Small in numbers, isolated in decaying suburbs, they aren't visible on any national scale until they are involved in something that really horrifies us, like a suicide pact, or parricide, or incest, or "satanic" sacrifice. For the most part, burnouts and dirtbags are anomic small town white boys and girls, just trying to get through the day. Their way of fighting back is to have enough fun to kill themselves before everything else does.

☻ ☻ ☻

Critical-Thinking Questions

1. What is it about the society in which the four young people lived that contributed to their suicide?

2. Do you think teen suicide is an issue all across the United States? Explain your view.

3. What might be done to prevent deaths like this?

Women and the Birth of Sociology

Patricia Madoo Lengermann
Jill Niebrugge-Brantley

Most beginning students of sociology know about Karl Marx, Max Weber, and Emile Durkheim; but Harriet Martineau, Ida Wells-Barnett, Anna Julia Cooper, Charlotte Perkins Gilman, and other women were also important founders of the discipline.

. . .

The history of sociology's theories is conventionally told as a history of white male agency—an account of the theoretical contributions of a "founding" generation of men, Auguste Comte, Herbert Spencer, and Karl Marx, writing in the middle of the nineteenth century, expanded by a second, "classic" generation of men, Emile Durkheim, Max Weber, Georg Simmel, George Herbert Mead, and Robert E. Park, who wrote between 1890 and 1930. This history is presented as an account of the natural way things occurred, a chronicle beyond the powers of human tellers to change. In contrast, we portray this history as a social construction arising out of the discipline's power arrangements, and like all histories, reflecting an ongoing conflict between exclusionary and inclusionary values and practices (Becker, 1971; Lemert, 1995; D. Smith, 1987). . . .

The claim that a group has been "written out" of history is different from the claim that a group has been "invisible." "Invisibility" sug-

Reprinted from *The Women Founders: Sociology and Theory, 1830–1930* (1998), McGraw–Hill Companies.

gests not being seen, that is, never having one's presence acknowledged as significant—a concept applied by many African Americans to their experience of marginalization (e.g., Collins, 1990; Cooper, 1892; Du Bois, 1903; Ellison, 1952; Lorde, 1984; Rollins, 1985). "Being written out" suggests having once been seen as a presence in a community and then having been erased from its record. For several reasons, the case of the fifteen women sociologists treated in this volume is an instance of erasure rather than invisibility. First, almost all these women were well-known public figures in their lifetime, larger than the fledgling discipline of sociology they helped create; like the work of Marx, Max Weber, or Durkheim, their work has relevance for all the social sciences. Second, they created social theory and did sociology in the same times and places as the male founders (see Figure 1). Third, they were widely recognized by their contemporaries, including male sociologists, as significant social analysts. Fourth, they all acted as members of a sociological community, meeting at least one of the following criteria: employment as a sociologist, membership in a national sociological association, publication framed by an explicit concern with sociological principles, self-identification as a sociologist and recognition by contemporaries as a sociologist (Käsler, 1981; Deegan, 1991). We introduce some of the evidence for these claims in the brief descriptions of the women that follow. . . .

Martineau—whose *Illustrations of Political Economy* (1832–1834) outsold even Charles Dickens (Hoecker-Drysdale 1992)—was Britain's preeminent woman of letters until her death, writing social analysis, journalism, history, novels, children's stories, and travel books. Long identified in the history of sociology for her 1853 translation and abridgement of Comte, she was herself writing sociology as early as 1834, drafting what would become the first major statement of method, *How to Observe Morals and Manners* (1838b) and testing her methodology in her classic study *Society in America* (1836). Addams was the founder of Hull-House, the famous Chicago social settlement; a major spokesperson for Progressive reform on behalf of immigrants, trade unions, women, children, working-class people, and African Americans; and consistently named in public

558

FIGURE 1   Lifelines of Women and Men Founders of Sociology

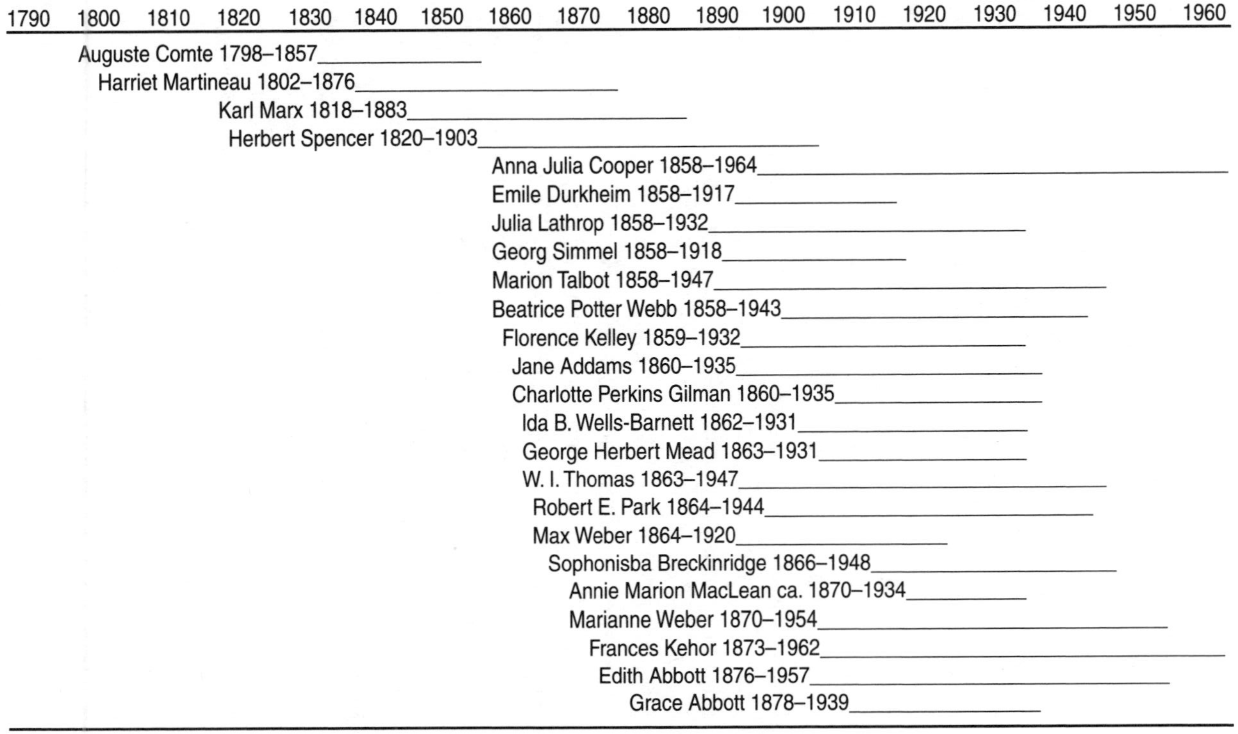

1790	1800	1810	1820	1830	1840	1850	1860	1870	1880	1890	1900	1910	1920	1930	1940	1950	1960

Auguste Comte 1798–1857

Harriet Martineau 1802–1876

Karl Marx 1818–1883

Herbert Spencer 1820–1903

Anna Julia Cooper 1858–1964

Emile Durkheim 1858–1917

Julia Lathrop 1858–1932

Georg Simmel 1858–1918

Marion Talbot 1858–1947

Beatrice Potter Webb 1858–1943

Florence Kelley 1859–1932

Jane Addams 1860–1935

Charlotte Perkins Gilman 1860–1935

Ida B. Wells-Barnett 1862–1931

George Herbert Mead 1863–1931

W. I. Thomas 1863–1947

Robert E. Park 1864–1944

Max Weber 1864–1920

Sophonisba Breckinridge 1866–1948

Annie Marion MacLean ca. 1870–1934

Marianne Weber 1870–1954

Frances Kehor 1873–1962

Edith Abbott 1876–1957

Grace Abbott 1878–1939

559

opinion polls as one of the most admired Americans (Davis, 1973; Daniel Levine, 1971). At Hull-House, she administered a major research institution, drawing on her experiences there to formulate a social theory in eight major books and some 200 articles. She self-identified as a sociologist; taught sociology; was a member of the American Sociological Society (ASS)—until 1959 the name of the American Sociological Association (ASA); published in the *American Journal of Sociology (AJS)*; and had significant relationships with Mead, Park, W. I. Thomas, Albion Small, and Ernest Burgess (Deegan, 1988). Gilman was widely regarded as the leading feminist intellectual of her day. *Her Women and Economics* (1898) went through nine printings by 1920, was translated into seven languages, and was the bible of many women's college student bodies (Ceplair, 1991). Besides the classic feminist novella *The Yellow Wallpaper* (1892) and some 2,000 pieces of journalism, poetry, and prose, she wrote six significant works of formal social theory, including *Women and Economics, Human Work* (1904), and *The Man-Made World* (1911). She also published in the *AJS*, was a member of the ASS, and maintained intellectual relationships with Lester Ward and E. A. Ross.

Wells-Barnett spearheaded national and international anti-lynching campaigns, writing major analyses of lynching—*Southern Horrors* (1892) and A Red Record (1895)—and carrying the battle to Britain, where she often spoke to crowds in the thousands. She was an active organizer for African American civil rights, helping to found the National Association for the Advancement of Colored People (NAACP). Cooper's major book *A Voice from the South* (1892) received superlative reviews from black and white publications alike, establishing her as a prominent intellectual and spokesperson for African American women; she was one of two women to address the world's first Pan-African Conference in London in 1900. Cooper and Wells-Barnett created a genuine American non-Marxian conflict theory in which they spoke of the sociological framing of their argument; but American racism made tentative any relationship between them and white professional sociology, although both knew and worked with black sociologist W. E. B. Du Bois. Marianne Weber lived at the center of German sociological circles and debated the ideas of both Simmel and her husband Max in her own writings. She was a leading figure in the German feminist movement, the first woman to be elected to a German parliament, and the author of nine books of social analysis and sociology including her monumental work on the legal position of women, *Ehefrau und Mutter in der Rechtsentwicklung* (*Marriage, Motherhood, and the Law*) (1907), and her collected essays, *Frauenfragen und Frauengedanken* (*Reflections on Women and Women's Issues*) (1919). She secured Max's position within sociology after his death by editing and publishing ten volumes of his work and writing her important interpretive biography of him.

Webb was tutored by Spencer, self-identified as a sociologist, taught sociology, worked as a social investigator on the major empirical study of her age (Charles Booth's *Life and Labour of the People of London*), and did her own independent investigations, leading to the socialist reform classic *The Co-operative Movement in Great Britain* (1891). With her husband Sidney, she researched and co-authored eleven voluminous works of empirical sociology that formed the blueprint for the British welfare state. All the members of the Chicago Women's School of Sociology (hereafter referred to as the Chicago Women's School or the Chicago Women) wrote prolifically as social analysis, all publishing in the *AJS*. Many were prominent public figures: Kelley headed the National Consumers' League (1899–1932); Lathrop (1912–20), and then Grace Abbott (1920–34), served as chief of the Children's Bureau, the highest-ranking woman in the federal government at that time; Edith Abbott and Breckinridge founded the University of Chicago's School of Social Service Administration (1922); Talbot was dean of women at the University of Chicago (1893–1925); Kellor was a founder and executive officer of the American Arbitration League (1926–53). Kelley knew Friedrich Engels, maintained a correspondence with him until his death, and did the first English translation of *The Condition of the Working Class in England in 1844*: MacLean studied with Small, Mead, and Charles Henderson; Kellor also studied with Henderson; Edith Abbott, Grace Abbott, and Breckinridge are all referenced in Park and Burgess's

Introduction to the Science of Sociology; Talbot served as an associate editor of the *AJS* from its founding by Small to her retirement in 1925.

These women knew each other or each other's work. Gilman, Webb, Weber, and Wells-Barnett all visited Hull-House, which was, of course, the working base for Addams and most of the Chicago Women. Many of them read Gilman's *Women and Economics*—Webb, Weber, Addams, Kelley, Lathrop, and Talbot. Addams published with Wells-Barnett on lynching on at least two occasions, one of which was in a remarkable issue of *Survey* in February of 1913 in which Addams, Wells-Barnett, Breckinridge, and Du Bois all analyze the problem of race.[1] Addams, Wells-Barnett, Kelley, and Breckinridge participated in the founding of the NAACP. Hull-House residents, including Addams, Lathrop, and Kelley, used Webb's *The Co-operative Movement in Great Britain* in preparation for their own venture into cooperative housing for working women. The persons most outside this network are Martineau, a full generation earlier than the rest of the women, and Cooper, whose life course rarely took her to Chicago. Yet Edith Abbott knew and responded to Martineau's work on women's employment in America, and Gilman refers to Martineau's struggle to overcome gender barriers to her career as a social analyst. And Cooper spoke in Chicago in 1893 at the white feminist Women's Congress, was active, as was Wells-Barnett, in the National Federation of Colored Women's Clubs and the African American settlement house movement, and wrote a sympathetic response to Gilman's suicide.

These women knew that they were part of a larger movement to create a science of society and had their own sense of what that science should be: a project of social critique in which research and theory had as a morally necessary focus the description, analysis, and correction of social inequality. The women vary in terms of the particular inequality focused on—gender, class, race, ethnicity, age, or combinations thereof; the relative balance between research and theory, and the choice of research strategy and theoretical method. Working out this commitment to critical social theory, these women engaged with sociology and the sociological community at the moment in which the discipline was itself emerging. Their varying relationships to that community thus reflect both the instability of sociology's emerging identity and the effects of gender, class, and race on access to what would become a formal academic enterprise, the province of educated white men. But at the moment these women were writing, sociology was as much their intellectual project as the men's; it is only in the retelling that they have disappeared.

Note

[1]The *Survey* was a magazine founded in the merger of several social work journals; it was edited by Paul U. Kellogg, and Addams served on its editorial board. This magazine served as a major vehicle for social reformers who saw themselves as engaged in sociology. It also offered a more popular version, *Survey Graphic*, because its editorial board took communication with a general public as a primary duty.

References

Becker, Ernest. 1971. *The Lost Science of Man*. New York: Braziller.

Ceplair, Larry (ed.). 1991. *Charlotte Perkins Gilman: A Non-Fiction Reader*. New York: Columbia University Press.

Collins, Randall. 1975. *Conflict Sociology*. New York: Academic Press.

Cooper, Anna Julia. 1892. *A Voice from the South by a Black Woman from the South*. Xenia, OH: Aldine Press.

Davis, Allen F. 1973. *American Heroine*. New York: Oxford University Press.

Deegan, Mary Jo. 1988. *Jane Addams and the Men of the Chicago School, 1892–1918*. New Brunswick, N.J. Transaction Books.

——— (ed.). 1991. *Women in Sociology: A Bio-Bibliographical Sourcebook*. Westport, CT: Greenwood Press.

Du Bois, W. E. B. 1903/1989. *The Souls of Black Folks*. New York: Bantam.

Ellison, Ralph. 1952/1972. *Invisible Man*. New York: Vintage Books.

Gilman, Charlotte Perkins. 1892/1973. *The Yellow Wallpaper 1892–1973*. New York: Feminist Press.

———. 1898. *Women and Economics*. Boston: Small and Maynard.

———. 1904. *Human Work*. New York: McClure and Phillips.

———. 1911. *The Man-Made World, or Our Androcentric Culture*. New York. Charlton Company.

Hoecker-Drysdale, Susan. 1992. *Harriet Martineau: First Woman Sociologist*. Oxford, England: Berg Publishers, Inc.

Käsler, Dirk. 1981. "Methodological Problems of a Sociological History of Early German Sociology." Paper presented at the Department of Education, University of Chicago, November 5.

Lemert, Charles. 1995. *Sociology after the Crisis*. Boulder, CO: Westview Press.

Levine, Daniel. 1971. *Jane Addams and the Liberal Tradition*. Madison: State Historical Society of Wisconsin.

Lorde, Audre. 1984. *Sister Outsider*. Trumansburg, NY: Crossings Press.

Martineu, Harriet. 1832–34. *Illustrations of Political Economy*. 9 vols. London: Charles Fox.

———. 1836/1837. *Society in America*. 2 vols. New York: Saunders and Otley.

———. 1838b. *How to Observe Morals and Manners*. London: Charles Knight and Company.

Rollins, Judith. 1985. *Between Women: Domestics and Their Employers*. Philadelphia: Temple University Press.

Smith, Dorothy E. 1979. "A Sociology for Women." In *The Prism of Sex: Essays in the Sociology of Knowledge*, ed. J. A. Sherman and E. T. Beck, pp. 135–87. Madison: University of Wisconsin Press.

———. 1987. *The Everyday World as Problematic: A Feminist Sociology*. Boston: Northeastern University Press.

Weber, Marianne. 1907. *Ehefrau und Mutter in der Rechtsentwicklung*. Tübingen: J. C. B. Mohr.

———. 1919. *Frauenfragen und Frauengedanken*, Tübingen: J. C. B. Mohr.

Wells-Barnett, Ida B. 1892/1969. *Southern Horrors*. Reprinted in *On Lynchings*, New York: Arno.

———. 1895. *A Red Record*. Chicago: Donohue and Henneberry.

☻ ☻ ☻

Critical-Thinking Questions

1. What does it mean to say that women have been "written out" of sociology's history? Why did this happen?

2. What issues or ideas did sociology's women founders have in common?

3. What is the importance today of recognizing the contributions of sociology's women founders?

The Importance of Social Research

Earl Babbie

How do we know what we know? Tradition, religion, laws, the media, personal experiences, and people in authority shape our everyday beliefs and behaviors. In this selection, Earl Babbie argues that social problems such as poverty could be diminished if policymakers and the general public based their responses on rigorous social science research results rather than on emotions and stereotypes.

. . .

We can't solve our social problems until we understand how they come about, persist. Social science research offers a way to examine and understand the operation of human social affairs. It provides points of view and technical procedures that uncover things that would otherwise escape our awareness. Often, as the cliché goes, things are not what they seem; social science research can make that clear. One example illustrates this fact.

Poverty is a persistent problem in the United States, and none of its intended solutions is more controversial than *welfare*. Although the program is intended to give the poor a helping hand while they reestablish their financial viability, many complain that it has the opposite effect.

Part of the public image of welfare in action was crystallized by Susan Sheehan (1976) in her book, *A Welfare Mother*, which describes

Reprinted from *Practice of Social Research*, Eighth Edition (1998), Cengage Learning.

the situation of a three-generation welfare family, suggesting that the welfare system trapped the poor rather than liberat[ed] them. Martin Anderson (1978:56) agreed with Sheehan's assessment and charged that the welfare system had established a caste system in America, "perhaps as much as one-tenth of this nation—a caste of people almost totally dependent on the state, with little hope or prospect of breaking free. Perhaps we should call them the Dependent Americans."

George Gilder (1990) has spoken for many who believe the poor are poor mainly because they refuse to work, saying the welfare system saps their incentive to take care of themselves. Ralph Segalman and David Marsland (1989:6–7) support the view that welfare has become an intergenerational way of life for the poor in welfare systems around the world. Children raised in welfare families, they assert, will likely live their adult lives on welfare:

> This conflict between the intent of welfare as a temporary aid (as so understood by most of the public) and welfare as a permanent right (as understood by the welfare bureaucracy and welfare state planners) has serious implications. The welfare state nations, by and large, have given up on the concept of client rehabilitation for self-sufficiency, an intent originally supported by most welfare state proponents. What was to have been a temporary condition has become a permanent cost on the welfare state. As a result, welfare discourages productivity and self-sufficiency and establishes a new mode of approved behaviour in the society—one of acceptance of dependency as the norm.

These negative views of the effects of the welfare system are widely shared by the general public, even among those basically sympathetic to the aims of the program. Greg Duncan (1984: 2–3) at the University of Michigan's Survey Research Center points out that census data would seem to confirm the impression that a hard core of the poor have become trapped in their poverty. Speaking of the percentage of the population living in poverty at any given time, he says,

Year-to-year changes in these fractions are typically less than 1 percent, and the Census survey's other measures show little change in the characteristic of the poor from one year to the next. They have shown repeatedly that the individuals who are poor are more likely to be in families headed by a woman, by someone with low education, and by blacks.

Evidence that one-eighth of the population was poor in two consecutive years, and that those poor shared similar characteristics, is consistent with an inference of absolutely no turnover in the poverty population. Moreover, the evidence seems to fit the stereotype that those families that are poor are likely to remain poor, and that there is a hard-core population of poor families for whom there is little hope of self-improvement.

Duncan continues, however, to warn that such snapshots of the population can conceal changes taking place. Specifically, an unchanging percentage of the population living in poverty does not necessarily mean the *same* families are poor from year to year. Theoretically, it could be a totally different set of families each year.

To determine the real nature of poverty and welfare, the University of Michigan undertook a "Panel Study of Income Dynamics" in which they followed the economic fate of 5,000 families from 1969 to 1978, or ten years, the period supposedly typified by Sheehan's "welfare mother." At the beginning, the researchers found that in 1978, 8.1 percent of these families were receiving some welfare benefits and 3.5 percent depended on welfare for more than half their income. Moreover, these percentages did not differ drastically over the ten-year period (Duncan 1984:75).

Looking beyond these surface data, however, the researchers found something you might not have expected. During the ten-year period, about one-fourth of the 5,000 families received welfare benefits at least once. However, only 8.7 percent of the families were ever dependent on welfare for more than half their income. *"Only a little over one-half of the individuals living in poverty in one year are found to be poor in the next, and considerably less than one-half of those who expe-*

rience poverty remain persistently poor over many years" (Duncan 1984:3; emphasis original).

Only 2 percent of the families received welfare each of the ten years, and less than 1 percent were continuously dependent on welfare for the ten years. Table 1 summarizes these findings.

These data paint a much different picture of poverty than people commonly assume. In a summary of his findings, Duncan (1984:4–5) says:

> While nearly one-quarter of the population received income from welfare sources at least once in the decade, only about 2 percent of all the population could be characterized as dependent upon this income for extended periods of time. Many families receiving welfare benefits at any given time were in the early stages of recovering from an economic crisis caused by the death, departure, or disability of a husband, a recovery that often lifted them out of welfare when they found full-time employment, or remarried, or both. Furthermore, most of the children raised in welfare families did not themselves receive welfare benefits after they left home and formed their own households.

TABLE 1   Incidence of Short- and Long-Run Welfare Receipt and Dependence, 1969–1978

	Percent of U.S. Population:	
	Receiving Any Welfare Income	*Dependent on Welfare for More than 50% of Family Income*
Welfare in 1978	8.1%	3.5%
Welfare in 1 or more years, 1969–78	25.2	8.7
Welfare in 5 or more years, 1969–78	8.3	3.5
Welfare in all 10 years, 1969–78	2.0	0.7
"Persistent welfare" (welfare in 8 or more years), 1969–78	4.4	2.0

Source: Greg J. Duncan, *Years of Poverty, Years of Plenty: The Changing Fortunes of American Workers and Families* (Ann Arbor: University of Michigan, 1984), 75.

Many of the things social scientists study—including [the issue of welfare] you've just read about—generate deep emotions and firm convictions in most people. This makes effective inquiry into the facts difficult at best; all too often, researchers manage only to confirm their initial prejudices. The special value of social science research methods is that they offer a way to address such issues with logical and observational rigor. They let us all pierce through our personal viewpoints and take a look at the world that lies beyond our own perspectives. And it is that "world beyond" that holds the solutions to the social problems we face today.

At a time of increased depression and disillusionment, we are continually tempted to turn away from confronting social problems and retreat into the concerns of our own self-interest. Social science research offers an opportunity to take on those problems and discover the experience of making a difference after all. The choice is yours; I invite you to take on the challenge.

References

Anderson, Martin. 1978. *Welfare: The political economy of welfare reform in the United States*. Stanford, Calif.: Hoover Institution Press.

Duncan, Greg J., with Richard D. Coe, et al. 1984. *Years of poverty, years of plenty: The changing fortunes of American workers and families*. Ann Arbor: Survey Research Center Institute.

Gilder, George. 1990. The nature of poverty. In *The American polity reader*, eds. A. Serow, W. Shannon, and E. Ladd, 658–63. New York: Norton.

Segalman, Ralph, and David Marsland. 1989. *Cradle to grave: Comparative perspectives on the state of welfare*. New York: St. Martin's Press.

Sheehan, Susan. 1976. *A welfare mother*. New York: Mentor.

☻ ☻ ☻

Critical-Thinking Questions

1. What does Babbie mean when he says that "things are not what they seem" when we read about controversial issues such as welfare?

2. Many people believe that welfare has become an intergenerational way of life. What data does Babbie present that challenge such beliefs?

3. In the classic selection ("The Case for Value-Free Sociology"), Max Weber asserts, "The primary task of a useful teacher is to teach [her/his] students to recognize 'inconvenient' facts—I mean facts that are inconvenient for their party opinions." Do you think some instructors (and students) feel pressure to conform to approved points of view, whether religious or political? Should faculty and students ignore research findings that contradict such perspectives?

Cultural Obsessions with Thinness: African American, Latina, and White Women

BECKY W. THOMPSON

According to the American Anorexia/Bulimia Association, 7 million women and 1 million men, ages ten to early twenties, suffer from eating disorders. An estimated 1,000 women die from anorexia every year. From an early age, girls are bombarded with messages that being thin will make them popular and happy and will attract a successful man. In this selection, Becky W. Thompson challenges the widely accepted belief that eating problems are largely limited to white, middle- and upper-class, heterosexual women. Instead of assuming that women are anorexic and bulimic because we live in a "culture of thinness," Thompson argues, eating problems may also be a response to poverty, sexual abuse, racism, heterosexism, social class inequality, and acculturation.

Reprinted from *Race, Class & Gender: Common Bonds, Different Voices*, edited by Esther Ngan-Ling Chow, Doris Wilkinson, and Maxine Baca-Zinn (1996), Sage Publications, Inc.

. . .

◉ Existing Research on Eating Problems

There are three theoretical models used to explain the epidemiology, etiology, and treatment of eating problems. The biomedical model offers important scientific research about possible physiological causes of eating problems and the physiological dangers of purging and starvation (Copeland, 1985; Spack, 1985). However, this model adopts medical treatment strategies that may disempower and traumatize women (Garner, 1985; Orbach, 1985). In addition, this model ignores many social, historical, and cultural factors that influence women's eating patterns. The psychological model identifies eating problems as "multidimensional disorders" that are influenced by biological, psychological, and cultural factors (Garfinkel & Garner, 1982). While useful in its exploration of effective therapeutic treatments, this model, like the biomedical one, tends to neglect women of color, lesbians, and working-class women.

The third model, offered by feminists, asserts that eating problems are gendered. This model explains why the vast majority of people with eating problems are women, how gender socialization and sexism may relate to eating problems, and how masculine models of psychological development have shaped theoretical interpretations. Feminists offer the *culture of thinness model* as a key reason why eating problems predominate among women. According to this model, thinness is a culturally, socially, and economically enforced requirement for female beauty. This imperative makes women vulnerable to cycles of dieting, weight loss, and subsequent weight gain, which may lead to anorexia nervosa and bulimia (Chernin, 1981; Orbach, 1978, 1985; Smead, 1984).

Feminists have rescued eating problems from the realm of individual psychopathology by showing how the difficulties are rooted in systematic and pervasive attempts to control women's body sizes and appetites. However, researchers have yet to give significant attention to how race, class, and sexuality influence women's understanding of their bodies and appetites. The handful of epidemiological studies that include African American women and Latinas casts doubt on the accuracy of the normative epidemiological portrait. The studies suggest that this portrait reflects which particular populations of women have been studied rather than actual prevalence (Anderson & Hay, 1985; Gray, Ford, & Kelly, 1987; Hsu, 1987; Nevo, 1985; Silber, 1986).

More important, this research shows that bias in research has consequences for women of color. Tomas Silber (1986) asserts that many well-trained professionals have either misdiagnosed or delayed their diagnoses of eating problems among African American and Latina women due to stereotypical thinking that these problems are restricted to white women. As a consequence, when African American women or Latinas are diagnosed, their eating problems tend to be more severe due to extended processes of starvation prior to intervention. In her autobiographical account of her eating problems, Retha Powers (1989), an African American woman, describes being told not to worry about her eating problems since "fat is more acceptable in the Black community" (p. 78). Stereotypical perceptions held by her peers and teachers of the "maternal Black woman" and the "persistent mammy–brickhouse Black woman image" (p. 134) made it difficult for Powers to find people who took her problems with food seriously.

Recent work by African American women reveals that eating problems often relate to women's struggles against a "simultaneity of oppressions" (Clarke, 1982; Naylor, 1985; White, 1991). Byllye Avery (1990), the founder of the National Black Women's Health Project, links the origins of eating problems among African American women to the daily stress of being undervalued and overburdened at home and at work. In Evelyn C. White's (1990) anthology, *The Black Woman's Health Book: Speaking for Ourselves,* Georgiana Arnold (1990) links her eating problems partly to racism and racial isolation during childhood.

Recent feminist research also identifies factors that are related to eating problems among lesbians (Brown, 1987; Dworkin, 1989;

Iazzetto, 1989; Schoenfielder & Wieser, 1983). In her clinical work, Brown (1987) found that lesbians who have internalized a high degree of homophobia are more likely to accept negative attitudes about fat than are lesbians who have examined their internalized homophobia. Autobiographical accounts by lesbians have also indicated that secrecy about eating problems among lesbians partly reflects their fear of being associated with a stigmatized illness ("What's Important," 1988).

Attention to African American women, Latinas, and lesbians paves the way for further research that explores the possible interface between facing multiple oppressions and the development of eating problems. In this way, this study is part of a larger feminist and sociological research agenda that seeks to understand how race, class, gender, nationality, and sexuality inform women's experiences and influence theory production.

❂ Methodology

I conducted eighteen life history interviews and administered lengthy questionnaires to explore eating problems among African American, Latina, and white women. I employed a snowball sample, a method in which potential respondents often first learn about the study from people who have already participated. . . .

Demographics of the Women in the Study

The eighteen women I interviewed included five African American women, five Latinas, and eight white women. Of these women, twelve are lesbian and six are heterosexual. Five women are Jewish, eight are Catholic, and five are Protestant. Three women grew up outside of the United States. The women represented a range of class backgrounds (both in terms of origin and current class status) and ranged in age from nineteen to forty-six years old (with a median age of 33.5 years).

The majority of the women reported having had a combination of eating problems (at least two of the following: bulimia, compulsive eating, anorexia nervosa, and/or extensive dieting). In addition, the particular types of eating problems often changed during a woman's life span. . . .

Two-thirds of the women have had eating problems for more than half of their lives, a finding that contradicts the stereotype of eating problems as transitory. The weight fluctuation among the women varied from 16 to 160 pounds, with an average fluctuation of 74 pounds. This drastic weight change illustrates the degree to which the women adjusted to major changes in body size at least once during their lives as they lost, gained, and lost weight again. The average age of onset was eleven years old, meaning that most of the women developed eating problems prior to puberty. Almost all of the women (88 percent) considered themselves as still having a problem with eating, although the majority believed they were well on the way to recovery.

◉ The Interface of Trauma and Eating Problems

One of the most striking findings in this study was the range of traumas the women associated with the origins of their eating problems, including racism, sexual abuse, poverty, sexism, emotional or physical abuse, heterosexism, class injuries, and acculturation.[1] The particular constellation of eating problems among the women did not vary with race, class, sexuality, or nationality. Women from various race and class backgrounds attributed the origins of their eating problems to sexual abuse, sexism, and emotional and/or physical abuse. Among some of the African American and Latina women, eating problems were also associated with poverty, racism, and class injuries. Heterosexism was a key factor in the onset of bulimia, compulsive eating, and extensive dieting among some of the lesbians. These oppressions are not the same nor are the injuries caused by them. And certainly, there are a variety of potentially harmful ways that women respond to oppression (such as using drugs, becoming a

576

workaholic, or committing suicide). However, for all these women, eating was a way of coping with trauma.

Sexual Abuse

Sexual abuse was the most common trauma that the women related to the origins of their eating problems. Until recently, there has been virtually no research exploring the possible relationship between these two phenomena. Since the mid-1980s, however, researchers have begun identifying connections between the two, a task that is part of a larger feminist critique of traditional psychoanalytic symptomatology (DeSalvo, 1989; Herman, 1981; Masson, 1984). Results of a number of incidence studies indicate that between one-third and two-thirds of women who have eating problems have been abused (Oppenheimer et al., 1985; Root & Fallon, 1988). In addition, a growing number of therapists and researchers have offered interpretations of the meaning and impact of eating problems for survivors of sexual abuse (Bass & Davis, 1988; Goldfarb, 1987; Iazzetto, 1989; Swink & Leveille, 1986). . . .

Among the women I interviewed, 61 percent were survivors of sexual abuse (eleven of the eighteen women), most of whom made connections between sexual abuse and the beginning of their eating problems. Binging was the most common method of coping identified by the survivors. Binging helped women "numb out" or anesthetize their feelings. Eating sedated, alleviated anxiety, and combated loneliness. Food was something that they could trust and was accessible whenever they needed it. Antonia (a pseudonym) is an Italian American woman who was first sexually abused by a male relative when she was four years old. Retrospectively, she knows that binging was a way she coped with the abuse. When the abuse began, and for many years subsequently, Antonia often woke up during the middle of the night with anxiety attacks or nightmares and would go straight to the kitchen cupboards to get food. Binging helped her block painful feelings because it put her back to sleep.

Like other women in the study who began binging when they were very young, Antonia was not always fully conscious as she binged. She described eating during the night as "sleepwalking. It was mostly desperate—like I had to have it." Describing why she ate after waking up with nightmares, Antonia said, "What else do you do? If you don't have any coping mechanisms, you eat." She said that binging made her "disappear," which made her feel protected. Like Antonia, most of the women were sexually abused before puberty; four of them before they were five years old. Given their youth, food was the most accessible and socially acceptable drug available to them. Because all of the women endured the psychological consequences alone, it is logical that they coped with tactics they could use alone as well.

One reason Antonia binged (rather than dieted) to cope with sexual abuse is that she saw little reason to try to be the small size girls were supposed to be. Growing up as one of the only Italian Americans in what she described as a "very WASP town," Antonia felt that everything from her weight and size to having dark hair on her upper lip were physical characteristics she was supposed to hide. From a young age she knew she "never embodied the essence of the good girl. I don't like her. I have never acted like her. I can't be her. I sort of gave up." For Antonia, her body was the physical entity that signified her outsider status. When the sexual abuse occurred, Antonia felt she had lost her body. In her mind, the body she lived in after the abuse was not really hers. By the time Antonia was eleven, her mother put her on diet pills. Antonia began to eat behind closed doors as she continued to cope with the psychological consequences of sexual abuse and feeling like a cultural outsider.

Extensive dieting and bulimia were also ways in which women responded to sexual abuse. Some women thought that the men had abused them because of their weight. They believed that if they were smaller, they might not have been abused. For example, when Elsa, an Argentine woman, was sexually abused at the age of eleven, she thought her chubby size was the reason the man was abusing her. Elsa said, "I had this notion that these old perverts liked these plump girls. You heard adults say this too. Sex and flesh being associated." Looking back on her childhood, Elsa believes she made fat the enemy partly due to the shame and guilt she felt about the incest. Her belief that fat was the source of her problems was also supported by her socialization. Raised by strict German governesses in an upper-class family, Elsa was taught that a woman's weight was a primary criterion for judging her worth. Her mother "was socially conscious of walking into places with a fat daughter and maybe people staring at her." Her father often referred to Elsa's body as "shot to hell." When asked to describe how she felt about her body when growing up, Elsa described being completely alienated from her body. She explained,

> Remember in school when they talk about the difference between body and soul? I always felt like my soul was skinny. My soul was free. My soul sort of flew. I was tied down by this big bag of rocks that was my body. I had to drag it around. It did pretty much what it wanted and I had a lot of trouble controlling it. It kept me from doing all the things that I dreamed of.

As is true for many women who have been abused, the split that Elsa described between her body and soul was an attempt to protect herself from the pain she believed her body caused her. In her mind, her fat body was what had "bashed in her dreams." Dieting became her solution but, as is true for many women in the study, this strategy soon led to cycles of binging and weight fluctuation.

Ruthie, a Puerto Rican woman who was sexually abused from twelve until sixteen years of age, described bulimia as a way she responded to sexual abuse. As a child, Ruthie liked her body. Like many Puerto Rican women of her mother's generation, Ruthie's mother did not want skinny children, interpreting that as a sign that they were sick or being fed improperly. Despite her mother's attempts to make her gain weight, Ruthie remained thin through puberty. When a male relative began sexually abusing her, Ruthie's sense of her body changed dramatically. Although she weighed only one hundred pounds, she began to feel fat and thought her size was causing the abuse. She had seen a movie on television about Romans who made themselves throw up and so she began doing it, in hopes that she could look like the "little kid" she was before the abuse began. Her symbolic attempt to protect herself by purging stands in stark contrast to the psychoanalytic explanation of eating problems as an "abnormal" repudiation of sexuality. In fact, her actions and those of many other survivors indicate a girl's logical attempt to protect herself (including her sexuality) by being a size and shape that does not seem as vulnerable to sexual assault. . . .

Poverty

Like sexual abuse, poverty is another injury that may make women vulnerable to eating problems. One woman I interviewed attributed her eating problems directly to the stress caused by poverty. Yolanda is a Black Cape Verdean mother who began eating compulsively when she was 27 years old. After leaving an abusive husband in her early twenties, Yolanda was forced to go on welfare. As a single mother with small children and few financial resources, she tried to support herself and her children on $539 a month. Yolanda began binging in the evenings after putting her children to bed. Eating was something she could do alone. It would calm her, help her deal with loneliness, and make her feel safe. Food was an accessible commodity that was cheap. She ate three boxes of macaroni and cheese when nothing else was available. As a single mother with little money, Yolanda felt as if her body was the only thing she had left. As she described it,

> I am here, [in my body] 'cause there is no where else for me to go. Where am I going to go? This is all I got . . . that probably contributes to putting on so much weight cause staying in your body, in your home, in yourself, you don't go out. You aren't around other people. . . . You hide and as long as you hide you don't have to face . . . nobody can see you eat. You are safe.

580

When she was eating, Yolanda felt a momentary reprieve from her worries. Binging not only became a logical solution because it was cheap and easy but also because she had grown up amid positive messages about eating. In her family, eating was a celebrated and joyful act. However, in adulthood, eating became a double-edged sword. While comforting her, binging also led to weight gain. During the three years Yolanda was on welfare, she gained seventy pounds.

Yolanda's story captures how poverty can be a precipitating factor in eating problems and high-lights the value of understanding how class inequalities may shape women's eating problems. As a single mother, her financial constraints mirrored those of most female heads of households. The dual hazards of a race- and sex-stratified labor market further limited her options (Higginbotham, 1986). In an article about Black women's health, Byllye Avery quotes a Black woman's explanation about why she eats compulsively (1990:7). The woman told Avery,

> I work for General Electric making batteries, and I know it's killing me. My old man is an alcoholic. My kids got babies. Things are not well with me. And one thing I know I can do when I come home is cook me a pot of food and sit down in front of the TV and eat it. And you can't take that away from me until you're ready to give me something in its place.

Like Yolanda, this woman identifies eating compulsively as a quick, accessible, and immediately satisfying way of coping with the daily stress caused by conditions she could not control. Connections between poverty and eating problems also show the limits of portraying eating problems as maladies of upper-class adolescent women.

The fact that many women use food to anesthetize themselves, rather than other drugs (even when they gained access to alcohol, marijuana, and other illegal drugs), is partly a function of gender socialization and the competing demands that women face. One of the physiological consequences of binge eating is a numbed state similar to that experienced by drinking. Troubles and tensions are covered over as a consequence of the body's defensive response to massive food intake. When food is eaten in that way, it effectively works like a drug with immediate and predictable effects. Yolanda said she binged late at night rather than getting drunk because she could still get up in the morning, get her children ready for school, and be clearheaded for the college classes she attended. By binging, she avoided the hang-over or sickness that results from alcohol or illegal drugs. In this way, food was her drug of choice, since it was possible for her to eat while she continued to care for her children, drive, cook, and study. Binging is also less expensive than drinking, a factor that is especially significant for poor women. . . .

Heterosexism

The life history interviews also uncovered new connections between heterosexism and eating problems. One of the most important recent feminist contributions has been identifying compulsory heterosexuality as an institution which truncates opportunities for heterosexual and lesbian women (Rich, 1986). All of the women interviewed for this study, both lesbian and heterosexual, were taught that heterosexuality was compulsory, although the versions of this enforcement were shaped by race and class. Expectations about heterosexuality were partly taught through messages that girls learned about eating and their bodies. In some homes, boys were given more food than girls, especially as teenagers, based on the rationale that girls need to be thin to attract boys. As the girls approached puberty, many were told to stop being athletic, begin wearing dresses, and watch their weight. For the women who weighed more than was considered acceptable, threats about their need to diet were laced with admonitions that being fat would ensure becoming an "old maid."

While compulsory heterosexuality influenced all of the women's emerging sense of their bodies and eating patterns, the women who linked heterosexism directly to the beginning of their eating problems were those who knew they were lesbians when very young and actively resisted heterosexual norms. One working-class Jewish woman, Martha, began compulsively eating when she was eleven

582

years old, the same year she started getting clues of her lesbian identity. In junior high school, as many of her female peers began dating boys, Martha began fantasizing about girls, which made her feel utterly alone. Confused and ashamed about her fantasies, Martha came home every day from school and binged. Binging was a way she drugged herself so that being alone was tolerable. Describing binging, she said, "It was the only thing I knew. I was looking for a comfort." Like many women, Martha binged because it softened painful feelings. Binging sedated her, lessened her anxiety, and induced sleep.

Martha's story also reveals ways that trauma can influence women's experience of their bodies. Like many other women, Martha had no sense of herself as connected to her body. When I asked Martha whether she saw herself as fat when she was growing up she said, "I didn't see myself as fat. I didn't see myself. I wasn't there. I get so sad about that because I missed so much." In the literature on eating problems, *body image* is the term that is typically used to describe a woman's experience of her body. This term connotes the act of imagining one's physical appearance. Typically, women with eating problems are assumed to have difficulties with their body image. However, the term body image does not adequately capture the complexity and range of bodily responses to trauma experienced by the women. Exposure to trauma did much more than distort the women's visual image of themselves. These traumas often jeopardized their capacity to consider themselves as having bodies at all. . . .

Racism and Class Injuries

For some of the Latinas and African American women, racism coupled with the stress resulting from class mobility related to the onset of their eating problems. Joselyn, an African American woman, remembered her white grandmother telling her she would never be as pretty as her cousins because they were lighter skinned. Her grandmother often humiliated Joselyn in front of others, as she made fun of Joselyn's body while she was naked and told her she was fat. As a young child, Joselyn began to think that although she could not change her skin color, she could at least try to be thin. When Joselyn was young, her grandmother was the only family member who objected to Joselyn's weight. However, her father also began encouraging his wife and daughter to be thin as the family's class standing began to change. When the family was working class, serving big meals, having chubby children, and keeping plenty of food in the house was a sign the family was doing well. But, as the family became mobile, Joselyn's father began insisting that Joselyn be thin. She remembered, "When my father's business began to bloom and my father was interacting more with white businessmen and seeing how they did business, suddenly thin became important. If you were a truly well-to-do family, then your family was slim and elegant."

As Joselyn's grandmother used Joselyn's body as territory for enforcing her own racism and prejudice about size, Joselyn's father used her body as the territory through which he channeled the demands he faced in the white-dominated business world. However, as Joselyn was pressured to diet, her father still served her large portions and bought treats for her and the neighborhood children. These contradictory messages made her feel confused about her body. As was true for many women in this study, Joselyn was told she was fat beginning when she was very young even though she was not overweight. And, like most of the women, Joselyn was put on diet pills and diets before even reaching puberty, beginning the cycles of dieting, compulsive eating, and bulimia.

The confusion about body size expectations that Joselyn associated with changes in class paralleled one Puerto Rican woman's association between her eating problems and the stress of assimilation as her family's class standing moved from poverty to working class. When Vera was very young, she was so thin that her mother took her to a doctor who prescribed appetite stimulants. However, by the time Vera was eight years old, her mother began trying to shame Vera into dieting. Looking back on it, Vera attributed her mother's change of heart to competition among extended family members that centered on "being white, being successful, being middle class, . . . and it was always, 'Ay Bendito. She is so fat. What happened?'"

The fact that some of the African American and Latina women associated the ambivalent messages about food and eating to their family's class mobility and/or the demands of assimilation while none of the eight white women expressed this (including those whose class was stable and changing) suggests that the added dimension of racism was connected to the imperative to be thin. In fact, the class expectations that their parents experienced exacerbated standards about weight that they inflicted on their daughters.

❧ Eating Problems as Survival Strategies

My research permits a reevaluation of many assumptions about eating problems. First, this work challenges the theoretical reliance on the culture-of-thinness model. Although all of the women I interviewed were manipulated and hurt by this imperative at some point in their lives, it is not the primary source of their problems. Even in the instances in which a culture of thinness was a precipitating factor in anorexia, bulimia, or binging, this influence occurred in concert with other oppressions.

Attributing the etiology of eating problems primarily to a woman's striving to attain a certain beauty ideal is also problematic because it labels a common way that women cope with pain as essentially appearance-based disorders. One blatant example of sexism is the notion that women's foremost worry is about their appearance. By focusing on the emphasis on slenderness, the eating problems literature falls into the same trap of assuming that the problems reflect women's "obsession" with appearance. Some women were raised in families and communities in which thinness was not considered a criterion for beauty. Yet they still developed eating problems. Other women were taught that women should be thin but their eating problems were not primarily in reaction to this imperative. Their eating strategies began as logical solutions to problems rather than problems themselves as they tried to cope with a variety of traumas.

Establishing links between eating problems and a range of oppressions invites a rethinking of both the groups of women who have been excluded from research and those whose lives have been the basis of theory formation. The construction of bulimia and anorexia nervosa as appearance-based disorders is rooted in a notion of femininity in which white middle- and upper-class women are portrayed as frivolous, obsessed with their bodies, and overly accepting of narrow gender roles. This portrayal fuels women's tremendous shame and guilt about eating problems—as signs of self-centered vanity. This construction of white middle- and upper-class women is intimately linked to the portrayal of working-class white women and women of color as their opposite: as somehow exempt from accepting the dominant standards of beauty or as one step away from being hungry and therefore not susceptible to eating problems. Identifying that women may binge to cope with poverty contrasts the notion that eating problems are class bound. Attending to the intricacies of race, class, sexuality, and gender pushes us to rethink the demeaning construction of middle-class femininity and establishes bulimia and anorexia nervosa as serious responses to injustices.

Note

[1] By trauma I mean a violating experience that has long-term emotional, physical, and/or spiritual consequences that may have immediate or delayed effects. One reason the term *trauma* is useful conceptually is its association with the diagnostic label Post Traumatic Stress Disorder (PTSD) (American Psychological Association, 1987). PTSD is one of the few clinical diagnostic categories that recognizes social problems (such as war or the Holocaust) as responsible for the symptoms identified (Trimble, 1985). This concept adapts well to the feminist assertion that a woman's symptoms cannot be understood as solely individual, considered outside of her social context, or prevented without significant changes in social conditions.

586

References

American Psychological Association. 1987. *Diagnostic and statistical manual of mental disorders*. 3rd ed. rev. Washington, D.C.: American Psychological Association.

Andersen, Arnold, and Andy Hay. 1985. Racial and socio-economic influences in anorexia nervosa and bulimia. *International Journal of Eating Disorders* 4: 479–87.

Arnold, Georgiana. 1990. Coming home: One Black woman's journey to health and fitness. In *The Black women's health book: Speaking for ourselves*, ed. Evelyn C. White. Seattle, Wash. Seal Press.

Avery, Byllye Y. 1990. Breathing life into ourselves: The evolution of the National Black Women's Health Project. In *The Black women's health book: Speaking for ourselves*, ed. Evelyn C. White. Seattle, Wash.: Seal Press.

Bass, Ellen, and Laura Davis. 1988. *The courage to heal: A guide for women survivors of child sexual abuse*. New York: Harper & Row.

Brown, Laura S. 1987. Lesbians, weight and eating: New analyses and perspectives. In Lesbian psychologies, ed. Boston Lesbian Psychologies Collective. Champaign: University of Illinois Press.

Chernin, Kim. 1981. *The obsession: Reflections on the tyranny of slenderness*. New York: Harper & Row.

Clarke, Cheryl. 1982. *Narratives*. New Brunswick, N.J.: Sister Books.

Copeland, Paul M. 1985. Neuroendocrine aspects of eating disorders. In *Theory and treatment of anorexia nervosa and bulimia: Biomedical, sociocultural and psychological perspectives*, ed. Steven Wiley Emmett. New York: Brunner/Mazel.

DeSalvo, Louise. 1989. *Virginia Woolf: The impact of childhood sexual abuse on her life and work*. Boston: Beacon.

Dworkin, Sari H. 1989. Not in man's image: Lesbians and the cultural oppression of body image. In *Loving boldly: Issues facing lesbians*, ed. Ester D. Rothblum and Ellen Close. New York: Harrington Park.

Garfinkel, Paul E., and David M. Garner. 1982. *Anorexia nervosa: A multidimensional perspective*. New York: Brunner/Mazel.

Garner, David. 1985. Iatrogenesis in anorexia nervosa and bulimia nervosa. *International Journal of Eating Disorders* 4: 701–26.

Goldfarb, Lori. 1987. Sexual abuse antecedent to anorexia nervosa, bulimia and compulsive overeating: Three case reports. *International Journal of Eating Disorders* 6: 675–80.

Gray, James, Kathryn Ford, and Lily M. Kelly. 1987. The prevalence of bulimia in a Black college population. *International Journal of Eating Disorders* 6: 733–40.

Herman, Judith. 1981. *Father–daughter incest*. Cambridge, Mass.: Harvard University Press.

Higginbotham, Elizabeth. 1986. We were never on a pedestal: Women of color continue to struggle with poverty, racism and sexism. In *For crying out loud*, ed. Rochelle Lefkowitz and Ann Withorn. Boston: Pilgrim.

Hsu, George. 1987. Are eating disorders becoming more common in Blacks? *International Journal of Eating Disorders* 6: 13–24.

Iazzetto, Demetria. 1989. When the body is not an easy place to be: Women's sexual abuse and eating problems. Ph.D. diss., Union for Experimenting Colleges and Universities, Cincinnati.

Masson, Jeffrey. 1984. *The assault on the truth: Freud's suppression of the seduction theory*. New York: Farrar, Strauss & Giroux.

Naylor, Gloria. 1985. *Linden Hills*. New York: Ticknor & Fields.

Nevo, Shoshana. 1985. Bulimic symptoms: Prevalence and ethnic differences among college women. *International Journal of Eating Disorders* 4: 151–68.

Oppenheimer, R., K. Howells, R. L. Palmer, and D. A. Chaloner. 1985. Adverse sexual experience in childhood and clinical eating disorders: A preliminary description. *Journal of Psychiatric Research* 19: 357–61.

Orbach, Susie. 1978. *Fat is a feminist issue*. New York: Paddington.

———. 1985. Accepting the symptom: A feminist psychoanalytic treatment of anorexia nervosa. In *Handbook of psychotherapy for anorexia nervosa and bulimia*, ed. David M. Garner and Paul E. Garfinkel. New York: Guilford.

Powers, Retha. 1989. Fat is a Black women's issue. *Essence* (October): 75, 78, 134, 136.

Rich, Adrienne. 1986. Compulsory heterosexuality and lesbian existence. In *Blood, bread and poetry*. New York: Norton.

Root, Maria P. P., and Patricia Fallon. 1988. The incidence of victimization experiences in a bulimic sample. *Journal of Interpersonal Violence* 3: 161–73.

Schoenfielder, Lisa, and Barbara Wieser, eds. 1983. *Shadow on a tightrope: Writings by women about fat liberation.* Iowa City: Aunt Lute Book Co.

Silber, Tomas. 1986. Anorexia nervosa in Blacks and Hispanics. *International Journal of Eating Disorders* 5: 121–28.

Smead, Valerie. 1984. Eating behaviors which may lead to and perpetuate anorexia nervosa, bulimarexia, and bulimia. *Women and Therapy* 3: 37–49.

Spack, Norman. 1985. Medical complications of anorexia nervosa and bulimia. In *Theory and treatment of anorexia nervosa and bulimia: Biomedical, sociocultural and psychological perspectives*, ed. Steven Wiley Emmett. New York: Brunner/Mazel.

Swink, Kathy, and Antoinette E. Leveille. 1986. From victim to survivor: A new look at the issues and recovery process for adult incest survivors. *Women and Therapy* 5: 119–43.

Trimble, Michael. 1985. Post-traumatic stress disorder: History of a concept. In *Trauma and its wake: The study and treatment of post-traumatic stress disorder*, ed. C. R. Figley. New York: Brunner/Mazel.

What's important is what you look like. 1988. *Gay Community News* (July): 24–30.

White, Evelyn C., ed. 1990. *The Black women's health book: Speaking for ourselves.* Seattle, Wash.: Seal Press.

———. 1991. Unhealthy appetites. *Essence* (September): 28, 30.

☻ ☻ ☻

Critical-Thinking Questions

1. How do the biomedical, psychological, and feminist models differ in explaining eating disorders?

2. Why does Thompson argue that eating problems are survival strategies to cope with sexism; heterosexism; and emotional, sexual, or physical abuse?

3. Thompson maintains that women's eating problems are a response to poverty, racism, acculturation, and social class inequality. How, then, might we explain the low rates of eating disorders among Black, ethnic, and low-income men?

India's Sacred Cow

Marvin Harris

Anthropologist Marvin Harris uses the approach of cultural ecology to investigate how exotic and seemingly inexplicable cultural patterns may turn out to be everyday strategies for human survival in a particular natural environment. In this article, he offers his own favorite example: Why do people in India—many of whom are hungry—refuse to eat beef from the "sacred cows" that are found most everywhere?

. . .

Whenever I get into discussions about the influence of practical and mundane factors on lifestyles, someone is sure to say, "But what about all those cows the hungry peasants in India refuse to eat?" The picture of a ragged farmer starving to death alongside a big fat cow conveys a reassuring sense of mystery to Western observers. In countless learned and popular allusions, it confirms our deepest conviction about how people with inscrutable Oriental minds ought to act. It is comforting to know—somewhat like "there will always be an England"—that in India spiritual values are more precious than life itself. And at the same time it makes us feel sad. How can we ever hope to understand people so different from ourselves? Westerners find the idea that there might be a practical explanation for Hindu love of the cow more upsetting than Hindus do. The sacred cow—how else can I say it?—is one of our favorite sacred cows.

Hindus venerate cows because cows are the symbol of everything that is alive. As Mary is to Christians the mother of God, the cow to Hindus is the mother of life. So there is no greater sacrilege for a

Reprinted from *Cows, Pigs, Wars, and Witches: The Riddles of Culture* (1974), Random House, Inc.

Hindu than killing a cow. Even the taking of human life lacks the symbolic meaning, the unutterable defilement, that is evoked by cow slaughter.

According to many experts, cow worship is the number one cause of India's hunger and poverty. Some Western-trained agronomists say that the taboo against cow slaughter is keeping 100 million "useless" animals alive. They claim that cow worship lowers the efficiency of agriculture because the useless animals contribute neither milk nor meat while competing for croplands and food-stuff with useful animals and hungry human beings. . . .

It does seem that there are enormous numbers of surplus, useless, and uneconomic animals, and that this situation is a direct result of irrational Hindu doctrines. Tourists on their way through Delhi, Calcutta, Madras, Bombay, and other Indian cities are astonished at the liberties enjoyed by stray cattle. The animals wander through the streets, browse off the stalls in the market place, break into private gardens, defecate all over the sidewalks, and snarl traffic by pausing to chew their cuds in the middle of busy intersections. In the countryside, the cattle congregate on the shoulders of every highway and spend much of their time taking leisurely walks down the railroad tracks.

To Western observers familiar with modern industrial techniques of agriculture and stock raising, cow love seems senseless, even suicidal. The efficiency expert yearns to get his hands on all those useless animals and ship them off to a proper fate. And yet one finds certain inconsistencies in the condemnation of cow love. When I began to wonder if there might be a practical explanation for the sacred cow, I came across an intriguing government report. It said that India had too many cows but too few oxen. With so many cows around, how could there be a shortage of oxen? Oxen and male water buffalo are the principal source of traction for plowing India's fields. For each farm of ten acres or less, one pair of oxen or water buffalo is considered adequate. A little arithmetic shows that as far as plowing is concerned, there is indeed a shortage rather than a surplus of animals. India has 60 million farms, but only 80 million traction animals. If each farm had its quota of two oxen or two water buffalo, there ought to be 120 million traction animals—that is, 40 million more than are actually available.

The shortage may not be quite so bad, since some farmers rent or borrow oxen from their neighbors. But the sharing of plow animals often proves impractical. Plowing must be coordinated with the monsoon rains, and by the time one farm has been plowed, the optimum moment for plowing another may already have passed. Also, after plowing is over, a farmer still needs his own pair of oxen to pull his oxcart, the mainstay of the bulk transport throughout rural India. Quite possibly private ownership of farms, livestock, plows, and oxcarts lowers the efficiency of Indian agriculture, but this, I soon realized, was not caused by cow love.

The shortage of draft animals is a terrible threat that hangs over most of India's peasant families. When an ox falls sick a poor farmer is in danger of losing his farm. If he has no replacement for it, he will have to borrow money at usurious rates. Millions of rural households have in fact lost all or part of their holdings and have gone into sharecropping or day labor as a result of such debts. Each year hundreds of thousands of destitute farmers end up migrating to the cities, which already teem with unemployed and homeless persons.

The Indian farmer who can't replace his sick or deceased ox is in much the same situation as an American farmer who can neither replace nor repair his broken tractor. But there is an important difference: Tractors are made by factories, but oxen are made by cows. A farmer who owns a cow owns a factory for making oxen. With or without cow love, this is a good reason for him not to be too anxious to sell his cow to the slaughterhouse. One also begins to see why Indian farmers might be willing to tolerate cows that give only 500 pounds of milk per year. If the main economic function of the zebu cow is to breed male traction animals, then there's no point in comparing her with specialized American dairy animals, whose main function is to produce milk. Still, the milk produced by zebu cows plays an important role in meeting the nutritional needs of many poor families. Even small amounts of milk products can improve the health of people who are forced to subsist on the edge of starvation.

Agriculture is part of a vast system of human and natural relationships. To judge isolated portions of this "ecosystem" in terms that are relevant to the conduct of American agribusiness leads to some very strange impressions. Cattle figure in the Indian ecosystem in ways that are easily overlooked or demeaned by observers from industrialized, high-energy societies. In the United States, chemicals have almost completely replaced animal manure as the principal source of farm fertilizer. American farmers stopped using manure when they began to plow with tractors rather than mules or horses. Since tractors excrete poisons rather than fertilizers, a commitment to large-scale machine farming is almost of necessity a commitment to the use of chemical fertilizers. And around the world today there has in fact grown up a vast integrated petrochemical-tractor-truck industrial complex that produces farm machinery, motorized transport, oil and gasoline, and chemical fertilizers and pesticides upon which new high-yield production techniques depend.

For better or worse, most of India's farmers cannot participate in this complex, not because they worship their cows, but because they can't afford to buy tractors. Like other underdeveloped nations, India can't build factories that are competitive with the facilities of the industrialized nations nor pay for large quantities of imported industrial products. To convert from animals and manure to tractors and petrochemicals would require the investment of incredible amounts of capital. Moreover, the inevitable effect of substituting costly machines for cheap animals is to reduce the number of people who can earn their living from agriculture and to force a corresponding increase in the size of the average farm. We know that the development of large-scale agribusiness in the United States has meant the virtual destruction of the small family farm. Less than 5 percent of U.S. families now live on farms, as compared with 60 percent about a hundred years ago. If agribusiness were to develop along similar lines in India, jobs and housing would soon have to be found for a quarter of a billion displaced peasants.

Since the suffering caused by unemployment and homelessness in India's cities is already intolerable, an additional massive build-up

594

of the urban population can only lead to unprecedented upheavals and catastrophes.

With this alternative in view, it becomes easier to understand low-energy, small-scale, animal-based systems. As I have already pointed out, cows and oxen provide low-energy substitutes for tractors and tractor factories. They also should be credited with carrying out the functions of a petrochemical industry. India's cattle annually excrete about 700 million tons of recoverable manure. Approximately half of this total is used as fertilizer, while most of the remainder is burned to provide heat for cooking. The annual quantity of heat liberated by this dung, the Indian housewife's main cooking fuel, is the thermal equivalent of 27 million tons of kerosene, 35 million tons of coal, or 68 million tons of wood. Since India has only small reserves of oil and coal and is already the victim of extensive deforestation, none of these fuels can be considered practical substitutes for cow dung. The thought of dung in the kitchen may not appeal to the average American, but Indian women regard it as a superior cooking fuel because it is finely adjusted to their domestic routines. Most Indian dishes are prepared with clarified butter known as *ghee,* for which cow dung is the preferred source of heat since it burns with a clean, slow, long-lasting flame that doesn't scorch the food. This enables the Indian housewife to start cooking her meals and to leave them unattended for several hours while she takes care of the children, helps out in the fields, or performs other chores. American housewives achieve a similar effect through a complex set of electronic controls that come as expensive options on late-model stoves.

Cow dung has at least one other major function. Mixed with water and made into a paste, it is used as a household flooring material. Smeared over a dirt floor and left to harden into a smooth surface, it keeps the dust down and can be swept clean with a broom.

Because cattle droppings have so many useful properties, every bit of dung is carefully collected. Village small fry are given the task of following the family cow around and of bringing home its daily petrochemical output. In the cities, sweeper castes enjoy a monopoly on the dung deposited by strays and earn their living by selling it to housewives. . . .

During droughts and famines, farmers are severely tempted to kill or sell their livestock. Those who succumb to this temptation seal their doom, even if they survive the drought, for when the rains come, they will be unable to plow their fields. I want to be even more emphatic: Massive slaughter of cattle under the duress of famine constitutes a much greater threat to aggregate welfare than any likely miscalculation by particular farmers concerning the usefulness of their animals during normal times. It seems probable that the sense of unutterable profanity elicited by cow slaughter has its roots in the excruciating contradiction between immediate needs and long-term conditions of survival. Cow love with its sacred symbols and holy doctrines protects the farmer against calculations that are "rational" only in the short term. To Western experts it looks as if "the Indian farmer would rather starve to death than eat his cow." . . . They don't realize that the farmer would rather eat his cow than starve, but that he will starve if he does eat it. . . .

Do I mean to say that cow love has no effect whatsoever on . . . the agricultural system? No. What I am saying is that cow love is an active element in a complex, finely articulated material and cultural order. Cow love mobilizes the latent capacity of human beings to persevere in a low-energy ecosystem in which there is little room for waste or indolence. Cow love contributes to the adaptive resilience of the human population by preserving temporarily dry or barren but still useful animals; by discouraging the growth of an energy-expensive beef industry; by protecting cattle that fatten in the public domain or at landlord's expense; and by preserving the recovery potential of the cattle population during droughts and famines. . . .

Wastefulness is more a characteristic of modern agribusiness than of traditional peasant economies. . . .

Automobiles and airplanes are faster than oxcarts, but they do not use energy more efficiently. In fact, more calories go up in useless heat and smoke during a single day of traffic jams in the United States than is wasted by all the cows of India during an entire year. The comparison is even less favorable when we consider the fact that the stalled vehicles are burning up irreplaceable reserves of petroleum that it took the earth tens of millions of years to accumulate. If you want to see a real sacred cow, go out and look at the family car.

◉ ◉ ◉

Critical-Thinking Questions

1. What evidence does Harris offer to support his argument that defining the cow as sacred is a necessary strategy for human survival in India?

2. If survival strategies make sense when we take a close look at them, why do they become so "encased" in elaborate cultural explanations?

3. Does India's recognition of the sacred cow help or hurt that nation's natural environment?

4. Following Harris's logic, can you think of reasons that people in some parts of the world (the Middle East, for instance) do not eat pork?

Unmarried with Children

KATHRYN EDIN AND MARIA KEFALAS

Since the late 1980s, one of the major changes in U.S. society has been a dramatic increase of unmarried mothers, especially at lower socioeconomic levels. Have these women given up on marriage, as most male, white, and middle-class observers have concluded? According to Kathryn Edin and Maria Kefalas, many of the single women who have children believe in marriage. They are still waiting for the right partner to fulfill their dreams of having a middle-class home with a devoted husband and father.

· · ·

Jen Burke, a white tenth-grade dropout who is seventeen years old, lives with her stepmother, her sister, and her sixteen-month-old son in a cramped but tidy row home in Philadelphia's beleaguered Kensington neighborhood. She is broke, on welfare, and struggling to complete her GED. Wouldn't she and her son have been better off if she had finished high school, found a job, and married her son's father first?

In 1950, when Jen's grandmother came of age, only one in twenty American children was born to an unmarried mother. Today, that rate is one in three—and they are usually born to those least likely to be able to support a child on their own. In our book, *Promises I Can Keep: Why Poor Women Put Motherhood Before Marriage,*[1] we discuss

_____

Reprinted from *Contexts* 4 (spring 2005), by permission of American Sociological Association.

the lives of 162 white, African American, and Puerto Rican low-income single mothers living in eight destitute neighborhoods across Philadelphia and its poorest industrial suburb, Camden. We spent five years chatting over kitchen tables and on front stoops, giving mothers like Jen the opportunity to speak to the question so many affluent Americans ask about them: Why do they have children while still young and unmarried when they will face such an uphill struggle to support them?

◉ Romance at Lightning Speed

Jen started having sex with her twenty-year-old boyfriend Rick just before her fifteenth birthday. A month and a half later, she was pregnant. "I didn't want to get pregnant," she claims. "*He* wanted me to get pregnant." "As soon as he met me, he wanted to have a kid with me," she explains. Though Jen's college-bound suburban peers would be appalled by such a declaration, on the streets of Jen's neighborhood, it is something of a badge of honor. "All those other girls he was with, he didn't want to have a baby with any of them," Jen boasts. "I asked him, 'Why did you choose me to have a kid when you could have a kid with any one of them?' He was like, 'I want to have a kid with *you*.'" Looking back, Jen says she now believes that the reason "he wanted me to have a kid that early is so that I didn't leave him."

In inner-city neighborhoods like Kensington, where child-bearing within marriage has become rare, romantic relationships like Jen and Rick's proceed at lightning speed. A young man's avowal, "I want to have a baby by you," is often part of the courtship ritual from the beginning. This is more than idle talk, as their first child is typically conceived within a year from the time a couple begins "kicking it." Yet while poor couples' pillow talk often revolves around dreams of shared children, the news of a pregnancy—the first indelible sign of the huge changes to come—puts these still-new relationships into overdrive. Suddenly, the would-be mother begins to scrutinize her mate as never before, wondering whether he can "get himself together"—find a job, settle down, and become a family man—in time.

Jen began pestering Rick to get a real job instead of picking up day-labor jobs at nearby construction sites. She also wanted him to stop hanging out with his ne'er-do-well friends, who had been getting him into serious trouble for more than a decade. Most of all, she wanted Rick to shed what she calls his "kiddie mentality"—his habit of spending money on alcohol and drugs rather than recognizing his growing financial obligations at home.

Rick did not try to deny paternity, as many would-be fathers do. Nor did he abandon or mistreat Jen, at least intentionally. But Rick, who had been in and out of juvenile detention since he was eight years old for everything from stealing cars to selling drugs, proved unable to stay away from his unsavory friends. At the beginning of her seventh month of pregnancy, an escapade that began as a drunken lark landed Rick in jail on a carjacking charge. Jen moved back home with her step-mother, applied for welfare, and spent the last two-and-a-half months of her pregnancy without Rick.

Rick sent penitent letters from jail. "I thought he changed by the letters he wrote me. I thought he changed a lot," she says. "He used to tell me that he loved me when he was in jail. . . . It was always gonna be me and him and the baby when he got out." Thus, when Rick's alleged victim failed to appear to testify and he was released just days before Colin's birth, the couple's reunion was a happy one. Often, the magic moment of childbirth calms the troubled waters of such relationships. New parents typically make amends and resolve to stay together for the sake of their child. When surveyed just after a child's birth, eight in ten unmarried parents say they are still together, and most plan to stay together and raise the child.

Promoting marriage among the poor has become the new war on poverty, Bush style. And it is true that the correlation between marital status and child poverty is strong. But poor single mothers already believe in marriage. Jen insists that she will walk down the aisle one day, though she admits it might not be with Rick. And demographers still project that more than seven in ten women who had a child outside of marriage will eventually wed someone. First, though, Jen wants to get a good job, finish school, and get her son out of Kensington.

Most poor, unmarried mothers and fathers readily admit that bearing children while poor and unmarried is not the ideal way to do things. Jen believes the best time to become a mother is "after you're out of school and you got a job, at least, when you're like twenty-one. . . . When you're ready to have kids, you should have everything ready, have your house, have a job, so when that baby comes, the baby can have its own room." Yet given their already limited economic prospects, the poor have little motivation to time their births as precisely as their middle-class counterparts do. The dreams of young people like Jen and Rick center on children at a time of life when their more affluent peers plan for college and careers. Poor girls coming of age in the inner city value children highly, anticipate them eagerly, and believe strongly that they are up to the job of mothering—even in difficult circumstances. Jen, for example, tells us, "People outside the neighborhood, they're like, 'You're fifteen! You're pregnant?' I'm like, it's not none of their business. I'm gonna be able to take care of my kid. They have nothing to worry about." Jen says she has concluded that "some people . . . are better at having kids at a younger age. . . . I think it's better for some people to have kids younger."

❂ When I Became a Mom

When we asked mothers like Jen what their lives would be like if they had not had children, we expected them to express regret over foregone opportunities for school and careers. Instead, most believe their children "saved" them. They describe their lives as spinning out of control before becoming pregnant—struggles with parents and peers, "wild," risky behavior, depression, and school failure. Jen speaks to this poignantly. "I was just real bad. I hung with a real bad crowd. I was doing pills. I was really depressed. . . . I was drinking. That was before I was pregnant." "I think," she reflects, "if I never had a baby or anything, . . . I would still be doing the things I was doing. I would

601

probably still be doing drugs. I'd probably still be drinking." Jen admits that when she first became pregnant, she was angry that she "couldn't be out no more. Couldn't be out with my friends. Couldn't do nothing." Now, though, she says, "I'm glad I have a son . . . because I would still be doing all that stuff."

Children offer poor youth like Jen a compelling sense of purpose. Jen paints a before-and-after picture of her life that was common among the mothers we interviewed. "Before, I didn't have nobody to take care of. I didn't have nothing left to go home for. . . . Now I have my son to take care of. I have him to go home for. . . . I don't have to go buy weed or drugs with my money. I could buy my son stuff with my money! . . . I have something to look up to now." Children also are a crucial source of relational intimacy, a self-made community of care. After a nasty fight with Rick, Jen recalls, "I was crying. My son came in the room. He was hugging me. He's sixteen months and he was hugging me with his little arms. He was really cute and happy, so I got happy. That's one of the good things. When you're sad, the baby's always gonna be there for you no matter what." Lately she has been thinking a lot about what her life was like back then, before the baby. "I thought about the stuff before I became a mom, what my life was like back then. I used to see pictures of me, and I would hide in every picture. This baby did so much for me. My son did a lot for me. He helped me a lot. I'm thankful that I had my baby."

Around the time of the birth, most unmarried parents claim they plan to get married eventually. Rick did not propose marriage when Jen's first child was born, but when she conceived a second time, at seventeen, Rick informed his dad, "It's time for me to get married. It's time for me to straighten up. This is the one I wanna be with. I had a baby with her, I'm gonna have another baby with her." Yet despite their intentions, few of these couples actually marry. Indeed, most break up well before their child enters preschool.

◉ *I'd Like to Get Married, but . . .*

The sharp decline in marriage in impoverished urban areas has led some to charge that the poor have abandoned the marriage norm. Yet we found few who had given up on the idea of marriage. But like their elite counterparts, disadvantaged women set a high financial bar for marriage. For the poor, marriage has become an elusive goal—one they feel ought to be reserved for those who can support a "white picket fence" lifestyle: a mortgage on a modest row home, a car and some furniture, some savings in the bank, and enough money left over to pay for a "decent" wedding. Jen's views on marriage provide a perfect case in point. "If I was gonna get married, I would want to be married like my Aunt Nancy and my Uncle Pat. They live in the mountains. She has a job. My Uncle Pat is a state trooper; he has lots of money. They live in the [Poconos]. It's real nice out there. Her kids go to Catholic school. . . . That's the kind of life I would want to have. If I get married, I would have a life like [theirs]." She adds, "And I would wanna have a big wedding, a real nice wedding."

Unlike the women of their mothers' and grandmothers' generations, young women like Jen are not merely content to rely on a man's earnings. Instead, they insist on being economically "set" in their own right before taking marriage vows. This is partly because they want a partnership of equals, and they believe money buys say-so in a relationship. Jen explains, "I'm not gonna just get into marrying him and not have my own house! Not have a job! I still wanna do a lot of things before I get married. He [already] tells me I can't do nothing. I can't go out. What's gonna happen when I marry him? He's gonna say he owns me!"

Economic independence is also insurance against a marriage gone bad. Jen explains, "I want to have everything ready, in case something goes wrong. . . . If we got a divorce, that would be my house. I bought that house, he can't kick me out or he can't take my kids from me." "That's what I want in case that ever happens. I know a lot of people that happened to. I don't want it to happen to me." These statements reveal that despite her desire to marry, Rick's role in the family's future is provisional at best. "We get along, but we fight a lot. If he's there, he's there, but if he's not, that's why I want a job . . . a job with computers . . . so I could afford my kids, could afford the house. . . . I don't want to be living off him. I want my kids to be living off me."

Why is Jen, who describes Rick as "the love of my life," so insistent on planning an exit strategy before she is willing to take the vows she firmly believes ought to last "forever?" If love is so sure, why does mistrust seem so palpable and strong? In relationships among poor couples like Jen and Rick, mistrust is often spawned by chronic violence and infidelity, drug and alcohol abuse, criminal activity, and the threat of imprisonment. In these tarnished corners of urban America, the stigma of a failed marriage is far worse than an out-of-wedlock birth. New mothers like Jen feel they must test the relationship over three, four, even five years' time. This is the only way, they believe, to ensure that their marriages will last.

Trust has been an enormous issue in Jen's relationship with Rick. "My son was born December 23rd, and [Rick] started cheating on me again . . . in March. He started cheating on me with some girl—Amanda. . . . Then it was another girl, another girl, another girl after. I didn't wanna believe it. My friends would come up to me and be like, 'Oh yeah, your boyfriend's cheating on you with this person.' I wouldn't believe it. . . . I would see him with them. He used to have hickies. He used to make up some excuse that he was drunk—that was always his excuse for everything." Things finally came to a head when Rick got another girl pregnant. "For a while, I forgave him for everything. Now, I don't forgive him for nothing." Now we begin to understand the source of Jen's hesitancy. "He wants me to marry him, [but] I'm not really sure. . . . If I can't trust him, I can't marry him, 'cause we would get a divorce. If you're gonna get married, you're supposed to be faithful!" she insists. To Jen and her peers, the worst thing that could happen is "to get married just to get divorced."

Given the economic challenges and often perilously low quality of the romantic relationships among unmarried parents, poor women may be right to be cautious about marriage. Five years after we first

604

spoke with her, we met with Jen again. We learned that Jen's second pregnancy ended in a miscarriage. We also learned that Rick was out of the picture—apparently for good. "You know that bar [down the street?] It happened in that bar. . . . They were in the bar, and this guy was like badmouthing [Rick's friend] Mikey, talking stuff to him or whatever. So Rick had to go get involved in it and start with this guy. . . . Then he goes outside and fights the guy [and] the guy dies of head trauma. They were all on drugs, they were all drinking, and things just got out of control, and that's what happened. He got fourteen to thirty years."

◉ These are Cards I Dealt Myself

Jen stuck with Rick for the first two and a half years of his prison sentence, but when another girl's name replaced her own on the visitors' list, Jen decided she was finished with him once and for all. Readers might be asking what Jen ever saw in a man like Rick. But Jen and Rick operate in a partner market where the better-off men go to the better-off women. The only way for someone like Jen to forge a satisfying relationship with a man is to find a diamond in the rough or improve her own economic position so that she can realistically compete for more upwardly mobile partners, which is what Jen is trying to do now. "There's this kid, Donny, he works at my job. He works on C shift. He's a supervisor! He's funny, three years older, and he's not a geek or anything, but he's not a real preppy good boy either. But he's not [a player like Rick] and them. He had a job, you know, so that's good. He doesn't do drugs or anything. And he asked my dad if he could take me out!"

These days, there is a new air of determination, even pride, about Jen. The aimless high school dropout pulls ten-hour shifts entering data at a warehouse distribution center Monday through Thursday. She has held the job for three years, and her aptitude and hard work have earned her a series of raises. Her current salary is higher than anyone in her household commands—$10.25 per hour, and she now gets two weeks of paid vacation, four personal days, sixty hours of sick time, and medical benefits. She has saved up the necessary $400 in tuition for a high school completion program that offers evening and weekend classes. Now all that stands between her and a diploma is a passing grade in mathematics, her least favorite subject. "My plan is to start college in January. [This month] I take my math test . . . so I can get my diploma," she confides.

Jen clearly sees how her life has improved since Rick's dramatic exit from the scene. "That's when I really started [to get better] because I didn't have to worry about what *he* was doing, didn't have to worry about him cheating on me, all this stuff. [It was] then I realized that I had to do what I had to do to take care of my son. . . . When he was there, I think that my whole life revolved around him, you know, so I always messed up somehow because I was so busy worrying about what *he* was doing. Like I would leave the [GED] programs I was in just to go home and see what he was doing. My mind was never concentrating." Now, she says, "a lot of people in my family look up to me now, because all my sisters dropped out from school, you know, nobody went back to school. I went back to school, you know? . . . I went back to school, and I plan to go to college, and a lot of people look up to me for that, you know? So that makes me happy . . . because five years ago nobody looked up to me. I was just like everybody else."

Yet the journey has not been easy. "Being a young mom, being fifteen, it's hard, hard, hard, you know." She says, "I have no life. . . . I work from 6:30 in the morning until 5:00 at night. I leave here at 5:30 in the morning. I don't get home until about 6:00 at night." Yet she measures her worth as a mother by the fact that she has managed to provide for her son largely on her own. "I don't depend on nobody. I might live with my dad and them, but I don't depend on them, you know." She continues, "There [used to] be days when I'd be so stressed out, like, 'I can't do this!' And I would just cry and cry and cry. . . . Then I look at Colin, and he'll be sleeping, and I'll just look at him and think I don't have no [reason to feel sorry for myself]. The cards I have I've dealt myself so I have to deal with it now. I'm older.

I can't change anything. He's my responsibility—he's nobody else's but mine—so I have to deal with that."

Becoming a mother transformed Jen's point of view on just about everything. She says, "I thought hanging on the corner drinking, getting high—I thought that was a good life, and I thought I could live that way for eternity, like sitting out with my friends. But it's not as fun once you have your own kid. . . . I think it changes [you]. I think, 'Would I want Colin to do that? Would I want my son to be like that . . .?' It was fun to me but it's not fun anymore. Half the people I hung with are either . . . Some have died from drug overdoses, some are in jail, and some people are just out there living the same life that they always lived, and they don't look really good. They look really bad." In the end, Jen believes, Colin's birth has brought far more good into her life than bad. "I know I could have waited [to have a child], but in a way I think Colin's the best thing that could have happened to me. . . . So I think I had my son for a purpose because I think Colin changed my life. He *saved* my life, really. My whole life revolves around Colin!"

❂ Promises I can Keep

There are unique themes in Jen's story—most fathers are only one or two, not five years older than the mothers of their children, and few fathers have as many glaring problems as Rick—but we heard most of these themes repeatedly in the stories of the 161 other poor, single mothers we came to know. Notably, poor women do not reject marriage; they revere it. Indeed, it is the conviction that marriage is forever that makes them think that divorce is worse than having a baby outside of marriage. Their children, far from being liabilities, provide crucial social-psychological resources—a strong sense of purpose and a profound source of intimacy. Jen and the other mothers we came to know are coming of age in an America that is profoundly unequal— where the gap between rich and poor continues to grow. This economic reality has convinced them that they have little to lose and, perhaps, something to gain by a seemingly "ill-timed" birth.

The lesson one draws from stories like Jen's is quite simple: Until poor young women have more access to jobs that lead to financial independence—until there is reason to hope for the rewarding life pathways that their privileged peers pursue—the poor will continue to have children far sooner than most Americans think they should, while still deferring marriage. Marital standards have risen for all Americans, and the poor want the same things that everyone now wants out of marriage. The poor want to marry too, but they insist on marrying well. This, in their view, is the only way to avoid an almost certain divorce. Like Jen, they are simply not willing to make promises they are not sure they can keep..

Note

1Kathryn Edin and Maria Kefalas. *Promises I Can Keep: Why Poor Women Put Motherhood Before Marriage* (University of California Press, 2005).

◉ ◉ ◉

Critical-Thinking Questions

1. Why does romance among many low-income women not result in marriage? How do these women differ from most middle-class women who have an out-of-wedlock baby?

2. Why is marriage for many low-income women an "elusive goal"? Consider, especially, the economic factors that these mothers describe as well as their expectations for a family provider in the future.

3. Do you agree or not with the women in this study that it's better to raise children as a single parent rather than marry a man who's not "marriage material"? Do you know any middle-class women (including yourself, your mother, relatives, or friends) who have made the same decisions?

Socialization and the Power of Advertising

JEAN KILBOURNE

Can parents just turn off the TV to protect their kids from the negative impact of advertising? No, claims Jean Kilbourne. Because advertising permeates our environment, she claims, "We cannot escape it." Advertisers customize ads for subscribers of the same magazine, attract children to Web sites with games and prizes, and bombard us with products on billboards, public transportation systems, and the sides of buildings, trucks, and shopping carts. As a result, Kilbourne argues, advertising continues to persuade people of all ages that the way to be happy is to buy, buy, buy.

. . .

If you're like most people, you think that advertising has no influence on you. This is what advertisers want you to believe. But, if that were true, why would companies spend over $200 billion a year on advertising? Why would they be willing to spend over $250,000 to produce an average television commercial and another $250,000 to air it? If they want to broadcast their commercial during the Super Bowl, they will gladly spend over a million dollars to produce it and over one and a half million to air it. After all, they might have the kind of success that Victoria's Secret did during the 1999 Super Bowl. When they paraded bra-and-panty-clad models across TV screens for a mere

Reprinted from *Deadly Persuasion: Why Women and Girls Must Fight the Addictive Power of Advertising* (1999), Simon & Schuster, Inc.

thirty seconds, 1 million people turned away from the game to log on to the Web site promoted in the ad. No influence? . . .

Through focus groups and depth interviews, psychological researchers can zero in on very specific target audiences—and their leaders. "Buy this twenty-four-year-old and get all his friends absolutely free," proclaims an ad for MTV directed to advertisers. MTV presents itself publicly as a place for rebels and nonconformists. Behind the scenes, however, it tells potential advertisers that its viewers are lemmings who will buy whatever they are told to buy.

The MTV ad gives us a somewhat different perspective on the concept of "peer pressure." Advertisers, especially those who advertise tobacco and alcohol, are forever claiming that advertising doesn't influence anyone, that kids smoke and drink because of peer pressure. Sure, such pressure exists and is an important influence, but a lot of it is created by advertising. Kids who exert peer pressure don't drop into high schools like Martians. They are kids who tend to be leaders, whom other kids follow for good or for bad. And they themselves are mightily influenced by advertising, sometimes very deliberately, as in the MTV ad. As an ad for *Seventeen* magazine, picturing a group of attractive young people, says, "Hip doesn't just happen. It starts at the source: *Seventeen*." In the global village, the "peers" are very much the same, regardless of nationality, ethnicity, culture. In the eyes of the media, the youths of the world are becoming a single, seamless, soulless target audience—often cynically labeled Generation X, or, for the newest wave of teens, Generation Y. "We're helping a soft drink company reach them, even if their parents can't," says [a newspaper ad] featuring a group of young people. The ad continues, "If you think authority figures have a hard time talking to Generation X, you should try being an advertiser," and goes on to suggest placing ads in the television sections of newspapers. . . .

Home pages on the World Wide Web hawk everything from potato chips to cereal to fast food—to drugs. Alcohol and tobacco companies, chafing under advertising restrictions in other media, have discovered they can find and woo young people without any problem on the Web. Indeed, children are especially vulnerable on the Internet, where advertising manipulates them, invades their privacy, and transforms them into customers without their knowledge. Although there are various initiatives pending, there are as yet no regulations against targeting children online. Marketers attract children to Web sites with games and contests, and then extract from them information that can be used in future sales pitches to the child and the child's family. They should be aware that this information might be misleading. My daughter recently checked the "less than $20,000" household income box because she was thinking of her allowance.

Some sites offer prizes to lure children into giving up the email addresses of their friends too. Online advertising targets children as young as four in an attempt to develop "brand loyalty" as early as possible. Companies unrelated to children's products have Web sites for children, such as Chevron's site, which features games, toys, and videos touting the importance of—surprise!—the oil industry. In this way, companies can create an image early on and can also gather marketing data. As one ad says to advertisers, "Beginning this August, Kidstar will be able to reach every kid on the planet. And you can, too."

The United States is one of the few industrialized nations in the world that thinks that children are legitimate targets for advertisers. Belgium, Denmark, Norway, and the Canadian province of Quebec ban all advertising to children on television and radio, and Sweden and Greece are pushing for an end to all advertising aimed at children throughout the European Union. An effort to pass similar legislation in the United States in the 1970s was squelched by a coalition of food and toy companies, broadcasters, and ad agencies. Children in America appear to have value primarily as new consumers. As an ad for juvenile and infant bedding and home accessories says, "Having children is so rewarding. You get to buy childish stuff and pretend it's for them." Our public policy—or lack thereof—on every children's issue, from education to drugs to teen suicide to child abuse, leaves many to conclude that we are a nation that hates its children.

However, the media care about them. The Turner Cartoon Network tells advertisers, "Today's kids influence over $130 billion of their parent's spending annually. Kids also spend $8 billion of their own money. That makes these little consumers big business." Not only are children influencing a lot of spending in the present, they are developing brand loyalty and the beginnings of an addiction to consumption that will serve corp-orations well in the future. According to Mike Searles, president of Kids 'R' Us, "If you own this child at an early age, you can own this child for years to come. Companies are saying, 'Hey, I want to own the kid younger and younger.' " No wonder Levi Strauss & Co. finds it worthwhile to send a direct mailing to seven- to twelve-year-old girls to learn about them when they are starting to form brand opinions. According to the senior advertising manager, "This is more of a long-term relationship that we're trying to explore." There may not seem much harm in this until we consider that the tobacco and alcohol industries are also interested in long-term relationships beginning in childhood—and are selling products that can indeed end up "owning" people.

Advertisers are willing to spend a great deal on psychological research that will help them target children more effectively. Nintendo U.S. has a research center which interviews at least fifteen hundred children every week. Kid Connection, a unit of the advertising agency Saatchi & Saatchi, has commissioned what the company calls "psychocultural youth research" studies from cultural anthropologists and clinical psychologists. In a recent study, psychologists interviewed young people between the ages of six and twenty and then analyzed their dreams, drawings, and reactions to symbols. Meanwhile, the anthropologists spent over five hundred hours watching other children use the Internet.

Children are easily influenced. Most little children can't tell the difference between the shows and the commercials (which basically means they are smarter than the rest of us). The toys sold during children's programs are often based on characters in the programs. Recently, the Center for Media Education asked the Federal Trade Commission to examine "kidola," a television marketing strategy in which toy companies promise to buy blocks of commercial time if a local broadcast station airs programs associated with their toys.

One company has initiated a program for advertisers to distribute samples, coupons, and promotional materials to a network of twenty-two thousand day care centers and 2 million preschool children. The editor-in-chief of *KidStyle*, a kids' fashion magazine that made its debut in 1997, said, "It's not going to be another parenting magazine. This will be a pictorial magazine focusing on products."

Perhaps most troubling, advertising is increasingly showing up in our schools, where ads are emblazoned on school buses, scoreboards, and book covers, where corporations provide "free" material for teachers, and where many children are a captive audience for the commercials on Channel One, a marketing program that gives video equipment to desperate schools in exchange for the right to broadcast a "news" program studded with commercials to all students every morning. Channel One is hardly free, however—it is estimated that it costs taxpayers $1.8 billion in lost classroom time. But it certainly is profitable for the owners who promise advertisers "the largest teen audience around" and "the undivided attention of millions of teenagers for twelve minutes a day." Another ad for Channel One boasts, "Our relationship with 8.1 million teenagers lasts for six years [rather remarkable considering most of theirs last for . . . like six days]." Imagine the public outcry if a political or religious group offered schools an information package with ten minutes of news and two minutes of political or religious persuasion. Yet we tend to think of commercial persuasion as somehow neutral, although it certainly promotes beliefs and behavior that have significant and sometimes harmful effects on the individual, the family, the society, and the environment.

"Reach him at the office," says an ad featuring a small boy in a business suit, which continues, "His first day job is kindergarten. Modern can put your sponsored educational materials in the lesson plan." Advertisers are reaching nearly 8 million public-school students each day.

Cash-strapped and underfunded schools accept this dance with the devil. And they are not alone. As many people become less and less willing to pay taxes to support public schools and other institutions and services, corporations are only too eager to pick up the slack—in exchange for a captive audience, of course. As one good corporate citizen, head of an outdoor advertising agency, suggested, "Perhaps fewer libraries would be closing their doors or reducing their services if they wrapped their buildings in tastefully done outdoor ads."

According to the Council for Aid to Education, the total amount corporations spend on "educational" programs from kindergarten through high school has increased from $5 million in 1965 to about $500 million today. The Seattle School Board recently voted to aggressively pursue advertising and corporate sponsorship. "There can be a Nike concert series and a Boeing valedictorian," said the head of the task force. We already have market-driven educational materials in our schools, such as Exxon's documentary on the beauty of the Alaskan coastline or the McDonald's Nutrition Chart and a kindergarten curriculum that teaches children to "Learn to Read through Recognizing Corporate Logos."

No wonder so many people fell for a "news item" in *Adbusters* (a Canadian magazine that critiques advertising and commercialism) about a new program called "Tattoo You Too!", which pays schools a fee in exchange for students willing to be tattooed with famous corporate logos, such as the Nike "swoosh" and the Guess question mark. Although the item was a spoof, it was believable enough to be picked up by some major media. I guess nothing about advertising seems unbelievable these days.

There are penalties for young people who resist this commercialization. In the spring of 1998 Mike Cameron, a senior at Greenbrier High School in Evans, Georgia, was suspended from school. Why? Did he bring a gun to school? Was he smoking in the boys' room? Did he assault a teacher? No. He wore a Pepsi shirt on a school-sponsored Coke day, an entire school day dedicated to an attempt to win ten thousand dollars in a national contest run by Coca-Cola.

Coke has several "partnerships" with schools around the country in which the company gives several million dollars to the school in exchange for a longterm contract giving Coke exclusive rights to

614

school vending machines. John Bushey, an area superintendent for thirteen schools in Colorado Springs who signs his correspondence "The Coke Dude," urged school officials to "get next year's volume up to 70,000 cases" and suggested letting students buy Coke throughout the day and putting vending machines "where they are accessible all day." Twenty years ago, teens drank almost twice as much milk as soda. Today they drink twice as much soda as milk. Some data suggest this contributes to broken bones while they are still teenagers and to osteoporosis in later life. . . .

◉ Advertising is Our Environment

Advertisers like to tell parents that they can always turn off the TV to protect their kids from any of the negative impact of advertising. This is like telling us that we can protect our children from air pollution by making sure they never breathe. Advertising is our *environment*. We swim in it as fish swim in water. We cannot escape it. Unless, of course, we keep our children home from school and blindfold them whenever they are outside of the house. And never let them play with other children. Even then, advertising's messages are inside our intimate relationships, our homes, our hearts, our heads.

Advertising not only appears on radio and television, in our magazines and newspapers, but also surrounds us on billboards, on the sides of buildings, plastered on our public transportation. Buses now in many cities are transformed into facsimiles of products, so that one boards a bus masquerading as a box of Dunkin' Donuts (followed, no doubt, by a Slimfast bus). The creators of this atrocity proudly tell us in their ad in *Advertising Age*, "In your face . . . all over the place!" Indeed.

Trucks carry advertising along with products as part of a marketing strategy. "I want every truck we have on the road making folks thirsty for Bud Light," says an ad in *Advertising Age*, which refers to a truck as a "valuable moving billboard." Given that almost half of all automobile crashes are alcohol-related, it's frightening to think of people becoming thirsty for Bud Light while driving their cars. A Spanish company has paid the drivers of seventy-five cars in Madrid to turn their cars into Pall Mall cigarette packages, and hopes to expand its operation throughout Spain. Imagine cars disguised as bottles of beer zipping along our highways. If we seek to escape all this by taking a plane, we become a captive audience for in-flight promotional videos.

Ads are on the videos we rent, the shopping carts we push through stores, the apples and hot dogs we buy, the online services we use, and the navigational screens of the luxury cars we drive. A new device allows advertisers to print their messages directly onto the sand of a beach. "This is my best idea ever—5,000 imprints of Skippy Peanut Butter jars covering the beach," crowed the inventor. Added the promotion director, "I'm here looking at thousands of families with kids. If they're on the beach thinking of Skippy, that's just what we want." Their next big idea is snow imprinting at ski resorts. In England the legendary white cliffs of Dover now serve as the backdrop for a laser-projected Adidas ad. American consumers have recently joined Europeans in being offered free phone calls if they will also listen to commercials. Conversations are interrupted by brief ads, tailored to match the age and social profiles of the conversants. And beer companies have experimented with messages posted over urinals, such as "Time for more Coors" or "Put used Bud here."

The average American is exposed to at least three thousand ads every day and will spend three years of his or her life watching television commercials. Advertising makes up about 70 percent of our newspapers and 40 percent of our mail. Of course, we don't pay direct attention to very many of these ads, but we are powerfully influenced, mostly on an unconscious level, by the experience of being immersed in an advertising culture, a market-driven culture, in which all our institutions, from political to religious to educational, are increasingly for sale to the highest bidder. According to Rance Crain, editor-in-chief of *Advertising Age*, the major publication of the advertising industry, "Only eight percent of an ad's message is received by the conscious mind; the rest is worked and reworked deep within the recesses of the brain, where a product's positioning and repositioning takes shape." It is in this sense that advertising is subliminal: not in the sense of hidden messages embedded in ice cubes, but in the sense that we aren't consciously aware of what advertising is doing.

Commercialism has no borders. There is barely any line left between advertising and the rest of the culture. The prestigious Museum of Fine Arts in Boston puts on a huge exhibit of Herb Ritts, fashion photographer, and draws one of the largest crowds in its history. In 1998 the museum's Monet show was the most popular exhibit in the world. Museum officials were especially pleased by results of a survey showing 74 percent of visitors recognized that the show's sponsor was Fleet Financial Group, which shelled out $1.2 million to underwrite the show.

Bob Dole plays on his defeat in the presidential election in ads for Air France and Viagra, while Ed Koch, former mayor of New York City, peddles Dunkin' Donuts' bagels. Dr. Jane Goodall, doyenne of primatology, appears with her chimpanzees in an ad for Home Box Office, and Sarah Ferguson, the former duchess of York, gets a million dollars for being the official spokeswoman for Weight Watchers (with a bonus if she keeps her weight down). . . .

The unintended effects of advertising are far more important and far more difficult to measure than those effects that are intended. The important question is not "Does this ad sell the product?" but rather "What else does this ad sell?" An ad for Gap khakis featuring a group of acrobatic swing dancers probably sold a lot of pants, which, of course, was the intention of the advertisers. But it also contributed to a rage for swing dancing. This is an innocuous example of advertising's powerful unintended effects. Swing dancing is not binge drinking, after all.

Advertising often sells a great deal more than products. It sells values, images, and concepts of love and sexuality, romance, success, and, perhaps most important, normalcy. To a great extent, it tells us who we are and who we should be. We are increasingly using brand names to create our identities. James Twitchell argues that the label of our shirt, the make of our car, and our favorite laundry detergent are filling the vacuum once occupied by religion, education, and our family name.

References

Angier, N. 1996. Who needs this ad most? *New York Times* (November 24): 4E.

Associated Press. 1998. Pepsi prank goes flat. *Boston Globe* (March 26): A3.

Austen, I. 1999. But first, another word from our sponsors. *New York Times* (February 18): E1, E8.

Bidlake, S. 1997. Commercials support free phone calls. *Advertising Age International* (September): 147, 149.

Carroll, J. 1996. Adventures into new territory. *Boston Globe* (November 24): D1, D5.

Cortissoz, A. 1998. For young people, swing's the thing. *Boston Globe* (July 25): A2, A10.

Crain, R. 1997. Who knows what ads lurk in the hearts of consumers? The inner mind knows. *Advertising Age* (June 9): 25.

Foreman, J. 1999. Sugar's "empty calories" pile up. *Boston Globe* (March 1): C1, C4.

Grunwald, M. 1997. Megamall sells stimulation. *Boston Globe* (December 9): A1, A26.

Harris, R. 1989. Children who dress for excess: Today's youngsters have become fixated with fashion. *Los Angeles Times* (November 12): A1.

Jacobson, M. F., and L. A. Mazur. 1995. *Marketing madness: A survival guide for a consumer society.* Boulder, Colo.: Westview Press.

Jhally, S. 1998. *Advertising and the end of the world* (a video). Northampton, Mass.: Media Education Foundation.

Kerwin, A. M. 1997. "KidStyle" crafts customized ad opportunities. *Advertising Age* (April 28): 46.

Koranteng, J. 1999. Sweden presses EU for further ad restrictions. *Advertising Age International* (April 12): 2.

Krol, C. 1998. Levi's reaches girls as they develop opinions on brands. *Advertising Age* (April 20): 29.

Lewis, M. 1997. Royal scam. *New York Times Magazine* (February 9): 22.

Liu, E. 1999. Remember when public space didn't carry brand names? *USA Today* (March 25): 15A.

McCarthy, C. 1990. In thingdom, laying waste our powers. *Washington Post* (November 11): F3.

McLaren, C. 1997. The babysitter's club. *Stay Free!* (Spring): 8–11.

Mohl, B. 1999. Lend them your ear, and your call is free. *Boston Globe* (January 13): AI, A10.

Monet show sets world record 1999. *Boston Globe* (February 2): E2.

Not for Sale! 1997. Oakland, Calif.: Center for Commercial-Free Public Education. (Spring).

Not for Sale! 1999. Oakland, Calif.: Center for Commercial-Free Public Education. (Winter).

Orlando, S. 1999. A material world: Defining ourselves by consumer goods. [Online]. Available: *http://www.sciencedaily.com/releases/1999/05/990518114815.htm.*

Reading, Writing . . . and TV commercials. 1999. *Enough!* 7(10) (Spring).

Rich, F. 1997. howdydoody.com. *New York Times* (June 8): E15.

Rosenberg, A. S. 1999. Ad ideas etched in sand. *Boston Globe* (February 1): A3.

Sharkey, J. 1998. Beach-blanket babel: Another reason to stay at the pool. *New York Times* (July 5): 2.

Twitchell, J. B. 1996. *Adcult USA: The triumph of advertising in American culture.* New York: Columbia University Press.

U.S. Department of Transportation. 1999. National Highway Traffic Safety Administration. [Online]. Available: *http://www.nhtsa.dot.gov/people/ncsa/FactPreve/alc96.html.*

Wallace, D. F. 1996. *Infinite jest.* Boston: Little Brown.

Weber, J. 1997. Selling to kids: At what price? *Boston Globe* (May 18): F4.

☻ ☻ ☻

Critical-Thinking Questions

1. Advertisers maintain that people rely on commercials and ads to make informed decisions about the products and services they buy. Using the material in this chapter, discuss whether you agree or disagree with advertisers' claims that they are providing a service to consumers by educating them about their market choices.

2. What does Kilbourne mean when she says that advertising "sells much more than products"? How, for example, does advertising influence our values and lifestyles? What about children's and adolescents' attitudes about tobacco, alcohol, food, and their self-image?

3. Belgium, Denmark, Norway, and other countries ban all television and radio advertising directed at children. Should the United States pass similar legislation?

Invisible Privilege

PAULA S. ROTHENBERG

In this article, mother and feminist scholar Paula Rothenberg explains how class and race affect friendship in the life of her daughter.

. . .

Perhaps it will be instructive to tell the story of the friendship between my daughter, Andrea, who is white and her onetime friend, Jewel, who is Black. Although it is simply the story of two little girls who managed to be best friends for a very brief time and is highly specific to them, it sheds light on the complex nature of relations across race/ethnicity and class in the suburbs.

Jewel and Andrea met in kindergarten and were kindred spirits from the start. Both were smart and spunky, and both loved to be silly. The girls wanted to play together after school, but that was easier said than done. They managed to trade phone numbers, but whenever I called Jewel's house her grandmother answered and said that Jewel's parents were not available and she was not able to make arrangements for a play date in their absence.

After several weeks of fruitless calls, persistence finally paid off; one day, Jewel's mother, Carol, called back. Yes, Jewel could play at our house after school as long as I didn't mind keeping her until after dinner. Her mother worked late and wouldn't be able to come by until 7:30 or so. Since that was no problem, I picked up both girls at school the very next day. What I remember about the visit was Jewel's amazement as she explored our house for the first time and discovered that we had more than one bathroom.

Reprinted from *Invisible Privilege: A Memoir About Race, Class, and Gender* (2000), by permission of University Press of Kansas.

After a series of other play dates and several conversations over coffee, Carol told me what I suspected. It was so difficult to reach her and so hard to coordinate play dates for the girls because Carol and her husband did not live in Montclair and Jewel managed to go to the Montclair public schools by claiming her grandmother's house as her residence.

This practice is not uncommon. Taxes in Montclair are very high, and many African-Americans who were raised in town and whose parents still live here can't afford either the price of a house or the taxes they would have to pay as residents. A common solution is to live in East Orange or some other surrounding community in a neighborhood where the schools are inferior but the taxes and property values are much lower and use a parent's or relative's address to claim residency and gain access to the Montclair school system.

Obviously people react to this subterfuge in different ways, depending largely on their race and their class. Many whites in town are angered by the fact that some children, mostly Black, who don't actually live in town attend the public schools, thereby raising their tax burden, while many Blacks see nothing very wrong with the practice. They question why education should be funded by local property taxes in the first place instead of on a statewide basis, which could ensure equal education for all children. Besides, having grown up here, they think of themselves as part of the town—quite apart from the technicality of their legal residence. While many of the white homeowner/tax payers are recent arrivals to Montclair, many of the African-Americans who resort to the subterfuge are members of families that have lived in the town for several generations. In many cases, they attended the same schools that their children now attend. What seems like a gross violation of law and justice to some of the whites, who focus on whether the parents of the children actually live in town, hardly seems that way to many of the African-Americans whose sense of family is much more inclusive. Children and grandchildren, cousins and nieces are understood to be part of the extended family of the relatives who are Montclair residents and taxpayers. These relatives care for the children at their homes on a regular basis, often having the children spend nights as well as days with them. The children's parents and other family members see the house itself as part of their extended residence, frequently eating and socializing with one another there, dropping in to use the phone or to help with home repairs. Legal residency often seems like a procedural technicality rather than an accurate indicator of who is part of town life. In fact, according to some criteria, these Black Montclairions, whose roots are firmly planted in the town, have more claim to being part of it than the newly arrived white professionals who simply sleep here, commuting to work in New York each day and spending their weekends playing golf at the country club in Glen Ridge.

When Carol finally gave me the family's address and phone number in another town, it was a real sign of trust. The first priority in her life was keeping Jewel in a good school system, arranging afternoon play dates with a white classmate was low on the list. But as the girls' friendship blossomed, Carol, like me, was eager to let them enjoy time together.

And then the inevitable happened. During one of the periodic efforts that the town officials make to track down children who are attending public school illegally, Jewel's illegal status was discovered. Carol never asked whether I had provided the school officials with the information—of course, I had not—but it's difficult to imagine that the idea didn't cross her mind. How could she ever be sure? Through some special arrangement, Jewel was allowed to finish up the school year, which was almost over. During the summer, her family moved out of their apartment and into a small house on the outskirts of Newark, about twenty minutes away. The following September, Jewel began attending parochial school. For her family, as for others like them, parochial school provided the only viable alternative to the inferior and dangerous public school near their home.

Jewel attended Andrea's birthday party that September, as she had in the past, and in January, Carol called to invite Andrea to Jewel's birthday party a week later. Andrea was thrilled with the prospect of seeing Jewel again and of visiting Jewel's house for the first time. She could talk of nothing else.

Jewel's new house was located in a fairly rundown Black neighborhood of small, single-family, urban-style homes. In spite of its appearance, I knew that it would be classified as a middle-class neighborhood by other Black families, since definitions of what counts as "middle class" are themselves race specific, and it is informal residential segregation that often determines how neighborhoods are defined and who gets to live in them. The front door of the house opened into a tiny living room that, in turn, opened into a larger, but still small, dining alcove. Sitting around a large wood table, filling all the space in the room, was a gaggle of aunts and uncles, grandparents and cousins. Apart from Jewel's young cousins, Andrea was the only child present, and she and I were the only white people. Conversation among the adults was friendly, if labored, with everyone trying hard to make us feel welcome. I tried hard not to cramp their good time.

But Andrea was very uncomfortable. Many of the social cues that she counted on to negotiate such events were missing, and she had not had the opportunity to learn the ones that were in place. People talked to each other in unfamiliar ways, and, at times, what I recognized as affectionate teasing must have sounded to her like sharp criticism or argument. She was frightened by how dark the house was and couldn't understand why only one lightbulb was burning on such a dark day. Coming from a world where people have enough money to use lighting as much for decoration as to be functional, she couldn't know that for most of the world, electric lights are a luxury or at least a carefully conserved resource.

A special point of pride for Jewel was the second toilet—literally a water closet—her dad had rigged up in the basement of the house to supplement the full bath upstairs. It consisted of a four-sided wooden cabinet set on a platform in the middle of a dark basement. The cabinet itself had no electric light, but some open space had been left between the ceiling and one side of the cabinet to allow light to enter. Jewel's pride was my daughter's terror. She went to the bathroom only after it was clear that one more postponement would have dire consequences, and she could use the bathroom at all only because I stayed in the cabinet with her.

As we drove home, I knew it was unlikely that the girls would continue their friendship. And in fact, they did not. It was just too difficult. Although Carol and I had tried to help the girls be friends, perhaps because we wanted the possibility of friendship for ourselves as well, the odds against it were too overwhelming and the differences separating the girls were just too great to bridge. In the end, personal relations occur within social contexts, and, in this case, it was unreasonable to expect two eight-year-old girls to be able to negotiate each other's worlds.

Different people will make different things out of this story. Some will see class as the villain here and argue, along with William Julius Wilson and others, that it is class, not race, that separates whites and Blacks today. This I think is an oversimplification. Jewel and Andrea carried with them the combined history of three hundred years of race, class, and gender oppression and privilege, and the differences created by them were just too great to overcome. For example, why was I able to live in the town and have legitimate access to the schools for my children while Jewel's mother, who had grown up there, could no longer claim access to her own community? Both Jewel's mother and I worked full time, but my job as a college teacher allowed me flexible hours with good pay. Carol worked in the accounting department of a large supermarket corporation in a job that often required her to stay until 11 p.m. Although both she and her husband worked full time, as did Andrea's father and I, their combined income was a fraction of ours. This was not surprising, since statistics indicate that in 1996 annual income for the typical Black family was about half of the $47,000 a year enjoyed by white families. In fact, according to a report issued by the White House's Council of Economic Advisers, Black and Hispanic family incomes are farther behind those of whites today than they were twenty years ago.* For so many years, while I was fortunate enough to be paying off a mortgage on a home I

New York Times, February 17, 1998, A18.

625

obtained because my in-laws could afford to provide a down payment, Carol and her husband were paying rent and working overtime to save up for a house. Their down payment ultimately bought them a poorly constructed home in a marginal urban neighborhood with inadequate schools, dirty streets, and food stores that overcharge. Some little white girl, a mirror image of my long-ago self, drives through those streets today, and her parents caution her to roll up her window and lock her door. They shake their heads over the way some people choose to live when nothing more than hard work and ability are required to earn us all a piece of the American dream. They do not know that for Jewel's family, this *is* their piece of the American dream and they have had to work very hard to achieve it. They do not understand that those of us who have more have drawn on the privileges of our race, our class, our gender, or some combination of them and have done so at the expense of the very people we denigrate.

◉ ◉ ◉

Critical-Thinking Questions

1. Why is privilege often invisible? What categories of people are more and less likely to be aware of privilege?

2. Why was Andrea so uncomfortable in Jewel's Newark home? Do you think people can overcome the type of social differences described here? Explain.

3. Can you identify elements of privilege in your own life? How have they affected your relationships with others?

You Just Don't Understand: Women and Men in Conversation

DEBORAH TANNEN

Many men and women complain with frustration that they communicate on different "wave lengths." Deborah Tannen, a sociolinguist, explains why men and women often talk past each other in a host of everyday situations.

. . .

I was sitting in a suburban living room, speaking to a women's group that had invited men to join them for the occasion of my talk about communication between women and men. During the discussion, one man was particularly talkative, full of lengthy comments and explanations. When I made the observation that women often complain that their husbands don't talk to them enough, this man volunteered that he heartily agreed. He gestured toward his wife, who had sat silently beside him on the couch throughout the evening, and said, "She's the talker in our family."

Everyone in the room burst into laughter. The man looked puzzled and hurt. "It's true," he explained. "When I come home from work, I usually have nothing to say, but she never runs out. If it weren't for her, we'd spend the whole evening in silence." Another

Reprinted from *You Just Don't Understand* (1990), HarperCollins, Inc.

woman expressed a similar paradox about her husband: "When we go out, he's the life of the party. If I happen to be in another room, I can always hear his voice above the others. But when we're home, he doesn't have that much to say. I do most of the talking."

Who talks more, women or men? According to the stereotype, women talk too much. Linguist Jennifer Coates notes some proverbs:

A woman's tongue wags like a lamb's tail.

Foxes are all tail and women are all tongue.

The North Sea will sooner be found wanting in water than a woman be at a loss for a word.

Throughout history, women have been punished for talking too much or in the wrong way. Linguist Connie Eble lists a variety of physical punishments used in Colonial America: Women were strapped to ducking stools and held underwater until they nearly drowned, put into the stocks with signs pinned to them, gagged, and silenced by a cleft stick applied to their tongues.

Though such institutionalized corporal punishments have given way to informal, often psychological ones, modern stereotypes are not much different from those expressed in the old proverbs. Women are believed to talk too much. Yet study after study finds that it is men who talk more at meetings, in mixed-group discussions, and in class-rooms where girls or young women sit next to boys or young men. For example, communications researchers Barbara and Gene Eakins tape recorded and studied seven university faculty meetings. They found that, with one exception, men spoke more often and, without exception, spoke for a longer time. The men's turns ranged from 10.66 to 17.07 seconds, while the women's turns ranged from 3 to 10 seconds. In other words, the women's longest turns were still shorter than the men's shortest turns.

When a public lecture is followed by questions from the floor, or a talk show host opens the phones, the first voice to be heard asking a question is almost always a man's. And when they ask questions or

628

offer comments from the audience, men tend to talk longer. Linguist Marjorie Swacker recorded question-and-answer sessions at academic conferences. Women were highly visible as speakers at the conferences studied; they presented 40.7 percent of the papers at the conferences studied and made up 42 percent of the audiences. But when it came to volunteering and being called on to ask questions, women contributed only 27.4 percent. Furthermore, the women's questions, on the average, took less than half as much time as the men's. (The mean was 23.1 seconds for women, 52.7 for men.) This happened, Swacker shows, because men (but not women) tended to preface their questions with statements, ask more than one question, and follow up the speaker's answer with another question or comment.

I have observed this pattern at my own lectures, which concern issues of direct relevance to women. Regardless of the proportion of women and men in the audience, men almost invariably ask the first question, more questions, and longer questions. In these situations, women often feel that men are talking too much. I recall one discussion period following a lecture I gave to a group assembled in a bookstore. The group was composed mostly of women, but most of the discussion was being conducted by men in the audience. At one point, a man sitting in the middle was talking at such great length that several women in the front rows began shifting in their seats and rolling their eyes at me. Ironically, what he was going on about was how frustrated he feels when he has to listen to women going on and on about topics he finds boring and unimportant.

◉ Rapport-Talk and Report-Talk

Who talks more, then, women or men? The seemingly contradictory evidence is reconciled by the difference between what I call *public* and *private speaking*. More men feel comfortable doing "public speaking," while more women feel comfortable doing "private speaking." Another way of capturing these differences is by using the terms *report-talk* and *rapport-talk*.

For most women, the language of conversation is primarily a language of rapport: a way of establishing connections and negotiating relationships. Emphasis is placed on displaying similarities and matching experiences. From childhood, girls criticize peers who try to stand out or appear better than others. People *feel* their closest connections at home, or in settings where they feel at home—with one or a few people they feel close to and comfortable with—in other words, during private speaking. But even the most public situations can be approached like private speaking.

For most men, talk is primarily a means to preserve independence and negotiate and maintain status in a hierarchical social order. This is done by exhibiting knowledge and skill, and by holding center stage through verbal performance such as storytelling, joking, or imparting information. From childhood, men learn to use talking as a way to get and keep attention. So they are more comfortable speaking in larger groups made up of people they know less well—in the broadest sense, "public speaking." But even the most private situations can be approached like public speaking, more like giving a report than establishing rapport.

❂ Private Speaking: The Wordy Woman and the Mute Man

What is the source of the stereotype that women talk a lot? Dale Spender suggests that most people feel instinctively (if not consciously) that women, like children, should be seen and not heard, so any amount of talk from them seems like too much. Studies have shown that if women and men talk equally in a group, people think the women talked more. So there is truth to Spender's view. But another explanation is that men think women talk a lot because they hear women talking in situations where men would not: on the telephone; or in social situations with friends, when they are not discussing topics that men find inherently interesting; or, like the couple at the women's group, at home alone—in other words, in private speaking.

630

Home is the setting for an American icon that features the silent man and the talkative woman. And this icon, which grows out of the different goals and habits I have been describing, explains why the complaint most often voiced by women about the men with whom they are intimate is "He doesn't talk to me"—and the second most frequent is "He doesn't listen to me."

A woman who wrote to Ann Landers is typical:

> My husband never speaks to me when he comes home from work. When I ask, "How did everything go today?" he says, "Rough . . ." or "It's a jungle out there." (We live in Jersey and he works in New York City.)
>
> It's a different story when we have guests or go visiting. Paul is the gabbiest guy in the crowd—a real spellbinder. He comes up with the most interesting stories. People hang on every word. I think to myself, "Why doesn't he ever tell *me* these things?"
>
> This has been going on for thirty-eight years. Paul started to go quiet on me after ten years of marriage. I could never figure out why. Can you solve the mystery?
>
> —The Invisible Woman

Ann Landers suggests that the husband may not want to talk because he is tired when he comes home from work. Yet women who work come home tired too, and they are nonetheless eager to tell their partners or friends everything that happened to them during the day and what these fleeting, daily dramas made them think and feel.

Sources as lofty as studies conducted by psychologists, as down to earth as letters written to advice columnists, and as sophisticated as movies and plays come up with the same insight: Men's silence at home is a disappointment to women. Again and again, women complain, "He seems to have everything to say to everyone else, and nothing to say to me."

The film *Divorce American Style* opens with a conversation in which Debbie Reynolds is claiming that she and Dick Van Dyke don't communicate, and he is protesting that he tells her everything that's on his mind. The doorbell interrupts their quarrel, and husband and wife compose themselves before opening the door to greet their guests with cheerful smiles.

Behind closed doors, many couples are having conversations like this. Like the character played by Debbie Reynolds, women feel men don't communicate. Like the husband played by Dick Van Dyke, men feel wrongly accused. How can she be convinced that he doesn't tell her anything, while he is equally convinced he tells her everything that's on his mind? How can women and men have such different ideas about the same conversations?

When something goes wrong, people look around for a source to blame: either the person they are trying to communicate with ("You're demanding, stubborn, self-centered") or the group that the other person belongs to ("All women are demanding"; "All men are self-centered"). Some generous-minded people blame the relationship ("We just can't communicate"). But underneath, or overlaid on these types of blame cast outward, most people believe that something is wrong with them.

If individual people or particular relationships were to blame, there wouldn't be so many different people having the same problems. The real problem is conversational style. Women and men have different ways of talking. Even with the best intentions, trying to settle the problem through talk can only make things worse if it is ways of talking that are causing trouble in the first place. . . .

❂ "Talk To Me!"

Women's dissatisfaction with men's silence at home is captured in the stock cartoon setting of a breakfast table at which a husband and wife are sitting: He's reading a newspaper; she's glaring at the back of the newspaper. In a Dagwood strip, Blondie complains, "Every morning all he sees is the newspaper! I'll bet you don't even know I'm here!" Dagwood reassures her, "Of course I know you're here. You're my wonderful wife and I love you very much." With this, he unseeingly pats the paw of the family dog, which the wife has put in her place before leaving the room. The cartoon strip shows that

632

Blondie is justified in feeling like the woman who wrote to Ann Landers: invisible.

Another cartoon shows a husband opening a newspaper and asking his wife, "Is there anything you would like to say to me before I begin reading the newspaper?" The reader knows that there isn't—but that as soon as he begins reading the paper, she will think of something. The cartoon highlights the difference in what women and men think talk is for: To him, talk is for information. So when his wife interrupts his reading, it must be to inform him of something that he needs to know. This being the case, she might as well tell him what she thinks he needs to know before he starts reading. But to her, talk is for interaction. Telling things is a way to show involvement, and listening is a way to show interest and caring. It is not an odd coincidence that she always thinks of things to tell him when he is reading. She feels the need for verbal interaction most keenly when he is (unaccountably, from her point of view) buried in the newspaper instead of talking to her.

Yet another cartoon shows a wedding cake that has, on top, in place of the plastic statues of bride and groom in tuxedo and gown, a breakfast scene in which an unshaven husband reads a newspaper across the table from his disgruntled wife. The cartoon reflects the enormous gulf between the romantic expectations of marriage, represented by the plastic couple in traditional wedding costume, and the often disappointing reality represented by the two sides of the newspaper at the breakfast table—the front, which he is reading, and the back, at which she is glaring.

These cartoons, and many others on the same theme, are funny because people recognize their own experience in them. What's not funny is that many women are deeply hurt when men don't talk to them at home, and many men are deeply frustrated by feeling they have disappointed their partners, without understanding how they failed or how else they could have behaved.

Some men are further frustrated because, as one put it, "When in the world am I supposed to read the morning paper?" If many women are incredulous that many men do not exchange personal information with their friends, this man is incredulous that many women do not bother to read the morning paper. To him, reading the paper is an essential part of his morning ritual, and his whole day is awry if he doesn't get to read it. In his words, reading the newspaper in the morning is as important to him as putting on makeup in the morning is to many women he knows. Yet many women, he observed, either don't subscribe to a paper or don't read it until they get home in the evening. "I find this very puzzling," he said. "I can't tell you how often I have picked up a woman's morning newspaper from her front door in the evening and handed it to her when she opened the door for me."

To this man (and I am sure many others), a woman who objects to his reading the morning paper is trying to keep him from doing something essential and harmless. It's a violation of his independence—his freedom of action. But when a woman who expects her partner to talk to her is disappointed that he doesn't, she perceives his behavior as a failure of intimacy: He's keeping things from her; he's lost interest in her; he's pulling away. A woman I will call Rebecca, who is generally quite happily married, told me that this is the one source of serious dissatisfaction with her husband, Stuart. Her term for his taciturnity is *stinginess of spirit*. She tells him what she is thinking, and he listens silently. She asks him what he is thinking, and he takes a long time to answer, "I don't know." In frustration she challenges, "Is there nothing on your mind?"

For Rebecca, who is accustomed to expressing her fleeting thoughts and opinions as they come to her, *saying* nothing means *thinking* nothing. But Stuart does not assume that his passing thoughts are worthy of utterance. He is not in the habit of uttering his fleeting ruminations, so just as Rebecca "naturally" speaks her thoughts, he "naturally" dismisses his as soon as they occur to him. Speaking them would give them more weight and significance than he feels they merit. All her life she has had practice in verbalizing her thoughts and feelings in private conversations with people she is close to; all his life he has had practice in dismissing his and keeping them to himself. . . .

☙ Public Speaking: The Talkative Man and the Silent Woman

So far I have been discussing the private scenes in which many men are silent and many women are talkative. But there are other scenes in which the roles are reversed. Returning to Rebecca and Stuart, we saw that when they are home alone, Rebecca's thoughts find their way into words effortlessly, whereas Stuart finds he can't come up with anything to say. The reverse happens when they are in other situations. For example, at a meeting of the neighborhood council or the parents' association at their children's school, it is Stuart who stands up and speaks. In that situation, it is Rebecca who is silent, her tongue tied by an acute awareness of all the negative reactions people could have to what she might say, all the mistakes she might make in trying to express her ideas. If she musters her courage and prepares to say something, she needs time to formulate it and then waits to be recognized by the chair. She cannot just jump up and start talking the way Stuart and some other men can.

Eleanor Smeal, president of the Fund for the Feminist Majority, was a guest on a call-in radio talk show, discussing abortion. No subject could be of more direct concern to women, yet during the hour-long show, all the callers except two were men. Diane Rehm, host of a radio talk show, expresses puzzlement that although the audience for her show is evenly split between women and men, 90 percent of the callers to the show are men. I am convinced that the reason is not that women are uninterested in the subjects discussed on the show. I would wager that women listeners are bringing up the subjects they heard on *The Diane Rehm Show* to their friends and family over lunch, tea, and dinner. But fewer of them call in because to do so would be putting themselves on display, claiming public attention for what they have to say, catapulting themselves onto center stage.

I myself have been the guest on innumerable radio and television talk shows. Perhaps I am unusual in being completely at ease in this mode of display. But perhaps I am not unusual at all, because although I am comfortable in the role of invited expert, I have never called in to a talk show I was listening to, although I have often had ideas to contribute. When I am the guest, my position of authority is granted before I begin to speak. Were I to call in, I would be claiming that right on my own. I would have to establish my credibility by explaining who I am, which might seem self-aggrandizing, or not explain who I am and risk having my comments ignored or not valued. For similar reasons, though I am comfortable lecturing to groups numbering in the thousands, I rarely ask questions following another lecturer's talk, unless I know both the subject and the group very well.

My own experience and that of talk show hosts seems to hold a clue to the difference in women's and men's attitudes toward talk: Many men are more comfortable than most women in using talk to claim attention. And this difference lies at the heart of the distinction between report-talk and rapport-talk.

☻ ☻ ☻

Critical-Thinking Questions

1. In general, who talks more, men or women? Who talks longer?

2. What is the difference between "report-talk" and "rapport-talk"? Between "private speaking" and "public speaking"?

3. In your opinion, is it possible to avoid some of the conflicts between report-talk and rapport-talk by developing a *shared* conversational style between men and women? Or is this unlikely?

The DOs and TABOOs of Body Language Around the World

ROGER E. AXTELL

In a world that grows smaller every year, it is easy to offend others simply by being ourselves—gestures that we take as innocent may be seen by someone else as deeply insulting. This selection suggests the extent of the problem and, in an age of global business dealings, the need to cultivate cultural sensitivity.

. . .

☻ Three Great Gaffes or One Country's Good Manners, Another's Grand Faux Pas

In Washington they call protocol "etiquette with a government expense account." But diplomacy isn't just for diplomats. How you behave in other people's countries reflects on more than you alone. It also brightens—or dims—the image of where you come from and whom you work for. The Ugly American about whom we used to

Reprinted from *The DOs and TABOOs around the World*, Third Edition (1993), John Wiley & Sons, Inc.

read so much may be dead, but here and there the ghost still wobbles out of the closet.

Three well-traveled Americans tell how even an old pro can sometimes make the wrong move in the wrong place at the wrong time.

A Partner in One of New York's Leading Private Banking Firms

When the board chairman is Lo Win Hao, do you smile brightly and say, "How do you do, Mr. Hao?" or "Mr. Lo"? Or "Mr. Win"?

> I traveled nine thousand miles to meet a client and arrived with my foot in my mouth. Determined to do things right, I'd memorized the names of the key men I was to see in Singapore. No easy job, inasmuch as the names all came in threes. So, of course, I couldn't resist showing off that I'd done my homework. I began by addressing top man Lo Win Hao with plenty of well placed Mr. Hao's—and sprinkled the rest of my remarks with a Mr. Chee this and a Mr. Woon that. Great show. Until a note was passed to me from one man I'd met before, in New York. Bad news. "Too friendly too soon, Mr. Long," it said. Where diffidence is next to godliness, there I was, calling a roomful of VIPs, in effect, Mr. Ed and Mr. Charlie. I'd remembered everybody's name—but forgotten that in Chinese the surname comes *first* and the given name *last.*

An Associate in Charge of Family Planning for an International Human Welfare Organization

The lady steps out in her dazzling new necklace and everybody dies laughing. (Or what not to wear to Togo on a Saturday night.)

638

From growing up in Cuba to joining the Peace Corps to my present work, I've spent most of my life in the Third World. So nobody should know better than I how to dress for it. Certainly one of the silliest mistakes an outsider can make is to dress up in "native" costume, whether it's a sari or a sombrero, unless you really know what you're doing. Yet, in Togo, when I found some of the most beautiful beads I'd ever seen, it never occurred to me not to wear them. While I was up-country, I seized the first grand occasion to flaunt my new find. What I didn't know is that locally the beads are worn not at the neck but at the waist—to hold up a sort of loincloth under the skirt. So, into the party I strutted, wearing around my neck what to every Togolese eye was part of a pair of underpants.

An Account Executive at an International Data Processing and Electronics Conglomerate

Even in a country run by generals, would you believe a runny nose could get you arrested?

A friend and I were coming into Colombia on business after a weekend in the Peruvian mountains touring Machu Picchu. What a sight that had been. And what a head cold the change in temperature had given my friend. As we proceeded through customs at the airport, he was wheezing and blowing into his handkerchief like an active volcano. Next thing I knew, two armed guards were lockstepping him through a door. I tried to intercede before the door slammed shut, but my spotty Spanish failed me completely. Inside a windowless room with the guards, so did his. He shouted in English. They shouted in Spanish. It was beginning to look like a bad day in Bogotá when a Colombian woman who had seen what happened burst into the room and finally achieved some

639

bilingual understanding. It seems all that sniffling in the land of the infamous coca leaf had convinced the guards that my friend was waltzing through their airport snorting cocaine.

☙ *Cuddly Ethnocentrics*

If only the world's customs inspectors could train their German shepherds to sniff out the invisible baggage we all manage to slip with us into foreign countries. They are like secret little land mines of the mind. Set to go off at the slightest quiver, they can sabotage a five-minute stroll down the Champs-Élysées or a $5 million tractor sale to Beijing. Three of our most popular national take-alongs:

Why Don't They Speak English?
For the same reason we don't speak Catalan or Urdu. The wonder, in fact, is that so many people do speak so many languages. Seldom is a Continental European fluent in fewer than three, often more. Africans grow up with language of the nation that once colonized theirs plus half a dozen different tribal dialects. Japan has three distinct Japanese languages, which even the lowliest street sweeper can understand. Middle Eastern businesspeople shift effortlessly from their native tongue(s) to Oxford English to Quai d'Orsay French. Yet most of the English-speaking world remains as cheerfully monolingual as Queen Victoria's parakeet. If there are any complaints, then, it is clear they should not be coming from the American/English-speaking traveler.

Take Me to Your Burger King
In Peoria a Persian does not go looking for pot-au-feu. Alone among travelers, Americans seem to embark like astronauts—sealed inside a cozy life-support system from home. Scrambled eggs. Rent-a-cars. Showers. TV. Nothing wrong with any of it back home, but to the rest of the universe it looks sadly like somebody trying to read a book with the cover closed. Experiment! Try the local specialties.

American Know-How to the Rescue!

Our brightest ideas have taken root all over the world—from assembling lines in Düsseldorf to silicon chips in Osaka to hybrid grains that are helping to nourish the Third World. Nonetheless, bigger, smarter, and faster do not inevitably add up to better. Indeed, the desire to take on shiny new American ways has been the downfall of nations whose cultures were already rich in art and technology when North America was still a glacier. As important as the idea itself is the way it is presented.

A U.S. doctor of public health recently back from West Africa offers an example of how to make the idea fit the ideology. "I don't just pop over and start handing out antimalarial pills on the corner," she says. "First I visit with the village chief. After he gives his blessing, I move in with the local witch doctor. After she shows me her techniques and I show her mine—and a few lives are saved—maybe then we can get the first native to swallow the first pill."

This is as true at the high-tech level as at the village dispensary. "What is all this drinking of green tea before the meeting with Mitsubishi?" The American way is to get right down to business. Yet if you look at Mitsubishi's bottom line, you have to wonder if green tea is such a bad idea after all.

It should come as no surprise that people surrounded by oceans rather than by other people end up ethnocentric. Even our biggest fans admit that America often strikes the rest of the world as a sweet-but-spoiled little darling, wanting desperately to please, but not paying too much attention to how it is done. Ever since the Marshall Plan, we seemed to believe that *our* games and *our* rules were the only ones in town. Any town. And that all else was the Heart of Darkness.

Take this scene in a Chinese cemetery. Watching a Chinese reverently placing fresh fruit on a grave, an American visitor asked, "When do you expect your ancestors to get up and eat the fruit?" The Chinese replied, "As soon as your ancestors get up and smell the flowers."

◉ Hands Across the Abyss

Our bad old habits are giving way to a new when-in-Rome awareness. Some corporations take it so seriously that they put employees into a crash course of overseas cultural immersion. AT&T, for instance, encourages—and pays for—the whole family of an executive on the way to a foreign assignment to enroll in classes given by experts in the mores and manners of other lands.

Among the areas that cry out loudest for international understanding are how to say people's names, eat, dress, and talk. Get those four basics right and the rest is a piece of kuchen.

Basic Rule #1: What's in a Name?

. . . The first transaction between even ordinary citizens—and the first chance to make an impression for better or worse—is, of course, an exchange of names. In America there usually is not very much to get wrong. And even if you do, so what?

Not so elsewhere. Especially in the Eastern Hemisphere, where name frequently denotes social rank or family status, a mistake can be an outright insult. So can switching to a given name without the other person's permission, even when you think the situation calls for it.

"What would you like me to call you?" is always the opening line of one overseas deputy director for an international telecommunications corporation. "Better to ask several times," he advises, "than to get it wrong." Even then, "I err on the side of formality until asked to 'Call me Joe.'" Another frequent traveler insists his company provide him with a list of key people he will meet, country by country, surnames underlined, to be memorized on the flight over.

Don't Trust the Rules

Just when you think you have broken the international name code, they switch the rules on you. Take Latin America. Most people's father's name used in conversation. In the Spanish-speaking countries the father's name comes first. Hence, Carlos Mendoza-Miller is called Mr. Mendoza. *But* in Portuguese-speaking Brazil it is the other way around, with the mother's name first.

In the Orient the Chinese system of surname first, given name last does not always apply. The Taiwanese, many of whom were educated in missionary schools, often have a Christian first name, which comes before any of the others—as in Tommy Ho Chin, who should be called Mr. Ho or, to his friends, Tommy Ho. Also, given names are often officially changed to initials, and a Y.Y. Lang is Y.Y.; never mind what it stands for. In Korea, which of a man's names takes a Mr. is determined by whether he is his father's first or second son. Although in Thailand names run backwards, Chinese style, the Mr. is put with the *given* name, and to a Thai it is just as important to be called by his given name as it is for a Japanese to be addressed by his surname. With the latter, incidentally, you can in a very friendly relationship respond to his using *your* first name by dropping the Mr. and adding *san* to his last name, as in Ishikawa-san.

Hello. Are you still there? Then get ready for the last installment of the name game, which is to disregard all of the above—sometimes. The reason is that many Easterners who deal regularly with the West are now changing the order of their names to un-confuse us. So, while to one another their names remain the same, to us the given name may come before the surname. Then again, it may not.

The safest course remains: Ask.

Basic Rule #2: Eat, Drink, and Be Wary

. . . [M]ealtime is no time for a thanks-but-no-thanks response. Acceptance of what is on your plate is tantamount to acceptance of host, country, and company. So, no matter how tough things may be to swallow, swallow. Or, as one veteran globe-girdler puts it, "Travel with a cast-iron stomach and eat everything everywhere."

Tastiness Is in the Eye of the Beholder

Often, what is offered constitutes your host country's proudest culinary achievements. What would we Americans think of a Frenchman who refused a bite of homemade apple pie or sizzling sirloin? Squeamishness comes not so much from the thing itself as from our unfamiliarity with it. After all, an oyster has remarkably the same look and consistency as a sheep's eye, and at first encounter a lobster would strike almost anybody as more a creature from science fiction than something you dip in melted butter and pop into your mouth.

Incidentally, in Saudi Arabia sheep's eyes are a delicacy, and in China it's bear's paw soup.

Perhaps the ultimate in exotic dining abroad befell a family planning expert on a trip for an international human welfare organization. It was a newly emerged African country where the national dish—in fact, the *only* dish eleven months of the year—is yam. The visitor's luck, however, was to be there the *other* month, when gorillas come in from the bush to steal the harvest. Being the only available protein, gorilla meat is as prized as sirloin is over here, and the village guest of honor was served a choice cut. Proudly, a platter of the usual mashed yams was placed before her—but with a roast gorilla hand thrusting artfully up from the center.

Is there any polite way out besides the back door?

Most experienced business travelers say no, at least not before taking at least a few bites. It helps, though, to slice whatever the item is very thin. This way, you minimize the texture—gristly, slimy, etc.— and the reminder of whence it came. Or, "Swallow it quickly," as one traveler recommends. "I still can't tell you what sheep's eyeballs taste like." As for dealing with taste, the old canard that "it tastes just like chicken" is often mercifully true. Even when the "it" is rodent, snake—or gorilla.

Another useful dodge is not knowing what you are eating. What's for dinner? Don't ask. Avoid poking around in the kitchen or looking at English-language menus. Your host will be flattered that you are following his lead, and who knows? Maybe it really is chicken in that stew. . . .

Bottoms Up—or Down?

Some countries seem to do it deliberately, some inadvertently, except for Islam, where they don't do it at all. Either way, getting visitors as tipsy as possible as fast as possible stands as a universal sign of hospitality, and refusal to play your part equals rebuff. Wherever you go, toasts are as reciprocal as handshakes: If one does, all do. "I don't drink, thank you" rarely gets you off gracefully. Neither does protesting that you must get up early. (So must everyone else.)

"I try to wangle a glass of wine instead of the local firewater," one itinerant American says. "The only trouble is, the wine is usually stronger than the hard stuff." Mao-tai, Chinese wine made from sorghum, is notorious for leaving the unsuspecting thoroughly shanghaied. The Georgian wine so popular in Russia is no ladylike little Chablis either. In Nordic lands proper form for the toast is to raise the glass in a sweeping arc from belt buckle to lips while locking stares with your host. It takes very few akvavit-with-beer-chasers before you both start seeing northern lights.

In Africa, where all the new countries were once old European colonies, it is often taken for granted that if you are white you must have whiskey or gin or whatever the colonials used to like. A traveler to a former French possession describes the dilemma of being served a large gourdful of Johnnie Walker Red at nine in the morning. The host was simply remembering how the French had always loved their Scotch. *When* they drank it and *how much* were details he had never noticed. Yet there was no saying no without giving offense. A few sips had to be taken and a promise made to finish the rest later.

Basic Rule #3: Clothes Can Also Unmake the Man

. . . Wherever you are, what you wear among strangers should not look strange to *them*. Which does not mean, "When in Morocco wear djellabas," etc. It means wear what you look natural in—and know how to wear—that also fits in with your surroundings.

645

For example, a woman dressed in a tailored suit, even with high heels and flowery blouse, looks startlingly masculine in a country full of diaphanous saris. More appropriate, then, is a silky, loose-fitting dress in a bright color—as opposed to blue serge or banker's gray.

In downtown Nairobi, a safari jacket looks as out of place as in London. With a few exceptions (where the weather is just too steamy for it), the general rule everywhere is that for business, for eating out, even for visiting people at home, you should be very buttoned up: conservative suit and tie for men, dress or skirt-suit for women. To be left in the closet until you go on an outdoor sight-seeing trek:

jeans, however haute couture

jogging shoes

tennis and T-shirts

tight-fitting sweaters (women)

open-to-the-navel shirts (men)

funny hats (both)

Where you *can* loosen up, it is best to do it the way the indigines do. In the Philippines men wear the barong tagalog—a loose, frilly, usually white or cream-colored shirt with tails out, no jacket or tie. In tropical Latin American countries the counterpart to the barong is called a *guayabera* and, except for formal occasions, is acceptable business attire. In Indonesia they wear *Batiks*—brightly patterned shirts that go tieless and jacketless everywhere. In Thailand the same is true for the collarless Thai silk shirt. In Japan dress is at least as formal as in Europe (dark suit and tie for a man, business suit or tailored dress for a woman) except at country inns (called *ryokans*), where even big-city corporations sometimes hold meetings. Here you are expected to wear a kimono. Not to daytime meetings but to dinner, no matter how formal. (Don't worry—the inn always provides the kimono.)

One thing you notice wherever you go is that polyester is the mark of the tourist. The less drip-dry you are, the more you look as if you have come to do serious business, even if it means multiple dry-cleaning bills along the way.

Take It Off or Put It On—Depending

What you do or do not wear can be worse than bad taste—ranging from insulting to unhygienic to positively sinful. Shoes are among the biggest offenders in the East, even if you wear a 5AAA. They are forbidden within Muslim mosques and Buddhist temples. Never wear them into Japanese homes or restaurants unless the owner insists, and in Indian and Indonesian homes, if the host goes shoeless, do likewise. And wherever you take your shoes off, remember to place them neatly together facing the door you came in. This is particularly important in Japan. . . .

In certain conservative Arab countries, the price for wearing the wrong thing can hurt more than feelings. Mullahs have been known to give a sharp whack with their walking sticks to any woman whom they consider immodestly dressed. Even at American-style hotels there, do not wear shorts, skirts above the knee, sleeveless blouses, or low necklines—much less a bikini at the pool.

☻ ☻ ☻

Critical-Thinking Questions

1. Historically, people in the United States have been rather indifferent to the dangers of inadvertently offending others. Why do you think this has been the case?

2. Have you ever offended others—or been offended—in the way depicted by Axtell? If so, how? How did you and others respond?

3. Can the type of cultural conflict Axtell describes occur right here in the United States? How?

McJobs: McDonaldization and the Workplace

George Ritzer

About a decade ago, George Ritzer coined the term "McDonaldization" to refer to a set of organizational principles— including efficiency, uniformity, predictability, and control— that play an important part in today's society. Here, he describes the way McDonald's and similar organizations control not just their workers, but also their customers.

. . .

In recent years the spread of McDonaldized systems has led to the creation of an enormous number of jobs. Unfortunately, the majority of them can be thought of as McDonaldized jobs, or "McJobs." While we usually associate these types of positions with fast-food restaurants, and in fact there are many such jobs in that setting (over 2.5 million people worked in that industry in the United States in 1992 [Van Giezen, 1994]), McJobs have spread throughout much of the economy with the growing impact of McDonaldization on work settings which had previously experienced relatively little rationalization.

It is worth outlining some of the basic realities of employment in the fast-food industry in the United States since those jobs serve as a model for employment in other McDonaldized settings (Van Giezen, 1994). The large number of people employed in fast-food restaurants

Reprinted from *The McDonaldization Thesis: Explorations and Extensions* (1998), Sage Publications, Inc.

accounts for over 40 percent of the approximately six million people employed in restaurants of all types. Fast-food restaurants rely heavily on teenage employees—almost 70 percent of their employees are twenty years of age or younger. For many, the fast-food restaurant is likely to be their first employer. It is estimated that the first job for one of every fifteen workers was at McDonald's; one of every eight Americans has worked at McDonald's at some time in his or her life. The vast majority of employees are part-time workers: The average work week in the fast-food industry is 29.5 hours. There is a high turnover rate: Only slightly more than half the employees remain on the job for a year or more. Minorities are overrepresented in these jobs—almost two-thirds of employees are women and nearly a quarter are non-white. These are low-paid occupations, with many earning the minimum wage, or slightly more. As a result, these jobs are greatly affected by changes in the minimum wage: An upward revision has an important effect on the income of these workers. However, there is a real danger that many workers would lose their positions as a result of such increases, especially in economically marginal fast-food restaurants.[1]

Although the McDonaldization of society is manifest at all levels and in all realms of the social world, the work world has played a particularly pivotal role in this. On the one hand, it is the main source of many of the precursors of McDonaldization, including bureaucracies, scientific management, assembly lines, and so on. More contemporaneously, the kinds of jobs, work procedures, and organizing principles that have made McDonald's so successful have affected the way in which many businesses now organize much of their work. In fact, it could well be argued that the primary root of the McDonaldization of the larger society is the work world. On the other hand, the McDonaldization of the larger society has, in turn, served to further rationalize the work world. We thus have a self-reinforcing and enriching process that is speeding the growth and spread of McDonaldization.

The process of McDonaldization is leading to the creation of more and more McJobs.[2] The service sector, especially at its lower end, is producing an enormous number of jobs, most of them requiring little or no skill. There is no better example of this than the mountain of jobs being produced by the fast-food industry. However, new occupational creation is not the only source of McJobs: Many extant low-level jobs are being McDonaldized. More strikingly, large numbers of middle-level jobs are also being deskilled and transformed into McJobs.

McJobs are characterized by the five dimensions of McDonaldization. The jobs tend to involve a series of simple tasks in which the emphasis is on performing each as efficiently as possible. Second, the time associated with many of the tasks is carefully calculated and the emphasis on the quantity of time a task should take tends to diminish the quality of the work from the point of view of the worker. That is, tasks are so simplified and streamlined that they provide little or no meaning to the worker. Third, the work is predictable: employees do and say essentially the same things hour after hour, day after day. Fourth, many nonhuman technologies are employed to control workers and reduce them to robotlike actions. Some technologies are in place, and others are in development, that will lead to the eventual replacement of many of these "human robots" with computerized robots. Finally, the rationalized McJobs lead to a variety of irrationalities, especially the dehumanization of work. The result is the extraordinarily high turnover rate described above and difficulty in maintaining an adequate supply of replacements.[3]

The claim is usually made by spokespeople for McDonaldized systems that they are offering a large number of entry-level positions that help give employees basic skills they will need in order to move up the occupational ladder within such systems (and many of them do). This is likely to be true in the instances in which the middle-level jobs to which they move—for example, shift leader, assistant manager, or manager of a fast-food restaurant—are also routinized and scripted. In fact, it turns out that this even holds for the positions held by the routinized and scripted instructors at [McDonald's training program at] Hamburger University who teach the managers, who teach the employees, and so on. However, the skills acquired in McJobs are not likely to prepare one for, help one to acquire, or help one to function well in, the far more desirable postindustrial occupations which are highly complex and require high levels of skill and education. Experience in routinized actions and scripted interactions do not help much when occupations require thought and creativity. . . .

At the cultural level, large numbers of people in the United States, and increasingly throughout much of the rest of the world, have come to value McDonaldization in general, as well as its fundamental characteristics. McDonaldization, as well as its various principles, has become part of our value system. That value system has, in turn, been translated into a series of principles that have been exported to, adopted by, and adapted to, a wide range of social settings. . . .

. . .For example, the behavior of customers at fast-food restaurants is being affected in much the same way as the behavior of those who work in those restaurants. . . .

The constraints on the behavior of employees and customers in McDonaldized systems are of both a structural and a cultural nature. Employees and customers find themselves in a variety of McDonaldized structures that demand that they behave in accord with the dictates of those structures. For example, the drive-through window associated with the fast-food restaurant (as well as other settings such as banks) structures both what customers in their cars and employees in their booths can and cannot do. They can efficiently exchange money for food, but their positions (in a car and a booth) and the press of other cars in the queue make any kind of personal interaction virtually impossible. Of course, many other kinds of behavior are either made possible, or prohibited, by such structures. In Giddens's (1984) terms, such structures are both enabling and constraining.

At a cultural level, both employees and customers are socialized into, and have internalized, the norms and values of working and living in a McDonaldized society. Employees are trained by managers or owners who are likely, themselves, to have been trained at an institution like McDonald's Hamburger University (Schaaf, 1994). Such institutions are as much concerned with inculcating norms and values as they are with the teaching of basic skills. For their part, customers are not required to attend Hamburger University, but they are "trained" by the employees themselves, by television advertisements, and by their own children who are often diligent students, teachers, and enforcers of the McDonald's way. This "training," like that of those employees who attend Hamburger University, is oriented not only to teaching the "skills" required to be a customer at a fast-food restaurant (e.g., how to queue up in order to order food), but also the norms and values of such settings as they apply to customers (e.g., customers are expected to dispose of their own debris; they are not expected to linger after eating). As a result of such formal and informal training, both employees and customers can be relied on to do what they are supposed to, and what is expected of them, with little or no personal supervision. . . .

. . . McJobs are not simply the deskilled jobs of our industrial past in new settings; they are jobs that have a variety of new and distinctive characteristics. . . . Industrial and McDonaldized jobs both tend to be highly routinized in terms of what people do on the job. However, one of the things that is distinctive about McDonaldized jobs, especially since so many of them involve work that requires interaction and communication, especially with consumers, is that what people say on the job is also highly routinized. To put this another way, McDonaldized jobs are tightly scripted: They are characterized by *both* routinized actions (for example, the way McDonald's hamburgers are to be put down on the grill and flipped [Love, 1986: 141–2]) and scripted interactions (examples include "May I help you?"; "Would you like a dessert to go with your meal?"; "Have a nice day!"). Scripts are crucial because, as Leidner (1993) points out, many of the workers in McDonaldized systems are interactive service workers. This means that they not only produce goods and provide services, but they often do so in interaction with customers.

The scripting of interaction leads to new depths in the deskilling of workers. Not only have employee actions been deskilled; employees' ability to speak and interact with customers is now being limited and controlled. There are not only scripts to handle general situations, but also a range of subscripts to deal with a variety of contingencies. Verbal and interactive skills are being taken away from employees and built into the scripts in much the same way that manual skills were

652

taken and built into various technologies. At one time distrusted in their ability to *do* the right thing, workers now find themselves no longer trusted to *say* the right thing. Once able to create distinctive interactive styles, and to adjust them to different circumstances, employees are now asked to follow scripts as mindlessly as possible. . . .

One very important, but rarely noted, aspect of the labor process in the fast-food restaurant and other McDonaldized systems is the extent to which customers are being led, perhaps even almost required, to perform a number of tasks without pay that were formerly performed by paid employees. For example, in the modern gasoline station the driver now does various things for free (pumps gas, cleans windows, checks oil, even pays through a computerized credit card system built into the pump) that were formerly done by paid attendants. In these and many other settings, McDonaldization has brought the customer *into* the labor process: The customer *is* the laborer! This has several advantages for employers, such as lower (even nonexistent) labor costs, the need for fewer employees, and less trouble with personnel prob-lems: Customers are far less likely to complain about a few seconds or minutes of tedious work than employees who devote a full work day to such tasks. Because of its advantages, as well as because customers are growing accustomed to and accepting of it, I think customers are likely to become even more involved in the labor process.

This is the most revolutionary development, at least as far as the labor process is concerned, associated with McDonaldization. As a result of this dramatic change, the analysis of the labor process must be extended to what customers do in McDonaldized systems. The distinction between customer and employee is eroding, or in post-modern terms "imploding," and one can envision more and more work settings in which customers are asked to do an increasing amount of "work." More dramatically, it is also likely that we will see more work settings in which there are no employees at all! In such settings customers, in interaction with nonhuman technologies, will do *all* of the human labor. A widespread example is the ATM in which customers (and the technology) do all of the work formerly done by bank tellers. More strikingly, we are beginning to see automated loan machines which dispense loans as high as $10,000 (Singletary, 1996). Again, customers and technologies do the work and, in the process, many loan-officer positions are eliminated. Similarly, the new automated gasoline pumps allow (or force) customers to do all of the required tasks; in some cases and at certain times (late at night) no employees at all are present.

In a sense, a key to the success of McDonaldized systems is that they have been able to supplement the exploitation of employees with the exploitation of customers. Lest we forget, Marx "put at the heart of his sociology—as no other sociology does—the theme of exploitation" (Worsley, 1982:115). In Marxian theory, the capitalists are seen as simply paying workers less than the value produced by the workers, and as keeping the rest for themselves. This dynamic continues in contemporary society, but capitalists have learned that they can ratchet up the level of exploitation not only by exploiting workers more, but also by exploiting a whole new group of people—consumers. In Marxian terms, customers create value in the tasks they perform for McDonaldized systems. And they are not simply paid less than the value they produce, they are paid *nothing at all*. In this way, customers are exploited to an even greater degree than workers. . . .

While no class within society is immune to McDonaldization, the lower classes are the most affected. They are the ones who are most likely to go to McDonaldized schools, live in inexpensive, mass-produced tract houses, and work in McDonaldized jobs. Those in the upper classes have much more of a chance of sending their children to non-McDonaldized schools, living in custom-built homes, and working in occupations in which they impose McDonaldization on others while avoiding it to a large degree themselves.

Also related to the social class issue . . . is the fact that the McDonaldization of a significant portion of the labor force does not mean that all, or even most, of the labor force is undergoing this process. In fact, the McDonaldization of some of the labor force is occurring at the same time that another large segment is moving in a postindustrial, that is, more highly skilled, direction (Hage & Powers,

1992). Being created in this sector of society are relatively high-status, well-paid occupations requiring high levels of education and training. In the main, these are far from McJobs and lack most, or all, of the dimensions discussed at the beginning of this [reading]. The growth of such postindustrial occupations parallels the concern in the labor process literature with flexible specialization occurring side by side with the deskilling of many other jobs. This points to a bifurcation in the class system. In spite of appearances, there is no contradiction here; McDonaldization and postindustrialization tend to occur in different sectors of the labor market. However, the spread of McJobs leads us to be dubious of the idea that we have moved into a new postindustrial era and have left behind the kind of deskilled jobs we associate with industrial society.

Notes

This chapter combines a paper, "McJobs," published in Rich Feller and Garry Walz (eds.), *Career Transitions in Turbulent Times* (Greensboro, N.C.: ERIC/CASS Publications, 1996) and the Invited Plenary Address, International Labour Process Conference, Blackpool, England, April, 1995.

[1]Although a study by Katz and Krueger (1992) indicates an employment *increase* accompanying a rise in the minimum wage.

[2]As we will see below, other kinds of high-status, high-paying postindustrial occupations are also growing.

[3]There are, of course, many other factors involved in turnover.

References

Giddens, Anthony. 1984. *The constitution of society: Outline of the theory of structuration*. Berkeley, Calif.: University of California Press.

Hage, Jerald, and Charles H. Powers. 1992. *Post-industrial lives: Roles and relationships in the 21st century*. Newbury Park, Calif.: Sage.

Leidner, Robin. 1993. *Fast food, fast talk: Service work and the routinization of everyday life*. Berkeley, Calif.: University of California Press.

Love, John. 1986. *McDonald's: Behind the arches*. Toronto: Bantam Books.

Schaaf, Dick. 1994. Inside Hamburger University. *Training*, December: 18–24.

Singletary, Michelle. 1996. Borrowing by the touch. *Washington Post*, 30 March: C1, C2.

Van Giezen, Robert W. 1994. Occupational wages in the fast-food restaurant industry. *Monthly Labor Review*, August: 24–30.

Worsley, Peter. 1982. *Marx and Marxism*. Chichester: Ellis Horwood.

☻ ☻ ☻

Critical-Thinking Questions

1. Describe ways in which McDonaldization is evident in a number of familiar settings (not just the workplace, but perhaps shopping malls and even the college campus). What elements of McDonaldization can you find?

2. In what ways does a McDonaldized setting control not just workers but customers as well? Why do organizations want to control customers?

3. Why does McDonaldization seem to appeal to many people? Do you think this process is good for society as a whole or harmful? Why?

Prostitution: A Worldwide Business of Sexual Exploitation

Melissa Farley

Some prostitutes and academic feminists contend that prostitution should be legalized: "Sex workers" would have greater autonomy over their earnings, they could report violence from pimps (men who economically benefit from a prostitute's earnings) and johns (customers), and international sex trafficking would decrease. Others, like Melissa Farley, argue that legalizing prostitution would legitimize and increase women's sexual exploitation around the world.

. . .

Prostitution is many kinds of violence against women, but it is often not clearly understood as such. Because prostitution/trafficking is so profitable, the factors that propel women into sex businesses, such as sexism, racism, poverty, and child abuse, are sometimes concealed. This article reviews evidence for the extreme violence that occurs in prostitution and the physical and psychological harm that results from that violence.

Reprinted from *Encyclopedia of Women and Gender* 2 (2001), Elsevier Ltd.

◉ Denial

Institutions such as prostitution and slavery, which have existed for thousands of years, are so deeply embedded in cultures that they become invisible. In Mauritania, for example, there are 90,000 Africans enslaved by Arabs. Human rights activists travel to Mauritania to report on slavery, but because they do not observe precisely the stereotype of what they think slavery should look like (for example, if they do not see bidding for shackled people on auction blocks), then they conclude that the Africans working in the fields in front of them are voluntary laborers who are receiving food and shelter as salary.

In a similar way, if observers do not see exactly what the stereotype of "harmful" prostitution is, for example, if they do not see a girl being trafficked at gunpoint from one state to another, or if all they see is a streetwise teenager who says, "I like this job, and besides, I'm making a lot of money," then they do not see the harm. Prostitution tourists go to the prostitution zones of Amsterdam, Atlanta, Phnom Penh, Moscow, or Havana and see smiling girls waving at them from glass cages or strip clubs. The customers decide that prostitution is a free choice.

If we describe women as "sex workers" then we are accepting conditions that in other employment would be correctly described as sexual harassment, sexual exploitation, or rape. If prostitution is transformed into "commercial sex work," then the brutal exploitation of those prostituted by pimps becomes an employer–employee relationship. And the predatory, pedophiliac purchase of a human being by the john becomes just an everyday business transaction.

The myth that prostitution is a free choice is a major obstacle to understanding the harm of prostitution. Most people in prostitution have few or no other options for obtaining the necessities of life. One woman, interviewed by Ine Vanwesenbeeck in the Netherlands, described prostitution as "volunteer slavery," clearly articulating both the appearance of choice and the overwhelming coercion behind that choice. Sexual exploitation seems to happen with the "consent" of those

658

involved. But real consent involves the option to make other choices. In prostitution, the conditions necessary for choice—physical safety, information, equal power with customers, and real alternatives—are absent. Women in prostitution tend to be the ones who have the fewest options.

The social and legal refusal to acknowledge the harm of prostitution is stunning. Normalization of prostitution by researchers, public health agencies, and the media is a significant barrier to addressing the harm of prostitution. In 1988, for example, the World Health Organization described prostitution as "dynamic and adaptive sex work, involving a transaction between seller and buyer of a sexual service." Continuing this trend a decade later, the International Labor Organization normalized prostitution as the "sex sector" of Asian economies despite citing surveys that indicated that, for example, in Indonesia, 96 percent of those interviewed wanted to leave prostitution if they could. Lin Lim commented, "many groups, sometimes including government officials, have an interest in maintaining the sex sector." Libertarian ideology obfuscates the harm of prostitution, defining it as a form of sex.

In the social sciences as well, the harm of prostitution becomes invisible. The psychological literature of the 1980s blamed battered women for their victimization, describing them as "masochistic," a theoretical perspective that was later rejected for lack of evidence. However, the notion that prostituted women (who are also battered women) have personality characteristics that lead to their victimization is still promoted. Karl Abraham saw prostitution as a woman's act of hostility against her father, based on an oedipal fixation. And the sexologists, from Alfred Kinsey to Havelock Ellis to Masters and Johnson, formulated their theories of human sexuality by observing johns with prostitutes, thus normalizing prostitution-like sexuality.

Since the 1980s, there has been huge growth in socially legitimized pimping in the United States: strip clubs, nude dancing, escort services, tanning salons, massage parlors, phone sex, and computer sex. Many people do not realize that these permutations of the commercial sex industry are, in fact, prostitution. The lines between prostitution and nonprostitution have become blurred. New employees may assume they are going to dance, waitress, or tend bar, but find that the real money comes from prostituting after work. Lisa Sanchez has pointed out that the amount of physical contact between dancers and customers has escalated since the 1980s, although earnings have decreased. In addition to watching a stage show, in most strip clubs, customers can buy either a table dance performance by the dancer directly in front of them or a lap dance where the dancer sits on the customer's lap while she wears few or no clothes and grinds her genitals against his. Although he is clothed, he usually expects ejaculation. Sometimes the table dance or lap dance is in front of the customer on the main floor of the club. It may also take place behind a curtain or in a private room. The more private the sexual performance, the more it costs, and the more likely that violent sexual harassment or rape will occur. Although the typical lap-dancing scenario does not involve skin-to-skin sexual contact, for a larger tip, some dancers allow customers to touch their genitals or they masturbate or fellate johns. Used condoms are often found in lap dance clubs.

Different kinds of exploitation and abuse overlap and combine to harm women. Catharine MacKinnon has pointed out that "a great many instances of sexual harassment in essence amount to solicitation for prostitution." The words used to humiliate prostituted women are the same verbal abuse used by men when they are beating up or raping nonprostituting women. Racially constructed ideas about women in sex tourism have a greater and greater effect on the ways women of color are treated at home. For example, Asian American women reported rapes after men viewed pornography of Asian women. A vast range of abuse makes up a continuum of violence in which women are first hurt in early childhood.

◉ Child Abuse and Prostitution

The prostitution of children is aggressively made invisible. For example, commenting that the connection between childhood sexual abuse and prostitution has been "exaggerated," Peter Davies and Rayah Feldman described the prostituted boys they interviewed in the United Kingdom as having an average age of under 18, with 97 percent of them younger than the legal age of consent. In other words, their interviewees were legally minors.

Another example of this invisibility is the common belief in Taiwan that the island's 100,000 child prostitutes want to prostitute because it pays for their "expensive tastes" in clothes and jewelry. Pimps are considered the children's bodyguards. Prejudice against indigenous people in Taiwan bolsters this denial of harm to their children, who comprise most of the children in prostitution.

In many parts of the world, a younger rather than older person is a preferred commodity, for several reasons. First, the culturally advocated pedophiliac sexuality in some countries (the Netherlands, India, the United States) channels men's sexual desire to younger and younger girls. Second, children are more easily controlled than adults by pimps and are more easily coerced by johns into behaviors that adults might resist. Third, there is the widespread but mistaken belief in some locales that younger children are safer for the customer since they are believed to be less likely to have HIV (Thailand, Zambia).

Most women over the age of 18 in prostitution began prostituting when they were adolescents. Adele du Plessis, a social worker who worked with homeless and prostituted children in Johannesburg, South Africa, reported that she could not refuse her agency's services to 21-year-olds because she understood them to be grownup child prostitutes. Estimates regarding the age of recruitment into prostitution vary, but early adolescence is the most frequently reported age of entry into any type of prostitution. Researcher Debra Boyer interviewed sixty women prostituting in escort, street, strip club, phone sex, and massage parlors (brothels) in Seattle, Washington. All of them began prostituting between the ages of 12 and 14. In another study, 89 percent had begun prostitution before the age of 16. Of 200 adult women in prostitution interviewed by Mimi Silbert, 78 percent began prostituting as juveniles and 68 percent began when they were younger than 16.

The artificial distinction between child and adult prostitution obscures the continuity between the two. On a continuum of violence and relative powerlessness, the prostitution of a 12-year-old is more horrific than the prostitution of a 20-year-old, not because the crimes committed against her are different, but because the younger person has less power. In other respects, the experiences of sexual exploitation, rape, verbal abuse, and social contempt are the same, whether the person being prostituted is the legal age of a child or the legal age of an adult. The antecedent poverty and attempts to escape from unbearable living conditions (violence at home or the economic violence of globalization) are similar in child and adult prostitution.

One woman interviewed by Boyer said, "We've all been molested. Over and over, and raped. We were all molested and sexually abused as children, don't you know that? We ran to get away. They didn't want us in the house anymore. We were thrown out, thrown away. We've been on the street since we were 12, 13, 14."

The chronic, systematic nature of violence against girls and women may be seen more clearly when incest is understood as child prostitution. Use of a child for sex by adults, with or without payment, is prostitution of the child. When a child is incestuously assaulted, the perpetrator's objectification of the child victim and his rationalization and denial are the same as those of the john in prostitution. Incest and prostitution cause similar physical and psychological symptoms in the victim.

Child sexual abuse is a primary risk factor for prostitution. Familial sexual abuse functions as a training ground for prostitution. One young woman told Mimi Silbert and Ayala Pines, "I started turning tricks to show my father what he made me." Andrea Dworkin described sexual abuse of children as "boot camp" for prostitution. Research and clinical reports have documented the widespread occurrence of childhood sexual abuse and chronic traumatization among prostituted women. From 60 percent to 90 percent of those in prostitution were sexually assaulted in childhood.

Multiple perpetrators of sexual abuse were common, as was physical abuse in childhood. Sixty-two percent of women in prostitution reported a history of physical abuse as children. Evelina Giobbe found that 90 percent of prostituted women had been physically battered in childhood; 74 percent were sexually abused in their families, with 50 percent also having been sexually abused by someone outside the family. Of 123 survivors of prostitution at the Council for Prostitution Alternatives in Portland, 85 percent reported a history of incest, 90 percent a history of physical abuse, and 98 percent a history of emotional abuse.

In the 1980s, Silbert and Pines published a number of groundbreaking studies that documented the role of child sexual abuse as an antecedent to prostitution. These authors and others have noted the role of pornography in the recruitment of children into prostitution and in teaching them how to act as prostitutes. Eighty percent of a group of prostituted women and girls in Vancouver, Canada, reported that while working as prostitutes, they had been upset by someone trying to coerce them into imitating pornography.

Prostituting adolescents grow up in neglectful, often violent families. Although not all sexually abused girls are recruited into prostitution, most of those in prostitution have a history of sexual abuse as children, usually by several people. For example, in a pilot study of prostituted women in Vancouver, Melissa Farley and Jackie Lynne reported that 88 percent of 40 women had been sexually assaulted as children, by an average of five perpetrators. This latter statistic (those assaulted by an average of five perpetrators) did not include those who responded to the question "If there was unwanted sexual touching or sexual contact between you and an adult, how many people in all?" with "tons" or "I can't count that high" or "I was too young to remember." Sixty-three percent of those whose experiences were recorded in this study were First Nations women.

Survivors directly link physical, sexual, and emotional abuse as children to later prostitution. Seventy percent of the adult women in prostitution in one study stated that their childhood sexual abuse affected their decision to become prostitutes. They described family abuse and neglect as not only causing direct physical and emotional harm, but also creating a cycle of victimization that affected their futures. For example, one woman interviewed by Joanna Phoenix stated that by the time she was 17, "all I knew was how to be raped, and how to be attacked, and how to be beaten up, and that's all I knew. So when he put me on the game [pimped her] I was too down in the dumps to do anything. All I knew was abuse."

When she is sexually abused, the child is reinforced via attention, food, and money for behaving sexually in the way the perpetrator wishes. The perpetrator's seductive manipulation of the child causes immense psychological harm. In addition, many children are threatened with violence if they do not perform sexually.

Angela Browne and David Finkelhor described traumatic sexualization as the inappropriate conditioning of the child's sexual responsiveness and the socialization of the child into faulty beliefs and assumptions about sexuality. Traumatic sexualization leaves the girl vulnerable to additional sexual exploitation and is a critical component of the grooming process for subsequent prostitution. Some of the consequences of childhood sexual abuse are behaviors that are prostitution-like; a common symptom of sexually abused children is sexualized behavior.

Sexual abuse may result in different behaviors at different stages of the child's development. Sexualized behaviors are likely to be prominent among sexually abused preschool-age children, submerge during the latency years, and then reemerge during adolescence as behavior described as promiscuity, prostitution, or sexual aggression.

Sexual abuse causes extreme damage to children's self-esteem. Frank Putnam noted that the child may incorporate the perpetrator's perspective, eventually viewing herself as good for nothing but sex, which is to say, she may adopt the perpetrator's view that she is a prostitute. According to John Briere, this constricted sense of self of the sexually abused child and the coercive refusal of the perpetrator to respect the child's physical boundaries may result in her subsequent difficulties in asserting boundaries, in impaired self-protection, and a greater likelihood of being further sexually victimized, including becoming involved in prostitution.

The powerlessness of having been sexually assaulted as a child may be related to the frequent discussions of control and power by women who are prostituting. The emotional and physical helplessness of the sexually abused child may be reenacted in the prostitution transaction, with vigilant attention to the tiniest shard of control. Payment of money for an unwanted sex act in prostitution may make the girl or woman feel more in control when compared to the same experience with no payment of money. For example, one woman said that at age 17, she felt safer and more in control turning tricks on the street than she did in her home with her stepfather who raped her.

Children commonly run away from homes in which they are being sexually abused. If there is no safe place to escape to, the child or adolescent is left extremely vulnerable to further sexual exploitation and assault. Mimi Silbert reported that 96 percent of the adults she interviewed had been runaway children before they began prostituting. Louie and colleagues found that more than half of fifty prostituting Asian girls aged 11 to 16 ran away because of family problems.

Children in prostitution are recruited from runaway and homeless populations. For example, John Lowman described the average Canadian prostitute as having entered prostitution between the ages of 13 and 19, usually after running away from home. Pimps exploit the vulnerability of runaway or thrown-out children in recruiting them to prostitution. In Vancouver, 46 percent of homeless girls had received offers of "assistance to help them work in prostitution." One 13-year old who had run away from home was given housing by a pimp, but only in exchange for prostituting.

A survey of 500 homeless youths by Barbara Lucas and Lena Hackett in Indianapolis found that at first only 14 percent acknowledged that they were "working as prostitutes." This survey reveals the importance of the wording of questions about prostitution. When the Indiana adolescents were later asked nonjudgmental questions about specific behaviors, they responded as follows: 32 percent said that they had sex to get money; 21 percent said they had sex for a place to stay overnight; 12 percent exchanged sex for food; 10 percent exchanged sex for drugs; and 6 percent exchanged sex for clothes. In other words, a total of 81 percent, not 14 percent of these 500 homeless adolescents, were prostituting. The following wordings for inquiry about prostitution are suggested: "Have you ever exchanged sex for money or clothes, food, housing, or drugs?" or "Have you ever worked in the commercial sex industry: dancing, escort, massage, prostitution, pornography, video, internet, or phone sex?"

Like heterosexual adolescent girls, gay male adolescents' prostitution behavior is likely to be a reenactment of earlier sexual abuse. Homophobia also plays a role in the prostituting of gay young men. Gay youth may have been thrown out of their homes because of their sexual orientation. Furthermore, in many cities, prostitution was the only available entry into the gay community; it was an activity where boys could "practice" being gay. Thus gay adolescent boys may develop an identity that links their sexual orientation to prostitution.

◉ Socioeconomic Contribution to Entry into Prostitution

According to Julia Davidson, "Prostitution is an institution in which one person has the social and economic power to transform another human being into the living embodiment of a masturbation fantasy." In addition to gender, poverty is a precondition for prostitution. The economic vulnerability and limited career options of poor women are significant factors in their recruitment into prostitution. Of 854 people in prostitution from nine countries (Canada, Colombia, Germany, Mexico, South Africa, Thailand, Turkey, United States, and Zambia), Melissa Farley and colleagues found that 75 percent were currently or previously homeless. PROMISE, a California agency serving women in prostitution, reported that 67 percent of those requesting services were currently or formerly homeless.

Lack of education was frequently a precursor to entering prostitution. Seventy percent of West Bengal Indian women wanted to escape prostitution, but the cultural and economic factors that channeled them into prostitution prevented that: a 6 percent literacy rate, beatings, starvation, rape by family members, and sexual exploitation at their jobs. As reported by Molly Chattopadhyay and her colleagues, women in most jobs in West Bengal, India, were required to permit sexual exploitation in order to stay employed. The most frequent reason given by these women for leaving their last job was that prostitution would provide "better pay for what they had to do anyway."

Racism and Colonialism in Prostitution

Women in prostitution are purchased for their appearance, including skin color and characteristics based on ethnic stereotyping. Throughout history, women have been enslaved and prostituted based on race and ethnicity, as well as gender and class.

Entire communities are affected by the racism that is entrenched in prostitution. For example, legal prostitution, such as strip clubs and stores that sell pornography (that is, pictures of women in prostitution) tends to be zoned into poor neighborhoods, which in many urban areas in the United States also tend to be neighborhoods of people of color. The insidious trauma of racism continually wears away at people of color and makes them vulnerable to stress disorders. Families who have been subjected to race and class discrimination may interface with street networks that normalize hustling for economic survival. Sex businesses create a hostile environment in which girls and women are continually harassed by pimps and johns. Women and girls are actively recruited by pimps and are harassed by johns driving through their neighborhoods. As Vednita Nelson pointed out, there is a sameness between the abduction into prostitution of African women by slavers and today's cruising of African American neighborhoods by johns searching for women to buy.

Compared to their numbers in the United States as a whole, women of color are overrepresented in prostitution. For example, in Minneapolis, a city that is 96 percent White European American, more than half of the women in strip club prostitution are women of color. Furthermore, African American women are arrested for prostitution solicitation at a higher rate than others charged with this crime.

Colonialism exploits not only natural resources, but also the people whose land contains those resources. Especially vulnerable to violence from wars or economic devastation, indigenous women are brutally exploited in prostitution (for example, Mayan women in Mexico City, Hmong women in Minneapolis, Karen women in Bangkok, and First Nations women in Vancouver).

Once in prostitution, women of color face barriers that prevent escape. Among these is an absence of culturally sensitive advocacy services. Other barriers faced by all women escaping prostitution are the lack of services that address emergency needs (for example, shelters, drug/alcohol detoxification, and treatment of acute posttraumatic stress disorder, or PTSD). There is a similar lack of services that address long-term needs, such as treatment of depression and chronic posttraumatic stress disorder (PTSD), vocational training, and long-term housing.

◉ Trafficking Is International Prostitution

Prostitution always involves marketing, and trafficking is the marketing of prostitution. Women in prostitution are transported to the most lucrative market. The United Nations estimated that two million women, girls, and boys were trafficked into prostitution in 1999. Trafficking (moving girls and women across international borders) can not exist without an acceptance of prostitution in the receiving country. Many governments protect commercial sex businesses because of the massive profits (estimated at $56 billion per year). For example, the International Labor Organization called on poor countries to take economic advantage of "the sex sector," that is, prostitution and trafficking. Governments frequently have chosen to protect the demand for prostitution, rather than adopting complex solutions, which would involve prevention through community education programs and penalization of traffickers, pimps, and customers. Governments have failed to address the root cause of prostitution, which is the unequal status of women.

In 1999, Thailand, Vietnam, China, Mexico, Russia, Ukraine, and the Czech Republic were primary source countries for trafficking of women into the United States. Source countries vary according to the economic desperation of women, promotion of prostitution/trafficking by corrupt government officials who issue passports and visas, and criminal connections in both the sending and the receiving country such

668

as gang-controlled massage parlors and the lack of laws to protect women who immigrate. The economic interdependence of countries and multinational corporations (globalization) promotes prostitution and trafficking by creating conditions for women to sell their own sexual exploitation at far better rates of pay than other forms of labor, according to Tanya Hernandez. Pimps and traffickers take advantage of the unequal status of women and girls in the source country by exploiting sexist and racist stereotypes of women as property, commodities, servants, and sexual objects.

Researcher Donna M. Hughes analyzed the ways in which economic devastation in Russia exacerbated preexisting gender inequality, promoting sex businesses including trafficking. Russian women have been scapegoated for keeping jobs that some believe they should have given up to men (the Russian Minister of Labor Melikyan stated that all women should be unemployed before a single man lost his job); domestic violence is at epidemic proportions; and sexual harassment on the job is commonplace. Under these conditions, almost any opportunity to leave Russia, even one that involves trafficking/prostitution, seems tolerable.

International prostitution includes prostitution tourism ("sex tourism"), arranged marriages with foreign women who are sexually objectified and kept in domestic servitude ("mail-order brides"), and recently, promotion of sexual exploitation by internet pimping and online prostitution, as described by Hughes.

The interconnectedness of racism and sexism in prostitution is vividly apparent in sex tourism. Colonialism in Asia and the Caribbean, according to Hernandez, promoted a view of women of color as natural-born sex workers, sexually promiscuous and immoral by nature. Over time, women of color came to be viewed as "exotic others," defined as inherently hypersexual on the basis of race and gender. The prostitution tourist, reading between the lines of travel brochures, denies the racist exploitation of women in "native cultures," as in Ryan Bishop and Lillian Robinson's analysis of the Thai sex business: "Indigenous Thai people are seen as Peter-Pan-like children who are sensual and never grow up. Thus travel brochures assure sex tourists that they are simply partaking of the Thai culture, which just happens to be 'overtly sexual.' "

Pervasive Violence in Prostitution

Prostitution is like rape. It's like when I was fifteen years old and I was raped. I used to experience leaving my body. I mean that's what I did when that man raped me. I looked up at the ceiling and I went to the ceiling and I numbed myself . . . because I didn't want to feel what I was feeling. I was very frightened. And while I was a prostitute I used to do that all the time. I would numb my feelings. I wouldn't even feel like I was in my body. I would actually leave my body and go somewhere else with my thoughts and with my feelings until he got off and it was over with. I don't know how else to explain it except that it felt like rape. It was rape to me. (Giobbe, 1991, p. 144)

Sexual violence and physical assault are normative experiences for women in prostitution. Silbert and Pines reported that 70 percent of women in prostitution were raped. The Council for Prostitution Alternatives in Portland reported that prostituted women were raped an average of once a week.

According to Ine Vanwesenbeeck, in the Netherlands, 60 percent of prostituted women suffered physical assaults, 70 percent experienced verbal threats of physical assault, 40 percent experienced sexual violence, and 40 percent had been forced into prostitution and/or sexual abuse by acquaintances. Most young women in prostitution were abused or beaten by pimps as well as johns. Eighty-five percent of women interviewed by Ruth Parriott had been raped in prostitution. Of 854 people in prostitution in nine countries, 71 percent had experienced physical assaults in prostitution, and 62 percent had been raped in prostitution, according to Farley and colleagues.

According to Jody Miller, 94 percent of those in street prostitution had experienced sexual assault and 75 percent had been raped by one or more johns. In spite of these reports of extreme violence, there is a widespread belief that the concept of rape does not apply to prostitutes. Some people assume that when a prostituted woman was raped, it was part of her job and that she deserved or even asked for the rape. Nothing could be farther from the truth.

Like battering, prostitution is domestic violence. Giobbe compared pimps and batterers and found similarities in the ways they used extreme physical violence to control women, the ways they forced women into social isolation, used minimization and denial, threats, intimidation, verbal and sexual abuse, and had an attitude of ownership. The techniques of physical violence used by pimps are often the same as those used by batterers and torturers.

The level of harassment and physical abuse of women in strip club prostitution has drastically increased in the past 20 years. Touching, grabbing, pinching, and fingering of dancers removes any boundary that previously existed between dancing, stripping, and prostitution. In 1998, Kelly Holsopple summarized the verbal, physical, and sexual abuse experienced by women in strip club prostitution, which included being grabbed on the breasts, buttocks, and genitals, as well as being kicked, bitten, slapped, spit on, and penetrated vaginally and anally during lap dancing.

◉ Trauma Symptoms among Women in Prostitution

Recruitment into prostitution begins with what Kathleen Barry has called seasoning: brutal violence designed to break the victim's will. After control is established, pimping tactics shift to brainwashing and other forms of psychological control. Pimps establish emotional dependency as quickly as possible, beginning with changing a girl's name. This obliterates her identity, separates her from her past, and isolates her from her community. The purpose of pimps' violence is to convince women of their worthlessness and social invisibility, as well as physically controlling them.

Escape from prostitution becomes more and more difficult as the woman is repeatedly overwhelmed with terror. She is forced to commit acts that are sexually humiliating and that cause her to betray her own principles. The contempt and violence aimed at her are eventually

671

internalized, resulting in a virulent self-hate that then makes it even more difficult to defend herself. Survivors report a sense of contamination, of being different from others, and self-loathing, which lasts many years after getting out of prostitution. Judith Herman and Lenore Terr have each described the complexity of repetitive behaviors found in survivors of chronic trauma. Traumatic reenactments of abuse are common, along with psychobiological dysfunction, including self-destructive thoughts and behaviors, self-contempt, feelings of shame and worthlessness, substance abuse, eating disorders, and sexual aversions or compulsions.

Dissociation is the psychological process of banishing traumatic events from consciousness. It is an emotional shutting down, which occurs during extreme stress among prisoners of war who are being tortured, among children who are being sexually assaulted, and among women who are being battered, raped, or prostituted. The emotional distancing necessary to survive rape and prostitution is the same technique used to endure familial sexual assault. Most women report that they cannot engage in prostitution unless they dissociate. Being drunk or high has been described as chemical dissociation.

One woman described the link between johns' behavior and her dissociation while she was prostituting in a strip club:

> You start changing yourself to fit a fantasy role of what they think a woman should be. In the real world, these women don't exist. They're not really looking at you. You become this empty shell. You're not you. You're not even there. (Farley, unpublished interview, 1998)

People in prostitution also suffer from posttraumatic stress disorder (PTSD). Symptoms of PTSD include anxiety, depression, insomnia, irritability, flashbacks, emotional numbing, and hyperalertness. Farley and colleagues found that 68 percent of 854 people in prostitution from nine countries met diagnostic criteria for PTSD, suggesting that the traumatic consequences of prostitution were similar across different cultures. The following are two examples of PTSD.

Saundra Sturdevant and Brenda Stolzfus interviewed an Okinawan woman who had been purchased by U.S. military personnel during the

Vietnam War. Many years later, she still became extremely agitated and had visions of sexual assault and persecution on the 15th and 30th of each month, the days that had been Army paydays. Another woman who spoke to Farley described symptoms of PTSD that were a consequence of violence in prostitution: "I wonder why I keep going to therapists and telling them I can't sleep, and I have nightmares. They pass right over the fact that I was a prostitute and I was beaten with two-by-four boards, I had my fingers and toes broken by a pimp, and I was raped more than 30 times. Why do they ignore that?"

Over time, the violence of prostitution, the constant humiliation, the social indignity, and the misogyny result in personality changes that Judith Herman has described as complex posttraumatic stress disorder (CPTSD). Symptoms of CPTSD include changes in consciousness and self-concept, changes in the ability to regulate emotions, shifts in systems of meaning, such as loss of faith, and an unremitting sense of despair. Sexual feelings are severely damaged in prostitution. Once out of prostitution, 76 percent of a group of women interviewed by Ruth Parriott reported that they had great difficulty with intimate relationships.

❧ Physical Health Consequences of Prostitution

Chronic health problems result from physical abuse and neglect in childhood, sexual assault, battering, untreated health problems, and overwhelming stress. Prostituted women suffer from all of these. Many of the chronic physical symptoms of women in prostitution are similar to the physical consequences of torture. In a 1985 study by the Canadian government, the death rate of those in prostitution was found to be 40 times higher than that of the general population.

A lack of attention to pervasive physical and sexual violence has resulted in failures of the health care system for all women. Those in prostitution lacked access to social and medical services that were available to other women. Fear of arrest and social contempt made it difficult for prostituted women to seek emergency shelter or medical treatment.

Although the majority of research on prostituted women's health from 1980 to 2000 focused exclusively on HIV or other sexually transmitted diseases (STDs), some research has addressed non-HIV-related health problems. Prostituted women had an increased risk of cervical cancer and chronic hepatitis. Incidence of abnormal Pap screens was several times higher than the state average in a Minnesota study of prostituted women's health. Childhood rape was associated with increased incidence of cervical dysplasia in Ann Coker and colleagues' study of women prisoners, many of whom had been in prostitution.

Half of the women interviewed in San Francisco in 1998 by Farley and Barkan reported physical health problems, including joint pain, cardiovascular symptoms, respiratory symptoms, neurological problems, and HIV (8 percent). Seventeen percent stated that, if it were accessible, they would request immediate hospital admission for drug addiction or emotional problems. Many acute and chronic problems were directly related to violence. In addition to poor nutrition, gastrointestinal problems, and pneumonia, Eleanor Miller reported that women in prostitution had bruises, broken bones, cuts, and abrasions that resulted from beatings and sexual assaults. One woman said about her health:

> I've had three broken arms, nose broken twice, [and] I'm partially deaf in one ear. . . . I have a small fragment of a bone floating in my head that gives me migraines. I've had a fractured skull. My legs ain't worth shit no more; my toes have been broken. My feet, bottom of my feet, have been burned; they've been whopped with a hot iron and clothes hanger . . . the hair on my pussy had been burned off at one time. . . . I have scars. I've been cut with a knife, beat with guns, two by fours. There hasn't been a place on my body that hasn't been bruised somehow, some way, some big, some small. (Giobbe, 1992, p. 126)

Frida Spiwak reported that 70 percent of 100 prostituted girls and women in Bogota had physical health problems. In addition to STDs, their diseases were those of poverty and despair: allergies, respiratory problems, and blindness caused by glue sniffing, migraines, symptoms of premature aging, dental problems, and complications from abortion.

Adolescent girls and boys in prostitution surveyed by D. Kelly Weisberg reported STDs, hepatitis, pregnancies, sore throats, flu, and repeated suicide attempts. Women who serviced more customers in prostitution reported more severe physical symptoms. The longer women were in prostitution, the more they suffered symptoms of STDs.

Globally, the incidence of HIV seropositivity among prostituted women and children is devastating. Homeless children are at highest risk for HIV, for example, in Romania and Colombia. Peter Piot noted that half of new AIDS cases are in the under-25 age group, and that girls are likely to become infected at a much younger age than boys, in part because of the acceptance of violence against women and girls in most cultures. . . .

❂ Criminal Justice Responses to Prostitution

It is commonly assumed that the greater the legal tolerance of prostitution, the easier it is to control public health. Public health in this context refers primarily to STDs in johns rather than to the psychological and physical health of prostituted women.

Legalized prostitution involves state, county, or city ordinances that regulate prostitution, for example, issuing zoning permits, requiring STD tests, and collecting taxes. In effect, the state operates as the pimp. In Nevada, state regulations determine geographic location and size of brothels, as well as activities of women outside the brothel. Prostituted women are only allowed into nearby towns from 1 to 4 p.m., are restricted to certain locations, and are even prohibited from talking to certain persons. Respondents in South Africa and Zambia were asked whether they thought they would be safer from sexual and physical assault if prostitution were legal. A significant majority (68 percent) said "no." The implication was that regardless of the legal status of prostitution, those in it knew that they would continue to experience violence.

The HIV epidemic has brought with it the advocacy of another legal approach to prostitution: decriminalization, or the cessation of enforcement of all laws against prostitution. Decriminalization of prostitution has been promoted by sex businesses as a way to remove the social stigma associated with prostitution. Decriminalization would normalize commercial sex, but it would not reduce the trauma and the humiliation of being prostituted. Compared to illegal prostitution, decriminalization would facilitate men's access to women and children.

Stating that "prostitution is not a desirable social phenomenon," the Swedish government in 1999 criminalized the behavior of pimps and johns but not those who were prostituting. Noting that "it is not reasonable to punish the person who sells a sexual service [because] in the majority of cases this person is a weaker partner who is exploited," the Swedish government allocated social welfare monies to "motivate prostitutes to seek help to leave their way of life." This progressive interventionist approach reflects the Swedish interest in counteracting growth of commercial sex businesses.

In the United States, although there is legislative concern about forced trafficking, there are few legal remedies for women who enter prostitution because of educational neglect, emotional abuse, or lack of economic alternatives. Some women in prostitution do not appear to have been forced or coerced. Public policies that offer legal, financial, and social assistance only to those who can prove violent force, or who are under age eighteen, or who crossed international borders, do not address the core of violence that is present in all types of prostitution. Legal responses to prostitution are inadequate if they fail to include johns, as well as pimps and traffickers, as perpetrators.

The state of Florida passed a remarkably progressive law that addresses some of the forces propelling girls and women into prostitution. The Florida law specifically prohibits inducement into prostitution by sexual abuse, by pornography, or by exploiting the need for food, shelter, safety, or affection.

◉ Conclusion

Commercial sex businesses are a multibillion dollar global market that includes strip clubs, massage parlors, phone sex, online prostitution, internet pimping of women and children, adult and child pornography, street, brothel, and escort prostitution. One's political perspective will determine whether prostitution is viewed primarily as a public health issue, as an issue of zoning and property values (which parts of town should house strip clubs and pornography stores?), as vocational choice, as sexual liberation, as freedom of speech (does the webmaster have the right to sell internet photographs of prostituted women being raped?), as petty crime, as domestic violence, or as human rights violation.

For the vast majority of the world's prostituted women, prostitution is the experience of being hunted, dominated, harassed, assaulted, and battered. Intrinsic to prostitution are numerous violations of human rights: sexual harassment, economic servitude, educational deprivation, job discrimination, domestic violence, racism, classism, vulnerability to frequent physical and sexual assault, and being subjected to body invasions that are equivalent to torture.

Demand creates supply in prostitution. Because men want to buy sex, prostitution is assumed to be inevitable, therefore "normal." Men's ambivalence about the purchase of women, however, is reflected in the scarcity of research interviews with johns and in their desire to remain hidden. In a series of interviews with johns conducted by women prostituting in message parlors, Elizabeth Plumridge noted that, on the one hand, the men believed that commercial sex was a mutually pleasurable exchange, and on the other hand, they asserted that payment of money removed all social and ethical obligations. A john interviewed by Neil McKeganey and Marina Barnard said: "It's like going to have your car done, you tell them what you want done, they don't ask, you tell them you want so and so done."

Programs that assist women in prostitution can not succeed in the long run unless social systems that keep women subordinate also change. Jacquelyn White and Mary Koss observed that violent behaviors against women have been associated with attitudes that promote men's beliefs that they are entitled to sexual access to women, that they are superior to women, and that they have a license for sexual aggression. Prostitution myths are a component of attitudes that normalize sexual violence. Martin Monto found that johns' acceptance of commodified sexuality was strongly associated with their acceptance of rape myths, violent sex, and less frequent use of condoms with women in prostitution. A widespread acceptance among men of what has been described as nonrelational sexuality may be a contributing factor to the normalization of prostitution. According to sociologist Kathleen Barry, in today's culture we do not distinguish sex that is exploitative or coercive from sex that is a positive human experience. This blurring results in what Barry has called the prostitution of human sexuality.

Prostitution must be exposed for what it really is: a particularly lethal form of male violence against women. The focus of research, prevention, and law enforcement in the next decades must be on the demand side of prostitution.

References

Abraham, K. 1953. *Selected papers on psychoanalysis.* New York: Basic Books.

Baldwin, M. A. 1999. A million dollars and an apology: Prostitution and public benefits claims. *Hastings Women's Law Journal,* Winter 1999, 189–224.

Barry, K. 1995. *The prostitution of sexuality.* New York: New York University Press.

Bishop, R., and L. S. Robinson. 1998. *Night market: Sexual cultures and the Thai economic miracle.* New York and London: Routledge.

Boyer, D., L. Chapman, and B. K. Marshall. 1993. Survival sex in King County: Helping women out. Seattle: *Report submitted to King County Women's Advisory Board, March 31, 1993.* Northwest Resource Associates.

Briere, J. 1992. *Child abuse trauma: Theory and treatment of the lasting effects.* Newbury Park: Sage.

Browne, A., and D. Finklehor. 1986. Impact of child sexual abuse: A review of the research. *Psychological Bulletin* 99(1): 66–77.

Burkett, E. 1997. God created me to be a slave. *New York Times Magazine* 12: 56–60.

Chattopadhyay, M., S. Bandyopadhyay, and C. Duttagupta. 1994. Biosocial factors influencing women to become prostitutes in India, *Social Biology* 41(3–4): 252–259.

Coker, A., N. Patel, S. Krishnaswami, W. Schmidt, and D. Richter. 1998. Childhood forced sex and cervical dysplasia among women prison inmates. *Violence Against Women* 4(5): 595–608.

Crowell, N. A., and A. W. Burgess (eds.). 1996. *Understanding violence against women.* Washington, D.C.: National Academy Press.

Davidson, J. O. 1998. *Prostitution, power, and freedom.* Ann Arbor: University of Michigan Press.

Davis, N. 1993. *Prostitution: An international handbook on trends, problems, and policies.* London: Greenwood Press.

Dworkin, A. 1997. *Prostitution and male supremacy in life and death.* New York: Free Press.

Farley, M., and H. Barkan. 1998. Prostitution, violence and posttraumatic stress disorder. *Women & Health* 27(3): 37–49.

Farley, M., I., Baral, M., Kiremire, and U. Sezgin, 1998. Prostitution in five countries: Violence and posttraumatic stress disorder. *Feminism & Psychology* 8(4): 415–26.

Finstad, L., and C. Hoigard, 1993. Norway. In *Prostitution: An international handbook on trends, problems, and policies,* ed. N. Davis. London: Greenwood Press.

Giobbe, E. 1991. Prostitution: Buying the right to rape. In *Rape and sexual assault III: A research handbook,* ed. A. W. Burgess. New York: Garland Press.

Giobbe, E. 1992. Juvenile prostitution: Profile of recruitment. In *Child trauma: Issues & research,* ed. A. W. Burgess. New York: Garland Press.

Giobbe, E. 1993. An analysis of individual, institutional and cultural pimping. *Michigan Journal of Gender & Law* 1: 33–57.

Giobbe, E., M., Harrigan, J. Ryan, and D. Gamache. 1990. *Prostitution: A matter of violence against women.* Minneapolis, Minn.: WHISPER.

Herman, J. L. 1992. *Trauma and recovery.* New York: Basic Books.

Hernandez, T. K. 2001. Sexual harassment and racial disparity: The mutual construction of gender and race. *Journal of Gender, Race & Justice* 4: 183.

Hoigard, C., and L. Finstad. 1986. *Backstreets: Prostitution, money and love.* University Park, Penn.: Pennsylvania State University Press.

Holsopple, K. 1998. Stripclubs according to strippers: Exposing workplace violence. Unpublished paper.

Hughes, D. M. 2000. The "Natasha" trade: The transnational shadow market of trafficking in women. *Journal of International Affairs* 53(2): 625–51.

Hughes, Donna M. 1999. *Pimps and predators on the Internet—Globalizing the sexual exploitation of women and children.* Kingston, Rhode Island: The Coalition Against Trafficking in Women.

Hunter, S. K. 1994. Prostitution is cruelty and abuse to women and children. *Michigan Journal of Gender and Law* 1: 1–14.

Lim, L. L., ed. 1998. *The sex sector: The economic and social bases of prostitution in Southeast Asia.* Geneva: International Labor Organization.

Louie, L., K. Joe, M. Luu, and B. Tong. 1991. Chinese American adolescent runaways. Paper presented at Annual Convention of the Asian American Psychological Association, San Francisco. August 1991.

Lowman, J. 1992. Canada. In *Prostitution: An international handbook on trends, problems, and policies,* ed. N. Davis, Westport, Conn.: Greenwood Press.

Lucas, B., and L. Hackerr. 1995. *Street youth: On their own in Indianapolis.* Health Foundation of Greater Indianapolis, Ind.

MacKinnon, C. A. 1993. Prostitution and civil rights. *Michigan Journal of Gender and Law* 1: 13–31.

MacKinnon, C. A., and A. Dworkin, 1997. In *harm's way: The pornography civil rights hearings.* Cambridge: Harvard University Press.

McKeganey, N., and M. Barnard. 1996. *Sex work on the streets: Prostitutes and their clients.* Buckingham, Scotland: Milton Keynes Open University Press.

Miller, E. M. 1986. *Street woman.* Philadelphia: Temple University Press.

Ministry of Labour in cooperation with the Ministry of Justice and the Ministry of Health and Social Affairs, Government of Sweden. (1998). Fact Sheet. Secretariat for Information and Communication, Ministry of Labour. Tel +46-8-405 11 55, Fax +46-8-405 12 98. Artiklne, A98.004.

Monto, M. 1999. *Prostitution and human commodification: A study of arrested clients of female street prostitutes.* Chicago: American Sociological Association.

Murphy, P. (1993). *Making the connections: Women, work and abuse: Dramatic insight into the lives of abuse victims and practical recommendations for their successful return to work.* Orlando, Fla.: Paul M. Deutsch Press.

Nelson, V. 1993. Prostitution: Where racism and sexism intersect. *Michigan Journal of Gender & Law* 1: 81–89.

Parriott, R. 1994. *Health experiences of twin cities women used in prostitution.* Minneapolis, Minn.: Unpublished survey initiated by WHISPER.

Piot, P. 1999. Remarks at United Nations Commission on the Status of Women, United Nations Press Release, March 3, New York.

Plumridge, E. W., J. W. Chetwynd, A. Reed, and S. J. Gifford. 1997. Discourses of emotionality in commercial sex: The missing client voice. *Feminism & Psychology* 7(2): 165–81.

Putnam, F. 1990. Disturbances of "self" in victims of childhood sexual abuse. In *Incest-related syndromes of adult psychopathology,* ed. R. Kluft, pp. 113–31. Washington, D.C: American Psychiatric Press.

Root, M. 1996. Women of color and traumatic stress in "domestic captivity": Gender and race as disempowering statuses. In *Ethnocultural aspects of posttraumatic stress disorder: Issues, research, and clinical applications.* eds. A. J. Mirsella, M. J. Friedman, E. T. Gerrity, and R. M. Scurfield. Washington, D.C.: American Psychological Assn.

Sanchez, L. 1998. Boundaries of legitimacy: Sex, violence, citizenship, and community in a local sexual economy. *Law and Social Inquiry* 22: 543–80.

Silbert, M. H., and A. M. Pines. 1983. Early sexual exploitation as an influence in prostitution. *Social Work* 28: 285–89.

Silbert, M. H., and A. M. Pines. 1984. Pornography and sexual abuse of women. *Sex Roles* 10(11–12): 857–68.

Special Committee on Pornography and Prostitution. 1985. *Pornography and Prostitution in Canada* 350.

Sturdevant, S., and B. Stolzfus. 1992. *Let the good times roll: Prostitution and the US military in Asia.* New York: The New Press.

Terr, L. C. 1991. Childhood traumas: An outline and overview. *American Journal of Psychiatry* 148: 10–20.

Vanwesenbeeck, I. 1994. *Prostitutes' well-being and risk.* Amsterdam: VU Boekhandel/Uitgeverij Press.

Weisberg, D. 1985. *Children of the night: A study of adolescent prostitution.* Lexington, Mass.: Lexington Books.

White, J. W., and M. P. Koss. 1993. Adolescent sexual aggression within heterosexual relationships: Prevalence, characteristics, and causes. In *The juvenile sex offender.* eds. H. E. Barbaree, W. L. Marshall, and D. R. Laws. New York: Guilford Press.

◉ ◉ ◉

Critical-Thinking Questions

1. Many people believe that prostitution is a free choice. Farley argues that this belief is false. Why? What is your view of this issue?

2. How does prostitution reflect an intersection of race, sex, and class oppression?

3. In terms of the legal status of prostitution, how do decriminalization and legalization differ? Why is Farley opposed to both? Do you agree or disagree with her position?

Understanding Sexual Orientation

ALFRED C. KINSEY
WARDELL B. POMEROY
CLYDE E. MARTIN

In 1948, Alfred Kinsey and his colleagues published the first modern study of sexuality in the United States—and raised plenty of eyebrows. For the first time, people began talking openly about sex, questioning many common stereotypes. Here Kinsey reports his finding that sexual orientation is not a matter of clear-cut differences between heterosexuals and homosexuals, but is better described as a continuum by which most people combine elements of both.

. . .

The Heterosexual-Homosexual Balance

Concerning patterns of sexual behavior, a great deal of the thinking done by scientists and laymen alike stems from the assumption that there are persons who are "heterosexual" and persons who are "homosexual," that these two types represent antitheses in the sexual world, and that there is only an insignificant class of "bisexuals" who occupy an intermediate position between the other groups. It is implied that every individual is innately—inherently—either heterosexual or homosexual. It is further implied that from the time of birth

Reprinted from *Sexual Behavior in the Human Male* (1948), The Kinsey Institute for Research in Sex, Gender, & Reproduction.

Heterosexual-homosexual rating scale

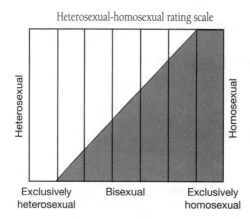

Exclusively   Bisexual   Exclusively
heterosexual   homosexual

one is fated to be one thing or the other, and that there is little chance for one to change his pattern in the course of a lifetime.

It is quite generally believed that one's preference for a sexual partner of one or the other sex is correlated with various physical and mental qualities, and with the total personality which makes a homosexual male or female physically, psychically, and perhaps spiritually distinct from a heterosexual individual. It is generally thought that these qualities make a homosexual person obvious and recognizable to anyone who has a sufficient understanding of such matters. Even psychiatrists discuss "the homosexual personality" and many of them believe that preferences for sexual partners of a particular sex are merely secondary manifestations of something that lies much deeper in the totality of that intangible which they call the personality.

It is commonly believed, for instance, that homosexual males are rarely robust physically, are uncoordinated or delicate in their movements, or perhaps graceful enough but not strong and vigorous in their physical expression. Fine skins, high-pitched voices, obvious hand movements, a feminine carriage of the hips, and peculiarities of walking gaits are supposed accompaniments of a preference for a male as a sexual partner. It is commonly believed that the homosexual male is artistically sensitive, emotionally unbalanced, temperamental to the point of being unpredictable, difficult to get along with, and undependable in

684

meeting specific obligations. In physical characters there have been attempts to show that the homosexual male has a considerable crop of hair and less often becomes bald, has teeth which are more like those of the female, a broader pelvis, larger genitalia, and a tendency toward being fat, and that he lacks a linea alba. The homosexual male is supposed to be less interested in athletics, more often interested in music and the arts, more often engaged in such occupations as bookkeeping, dress design, window display, hairdressing, acting, radio work, nursing, religious service, and social work. The converse to all of these is supposed to represent the typical heterosexual male. Many a clinician attaches considerable weight to these things in diagnosing the basic heterosexuality or homosexuality of his patients. The characterizations are so distinct that they seem to leave little room for doubt that homosexual and heterosexual represent two very distinct types of males. . . .

It should be pointed out that scientific judgments on this point have been based on little more than the same sorts of impressions which the general public has had concerning homosexual persons. But before any sufficient study can be made of such possible correlations between patterns of sexual behavior and other qualities in the individual, it is necessary to understand the incidences and frequencies of the homosexual in the population as a whole, and the relation of the homosexual activity to the rest of the sexual pattern in each individual's history.

The histories which have been available in the present study make it apparent that the heterosexuality or homosexuality of many individuals is not an all-or-none proposition. It is true that there are persons in the population whose histories are exclusively heterosexual, both in regard to their overt experience and in regard to their psychic reactions. And there are individuals in the population whose histories are exclusively homosexual, both in experience and in psychic reactions. But the record also shows that there is a considerable portion of the population whose members have combined, within their individual histories, both homosexual and heterosexual experience and/or psychic responses. There are some whose heterosexual experiences predominate, there are some whose homosexual experiences predominate, there are some who have had quite equal amounts of both types of experience.

Some of the males who are involved in one type of relation at one period in their lives may have only the other type of relation at some later period. There may be considerable fluctuation of patterns from time to time. Some males may be involved in both heterosexual and homosexual activities within the same period of time. For instance, there are some who engage in both heterosexual and homosexual activities in the same year, or in the same month or week, or even in the same day. There are not a few individuals who engage in group activities in which they may make simultaneous contact with partners of both sexes.

Males do not represent two discrete populations, heterosexual and homosexual. The world is not to be divided into sheep and goats. Not all things are black nor all things white. It is a fundamental of taxonomy that nature rarely deals with discrete categories. Only the human mind invents categories and tries to force facts into separated pigeon-holes. The living world is a continuum in each and every one of its aspects. The sooner we learn this concerning human sexual behavior the sooner we shall reach a sound understanding of the realities of sex.

◉ ◉ ◉

Critical-Thinking Questions

1. Why do you think people have long thought of heterosexuality and homosexuality as opposite and mutually exclusive (that is, only in terms of "exclusively heterosexual" or "exclusively homosexual" in the figure on page 194)?

2. Kinsey suggests that anyone's sexual orientation may well change over time. Do you agree? Why or why not?

3. Why do people tend to label someone with any degree of homosexual experience as a "homosexual"? (After all, we don't do the same in the case of any heterosexual experience.)

The Uses of Global Poverty: How Economic Inequality Benefits the West

DAINA STUKULIS EGLITIS

In his 1971 article, Herbert Gans used a variant of functionalist theory to argue that poverty serves particular functions or purposes in American society. The logical conclusion from Gans's research is that poverty cannot be eliminated without society's needing to find other ways to serve those functions or purposes. The article was heavily criticized. Many contended that it served no purpose other than to rationalize the existence of poverty, and that such a thesis would jeopardize poverty-relief programs. Over thirty years later, poverty is still an issue in America. Economic, political, and social relations, however, have become more heavily globalized and interconnected, and in this selection, Daina Stukulis Eglitis examines global poverty using Gans's theoretical perspective and presents eleven functions of global poverty.

In the global village, there stand a wide variety of homes, from the stately mansion on the hill, to the modest abode blessed with electricity and running water, to the adequate but unheated (or uncooled) hut, to the flood-prone, tattered shanty cobbled together from gathered scrap. Those who live on the hill are aware of their neighbors, as their neighbors are aware of them. Most inhabitants of the global village recognize that wealth and the accompanying opportunities for education, health care, and consumption are not evenly divided and that a substantial gap exists between the more and less materially blessed populations. Not everyone agrees on why that is the case.

Consider the following comparisons of life in the global village: In 1999, the gross national income in purchasing power parity (GNI PPP)[1] in the

United States was $31,910. In Germany the figure was $23,510, and in Australia, $23,850. By contrast, the GNI PPP of China was $3,550, in Indonesia it was $2,660, and in Pakistan, $1,860. On the bottom tier of states, we find countries like Nigeria with a GNI of $770 and Sierra Leone with just $440. If we use the GNI PPP as a yardstick of economic power and the well-being of populations, we may begin to construct a picture of a global system characterized by the massive maldistribution of wealth, economic security, and purchasing power. Our village is one characterized by deep and fundamental stratification.

What have been the responses of well-off states to this global class system with its extremes of wealth and poverty? Not surprisingly, perhaps, political rhetoric has consistently elevated the goal of spreading the prosperity enjoyed by the advanced industrial states of the West around the globe. In remarks made at the United States Coast Guard Academy commencement ceremony in 1989, President George Bush phrased it this way: "What is it that we want to see? It is a growing community of democracies anchoring international peace and stability, and a dynamic free-market system generating prosperity and progress on a global scale. . . . If we succeed, the next decade and the century beyond will be an era of unparalleled growth, an era which sees the flourishing of freedom, peace, and prosperity around the world."

If shared global prosperity was the goal, it seems safe to say that while there was some modest progress made in areas like Latin America, Eastern Europe, and parts of Asia, "we" did not really succeed, because the global wealth gap is still massive and growing. The rich countries remain rich, and the poor countries, for the most part, remain trapped in desperate, dire poverty. This has not changed.

Another thing that has not changed is the rhetorical commitment to spreading the wealth. In a speech in Coventry, England, in December 2000, President Bill Clinton laid out a "prescription for how the United States might help close the gap between rich and poor nations." And in his farewell address to the nation in January 2001, the President declared that "the global gap requires more than compassion. It requires action."

As of 2002, President George W. Bush has not addressed the question of non-Western development specifically, though it seems relatively safe to say that he too will join the political chorus of support for global prosperity, although his administration seems destined to be defined by a focus on war rather than development.

Western rhetoric, assistance programs, and advice seem to support the goal of global prosperity and its extension to the 1.3 billion who live on less than $1 per day and those millions or even billions more who eke out a sparse existence just above the threshold of absolute poverty. But the reality of prosperity has touched only a relative few countries, while the struggle to meet basic needs touches many more. Social indicators like the GNI PPP highlight the differences we find in our village. But what explains them? Why does global poverty exist and persist? Why does a global class system with a thin layer of rich states and a broad strata of poor countries exist and persist? What explains why some villagers inhabit houses on the mount while others squat in mud huts below? Possible answers are many. This article explores one way of understanding the yawning gap between the planet's wealthiest and poorest states.

In 1971, sociologist Herbert Gans published an article entitled "The Uses of Poverty: The Poor Pay All."[2] In the article, Gans utilized a conservative theoretical perspective in sociology, functionalism, to inquire about the persistence of poverty in America. The functionalist perspective takes as its starting point the position that essentially all institutions and social phenomena that exist in society contribute in some manner to that society—that is, they are functional for society. If they did not contribute to the social order, the functionalists maintain, they would disappear. Using this perspective, functionalists may inquire about, for instance, the functions, both obvious and hidden (or manifest and latent, to use sociologist Robert Merton's terms), of institutions like the education system or the family or social phenomena like punishment for deviance. These social theorists assume that institutions or phenomena exist because they are functional, and hence their guiding question is, What function do they serve?

Gans posed a similar question about poverty, asking, What are the uses of poverty? Clearly, the notion that poverty is functional for society as a whole is ludicrous: Who would suggest that it is functional for those who endure economic deprivation? So Gans offered a modified functionalist analysis: ". . . instead of identifying functions for an entire social system, I shall identify them for the interest groups, socioeconomic classes, and other population aggregates with shared values that 'inhabit' a social system. I suspect that in a modern heterogeneous society, few phenomena are functional or dysfunctional for the society as a whole, and that most result in benefits to some groups and costs to others."

Gans sought to explain the existence and persistence of poverty in modern, wealthy America by highlighting the way that the existence of poverty has benefits for the nonpoor—not just "evil" individuals like the loan shark or the slum lord, but for "normal" members of nonpoor classes. He identified thirteen "uses" of poverty, including the notions that the existence of a poor class "ensures that society's 'dirty work' will be done," that "the poor buy goods others do not want and thus prolong the economic usefulness of such goods," and "the poor can be identified and punished as alleged or real deviants in order to uphold the legitimacy of conventional norms." He was not arguing that poverty is good. He was suggesting that understanding poverty's existence and persistence means recognizing that the poor have positive social and economic functions for the nonpoor. Thus, one would conclude that the elimination of poverty, while elevated as a societal goal, would be, in practice, costly to the nonpoor.

While Gans's theoretically based inquiry into poverty was focused on America's poor, the same question might be asked about the existence of global poverty: What are the "uses" of global poverty for the better-off countries of the world economic system? The purpose of such an inquiry would be, as it was in Gans's inquiry, not to use a functionalist analysis to legitimate poverty or the highly skewed distribution of wealth in the global system, but to contribute to a deeper understanding of why it continues to exist by explaining how its persistence confers benefits on well-off states and their inhabitants.

The argument is not that advanced states are consciously conspiring to keep the poor states destitute: Well-off countries have historically sought to offer help to less developed countries. In reality, however, there are limited incentives for the better-off states to support the full industrial and technological (and even democratic) development of all the states in the global system. To the degree that the existence of a class of poor states is positively functional for wealthy states, we can begin to imagine why development and assistance programs that help ensure survival, but not prosperity, for poor populations are quite characteristic of Western policy.

This article notes eleven "uses" of global poverty. Global poverty is not, from this perspective, functional for the global community as a whole. The notion that the poverty of billions who live in economically marginal states is globally "useful" would be absurd. But it is not absurd to ask how the existence of a class of poor states serves wealthy states. In fact, asking such a question might contribute to a better understanding of the dual phenomena of global poverty and the global "class" system.

690

◉ Point 1: The existence of global poverty helps ensure the wealth of affordable goods for Western consumers.

The cornucopia of decently priced goods of reasonable quality enjoyed by Western consumers is underpinned by the low-wage work done in low-income countries. The labels on the clothing you are wearing right now likely contain the familiar words "Made in China" or perhaps "Made in Pakistan." Your clothing is probably of reasonable quality, and you likely paid a reasonable (but not necessarily cheap) price for it.

The Western consumer of textiles such as off-the-rack clothing is a beneficiary of a globalized manufacturing process that has seen the movement of manufacturing to low-wage areas located in poor states that provide ready pools of workers needy enough to labor for a pittance. In China, the average hourly wage of apparel workers is about 23 cents. This benefits the consumer of that apparel. The worker herself (workers in this industry are usually female) derives less benefit: The average hourly wage needed to meet basic needs in China, according to Women's Edge, an advocacy group, is 87 cents.[3]

Another way that the impoverished workers of the third world help reduce the cost of goods coming to Western consumers is through their agricultural labor. For instance, the comparably (and sometimes illegally) low wages paid to many poor migrant farm workers from Mexico and Central America in states like California contribute to America's ample and reasonably priced food supply.

Stories about low-wage workers in developing countries have, in recent years, emerged in the Western press and provoked some expressions of outrage and the formation of groups like United Students Against Sweatshops. These expressions have been small and limited. Imagine, however, the outrage if popular sports shoes, already pricey, climbed another $50 in cost as a result of manufacturers opting for well-paid, unionized labor. Or imagine if the price of a head of iceberg lettuce, America's favorite vegetable, suddenly doubled in price to $3.00. Which outrage would be more potent?

691

◉ Point 2: The existence of global poverty benefits Western companies and shareholders in the form of increased profit margins.

Labor costs typically constitute a high percentage of a company's expenditures. By reducing labor costs, companies can both keep prices reasonable (which benefits, as noted, the consumer) and raise profit margins. Not surprisingly, then, companies are not likely to locate in—and are more likely to leave—locations where wages are relatively high. The use of poor female workers in the third world is, in this respect, especially "beneficial" to companies. Women comprise about 80 percent of workers in Export Processing Zones and are often paid 20 percent to 50 percent less than male counterparts. The less costly the workforce, the greater the opportunity for profit. Not coincidentally, countries with an ample supply of poor workers willing to work for miserable wages are also countries with lax safety and environmental regulations, which also keeps down the costs to the Western employer and pushes up the profits. Hence, companies benefit directly from the existence of economically deprived would-be workers willing (or not in a position to be unwilling) to work for paltry wages in potentially hazardous, or at least very unpleasant, conditions.

◉ Point 3: The existence of global poverty fosters access to resources in poor states that are needed in or desired by the West.

Poor states may sell raw goods at low prices to Western states, which can transform the resource into a more valuable finished product. The position of the poor states in the world economy makes it less likely that they can derive the full benefit of the resources they possess for the government and people. The case of oil in resource-rich but desperately poor Nigeria is an example. Seven major foreign oil companies operate in Nigeria, all representing interests in wealthy states. The vast majority of benefits from Nigeria's oil has accrued not to the country's people, but to the companies (and consumers) of the wealthy states. There is no attempt to hide this: John Connor, head of Texaco's worldwide exploration and production, talking about a massive oil strike in January 2000, stated that the successful conclusion of the well test "sets the stage for development of a world-class project that will add substantially to the company's resource base."[4] Clearly the failure of Nigeria's people to benefit from the country's resources is also linked to a succession of corrupt governments, but the poverty of the masses and the powerful position of oil companies help to ensure that resistance to exploitation of resources for the benefit of non-Nigerian interests will be marginal.

◉ Point 4: The existence of global poverty helps support Western medical advances.

The poor provide a pool of guinea pigs for the testing of medicines developed for use primarily in the West. The beneficiaries are not the poor themselves consumers of advanced medicine (60 percent of profits are made in the United States, which leads the world in drug consumption) and the pharmaceutical companies, which stand astride a $350 billion (and growing) industry. A series of reports in the *Washington Post* in December 2000 documents the disturbing practice of conducting drug trials on ill inhabitants of poor states. For instance, an unapproved antibiotic was tested by a major pharmaceutical company on sick children during a meningitis epidemic in Nigeria. The country's lax regulatory oversight, the sense among some doctors that they could not object to experiment conditions for political or economic reasons, the dearth of alternative health care options, combined with the desire of the company to rapidly prepare for the market a potential "blockbuster" drug underpinned a situation in which disease victims were treated as test subjects rather than patients. This case highlights the way that non-poor states actually benefit from the existence of poor states with struggling, sick populations. A reporter for the series noted that "companies use the tests to produce new product and revenue streams, but they are also responding to pressure from regulators, Congress, and lobbyists for disease victims to develop new medicines quickly. By providing huge pools of human subjects, foreign trials help speed new drugs to the marketplace—where they will be sold mainly to patients in wealthy countries."[5]

◉ Point 5: The existence of global poverty contributes to the advancement of Western economies and societies with the human capital of poor states.

Poorer states like India have become intellectual feeders of well-educated and bright individuals whose skills cannot be fully rewarded in less developed states. The magnetic draw of a better life in economies that amply reward their human capital pulls the brightest minds from their countries of origin, a process referred to as "brain drain." Advanced economies such as the United States and England are beneficiaries of brain drain. The United States has moved to take advantage of the pool of highly educated workers from the developing world: Congress has passed legislation increasing the number of H-1B visas, or "high-tech visas," to bring up to 600,000 workers to the United States over the next several years. The United States and England offer attractive opportunities to highly educated workers from poorer states. Notably, high-tech companies often pay the foreign workers less than their domestic equivalents would demand.

◉ Point 6: The existence of global poverty may contribute to the pacification of the Western proletariat, or "Workers of the World, A Blue Light Special!"

To some degree, the broad availability of good, inexpensive merchandise may help obscure class divisions in the West, at least in the arena of consumption. It is clear that those with greater wealth can consume more high-quality goods, but low-end "designer" merchandise is accessible to the less well-off in cathedrals of consumption such as Wal-Mart. At K-Mart, for instance, Martha Stewart peddles her wares, intended to transform "home-making chores . . . into what we like to call 'domestic art.'" Thanks in part to the low-wage workers in places like China, these goods are available to the unwashed masses (now washed by Martha's smart and cozy towels) as well as to better-situated homemakers. Consumption appears to be one of the great equalizers of modern society. (It is worth noting, though, that many members of the Western working class are also "victims" of global poverty, since many jobs have gone abroad to low-wage areas, leaving behind, for less educated workers, positions in the less remunerative and less secure service industry or leaving former industrial workers jobless.)

❧ Point 7: Global poverty benefits the West because poor countries make optimal dumping grounds for goods that are dangerous, expired, or illegal.

Wealthy countries and their inhabitants may utilize poorer states as repositories for dangerous or unwanted material such as nuclear waste. The desperation of cash-strapped states benefits better-off countries, which might otherwise have difficulty ridding themselves of the dangerous by-products of their industrial and consumer economies. For instance, in December 2000, the Russian Parliament, in an initial vote on the issue, overwhelmingly supported the amendment of an environmental law to permit the importation of foreign nuclear waste. The alteration of the law was supported by the Atomic Ministry of the Russian Federation, which suggested that over the next decade, Russia might earn up to $21 billion from the importation of spent nuclear fuel from states like Japan, Germany, and South Korea. Likely repositories of the radioactive refuse are Mayak and Krasnoyarsk, already among the most contaminated sites on the planet.

India has also emerged as a dumping ground for hazardous junk from the world's industrial giants. The western Indian city of Alang, for instance, is host to the world's largest shipbreaking yard, where Western-owned ships are sent for dismantling and, ostensibly, recycling. The process of "breaking" the old vessels, however, endangers workers and the environment because it releases asbestos, PCBs, and other toxic wastes.[6]

❂ Point 8: The existence of global poverty provides jobs for specialists employed to assist, advise, and study the world's poor and to protect the "better-off" from them.

Within this group of specialists we find people in a variety of professions. There are those who are professional development workers, operating through organizations like the United States Agency for International Development (USAID) to further "America's foreign policy interests in expanding democracy and free markets while improving the lives of the citizens of the developing world."[7] The Peace Corps is also built around the goal of bringing Western "know-how" to the poor with volunteer programs that promote entrepreneurship and agricultural development.

Academics in fields as diverse as economics, sociology, international affairs, political science, and anthropology study, write about, and "decipher" the lives of the poor and the condition of poor states. Texts on development, articles debating why poverty persists, and books from university presses are only some of the products of this research. Journalists and novelists can build careers around bringing colorful, compelling representations of the poor to the warm living rooms of literate, well-off consumers. Still others are charged with the task of protecting wealthy states from "invasions" of the poor: U.S. border patrols, for instance, employ thousands to keep those seeking better fortunes out of U.S. territory.

❂ Point 9: Global poverty benefits inhabitants of wealthy countries, who can feel good about helping the global poor through charitable work and charitable giving.

From the celebrity-studded musical production "We are the World" to trick-or-treating for UNICEF, those who inhabit the wealthy corners of the world feel good about themselves for sharing their good fortune. The Web site of World Vision, a faith-based charity that offers the opportunity to sponsor poor children, features a speak-out area for contributors. On that site, a young Canadian sponsor wrote, "A few days ago I woke up early and turned the TV on . . . looking at those children made me realize I could help them. I thought if I had enough money to pay for the Internet, cell phone, and a couple of other things I didn't need, I said to myself, [then] why not give that money to people who need it instead of spending it all in (sic) luxury and things that are not really important. . . . I immediately picked up the phone and called to sponsor a child! I am happy. I can help someone who needs it!"[8]

Apparently, we need not feel guilt about consuming many times what the unfortunate inhabitants of the world's poor states do if only we are willing to give up a few of our luxuries to help them. Indeed, not only do the poor not inspire guilt, they may inspire positive feelings: As the World Vision writer notes, she feels "happy" because she can "help someone who needs it." No less a figure than the world's richest man, Bill Gates, is also "dedicated to improving people's lives by sharing advances in health and learning with the global community" through the Gates Foundation.[9]

A related point is that the poor we see on television or hear about in news or music give those of us in wealthy countries the opportunity to feel good about ourselves, regardless of our position in the socioeconomic structure of our own states. Consider the memorable lines from the 1985 Band-Aid song, "Do They Know It's Christmas?" which was produced by British pop artist Bob Geldof as a charitable act to raise money for Ethiopia's famine victims: "And the Christmas bells that ring there are the clanging chimes of doom. Well, tonight, thank God, it's them instead of you." Indeed, even the underpaid blue- or pink-collar worker in the West can relate to that sentiment.

❧ Point 10: The poverty of less developed states makes possible the massive flow of resources westward.

Imagine if large and largely poor countries like China, Nigeria, and India consumed at U.S. rates. At present, Americans consume a tremendously disproportionate share of the world's resources. With their profligate use of all

697

manner of resources, most notably fossil fuels, Americans are the greediest consumers of natural resources on the planet. On both an absolute and per capita basis, most world resources flow westward. Notably, on October 4, 2000, article in the *Seattle Times* reported that bicycles, long a characteristic and popular means of transport for Chinese commuters, are losing popularity: "Increasingly, young Chinese are not even bothering to learn to ride bikes, because growing wealth has unlashed a plethora of transportation choices, public and private."[10] The new transportation of choice is still largely public buses or private taxis; the Chinese have not yet graduated to mass private cars. But it is interesting to ponder whether there would be enough (affordable) oil for everyone if the Chinese, with their growing population and prosperity, became a country of two-vehicle families or developed a taste and market for gas-guzzling sports utility vehicles. In this case, the West likely benefits from the fact that few can afford (at least at present) to consume at the rate its people do.

◉ Point 11: The poorer countries, which reproduce at rates higher than Western states, are useful scapegoats for real and potential global environmental threats.

What is the bigger environmental threat to our planet? Is it the rapid growth of the populations of developing states or the rapid consumption of resources by the much smaller populations of developed states? The overdevelopment of the West may well be the bigger threat, though the growth of populations in third-world countries, which is often linked to conditions of underdevelopment, such as a lack of birth control and the need to have "extra" children as a hedge against high child mortality rates, makes an attractive alternative explanation for those who would not wish to fault the SUV-driving, disposable-diaper using, BBQ-loving American consumer for threats to the global environment. While some Western policymakers express concern about the environmental threats emerging from rapid population growth or the use of "dirty" technology in developing states, there is comparably little serious attention given to the global threat presented by the profligate consumption by Western states. The poor divert attention from the environmental problems caused by Western overconsumption.

698

I have talked about eleven ways that the continued existence of global poverty benefits those who reside in wealthy states. The argument I have offered to explain the persistence of a strata of poor states and the yawning global gap highlights the idea that while global poverty (and the status quo) is beneficial to the wealthy West, serious steps to alleviate it will not be taken.

It is surely the case that poverty does not have to exist. But while we in the West derive the benefits and bonuses of these economic inequalities, it seems likely that our efforts to support, advise, and assist the less developed states will remain at levels that are financially and politically convenient and feasible, and will target survival rather than true prosperity for those outside our gated, privileged, greedy Western neighborhood. In Gans's words, "Phenomena like poverty can be eliminated only when they become dysfunctional for the affluent or powerful, or when powerless can obtain enough power to change society."

Endnotes

[1] The figures in this paragraph come from the Population Reference Bureau Web site (*http://www.prb.org*), which provides excellent demographic data. According to the PRB, the "GNI PPP per capita is gross national income in purchasing power parity divided by mid-year population. . . . GNI PPP refers to gross national income converted to 'international' dollars using a purchasing power parity conversion factor. International dollars indicate the amount of goods or services one could buy in the United States with a given amount of money. GNI PPP provides an indicator of the welfare of people that is comparable across countries free of price and exchange rate distortions that occur when GNI is converted using market exchange rates."

[2] *Social Policy,* July/August 1971.

[3] Information on issues of trade and Chinese women is available at *http://www.womensedge.org*. The information cited is from the April 2000 Web issue of *Notes from the Edge.*

[4] "Texaco in massive oil strike in Nigeria" in *The Namibian,* available online at *http://www.namibian.com.ma/Netstories/2000/January/Marketplace/texaco.html.*

[5] Stephens, Joe, "As Drug Testing Spreads, Profits and Lives Hang in Balance," *The Washington Post* 17, (December 2000): A1.

[6] Information on both issues is available at the Web site of the environmental group Greenpeace at *http://www.greenpeace.org.*

[7] The Web site address is *http://www.usaid.gov.*

[8]The charity's Web site address is *http://www.worldvision.org.*

[9]The foundation is at *http://www.gatesfoundation.org.*

[10]The article is cited at the Web site of the Competitive Enterprise Institute: *http://www.cei.org/CHNReader.asp? ID=1227.*

❂ ❂ ❂

Questions

1. What are the key premises of functionalist theory?

2. In what way does Eglitis's research rely on a "modified" functionalist perspective?

3. Which of the author's eleven "uses" of global poverty do you find most convincing? Why?

4. Can you categorize or classify Eglitis's points in a way that might generalize the uses of global poverty (e.g., economic, political)?

5. Find and read Herbert Gans's 1971 article, "The Uses of Poverty: The Poor Pay All," *Social Policy* July/August. How are the functions portrayed by Gans in 1971 similar to or different from those discussed by Eglitis in 2004? Explain.

"Night to His Day": The Social Construction of Gender

JUDITH LORBER

In this article, Judith Lorber focuses on something that most people take for granted—gender. She explains how gender is socially constructed and how cultural expectations of what constitutes appropriate masculine and feminine behavior vary from one culture to another. After you have completed this article, you will not only understand how gender is socially constructed, but how we become gendered.

*T*alking about gender for most people is the equivalent of fish talking about water. Gender is so much the routine ground of everyday activities that questioning its taken-for-granted assumptions and presuppositions is like thinking about whether the sun will come up. Gender is so pervasive that in our society we assume it is bred into our genes. Most people find it hard to believe that gender is constantly created and re-created out of human interaction, out of social life, and is the texture and order of that social life. Yet gender, like culture, is a human production that depends on everyone constantly "doing gender" (West & Zimmerman, 1987).

And everyone "does gender" without thinking about it. Today, on the subway, I saw a well-dressed man with a year-old child in a stroller. Yesterday, on a bus, I saw a man with a tiny baby in a carrier on his chest. Seeing men taking care of small children in public is increasingly common—at least in New York City. But both men are quite obviously stared at—and smiled at, approvingly. Everyone was doing gender—the men who were changing the role of fathers and the other passengers, who were applauding them silently. But there was more gendering going on that probably fewer people noticed. The baby was wearing a white crocheted cap and white clothes. You couldn't tell if it was a boy or a girl. The child in the stroller was wearing a dark blue T-shirt and dark print pants. As they started to leave the train, the father put a Yankees baseball cap on the child's head. Ah, a boy, I thought. Then I noticed the gleam of tiny earrings in the child's ears, and as they got off, I saw the little flowered sneakers and lace-trimmed socks. Not a boy after all. Gender done.

Gender is such a familiar part of daily life that it usually takes a deliberate disruption of our expectations of how women and men are supposed to act to pay attention to how it is produced. Gender signs and signals are so ubiquitous that we usually fail to note them—unless they are missing or ambiguous. Then we are uncomfortable until we have successfully placed the other person in a gender status; otherwise, we feel socially dislocated. In our society, in addition to man and woman, the status can be *transvestite* (a person who dresses in opposite-gender clothes) and *transsexual* (a person who has had sex-change surgery). Transvestites and transsexuals carefully construct their gender status by dressing, speaking, walking, gesturing in the ways prescribed for women or men—whichever they want to be taken for—and so does any "normal" person.

For the individual, gender construction starts with assignment to a sex category on the basis of what the genitalia look like at birth.[1] Then babies are dressed or adorned in a way that displays the category because parents don't want to be constantly asked whether their baby is a girl or a boy. A sex category becomes a gender status through naming, dress, and the use of other gender markers. Once a child's gender is evident, others treat those in one gender differently from those in the other, and the children respond to the different treatment by feeling different and behaving differently. As soon as they can talk, they start to refer to themselves as members of their gender. Sex doesn't come into play again until puberty, but by that time, sexual feelings and desires and practices have been shaped by gendered norms and expectations. Adolescent boys and girls approach and avoid each other in an elaborately scripted and gendered mating dance. Parenting is gendered, with different expectations for mothers and for fathers, and people of different genders work at different kinds of jobs. The work adults do as mothers and fathers and as low-level workers and high-level bosses, shapes women's and men's life experiences, and these experiences produce different feelings, consciousness, relationships, skills—ways of being that we call feminine or masculine. All of these processes constitute the social construction of gender.

Gendered roles change—today fathers are taking care of little children, girls and boys are wearing unisex clothing and getting the same education, women and men are working at the same jobs. Although many traditional

702

social groups are quite strict about maintaining gender differences, in other social groups they seem to be blurring. Then why the one-year-old's earrings? Why is it still so important to mark a child as a girl or a boy, to make sure she is not taken for a boy or he for a girl? What would happen if they were? They would, quite literally, have changed places in their social world.

To explain why gendering is done from birth, constantly and by everyone, we have to look not only at the way individuals experience gender but at gender as a social institution. As a social institution, gender is one of the major ways that human beings organize their lives. Human society depends on a predictable division of labor, a designated allocation of scarce goods, assigned responsibility for children and others who cannot care for themselves, common values and their systematic transmission to new members, legitimate leadership, music, art, stories, games, and other symbolic productions. One way of choosing people for the different tasks of society is on the basis of their talents, motivations, and competence—their demonstrated achievements. The other way is on the basis of gender, race, ethnicity—ascribed membership in a category of people. Although societies vary in the extent to which they use one or the other of these ways of allocating people to work and to carry out other responsibilities, every society uses gender and age grades. Every society classifies people as "girl and boy children," "girls and boys ready to be married," and "fully adult women and men," constructs similarities among them and differences between them, and assigns them to different roles and responsibilities. Personality characteristics, feelings, motivations, and ambitions flow from these different life experiences so that the members of these different groups become different kinds of people. The process of gendering and its outcome are legitimated by religion, law, science, and the society's entire set of values.

· · ·

Western society's values legitimate gendering by claiming that it all comes from physiology—female and male procreative differences. But gender and sex are not equivalent, and gender as a social construction does not flow automatically from genitalia and reproductive organs, the main physiological differences of females and males. In the construction of ascribed social statuses, physiological differences such as sex, stage of development, color of skin, and size are crude markers. They are not the source of the social statuses of gender, age grade, and race. Social statuses are carefully constructed through prescribed processes of teaching, learning, emulation, and enforcement. Whatever genes, hormones, and biological evolution contribute to human social institutions is materially as well as qualitatively transformed by

703

social practices. Every social institution has a material base, but culture and social practices transform that base into something with qualitatively different patterns and constraints. The economy is much more than producing food and goods and distributing them to eaters and users; family and kinship are not the equivalent of having sex and procreating; morals and religions cannot be equated with the fears and ecstasies of the brain; language goes far beyond the sounds produced by tongue and larynx. No one eats "money" or "credit"; the concepts of "god" and "angels" are the subjects of theological disquisitions; not only words but objects, such as their flag, "speak" to the citizens of a country.

Similarly, gender cannot be equated with biological and physiological differences between human females and males. The building blocks of gender are *socially constructed statuses*. Western societies have only two genders, "man" and "woman." Some societies have three genders—men, women, and *berdaches* or *hijras* or *xaniths*. Berdaches, hijras, and xaniths are biological males who behave, dress, work, and are treated in most respects as social women; they are therefore not men, nor are they female women; they are, in our language, "male women."[2] There are African and American Indian societies that have a gender status called *manly hearted women*—biological females who work, marry, and parent as men; their social status is "female men" (Amadiume, 1987; Blackwood, 1984). They do not have to behave or dress as men to have the social responsibilities and prerogatives of husbands and fathers; what makes them men is enough wealth to buy a wife.

Modern Western societies' *transsexuals* and *transvestites* are the nearest equivalent of these crossover genders, but they are not institutionalized as third genders (Bolin, 1987). Transsexuals are biological males and females who have sex-change operations to alter their genitalia. They do so in order to bring their physical anatomy in congruence with the way they want to live and with their own sense of gender identity. They do not become a third gender; they change genders. Transvestites are males who live as women and females who live as men but do not intend to have sex-change surgery. Their dress, appearance, and mannerisms fall within the range of what is expected from members of the opposite gender, so that they "pass." They also change genders, sometimes temporarily, some for most of their lives. Transvestite women have fought in wars as men soldiers as recently as the nineteenth century; some married women, and others went back to being women and married men once the war was over.[3] Some were discovered when their wounds were treated; others not until they died. In order to work as a jazz musician, a man's occupation, Billy Tipton, a woman, lived most of her life as a man.

704

She died recently at seventy-four, leaving a wife and three adopted sons for whom she was husband and father, and musicians with whom she had played and traveled, for whom she was "one of the boys" (*New York Times,* 1989).[4] There have been many other such occurrences of women passing as men who do more prestigious or lucrative men's work (Matthaei, 1982, p. 192–93).[5]

Genders, therefore, are not attached to a biological substratum. Gender boundaries are breachable, and individual and socially organized shifts from one gender to another call attention to "cultural, social, or aesthetic dissonances" (Garber, 1992, p. 16). These odd or deviant or third genders show us what we ordinarily take for granted—that people have to learn to be women and men. Because transvestism is direct evidence of how gender is constructed, Marjorie Garber claims it as "extraordinary power . . . to disrupt, expose, and challenge, putting in question the very notion of the 'original' and of stable identity" (1992, 16).

● *Gender Bending*

It is difficult to see how gender is constructed because we take it for granted that it's all biology, or hormones, or human nature. The differences between women and men seem to be self-evident, and we think they would occur no matter what society did. But in actuality, human females and males are physiologically more similar in appearance than are the two sexes of many species of animals and are more alike than different in traits and behavior (C. F. Epstein, 1988). Without the deliberate use of gendered clothing, hairstyles, jewelry, and cosmetics, women and men would look far more alike.[6] Even societies that do not cover women's breasts have gender-identifying clothing, scarification, jewelry, and hairstyles.

The ease with which many transvestite women pass as men and transvestite men as women is corroborated by the common gender misidentification in Westernized societies of people in jeans, T-shirts, and sneakers. Men with long hair may be addressed as "miss," and women with short hair are often taken for men unless they offset the potential ambiguity with deliberate gender markers (Devor, 1987, 1989). Jan Morris, in *Conundrum,* an autobiographical account of events just before and just after a sex-change operation, described how easy it was to shift back and forth from being a man to being a woman when testing how it would feel to change gender status. During this time, Morris still had a penis and wore more or less unisex clothing; the context alone made the man and the woman:

Sometimes the arena of my ambivalence was uncomfortably small. At the Travellers' Club, for example, I was obviously known as a man or sorts—women were only allowed on the premises at all during a few hours of the day, and even then were hidden away as far as possible in lesser rooms or alcoves. But I had another club, only a few hundred yards away, where I was known only as a woman, and often I went directly from one to the other, imperceptibly changing roles on the way—"Cheerio, sir," the porter would say at one club, and "Hello, madam," the porter would greet me at the other. (1975, p. 132)

Gender shifts are actually a common phenomenon in public roles as well. Queen Elizabeth II of England bore children, but when she went to Saudi Arabia on a state visit, she was considered an honorary man so that she could confer and dine with the men who were heads of a state that forbids unrelated men and women to have face-to-unveiled-face contact. In contemporary Egypt, lower-class women who run restaurants or shops dress in men's clothing and engage in unfeminine aggressive behavior, and middle-class educated women of professional or managerial status can take positions of authority (Rugh, 1986, p. 131). In these situations, there is an important status change: These women are treated by the others in the situation as if they are men. From their own point of view, they are still women. From the social perspective, however, they are men.[7]

In many cultures, gender bending is prevalent in theater or dance—the Japanese kabuki are men actors who play both women and men; in Shakespeare's theater company, there were no actresses—Juliet and Lady Macbeth were played by boys. Shakespeare's comedies are full of witty comments on gender shifts. Women characters frequently masquerade as young men, and other women characters fall in love with them; the boys playing these masquerading women, meanwhile, are acting out pining for the love of men characters.[8]

• • •

But despite the ease with which gender boundaries can be traversed in work, in social relationships, and in cultural productions, gender statuses remain. Transvestites and transsexuals do not challenge the social construction of gender. Their goal is to be feminine women and masculine men (Kando, 1973). Those who do not want to change their anatomy but do want to change their gender behavior fare less well in establishing their social identity. . . .

Paradoxically, then, bending gender rules and passing between genders does not erode but rather preserves gender boundaries. In societies with only

706

two genders, the gender dichotomy is not disturbed by transvestites, because others feel that a transvestite is only transitorily ambiguous—is "really a man or woman underneath." After sex-change surgery, transsexuals end up in a conventional gender status—a "man" or a "woman" with the appropriate genitals (Eichler, 1989). When women dress as men for business reasons, they are indicating that in that situation, they want to be treated the way men are treated; when they dress as women, they want to be treated as women:

> By their male dress, female entrepreneurs signal their desire to suspend the expectations of accepted feminine conduct without losing respect and reputation. By wearing what is "unattractive" they signify that they are not intending to display their physical charms while engaging in public activity. Their loud, aggressive banter contrasts with the modest demeanor that attracts men. . . . Overt signalling of a suspension of the rules preserves normal conduct from eroding expectations. (Rugh, 1986, p. 131)

❧ For Individuals, Gender Means Sameness

Although the possible combinations of genitalia, body shapes, clothing, mannerisms, sexuality, and roles could produce infinite varieties in human beings, the social institution of gender depends on the production and maintenance of a limited number of gender statuses and of making the members of these statuses similar to each other. Individuals are born sexed but not gendered, and they have to be taught to be masculine or feminine.[9] As Simone de Beauvoir said: "One is not born, but rather becomes, a woman. . . . ; it is civilization as a whole that produces this creature . . . which is described as feminine." (1952, p. 267).

Children learn to walk, talk, and gesture the way their social group says girls and boys should. Ray Birdwhistell, in his analysis of body motion as human communication, calls these learned gender displays *tertiary* sex characteristics and argues that they are needed to distinguish genders because humans are a weakly dimorphic species—their only sex markers are genitalia (1970, p. 39–46). Clothing, paradoxically, often hides the sex but displays the gender.

In early childhood, humans develop gendered personality structures and sexual orientations through their interactions with parents of the same and opposite gender. As adolescents, they conduct their sexual behavior according to gendered scripts. Schools, parents, peers, and the mass media

707

guide young people into gendered work and family roles. As adults, they take on a gendered social status in their society's stratification system. Gender is thus both ascribed and achieved (West & Zimmerman, 1987).

The achievement of gender was most dramatically revealed in a case of an accidental transsexual—a baby boy whose penis was destroyed in the course of a botched circumcision when he was seven months old (Money & Ehrhardt, 1972, p. 118–23). The child's sex category was changed to "female," and a vagina was surgically constructed when the child was seventeen months old. The parents were advised that they could successfully raise the child, one of identical twins, as a girl. Physicians assured them that the child was too young to have formed a gender identity. Children's sense of which gender they belong to usually develops around the age of three, at the time that they start to group objects and recognize that the people around them also fit into categories—big, little; pink-skinned, brown-skinned; boys, girls. Three has also been the age when children's appearance is ritually gendered, usually by cutting a boy's hair or dressing him in distinctively masculine clothing. In Victorian times, English boys wore dresses up to the age of three, when they were put into short pants. (Garber, 1992, p. 1–2)

The parents of the accidental transsexual bent over backward to feminize the child—and succeeded. Frilly dresses, hair ribbons, and jewelry created a pride in looks, neatness, and "daintiness." More significant, the child's dominance was also feminized:

> The girl had many tomboyish traits, such as abundant physical energy, a high level of activity, stubbornness, and being often the dominant one in a girls' group. Her mother tried to modify her tomboyishness: ". . . I teach her to be more polite and quiet. I always wanted those virtues. I never did manage, but I'm going to try to manage them to—my daughter—to be more quiet and ladylike." From the beginning the girl had been the dominant twin. By the age of three, her dominance over her brother was, as her mother described it, that of a mother hen. The boy in turn took up for his sister, if anyone threatened her. (Money & Ehrhardt, 1972, 122)

This child was not a tomboy because of male genes or hormones; according to her mother, she herself had also been a tomboy. What the mother had learned poorly while growing up as a "natural" female she insisted that her physically reconstructed son-daughter learn well. For both mother and child, the social construction of gender overrode any possibly inborn traits.

People go along with the imposition of gender norms because the weight of morality as well as immediate social pressure enforces them. Consider how many instructions for properly gendered behavior are packed into this mother's admonition to her daughter: "This is how to hem a dress when you see the hem coming down and so to prevent yourself from looking like the slut I know you are so bent on becoming" (Kincaid, 1978).

Gender norms are inscribed in the way people move, gesture, and even eat. In one African society, men were supposed to eat with their "whole mouth, wholeheartedly, and not, like women, just with the lips, that is half-heartedly, with reservation and restraint" (Bordieu, [1980] 1990, p. 70). Men and women in this society learned to walk in ways that proclaimed their different positions in the society:

> The manly man . . . stands up straight into the face of the person he approaches, or wishes to welcome. Ever on the alert, because ever threatened, he misses nothing of what happens around him. . . . Conversely, a well brought-up woman . . . is expected to walk with a slight stoop, avoiding every misplaced movement of her body, her head or her arms, looking down, keeping her eyes on the spot where she will next put her foot, especially if she happens to have to walk past the men's assembly. (70)

Many cultures go beyond clothing, gestures, and demeanor in gendering children. They inscribe gender directly into bodies. In traditional Chinese society, mothers bound their daughters' feet into three-inch stumps to enhance their sexual attractiveness. Jewish fathers circumcise their infant sons to show their covenant with God. Women in African societies remove the clitoris of prepubescent girls, scrape their labia, and make the lips grow together to preserve their chastity and ensure their marriageability. In Western societies, women augment their breast size with silicone and reconstruct their faces with cosmetic surgery to conform to cultural ideals of feminine beauty. . . .

Most parents create a gendered world for their newborn by naming, birth announcements, and dress. Children's relationships with same-gendered and different-gendered caretakers structure their self-identifications and personalities. Through cognitive development, children extract and apply to their own actions the appropriate behavior for those who belong in their own gender, as well as race, religion, ethnic group, and social class, rejecting what is not appropriate. If their social categories are highly valued, they value themselves highly; if their social categories are low status, they lose self-esteem (Chodorow, 1974). Many feminist parents who want to raise androgynous children soon lose their children to the pull of gendered norms (T. Gordon, 1990, p. 87–90). My son attended a carefully nonsexist elementary school, which didn't even have girls' and boys' bathrooms. When he was seven or eight years old, I attended a class play about "squares" and "circles"

709

and their need for each other and noticed that all the girl squares and circles wore makeup, but none of the boy squares and circles did. I asked the teacher about it after the play, and she said, "Bobby said he was not going to wear makeup, and he is a powerful child, so none of the boys would either." In a long discussion about conformity, my son confronted me with the question of who the conformists were, the boys who followed their leader or the girls who listened to the woman teacher. In actuality, they both were, because they both followed same-gender leaders and acted in gender-appropriate ways. (Actors may wear makeup, but real boys don't.)

For human beings there is no essential femaleness or maleness, femininity or masculinity, womanhood or manhood, but once gender is ascribed, the social order constructs and holds individuals to strongly gendered norms and expectations. Individuals may vary on many of the components of gender and may shift genders temporarily or permanently, but they must fit into the limited number of gender statuses their society recognizes. In the process, they re-create their society's version of women and men: "If we do gender appropriately, we simultaneously sustain, reproduce, and render legitimate the institutional arrangements. . . . If we fail to do gender appropriately, we as individuals—not the institutional arrangements—may be called to account (for our character, motives, and predispositions)" (West & Zimmerman, 1987, p. 146).

The gendered practices of everyday life reproduce a society's view of how women and men should act (Bourdieu, [1980], 1990). Gendered social arrangements are justified by religion and cultural productions and backed by law, but the most powerful means of sustaining the moral hegemony of the dominant gender ideology is that the process is made invisible; any possible alternatives are virtually unthinkable (Foucault, 1972; Gramsci, 1971).

❧ For Society, Gender Means Difference

The persuasiveness of gender as a way of structuring social life demands that gender statuses be clearly differentiated. Varied talents, sexual preferences, identities, personalities, interests, and ways of interacting fragment the individual's bodily and social experiences. Nonetheless, these are organized in Western cultures into two and only two socially and legally recognized gender statuses, "man" and "woman."[10] In the social construction of gender, it does not matter what men and women actually do; it does not even matter if

710

they do exactly the same thing. The social institution of gender insists only that what they do is *perceived* as different.

If men and women are doing the same tasks, they are usually spatially segregated to maintain gender separation, and often the tasks are given different job titles as well, such as executive secretary and administrative assistant (Reskin, 1988). If the differences between women and men begin to blur, society's "sameness taboo" goes into action (G. Rubin, 1975, p. 178). At a rock and roll dance at West Point in 1976, the year women were admitted to the prestigious military academy for the first time, the school's administrators "were reportedly perturbed by the sight of mirror-image couples dancing in short hair and dress gray trousers," and a rule was established that women cadets could dance at these events only if they wore skirts (Barkalow & Raab, 1970, p. 53). Women recruits in the U.S. Marine Corps are required to wear makeup—at a minimum, lipstick and eye shadow—and they have to take classes in makeup, hair care, poise, and etiquette. This feminization is part of a deliberate policy of making them clearly distinguishable from men Marines. Christine Williams quotes a twenty-five-year-old woman drill instructor as saying: "A lot of the recruits who come here don't wear makeup; they're tomboyish or athletic. A lot of them have the preconceived idea that going into the military means they can still be a tomboy. They don't realize that you are a *Woman* Marine" (1989, p. 76–77).[11]

If gender differences were genetic, physiological, or hormonal, gender bending and gender ambiguity would occur only in hermaphrodites, who are born with chromosomes and genitalia that are not clearly female or male. Since gender differences are socially constructed, all men and all women can enact the behavior of the other, because they know the other's social script: "'Man' and 'woman' are at once empty and overflowing categories. Empty because they have no ultimate, transcendental meaning. Overflowing because even when they appear to be fixed, they still contain within them alternative, denied, or suppressed definitions" (J. W. Scott, 1988a, p. 49). Nonetheless, though individuals may be able to shift gender statuses, the gender boundaries have to hold, or the whole gendered social order will come crashing down.

Paradoxically, it is the social importance of gender statuses and their external markers—clothing, mannerisms, and spatial segregation—that makes gender bending or gender crossing possible—or even necessary. The social viability of differentiated gender statuses produces the need or desire to shift statuses. Without gender differentiation, transvestitism and transsexuality could be meaningless. You couldn't dress in the opposite gender's clothing if all clothing were unisex. There would be no need to reconstruct genitalia to match identity if interests and life-styles were not gendered. There would be no need for women to pass as men to do certain kinds of work if jobs were not typed as "women's work" and "men's work." Women would not have to dress as men in public life in order to give orders or aggressively bargain with customers.

Gender boundaries are preserved when transsexuals create congruous autobiographies of always having felt like what they are now. The transvestite's story also "recuperates social and sexual norms" (Garber, 1992, p. 69). In the transvestite's normalized narrative, he or she "is 'compelled' by social and economic forces to disguise himself or herself in order to get a job, escape repression, or gain artistic or political 'freedom'" (Garber, 1992, p. 70). The "true identity," when revealed, causes amazement over how easily and successfully the person passed as a member of the opposite gender, not a suspicion that gender itself is something of a put-on.

· · ·

Endnotes

[1] In cases of ambiguity in countries with modern medicine, surgery is usually performed to make the genitalia more clearly male or female.

[2] On the hijras of India, see Nanda 1990; on the xaniths of Oman, Wikan 1982, 168–86; on the American Indian berdaches, W. L. Williams 1986. Other societies that have similar institutionalized third-gender men are the Koniag of Alaska, the Tanala of Madagascar, the Mesakin of Nuba, and the Chukchee of Siberia (Wikan 1982, 1970).

[3] Durova 1989; Freeman and Bond 1992; Wheelwright 1989.

[4] Gender segregation of work in popular music still has not changed very much, according to Groce and Cooper 1989, despite considerable androgyny in some very popular figures. See Garber 1992 on the androgyny. She discusses Tipton on pp. 67–70.

[5] In the nineteenth century, not only did these women get men's wages, but they also "had male privileges and could do all manner of things other women could not: open a bank account, write checks, own property, go anywhere unaccompanied, vote in elections" (Faderman 1991, 44).

[6] When unisex clothing and men wearing long hair came into vogue in the United States in the mid-1960s, beards and mustaches for men also came into style again as gender identifications.

[7]For other accounts of women being treated as men in Islamic countries, as well as accounts of women and men cross-dressing in these countries, see Garber 1992, 304–52.

[8]Dollimore 1986; Garber 1992, 32–40; Greenblatt 1987, 66–93; Howard 1988. For Renaissance accounts of sexual relations with women and men of ambiguous sex, see Laqueur 1990a, 134–39. For modern accounts of women passing as men that other women find sexually attractive, see Devor 1989, 136–37; Wheelwright 1989, 53–59.

[9]For an account of how a potential man-to-woman transsexual learned to be feminine, see Garfinkel 1967, 116–85, 285–88. For a gloss on this account that points out how, throughout his encounter with Agnes, Garfinkel failed to see how he himself was constructing his own masculinity, see Rogers 1992.

[10]Other societies recognize more than two categories, but usually no more than three or four (Jacobs and Roberts 1989).

[11]The taboo on males and females looking alike reflects the U.S. military's homophobia (Bérubé 1989). If you can't tell those with a penis from those with a vagina, how are you going to determine whether their sexual interest is heterosexual or homosexual unless you watch them having sexual relations?

References

Amadiume, I. (1987). *Male daughters, female husbands: Gender and sex in an African society.* London: Zed Books.

Barkalow, C., & Raab, A. (1990). *In the men's house.* New York: Poseidon Press.

Bérubé, A. (1989). Marching to a different drummer: Gay and lesbian GIs in World War II. In Duberman, Vicinus, & Chauncey (Eds.).

Birdwhistell, R. L. (1970). *Kinesics and context: Essays on body motion communication.* Philadelphia: University of Pennsylvania Press.

Blackwood, E. (1984). Sexuality and gender in certain Native American tribes: The case of cross-gender females. *Signs, 10,* 27–42.

Bolin, A. (1987). Transsexualism and the limits of the traditional analysis. *American Behavioral Scientist, 31,* 41–65.

Bourdieu, P. (1989). Social space and symbolic power. *Sociological Theory, 7,* 14–25.

Bourdieu, P. [1980]. (1990). *The logic of practice.* Stanford, CA: Stanford University Press.

Chodorow, N. (1974). Family structure and feminine personality. In Rosaldo & Lamphere (Eds.).

De Beauvoir, S. (1953). *The second sex* (H. M. Parshley, Trans.). New York: Knopf.

713

Devor, H. (1987). Gender blending females: Women and sometimes men. *American Behavioral Scientist, 31,* 12–40.

Devor, H. (1989). *Gender blending: Confronting the limits of duality.* Bloomington: Indiana University Press.

Dollimore, J. (1986). Subjectivity, sexuality, and transgression: The Jacobean connection. *Renaissance Drama, n.s., 17,* 53–81.

Durova, N. (1989). *The cavalry maiden: Journals of a Russian officer in the Napoleonic Wars* (M. F. Zirn, Trans.). Bloomington: Indiana University Press.

Eichler, M. (1989). Sex change operations: The last bulwark of the double standard. In L. Richardson & V. Taylor (Eds.), *Feminist frontiers II.* New York: Random House.

Epstein, C. F. (1988). *Deceptive distinctions: Sex, gender and the social order.* New Haven, CT: Yale University Press.

Faderman, L. (1991). *Odd girls and twilight lovers: A history of lesbian life in twentieth-century America.* New York: Columbia University Press.

Foucault, M. (1972). *The archeology of knowledge and the discourse on language* (A. M. S. Smith, Trans.). New York: Pantheon.

Freeman, L., & Bond, A. H. (1992). *America's first woman warrior: The courage of Deborah Sampson.* New York: Paragon.

Garber, M. (1992). *Vested interests: Cross-dressing and cultural anxiety.* New York and London: Routledge.

Garfinkel, H. (1967). *Studies in ethnomethodology.* Englewood Cliffs, NJ: Prentice-Hall.

Gordon, T. (1990). *Feminist mothers.* New York: New York University Press.

Gramsci, A. (1971). *Selections from the prison notebooks* (Q. Hoare & G. N. Smith, Trans. and Eds.). New York: International Publishers.

Greenblatt, S. (1987). *Shakespearean negotiations: The circulation of social energy in Renaissance England.* Berkeley: University of California Press.

Groce, S. B., & Cooper, M. (1990). Just me and the boys? Women in local-level rock and roll. *Gender & Society, 4,* 220–229.

Howard, J. E. (1988). Cross-dressing, the theater, and gender struggle in early modern England. *Shakespeare Quarterly, 39,* 418–441.

Jacobs, S. E., & Roberts, C. (1989). Sex, sexuality, gender, and gender variance. In S. Morgen (Ed.), *Gender and anthropology.* Washington, DC: American Anthropological Association.

Kando, T. (1973). *Sex change: The achievement of gender identity among feminized transsexuals.* Springfield, IL: Charles C. Thomas.

Kincaid, J. (1978, June 26). Girl. *The New Yorker.*

Laqueur, T. (1990a). *Making sex: Body and gender from the Greeks to Freud*. Cambridge, MA: Harvard University Press.

Laqueur, T. (1990b). The facts of fatherhood. In M. Hirsch & E. F. Keller (Eds.), *Conflicts in feminism*. New York and London: Routledge.

Larrington, C. (Ed.). (1992). *The feminist companion to mythology*. London: Pandora Press.

Larwood, L., Stromberg, A. H., & Gutek, B. A. (Eds.). (1985). *Women and work: An annual review* (Vol. 1). Newbury Park, CA: Sage.

Lasker, J. N., & Borg, S. (1987). *In search of parenthood*. Boston: Beacon Press.

Laslett, B., & Brenner, J. (1989). Gender and social reproduction: Historical perspectives. *Annual Review of Sociology, 15,* 381–404.

Laslett, P. (1977). *Family life and illicit love in earlier generations*. Cambridge: Cambridge University Press.

Lavine, L. (1986). Men in women's clothing: Anti-theatricality and effeminization from 1579 to 1642. *Criticism, 28,* 121–143.

Laws, J. L. (1975). The psychology of tokenism: An analysis. *Sex Roles, 1,* 51–67.

Laws, J. L., & Schwartz, P. (1977). *Sexual scripts: The social construction of female sexuality*. New York: Holt, Rinehart and Winston.

Matthaei, J. A. (1982). *An economic history of women's work in America*. New York: Schocken.

Morris, J. (1975). *Conundrum*. New York: Signet.

Nanda, S. (1990). *Neither man nor woman: The hijiras of India*. Belmont, CA: Wadsworth.

New York Times. (1989a, February 2). Musician's death at 74 reveals he was a man.

Reskin, B. F. (1988). Bringing the men back in: Sex differentiation and the devaluation of women's work. *Gender & Society, 2,* 58–81.

Richardson, L., & Taylor, V. (Eds.). (1989). *Feminist frontiers II*. New York: Random House.

Rogers, M. F. (1992). They were all passing: Agnes, Garfinkel, and company. *Gender & Society, 6,* 169–191.

Rubin, G. (1975). The traffic in women: Notes on the political economy of sex. In R. R. Reiter (Ed.), *Toward an anthropology of women*. New York: Monthly Review Press.

Rugh, A. B. (1986). *Reveal and conceal; Dress in contemporary Egypt*. Syracuse, NY: Syracuse University Press.

Scott, J. W. (1988a). *Gender and the politics of history*. New York: Columbia University Press.

West, C., & Zimmerman, D. (1987). Doing gender. *Gender & Society, 1,* 125–151.

Wheelwright, J. (1989). *Amazons and military maids: Women who cross-dressed in pursuit of life, liberty and happiness.* London: Pandora Press.

Wikam, U. (1982). *Behind the veil in Arabia: Women in Oman.* Baltimore, MD: Johns Hopkins University Press.

Williams, C. L. (1989). *Gender differences at work: Women and men in nontraditional occupations.* Berkeley: University of California Press.

Williams, W. L. (1986). *The spirit and the flesh: Sexual diversity in American Indian culture.* Boston: Beacon Press.

◉ ◉ ◉

Questions

1. What is gender? Why do many people believe that it is innate?

2. What is meant by the social construction of gender? How is gender socially constructed in everyday life?

3. What does Lorber mean when she says that people "do gender"? Why is doing gender important? How do *you* do gender?

4. What are third genders? Is there an equivalent of this in Western societies?

5. What is gender bending? Why is it beneficial for a society to have some members who are gender benders?

6. Lorber says that "it does not matter what men and women actually do; it does not matter if they do exactly the same thing. The social institution of gender insists only that what they do is *perceived* as different." Explain what she means by this statement and give an example.

How Subtle Sex Discrimination Works

Nijole V. Benokraitis

There are many forms of sex discrimination. Blatant sex discrimination is typically intentional, quite visible, and easily documented. Covert sex discrimination is hidden, purposeful, and difficult to prove. This selection discusses subtle sex discrimination—behavior, often unnoticed, that people have internalized as "normal," "natural," or customary.

. . .

Subtle sex discrimination refers to the unequal and harmful treatment of women that is typically less visible and obvious than blatant sex discrimination. It is often not noticed because most people have internalized subtle sexist behavior as "normal," "natural," or acceptable. Subtle sex discrimination can be relatively innocent or manipulative, intentional or unintentional, well-meaning or malicious. Subtle sex discrimination is difficult to document because many people do not perceive it as serious or harmful. In addition, subtle sex discrimination is often more complex than it appears: What is discrimination to many women may not seem discriminatory to many men or even women. . . .

☙ Condescending Chivalry

Condescending chivalry refers to superficially courteous behavior that is protective and paternalistic, but treats women as subordinates.

Reprinted from *Subtle Sexism: Current Practices and Prospects for Change* (1997), Sage Publications, Inc.

Sometimes the chivalry is well-intentioned because it "protects" women from criticism. For example, "A male boss will haul a guy aside and just kick ass if the [male] subordinate performs badly in front of a client" but may not say anything to a female subordinate (Fraker, 1984). Not providing such criticism may seem benevolent in the short term, but it will handicap an employee's performance in the long run. . . .

Thus, chivalrous behavior can signal status inequality. According to some researchers, outmoded attitudes—on the parts of both men and women—are preventing many qualified women from breaking into top jobs as school superintendents. Unlike their male counterparts, female candidates still get such questions from school board members as "How would your husband feel about your moving?" "Can you deal with a district where the administrators are mostly men?" and "Can you handle tough discipline problems?" According to researchers, the oppressive chivalry continues after a woman is hired. Female school superintendents often face greater scrutiny, for example, when it comes to such "masculine" tasks as finances and maintenance issues (see Nakashima, 1996).

Supportive Discouragement

Supportive discouragement refers to a form of subtle sex discrimination where women receive mixed messages about their abilities, intelligence, or accomplishments. One form of supportive discouragement involves encouraging women to succeed in general but not rewarding their actual achievements because the latter may not reflect traditionally male interests:

> . . . [H]aving served on several search committees, I'm aware of how often feminist (or even woman-topic) dissertations are dismissed as "jargony," "trendy," etc. . . . I'm not really sure if feminism is still seen as a "fly-by-night" sort of discipline, but the accusation is a difficult one to argue because the people who make it will assure you until they're blue in the face (or you are) that they would love to hire a woman, are not

opposed to feminism, etc. But it's only "this" dissertation, you see, they are opposed to. . . . (E-mail correspondence, 1996)

Another form of supportive discouragement encourages women to be ambitious and successful but places numerous obstacles in their paths, which either limit or derail the progress. Consider the following example from a colleague in the United Kingdom:

> One of the largest departments in our College is the Access department which offers part-time courses for people with no formal qualifications who wish to enter higher education or return to work. I would say that about 70 percent of these students are female and intend to go into teaching or similar work. The College refuses to implement a crèche or other day-care on the basis that it would be too expensive; staffing would cost almost nothing as the College runs courses for Nursery Nurses, childcare workers, etc. This despite the fact that of the people who are offered places on the Access course and turn it down, 80 percent give lack of child care as the main reason. Of this 80 percent, 92 percent are women. The courses are also run in some of the worst accommodations on site—"temporary" buildings which have been there for about twenty years and which are in a terrible state. The Chemistry department (not many women here) has, however, had at least three major renovations in the last ten years. It certainly makes clear to the many women on the Access course the opinion the College management has of their relative importance. (E-mail correspondence, 1996)

❂ Friendly Harassment

Friendly harassment refers to sexually oriented behavior that, at face value, looks harmless or even playful. If it creates discomfort, embarrassment, or humiliation, however, it is a form of subtle discrimination. According to some female students at Stanford Medical School, for example, it is in such traditionally male-taught courses as those in surgery and internal medicine that many women encounter the most offensive sexual jokes. A fourth-year student said that many of her days "are spent fending off stupid little comments," many of them sexual, from male residents and doctors. She hesitated to complain, however, because good evaluations from professors are essential to get a good residency (Gose, 1995).

When women don't laugh at "stupid little jokes," moreover, they are often accused of not having a sense of humor:

> In response to a question from a friend of mine (a female graduate student) regarding how to comport herself at a job interview, a male faculty adviser responds, "Just flirt!" When I recount the incident to a male friend (junior faculty in another field at another institution), he responds: "Maybe it was a joke. Lighten up!" The primary sexism of the first remark gets echoed in the secondary sexism of the second remark, which trivializes the offense and the indignation ["no sense of humor"]. (E-mail correspondence, 1996)

Humor and jokes serve a number of functions: They reinforce group solidarity; define the defiant/outsider group; educate; save face; ingratiate; express caring for others; provide a safety valve for discussing taboo topics; maintain status inequality; silence or embarrass people; and provide tension release, hostility, and anger toward any group that is seen as marginal, inferior, or threatening. A single joke can serve several of these functions.

Although women's humor can be a powerful tool for changing stereotypes about females, much of men's sexual humor expresses male dominance over women, negates their personhood, and tries to silence women: "There are whole categories of jokes about women for which there are no male parallels: prostitute jokes, mother-in-law jokes, dumb blonde jokes, woman driver jokes, Jewish mother jokes" (Crawford, 1995:138). Women often don't laugh at many of these jokes not because they don't have a sense of humor, but because the "jokes" are hostile, aggressive, and demeaning. . . .

◉ Subjective Objectification

Subjective objectification refers to a form of subtle sex discrimination that treats women as children, possessions, or sex objects. Women are often punished like children—their "allowances" may be taken away, they may be forbidden to associate with their friends, their physical mobility may be limited, they may be given curfews, or they may be threatened with punishment similar to that of children. . . .

Our culture is continuously bombarded with images of women as little more than sexual body parts. The Media Action Alliance, which publishes the *Action Agenda* newsletter, is constantly filled with examples of posters, ads, videos, and other media materials that glorify violence against women and exploitation of women's bodies. It has been estimated that the average teenager sees between 1,900 and 2,400 sex-related messages per year on television alone (Brown, Childers, & Waszik, 1990). Many of the images, including those in films targeted at adolescents, treat women's bodies as trophies: Boys compete to be the first to "score," to achieve the most sexual conquests, and to "make it" with the sexiest teenage girls (see Whatley, 1994).

A frightening result of such competition can include rape and other sexual assaults on women. Consider the "Spur Posse" case in California. In 1993 eight members of a suburban high school, many of them top athletes at the school, created a clique called the "Spur Posse." Their primary goal was to "score" with as many girls as possible. They kept track of the girls with whom they had intercourse, and some bragged that their individual tallies ran into the sixties. In at least seven cases, girls from ten to sixteen years old said they had been raped. Some of the parents condoned their sons' behavior. One father, in fact, boasted to reporters that the assaults were not rape but indicators of his son's virility and sexual prowess (Seligmann, 1993).

This bizarre perception of women as possessions and trophies follows many boys into adulthood. According to Brooks (1995:3–4), what he refers to as "the Centerfold Syndrome" represents "one of the most malignant forces in contemporary relationships between men

721

and women." One of the elements of the Centerfold Syndrome is objectification:

> Women become objects as men become objectifiers. As the culture has granted men the right and privilege of looking at women, women have been expected to accept the role of stimulators of men's visual interest, with their bodies becoming objects that can be lined up, compared, and rated. . . . Objective physical aspects are critical: Size, shape, and harmony of body parts are more important than a woman's human qualities. . . . Men talk of their attraction to women in dehumanizing terms based on the body part of their obsession—"I'm a leg man," or "I'm an ass man."

Brooks notes that one of the most harmful effects of such objectification is that real women become more complicated, less appealing, and even ugly: "Stretch marks, varicose veins, sagging breasts, and cellulite-marked legs, common phenomena for real female bodies, may be viewed as repugnant by men who see women as objects" (p. 5). As a result, Centerfold Syndrome men may be sexually and emotionally inexpressive with the most important women in their lives.

☻ Radiant Devaluation

Although women are less likely to be openly maligned or insulted than in the past, they are devalued more subtly but just as effectively. Often, the devaluation is done in glowing terms (Benokraitis & Feagin, 1995:102):

> A psychologist, one of the most popular instructors in her college, said she would get good teaching evaluations from her male chair but that the positive review would be couched in sex-stereotypical rather than professional terms—she was described as being "mama-ish" and as having a "charming" approach to teaching. Being "mama-ish" and "charming" are *not* the criteria used by tenure and promotion committees.

722

On a much broader scale, some scholars contend that the most recent devaluations have focused on antifeminist intellectual harassment through the use of "vilification and distortion or even violence to repress certain areas of research and forms of inquiry" (Clark et al., 1996:x). Attacks on feminists and feminist scholarship are nothing new. What has changed, however, is that much of the "newest wave of antifeminism cloaks itself in the vestments of feminism: the new antifeminists are women who, claiming to be feminists themselves, now maintain they are rescuing the women's movement from those who have led it astray" (Ginsburg & Lennox, 1996:170). Many of these devaluators have impressive academic credentials, are articulate, have been supported by conservative corporate foundations, and have found a receptive audience in the mainstream media and many publishing companies, which see antifeminism as a "hot commodity" because it is so profitable. Blaming feminism for such (real or imagined) ailments as the deterioration of relationships between the sexes and the presumed dissolution of the family—especially when the criticism comes from well-educated, self-proclaimed feminists—sells a lot of books.

❧ Liberated Sexism

Liberated sexism refers to the process that, at face value, appears to be treating women and men equally but that, in practice, increases men's freedom while placing greater burdens on women. One of the best examples of liberated sexism is work overloads both within the home and at the job site. Since the 1970s, increasing numbers of women have found themselves with two jobs—one inside and one outside the home. Ironically, women working these "double days" are often referred to as "liberated women." But liberated from what?

Shared parenting reflects more rhetoric than reality. In a national study, Bianchi (1990) found that more than 60 percent of divorced fathers either did not visit their children, or did not visit them and had no telephone or mail contact with them over a one-year period. Employed mothers with preschool-age children spend twenty-four hours more a week in child-care activities than do their husbands.

723

Because the husband's job typically takes priority over his wife's (his salary is usually much higher), nearly nine out of ten mothers care for their children when they are sick, compared with only one out of ten working fathers (DeStefano & Colasanto, 1990). Although in one survey 56 percent of male employees said they were interested in flexible work schedules that would allow them more family time, in reality fewer than 1 percent take advantage of the unpaid paternity leaves that some 30 percent of companies offer today. The Family and Medical Leave Act, which was signed into law by President Clinton in 1993, allows workers of employers with fifty or more employees to take up to twelve weeks of unpaid leave following the birth or adoption of a child. Most men fear the career repercussions of taking paternity leaves or can't afford unpaid leaves financially, however (see Sommer, 1994). . . .

◉ Considerate Domination

Men often occupy preeminent positions and control important decision-making functions. . . . Men's dominance is built into our language, laws, and customs in both formal and informal ways. The dominance is accepted because it has been internalized and is often portrayed as "collegial," authoritative, or mutually beneficial.

Most of us take for granted that the expert and dominant cast of characters in the media are men. The media routinely ignore women or present them as second-class citizens. A recent survey of the front-page stories of twenty national and local newspapers found that although women make up 52 percent of the population, they show up just 13 percent of the time in the prime news spots. Even the stories about breast implants quoted men more often than women. Two-thirds of the bylines on front pages were male, and three-quarters of the opinions on op-ed pages were by men. Fewer than a third of the photographs on front pages featured women. Since the old "women's sections" are now more unisex and focus on both men and women, news about and by women has lost space even in these lifestyle sections (Goodman, 1992; see also Overholser, 1996).

Television news is not much better. In a study of the content of evening news programs on CBS, NBC, and ABC, Rakow and Kranich (1991) found that women as on-camera sources of information were used in less than 15 percent of the cases. When women did speak, they were usually passive reactors to public events as housewife or wife of the man in the news rather than participants or experts. Even in critical analyses of issues that affect more women than men, women may not appear on the screen. For example, a lengthy story on CBS on welfare reform did not use any women or feminist sources. . . .

❀ Collegial Exclusion

One of the most familiar forms of subtle sexism is collegial exclusion, whereby women are made to feel invisible or unimportant through physical, social, or professional isolation. When Hall and Sandler's pamphlet, "The Classroom Climate: A Chilly One for Women?" was published in 1982, it was an instant success. Among other reasons, Sandler and Hall articulated the feelings that many women had experienced in higher education of being ignored, not having female role models, or being excluded from classroom discussions and activities. Since then, many studies have documented women's exclusion from classroom discourse, textbooks, and other academic activities (see, for example, Ginorio, 1995; Lewis, 1990; Maher & Tetreault, 1994; Peterson & Kroner, 1992).

Although there has been greater awareness of exclusion, it's not evident that there has been much change since 1982. At Stanford Medical School, for example, "The male body has been used as the standard, and the woman's body has been seen as a variation on that theme," says a third-year female student. Several women once heard a professor dismiss the clitoris with five words: "like the penis, just shorter" (Gose, 1995:A50). At Yale and American University law schools, female students' complaints are strikingly similar to those that Hall and Sandler described in 1982: Women feel their speech is stifled in class; professors respond more positively to comments by men, even if a woman voiced the same idea first; male students, even friends, ignore women's comments on legal issues and talk around them; male students and faculty devalue women's opinions; and men don't hear what women say (Torry, 1995).

When I asked the subscribers of the Women's Studies e-mail discussion list if they or someone they knew had ever experienced subtle sexism, many of the responses (from both the United States and Europe) described collegial exclusion. Here are a few examples:

Just got back from a national conference and heard a female college president relate her experiences at meetings with other college presidents in the state. She was the only female present at the meetings and found that her suggestions/insights were ignored by her male colleagues. However, when the same suggestions later came from one of them, they were acknowledged. She finally took to writing her suggestions on the chalkboard. They couldn't be ignored that way—or at least not for long.

There was a series of women-only staff development meetings set up by one of the more senior women (there are few), but the "only" time that could be found for this was on Monday at 6:00 p.m. Other staff development meetings are held at lunchtime with time off for anybody who wants to go.

Women often feel they're isolated. . . . Many women begin with great promise but are demoralized and cut off from support . . . I'm referring to women who are cut off from support in ways it's hard to explain . . . often the only women in their departments . . . although some are in departments with other untenured women but the Old White Guys have the power. [The women] often are lacking a real (feminist) community.

References

Benokraitis, N. V., and J. R. Feagin. 1995. *Modern sexism: Blatant, subtle, and covert discrimination*. Englewood Cliffs, N.J.: Prentice Hall.

Bianchi, S. 1990. America's children: Mixed prospects. *Population Bulletin*, 45: 3–41.

Brooks, G. R. 1995. *The centerfold syndrome: How men can overcome objectification and achieve intimacy with women.* San Francisco, Calif.: Jossey-Bass.

Brown, J. D., K. W. Childers, and C. S. Waszik. 1990. Television and adolescent sexuality. *Journal of Adolescent Health Care,* 11: 62–70.

Clark, V., S. N. Garner, M. Higonnet, and K. H. Katrak, eds. 1996. *Antifeminism in the academy.* New York: Routledge.

Crawford, M. 1995. *Talking difference: On gender and language.* Thousand Oaks, Calif.: Sage.

DeStefano, L., and D. Colasanto. 1990. Unlike 1975, today most Americans think men have it better. *Gallup Poll Monthly,* (February): 25–36.

Fraker, S. 1984. Why top jobs elude female executives. *Fortune,* (April 16): 46.

Ginorio, A. B. 1995. *Warming the climate for women in academic science.* Washington, D.C.: Association of American Colleges and Universities.

Ginsburg, E., and S. Lennox. 1996. Antifeminism in scholarship and publishing. In *Antifeminism in the academy,* eds. V. Clark, S. N. Garner, M. Higonnet, and K. H. Katrak, 169–200. New York: Routledge.

Goodman, E. 1992. A woman's place is in the paper. *Baltimore Sun,* (April 7):15A.

Gose, B. 1995. Women's place in medicine. *Chronicle of Higher Education,* (November 3): A49.

Lewis, M. 1990. Interrupting patriarchy: Politics, resistance, and transformation in the feminist classroom. *Harvard Educational Review,* 60: 472.

Maher, F. A., and M. K. T. Tetreault. 1994. *The feminist classroom.* New York: Basic Books.

Nakashima, E. 1996. When it comes to top school jobs, women learn it's tough to get ahead. *Washington Post,* (April 21): B1, B5.

Overholser, G. 1996. Front page story: Women. *Washington Post,* (April 21): C6.

Peterson, S. B., and T. Kroner. 1992. Gender biases in textbooks for introductory psychology and human development. *Psychology of Women Quarterly,* 16: 17–36.

Rakow, L. F., and K. Kranich. 1991. Woman as sign in television news. *Journal of Communication,* 41: 8–23.

727

Seligmann, J. 1993. A town's divided loyalties. *Newsweek,* (April 12): 29.

Sommer, M. 1994. Welcome cribside, Dad. *Christian Science Monitor,* (June 28): 19.

Torry, S. 1995. Voice of concern grows louder on gender bias issue. *Washington Post,* (November 20): 7.

Whatley, M. H. 1994. Keeping adolescents in the picture: Construction of adolescent sexuality in textbook images and popular films. In *Sexual culture and the construction of adolescent identities,* ed. J. M. Irvine, 183–205. Philadelphia: Temple University Press.

☻ ☻ ☻

Critical-Thinking Questions

1. Why are the various categories of subtle sex discrimination presented as oxymorons? How does subtle sexism differ from more blatant forms of discrimination?

2. Can you identify situations in which you have experienced subtle sex discrimination? Have you ever discriminated in this way against others?

3. What are the individual and organizational costs of subtle sex discrimination? What remedies might be effective in decreasing this form of inequality?

Controlling Images and Black Women's Oppression

PATRICIA HILL COLLINS

As W. E. B. Du Bois noted, many victims of racial prejudice and stereotypes often experience inevitable self-questioning and self-disparagement. Recently, feminists have argued that women of color typically confront gendered racism—a combination of both racism and sexism. In the following selection, Patricia Hill Collins shows how negative images of black women have provided an ideological justification for race, gender, and class inequality.

• • •

"Black women emerged from slavery firmly enshrined in the consciousness of white America as 'Mammy' and the 'bad black woman,'" contends Cheryl Gilkes (1983:294). The dominant ideology of the slave era fostered the creation of four interrelated, socially constructed controlling images of Black womanhood, each reflecting the dominant group's interest in maintaining Black women's subordination. Given that both Black and white women were important to slavery's continuation, the prevailing ideology functioned to mask contradictions in social relations affecting all women. According to the cult of true womanhood, "true" women possessed four cardinal virtues: piety, purity, submissiveness, and domesticity. Elite white

Reprinted from *Seeing Ourselves*, edited by J.J. Macionis and N.V. Benokraitis (2004), Prentice-Hall, Inc.

women and those of the emerging middle class were encouraged to aspire to these virtues. African American women encountered a different set of controlling images. The sexual ideology of the period as is the case today "confirmed the differing material circumstances of these two groups of women . . . by balancing opposing definitions of womanhood and motherhood, each depend ent on the other for its existence" (Carby, 1987:25).

The first controlling image applied to African American women is that of the mammy—the faithful, obedient domestic servant. Created to justify the economic exploitation of house slaves and sustained to explain Black women's long-standing restriction to domestic service, the mammy image represents the normative yardstick used to evaluate all Black women's behavior. By loving, nurturing, and caring for her white children and "family" better than her own, the mammy symbolizes the dominant group's perception of the ideal Black female relationship to elite white male power. Even though she may be well loved and may wield considerable authority in her white "family," the mammy still knows her "place" as obedient servant. She has accepted her subordination.

Black women intellectuals have aggressively deconstructed the image of African American women as contented mammies by challenging traditional views of Black women domestics (Dill, 1980, 1988; Clark-Lewis, 1985; Rollins, 1985). Literary critic Trudier Harris's (1982) volume *From Mammies to Militants: Domestics in Black American Literature* investigates prominent differences in how Black women have been portrayed by others in literature and how they portray themselves. In her work on the difficulties faced by Black women leaders, Rhetaugh Dumas (1980) describes how Black women executives are hampered by being treated as mammies and penalized if they do not appear warm and nurturing. But despite these works, the mammy image lives on in scholarly and popular culture. Audre Lorde's account of a shopping trip offers a powerful example of its tenacity: "I wheel my two-year-old daughter in a shopping cart through a supermarket in . . . 1967, and a little white girl riding past in her mother's cart calls out excitedly, 'Oh look, Mommy, a baby maid!'" (1984:126).[1]

The mammy image is central to interlocking systems of race, gender, and class oppression. Since efforts to control African American family life require perpetuating the symbolic structures of racial oppression, the mammy image is important because it aims to shape Black women's behavior as mothers. As the members of African American families who are most familiar with the skills needed for Black accommodation, Black women are encouraged to transmit to their own children the deference behavior many are forced to exhibit in mammy roles. By teaching Black children their assigned place in white power structures, Black women who internalize the mammy image potentially become effective conduits for perpetuating racial oppression. In addition, employing mammies buttresses the racial superiority of white women employers and weds them more closely to their fathers, husbands, and sons as sources of elite white male power (Rollins, 1985).

The mammy image also serves a symbolic function in maintaining gender oppression. Black feminist critic Barbara Christian argues that images of Black womanhood serve as a reservoir for the fears of Western culture, "a dumping ground for those female functions a basically Puritan society could not confront" (1985:2). Juxtaposed against the image of white women promulgated through the cult of true womanhood, the mammy image as the Other symbolizes the oppositional difference of mind/body and culture/nature thought to distinguish Black women from everyone else. Christian comments on the mammy's gender significance: "All the functions of mammy are magnificently physical. They involve the body as sensuous, as funky, the part of women that white southern America was profoundly afraid of. Mammy, then, harmless in her position of slave, unable because of her all-giving nature to do harm, is needed as an image, a surrogate to contain all those fears of the physical female" (1985:2). The mammy image buttresses the ideology of the cult of true womanhood, one in which sexuality and fertility are severed. "Good" white mothers are expected to deny their female sexuality and devote their attention to the moral development of their offspring. In contrast, the mammy image is one

731

of an asexual woman, a surrogate mother in blackface devoted to the development of a white family.

No matter how loved they were by their white "families," Black women domestic workers remained poor because they were economically exploited. The restructured post–World War II economy in which African American women moved from service in private homes to jobs in the low-paid service sector has produced comparable economic exploitation. Removing Black women's labor from African American families and exploiting it denies Black extended family units the benefits of either decent wages or Black women's unpaid labor in their homes. Moreover, many white families in both the middle class and working class are able to maintain their class position because they have long used Black women as a source of cheap labor (Rollins, 1985; Byerly, 1986). The mammy image is designed to mask this economic exploitation of social class (King, 1973).

For reasons of economic survival, African American women may play the mammy role in paid work settings. But within African American communities these same women often teach their own children something quite different. Bonnie Thornton Dill's (1980) work on child-rearing patterns among Black domestics shows that while the participants in her study showed deference behavior at work, they discouraged their children from believing that they should be deferent to whites and encouraged their children to avoid domestic work. Barbara Christian's analysis of the mammy in Black slave narratives reveals that, "unlike the white southern image of mammy, she is cunning, prone to poisoning her master, and not at all content with her lot" (1985:5).

The fact that the mammy image cannot control Black women's behavior as mothers is tied to the creation of the second controlling image of Black womanhood. Though a more recent phenomenon, the image of the Black matriarch fulfills similar functions in explaining Black women's placement in interlocking systems of race, gender, and class oppression. Ironically, Black scholars such as William E. B. Du Bois (1969) and E. Franklin Frazier (1948) described the connections among higher rates of female-headed households in African American communities, the importance that women assume in Black family networks, and the persistence of Black poverty. However, neither scholar interpreted Black women's centrality in Black families as a *cause* of African American social class status. Both saw so-called matriarchal families as an *outcome* of racial oppression and poverty. During the eras when Du Bois and Frazier wrote, the oppression of African Americans was so total that control was maintained without the controlling image of matriarch. But what began as a muted theme in the works of these earlier Black scholars grew into a full-blown racialized image in the 1960s, a time of significant political and economic mobility for African Americans. Racialization involves attaching racial meaning to a previously racially unclassified relationship, social practice, or group (Omi & Winant, 1986). Prior to the 1960s, female-headed households were certainly higher in African American communities, but an ideology racializing female-headedness as a causal feature of Black poverty had not emerged. Moreover, "the public depiction of Black women as unfeminine, castrating matriarchs came at precisely the same moment that the feminist movement was advancing its public critique of American patriarchy" (Gilkes, 1983:296).

While the mammy typifies the Black mother figure in white homes, the matriarch symbolizes the mother figure in Black homes. Just as the mammy represents the "good" Black mother, the matriarch symbolizes the "bad" Black mother. The modern Black matriarchy thesis contends that African American women fail to fulfill their traditional "womanly" duties (Moynihan, 1965). Spending too much time away from home, these working mothers ostensibly cannot properly supervise their children and are a major contributing factor to their children's school failure. As overly aggressive, unfeminine women, Black matriarchs allegedly emasculate their lovers and husbands. These men, understandably, either desert their partners or refuse to marry the mothers of their children. From an elite white male standpoint, the matriarch is essentially a failed mammy, a negative stigma applied to those African American women who dared to violate the image of the submissive, hard-working servant.

733

Black women intellectuals examining the role of women in African American families discover few matriarchs and even fewer mammies (Hale, 1980; Myers, 1980; Sudarkasa, 1981; Dill, 1988). Instead they portray African American mothers as complex individuals who often show tremendous strength under adverse conditions. In *A Raisin in the Sun*, the first play presented on Broadway written by a Black woman, Lorraine Hansberry (1959) examines the struggles of widow Lena Younger to actualize her dream of purchasing a home for her family. In *Brown Girl, Brownstones*, novelist Paule Marshall (1959) presents Mrs. Boyce, a Black mother negotiating a series of relationships with her husband, her daughters, the women in her community, and the work she must perform outside her home. Ann Allen Shockley's *Loving Her* (1974) depicts the struggle of a lesbian mother trying to balance her needs for self-actualization with the pressures of childrearing in the homophobic community. Like these fictional analyses, Black women's scholarship on Black single mothers also challenges the matriarchy thesis (Ladner, 1972; McCray, 1980; Lorde, 1984; McAdoo, 1985; Brewer, 1988).

Like the mammy, the image of the matriarch is central to interlocking systems of race, gender, and class oppression. Portraying African American women as matriarchs allows the dominant group to blame Black women for the success or failure of Black children. Assuming that Black poverty is passed on intergenerationally via value transmission in families, an elite white male standpoint suggests that Black children lack the attention and care allegedly lavished on white, middle-class children and that this deficiency seriously retards Black children's achievement. Such a view diverts attention from the political and economic inequality affecting Black mothers and children and suggests that anyone can rise from poverty if he or she only received good values at home. Those African Americans who remain poor are blamed for their own victimization. Using Black women's performance as mothers to explain Black economic subordination links gender ideology to explanations of class subordination.

The source of the matriarch's failure is her inability to model appropriate gender behavior. In the post–World War II era, increasing numbers of white women entered the labor market, limited their fertility, and generally challenged their proscribed roles in white patriarchal institutions. The image of the Black matriarch emerged at that time as a powerful symbol for both Black and white women of what can go wrong if white patriarchal power is challenged. Aggressive, assertive women are penalized—they are abandoned by their men, end up impoverished, and are stigmatized as being unfeminine.

The image of the matriarch also supports racial oppression. Much social science research implicitly uses gender relations in African American communities as one putative measure of Black cultural disadvantage. For example, the Moynihan Report (1965) contends that slavery destroyed Black families by creating reversed roles for men and women. Black family structures are seen as being deviant because they challenge the patriarchal assumptions underpinning the construct of the ideal "family." Moreover, the absence of Black patriarchy is used as evidence for Black cultural inferiority (Collins, 1989). Black women's failure to conform to the cult of true womanhood can then be identified as one fundamental source of Black cultural deficiency. Cheryl Gilkes posits that the emergence of the matriarchal image occurred as a counterideology to efforts by African Americans and women who were confronting interlocking systems of race, gender, and class oppression: "The image of dangerous Black women who are also deviant castrating mothers divided the Black community at the critical period in the Black liberation struggle and created a wider gap between the worlds of Black and white women at a critical period in women's history" (1983:297).

Taken together, images of the mammy and the matriarch place African American women in an untenable position. For Black women workers in domestic work and other occupations requiring long hours and/or substantial emotional labor, becoming the ideal mammy means precious time and energy spent away from husbands and children. But being employed when Black men have difficulty finding steady work exposes African American women to the charge that Black women emasculate Black men by failing to be submissive, dependent, "feminine" women. Moreover, Black women's financial contributions to Black family well-being have also been cited as evidence supporting the matriarchy thesis (Moynihan, 1965). Many Black women are the sole support of their families, and labeling these women "matriarchs" erodes their self-confidence and ability to confront oppression. In essence, African American women who must work are labeled mammies, then are stigmatized again as matriarchs for being strong figures in their own homes.

A third, externally defined, controlling image of Black womanhood—that of the welfare mother—appears tied to Black women's increasing dependence on the post–World War II welfare state. Essentially an updated version of the breeder woman image created during slavery, this image provides an ideological justification for efforts to harness Black women's fertility to the needs of a changing political economy.

During slavery the breeder woman image portrayed Black women as more suitable for having children than white women. By claiming that Black women were able to produce children as easily as animals, this objectification of Black women as the Other provided justification for interference in the reproductive rights of enslaved Africans. Slaveowners wanted enslaved Africans to "breed" because every slave child born represented a valuable unit of property, another unit of labor, and, if female, the prospects for more slaves. The externally defined, controlling image of the breeder woman served to justify slaveowner intrusion into Black women's decisions about fertility (King, 1973; Davis, 1981).

The post–World War II political economy has offered African Americans rights not available in former historical periods (Fusfeld & Bates, 1984; Wilson, 1987). African Americans have successfully acquired basic political and economic protections from a greatly expanded welfare state, particularly Social Security, Aid to Families with Dependent Children, unemployment compensation, affirmative action, voting rights, antidiscrimination legislation, and the minimum wage. In spite of sustained opposition by Republican administrations in the 1980s, these programs allow many African

Americans to reject the subsistence-level, exploitative jobs held by their parents and grandparents. Job export, deskilling, and increased use of illegal immigrants have all been used to replace the loss of cheap, docile Black labor (Braverman, 1974; Gordon et al., 1982; Nash & Fernandez-Kelly, 1983). The large numbers of undereducated, unemployed African Americans, most of whom are women and children, who inhabit inner cities cannot be forced to work. From the standpoint of the dominant group, they no longer represent cheap labor but instead signify a costly threat to political and economic stability.

Controlling Black women's fertility in such a political economy becomes important. The image of the welfare mother fulfills this function by labeling as unnecessary and even dangerous to the values of the country the fertility of women who are not white and middle class. A closer look at this controlling image reveals that it shares some important features with its mammy and matriarch counterparts. Like the matriarch, the welfare mother is labeled a bad mother. But unlike the matriarch, she is not too aggressive—on the contrary, she is not aggressive enough. While the matriarch's unavailability contributed to her children's poor socialization, the welfare mother's accessibility is deemed the problem. She is portrayed as being content to sit around and collect welfare, shunning work and passing on her bad values to her offspring. The image of the welfare mother represents another failed mammy, one who is unwilling to become "de mule uh de world."

The image of the welfare mother provides ideological justifications for interlocking systems of race, gender, and class oppression. African Americans can be racially stereotyped as being lazy by blaming Black welfare mothers for failing to pass on the work ethic. Moreover, the welfare mother has no male authority figure to assist her. Typically portrayed as an unwed mother, she violates one cardinal tenet of Eurocentric masculinist thought: She is a woman alone. As a result, her treatment reinforces the dominant gender ideology positing that a woman's true worth and financial security should occur through heterosexual marriage. Finally, in the post–World War II political economy, one of every three African American families is officially classified as poor. With such high levels of Black poverty, welfare state policies supporting poor Black mothers and their children have become increasingly expensive. Creating the controlling image of the welfare mother and stigmatizing her as the cause of her own poverty and that of African American communities shifts the angle of vision away from structural sources of poverty and blames the victims themselves. The image of the welfare mother thus provides ideological justification for the dominant group's interest in limiting the fertility of Black mothers who are seen as producing too many economically unproductive children (Davis, 1981).

The fourth controlling image—the Jezebel, whore, or sexually aggressive woman—is central in the nexus of elite white male images of Black womanhood because efforts to control Black women's sexuality lie at the heart of Black women's oppression. The image of Jezebel originated under slavery when Black women were portrayed as being, to use Jewelle Gomez's words, "sexually aggressive wet nurses" (Clarke et al., 1983:99). Jezebel's function was to relegate all Black women to the category of sexually aggressive women, thus providing a powerful rationale for the widespread sexual assaults by white men typically reported by Black slave women (Davis, 1981; Hooks, 1981; White, 1985). Yet Jezebel served another function. If Black slave women could be portrayed as having excessive sexual appetites, then increased fertility should be the expected outcome. By suppressing the nurturing that African American women might give their own children which would strengthen Black family networks, and by forcing Black women to work in the field or "wet nurse" white children, slaveowners effectively tied the controlling images of Jezebel and Mammy to the economic exploitation inherent in the institution of slavery.

The fourth image of the sexually denigrated Black woman is the foundation underlying elite white male conceptualizations of the mammy, matriarch, and welfare mother. Connecting all three is the common theme of Black women's sexuality. Each image transmits clear messages about the proper links among female sexuality, fertility, and Black women's roles in the political economy. For example, the mammy, the only somewhat positive figure, is a desexed individual. The mammy is typically portrayed as overweight, dark, and with characteristically African features—in brief, as an unsuitable sexual partner for white men. She is asexual and therefore is free to become a surrogate mother to the children she acquired not through her own sexuality. The mammy represents the clearest example of the split between sexuality and motherhood present in Eurocentric masculinist thought. In contrast, both the matriarch and the welfare mother are sexual beings. But their sexuality is linked to their fertility, and this link forms one fundamental reason they are negative images. The matriarch represents the sexually aggressive woman, one who emasculates Black men because she will not permit them to assume roles as Black patriarchs. She refuses to be passive and thus is stigmatized. Similarly, the welfare mother represents a woman of low morals and uncontrolled sexuality, factors identified as the cause of her impoverished state. In both cases Black female control over sexuality and fertility is conceptualized as antithetical to elite white male interests.

Taken together, these four prevailing interpretations of Black womanhood form a nexus of elite white male interpretations of Black female sexuality and fertility. Moreover, by meshing smoothly with systems of race, class, and gender oppression, they provide effective ideological justifications for racial oppression, the politics of gender subordination, and the economic exploitation inherent in capitalist economies.

Note

[1]Brittan and Maynard (1984) note that ideology (1) is common sense and obvious; (2) appears natural, inevitable, and universal; (3) shapes lived experience and behavior; (4) is sedimented in people's consciousness; and (5) consists of a system of ideas embedded in the social system as a whole. This example captures all dimensions of how racism and sexism function ideologically. The status of Black woman as servant is so "common sense" that even a child knows it. That the child saw a Black female child as a baby maid speaks to the naturalization dimension and to the

persistence of controlling images in individual consciousness and the social system overall.

References

Braverman, H. 1974. *Labor and monopoly capital*. New York: Monthly Review Press.

Brewer, R. 1988. Black women in poverty: Some comments on female-headed families. *Signs*, 13(2): 331–39.

Brittan, A., and M. Maynard. 1984. *Sexism, racism and oppression*. New York: Basil Blackwell.

Byerly, V. 1986. *Hard times cotton mills girls*. Ithaca, N.Y.: Cornell University Press.

Carby, H. 1987. *Reconstructing womanhood: The emergence of the Afro-American woman novelist*. New York: Oxford.

Christian, B. 1985. *Black feminist criticism: Perspectives on black women writers*. New York: Pergamon.

Clarke, C., J. L. Gomez, E. Hammonds, B. Johnson, and L. Powell. 1983. Conversations and questions: Black women on black women writers. *Conditions: Nine*, 3(3): 88–137.

Clark-Lewis, E. 1985. *"This work had a' end": The transition from live-in to day work*. Southern Women: The Intersection of Race, Class and Gender. Working Paper #2. Memphis, Tenn.: Center for Research on Women, Memphis State University.

Collins, P. H. 1989. A comparison of two works on black family life. *Signs*, 14(4): 875–84.

Davis, A. Y. 1981. *Women, race and class*. New York: Random House.

Dill, B. T. 1980. 'The means to put my children through': Child-rearing goals and strategies among black female domestic servants. In *The Black woman*, ed. L. F. Rodgers-Rose, 107–23. Beverly Hills, Calif.: Sage.

———. 1988a. 'Making your job good yourself': Domestic service and the construction of personal dignity. In *Women and the politics of empowerment*, eds. A. Bookman and S. Morgen, 33–52. Philadelphia: Temple University Press.

———. 1988b. Our mothers' grief: Racial ethnic women and the maintenance of families. *Journal of Family History*, 13(4): 415–31.

Du Bois, W. E. B. 1969. *The Negro American family*. New York: Negro Universities Press.

Dumas, R. G. 1980. Dilemmas of Black females in leadership. In *The Black woman*, ed. L. F. Rodgers-Rose, 203–15. Beverly Hills, Calif.: Sage.

Frazier, E. F. 1948. *The Negro family in the United States*. New York: Dryden Press.

Fusfeld, D. R., and T. Bates. 1984. *The political economy of the urban ghetto*. Carbondale: Southern Illinois University Press.

Gilkes, C. T. 1983. From slavery to social welfare: Racism and the control of Black women. In *Class, race, and sex: The dynamics of control*, eds. A. Swerdlow and H. Lessinger, 288–300. Boston: G. K. Hall.

Gordon, D. M., R. Edwards, and M. Reich. 1982. *Segmented work, divided workers*. New York: Cambridge University Press.

Hale, J. 1980. The Black woman and child rearing. In *The Black woman*, ed. L. F. Rodgers-Rose, 79–88. Beverly Hills, Calif.: Sage.

Hansberry, L. 1959. *A raisin in the sun*. New York: Signet.

Harris, T. 1982. *From mammies to militants: Domestics in Black American literature*. Philadelphia: Temple University Press.

Hooks, B. 1981. *Ain't I a woman: Black women and feminism*. Boston: South End Press.

King, M. 1973. The politics of sexual stereotypes. *Black Scholar*, 4(6–7): 12–23.

Ladner, J. 1972. *Tomorrow's tomorrow*. Garden City, N.Y.: Doubleday.

Lorde, A. 1984. *Sister outsider*. Trumansberg, N.Y.: The Crossing Press.

Marshall, P. 1959. *Brown girl, brownstones*. New York: Avon.

McAdoo, H. P. 1985. Strategies used by Black single mothers against stress. *Review of Black Political Economy*, 14(2–3): 153–66.

McCray, C. A. 1980. The Black woman and family roles. In *The Black woman*, ed. L. F. Rodgers-Rose, 67–78. Beverly Hills, Calif.: Sage.

Moynihan, D. P. 1965. *The negro family: The case for national action*. Washington, D.C.: GPO.

Myers, L. W. 1980. *Black women: Do they cope better?* Englewood Cliffs, N.J.: Prentice Hall.

Nash, J., and M. P. Fernandez-Kelly, eds. 1983. *Women, men, and the international division of labor*. Albany: State University of New York.

Omi, M., and H. Winant. 1986. *Racial formation in the United States: From the 1960s to the 1980s*. New York: Routledge.

Rollins, J. 1985. *Between women: Domestics and their employers*. Philadelphia: Temple University Press.

Shockley, A. A. 1974. *Loving her*. Tallahassee, Fla.: Naiad Press.

Sudarkasa, N. 1981. Interpreting the African heritage in Afro-American family organization. In *Black families*, ed. H. P. McAdoo, 37–53. Beverly Hills, Calif.: Sage.

White, D. G. 1985. *Ar'n't I a woman? Female slaves in the plantation south*. New York: W. W. Norton.

Wilson, W. J. 1987. *The truly disadvantaged: The inner city, the underclass, and public policy*. Chicago: University of Chicago Press.

◉ ◉ ◉

Critical-Thinking Questions

1. Describe the four negative images of Black women. How have these images reinforced an "interlocking system" of Black women's oppression?

2. Collins argues that the controlling images "are designed to make racism, sexism, and poverty appear to be natural, normal, and an inevitable part of everyday life." Do you agree or disagree with this statement? Support your position.

3. Do women of other categories (such as Asians, Latinas, and Native Americans) face similar or different stereotypes?

How Did Jews Become White Folks?

KAREN B. BRODKIN

One way to see how societies construct race and ethnicity is to look at the historical experiences of particular categories of people in the United States. A century ago, the author of this selection explains, Jews and other European immigrants were defined as nonwhite. After World War II, however, Jews were included among "white folks."

. . .

The American nation was founded and developed by the Nordic race, but if a few more million members of the Alpine, Mediterranean, and Semitic races are poured among us, the result must inevitably be a hybrid race of people as worthless and futile as the good-for-nothing mongrels of Central America and Southeastern Europe.

(Kenneth Roberts, quoted in Carlson
& Colburn, 1972:312)

It is clear that Kenneth Roberts did not think of my ancestors as white like him. The late nineteenth and early decades of the twentieth centuries saw a steady stream of warnings by scientists, policymakers, and the popular press that "mongrelization" of the Nordic or Anglo-Saxon race—the real Americans—by inferior European races (as well as inferior non-European ones) was destroying the fabric of the nation. I continue to be surprised to read that America did not always regard

Reprinted from *How Did Jews Become White Folks & What That Says About Race in America* (1998), Rutgers University Press.

its immigrant European workers as white, that they thought people from different nations were biologically different. My parents, who are first-generation U.S.-born Eastern European Jews, are not surprised. They expect anti-Semitism to be part of the fabric of daily life, much as I expect racism to be part of it. They came of age in a Jewish world in the 1920s and 1930s at the peak of anti-Semitism in the United States (Gerber, 1986a). . . .

It is certainly true that the United States has a history of anti-Semitism and of beliefs that Jews were members of an inferior race. But Jews were hardly alone. American anti-Semitism was part of a broader pattern of late-nineteenth-century racism against all southern and eastern European immigrants, as well as against Asian immigrants. These views justified all sorts of discriminatory treatment, including closing the doors to immigration from Europe and Asia in the 1920s.[1] This picture changed radically after World War II. Suddenly the same folks who promoted nativism and xenophobia were eager to believe that the Euro-origin people whom they had deported, reviled as members of inferior races, and prevented from immigrating only a few years earlier were now model middle-class white suburban citizens.

It was not an educational epiphany that made those in power change their hearts, their minds, and our race. Instead, it was the biggest and best affirmative action program in the history of our nation, and it was for Euromales. There are similarities and differences in the ways each of the European immigrant groups became "whitened." I want to tell the story in a way that links anti-Semitism to other varieties of anti-European racism, because this foregrounds what Jews shared with other Euroimmigrants and shows changing notions of whiteness to be part of America's larger system of institutional racism.

◉ Euroraces

The U.S. "discovery" that Europe had inferior and superior races came in response to the great waves of immigration from southern and eastern Europe in the late nineteenth century. Before that time, European immigrants—including Jews—had been largely assimilated into the white population. The 23 million European immigrants who came to work in U.S. cities after 1880 were too many and too concentrated to disperse and blend. Instead, they piled up in the country's most dilapidated urban areas, where they built new kinds of working-class ethnic communities. Since immigrants and their children made up more than 70 percent of the population of most of the country's largest cities, urban America came to take on a distinctly immigrant flavor. The golden age of industrialization in the United States was also the golden age of class struggle between the captains of the new industrial empires and the masses of manual workers whose labor made them rich. As the majority of mining and manufacturing workers, immigrants were visibly major players in these struggles (Higham, 1955:226; Steinberg, 1989:36).[2]

The Red Scare of 1919 clearly linked anti-immigrant to anti-working-class sentiment—to the extent that the Seattle general strike of native-born workers was blamed on foreign agitators. The Red Scare was fueled by economic depression, a massive postwar strike wave, the Russian revolution, and a new wave of postwar immigration. Strikers in steel, and the garment and textile workers in New York and New England, were mainly new immigrants. "As part of a fierce counteroffensive, employers inflamed the historic identification of class conflict with immigrant radicalism." Anticommunism and anti-immigrant sentiment came together in the Palmer raids and deportation of immigrant working-class activists. There was real fear of revolution. One of President Wilson's aides feared it was "the first appearance of the soviet in this country" (Higham, 1955:226).

Not surprisingly, the belief in European races took root most deeply among the wealthy U.S.-born Protestant elite, who feared a hostile and seemingly unassimilable working class. By the end of the nineteenth century, Senator Henry Cabot Lodge pressed Congress to cut off immigration to the United States; Teddy Roosevelt raised the alarm of "race suicide" and took Anglo-Saxon women to task for allowing "native" stock to be outbred by inferior immigrants. In the twentieth century, these fears gained a great deal of social legitimacy thanks to the efforts of an influential network of aristocrats and scientists who developed theories of eugenics—breeding for a "better" humanity—and scientific racism. Key to these efforts was Madison Grant's influential *Passing of the Great Race,* in which he shared his discovery that there were three or four major European races ranging from the superior Nordics of northwestern Europe to the inferior southern and eastern races of Alpines, Mediterraneans, and, worst of all, Jews, who seemed to be everywhere in his native New York City. Grant's nightmare was race mixing among Europeans. For him, "the cross between any of the three European races and a Jew is a Jew" (quoted in Higham, 1955:156). He didn't have good things to say about Alpine or Mediterranean "races" either. For Grant, race and class were interwoven: The upper class was racially pure Nordic, and the lower classes came from the lower races.

Far from being on the fringe, Grant's views resonated with those of the nonimmigrant middle class. A *New York Times* reporter wrote of his visit to the Lower East Side:

> This neighborhood, peopled almost entirely by the people who claim to have been driven from Poland and Russia, is the eyesore of New York and perhaps the filthiest place on the western continent. It is impossible for a Christian to live there because he will be driven out, either by blows or the dirt and stench. Cleanliness is an unknown quantity to these people. They cannot be lifted up to a higher plane because they do not want to be. If the cholera should ever get among these people, they would scatter its germs as a sower does grain. (quoted in Schoener, 1967:58)[3]

Such views were well within the mainstream of the early twentieth-century scientific community. Grant and eugenicist Charles B. Davenport organized the Galton Society in 1918 in order to foster research and to otherwise promote eugenics and immigration restriction.[4] Lewis Terman, Henry Goddard, and Robert Yerkes, developers of the so-called intelligence test, believed firmly that southeastern European immigrants, African Americans, American Indians, and Mexicans were "feebleminded." And indeed, more than 80 percent of the immigrants whom Goddard tested at Ellis Island in 1912 turned out to be just that. Racism fused with eugenics in scientific circles, and the eugenics circles overlapped with the nativism of WASP aristocrats. During World War I, racism shaped the army's development of a mass intelligence test. Psychologist Robert Yerkes, who developed the test, became an even stronger advocate of eugenics after the war. Writing in the *Atlantic Monthly* in 1923, he noted:

> If we may safely judge by the army measurements of intelligence, races are quite as significantly different as individuals. . . [and] almost as great as the intellectual difference between negro and white in the army are the differences between white racial groups. . . .
>
> For the past ten years or so the intellectual status of immigrants has been disquietingly low. Perhaps this is because of the dominance of the Mediterranean races, as contrasted with the Nordic and Alpine. (quoted in Carlson & Colburn, 1972:333–34)

By the 1920s, scientific racism sanctified the notion that real Americans were white and real whites came from northwest Europe. Racism animated laws excluding and expelling Chinese in 1882, and then closing the door to immigration by virtually all Asians and most Europeans in 1924 (Saxton, 1971, 1990). Northwestern European ancestry as a requisite for whiteness was set in legal concrete when the Supreme Court denied Bhagat Singh Thind the right to become a naturalized citizen under a 1790 federal law that allowed whites the right to become naturalized citizens. Thind argued that Asian Indians were the real Aryans and Caucasians, and therefore white. The Court countered that the United States only wanted blond Aryans and Caucasians, "that the blond Scandinavian and the brown Hindu have a common ancestor in the dim reaches of antiquity, but the average man knows perfectly well that there are unmistakable and profound differences between them today" (Takaki, 1989:298–99). A narrowly defined white, Christian race was also built into the 1705 Virginia "Act concerning servants and slaves." This statute stated "that no negroes, mulattos and Indians or other infidels or jews, Moors, Mahometans or other infidels shall, at any time, purchase any christian servant, nor any other except of their own complexion" (Martyn, 1979:111).[5]

The 1930 census added its voice, distinguishing not only immigrant from "native" whites, but also native whites of native white parentage, and native whites of immigrant (or mixed) parentage. In distinguishing immigrant (southern and eastern Europeans) from "native" (northwestern Europeans), the census reflected the racial distinctions of the eugenicist-inspired intelligence tests.[6]

Racism and anti-immigrant sentiment in general and anti-Semitism in particular flourished in higher education. Jews were the first of the Euroimmigrant groups to enter colleges in significant numbers, so it wasn't surprising that they faced the brunt of discrimination there.[7] The Protestant elite complained that Jews were unwashed, uncouth, unrefined, loud, and pushy. Harvard University President A. Lawrence Lowell, who was also a vice president of the Immigration Restriction League, was openly opposed to Jews at Harvard. The Seven Sisters schools had a reputation for "flagrant discrimination." M. Carey Thomas, Bryn Mawr president, may have been a feminist of a kind, but she also was an admirer of scientific racism and an advocate of immigration restriction. She "blocked both the admission of black students and the promotion of Jewish instructors" (Synott, 1986:233, 238–39, 249–50).

Anti-Semitic patterns set by these elite schools influenced standards of other schools, made anti-Semitism acceptable, and "made the aura of exclusivity a desirable commodity for the college-seeking clientele" (Synott, 1986:250; and see Karabel, 1984; Silberman, 1985; Steinberg, 1989: chaps. 5, 9). Fear that colleges "might soon be overrun by Jews" were publicly expressed at a 1918 meeting of the Association of New England Deans. In 1919 Columbia University took steps to decrease the number of entering Jews by a set of practices that soon came to be widely adopted. The school developed a psychological test based on the World War I army intelligence tests to measure "innate ability—and middle-class home environment" and redesigned the admission application to ask for religion, father's name and birthplace, a photo, and a personal interview (Synott, 1986:239–40). Other techniques for excluding Jews, like a fixed class size, a chapel requirement, and preference for children of alumni, were less obvious. Sociologist

Jerome Karabel (1984) has argued that these exclusionary efforts provided the basis for contemporary criteria for college admission that mix grades and test scores with criteria for well-roundedness and character, as well as affirmative action for athletes and children of alumni, which allowed schools to select more affluent Protestants. Their proliferation in the 1920s caused the intended drop in the number of Jewish students in law, dental, and medical schools and also saw the imposition of quotas in engineering, pharmacy, and veterinary schools.[8] . . .

☻ Euroethnics Into Whites

By the time I was an adolescent, Jews were just as white as the next white person. Until I was eight, I was a Jew in a world of Jews. Everyone on Avenue Z in Sheepshead Bay was Jewish. I spent my days playing and going to school on three blocks of Avenue Z, and visiting my grandparents in the nearby Jewish neighborhoods of Brighton Beach and Coney Island. There were plenty of Italians in my neighborhood, but they lived around the corner. They were a kind of Jew, but on the margins of my social horizons. Portuguese were even more distant, at the end of the bus ride, at Sheepshead Bay. The schul, or temple, was on Avenue Z, and I begged my father to take me like all the other fathers took their kids, but religion wasn't part of my fam-ily's Judaism. Just how Jewish my neighborhood was hit me in first grade when I was one of two kids in my class to go to school on Rosh Hashanah. My teacher was shocked—she was Jewish too—and I was embarrassed to tears when she sent me home. I was never again sent to school on Jewish holidays. We left that world in 1949 when we moved to Valley Stream, Long Island, which was Protestant, Republican, and even had farms until Irish, Italian, and Jewish exurbanites like us gave it a more suburban and Democratic flavor. Neither religion nor ethnicity separated us at school or in the neighborhood. Except temporarily. In elementary school years, I remember a fair number of dirt-bomb (a good suburban weapon) wars on the block. Periodically one of the Catholic boys would accuse me or my brother of killing his God, to which we would reply, "Did not" and start lobbing dirt-bombs. Sometimes he would get his friends from Catholic school, and I would get mine from public school kids on the block, some of whom were Catholic. Hostilities lasted no more than a couple of hours and punctuated an otherwise friendly relationship. They ended by junior high years, when other things became more important. Jews, Catholics, and Protestants, Italians, Irish, Poles, and "English" (I don't remember hearing WASP as a kid) were mixed up on the block and in school. We thought of ourselves as middle class and very enlightened because our ethnic backgrounds seemed so irrelevant to high school culture. We didn't see race (we thought), and racism was not part of our peer consciousness, nor were the immigrant or working-class histories of our families.

Like most chicken and egg problems, it's hard to know which came first. Did Jews and other Euroethnics become white because they became middle class? That is, did money whiten? Or did being incorporated in an expanded version of whiteness open up the economic doors to a middle-class status? Clearly, both tendencies were at work. Some of the changes set in motion during the war against fascism led to a more inclusive version of whiteness. Anti-Semitism and anti-European racism lost respectability. The 1940 census no longer distinguished native whites of native parentage from those, like my parents, of immigrant parentage, so that Euroimmigrants and their children were more securely white by submersion in an expanded notion of whiteness. (This census also changed the race of Mexicans to white [U.S. Bureau of the Census, 1940:4].) Theories of nurture and culture replaced theories of nature and biology. Instead of dirty and dangerous races who would destroy U.S. democracy, immigrants became ethnic groups whose children had successfully assimilated into the mainstream and risen to the middle class. In this new myth, Euroethnic suburbs like mine became the measure of U.S. democracy's victory over racism. Jewish mobility became a new Horatio Alger story. In time and with hard work, every ethnic group would get a piece of the pie, and the United States would be a nation with equal opportunity for all its people to become part of a prosperous middle-class majority. And it seemed that Euroethnic immigrants and their children were delighted to join middle America.[9]

750

This is not to say that anti-Semitism disappeared after World War II, only that it fell from fashion and was driven underground. . . .

Although changing views on who was white made it easier for Euroethnics to become middle class, it was also the case that economic prosperity played a very powerful role in the whitening process. Economic mobility of Jews and other Euroethnics rested ultimately on U.S. postwar economic prosperity with its enormously expanded need for professional, technical, and managerial labor, and on government assistance in providing it. The United States emerged from the war with the strongest economy in the world. Real wages rose between 1946 and 1960, increasing buying power a hefty 22 percent and giving most Americans some discretionary income (Nash et al., 1986:885–86). U.S. manufacturing, banking, and business services became increasingly dominated by large corporations, and these grew into multinational corporations. Their organizational centers lay in big, new urban headquarters that demanded growing numbers of technical and managerial workers. The postwar period was a historic moment for real class mobility and for the affluence we have erroneously come to believe was the U.S. norm. It was a time when the old white and the newly white masses became middle class.

The GI Bill of Rights, as the 1944 Serviceman's Readjustment Act was known, was arguably the most massive affirmative action program in U.S. history. It was created to develop needed labor-force skills, and to provide those who had them with a life-style that reflected their value to the economy. The GI benefits ultimately extended to 16 million GIs (veterans of the Korean War as well) included priority in jobs—that is, preferential hiring, but no one objected to it then—financial support during the job search; small loans for starting up businesses; and, most important, low-interest home loans and educational benefits, which included tuition and living expenses (Brown, 1946; Hurd, 1946; Mosch, 1975; *Postwar Jobs for Veterans*, 1945; Willenz, 1983). This legislation was rightly regarded as one of the most revolutionary postwar programs. I call it affirmative action because it was aimed at and disproportionately helped male, Euro-origin GIs.

GI benefits, like the New Deal affirmative action programs before them and the 1960s affirmative action programs after them, were responses to protest. Business executives and the general public believed that the war economy had only temporarily halted the Great Depression. Many feared its return and a return to the labor strife and radicalism of the 1930s (Eichler, 1982:4; Nash et al., 1986:885). "[M]emories of the Depression remained vivid and many people suffered from what Davis Ross has aptly called 'depression psychosis'— the fear that the war would inevitably be followed by layoffs and mass unemployment" (Wynn, 1976:15).

It was a reasonable fear. The 11 million military personnel who were demobilized in the 1940s represented a quarter of the U.S. labor force (Mosch, 1975:1, 20). In addition, ending war production brought a huge number of layoffs, growing unemployment, and a high rate of inflation. To recoup wartime losses in real wages caused by inflation as well as by the unions' no-strike pledge in support of the war effort, workers staged a massive wave of strikes in 1946. More workers went out on strike that year than ever before, and there were strikes in all the heavy industries: railroads, coal mining, auto, steel, and electrical. For a brief moment, it looked like class struggle all over again. But government and business leaders had learned from the experience of bitter labor struggles after World War I just how important it was to assist demobilized soldiers. The GI Bill resulted from their determination to avoid those mistakes this time. The biggest benefits of this legislation were for college and technical school education, and for very cheap home mortgages.

❂ Education and Occupation

It is important to remember that prior to the war, a college degree was still very much a "mark of the upper class" (Willenz, 1983:165). Colleges were largely finishing schools for Protestant elites. Before the postwar boom, schools could not begin to accommodate the American masses. Even in New York City before the 1930s, neither the public schools nor City College had room for more than a tiny fraction of potential immigrant students.

Not so after the war. The almost 8 million GIs who took advantage of their educational benefits under the GI bill caused "the greatest wave of college building in American history" (Nash et al., 1986:885). White male GIs were able to take advantage of their educational benefits for college and technical training, so they were particularly well positioned to seize the opportunities provided by the new demands for professional, managerial, and technical labor. "It has been well documented that the GI educational benefits transformed American higher education and raised the educational level of that generation and generations to come. With many provisions for assistance in upgrading their educational attainments, veterans pulled ahead of nonveterans in earning capacity. In the long run it was the nonveterans who had fewer opportunities" (Willenz, 1983:165).[10]

Just how valuable a college education was for white men's occupational mobility can be seen in John Keller's study of who benefited from the metamorphosis of California's Santa Clara Valley into Silicon Valley. Formerly an agricultural region, in the 1950s the area became the scene of explosive growth in the semiconductor electronics industry. This industry epitomized the postwar economy and occupational structure. It owed its existence directly to the military and to the National Aeronautics and Space Administration (NASA), who were its major funders and its major markets. It had an increasingly white-collar workforce. White men, who were the initial production workers in the 1950s, quickly transformed themselves into a technical and professional workforce thanks largely to GI benefits and the new junior college training programs designed to meet the industry's growing workforce needs. Keller notes that "62 percent of enrollees at San Jose Junior College (later renamed San Jose City College) came from blue-collar families, and 55 percent of all job placements were as electronics technicians in the industrial and service sectors of the county economy" (1983:363). As white men left assembly work and the industry expanded between 1950 and 1960, they were replaced initially by Latinas and African American women, who were joined after 1970 by new immigrant women. Inmigrating men tended to work in the better-paid unionized industries that grew up in the area.

Postwar expansion made college accessible to the mass of Euromales in general and to Jews in particular. My generation's "Think what you could have been!" answer to our parents became our reality as quotas and old occupational barriers fell and new fields opened up to Jews. The most striking result was a sharp decline in Jewish small businesses and a skyrocketing of Jewish professionals. For example, as quotas in medical schools fell, the numbers of Jewish doctors mushroomed. If Boston is an indication, just over 1 percent of all Jewish men before the war were doctors compared to 16 percent of the postwar generation (Silberman, 1985:124, and see 118–26). A similar Jewish mass movement took place into college and university faculties, especially in "new and expanding fields in the social and natural sciences" (Steinberg, 1989:137).[11] Although these Jewish college professors tended to be sons of businesspersons and professionals, the postwar boom saw the first large-scale class mobility among Jewish men. Sons of working-class Jews now went to college and became professionals themselves; according to the Boston survey, almost two-thirds of them. This compared favorably with three-quarters of the sons of professional fathers (Silberman, 1985: 121–22).[12]

Even more significantly, the postwar boom transformed the U.S. class structure—or at least its status structure—so that the middle class expanded to encompass most of the population. Before the war, most Jews, like most other Americans, were working class. Already upwardly mobile before the war relative to other immigrants, Jews floated high on this rising economic tide, and most of them entered the middle class. Still, even the high tide missed some Jews. As late as 1973, some 15 percent of New York's Jews were poor or near-poor, and in the 1960s, almost 25 percent of employed Jewish men remained manual workers (Steinberg, 1989:89–90).

Educational and occupational GI benefits really constituted affirmative action programs for white males because they were decidedly not extended to African Americans or to women of any race. White male privilege was shaped against the backdrop of wartime racism and postwar sexism. During and after the war, there was an upsurge in white racist violence against black servicemen in public schools, and in the KKK, which spread to California and New York (Dalfiume, 1969:133–34). The number of lynchings rose during the war, and in 1943 there were antiblack race riots in several large northern cities.

Although there was a wartime labor shortage, black people were discriminated against in access to well-paid defense industry jobs and in housing. In 1946 there were white riots against African Americans across the South, and in Chicago and Philadelphia as well. Gains made as a result of the wartime Civil Rights movement, especially employment in defense-related industries, were lost with peacetime conversion as black workers were the first fired, often in violation of seniority (Wynn, 1976:114, 116). White women were also laid off, ostensibly to make jobs for demobilized servicemen, and in the long run women lost most of the gains they had made in wartime (Kessler-Harris, 1982). We now know that women did not leave the labor force in any significant numbers but instead were forced to find inferior jobs, largely nonunion, part-time, and clerical.

Theoretically available to all veterans, in practice women and black veterans did not get anywhere near their share of GI benefits. Because women's units were not treated as part of the military, women in them were not considered veterans and were ineligible for Veterans' Administration (VA) benefits (Willenz, 1983:168). The barriers that almost completely shut African American GIs out of their benefits were more complex. In Wynn's portrait (1976:115), black GIs anticipated starting new lives, just like their white counterparts. Over 43 percent hoped to return to school and most expected to relocate, to find better jobs in new lines of work. The exodus from the South toward the North and far West was particularly large. So it wasn't a question of any lack of ambition on the part of African American GIs.

Rather, the military, the Veterans' Administration, the U.S. Employment Service, and the Federal Housing Administration (FHA) effectively denied African American GIs access to their benefits and to the new educational, occupational, and residential opportunities. Black GIs who served in the thoroughly segregated armed forces during World War II served under white officers, usually southerners (Binkin & Eitelberg, 1982; Dalfiume, 1969; Foner, 1974; Johnson, 1967; Nalty & MacGregor, 1981). African American soldiers were disproportionately given dishonorable discharges, which denied them veterans' rights under the GI Bill. Thus between August and November 1946, 21 percent of white soldiers and 39 percent of black soldiers were dishonorably discharged. Those who did get an honorable discharge then faced the Veterans' Administration and the U.S. Employment Service. The latter, which was responsible for job placements, employed very few African Americans, especially in the South. This meant that black veterans did not receive much employment information, and that the offers they did receive were for low-paid and menial jobs. "In one survey of fifty cities, the movement of blacks into peacetime employment was found to be lagging far behind that of white veterans: in Arkansas 95 percent of the placements made by the USES for Afro Americans were in service or unskilled jobs" (Nalty and MacGregor, 1981:218, and see 60–61). African Americans were also less likely than whites, regardless of GI status, to gain new jobs commensurate with their wartime jobs, and they suffered more heavily. For example, in San Francisco by 1948, Black Americans "had dropped back halfway to their pre-war employment status" (Wynn, 1976:114, 116).[13]

Black GIs faced discrimination in the educational system as well. Despite the end of restrictions on Jews and other Euroethnics, African Americans were not welcome in white colleges. Black colleges were overcrowded, and the combination of segregation and prejudice made for few alternatives. About 20,000 black veterans attended college by 1947, most in black colleges, but almost as many, 15,000, could not gain entry. Predictably, the disproportionately few African Americans who did gain access to their educational benefits were able, like their white counterparts, to become doctors and engineers, and to enter the black middle class (Walker, 1970).

. . . The record is very clear that instead of seizing the opportunity to end institutionalized racism, the federal government did its best to shut and double seal the postwar window of opportunity in African Americans' faces. It consistently refused to combat segregation in the social institutions that were key for upward mobility: education, housing, and employment. Moreover, federal programs that were themselves designed to assist demobilized GIs and young families systematically discriminated against African Americans. Such programs reinforced white/nonwhite racial distinctions even as intrawhite racialization was falling out of fashion. This other side of

756

the coin, that white men of northwestern and southeastern European ancestry were treated equally in theory and in practice with regard to the benefits they received, was part of the larger postwar whitening of Jews and other eastern and southern Europeans.

The myth that Jews pulled themselves up by their own bootstraps ignores the fact that it took federal programs to create the conditions whereby the abilities of Jews and other European immigrants could be recognized and rewarded rather than denigrated and denied. The GI Bill and FHA and VA mortgages were forms of affirmative action that allowed male Jews and other Euro-American men to become suburban homeowners and to get the training that allowed them— but not women vets or war workers—to become professionals, technicians, salesmen, and managers in a growing economy. Jews' and other white ethnics' upward mobility was the result of programs that allowed us to float on a rising economic tide. To African Americans, the government offered the cement boots of segregation, redlining, urban renewal, and discrimination.

Those racially skewed gains have been passed across the generations, so that racial inequality seems to maintain itself "naturally," even after legal segregation ended. Today, in a shrinking economy where downward mobility is the norm, the children and grandchildren of the postwar beneficiaries of the economic boom have some precious advantages. For example, having parents who own their own homes or who have decent retirement benefits can make a real difference in young people's ability to take on huge college loans or to come up with a down payment for a house. Even this simple inheritance helps perpetuate the gap between whites and nonwhites. Sure Jews needed ability, but ability was not enough to make it. The same applies even more in today's long recession.

Notes

This is a revised and expanded version of a paper published in *Jewish Currents* in June 1992 and delivered at the 1992 meetings of the American Anthropological Association in the session *Blacks and Jews, 1992: Reaching across the Cultural Boundaries* organized by Angela Gilliam. I would like to thank Emily Abel, Katya Gibel Azoulay, Edna Bonacich, Angela Gilliam,

Isabelle Gunning, Valerie Matsumoto, Regina Morantz-Sanchez, Roger Sanjek, Rabbi Chaim Seidler-Feller, Janet Silverstein, and Eloise Klein Healy's writing group for uncovering wonderful sources and for critical readings along the way.

[1] Indeed, Boasian and Du Boisian anthropology developed in active political opposition to this nativism: on Du Bois, see Harrison & Nonini, 1992.

[2] On immigrants as part of the industrial workforce, see Steinberg, 1989:36.

[3] I thank Roger Sanjek for providing me with this source.

[4] It was intended, as Davenport wrote to the president of the American Museum of Natural History, Henry Fairfield Osborne, as "an anthropological society . . . with a central governing body, self-elected and self-perpetuating, and very limited in members, and also confined to native Americans who are anthropologically, socially and politically sound, no Bolsheviki need apply" (Barkan, 1991:67–68).

[5] I thank Valerie Matsumoto for telling me about the Thind case and Katya Gibel Azoulay for providing this information to me on the Virginia statute.

[6] "The distinction between white and colored" has been "the only racial classification which has been carried through all the 15 censuses." "Colored" consisted of "Negroes" and "other races": Mexican, Indian, Chinese, Japanese, Filipino, Hindu, Korean, Hawaiian, Malay, Siamese, and Samoan. (U.S. Bureau of the Census, 1930:25, 26).

[7] For why Jews entered colleges earlier than other immigrants, and for a challenge to views that attribute it to Jewish culture, see Steinberg, 1989.

[8] Although quotas on Jews persisted into the 1950s in some of the elite schools, they were much attenuated, as the postwar college-building boom gave the coup-de-grace to the gentleman's finishing school.

[9] Indeed, Jewish social scientists were prominent in creating this ideology of the United States as a meritocracy. Most prominent of course was Nathan Glazer, but among them also were Charles Silberman and Marshall Sklare.

[10] The belief was widespread that "the GI Bill . . . helped millions of families move into the middle class" (Nash et al., 1986:885). A study that compares mobility among veterans and nonveterans provides a kind of confirmation. In an unnamed small city in Illinois, Havighurst and his

758

colleagues (1951) found no significant difference between veterans and nonveterans, but this was because apparently very few veterans used any of their GI benefits.

[11]Interestingly, Steinberg (1989:149) shows that Jewish professionals tended to be children of small-business owners, but their Catholic counterparts tended to be children of workers.

[12]None of the Jewish surveys seem to have asked what women were doing. Silberman (1985) claims that Jewish women stayed out of the labor force prior to the 1970s, but if my parents' circle is any indication, there were plenty of working professional women.

[13]African Americans and Japanese Americans were the main target of wartime racism (see Murray, 1992). By contrast, there were virtually no anti-German American or anti-Italian American policies in World War II (see Takaki, 1989:357–406).

References

Barkan, Elazar. 1991. *The retreat of scientific racism: Changing concepts of race in Britain and the United States between the world wars.* Cambridge: Cambridge University Press.

Binkin, Martin, and Mark J. Eitelberg. 1982. *Blacks and the military.* Washington, D.C.: Brookings.

Brown, Francis J. 1946. *Educational opportunities for veterans.* Washington, D.C.: Public Affairs Press, American Council on Public Affairs.

Carlson, Lewis H., and George A. Colburn. 1972. *In their place: White America defines her minorities, 1850–1950.* New York: Wiley.

Dalfiume, Richard M. 1969. *Desegregation of the U.S. armed forces: Fighting on two fronts, 1939–1953.* Columbia: University of Missouri Press.

Eichler, Ned. 1982. *The merchant builders.* Cambridge, Mass.: MIT Press.

Foner, Jack. 1974. *Blacks and the military in American history: A new perspective.* New York: Praeger.

Gerber, David. 1986a. Introduction. In *Anti-Semitism in American history,* ed. Gerber, 3–56.

———, ed. 1986b. *Anti-Semitism in American history.* Urbana: University of Illinois Press.

Harrison, Faye V., and Donald Nonini, eds. 1992. *Critique of anthropology* (special issue on W. E. B. Du Bois and anthropology), 12(3).

Havighurst, Robert J., John W. Baughman, Walter H. Eaton, and Ernest W. Burgess. 1951. *The American veteran back home: A study of veteran readjustment.* New York: Longmans, Green.

Higham, John. 1955. *Strangers in the land.* New Brunswick: Rutgers University Press.

Hurd, Charles. 1946. *The veterans' program: A complete guide to its benefits, rights, and options.* New York: McGraw-Hill.

Johnson, Jesse J. 1967. *Ebony brass: An autobiography of Negro frustration amid aspiration.* New York: Frederick.

Karabel, Jerome. 1984. Status-group struggle, organizational interests, and the limits of institutional autonomy. *Theory and Society,* 13: 1–40.

Kessler-Harris, Alice. 1982. *Out to work: A history of wage-earning women in the United States.* New York: Oxford University Press.

Martyn, Byron Curti. 1979. Racism in the U.S.: A history of anti-miscegenation legislation and litigation. Ph.D. diss., University of Southern California.

Mosch, Theodore R. 1975. *The GI bill: A breakthrough in educational and social policy in the United States.* Hicksville, N.Y.: Exposition.

Murray, Alice Yang. 1992. Japanese Americans, redress, and reparations: A study of community, family, and gender, 1940–1990. Ph.D. diss., Stanford University.

Nalty, Bernard C., and Morris J. MacGregor, eds. 1981. *Blacks in the military: Essential documents.* Wilmington, Del.: Scholarly Resources.

Nash, Gary B., Julie Roy Jeffrey, John R. Howe, Allen F. Davis, Peter J. Frederick, and Allen M. Winkler. 1986. *The American people: Creating a nation and a society.* New York: Harper and Row.

Postwar jobs for veterans. 1945. *Annals of the American Academy of Political and Social Science,* 238 (March).

Saxton, Alexander. 1971. *The indispensible enemy.* Berkeley and Los Angeles: University of California Press.

———. 1990. *The rise and fall of the White Republic.* London: Verso.

Schoener, Allon. 1967. *Portal to America: The Lower East Side, 1870–1925.* New York: Holt, Rinehart and Winston.

Silberman, Charles. 1985. *A certain people: American Jews and their lives today.* New York: Summit.

Steinberg, Stephen. 1989. *The ethnic myth: Race, ethnicity, and class in America.* 2d ed. Boston: Beacon.

Synott, Marcia Graham. 1986. Anti-Semitism and American universities: Did quotas follow the Jews? In *Anti-Semitism in American history,* ed. David A. Gerber, 233–74.

Takaki, Ronald. 1989. *Strangers from a different shore.* Boston: Little, Brown.

U.S. Bureau of the Census. 1930. *Fifteenth census of the United States.* Vol. 2. Washington, D.C.: U.S. Government Printing Office.

———. 1940. *Sixteenth census of the United States.* Vol. 2. Washington, D.C.: U.S. Government Printing Office.

Walker, Olive. 1970. The Windsor Hills School story. *Integrated Education: Race and Schools,* 8(3): 4–9.

Willenz, June A. 1983. *Women veterans: America's forgotten heroines.* New York: Continuum.

Wynn, Neil A. 1976. *The Afro-American and the Second World War.* London: Elek.

◉ ◉ ◉

Critical-Thinking Questions

1. What specific evidence does the author present to demonstrate that race and ethnicity are socially constructed concepts?

2. How fair is it to say that Jews became successful due to their own abilities and efforts? To what degree did government programs play a part in this upward mobility?

3. According to the author, how do the historical experiences of Jews differ from those of African Americans?

When Work Disappears

WILLIAM JULIUS WILSON

In this article, William Julius Wilson addresses the effect of joblessness on inner-city neighborhoods. He contends that there are several driving forces—such as deindustrialization, globalization of the economy, and a shifting of jobs from inner cities to suburbs—that have contributed to joblessness. He also argues that specific local and federal policies have amplified the problem by promoting the exodus of jobs and providing little relief to the distressed neighborhoods left behind.

The disappearance of work in many inner-city neighborhoods is partly related to the nationwide decline in the fortunes of low-skilled workers. Although the growing wage inequality has hurt both low-skilled men and women, the problem of declining employment has been concentrated among low-skilled men. In 1987–89, a low-skilled male worker was jobless eight and a half weeks longer than he would have been in 1967–69. Moreover, the proportion of men who "permanently" dropped out of the labor force was more than twice as high in the late 1980s than it had been in the late 1960s. A precipitous drop in real wages—that is, wages adjusted for inflation—has accompanied the increases in joblessness among low-income workers. If you arrange all wages into five groups according to wage percentile (from highest to lowest), you see that men in the bottom fifth of this income distribution experienced more than a 30 percent drop in real wages between 1970 and 1989.

Excerpt from *When Work Disappears: The World of the New Urban Poor*, by William Julius Wilson, 1996, Knopf. pp. 25–50, 283–307.

Even the low-skilled workers who are consistently employed face problems of economic advancement. Job ladders—opportunities for promotion within firms—have eroded, and many less-skilled workers stagnate in dead-end, low-paying positions. This suggests that the chances of improving one's earnings by changing jobs have declined: if jobs inside a firm have become less available to the experienced workers in that firm, they are probably even more difficult for outsiders to obtain.

But there is a paradox here. Despite the increasing economic marginality of low-wage workers, unemployment dipped below 6 percent in 1994 and early 1995, many workers are holding more than one job, and overtime work has reached a record high. Yet while tens of millions of new jobs have been created in the past two decades, men who are well below retirement age are working less than they did two decades ago—and a growing percentage are neither working nor looking for work. The proportion of male workers in the prime of their life (between the ages of 22 and 58) who worked in a given decade full-time, year-round, in at least eight out of ten years declined from 79 percent during the 1970s to 71 percent in the 1980s. While the American economy saw a rapid expansion in high technology and services, especially advanced services, growth in blue-collar factory, transportation, and construction jobs, traditionally held by men, has not kept pace with the rise in the working-age population. These men are working less as a result.

The growth of a nonworking class of prime-age males along with a larger number of those who are often unemployed, who work part-time, or who work in temporary jobs is concentrated among the poorly educated, the school dropouts, and minorities. In the 1970s, two-thirds of prime-age male workers with less than a high school education worked full-time, year-round, in eight out of ten years. During the 1980s, only half did so. Prime-age black men experienced a similar sharp decline. Seven out of ten of all black men worked full-time, year-round, in eight out of ten years in the 1970s, but only half did so in the 1980s. The figures for those who reside in the inner city are obviously even lower. . . .

763

These changes are related to the decline of the mass production system in the United States. The traditional American economy featured rapid growth in productivity and living standards. The mass production system benefited from large quantities of cheap natural resources, economies of scale, and processes that generated higher uses of productivity through shifts in market forces from agriculture to manufacturing and that caused improvements in one industry (for example, reduced steel costs) to lead to advancements in others (for example, higher sales and greater economies of scale in the automobile industry). In this system plenty of blue-collar jobs were available to workers with little formal education. Today, most of the new jobs for workers with limited education and experience are in the service sector. . . .

. . .

Joblessness and declining wages are also related to the recent growth in ghetto poverty. The most dramatic increases in ghetto poverty occurred between 1970 and 1980, and they were mostly confined to the large industrial metropolises of the Northeast and Midwest, regions that experienced massive industrial restructuring and loss of blue-collar jobs during that decade. But the rise in ghetto poverty was not the only problem. Industrial restructuring had devastating effects on the social organization of many inner-city neighborhoods in these regions. The fate of the West Side black community of North Lawndale vividly exemplifies the cumulative process of economic and social dislocation that has swept through Chicago's inner city.

After more than a quarter century of continuous deterioration, North Lawndale resembles a war zone. Since 1960, nearly half of its housing stock has disappeared; the remaining units are mostly rundown or dilapidated. Two large factories anchored the economy of this West Side neighborhood in its good days—the Hawthorne plant of Western Electric, which employed over 43,000 workers; and an International Harvester plant with 14,000 workers. The world headquarters for Sears, Roebuck and Company was located there, providing another 10,000 jobs. The neighborhood also had a Copenhagen snuff plant, a Sunbeam factory, and a Zenith factory, a Dell Farm food market, an Alden's catalog store, and a U.S. Post Office bulk station. But conditions rapidly changed. Harvester closed its doors in the late 1960s. Sears moved most of its offices to the Loop in downtown Chicago in 1973; a catalog distribution center with a workforce of 3,000 initially remained in the neighborhood but was relocated outside of the state of Illinois in 1987. The Hawthorne plant gradually phased out its operations and finally shut down in 1984.

The departure of the big plants triggered the demise or exodus of the smaller stores, the banks, and other businesses that relied on the wages paid by the large employers. "To make matters worse, scores of stores were forced out of business or pushed out of the neighborhoods by insurance companies in the wake of the 1968 riots that swept through Chicago's West Side after the assassination of Dr. Martin Luther King, Jr. Others were simply burned or abandoned. It has been estimated that the community lost 75 percent of its business establishments from 1960 to 1970 alone." In 1986, North Lawndale, with a population of over 66,000, had only one bank and one supermarket; but it was also home to forty-eight state lottery agents, fifty currency exchanges, and ninety-nine licensed liquor stores and bars.

The impact of industrial restructuring on inner-city employment is dearly apparent to urban blacks. The UPFLS survey posed the following question: "Over the past five or ten years, how many friends of yours have lost their jobs because the place where they worked shut down—would you say none, a few, some, or most?" Only 26 percent of the black residents in our sample reported that none of their friends had lost jobs because their workplace shut down. Indeed, both black men and black women were more likely to report that their friends had lost jobs because of plant closings than were the Mexicans and the other ethnic groups in our study. Moreover, nearly half of the employed black fathers and mothers in the UPFLS survey stated that they considered themselves to be at high risk of losing their jobs because of plant shutdowns. Significantly fewer Hispanic and white parents felt this way.

Some of the inner-city neighborhoods have experienced more visible job losses than others. But residents of the inner city are keenly aware of the rapid depletion of job opportunities. A 33-year-old unmarried black male of North Lawndale who is employed as a clerical worker stated: "Because of the way the economy is structured, we're losing more jobs. Chicago is losing jobs by the thousands. There just aren't any starting companies here and it's harder to find a job compared to what it was years ago."

A similar view was expressed by a 41-year-old black female, also from North Lawndale, who works as a nurse's aide:

> Chicago is really full of peoples. Everybody can't get a good job. They don't have enough good jobs to provide for everybody. I don't think they have enough jobs period. . . . And all the factories and the places, they closed up and moved out of the city and stuff like that, you know. I guess it's one of the reasons they haven't got too many jobs now, 'cause a lot of the jobs now, factories and business, they're done moved out. So that way it's less jobs for lot of peoples.

Respondents from other neighborhoods also reported on the impact of industrial restructuring. According to a 33-year-old South Side janitor:

> The machines are putting a lot of people out of jobs. I worked for *Time* magazine for seven years on a videograph printer and they come along with the Abedic printer, it cost them half a million dollars: they did what we did in half the time, eliminated two shifts.

"Jobs were plentiful in the past," stated a 79-year-old unemployed black male who lives in one of the poorest neighborhoods on the South Side.

> You could walk out of the house and get a job. Maybe not what you want but you could get a job. Now, you can't find anything. A lot of people in this neighborhood, they want to work but they can't get work. A few, but a very few, they just

don't want to work. The majority they want to work but they can't find work.

Finally, a 41-year-old hospital worker from another impoverished South Side neighborhood associated declining employment opportunities with decreasing skill levels:

> Well, most of the jobs have moved out of Chicago. Factory jobs have moved out. There are no jobs here. Not like it was 20, 30 years ago. And people aren't skilled enough for the jobs that are here. You don't have enough skilled and educated people to fill them.

The increasing suburbanization of employment has accompanied industrial restructuring and has further exacerbated the problems of inner-city joblessness and restricted access to jobs. "Metropolitan areas captured nearly 90 percent of the nation's employment growth; much of this growth occurred in booming 'edge cities' at the metropolitan periphery. By 1990, many of these 'edge cities' had more office space and retail sales than the metropolitan downtowns." Over the last two decades, 60 percent of the new jobs created in the Chicago metropolitan area have been located in the northwest suburbs of Cook and Du Page counties. African-Americans constitute less than 2 percent of the population in these areas.

In *The Truly Disadvantaged,* I maintained that one result of these changes for many urban blacks has been a growing mismatch between the suburban location of employment and minorities' residence in the inner city. Although studies based on data collected before 1970 showed no consistent or convincing effects on black employment as a consequence of this spatial mismatch, the employment of inner-city blacks relative to suburban blacks has clearly deteriorated since then. Recent research, conducted mainly by urban and labor economists, strongly shows that the decentralization of employment is continuing and that employment in manufacturing, most of which is already suburbanized, has decreased in central cities, particularly in the Northeast and Midwest. As Farrell Bloch, an economic and statistical consultant, points out, "Not only has the number of manufacturing jobs been decreasing, but new plants now tend to locate in the suburbs to take advantage of cheap land, access to highways, and low crime rates; in addition, businesses shun urban locations to avoid buying land from several different owners, paying high demolition costs for old buildings, and arranging parking for employees and customers."

Blacks living in central cities have less access to employment, as measured by the ratio of jobs to people and the average travel time to and from work than do central-city whites. Moreover, unlike most other groups of workers across the urban/suburban divide, less educated central-city blacks receive lower wages than suburban blacks who have similar levels of education. And the decline in earnings of central-city blacks is related to the decentralization of employment—that is, the movement of jobs from the cities to the suburbs—in metropolitan areas

But are the differences in employment between city and suburban blacks mainly the result of changes in the location of jobs? It is possible that in recent years the migration of blacks to the suburbs has become much more selective than in earlier years, so much so that the changes attributed to job location are actually caused by this selective migration. The pattern of black migration to the suburbs in the 1970s was similar to that of whites during the 1950s and 1960s in the sense that it was concentrated among the better-educated and younger city residents. However, in the 1970s this was even more true for blacks, creating a situation in which the education and income gaps between city and suburban blacks seemed to expand at the same time that the differences between city and suburban whites seemed to contract. Accordingly, if one were to take into account differences in education, family background, and so on, how much of the employment gap between city and suburbs would remain?

This question was addressed in a study of the Gautreaux program in Chicago. The Gautreaux program was created under a 1976 court order resulting from a judicial finding of widespread discrimination in the public housing projects of Chicago. The program has relocated more than 4,000 residents from public housing into subsidized housing in neighborhoods throughout the Greater Chicago area. The design of the program permitted the researchers, James E. Rosenbaum and Susan J. Popkin, to contrast systematically the employment experiences of a group of low-income blacks who had been assigned private apartments in the suburbs with the experiences of a control group with similar characteristics and histories who had been assigned private apartments in the city. Their findings support the spatial mismatch hypothesis. After taking into account the personal characteristics of the respondents (including family background, family circumstances, levels of human capital, motivation, length of time since the respondent first enrolled in the Gautreaux program), Rosenbaum and Popkin found that those who moved to apartments in the suburbs were significantly more likely to have a job after the move than those placed in the city. When asked what makes it easier to obtain employment in the suburbs, nearly all the suburban respondents mentioned the high availability of jobs.

The African-Americans surveyed in the UPFLS clearly recognized a spatial mismatch of jobs. Both black men and black women saw greater job prospects outside the city. For example, only one-third of black fathers from areas with poverty rates of at least 30 percent reported that their best opportunities for employment were to be found in the city. Nearly two-thirds of whites and Puerto Ricans and over half of Mexicans living in similar neighborhoods felt this way. Getting to suburban jobs is especially problematic for the jobless individuals in the UPFLS because only 28 percent have access to an automobile. This rate falls even further to 18 percent for those living in the ghetto areas.

Among two-car middle-class, and affluent families, commuting is accepted as a fact of fife; but it occurs in a context of safe school environments for children, more available and accessible day care, and higher incomes to support mobile, away-from-home lifestyles. In a multitiered job market that requires substantial resources for participation, most inner-city minorities must rely on public transportation systems that rarely provide easy and quick access to suburban locations. A 32-year-old unemployed South Side welfare mother described the problem this way:

> There's not enough jobs. I thinks Chicago's the only city that does not have a lot of opportunities opening in it. There's not enough factories, there's not enough work. Most all the good jobs are in the suburbs. Sometimes it's hard for the people in the city to get to the suburbs, because everybody don't own a car. Everybody don't drive.

After commenting on the lack of jobs in his area, a 29-year-old unemployed South Side black male continued:

> You gotta go out in the suburbs, but I can't get out there. The bus go out there but you don't want to catch the bus out there, going two hours each ways. If you have to be at work at eight that mean you have to leave for work at six, that mean you have to get up at five to be at work at eight. Then when wintertime come you be in trouble.

Another unemployed South Side black male had this to say: "Most of the time . . . the places be too far and you need transportation and I don't have none right now. If I had some I'd probably be able to get one [a job]. If I had a car and went way into the suburbs, 'cause there ain't none in the city." This perception was echoed by an 18-year-old unemployed West Side black male:

> They are most likely hiring in the suburbs. Recently, I think about two years ago, I had a job but they say that I need some transportation and they say that the bus out in the suburbs run at a certain time. So I had to pass that job up because I did not have no transport.

An unemployed unmarried welfare mother of two from the West Side likewise stated:

> Well, I'm goin' to tell you: most jobs, more jobs are in the suburbs. It's where the good jobs and stuff is but you gotta have transportation to get there and it's hard to be gettin' out

there in the suburbs. Some people don't know where the suburbs is, some people get lost out there. It is really hard, but
some make a way.

One employed factory worker from the West Side who works a
night shift described the situation this way:

> From what I, I see, you know, it's hard to find a good job in
> the inner city 'cause so many people moving, you know, west
> to the suburbs and out of state. . . . Some people turn jobs
> down because they don't have no way of getting out there.
> . . . I just see some people just going to work—and they seem
> like they the type who just used to—they coming all the way
> from the city and go on all the way to the suburbs and, you
> know, you can see 'em all bundled and—catching one bus
> and the next bus. They just used to doing that.

But the problem is not simply one of transportation and the
length of commuting time. There is also the problem of the travel
expense and of whether the long trek to the suburbs is actually worth
it in terms of the income earned—after all, owning a car creates
expenses far beyond the purchase price, including insurance, which
is much more costly for city dwellers than it is for suburban
motorists. "If you work in the suburbs you gotta have a car," stated
an unmarried welfare mother of three children who lives on
Chicago's West Side, "then you gotta buy gas. You spending more getting to the suburbs to work, than you is getting paid, so you still ain't
getting nowhere."

Indeed, one unemployed 36-year-old black man from the West
Side of Chicago actually quit his suburban job because of the transportation problem. "It was more expensive going to work in
Naperville, transportation and all, and it wasn't worth it. . . . I was
spending more money getting to work than I earned working."

If transportation poses a problem for those who have to commute
to work from the inner city to the suburbs, it can also hinder poor
ghetto residents' ability to travel to the suburbs just to seek employment. For example, one unemployed man who lives on the South

Side had just gone to O'Hare Airport looking for work with no luck. His complaint: "The money I spent yesterday, I coulda kept that in my pocket—I coulda kept that. 'Cause you know I musta spent about $7 or somethin'. I coulda kept that."

Finally, in addition to enduring the search-and-travel costs, inner-city, black workers often confront racial harassment when they enter suburban communities. A 38-year-old South Side divorced mother of two children who works as a hotel cashier described the problems experienced by her son and his coworker in one of Chicago's suburbs:

> My son, who works in Carol Stream, an all-white communi-ty, they've been stopped by a policeman two or three times asking them why they're in the community. And they're try-ing to go to work. They want everyone to stay in their own place. That's what society wants. And they followed them all the way to work to make sure. 'Cause it's an all-white neigh-borhood. But there're no jobs in the black neighborhoods. They got to go way out there to get a job.

These informal observations on the difficulties and cost of travel to suburban employment are consistent with the results of a recent study by the labor economists Harry J. Holzer, Keith R. Ihlandfeldt, and David L. Sjoquist. In addition to finding that the lack of auto-mobile ownership among inner-city blacks contributed significantly to their lower wages and lower rate of employment, these authors also reported that African-Americans "spend more time traveling to work than whites," that "the time cost per mile traveled is . . . signif-icantly higher for blacks," and that the resulting gains are relatively small. Overall, their results suggest that the amount of time and money spent in commuting, when compared with the actual income that accrues to inner-city blacks in low-skill jobs in the suburbs, acts to discourage poor people from seeking employment far from their own neighborhoods. Holzer and his colleagues concluded that it was quite rational for blacks to reject these search-and-travel choices when assessing their position in the job market.

Changes in the industrial and occupational mix, including the removal of jobs from urban centers to suburban corridors, represent external factors that have helped to elevate joblessness among inner-city blacks. But important social and demographic changes within the inner city are also associated with the escalating rates of neighborhood joblessness, and we shall consider these next.

· · ·

One of the important demographic shifts that had an impact on the upturn in the jobless rate has been the change in the age structure of inner-city ghetto neighborhoods. Let us . . . examine the three Bronzeville neighborhoods of Douglas Grand Boulevard, and Washington Park. . . . [T]he proportion of those in the age categories (20–64) that roughly approximate the prime-age workforce has declined in all three neighborhoods since 1950, whereas the proportion in the age category 65 and over has increased. Of the adults age 20 and over, the proportion in the prime-age categories declined by 17 percent in Grand Boulevard, 16 percent in Douglas, and 12 percent in Washington Park between 1950 and 1990. The smaller the percentage of prime-age adults in a population, the lower the proportion of residents who are likely to be employed. The proportion of residents in the age category 5–19 increased sharply in each neighborhood from 1950 to 1990, suggesting that the growth in the proportion of teenagers also contributed to the rise in the jobless rate. However, if we consider the fact that male employment in these neighborhoods declined by a phenomenal 46 percent between 1950 and 1960, these demographic changes obviously can account for only a fraction, albeit a significant fraction, of the high proportion of the area's jobless adults.

The rise in the proportion of jobless adults in the Bronzeville neighborhoods has been accompanied by an incredible depopulation—a decline of 66 percent in the three neighborhoods combined—that magnifies the problems of the new poverty neighborhoods. As the population drops and the proportion of nonworking adults rises, basic neighborhood institutions are more difficult to maintain: stores, banks, credit institutions, restaurants, dry

773

cleaners, gas stations, medical doctors, and so on lose regular and potential patrons. Churches experience dwindling numbers of parishioners and shrinking resources; recreational facilities, block clubs, community groups, and other informal organizations also suffer. As these organizations decline, the means of formal and informal social control in the neighborhood become weaker. Levels of crime and street violence increase as a result, leading to further deterioration of the neighborhood.

The more rapid the neighborhood deterioration, the greater the institutional disinvestment. In the 1960s and 1970s, neighborhoods plagued by heavy abandonment were frequently "redlined" (identified as areas that should not receive or be recommended for mortgage loans or insurance); this paralyzed the housing market, lowered property values, and further encouraged landlord abandonment. The enactment of federal and state community reinvestment legislation in the 1970s curbed the practice of open redlining. Nonetheless, "prudent lenders will exercise increased caution in advancing mortgages, particularly in neighborhoods marked by strong indication of owner disinvestment and early abandonment."

As the neighborhood disintegrates, those who are able to leave depart in increasing numbers; among these are many working- and middle-class families. The lower population density in turn creates additional problems. Abandoned buildings increase and often serve as havens for crack use and other illegal enterprises that give criminals footholds in the community. Precipitous declines in density also make it even more difficult to sustain or develop a sense of community. The feeling of safety in numbers is completely lacking in such neighborhoods.

Although changes in the economy (industrial restructuring and reorganization) and changes in the class, racial, and demographic composition of inner-city ghetto neighborhoods are important factors in the shift from institutional to jobless ghettos since 1970, we ought not to lose sight of the fact that this process actually began immediately following World War II.

The federal government contributed to the early decay of inner-city neighborhoods by withholding mortgage capital and by making it difficult for urban areas to retain or attract families able to purchase their own homes. Spurred on by massive mortgage foreclosures during the Great Depression, the federal government in the 1940s began underwriting mortgages in an effort to enable citizens to become homeowners. But the mortgage program was selectively administered by the Federal Housing Administration (FHA), and urban neighborhoods considered poor risks were redlined—an action that excluded virtually all the black neighborhoods and many neighborhoods with a considerable number of European immigrants. It was not until the 1960s that the FHA discontinued its racial restrictions on mortgages.

By manipulating market incentives, the federal government drew middle-class whites to the suburbs and, in effect, trapped blacks in the inner cities. Beginning in the 1950s, the suburbanization of the middle class was also facilitated by a federal transportation and highway policy, including the building of freeway networks through the hearts of many cities, mortgages for veterans, mortgage-interest tax exemptions, and the quick, cheap production of massive amounts of tract housing.

In the nineteenth and early twentieth centuries, with the offer of municipal services as an inducement, cities tended to annex their suburbs. But the relations between cities and suburbs in the United States began to change following a century-long influx of poor migrants who required expensive services and paid relatively little in taxes. Annexation largely ended in the mid-twentieth century as suburbs began to resist incorporation successfully. Suburban communities also drew tighter boundaries through the manipulation of zoning laws and discriminatory land-use controls and site-selection practices, making it difficult for inner-city racial minorities to penetrate.

As separate political jurisdictions, suburbs exercised a great deal of autonomy in their use of zoning, land-use policies, covenants, and deed restrictions. In the face of mounting pressures calling for integration in the 1960s, "suburbs chose to diversify by race rather than class. They retained zoning and other restrictions that allowed only affluent blacks (and in some instances Jews) to enter, thereby intensifying the concentration and isolation of the urban poor."

Other government policies also contributed to the growth of jobless ghettos, both directly and indirectly. Many black communities were uprooted by urban renewal and forced migration. The construction of freeway and highway networks through the hearts of many cities in the 1950s produced the most dramatic changes, as many viable low-income communities were destroyed. These networks not only encouraged relocation from the cities to the suburbs, "they also created barriers between the sections of the cities, walling off poor and minority neighborhoods from central business districts. Like urban renewal, highway and expressway construction also displaced many poor people from their homes."

Federal housing policy also contributed to the gradual shift to jobless ghettos. Indeed, the lack of federal action to fight extensive segregation against African-Americans in urban housing markets and acquiescence to the opposition of organized neighborhood groups to the construction of public housing in their communities have resulted in massive segregated housing projects. The federal public housing program evolved in two policy stages that represented two distinct styles. The Wagner Housing Act of 1937 initiated the first stage. Concerned that the construction of public housing might depress private rent levels, groups such as the U.S. Building and Loan League and the National Association of Real Estate Boards successfully lobbied Congress to require, by law, that for each new unit of public housing one "unsafe or unsanitary" unit of public housing be destroyed. As Alark Condon points out, "This policy increased employment in the urban construction market while insulating private rent levels by barring the expansion of the housing stock available to low-income families."

The early years of the public housing program produced positive results. Initially, the program mainly served intact families temporarily displaced by the Depression or in need of housing after the end of World War II. For many of these families, public housing was the first step on the road toward economic recovery. Their stay in the projects was relatively brief. The economic mobility of these families "contributed to the sociological stability of the first public housing communities, and explains the program's initial success."

The passage of the Housing Act of 1949 marked the beginning of the second policy stage. It instituted and funded the urban renewal program designed to eradicate urban slums. "Public housing was now meant to collect the ghetto residents left homeless by the urban renewal bulldozers." A new, lower-income ceiling for public housing residency was established by the federal Public Housing Authority, and families with incomes above that ceiling were evicted, thereby restricting access to public housing to the most economically disadvantaged segments of the population.

This change in federal housing policy coincided with the mass migration of African-Americans from the rural South to the cities of the Northeast and Midwest. Since smaller suburban communities refused to permit the construction of public housing, the units were overwhelmingly concentrated in the overcrowded and deteriorating inner-city ghettos—the poorest and least socially organized sections of the city and the metropolitan area. "This growing population of politically weak urban poor was unable to counteract the desires of vocal middle- and working-class whites for segregated housing," housing that would keep blacks out of white neighborhoods. In short, public housing represents a federally funded institution that has isolated families by race and class for decades, and has therefore contributed to the growing concentration of jobless families in the inner-city ghettos in recent years.

Also, since 1980, a fundamental shift in the federal government's support for basic urban programs has aggravated the problems of joblessness and social organization in the new poverty neighborhoods. The Reagan and Bush administrations—proponents of the New Federalism—sharply cut spending on direct aid to cities, including general revenue sharing, urban mass transit, public service jobs and job training, compensatory education, social service block grants, local public works, economic development assistance, and urban development action grants. In 1980 the federal contribution to city budgets was 18 percent, by 1990 it had dropped to 6.4 percent. In addition, the economic recession which began in the Northeast in 1989 and lasted until the early 1990s sharply reduced those revenues that the cities themselves generated, thereby creating budget deficits that resulted in further cutbacks in basic services and programs along with increases in local taxes.

For many cities, especially the older cities of the East and Midwest, the combination of the New Federalism and the recession led to the worst fiscal and service crisis since the Depression. Cities have become increasingly underserviced, and many have been on the brink of bankruptcy. They have therefore not been in a position to combat effectively three unhealthy social conditions that have emerged or become prominent since 1980: (1) the prevalence of crack-cocaine addiction and the violent crime associated with it; (2) the AIDS epidemic and its escalating public health costs; and (3) the sharp rise in the homeless population not only for individuals but for whole families as well.

Although drug addiction and its attendant violence, AIDS and its toll on public health resources, and homelessness are found in many American communities, their impact on the ghetto is profound. These communities, whose residents have been pushed to the margins of society, have few resources with which to combat these social ills that arose in the 1980s. Fiscally strapped cities have watched helplessly as these problems—exacerbated by the new poverty, the decline of social organization in the jobless neighborhoods, and the reduction of social services—have made the city at large seem a dangerous and threatening place in which to live. Accordingly, working- and middle-class urban residents continue to relocate in the suburbs. Thus, while joblessness and related social problems are on the rise in inner-city neighborhoods, especially in those that represent the new poverty areas, the larger city has fewer and fewer resources with which to combat them.

Finally, policymakers indirectly contributed to the emergence of jobless ghettos by making decisions that have decreased the attractiveness of low-paying jobs and accelerated the relative decline in

778

wages for low-income workers. In particular, in the absence of an effective labor-market policy, they have tolerated industry practices that undermine worker security, such as the reduction in benefits and the rise of involuntary part-time employment, and they have "allowed the minimum wage to erode to its second-lowest level in purchasing power in 40 years." After adjusting for inflation, "the minimum wage is 26 percent below its average level in the 1970s." Moreover, they virtually eliminated AFDC benefits for families in which a mother is employed at least half-time. In the early 1970s, a working mother with two children whose wages equaled 75 percent of the amount designated as the poverty line could receive AFDC benefits as a wage supplement in forty-nine states; in 1995 only those in three states could. . . . [E]ven with the expansion of the earned income tax credit (a wage subsidy for the working poor) such policies make it difficult for poor workers to support their families and protect their children. The erosion of wages and benefits force many low-income workers in the inner city to move or remain on welfare.

References

Block, F. (1994). *Antidiscrimination law and minority employment: recruitment practices and regulatory constraints.* Chicago: University of Chicago Press.

Condon, M. (1991). Public housing, crime and the urban labor market: A study of black youths in Chicago. Working paper series, Malcolm Wiener Center for Social Policy, John F. Kennedy School of Government, Harvard University, March, no. H-91-3.

Holzer, H. J., Ihlanfeldt, K. R., and Sjoquist, D. L. (1994). "Work, search and travel among white and black youth." *Journal of Urban Economics,* 35:320–45.

Rosenbaum, J. E., and Popkin, S. J. (1991). Employment and earnings of low-income blacks who move to middle-class suburbs." In C. Jencks & P. E. Peterson (Eds.), *The urban underclass.* (pp. 342–356.) Washington, D.C.: Brookings Institute.

Wilson, W. J. (1987). *The truly disadvantaged: The inner city, the underclass, and public policy.* Chicago: University of Chicago Press.

⊙ ⊙ ⊙

Questions

1. What key factors does Wilson contend have contributed to the plight of inner-city neighborhoods?

2. What are some consequences, for inner-city neighborhoods, of the shifting of jobs out to the suburbs?

3. What factors complicate the ability of inner-city residents to work in the suburbs?

4. Race is clearly part of the social dynamic discussed by Wilson. How does race affect the processes he discusses?

5. How do certain federal policies contribute to the plight of inner-city neighborhoods?

6. Given the structural and cultural dynamics discussed by Wilson, what policies do you think might help reverse the current trend?

"His" and "Her" Marriage

Jessie Bernard

Social scientists have found that men and women are not joined at the hip by a wedding ceremony. Rather, their subsequent lives differ in terms of gender roles, power, and ways of communicating. Bernard was among the first sociologists to point out that marriage has a different meaning for women and men. As this selection shows, spouses rarely define reality in the same way, even with regard to simple routines such as sweeping the floor or mowing the lawn.

. . .

. . . [T]here is by now a very considerable body of well-authenticated research to show that there really are two marriages in every marital union, and that they do not always coincide.

☉ "His" and "Her" Marriages

. . . [T]he differences in the marriages of husbands and wives have come under the careful scrutiny of a score of researchers. They have found that when they ask husbands and wives identical questions about the union, they often get quite different replies. There is usually agreement on the number of children they have and a few other such verifiable items, although not, for example, on length of premarital acquaintance and of engagement, on age at marriage, and interval

Reprinted from *The Future of Marriage*, Yale University Press.

Edward Hopper (1882–1967), *Room in New York*, 1932. Oil on Canvas, 29 × 36 in. Sheldon Memorial Art Gallery, University of Nebraska-Lincoln. F. M. Hall Collection, 1932. H-166.

between marriage and birth of first child. Indeed, with respect to even such basic components of the marriage as frequency of sexual relations, social interaction, household tasks, and decision making, they seem to be reporting on different marriages. As, I think, they are.

In the area of sexual relations, for example, Kinsey and his associates found different responses in from one- to two-thirds of the couples they studied. Kinsey interpreted these differences in terms of selective perception. In the generation he was studying, husbands wanted sexual relations oftener than the wives did, thus "the females may be overestimating the actual frequencies" and "the husbands . . . are probably underestimating the frequencies." The differences might also have been vestiges of the probable situation earlier in the marriage when the desired frequency of sexual relations was about six to seven times greater among husbands than among wives. This difference may have become so impressed on the spouses that it remained in their minds even after the difference itself had disappeared or even been reversed. In a sample of happily married, middle-class couples a generation later, Harold Feldman found that both spouses attributed to their mates more influence in the area of sex than they did to themselves.

Companionship, as reflected in talking together, he found, was another area where differences showed up. Replies differed on three-fourths of all the items studied, including the topics talked about, the amount of time spent talking with each other, and which partner initiated conversation. Both partners claimed that whereas they talked more about topics of interest to their mates, their mates initiated conversations about topics primarily of interest to themselves. Harold Feldman concluded that projection in terms of needs was distorting even simple, everyday events, and lack of communication was permitting the distortions to continue. It seemed to him that "if these sex differences can occur so often among these generally well-satisfied couples, it would not be surprising to find even less consensus and more distortion in other less satisfied couples."

Although, by and large, husbands and wives tend to become more alike with age, in this study of middle-class couples, differences increased with length of marriage rather than decreased, as one might logically have expected. More couples in the later than in the earlier years, for example, had differing pictures in their heads about how often they laughed together, discussed together, exchanged ideas, or worked together on projects, and about how well things were going between them.

The special nature of sex and the amorphousness of social interaction help to explain why differences in response might occur. But household tasks? They are fairly objective and clear-cut and not all that emotion-laden. Yet even here there are his-and-her versions. Since the division of labor in the household is becoming increasingly an issue in marriage, the uncovering of differing replies in this area is especially relevant. Hard as it is to believe, Granbois and Willett tell us that more than half of the partners in one sample disagreed on who kept track of money and bills. On the question, who mows the lawn? more than a fourth disagreed. Even family income was not universally agreed on.

These differences about sexual relations, companionship, and domestic duties tell us a great deal about the two marriages. But power or decision making can cover all aspects of a relationship. The question of who makes decisions or who exercises power has therefore attracted a great deal of research attention. If we were interested in who really had the power or who really made the decisions, the research would be hopeless. Would it be possible to draw any conclusion from a situation in which both partners agree that the husband ordered the wife to make all the decisions? Still, an enormous literature documents the quest of researchers for answers to the question of marital power. The major contribution it has made has been to reveal the existence of differences in replies between husbands and wives.

The presence of such inconsistent replies did not at first cause much concern. The researchers apologized for them but interpreted them as due to methodological inadequacies; if only they could find a better way to approach the problem, the differences would disappear. Alternatively, the use of only the wife's responses, which were more easily available, was justified on the grounds that differences in one direction between the partners in one marriage compensated for differences in another direction between the partners in another marriage and thus canceled them out. As, indeed, they did. For when Granbois and Willett, two market researchers, analyzed the replies of husbands and wives separately, the overall picture was in fact the same for both wives and husbands. Such canceling out of differences in the total sample, however, concealed almost as much as it revealed about the individual couples who composed it. Granbois and Willett concluded, as Kinsey had earlier, that the "discrepancies . . . reflect differing perceptions on the part of responding partners." And this was the heart of the matter.

Differing reactions to common situations, it should be noted, are not at all uncommon. They are recognized in the folk wisdom embedded in the story of the blind men all giving different replies to questions on the nature of the elephant. One of the oldest experiments in juridical psychology demonstrates how different the statements of witnesses of the same act can be. Even in laboratory studies, it takes intensive training of raters to make it possible for them to arrive at agreement on the behavior they observe.

It has long been known that people with different backgrounds see things differently. We know, for example, that poor children perceive coins as larger than do children from more affluent homes. Boys and

784

girls perceive differently. A good deal of the foundation for projective tests rests on the different ways in which individuals see identical stimuli. And this perception—or, as the sociologists put it, definition of the situation—is reality for them. In this sense, the realities of the husband's marriage are different from those of the wife's.

Finally, one of the most perceptive of the researchers, Constantina Safilios-Rothschild, asked the crucial question: Was what they were getting, even with the best research techniques, family sociology or wives' family sociology? She answered her own question: What the researchers who relied on wives' replies exclusively were reporting on was the wife's marriage. The husband's was not necessarily the same. There were, in fact, two marriages present:

> One explanation of discrepancies between the responses of husbands and wives may be the possibility of two "realities," the husband's subjective reality and the wife's subjective reality—two perspectives which do not always coincide. Each spouse perceives "facts" and situations differently according to his own needs, values, attitudes, and beliefs. An "objective" reality could possibly exist only in the trained observer's evaluation, if it does exist at all.

Interpreting the different replies of husbands and wives in terms of selective perception, projection of needs, values, attitudes, and beliefs, or different definitions of the situation, by no means renders them trivial or incidental or justifies dis-missing or ignoring them. They are, rather, fundamental for an understanding of the two marriages, his and hers, and we ignore them at the peril of serious misunderstanding of marriage, present as well as future.

⊕ Is there an Objective Reality in Marriage?

Whether or not husbands and wives perceive differently or define situations differently, still sexual relations are taking place, companionship is or is not occurring, tasks about the house are being performed, and decisions are being made every day by someone. In this sense, some sort of "reality" does exist. David Olson went to the laboratory to see if he could uncover it.

He first asked young couples expecting babies such questions as these: Which one of them would decide whether to buy insurance for the newborn child? Which one would decide the husband's part in diaper changing? Which one would decide whether the new mother would return to work or to school? When there were differences in the answers each gave individually on the questionnaire, he set up a situation in which together they had to arrive at a decision in his laboratory. He could then compare the results of the questionnaire with the results in the simulated situation. He found neither spouse's questionnaire response any more accurate than the other's; that is, neither conformed better to the behavioral "reality" of the laboratory than the other did.

The most interesting thing, however, was that husbands, as shown on their questionnaire response, perceived themselves as having more power than they actually did have in the laboratory "reality," and wives perceived that they had less. Thus, whereas three-fourths (73 percent) of the husbands overestimated their power in decision making, 70 percent of the wives underestimated theirs. Turk and Bell found similar results in Canada. Both spouses tend to attribute decision-making power to the one who has the "right" to make the decision. Their replies, that is, conform to the model of marriage that has characterized civilized mankind for millennia. It is this model rather than their own actual behavior that husbands and wives tend to perceive.

We are now zeroing in on the basic reality. We can remove the quotation marks. For there is, in fact, an objective reality in marriage. It is a reality that resides in the cultural—legal, moral, and conventional—prescriptions and proscriptions and, hence, expectations that constitute marriage. It is the reality that is reflected in the minds of the spouses themselves. The differences between the marriages of husbands and of wives are structural realities, and it is these structural differences that constitute the basis for the different psychological realities.

786

◉ The Authority Structure of Marriage

Authority is an institutional phenomenon; it is strongly bound up with faith. It must be believed in; it cannot be enforced unless it also has power. Authority resides not in the person on whom it is conferred by the group or society, but in the recognition and acceptance it elicits in others. Power, on the other hand, may dispense with the prop of authority. It may take the form of the ability to coerce or to veto; it is often personal, charismatic, not institutional. This kind of personal power is self-enforcing. It does not require shoring up by access to force. In fact, it may even operate subversively. A woman with this kind of power may or may not know that she possesses it. If she does know she has it, she will probably disguise her exercise of it.

In the West, the institutional structure of marriage has invested the husband with authority and backed it by the power of church and state. The marriages of wives have thus been officially dominated by the husband. Hebrew, Christian, and Islamic versions of deity were in complete accord on this matter. The laws, written or unwritten, religious or civil, which have defined the marital union have been based on male conceptions, and they have undergirded male authority.

Adam came first. Eve was created to supply him with companionship, not vice versa. And God himself had told her that Adam would rule over her; her wishes had to conform to his. The New Testament authors agreed. Women were created for men, not men for women; women were therefore commanded to be obedient. If they wanted to learn anything, let them ask their husbands in private, for it was shameful for them to talk in the church. They should submit themselves to their husbands, because husbands were superior to wives; and wives should be as subject to their husbands as the church was to Christ. Timothy wrapped it all up: "Let the woman learn in silence with all subjection. But I suffer not a woman to teach, nor to usurp authority over the man, but to be in silence." Male Jews continued for millennia to thank God three times a day that they were not women. And the Koran teaches women that men are naturally their superiors because God made them that way; naturally, their own status is one of subordination.

The state as well as the church had the same conception of marriage, assigning to the husband and father control over his dependents, including his wife. Sometimes this power was well-nigh absolute, as in the case of the Roman *patria potestas*—or the English common law, which flatly said, "The husband and wife are as one and that one is the husband." There are rules still lingering today with the same, though less extreme, slant. Diane B. Schulder has summarized the legal framework of the wife's marriage as laid down in the common law:

> The legal responsibilities of a wife are to live in the home established by her husband; to perform the domestic chores (cleaning, cooking, washing, etc.) necessary to help maintain that home; to care for her husband and children. . . . A husband may force his wife to have sexual relations as long as his demands are reasonable and her health is not endangered. . . . The law allows a wife to take a job if she wishes. However, she must see that her domestic chores are completed, and, if there are children, that they receive proper care during her absence.

A wife is not entitled to payment for household work; and some jurisdictions in the United States expressly deny payment for it. In some states, the wife's earnings are under the control of her husband, and in four, special court approval and in some cases husband's consent are required if a wife wishes to start a business of her own.

The male counterpart to these obligations includes that of supporting his wife. He may not disinherit her. She has a third interest in property owned by him, even if it is held in his name only. Her name is required when he sells property.

Not only divine and civil law but also rules of etiquette have defined authority as a husband's prerogative. One of the first books published in England was a *Boke of Good Manners*, translated from the French of Jacques Le Grand in 1487, which included a chapter on "How

Wymmen Ought to Be Gouerned." The thirty-third rule of Plutarch's *Rules for Husbands and Wives* was that women should obey their husbands; if they "try to rule over their husbands they make a worse mistake than the husbands do who let themselves be ruled." The husband's rule should not, of course, be brutal; he should not rule his wife "as a master does his chattel, but as the soul governs the body, by feeling with her and being linked to her by affection." Wives, according to Richard Baxter, a seventeenth-century English divine, had to obey even a wicked husband, the only exception being that a wife need not obey a husband if he ordered her to change her religion. But, again, like Plutarch, Baxter warned that the husband should love his wife; his authority should not be so coercive or so harsh as to destroy love. Among his twelve rules for carrying out the duties of conjugal love, however, was one to the effect that love must not be so imprudent as to destroy authority.

As late as the nineteenth century, Tocqueville noted that in the United States the ideals of democracy did not apply between husbands and wives:

> Nor have the Americans ever supposed that one consequence of democratic principles is the subversion of marital power, or the confusion of the natural authorities in families. They hold that every association must have a head in order to accomplish its objective, and that the natural head of the conjugal association is man. They do not therefore deny him the right of directing his partner; and they maintain, that in the smaller association of husband and wife, as well as in the great social community, the object of democracy is to regulate and legalize the powers which are necessary, not to subvert all power.
>
> This opinion is not peculiar to men and contested by women; I never observed that the women of America consider conjugal authority as an unfortunate usurpation [by men] of their rights, nor that they thought themselves degraded by submitting to it. It appears to me, on the contrary, that they attach a sort of pride to the voluntary surrender of their own

will, and make it their boast to bend themselves to the yoke, not to shake it off.

The point here is not to document once more the specific ways (religious, legal, moral, traditional) in which male authority has been built into the marital union—that has been done a great many times—but merely to illustrate how different (structurally or "objectively" as well as perceptually or "subjectively") the wife's marriage has actually been from the husband's throughout history.

❧ The Subversiveness of Nature

The rationale for male authority rested not only on biblical grounds but also on nature or natural law, on the generally accepted natural superiority of men. For nothing could be more self-evident than that the patriarchal conception of marriage, in which the husband was unequivocally the boss, was natural, resting as it did on the unchallenged superiority of males.

Actually, nature, if not deity, is subversive. Power, or the ability to coerce or to veto, is widely distributed in both sexes, among women as well as among men. And whatever the theoretical or conceptual picture may have been, the actual, day-by-day relationships between husbands and wives have been determined by the men and women themselves. All that the institutional machinery could do was to confer authority; it could not create personal power, for such power cannot be conferred, and women can generate it as well as men. . . . Thus, keeping women in their place has been a universal problem, in spite of the fact that almost without exception institutional patterns give men positions of superiority over them.

If the sexes were, in fact, categorically distinct, with no overlapping, so that no man was inferior to any woman or any woman superior to any man, or vice versa, marriage would have been a great deal simpler. But there is no such sharp cleavage between the sexes except with respect to the presence or absence of certain organs. With all the other characteristics of each sex, there is greater or less overlapping, some men being more "feminine" than the average woman and some women more "masculine" than the average man. The structure of families and societies reflects the positions assigned to men and women. The bottom stratum includes children, slaves, servants, and outcasts of all kinds, males as well as females. As one ascends the structural hierarchy, the proportion of males increases, so that at the apex there are only males.

When societies fall back on the lazy expedient—as all societies everywhere have done—of allocating the rewards and punishments of life on the basis of sex, they are bound to create a host of anomalies, square pegs in round holes, societal misfits. Roles have been allocated on the basis of sex which did not fit a sizable number of both sexes— women, for example, who chafed at subordinate status and men who could not master superordinate status. The history of the relations of the sexes is replete with examples of such misfits. Unless a modus vivendi is arrived at, unhappy marriages are the result.

There is, though, a difference between the exercise of power by husbands and by wives. When women exert power, they are not rewarded; they may even be punished. They are "deviant." Turk and Bell note that "wives who . . . have the greater influence in decision making may experience guilt over this fact." They must therefore dissemble to maintain the illusion, even to themselves, that they are subservient. They tend to feel less powerful than they are because they *ought* to be.

When men exert power, on the other hand, they are rewarded; it is the natural expression of authority. They feel no guilt about it. The prestige of authority goes to the husband whether or not he is actually the one who exercises it. It is not often even noticed when the wife does so. She sees to it that it is not.

There are two marriages, then, in every marital union, his and hers. And his . . . is better than hers. The questions, therefore, are these: In what direction will they change in the future? Will one change more than the other? Will they tend to converge or to diverge? Will the future continue to favor the husband's marriage? And if the wife's marriage is improved, will it cost the husband's anything, or will his benefit along with hers?

791

☻ ☻ ☻

Critical-Thinking Questions

1. What evidence does Bernard offer to support her conclusion that there are "his" and "her" marriages rather than "our" marriage?

2. Does the traditional inequality of men and women support or undermine marital roles? How?

3. What are the consequences for marriage of the gradual process by which the two sexes are becoming more socially equal?

The Mommy Myth

Susan J. Douglas
Meredith W. Michaels

Many people feel that women have many more choices today than in the past: They can earn a college degree, forge rewarding careers, and successfully juggle work and domestic responsibilities. In contrast, Susan Douglas and Meredith Michaels contend that the media's obsession with "celebrity moms" and mythical images of motherhood make most mothers feel inadequate and unsure of themselves.

. . .

It's 5:22 P.M. You're in the grocery checkout line. Your three-year-old is writhing on the floor, screaming, because you have refused to buy her a Teletubby pinwheel. Your six-year-old is whining, repeatedly, in a voice that could saw through cement, "But mommy, puleeze, puleeze" because you have not bought him the latest "Lunchables," which features, as the four food groups, Cheetos, a Snickers, Cheez Whiz, and Twizzlers. Your teenager, who has not spoken a single word in the past four days except, "You've ruined my life," followed by "Everyone else has one," is out in the car, sulking, with the new rap-metal band Piss on the Parentals blasting through the headphones of a Discman.

To distract yourself, and to avoid the glares of other shoppers who have already deemed you the worst mother in America, you leaf through *People* magazine. Inside, Uma Thurman gushes "Motherhood Is Sexy."[1] Moving on to *Good Housekeeping,* Vanna White says of her child, "When I hear his cry at six-thirty in the morning, I have a smile on my face, and

Reprinted from *The Mommy Myth: The Idealization of Motherhood and How It Has Undermined Women* (2004), Simon & Schuster, Inc.

I'm not an early riser."[2] Another unexpected source of earth-mother wisdom, the newly maternal Pamela Lee, also confides to *People,* "I just love getting up with him in the middle of the night to feed him or soothe him."[3] Brought back to reality by stereophonic whining, you indeed feel as sexy as Rush Limbaugh in a thong.

You drag your sorry ass home. Now, if you were a "good" mom, you'd joyfully empty the shopping bags and transform the process of putting the groceries away into a fun game your kids love to play (upbeat Raffi songs would provide a lilting soundtrack). Then, while you steamed the broccoli and poached the chicken breasts in Vouvray and Evian water, you and the kids would also be doing jigsaw puzzles in the shape of the United Arab Emirates so they learned some geography. Your cheerful teenager would say, "Gee, Mom, you gave me the best advice on that last homework assignment." When your husband arrives, he is so overcome with admiration for how well you do it all that he looks lovingly into your eyes, kisses you, and presents you with a diamond anniversary bracelet. He then announces that he has gone on flex time for the next two years so that he can split childcare duties with you fifty-fifty. The children, chattering away happily, help set the table, and then eat their broccoli. After dinner, you all go out and stencil the driveway with autumn leaves.

But maybe this sounds slightly more familiar. "I won't unpack the groceries! You can't make me," bellows your child as he runs to his room, knocking down a lamp on the way. "Eewee—gross out!" he yells and you discover that the cat has barfed on his bed. You have fifteen minutes to make dinner because there's a school play in half an hour. While the children fight over whether to watch *Hot Couples* or people eating larvae on *Fear Factor,* you zap some Prego spaghetti sauce in the microwave and boil some pasta. *You* set the table. "Mommy, Mommy, Sam losted my hamster," your daughter wails. Your ex-husband calls to say he won't be taking the kids this weekend after all because his new wife, Buffy, twenty-three, has to go on a modeling shoot in Virgin Gorda for the *Sports Illustrated* swimsuit issue, and "she really needs me with her." You go to the TV room to discover the kids watching transvestites punching each other out on *Jerry Springer. . . .*

If you're like us—mothers with an attitude problem—you may be getting increasingly irritable about this chasm between the ridiculous, honey-hued ideals of perfect motherhood in the mass media and the reality of mothers' everyday lives. And you may also be worn down by media images that suggest that however much you do for and love your kids, it is never enough. The love we feel for our kids, the joyful times we have with them, are repackaged into unattainable images of infinite patience and constant adoration so that we fear, as Kristin van Ogtrop put it movingly in *The Bitch in the House,* "I will love my children, but my love for them will always be imperfect."[4]

From the moment we get up until the moment we collapse in bed at night, the media are out there, calling to us, yelling, "Hey you! Yeah, you! Are you *really* raising your kids right?" Whether it's the cover of *Redbook* or *Parents* demanding "Are You a Sensitive Mother?" "Is Your Child Eating Enough?" "Is Your Baby Normal?" (and exhorting us to enter its pages and have great sex at 25, 35, or 85), the nightly news warning us about missing children, a movie trailer hyping a film about a cross-dressing dad who's way more fun than his stinky, careerist wife (*Mrs. Doubtfire*), or Dr. Laura telling some poor mother who works forty hours a week that she's neglectful, the siren song blending seduction and accusation is there all the time. Mothers are subjected to an onslaught of beatific imagery, romantic fantasies, self-righteous sermons, psychological warnings, terrifying movies about losing their children, even more terrifying news stories about abducted and abused children, and totally unrealistic advice about how to be the most perfect and revered mom in the neighborhood, maybe even in the whole country. (Even *Working Mother*—which should have known better—had a "Working Mother of the Year Contest." When Jill Kirschenbaum became the editor in 2001, one of the first things she did was dump this feature, noting that motherhood should not be a "competitive sport.") We are urged to be fun-loving, spontaneous, and relaxed, yet, at the same time, scared out of our minds that our kids could be killed at any moment. No wonder 81 percent of women in a recent poll said it's harder to be a mother now than it was twenty or thirty years ago, and 56 percent felt mothers were doing a worse job today than mothers back then.[5] Even mothers who deliberately avoid TV and magazines, or who pride themselves on seeing through them, have trouble escaping the standards of perfection, and the sense of threat, that the media ceaselessly atomize into the air we breathe.

We are both mothers, and we adore our kids—for example, neither one of us has ever locked them up in dog crates in the basement (although we have, of course, been tempted). The smell of a new baby's head, tucking a child in at night, receiving homemade, hand-scrawled birthday cards, heart-to-hearts with a teenager after a date, seeing *them* become parents—these are joys parents treasure. But like increasing numbers of women, we are fed up with the myth—shamelessly hawked by the media—that motherhood is eternally fulfilling and rewarding, that it is *always* the best and most important thing you do, that there is only a narrowly prescribed way to do it right, and that if you don't love each and every second of it there's something really wrong with you. At the same time, the two of us still have been complete suckers, buying those black-and-white mobiles that allegedly turn your baby into Einstein Jr., feeling guilty for sending in store-bought cookies to the class bake sale instead of homemade like the "good" moms, staying up until 2:30 A.M. making our kids' Halloween costumes, driving to the Multiplex 18 at midnight to pick up teenagers so they won't miss the latest outing with their friends. We know that building a scale model of Versailles out of mashed potatoes may not be quite as crucial to good mothering as *Martha Stewart Living* suggests. Yet here we are, cowed by that most tyrannical of our cultural icons, Perfect Mom. So, like millions of women, we buy into these absurd ideals at the same time that we resent them and think they are utterly ridiculous and oppressive. After all, our parents—the group Tom Brokaw has labeled "the greatest generation"—had parents who whooped them on the behind, screamed stuff at them like "I'll tear you limb from limb," told them babies came from cabbage patches, never drove them four hours to a soccer match, and yet they seemed to have nonetheless saved the western world.

This book is about the rise in the media of what we are calling the "new momism": the insistence that no woman is truly complete or fulfilled unless she has kids, that women remain the best primary caretakers of children, and that to be a remotely decent mother, a woman has to devote her entire physical, psychological, emotional, and intellectual being, 24/7, to her children. The new momism is a highly romanticized and yet demanding view of motherhood in which the standards for success are impossible to meet. The term "momism" was initially coined by the journalist Philip Wylie in his highly influential 1942 bestseller *Generation of Vipers,* and it was a very derogatory term. Drawing from Freud (who else?), Wylie attacked the mothers of America as being so smothering, overprotective, and invested in their kids, especially their sons, that they turned them into dysfunctional, sniveling weaklings, maternal slaves chained to the apron strings, unable to fight for their country or even stand on their own two feet.[6] We seek to reclaim this term, rip it from its misogynistic origins, and apply it to an ideology that has snowballed since the 1980s and seeks to return women to the Stone Age.

The "new momism" is a set of ideals, norms, and practices, most frequently and powerfully represented in the media, that seem on the surface to celebrate motherhood, but which in reality promulgate standards of perfection that are beyond your reach. The new momism is the direct descendant and latest version of what Betty Friedan famously labeled the "feminine mystique" back in the 1960s. The new momism *seems* to be much more hip and progressive than the feminine mystique, because now, of course, mothers can and do work outside the home, have their own ambitions and money, raise kids on their own, or freely choose to stay at home with their kids rather than being forced to. And unlike the feminine mystique, the notion that women should be subservient to men is not an accepted tenet of the new momism. Central to the new momism, in fact, is the feminist insistence that woman have choices, that they are active agents in control of their own destiny, that they have autonomy. But here's where the distortion of feminism occurs. The only truly enlightened choice to make as a woman, the one that proves, first, that you are a "real" woman, and second, that you are a decent, worthy one, is to become a "mom" and to bring to child rearing a combination of selflessness and professionalism that would involve the cross clon-ing of Mother

Teresa with Donna Shalala. Thus the new momism is deeply contradictory: It both draws from and repudiates feminism.

The fulcrum of the new momism is the rise of a really pernicious ideal in the late twentieth century that the sociologist Sharon Hays has perfectly labeled "intensive mothering."[7] It is no longer okay, as it was even during the heyday of June Cleaver, to let (or make) your kids walk to school, tell them to stop bugging you and go outside and play, or, God forbid, serve them something like Tang, once the preferred beverage of the astronauts, for breakfast. Of course many of our mothers baked us cookies, served as Brownie troop leaders, and chaperoned class trips to Elf Land. But today, the standards of good motherhood are really over the top. And they've gone through the roof at the same time that there has been a real decline in leisure time for most Americans.[8] The yuppie work ethic of the 1980s, which insisted that even when you were off the job you should be working—on your abs, your connections, your portfolio, whatever—absolutely conquered motherhood. As the actress Patricia Heaton jokes in *Motherhood & Hollywood,* now mothers are supposed to "sneak echinacea" into the "freshly squeezed, organically grown orange juice" we've made for our kids and teach them to "download research for their kindergarten report on 'My Family Tree—The Early Roman Years.'"[9]

Intensive mothering insists that mothers acquire professional-level skills such as those of a therapist, pediatrician ("Dr. Mom"), consumer products safety inspector, and teacher, and that they lavish every ounce of physical vitality they have, the monetary equivalent of the gross domestic product of Australia, and, most of all, every single bit of their emotional, mental, and psychic energy on their kids. We must learn to put on the masquerade of the doting, self-sacrificing mother and wear it at all times. With intensive mothering, everyone watches us, we watch ourselves and other mothers, and we watch ourselves watching ourselves. How many of you know someone who swatted her child on the behind in a supermarket because he was, say, opening a pack of razor blades in the toiletries aisle, only to be accosted by someone she never met who threatened to put her up on child-abuse charges? In 1997, one mother was arrested for child neglect because she left a ten-

798

year-old and a four-year-old home for an hour and a half while she went to the supermarket.[10] Motherhood has become a psychological police state.

Intensive mothering is the ultimate female Olympics: We are all in powerful competition with each other, in constant danger of being trumped by the mom down the street, or in the magazine we're reading. The competition isn't just over who's a good mother—it's over who's the best. We compete with each other; we compete with ourselves. The best mothers always put their kids' needs before their own, period. The best mothers are the main caregivers. For the best mothers, their kids are the center of the universe. The best mothers always smile. They always understand. They are never tired. They never lose their temper. They never say, "Go to the neighbor's house and play while Mommy has a beer." Their love for their children is boundless, unflagging, flawless, total. Mothers today cannot just respond to their kids' needs, they must predict them—and with the telepathic accuracy of Houdini. They must memorize verbatim the books of all the child-care experts and know which approaches are developmentally appropriate at different ages. They are supposed to treat their two-year-olds with "respect." If mothers screw up and fail to do this on any given day, they should apologize to their kids, because any misstep leads to permanent psychological and/or physical damage. Anyone who questions whether this is *the* best and *the* necessary way to raise kids is an insensitive, ignorant brute. This is just common sense, right?[11]

The new momism has become unavoidable, unless you raise your kids in a yurt on the tundra, for one basic reason: Motherhood became one of the biggest media obsessions of the last three decades, exploding especially in the mid-1980s and continuing unabated to the present. Women have been deluged by an ever-thickening mudslide of maternal media advice, programming, and marketing that powerfully shapes how we mothers feel about our relationships with our own kids and, indeed, how we feel about ourselves. These media representations have changed over time, cutting mothers some real slack in the 1970s, and then increasingly closing the vise in the late 1980s and after, despite important rebellions by Roseanne and others. People don't usually notice that motherhood has been such a major media fixation, revolted or hooked as they've been over the years by other media excesses like the O. J. Simpson trials, the Lewinsky-Clinton imbroglio, the Elian Gonzalez carnival, *Survivor,* or the 2002 Washington-area sniper killings in which "profilers" who knew as much as SpongeBob SquarePants nonetheless got on TV to tell us what the killer was thinking.

But make no mistake about it—mothers and motherhood came under unprecedented media surveillance in the 1980s and beyond. And since the media traffic in extremes, in anomalies—the rich, the deviant, the exemplary, the criminal, the gorgeous—they emphasize fear and dread on the one hand and promote impossible ideals on the other. In the process, *Good Housekeeping, People,* E!, Lifetime, *Entertainment Tonight,* and *NBC Nightly News* built an interlocking, cumulative image of the dedicated, doting "mom" versus the delinquent, bad "mother." There have been, since the early 1980s, several overlapping media frameworks that have fueled the new momism. First, the media warned mothers about the external threats to their kids from abductors and the like. Then the "family values" crowd made it clear that supporting the family was not part of the government's responsibility. By the late 1980s, stories about welfare and crack mothers emphasized the internal threats to children from mothers themselves. And finally, the media brouhaha over the "Mommy Track" reaffirmed that businesses could not or would not budge much to accommodate the care of children. Together, and over time, these frameworks produced a prevailing common sense that only you, the individual mother, are responsible for your child's welfare: The buck stops with you, period, and you'd better be a superstar.

Of course there has been a revolution in fatherhood over the past thirty years, and millions of men today tend to the details of child rearing in ways their own fathers rarely did. Feminism prompted women to insist that men change diapers and pack school lunches, but it also gave men permission to become more involved with their kids in ways they have found to be deeply satisfying. And between images of cuddly, New Age dads with babies asleep on their chests (think old Folger's ads),

800

movies about hunky men and a baby (or clueless ones who shrink the kids), and sensational news stories about "deadbeat dads" and men who beat up their sons' hockey coaches, fathers too have been subject to a media "dad patrol." But it pales in comparison to the new momism. After all, a dad who knows the name of his kids' pediatrician and reads them stories at night is still regarded as a saint; a mother who doesn't is a sinner.

Once you identify it, you see the new momism everywhere. The recent spate of magazines for "parents" (i.e., mothers) bombard the anxiety-induced mothers of America with reassurances that they can (after a $100,000 raise and a personality transplant) produce bright, motivated, focused, fun-loving, sensitive, cooperative, confident, contented kids just like the clean, obedient ones on the cover. The frenzied hypernatalism of the women's magazines alone (and that includes *People, Us,* and *InStyle*), with their endless parade of perfect, "sexy" celebrity moms who've had babies, adopted babies, been to sperm banks, frozen their eggs for future use, hatched the frozen eggs, had more babies, or adopted a small Tibetan village, all to satisfy their "baby lust," is enough to make you want to get your tubes tied. (These profiles always insist that celebs all love being "moms" much, much more than they do their work, let alone being rich and famous, and that they'd spend every second with their kids if they didn't have that pesky blockbuster movie to finish.) Women without children, wherever they look, are besieged by ridiculously romantic images that insist that having children is the most joyous, fulfilling experience in the galaxy, and if they don't have a small drooling creature who likes to stick forks in electrical outlets, they are leading bankrupt, empty lives. Images of ideal moms and their miracle babies are everywhere, like leeches in the Amazon, impossible to dislodge and sucking us dry.

There is also the ceaseless outpouring of books on toilet training, separating one sibling's fist from another sibling's eye socket, expressing breast milk while reading a legal brief, helping preschoolers to "own" their feelings, getting Joshua to do his homework, and raising teenage boys so they become Sensitive New Age Guys instead of rooftop snipers or Chippendale dancers. Over eight hundred books on motherhood were published between 1970 and 2000; only twenty-seven of these came out between 1970 and 1980, so the real avalanche happened in the past twenty years.[12] We've learned about the perils of "the hurried child" and "hyperparenting," in which we schedule our kids with so many enriching activities that they make the secretary of state look like a couch spud. But the unhurried child probably plays too much Nintendo and is out in the garage building pipe bombs, so you can't underschedule them either.

Then there's the Martha Stewartization of America, in which we are meant to sculpt the carrots we put in our kids' lunches into the shape of peonies and build funhouses for them in the backyard; this has raised the bar to even more ridiculous levels than during the June Cleaver era. Most women know that there was a massive public relations campaign during World War II to get women into the workforce, and then one right after the war to get them to go back to the kitchen. But we haven't fully focused on the fact that another, more subtle, sometimes unintentional, more long-term propaganda campaign began in the 1980s to redomesticate the women of America through motherhood.[13] Why aren't all the mothers of America leaning out their windows yelling "I'm mad as hell and I'm not going to take it anymore"?

Notes

[1]*People,* September 21, 1998.

[2]*Good Housekeeping,* January 1995.

[3]*People,* July 8, 1996.

[4]Kristin van Ogtrop, "Attila the Honey I'm Home," *The Bitch in the House* (New York: William Morrow, 2002), p. 169.

[5]"Motherhood Today—A Tougher Job, Less Ably Done," The Pew Research Center for the People & the Press, March 1997.

[6]Philip Wylie, *Generation of Vipers* (New York: Holt, Rinehart and Winston, 1942). See also Ruth Feldstein's excellent discussion of momism in *Motherhood in Black and White: Race and Sex in American Liberalism, 1930–1965* (Ithaca: Cornell University Press, 2000), especially chapter 2.

[7]Hays's book is must reading for all mothers, and we are indebted to her analysis of intensive mothering, from which this discussion draws. Sharon Hays, *The Cultural Contradictions of Motherhood* (New Haven: Yale University Press, 1996), p. 4.

[8]For an account of the decline in leisure time see Juliet B. Schorr, *The Overworked American* (New York: Basic Books, 1992).

[9]Patricia Heaton, *Motherhood & Hollywood* (New York: Villard Books, 2002), pp. 48–49.

[10]See Katha Pollitt's terrific piece "Killer Moms, Working Nannies" in *The Nation,* November 24, 1997, p. 9.

[11]Hays, pp. 4–9.

[12]Based on an On-line Computer Library Center, Inc., search under the word *motherhood,* from 1970–2000.

[13]Susan Faludi, in her instant classic *Backlash,* made this point, too, but the book focused on the various and multiple forms of backlash, and we will be focusing only on the use of motherhood here.

☻ ☻ ☻

Critical-Thinking Questions

1. What is the "new momism"? According to Douglas and Michaels, why has the new momism been unhealthy for women, men, and children? On the other hand, how does the new momism benefit men and children?

2. Think about the television programs you watch and the ads you see in magazines. How many portray mothers realistically— especially working mothers who aren't "celebrity moms"?

3. Do you think that the authors' views are wrong or offensive because they trivialize motherhood? Or do you agree with Douglas and Michaels that we tend to worship an unrealistic image of the "perfect mother"?

Female Genital Mutilation

Efua Dorkenoo
Scilla Elworthy

*In recent decades, numerous women's organizations around the
In recent decades, numerous women's organizations around the
world have focused on a variety of health-related issues and
problems, including domestic violence, rape, sexual harassment,
and poverty. In this selection, Efua Dorkenoo and Scilla
Elworthy examine the complex cultural issues surrounding
female genital mutilation, a practice that has received international attention since the early 1990s.*

. . .

☻ The Facts

. . . [F]emale genital mutilation covers four types of operation:

1. *Circumcision*, or cutting of the prepuce or hood of the clitoris,
   known in Muslim countries as Sunna (tradition). This, the
   mildest type, affects only a small proportion of the millions of
   women concerned. It is the only type of mutilation that can correctly be called circumcision, though there has been a tendency
   to group all kinds of mutilations under the misleading term
   'female circumcision.'

2. *Excision*, meaning the cutting of the clitoris and of all or part of
   the labia minora.

Reprinted from *Female Genital Mutation: Proposals for Change, an MRG Report*,
Minority Rights Group.

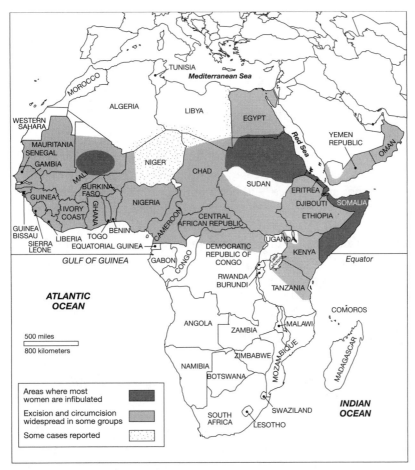

Female Genital Mutilation in Africa

3. *Infibulation*, the cutting of the clitoris, labia minora, and at least part of the labia majora. The two sides of the vulva are then pinned together by silk or catgut sutures, or with thorns, thus obliterating the vaginal introitus except for a very small opening, preserved by the insertion of a tiny piece of wood or a reed for the passage of urine or menstrual blood. These operations are done with special

805

knives, with razor blades or pieces of glass. The girl's legs are then bound together from hip to ankle and she is kept immobile for up to forty days to permit the formation of scar tissue.

4. *Intermediate*, meaning the removal of the clitoris and some parts of the labia minora or the whole of it. Various degrees are done according to the demands of the girl's relatives. . . .

Most frequently these operations are performed by an old woman of the village or by a traditional birth attendant and only rarely by qualified nurses or doctors. The age at which the mutilations are carried out varies from area to area, and according to whether legislation against the practice is foreseen or not. It varies from a few days old (for example, the Jewish Falashas in Ethiopia, and the nomads of the Sudan) to about seven years (as in Egypt and many countries of Central Africa) or—more rarely—adolescence, as among the Ibo of Nigeria. Most experts are agreed that the age of mutilation is becoming younger, and has less and less to do with initiation into adulthood.[1]

Physical Consequences

Health risks and complications depend on the gravity of the mutilation, hygienic conditions, the skill and eyesight of the operator, and the struggles of the child. Whether immediate or long term, they are grave.[2] Death from bleeding is not uncommon, while long-term complications include chronic infections of the uterus and vagina, painful menstruation, severe pain during intercourse, sterility, and complications during childbirth. Though evidence has yet to be collected, it is also likely that bleeding or open wounds increase the likelihood of HIV transmission and AIDS.

There is great difficulty in obtaining accurate research on the sexual experiences of mutilated women, because the majority are reluctant to speak on the subject and are generally ambivalent on questions of sexual enjoyment.[3] However, in all types of mutilation, even the "mildest" clitoridectomy, a part of a woman's body containing nerves of vital importance to sexual pleasure is amputated.

Psychological Consequences

Even less research has been done to date on the psychological consequences of these traditions. However, many personal accounts and research findings contain repeated references to anxiety prior to the operation, terror at the moment of being seized by an aunt or village matron, unbearable pain, and the subsequent sense of humiliation and of being betrayed by parents, especially the mother. On the other hand, there are references to special clothes and good food associated with the event, to the pride felt in being like everyone else, in being "made clean," in having suffered without screaming.

To be different clearly produces anxiety and mental conflict. An unexcised, non-infibulated girl is despised and made the target of ridicule, and no one in her community will marry her. Thus what is clearly understood to be her life's work, namely marriage and childbearing, is denied her. So, in tight-knit village societies where mutilation is the rule, it will be the exceptional girl who will suffer psychologically, unless she has another very strong identity which she has lost.[4]

There is no doubt that genital mutilation would have overwhelming psychological effects on an unmotivated girl, unsupported by her family, village, peers, and community. To those from other cultures unfamiliar with the force of this particular community identity, the very concept of amputation of the genitals carries a shock value which does not exist for most women in the areas concerned. For them, not to amputate would be shocking.

These observations concern social-psychological factors rather than the central question, namely, what effects do these traumatic operations have on little girls at the moment of operation and as they grow up? The fact is that we simply don't know. We do not know what it means to a girl or woman when her central organ of sensory pleasure is cut off, when her life-giving canal is stitched up amid blood and fear and secrecy, while she is forcibly held down and told that if she screams she will cause the death of her mother or bring shame on the family.

807

◉ The Practice

The Area Covered

The countries where one or more forms of female genital mutilation are practised number more than twenty in Africa, from the Atlantic to the Red Sea, the Indian Ocean, and the eastern Mediterranean. Outside Africa, excision is also practised in Oman, South Yemen, and in the United Arab Emirates (UAE). Circumcision is practised by the Muslim populations of Indonesia and Malaysia and by Bohra Muslims in India, Pakistan and East Africa.[5]

On the map of Africa, an uninterrupted belt is formed across the centre of the continent, which then expands up the length of the Nile. This belt, with the exception of the Egyptian buckle, corresponds strikingly with the pattern of countries that have the highest child mortality rates (more than 30 percent for children from one to four years of age).[6] These levels reflect deficiencies of medical care, of clean drinking water, of sanitary infrastructure, and of adequate nutrition in most of the countries.

The gravity of the mutilations varies from country to country. Infibulation is reported to affect nearly all the female population of Somalia, Djibouti, and the Sudan (except the non-Muslim population of southern Sudan), southern Egypt, the Red Sea coast of Ethiopia, northern Kenya, northern Nigeria, and some parts of Mali. The most recent estimate of women mutilated is 74 million.[7]

Ethnic groups closely situated geographically are by no means affected in the same way: For example, in Kenya, the Kikuyu practise excision and the Luo do not; in Nigeria, the Yoruba, the Ibo, and the Hausa do, but not the Nupes or the Fulanis; in Senegal, the Woloff have no practice of mutilation. There are many other examples.

As the subject of female genital mutilation began to be eligible at least for discussion, reports of genital operations on nonconsenting females have appeared from many unexpected parts of the world. During the 1980s, women in Sweden were shocked by accounts of mutilations performed in Swedish hospitals on daughters of immigrants. In France, women from Mali and Senegal have been reported to bring an *exciseuse* to France once a year to operate on their daughters in their apartments.[8] In July 1982 a Malian infant died of an excision performed by a professional circumciser, who then fled to Mali. In the same year, reports appeared in the British press that excision for nonmedical reasons had been performed in a London private clinic.

Legislation

In Africa

Formal legislation forbidding genital mutilation, or more precisely infibulation, exists in the Sudan. A law first enacted in 1946 allows for a term of imprisonment up to five years and/or a fine. However, it is not an offence (under Article 284 of the Sudan Penal Code for 1974) "merely to remove the free and projecting part of the clitoris."

Many references have been made to legislation in Egypt, but after researching the available materials, all that has been traced is a resolution signed by the Minister of Health in 1959, recommending only partial clitoridectomy for those who want an operation, to be performed only by doctors.[9]

In late 1978, largely due to the efforts of the Somali Women's Democratic Organization (SWDO), Somalia set up a commission to abolish infibulation. In 1988 at a seminar held in Mogadishu, it was recommended that SWDO should propose a bill to the competent authorities to eradicate all forms of female genital mutilation.

In September 1982, President Arap Moi took steps to ban the practices in Kenya, following reports of the deaths of fourteen children after excision. A traditional practitioner found to be carrying out this operation can be arrested under the Chiefs Act and brought before the law.

Official declarations against female genital mutilation were made by the late Captain Thomas Sankara and Abdou Diouf, the heads of state in Burkina Faso and Senegal respectively.

In Western Countries

A law prohibiting female excision, whether consent has been given or not, came into force in Sweden in July 1982, carrying a two-year sentence. In Norway, in 1985, all hospitals were alerted to the practice. Belgium has incorporated a ban on the practice. Several states in the U.S.A. have incorporated female genital mutilation into their criminal code.

In the U.K., specific legislation prohibiting female circumcision came into force at the end of 1985. A person found guilty of an offence is liable to up to five years' imprisonment or to a fine. Female genital mutilation has been incorporated into child protection procedures at local authority levels. As yet no person has been committed in the English courts for female circumcision, but since 1989 there have been at least seven local authority legal interventions which prevented parents from sexually mutilating their daughters or wards.

France does not have specific legislation on female sexual mutilation but under Article 312–3 of the French Penal Code, female genital mutilation can be considered as a criminal offence. Under this code, anybody who exercises violence or seriously assaults a child less than fifteen years old can be punished with imprisonment from ten to twenty years, if the act of violence results in a mutilation, amputation of a limb, the loss of an eye or other parts of the body, or has unintentionally caused the death of the child.

In 1989, a mother who had paid a traditional woman exciser to excise her week-old daughter, in 1984, was convicted and given a three-year suspended jail sentence. In 1991 a traditional exciser was jailed for five years in France.

Contemporary Practices

Opinions are very divided as to whether the practice is disappearing because of legislation or social and economic changes. Esther Ogunmodede, for instance, believes that in Nigeria, Africa's most populous country, the tradition is disappearing but extremely slowly, with millions of excisions still taking place. She reports that in areas where the operations are done on girls of marriageable age, they are

810

"running away from home to avoid the razor." This confirms Fran Hosken's assertion that operations are being done at earlier and earlier ages, in order that the children should be "too young to resist." Fran Hosken does not think that the custom is dying out, and she indisputably has the best published range of information concerning all the countries where the practice is known.

An interesting development took place in Ethiopia during the years of civil warfare which only ended in 1991. When the Eritrean People's Liberation Front (EPLF) occupied large areas from January 1977 to December 1978, among many other reforms they categorically and successfully forbade genital mutilation and forced marriage. In fact, the reason given for the large numbers of young women in the EPLF army was that they were running away from home in other parts of Ethiopia to avoid forced marriage and the knife.[10] Although it appears the practice continues in remote areas, because the consciousness of Eritrean women has changed dramatically during the war years, it is easier to persuade men and women to let go of this practice.

Since 1983, the number of educational programmes initiated to raise public awareness of the health risk associated with female genital mutilation at local, national, and international levels have increased. The media have played a major role in bringing this issue from the domestic to the public domain. As a result of these efforts it can be said that the taboo surrounding even public mention of the practice has at last been broken. There is an increase in public awareness of the harmful effects of female genital mutilation.

It has been noted that female genital mutilation is becoming unpopular amongst the urban elite in some African countries. In Sierra Leone, for example, Koso-Thomas claims that urban men are willing to marry uncircumcised women, in particular when the marriage is not pre-arranged.[11]

In general, among urban educated women, reasons often cited against female genital mutilation include the pointlessness of mutilation, health risks, and reduction of sexual sensitivity. The last reason points to a changing attitude towards women's fundamental human rights amongst urban Africans.

In the main, the practice continues to be widespread among large sectors and groups within Africa. Those in favour of the practice are noted in the 1986 U.N. study to be a passive majority who refer back to traditional society, without necessarily sharing that society's values.[12] In some cases, the practice appears to be spreading to population groups who traditionally never practised female genital mutilation, as observed with city women in Wau, Sudan, who regard it as fashionable, and among converted Muslim women in southern Sudan who marry northern Sudanese men.[13] Furthermore, even in areas where some groups are turning against the practice, the absolute numbers affected may be increasing. Rapid population growth in Africa means greater numbers of female children are born, who in turn are exposed to the risk of mutilation.

◉ The Issues

Female genital mutilation is a complex issue, for it involves deep-seated cultural practices which affect millions of people. However, it can be divided into (at least) four distinct issues.

Rights of Women

Female genital mutilation is an extreme example of the general subjugation of women, sufficiently extreme and horrifying to make women and men question the basis of what is done to women, what women have accepted and why, in the name of society and tradition.

The burning of Indian widows and the binding of the feet of Chinese girl children are other striking examples, sharp enough and strange enough to throw a spotlight on other less obvious ways in which women the world over submit to oppression. It is important to remember that all these practices are, or were, preserved under centuries of tradition, and that foot-binding was only definitively stopped by a massive social and political revolution (replacing the many traditions which it swept away by offering an entirely new social system, revolutionary in many aspects: land ownership, class system, education, sex equality, etc.) which had been preceded by years of patient work by reformers.

Thus, to be successful, campaigns on female genital mutilation should consider carefully not only eliminating but also replacing the custom. (The example of Eritrea, previously quoted, is illuminating here.) Furthermore, such success may be predicated on long-term changes in attitudes and ideologies by both men and women.

A major international expression of the goal of equal rights for women was taken in December 1979, when the U.N. General Assembly adopted the Convention on the Elimination of All Forms of Discrimination Against Women. This came into force in September 1981. The comprehensive convention calls for equal rights for women, regardless of their marital status, in all fields: political, economic, social, cultural and, civil. Article 5(a) obliges states' parties to take:

> . . . all appropriate measures to modify the social and cultur-
> al patterns of conduct of men and women, with a view to
> achieving the elimination of prejudices and customary and
> all other practices which are based on the idea of the inferi-
> ority or superiority of either of the sexes or on stereotyped
> roles for men and women.

To succeed in abolishing such practices will demand fundamental attitudinal shifts in the way that society perceives the human rights of women. The starting point for change should be educational programmes that assist women to recognize their fundamental human rights. This is where UNESCO, the U.N. Centre for Human Rights, and international agencies could help by supporting awareness-building programmes.

Rights of Children

An adult is free to submit her or himself to a ritual or tradition, but a child, having no formed judgement, does not consent but simply undergoes the operation (which in this case is irrevocable) while she is totally vulnerablle. The descriptions available of the reactions of children—panic and shock from extreme pain, biting through the tongue, convulsions, necessity for six adults to hold down an eight-year-old, and death—indicate a practice comparable to torture.

Many countries signatory to Article 5 of the Universal Declaration of Human Rights (which provides that no one shall be subjected to torture, or to cruel, inhuman, or degrading treatment) violate that clause. Those violations are discussed and sometimes condemned by various U.N. commissions. Female genital mutilation, however, is a question of torture inflicted not on adults but on girl children, and the reasons given are not concerned with either political conviction or military necessity but are solely in the name of tradition.

The Declaration of the Rights of Children, adopted in 1959 by the General Assembly, asserts that children should have the possibility to develop physically in a healthy and normal way in conditions of liberty and dignity. They should have adequate medical attention and be protected from all forms of cruelty.

It is the opinion of Renée Bridel, of the Fédération Internationale des Femmes de Carrières Juridiques, that "One cannot but consider Member States which tolerate these practices as infringing their obligations as assumed under the terms of the Charter [of the U.N.].[14]

In September 1990, the United Nations Convention on the Rights of the Child went into force. It became part of international human rights law. Under Article 24(3) it states that "States Parties shall take all effective and appropriate measures with a view to abolishing traditional practices prejudicial to the health of children." This crucial article should not merely remain a paper provision, to be given lip service by those entrusted to implement it. Members of the U.N. should work at translating its provisions into specific implementation programmes at grassroots level. Much could be learned (by African states in particular) from countries with established child protection systems.

The Right to Good Health

No reputable medical practitioner insists that mutilation is good for the physical or mental health of girls and women, and a growing number offer research indicating its grave permanent damage to health and underlining the risks of death. Medical facts, carefully explained, may be the way to discourage the practice, since these facts are almost always the contrary of what is believed, and can be shown and demonstrated.

Those U.N. agencies and government departments specifically entrusted with the health needs of women and children must realize that it is their responsibility to support positive and specific preventative programmes against female genital mutilation, for while the practice continues the quality of life and health will inevitably suffer. However, this approach, if presented out of context, ignores the force of societal pressures which drive women to perform these operations, regardless of risk, in order to guarantee marriage for their daughters and to conform to severe codes of female behaviour laid down by male-dominated societies.

The Right to Development

The practice of female genital mutilation must be seen in the context of underdevelopment,[15] and the realities of life for the most vulnerable and exploited sectors—women and children. International political and economic forces have frequently prevented development programmes from meeting the basic needs of rural populations. With no access to education or resources, and with no effective power base, the rural and urban poor cling to traditions as a survival mechanism in time of socioeconomic change.

In societies where marriage for a woman is her only means of survival, and where some form of excision is a prerequisite for marriage, persuading her to relinquish the practice for herself or for her children is an extraordinarily difficult task. Female (and some male) African analysts of development strategies are today constantly urging that the overall deteriorating conditions in which poor women live be made a major focus for change, for unless development affects their lives for the better, traditional practices are unlikely to change.

☻ Directions for the Future

The mutilation of female genitals has been practised in many areas for centuries. The greatest determination, combined with sensitivity and understanding of local conditions, will be needed if it is to be abolished. In every country and region where operations are carried out, the situation is different, as is the political will, whether at local or national levels. In Western countries the way forward is relatively clear. In Africa the problem is more profound and the economic and political conditions vastly more difficult, while international agencies have hardly begun to explore their potential role.

What all three have in common is that, to date, nearly all programmes have been individual or *ad hoc* efforts, with little integration into other structures, with minimal evaluation or monitoring, and lacking in long-term goals and strategies. To achieve real change will require more resources, more detailed planning, and more real, sustained commitment from governments and international organizations.

Notes

[1]Fran Hosken, *The Hosken Report—Genital and Sexual Mutilation of Females* (third enlarged/revised edition, Autumn, 1982, published by Women's International Network News, 187 Grant St., Lexington, Mass. 02173, USA). This is the most detailed and comprehensive collection of information available.

[2]The consequences of sexual mutilations on the health of women have been studied by Dr. Ahmed Abu-el-Futuh Shandall, Lecturer in the Department of Obstetrics and Gynaecology at the University of Khartoum, in a paper entitled, "Circumcision and Infibulation of Females" (*Sudanese Medical Journal,* Vol. 5, No. 4, 1967); and by Dr. J.A. Verzin, in an article entitled "The Sequelae of Female Circumcision," (*Tropical Doctor,* October, 1975). A bibliography on the subject has been prepared by Dr. R. Cook for the World Health Organization.

[3]Readers interested to read more about research on the sexual experience of circumcised women may want to read Hanny Lightfoot-Klein, *Prisoners of Ritual: An Odyssey into Female Genital Mutilation in Africa* (New York: The Haworth Press, 1989).

[4]These feelings of rejection are clearly articulated by Kenyan girls in "The Silence over Female Circumcision in Kenya," in *Viva*, August, 1978.

[5]Q.R. Ghadially, "Ali for 'Izzat': The Practice of Female Circumcision among Bohra Muslims," *Manushi*, No. 66, New Delhi, India, 1991.

[6]See map of Childhood Mortality in the World, 1977 (Health Sector Policy Paper, World Bank, Washington, D.C., 1980).

[7]See Hosken for details and estimates of ethnic groups involved.

[8]*F Magazine*, No. 4, March, 1979, and No. 31, October, 1980.

[9]Marie Assaad, *Female Circumcision in Egypt—Current Research and Social Implications* (American University in Cairo, 1979), p. 12.

[10]"Social Transformation of Eritrean Society," paper presented to the People's Tribunal, Milan, 24–26 May 1980, by Mary Dines of Rights and Justice.

[11]Koso-Thomas, *The Circumcision of Women: A Strategy for Elimination* (London: Zed Books, 1987).

[12]UN Commission on Human Rights, Report of the Working Group on Traditional Practices Affecting Women and Children, 1986.

[13]Ellen Ismail et al., *Women of the Sudan* (Bendestorf, Germany: EIS, 1990).

[14]*L'enfant mutilé* by Renée Bridel, delegate of the FIFCJ to the UN, Geneva, 1978. See also Raqiya Haji Dualeh Abdalla, Sisters in Affliction (London: Zed Press, 1982) and Asma El Dareer, Woman, Why Do You Weep? (London: Zed Press, 1982).

[15]Belkis Woldes Giorgis, *Female Circumcision in Africa*, ST/ECA/ATRCW 81/02.

◉ ◉ ◉

Critical-Thinking Questions

1. What are the four types of female genital mutilation? How widespread are these practices?

2. What do Dorkenoo and Elworthy mean when they describe female genital mutilation as a "complex" issue? Do they feel that this practice can be abolished or not?

3. Many Western countries have denounced female genital mutilation as barbaric. But what about comparable practices in the United States and other Western nations? Even though they are voluntary, are silicone breast transplants, facelifts, or liposuction more "civilized" in making women's bodies more acceptable to men?

Urban Sprawl: The Formation of Edge Cities

JOHN J. MACIONIS
VINCENT N. PARRILLO

A century ago, industrialization changed the shape of cities by concentrating population and construction in densely packed central cities. In recent years, cities are changing once again, this time spreading outward and creating what analysts call "edge cities."

. . .

Urban Sprawl: The Formation of Edge Cities

Not since the expansion of small cities into huge metropolises a century ago have we seen as profound a change in our urban world as the emergence of edge cities. An *edge city* is a new, sprawling, middle-class, automobile-dependent center typically located at the fringe of an older urban area, at the intersection of major highways, where little except villages or farmland existed three decades earlier.

In the second half of the twentieth century, North Americans went through three waves of centrifugal movement away from the older cities. First came the suburbanization of North America, most notably after World War II, as people moved into new homes beyond

Reprinted from *Cities and Urban Life* (2000), Pearson Education.

city boundaries. Next came the malling of North America, particularly in the 1960s and 1970s, when we moved our stores out to where we lived. And now, says Joel Garreau (1991), we have moved our means of creating wealth, the essence of urbanism—our jobs—out to where most of us have lived and shopped for two generations. This has led to the rise of edge cities, resulting in profound changes in the ways we live, work, and play. Garreau (1991:8–9) describes the new urban form this way:

> . . . For my sins I once spent a fair chunk of a Christmas season in Tysons Corner, Virginia, stopping people as they hurried about their holiday tasks, asking them what they thought of their brave new world. The words I recorded were searing. They described the area as plastic, a hodgepodge, Disneyland (used as a pejorative), and sterile. They said it lacked livability, civilization, community, neighborhood, and even a soul.
>
> These responses are frightening, if Edge City is the laboratory of how civilized and livable urban Americans will be well into the next century. Right now, it is vertigo-inducing. It may have all the complexity, diversity, and size of a downtown. But it can cover dozens of square miles, and juxtapose schools and freeways and atria and shimmering parking lots with corporate lawns and Day-Glo-orange helicopter wind socks. Its logic takes a while to decode.
>
> Will we ever be proud of this place? Will we ever drag our visiting relatives out to show off our Edge City, our shining city on the hill? Will we ever feel—for this generation and the ones that follow—that it's a good place to be young? To be old? To fall in love? To have a Fourth of July parade? Will it ever be the place we want to call home?

It is the evolution of edge cities in the past quarter-century that helps explain the increases in population in nonmetropolitan areas. Garreau suggests that North Americans have reinvented the city in the past two decades and that these new urban agglomerations are now the future. Numbering over 200 in the United States, these edge cities with their malls and office parks now dominate the nation's retail trade and office facilities. . . .

Edge cities are appearing in Canada as well as in the United States, but apparently for different reasons. Unlike the United States, the Canadian government does not provide suburb-enhancing tax deductions for home mortgages, and it has greater control over planning and development. In Canada also, there is a greater emphasis on mass transit; a relative lack of freeways; vibrant, bustling urban centers; and a relative lack of racial problems. Nevertheless, edge cities are flourishing. Toronto, for example, has only 46 percent of the area's market. The rest is found in the nine edge cities growing up around it. These are Midtown–Yorkville and North York–North Yonge to the north; Mississauga, the Downsview Airport area, and the Etobicoke– 427 area to the west; and the Don Valley Parkway– 401 area, Markham–404 area, Eglington–Don Mills area, and Scarborough to the east.

Joel Garreau (1991:5) points out that attract edge cities have become the dominant form:

> By any functional urban standard—tall buildings, bright lights, office space that represents whitecollar jobs, shopping, entertainment, prestigious hotels, corporate headquarters, hospitals with CAT scans, even population—each Edge City is larger than down-town Portland, Oregon, or Portland, Maine, or Tampa, or Tucson. Already, two-thirds of all [North] American office facilities are in Edge Cities, and 80 percent of them have materialized in only the last two decades.

Characteristics and Commonalities

Garreau identified over 200 new edge cities in the United States and Canada, giving him a comparative base for analysis. Garreau (1991:425) concluded that this fledgling urban form, despite a sprawling, apparently chaotic evolution, actually possesses specific characteristics. A full-blown edge city contains

- At least 5 million square feet of leasable office space;

- At least 600,000 square feet of retail space (the equivalent of an average mall of three large stores and 80 to 100 shops and boutiques);
- An increasing population each weekday morning, marking it as primarily a work center, not a residential suburb;
- A local perception as a single-end destination for mixed use—jobs, shopping, and entertainment.

What one cannot find, however, is a clearly defined territorial boundary, for edge cities do not have the same look (the compactness of closely adjacent buildings and high pedestrian traffic), political organization (elected officials or civic codes), or even visual clues of older cities (signs, edges) to mark their perimeters. As Garreau (1991:6) explains:

> The reasons these places are tricky to define is that they rarely have a mayor or a city council, and just about never match boundaries on a map. We're still in the process of giving each Edge City its name—a project, incidentally, that could use more flair. In New Jersey, for example, there is one with only the laconic designation "287 and 78." The reason there are no "Welcome to" signs at Edge City is that it is a judgment call where it begins and ends.

A common feature of edge cities is that they have sprouted far from the old downtowns, in locales where, thirty years ago, little existed save villages and farmland. They typically evolve adjacent to two or more major highways, usually with shopping malls serving as anchor points. . . .

Types of Edge Cities

Edge cities fall into one of three major categories: (1) uptowns, built on top of preautomobile settlements, such as Pasadena, California, or Arlington, Virginia; (2) boomers, the typical edge city located at the intersection of two major highways and almost always centered on a mall, and (3) greenfields, a master-planned city by one developer on thousands of farmland acres, such as Irvine, California, and Las Colinas, near the Dallas-Fort Worth airport (Garreau, 1991:115):

Because boomers, the most common form of edge cities, have grown so profusely throughout North America, urbanists identify three subcategories of them. The strip boomer city is usually only a few hundred yards wide but extends for miles along a major highway. Most representative are the strips along Route 1 in Princeton, Route 128 near the Mass Pike outside Boston, and I-270 in Montgomery County, Maryland, in the Washington, D.C., region. All three suffer severe traffic congestion because of their extended shapes. The node boomer city is relatively dense and contained, such as The Galleria area near Houston, Tysons Corner in Virginia, and the Midtown-Yorkville and North York-North Yonge areas in Toronto. The pig-in-the-python boomer city is a cross between the previous two types. It is a strip that develops one or several nodes along it, such as the Lodge Freeway in Southfield, northwest of Detroit, or King of Prussia, Pennsylvania, northwest of Philadelphia.

Evolving Middle-Class Centers

The majority of metropolitan North Americans now work, shop, and live in and around the 200-plus "new hearths of our civilization." Shopping malls function as the village squares for these new urban centers. Adjacent are the hotels, office buildings, and corporate headquarters, whose tall buildings are not side by side as in a downtown, but instead are located on campuslike settings of grass and trees, gazing at one another at a respectful distance. Surrounding this broad center of employment and shopping are the single-family suburban homes whose occupants now outnumber those living next to the old downtowns.

The rise of edge cities is essentially a function of social class, not race. They are evolving in metropolitan areas with low black populations (Denver, Minneapolis, Seattle, Toronto) as well as in metropolitan areas with high black populations (Atlanta, Chicago, New York, Washington). In the latter, middle-class African Americans (presently about one-third of the total U.S. black population) are just as likely to be part of edge cities as are middle-class whites. Just as the skin of the middle-class North American comes in various hues—brown, black, shades of tan, and white—so too do edge cities reflect this reality.

The edge city, however, has been criticized as plastic and sterile, lacking in livability, civilization, community, neighborhood—in short, having little urban soul (Garreau, 1991:8). It is, however, an unfinished new city form and we do not yet know if, in its maturity, this ugly duckling will emerge as a splendid swan. Whatever its ultimate shape, we do know that the

> Edge City acculturates immigrants, provides child care, and offers safety. It is, on average, an improvement in per capita fuel efficiency over the old suburbia– downtown arrangement, since it moves everything closer to the homes of the middle class.
>
> That is why Edge City is the crucible of [North] America's urban future. Having become the place in which the majority of [North] Americans now live, learn, work, shop, play, pray, and die, Edge City will be the forge of the fabled [North] American way of life well into the twenty-first century.

And edge cities are appearing worldwide as well. They now mark the fringes of Bangkok, Beijing, London, Paris, and Sydney. Increased affluence, the desire for more individual transportation, greater use of computers and telecommunications requiring air climate control, and the existence of world financial centers requiring trading floors of at least 20,000 square feet are some of the important elements shaping the growth of edge cities in urban areas throughout the world.

Three Edge City Variations

Not all edge cities are alike, nor does their evolution occur for the same reasons everywhere. The following examples illustrate how the edge city can serve as its own motivation, emerge as a solution to a problem, or simply become the problem.

Edge City as Motivator

By 1990, Oshawa Centre, one of the oldest shopping malls in Ontario, Canada, was showing its age. Originally built for the town's blue-collar population, the place was dark and ugly, some of the stores had out-door-facing windows and doors plastered with newspaper and card-board, and its sales and rental value were declining. Not anymore. The Toronto-based Cambridge Shopping Centres purchased it in 1991 for $145 million. It did so because Garreau had written in *Edge City* that shopping malls usually function as the village squares of the new urban centers. "So, taking that theory," said Ronald Charbon, Cambridge's director of strategic market information, "we said, 'Where are the next edge cities going to occur? Where is the next wave of growth going to occur in the greater metropolitan Toronto area? And are any of our shopping centres sufficiently located to capitalize on that growth?' " (cited in Berman, 1997).

Using census tracts and surveys, Cambridge amassed a population profile of the area, discovering that areas surrounding Oshawa were white-collar and that projections of the area's growth rate were almost three times that in the Greater Toronto Area. So the company took the gamble, invested $40 million in a major facelift, and re-cruited upscale stores. However, that was only one part of a sophisticated strategy to turn Oshawa Centre (as Garreau described other edge cities) into a village square. Cambridge secured government approval to construct six modest-sized office towers over a twenty-five-year period. The Oshawa Centre is thus in the midst of a massive transformation from a jerry-built suburban mall into a mixed-use development that includes retail, business, government, and community services, all inspired by Garreau's book.

Edge City as the Solution

Since incorporating in 1956, Schaumburg, Illinois, has been what Judy Pasternak (1998) called "the ultimate faceless postwar suburb." Located twenty-six miles northwest of Chicago, the town is home to nearly 74,000 people living in townhouses and subdivisions and shopping in one or more of the sixty-five shopping centers that line its streets. Along its expressway, glassy office towers provide a solid employment base. The one thing lacking in Schaumburg, though, is that it has no center, no downtown, no place to walk to or for people to gather. In fact, it hadn't had a town center since 1875.

That is now changing. The local government tore down a faded strip mall on a thirty-acre site to make way for a downtown center called "Town Square." But this place is no small-town core like the downtowns of older suburbs that developed around train depots generations ago. There are no retail stores lining Main Street. In fact, there is no Main Street. Instead, a supermarket and a cluster of retail stores border a large parking lot, giving this area the look of a shopping center. Nearby is a new library, a brick clock tower, a green wrought-iron gazebo, a pond, curved benches, and a chain restaurant. "It's plastic," grumbled one store owner. Others, however, are more optimistic, hoping that this shopping area—with plenty of parking, strolling amenities, and mixed-use development—will allow community to blossom where none had existed before (Pasternak, 1998).

Edge City as the Problem

The more that Tysons Corner, Virginia—one of Joel Garreau's prime examples of an edge city—continues to grow and thrive economically, the more it remains an object of derisive commentary by architects, city planners, design critics, and urban scholars. Indeed, finding ways to "fix" Tysons Corner has been the goal of several planning studies sponsored by academic institutions, professional groups, and Fairfax County, home to this edge city. Tysons Corner today is larger, in both geographic size and employment, than many U.S. central cities, with over 80,000 jobs and 12,000 residents sharing a few hundred acres of former farmland. Moreover, five new office building projects that will add 10,000 jobs (and perhaps almost as many automobile trips) are under construction, and zoning allows for an additional 20 million square feet of commercial space. Incredibly, though, Metrorail does not go there, making road transit the only means of transportation (Lewis, 1999).

Clearly, mass transit would greatly alleviate the traffic congestion. During weekday rush hours and weekend shopping times, backups are horrendous. Recommendations include creating an elevated rail system looping around Tysons Corner, as well as a link between Tysons and the regional Metrorail network. But much more is needed. Tysons is not pedestrian-friendly, for there are few sidewalks or signalized crosswalks, which are critical for safely traversing the extraordinarily wide, traffic-choked roads, making walking around Tysons virtually impossible.

Even if traffic congestion could be reduced and pedestrian traffic encouraged, the aesthetic and visual deficiencies, the visual chaos and formlessness would still remain. In the interest of bringing a bit of visual order to Tysons Corner, a county task force developed a plan a few years ago to address streetscapes, pedestrian walkways, site planning of buildings, and open space. Still, Tysons has no civic focus, or heart, and so planners propose a "town center" as a way to "give Tysons more soul." Such an undertaking is still several years away, however. In the meantime, Tysons continues to be emblematic of how poorly we have planned, zoned, and developed much of the landscape girdling our cities since the end of World War II (Lewis, 1999).

References

Berman, D. 1997. Shopping on the edge. *Canadian Business*, (October 31): 72–79.

Garreau, J. 1991. *Edge city*. New York: Doubleday.

Lewis, R. K. 1999. Saving Tyson's Corner: Plans, but little progress. *Washington Post*, (March 20): G3.

Pasternak, J. 1998. "Edge City" is attempting to build a center. *Los Angeles Times*, (January 1): 5.

◉ ◉ ◉

Questions

1. What three waves of outward movement from central cities in the United States marked the second half of the twentieth century?

2. In what ways do today's edge cities differ from the old "downtown" cities of a century ago?

3. Why do some critics claim that edge cities are not socially healthy places to live? Do you agree? Why, or why not?

"The American Paradox: Spiritual Hunger in an Age of Plenty

DAVID G. MYERS

Has life in the United States improved over the course of recent decades? According to David Myers, we live in the best of times because there has never been more material affluence. Yet we also live in the worst of times because many indicators of social health—including the rates of divorce, teen suicide, and violent crime—rose dramatically after 1960.

. . .

It was the best of times, it was the worst of times, it was the age of wisdom, it was the age of foolishness, it was the epoch of belief, it was the epoch of incredulity, it was the season of Light, it was the season of Darkness, it was the spring of hope, it was the winter of despair, we had everything before us, we had nothing before us, we were all going direct to Heaven, we were all going direct the other way.

—CHARLES DICKENS, *A Tale of Two Cities*

We Americans embody a paradox. We read and hear it all around us. There are those who rightly claim, "We've never had it so good. Things

Reprinted from *The American Paradox: Spiritual Hunger in an Age of Plenty* (2001), Yale University Press.

are going *great* in this country!" And they are right. But then there are those who wring their hands and just as rightly worry that our civilization could collapse on its decaying moral infrastructure. The best of times, the worst of times. Wisdom, foolishness. Light, darkness. Hope, despair. Dickens' words fit.

What are we to make of this seeming paradox? How can this be both the best and worst of times? And where do we go from here?

It is the Best of Times

We are fortunate to be living when we do. Moments ago, I made a cup of tea in a microwave oven, sat down in a comfortable ergonomic office chair in my climate-controlled office, turned on my personal computer, and answered electronic mail from friends in Hong Kong and Scotland. Planning for tomorrow's trip, I check the Seattle weather forecast via the Web, then leap to a University of California survey archive to glean information for this [reading]. Gazing through my double-glazed window, I look across a landscaped courtyard to a state-of-the-art library that feeds to my desktop screen information hidden among millions of published articles. What a different world from the one I was born into barely half a century ago—a world without broadcast television, fax machines, computers, jets, or cell phones. . . .

Ethnic strife and hate crimes still haunt humanity, but in our part of the world bigotry is more gauche and diversity more accepted than ever before. The environment is under assault, but we have awakened to the perils of deforestation, ozone depletion, and global warming and are taking steps to contain the damage. (We middle-aged adults drive cars that get twice the mileage and produce a twentieth the pollution of our first cars.) Our economy has produced a growing underclass. Yet our average disposable income in constant dollars is more than double that of the mid-1950s. This enables our having, among the other accouterments of our unprecedented national wealth, twice as many cars per person today as then and our eating out two and a half times as often.

830

More good news is bursting from all around:

- Although population has doubled since World War II, food production has tripled and food is cheaper than ever before.
- Welfare rolls are shrinking as joblessness reaches a quarter-century low.
- Inflation—the "cruelest tax"—is at a thirty-year low, interest rates have moderated, the dollar rides strong, and the stock market has touched undreamed-of heights.
- The prices of cars, air travel, gasoline, and hamburgers are at record real-dollar lows. The half gallon of milk that cost the average American thirty-nine minutes of work in 1919 now requires only seven minutes.
- The national budget, faster than anyone dared expect, has a substantial *surplus*.
- Since the early 1990s, the AIDS death rate has plummeted.
- Over the past half century, performance on intelligence tests has been rising, and race and class differences have lessened somewhat.
- Heavy drinking rates, hard liquor consumption, and drunken driving fatalities are declining.
- New drugs are shrinking our tumors and enlarging our sexual potency.

And would any of us really wish to have braved the family life of a century ago? Without indoor plumbing? With less electricity generated each year than we now consume in a day? When trivial infections might take a life and when people feared the two leading causes of death—tuberculosis and pneumonia? (From 1900 to the present, life expectancy has risen from forty-seven to seventy-six years.)

In 1999, Joyce and Paul Bowler—a couple with a keen interest in past ways of life—were selected from among 450 applicants to Britain's Channel 4 network to spend three months with four of their children living the middle-class life of 1900 (which at the time must have seemed like a cuppa tea compared to working-class life). After just a week of rising at 5:30 each morning, preparing food like the Victorians, wearing corsets, shampooing with a mixture of egg, lemon, borax, and camphor, and playing parlor games by gaslight at night, they were "close to calling it quits." They endured. But lacking a surrounding community of other "Victorian" families, the realities of life in the early 1900s lacked the romantic appeal of *Upstairs Downstairs*.

In *The Way We Never Were: American Families and the Nostalgia Trap,* Stephanie Coontz reminds us of the way families *really* were.

Children were exploited. In Pennsylvania mines at the turn of the twentieth century, 120,000 children were at work, most of whom started laboring by age eleven. Children were one-fourth of the workers in southern textile mills. Seven-year-olds sometimes worked twelve-hour shifts before falling asleep on the job and being carried to bed unwashed.

Families were often broken—by death. In colonial times, mortality reduced the average length of marriage to a dozen years. Four in ten children lost a parent by age twenty-one. As late as 1940, one in ten children did not live with either parent, more than double today's one in twenty-five. In 1850, when only 2 percent of the population lived past sixty-five and many people were migrating, few children had ties with their grandparents. Today, "for the first time in history," notes sociologist Arlene Skolnick, "the average couple has more parents living than it has children. It is also the first era when most of the parent–child relationship takes place after the child becomes an adult." Before 1900, only four in ten women married, raised children, and enjoyed the empty nest with their spouse—because most women either died before marriage, never married, died before children were born or grown, or were widowed before age fifty. And consider the poems unwritten, the music never composed, the philosophy never completed, because Keats died at twenty-five, Mozart at thirty-five, Pascal at thirty-nine.

The social safety net had gaping holes. At the beginning of the twentieth century, we had no social security system. Divorced fathers were not obligated to pay child support. One in five children lived in orphanages, often because their impoverished parents could not support them.

Most people had limited educational opportunities. In the bad old days of a century ago, only half of five- to nineteen-year-olds were in school (compared with more than 90 percent today). Only 3.5 percent of eighteen-year-olds were graduating from high school. Today, eight in ten adults have at least a high school education.

Women had restricted opportunities. A half century ago, only one in five Americans approved "of a married woman earning money in business or industry if she has a husband capable of supporting her." Today, 80 percent approve. Thus, six in ten married women are now in the paid workforce—up from four in ten a half century ago and one in seven a century ago. With greater economic independence, today's women are more likely to marry for love and less likely to endure abuse out of economic need. America's married women, whether employed or not, still devote twice as many hours to household tasks as do their husbands. But men's participation has doubled since 1965, putting them more often in front of the stove, behind the vacuum cleaner, and over the diaper-changing table. Today's men and women are more likely to share opportunities, responsibilities, and power.

Minorities were shunned. Within the memory of many living individuals, some public accommodations offered "colored" and "white" toilets, those with disabilities were ignored, and gays and lesbians hid from public loathing. If we have not yet achieved "the Great Society," we have improved upon yesterday's unjust society.

Ergo, however great our present problems, the past is no golden age to which we would willingly return if only we could. Yesterday was not the best of times, *today* is the best of times. Seen in the rose-tinted rearview mirror, yesterday may *seem* like a golden age. But even the wholesome 1950s was the decade of McCarthyism, segregation, the Korean War, and air-raid drills and bomb shelters. Golden ages do happen, notes political scientist John Mueller. "But we are never actually *in* them," because "no matter how much better the present gets, the past gets better faster in reflection."

In his own golden age of life, my optimistic friend Sir John Templeton is one who does see the present as the best of times. In *Is Progress Speeding Up?* he concludes that things are not only getting better, they are getting better faster than ever, making this "a wonderful time to be alive!"

How true. Yet there is more to the story.

◉ It is the Worst of Times

We are better paid, better fed, better housed, better educated, and healthier than ever before, and with more human rights, faster communication, and more convenient transportation than we have ever known. Ironically, however, for thirty-plus years—from 1960 until the early 1990s—America slid into a deepening social recession that dwarfed the comparatively milder and briefer economic recessions that often dominated our news and politics. Had you fallen asleep in 1960 and awakened in the 1990s, would you—overwhelmed by all the good tidings—feel pleased at the cultural shift? Here are some other facts that would greet you. Since 1960, as we will see,

- The divorce rate has doubled.
- The teen suicide rate has tripled.
- The recorded violent crime rate has quadrupled.
- The prison population has quintupled.
- The percentage of babies born to unmarried parents has (excuse the pun) sextupled.
- Cohabitation (a predictor of future divorce) has increased sevenfold.
- Depression has soared—to ten times the pre-World War II level, by one estimate.

The National Commission on Civic Renewal combined social trends such as these in creating its 1998 "Index of National Civic Health"—which has plunged southward since 1960. Bertrand Russell once said that the mark of a civilized human is the capacity to read a

834

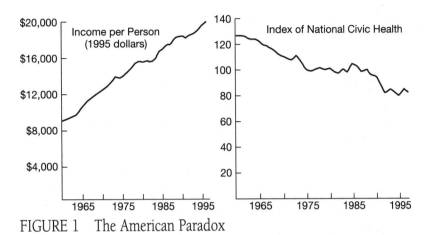

FIGURE 1   The American Paradox

column of numbers and weep. Can we weep for all the crushed lives behind these numbers? It is hard to argue with Al Gore: "The accumulation of material goods is at an all-time high, but so is the number of people who feel an emptiness in their lives."

At the epicenter of America's social recession are children and youth. Writing with Elizabeth Gilman, Yale psychologist Edward Zigler, co-founder of Head Start, reported a consensus among researchers: "In the past thirty years of monitoring the indicators of child well-being, never have the indicators looked so negative." Across America, children are having children and men are fathering children with little commitment to mother or child. In 1960 just over one in ten children did not live with two parents. Today, a third do not. In a recent survey, American Psychological Association members rated "the decline of the nuclear family" as today's number-one threat to mental health. Urie Bronfenbrenner, a respected developmental psychologist, describes the trends starkly: "The present state of children and families in the United States represents the greatest domestic problem our nation has faced since the founding of the Republic. It is sapping our very roots." Speaking to the National Press Club in late 1998, American Psychological Association president Martin Seligman was struck by a "serious paradox": "Every statistic we have on the 'objective' well-being of young Americans is going north. And every statistic we have on their demoralization, on depression, is going in the other direction."

Facing this cultural erosion, can we—without yearning for an unreal past or squashing basic liberties—expose the corrosive social forces at work and renew our social fabric? And what are the corrosive forces? How is it that things could have gone so well materially and so poorly socially? In other ways, too, these are hardly the best of times, notes Cornell economist Robert Frank in *Luxury Fever*. Americans are spending more hours at work, fewer hours sleeping, and fewer hours with friends and family. "Traffic has grown considerably more congested; savings rates have fallen precipitously; personal bankruptcy filings are at an all-time high; and there is at least a widespread perception that employment security has fallen sharply."

Radical Individualism

Part of the explanation lies in the radical individualism familiar to us in contemporary America's pop psychology and libertarian values. Do your own thing. Seek your own bliss. Challenge authority. If it feels good, do it. Shun conformity. Don't force your values on others. Assert your personal rights (to own guns, sell pornography, do business free of regulations). Protect your privacy. Cut taxes and raise executive pay (personal income takes priority over the common good). To love others, first love yourself. Listen to your own heart. Prefer solo spirituality to communal religion. Be self-sufficient. Expect others likewise to believe in themselves and to make it on their own. Such sentiments define the heart of economic and social individualism, which finds its peak expression in modern America.

The celebration and defense of personal liberty lies at the heart of the old American dream. It drives our free market economy and underlies our respect for the rights of all. In democratic countries that guarantee what Americans consider basic freedoms, people live more happily than in those that don't. Migration patterns testify to this reality. Yet for today's radical individualism, we pay a price:

836

a social recession that imperils children, corrodes civility, and diminishes happiness. When individualism is taken to an extreme, individuals become its ironic casualties.

To cope with the casualties at the base of the social cliffs, we can expand our social ambulance services. Or we can . . . build guardrails at the top. We can dream a new American dream—one that renews our social ecology with values and policies that balance "me thinking" with "we thinking."

What Is the New American Dream?

To counter radical individualism and cultural corrosion, a new, inclusive social renewal movement is emerging: one that affirms liberals' indictment of the demoralizing effects of poverty and conservatives' indictment of toxic media models; one that welcomes liberals' support for family-friendly workplaces and conservatives' support for committed relationships; one that agrees with liberals' advocacy for children in all sorts of families and conservatives' support for marriage and coparenting. Viewing the contest between liberal and conservative ideas, we can respond like the Dodo in *Alice's Adventures in Wonderland*: "*Everyone* has won and *all* must have prizes!"

Without suppressing our differences do we not—whether self-described liberals or conservatives—share a vision of a better world? Is it not one that rewards initiative but restrains exploitative greed? that balances individual rights with communal well-being? that respects diversity while embracing unifying ideals? that is tolerant of other cultures without being indifferent to moral issues? that protects and heals our degrading physical and social environments? In our utopian social world, adults and children will together enjoy their routines and traditions. They will have close relationships with extended family and with supportive neighbors. Children will live without fear for their safety or the breakup of their families. Fathers and mothers will jointly nurture their children; to say "He fathered the child" will parallel the meaning of "She mothered the child." Free yet responsible media will entertain us with stories and images that exemplify heroism, compassion, and committed love. Reasonable and rooted moral judgments will motivate compassionate acts and enable noble and satisfying lives.

Mapping the Quest

This dreamed-of world is, as yet, far from our real world. Still facing a large gap between the ideal and real, the advent of the new millennium is a fitting time to confront the reality of America's post-1960 social recession, to identify its roots, and to celebrate the quest for a healthier and happier American culture.

☻ ☻ ☻

Critical-Thinking Questions

1. In what sense are we in the United States today living in "the best of times"? In what ways has life been getting worse?

2. What role does "radical individualism" play in these trends?

3. What do you think we might do to improve the social health of the United States? Why?

Retelling Selves Through Visual Narratives: The Reciprocity of Culture and Identity[1]

TRACY XAVIA KARNER, UNIVERSITY OF HOUSTON

> *If I attempt to watch a movie about Vietnam, I search for the identity, for me in the movie and none of them tell [my] story (Dan).*

· · ·

Exploring narratives of visual images provides an intriguing view for the social scientist. Paying attention to the referencing of images and media representations as a means of communicating an expression of one's identity is illuminative. This personal internalization and articulation of cultural products provides a window from which to study the reciprocity of culture and identity. Though sociology has a long, but forgotten, history of interest in the visual (Ball and Smith 1992), most cultural analysis has been found in other disciplines until recently. The emerging and active field of visual sociology, though still in the process of defining its purview, holds two core tenets: "reference to the camera and its uses; and, a discussion of the analytic purpose of the user" (Grady 1996:11). This project both holds to these premises and expands them, by focusing on the interpretation of cinemat-

Reprinted from *Communication and Cognition* (1998).

ic Hollywood images of Vietnam veterans by those they portray. Thus, the reference to the camera is integral to film and television representations. Furthermore, the analytic purpose of the user of that camera and its product is interpreted in the veterans' narratives. Indeed, the veterans themselves become a "user" of the cultural image with their own analytic purposes and agendas.

Analyzing visual images in this way is an enlarged form of visual sociology. Unlike the scholars who take photographs or videos (collecting the data) or analyze preexisting images (interpreting the data), my interest is in how individuals understand and utilize media productions in explaining and understanding their own lives. This mediation of the visual by the individual also has consequences for their behavior as well. The veterans often mentioned the glamorization they saw during their childhoods' of World War II in the news reels, and this picture of war was what they expected to find in Vietnam. Thus, the images influenced the veterans' decisions to join, and for some, to volunteer for combat which created unexpected, and often overwhelming, consequences for their lives. These veteran narratives provide a startling example of the importance of the visual in individual lives.

❂ The Search for a Meaningful Narrative

As life stories are created within, and dependent upon, broader social narratives, it is important to explore representations of the Vietnam experience. The Vietnam war, like any other event, is subject to the narrative processes of meaning construction, deconstruction, and reconstruction. Some have contended that the war in Vietnam, in American society, has been subject to a disproportionate amount of rewritings and then even, rewritings of the rewritings (Robinson 1992: 60). This continual revision of an era in our nation's history and a stultifying portion of many individuals' recollections has certainly been a prominent theme in American culture for the last fifteen

840

years. Journalists, writers, and historians place Vietnam in a unique position in American history, suggesting that its full impact on the American consciousness has yet to be appraised (Krasteva 1992: 165). "What made Vietnam different from other wars also made it more difficult . . . to fit into a pre-constructed social or psychological niche—there was nothing in the American myth of wars and heroes that could encompass the experience that was `the 'Nam'" (Shell 1989: 61). Thus the need to rewrite and rework Vietnam for a cohesive, sense-making story continues. Wagner-Pacifici and Schwartz (1991: 384) argue that when experiences clash with prior social assumptions "individual and institutional discourses must realign their terms or remain incapable of making that war understandable." However, in spite of the variety of cultural and social retellings of Vietnam, the war in Southeast Asia still remains beyond a satisfying understanding for many Americans.

In the pages that follow, I outline the cultural resources, specifically the media images that were meaningful in the narratives of Vietnam veterans who had been diagnosed with Post Traumatic Stress Disorder (PTSD). In addition, I explore the relationship of these images to Vietnam veterans' self-identity. As part of their treatment for PTSD, these men were called upon to retell their lives in the process of confronting and tracing the variety of social pressures, myths, and images that helped to shape their sense of self.

The data that form the basis of this study are drawn from intensive interviews with Vietnam combat veterans and participant observation on a PTSD unit[2] of a VA Hospital (see Karner 1994). In the Midwest institutional setting, one half of the inpatient population—15 veterans— were interviewed one to four times each, and were observed in a variety of hospital settings. In addition, I interviewed hospital staff, sat in on staff meetings, and had access to autobiographies written by the veterans as they entered the hospital. During the study, all the patients were Vietnam veterans and one was also a Gulf War veteran. All but one of the men interviewed were white, one was African American. The veterans ranged in age from 38 to 47 years and all were from Midwestern states. Only one veteran had been drafted—the majority had enlisted and many had volunteered specifically for combat duty.

841

The interviews focused on life history narratives and not on visual images of Vietnam veterans available in the society. Rather, the veterans would use examples from television and film to clarify and illustrate different aspects of their experiences. Other times they would draw on these Hollywood-produced cultural images to explain non-veteran understandings and subsequent treatment of the veterans. All these comments were volunteered in the course of talking about their lives. Thus, for the purposes of this paper, I will be using the veterans' narratives as interpretive data for analyzing the role of moving images in identity formation and expression.

❂ Cultural Narratives of Vietnam

Cultural dramatizations of Vietnam abound in a variety of creative forms. Scholars, journalists, fiction writers, participants, and observers have written much on the American involvement in Vietnam. It has been historically chronicled as a military story, most notably by Karnow (1983); explored as a significant socio-political influence by Hodgson (1976); identified as the basis of the student movements, both nationally by Gitlin (1987) and internationally by Fraser (1988); and has been the subject of many literary and cinematographic works. Numerous individuals have written their own autobiographical portrait of the war (see Kovic 1976; Mason 1981; and O'Brien 1973). Others have collected the oral histories of those who went to Vietnam (Walker 1985; Pratt 1984; Marshall 1987; Hansen et al. 1992). However, these compilations focus mainly on the Vietnam war experiences with little emphasis on life events before or after combat.

Krasteva asserts that these authors are demonstrating and exploring their own sense of ambiguity and uncertainty in writing about Vietnam.

> In creating and educating himself in the text, the author creates and educates his reader. Every novel about Vietnam is a book within a book, about the war, about the protagonist's

journey to himself and through national history, and finally about the writing of the novel itself" (1992: 166).

Thus Krasteva points to the process whereby the self is illuminated through interaction with available cultural forms and "tries on" social ideals. This measuring of self among narrative possibilities, each with an attendant reward or stigma, is at the crux of identity creation.

Lomperis (1987: 153) contends "that the essential truth of the Vietnam war can be understood" within the fiction it has inspired. Finding personal narratives unable to convey the complexity of the war, he looks to the totalizing views that perhaps are only available within the imagination, literary or otherwise. Langer (1991: 204) concurs, "art may in fact achieve what life cannot"—a coherent, meaningful narrative. Such popular culture representations can be seen as part of the "ongoing dialogue between members of that culture, shaping and being shaped by their individual anxieties and fears" (Tal 1989: 161). Thus, the cultural search for an all-encompassing, meaning creating narrative—a kind of sacred canopy, in Peter Berger's terms—may be destined to fail and, ironically, to create more confusion than it alleviates.

❧ Visual and Experiential Narratives of Vietnam Veterans

During the war, images of the soldiers in Vietnam permeated the culture, predominantly through the news media. "One-day relay of film and other forms of rapid dissemination gave much of what Americans watched on the evening news an immediacy and intensity that was new and that forever shaped America's experience of warfare" (Anderegg 1991: 2). The images of Vietnam that occupied the evening news were viewed in a context of journalistic "objectivity," which denied any of the utilized techniques of image construction: camera angles, framing, cutting, decontextualizing, or editorializing. The daily "living room war" was seen as an "unmediated" picture of reality and an impartial "window on the world" (Berg 1990: 44-5).

One veteran interviewed, Tommy[3], traced the origin of society's dislike of Vietnam veterans to the nightly news casts.

> Well, I think the news media hurt us. If you want me to be real honest. . . . 'Cause it was a five-six o'clock day war—everyday. And that was wrong. They shouldn't a been able to show the stuff they did. . . . No it shouldn't a been a secret, but it wasn't, it shouldn't have been showed the way it was. You know, they shouldn't a showed all the bullshit they did. All the dying and death because the people got used to it and people got tired of it. They didn't really get used to it, they got tired of seeing that shit on the news every night. . . . No, I didn't want them to see the stuff. If it was up to me I don't think they couldn't deal with it in the first place. [To] see somebody die on TV, it's like a goddamned movie. You get tired of the same ring-arounds and lot of things. You can't handle it.

Tommy saw the media images, presented without adequate combat contextualization, as inaccurate and dishonest, providing society with a distorted reality that they could not "handle." In part, Tommy was protective, believing that it was his place as a soldier to "handle" the atrocities of war whereas the average citizen should not have been expected to comprehend such matters. He continued.

> That was our job. That was our job [to handle it]. . . . 'Cause they don't know what the hell's going down. They aren't out there everyday—living, dying, bleeding to death. They don't really understand. You can't comprehend for it unless you're there. What it's like. Walking for days without water. Drinking out of goddamned mud holes, your lips busted open, your clothes falling off you because they're so god-damned rotten. Stuff like that. People don't understand that. Not in this [American] society.

More visual representations were made of the Vietnam War than any other war in American history (Anderegg 1991: 2-3). However, the *Green Berets* (1968) was the only dramatic film about the conflict

844

made during the war. The rest were produced after the war had ended. Thus, there were none of the propaganda films[4] that had been prevalent during earlier wars so there were virtually no promilitary cultural representations and certainly no heroic images. The majority of information about, and perceptions of, the war and the individuals fighting were available only through the television news. With this monopoly on information also came an unparalleled power— "the power to decide what the war means" (Delli Carpini 1990: 125). Vietnam was television's first war and the reporters and cameramen set about extending their technology into the battlefield. As early as 1965, CBS and NBC began increasing their Saigon bureaus and by 1967, the three networks together were spending around $5 million to cover the war. Vietnam meant ratings and the networks competed for the best footage. Producers preferred to air anonymous and "timeless" combat stories of "recent fighting" instead of film of a specific battle; film of Americans rather than South Vietnamese; and actions where the American forces were successful (Hodgson 1976: 149-50). This practice allowed the Americans at home to watch firefights, napalm bombings, and search and destroy missions in sound byte format every evening.

After the war ended and all the troops returned stateside, Vietnam faded from the news and the media discussion of the war diminished. For a few years, Vietnam and its veterans were symbolically erased by this nonrepresentation. Losing or withdrawing from a military intervention was a new experience for the United States; there were no precedents to follow. There were no heroic homecomings[5] and social silence prevailed. In 1975 each of the television networks attempted a summarizing documentary of the war, but they were poorly received. While the anguish of Vietnam remained too sensitive a topic, images of veterans eventually began showing up on television sitcoms. In the early 1970s, television portrayed the veteran as a "strung-out, criminal psychotic who could go off at the sound of a backfire" (Berg 1990: 45). Veterans were shown as a threat to civilized law and order, acting out the criminality and brutality that had been perceived as normal in combat.

These social portraits furnished the veterans with concrete representations of who they were perceived to be and also dramatized the role society had designated for them. Thus cultural narratives of television, films, and books communicate the nature of social relations and the appropriate roles each is supposed to play. In analyzing such imagery, information that was transmitted directly was often less significant than the "messages that may be implicit in the ways in which social life is arranged, in rituals, and in the choice of words in discourse" (Wuthnow 1987: 15). When Vietnam veterans looked into the social mirror for their image, they saw madmen, villains, and losers. Kurt spoke with aggravation about an episode of Hunter, a television police drama, where the rapist and murderer was a Vietnam veteran.

> Don't condemn us. Don't put out the bullshit movies of the killer.
> . . . Three months ago that TV show, Hunter—that police story.
> . . . I was watching it [and] I put a stapler through my TV. . . .
> This guy was killing women, then raping them. Alright. So he's
> done three. Now the forth one, Hunter was called in before they
> took the body away. And she was laying on the bed, and you
> could see part of her head. And her hand would stick out like this,
> clenched. So Hunter noticed something in her hand, so he
> unclenches the hand. What does he come up with was a Vietnam
> campaign ribbon. So in other words this girl ripped [it] off a
> Vietnam vet. . . . The news media's the same way. They're the ones
> that hurt us.

Kurt experienced the media representations as another victimization—as society "downgrading us again."

It wasn't until the late 1970s that Hollywood films began to focus on the Vietnam war directly. Over the years, several cinematic genres have been identified. The early Vietnam films glorified American military power and righteousness (*The Quiet Americans* in 1957 and *Green Berets* in 1968). The movies of the 1970s were for the most part antiwar, typified in *Coming Home* (1978) and *The Deer Hunter* (1978) representing Vietnam as a personal tragedy. *First Blood* (1982) and *Missing in Action* (1984) began the Stallone/Norris genre films of the early 1980s that attempted to refight the war and refigure the warrior as hero. Later movies sought to bring the veterans home psychologically with *Jackknife* (1988) and *In Country* (1989). By the early 1990s, films like *Article 49* and *Jacobs' Ladder* started to dramatize the veterans' problematic relationship with the Veteran's Administration.

Within each of the movies about Vietnam was an attempt to understand the whole of the national and personal experience of the war. They were narrative fictions that attempted to encompass a historical event and rewrite it with symbols and mythic imagery. "Film has established itself as a major medium by which our culture reflects and shapes its reality with a speed and a scope previously unimagined or experienced" (Taylor 1990: 186). In particular, Vietnam films "strive to find something redeeming to say about this war," echoing the public's and the veterans' interest in arriving at some rationale for what occurred (Dittmar and Michaud 1990: 7). Like other veterans, Dan assessed the validity of these cultural representations of the Vietnam experience in terms of the extent to which they portrayed his own story and experience.

> If I attempt to watch a movie about Vietnam, I search for the identity, for me in the movie and none of them tell the story.
> . . . I watched quite a few. The closest one, and really wasn't that close, was *Platoon* for me. But even then, the main thing about it was the kid saying, "Grandma, I think I'm here to stay."

Although Dan said he had difficulty watching other kinds of media violence, he described an almost compulsive desire to watch movies about Vietnam in their entirety.

Similarly David watched "battle flicks" and said that he had seen all those set in Vietnam. Unlike Dan, David reported no emotional problems in viewing them. He watched, he said, "just to see how much of it relates to me. . . . Some do, most of them don't. . . . I watched 'cause I was there. Now I could tell the differences from the movie or the real thing. . . . [It's about] 70/30—70 [percent] off, 30 [percent] on."

The primacy of personal experience seems to be prized among those veterans who do watch Vietnam films. Larry recalled the first time he had seen John Wayne in the *Green Berets*. "I just laughed at it, wasn't nothing whatsoever realistic about it," Larry chortled, "you got to stay real far apart in the daytime, you don't stay close to each other, you got to take your time through the jungles, you don't run through them." Later, Larry was able to find a film that he could identify with, "There's one . . . it really what I done most. . . . It's been out a couple, three years, Sergeant Charlie something.[6] . . It was about a [squad] that was always on patrol and what they encountered, walking through the villages and stuff. It's more what I was exposed to." Larry continued to explain that he no longer really wanted to watch these movies, because "quite often I see it at night in my sleep."

In contrast, Mangum found Vietnam films frustrating. The absence of a portrayal of his job on a riverboat, in Mangum's mind, rendered his tour invisible.

> I look at these movies they make. They show the Marines. They show the Air Force. They show the Army. Only part of the Navy they show is aircraft carriers that the aircraft on, they have never yet showed us going up and down the rivers.
> . . . And I tell my son, *I guess I didn't do anything over there* (emphasis added).

Mangum could not find himself in the social mirror and therefore could not find any validation for his experience. His aggravation was so intense that he was unable to watch more than brief "sketches" of the films. He said, "I can watch it until they start the killing, then I'm through with it." Before Vietnam, Mangum liked westerns and horror shows, but after combat he could no longer handle the violence of these genres either.

Mangum was an exception among the veterans in this study. Some, like Ramsey and Chris, claimed not to have seen any films, whereas all the other veterans had and said they did identify with some aspects of certain films. Mangum's experience, alone, was missing within the cultural resources available. Perhaps his representa-

848

tional absence was more symbolically accurate as most films try to create some sense of order by way of a linear narrative that imposes a "truth" about the war or an implied image of the "reality" of Vietnam. As a society, we expect Vietnam films not only to show us "what it was like" but also to address what Americans were fighting for and what went wrong (Taylor 1990: 204). Without such a representation of Mangum's riverboat experience, he was afforded no cinematic resources to answer those questions for himself.

John differed greatly from Mangum in his viewing habits, though both had hoped to find the same sense making social answers. John considered that forcing himself to sit through Vietnam images film after film, he was doing his own version of psychotherapy. "I guess by bringing it up and bringing it out," John explained, "I know in my own mind I have to sit and watch this stuff to where I can come to grips with it." John enumerated an extensive videotape collection that he owned. He had found viewing them emotionally difficult, but he would force himself to watch and re-watch different tapes and scenes. "I sit crying," John admitted, "I get them on video, that way I can shut off, turn off what I don't want to see, if I want to see how it happened, if I want to see something again, to try and figure out their line of thinking." John utilized the media representations to help reconcile himself with what he had done and seen and hoped to reframe as heroic. He liked the movies that came closest to his experience—*Full Metal Jacket, Platoon, and Fourth of July.*

Besides the films, John had religiously watched the CBS television series, *Tour of Duty* (1987-90), which valorized and privileged the experience of the individual soldiers in Vietnam while remaining apolitical and staying away from some of the larger issues of why Americans were there and what the objectives had been. Using traditional themes and narratives drawn mainly from the genre of Westerns, the show dramatized the "interpersonal struggle between men of mixed class and race surviving the threat of a harsh, primal environment and savage native aggressors through the exercise of individual initiative, heroism, brotherhood, and dedication to a just cause" (Miller 1991: 170). In some ways the series was able to do what John had wished he had been able to do—it reconstructed the

soldier as heroic within conventional American mythology and satis-
factorily resolved all the difficulties and conflicts that faced him in
Vietnam through military patriarchy (Anderegg 1991: 10). Television
series format usually consists of an episodic closure of a specific
weekly theme, a pattern that enhanced the resolution process. John
watched the show searching for his own closure and understanding.

> That show probably helped me more than, I think it ran a
> year and a half maybe two years that I watched it, probably
> helped me more than all the counseling I think could have
> came to . . . because for one thing it was so real. You know,
> you could relate to it—it was what they was going through
> on this TV series. My wife would look at me and say, "stuff
> like that really happen over there?" and I'd say, "yeah, I've
> been in circumstances just like it." And she'd say, "well God,
> no wonder your mind's so screwed up John, I don't know
> how you handled it." Sit here and get drunk that's how I han-
> dled it, but it's, I was really taken back when I'd found out
> that they'd cancelled it, 'cause I mean, how can I put this,
> women have their soap operas and everything that they, well
> *Tour of Duty* was mine. . . . It was real, it was, I mean it was-
> n't real, it was a TV show, but capturing the veterans' atten-
> tion as to actual sequences in combat, in the way that they
> handled the stress situations and everything at the time, it
> was just like a chapter out of my life, seen it. . . . Like I could
> see what they was gonna do on TV, and I be thinking no man
> I tried that—that don't work, do something else and they'd
> always get it worked out. It was just, well it's like I could
> have wrote the program and directed it. . . . Yeah I'd lived it,
> it wasn't a TV show, I'd lived it.

Most of what Americans currently know about the Vietnam War has
come from the movies and television representations of the conflict
(Taylor 1990: 186). The majority of these veterans were familiar with
the media stereotypes and were influenced by them even if they had-
n't viewed them directly. These images stand as dramatizations of the
social order—specifying appropriate roles for Vietnam veterans. And

the veteran was left with his own boyhood ideals, his own recollections of combat, and his own experience of judgment and alienation. From the different notions, he needed to construct some sense or meaning for himself. Most of the social resources granted him were guilt laden, shameful, and inadequate to his needs. Thus many men had fallen into a confused silence.

These veterans felt rejected by society and, in turn, rejected society. Media images had an impact on the nonveteran public as well as on the veterans. In the face of such powerful and pervasive denunciations, veterans' strivings for acceptance were eventually abandoned and followed by resignation to defeat and withdrawal from almost all social interactions. For Marty, his estrangement was at the most basic level of mere communication.

> I try to relate to people and I make concerted efforts to try to put my war experience away and to try to learn about other people. And I try to get involved with what they're involved with and become . . . like normal. But I always find myself, that . . . it's almost seems superficial like your life is like, they don't know what to do and I don't know how to, how to blend with these folks. And that all comes from me. It's not their fault.

These Vietnam veterans all described a sense of not fitting into society anymore. Bill remembered being treated "strange" by people in his community. "[They] would more or less turn their back on me or act like I wasn't even there. They never said hello, welcome home, good to see you made [it], good job, nothing." Larry said that "telling somebody that you were a Vietnam veteran was like telling you had a disease or something." Mangum said that disclosing his Vietnam veteran status caused people to "just kind of ease off from you." In addition to the social stigma, many believed that their combat experience had changed them so deeply that they could never fully "come home." Their "combat self" predominated and they could no longer adopt a innocent approach to life. Emotionally, they felt tainted by their participation and needed to maintain a more "authentic" lifestyle than our consumer culture advocates. "I don't live for

851

society," Bill acknowledged, "I live for myself." Whatever their particular view of displacement, it was strong enough to sustain their sense of difference and prevent an emotional closure to their tours of duty.

◉ Retelling Selves Through Culture— Retelling Culture Through Self Narratives

Identity formation can be conceived of as a "dialectic between internal identification and external ascription" and thus contingent on the social field of meaning within which it is fashioned (Nagel 1994: 10). Broad cultural understandings of what it means to be a veteran or to have participated in a war provide the ascriptive arena for the individual internalizing such roles. "Stories of war and politics structure individual and collective experiences in ways that set the horizon for human expectations" (Elshtain 1987: 48). Such stories of social meanings are dynamic, emergent constructs derived from communicative human interaction. Social actors draw from this acknowledged repertoire of cultural symbols and shared knowledge when engaging others in an exchange of communication and acquiring identities. Each moment of such an exchange contains the existing social meanings and attendant identities that are being reinvigorated, reexamined, elaborated, and/or transformed with each usage. Thus meaning, by the very nature of its construction, is comprised of fragments of understanding held only briefly by the participants until they evolve to another interpretive segment.

My analysis has been both sociological and cultural. The exploration of the semiotic webs of significance within which individuals create, recreate, and act out their lives provides the core of this text. The available social and cultural resources internalized to construct selves and expressed in narrative form illuminate the interplay between visual and experiential retellings. The desire for coherence and making sense of experience can be traced within the foundation of all identity constructs as meaning is the goal of narrative formations. Indeed, such meaning structures and expressions of moral order may be seen as more pronounced within the chaotic ambiguity of Vietnam. The contradictions of combat facilitate a more anomic field within which the individual must attempt to recreate new structures of meaning as the traditional myths and images become inadequate. An awareness of the dynamics of these social processes can broaden our understanding of Vietnam and its veterans, as well as the impact of culture on self and self on culture.

Notes

[1]The author gratefully acknowledges the insightful comments of Norman Yetman, Carol Warren, and Joane Nagel on earlier drafts of this work. Additionally, Debra McAferty provided much appreciated word processing support.

[2]Using the midwestern Veteran's Administration Hospital unit as the primary research setting does have some drawbacks. The unit had never had a woman veteran apply for treatment, and the inpatient population was mostly white. Thus, I found myself approaching the common criticism of studying mainly white males. With this in mind, I have tried to avoid typifications about white men in general as well as generalizing from these respondents in any absolute manner. Rather, I utilize their narratives to illuminate themes and conceptual approaches to the Vietnam war.

Situating my research within a therapeutic community raised several additional issues. The difference between the veterans with a PTSD diagnosis included in this study from other Vietnam combat veterans can only be speculated upon and is well beyond the scope of this project because there was no comparative "control group" available. However, previous studies contended that PTSD symptoms are more prevalent among Vietnam veterans than veterans of other wars. Kulka et al. (1990) estimated that over one-third of all male Vietnam theater veterans will experience PTSD at least once in their lifetime. When the rate of PTSD is compared to combat exposure, Egendorf et al. (1981) reported that 33 percent of Vietnam veterans who saw heavy combat claim to have experienced PTSD symptoms. Even more startling was a random screening of nonpsychiatric Vietnam combat and POW

853

veterans while inpatients for medical treatment that revealed that 46 percent experienced PTSD (Blake et al. 1990). Such frequencies of PTSD symptoms among Vietnam combat veterans suggest that the experience of the men seeking treatment at the VA may not be unique among Vietnam veterans. However, the question of why the men included in this study have voluntarily sought treatment and others do not still remains.

For a further discussion, see also, Tracy X. Karner "Masculinity, Trauma, and Identity: Life Narratives of Vietnam Veterans with Post Traumatic Stress Disorder," an unpublished dissertation (University of Kansas, 1994).

[3]Veterans are referred to by pseudonyms of their own choosing and all identifying aspects of their narratives have been changed to protect their confidentiality. Also, the different forms of data utilized within this research study are denoted as follows: excerpts from my field notes are labeled (FN); veteran quotes from the interviews are cited with their pseudonym; material from their autobiographies is distinguished with an "a" after their pseudonym—for example, (Ramsey.a).

[4]The exception to this was The *Quiet Americans* made prior to the war intensifying in 1957.

[5]There was a belated national welcome home celebration in 1985 under the Reagan presidency. Berg and Rowe (1991: 10) mentioned this with cynicism, explaining the celebration as the mark of a new cultural use for Vietnam veterans. The stereotyped media image was refigured into a wise consultant with special knowledge, training and skills that could be applied to the urban social problems of our society. Thus Vietnam veterans began to be seen as good guys in crime fighting television series, such as Miami Vice and Magnum, P.I.

[6]I believe Larry was referring to 84 Charlie Mopic which is about a camera crew that follows a squad through the jungle on patrol.

References

Anderegg, Michael. 1991. "Hollywood and Vietnam: John Wayne and Jane Fonda as Discourse," pp. 15–32 in *Inventing Vietnam: The War in Film and Television*. Philadelphia: Temple University Press.

Ball, Michael S. and Gregory W.H. Smith. 1992. *Analyzing Visual Data*. Newbury Park, CA: Sage Publications.

Berg, Rick. 1990. "Losing Vietnam: Covering the War in an Age of Technology," pp. 41–68 in *From Hanoi to Hollywood: The Vietnam War in American Film* (Linda Dittmar and Gene Michaud, editors). New Brunswick and London: Rutgers University Press.

Delli Carpini, Michael X. 1990. "Vietnam and the Press" pp. 125–56 in *The Legacy: The Vietnam War in the American Imagination* (D. Michael Shafer, editor). Boston: Beacon Press.

Dittmar, Linda and Gene Michaud. 1990. "America's War Films: Marching Toward Denial," pp. 1–18 in *From Hanoi to Hollywood: The Vietnam War in American Film* (Linda Dittmar and Gene Michaud, editors). New Brunswick and London: Rutgers University Press.

Elshtain, Jean B. 1987. *Women and War*. New York: Basic Books.

Fraser Ronald, 1988. *1968: A Student Generation in Revolt*. New York: Pantheon Books.

Gitlin, Todd. 1987. *The Sixties: Years of Hope, Days of Rage*. New York: Bantam Books.

Grady, John. 1996. "The Scope of Visual Sociology," *Visual Sociology*, 11(2): 10–24.

Hansen, J.T., A. Susan Owen, and Michael P. Madden. 1992. *Parallels: The Soldiers' Knowledge and the Oral History of Contemporary Warefare*. New York: Aldine de Gruyter.

Hodgson, Godfrey. 1976. *America in Our Time*. New York: Vintage Books.

Karner, Tracy X. 1994. "Masculinity, Trauma, and Identity: Life Narratives of Vietnam Veterans with Post Traumatic Stress Disorder," an unpublished dissertation. University of Kansas.

Karnow, Stanley. 1983. *Vietnam: A History*. New York: Penguin Books.

Kovic, Ron. 1976. *Born on the Fourth of July*. New York: McGraw-Hill.

Krasteva, Yonka K. 1992. "Rediscovering America in Personal Narratives about Vietnam," *North Dakota Quarterly* 60(1): 161–73.

Langer, Lawrence L. 1991. *Holocaust Testimonies: The Ruins of Memory*. New Haven: Yale University Press.

Lomperis, Timothy. 1987. *Reading the Wind: The Literature of the Vietnam War*. Durham: Duke University Press.

Marshall, Katherine. 1987. *In the Combat Zone: An Oral History of American Women in Vietnam, 1966–1975*. New York: Little, Brown.

Mason, Robert. 1981. *Chickenhawk*. New York: Viking.

Miller, Daniel. 1991. "Primetime Television's Tour of Duty," pp. 166-89 in *Inventing Vietnam: The War in Film and Television*. Philadelphia: Temple University Press.

Nagel, Joane. 1994. *American Indian Ethnic Renewal*. Oxford: Oxford University Press.

O'Brien, Tim. 1973. *If I Die in a Combat Zone*. New York: Delacorte.

Pratt, James C. 1984. *Vietnam Voices*. New York: Viking.

Robinson, Lillian S. 1992. "The Vietnam Syndrome," *The Nation* 60–62.

Shell, Cheryl A. 1989. "Making Sense of Vietnam and Telling the Real Story: Military Women in the Combat Zone," *Vietnam Generation* 1(3-4): 59–67.

Tal, Kali. 1989. "On the Cover of the Rolling Stone: Toward a Theory of Cultural Therapy," *Vietnam Generation* 1(1): 157–64.

Taylor, Bruce. 1990. "The Vietnam War Movie" pp. 186–206 in *The Legacy: The Vietnam War in the American Imagination* (D. Michael Shafer, editor). Boston: Beacon Press.

Wagner-Pacifici, Robin and Barry Schwartz. 1991. "The Vietnam Veteran Memorial: Commemorating a Difficult Past," *American Journal of Sociology* 97(2): 376–420.

Walker, Keith. 1986. *A Piece of My Heart: The Stories of Twenty-Six American Women Who Served in Vietnam*. New York: Ballantine..

Wuthnow, Robert. 1987. *Meaning and Moral Order: Explorations in Cultural Analysis*. Berkeley: University of California.

Rock 'n' Roll Experiences in Middle Age

JOSEPH A. KOTARBA, UNIVERSITY OF HOUSTON

Although many observers still assume that rock 'n' roll is essentially a feature of youth culture, the author argues that it is a key feature of adult culture and a primary source of everyday meanings for the first generation raised on it. The concept of the existential self, which focuses on the situational and evolving aspects of individuality in a rapidly changing social world, informs several qualitative studies to produce the following ways to characterize personal rock 'n' roll experiences: the e-self, the self as lover, the self as parent, the self as believer, and the self as political actor.

. . .

The social science literature traditionally focuses on popular music experiences among young audiences. Specifically, the focus is on the rock 'n' roll idiom as a feature of adolescent culture and, therefore, of teenagers' everyday life experience. As Simon Frith (1981) noted in his famous sociological text, *Sound Effects*, rock 'n' roll music has been fundamental to the experience of growing upever since the end of World War II. Similarly, sociologists have demonstrated increasing interest in rock 'n' roll music as an indicator of dramatic changes occurring in the social and cultural worlds of teenagers. We can trace this interest at least as far back as David Riesman's (1950) classic

Reprinted from *American Behavioral Scientist* 48, no.11 (July 2005), Sage Publications, Inc.

examination of the emergence of the other-directed personality in post–World War II American society. The new middle class was marked by a weakening of parental control, a preoccupation with consumption, and a shift in the meaning of leisure resulting in the masses'—the lonely crowd—desperately trying to have fun. The time was ripe for the emergence of a youth culture defined by what has come to be known as rock 'n' roll music.

The rock 'n' roll industry continues to expand dramatically—beyond multibillion dollar annual sales, globalization, CDs, MP3 technology, and the Internet. Yet lay and scholarly observers have generally ignored or underplayed an important element of social and cultural change: rock 'n' roll is no longer limited to, nor solely the possession of, teenagers. The original generation of rock 'n' rollers—the baby boomers—are now parents and in some cases, grandparents. The music and musical culture they grew up with has stayed with them, becoming the soundtrack of American culture.

I define *rock 'n' roll music* very broadly as popular music that (a) is created for and marketed toward young peopleor people who consume music according to youthful tastes and values, (b) is primarily guitar driven and amplified, (c) has its musicological origins in African American musical styles, (d) is usually danceable, and (e) sounds best when played or performed loudly (Kotarba, 1994a). I define *rock 'n' roll* broadly to include all varieties of pop music that have evolved from it (e.g., heavy metal, pop, New Age, Christian pop). All told, rock 'n' roll music is arguably the preeminent form of popular music in our society.

The purpose of this article is to survey the many ways rock 'n' roll pervades the everyday lives of adults in American society. In commonsense terms, I examine what happened to the first, complete generation of rock 'n' roll fans—the baby boomer generation now in late middle age. I argue that rock 'n' roll music continues to serve as a critical meaning resource for its adult fans as they continuously experience the becoming-of-self throughout life.

◉ Sociological Analysis of Rock 'n' Roll

Four moments in the sociological analysis of rock 'n' roll closely parallel the historical development of rock 'n' roll itself during the past 50 years. I briefly trace these four moments to show their relevance to understanding adult experiences of this phenomenon.[1]

The first moment of rock 'n' roll occurred during the 1950s, when the idea of *teenagers* emerged within general American culture and scholarly observers forged the concept of *youth culture* to explain this strange yet wondrous new cohort. Whereas it is clear that cultural and musicological roots of rock 'n' roll can be traced back at least several decades (Friedlander, 1996), these roots were post–World War II. The sociologist James Coleman (1961) conceptualized rock 'n' roll music as a key feature of this youth culture. He argued that teenagers used popular music to stratify, organize, and manage each other and that rock 'n' roll was a tool of working-class kids. When considering adult experiences, the concept of youth culture may be useful to the degree that its substantive contents and values are available to adults today as the making of youthful styles to apply to adult circumstances.

The second moment of rock 'n' roll occurred during the late 1960s and 1970s. Rock 'n' roll music grew to become a cultural entity much greater than merely the beat for sock hops or the drive-in. It took on broader political implications through its links to the civil rights and antiwar movements. In the second moment, sociologists such as Frith (1981) and George Lewis (1983) conceptualized rock 'n' roll as *popular culture*—the product of the popular culture industry in capitalistic society. They also acknowledged the fact that the rock 'n' roll audience was much more diverse than the notion of *youth* implies. Experientially, there were White, Black, gay, men's, and women's rock 'n' roll(s) and subsequently, markets. Viewing rock 'n' roll music among adults as popular culture may be useful to the degree that the adult culture of rock 'n' roll reflects similar diversity.

The third moment of rock 'n' roll occurred in the 1970s

and 1980s when rock 'n' roll lost some of its critical appeal and became increasingly entrenched in and controlled by the entertainment industry. The ensuing revolt against corporate rock 'n' roll, especially in terms of the new wave and punk movements in England, led British scholars such as Dick Hebdige (1979) and others from the Birmingham school to conceptualize rock 'n' roll as *subculture*. Subcultural theory denotes marginality and resistance to an authority, hegemonic or otherwise. The image of Bill Clinton jamming on a saxophone at an inauguration party makes the existence of meaningful resistance among adult rock 'n' rollers problematic.[2]

The fourth moment of rock 'n' roll began in the 1980s and 1990s, when sociologists joined other scholarly observers to conceptualize rock 'n' roll simply as *culture* (e.g., Kaplan, 1987). They saw rock 'n' roll as one feature of a postindustrial or postmodern culture undergoing radical transformation. The generational boundaries that so obviously delineated youth from their parents were cracking. Lawrence Grossberg (1992), for example, proclaimed the death of rock 'n' roll insofar as it no longer functions to empower teenagers by differentiating them from their parents and other adults. By the 1990s, cross-generational pop music (e.g., Billy Joel, Madonna) that could be enjoyed by everyone had started to supplant rock 'n' roll as the dominant soundtrack in American culture, whereas rap music has taken over much of rock 'n' roll's political role. Yet rock 'n' roll has not simply died. Rock 'n' roll acts of an earlier era continue to draw loyal audiences, whereas contemporary rock 'n' roll has dissolved into the pastiche of popular music that results in White rappers such as Eminem, rock and rapper groups such as Limp Bizkit, and pop acts such as Britney Spears and her myriad of clones. Why, then, have so many adults not outgrown rock 'n' roll?

❂ The Becoming-of-Self

The existential sociological concept of *the becoming-of-self* is a useful guide in seeking the sociological answers to this question. Existential social thought views the self "as a unique experience of being within the context of contemporary social conditions, an experience most

860

notably marked by an incessant sense of becoming and an active participation in social change" (Kotarba, 1984, p. 223). The incessant sense of becoming is a reflection of the contemporary need for the individual to be prepared to reshape meanings of self in response to the dictates of a rapidly changing social world. The well-integrated self accepts the reality of change and welcomes new ideas, new experiences, and reformulations of old ideas and experiences that help one adapt to change (Kotarba, 1987).

The idea of becoming is one of the most important ideas in existentialist thought across disciplines because it places responsibility for fashioning a self on the individual. Whereas Jean-Paul Sartre (1945) argued dramatically that we are condemned to be free and to choose who we are to become, Maurice Merleau-Ponty (1962) insisted more moderately and sociologically that we must ground our becoming-of-self in the real world to cope effectively with it. Thus, an effective strategy for becoming begins with a foundation of personal experience and the constraints of social structure, while evolving in terms of the resources presented by culture. I argue that middle-aged Americans work with a self built to some degree on the meanings provided by the rock 'n' roll idiom, and they continue to nurture the self within the ever-present cultural context of rock 'n' roll.

Douglas (1984) noted that there are, in fact, two analytically distinct stages of becoming-of-self with which the modern actor contends. The first is the need to eliminate or control threats to the basic security of self (e.g., meaninglessness, isolation from others, shame, death). Although existential psychotherapists such as Yalom (1980) have argued that chronic insecurity—or neurosis—is pervasive in our society, Douglas argued sociologically that it is more common for the sense of security to vary biographically, situationally, and developmentally. In general, adults try to shape everyday life experiences to avoid basic threats to the self. Basic threats to the adult self in our society would include divorce, the loss of a job, the loss of children (e.g., the empty-nest syndrome), illness, disability, and poverty. The second stage of becoming-of-self involves growth of the sense of self. Growth occurs when the individual seeks new experiences as media for innovative and potentially rewarding meanings

861

for self (Kotarba, 1987). It is through growth, or self-actualization as it is often referred to today, that life becomes rich, rewarding, full, and manageable.

Accordingly, adult fans nurture their interest in and experience with rock 'n' roll music for two reasons. On one hand, keeping up with the music and the culture that were so important to them when growing up helps them maintain continuity with the past and, thus, solidify the sense of self security. On the other hand, working hard to keep rock 'n' roll current and relevant to their lives helps adults grow as parents, as spiritual beings, and as friends.

The concept of the *existential self* tells us that the experience of individuality is never complete; the answer to the question Who am I? is always tentative. In the postmodern world, the mass media—including popular music—serve as increasingly important audiences to the self. The self is situational and mutable (Zurcher, 1977). One can be various selves as the fast-paced, ever-changing, uncertain postmodern society requires. In the remainder of this article, I provide a working inventory of the various adult experiences of self—common in everyday life—predicated by or embedded in the rock 'n' roll idiom.

☻ Methodology

This article is based on several studies of popular music conducted during the course of 15 years. These studies have used a range of symbolic interactionist–inspired, qualitative methods—including conversational interviews with artists, fans, and others—participant observation of rock 'n' roll concerts and events, the analysis of popular music materials and documents, and the active production of rock 'n' roll events.

I refer to my style of research on this topic as *ethnographic tourism* (Kotarba, 1994b). It is ethnographic to the degree that it attempts to describe rock 'n' roll phenomena in terms of the natural situations in which they occur and in terms of the language, feelings, and perceptions of the individuals who experience them. This research can be viewed metaphorically as tourism because it is an attempt to approach rock 'n' roll phenomena with wonder and discovery. This analytical distancing of researcher from phenomena is important because the author is a member of the population in question and as a typical rock 'n' roller, could be too easily tempted to claim experience with and expertise in rock 'n' roll.

❂ The E-Self

As the rock 'n' roll fan ages, many of the attractive aspects of the earlier self are more difficult to maintain. There is a tendency for youthfulness, energy, risk taking, appearance, sensuality, and other aspects of the adolescent or young-adult self to become either less available or less desirable. Our culture does, however, provide a self-identity that resonates with the affluence of middle age, as well as with the continuing need to establish status/self-esteem. The e-self refers to an experience of individuality in which the affective and philosophical self-resources of rock 'n' roll media are displaced or at least supplemented by the increasingly technological and commodified aspects of the media. For the middle-aged fan, what you play your music on can be at least as, if not more, important than what you play.

Middle age results in less concert attendance and more music experience in the comfort of home, automobile, and for the energetic, on the jogging trail. A content analysis of an issue of *Wired* (2004), a magazine that is geared toward the affluent and technologically interested middle-aged person, discloses the strategy of marketing rock 'n' roll to its audience. There are ads for sophisticated cell phones that allow the consumer to "keep rockin' with your favorite MP3s." The promotion for "THEWIREDAUCTION" on eBay, which benefits a children's foundation, includes a "limited edition series precision bass guitar signed by Sting," among other high-end music items. The ad for the Bose Music intelligent playback system highlights "its unique ability to listen to the music you play and learn your preferences based on your likes, dislikes, or even your mood at the moment." There are numerous ads for satellite radio systems and the luxury sport-utility vehicles that include them as standard equipment.

863

Such marketing sometimes resonates with the adults it targets. George is a 51-year-old Anglo electrical engineer who just installed a satellite radio system in his Lexus sedan. He sees two benefits of his musical purchase: "I don't have to mess with CDs or radio anymore. I get to play only the music I like to hear. . . . There are stations dedicated just to '80s heavy metal. Cool." George has effectively eliminated the hassles of concert crowds and debates about musical tastes with peers. High technology puts his e-self in control of his musical environment. George can experience his music with the aura of cultural independence that affluent adults seek.

❧ The Self as Lover

A significant aspect of the continuous popularity of rock 'n' roll music is its use in helping make sense of others, especially in intimate relationships. Numerous observers have correctly identified the sexist messages present in rock 'n' roll (e.g., McRobbie, 1978). A postmodern existentialist view, however, highlights the fact that rock 'n' roll music displays an open-ended horizon of meaning for its audiences. What a rock 'n' roll music performance means is largely a function of the situation in which it is experienced and the particular self-needs of the audience member (Kotarba, 1994a). As time passes, the rock 'n' roll audience matures, biographies evolve, men's and women's relationships change, popular music commodities come and go, cultural themes available through the media advance, and we would expect the actual lived experience of popular music to change.

A particular self-need of the mature rock 'n' roll fan is to interpret romantic phenomena. This can happen two ways. First, fans can (re)interpret music to fit romantic needs. In my autobiographical writing as a rock 'n' roll fan (Kotarba, 1997), I described the way I used Dion's "Runaround Sue" to account for the way a girl back in eighth grade rejected my very timid show of affection in favor of those of an older boy. Like the Sue in the song, my Sue was a "bad" girl and I was merely a victim of her wiles. Twenty-five years later, at a class reunion, I used the same song as the basis for a conversation with the same Sue. We laughed about the silliness of those grammar

864

school days, but my heartbeat jumped a bit when she admitted that she really did like me back then but was too shy to tell me!

Second, fans can gravitate toward music that can be perceived as romantic. Autobiographically, "Smokey" Robinson and the Miracles' "Tracks of My Tears" was a constant play on my 45 record player in 1965 when it put comforting words to yet another heartbreak in my life. My guess is that I would not have been drawn as much to this new record if I did not have a personal need for its plaintive prose. In general, fans gravitate toward music that fits their everyday life concerns.

Baby boomers use rock 'n' roll materials for a range of romantic purposes. They use music (e.g., CDs) as birthday and Christmas gifts. They use music to help them appreciate other media such as films and television. One of the more interesting romantic uses of rock 'n' roll music is the our-song phenomenon, where a musical performance serves to define a relationship. Our-songs are clearly not limited to baby boomers. Preadolescents, for example, commonly choose songs that remind them of a boy or a girl but are often too shy to disclose this fact to the other!

For mature rock 'n' roll fans, the our-song can function at least two ways. First, it provides meaning for benchmark events in the relationship. Shirley is a 52-year-old, Latina sales person who is a big Los Lobos fan. She builds anniversary activities around one particular song she and her husband both enjoy:

> We fell in love with "Nadie Quiere Sufrir" at a Los Lobos concert when we were still just dating. It is a very pretty waltz that actually comes from an Edith Piaf song. . . . I make sure the CD [with the song] is in the car when we drive to [our anniversary] dinner. He bought me the CD for our anniversary a few years ago. . . . Oh, I guess it just makes us feel young again.

Second, the our-song can help the person feel like a lover. As couples age and perhaps find themselves feeling and acting less romantic with time, the our-song can function as a quick fix. Rob is a 58-year-old, Anglo executive who has maintained a serious relationship with

Tommy, a 47-year-old artist, for about 15 years. Their song is Queen's "Bohemian Rhapsody":

> There will never be another Freddie Mercury. It was really special to have our own gay rock icon. . . . I surprise Tommy by playing "Bohemian Rhapsody" now and again. Tommy is still thrilled that I remember it. . . . Why? Well, it's one of those songs that make you feel good, to feel that you can be gay and a rocker at the same time. . . . I like doing things for Tommy. We are just so busy with our careers, 'makes us feel like an old married couple!

Needless to say, the rock 'n' roll industry is aware of the market here for its goods and services. One of the more recent examples is the advent and growing popularity of rock 'n' roll cruises. Carnival Cruise Lines offered the following "Rock 'n' Roll Cruise Vacation" in an online ad:

> What could be cooler than a seven-day Caribbean cruise with legendary big-hair 1970s/80s rockers Journey, Styx and REO Speedwagon? Well . . . we'll reserve comment. But, if your idea of a totally awesome vacation is a seven-day cruise with legendary big-hair 1970s/80s rockers Journey, Styx and REO Speedwagon, you're in luck. (Rock 'n' Roll Holiday Escape, 2004)

❂ The Self as Parent

The impact of rock 'n' roll on one's self as parent is possibly the most pervasive aspect of the personal rock 'n' roll experience. Baby boomers grew up experiencing music as a major medium for communicating with parents. Managing music illustrates one's skill at parenting, as well as one's style of parenting.

Standard scholarly and journalistic wisdom on rock 'n' roll argues that it has functioned largely to help establish adolescence as a distinct stage in the life cycle while serving as a weapon in conflicts between adults and adolescents. The mass media have long contributed to this overstated, overromanticized view of rock 'n' roll and adolescence. The rebellious imagery of Elvis Presley, for example, portrays a prevailing cultural myth that links rock 'n' roll with youthful rebellion, unbridled sexuality, cross-ethnic intimacy, and a wide range of delinquent activities (Garafolo, 2002). The film *Footloose* (Ross, 1984) portrays the plausible scenario in which fundamentally conservative, small-town adults view rock 'n' roll as an evil influence on their teenagers. Rock 'n' roll is portrayed in the film as the gauntlet that forces teenagers to choose between good and evil by choosing their parents or dancing.

These cultural images support an ideological vision of youth culture that overemphasizes the independence and rebellion of teenagers. A postmodernist existentialist reading of this history finds much more diversity within youth culture (Kotarba, 2002a). The kids on the *American Bandstand* television show in the 1950s and early 1960s were all-American kids. They dressed modestly and neatly. They all chewed Beechnut gum, provided by the sponsor of the program. And above all, they were extremely well behaved. The boys and girls, especially the "regulars," tended to match up as boyfriends and girlfriends, not as potentially promiscuous dates and mates. *American Bandstand* probably represented many teenagers in American society at that time. And teenagers could not participate in activities like *American Bandstand* without the approval, if not support, of their parents. After all, someone had to drive the kids to the studio or at least give them permission and money to take the bus there, just as someone had to provide the television and permit watching *American Bandstand* at home.

Baby boomers appear more likely to be cautious supporters of their children's rock 'n' roll activities than outright critics. This somewhat passive if not permissive style of parenting is not new to baby boomers; in fact, they learned it from their parents. For every Elvis Presley fan in the 1950s and 1960s whose parents threatened disowning, there was an *American Bandstand* fan whose parent (mom?) was likely to sit next to her in front of the TV and watch Fabian and Frankie Avalon make all the girls sigh (Stuessy & Lipscomb, 1999).

There is a greater tendency among parents—apparently across

867

ethnic groups and social classes—to manage rock 'n' roll as though their teenagers are children who need to be nurtured and protected rather than as adolescents who must be controlled, sanctioned, and feared. At a recent Metallica concert in Houston, for example, numerous teenagers indicated that their parents did not approve of heavy metal music for various reasons (e.g., volume, distortion, immorality, potential affiliation with evils such as satanism). Yet these same parents carpooled their teenagers and friends to the Astrodome on a school day and in most cases, bought or provided the money for tickets. A similar situation exists among African American and Hispanic parents in terms of the popularity of rap music among their teenagers (Kotarba, 1994b). Mass media–generated images of obstinate if not rebellious youth generally ignore the reflexive relationship between teenagers and their parents. As long as teenagers live at home as legal, financial, and moral dependents—that is, as children—their parents provide the resources for creating rock 'n' roll identities (e.g., allowances, free time, and fashionable hip-hop clothing). Parents then respond to the identities they helped create by controlling, criticizing, sanctioning, and punishing their teenagers for living out their rock 'n' roll–inspired identities—responding to them as if they were autonomous, responsible adults.

Baby boomer parents often share their music with their children. Sociologically, much of this sharing is functional and positive: Rock 'n' roll helps integrate families. Rock 'n' roll has always served as a special commonality between mothers and daughters. They shared Elvis Presley in the 1950s, the Beatles in the 1960s, and Neil Diamond in the 1970s. In the feminist era of the 1980s and 1990s, however, the object of sharing shifted to other women. Madonna is the case in point.

Madonna represents a rock 'n' roll phenomenon that is attractive to both mothers and daughters. Madonna is a multifaceted star whose appeal rests on lifestyle, clothing style, and attitude as well as musical performance. During the Houston stop on the "Like a Virgin" tour, I interviewed a number of mother-daughter pairs who attended. The pairs typically were dressed alike, in outfits such as black bustier and short black skirts, with matching jewelry. During the interviews, they talked about Madonna in similar ways and appeared more like friends than family. In virtually all cases, they noted a distinct lack of true appreciation of Madonna by the men in their lives (e.g., fathers, husbands, brothers, and boyfriends who may look at Madonna and see only a sex object). And in most cases, the mothers indicated that Madonna served to bring them closer to their daughters. A currently fashionable style of music shared by mothers and daughters is the boy group: 'N Sync, Backstreet Boys, O Town, and so forth.

Fathers and sons also use rock 'n' roll music to bond, but in different ways than one might expect. Fathers who learned to play guitar in the 1960s or 1970s teach their sons how to play. Sharing music is difficult, as the younger generation today continues the traditional ideological belief that their music is better than that of their parents. Fathers and sons are considerably more vehement than women in their allegiance to their generation's music. During our study of the rave phenomenon in Houston (Kotarba, 1993, 2003), we heard one 16-year-old boy exclaim, "I hate my dad's music. He listens to that old shit, like Led Zeppelin." On the other hand, recent trends such as rave (i.e., dance parties held in clandestine locations to the beat of loud synthesized music) display a renaissance of the 1960s counterculture. Psychedelia is "in," for example, with LSD as the drug of choice and lighting provided by mood lamps. Teenagers see rave as a way of retrieving the romance and simplicity of the 1960s. In a way, these kids accept their parents' claim that growing up in the 1960s was special. Another example is Deadhead fathers and their sons sharing the Grateful Dead experience.

Rock 'n' roll fits well with the burgeoning family leisure and vacation industry. Family theme parks typically have some attraction related to rock 'n' roll, such as the complete mock-up of a 1950s small-town main street in the Fiesta Texas amusement park in San Antonio. The artists performing at the amphitheaters in the Six Flags parks have included, during the course of several years, REO Speedwagon, an Eagles reunion band, and a KISS reunion band. The concept "family entertainment" in the 1950s, 1960s, and 1970s referred to phenomena such as wholesome television programming, Walt Disney films, and home games, whereas today it increasingly refers to rock 'n' roll. The rock 'n' roll presented usually addresses a common denominator acceptable to both parents and children, such as rockabilly or 1980s power pop (e.g., Lynyrd Skynyrd, Van Halen, Cheap Trick, Aerosmith).

◎ The Self as Believer

As we have seen, baby boomers' early experiences of rock 'n' roll music were complex. They learned to love, play, dissent, and belong through the idiom. They also experienced spirituality (Seay & Neely, 1986). In adulthood, the spiritual dimension of rock 'n' roll continues to affect the self as believer. The lyrics and mood created by such performers as Van Morrison (*Astral Weeks*) and U2 (*The Joshua Tree*) provide baby boomers with nonsectarian yet religion-friendly soundtracks. New Age Music, such as that produced by Windham Hill, functions the same way.

Rock 'n' roll music has also had a direct influence on spirituality by helping shape organized religious ceremonies and rituals to fit the tastes of the adult member. For example, Catholic baby boomers grew up at a time when the Church, largely as a result of the Vatican II Council, encouraged parishes to make use of local musical styles and talent. Witness the emergence of the rock 'n' roll mass in the 1970s. Today, the very popular style of praise and worship music, with its electronic keyboard and modern melodies, is infiltrating Catholic liturgy.

An integral segment of the self as parent is moral if not religious or spiritual socialization. Rock 'n' roll functions as a mechanism for teaching religious beliefs and values in many families, whether or not rock 'n' roll is compatible with the particular family's religious orientation. For mainstream Protestant denominations, rock 'n' roll increasingly fits with the faith. For example, when Amy Grant played Houston several years back, her music was loud and fast (e.g., seven piece band with double drummers and double lead guitars). Parents accompanying their children to the concert peppered the audience. One father, in his 30s, brought his wife and 10-year-old daughter to the concert (which he learned aboutat his Lutheran church). When I

870

asked him about the compatibility of Christian rock music with Christianity, he stated,

> We love Amy Grant. She is married and tours with her husband, which is not the case with regular rock stars. Her songs are full of Christian messages. Any way you can get the message of Christ to your kids is OK with us.

The variety of Christian rock 'n' role styles is growing. A particularly intriguing version is Christian heavy metal (Kotarba, 1991). One rock club in Houston routinely books Christian heavy metal bands on Sunday evenings. One evening, they booked a Christian speed metal band, which played extremely loud and fast music about Christ. I talked to several parents who accompanied their children to the concert. The parents were very polite, clean-cut, middle-class, Southern Baptists surrounded by a sea of punk rockers and headbangers. They struck me as being much like the parents of the *American Bandstand* generation discussed above. They created the opportunity for their teenagers to attend the concert by carpooling them and their friends in from the suburbs. They hoped that the message emanating from the longhaired rockers was indeed Christian, but they wanted to see for themselves that Satan was not infiltrating the event.

Certain Christian denominations, such as the Assemblies of God Church, tend to view rock 'n' roll of any kind as evil, whether under the guise of Christian rock or not. Parents in this faith focus their attention on rock 'n' roll as a way of establishing moral boundaries for their children. For example, a very popular video among Assemblies of God youth ministers is called *Rock and Roll: A Search for God*. The producer, Eric Holmberg (n.d.), displayed numerous rock album covers to illustrate his argument that rockers, especially heavy metal rockers, advertently or inadvertently proclaim satanic messages. For fundamentalist parents, rock 'n' roll functions as a convenient and accessible way of teaching their children clearly and directly that Satan and evil are present in today's world and can take various attractive forms. Ironically, Christian rock and satanic rock dramatically illustrate the ongoing battle between good and evil for many Christians.

◉ The Self as Political Actor

Rock 'n' roll music serves as a soundtrack for the situations in which baby boomers perceive themselves as political actors. Rock 'n' roll can add both atmosphere and meaning to political events. For example, New York punk poet and singer Patti Smith performed a concert in Houston on March 28, 2003—right at the beginning of the war in Iraq. The concert was originally scheduled simply to support an exhibit of her art displayed at the Museum of Contemporary Arts. The audience was overwhelmingly middle-aged people, dressed up in their jeans and long (hippie) skirts. Through conversations with numerous fans after the concert, it was clear that they enjoyed the concert. Patti Smith's poetry and songs (e.g., "People Have the Power") gave them a relevant and identifiable venue for sharing their overwhelmingly negative feelings about the war.

Families also use rock 'n' roll to relay a sense of political history to their children. For example, every year on Memorial Day in Houston, various veterans organizations sponsor a concert and rally at the Miller Outdoor Theater. Most of the veterans present fought in the Vietnam and Gulf Wars, wars for which rock 'n' roll served as the musical soundtrack. Most of the veterans bring their children to the event. Among all the messages and information available to the kids is the type of music popular during the wars. A popular band regularly invited to perform is the Guess Who, whose "American Woman" was a major anthem among soldiers. I have observed fathers explaining the song to their teenaged and preteen children, who would otherwise view it as just another of dad's old songs. The fathers explain that the song had different meanings for different men. For some, it reminded them of girlfriends back home who broke up with them during the war. For others, the title was enough to remind them of their faithful girlfriends back home. For still others, the song reminded them of the occasions when they were sitting around camp, smoking pot and listening to any American rock 'n' roll songs available as a way of bridging the many miles between them and home. In Houston, Juneteenth and Cinco de Mayo activities function much the same way for African American and Hispanic families, respectively. In summary, rock 'n' roll music is vital to maintaining a sense of the political self because many baby boomers learned their politics—and how to be and feel political—from Country Joe McDonald (and the Fish), Jimi Hendrix, and the Grateful Dead.

◉ Conclusion

I have described several contemporary experiences of self to illustrate the ways the rock 'n' roll idiom has remained a major cultural force in the everyday lives of mature fans. There are obviously other experiences. Furthermore, these experiences are not limited to fans. Rock 'n' roll music is also a preeminent aspect of the musician's self who performed rock 'n' roll music many years ago and who continues to perform. These musicians redirect their careers in directions more comfortable if not more profitable. Kinky Friedman comes to mind. He was a Texas-based bandleader in the 1970s (the infamous Texas Jew Boys). He now performs acoustically in small clubs while managing a very successful line of men's clothing and authoring popular mystery novels. As time passes, rock 'n' roll provides resources for the aging self (Kotarba, 2002b). In my interviews, I routinely hear respondents note how the recent deaths of middle-aged rock 'n' roll artists, such as Robert Palmer and George Harrison, are disturbing because these afflictions may be more the result of aging than the excessive lifestyles associated with the premature deaths of artists such as Janice Joplin, Jimmy Hendrix, and Jim Morrison. It will be interesting, then, to see the various ways in which baby boomers draw on the rock 'n' roll idiom as they move beyond middle age. For example, what new meanings will aging boomers attach to the rock 'n' roll idiom? What place will rock 'n' roll have in the grandparent-grandchild relationship? Attending to such questions will highlight the role that music plays in the ongoing becoming-of-self.

Notes

Author's Note: Much of the research reported in this article was supported by grants from the National Institute on Drug Abuse, the Texas Commission on the Arts, the Cultural Arts Council of Houston and Harris County, and the National Endowment for the Arts.

[1]A detailed discussion of the four moments in rock 'n' roll and the sociological analysis of rock 'n' roll is found in Kotarba (2002a).

[2]Scene theory appears to be a promising refinement of subculture theory (Bennett & Peterson, 2004),as its core concept of "scene" suggests the possibility that contemporary adults may be able to maintain lifelong interests in rock 'n' roll while assimilating these interests into their otherwise complex and multifaceted lifestyles and self-identities.

References

Bennett, A., Peterson, R. A. (Eds.). (2004). *Music scenes.* Nashville, TN: Vanderbilt University Press.

Coleman, J. S. (1961). *The adolescent society.* Glencoe, IL: Free Press.

Douglas, J. D. (1984). The emergence, security, and growth of the sense of self. In J. A. Kotarba & A. Fontana (Eds.), *The existential self and society* (pp. 69–99). Chicago: University of Chicago Press.

Friedlander, P. (1996). *Rock and roll.* Boulder, CO: Westview.

Frith, S. (1981). *Sound effects.* New York: Pantheon.

Garafolo, R. (2002). *Rockin' out.* Upper Saddle River, NJ: Pearson.

Grossberg, L. (1992). Rock and roll in search of an audience. In J. Lull (Ed.), *Popularmusic and communication* (pp. 175–197). Newbury Park, CA: Sage.

Hebdige, D. (1979). *Subculture: The meaning of style.* New York: Methuen.

Holmberg, E. (Producer). (n.d.). *Rock and roll: A search for God.* Pittsburgh, PA: Reel to Real Ministries. Available from American Portrait Films Web site at http://www.amport.com/eric-h.htm

Kaplan, E. A. (1987). *Rocking around the clock.* New York: Routledge.

Kotarba, J. A. (1984). The existential self and society. In J. A. Kotarba & A. Fontana (Eds.), *The existential self and society* (pp. 222–234). Chicago: University of Chicago Press.

Kotarba, J. A. (1987). Adolescents and rock 'n' roll. *Youth and Society, 18,* 323–325.

Kotarba, J. A. (1991). Postmodernism, ethnography and culture. *Studies in Symbolic Interaction, 12,* 45–52.

Kotarba, J. A. (1993, October). The rave scene in Houston, Texas. In *Research briefs* (Report to the Texas Commission on Alcohol and Drug Abuse). Austin: Texas Commission on Alcohol and Drug Abuse.

Kotarba, J. A. (1994a). The postmodernization of rock music. In J. Epstein (Ed.), *Adolescents and their music* (pp. 141–163). New York: Garland.

Kotarba, J. A. (1994b). The positive functions of rock and roll music. In J. Best (Ed.), *Troubling children* (pp. 155–170). New York: Aldine.

Kotarba, J. A. (1997). Reading the male experience of rock music. *Culture Studies, 2,* 265–277.

Kotarba, J. A. (2002a). Baby boomer rock 'n' roll fans and the becoming of self. In J. A. Kotarba & J. M. Johnson (Eds.), *Postmodern existential sociology* (pp. 103–126). Walnut Creek, CA: AltaMira.

Kotarba, J. A. (2002b). Rock 'n' roll music as a timepiece. *Symbolic Interaction, 25,* 397–404.

Kotarba, J. A. (2003, July). *Popular music as a medium for on-line, club drug interaction* (Report for the project Technology, Youth and the Proliferation of Drug Use). Bethesda, MD: National Institute on Drug Abuse.

Lewis, G. (1983). The meaning's inn the music. *Theory, Culture and Society, 3,* 133–141.

McRobbie, A. (1978). Working class girls and the culture of femininity. In Women's Studies Group (Eds.), *Women take issue* (pp. 34–54). London: Hutchinson.

Merleau-Ponty, M. (1962). *Phenomenology of perception.* London:Routledge.

Riesman, D. (1950). *The lonely crowd.* New Haven, CT: Yale University Press.

Rock 'n' Roll Holiday Escape. (2004, October 18). *Thank you for spending a week cruising the Caribbean with 3 of rock's biggest artists.* Available from http://www.rrholidayescape.com

Ross, H. (Director). (1984). *Footloose* [Motion picture].United States: United International Picture.

Sartre, J. P. (1945). *The age of reason*. Paris: Gallimard.

Seay, D., & Neely, M. (1986). *Stairway to heaven*. New York: Ballantine.

Stuessy J., & Lipscomb, S. (1999). *Rock and roll*. Upper Saddle River, NJ: Prentice Hall.

Wired. (2004, October). [Advertisements throughout issue]. *12*(10).

Yalom, I. D. (1980). *Existential psychotherapy*. New York: Basic Books.

Zurcher, L. (1977). *The mutable self*. Beverly Hills, CA: Sage.

JOSEPH A. KOTARBA is professor of sociology at the University of Houston and a former president of the Society for the Study of Symbolic Interaction. His recent publications in culture and popular music studies include Postmodern Existential Sociology *(coedited with John M. Johnson, AltaMira, 2002) and "Popular Music as a Timepiece" in the journal* Symbolic Interaction *(2002), and he is coediting (with Phillip Vannini) a special issue of* Symbolic Interaction *on popular music and everyday life (2005). He has produced a video ethnography titled* Our Parents' Music *(2003) and is studying the emergence of youth culture in the high school setting.*

Beauty Work: Individual and Institutional Rewards, the Reproduction of Gender, and Questions of Agency

Samantha Kwan, University of Houston

Mary Nell Trautner, University at Buffalo, SUNY

Physical attractiveness is associated with a number of positive outcomes, including employment benefits such as hiring, wages, and promotion, and is correlated with social and personal rewards such as work satisfaction, positive perceptions of others, and higher self-esteem. As a result, individuals perform various forms of beauty work, thus reproducing and strengthening a social system that privileges youth and attractiveness. In this article, we explore the beauty work practices that people perform. We begin with an examination of the cultural context in which beauty work occurs, including the individual, social, and institutional rewards accompanying physical attractiveness, and then review the practices themselves. Because these rewards and practices contribute in part to the reproduction of social relations and norms, we then turn to the gender dimensions of beauty work, along with its unique

Reprinted from *Sociology Compass* 3, no.1 (2008), John Wiley & Sons, Inc.

racial embodiment. Throughout, we raise the issue of individual agency in beauty work. Finally, we conclude with suggestions for future research.

. . .

Cultural representations of beauty in contemporary Western societies are, by and large, homogeneous, emphasizing a feminine ideal of slenderness and firmness (Bordo 2003; Hesse-Biber 1996; Kilbourne 1999) and a masculine ideal of strength and muscularity (Bordo 1999; Pope et al. 2000). These hegemonic beauty ideals embrace youth and privilege whiteness as embodied in fair skin, eye color, and hair texture (see Collins 1991). While competing discourses theorize whether these ideals are socially constructed (e.g., Wolf 1991) or stem from our evolutionary psychology (e.g., Etcoff 1999), there is little dispute about their prevalence. Images of male and female hegemonic beauty are ubiquitous.

Various beauty practices accompany these cultural beauty norms. Recently, Gimlin (2007) distinguishes among several types of 'body work', including work performed on oneself and work performed on others, also called 'body labor' (Kang 2003). While both types of body work include appearance-related practices, they also include a wide range of experiences, from the embodied display of workplace sexuality to female care work performed in the domestic sphere. These two types of body work thus capture an array of social processes concerning the body. In contrast, *beauty work* and *beauty labor* are narrower terms that reflect specific appearance and beauty practices performed on oneself and on others, respectively (see Roth and Neal 2006).

In this article, we focus on *beauty work* and explore beauty practices as work that individuals perform on themselves to elicit certain benefits within a specific social hierarchy. We begin with an examination of the cultural context in which beauty work occurs, including the individual and institutional rewards accompanying physical attractiveness. We then discuss specific beauty work practices.

Because these rewards and practices contribute in part to the reproduction of social relations and norms, we then turn to the gender dimensions of beauty work, along with its unique racial embodiment. Throughout, we discuss a key theme in the literature—the issue of agency—and conclude with suggestions for future research.

◉ Why Beauty Work Matters: Stereotypes and their Individual Impacts

Beauty work occurs within a social system that distributes rewards and sanctions based partially on appearance. Early studies show that perceptions of beautiful people are generally positive and, as a whole, individuals associate positive traits with physically attractive persons. An oft-cited phrase in the literature, 'what is beautiful is good', sums up these perceptions. For example, individuals often assume that physically attractive people lead happier and more successful lives than less attractive persons (Dion et al. 1972). Beauty is also equated with talent (Landy and Sigall 1974). Individuals are more likely to evaluate work performed by physically attractive people favorably, a particularly pronounced observation when work is below par. As Landy and Sigall observe: 'You may be able to get away with inferior work if you are beautiful' (1974, 302). Simply stated, physical attractiveness confers status and is an important status characteristic that favorably shapes expectations (Webster and Driskell 1983; for other reviews, see Adams 1982; Hatfield and Sprecher 1986). Scholars fittingly refer to this as a 'halo effect' and explain it in part through implicit personality theory (see Schneider 1973). This theory states that individuals sometimes infer peripheral attributes based on central attributes such as attractiveness.

While a large body of literature supports the beauty-as-good thesis, research also points to several disadvantages that come with being beautiful. Alongside the beauty-as-socially competent stereotype is the perception that beauty also signifies vanity and self-centeredness.

879

For example, despite finding general support for the beauty-as-good thesis, Dermer and Thiel (1975) report that individuals expect attractive women to be more conceited and likely to engage in adultery. Their research highlights the importance of beauty's social context. As they theorize, a woman stereotyped as professionally competent may have the best chance of getting a sales job, but if considered conceited or adulterous, she may encounter difficulties prosecuting a rapist (1975, 1175).

Subsequent research, however, questions the strength of this thesis. While the meta-analysis of Eagly et al. (1991) confirms the predicted effects of beauty, they concurrently note that the magnitude of the effect is moderate and varies considerably across studies. They also report that the strength of beauty's power is contingent upon the type of inference a perceiver makes. While physical attractiveness induces strong inferences about social competence, it is weaker for potency, adjustment, and intellectual competence. Additionally, their statistical review found no effect of beauty on integrity and concern for others. These nuances partially support Feingold's (1992) meta-analysis indicating that study methodology matters. So while the experimental literature shows that individuals associate desirable social traits (e.g., sociable, mentally healthy, and intelligent) with physically attractive people, correlation studies show generally trivial relationships on personality measures. In sum, the beauty stereotype is present, but it varies in magnitude and by the trait inferred.

Beyond perceptions are the real effects of beauty on life outcomes. Attractive people are in fact treated better and experience desirable social outcomes. Appearance matters on both an individual and institutional level. For example, experimental research on exchange theory and the prisoner's dilemma illustrates that beauty has a double advantage (Mulford et al. 1998). Subjects expect more cooperation from others they view as attractive and, moreover, choose to interact more often with such individuals. Attractive individuals thus have more opportunities for social exchange and these opportunities turn out to be with people who are relatively inclined to cooperate. As a result, beautiful individuals are more likely to encounter opportunities for successful interactions.

Classic studies on interactions also find that physical attractiveness comes with greater peer acceptance (Dion and Berscheid 1974; Kleck et al. 1974) and that attractive individuals possess greater interpersonal influence and elicit greater opinion agreement than unattractive individuals, particularly with opposite sex peers (Dion and Stein 1978; Horai et al. 1974). Additionally, a communicator's attractiveness influences opinion change and under some conditions more so than a communicator's expertise, although beauty's persuasiveness may only be evident when there is an overt expression of persuasion intent (Mills and Aronson 1965; Mills and Harvey 1972). Physically attractive people are also more memorable and likely to elicit favorable reactions from other communicants such as being looked upon and smiled at (Kleck and Rubenstein 1975). It is noteworthy that the relationship between physical attractiveness and personality traits works in both directions (see Webster and Driskell 1983). Not only is there a certain persuasiveness that comes with attractiveness, but individuals may actually judge the attractiveness of others with whom they interact based on whether their views resonate with their own.

Conversely, unattractive individuals are subject to stigma, stereotyping, and discrimination. Like race or gender, appearance is a visible and diffuse status characteristic (Berger et al. 1977; Webster and Driskell 1983) and deviation from beauty ideals can lead to stigma and a spoiled identity (Goffman 1963). There is much discussion in the literature about the stigma of, for example, disability, disfigurement, and body size. Susman's (1993) review points out that while the stigma of disability remains, these imputations are losing force. Others writing about deformities argue that, while disadvantaging stigmas are present, physical abnormalities such as craniofacial disfigurement, may actually elicit pro-social behavior from others through a 'kindness to the disadvantaged' reaction—a reaction that unattractive, but otherwise normal, individuals do not elicit (Reis and Hodgins 1995). Finally, Puhl and Brownell's (2001) review documents the widespread occurrence of size-based bias, stereotyping, and discrimination in many arenas of social life (on weight stigma and discrimination, see also Allon 1982; Sobal 2004; Solovay 2000).

◎ Social Institutions and the Advantages of Beauty

While beauty matters on an individual level, it also matters on an institutional level. Physical attractiveness affects individual prospects in social institutions such as work, education, and marriage. Again, beauty translates into social rewards. For example, some organizations may communicate, both overtly and subtly, organizational 'image norms'. Abercrombie & Fitch's legal trouble in the early 2000s stemmed in part from the company's desire to hire employees who embody the 'A & F Look'. This policy led to the termination, or transfer to less visible positions, of employees who did not fit this look.[1] Organizational manipulation of appearance for clientele and profit is evident in other organizations as well, including sex organizations such as exotic dance clubs (Trautner 2005).

There is some dispute over what researchers call a Lack of Fit Model (Heilman 1983). According to this model, 'a perceiver makes inferences about attributes and characteristics of an individual based upon stereotypes (e.g., sex, attractiveness), and then evaluates the individual on the degree to which these attributes match the perceived requirements of a job' (Hosoda et al. 2003, 435). Early research by Heilman et al. supports the model, showing that an attractiveness bias occurs based on an employee's gender and the perceived nature of the job as masculine or feminine (Heilman and Saruwatari 1979; Heilman and Stopeck 1985; the model has also been used to explain obesity discrimination, see Polinko and Popovich 2001). However, other work suggests otherwise. Specifically, Drogosz and Levy's (1996) empirical analysis explicitly rejects the model. They find that attractiveness is an asset regardless of job type or employee's gender. Moreover, a more recent meta-analysis of 27 experimental studies finds that attractiveness matters as much for men as for women, that attractiveness bias does not differ by amount of job-relevant information provided, and that attractiveness is an asset affecting many stages of the employment process including hiring, performance evaluation, and promotion (Hosoda et al. 2003).

The employment benefits of attractiveness ultimately lead to financial advantages. A study of MBA graduates found that facially attractive men start with higher salaries and continued to earn more over time (Frieze et al. 1991). While this study observed no effect on initial salaries for women, more attractive women eventually earned more in their jobs. Others have documented a hierarchy of earnings by appearance (plain-looking, average-looking, and good-looking; Hammermesh and Biddle 1994) and a positive correlation between appearance and both family and personal income (Umberson and Hughes 1987). Conley and Glauber's (2005) recent analysis demonstrates the adverse effects of weight on economic outcomes. They report that increases in women's body mass result in a decrease in family income and later occupational prestige. Research also shows that unattractive women generally have lower labor-force participation rates (Hammermesh and Biddle 1994). Discussed below in the section on beauty work practices, it is thus unsurprising that working women claim they perform beauty work, like putting on makeup, in part to appear competent in the workplace (Dellinger and Williams 1997; on body management in the workplace, also see Gimlin 2007).

Similarly, appearance is connected to success in the educational arena. First, attractiveness affects teacher's perceptions. Studies report an association between attractiveness and a teacher's evaluation of a child's intelligence (Clifford and Walster 1973). Evaluations of an attractive child's transgression are also less negative and less likely to be seen as reflecting an enduring disposition to antisocial behavior than that of an unattractive child (Dion 1972). Second, physical attractiveness impacts actual educational attainment. There is a positive relationship between attractiveness and education level and grades (Felson 1980; Umberson and Hughes 1987). Research with obese students also finds that they encounter difficulty at all levels of the educational system and during the college application process (see Puhl and Brownell 2001; Solovay 2000). At the front of the classroom, one naturalistic study even found that appearance matters for both female and male professors; professors' appearances positively correlate with their teaching evaluations (Riniolo et al. 2006).

Given the centrality of physical attractiveness in mate selection, it is not unexpected that physical appearance affects dating and marriage prospects. Initial studies focused on the Matching Hypothesis that predicts individuals will choose to date others who approximate their own level of social desirability. Results were equivocal, showing that, on the one hand, individuals seek attractive dates regardless of own physical attractiveness (e.g., Walster et al. 1966) and, on the other, individuals match potential dates by physical attractiveness level (e.g., Berscheid et al. 1971). Research also shows that women's attractiveness and body mass negatively influences the probability of marriage (Conley and Glauber 2005; Udry and Eckland 1984). Importantly, appearance correlates with mobility through marriage. Physical attractiveness is an important variable to upward mobility for women, playing a key role in marriage to high-status men (Elder 1969). That is, more attractive women marry highly educated husbands with higher incomes (Udry and Eckland 1984). As researchers claim: 'Women face an additional economic penalty for bad looks in the form of marriage to husbands whose potential earnings abilities are lower' (Hammermesh and Biddle 1994, 1189).

Institutionalized advantages of beauty are apparent in other arenas of social life beyond work, education, and marriage. In sport, beauty influences success including wins, the distribution of sponsorships, and media exposure (Hilliard 1984; Lowe 1998; Messner 2002). Research in health care administration indicates that unattractive individuals may receive poorer treatment. For example, physician surveys find that obesity is a condition many physicians respond to negatively and associate negative stereotypes to, including laziness and a lack of self-control (Klein et al. 1982; Price et al. 1987). In the mental health arena, studies show that mental health practitioners may consider attractive people better adjusted and see them as having better self concepts and a better prognosis for recovery than unattractive individuals (Cash et al. 1977; Hobfoll and Penner 1978).

Finally, in law, extensive research maintains that attractiveness matters. As Hatfield and Sprecher summarize in their review, 'good-looking defendants have several advantages: (i) They are less likely to be caught; (ii) If caught, they are less likely to be reported; (iii) If their case comes to court, judges and jurors are more likely to be lenient' (1986, 91). In light of this plethora of individual and institutional effects, predictably, even when controlling for race, age, and other relevant covariates, attractiveness correlates positively with happiness and negatively with stress (Umberson and Hughes 1987). The social reality for attractive individuals is that they generally report better overall social and psychological outcomes.

◉ Beauty Work Practices

The social rewards and benefits that accompany physical attractiveness provide strong incentive to participate in beauty work practices. This work ranges from mundane acts like putting on makeup to extraordinary decisions like undertaking cosmetic surgery. Because women's appearances are more carefully scripted and scrutinized than are men's (Jackson 1992; Weitz 2001), most academic studies have focused on the appearance-related practices of women. Women are conditioned to think about their appearance and to make changes to their appearance in pursuit of achieving the perfection associated with the hegemonic beauty ideal (Chapkis 1986; Gimlin 2002). Even women who reject hegemonic beauty ideals participate in some forms of beauty work, perhaps to achieve a different ideal (for example, pursuing ideals associated with particular subcultures like punks or goths, or wanting to achieve a 'natural' look or a 'lesbian' appearance). For this reason, we focus our attention in this article on beauty work performed by women. However, it is important to note that researchers are beginning to turn their attention to men and the beauty work that they perform as well (e.g., Andersen et al. 2000; Bell and McNaughton 2007; Bordo 1999; Monaghan 2008; Pope et al. 2000).

Women are held accountable for numerous appearance norms, including, among others, those related to their hair, makeup, body hair, body size and shape, clothing, and nails (Chapkis 1986; Gimlin

1996). The basic assumption that underlies all of these norms is that women's bodies must be altered in some way—that their natural state is unacceptable. And if women are unable to perform beauty work on their own to achieve these ideals, a large cosmetic surgery industry exists to support their endeavors. In the section below, we discuss appearance norms and beauty work practices surrounding three key areas of women's appearance: hair (and body hair), makeup, and body shape/size.

Hair and Body Hair

One particularly important part of a person's appearance, especially for women, is their hair (Gimlin 1996). While ideals associated with hair vary by race, social class, and region, hegemonic norms prescribe that women's hair be long, blonde, and intentionally styled (Weitz 2001). Women are aware of these norms and make choices as to whether they will accommodate or resist them. For example, Weitz (2001) examined the ways in which women's hair conveys messages about conformity, power, docility, or resistance. Based on in-depth interviews, she finds that women are able to use their hair (through the style, length, color, etc.) to gain power in both personal and professional settings. The majority of women emphasized attractiveness and accommodation to mainstream ideals in their appearance—what Weitz refers to as a 'traditional' strategy to gain power through their hair.

Gimlin (1996) and Weitz (2001) both find that women can use their hair to influence other people's perceptions of them, as well as to modify their own personalities and behaviors. Many of the women described the power they felt in being attractive to men, regardless of their own sexual orientation. One lesbian woman in Weitz's sample, for example, felt that her long hair helped her to 'pass' as heterosexual, which she felt helped her in the workplace. Another woman dyed her hair red, claiming that not only did it make people see her differently ('I started getting noticed a little bit more'), but that she also changed her own behavior to conform more closely with what she saw as characteristic of 'red-headed women' ('I stopped waiting to be asked,' and 'I decided I was going to quit being what I thought other people wanted me to be').

Not all beauty work, however, is in service to hegemonic beauty ideals. Weitz found that some women resisted these ideals, employing more non-traditional strategies to gain power through their hair. For instance, several women described cutting their hair short in order to be taken more seriously in the workforce, noting the contradiction between 'professionalism' and hegemonic femininity ('I'm not going to get through life by being girly,' one woman said). Others used their hair to make political, religious, or social statements. One African-American woman stated that her dreadlocks allowed her to express pride in her cultural heritage and to make a statement about 'the realities of cultural alienation, cultural marginalization, cultural invisibility, discrimination, injustice, all of that' (2001, 680). Women also used their hair to assert a specific identity, such as a lesbian or Muslim identity.

Body Hair Removal

US and Western cultural appearance norms prescribe that women remove and/or vigilantly maintain their body hair (Tiggemann and Lewis 2004; Toerien and Wilkinson 2003). This includes primarily leg, facial, and underarm hair and, increasingly, the partial or full removal of pubic hair (Toerien et al. 2005). Basow (1991) and others argue that this hairlessness ideal essentially de-emphasizes women's adult status and sexuality by returning them to a pre-adolescent state.

Adherence to the hairlessness norm is widespread among Western women. Studies conducted in the United States, the United Kingdom, and Australia find that over 90 percent of women remove their leg and underarm hair on a regular basis (Basow 1991 reports figures closer to 80 percent, as she oversampled lesbians and older adults in her US study; Tiggemann and Lewis 2004; Toerien et al. 2005). Of the women sampled in Toerien et al.'s (2005) British study, 85 percent reported removing some or all of their pubic hair and 82 percent reported manipulating their eyebrows. These women also reported a range of other sites for hair removal: 12 percent removed hair from their breasts, 11 percent from their stomach, 8 percent from their arms, 2 percent from their toes, and a smattering of participants listed fingers, knuckles, hands, neck, back, feet, and nostrils.

Common reasons for *initially* removing leg and underarm hair related to social norms and social acceptability (e.g., 'it was the thing to do' or 'women are supposed to shave'; Basow 1991). The main reasons women *continued* to adhere to the hairlessness ideal related to femininity and conventional attractiveness (e.g., 'I like the soft/silky feeling' or 'men prefer women without ... hair'). Later studies found that women who do not remove body hair are not only rated as unattractive, but also as less intelligent, less happy, and less sociable than women who do shave their legs and underarms (Basow and Braman 1998; Tiggemann and Lewis 2004).

Makeup

Women are also held accountable for complying with makeup norms, in both their personal and professional lives. Based on in-depth interviews with professional women, Dellinger and Williams (1997) find that the use of makeup elicits several benefits for women. First, when women wear makeup to work, others perceived them as well-rested and having an overall healthy appearance. When women who usually wear makeup show up to work without it, co-workers also subject them to questions about their health and/or energy level (e.g., 'Do you feel alright?'). Thus, the use of makeup can function to help women avoid negative attention. Likewise, women who usually did not wear makeup to work received positive attention on those occasions when they did. Both reactions to the use—or non-use—of makeup reinforce the norm that makeup is an integral part of looking healthy, energized, and well-rested (Dellinger and Williams 1997).

The use of makeup also marks women as heterosexual. In Dellinger's and Williams' (1997) study, the use of makeup was interpreted as showing respect for, or caring for, men and their opinions. All of the lesbian women they interviewed (25 percent of their sample) noted a connection between wearing makeup and being perceived as heterosexual. This connection is perhaps even more pronounced among women athletes, regardless of their sexuality, who actively use makeup to guard against people's assumptions that they are lesbians (Blinde and Taub 1992; Cahn 1994; Hilliard 1984; Lowe 1998). Thus, like dyeing or styling hair, wearing makeup has the added function of allowing lesbians to 'pass' for straight while also allowing straight women to be free from questions about their heterosexuality.

Finally, many of the women interviewed by Dellinger and Williams (1997) felt that wearing makeup at work enhanced their credibility. Certainly, women who worked in the 'appearance industry' as hairstylists or in cosmetic retail felt that their use of makeup added to their credibility and competence in helping other women with their appearances. As one woman put it, 'you can't look like crap and tell somebody how they should look and expect them to believe you if you look like shit' (1997, 165). Other women also felt that makeup increased their perceived competence and credibility. Wearing makeup for them was seen as part of 'looking professional'. Young women can use makeup to try to look older (and thus more credible), older women can use makeup to appear younger (and thus more competent), and women of color can use makeup to signal that they 'fit in' with the norms of the dominant culture.

Body Size and Body Shape

Given the prevalence of a thin and firm body ideal for women and a firm ideal for men in western culture, much beauty work today focuses on altering body size and shape. Because the cultural ideal is generally unattainable and has debilitating effects on women, including their mental and physical health (see, e.g., Sprague-Zones 1997), some feminists refer to it as a 'tyranny of slenderness' (Chernin 1994) and a 'beauty myth' (Wolf 1991). This myth, they critique, reproduces gender hierarchies and is a form of patriarchal oppression. According to Wolf, women's fixation on thinness is akin to self-starvation, contributes to lowered self-esteem, and diverts women's attention from social advancement. In her Foucauldian analysis, Bordo (2003) also argues that these practices stem, not solely from direct repression, but from more subtle forms of surveillance including self-surveillance, surveillance by men, and surveillance by other women. We elaborate on the relationship between beauty work and the reproduction of gender norms in the following section.

Like other forms of beauty work, much of the literature on weight loss practices focuses on women. This is consistent with the high rates of female body dissatisfaction documented (Feingold and Mazzella 1998). Body weight concerns are so prevalent that some scholars label it a 'normative discontent' for women (Rodin et al. 1985). Dieting practices vary and include techniques such as reduced calorie consumption, vomiting, diet pills, and fad diets (Ogden 1992). Women have also turned to surgery to alter body size and shape and, in fact, most weight loss surgery patients are women (Santry et al. 2005).

Studies exploring the perspectives of women who undertake cosmetic surgery illuminate a central tension between free will and cooptation. While female beauty norms can be interpreted as an oppressive tool and beauty work as a form of compliance or cooptation, Davis (1991) observes that women's agency is actual central to these practices. Her analysis of Dutch cosmetic surgery patients indicates that women are neither mistaken nor misguided in their endeavors. Instead, abandoning the simplistic notion that women are victims of beauty constraints, Davis argues that women actively pursue cosmetic surgery so that they can regain control of their lives, feel normal, or even right the wrong of an ongoing suffering. In this way, they are far from 'cultural dopes'. Similarly, in her interviews with women who participated in cosmetic surgery, Gimlin (2000) documents the importance women attach to having 'freely chosen' to undergo surgery. The surgery enables women to reposition their bodies as normal, even if it simultaneously requires accounting for charges of inauthenticity.

☻ Beauty Work and the Reproduction of Gender

These practices illuminate the importance of social norms and constraints. Moreover, they highlight a notable gender dimension. We have already alluded to this double standard of beauty. While attractiveness matters for men, for women it is essential, nearly compulsory. We observe this double standard especially with regard to weight and aging. So while there is substantial evidence that large individuals encounter stigma (e.g., Puhl and Brownell 2001), this is especially the case for large women. Because ideologies of weight closely parallel ideologies of womanhood, women experience extraordinary pressure to conform to body ideals and are stigmatized even more so than men when they do not conform (McKinley 1999). The effects are not inconsequential. For example, obese women face downward social and economic mobility (Rothblum 1992), suffer greater economic penalties that obese men do not (Conley and Glauber 2005; Register and Williams 1990), and are more negatively stigmatized as less sexually attractive mates than obese men (Regan 1996). Moreover, as men age and deviate from the youthful beauty ideal, they are given more social latitude than women. So even when aging accompanies diminished attractiveness for both women and men, this decline is greater for women (Deutsch et al. 1986). Not surprisingly, beauty work is much more prevalent among women. Preoccupation with body is so prevalent that young girls' 'fat talk' is a form of beauty work in itself, even as it fulfills a female bonding function (Nichter 2000).

Women face several contradictions when they perform beauty work. If she fails at beauty conformity, she is powerless and condemned as ugly; if she is successful, she is still powerless in a regime that defines her value and worth by her appearance (Tseëlon 1993). It is a double bind. In her conformity attempts, she also reinforces economic structures and a multi-billion dollar-a-year beauty industry profits nicely from her efforts (Fraser 1998). Moreover, hegemonic beauty ideals are not only unrealistic, they are made to seem natural

891

for women. 'She is expected to embody a ìtimelessë cultural fantasy that is removed from the diverse and changing world of the living. But her special beauty is not really innate, and it takes a lot of effort to maintain' (Tseëlon 1993, 319). Women's effortless authentic beauty is thus far from it. Beauty work is in large part this process of transforming the natural body to fit the cultural ideal, altogether while concealing the process and making it seem natural. Dull and West (1991) observe this phenomenon in their interviews with cosmetic surgeons and patients. Surgeons and patients consider women's pursuit of aesthetic improvement as 'normal' or 'natural'. However, because it is considered less so for men, men's surgery discourses center around instrumental reasons such as job-related concerns. In similar vein, as women age, they laud the natural unmodified body yet nevertheless engage in beauty work, endeavoring to produce a 'natural look' through their beauty regimens (Clarke and Griffin 2007).

The salience of beauty for women stems in part from Western culture's emphasis on the female body. Mass media images of feminine beauty, however unrealistic, are pervasive and objectify and commodify women's bodies (Kilbourne 1999). From an early age, cultural artifacts, from advertisements to children's fairy tales, expose young girls to the feminine beauty ideal (Baker-Sperry and Grauerholz 2003). These images reinforce what Connell (1987) refers to as 'emphasized femininity', a femininity that is complicit to gender inequality and is organized around men's desires and interests. This emphasized femininity teaches young girls and women that their appearance is central to self and success. Indeed research shows that a woman's body and appearance closely tie to her self-definition and self-esteem (e.g., Tiggemann 1994). One study reports that physical appearance is actually the most important predictor of self-evaluation by college and high school girls (Jackson et al. 1994). Women may even come to define themselves—and other women—in terms of this objectification and 'male gaze' (Berger 1972; Frederickson and Roberts 1997; McKinley 1999; McKinley and Hyde 1996; Mulvey 1989).

Furthermore, the rules of femininity are transmitted through mass media and other visual images (Bordo 2003). Power and social relations are written on the body as text. In Bordo's words, 'we learn the rules directly through bodily discourse: through images that tell us what clothes, body shape, facial expression, movements, and behavior are required' (2003, 170). Even when these rules contradict and gender norms are ambiguous, their bodily inscription is apparent. The female anorexic is exemplary. She embraces with vehemence both a domestic conception of fragility, powerless, and containment, alongside the masculine ideals of self-control and mastery. Through self-regulation and other surveillance techniques, women monitor and discipline their bodies in ways that reproduce the social order. So despite the diversity and complexity of cultural images and ideals, a homogenizing and normalizing tendency occurs (Bordo 2003). In this way, women's beauty work, whether it is donning makeup, hair styling, and/or dieting, is a way of 'doing gender' (West and Zimmerman 1987). The body is a text for expressing and reproducing gender hierarchies.

While cultural gender bias means beauty work is more prevalent among women, men too participate in appearance-related work. In recent years, there has been a rise in what Pope et al. (2000) refer to as the Adonis Complex. The sale of men's beauty products, gym equipment, and fitness memberships all point to men's growing concern for their appearance. According to these authors, two important impetuses account for this rise. First, the commonplace of anabolic steroids by the 1980s, along with the Hollywood bodies built from its usage, changed the cultural landscape and enabled young men to surpass the boundaries of physiology. Second, women's growing equality threatened men's social position, leading them to seek alternative arenas and avenues to enact masculinity. The leading cultural construction of masculinity, or hegemonic masculinity (Connell 1995), dictates that 'real men' possess, among other characteristics, strength, control, and autonomy. When women's equality threatens masculinity, control over the body through beauty work such as weight training and body building becomes a way of regaining control. Again, similar to women's feminine beauty work, men's displays of muscularity can help sustain dominant cultural hierarchies and social relations.

893

◉ Race, Body Satisfaction, and Beauty Work

There is an important racial dimension to beauty norms and beauty work. Simply stated, the Western beauty aesthetic is a white ideal defined in opposition to the black body (Collins 1991). As Collins (1991) points out, the black body is the Other and it is this Other that the beauty ideal defines itself in opposition to (see also Young 1990). In her words, '[b]lue-eyed, blond, thin women could not be considered beautiful without the Other—Black women with classical African features of dark skin, broad noses, full lips, and kinky hair' (1991, 79). Moreover, depictions of the Eurocentric beauty ideal come alongside negative, stereotypical, and controlling images of black women's bodies (Collins 1991). These cultural depictions lead to important racial and ethnic differences in body dissatisfaction and beauty work.

While there is some evidence that African-American women idealize Eurocentric features such as lighter skin color (Bond and Cash 1992), studies generally confirm that body dissatisfaction is lower among African-American women and that, as a whole, there is a more flexible standard of beauty in black communities.[2] For example, Milkie's (1999) interviews with white and minority girls found that minority girls' lack of identification with 'white' media images serves as a buffer to their harmful effects on self-concept. Research by Parker et al. (1995) reports that African-American girls' sense of beauty comes from 'looking good' or making what 'you've got work for you'. This is in contrast to white adolescent girls who voice body dissatisfaction and affix themselves to a more rigid conception of beauty. In Lovejoy's (2001) excellent review, she also notes that black women subscribe to an alternative aesthetic. This aesthetic enables them to combat social stigmatization and is a form of cultural resistance. A more flexible and egalitarian aesthetic found in black communities thus celebrates uniqueness and harmony in diversity (Collins 1991). This black aesthetic encourages self-acceptance among African-American girls and women, leading to higher levels of body satisfaction.

894

Despite black women's positive body image, Lovejoy (2001) cautions that greater body acceptance may lead to a denial of psychological and physical health problems such as obesity and compulsive overeating. Thompson (1992, 1994) has also written about eating disorders among African American. Importantly, she critiques feminist theories that explain eating disorders as an extension of compulsory thinness for women. Her life history interviews with African-American, Latina, and white women suggest that these behaviors often serve as coping strategies for serious traumas including sexual abuse, racism, and poverty.

Studies of Asian-American women report greater resemblance to whites than blacks and an idealization of the white beauty ideal. For example, Evans and McConnell (2003) exposed three groups of women (Asian, black, and white) to idealized images and found that, while black women did not find mainstream standards relevant to themselves, Asian and white women were more likely to endorse mainstream beauty standards. Lee and Zhan's (1998) review also finds an idealized Caucasian identification among Asian-American youth and general dissatisfaction among Asian-American youths about their appearance. Similarly, Kaw (1993) observes a predominance of nose implants and double-eyelid surgery among Asian-American women. She argues that these alterations are an attempt to escape persisting racial prejudice that correlates stereotypical genetic physical features such as 'slanty eyes' and a 'flat nose' with negative behavioral characteristics such as passivity. As a whole, there is some evidence that hegemonic Western beauty norms contribute to Asian-American women's body dissatisfaction, leading to normalizing beauty work (Kawamura 2002).

Researchers have also studied beauty work and dissatisfaction among Hispanics. Altabe and O'Garo (2002) note that Hispanic communities' emphasis on a traditional feminine role, along with a cultural fatalism that suppresses interpersonal conflict and defiance, may exacerbate body dissatisfaction among young Latinas. Researchers have also studied the role of acculturation finding that, at times, it plays an important role in eating disorders; for example, immigration to the United States prior to puberty is a risk factor (Lopez et al.

1995), while at other times, it is unrelated (Joiner and Kashubeck 1996). Grabe and Hyde best capture the position of beauty work and body dissatisfaction among Latinas when they state, 'unlike the consistent differences reported in the Black-White literature, recent research regarding differences in body dissatisfaction between Hispanic and White women has been mixed' (2006, 624).

Because most empirical research focuses on women, relatively few studies have examined racial/ethnic differences in body image for men. However, Ricciardelli et al. (2007) recently, systematically, and comprehensively reviewed the research on men across several body work variables. Specifically, they consider body image, weight loss strategies and binge eating, weight/muscle gain strategies and steroids for several cultural groups in the United States, including blacks, Hispanics, Asians, Native Americans, Pacific Islanders, and Middle Easterners. They conclude that men from minority ethnic groups engage in more extreme body transformation strategies and binge eating than do white men. Moreover, they suggest that, for men, several variables moderate and/or mediate the relationship between culture and body image. These include acculturation, socio-economic status, media exposure, and the internalization of the muscular ideal.

◉ Conclusion

In Western cultures that hold the beautiful body in high esteem, individuals perform various forms of beauty work, thus reproducing and strengthening this social hierarchy. Social structures that confer both individual and institutional rewards to physically attractive individuals encourage these practices. Not only do individuals associate positive traits with beautiful persons, physically attractive people hold a communication advantage in social interactions and are more likely to experience employment, educational, and marital success compared to unattractive persons. While both women and men perform beauty work, in light of the double standard of beauty, beauty work plays a more central role in women's lives. There are also important racial and ethnic group variations in body satisfaction and beauty work practices.

Despite the cultural hierarchy that clearly allocates benefits and privileges to the beautiful, resistance practices are evident. For example, Butler (1990) shows how drag is one way of subverting normative constructions of sex and gender, creating 'gender trouble' (see also Bornstein 1994). Subcultural bodily practices such as scarification enable the reclaiming of the female body (Pitts 1998). Resistance to, and the subversion of, the thin ideal comes in many forms including what Lebesco (2001, 2004) describes as 'queering corpulent bodies/politics' that involves rejecting essentialist approaches to fat (2001, 84). Some have even argued that cosmetic surgery is a possible tool to subvert dominant patriarchal ideals of feminine beauty by highlighting the artificial nature of the body (Balasmo 1996; Morgan 1991; for a review of this perspective, see Negrin 2002).

There are several ways of understanding the relationship between cultural norms and beauty work. On the one hand, individuals who participate in body modification practices can be thought of as 'cultural dopes,' passively adopting hegemonic beauty norms. In this vein, beauty work, especially for women, is a form of complicity. The homogenizing and normalizing effects of hegemonic cultural norms are successful (Bordo 2003; Foucault 1979). Through self-regulation and other mechanisms, docile bodies emerge. In this line of thinking, willing participants need consciousness-raising to understand how their actions play into larger systems of domination. Body acceptance thus becomes crucial to women's advancement (Chapkis 1986).

On the other hand, it is possible to understand individuals as active agents who perform beauty work to consciously reap certain rewards and avoid stigma. As discussed previously, cosmetic surgery undertakers see surgery as a way of regaining control of one's life, feeling normal, and righting the wrong of suffering (Davis 1995; see also Gimlin 2000; Kaw 1993). Dellinger and Williams' (1997) interviews indicate that women feel they need makeup to appear healthy, heterosexual, and competent in the workplace. These researchers also report that women sometimes 'transform the meanings attached to their own use of makeup' (1997, 168), documenting several positive functions of makeup. At times, makeup is a topic of conversation that bonds women and it also symbolizes a woman's time for herself (Dellinger and Williams 1997). Delano (2000) too observes that, for some women, wearing makeup may be an act of agency. During World War II, American women used makeup in part to disrupt wartime's masculine code of power.

As these cases illustrate, individuals are far from simply cultural dopes. Instead, they negotiate their experiences within structural constraints and employ beauty work in the active pursuit of some goal, whether it is happiness, success, or resistance. Gagné and McGaughey's (2002) in-depth interviews with elective mammoplasty patients point to a middle-ground where patients exercise agency within cultural constraints (also see Negrin 2002). That is, beauty practices can be empowering while simultaneously reinforcing oppressive hegemonic ideals. These practices can sustain and reproduce the social order. Weitz (2001) draws a similar conclusion in her study of hair. While women who use traditional means of seeking power through conventional attractiveness 'are actively and rationally making choices based on a realistic assessment of how they can best obtain their goals' (2001, 675), they do little to challenge the broader ideologies that support women's appearance as the primary means through which they are valued. Even women who reject elements of the hegemonic ideals reinforce the importance of appearance. In addition, they may gain personal power at the expense of other women.

Our review of the beauty work literature highlights widespread beauty practices, particularly among women, in a society that rewards beauty and sanctions ugliness. However, it also illuminates several areas of research that currently remain un- or under-explored. First, while much work focuses on how physical attractiveness affects perceptions and social outcomes at both the individual and institutional levels, given the importance of intersecting status characteristics (Collins 1991), it would be valuable for researchers to conduct empirical analyses on how race, gender, and class (among other characteristics) interact with beauty to shape perceptions and outcomes. For instance, how do advantageous and disadvantageous characteristics operate simultaneously? What are their meanings for self and identity, psychological well-being, and other social out-comes? For example, while age usually brings higher income, beauty as an asset declines with age. What mechanisms are at work in these situations? How do these competing characteristics intersect and interact?[3] Second, while a dialogue has begun about men's bodies, their performance of beauty work, and the rise of the Adonis Complex, we acknowledge that the widespread focus on women's beauty work has resulted in a dearth of literature on men. As such, we encourage continued theoretical and empirical attention on men's practices. Third, while researchers are moving past a one-dimension-al focus on women to examine other diffuse status characteristics such as race and ethnicity, most of this literature has focused on large minority groups such as blacks, Asians, and Hispanics. This has come at the cost of other groups such as Native Americans, Middle-Easterners, and multi-racial individuals. Indeed these groups provide a unique episte-mological standpoint on beauty work that merit in-depth exploration. Finally, an ideological shift towards public sociol-ogy beseeches us as researchers to take our study of social life one step further and contemplate how our work fits into practical and positive social change. As such, we encourage researchers not only to investigate the concrete manifestations of western culture's hierarchy of beauty, but to explore how both formal and informal policy can be enacted to subvert this hierarchy and/or to eliminate stigma, bias, and discrimination for beauty nonconformists.

◉ Short Biography

Samantha Kwan, PhD, is an Assistant Professor of Sociology and a Women's Studies faculty affiliate at the University of Houston. She received her doctorate in sociology from the University of Arizona in 2007. Her research interests are in the areas of gender, body, and cul-ture. Her current work focuses on contested meanings about body, health, and weight; cosmetic surgery; and the relationship between religion and body work. She teaches various courses at the University of Houston including the sociology of gender, research methods, and criminology.

Mary Nell Trautner, PhD, is an Assistant Professor of Sociology at the University at Buffalo, SUNY. She received her doctorate in sociology from the University of Arizona in 2006. Her research and teaching interests are in the areas of law and society, gender, organizations, and labor and labor movements. Her current work focuses on legal decision making and public policy, specifically how tort reform impacts how personal injury lawyers decide which cases to accept and which to decline. Her articles have appeared in Gender & Society, Social Forces, and Working USA.

Notes

[1]Appearance/image is not federally protected. In the A & F case, plaintiffs had recourse because of the interrelationship between appearance discrimination and race/sex discrimination. The consent decree stated that the company cannot discriminate by race or sex under the auspice of a marketing strategy for a particular look. In 2004, the US Equal Employment Opportunity Commission (EEOC) agreed to a mutual resolution of the lawsuit for $50 million (U.S. EEOC Press Release November 16, 2004).

[2]Grabe and Hyde (2006) question whether there are large differences in dissatisfaction among white and non-white women. Their recent meta-analysis indicates that, while there are differences among these groups, these differences are small.

[3]We thank David Shulman for bringing this paradox to our attention.

References

Adams, Gerald R. 1982. 'Physical Attractiveness.' pp. 253–304 in *In the Eye of the Beholder*, edited by Arthur Miller. New York, NY: Praeger.

Allon, Natalie 1982. 'The Stigma of Overweight in Everyday Life.' p. 130–74 in *Psychological Aspects of Obesity: A Handbook*, edited by Benjamin B. Wolman. New York, NY: Va n Nostrand Reinhold.

Altabe, Madeline and Keisha-Gaye N. O'Garo 2002. 'Hispanic Body Images.' pp. 250–6 in *Body Image: A Handbook of Theory, Research, and Clinical Practice*, edited by Thomas F. Cash and Thomas Pruzinsky. New York, NY: Guilford Press.

Andersen, Arnold, Leigh Cohn and To m Holbrook 2000. *Making Weight: Men's Conflicts with Food, Weight, Shape, and Appearance*. Carlsbad, CA: Gurze Books.

Baker-Sperry, Lori and Liz Grauerholz 2003. 'The Pervasiveness and Persistence of the Feminine Beauty Ideal in Children's Fairy Tales.' *Gender & Society* 17: 711–26.

Balasmo, Anne 1996. *Technologies of the Gendered Body: Reading Cyborg Women*. Durham, NC: Duke University Press.

Basow, Susan A. 1991. 'The Hairless Ideal: Women and Their Body Hair.' *Psychology of Women Quarterly* 15: 83 –96.

Basow, Susan A. and Amie C. Braman 1998. 'Women and Body Hair: Social Perceptions and Attitudes.' *Psychology of Women Quarterly* 22: 637–45.

Bell, Kirsten and Darlene McNaughton 2007. 'Feminism and the Invisible Fat Man.' *Body & Society* 13: 107–31.

Berger John. 1972. *Ways of Seeing*. London, UK: Penguin.

Berger, Joseph, H. Famit Fisek, Robert Z. Norman and Morris Zelditch Jr. 1977. *Status Characteristics and Social Interaction: An Expectation-States Approach*. New York, NY: Elsevier Scientific Publishing Co.

Berscheid, Ellen, Karen Dion, Elaine Walster and G. William Walster 1971. 'Physical Attractiveness and Dating Choice: A test of the Matching Hypothesis.' *Journal of Experimental Social Psychology* 7: 173–89.

Blinde, Elaine M. and Diane E. Taub 1992. 'Women Athletes as Falsely Accused Deviants: Managing the Lesbian Stigma.' *The Sociological Quarterly* 33: 521–33.

Bond, Selena and Thomas F. Cash 1992. 'Black Beauty: Skin Color and Body Images among African-American College Women.' *Journal of Applied Social Psychology* 22: 874–88.

Bordo, Susan 1999. *The Male Body: A New Look at Men in Public and in Private*. New York, NY: Farrar, Straus and Giroux.

Bordo, Susan 2003. *Unbearable Weight: Feminism, Western Culture & the Body*. Berkeley, CA: University of California Press.

Bornstein, Kate 1994. *Gender Outlaw: On Men, Women, and the Rest of Us*. New York, NY: Routledge.

Butler, Judith 1990. *Gender Trouble: Feminism and the Subversion of Identity*. Second edition. New York, NY: Routledge.

901

Cahn, Susan 1994. *Coming On Strong: Gender and Sexuality in Twentieth Century Women's Sport*. New York, NY: Free Press.

Cash, Thomas F., Jo Anne Kehr, James Polyson and Valerie Freeman 1977. 'Role of Physical Attractiveness in Peer Attribution of Psychological Disturbance.' *Journal of Consulting and Clinical* Psychology 45: 987–93.

Chapkis, Wendy 1986. Beauty Secrets: *Women and the Politics of Appearance*. Boston, MA: South End Press.

Chernin, Kim 1994. *The Obsession: Reflections on the Tyranny of Slenderness*. New York, NY: Harper Perennial.

Clarke, Laura Hurd and Meredith Griffin 2007. 'The Body Natural and the Body Unnatural: Beauty Work and Aging.' Journal of Aging Studies 21: 187–201.

Clifford, Margaret M. and Elaine Walster 1973. 'The Effect of Physical Attractiveness on Teacher Expectations.' *Sociology of Education* 46: 248 –58.

Collins, Patricia Hill 1991. *Black Feminist Thought; Knowledge, Consciousness, and the Politics of Empowerment*. New York, NY: Routledge.

Conley, Dalton and Rebecca Glauber May 2005. 'Gender, Body Mass and Economic Status.' *National Bureau of Economic Research Working Paper Series*. Cambridge, MA: National Bureau of Economic Research.

Connell, R. W. 1987. *Gender and Power*. Stanford, CA: Stanford University Press.

Connell, R. W. 1995. *Masculinities*. Berkeley, CA: University of California Press.

Davis, Kathy 1991. 'Remaking the She-Devil: A Critical Look at Feminist Approaches to Beauty.' *Hypatia* 6 (2): 21–43.

Davis, Kathy 1995. *Reshaping the Female Body: The Dilemma of Cosmetic Surgery*. New York, NY: Routledge.

Delano, Page D. 2000. 'Making Up for War: Sexuality and Citizenship in Wartime Culture.' *Feminist Studies* 26: 33–68.

Dellinger, Kirsten and Christine L. Williams 1997. 'Makeup at Work: Negotiating Appearance Rules in the Workplace.' *Gender & Society* 11: 151–77.

Dermer, Marshall and Darrel L. Thiel 1975. 'When Beauty May Fail.' *Journal of Personality and Social Psychology* 31: 1168 –76.

Deutsch, Francine M., Carla M. Zalenski and Mary E. Clark 1986. 'Is There a Double Standard of Aging?' *Journal of Applied Social Psychology* 16: 771–85.

Dion, Karen and Ellen Berscheid 1974. 'Physical Attractiveness and Perception in Children.' *Sociometry* 37: 1–12.

Dion, Karen and Steven Stein 1978. 'Physical Attractiveness and Interpersonal Influence.' *Journal of Experimental Social Psychology* 14: 97–108.

Dion, Karen, Ellen Berscheid and Elaine Walster 1972. 'What Is Beautiful Is Good.' *Journal of Personality and Social Psychology* 24: 285–90.

Dion, Karen 1972. 'Physical Attractiveness and Evaluation of Children's Transgressions.' *Journal of Personality and Social Psychology* 24: 207–13.

Drogosz, Lisa M. and Paul E. Levy 1996. 'Another Look at the Effects of Appearance, Gender, and Job Type on Performance-Based Decision' *Psychology of Women Quarterly* 20: 437–445.

Dull, Diane and Candace West 1991. 'Accounting for Cosmetic Surgery: The Accomplishment of Gender.' *Social Problems* 38: 54–70.

Eagly, Alice H., Richard D. Ashmore, Mona G. Makhijani and Laura C. Longo 1991. 'What Is Beautiful Is Good, but . . . : A Meta-Analytic Review of Research on the Physical Attractiveness Stereotype.' *Psychological Bulletin* 110: 109–28.

Elder, Glen 1969. 'Appearance and Education in Marriage Mobility.' *American Sociological Review* 34: 519–33.

Etcoff, Nancy 1999. *Survival of the Prettiest: The Science of Beauty*. New York, NY: Doubleday.

Evans, Peggy Chin and Allen R. McConnell 2003. 'Do Racial Minorities Respond in the Same Way to Mainstream Beauty Standards? Social Comparison Processes in Asian, Black, and White Women.' *Self and Identity* 2: 153–67.

Feingold, Alan and Ronald Mazzella 1998. 'Gender Differences in Body Image are Increasing.' *Psychological Science* 9: 190–5.

Feingold, Alan 1992. 'Good-Looking People Are Not What We Think.' *Psychological Bulletin* 111: 304–41.

Felson, Richard B. 1980. 'Physical Attractiveness, Grades, and Teachers' Attributions.' *Representative Research in Social Psychology* 11: 64–71.

Foucault, Michel 1979. *Discipline and Punish*. New York, NY: Vintage.

Fraser, Laura 1998. *Losing It: America's Obsession with Weight and the Industry that Feeds on It*. New York, NY: Dutton.

Frederickson, Barbara L. and Tomi-Ann Roberts 1997. 'Objectification Theory: Towards Understanding Women's Lived Experiences and Mental Health Risks.' *Psychology of Women Quarterly* 21: 173–206.

Frieze, Irene Hanson, Josephine E. Olson and June Russell 1991. 'Attractiveness and Income for Men and Women in Management.' *Journal of Applied Social Psychology* 21: 1039–57.

Gagné, Patricia and Deanna McGaughey 2002. 'Designing Women: Cultural Hegemony and the Exercise of Power Among Women Who have Undergone Elective Mamoplasty.' *Gender & Society* 16: 814–38.

Gimlin, Debra L. 1996. 'Pamela's Place: Power and Negotiation in the Hair Salon.' *Gender & Society* 10: 505 –26.

Gimlin, Debra L. 2000. 'Cosmetic Surgery: Beauty as Commodity.' *Qualitative Sociology* 23: 77– 98.

Gimlin, Debra L. 2002. *Body Work: Beauty and Self-Image in American Culture*. Berkeley, CA: University of California Press.

Gimlin, Debra L. 2007. 'What Is "Body Work"? A Review of the Literature.' *Sociology Compass* 1: 353–70.

Goffman, Erving 1963. *Stigma: Notes on the Management of Spoiled Identity*. Englewood Cliffs, NJ: Prentice-Hall.

Grabe, Shelly and Janet Shibley Hyde 2006. 'Ethnicity and Body Dissatisfaction among Women in the United States: A Meta-Analysis.' *Psychological Bulletin* 132: 622–40.

Hammermesh, Daniel S. and Jeff E. Biddle 1994. 'Beauty and the Labor Market.' *American Economic Review* 84: 1174–94.

Hatfield, Elaine and Susan Sprecher 1986. *Mirror, Mirror: The Importance of Looks in Everyday Life*. New York, NY: State University of New York Press.

Heilman, Madeline E. 1983. 'Sex Bias in Work Settings: The Lack of Fit Model.' *Research in Organizational Behavior* 5: 269–98.

Heilman, Madeline E. and Lois R. Saruwatari 1979. 'When Beauty Is Beastly: The Effects of Appearance and Sex on Evaluations of Job Applications for Managerial and Nonmanagerial Jobs.' *Organizational Behavior and Human Performance* 23: 360–72.

Heilman, Madeline E. and Melanie E. Stopeck 1985. 'Being Attractive, Advantage or Disadvantage? Performance-Based Evaluations and Recommended Personnel Actions as a Function of Appearance, Sex, and Job Type.' *Organizational Behavior and Human Decision Processes* 35: 202–15.

Hesse-Biber, Sharlene 1996. *Am I Thin Enough Yet? The Cult of Thinness and the Commercialization of Identity*. New York, NY: Oxford University Press.

Hilliard, Dan C. 1984. 'Media Images of Male and Female Professional Athletes: An Interpretive Analysis of Magazine Articles.' *Sociology of Sport Journal* 1: 251– 62.

Hobfoll, Steven E. and Louis A. Penner 1978. 'Effect of Physical Attractiveness on Therapists' Initial Judgments of Person's Self Concept.' *Journal of Consulting and Clinical Psychology* 46: 200–1.

Horai, Joann, Nicholas Naccari and Elliot Fatoullah 1974. 'The Effects of Expertise and Physical Attractiveness upon Opinion Agreement and Liking.' *Sociometry* 37: 601–6.

Hosoda, Megumi, Eugene F. Stone-Romero and Gwen Coats 2003. 'The Effects of Physical Attractiveness on Job-Related Outcomes: A Meta-Analysis of Experimental Studies.' *Personnel Psychology* 56: 431– 62.

Jackson, Linda A., Carole N. Hodge and Julie M. Ingram 1994. 'Gender and Self-Concept: A Reexamination of Stereotypic Differences and the Role of Gender Attitudes.' *Sex Roles* 30: 615–30.

Jackson, Linda 1992. *Physical Appearance and Gender: Sociobiological and Sociocultural Perspectives*. Albany, NY: State University of New York Press.

Joiner, Greg W. and Susan Kashubeck 1996. 'Acculturation, Body Image, Self-Esteem, and Eating-Disorder Symptomology in Adolescent Mexican American Women.' *Psychology of Women Quarterly* 20: 419–35.

Kang, Milliann 2003. 'The Managed Hand: the Commercialization of Bodies and Emotions in Korean Immigrant-Owned Nail Salons.' *Gender & Society* 17: 820–39.

Kaw, Eugenia 1993. 'Medicalization of Racial Features: Asian American Women and Cosmetic Surgery.' *Medical Anthropology* Quarterly 7: 74– 89.

Kawamura, Kathleen Y. 2002. 'Asian American Body Images.' pp. 243–2439 in *Body Image: A Handbook of Theory, Research, and Clinical Practice*, edited by Thomas F. Cash and Thomas Pruzinsky. New York, NY: Guilford Press.

Kilbourne, Jean 1999. *Can't Buy My Love: How Advertising Changes the Way We Think and Feel*. New York, NY: Touchstone Press.

Kleck, Robert E. and Carin Rubenstein 1975. 'Physical Attractiveness, Perceived Attitude Similarity, and Interpersonal Attraction in an Opposite-Sex Encounter.' *Journal of Personality and Social Psychology* 31: 107–14.

Kleck, Robert E., Stephen A. Richardson and Linda Ronald 1974. 'Physical Appearance Cues and Interpersonal Attraction in Children.' *Child Development* 45: 305–10.

Klein, David, Jackob Najman, Arthur F. Kohrman and Clarke Munro 1982. 'Patient Characteristics that Elicit Negative Responses from Family Physicians.' *Journal of Family Practice* 14: 881–8.

Landy, David and Harold Sigall 1974. 'Beauty Is Talent: Task Evaluation as a Function of the Performer's Physical Attractiveness.' *Journal of Personality and Social Psychology* 39: 299–304.

Lebesco, Kathleen 2001. 'Queering Fat Bodies/Politics.' pp. 74–87 in *Bodies Out of Bounds: Fatness and Transgression*, edited by Kane Evans Braziel and Kathleen LeBesco. Berkeley, CA: University of California Press.

Lebesco, Kathleen 2004. *Revolting Bodies: The Struggle to Redefine Fat Identity*. Boston, MA: University of Massachusetts Press.

Lee, Lee C. and Ginny Zhan 1998. 'Psychological Status of Children and Youths.' pp. 137–163 in *Handbook of Asian American Psychology*, edited by Lee C. Lee and Nolan W. S. Zane. Thousand Oaks, CA: Sage.

Lopez, Ester, Glen Garry Blix and Arlene Gray Blix 1995. 'Body Image of Latinas Compared to Body Image of Non-Latina White Women.' *Health Values: The Journal of Health Behavior, Education & Promotion* 19: 3–10.

Lovejoy, Meg 2001. 'Disturbances in the Social Body: Differences in Body Image and Eating Problems among African American and White Women.' *Gender & Society* 15: 239–61.

Lowe, Maria R. 1998. *Women of Steel: Female Bodybuilders and the Struggle for Self-Definition*. New York, NY: New York University Press.

McKinley, Nita Mary and Janet Shibley Hyde 1996. 'The Objectified Body Consciousness Scale.' *Psychology of Women Quarterly* 20: 181–215.

McKinley, Nita Mary 1999. 'Ideal Weight/Ideal Women: Society Constructs the Female.' pp. 97–115 in *Weighty Issues: Fatness and Thinness as Social Problems*, edited by Jeffery Sobal and Donna Maurer. New York, NY: Aldine de Gruyter.

Messner, Michael A. 2002. *Taking the Field: Men, Women, and Sports*. Minneapolis, MN: University of Minnesota Press.

Milkie, Melissa 1999. 'Social Comparisons, Reflected Appraisals, and Mass Media: The Impact of Pervasive Beauty Images on Black and White Girls' Self-Concepts.' *Social Psychology Quarterly* 62: 190–210.

Mills, Judson and Elliot Aronson 1965. 'Opinion Change as a Function of the Communicator's Attractiveness and Desire to Influence.' *Journal of Personality and Social Psychology* 1: 173–7.

Mills, Judson and John Harvey 1972. 'Opinion Change as a Function of When Information about the Communicator Is Received and Whether he is Attractive or Expert.' *Journal of Personality and Social Psychology* 21: 52–5.

Monaghan, Lee 2008. *Men and the War on Obesity: A Sociological Study*. New York, NY: Routledge.

Morgan, Kathryn 1991. 'Women and the Knife: Cosmetic Surgery and the Colonization of Women's Bodies.' *Hypatia* 6: 25–53.

Mulford, Matthew, John Orbell, Catherine Shatto and Jean Stockard 1998. 'Physical Attractiveness, Opportunity, and Success in Everyday Exchange.' *American Journal of Sociology* 103: 1565–92.

Mulvey, Laura 1989. *Visual Pleasures and Narrative Cinema*. Bloomington, IN: Indianapolis University Press.

Negrin, Llewellyn 2002. 'Cosmetic Surgery and the Eclipse of Identity.' *Body & Society* 8: 21–42.

Nichter, Mimi 2000. *Fat Talk: What Girls and Their Parents Say About Dieting*. Cambridge, MA: Harvard University Press.

Ogden, Jane 1992. *Fat Chance! The Myth of Dieting Explained*. London, UK: Routledge.

Parker, Sheila, Mimi Nichter, Mark Nichter, Nancy Nuckovic, Colette Sims and Cheryl Ritenbaugh 1995. 'Body Image and Weight Concerns among African American and White Adolescent Females: Differences that Make a Difference.' *Human Organization* 54: 103–14.

907

Pitts, Victoria 1998. ' "Reclaiming" the Female Body: Embodied Identity Work, Resistance, and the Grotesque.' *Body & Society* 4: 67–84.

Polinko, Natalie K. and Paula M. Popvich 2001. 'Evil Thoughts But Angelic Actions: Responses to Overweight Job Applicants.' *Journal of Applied Social Psychology* 31: 904–24.

Pope, Harrison G. Jr., Katharine A. Phillips and Roberto Olivardia 2000. *The Adonis Complex: The Secret Crisis of Male Body Obsession.* New York, NY: The Free Press.

Price, James H., Sharon M. Desmond, R. A. Krol, F. F. Snyder and Janelle K. O'Connell 1987. 'Family Practice Physicians' Beliefs, Attitudes, and Practices Regarding Obesity.' *American Journal of Preventive Medicine* 3: 339–345.

Puhl, Rebecca and Kelly D. Brownell 2001. 'Bias, Discrimination, and Obesity.' Obesity Research 9: 788–805.

Regan, Pamela C. 1996. 'Sexual Outcasts: The Perceived Impact of Body Weight and Gender on Sexuality.' *Journal of Applied Social Psychology* 25: 1803–1813.

Register, Charles A. and Donald R. Williams 1990. 'Wage Effects of Obesity among Young Workers.' *Social Science Quarterly* 71: 130 –141.

Reis, Harry T. and Holley S. Hodgins 1995. 'Reactions to Craniofacial Disfigurement: Lessons from the Physical Attractiveness and Stigma Literatures.' pp. 177–198 in *Craniofacial Anomalies: Psychological Perspectives*, edited by Rebecca Eder. New York, NY: Springer-Verlag.

Ricciardelli, Lina A., Marita P. McCabe, Robert J. Williams and J. Kevin Thompson 2007. 'The Role of Ethnicity and Culture in Body Image and Disordered Eating Among Males.' *Clinical Psychology Review* 27: 582–606.

Riniolo, Todd C. Katherine C. Johnson, Tracy R. Sherman and Julie A. Misso 2006. 'Hot or Not: Do Professors Perceived as Physically Attractive Receive Higher Student Evaluations?' *Journal of General Psychology* 133: 19 –35.

Rodin, Judith, Lisa R. Silberstein and Ruth H. Streigel-Moore 1985. 'Women and Weight: A Normative Discontent.' pp. 267–307 in *Nebraska Symposium on Motivation: Psychology and Gender*, edited by Theo B. Sondregger. Lincoln, NE: University of Nebraska Press.

Roth, Louise and Rachael Neal 2006. *Peaches and Cream: Women Respond to White Images of Beauty*. Unpublished manuscript, Department of Sociology, University of Arizona.

Rothblum, Ester D. 1992. 'The Stigma of Women's Weight: Social and Economic Realities.' *Feminism and Psychology* 2: 61–73.

Santry, Heena P. , Daniel L. Gillen and Diane S. Lauderdale 2005. 'Trends in Bariatric Surgical Procedures.' *Journal of the American Medical Association* 294: 1909 –17.

Schneider, David J. 1973. 'Implicit Personality Theory: A Review.' *Psychological Bulletin* 79: 294–309.

Sobal, Jeffery 2004. 'Sociological Analysis of the Stigmatisation of Obesity.' pp. 187–204 in *A Sociology of Food and Nutrition: The Social Appetite*, edited by John Germov and Lauren Williams. Oxford, UK: Oxford University Press.

Solovay, Sondra 2000. *Tipping the Scales of Injustice: Fighting Weight-Based Discrimination*. Amherst, NY: Prometheus Books.

Sprague-Zones, Jane 1997. 'Beauty Myths and Realities and their Impact on Women's Health.' pp. 249–75 in *Women's Health: Complexities and Differences*, edited by Cheryl B. Ruzek, Virginia L. Oleson and Adele E. Clarke. Columbus, OH: Ohio State University Press.

Susman, Joan 1993. 'Disability, Stigma, and Deviance.' *Social Science & Medicine* 38: 15–22.

Thompson, Becky W. 1992. '"A Way Outa no Way": Eating Problems Among African-American, Latina, and White Women.' *Gender & Society* 6: 546–61.

Thompson, Becky W. 1994. *A Hunger So Wide and So Deep: A Multiracial View of Women's Eating Problems*. Minneapolis, MN: University of Minnesota Press.

Tiggemann, Marika and Christine Lewis 2004. 'Attitudes Toward Women's Body Hair: Relationship with Disgust Sensitivity.' *Psychology of Women Quarterly* 28: 381–7.

Tiggemann, Marika 1994. 'Gender Differences in the Interrelationship Between Weight Dissatisfaction, Restraint, and Self-Esteem.' *Sex Roles* 30: 319 –30.

Toerien, Merran and Sue Wilkinson 2003. 'Gender and Body Hair: Constructing the Feminine Woman.' *Women's Studies International Forum* 26: 333–44.

Toerien, Merran, Sue Wilkinson and Precilla Y. L. Choi 2005. 'Body Hair Removal: The "Mundane" Production of Normative Femininity.' *Sex Roles* 52: 399–406.

Trautner, Mary Nell 2005. 'Doing Gender, Doing Class: The Performance of Sexuality in Exotic Dance Clubs.' *Gender & Society* 19: 771–88.

Tse'lon, Efrat 1993. 'The Ideology of Beauty.' pp. 319–23 in *Recent Trends in Theoretical Psychology*, Volume III, edited by Henderikus J. Stam, Leendert P. Mos, Warren Thorngate and Bernie Kaplan. New York, NY: Springer-Verlag.

U.S. Equal Employment Opportunity Commission November 16, 2004. *EEOC Agrees to Landmark Resolution of Discrimination Case Against Abercrombie & Fitch.* Retrieved March 15, 2008 (http://www.eeoc.gov/press/11-18-04.html).

Udry, J. Richard and Bruce K. Eckland 1984. 'The Benefits of Being Attractive: Differential Payoffs for Men and Women.' *Psychological Reports* 54: 47–56.

Umberson, Debra and Michael Hughes 1987. 'The Impact of Physical Attractiveness on Achievement and Psychological Well-Being.' *Social Psychology Quarterly* 50: 227–36.

Walster Elaine, Vera Aronson, Darcy Abrahams and L. Rottman 1966. 'Importance of Physical Attractiveness in Dating Behavior.' *Journal of Personality and Social Psychology* 4: 508 –516.

Webster, Murray Jr. and James E. Driskell 1983. 'Beauty as Status'. *American Journal of Sociology* 89: 140–65.

Weitz, Rose 2001. 'Women and Their Hair: Seeking Power through Resistance and Accommodation.' *Gender & Society* 15: 667–86.

West, Candace and Don H. Zimmerman 1987. 'Doing Gender.' *Gender & Society* 1: 125–51.

Wolf, Naomi 1991. *The Beauty Myth*. New York, NY: W. Morrow.

Young, Iris Marion 1990. *Justice and the Politics of Difference*. Princeton, NJ: Princeton University Press.

INDEX